T0189695

Lecture Notes in Artificial Intelligence   10458

Subseries of Lecture Notes in Computer Science

LNAI Series Editors

Randy Goebel
University of Alberta, Edmonton, Canada
Yuzuru Tanaka
Hokkaido University, Sapporo, Japan
Wolfgang Wahlster
DFKI and Saarland University, Saarbrücken, Germany

LNAI Founding Series Editor

Joerg Siekmann
DFKI and Saarland University, Saarbrücken, Germany

More information about this series at http://www.springer.com/series/1244

Alexey Karpov · Rodmonga Potapova
Iosif Mporas (Eds.)

Speech and Computer

19th International Conference, SPECOM 2017
Hatfield, UK, September 12–16, 2017
Proceedings

Editors
Alexey Karpov (iD)
SPIIRAS
Saint Petersburg
Russia

Iosif Mporas (iD)
University of Hertfordshire
Hatfield
UK

Rodmonga Potapova (iD)
Moscow State Linguistic University
Moscow
Russia

ISSN 0302-9743 ISSN 1611-3349 (electronic)
Lecture Notes in Artificial Intelligence
ISBN 978-3-319-66428-6 ISBN 978-3-319-66429-3 (eBook)
DOI 10.1007/978-3-319-66429-3

Library of Congress Control Number: 2017949519

LNCS Sublibrary: SL7 – Artificial Intelligence

© Springer International Publishing AG 2017
This work is subject to copyright. All rights are reserved by the Publisher, whether the whole or part of the material is concerned, specifically the rights of translation, reprinting, reuse of illustrations, recitation, broadcasting, reproduction on microfilms or in any other physical way, and transmission or information storage and retrieval, electronic adaptation, computer software, or by similar or dissimilar methodology now known or hereafter developed.
The use of general descriptive names, registered names, trademarks, service marks, etc. in this publication does not imply, even in the absence of a specific statement, that such names are exempt from the relevant protective laws and regulations and therefore free for general use.
The publisher, the authors and the editors are safe to assume that the advice and information in this book are believed to be true and accurate at the date of publication. Neither the publisher nor the authors or the editors give a warranty, express or implied, with respect to the material contained herein or for any errors or omissions that may have been made. The publisher remains neutral with regard to jurisdictional claims in published maps and institutional affiliations.

Printed on acid-free paper

This Springer imprint is published by Springer Nature
The registered company is Springer International Publishing AG
The registered company address is: Gewerbestrasse 11, 6330 Cham, Switzerland

Preface

The Speech and Computer International Conference (SPECOM) has become a regular event since the first SPECOM, which was held in St. Petersburg, Russian Federation, in 1996. Twenty one years ago, SPECOM was established by the St. Petersburg Institute for Informatics and Automation of the Russian Academy of Sciences and State Pedagogical University of Russia thanks to the efforts of Prof. Yuri Kosarev and Prof. Rajmund Piotrowski.

SPECOM is a conference with a long tradition that attracts researchers in the area of computer speech processing (recognition, synthesis, understanding, etc.) and related domains (including signal processing, language and text processing, computational paralinguistics, multi-modal speech processing, and human–computer interaction). The SPECOM International Conference is an ideal platform for know-how exchange – especially for experts working on Slavic and other highly inflectional languages – including both under-resourced and regular well-resourced languages.

In its long history, the SPECOM conference has been organized alternately by the St. Petersburg Institute for Informatics and Automation of the Russian Academy of Sciences (SPIIRAS) and by the Moscow State Linguistic University (MSLU) in their home cities. Furthermore, in 1997 it was organized by the Cluj-Napoca Subsidiary of the Research Institute for Computer Technique (Romania), in 2005 by the University of Patras (in Patras, Greece), in 2011 by the Kazan Federal University (Russian Federation, Republic of Tatarstan), in 2013 by the University of West Bohemia (in Pilsen, Czech Republic), and in 2014 by the University of Novi Sad (Serbia), in 2015 by the University of Patras (in Athens, Greece), and in 2016 by the Budapest University of Technology and Economics (in Budapest, Hungary).

SPECOM 2017 was the 19th event in the series and this time it was organized by the University of Hertfordshire, in cooperation with the St. Petersburg Institute for Informatics and Automation of the Russian Academy of Sciences (SPIIRAS), Moscow State Linguistic University (MSLU), and St. Petersburg National Research University of Information Technologies, Mechanics and Optics (ITMO University). The conference was held jointly with the Second International Conference on Interactive Collaborative Robotics (ICR) – where problems and modern solutions of human–robot interaction were discussed – during September 12–16, 2017 at the College Lane campus of the University of Hertfordshire, which is located in Hatfield, UK 20 miles (30 kilometres) north of London, just 20 minutes by train from London's King's Cross station.

During the conference two invited talks were given by Prof. Mark J.F. Gales (Engineering Department, University of Cambridge, UK) and Prof. Björn W. Schuller (University of Passau, Germany and Imperial College London, UK) on the latest achievements in speech technology, automatic speech recognition, keyword spotting speaker analysis and computational paralinguistics. The invited papers are published as a first part of the SPECOM 2017 proceedings.

This volume contains a collection of submitted papers presented at the conference, which were thoroughly reviewed by members of the Program Committee consisting of above 100 top specialists in the conference topic areas. A total of 80 accepted papers out of 150 submitted for SPECOM and ICR were selected by the Program Committee for presentation at the conference and for inclusion in this book. Theoretical and more general contributions were presented in common (plenary) sessions. Problem-oriented sessions as well as panel discussions brought together specialists in limited problem areas with the aim of exchanging knowledge and skills resulting from research projects of all kinds. This year, except the regular technical sessions, three special sessions were organized on (i) Natural Language Processing for Social Media Analysis, (ii) Multilingual and Low-Resourced Languages Speech Processing in Human-Computer Interaction, and (iii) Real-Life Challenges in Voice and Multimodal Biometrics.

We would like to express our gratitude to the authors for providing their papers on time, to the members of the conference Program Committee and the organizers of the special sessions for their careful reviews and paper selection, and to the editors and correctors for their hard work in preparing this volume. Special thanks are due to the members of the Organizing Committee for their tireless effort and enthusiasm during the conference organization.

September 2017

Alexey Karpov
Rodmonga Potapova
Iosif Mporas

Organization

The conference SPECOM 2017 was organized by the University of Hertfordshire, in cooperation with the St. Petersburg Institute for Informatics and Automation of the Russian Academy of Sciences (SPIIRAS), Moscow State Linguistic University (MSLU), and St. Petersburg National Research University of Information Technologies, Mechanics and Optics (ITMO University). SPECOM 2017 was sponsored by ASM Solutions Ltd. (Moscow, Russia). The conference website is: http://specom.nw.ru/sites/2017.

General Co-chairs

Iosif Mporas   University of Hertfordshire, UK
Rodmonga Potapova   MSLU, Russia
Andrey Ronzhin   SPIIRAS, Russia

Program Committee Chair

Alexey Karpov   SPIIRAS, Russia

Program Committee

Shyam Agrawal, India
Tanel Alumae, Estonia
Ebru Arisoy, Turkey
Elias Azarov, Belarus
Gerard Bailly, France
Andrey Barabanov, Russia
Anton Batliner, Germany
Marie-Luce Bourguet, UK
Nick Campbell, Ireland
Eric Castelli, Vietnam
Vladimiir Chuchupal, Russia
Dirk van Compernolle, Belgium
Marelie Davel, South Africa
Vlado Delic, Serbia
Olivier Deroo, Belgium
Keelan Evanini, USA
Nicholas Evans, France
Vera Evdokimova, Russia
Nikos Fakotakis, Greece
Mauro Falcone, Italy

Vasiliki Foufi, Switzerland
Peter French, UK
Mark Gales, UK
Philip Garner, Switzerland
Theodoros Giannakopoulos, Greece
Gabor Gosztolya, Hungary
Abualsoud Hanani, Palestine
Charl van Heerden, South Africa
Ivan Himawan, Australia
Ruediger Hoffmann, Germany
Marek Hruz, Czech Republic
Alexei Ivanov, USA
Kristiina Jokinen, Finland
Oliver Jokisch, Germany
Alexey Karpov, Russia
Heysem Kaya, Turkey
Andreas Kerren, Sweden
Tomi Kinnunen, Finland
Irina Kipyatkova, Russia
Kate Knill, UK

Daniil Kocharov, Russia
Liliya Komalova, Russia
Theodoros Kostoulas, Switzerland
Constantine Kotropoulos, Greece
Georgios Kouroupetroglou, Greece
Alexandros Lazaridis, Switzerland
Benjamin Lecouteux, France
Boris Lobanov, Belarus
Elena Lyakso, Russia
Fragkiskos Malliaros, USA
Konstantin Markov, Japan
Yuri Matveev, Russia
Lily Meng, UK
Roman Meshcheryakov, Russia
Peter Mihajlik, Hungary
Wolfgang Minker, Germany
Bernd Möbius, Germany
Konstantinos Moustakas, Greece
Iosif Mporas, UK
Hema Murthy, India
Maryam Najafian, USA
Satoshi Nakamura, Japan
Marina Nastasenko, Russia
Géza Németh, Hungary
Thomas Niesler, South Africa
Stavros Ntalampiras, Italy
Carita Paradis, Sweden
Hemant Patil, India
Alexander Petrovsky, Belarus
Alexey Petrovsky, Russia
Branislav Popović, Serbia
Vsevolod Potapov, Russia
Rodmonga Potapova, Russia

Blaise Potard, UK
Fabio Rinaldi, Switzerland
Andrey Ronzhin, Russia
Paolo Rosso, Spain
Milan Rusko, Slovakia
Saeid Safavi, UK
Sakriani Sakti, Japan
Albert Ali Salah, Turkey
Murat Saraclar, Turkey
Björn Schuller, Germany
James Scobbie, UK
Vasiliki Simaki, Sweden
Pavel Skrelin, Russia
Victor Sorokin, Russia
Efstathios Stamatatos, Greece
Stefan Steidl, Germany
Mikhail Stolbov, Russia
Sebastian Stüker, Germany
Yannis Stylianou, Greece
György Szaszák, Hungary
Zheng-Hua Tan, Denmark
Laszlo Toth, Hungary
Isabel Trancoso, Portugal
Khiet Truong, The Netherlands
Stavros Tsakalidis, USA
Vasilisa Verkhodanova, Russia
Klara Vicsi, Hungary
Wenwu Wang, UK
Christian Wellekens, France
Andreas Wendemuth, Germany
Hossein Zeinali, Iran
Miloš Železný, Czech Republic

Organizing Committee

Iosif Mporas (Chair)
Alexey Karpov
Irina Kipyatkova
Dana Kovach
Yuri Matveev

Ekaterina Miroshnikova
Rodmonga Potapova
Andrey Ronzhin
Dmitry Ryumin
Anton Saveliev

Contents

Invited Talks

Low-Resource Speech Recognition and Keyword-Spotting

Mark J.F. Gales(✉), Kate M. Knill, and Anton Ragni

Engineering Department, Cambridge University, Trumpington Street, Cambridge, UK
{mjfg,kate.knill,ar257}@eng.cam.ac.uk

Abstract. The IARPA Babel program ran from March 2012 to November 2016. The aim of the program was to develop agile and robust speech technology that can be rapidly applied to any human language in order to provide effective search capability on large quantities of real world data. This paper will describe some of the developments in speech recognition and keyword-spotting during the lifetime of the project. Two technical areas will be briefly discussed with a focus on techniques developed at Cambridge University: the application of deep learning for low-resource speech recognition; and efficient approaches for keyword spotting. Finally a brief analysis of the Babel speech language characteristics and language performance will be presented.

Keywords: Prosody perception · Narrow versus broad focus · Japanese learners of English · L2 acquisition

1 Introduction

In recent years there has been an increasing interest in Automatic Speech Recognition (ASR) and Key Word Spotting (KWS) for low resource languages. One of the driving forces for this research direction was the IARPA Babel project [13] which ran from March 2012 until November 2016. To quote from the BAA:

> "The Babel Program will develop agile and robust speech recognition technology that can be rapidly applied to any human language in order to provide effective search capability for analysts to efficiently process massive amounts of real-world recorded speech."

The particular form of speech technology assessed as a realisation of this aim was Key Word, or phrase, Spotting (KWS). The funding for, and evaluations of, the project was split into four phases, a base period (BP) followed by three "option" periods (OP1, OP2 and OP3). During the project 25 languages were released spanning a wide range of language groups, writing schemes, and linguistic attributes. Conversational telephone speech data was recorded either directly, or using a microphone. Each side of the conversation was recorded separately.

    Language packs were released for each language with various quantities of data:

© Springer International Publishing AG 2017
A. Karpov et al. (Eds.): SPECOM 2017, LNAI 10458, pp. 3–19, 2017.
DOI: 10.1007/978-3-319-66429-3_1

- **Full Language Pack** (FLP): 40–80 h of transcribed audio data;
- **Limited Language Pack** (LLP): 10 h of transcribed audio data, selected from a subset of conversation sides in the FLP;
- **Very Limited Language Pack** (VLLP): 3 h of transcribed audio data, selected from all sides in the FLP. This was a baseline for active learning approaches.

In addition untranscribed audio data was made available, yielding approximately 100–150 h of audio data in total per language. For each phase of the programme the evaluation concentrated on different configurations: BP FLP; OP1 LLP; OP2 VLLP; and OP3 FLP. The results presented in this paper are based on the FLP configuration as this was the focus in the final phase of the project.

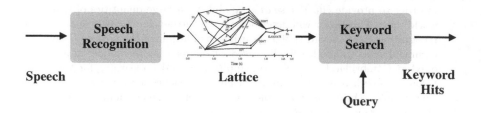

Fig. 1. Key word, or phrase, spotting pipeline

The vast majority of systems developed followed the pipeline shown in Fig. 1. An Automatic Speech Recognition (ASR) system is initially run to generate lattices, with nodes at phone, morph or word level. Using lattices to propagate information from the ASR system to the KWS stage makes the system less sensitive to errors; words and phrases can be found even if they do not appear in the 1-best ASR output. Given the quantities of data available in these low resource scenarios the Word Error Rates (WERs) can be very high, 30% to 70%, which means that very rich deep lattices are required for high performance KWS.

Error mitigation between the ASR and search module is only one of the problems that must be dealt with. Current state of the art speech recognition systems are based around deep learning [16]. These approaches operate best when there are large quantities of training data, the opposite of the situation in the Babel project. To address this problem approaches have been developed for both the acoustic and language models used in the majority of ASR systems; examples of these will be discussed in Sect. 2. Another factor that impacts the development of low-resource systems is the lack of linguistic resources. Unlike more frequently investigated languages, there are unlikely to be well defined lexicons, morphological analysers or parts of speech taggers. To address this the impact of using purely graphemic systems [17,18] on a range of languages using both Latin and non-Latin scripts is discussed. In addition, approaches for system combination for both ASR [6,8,27] and KWS [19,22,28,30] and their impact in a low-resource scenario will be described.

One of the interesting aspects of the Babel data is that there are 25 languages with a wide range of attributes, with all the data collected and annotated in a consistent fashion on a highly challenging task. The final part of this paper discusses the performance over a number of these languages in a consistent configuration.

For the Babel project the performance of the system was evaluated in two ways. The primary metric reflected KWS performance. The Term Weighted Value (TWV) [9] is defined as

$$TWV(\theta) = 1 - [P_{miss}(\theta) + \beta P_{fa}(\theta)] \tag{1}$$

where $P_{miss}(\theta)$ and $P_{fa}(\theta)$ denote the probability of miss and false alarm, respectively, and β is 999.9. For the evaluation a single threshold was required to be specified. To avoid the impact of threshold selection, in this paper the Maximum TWV (MTWV) score is given which is the maximum TWV achievable for that system. The second metric used is related to the WER for ASR. As the specification of a word can be poorly defined for some languages, the metric used is the Token Error Rate (TER). This is defined in the same way as the WER, but with the generalisation of handling tokens rather than words. For most languages TER and WER are the same.

2   Low-Resource Speech Recognition

Speech recognition for low-resource languages has followed the same directions as more general speech technology. Deep learning is a central aspect of all components of these systems: feature extraction [12,15]; acoustic modelling [16]; and language modelling [21]. To address the lack of training data, however, a number of modifications have been made to the standard pipeline. These approaches include data augmentation [5,14,23]; the use of web data [20]; extensive system combination [31]; and the use of multiple languages [4,24]. Furthermore the concept of *low resource* can be applied beyond the availability of training data to include linguistic resources such as an accurate lexicon.

This section briefly describes some of the approaches adopted for implementing the lexicon, acoustic and language models in those low-resource scenarios at CUED to support the evaluation systems developed over the Babel programme [11,25,26]. For the sake of brevity the baseline ASR system will not be described in detail. For details of the systems used see the associated references.

2.1   Graphemic Lexicon

For the OP2 and OP3 evaluations no phonetic lexicon was supplied. To address this a graphemic lexicon was used. Here, the spelling of the word is used to directly determine the sub-word units. Prior to the Babel program, most graphemic systems have been built either for Latin script languages or the script has been converted to Romanised form before creation of the graphemic lexicon, e.g. [17,18]. One of the challenges was to examine whether a graphemic system could be applied to a wide range of languages with minimal, or preferably no knowledge of phonology of the language.

The approach adopted at CUED to constructing graphemic systems was to use the attributes of unicode [1] to define the attributes of each of the *graphemes*. These attributes are then used to map the character into a root grapheme and associated attributes [10]. For example, for Kazakh, which is a mixture of Cyrillic and Latin scripts, a subset of the graphemes associated with the letter "I" are

i G6;D2D3D6   LATIN SMALL LETTER I
I G6;D8D3D6   LATIN CAPITAL LETTER I
и G6;D1D2D3   CYRILLIC SMALL LETTER I
ѝ G6;D1D2D3D4 CYRILLIC SMALL LETTER I WITH GRAVE
й G6;D1D2D3D5 CYRILLIC SMALL LETTER SHORT I

where the following attributes are defined

D1 CYRILLIC D2 SMALL D3 LETTER D4 WITH GRAVE
D5 SHORT   D6 LATIN D8 CAPITAL

All graphemes are thus mapped into a set of core graphemes, and attributes associated with the set of graphemes. This mimics the set of attributes associated with phones that can be obtained for all phones using, for example, X-SAMPA phonetic look-up tables.

The above scheme has assumed that all unicode characters have a distinct acoustic realisation. Unicode characters that do not have an acoustic realisation, or alter the realisation of an adjoining grapheme, can be split into two distinct groups. The first set are language-dependent graphemes, and are related to diacritics, but written as separate unicode characters, denoted by the word SIGN in the character descriptor. Note VOWEL SIGN characters in for example Abugida written languages are kept as separate symbols with acoustic realisations. In addition to the unicode attributes additional markers indicating the position of the grapheme in the word (beginning/middle/end) was added.

Table 1. Babel FLP Tandem-SAT Performance: with confusion network (CN) decoding and CNC CN-combination

Language	Id	Script	TER (%)		
			Phon	Grph	CNC
Tok Pisin	207	Latin	40.6	41.1	39.4
Kazakh	302	Cyrillic/Latin	53.5	52.7	51.5
Telugu	303	Telugu	69.1	69.5	67.5

Table 1 contrasts the performance of three OP2 languages with scripts ranging from Latin (Tok Pisin) mixed Latin and Cyrillic (Kazakh) to Telugu (Telugu). The performance of the graphemic and the phonetic system is comparable even though no phonetic information was used for the graphemic system. Additionally the combination of the phonetic and graphemic systems using Confusion Network Combination (CNC) [7] shows consistent gains.

2.2   Stimulated Training of Neural Networks

One of the issues with the standard training of neural networks is that the nodes are not interpretable. This lack of interpretability can cause issues for speaker adaptation and network generalisation as it is difficult to relate weights from the network to each other. To address this problem *stimulated network training* has been proposed [25, 29, 32]. The aim of stimulated training is to train networks where nodes with similar activation functions are grouped together. The Babel program, requiring low resources systems, should be suited to this form of training.

In stimulated training a phone (or grapheme) dependent prior distribution is defined over the normalised activation function outputs for each of the layers. The nodes in each layer are reorganised into a grid, so that each node, i, of a layer is represented as a point in a two dimensional *network-grid* space, s_i. A point in this network-grid space is also associated with each phone s_p. It is then possible to define a normalised distance from every node to the correct phone position. These normalised distances are used as a prior over the distribution of the activation function values for a layer. This prior encourages activation functions in the same locality to have the same normalised output.

To implement stimulated training, a regularisation term, $\mathcal{R}(\lambda)$, is added to the training criterion

$$\mathcal{F}(\lambda) = \mathcal{L}(\lambda) + \alpha \mathcal{R}(\lambda)$$

where $\mathcal{L}(\lambda)$ is the standard training criterion for parameters λ, for an L hidden-layer network $\lambda = \{\mathbf{W}^{(1)}, \dots, \mathbf{W}^{(L)}\}$, α determines the contribution of the prior, $\mathcal{R}(\lambda)$. Here $\mathcal{R}(\lambda)$ is based on the KL-divergence of the prior distribution over the normalised activation, $g(s_i, \hat{s}_{p_t})$ and the current distribution, $\overline{h}_{ti}^{(l)}$. Thus

$$\mathcal{R}(\lambda) = \sum_t \sum_l \sum_i g(s_i, \hat{s}_{p_t}) \log \left(\frac{g(s_i, \hat{s}_{p_t})}{\overline{h}_{ti}^{(l)}} \right)$$

where the two distributions are defined as:

1. *phone-specific activation distribution prior:* $g(s_i, \hat{s}_{p_t})$ is the normalised distance of a node and the current active-phone position. For these experiments:

$$g(s_i, \hat{s}_{p_t}) = \frac{\exp\left(-\frac{1}{2}||s_i - \hat{s}_{p_t}||^2\right)}{\sum_j \exp\left(-\frac{1}{2}||s_j - \hat{s}_{p_t}||^2\right)}$$

where s_i the position in the network-grid space of node i, $\hat{s}_{p_t}$ the position in the network-grid space of the "correct" phone at time t. The denominator summation is over all nodes in network layer l.

2. *network activation distribution:* $\overline{h}_{ti}^{(l)}$ is the normalised activation function output for node i of layer l at time instance t

$$\overline{h}_{ti}^{(l)} = \frac{\beta_i^{(l)} h_{ti}^{(l)}}{\sum_j \beta_j^{(l)} h_{tj}^{(l)}}; \quad \beta_i^{(l)} = \sqrt{\sum_k w_{ik}^{(l+1)2}}$$

$h_{ti}^{(l)}$ is the output activation function value for node i of layer l at time instance t and $w_{ik}^{(l)}$ is the weight connection from node i of layer l to node k of layer $l+1$. $\beta_i^{(l)}$ is used to reflect the impact that the activation function has on the following layer, $l+1$ and has been found to be important for stimulated training.

This form of prior can be applied to any form of network. To generate the position of the correct grapheme, t-SNE was applied [32].

Fig. 2. Example of the impact of stimulated training for a particular instance of the phone /ay/. The left plot is the position of the stimulation points (/ay/ circled), the center plot standard, unstimulated, training, the right plot stimulated training

Figure 2 shows the impact of stimulated training using phone stimulation points on network training. The stimulation points, left figure, were obtained using t-SNE projections of phone feature means. The center plot shows the (scaled) network activation functions for hidden layer 3 (of 5) with standard training and has no structure in the node activation function values. This is expected for a randomly initialised distributed representation. The right plot shows the impact of stimulated training. Structure is clearly visible in the form of the activation functions[1].

Table 2 shows the impact of stimulated training on both ASR and KWS performance. For these results both Tandem and Hybrid systems were combined using joint decoding with stimulated training only being applied to the Hybrid systems. See [25] for additional system configurations and results. For all language investigated stimulated training gave performance gains for both ASR and KWS.

---

[1] For a complete movie of the activation functions for stimulated training see: http://mi.eng.cam.ac.uk/~mjfg/bneStimu.avi.

Table 2. Impact of stimulated training on ASR and KWS performance for the OP3 languages

Language	Id	Stimulated Training	TER (%)	MTWV		
				iv	oov	tot
Amharic	307	✗	41.1	0.6500	0.5828	0.6402
		✓	40.8	0.6619	0.5935	0.6521
Javanese	402	✗	50.9	0.4991	0.4448	0.4924
		✓	50.7	0.5024	0.4679	0.4993

2.3 Web Data and RNN Language Models

One of the major issues associated with low-resource languages is the lack of appropriate language model training data. This has two immediate impacts. First if only 40–80 h of transcriptions are available the resulting vocabulary will be very small resulting in high OOV rates for both ASR and KWS. Second the robustness of the estimates of the language model probabilities will be poor. To address this problem the web was "scraped" for data of the target language [20,34]. This allows large amounts of training data to be collected for many languages, with some exceptions such as Dholou. For example for Pashto the amount of data available from the FLP was 535 K words, but 105M words could be collected from the web.

Unfortunately the availability of large amounts of data introduces two additional problems. Current state-of-the-art language models are built using Recurrent Neural Networks (RNNs) [21]. These models can take a significant amount of time to train on large amounts of data. To enable rapid deployment of systems it is necessary to improve the training time. Second the data collected from the web is typically poorly matched to the target domain, CTS. To address these problems modified training criteria were examined and "fine-tuning" to the FLP data used [3].

The standard training criterion for training neural network language models, including RNN LMs is based on cross-entropy. For word sequence $\omega_{1:L} = \omega_1, \ldots, \omega_L$, the following criterion is optimised.

$$\mathcal{F}_{\text{ce}} = -\frac{1}{L} \sum_{i=1}^{L} \log \left(P(\omega_i | \tilde{\boldsymbol{h}}_{i-1}) \right)$$

Though this can be efficiently implemented using GPUs if the output layer, the prediction vocabulary size, is not large. As the size of the output vocabulary increases the computational cost is dominated the softmax normalisation term $Z(\tilde{\boldsymbol{h}}_{i-1})$

$$P(\omega_i | \tilde{\boldsymbol{h}}_{i-1}) = \frac{1}{Z(\tilde{\boldsymbol{h}}_{i-1})} \exp \left(\boldsymbol{w}_{f(\omega_i)}^{\mathsf{T}} \tilde{\boldsymbol{h}}_{i-1} \right)$$

This impacts both the training and decoding. For the word-based systems the vocabulary associated when including the web-data, was very large, for Pashto 273 K words. Training the RNNLM using CE, the standard criterion, and then fine-tuning to the FLP data, is impractical for the surprise language evaluation as both training and recognition is very slow. To address this problem two different training criteria were investigated:

- *variance regularisation* (VR): this ensures that the normalisation term (in the prediction) is approximately constant for all word histories. An additional regularisation term is added to the standard cross-entropy (CE) criterion, $\mathcal{F}_{ce}$. The following criterion is optimised

$$\mathcal{F}_{vr} = \mathcal{F}_{ce} + \frac{\gamma}{2}\frac{1}{L}\sum_{i=1}^{L}\left(\log(Z(\tilde{\boldsymbol{h}}_{i-1})) - \overline{\log(Z)}\right)^2$$

If all the normalisation terms for all histories are constrained to be the same, it is therefore not necessary to compute it during recognition time, improving decoding time significantly;
- *noise contrastive estimation* (NCE): this trains a discriminative model between classifying the word sequences and noise samples often generated by a unigram language model. Here the following discriminative criterion is optimised

$$\mathcal{F}_{nce} = -\frac{1}{L}\sum_{i=1}^{L}\left(\log(P(y_i = \text{T}|\omega_i, \tilde{\boldsymbol{h}}_{i-1}) + \sum_{j=1}^{k}\log(P(y_i = \text{F}|\hat{\omega}_{ij}, \tilde{\boldsymbol{h}}_{i-1})\right)$$

where $\hat{\omega}_{ij}$ are *noise samples* for ω_i, often generated by a uni-gram language-model. In this model it is not necessary to estimate the normalisation term during training or recognition.

Table 3 shows the impact of web-data on the ASR and KWS systems. For details of the system configurations see [3]. The first line is the performance when only using the FLP data to train an tri-gram language model. Comparing the first and second lines, where a language model component trained on the web-data was used, shows that the use of the web-data had little impact on ASR performance.

Table 3. Impact of web RNN LMs on KWS performance on Pashto. The RNN-Criterion is either used for initial training (Trn) or fine-tuning (F-T)

Language	Id	Vocab	RNN Crit		Time (hrs)		TER (%)	MTWV		
			Trn	F-T	Train	Rescore		iv	oov	tot
Pashto	104	14.4K	—		—		44.1	0.4808	0.2412	0.4541
			—		—		43.8	0.4828	0.4083	0.4750
		376.3K	CE	CE	125.0	23.0	42.8	0.4975	0.4048	0.4871
			NCE	VR	10.7	2.0	43.0	0.4975	0.3953	0.4862

However the KWS performance is significantly better. The main reason for this is the performance on OOV KWS terms (as defined by the FLP), as the increased vocabulary reduces the need to use "phone" search for the KWS system.

Table 3 also shows the impact of including an RNNLM in the system. For both configurations the RNNLM was initially trained on all the data and then fine-tuned to the FLP data. Line three of the table shows the performance when CE is used for both stages. Gains can be see for both ASR and KWS performance. However examining both the training and lattice rescoring times shows that it takes over 5 days to train the system. Using NCE for initial training, and then VR to fine-tune, reduced this training time by more than an order-of-magnitude, and similarly for the deciding time.

3   Improved ASR and KWS Efficiency Research at CUED

As previously discussed to minimise the impact of error propagation from the ASR system to the KWS very large lattices are created. Additionally to maximise performance multiple systems need to be combined together to yield the final result. The combination of the two can result in significant computational cost when handling large quantities of data. This section briefly describes two approaches that were used at CUED to reduce the computational cost: unique arc-per-second pruning to reduce the size of the lattices; and model-merging to reduce the number of ASR and KWS runs.

3.1   Unique-Arcs Per-Second Pruning

There are two contradictory requirements for the lattices that are used for KWS. First they should be large and diverse, containing multiple competing paths. Second, they should be compact so that the speed of KWS is fast. There have been a number of approaches adopted to balance these two, including confusion network based KWS and ensuring that all words in the best path for all word sequences are kept. An alternative approach that is to control the distribution of the number of unique arcs at each time instance. It is possible to apply this process during decoding, or on lattices. The basic process is:

For each selected time instance:

- for each word (unique arc) rank order all arcs by score for that word;
- rank order all words by the best arc score for that word;
- prune arcs so that the selected distribution over words (unique arcs) is satisfied, ensuring that connections to all arcs in the previous pruning time instance are maintained.

This approach is highly flexible as it is possible to control the size of lattice by varying the target unique-arcs-per-second distribution. Figure 3 shows the impact of UAPS pruning. The top figure shows the total number of arcs in a

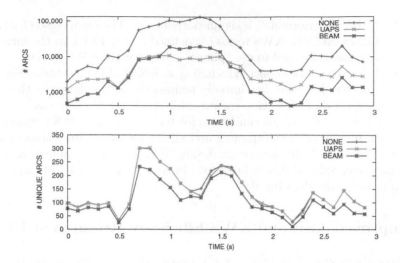

Fig. 3. Illustration of unique-arcs-per-second pruning for a sentence

lattice. The lower figure shows the number of unique arcs. The standard beam-pruning and UAPS pruning are configured to yield the same lattice size for the utterance. It is clear from the diagram that UAPS pruning maintains the number of unique arcs of the original unpruned system, but at a significantly smaller lattice size.

All the CUED evaluation systems for OP2 and OP3 were based on UAPS pruning. Typically the size of lattices was reduced by an order of magnitude, with no impact on KWS performance.

Table 4. Example lattice size (arcs/second) of the original lattices and after unique-arcs per-second pruning

Language	Id	Arcs/Sec	
		Decode	UAPS
Mongolian	401	88,479	17,623
Javanese	402	41,880	11,109

Table 4 shows the sizes of lattice generated from the decoding process and after UAPS for two of the OP3 languages. For these systems the number of unique arcs is approximately the same. The size of lattices after UAPS are approximately an order of magnitude smaller, dramatically improving time/memory requirements for KWS.

3.2   Model Merging or Posting-List Merging

As previously discussed one important approach to improve the performance of both ASR and KWS is to perform system combination. Here multiple, preferably complementary systems, are combined together to yield the final result. An important consideration for these approaches is the computational load. The simplest approach is to run all the systems separately and combine the final outputs together. This is the approach adopted with ROVER [8] and CNC [7] for ASR, and posting-list merging for KWS [19]. If four systems were to be combined this would requiter four ASR decodes, followed by four KWS runs.

To reduce the computational load it is possible to combine the multiple systems together. The approach adopted at CUED for the Babel programme was log-linear model-combination [2,33]. Here the log-likelihood of a particular observation $\mathbf{o}_t$ for state $\mathbf{s}$ is given by

$$\log(p(\mathbf{o}_t|\mathbf{s})) = \frac{1}{Z(\mathbf{o}_t)} \exp \left(\sum_{m=1}^{M} \alpha_m \log(p(\mathbf{o}_t|\mathbf{s}; \boldsymbol{\lambda}^{(m)})) \right)$$

where $\log(p(\mathbf{o}_t|\mathbf{s}; \boldsymbol{\lambda}^{(m)}))$ is the log-likelihood from model m and α_m is the related weight. Only a single decode and lattice generation, and KWS search are performed. As the normalisation term, $Z(\mathbf{o}_t)$, is only a function of the observation it does not impact the rank ordering in decoding. Thus the weight for each model α_m can be hand selected and used for decoding. This was the approach adopted here [31].

An interesting question is the nature of the systems to combine. For OP2 evaluation systems Tandem and Hybrid systems were combined. For OP3 multiple multi-lingual bottleneck features (BN) were made available from Aachen (A28) and IBM (I28), see [4] for details. Two configurations were compared. First the use of joint decoding between Tandem and Hybrid systems for each of the BN features (labelled A28 and I28) and then output combination (CNC for ASR and posting-list merging for KWS), or joint decoding using all fours models was investigated. The weights for the models were empirically selected, but consistent for all languages.

The performance of various configurations is shown in Table 5. Though performing two separate runs and then two KW searches yielded better performance (for KWS) for all languages the differences were not large compared to the memory and computational loads. For the final evaluation joint decoding over all four systems was used for efficiency.

4   Language Analysis and Prediction

There is a wide range of performance over the languages distributed in the BP, OP1, OP2 and OP3. One of the interesting aspects of these language packs is that they are consistently annotated and are associated with challenging data,

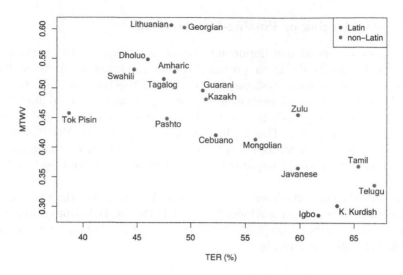

Fig. 4. Summary plot (MTWV vs TER) for FLP systems in a single graphemic system OP2 configuration

CTS. An interesting question is whether it is possible to predict the performance for a particular language without having to build a full system.

As a starting point for the analysis a sub-set of languages were all built using a consistent, relatively advanced graphemic lexicon configuration that was used for the OP2 FLP evaluation [31]. The subset was selected to give a spread over the language groups and interesting language pairs for analysis. For example: the Dravidian Languages, Tamil and Telugu generally performed poorly; members of the Niger-Kongo languages, Swahili, Zulu and Igbo, were selected as there was a large performance difference (ASR/KWS) between Swahili and Zulu, and the opportunity to predict Igbo. Figure 4 shows the plot of MTWV against TER for all these languages. It can be seen that MTWV and TER are negatively correlated, with some outliers: Tok Pisin has a worse than expected KWS performance given the TER; Zulu, Lithuanian and Georgian have a better

Table 5. Performance of the OP2 joint decoding configuration using the Aachen BN features (A28) and the IBM BN features (I28), ⊕ indicates CNC/posting-list merging, ⊗ indicated joint decoding

Language	Id	System comb.	TER (%)	MTWV		
				iv	oov	tot
Javanese	402	A28	52.5	0.4787	0.4379	0.4736
		I28	52.1	0.4763	0.4283	0.4712
		A28⊕I28	50.9	0.4991	0.4448	0.4924
		A28⊗I28	50.9	0.4979	0.4843	0.4970

KWS performance than expected. What is also interesting is the wide spread of performance ranging from 65% to 40% TER for ASR, and 0.30 to 0.60 MTWV for KWS.

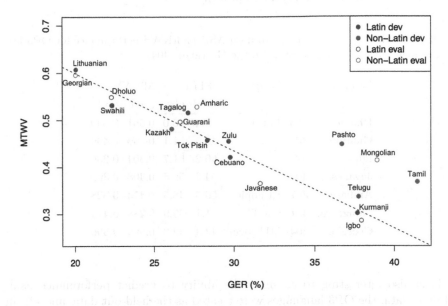

Fig. 5. Summary plot (MTWV vs Graphemic Error Rate (GER)) for FLP systems in an OP2 graphemic system configuration. Blue indicates Latin script alphabet. Best fit line computed using the 7 dev Latin script languages (Color figure online)

A range of attributes (including SNR, number of words/phones, OOV, LM perplexity) from the languages were evaluated to see whether performance could be predicted using language attributes rather than building systems. Unfortunately none of these showed strong correlations with the final performance. One issue that impacts this form of analysis is the level of inter-annotator dis-agreement (WER), which can vary considerably over languages: Tamil ≈ 25%; Lithuanian ≈ 10%. Rather than looking at general language attributes, the ability to predict final ASR and KWS performance from a simple initial ASR build was investigated. The most informative attribute was Graphemic Error Rate (GER)[2] calculated from a simple maximum likelihood PLP-based, speaker-independent, graphemic system on the training data. The system is relatively fast to train, and no held-out data is required. Additionally inter-annotator inconsistencies are implicitly handled. Figure 5 shows MTWV against GER. For all the Latin script languages there is a strong correlation between GER and MTWV. The previous outlier Latin script languages, Tok Pisin, Zulu and Lithuanian, are now in-line with predictions.

---

[2] All markers such as accents are stripped from the grapheme to yield the root grapheme. Thus Latin scripts have 26 graphemes. These accuracies include silence at the beginning and end of sentences, and between all words.

As the grapheme accuracy will depend on the number of graphemes the non-Latin script languages marked in red (Kazakh, Tamil, Telugu and Pashto) are not considered. These are expected to have a higher grapheme error rate as there are more graphemes present (Kazakh is an exception).

Table 6. Predictions of OP2 configuration ASR and KWS performance for OP3 languages, including OP3 evaluation language Georgian (404)

Language	Id	Script	%TER		MTWV	
			pred	obs	pred	obs
Dholuo	403	Latin	45.4	46.0	0.561	0.549
Guarani	305		49.5	51.1	0.490	0.496
Igbo	306		60.2	61.7	0.304	0.286
Javanese	402		54.2	59.8	0.408	0.362
Amharic	307	Ethiopic	50.5	48.5	0.473	0.528
Mongolian	401	Cyrillic	61.1	55.9	0.288	0.414
Georgian	404	Mkhedruli	43.3	49.2	0.599	0.596

It is also interesting to examine the ability to predict performance using held-out data. the OP3 languages were treated as the held-out data, and all the remaining Latin script languages used to generator a predictor. For MTWV this is the dotted line in Fig. 5. Similarly a linear predictor for TER was generated. Table 6 shows the resulting predictions, and actual observed values. For the Latin script it can be seen that GER is a good predictor for MTWV and indicative for TER.

5   Conclusions

This paper has briefly outlined some of the approaches developed at Cambridge University to handle low-resource keyword-spotting and speech recognition under the Babel programme. Two distinct areas are discussed low-resource speech recognition and efficient low-resource keyword-spotting. The final section of the paper briefly examines the performance on a wide-range of languages in a consistent configuration and how to predict performance.

Though significant advances were made during the Babel programme on low-resource speech processing, it still remains a highly challenging area. The current ability to leverage data across languages is limited despite the fact that there is a common acoustic generation process for all languages, human physiology. Additionally many languages have common syntactic and semantic structure. Extracting these, and leveraging connections is still not addressed.

Acknowledgements. This work was supported in part by the Intelligence Advanced Research Projects Activity (IARPA) via Department of Defense U.S. Army Research Laboratory (DoD/ARL) contract number W911NF-12-C-0012. The U.S. Government is authorized to reproduce and distribute reprints for Governmental purposes notwithstanding any copyright annotation thereon. Disclaimer: The views and conclusions contained herein are those of the authors and should not be interpreted as necessarily representing the official policies or endorsements, either expressed or implied, of IARPA, DoD/ARL, or the U.S. Government. This work made use of data provided by IARPA The following data was used in the FLP configuration:

IARPA-babel106-v0.2f,   IARPA-babel202b-v1.0d,   IARPA-babel204b-v1.1b, IARPA-babel205b-v1.0a, IARPA-babel206b-v0.1d, IARPA-babel207b-v1.0a, IARPA-babel301b-v1.0b, IARPA-babel302b-v1.0a, IARPA-babel303b-v1.0a, IARPA-babel 304b-v1.0b, IARPA-babel104b-v0.4bY, IARPA-babel306b-v2.0c, IARPA- babel401b-v2.0b, IARPA-babel402b-v1.0b, IARPA-babel403b-v1.0b, IARPA-babel404b-v1.0a, ...

The authors would like to thank the contributions of all the members of the CUED Babel team during the project. In particular Dr X. Chen, J. Vasilakes, Dr H. Wang and Dr S. Rath who directly worked on the evaluation systems and during the "interesting" Babel evaluation periods. The authors would also like to thank all the members of the LORELEI team, in particular the IBM and RWTH Aachen Babel teams.

References

1. The unicode consortium. http://www.unicode.org. Accessed 30 Sep 2014
2. Beyerlein, P.: Discriminative model combination. In: Proceedings of ASRU (1997)
3. Chen, X., Ragni, A., Liu, X., Vasilakes, J., Knill, K.M., Gales, M.J.: Recurrent neural network language models for keyword search. In: ICASSP (2017)
4. Cui, J., Kingsbury, B., Ramabhadran, B., Sethy, A., Audhkhasi, K., Cui, X., Kislal, E., Mangu, L., Nussbaum-Thom, M., Picheny, M., et al.: Multilingual representations for low resource speech recognition and keyword search. In: 2015 IEEE Workshop on Automatic Speech Recognition and Understanding (ASRU), pp. 259–266. IEEE (2015)
5. Cui, X., Goel, V., Kingsbury, B.: Data augmentation for deep neural network acoustic modeling. IEEE/ACM Trans. Audio Speech Lang. Process. (TASLP) **23**(9), 1469–1477 (2015)
6. Evermann, G., Woodland, P.C.: Large vocabulary decoding and confidence estimation using word posterior probabilities. In: Proceedings of ICASSP (2000)
7. Evermann, G., Woodland, P.: Posterior probability decoding, confidence estimation and system combination. In: Proceedings of Speech Transcription Workshop, vol. 27, p. 78, Baltimore (2000)
8. Fiscus, J.G.: A post-processing system to yield reduced word error rates: recogniser output voting error reduction (ROVER). In: Proceedings of ASRU (1997)
9. Fiscus, J.G., et al.: Results of the 2006 spoken term detection evaluation. In: Proceedings of ACM SIGIR Workshop on Searching Spontaneous Conversational Speech (2007)
10. Gales, M.J., Knill, K.M., Ragni, A.: Unicode-based graphemic systems for limited resource languages. In: ICASSP, pp. 5186–5190. IEEE (2015)

11. Gales, M.J., Knill, K.M., Ragni, A., Rath, S.P.: Speech recognition and keyword spotting for low-resource languages: Babel project research at cued. In: SLTU. pp. 16–23 (2014)
12. Grezl, F., Karafiat, M., Janda, M.: Study of probabilistic and bottle-neck features in multilingual environment. In: Proceedings of ASRU (2011)
13. Harper, M.: IARPA Babel Program. http://www.iarpa.gov/Programs/ia/Babel/babel.html
14. Hartmann, W., Ng, T., Hsiao, R., Tsakalidis, S., Schwartz, R.: Two-stage data augmentation for low-resourced speech recognition. In: Interspeech 2016, pp. 2378–2382 (2016)
15. Hermansky, H., Ellis, D., Sharma, S.: Tandem connectionist feature extraction for conventional HMM systems. In: Proceedings of ICASSP (2000)
16. Hinton, G., Deng, L., et al.: Deep neural networks for acoustic modeling in speech recognition. IEEE Signal Process. Mag. 29(6), 82–97 (2012)
17. Kanthak, S., Ney, H.: Context-dependent acoustic modelling using graphemes for large-vocabulary speech recognition. In: Proceedings of ICASSP (2002)
18. Killer, M., Stüker, S., Schultz, T.: Grapheme based speech recognition. In: Proceedings of EUROSPEECH (2003)
19. Mamou, J., Cui, J., Cui, X., Gales, M.J., Kingsbury, B., Knill, K., Mangu, L., Nolden, D., Picheny, M., Ramabhadran, B., et al.: System combination and score normalization for spoken term detection. In: ICASSP, pp. 8272–8276. IEEE (2013)
20. Mendels, G., Cooper, E., Soto, V., Hirschberg, J., Gales, M.J., Knill, K.M., Ragni, A., Wang, H.: Improving speech recognition and keyword search for low resource languages using web data. In: INTERSPEECH, pp. 829–833 (2015)
21. Mikolov, T., Karafiát, M., Burget, L., Cernockỳ, J., Khudanpur, S.: Recurrent neural network based language model. In: Interspeech, vol. 2, p. 3 (2010)
22. Miller, D.R.H., Kleber, M., et al.: Rapid and accurate spoken term detection. In: Proceedings of Interspeech (2007)
23. Ragni, A., Knill, K.M., Rath, S.P., Gales, M.J.F.: Data augmentation for low resource languages. In: Proceedings of InterSpeech (2014)
24. Ragni, A., Dakin, E., Chen, X., Gales, M.J., Knill, K.M.: Multi-language neural network language models. Interspeech 8, 3042–3046 (2016)
25. Ragni, A., Wu, C., Gales, M.J., Vasilakes, J., Knill, K.M.: Stimulated training for automatic speech recognition and keyword search in limited resource conditions. In: ICASSP (2017)
26. Rath, S.P., Knill, K.M., Ragni, A., Gales, M.J.: Combining tandem and hybrid systems for improved speech recognition and keyword spotting on low resource languages. In: INTERSPEECH, pp. 835–839 (2014)
27. Swietojanski, P., Ghoshal, A., Renals, S.: Revisiting hybrid and gmm-hmm system combination techniques. In: ICASSP, pp. 6744–6748. IEEE (2013)
28. Szoke, I., Burget, L., Cernocky, J., Fapso, M.: Sub-word modeling of out of vocabulary words in spoken term detection. In: Proceedings of SLT (2008)
29. Tan, S., Sim, K.C., Gales, M.: Improving the interpretability of deep neural networks with stimulated learning. In: 2015 IEEE Workshop on Automatic Speech Recognition and Understanding (ASRU), pp. 617–623. IEEE (2015)
30. Vergyri, D., Shafran, I., et al.: The SRI/OGI 2006 spoken term detection system. In: Proceedings of Interspeech (2007)

31. Wang, H., Ragni, A., Gales, M.J., Knill, K.M., Woodland, P.C., Zhang, C.: Joint decoding of tandem and hybrid systems for improved keyword spotting on low resource languages. In: INTERSPEECH, pp. 3660–3664 (2015)
32. Wu, C., Karanasou, P., Gales, M.J., Sim, K.C.: Stimulated deep neural network for speech recognition. In: Proceedings of Interspeech, pp. 400–404 (2016)
33. Yang, J., Zhang, C., Ragni, A., Gales, M.J., Woodland, P.C.: System combination with log-linear models. In: ICASSP, pp. 5675–5679. IEEE (2016)
34. Zhang, L., Karakos, D., Hartmann, W., Hsiao, R., Schwartz, R., Tsakalidis, S.: Enhancing low resource keyword spotting with automatically retrieved web documents. In: Interspeech (2015)

Big Data, Deep Learning – At the Edge of X-Ray Speaker Analysis

Björn W. Schuller[1,2,3](✉)

[1] Department of Computing, Imperial College London, London SW7 2AZ, UK
bjoern.schuller@imperial.ac.uk
[2] Chair of Complex and Intelligent Systems,
University of Passau, 94032 Passau, Germany
[3] audEERING GmbH, 82205 Gilching, Germany
http://www.schuller.one

Abstract. With two years, one has roughly heard a thousand hours of speech – with ten years, around ten thousand. Similarly, an automatic speech recogniser's data hunger these days is often fed in these dimensions. In stark contrast, however, only few databases to train a speaker analysis system contain more than ten hours of speech. Yet, these systems are ideally expected to recognise the states and traits of speakers independent of the person, spoken content, language, cultural background, and acoustic disturbances at human parity or even super-human levels. While this is not reached at the time for many tasks such as speaker emotion recognition, deep learning – often described to lead to 'dramatic improvements' – in combination with sufficient learning data satisfying the 'deep data cravings' holds the promise to get us there. Luckily, every second, more than five hours of video are uploaded to the web and several hundreds of hours of audio and video communication in most languages of the world take place. If only a fraction of these data would be shared and labelled reliably, 'x-ray'-alike automatic speaker analysis could be around the corner for next gen human-computer interaction, mobile health applications, and many further benefits to society. In this light, first, a solution towards utmost efficient exploitation of the 'big' (unlabelled) data available is presented. Small-world modelling in combination with unsupervised learning help to rapidly identify potential target data of interest. Then, gamified dynamic cooperative crowdsourcing turn its labelling into an entertaining experience, while reducing the amount of required labels to a minimum by learning alongside the target task also the labellers' behaviour and reliability. Further, increasingly autonomous deep holistic end-to-end learning solutions are presented for the task at hand. Benchmarks are given from the nine research challenges co-organised by the author over the years at the annual Interspeech conference since 2009. The concluding discussion will contain some crystal ball gazing alongside practical hints not missing out on ethical aspects.

Keywords: Computational paralinguistics · Automatic speaker analysis · Big data · Deep learning

© Springer International Publishing AG 2017
A. Karpov et al. (Eds.): SPECOM 2017, LNAI 10458, pp. 20–34, 2017.
DOI: 10.1007/978-3-319-66429-3_2

1   Introduction

X-radiation – here in the sense of Röntgen radiation is composed of x-rays, which have largely become synonymous of enabling seeing usually hidden aspects via empowering technology. The field of automatic speaker analysis or 'Computational Paralinguistics' dealing with the automatic characterisation of speakers (or authors of written text) such as by assessing states and traits from the voice acoustics and textual cues of an individual is hardly connoted with such 'see-through' abilities in a figurative sense, yet. This comes, as even those tasks which are directly accessible to a human listener can still pose problems to a machine such as when aiming at recognition of human emotion. However, largely unnoticed by the broad public, computers can indeed already provide 'x-ray alike' speaker analysis empowering humans beyond their natural skill-set in terms of listening such as when automatically estimating height or weight of a speaker [3,33] down to a few centimetres or kilograms of error, despite such tasks clearly being challenging [21] also for humans [52].

To be fair, however, humans have an impressive amount of data available to learn on speech and speaker characteristics contained in the signal – simply, as they are constantly exposed to it. Likewise, at the age of just two years, we roughly heard already as much as some thousand hours of speech. At the age of ten years, this has already increased to around ten thousand hours of speech heard [29]. Obviously, these do not come with 'labels' – rather, we learn reinforced and from the situational context on 'recognising', understanding, and analysing the speaker characteristics as conveyed in the speech signal. At the same time, we synthesise speech and learn also from coupling analysis and synthesis efforts.

In terms of sheer amount of data, an automatic speech recogniser's data hunger is these days often fed in similar dimensions. And in fact, also speech recognition engines increasingly learn in weakly supervised ways, exploiting also unlabelled speech data to go from some one or two thousand hours of training material to the order of tens of thousands [53].

This is in stark contrast to the situation in Computational Paralinguistics. There, only few databases allow to train a speaker analysis system based on more than ten hours of speech – ten hours of speech vs several thousand. Yet, expectations are high as to what these systems ideally should be able to recognise: The tasks are often ambiguous such as automatic recognition of emotion or likability or the perceived personality of a speaker – all subjective and therefore ambiguous tasks. At the same time, recognition should be reliable independent of the person, i. e., work also for unknown speakers. Then, such automatic assessment of speaker characteristics should also work independent of the spoken content and by that ideally also independent of the spoken language, i. e., as for the acoustic analysis, there should be no requirement for prompted speech. A potentially even higher depending on the type of information that shall be extracted from spoken language is the desired indifference to varying cultural backgrounds. Then, acoustic disturbances including severe cases such as multiple speakers speaking overlapping should not be in the way of reliable assessment – best at human parity or even super-human levels such as when attempting automatic recognition of heart-beat down to a few beats of error [19], or recognition of diverse health conditions which at best a trained human could hear from the voice, or even earlier on in terms of age of the affected individual than a human could [32].

Likewise, having only a few hours of learning material at hand, it is not surprising that some automatic recognition tasks have not yet reached or surpassed human parity – an example being the above named emotion recognition from voice acoustics [40,57]. However, the recent advances in processing power, and machine learning methods – most notably deep learning which is often described to lead to 'dramatic improvements' [10] – in combination with sufficient amounts of learning data that can satisfy the 'deep data cravings' [6] that come with deep neural network approaches hold the promise to reach the point of super-human level on most or even all Computational Paralinguistics tasks likely already in the near future.

As to the amount of data available, luckily, every second, more than five hours of video are uploaded to the web. YouTube alone reached 70 million hours of video material by March 2015[1]. This is added by several hundreds of hours of audio and video communication in most languages of the world taking place. If only a fraction of these data would be shared and labelled reliably, 'x-ray'-alike automatic speaker analysis could be around the corner for next gen human-computer interaction, mobile health applications, and many further benefits to society.

In this context, the remainder of this paper is laid out as follows: first, a solution towards utmost efficient exploitation of the 'big' (unlabelled) data available is presented in Sect. 2. Small-world modelling in combination with unsupervised learning help to rapidly identify potential target data of interest. Then, gamified dynamic cooperative crowdsourcing aim at turning its labelling into an entertaining experience, while reducing the amount of required labels to a minimum by learning alongside the target task also the labellers' behaviour and reliability. Subsequently, Sect. 3 introduces increasingly autonomous deep holistic end-to-end learning solutions for the rich speaker analysis. Demonstrating the performance of today's engines, benchmarks are then given in Sect. 4. These stem from the nine research challenges dealing with Computational Paralinguistics held over the years at Interspeech. The concluding discussion will contain some crystal ball gazing alongside practical hints not missing out on ethical aspects.

2   Big Data, Little Labels – Efficiency Matters

While it was outlined above that there is sufficient data for most tasks of interest in Computational Paralinguistics owing to the rich amounts of videos available on social media, it is mostly the labels that lack. Certainly, some tasks of speaker analysis will be hard to find on social media or in conversations of millions of users, such as those dealing with rare diseases or disorders. For others, it may be hard to obtain a 'ground truth' such as accurate height of speakers, accurate heart rate of speakers, etc., from social media and human labelling alone.

---

[1] https://www.youtube.com/yt/press/de/statistics.html – accessed 1 June 2017.

However, for practically any task dealing with perceived speaker characteristics and some more, exploiting the data in combination with efficient human labelling mechanisms seems a promising avenue. For the remaining tasks, purely semi-supervised or unsupervised learning approaches may still benefit from sheer endless amounts of speech available [36]. In the ongoing, different ways of reaching utmost efficiency in exploiting big speech data are laid out.

2.1 Network Analysis for Pre-selection of Social Media Data

It seems obvious that labelling social multimedia needs some efficient pre-selection on 'where to start' looking at, e. g., the above named more than 70 million hours of video material available on YouTube alone. At the age of 80, we roughly lived 700 000 hours, i. e., around 1 % of the available video time on YouTube in March 2015. Entering a search term such as 'joy' in a social multimedia platform is unfortunately insufficient to quickly lead to a selection of suited videos (or directly audio streams such as by services as SoundCloud) containing joyful speech, as the retrieved videos may deal with anything related to joy such as movies, songs, etc. that somehow related to joy. This makes it evident that some smart pre-filtering is needed. Such smart pre-filtering could be realised by a 'complex network analysis' to quickly retrieve related videos from social multimedia platforms. Such platforms usually have their own suggestion on the next best related videos to watch, which could be exploited to identify next best options for more data. Unfortunately, the algorithms behind these recommendations are usually unknown, but they are mostly based on the title and description as well as more general (textual) meta-data as well as 'social' data including the viewing statistics including demographic aspects, number of likes/dislikes given by viewers, and related search queries of the users [7]. In particular, the social aspects can be unrelated or even counter-productive if establishing a database for machine learning, as they will likely lead to a biased set of data. Based on existing recommendations, one can aim to reach more suited candidates of videos by providing one's own network analysis to identify relevant videos for database establishment. This can, for example, be based on the assumption of high similarity of videos. An option is then to use interconnections of videos as generated by the social media platform's recommendations such as by small-world models and graph-based analysis finding cliques in the graph. Ideally, some content-based verification check is additionally implemented verifying coarsely that the found videos at least likely contain the desired speech samples. This can contain a speech activity detection engine or even some comparison against an initial or several initial exemplary audio streams.

2.2 Game's On! – Making Crowdsourcing Fun – Seriously

Whether freshly recorded or retrieved from social media, the speech and audio or language data next has to be annotated. Crowdsourcing can be a highly efficient way to label data, but it has also been questioned in terms of ethical aspects [1]. Such concerns touch upon whether the crowd workers are potentially exploited [11], or "ethical norms of privacy" could be violated – potentially even knowingly by the crowd workers [18]. In addition, unreliable raters can be a severe problem adding noise to the labels [48]. In rather subjective tasks such as observed emotion or perceived personality, it can be particularly difficult to estimate the reliability of raters. Likewise, motivating the crowd worker seems an interesting option for example by gamification of the labour to turn it into fun aiming at lowering the risks of exploitation and unreliable labelling [30]. This may include social elements such as competing against other crowd workers on a leaderboard or in one vs one challenges, a point system and 'badges' or levels such as 'master rater', 'grand master', etc. An exemplary existing platform in the field is given by the iHEARu-PLAY platform [16]. More interestingly, crowd workers could experience how their work empowers Artificial Intelligence by having a gamified crowd-sourcing platform train models exclusively from their labels (or by improving existing systems with their labels) and have these compete against other crowd-workers' engines trained on their respective labels. In automatic speaker analysis, this would mean training engines based on different crowd-workers' labels and having them compete, e. g., on well-defined test-beds such as the challenges introduced in Sect. 4.

2.3   Cooperative Learning: The Matrix Needs Us

Aiming to reduce human labelling effort has long since led to the idea of self-learning by machines such as by unsupervised, semi-supervised, or reinforcement learning. This could be shown successful in Computational Paralinguistics tasks starting with the recognition of emotion [64] or the confidence estimation in emotion recognition results [9] exploiting unlabelled data and even earlier on in textual cues' exploitation [14] in sentiment analysis. Purely self-learning hardly seems unsuited, as the risk to run into stagnation of improvement despite adding exponentially more unlabelled data can be high. Furthermore, models could of course also become corrupted by purely semi-supervised learning, if no proper control mechanisms of model performance are in place to monitor the development of the models when adding increasingly more machine-labelled data for model training. Thus, even when aiming at 'never-ending learning' [27], it seems wise to keep the human in the loop by combining semi-supervised learning with active learning – an idea which has been considered early on in general machine learning [66], but only more recently in Computational Paralinguistics [63]. Likewise, rather than to harvest energy from us human beings – a sinister view on future Artificial Intelligence (AI) exploiting mankind taken in Hollywood's "The Matrix" trilogy at the last turn of millennium – AI will indeed profit from human labels.

Active learning, i. e., pre-selecting most informative instances for labelling by humans, has thereby mostly been shown to work well in simulations with 'oracle' labels. This means, experiments were carried out on fully labelled databases blinding part of the labels and revealing them only if the data has been selected for active learning. This may be overly optimistic, as the data likewise has been labelled under comparably controlled conditions, i. e., by the same individuals on a small dataset in a short time window. However, recently it has been shown that the idea also works well in a crowdsourcing framework for Computational Paralinguistics tasks [17]. In future solutions, learning the labellers, i. e., 'being careful whom to trust when' [48] can play an increasingly important role when it comes to crowdsourcing-based annotation in an active learning manner [58]. This can also help increase efficiency when learning profiles of cross-labeller reliability to get to know optimal patterns of which combination of crowd-workers best to ask to reduce labelling efforts required.

3 Deep Learning, Broad Tasks – Holism Matters

A state-of-the-art (group of) approach(es) to best exploit 'big' data is given by the family of deep learning algorithms that provide a sufficient number of free parameters to be learnt to model complex arbitrary functions for classification or regression of highly non-linear problems [6] in efficient ways. Further, going 'broad' in the sense of widening up of the speaker characteristics targeted – ideally in full parallel – becomes possible with sufficient data. Below, it is argued that this will be beneficial even if interested in only one aspect of the speaker to reduce confusion with effects that other characteristics of the speaker may have on speech acoustics or the choice of words.

3.1 Deep Learning in Computational Paralinguistics

Deep learning has a long tradition in the field of Computational Paralinguistics: the first paper using long-short term memory (LSTM) recurrent neural networks (RNNs) for speech emotion recognition dates back some almost ten years [54], the first to use a deep architecture based on restricted Boltzmann machines – again for speech emotion recognition – appeared some three years later [45]. More recently appeared first works on convolutional neural networks (CNNs) for – speech emotion recognition [26]. However, only last year, the first true end-to-end Computational Paralinguistics system using convolutional layers ahead of LSTM layers [50] appeared. Also there, the task was emotion recognition from speech, making emotion recognition the pioneering task when it comes to deep learning in Computational Paralinguistics. This seems to hold also for one of the latest trends in deep learning – the use of generative adversarial networks [4].

In fact, largely independent of this development in deep learning exploiting acoustic information in Computational Paralinguistics, deep learning is increasingly used in the analysis of textual cues.

LSTM RNNs are for example used in sentiment analysis from textual cues [38,65]. Alternatively, gated recurrent units have been considered to the same task in [47].

CNNs are for example applied for personality analysis [25,35], computation of sentiment [35,46,65], and emotion features [35], or dialect and variety recognition [15].

Adversarial network inspirations can be found on sentiment tasks as well in [22,28].

3.2   Learning End-to-End

The learning of feature representations from the data seems attractive in a field that has been coined by huge efforts put into the design of acoustic features over the years. Indeed, as outlined above, last year first efforts in doing so were successfully reported [50]. In the work, the authors train an emotion recogniser to learn directly from the raw audio signal waveform. Furthermore, via correlation analysis, they show that the network seems to learn features that relate to the 'traditional' ones extracted by experts such as functionals of the fundamental frequency or energy contours. In [39], this is broadened up to three more paralinguistic tasks providing a benchmark of a challenge event by end-to-end learning among other ways of establishing a benchmark. While the approach is not always superior to traditional methods in these works, it shows that indeed, meaningful feature representations can be learnt from the data. One can assume that given the above named small size of corpora is the major bottleneck when it comes to reaching much more competitive results.

3.3   Borrowing Pre-trained Models from Computer Vision

This bottleneck of little data for pre-training is yet overcome in computer vision, where large pre-trained netowrks such as AlexNet [20] or VGG19 [43] exist. In [2], these are for the first time exploited for Computational Paralinguistics showing the power of the approach on the Interspeech 2017 Computational Paralinguistic Challenge's [39] snoring sub-challenge: image classification CNN descriptors are extracted from audio spectrograms called "deep spectrum features" in the paper. They are extracted by forwarding the audio spectrograms through the very deep task-independent pre-trained CNNs named previously to build up feature vectors. In this first paper, the authors evaluate the use of different spectrogram colour maps and different CNN topologies. They beat the conventionally established baseline in the challenge by a large margin, which the authors can further increase by suited feature selection by competitive swarm optimisation in [13], rendering this approach highly promising and likely supporting the claim that it is mostly about the amounts of data needed to fully exploit deep learning in Computational Paralinguistics.

3.4   Going Broad – Holistic Speaker Analysis

As the characteristics of a speaker are usually 'all present' or 'all on' more or less at the same time, it appears crucial to address them in parallel rather than one by one in isolation ignorant to potential other ones. This seems relevant even if one is only interested in one speaker characteristic, e. g., emotion of the speaker, to avoid confusion by interfering other speaker states or traits such as being tired, intoxicated by alcohol, being under a certain cognitive load, or simply with one's personality type. There are only a few approaches, yet, considering this mutual dependency of speaker characteristics, mostly based on multi-task learning with neural networks. Examples in acoustic speech information exploitation include simultaneous assessment of age, gender, height, and race recognition [41], age, height, weight, and smoking habits recognition at the same time [34], emotion, likability, and personality assessment in one pass [62], commonly targeting deception and sincerity [60] or drowsiness and alcohol intoxication [61] in the recognition, as well as assessment of several emotion dimensions or representations in parallel [12,55,56,59], and aiming at speaker verification [5] co-learning other aspects.

Similar approaches can be found in text-based information exploitation [22].

4   Where Are We on Automatic Speaker Analysis?

The above sections laid out options for future improvement of Computational Paralinguistics, mainly by collection of more data and training deeper and 'broader' models to best exploit these data. But what are current performances? To provide an impression of what today's speaker analysis systems can reach in a nutshell, Table 1 shows the baseline results of the Interspeech challenges centred on Computational Paralinguistics. Since 2013, these are running under the unified name of Interspeech Computational Paralinguistics Challenge or INTERSPEECH COMPARE for short. Previous events were the 2009 Emotion Challenge, the 2010 Paralinguistic Challenge, and the 2011 and 2012 Speaker State and Speaker Trait Challenges[2].

In these challenges, weight is put on realism in the sense of assessing the speaker from a short snippet of audio only (usually around one to a few seconds), independent of the speaker, in mostly real-world conditions such as telephone or broadcast speech. Different measures were used over the different tasks in the 'sub-challenges' per year respecting the different type of representation or task such as classification, regression, or detection. Explanations on these are given in the caption.

The baselines have been established under somewhat similar conditions over the years based on the openSMILE toolkit[3] for large-scale acoustic feature space brute forcing with standardised feature sets (which, however, grew over the years from 384 features (2009) over 1 582 (2010), 3 996 (2011), 6 125 (2012), to 6 373 (since 2013) features on 'functional' level – partially, however, also directly (lower numbers of) low-level-descriptors on frame level were used), and WEKA[4] (mostly using Support Vector Machines). In 2017, openXBOW[5] and end-to-end learning based on TensorFlow[6], were used in addition in a fusion of methods.

From the table, one can mainly see two things: an astonishing range of speaker characteristics can be automatically extracted significantly above chance level –

---

[2] See http://compare.openaudio.eu/ for details on these events.
[3] http://audeering.com/technology/opensmile/.
[4] http://www.cs.waikato.ac.nz/ml/weka/.
[5] http://github.com/openXBOW/openXBOW/.
[6] http://www.tensorflow.org/.

Table 1. Interspeech Computational Paralinguistics Challange series (ComParE) baseline results over the years following similar brute-force open-source focussed computation by openSMILE and WEKA (in 2017, openXBOW and end-to-end deep learning have been used in addition) as seen in the challenge by sub-challenge. Given are the year the challenge was held, the name of the sub-challenge usually clearly representing the task targeted ("Pathology", however, deals with intelligibility of head and neck cancer patients before and after chemo-radiation treatment), the modelling (column "Model") of the task either naming the number of distinct classes to recognise, or the interval (marked by $[\cdots]$) in case of a regression task, or "x" in case several (classification) tasks had to be addressed, and the baseline results (column "Base"). Different evaluation measures were used for competition depending on the type of task and modelling of it as *classification* (result given in terms of percentage of unweighted accuracy (% UA), i.e., added recall per class divided by the number of classes to cope with imbalance across classes in the sense of chance-normalisation), *regression* (shown is the correlation coefficient (CC (2010)/ρ (else)) – marked by $^+$) or *detection* task (given is the percentage of unweighted average area under the curve (% UAAUC) – marked by *)

Year	Sub-challenge	Model	Base
2017	Addressee	2	70.2
	Cold	2	71.0
	Snoring	4	58.5
2016	Deception	2	68.3
	Sincerity	[0,1]	.602$^+$
	Native Language	11	47.5
2015	Degree of Nativeness	[0,1]	.425$^+$
	Parkinson's Condition	[0,100]	.390$^+$
	Eating Condition	7	65.9
2014	Cognitive Load	3	61.6
	Physical Load	2	71.9
2013	Social Signals	2×2	83.3*
	Conflict	2	80.8
	Emotion	12	40.9
	Autism	4	67.1
2012	Personality	5×2	68.3
	Likability	2	59.0
	Pathology	2	68.9
2011	Intoxication	2	65.9
	Sleepiness	2	70.3
2010	Age	4	48.91
	Gender	3	81.21
	Interest	[−1,1]	.421$^+$
2009	Emotion	5	38.2
		2	67.7

sometimes already at super-human level such as in the case of intoxication or some pathologies –, yet leaving head room for improvement for several others if not all.

Note that in this series, both, acoustic and textual cues can mostly be exploited unless – in rare cases – the data of a sub-challenge features prompted speech. However, other challenges exist focussing on textual cues such as the annual author profiling task at PAN within the CLEF framework (cf. e. g., [37] for the latest edition), or the affective text [44], sentiment analysis [31], and other tasks in SemEval.

5   Conclusions and Perspectives

Concluding this contribution, a short summary is given followed by some perspectives.

5.1   Conclusions

Current-state performances based on the Interspeech challenge series on Computational Paralinguistics over nine years have been shown that demonstrated the richness of speaker characteristics that can be automatically accessed already by today. At the same time, these results showed the room left over for future improvements. To address this issue, an argument was made to go 'broader' in automatic speaker analysis in terms of assessment of multiple characteristics of a speaker in full parallel to avoid confusion due to co-influence of these. Further, deep learning has been named as current promising solution for modelling in terms of machine learning. As particular advantage, this allows the learning of the feature representation directly from the data – an interesting and valuable aspect in a field that is ever-since marked by major efforts going into the design of optimal feature representations. As such going 'deep and broad' requires 'big' training data, avenues towards efficient exploitation of 'big' social multimedia data in combination with gamified crowd-sourcing were shown. These included efficiency-optimising measures by smart pre-selection of instances and combined active and semi-supervised learning mechanisms to avoid human involvement in labelling as much as possible. Alternatively, exploitation of pre-trained networks on 'big' image data was named to analyse speech data based on image-related representations such as spectograms or scalograms and alike in potential future efforts. However, for some under-resourced special types of data, such as of vulnerable parts of the population [24], 'conventional' collection of data will still be required.

5.2   Some Crystal-Ball Gazing

Putting the above together in a 'life-long learning' [42] Computational Paralinguistics system supported by the crowd during 24/7 learning efforts based on big social media and contributed data, we may soon witness passing the 'edge' of 'x-ray speaker analysis', i. e., soon see super-human level automatic speaker analysis for an astonishingly broad range of speaker characteristics.

Further supporting approaches not mentioned here include transfer learning [23], reinforcement learning [49], and tighter coupling of generative and discriminative approaches [51] or synthesis and analysis of speaker states and traits, to name but three of the most promising aspects.

Once reaching such abilities, ethical, legal, and societal implications (ELSI) will play an important role [8] if such technology is increasingly used in human-decision support such as in automatic job interviews, tele-diagnosis in health care, or monitoring of customers, and employees, to name again but three use-cases. It will be of crucial importance to invest efforts into privacy protection, reliable and meaningful automatic confidence measure provision to explain the certainty and trust one should have in the automatic assessments, and account-able communication of the 'possible' to the general public such as in down-toning trust in deception recognition, if it only works at – say – some 70 % accuracy as shown in the table above. This will require organisation of future challenges in the research community as well as ensuring widest possible spread of the word.

May we soon experience powerful and reliable automatic speaker analysis and Computational Paralinguistics applied in the best possible ways only to benefit society at large in everyday problem solving and increase of wellbeing.

Acknowledgment. The author acknowledges funding from the European Research Council within the European Union's 7th Framework Programme under grant agreement no. 338164 (Starting Grant Intelligent systems' Holistic Evolving Analysis of Real-life Universal speaker characteristics (iHEARu)) and the European Union's Horizon 2020 Framework Programme under grant agreement no. 645378 (Research Innovation Action Artificial Retrieval of Information Assistants - Virtual Agents with Linguistic Understanding, Social skills, and Personalised Aspects (ARIA-VALUSPA)). The responsobility lies with the author. The author would further like to thank his team colleague Anton Batliner at University of Passau/Germany as well as Stefan Steidl at FAU Erlangen/Germany and all other co-organisers and participants over the years for running the Interspeech Computational Paralinguistics related challenge events and turning them into a meaningful benchmark.

References

1. Adda, G., Besacier, L., Couillault, A., Fort, K., Mariani, J., De Mazancourt, H.: "Where the data are coming from?" ethics, crowdsourcing and traceability for big data in human language technology. In: Proceedings Crowdsourcing and Human Computation Multidisciplinary Workshop, Paris, France (2014)
2. Amiriparian, S., Gerczuk, M., Ottl, S., Cummins, N., Freitag, M., Pugachevskiy, S., Schuller, B.: Snore sound classification using image-based deep spectrum features. In: Proceedings INTERSPEECH, 5 p. ISCA, Stockholm (2017)
3. Arsikere, H., Lulich, S.M., Alwan, A.: Estimating speaker height and subglottal resonances using mfccs and gmms. IEEE Signal Process. Lett. **21**(2), 159–162 (2014)

4. Chang, J., Scherer, S.: Learning representations of emotional speech with deep convolutional generative adversarial networks. arXiv preprint (2017). arXiv:1705.02394
5. Chen, N., Qian, Y., Yu, K.: Multi-task learning for text-dependent speaker verification. In: Proceedings INTERSPEECH, 5 p. ISCA, Dresden, Germany (2015)
6. Chen, X.W., Lin, X.: Big data deep learning: challenges and perspectives. IEEE Access **2**, 514–525 (2014)
7. Covington, P., Adams, J., Sargin, E.: Deep neural networks for youtube recommendations. In: Proceedings 10th ACM Conference on Recommender Systems (RecSys), pp. 191–198. ACM, Boston (2016)
8. Davis, K.: Ethics of Big Data: Balancing risk and innovation. O'Reilly Media Inc., Newton (2012)
9. Deng, J., Schuller, B.: Confidence measures in speech emotion recognition based on semi-supervised learning. In: Proceedings of INTERSPEECH, 5 p. ISCA, Portland (2012)
10. Deng, L., Li, J., Huang, J.T., Yao, K., Yu, D., Seide, F., Seltzer, M., Zweig, G., He, X., Williams, J., et al.: Recent advances in deep learning for speech research at microsoft. In: Proceedings ICASSP, pp. 8604–8608. IEEE, Vancouver (2013)
11. Deng, X.N., Joshi, K.: Is crowdsourcing a source of worker empowerment or exploitation? understanding crowd workers perceptions of crowdsourcing career (2013)
12. Eyben, F., Wöllmer, M., Schuller, B.: A Multi-task approach to continuous five-dimensional affect sensing in natural speech. ACM Trans. Interact. Intell. Syst. Spec. Issue Affect. Interact. Nat. Environ. **2**(1), 6 (2012)
13. Freitag, M., Amiriparian, S., Cummins, N., Gerczuk, M., Schuller, B.: An 'end-to-evolution' hybrid approach for snore sound classification. In: Proceedings INTERSPEECH, 5 p. ISCA, Stockholm (2017)
14. Goldberg, A.B., Zhu, X.: Seeing stars when there aren't many stars: graph-based semi-supervised learning for sentiment categorization. In: Proceedings 1st Workshop on Graph Based Methods for Natural Language Processing, pp. 45–52. ACL, Stroudsburg (2006)
15. Guggilla, C.: Discrimination between similar languages, varieties and dialects using cnn-and lstm-based deep neural networks. VarDial **3**, 185 (2016)
16. Hantke, S., Eyben, F., Appel, T., Schuller, B.: ihearu-play: Introducing a game for crowdsourced data collection for affective computing. In: Proceedings 6th biannual Conference on Affective Computing and Intelligent Interaction (ACII), pp. 891–897. aaac/IEEE, Xi'An (2015)
17. Hantke, S., Zhang, Z., Schuller, B.: Towards intelligent crowdsourcing for audio data annotation: integrating active learning in the real world. In: Proceedings INTERSPEECH, 5 p. ISCA, Stockholm, Sweden (2017)
18. Harris, C.G., Srinivasan, P.: Crowdsourcing and ethics. In: Altshuler, Y., Elovici, Y., Cremers, A.B., Aharony, N., Pentland, A. (eds.) Security and Privacy in Social Networks, pp. 67–83. Springer, Heidelberg (2013)
19. Kranjec, J., Beguš, S., Geršak, G., Drnovšek, J.: Non-contact heart rate and heart rate variability measurements: a review. Biomed. Signal Process. Control **13**, 102–112 (2014)
20. Krizhevsky, A., Sutskever, I., Hinton, G.E.: Imagenet classification with deep convolutional neural networks. In: Advances in neural information processing systems, pp. 1097–1105 (2012)
21. Künzel, H.J.: How well does average fundamental frequency correlate with speaker height and weight? Phonetica **46**(1–3), 117–125 (1989)

22. Liu, P., Qiu, X., Huang, X.: Adversarial multi-task learning for text classification. arXiv preprint (2017). arXiv:1704.05742
23. Lu, J., Behbood, V., Hao, P., Zuo, H., Xue, S., Zhang, G.: Transfer learning using computational intelligence: a survey. Knowl. Based Syst. **80**, 14–23 (2015)
24. Lyakso, E., Frolova, O., Dmitrieva, E., Grigorev, A., Kaya, H., Salah, A.A., Karpov, A.: EmoChildRu: emotional child russian speech corpus. In: Ronzhin, A., Potapova, R., Fakotakis, N. (eds.) SPECOM 2015. LNCS, vol. 9319, pp. 144–152. Springer, Cham (2015). doi:10.1007/978-3-319-23132-7_18
25. Majumder, N., Poria, S., Gelbukh, A., Cambria, E.: Deep learning-based document modeling for personality detection from text. IEEE Intell. Syst. **32**(2), 74–79 (2017)
26. Mao, Q., Dong, M., Huang, Z., Zhan, Y.: Learning salient features for speech emotion recognition using convolutional neural networks. IEEE Trans. Multimedia **16**(8), 2203–2213 (2014)
27. Mitchell, T.M., Cohen, W., Hruschka, E., Talukdar, P., Betteridge, J., Carlson, A., Mishra, B.D., Gardner, M., Kisiel, B., Krishnamurthy, J., et al.: Never-ending learning. In: Proceedings 29th AAAI Conference on Artificial Intelligence. AAAI, Austin (2015)
28. Miyato, T., Dai, A.M., Goodfellow, I.: Virtual adversarial training for semi-supervised text classification. Stat **1050**, 25 (2016)
29. Moore, R.K.: A comparison of the data requirements of automatic speech recognition systems and human listeners. In: Proceedings INTERSPEECH, pp. 2582–2584, Geneva, Switzerland (2003)
30. Morschheuser, B., Hamari, J., Koivisto, J.: Gamification in crowdsourcing: A review. In: Proceedings 49th Hawaii International Conference on System Sciences (HICSS). pp. 4375–4384. IEEE (2016)
31. Nakov, P., Ritter, A., Rosenthal, S., Sebastiani, F., Stoyanov, V.: Semeval-2016 task 4: sentiment analysis in twitter. In: Proceedings International Workshop on Semantic Evaluations (SemEval), pp. 1–18 (2016)
32. Pokorny, F., Schuller, B., Marschik, P., Brückner, R., Nyström, P., Cummins, N., Bölte, S., Einspieler, C., Falck-Ytter, T.: Earlier identification of children with autism spectrum disorder: an automatic vocalisation-based approach. In: Proceedings INTERSPEECH, 5 p. ISCA, Stockholm (2017)
33. Poorjam, A.H., Bahari, M.H., Vasilakakis, V., et al.: Height estimation from speech signals using i-vectors and least-squares support vector regression. In: Proceedings 38th International Conference on Telecommunications and Signal Processing (TSP), pp. 1–5. IEEE, Prague (2015)
34. Poorjam, A.H., Bahari, M.H., et al.: Multitask speaker profiling for estimating age, height, weight and smoking habits from spontaneous telephone speech signals. In: Proceedings 4th International eConference on Computer and Knowledge Engineering (ICCKE). pp. 7–12. IEEE, Mashhad (2014)
35. Poria, S., Cambria, E., Hazarika, D., Vij, P.: A deeper look into sarcastic tweets using deep convolutional neural networks. arXiv preprint (2016). arXiv:1610.08815
36. Raina, R., Battle, A., Lee, H., Packer, B., Ng, A.Y.: Self-taught learning: transfer learning from unlabeled data. In: Proceedings 24th International Conference on Machine learning. pp. 759–766. ACM, Corvallis, OR (2007)
37. Rangel, F., Rosso, P., Verhoeven, B., Daelemans, W., Potthast, M., Stein, B.: Overview of the 4th author profiling task at pan 2016: cross-genre evaluations. Working Notes Papers of the CLEF (2016)
38. Schuller, B., Mousa, A.E.D., Vryniotis, V.: Sentiment analysis and opinion mining: on optimal parameters and performances. Wiley Interdisc. Rev. Data Min. Knowl. Disc. **5**(5), 255–263 (2015)

39. Schuller, B., Steidl, S., Batliner, A., Bergelson, E., Krajewski, J., Janott, C., Amatuni, A., Casillas, M., Seidl, A., Soderstrom, M., Warlaumont, A., Hidalgo, G., Schnieder, S., Heiser, C., Hohenhorst, W., Herzog, M., Schmitt, M., Qian, K., Zhang, Y., Trigeorgis, G., Tzirakis, P., Zafeiriou, S.: The INTERSPEECH 2017 computational paralinguistics challenge: addressee, Cold and Snoring.. In: Proceedings INTERSPEECH, 5 p. ISCA, Stockholm (2017)
40. Schuller, B., Vlasenko, B., Eyben, F., Wollmer, M., Stuhlsatz, A., Wendemuth, A., Rigoll, G.: Cross-corpus acoustic emotion recognition: variances and strategies. IEEE Trans. Affect. Comput. 1(2), 119–131 (2010)
41. Schuller, B., Wöllmer, M., Eyben, F., Rigoll, G., Arsić, D.: Semantic speech tagging: towards combined analysis of speaker traits. In: Proceedings AES 42nd International Conference, pp. 89–97. AES, Ilmenau (2011)
42. Silver, D.L., Yang, Q., Li, L.: Lifelong machine learning systems: Beyond learning algorithms. In: Proceedings AAAI spring symposium series. AAAI, Palo Alto (2013)
43. Simonyan, K., Zisserman, A.: Very deep convolutional networks for large-scale image recognition. arXiv preprint (2014). arXiv:1409.1556
44. Strapparava, C., Mihalcea, R.: Semeval-2007 task 14: Affective text. In: Proceedings 4th International Workshop on Semantic Evaluations (SemEval), pp. 70–74. ACL, Swarthmore (2007)
45. Stuhlsatz, A., Meyer, C., Eyben, F., Zielke, T., Meier, G., Schuller, B.: Deep neural networks for acoustic emotion recognition: raising the benchmarks. In: Proceedings ICASSP, pp. 5688–5691. IEEE, Prague (2011)
46. Sun, X., Gao, F., Li, C., Ren, F.: Chinese microblog sentiment classification based on convolution neural network with content extension method. In: Proceedings 6th Biannual Conference on Affective Computing and Intelligent Interaction (ACII), pp. 408–414. aaac/IEEE, Xi'an (2015)
47. Tang, D., Qin, B., Liu, T.: Document modeling with gated recurrent neural network for sentiment classification. In: Proceedings Conference on Empirical Methods in Natural Language Processing (EMNLP). pp. 1422–1432. ACL, Lisbon, Portugal (2015)
48. Tarasov, A., Delany, S.J., Mac Namee, B.: Dynamic estimation of worker reliability in crowdsourcing for regression tasks: making it work. Expert Syst. Appl. 41(14), 6190–6210 (2014)
49. Taylor, M.E., Stone, P.: Transfer learning for reinforcement learning domains: a survey. J. Mach. Learn. Res. 10, 1633–1685 (2009)
50. Trigeorgis, G., Ringeval, F., Brückner, R., Marchi, E., Nicolaou, M., Schuller, B., Zafeiriou, S.: Adieu features? end-to-end speech emotion recognition using a deep convolutional recurrent network. In: Proceedings ICASSP, pp. 5200–5204. IEEE, Shanghai (2016)
51. Tzeng, E., Hoffman, J., Saenko, K., Darrell, T.: Adversarial discriminative domain adaptation (workshop extended abstract) (2017)
52. Van Dommelen, W.A., Moxness, B.H.: Acoustic parameters in speaker height and weight identification: sex-specific behaviour. Lang. Speech 38(3), 267–287 (1995)
53. Walker, S., Pedersen, M., Orife, I., Flaks, J.: Semi-supervised model training for unbounded conversational speech recognition. arXiv preprint (2017). arXiv:1705.09724
54. Wöllmer, M., Eyben, F., Reiter, S., Schuller, B., Cox, C., Douglas-Cowie, E., Cowie, R.: Abandoning emotion classes - towards continuous emotion recognition with modelling of long-range dependencies. In: Proceedings INTERSPEECH, pp. 597–600. ISCA, Brisbane (2008)

55. Xia, R., Liu, Y.: Leveraging valence and activation information via multi-task learning for categorical emotion recognition. In: Proceedings ICASSP, pp. 5301–5305. IEEE, Brisbane (2015)
56. Zhang, B., Provost, E.M., Essi, G.: Cross-corpus acoustic emotion recognition from singing and speaking: a multi-task learning approach. In: Proceedings ICASSP, pp. 5805–5809. IEEE, Shanghai (2016)
57. Zhang, B., Provost, E.M., Essl, G.: Cross-corpus acoustic emotion recognition with multi-task learning: seeking common ground while preserving differences. IEEE Trans. Affect. Comput. (2017)
58. Zhang, Y., Coutinho, E., Zhang, Z., Adam, M., Schuller, B.: On rater reliability and agreement based dynamic active learning. In: Proceedings 6th Biannual Conference on Affective Computing and Intelligent Interaction (ACII), pp. 70–76. aaac/IEEE, Xi'an (2015)
59. Zhang, Y., Liu, Y., Weninger, F., Schuller, B.: Multi-task deep neural network with shared hidden layers: breaking down the wall between emotion representations. In: Proceedings ICASSP, pp. 4990–4994. IEEE, New Orleans (2017)
60. Zhang, Y., Weninger, F., Ren, Z., Schuller, B.: Sincerity and deception in speech: two sides of the same coin? a transfer- and multi-task learning perspective. In: Proceedings INTERSPEECH, pp. 2041–2045. ISCA, San Francisco (2016)
61. Zhang, Y., Weninger, F., Schuller, B.: Cross-domain classification of drowsiness in speech: the case of alcohol intoxication and sleep deprivation. In: Proceedings INTERSPEECH, 5 p. ISCA, Stockholm (2017)
62. Zhang, Y., Zhou, Y., Shen, J., Schuller, B.: Semi-autonomous data enrichment based on cross-task labelling of missing targets for holistic speech analysis. In: Proceedings ICASSP, pp. 6090–6094. IEEE, Shanghai (2016)
63. Zhang, Z., Coutinho, E., Deng, J., Schuller, B.: Cooperative learning and its application to emotion recognition from speech. IEEE/ACM Trans. Audio Speech Lang. Process. 23(1), 115–126 (2015)
64. Zhang, Z., Weninger, F., Wöllmer, M., Schuller, B.: Unsupervised learning in cross-corpus acoustic emotion recognition. In: Proceedings ASRU, pp. 523–528. IEEE, Big Island (2011)
65. Zhou, C., Sun, C., Liu, Z., Lau, F.: A c-lstm neural network for text classification. arXiv preprint (2015). arXiv:1511.08630
66. Zhu, X., Lafferty, J., Ghahramani, Z.: Combining active learning and semi-supervised learning using gaussian fields and harmonic functions. In: Proceedings ICML 2003 Workshop on the Continuum From Labeled to Unlabeled Data in Machine Learning and Data Mining, vol. 3, Washington, DC (2003)

Conference Papers

Conference Papers

A Comparison of Covariance Matrix and i-vector Based Speaker Recognition

Nikša Jakovljević$^{(\boxtimes)}$, Ivan Jokić, Slobodan Jošić, and Vlado Delić

Faculty of Technical Sciences, University of Novi Sad, Novi Sad, Serbia
{jakovnik,ivan.jokic,slobodan.josic,vdelic}@uns.ac.rs

Abstract. The paper presents results of an evaluation of covariance matrix and i-vector based speaker identification methods on Serbian S70W100s120 database. Open set speaker identification evaluation scheme was adopted. The number of target speakers and the number of impostors were 20 and 60 respectively. Additional utterances from 41 speakers were used for training. Amount of data for modeling a target speaker was limited to about 4 s of speech. In this study, the i-vector base approach showed significantly better performance (equal error rate EER ~5%) than the covariance matrix based approach (EER ~16%). This small EER for the i-vector based approach was obtained after substantial reduction of the number of the parameters in universal background model, i-vector transformation matrix and Gaussian probabilistic linear discriminant analysis that is typically reported in the papers. Additionally, these experiments showed that cepstral mean and variance normalization can deteriorate EER in case of a single channel.

Keywords: Speaker identification · i-vector · G-PLDA · Covariance matrix · S70W100s120

1 Introduction

Automatic speaker identification (ASI) is a task to discover a speaker identity from its voice. It provides medium accuracy comparing to other biometrics [1], but it has a few advantages that allow its widespread usage. The first one is the fact that speech is a natural gesture and user acceptance is high. The hardware costs are low and in many cases microphone and sound-card are built-in devices. Finally, there is no physical contact to record the biometric sample and the rate of failure to enroll is low [1].

To compare different automatic speaker recognition systems National Institute of Standards and Technology (NIST) has organized their evaluations every 2 years since 1996. In each evaluation the task was different, and with years it became more complicated and closer to the real conditions [2]. The systems showed high performance (equal error rate EER is below 2% [3]) since they were trained on a lot of data in conditions close to the evaluation data. It is interesting to test behaviors of these well-proven systems when little training and development data is available in new unknown conditions (language, speaking style, etc.) [2]. An evaluation on database containing different acoustic conditions was organized by Speech Technology and Research Laboratory (SRI). The best system has achieved EER close to 6% [4].

© Springer International Publishing AG 2017
A. Karpov et al. (Eds.): SPECOM 2017, LNAI 10458, pp. 37–45, 2017.
DOI: 10.1007/978-3-319-66429-3_3

The aim of this study is to evaluate one of the well-performed systems in NIST challenges [5] in case of limited training dataset (total duration of speech is about 36 min) and to compare it with the algorithm that was developed at the University of Novi Sad [6]. In the last decade systems based on i-vectors extracted from mel-frequency cepstral coefficients (MFCCs) or perceptual linear prediction (PLP) or bottle neck (BN) features in combination with linear discriminant analysis (LDA) or near discriminant analysis (NDA) and probabilistic linear discriminant analysis (PLDA) [3, 7–10]. Deep neural networks did not take into consideration since the amount of training data was insufficient for good parameter estimation.

Detailed descriptions of analyzed methods are presented in Sect. 2. Information about used corpus is given in Sect. 3, and appropriate evaluation results of examined systems are shown in Sect. 4. The conclusion contains the most prominent remarks, and directions for the future research.

2 Algorithms

2.1 Covariance Matrix Based Speaker Identification

This approach is relative simple and computationally efficient. Each target speaker is modeled by the covariance matrix of MFCCs estimated on its training data [6]. For an unknown (test) utterance the same covariance matrix is estimated and normalized l_1 distances between it and covariance matrices of target speakers are calculated. If the smallest distance between covariance matrices is less than a given threshold, algorithm assigns the utterance to the closest target speaker, otherwise it assigns to an imposter.

The first step is MFCCs extraction on short overlapped windowed segments of the speech signal. During the extraction, the spectrum of a signal is divided into N_b overlapped bands being equally spaced in mel scale. The shape of the band pass filters being used in this spectrum division is piece-wise exponential, defined by following equation:

$$A_n(k) = \begin{cases} e^{a(k-k_{c,n})}, & k_{l,n} \leq k \leq k_{c,n}, \\ e^{-a(k-k_{c,n})}, & k_{c,n} < k \leq k_{u,n}, \end{cases} \tag{1}$$

where: $k_{l,n}$ and $k_{u,n}$ are lower and upper cutoff frequencies of n-th filter, $k_{c,n} = 0.5 (k_{l,n} + k_{u,n})$, a is steepness factor, and k is discrete frequency [11]. In [6] is reported that the system used this shape of band-pass filters showed better recognition accuracy than the system used typical triangular shaped filters.

MFCC are determined by

$$c_m = \sum_{n=1}^{N_b} \log(E_n) \cdot \cos\left[m \cdot \left(n - \frac{1}{2}\right)\right], \quad m = 1, 2, \ldots, M, \tag{2}$$

where: E_n is energy in the n-th band, and M is the number of cepstral coefficients.

A speaker is modeled by its covariance matrix which is defined as:

$$\Sigma_s = \frac{1}{T-1}\sum_{t=1}^{T}(\mathbf{c}_{s,t} - \boldsymbol{\mu}_s)(\mathbf{c}_{s,t} - \boldsymbol{\mu}_s)^T, \tag{3}$$

where: $\mathbf{c}_{s,t}$ is t-th feature vectors belonging to the speaker s, T is the total number of the feature vectors for the speaker s and:

$$\boldsymbol{\mu}_s = \frac{1}{T}\sum_{t=1}^{T}\mathbf{c}_{s,t}, \tag{4}$$

For a test utterance covariance matrix Σ_{test} is calculated using (3) and (4) where $\mathbf{c}_{s,t}$ represents speech feature vectors in the test utterance. The distance between a target speaker s and test utterance is calculated by:

$$d(\text{test}, s) = \frac{1}{M^2}\sum_{i=1}^{M}\sum_{j=1}^{M}|\Sigma_{\text{test},i,j} - \Sigma_{s,i,j}|, \tag{5}$$

If the smallest distance $d(\text{test},s)$ over all target speakers is less than the given threshold algorithm assigns the test utterance to the closest target speaker, otherwise it assigns to an imposter.

2.2 i-vector Based Speaker Identification

The-state-of-the-art approach in speaker identification is i-vectors [12]. In this approach, high-dimensional feature vector in Gaussian mixture model (GMM) space is reduced to low-dimensional feature space preserving most of relevant information for speaker recognition. The extraction of relevant information is based on joint factor analysis [13].

The first step is extraction of MFCCs from an utterance. Usually, the silent segments are rejected from further processing, and cepstral mean and variance normalization (CMVN) are applied to remove convolutional distortions caused by channel.

The MFCCs (with their first and second time derivatives) are aligned with components of GMM of the universal background model (UBM) to form a super-vector $\mathbf{f}_s = [\mathbf{f}_s^{(1)T}, \mathbf{f}_s^{(2)T}, \ldots, \mathbf{f}_s^{(C)T}]^T$ using following equation:

$$\mathbf{f}_s^{(c)} = \left(\boldsymbol{\Sigma}^{(c)}\right)^{-1}\sum_{t=1}^{T}\gamma_t^{(c)}(\mathbf{c}_t - \boldsymbol{\mu}^{(c)}), \quad c = 1, 2, \ldots, C, \tag{6}$$

where: $\mathbf{c}_t$ is the feature vector at time t, $\gamma_t^{(c)}$ is occupation probability that feature vector $\mathbf{c}_t$ belongs to the c-th Gaussian component described by mean $\boldsymbol{\mu}^{(c)}$ and covariance $\boldsymbol{\Sigma}^{(c)}$, and C is the number of the components in the GMM of UBM.

The i-vector for given feature sequence can be obtained using following equation:

$$\mathbf{w} = \left(\mathbf{I}_{L \times L} + \sum_{c=1}^{C} N^{(c)} \mathbf{T}^{(c)T} \left(\mathbf{\Sigma}^{(c)}\right)^{-1} \mathbf{T}^{(c)}\right)^{-1} \mathbf{T}^{T} \mathbf{f}_{s}, \qquad (7)$$

where: $\mathbf{T} = [\mathbf{T}^{(1)T}, \mathbf{T}^{(2)T}, \ldots, \mathbf{T}^{(C)T}]^{T}$ is a low-rank matrix representing L bases that span subspace with important variability in super-vector space, and

$$N^{(c)} = \sum_{t=1}^{T} \gamma_{t}^{(c)}, \quad c = 1, 2, \ldots, C, \qquad (8)$$

Additionally, LDA can be applied to remove correlations between features in the i-vector $\mathbf{w}$ [5, 12], and Gaussian probabilistic linear discriminant analysis (G-PLDA) [10] to eliminate variations caused by channel.

In this paper two type of scores were evaluated. The first type of score was defined for G-PLDA as following:

$$SCR_1 = \mathbf{v}_{test}^{T} \mathbf{Q} \mathbf{v}_{test} + \mathbf{v}_{s}^{T} \mathbf{Q} \mathbf{v}_{s} + 2\mathbf{v}_{test}^{T} \mathbf{P} \mathbf{v}_{s}, \qquad (9)$$

with

$$\mathbf{Q} = \mathbf{\Sigma}_{tot}^{-1} - \left(\mathbf{\Sigma}_{tot} - \mathbf{\Sigma}_{ac} \mathbf{\Sigma}_{tot}^{-1} \mathbf{\Sigma}_{ac}\right)^{-1}, \qquad (10)$$

$$\mathbf{P} = \mathbf{\Sigma}_{tot}^{-1} \mathbf{\Sigma}_{ac} \left(\mathbf{\Sigma}_{tot} - \mathbf{\Sigma}_{ac} \mathbf{\Sigma}_{tot}^{-1} \mathbf{\Sigma}_{ac}\right)^{-1}, \qquad (11)$$

$$\mathbf{\Sigma}_{tot} = \mathbf{\Phi} \mathbf{\Phi}^{T} + \mathbf{\Sigma}_{\varepsilon}, \qquad (12)$$

$$\mathbf{\Sigma}_{ac} = \mathbf{\Phi} \mathbf{\Phi}^{T}, \qquad (13)$$

where: $\mathbf{v}_{test}$ and $\mathbf{v}_{s}$ are zero centered i-vectors after LDA transformation for test sequence and a target speaker s respectively, $\mathbf{\Phi}$ is a low-rank matrix representing J bases that spans speaker-specific subspace, and $\mathbf{\Sigma}_{\varepsilon}$ is covariance describing residual term in modified G-PLDA model [10]. Typically, the J is the same as the dimension of input vector $\mathbf{v}$.

The second type of score was defined as cosine distance [5] between i-vectors transformed by LDA i.e.:

$$SCR_2 = \frac{\mathbf{v}_{test}^{T} \mathbf{v}_{s}}{\|\mathbf{v}_{test}\| \|\mathbf{v}_{s}\|}, \qquad (14)$$

We used MSR Identity toolbox [14] in combination with voicebox speech processing toolbox [15] as a starting point in the experiments with i-vectors.

3 Speech Database

This study is based on the S70W100s120 full-spectrum speech database recorded in the studio conditions [16]. It contains utterances spoken by 121 Serbian native speakers with total duration of about 110 min of speech (without pauses). Each speaker spoken his/her name, 60 words related to military terminology (e.g.: group, understand, direction, reception, weather etc.) and 10 digits. The database is relatively small and to reduce variability in performance estimation 3 different partitions were used for training and evaluation. In each of these partitions, 20 speakers (10 male and 10 female) were randomly chosen to be target speakers and 60 to be impostors. To train the model of a target speaker about 4.5 s of speech were used. The word sequence used for training of a target speaker model was the same for all target speakers. Utterances of the imposters were used only in the test phase. Total duration of the test set in each partition was about 64 min (13 utterances per target speaker and 14 utterances per impostor). The word content in the 13 test utterances for target speakers and impostors were the same, and impostors had additional utterance containing words that were used in training of target speaker models. To increase the number of training samples for estimation of the parameters of universal background model and i-vector transformations, utterances of 41 speakers were used as additional data. The total duration of the training set in each partition was about 36 min.

4 Results

An exhaustive research of the method based on covariance matrix is presented in [6]. In this study, only the parameters of the model that showed the highest accuracy (about 93.4%) in [6] were examined. Extraction of MFCCs was done every 10 ms on 25 ms frame using Hamming window. During the extraction, the spectrum was divided into $N = 20$ bands. Bands were 300 mel wide, and adjacent bands were overlapped by 150 mel. Bandpass filters used for spectrum division were piece-wise exponential with a steepest factor $a = 2$. The number of MFCCs was 18. It should be noted that in this evaluation, the test set was open (it included the impostors), and to model target speakers only single utterance (about 4.5 s of speech) were used. The equal error rate (EER) of this speaker recognition system in this study was 16.0%, which represents serious degradation comparing to the results presented in [6]. It can be explained by difficulty of the problem presented here – lack of training data and open test set.

As a starting point for experiments with i-vector we used parameters proposed in [5]. Initial feature vectors were 19 MFCCs, log energy and their delta and delta-delta features. Features vectors were extracted every 10 ms on the 25 ms frame using full spectrum (up to 11025 Hz) divided into 57 mel equidistant and overlapped bands. To calculate delta and delta-delta features 5 frame long window were used. To extract only speech frames Sohn [17] voice activity detector was used. CMVN were used only on the speech frames as it was suggested in [5]. The number of the components in UBM in [5] was 2048 and the volume of the training set was about 300 h. In this study, the volume of the training set was significantly smaller (36 min), thus the number of the components was significantly lower. The number of the components of UBM (C) were varied from 16 up to 512, and the dimension of i-vector (L) varied from 100 to 400. Dimension of the vector after LDA and G-PLDA (J) was 40 or 60, since the number of different speakers (classes) in our train set was 61.

The obtained EERs for different parameters were presented in Fig. 1 (variation in L and J are coded by different colors). One can see that the best results (EER about 11%) were obtained for C equal to 32 or 64, L equal to 100 and J equal to 40. This can be explained by significantly smaller training set than in [5] and insufficient amount of data for robust parameter estimation. The obtained results with number of parameters close to those in [5] shows higher EER than covariance based algorithm (EER over 22% compared to 16%). However, reduction of the number of parameters leads to decrease of EER below 16%.

All records in our database were done with the same equipment, thus the channel effects are the same in all utterances. To explore the effects of CMVN, previous tests were repeated without CMVN. The obtained results are presented in Fig. 2 (the labels are the same as in Fig. 1). Elimination of CMVN resulted in significant decrease of EER for each configuration. As in the previous case, when the number of the parameters is close to those described in [5] EER is greater than EER of covariance based system, but the difference is not so significant. If the number of parameters is significantly lower, than the smallest EER is between 6 and 7%. It should be noted that the smallest EER was obtained for the same configuration as in the previous case.

Experiments with models based on covariance matrix presented in [6] showed that static MFCCs are sufficient for speaker recognition. This was a motivation for the third set of experiments, where feature vectors contained only 18 and 19 MFCCs (without

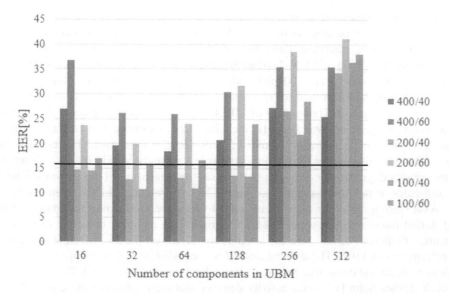

Fig. 1. EERs of different systems based on i-vectors. Input features are 19 MFCC, log energy, and theirs first and second time derivatives which are normalized by CMVN. Dimensions of an i-vector (L) and a vector after LDA and PLDA (J) are coded by colors (L/J). Horizontal black line represents EER level for covariance matrix based approach

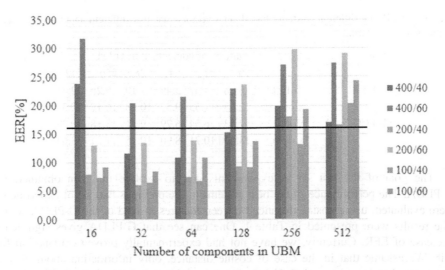

Fig. 2. EERs of different systems based on i-vectors but input features are not normalized by CMVN. Input features are 19 MFCC, log energy, and theirs first and second time derivatives. Dimensions of an i-vector (*L*) and a vector after LDA and PLDA (*J*) are coded by colors (*L/J*). Horizontal black line represents EER level for covariance matrix based approach

energy). Dimensions of i-vector and its transformed version (*L* and *J*) were fixed to 100 and 40 respectively. These values were chosen, since in the previous two experiments they gave the smallest EER. The obtained EERs are presented in Fig. 3 along with the EERs for the best systems in the second set of experiments, for an easier comparison. One can see that in i-vector approach static features are sufficient for speaker recognition. The additional decrease of EER in this case can be explained by robust feature extraction in reduced feature space.

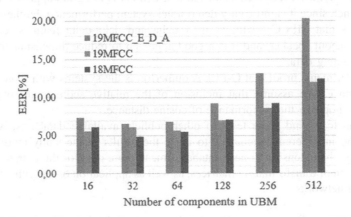

Fig. 3. EERs of different systems based on i-vectors where the input features are 19 MFCC, log energy, and theirs first and second time derivatives, only 19 MFCC and 18 MFCC. In the all cases CMVN is not applied

Table 1. EERs of different systems based on i-vectors that use different input features and different score criteria

Feature	Score	Number of component in UBM					
		16	32	64	128	256	512
18 MFCC	G-PLDA	6.08	4.87	5.49	7.10	9.26	12.41
	Cosine	12.73	11.55	9.57	10.88	10.17	10.31
19MFCC_E_D_A	G-PLDA	7.33	6.54	6.79	9.21	13.18	20.29
	Cosine	13.43	10.71	8.90	10.25	11.21	13.63

The goal of the last set of experiments was to explore the gain obtained by G-PLDA. The performance of the best systems in the previous two set of experiments were evaluated, using cosine distance between features instead of the G-PLDA score. The results were presented in Table 1. One can see that G-PLDA gives significant decrease of EER. Currently, we have not had experimentally proved explanation for this. We assume that in the case of cosine distance, only information about closest target speaker is used, and G-PLDA score exploits information about other target speakers indirectly through Φ and Σ_ε matrices.

5   Conclusions and Further Research

In this paper, we presented results of speaker recognition in case of small amount of training data (about 4 s to train model, and 36 min to estimate parameters of UBM, i-vector transformation matrix, LDA and G-PLDA). We have shown that the number of parameters being typical in NIST challenges is high and these models have modest accuracy (their EERs are greater than the EER of the simpler one system based on covariance matrix). Reduction of the number of parameters of i-vectors decrease EERs, and these i-vector based systems outperform the system based on covariance matrix.

Additionally, the experiments showed that CMVN is not good approach in case of single channel, since it significantly deteriorates system performance. Furthermore, this study shows that MFCCs (without their delta and delta-delta features) contain all information about speaker, and it is a good approach to reduce dimensionality in case of scarce training data.

The experiments proof that G-PLDA outperforms the systems with score based on cosine distance. We assume that inclusion of the relative score to the other target speaker can improve the performance of cosine distance.

We plan to extend these tests to other publicly available databases, with more speakers and in different languages, to make the results of the study more relevant. Additionally, the extension to new databases mean more data for the training of UBM and estimation of transformation matrices, as well as application of algorithms based on deep neural networks.

Acknowledgments. This research work has been supported by the Ministry of Education, Science and Technological Development of the Republic of Serbia, and it has been realized as a part of the research project TR 32035 and EUREKA project DANSPLAT (project ID 9944).

References

1. Hennerbert, J.: Speaker recognition, overview. In: Encyclopedia of Biometrics. Springer Science + Business Media, New York (2009)
2. Gonzalez-Rodriguez, J.: Evaluating automatic speaker recognition systems: an overview of the NIST speaker recognition evaluations (1996–2014). Loquens 1(1), e007 (2014)
3. Kohler, T.: The 2010 NIST Speaker Recognition Evaluation. http://archive.signalprocessing society.org/technical-committees/list/sl-tc/spl-nl/2010-07/NIST-SRE/. Accessed Mar 2017
4. McLaren, M., Ferrer, L., Castán, D., Lawson, A.: The 2016 speakers in the wild speaker recognition evaluation. In: INTERSPEECH 2016, San Francisco, CA, USA, pp. 823–827 (2016)
5. Matejka, P., Glembek, O., Castalado, F., Alam, M.J., Plchot, O., Kenny, P., Burget, L., Černocky, J.: Full-covariance UBM and heavy-tailed PLDA in i-vector speaker verification. In: ICASSP 2011, Prague, Czech Republic, pp. 4828–4831 (2011)
6. Jokić, I., Delić, V., Jokić, S., Perić, Z.: Automatic speaker recognition dependency on both the shape of auditory critical bands and speaker discriminative MFCCs. Adv. Electr. Comput. Eng. 15(4), 25–32 (2015)
7. Novotny, O., Matejka, P., Plchot, O., Glembek, O., Burget, L., Černocky, J.: Analysis of speaker recognition systems in realistic scenarios of the SITW 2016 challenge. In: INTERSPEECH 2016, San Francisco, CA, USA, pp. 828–832 (2016)
8. Sadjadi, S., Ganapathy, S., Pelecanos, J.: The IBM speaker recognition system: recent advances and error analysis. In: INTERSPEECH 2016, San Francisco, CA, USA, pp. 3633–3637 (2016)
9. Hasan, T., Liu, G., Sadjadi, S.O., Shokouhi, N., Boril, H., Ziaei, A., Misra, A., Godin, K.W., Hansen, J.: UTD-CRSS systems for 2012 NIST speaker recognition evaluation. In: ICASSP 2013, Vancouver, BC, Canada, pp. 6783–6787 (2013)
10. Garcia-Romero, D., Espy-Wilson, C: Analysis of i-vector length normalization in speaker recognition systems. In: INTERSPEECH 2011, Florence, Italy, pp. 249–252 (2011)
11. Wildermoth, B.: Text-Independent Speaker Recognition Using Source Based Features. Master thesis, Griffith University, Australia (2001)
12. Gelembek, O., Burget, L., Matejka, P., Karafiat, M., Kenny, P.: Simplification and optimization of i-vector extraction. In: ICASSP 2011, Prague, Czech Republic, pp. 4516–4519 (2011)
13. Kenny, P.: Joint factor analysis of speaker and session variability: Theory and algorithms. Technical report CRIM-06/08-13, CRIM, Montreal (2005)
14. Sadjadi, S., Slaney, M., Heck, L.: MSR Identity Toolbox: A MATLAB Toolbox for Speaker Recognition Research. Technical report, Microsoft Research, Conversational Systems Research Center (2013)
15. Brookes, M.: VOICEBOX. http://www.ee.ic.ac.uk/hp/staff/dmb/voicebox/voicebox.html
16. Delić, V., Sečujski, M., Jakovljević, N., Pekar, D., Mišković, D., Popović, B., Ostrogonac, S., Bojanić, M., Knežević, D.: Speech and language resources within speech recognition and synthesis systems for Serbian and Kindred South Slavic Languages. In: Železný, M., Habernal, I., Ronzhin, A. (eds.) SPECOM 2013. LNCS, vol. 8113, pp. 319–326. Springer, Cham (2013). doi:10.1007/978-3-319-01931-4_42

A Trainable Method for the Phonetic Similarity Search in German Proper Names

Oliver Jokisch[1(✉)] and Horst-Udo Hain[2]

[1] Leipzig University of Telecommunications (HfTL), Leipzig, Germany
jokisch@hft-leipzig.de
[2] GWT-TUD GmbH, Dresden, Germany
udo.hain@bluesilisk.de

Abstract. Efficient methods for the similarity search in word databases play a significant role in various applications such as the robust search or indexing of names and addresses, spell-checking algorithms or the monitoring of trademark rights. The underlying distance measures are associated with similarity criteria of the users, and phonetic-based search algorithms are well-established since decades. Nonetheless, rule-based phonetic algorithms exhibit some weak points, e.g. their strong language dependency, the search overhead by tolerance or the risk of missing valid matches vice versa, which causes a pseudo-phonetic functionality in some cases. In contrast, we suggest a novel, adaptive method for similarity search in words, which is based on a trainable grapheme-to-phoneme (G2P) converter that generates most likely and widely correct pronunciations. Only as a second step, the similarity search in the phonemic reference data is performed by involving a conventional string metric such as the Levenshtein distance (LD). The G2P algorithm achieves a string accuracy of up to 99.5% in a German pronunciation lexicon and can be trained for different languages or specific domains such as proper names. The similarity tolerance can be easily adjusted by parameters like the admissible number or likability of pronunciation variants as well as by the phonemic or graphemic LD. As a proof of concept, we compare the G2P-based search method on a German surname database and a telephone book including first name, surname and street name to similarity matches by the conventional Cologne phonetic (Kölner Phonetik, KP) algorithm.

Keywords: Phonetic similarity search · Trainable G2P · Levenshtein distance

1 Introduction and Previous Studies

Similarity search is a well-established discipline in information retrieval, including phonetic or pseudo-phonetic similarity search in name databases [6]. The practical use of rule-based methods such as Soundex [9], its derivatives or similar methods like Cologne phonetics [15] e.g. in the Automated Information Process

© Springer International Publishing AG 2017
A. Karpov et al. (Eds.): SPECOM 2017, LNAI 10458, pp. 46–55, 2017.
DOI: 10.1007/978-3-319-66429-3_4

(Automatisiertes Auskunftsverfahren, AAV) [16,17] between German authorities and telecommunication providers poses some challenges – the similarity search is highly language and domain dependent, does not necessarily match the subjective distance metric of professional users and involves false-positive and false-negative matches, i.e. overhead or lack of relevant data. As an example within a matching list of German surnames, "Meier", "Maier" and "Meyer" would be relevant (true-positives), whereas "Müller" is a false-positive. Vice versa, in a rejection list, "Maler" would be a true-negative, "Mayer" a false-negative, and the categorization of the surname "Mai" is depending on the users' metric.

Beside phonetic techniques, further approaches for similarity search can be used, such as regular expressions or distance measures between letter sequences. A collection of algorithms can be found in different projects, e.g. Stringmetric [8], clj-fuzzy [14] or Talisman [20]. Qualitative aspects of such methods are recently discussed in comparative studies, e.g. for Slavic languages or Hindi [10,18,19], but only a few studies deal with the quantitative comparison and appropriateness of the distance metric [11,24]. In [11], a small test set of 25 words showed success rates of 0.88 for Soundex and 0.72 for Metaphone [12]. Sophisticated experiments on five methods in a large database [24] resulted in precisions (level of usability) from 0.36 (Soundex-6) to 0.47 (MidEPhone-6) and in recalls (level of completeness) from 0.56 (Soundex-6) to 0.81 (MidEPhone-6), underlining the mentioned challenges. Additionally, widely rule-based similarity search paradigms contrast the success of learning methods in language and speech processing. In [3], Double Metaphone [13] was used for pre-processing in a speech recognizer, demonstrating the potential of phonetic similarity indexing in trainable systems.

Addressing the precision problem, we propose a novel method starting with a more adequate grapheme-to-phoneme (G2P) conversion known from speech synthesis. Although G2P algorithms were also rule-based initially, meanwhile trainable, e.g. neural network-based algorithms as in [5] have been established. To enable variance in the search strings and to achieve necessary recall rates, we then suggest an edit-distance measure such as the Levenshtein one [7] in a second stage. Section 2 presents the databases, phonetic algorithms, distance measures and our experimental setup. In Sect. 3, we summarize and discuss the experimental results, followed by the conclusion and outlook in Sect. 4.

2   Methods

2.1   Data

For legal and commercial reasons, we could not use real-world data e.g. from telecommunication providers and thus analyzed following accessible databases:

- Pronunciation lexicon CELEX-2 [1] with 51,728 German lemmas and 365,530 inflected forms as a phonetic reference and to train the G2P algorithm,
- Family names from a Web collection of 69,170 death certificates (in German "Totenzettel", TZ) [22] for a variance analysis in proper names,

- Subsets of the telephone book 2016–2017 (TB) [21] from the four German municipalities Hesseneck, Breisach, Spremberg and Berlin-Neukölln with minimal 194 and a maximum of 8,042 entries including regional and loanword peculiarities for proper name statistics.

The name databases TZ and TB do not include any phonetic transcription for analysis, training or testing of similarity search. To avoid both, inaccurate automatic or elaborate manual annotations within the reported survey, the standard pronunciation lexicon CELEX-2 for German is used, which is also available in other major languages, facilitating a multilingual transfer of our findings. The TB subsets are random in the following intention:

- Hesseneck, smallest municipality in Hessen as a village in German's center,
- Breisach, city in the border area with France including French names,
- Spremberg, Sorbian settlement close to Poland with Slavic loanwords,
- Berlin-Neukölln, multicultural neighborhood e.g. including Turkish names.

2.2   Search Principle and Algorithms

Cologne Phonetics (in German Kölner Phonetik, KP) was suggested by Postel [15] to index phonetically similar words during the search in German personal data. KP works alike Soundex, whereby the graphemes are coded into digits from 0 to 8 with regard to their context. The maximal context is 1 (neighbored letter). Contrary to Soundex, the KP code does not have a limited length. Repeated symbols (code digits) and vowels (code 0) are deleted in a second step. With regard to minor shortcomings in the original version and existing implementations, we use a slightly modified version of KP, shown in Table 1.

Considering the 23 rules, the calculation effort is low but the indexing involves a weak causality which comes along with a significant overhead of potential similarity matches like in Soundex. The KP code for the example name "Müller-Lüdenscheidt" results to: 60550750206880022 → 6050750206802 → 65752682.

Trainable Grapheme-to-Phoneme Converter. In text-to-speech synthesis, training-based algorithms for grapheme-to-phoneme (G2P) conversion such as [4,5] are meanwhile well-studied, and they are simplifying the adaptation to new languages or application domains. Subsequently, we intend to use G2P in the optimization of phonetic similarity search and indexing. G2P algorithms are aiming at the generation of the most likely phoneme sequence for a given grapheme (letter) sequence including additional information (language, lexicon, syllable limiters, real-world knowledge), usually based on the Speech Assessment Methods Phonetic Alphabet (SAMPA) or its derivatives [23]. Many languages like German involve a mapping from m letters to n phonemes, i.e. there is no 1:1 mapping, cf. the German words "Schutz" → [S U ts] versus "Axt" → [a ks t].

In this study, we use the trainable Sequitur G2P system from Bisani and Ney 2008 [2]. With appropriate training data – usually a few 10,000 phonetically annotated lexicon entries – a high transcription quality with word error rates

Table 1. Kölner Phonetik (KP) – slightly modified version, based on [15]

Grapheme	Context	Code
A, E, I, J, O, U, Y		0
H	without context (isolated word "'H"')	
	any context (non-empty)	–
B		1
P	not before H	
D, T	not before C, S, Z	2
F, V, W		3
P	before H	
G, K, Q		
C	in initial sound before A, H, K, L, O, Q, R, U, X	4
	before A, H, K, O, Q, U, X except after S, Z	
X	not after C, K, Q	48
L		5
M, N		6
R		7
S, Z		
C	after S, Z	8
	in initial sound, except before A, H, K, L, O, Q, R, U, X	
	not before A, H, K, O, Q, U, Y	
D, T	before C, S, Z	
X	after C, K, Q	

(WER) of less than 1% can be achieved. We trainined the Sequitur G2P with the pronunciation lexicon CELEX2 and reached an acceptable WER <0.5% in the test probe, which enables an alternative baseline technology for a really sound-related indexing versus *pseudo-phonetic* methods like Soundex or KP. The challenges in this approach are posed by:

- Coding errors in proper names with deviation from standard pronunciation (e.g. by cross-lingual effects),
- Obtaining the appropriate amount of training data for a new application domain or language including manual corrections,
- The higher calculation complexity in both, training and working phases, compared to rule-based methods like Soundex or KP.

Table 2 demonstrates typical G2P transcription examples extended by the English name "Britney Spears" for comparison and sorted by their probabilities P that serve as our confidence measure for the concerning phoneme sequence. The obviously optimal transcription results are marked green.

For the names "Meier" and "Maier" only a single SAMPA result is generated [m aI 6], also reflected by the high confidence (probability $P_{0,meier}$=0.9987 and $P_{0,maier}$=0.9587 respectively). Regarding "Mayer" the phonetically preferred variant [m aI 6] ranks only at 2, but [m aI @ r] at rank 1 and the following variants are also acceptable. The name "Meyer" leads to 25 transcription proposals. The best variant also reaches rank 1 but with a low probability of $P_{0,meyer}$ = 0.1381. This result corresponds with the fact that the regarding grapheme sequence "Meyer" is rather untypical in standard German and not part of the training data. Although the English name "Britney Spears" was not included in the training data, our trained G2P converter produces logical output with regard to German rules such as [b r I t n aI] or [b r I t n i:] as well as [S p e: a: r s].

Table 2. Selected G2P results including the probability of the variants

Name	Variant	Probability	G2P result
Meier	1	0.9987	m aI 6
Maier	1	0.9587	m aI 6
Mayer	1	0.4502	m aI @ r
	2	0.3560	m aI 6
	3	0.0422	m aI e: r
Meyer	1	0.1381	m aI 6
	2	0.1157	m i: 6
	..	..	..
	25	0.0065	m E Y e: r
Britney	1	0.2783	b r I t n aI
	2	0.2331	b r I t n i:
	3	0.0731	b r I t n e: Y
Spears	1	0.9384	S p e: a: r s

Levenshtein Distance. The names "Meier" and "Maier" have an identical KP code of 67. The most probable G2P result [m aI 6] is identical too, which leads to a similarity decision in both pathways. In contrast, "Mayer" and "Neuer" (also generating KP codes of 67) result in the different phoneme sequences [m aI @ r] (most probable G2P result) and [n OY 6]. In this example, KP is covering three name variants correctly. The match "Neuer" can be considered as false-positive in the similarity search. G2P works phonetically correct and does not generate this overhead but finds only the first two variants. Thus it requires a certain tolerance scheme by an appropriate distance metric to ignore slight variations in the phoneme string if necessary (like the listeners' tolerance with regard to the speakers' pronunciation). In literature, several distance measures are proposed. For this study, we selected the robust and demonstrative Levenshtein distance (LD) [7] – the minimal number of insertions, deletions or substitutions to convert a string into another. Identical strings lead to a LD of zero. The LD can be calculated recursively, whereby u and v denominate the strings:

$$m = |u|, \; n = |v|$$
$$D_{0,0} = 0, \; D_{i,0} = i, \; D_{0,j} = j$$
$$D_{i,j} = \min \begin{cases} D_{i-1,j-1} +0 \text{ if } u_i = v_i \\ D_{i-1,j-1} +1 \text{ substitution} \\ D_{i,j-1} \quad +1 \text{ insertion} \\ D_{i-1,j} \quad +1 \text{ deletion} \end{cases}$$
$$1 \le i \le m, \; 1 \le j \le n.$$

If we accept in our previous example a Levenshtein distance $LD \le 2$ among the three phoneme strings [m aI 6], [m aI @ r] and [n OY 6], all four names "Meier", "Maier", "Mayer" und "Neuer" would be considered similar (i.e. receiving the same index), and KP and G2P-based results were identical. On graphemic string level (letter sequence) the distance measure leads to $LD = 1 \ldots 3$ however.

A combination of the described G2P algorithm from m most likely phoneme outputs with a phonemic LD of n is named G2P[m][n] method in the following e. g. G2P10, G2P11 or G2P32.

3 Experimental Results and Discussion

3.1 Case Examples from TZ Data

The rule-based KP algorithms delivers the code 04767 for the random surname "Achorner", which implies 11 matches across the 69,170 entries in the TZ database: "Achhorner", "Achrainer", "Achreiner", "Aigriner", "Eckkramer", "Hochgerner", "Hochrainer","Hochreiner", "Jackermeier", "Jägermayr" and "Jägermeier".

A subjective assessment would claim three similarity matches (27.3%, marked green) as true-positive in a narrow sense. Two further matches show an eventually acceptable similarity (18.2%), and six names (54.5%, marked red) are clearly false-positive with a significant deviation, unseen their identical KP code.

Another random, one-syllable surname "Münz" shows even 66 KP matches in TZ with an estimated false-positive overhead of 78.8%. The corresponding low precision hints at the weak causality of the KP method. In this context, the completeness of the matches (recall rate) is also questionable, but a manual recall measure over the whole TZ database would be elaborate.

3.2 Influence of Phonetic Variants and Phonemic Metric

KP and Soundex (as reference for non-appropriate German indexing) are tested versus different G2P[m][n] variants on the phonemic side. KP produces numerous matches in the TZ data with a maximum of 310 – a remarkable portion of 27.2% names has 50 or more matches, in Soundex even 35.1%. G2P31 generates far less matches (5.2% with ≥ 50 matches). The *most intolerant* G2P10 method finds no match for 88.7% of the names, which seems not functional for a typical user metric or application. The frequency distributions are reflected in Fig. 1.

3.3 Experiments on Graphemic Metric

Beside phonemic measures, the similarity metric can be also considered on the side of the letter sequence (grapheme string). The G2P10 variant *without phonemic tolerance* ($LD = 0$) creates a maximal graphemic LD of 5 over all matches in the TZ data, e.g. between the matching names "Cox" and "Koksch". G2P11 allows graphemic distances up to 6 like in "Berthel" versus "Schärtel", while KP matches reach a maximal distance of 12 as in "Einzinger" versus "Handschuhmacher" with almost no similarity. Figure 2 illustrates the absolute frequency of matches over all TZ entries as a function of the graphemic Levenshtein distance and the search method. In KP and Soundex, the maximum of matches is corresponding with a graphemic $LD = 4$, while G2P31 achieves the maximum at $LD = 2$.

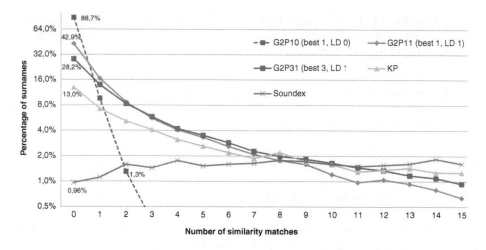

Fig. 1. Percentage of surnames in the TZ data for the selected interval 0 . . . 15 matches

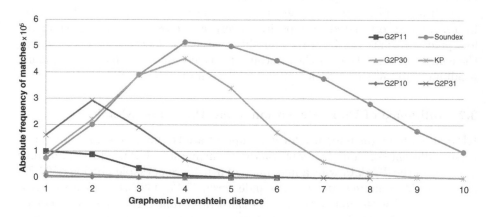

Fig. 2. Absolute frequency of matches in the TZ data as a function of the graphemic Levenshtein distance in the selected interval 1 . . . 10

Depending on users' metric and typical word lengths, we expect a distribution optimum in between ($LD = 2 \ldots 4$), which characterizes a large proportion of the KP and Soundex results as potential overhead. Both, phonemic and graphemic plots support the concept of our proposed G2P-based method with regard to a specific training and the adaptivity. For an optimization, further G2P[m][n] variants need to be analyzed, which has not been the target of the current study.

3.4   Case Examples from TB Data

Table 3 demonstrates the search of two frequent first names in the TB subset Berlin-Neukölln. For the examples "Klaus" or "Jürgen" and contrary to

Table 3. Examples of similarity search in first names of the TB subset Berlin-Neukölln

Name	Method	Precision	Matches
klaus	KP	0.500	**claus** gilles gülsah keles **klaus klaus_o**
	G2P10	1.000	**claus klaus**
	G2P11	1.000	**claus klaus klaus_o**
	G2P12	0.600	blas **claus** keles **klaus klaus_o**
jürgen	KP	0.500	ercan ercümen **jörgen jürgen**
	G2P10	1.000	**jürgen**
	G2P11	1.000	**jörgen jürgen**
	G2P12	1.000	**jörgen jürgen**
	G2P13	0.095	carmen eugen gorden gülten gürkan gürsel hagen jochen julien **jörgen** jörn **jürgen** karen maren ..

the G2P1[0..2] variants, the KP method delivers confusions with other foreign (e.g. Turkish) names. G2P13 also creates matching overhead, although some variants appear plausible, such as "Gürkan" versus "Jürgen". Table 4 presents two

Table 4. Examples of similarity search in surnames of the TB subset Spremberg

Name	Method	Precision	Matches
nowotnik	KP	1.000	**nowothnick nowotnig nowotnik**
	G2P10	1.000	**nowothnick nowotnik**
	G2P11	1.000	**nowothnick nowotnig nowotnik**
	G2P12	0.600	nothnick nothnik **nowothnick nowotnig nowotnik**
	G2P13	0.571	**nowotnick** nothnick nothnik **nowothnick nowotnig nowotnik** sarodnik
noack	KP	0.143	maak macha mank manka manke mikucki moch mock mucha mönnig mücke **noack nohke** nuck
	G2P10	1.000	**noack**
	G2P11	1.000	**noack noatschk**
	G2P12	0.222	back bork flack koal koall koark koßack nath **noack noatschk** noel **nohke nowak** nowka nuck roick ..

Table 5. Street name matches by G2P12 in TB subsets (graphemic LD in parenthesis)

Street name	Matches
am werd	am wald(2), werd(3)
amselweg	angelweg(2)
an den gärten	in den gärten(1)
birkenweg	finkenweg(2), kirchenweg(3)
breisacher straße	neu-breisacher-straße(5)
buckower weg	muckrower weg(2)
burgstraße	bergstraße(1), erkstraße(3), turnstraße(2), werkstraße(3)

further examples for Slavic surnames. All methods deliver reasonable matches but the G2P-based variants outperform KP in terms of precision and recall. Beyond the true-positive matches (marked bold), further variants are plausible and can be considered also true, depending on the assumed similarity metric. Complementary, Table 5 shows some examples of matching street names in the TB subsets including the resulting graphemic LD in parenthesis.

4   Conclusions and Outlook

We achieved a comparable performance in both, unstructured surname data (TZ) and selected telephone book entries (TB). The rule-based KP method has a good benefit-cost ratio. Nevertheless, it can not be adjusted and creates more false-positive matches, i.e. overhead e.g. in loanwords. The proposed G2P-based method involves extensive training data and calculation complexity in the working phase, but the variants enable flexibility regarding a given distance metric. The completeness of the matches (recall measure) was not surveyed in this contribution.

The further research should be mainly dedicated to an objective, user-oriented or application-driven, similarity metric, which might combine amongst others phonemic, graphemic or even perceptive features, bearing in mind different e.g. weighted-distance measures.

Acknowledgements. We would like to thank Haya Hadidi and Tristan Münz from the Federal Network Agency of Germany (Bundesnetzagentur) for initiating this research and their practical hints on AAV procedures. Further thanks goes to Viktor Iaroshenko from HfT Leipzig and to Gabor Pintér from Kobe University in Japan for their project support and advice.

References

1. Baayen, R., Piepenbrock, R., Gulikers, L.: CELEX2 lexical database of German (Version 2.0). Linguistic Data Consortium Philadelphia (1995). https://catalog.ldc.upenn.edu/ldc96l14. Accessed 12 Oct 2016
2. Bisani, M., Ney, H.: Joint-sequence models for grapheme-to-phoneme conversion. Speech Commun. **50**(5), 434–451 (2008). https://www-i6.informatik.rwth-aachen.de/web/Software/g2p.html, gPL software
3. D'Haro, L.F., Banchs, R.E.: Automatic correction of ASR outputs by using machine translation. In: Interspeech 2016, San Francisco, pp. 3469–3473 (2016). http://dx.doi.org/10.21437/Interspeech.2016-299
4. Hain, H.-U.: Graphem-Phonem-Konvertierung, Patent DE 100 42 944 C2 (2003). (in German)
5. Hain, H.-U.: Phonetische Transkription für ein multilinguales Sprachsynthesesystem. PhD thesis, TU Dresden (2004). (in German)
6. Kessler, B.: Phonetic comparison algorithms. Trans. Philol. Soc. **103**(2), 243–260 (2005)
7. Levenshtein, V.I.: Binary codes capable of correcting deletions, insertions, and reversals. Dokl. Akad. Nauk SSSR **163**(4), 845–848 (1965). (in Russian)

8. Madden, R.: (2013). https://github.com/rockymadden/stringmetric/. Accessed 03 Apr 2017
9. Odell, M.K., Russell, R.C.: US patents 1 261 167 and 1 435 683 (1918, 1922). https://en.wikipedia.org/wiki/Soundex
10. Pardeshi, J.B., Nandwalkar, B.R.: Survey on rule based phonetic search for slavic surnames. J. Comput. Technol. Appl. **7**(1), 65–68 (2016)
11. Parmar, V.P., Kumbharana, C.K.: Study existing various phonetic algorithms and designing and development of a working model for the new developed algorithm and comparison by implementing it with existing algorithms. J. Comput. Appl. **98**(19), 45–49 (2014)
12. Philips, L.: Hanging on the metaphone. J. Comput. Lang. **7**(12), 39–44 (1990)
13. Philips, L.: The double metaphone search algorithm. C/C++ Users J. **18**(6), 38–43 (2000)
14. Plique, G.: (2014). http://yomguithereal.github.io/clj-fuzzy/. Accessed 03 Apr 2017
15. Postel, H.J.: Die Kölner Phonetik. Ein Verfahren zur Identifizierung von Personennamen auf der Grundlage der Gestaltanalyse. IBM-Nachrichten **19**, 925–931 (1969). (in German)
16. Interface for data exchange in automated information process according to §112 TKG between Federal Network Agency and beneficiary (SBS, in German). Version 1.0, 27 October (2015). https://www.bundesnetzagentur.de/DE/Sachgebiete/ Telekommunikation/Unternehmen_Institutionen/Anbieterpflichten/Oeffentliche Sicherheit/AutomatisiertesAuskunftsverfahren/Automatisiertesauskunftsverfahren -node.html. Accessed 10 Dec 2016
17. Interface for data exchange in automated information process according to Section 112 TKG between Federal Network Agency and obligor (SBV, in German). Version 1.1 (Draft), 04 January (2016). https://www.bundesnetzagentur.de/DE/ Sachgebiete/Telekommunikation/Unternehmen_Institutionen/Anbieterpflichten/ OeffentlicheSicherheit/AutomatisiertesAuskunftsverfahren/Automatisiertesaus kunftsverfahren-node.html. Accessed 10 Dec 2016
18. Shah, R., Singh, D.K.: Analysis and comparative study on phonetic matching techniques. Int. J. Comput. Appl. **87**(9), 14–17 (2014)
19. Shah, R., Singh, D.K.: Improvement of Soundex algorithm for Indian language based on phonetic matching. Int. J. Comput. Sci. Eng. Appl. (IJCSEA) **4**(3), 31–39 (2014)
20. http://yomguithereal.github.io/talisman/phonetics/. Accessed 03 Apr 2017
21. Das Telefonbuch Deutschland. https://www.telefoncd.de/DasTelefonbuch-CD-mit-Rueckwaertssuche.html (2016). German phone book DVD 2016–17, data status 01 September 2016
22. Supraregional collection of German family names from death certificates. Verein für Computergenealogie, Erkrath (2016). www.familienanzeigen.org/totzfanamen. php. Accessed 12 Oct 2016
23. Wells, J.: SAMPA - computer readable phonetic alphabet (1997). http://www. phon.ucl.ac.uk/home/sampa/. Accessed 10 Jan 2017
24. Zahoranský, D., Polasek, I.: Text search of surnames in some slavic and other morphologically rich languages using rule based phonetic algorithms. IEEE/ACM Trans. Audio Speech Lang. Process. **23**(3), 553–563 (2015)

Acoustic and Perceptual Correlates of Vowel Articulation in Parkinson's Disease With and Without Mild Cognitive Impairment: A Pilot Study

Michaela Strinzel[1]([envelope]), Vasilisa Verkhodanova[2], Fedor Jalvingh[3,4], Roel Jonkers[4], and Matt Coler[2]

[1] European Master in Clinical Linguistics, University of Groningen,
Groningen, The Netherlands
michaela_strinzel@yahoo.de

[2] University of Groningen, Campus Fryslân, Leeuwarden, The Netherlands
v.verkhodanova@rug.nl, m.coler@rug.nl

[3] Geriatric Clinic Vechta, St. Marienhospital - Vechta, Vechta, Germany
f.c.jalvingh@rug.nl

[4] Center for Language and Cognition, University of Groningen,
Groningen, The Netherlands
r.jonkers@rug.nl

Abstract. This pilot study investigates the added acoustic and perceptual effect of cognitive impairment on vowel articulation precision in individuals with Parkinson's Disease (PD). We compared PD patients with and without Mild Cognitive Impairments (MCI) to elderly healthy controls on various acoustic measurements of the first and second formants of the vowels /i, u, aː, ɪ, ʊ, a/, extracted from spontaneous speech recordings. In addition, 15 naïve listeners performed intelligibility ratings on segments of the spontaneous speech. Results show a centralization of vowel formant frequencies, an increased formant frequency variability and reduced intelligibility in individuals with PD compared to controls. Acoustic and perceptual effects of cognitive impairments on vowel articulation precision were only found for the male speakers.

Keywords: Parkinson's Disease · Hypokinetic dysarthria · Mild cognitive impairments · Vowel articulation · Acoustic analysis · Speech intelligibility

1 Introduction

Parkinson's Disease (PD) is a complex neurodegenerative disease that is characterized by motor impairments [1,5]. However, a growing body of research shows that non-motor symptoms are common and clinically significant features in PD as well. These non-motor symptoms include first and foremost Mild Cognitive Impairment (MCI) and dementia. Cognitive impairments are prevalent in

© Springer International Publishing AG 2017
A. Karpov et al. (Eds.): SPECOM 2017, LNAI 10458, pp. 56–64, 2017.
DOI: 10.1007/978-3-319-66429-3_5

approximately 30% of the individuals with PD [1, 12] and have been found to significantly contribute to disability and reduced quality of life in PD patients. The pattern of cognitive deteriorations in PD is heterogeneous but typically comprises memory-based impairments, executive dysfunctions, visual-spatial impairments and attentional deficits [10]. Although there is evidence indicating a positive correlation between motor and cognitive symptoms [11], to the best of our knowledge no study has yet investigated which effect (if any) cognitive impairments have on speech motor disorders in PD.

Up to 90% of the individuals with PD manifest the speech motor disorder referred to as hypokinetic dysarthria. Apart from respiratory, phonatory and prosodic abnormalities a common feature of dysarthria in PD is imprecise vowel articulation. Individuals with PD are limited in the execution of articulatory movements. Accordingly, voluntary motions of lips, jaw and tongue tend to be smaller and slower than that of healthy controls [3]. A typical consequence is articulatory "undershooting" [3], i.e. the reduced ability to achieve a certain vowel target. As a result, vowels are produced more centralized and become less distinct from each other. This contributes to reduced speech intelligibility [8]. A common method to represent this phenomenon is with the vowel space area (VSA) based on F1/F2 values of the corner vowels. However, findings on the VSA have been inconsistent. While the VSA separated dysarthric from non-pathological speech in some studies [7], it yielded no significant differences in other studies [17,20]. Ratio based vowel measurements such as the F2 ratio of the vowels /i/ and /u/ or the vowel articulation index (VAI) [14,16] have been found to be more sensitive towards speech impairments and less sensitive towards interspeaker variability than the VSA [16,18]. Apart from vowel space metrics, measurements of formant frequency overlap and a speaker's relative stability of reaching a vowel target seem to account for speech intelligibility as well [8].

Speech motor control requires more attention in individuals with PD than in healthy individuals and it is more likely to deteriorate as the complexity of a verbal task increases [4,19]. Consequently, the characteristics of dysarthria differ depending on the type of verbal task that is performed [13,15]. In particular spontaneous speech shows significantly different phonetic features compared to non-spontaneous speech in individuals with PD [6]. Presumably due to the attention devoted to cognitive and linguistic processing, the control of articulatory movements decreases during spontaneous speech. A recent study by Rusz et al. [15] suggests that spontaneous speech is preferable to other speech tasks in detecting imprecise vowel articulation in Czech speakers with PD. Since acoustic studies on articulatory performance of PD during spontaneous speech are scarce we aimed to replicate Rusz et al.'s findings for German speakers. In addition, we were interested in whether cognitive impairments would influence vowel articulation precision in PD. One of the features of cognitive impairments in PD is a reduced attention capacity. We therefore hypothesize that the control of articulatory precision during spontaneous speech is more compromised in individuals with PD and additional cognitive impairments than in individuals with PD only. We expect this pattern to be reflected by acoustic vowel measurements.

This study addresses three research questions: (1) Are the results from Rusz. et al. replicable for German, i.e. is spontaneous speech sensitive enough to acoustically detect vowel articulation imprecision in PD? (2) Which acoustic measurement is the most efficient in separating dysarthric from non-pathological speech? (3) Does MCI in PD have an additional acoustic and/or auditory perceivable effect on vowel articulation precision in spontaneous speech?

2   Methods

2.1   Participants

A total of 23 German native speakers participated in this study. The participants were split into three groups. The first group included 8 individuals who were clinically diagnosed with idiopathic PD (hereafter PD group). None of these individuals exhibited cognitive impairments as assessed with the Minimal Mental State Examination (MMSE). The second group was comprised of 6 individuals clinically diagnosed with idiopathic PD and MCI (hereafter MCI group). The third group was made up of 9 elderly healthy controls (hereafter HC group) without a history of neurological disorders. Table 1 summarizes the demographic data of each group.

All participants gave their written informed consent to the speech task and the recording procedure.

Table 1. Summary of group demographics. Age and duration of disease are given in years

		PD	MCI	HC
Male: Female		5:3	4:2	5:4
Age	M	76	81.8	74
	SD	6	2.5	5.9
Duration of disease	M	12	5.7	-
	SD	4.1	2.4	-
MMSE	M	29	24.5	29.8
	SD	1	1.9	0.4

2.2   Speech Task and Recording Procedure

Participant monologues were audio-recorded during a conversational interview with open-ended questions on a familiar topic such as hobbies, daily routines, family or prior jobs. Recordings were made with a Zoom H2 Recorder with 16-bit quantization and a sampling frequency of 44.1 kHz. The recordings were administered in an identical manner for each participant.

2.3 Annotation

For each monologue the occurrence of the three corner vowels /aː, i, u/ and their respectively short or lax counterparts /a, ɪ, ʊ/ was manually segmented and annotated based on visual observation of the waveform and the wideband spectrogram in Praat [2]. All annotation work was done by the same trained German native speaker to keep segmentations and annotation consistent. Given the characteristics of continuous speech we established criteria according to which suitable vowels were selected:

1. Only vowels occurring in intelligible, phonated words were annotated.
2. Only vowels with a stable part of at least 40 ms were selected. This stable part was the central part of each vowel, starting at least one period after vowel onset and ending one period before vowel offset.
3. Vowels preceded by a voiced sound were only selected if that sound matched the respective vowel's place of articulation, to ensure that formant transitions and co-articulation did not affect the vowel.
4. Vowels immediately following nasals, glides or other vowels were not selected.

2.4 Acoustic Analysis

Acoustic measures were obtained with the speech-analysis software Praat [2]. Automatic scripts were run to determine the formant frequencies of F1 and F2 in Hertz (Hz) from the entire duration of the stable part of each selected vowel.

With the obtained formant frequencies we computed the following five vowel measurements: (1) vowel formant contrasts for each speaker, (2) F1 and F2 variability within each speaker, (3) the vowel space area (VSA), (4) the vowel articulation index (VAI) and (5) the F2 ratio of the vowels /i, ɪ/ and /u, ʊ/.

To measure the vowel contrast for each speaker individually, we run ANOVAs and subsequent *post hoc* comparisons with the dependent variables F1 and F2 frequencies and vowel as independent variable. This measurement serves as an index of whether the formant frequencies of different vowels are distinct or not. We expected F1 frequencies to differ between the vowels /a, aː/ and /i, ɪ, u, ʊ/ and F2 frequencies between /i, ɪ/ and /a, aː, u, ʊ/. Accordingly, we expressed this measurement as a ratio of expected contrasts to observed contrasts, with a ratio of 1.0 indicating full contrasts between vowels and a lower ratio indicating reduced vowel contrasts.

The F1 and F2 variabilities were computed for each speaker individually as the mean standard deviation of each vowel respectively. According to Kim et al. [8] this measurement reflects a speaker's relative stability of achieving vowel targets. For VSA, VAI and the F2 ratio the formant frequencies were averaged over vowel and speaker. VSA is expressed as the following formula [9]:

$$VSA = 0.5 \times |F1i \times (F2a - F2u) + F1a \times (F2u - F2i) + F1u \times (F2i - F2a)|. \quad (1)$$

The VAI calculation was based on that of Roy et al. [14]:

$$VAI = \frac{F1a + F2i}{F1i + F1u + F2a + F2u}. \quad (2)$$

2.5 Intelligibility Rating

As a rough measure of speech impairment severity, the intelligibility of each participant's speech was rated by 15 naïve listeners. The listeners were German native speakers, between 20 and 40 years of age who had no training in phonetics or background related to speech pathologies.

For the intelligibility ratings two words and two short phrases were randomly selected from each monologue resulting in 46 words and 46 phrases in total. Both words and phrases included at least one of the selected vowels. The listeners were instructed to rate the intelligibility of each word and phrase on a scale from 1 (very poor intelligibility) to 6 (very high intelligibility). No time restrictions were imposed on the rating tasks and listeners were allowed to listen to the words and phrases as many times as needed.

3 Results

Table 2 summarizes the results of the vowel measurements and averaged intelligibility rating scores for each group divided by gender. For the male groups we found the predicted pattern of vowel articulation precision: the MCI group yielded lower values for VSA, VAI, F2 ratio and formant frequency contrasts than the PD and the HC group. As expected, higher values were found in the formant frequency variabilities for the MCI group compared to the PD and HC group. The vowel measurement results of the female groups are more ambiguous: the female MCI group scored lowest only in the VAI. In all other measures, except for the F2-Contrast, the PD group performed poorest among the female participants.

Kruskal-Wallis rank sum tests for non-parametric data were conducted to determine group differences across the data. The overall comparison of individuals with PD (including both PD group and MCI group) and healthy controls yielded significant differences for the measurements VAI ($H(2) = 4.6$, $p < .05$) and F1-Contrast ($H(2)$, $p < .05$). When MCI was included as a factor subsequent *post hoc* tests showed a significant difference between the F2-Variability values of the MCI group and the healthy controls. To assess how this finding was related to gender differences, we ran separate analyses for the male and female participants.

All male participants' vowel measurements (except for the F1-Variability measures) confirm the expected pattern of decrease of vowel space, formant contrasts and stability of achieving vowel targets in the MCI group compared to the PD and HC group (see Fig. 1). This finding is further reflected by a lower intelligibility score for the MCI group. Kruskal-Wallis tests were run to assess the significance of the observed trend. Significant differences were found for the vowel measurements VAI ($H(2) = 6.2$, $p < .05$), F1-Contrast ($H(2) = 6$, $p < .05$) and F2-Variability ($H(2) = 8$, $p < .05$). Subsequent *post hoc* analyses revealed that differences between the MCI group and the HC group accounted for the significance. The PD group did not differ from the MCI or the HC group.

Table 2. Summary of vowel measurements for each group divided by gender, where F2-ratio is ratio of /i/ and /u/, F1-cntr and F2-cntr are F1 and F2 contrasts (as ratios), F1-var and F2-var are F1 and F2 variabilities (mean(sd)), I-scores is intelligibility scores

		Vowel measurements							I-Scores
	Group	VSA	VAI	F2-ratio	F1-cntr	F2-cntr	F1-var	F2-var	
Male	**HC M**	105105	0.86	1.76	1	0.93	50	162	5.2
	SD	63348	0.09	0.42	0	0.15	4.5	41	
	PD M	60707	0.74	1.43	0.83	0.7	48	139	4.1
	SD	76967	0.09	0.46	0.24	0.33	12	29	
	MCI M	42742	0.72	1.35	0.38	0.56	118	297	3.2
	SD	19217	0.04	0.12	0.49	0.36	116	95	
Female	**HC M**	246025	1.00	2.42	1	1	42	130	5.3
	SD	30710	0.04	0.23	0	0	5.5	31	
	PD M	194988	0.96	2.13	0.79	1	68	227	4.3
	SD	97948	0.11	0.57	0.36	0	36	44	
	MCI M	221496	0.94	2.39	1	1	48	167	4.1
	SD	89311	0.02	0.33	0	0	7.4	31	

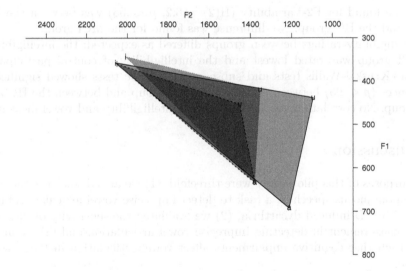

Fig. 1. Male vowel space areas. VSAs with dotted lines reflect the PD group, VSAs with scattered lines reflect the MCI group and solid lined VSAs the HC group

For the female participants, however, the pattern of vowel measurement results was less consistent (see Fig. 2). Although the intelligibility scores for the three female groups show the expected trend, with the MCI group being the least intelligible one, the PD group performed poorest in almost all vowel measurements (expect for VAI and F2-Contrast). Accordingly, the significant

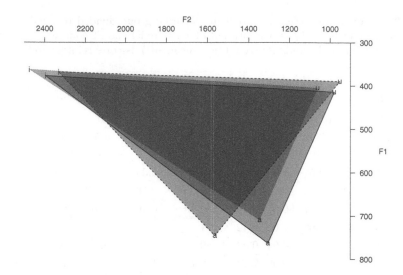

Fig. 2. Female vowel space areas. VSAs with dotted lines reflect the PD group, VSAs with scattered lines reflect the MCI group and solid lined VSAs the HC group

difference found for F2-Variability (H(2) = 6.2, $p < .05$) was between the PD group and the HC group. No difference was found for the MCI group.

Intelligibility ratings between groups differed as expected: the intelligibility of MCI group was rated lowest and the intelligibility of control participants highest. Kruskal-Wallis tests and subsequent *post hoc* tests showed significant differences ($p < .05$) between the HC and MCI group and between the HC and PD group. No correlation was found between intelligibility and vowel measures.

4   Discussion

The purposes of this pilot study were threefold: (1) we aimed to assess the utility of spontaneous speech as a task to detect imprecise vowel articulation often attested in PD-induced dysarthria, (2) we evaluated the sensitivity of different vowel measurement in detecting imprecise vowel articulation and (3) we investigated whether cognitive impairments affect vowel articulation in Parkinson's Disease.

The results are in line with a previous study by Rusz et al. [15], indicating that acoustic analysis of spontaneous speech is sensitive enough to separate impaired from non-pathological speech at the group level. Even with a small sample size as in this study, we were able to acoustically detect imprecise vowel articulation. Vowel measurements that proved to be most sensitive in this study were the vowel articulation index (VAI) and the F1-Contrast. While the first measurement is related to vowel space, the F1-Contrast is an index of how distinct a speaker's formant frequencies between different vowels are. Moreover, the separate analyses for men and women yielded significant effects of the F2-Variability measurement, which reflects a speaker's steadiness in achieving vowel targets [8]. The effects of cognitive impairments on Parkinsonian speech, however, remain inconclusive. As speech motor control requires more attention capacity in individuals with PD than in healthy individuals, we expected individuals with PD and additional cognitive impairments to exhibit less precise vowel articulation than individuals with PD only, because of their reduced attention capacity. While vowel measurements and intelligibility rating showed the expected trend for male participants, the pattern of vowel measurements and intelligibility rating was less clear for the female speakers.

The lack of clarity could be attributable to in-group variation relative to the scarcity of data, especially among the female speakers. Although this study focused on vowel articulation precision, we stress that metrics of vowel articulation should not be treated as single parameter to differentiate dysarthric from healthy speech and to investigate the effects of cognitive decline. Thus, future research should include a larger sample size, more balanced sets of groups and further acoustic measurements to better understand the effects of cognitive impairment on speech motor control in PD.

5   Conclusion

With this pilot study we demonstrated the adequacy of acoustic analysis as a methodological approach to detect cognitive decline in PD. The main contribution of this study are primary data that indicate a potential, negative effect of cognitive impairment on the speech impairment dysarthria in individuals with PD. This effect is acoustically measurable and auditory perceivable.

Acknowledgments. This study has been supported by the Research Assistants Programme of the Faculty of Arts, University of Groningen.

References

1. Aarsland, D., Kurz, M.W.: The epidemiology of dementia associated with Parkinson's Disease. J. Neurol. Sci. **289**(1), 18–22 (2010)
2. Boersma, P., Weenink, D.: Praat: doing phonetics by computer [computer program], version 6.0. 14 (2017)
3. Forrest, K., Weismer, G., Turner, G.S.: Kinematic, acoustic, and perceptual analyses of connected speech produced by parkinsonian and normal geriatric adults. J. Acoust. Soc. Am. **85**(6), 2608–2622 (1989)
4. Ho, A.K., Iansek, R., Bradshaw, J.L.: The effect of a concurrent task on parkinsonian speech. J. Clin. Exp. Neuropsychol. **24**(1), 36–47 (2002)
5. Kalia, L., Lang, A.: Parkinson's Disease. Lancet **386**(9996), 896–912 (2015)
6. Kempler, D., Van Lancker, D.: Effect of speech task on intelligibility in dysarthria: a case study of Parkinson's Disease. Brain Lang. **80**(3), 449–464 (2002)
7. Kent, R.D., Kim, Y.J.: Toward an acoustic typology of motor speech disorders. Clin. Linguist. Phonetics **17**(6), 427–445 (2003)

8. Kim, H., Hasegawa-Johnson, M., Perlman, A.: Vowel contrast and speech intelligibility in dysarthria. Folia Phoniatr. Logop. **63**(4), 187–194 (2011)
9. Liu, H.M., Tsao, F.M., Kuhl, P.K.: The effect of reduced vowel working space on speech intelligibility in mandarin-speaking young adults with cerebral palsy. J. Acoust. Soc. Am. **117**(6), 3879–3889 (2005)
10. Meireles, J., Massano, J.: Cognitive impairment and dementia in Parkinson's Disease: clinical features, diagnosis, and management. Front. Neurol. **3**, 88 (2012)
11. Papapetropoulos, S., Ellul, J., Polychronopoulos, P., Chroni, E.: A registry-based, case-control investigation of Parkinson's Disease with and without cognitive impairment. Eur. J. Neurol. **11**(5), 347–351 (2004)
12. Riedel, O., Klotsche, J., Spottke, A., Deuschl, G., Förstl, H., Henn, F., Heuser, I., Oertel, W., Reichmann, H., Riederer, P., et al.: Cognitive impairment in 873 patients with idiopathic Parkinson's Disease. J. Neurol. **255**(2), 255–264 (2008)
13. Rosen, K.M., Kent, R.D., Duffy, J.R.: Task-based profile of vocal intensity decline in Parkinson's Disease. Folia Phoniatr. Logop. **57**(1), 28–37 (2005)
14. Roy, N., Nissen, S.L., Dromey, C., Sapir, S.: Articulatory changes in muscle tension dysphonia: evidence of vowel space expansion following manual circumlaryngeal therapy. J. Commun. Disord. **42**(2), 124–135 (2009)
15. Rusz, J., Cmejla, R., Tykalova, T., Ruzickova, H., Klempir, J., Majerova, V., Picmausova, J., Roth, J., Ruzicka, E.: Imprecise vowel articulation as a potential early marker of Parkinson's Disease: effect of speaking task. J. Acoust. Soc. Am. **134**(3), 2171–2181 (2013)
16. Sapir, S., Ramig, L.O., Spielman, J.L., Fox, C.: Formant centralization ratio: a proposal for a new acoustic measure of dysarthric speech. J. Speech Lang. Hear. Res. **53**(1), 114–125 (2010)
17. Sapir, S., Spielman, J.L., Ramig, L.O., Story, B.H., Fox, C.: Effects of intensive voice treatment (the lee silverman voice treatment [lsvt]) on vowel articulation in dysarthric individuals with idiopathic Parkinson's Disease: acoustic and perceptual findings. J. Speech Lang. Hear. Res. **50**(4), 899–912 (2007)
18. Skodda, S., Grönheit, W., Schlegel, U.: Impairment of vowel articulation as a possible marker of disease progression in Parkinson's Disease. PloS One **7**(2), e32132 (2012)
19. Walsh, B., Smith, A.: Linguistic complexity, speech production, and comprehension in Parkinson's Disease: behavioral and physiological indices. J. Speech Lang. Hear. Res. **54**(3), 787–802 (2011)
20. Weismer, G., Jeng, J.Y., Laures, J.S., Kent, R.D., Kent, J.F.: Acoustic and intelligibility characteristics of sentence production in neurogenic speech disorders. Folia Phoniat. Logop. **53**(1), 1–18 (2000)

Acoustic Cues for the Perceptual Assessment of Surround Sound

Ingo Siegert[1](✉), Oliver Jokisch[2](✉), Alicia Flores Lotz[1], Franziska Trojahn[2], Martin Meszaros[2], and Michael Maruschke[2]

[1] Cognitive Systems Group,
Institute of Information and Communication Engineering,
Otto von Guericke University, 39016 Magdeburg, Germany
{ingo.siegert,alicia.lotz}@ovgu.de
[2] Institute of Communications Engineering,
Leipzig University of Telecommunications, 04277 Leipzig, Germany
{jokisch,maruschke}@hftl.de

Abstract. Speech and audio codecs are implemented in a variety of multimedia applications, and multichannel sound is offered by first streaming or cloud-based services. Beside the objective of perceptual quality, coding-related research is focused on low bitrate and minimal latency. The IETF-standardized Opus codec provides a high perceptual quality, low latency and the capability of coding multiple channels in various audio bandwidths up to Fullband (20 kHz). In a previous perceptual study on Opus-processed 5.1 surround sound, uncompressed and degraded stimuli were rated on a five-point degradation category scale (DMOS) for six channels at total bitrates between 96 and 192 kbit/s. This study revealed that the perceived quality depends on the music characteristics. In the current study we analyze spectral and music-feature differences between those five music stimuli at three coding bitrates and uncompressed sound to identify objective causes for perceptual differences. The results show that samples with *annoying* audible degradations involve higher spectral differences within the LFE channel as well as highly uncorrelated LSPs.

Keywords: Opus · Music coding · Surround sound · Spectral features · Perception

1 Introduction

The increase in different kinds of multimedia applications necessitates speech and audio codecs with different profiles. Recently, the demand for low delay and high quality audio applications, such as remote cloud gaming, has been strongly increasing, as well as the interest in codecs providing high audio quality, low bitrates and minimum latency. Furthermore, several streaming and cloud-based applications already use or would like to offer multichannel sound [22].

© Springer International Publishing AG 2017
A. Karpov et al. (Eds.): SPECOM 2017, LNAI 10458, pp. 65–75, 2017.
DOI: 10.1007/978-3-319-66429-3_6

Opus [21] represents an audio codec that fulfills such demands and offers high quality and low delay together with the capability of incorporating multiple channels. It supports several audio-frequency bandwidths and is suitable for various real-time audio signals including speech and music [15].

In [15], the usability of the Opus codec for real world scenarios was confirmed. Among other applications, this makes it possible for Video on Demand (VoD) services, like Netflix or Amazon Prime Video, to offer surround sound using the web browser embedded Opus audio codec. Using surround sound, the available bitrate has to be divided by the number of audio channels needed. In a previous study [19], we analyzed the perceived quality of degraded surround sound coded with Opus at different bitrates. The current contribution extends this investigation by analyzing quantifiable parameters that can explain observed differences in the perceived quality. Therefore, the spectral difference measured by the Compression Error Rate (CER) and the identified degraded features showing the greatest degradation from the original audio using statistical analyzes are investigated.

Our study is structured as follows: Sect. 2 presents related research. In Sect. 3, we summarize the test samples and the perception test setup used in [19]. Section 4 describes the methods for calculating spectral differences and the identification of feature modifications. Subsequently, our results are presented in Sect. 5. Section 6 concludes the paper and presents an outlook.

2   Previous Studies

Although the demand of multichannel sound is increasing, only few research is dedicated to this field. For interactive applications, cloud gaming and multimedia streaming, a good Quality of Experience (QoE) has to be guaranteed. Hence codecs have to be used that offer low transmission time, good compression quality and supporting multichannel audio.

A perceptual evaluation of cloud gaming under different network conditions showed that a Round Trip Time (RTT) of more than 160 ms leads to a noticeable degradation of the user's QoE [10]. One aspect, contributing to the RTT, is the algorithmic delay of involved compression algorithms. In several studies the amount of delay introduced by audio codecs is investigated [11,13] stating that well-known codecs like AAC or MP3 are not suitable for real-time scenarios, although they support multichannel audio.

Furthermore, the QoE is influenced by the overall listening impression. In several listening tests, the quality of different speech and audio codecs is compared [7,16,20]. The performance of Opus surpassed the performance of all other audio codecs in these tests, especially in the higher bands if applicable. Studies including the Enhanced Voice Services (EVS) codec, showed that both, Opus and EVS, provide equal coding abilities [14] with a slight advantage for EVS [17]. Nonetheless, EVS does not support multichannel sound [1]. Another study, analyzing the representation of prosodic aspects and tonal features, illustrated only small perceptual assessment differences between original and Opus-compressed speech stimuli – also hinting at a good applicability of Opus to further tonal structures [2]. Summarizing the initial requirements for interactive applications and the reported results so far, only Opus seems to fulfill all demands. Opus was designed as an all-purpose interactive speech and audio codec, standardized in RFC 6716 by the Internet Engineering Task Force (IETF) [21]. It has a very short coding latency between 5 and 66.5 ms – depending on the framesize – and variable bitrates in the range of 6 to 510 kbit/s. Additionally, Opus supports a maximum of 255 audio channels which makes it is suitable for multiple scenarios like Voice over IP, video conferencing, streaming multichannel music or providing surround sound in movies as well as for interactive multichannel audio scenarios like remote real-time jamming and cloud gaming. All mentioned studies, except for the preceding one [19], included just mono or stereo samples. Consequently, assessments on the multichannel or surround coding quality, especially reasons which explain the perceived differences, are missing.

3   Experimental Design

3.1   Test Data

The experimental design follows the description in [19]. Five surround sound samples coded with Opus (libopus 1.1.3) at different bitrates are utilized in order to survey the multichannel quality of Opus. Four samples are taken from [12] having a bit depth of 24 bit and a sample rate of 96 kHz, originally encoded with Free Lossless Audio Codec (FLAC). The fifth sample was featured on [3] as Dolby True HD (lossless) at 24 bit and 48 kHz. Further sample details are described in Table 1. We are aware that the selected test samples mostly cover classical music, but due to the limited availability of free to use surround sound samples, we chose these samples to guarantee reproducibility. In order to replicate the listening evaluations of [19], the same excerpts of about 15 seconds length from the samples were used. In total, our test set comprises 20 audio samples and includes three different coding bitrates as well as the Fullband reference.

Table 1. Overview of utilized surround music samples

ID	Title	Artist	Composer	Source
1 Soprano	Recitative from Cantata RV 679	T. Wik and Barokkanerne	A. Vivaldi	Period instr.
2 Piano	Living	J.G. Hoff	J.G. Hoff	piano
3 Quartet	String Quart. in D, Op. 76, No. 5 Finale, Preston	Engegård Quartet	J. Haydn	string instr.
4 Ensemble	Frank bridge variations - romance	Trondheim-Solistene	B. Britten	String instr.
5 Unfold	Dolby Atmos unfold	Unknown	Unknown	Synthetic

3.2 Perception Experiment

To evaluate the QoE, we selected the Degradation Category Rating (DCR) method as described in [9]. Listeners rate the degradation of an audio sample compared to a quality reference on a five point scale. The results are displayed on a five point Degradation Mean Opinion Score (DMOS) scale ranging from 1 *Degradation is very annoying* to 5 *Degradation is inaudible*. We opted for DCR because it can detect small impairments and minimizes the influence of personal taste in music or loudspeaker characteristics. The loudspeakers were placed as described in [8,19].

A maximum of five subjects participated in the listening test at the same time. The assessment study included 27 naive students from Leipzig University of Telecommunications, 6 female and 21 male students, aged between 18 and 30 years (mean of 23.1 years). Before each session, participants were trained with four audio examples. During the assessment an additional hidden reference was used.

4   Analysis Methods

4.1 Spectral Difference

To qualitatively analyze changes in the spectral domain, we calculated the CER, introduced in [18]. The CER uses spectrograms with a window size of 200 samples and an overlap of 80 samples to express the samples' variations. The mean squared error of the absolute error for each window of the standardized spectrograms is determined. The CER is then computed by calculating its mean over all windows. To produce comparable results across all used test samples, three different CER measures are reported regarding different channel combinations. First, to compare the overall differences, the CER is normalized by the averaged maximum error over all samples and channels. Second, the CER is normalized by the averaged maximum error using only the samples of the Low Frequency Effects (LFE) channel to identify the LFE's influence on the CER. Finally, to eliminate the influence of the LFE channel on the CER, it is normalized by the averaged maximum error using samples of all channels excluding the LFE channel. In all cases, the CER values range from 1 ("no difference") to 0 ("max. difference").

4.2 Identification of Degraded Acoustic Features

To determine features responsible for the perceived degradation, we first conducted a feature extraction using *openSMILE* [4]. As features we applied 28 Low-Level Descriptors (LLDs) that have been used successfully for music classification [5]. These 28 LLDs comprise loudness, Zero-Crossing Rate (ZCR), pitch envelope (F0env), linear Harmonics to Noise Ratio (HMR), auditory spectrum, eight Line Spectral Pairs (LSPs), 95% spectral Roll-Off point, spectral centroid, spectral entropy, spectral variance and Mel-Frequency Cepstral Coefficients (MFCCs) 0 to 12. For reproducibility, we used the feature names supplied by *openSMILE* in the results section. To identify the feature degradation, we compared all features of the compressed samples with their uncompressed counterparts by applying a Pearson correlation to each LLD. This correlation was performed for each channel of a sample independently. Afterwards, a majority voting of the identified features was applied over all channels, only over the LFE channel or over all channels excluding LFE, within each sample. The threshold for the correlation was varied between 0.75 and 0.95. Features with a correlation coefficient below a chosen threshold in the majority of the selected channels of a sample were labeled as "degraded".

5 Results

5.1 Perceptual Assessment

Figure 1 shows the averaged quality scores over all music samples for the bitrates 96, 128 and 192 kbit/s as well as the subjective quality for each audio sample at all bitrates. As reference, the mean ratings of all uncompressed audio files are also shown. The rating of the reference with an average DMOS of 4.33 illustrates the challenging test conditions and the critical absolute ratings of our subjects. From the reference to the highest compressed bitrate (192 kbit/s), a significant drop of 0.4 for the average DMOS can be observed. The graph proceeds to decrease almost linearly and the DMOS reaches its lowest value of 3.37 at 96 kbit/s. On average, the degradation ranges from *slightly annoying* to *not annoying but audible*. Hence, the audio quality is at least acceptable at all tested bitrates.

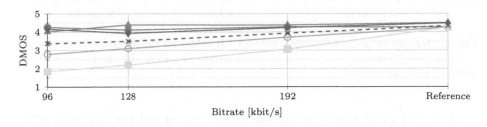

Fig. 1. Perceived overall averaged quality (- ∗ -) and perceived quality depending on music characteristics (—⊖— *Soprano*, —▲— *Piano*, —■— *Quartet*, —◆— *Ensemble*, and —●— *Unfold*)

Regarding the subjective quality for each audio sample, it is apparent that *Soprano* and *Quartet* are remarkably lower than the results of the three other samples as well as the average DMOS. For 96 and 128 kbit/s both are evaluated as *(slightly) annoying*. The samples for *Unfold*, *Ensemble*, and *Piano* are nearly constantly assessed over all considered bitrates. With only one exception for *Ensemble* at 128 kbit/s, the DMOS is always above 4, which means an *audible but not annoying* degradation.

Since the music examples represent different styles, it can be assumed that the compression affected them differently, which should be measurable within the spectral quality as well as in the acoustic characteristics. We further assume that if we identify peculiarities only observable within *Soprano* and *Quartet*, these characteristics are responsible for the perceived lower QoE.

5.2 Spectral Difference

As first measure to identify quantifiable parameters, we analyzed the CER as described in Sect. 4.1. The results incorporating different channels for each test sample are depicted in Fig. 2. Analyzing the average CER over all channels (Fig. 2a), it can be seen that although a large compression has been conducted, the overall CER is very close to 1 and thus only a small spectral difference is present. But the CER for the two samples with a perceived *slightly annoying* degradation is marginally below the other three test samples, and it has a very high standard deviation in comparison to the three other samples. Thus, we can assume that the CER values between the different channels diverge significantly.

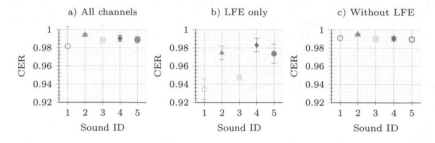

Fig. 2. Mean and standard deviation of the CER values for the different music characteristics (—⊙— *Soprano*, —▲— *Piano*, —■— *Quartet*, —◆— *Ensemble*, and —●— *Unfold*) averaged over all bitrates

Analyzing the channels' individual CER, we identified the LFE channel as the cause. This can be seen in (Fig. 2b). For *Soprano* and *Quartet*, the LFE channels' CER values are significantly below those of the three remaining test samples. It has to be remarked that all samples except *Quartet* have a noticeable standard deviation.

To substantiate this statement, we also depicted the average CER for each test sample using all channels except the LFE channel (Fig. 2c). It can be seen that for this case, the CER values are very similar with a slightly higher standard deviation. Thus, for both samples evaluated with a low QoE, the LFE channel is significantly deviant.

The LFE channel is used to transmit deep, low-pitched sounds ranging between 3 and 120 Hz. After coding, the acoustic parts transmitted over the LFE were perceived as more flatten and synthetic. We assume that for the *Soprano* and *Quartet*, where distinct easy separable sound sources are present, changes in the LFE channel are more distracting. The acoustic impression of the *Unfold* and *Ensemble* samples is wider and fuller. Therefore, the degradation of the LFE channel is of less consequence. With the *Piano* sample, high tones are more dominant, and only a few are present in the LFE channel.

5.3   Identified Degraded Acoustic Features

The identification of degraded acoustic features used the statistical analysis described in Sect. 4.2. We investigated both, the number of identified degraded features depending on the chosen threshold and the specific identified degraded features. According to our findings in the previous section, we analyzed the influence of the LFE channel. Therefore, we conducted the analysis in three conditions: (1) by using all channels, (2) only the LFE channel, and (3) all channels except for LFE. Regarding the last analysis, using only the LFE channel, we can state that for all samples nearly all features are identified as degraded. This means no statements regarding the perceived quality can be derived.

	Ensemble			Soprano			Piano			Quartet			Unfold		
δ\b	96	128	192	96	128	192	96	128	192	96	128	192	96	128	192
0.95	8	8	8	13	13	13	8	8	8	19	16	14	17	16	16
0.9	7	7	6	11	11	11	7	5	5	11	11	11	12	11	10
0.85	6	6	5	8	8	8	5	4	4	9	9	9	10	9	5
0.80	5	5	4	7	7	7	2	2	1	9	9	9	8	5	3
0.75	4	3	3	6	6	6	1	1	1	8	8	8	3	3	3

Fig. 3. Number of identified degraded features for each sample using all channels for different correlation thresholds (δ) and bitrates (b in kbit/s)

	Ensemble			Soprano			Piano			Quartet			Unfold		
δ\b	96	128	192	96	128	192	96	128	192	96	128	192	96	128	192
0.95	6	6	6	12	12	12	6	6	5	14	14	14	21	19	14
0.9	6	6	4	11	11	11	3	3	3	12	12	11	7	5	5
0.85	3	3	2	9	9	9	3	3	3	7	7	7	3	2	2
0.80	2	2	2	6	6	6	2	2	1	4	4	4	2	2	2
0.75	2	2	2	5	5	5	1	1	1	3	3	3	2	2	2

Fig. 4. Number of identified degraded features for each sample using all channels except LFE for different correlation thresholds (δ) and bitrates (b in kbit/s)

Figure 3 depicts the number of identified features below the given correlation threshold per sample over all channels. Figure 4 depicts the number of identified features below the given correlation threshold per sample over all channels excluding LFE. It can be seen that in both cases, the average number of identified degraded features for *Soprano* and *Quartet* is remarkably higher than for the other three samples. Especially, if excluding the LFE channel, this observation becomes evident. Although, the *Unfold* sample has the highest absolute number of identified degraded features, this number is decreasing very fast for

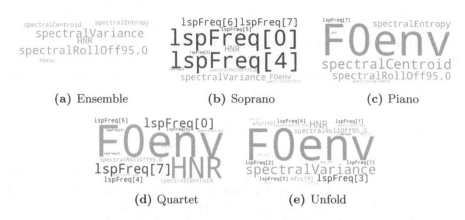

(a) Ensemble   (b) Soprano   (c) Piano

(d) Quartet   (e) Unfold

Fig. 5. Word clouds of identified modified acoustic features for each sample combined over all bitrates and correlation coefficients. Features frequently occurring in *Soprano* and *Quartet* are highlighted

declining correlation thresholds. Thus, beside the influence of the LFE channel on the perceived quality, we can also find an influence in the number of degraded features.

Additionally, we analyzed the degraded acoustic characteristics in detail. Figure 5 depicts the degraded features identified for each sample over all bitrates and correlation coefficients in individual word clouds. For this, we used all channels except LFE, see Fig. 4. It can bee seen that features related to the overall acoustic brightness, like spectral centroid, spectral variance and spectral roll-off, as well as the pitch contour and HMR, are identified as degraded for all samples. Thus, it can be assumed that the acoustic impression is narrowed, which is to some extent compensated by the surround sound setting and furthermore does not influence the DMOS assessment.

Regarding the two examples where the listening evaluation identified an *annoying* degradation, also the feature assessment found abnormalities that are unique. Only for *Soprano* and *Quartet*, LSPs are identified as degraded for all bitrates (and all correlation coefficients). Interestingly, the MFCCs were not degraded. Reasons for that have to be analyzed in further research. LSPs represent Linear Predictive Coding Coefficient (LPCC) and have a smaller sensitivity to quantization noise than direct LPCCs and therefore are often used in speech coding, such as the SILK mode of the Opus codec. We assume that the degradation of LSPs causes changes in the tonal representation of the music pieces and lead to audible dissonances. These dissonances are perceived as distractive. Noticeably, in the *Unfold* sample both, LSPs and MFCCs are also degraded, but only for correlation coefficients of 0.9 and above or for the sample coded at 96 kbit/s (not indicated within the plot). Since all coded samples of *Unfold* are not perceived with the same good quality, we assume that these slight changes might be beyond the auditory resolution of human listeners [6].

6   Conclusion and Outlook

We surveyed various spectral and music features in compressed 5.1 surround sound to explain perceptual assessment differences discovered in a previous study [19]. The same surround sound samples with varying bitrates between 96 and 192 kbit/s as in the previous study were used. Our extensive spectral and music-feature analysis shows a remarkable correlation with perceptual findings, in particular concerning the results for *slightly annoying* audible degradations (DMOS rating of 3.0 and below) in the music stimuli.

We detected a strong correlation between spectral differences in the LFE channel and the subjective quality assessments. The two samples having a significant higher difference within the LFE channel, were previously assessed with an *annoying audible* degradation. Therefore, it can be assumed that higher differences within the LFE channel are accounting for the QoE degradation.

Furthermore, these two samples also showed peculiarities regarding the degraded music-related LLDs. First of all, a higher number of LLDs is degraded in the two samples regardless of the bitrate. Moreover, also the type of degraded LLDs is remarkably different. Especially in those samples, the LSPs are identified as degraded. Therefore, we suggest that degradations within the LSPs contribute to the perceived *slightly annoying audible* degradation. As these peculiarities are observed in two different samples perceived as *slightly annoying*, it can be assumed that they are responsible for the audible degradation, but further listening evaluations are needed to confirm this assumption.

The future research will be dedicated to common metrics to cover both, the subjective perceptual assessment and corresponding objective signal features such as spectral or music-feature measures. Therefore, listener evaluations with additional stimuli, also comprising non classical samples, will be conducted. The selection of samples will also take into account the observed spectral differences. On top of that, we will evaluate further high-quality multi-channel music codecs without a low-latency capability like AC3, DTS and Dolby True HD to obtain an overall impression in the multimedia-streaming domain.

Acknowledgments. This work was partly carried out within the Transregional Collaborative Research Centre SFB/TRR 62 "Companion Technology for Cognitive Technical Systems" funded by the German Research Foundation (DFG) (www.sfb-trr-62.de).

References

1. Dietz, M., Multrus, M., Eksler, V., Malenovsky, V., Norvell, E., Pobloth, H., Miao, L., Wang, Z., Laaksonen, L., Vasilache, A., Kamamoto, Y., Kikuiri, K., Ragot, S., Faure, J., Ehara, H., Rajendran, V., Atti, V., Sung, H., Oh, E., Yuan, H., Zhu, C.: Overview of the EVS codec architecture. In: 2015 IEEE International Conference on Acoustics, Speech and Signal Processing (ICASSP), pp. 5698–5702 (2015)
2. Dobbriner, J., Jokisch, O., Maruschke, M.: Assessment of prosodic attributes in codec-compressed speech. In: Draxler, C., Kleber, F. (eds.) Proceedings of 12th Conference Phonetik und Phonologie im deutschsprachigen Raum (P&P), Munich, Germany, vol. 12, pp. 35–39. LMU Munich, October 2016

3. Dolby Laboratories Inc.: Dolby Atmos Demonstration Disc, August 2014
4. Eyben, F., Wöllmer, M., Schuller, B.: OpenSMILE - The Munich versatile and fast open-source audio feature extractor. In: Proceedings of the ACM MM-2010, p. s.p., Firenze, Italy (2010)
5. Eyben, F., Schuller, B.: Music classification with the Munich openSMILE toolkit. In: Proceedings of Annual Meeting of the MIREX 2010 Community as Part of the 11th International Conference on Music Information Retrieval, p. s.p., Utrecht, Netherlands, August 2010
6. Fastl, H., Zwicker, E.: Psychoacoustics. Facts and Models. Springer, Berlin (2007)
7. Hoene, C., Valin, J.M., Vos, K., Skoglund, J.: Summary of Opus listening test results draft-valin-codec-results-03. Internet-draft, IETF (2013). https://tools.ietf.org/html/draft-ietf-codec-results-03
8. ITU-R: Multichannel stereophonic sound system with and without accompanying picture. REC BS.775-3, International Telecommunication Union (Radiocommunication Sector), August 2012. http://www.itu.int/rec/R-REC-BS.775-3-201208-I/en
9. ITU-T: Methods for objective and subjective assessment of quality- Methods for subjective determination of transmissen quality. REC P.800, International Telecommunication Union (Telecommunication Standardization Sector), August 1996. http://www.itu.int/rec/T-REC-P.800-199608-I/en
10. Jarschel, M., Schlosser, D., Scheuring, S., Hoßfeld, T.: An evaluation of QoE in cloud gaming based on subjective tests. In: Fifth International Conference on Innovative Mobile and Internet Services in Ubiquitous Computing, pp. 330–335, Seoul, Korea (2011)
11. Jokisch, O., Maruschke, M.: Audio and speech coding/transcoding in web real-time communication. In: International Symposium on Human Life Design (HLD 2016), p. s.p., Kanazawa, Japan (2016)
12. Lindberg Lyd AS. 2L - the Nordic sound: HiRes Test Bench (online available). http://www.2l.no/hires/index.html. Accessed 15 Jan 2017
13. Lutzky, M., Schuller, G., Gayer, M., Krämer, U., Wabnik, S.: A guideline to audio codec delay. In: AES 116th Convention, Berlin, Germany, pp. 8–11 (2004)
14. Maruschke, M., Jokisch, O., Meszaros, M., Trojahn, F., Hoffmann, M.: Quality assessment of two fullband audio codecs supporting real-time communication. In: Ronzhin, A., Potapova, R., Németh, G. (eds.) SPECOM 2016. LNCS (LNAI), vol. 9811, pp. 571–579. Springer, Cham (2016). doi:10.1007/978-3-319-43958-7_69
15. Maruschke, M., Jokisch, O., Meszaros, M., Iaroshenko, V.: Review of the Opus Codec in a WebRTC scenario for audio and speech communication. In: Ronzhin, A., Potapova, R., Fakotakis, N. (eds.) SPECOM 2015. LNCS (LNAI), vol. 9319, pp. 348–355. Springer, Cham (2015). doi:10.1007/978-3-319-23132-7_43
16. Rämö, A., Toukomaa, H.: Voice quality characterization of IETF Opus codec. In: Proceedings of the INTERSPEECH-2011, pp. 2541–2544, Florence, Italy (2011)
17. Rämö, A., Toukomaa, H.: Subjective qualitiy evaluation of the 3Gpp. EVS codec. In: Proceedings of the 40th IEEE ICASSP, pp. 5157–5161, Brisbane, Australia (2015)
18. Siegert, I., Lotz, A.F., l. Duong, L., Wendemuth, A.: Measuring the impact of audio compression on the spectral quality of speech data. In: Elektronische Sprachsignalverarbeitung 2016. Studientexte zur Sprachkommunikation, vol. 81, pp. 229–236, Leipzig, Germany (2016)

19. Trojahn, F., Meszaros, M., Maruschke, M., Jokisch, O.: Surround sound processed by Opus codec: a perceptual quality assessment. In: Elektronische Sprachsignalverarbeitung 2017. Tagungsband der 28. Konferenz. Studientexte zur Sprachkommunikation, vol. 86, pp. 300–307. TUDpress, Saarbrücken, Germany (2017)
20. Valin, J.M., Maxwell, G., Terriberry, T., Vos, K.: High-quality, low-delay music coding in the Opus codec. In: Proceedings of the 135th Audio Engineering Society Convention, p. s.p. Audio Engineering Society, New York, USA, October 2013
21. Valin, J., Vos, K., Terriberry, T.: Definition of the Opus audio codec. RFC 6716. http://tools.ietf.org/html/rfc6716
22. Zion Market Research Blog: Sound Bar Market: Rising events in corporate, film industry, sports and others increase the demand of sound bar systems, November 2016

Acoustic Modeling in the STC Keyword Search System for OpenKWS 2016 Evaluation

Ivan Medennikov[1,2]([✉]), Aleksei Romanenko[1,2], Alexey Prudnikov[1],
Valentin Mendelev[1,2], Yuri Khokhlov[1], Maxim Korenevsky[1,2],
Natalia Tomashenko[1,2], and Alexander Zatvornitskiy[1,2]

[1] STC-innovations Ltd., St. Petersburg, Russia
{medennikov,romanenko,mendelev,khokhlov,korenevsky,tomashenko-n,
zatvornitskiy}@speechpro.com, alexey.prudnikov@corp.mail.ru
[2] ITMO University, St. Petersburg, Russia

Abstract. This paper describes in detail the acoustic modeling part of the keyword search system developed in the Speech Technology Center (STC) for the OpenKWS 2016 evaluation. The key idea was to utilize diversity of both sound representations and acoustic model architectures in the system. For the former, we extended speaker-dependent bottleneck (SDBN) approach to the multilingual case, which is the main contribution of the paper. Two types of multilingual SDBN features were applied in addition to conventional spectral and cepstral features. The acoustic model architectures employed in the final system are based on deep feedforward and recurrent neural networks. We also applied speaker adaptation of acoustic models using multilingual i-vectors, speed perturbation based data augmentation and semi-supervised training. Final STC system comprised 9 acoustic models, which allowed it to achieve strong performance and to be among the top three systems in the evaluation.

Keywords: Acoustic models · Low-resource speech recognition · Multilingual speaker-dependent bottleneck features · OpenKWS 2016

1 Introduction

In recent years a lot of effort in the automatic speech recognition (ASR) area have been devoted to creating ASR systems for low-resource languages. One of such efforts is the annual OpenKWS evaluation organized as a part of IARPA Babel program [1] to assess progress in rapid developing of keyword search (KWS) systems for new languages with limited amount of training data. STC team participated in the OpenKWS 2016 evaluation [2] dealing with Georgian as a "surprise" language.

Alexey Prudnikov—Mail.ru Group, St. Petersburg, Russia
Natalia Tomashenko—LIUM University of Le Mans, France.

© Springer International Publishing AG 2017
A. Karpov et al. (Eds.): SPECOM 2017, LNAI 10458, pp. 76–86, 2017.
DOI: 10.1007/978-3-319-66429-3_7

The acoustic modeling part is one of the most important components of modern automatic speech recognition systems. Building a strong and robust acoustic model for a low-resource language is a very challenging task. This paper details the acoustic modeling part of the STC keyword search system for the OpenKWS 2016 evaluation. The other parts of the system are described in [3,4].

Recent works on low-resource ASR and KWS have shown great success of the approach based on combination of many different acoustic models in the system [5–7]. This motivated us to utilize diversity of both sound representations and acoustic model architectures in our system.

Multilingual bottleneck features are widely used in modern low-resource speech recognition systems because it is the way to increase training dataset and thus to improve system robustness. In our previous papers [8–11] we proposed speaker-dependent bottleneck (SDBN) features. These features are extracted from the Deep Neural Network (DNN) adapted to speaker using i-vectors [13]. In [12], SDBN approach have been applied with Deep Maxout Networks (DMN). It was shown that SDBN features allow to achieve strong results in terms of Word Error Rate (WER) for Russian and English conversational telephone speech recognition. In this paper we extend SDBN approach to the multilingual case with the use of multilingual i-vectors.

Our system employs 2 types of multilingual SDBN features in addition to conventional perceptual linear prediction (PLP) features, mel frequency cepstral coefficients (MFCC) and log mel filterbank energy (FBANK) features. The applied acoustic model architectures included DNN, DMN trained using annealed dropout regularization [14], Time-Delay Neural Network (TDNN) [15] and Bidirectional Long Short-Term Memory Recurrent Neural Network (BLSTM) with projection layers [16]. In addition, the following acoustic modeling techniques were applied: speaker adaptation of acoustic models using multilingual i-vectors [13], speed perturbation based data augmentation [17] and semi-supervised training of acoustic model [18] using untranscribed data.

The rest of the paper is organized as follows. Section 2 presents multilingual speaker-dependent bottleneck features. Experiments on building SDBN features and training of acoustic models on Georgian language are described in Sect. 3. Finally, Sect. 4 summarizes our results.

2   Multilingual Speaker-Dependent Bottleneck Features

In this section we present an extension of SDBN approach [8–11] to the multitask case. Our goal is to construct robust speaker-adapted features with the use of several speech datasets which differ in their nature, e.g. language or recording conditions. The presented approach is described in detail in the context of the multilingual training. However, it can be easily applied to other multi-task training setups. The scheme of the multilingual SDBN approach is presented in Fig. 1.

The first stage is building the multilingual i-vectors [19]—low-dimensional vectors containing information about the speaker and the acoustic environment on the recording. I-vectors are widely used in speaker and language recognition tasks [19–21]. Universal Background Model (UBM) based i-vectors extractors trained using cepstral features are commonly used. However, recently it was shown that i-vectors extracted using high-level bottleneck features significantly outperform traditional MFCC based i-vectors in language recognition tasks [21]. Thus we suppose that multilingual speaker-independent bottleneck (SIBN) features will be more suitable for i-vectors extractor training than MFCC. The procedure of multilingual SIBN features extraction is almost the same as for multilingual SDBN features which is described below. The only difference is that the network retraining with i-vectors is not performed for SIBN features.

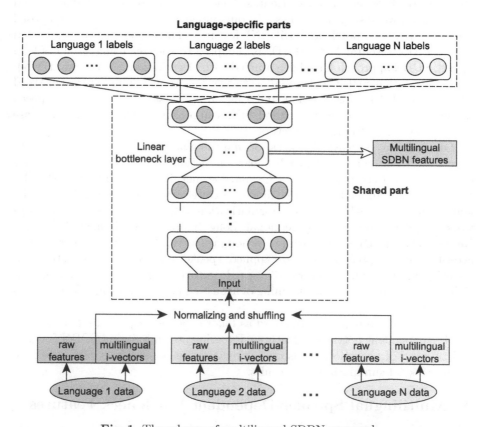

Fig. 1. The scheme of multilingual SDBN approach

Prior to bottleneck extractor training, it is necessary to train the acoustic models for each dataset and generate phone or senone alignment of each dataset with a corresponding acoustic model. We propose the multilingual SDBN extractor training scheme consisting of the following steps:

1. Training of speaker-independent neural network in a multi-task manner [22] with 5–7 layers in shared part and one language-specific part per language.

Each language-specific part of the network consists of softmax layer with corresponding language phones or senones as labels. We recommend to perform greedy layer-wise pretraining of the DNN based extractor. On the other hand, the DMN based extractor training with annealed dropout regularization [14] does not require any pretraining.

2. Retraining of the network from the first step using input feature vector concatenated with the corresponding i-vector. The regularizing term

$$R = \lambda \sum_{l=1}^{L} \sum_{i=1}^{N_l} \sum_{j=1}^{N_{l-1}} (\mathbf{W}_{ij}^l - \bar{\mathbf{W}}_{ij}^l)^2 \qquad (1)$$

is added to the Cross-Entropy (CE) loss function for penalizing parameters deviation from the source model values. Here $\mathbf{W}^l$ and $\bar{\mathbf{W}}^l$ are weight matrices of l-th layer ($1 \leq l \leq L$) of the current and the source neural networks, N_l is the size of l-th layer, and N_0 is the dimension of the input feature vector.

3. Transformation of the last hidden layer of the shared part of the speaker-dependent neural network obtained on the previous step into two layers. The first one is a bottleneck layer with the weight matrix $\mathbf{W}_{bn}$, a zero bias vector and the linear activation function. The second one is a non-linear layer with the dimension equal of that of the source layer, with the weight matrix $\mathbf{W}_{out}$, the original bias vector $\mathbf{b}$, activation function f and the dimension of the source layer.

$$\mathbf{y} = f(\mathbf{W}\mathbf{x} + \mathbf{b}) \approx f(\mathbf{W}_{out}(\mathbf{W}_{bn}\mathbf{x} + \mathbf{0}) + \mathbf{b}). \qquad (2)$$

These layers are formed by applying Singular Value Decomposition (SVD) to the weight matrix $\mathbf{W}$ of the source layer:

$$\mathbf{W} = \mathbf{U}\mathbf{S}\mathbf{V}^T \approx \tilde{\mathbf{U}}_{bn}\tilde{\mathbf{V}}_{bn}^T = \mathbf{W}_{out}\mathbf{W}_{bn}, \qquad (3)$$

where bn denotes the reduced dimension.

4. Retraining the network formed at the previous step using the penalty (1) for parameters deviation from the original values.

5. Extracting multilingual SDBN features from the bottleneck layer of the shared part of the resulting neural network.

The training procedure listed above is performed using the CE criterion. Each minibatch consists of training examples for one language only. The language corresponding to the current minibatch is chosen with the probability determined as number of unprocessed minibatches for this language divided by the total number of unprocessed minibatches. We also recommend to apply global per-frame input features normalization to zero mean and unit variance with normalizing coefficients computed over all languages data.

The proposed multilingual SDBN features can be used in both Gaussian Mixture Model (GMM) and DNN/DMN based acoustic models.

3   Experiments

3.1   Experimental Setup

All experiments were performed using the Kaldi ASR Toolkit [23] as well as our proprietary training tools. Extractors of multilingual i-vectors and bottleneck features were trained using build datasets for 18 languages from the IARPA Babel Program language collection with the total amount of 860 h. Acoustic models for Georgian language were trained on 40 h of transcribed and 40 h of untranscribed data from the Georgian language pack (IARPA-babel404b-v1.0a).

Speech recognition of the 10-hour Georgian development set was carried out with the 3-gram language model (LM). This model was obtained as a linear interpolation of 3 models: the first one was trained on the transcriptions of the 40 h acoustic training data; the second one was built on text data artificially generated by a character-based recurrent neural network LM [24]; the third one was trained on 380 Mb of Web texts (BBN part) provided by the organizers. Interpolation weights of these models were 0.6, 0.1 and 0.3 respectively. The resulting LM contained 4M n-grams and 260 K words, out-of-vocabulary words rate on the development set was 4.4%. Detailed description of the language models used in our system can be found in [3]. The produced word lattices were used for proxies-based keyword search which is implemented in Kaldi [25].

The used speech recognition and keyword search performance metrics are Word Error Rate (WER) and Actual Term Weighted Value (ATWV) respectively. The details on the metrics can be found in the OpenKWS 2016 evaluation plan [2]. ATWV scores are reported for in-vocabulary part of the official development keywords list.

3.2   Extractors Training

In this subsection we describe our experiments on building the multilingual SDBN features extractors according to the approach presented in Sect. 2.

In order to obtain senone alignments for each of the 18 languages, we trained an acoustic models based on Gaussian Mixture Model and Hidden Markov Model (GMM-HMM) for each of them using Kaldi *babel/s5c* recipe. 13-dimensional Perceptual Linear Prediction (PLP) coefficients combined with 3 pitch values were used in these models. Each of these acoustic models was trained using feature-space Maximum Likelihood Linear Regression (fMLLR) [26] speaker adaptation and had about 5 K senones and 75 K Gaussians.

The DNN-based extractor of multilingual SIBN features was trained using PLP + pitch features, appended with first and second order derivatives, spliced with a temporal context of 11 frames. The shared part of the network had 6×1024 hidden layers with sigmoid activation function and 80-dimensional linear bottleneck layer placed before the last hidden layer. The training was initialized with greedy layer-wise pretraining.

The constructed multilingual SIBN features were applied to train the extractor of 200-dimensional i-vectors, which was based on the Universal Background Model (UBM) with 2048 Gaussians.

Then, 2 extractors of multilingual SDBN features were trained. The first one used the same features and topology as the SIBN extractor, with the only difference in the presence of i-vectors as part of the input vectors.

The second SDBN extractor based on DMN was trained using 40-dimensional log mel filterbank energy (FBANK) features combined with 3 pitch values, spliced with a temporal context of 11 frames. The shared part consisted of 10×1024 maxout hidden layers with group size of 2. The training was carried out without pretraining using the annealed dropout regularization [14]. The dropout rate decreased uniformly from the starting value (0.5 for step 1, 0.25 for steps 2 and 4 of the training scheme described in Sect. 2) during the first epoch to the final value of 0.05 at the 25-th epoch.

All bottleneck extractors were trained using Nesterov Accelerated Gradient algorithm [27] with the momentum value of 0.7. Initial learning rate was 0.5 for speaker-independent training (step 1) and 0.1 for the retraining with i-vectors (step 2) and bottleneck layer (step 4). Per-speaker mean normalization followed by the global per-frame zero mean and unit variance normalization of the input features was applied.

The described extraction scheme of the multilingual bottleneck features and i-vectors is illustrated in Fig. 2.

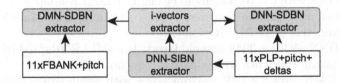

Fig. 2. Bottleneck features and i-vectors extraction scheme

Table 1 demonstrates the performance of the extractors in terms of Frame Error Rate (FER) on 10-hour development datasets for 6 of 18 languages used in the multilingual training. It should be noted that DMN-based extractor input features do not contain time derivatives, thus it cannot be fairly compared with the DNN-based extractors in terms of FER. In order to perform fair extractors comparison as well as to analyze the impact of the training data amount, we also trained the DNN and DMN based extractors on the same features using the subset of 6 languages with the total amount of 300 h.

The results of the comparison show that increasing data amount from 300 to 860 h improves FER only slightly. On the other hand, the DNN-SDBN extractor significantly outperforms the DNN-SIBN one.

3.3 Acoustic Models Training

Experiments on Georgian language were started with building of grapheme based ASR system using the Kaldi *babel/s5c* recipe. GMM-HMM acoustic model with

Table 1. Extractors comparison in terms of Frame Error Rate

Extractor	Languages	Features	Amharic	Haitian	Igbo	Kazakh	Lao	Zulu
DNN-SIBN	6	PLP	54.24	54.96	58.52	52.20	48.29	57.42
DMN-SIBN	6	PLP	53.43	53.92	57.71	51.34	47.33	56.70
DNN-SIBN	18	PLP	53.86	54.81	58.32	51.66	47.84	57.20
DNN-SDBN	18	PLP + i-vec	51.90	51.96	56.83	50.38	46.09	56.24
DMN-SDBN	18	FBANK + i-vec	54.85	55.96	59.37	53.15	49.30	59.17

5 K senones and 75 K Gaussians trained using fMLLR based speaker adaptation on PLP + pitch features was considered as a baseline.

In order to evaluate the multilingual bottleneck features constructed in Subsect. 3.2, we trained GMM-HMM acoustic models without fMLLR adaptation and with it on DNN-SIBN, DNN-SDBN and DMN-SDBN features. The numbers of Gaussians and senones were the same as for the baseline GMM. We also trained Subspace GMM acoustic model [28] on DNN-SDBN features with fMLLR speaker adaptation.

Furthermore, we trained 9 acoustic models based on neural networks:

1. **DNN_1**: DNN with 6×1024 sigmoid layers; $11 \times$ fMLLR-adapted LDA-MLLT transformed PLP + pitch features; sequence training with state-level Minimum Bayes Risk (sMBR) criterion [29].
2. **DNN_2**: DNN with 4×2048 sigmoid layers; $31 \times$ fMLLR-adapted DNN-SDBN features taking every 5th frame; sMBR sequence training.
3. **DMN_3**: DMN with 6×1536 maxout layers with group size of 2; $31 \times$ DMN-SDBN features taking every 5th frame; cross-entropy training with annealed dropout regularization followed by sMBR sequence training.
4. **DMN_4**: the same as **DMN_3**, but training was initialized with the shared part of multilingual DMN (18 langs). This multilingual DMN was trained on $31 \times$ DMN-SDBN features taking every 5th frame using the first step of the multilingual SDBN extractor training scheme described in Sect. 2.
5. **$TDNN_5$**: Time Delay Neural Network (TDNN) [15] with 4×1024 ReLU layers trained using the Kaldi *swbd/s5c* recipe; $5 \times$ MFCC + pitch features concatenated with i-vector; CE criterion.
6. **$BLSTM_6$**: Bidirectional Long Short-Term Memory recurrent neural network (BLSTM) with projection layers [16]; 3×512(cell,hidden) $\times 128$(recurrent proj.,non-recurrent proj.) hidden layers; $5 \times$ FBANK + pitch features concatenated with i-vector; CE criterion.
7. **DNN_7**: DNN with 6×1024 sigmoid layers; $11 \times$ PLP + pitch features concatenated with i-vector; training initialization with the shared part of multilingual DNN (18 langs); CE criterion.
8. **DMN_8**: DMN with 10×1024 maxout layers with group size of 2; $11 \times$ FBANK + pitch features concatenated with i-vector; training initialization with the shared part of multilingual DMN (18 langs); CE training with annealed dropout regularization.

9. **DMN$_9$**: DMN with semi-supervised learning. 40 h of untranscribed training data were recognized using the best acoustic model in terms of WER (**DMN$_3$**). Training utterances were constructed using the following procedure. The next word was added to the existing word sequence if the average confidence score of the resulting sequence was higher than the threshold. Otherwise, the existing word sequence had been finalized and the construction of the next word sequence was started from the first following word with confidence score higher than the threshold. Time boundaries of word sequences were taken from the recognition result. Following this procedure, around 55% of untranscribed data with automatically generated transcriptions were included into the training set. Training procedure was the same as for **DMN$_8$** model.

All these models except the first one were trained with the use of speed perturbed data [17] (two additional copies of the training data were created by adjusting the speed by $+-10\%$ of the original value). The **DNN$_1$** model was trained using senone alignments generated by the baseline GMM; The **DNN$_2$**, **DMN$_3$** and **DMN$_4$** models were trained on senone alignments generated by the best of GMM on SDBN features; senone alignments for the other models were prepared using the **DNN$_2$** model.

The performance of the acoustic models and of their keywords lists level combination is reported in Table 2. The combination was carried out using the Kaldi implementation which performs weighted combination of non-normalized keywords lists produced by different systems. Our results were obtained with equal combination weights. Detailed explanation of the combining procedure can be found in [30].

Table 2. Performance of acoustic models and their keywords lists level combination

Acoustic Model	ATWV	WER,%	Acoustic Model	ATWV	WER,%
GMM baseline	0.490	56.2	DNN$_1$	0.643	44.2
GMM DNN-SIBN	0.514	53.7	DNN$_2$	0.634	41.5
+fMLLR	0.569	49.5	DMN$_3$	0.675	**39.4**
GMM DNN-SDBN	0.570	49.5	DMN$_4$	0.660	44.3
+fMLLR	0.591	47.1	TDNN$_5$	0.658	42.3
GMM DMN-SDBN	0.585	49.1	BLSTM$_6$	0.652	41.1
+fMLLR	0.614	47.0	DNN$_7$	0.669	43.0
SGMM DNN-SDBN	0.606	45.4	DMN$_8$	0.680	42.4
			DMN$_9$	**0.685**	41.8
			combination	0.749	—

4 Discussion and Conclusions

The results given in Table 2 show that the multilingual SDBN features clearly outperformed speaker-independent multilingual bottleneck features for GMM-HMM acoustic models. Moreover, fMLLR speaker adaptation performed well for SDBN features, despite their inherent speaker-adapted nature. It is interesting that, for both DNN and DMN model types, SDBN features shown significantly better WER than for the raw features, while ATWV scores were comparable or worse.

The combination of the models outperformed any single model by a big margin. DMN based models showed the best performance, although DNN, TDNN and BLSTM based ones also provided significant contribution into the final combination result. On the other hand, GMM and SGMM demonstrated poor results in comparison with neural networks based models, and did not improve the result of the combination.

Thus, final system included 9 neural network based acoustic models which were combined on the level of keywords lists. Largely due to strong acoustic modeling part, our system achieved high ATWV score of 0.821 and was among the top three systems in the OpenKWS 2016 evaluation.

Acknowledgements. This work was financially supported by the Ministry of Education and Science of the Russian Federation, Contract 14.579.21.0121 (ID RFMEFI57915X0121).

This effort uses the IARPA Babel Program language collection release IARPA-babel{101b-v0.4c, 102b-v0.5a, 103b-v0.4b, 201b-v0.2b, 203b-v3.1a, 205b-v1.0a, 206b-v0.1e, 207b-v1.0e, 301b-v2.0b, 302b-v1.0a, 303b-v1.0a, 304b-v1.0b, 305b-v1.0c, 306b-v2.0c, 307b-v1.0b, 401b-v2.0b, 402b-v1.0b, 403b-v1.0b, 404b-v1.0a}, set of training transcriptions and BBN part of clean web data for Georgian language.

References

1. IARPA Babel program, https://www.iarpa.gov/index.php/research-programs/babel
2. OpenKWS 2016 Evaluation Plan, https://www.nist.gov/sites/default/files/documents/itl/iad/mig/KWS16-evalplan-v04.pdf
3. Khokhlov, Y., Medennikov, I., Mendelev, V., et al.: The STC keyword search system For OpenKWS 2016 evaluation. In: INTERSPEECH 2017 (accepted 2017)
4. Khokhlov, Y., Tomashenko, N., et al.: Fast and accurate OOV decoder on high-level features. In: INTERSPEECH 2017 (accepted 2017)
5. Lee, W., Kim, J., Lane, I.: Multi-stream combination for LVCSR and keyword search on GPU-accelerated platforms. In: ICASSP 2014, pp. 3296–3300 (2014)
6. Cai, M., et al.: High-performance Swahili keyword search with very limited language pack: the THUEE system for the OpenKWS15 evaluation. In: ASRU 2015, pp. 215–222 (2015)
7. Hartmann, W., et al.: Comparison of multiple system combination techniques for keyword spotting. In: INTERSPEECH 2016, pp. 1913–1917 (2016)

8. Prudnikov, A., Medennikov, I., Mendelev, V., Korenevsky, M., Khokhlov, Y.: Improving acoustic models for russian spontaneous speech recognition. In: Ronzhin, A., Potapova, R., Fakotakis, N. (eds.) SPECOM 2015. LNCS (LNAI), vol. 9319, pp. 234–242. Springer, Cham (2015). doi:10.1007/978-3-319-23132-7_29

9. Medennikov, I., Prudnikov, A.: Advances in STC russian spontaneous speech recognition system. In: Ronzhin, A., Potapova, R., Németh, G. (eds.) SPECOM 2016. LNCS (LNAI), vol. 9811, pp. 116–123. Springer, Cham (2016). doi:10.1007/978-3-319-43958-7_13

10. Medennikov, I.P.: Speaker-dependent features for spontaneous speech recognition. Sci. Tech. J. Inf. Technol. Mech. Opt. $16(1)$, 195–197 (2016). doi:10.17586/2226-1494-2016-16-1-195-197

11. Medennikov, I., Prudnikov, A., Zatvornitskiy, A.: Improving english conversational telephone speech recognition. In: INTERSPEECH 2016, pp. 2–6 (2016)

12. Prudnikov, A., Korenevsky, M.: Training maxout neural networks for speech recognition tasks. In: Sojka, P., Horák, A., Kopeček, I., Pala, K. (eds.) TSD 2016. LNCS (LNAI), vol. 9924, pp. 443–451. Springer, Cham (2016). doi:10.1007/978-3-319-45510-5_51

13. Saon, G., Soltau, H., Nahamoo, D., Picheny, M.: Speaker adaptation of neural network acoustic models using i-vectors. In: ASRU 2013, pp. 55–59 (2013)

14. Rennie, S.J., Goel, V., Thomas, S.: Annealed dropout training of deep networks. In: 2014 IEEE Workshop on Spoken Language Technology (SLT), pp. 159–164 (2014)

15. Peddinti, V., Povey, D., Khudanpur, S.: A time delay neural network architecture for efficient modeling of long temporal contexts. In: INTERSPEECH 2015, pp. 2440–2444 (2015)

16. Sak, H., Senior, A., Beaufays, F.: Long short-term memory recurrent neural network architectures for large scale acoustic modeling. In: INTERSPEECH 2014 (2014)

17. Ko, T., Peddinti, V., Povey, D., Khudanpur, S.: Audio augmentation for speech recognition. In: INTERSPEECH 2015 (2015)

18. Vesely, K., Hannemann, M., Burget, L.: Semi-supervised training of deep neural networks. In: ASRU 2013, pp. 267–272 (2013)

19. Dehak, N., et al.: Front-end factor analysis for speaker verification. IEEE Trans. Audio Speech Lang. Process. $19(4)$, 788–798 (2010)

20. Kozlov, A., Kudashev, O., Matveev, Y., Pekhovsky, T., Simonchik, K., Shulipa, A.: SVID speaker recognition system for NIST SRE 2012. In: Železný, M., Habernal, I., Ronzhin, A. (eds.) SPECOM 2013. LNCS (LNAI), vol. 8113, pp. 278–285. Springer, Cham (2013). doi:10.1007/978-3-319-01931-4_37

21. Lee, K.A., et al.: The 2015 NIST Language Recognition Evaluation: the Shared View of I2R, Fantastic4 and SingaMS. In: INTERSPEECH 2016, pp. 3211–3215 (2016)

22. Caruana, R.: Multitask learning. Mac. Learn. $28(1)$, 41–75 (1997)

23. Povey, D., et al.: The kaldi speech recognition toolkit. In: ASRU 2011, pp. 1–4 (2011)

24. Karpathy, A.: The Unreasonable Effectiveness of Recurrent Neural Networks, http://karpathy.github.io/2015/05/21/rnn-effectiveness

25. Chen, G., Yilmaz, O., Trmal, J., Povey, D.: Khudanpur, S: Using proxies for OOV keywords in the keyword search task. In: ASRU 2013, pp. 416–421 (2013)

26. Gales, M.J.F.: Maximum likelihood linear transformations for HMM-based speech recognition. Comput. Speech Lang. 12, 75–98 (1998)

27. Sutskever, I., Martens, J., Dahl, G., Hinton, G.: On the importance of momentum and initialization in deep learning. In: 30th International Conference on Machine Learning (2013)
28. Povey, D., et al.: The subspace Gaussian mixture model–a structured model for speech recognition. Comput. Speech Lang. **25**(2), 404–439 (2011)
29. Vesely, K., Ghoshal, A., Burget, L., Povey, D.: Sequence-discriminative training of deep neural networks. In: INTERSPEECH 2013, pp. 2345–2349 (2013)
30. Trmal, J., et al.: A keyword search system using open source software. In: 2014 IEEE Workshop on Spoken Language Technology (2014)

Adaptation Approaches for Pronunciation Scoring with Sparse Training Data

Federico Landini[1](✉), Luciana Ferrer[2], and Horacio Franco[3]

[1] Departamento de Computación, FCEN, Universidad de Buenos Aires,
Buenos Aires, Argentina
fnlandini@dc.uba.ar
[2] Instituto de Investigación en Ciencias de la Computación (ICC),
UBA-CONICET, Buenos Aires, Argentina
lferrer@dc.uba.ar
[3] Speech Technology and Research Laboratory, SRI International,
Menlo Park CA, USA
horacio.franco@sri.com

Abstract. In Computer Assisted Language Learning systems, pronunciation scoring consists in providing a score grading the overall pronunciation quality of the speech uttered by a student. In this work, a log-likelihood ratio obtained with respect to two automatic speech recognition (ASR) models was used as score. One model represents native pronunciation while the other one captures non-native pronunciation. Different approaches to obtain each model and different amounts of training data were analyzed. The best results were obtained training an ASR system using a separate large corpus without pronunciation quality annotations and then adapting it to the native and non-native data, sequentially. Nevertheless, when models are trained directly on the native and non-native data, pronunciation scoring performance is similar. This is a surprising result considering that word error rates for these models are significantly worse, indicating that ASR performance is not a good predictor of pronunciation scoring performance on this system.

Keywords: Computer-assisted language learning · Pronunciation scoring · Log-likelihood ratio · MAP adaptation

1 Introduction

Computer Assisted Language Learning (CALL) systems allow students of second languages to develop different abilities. In this work we focus our attention on the pronunciation scoring task, which consists in providing a score grading the overall pronunciation quality of speech uttered by a student.

Although many programs offer evaluation of the pronunciation independently of the native language of the learner, different pronunciation errors are produced by students with different native language (L1) and target language (L2) pairs. In this work we focus on a pronunciation scoring system that takes into account

© Springer International Publishing AG 2017
A. Karpov et al. (Eds.): SPECOM 2017, LNAI 10458, pp. 87–97, 2017.
DOI: 10.1007/978-3-319-66429-3_8

the native language of the learner, allowing for more accurate models than those that are independent of the L1. However, this accuracy is possible at the expense of having enough data annotated for pronunciation quality for the specific target population. Since this kind of data is scarcely available and expensive to collect, we focus on techniques to optimize system performance under data sparsity constraints.

Some of the best systems for pronunciation assessment have been based on automatic speech recognition (ASR) technology, using as score the log-likelihood ratio (LLR) between an ASR model representing native pronunciations and another model representing non-native pronunciation [3,5,6]. This approach was successfully used for the first time in [3] for pronunciation scoring, where the native model was obtained using a pronunciation network consisting of native phones for each word and the non-native model using a pronunciation network consisting of non-native phones. The LLR approach was later successfully used for the task of mispronunciation detection in [5] at phone level and [6] at word level. In these two works, different gaussian mixture models (GMM) were trained for the native and non-native pronunciation for each phone. These models were obtained adapting a base GMM model trained with both native and non-native pronunciations to native and non-native pronunciations, respectively. This approach for obtaining the models produced better results than obtaining the native and non-native models by training them from scratch.

In this work we used the LLR between two ASR models as in [3], capturing the native and non-native pronunciations through adaptation as in [5]. Considering that annotated data for a certain L1 population speaking a specific L2 is usually sparse, we investigate different approaches for obtaining the native and non-native ASR models through adaptation, which we postulate should result on more robust models in this scenario. We further assume that the transcriptions are available at scoring time and that a separate large dataset without pronunciation quality annotations is available for training a base ASR model to which to adapt. We evaluated different adaptation schemes: a parallel approach where native and nonnative models are obtained simultaneously from a base model as in [5], and a sequential approach where the non-native model is obtained by adapting the native model to the non-native speakers. We considered three different base models: one trained with both native and non-native speakers, one trained with the separate large corpus, and one trained with the separate corpus and adapted to native and non-native speakers. We also considered training the two models from scratch without a base model to adapt to.

Our experiments showed that the best results are obtained with the sequential adaptation approach using an ASR base model trained with a separate large corpus. However, the advantage of this approach on pronunciation scoring performance over training the models from scratch is small compared to the advantage it gives on word error rate when the models are used for ASR.

2   Method

The pronunciation scoring system in this work computes the score as the log-likelihood ratio between a native and a non-native ASR model (Fig. 1). Each log-likelihood is given by the logarithm of the probability of the features given the optimal path over the HMM states obtained when forced-aligning the features extracted from the signal to the transcription of the speech in the utterance. When subtracting the log-likelihood obtained with the native model from the log-likelihood obtained using the non-native model we obtain the LLR (Fig. 1).

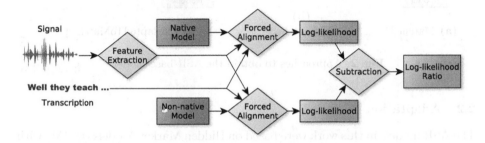

Fig. 1. LLR-based pronunciation scoring system

In this work we evaluated different approaches for obtaining the native and non-native models using adaptation, since this approach was shown in [5] to give better results than training the models from scratch. We compared three approaches to obtain an ASR base model from which to obtain the native and non-native models through MAP adaptation. Then, two different adaptation schemes and two approaches that do not rely on a base model were evaluated.

We assumed two datasets are available, one relatively small set acoustically matched to the testing data with transcriptions and pronunciation quality labels, and a larger set acoustically mismatched to the testing data with transcriptions but no pronunciation quality labels. This is an usual scenario for pronunciation scoring, since large sets are available for ASR training in many languages, while large datasets labelled for pronunciation quality are much harder to obtain, specially when targeting a specific L1 population.

2.1   ASR-Based Models

In [5], GMM base models were trained first using all samples ignoring the class (native or non-native) they belonged to. In this work we used this approach (which we call Matched, Fig. 2a) to obtain an ASR base model. The second approach (Mismatched, Fig. 2b), used a separate but larger acoustically mismatched corpus. Finally, the third approach (AdaptedToMatched, Fig. 2c) adapted the model obtained as in the Mismatched approach using both native and non-native speakers in the matched dataset in order to obtain a model acoustically matched to the test data.

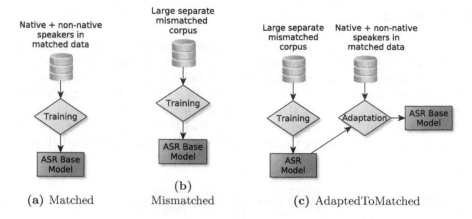

Fig. 2. Approaches to obtain the ASR base models

2.2 Adaptation

The ASR models in this work were based on Hidden Markov Models (HMM) with GMM-based states. The adaptation of the models was done using the maximum a posteriori approach on the GMM means (MAP, [2]). The adapted mean of the GMM component k of state i in the HMM, is given by

$$\widetilde{\mu}_{ik} = \frac{\tau \mu_{ik} + \sum_t c_{ikt} x_t}{\tau + \sum_t c_{ikt}}, \tag{1}$$

where τ is a hyperparameter that measures the "strength" of belief in the prior, c_{ikt} is the probability of the mixture component k in state i given observation x_t and μ_{ik} is the mean of the base model. The second term in the numerator corresponds to the "new" mean, obtained as the weighted mean of the samples found to belong to the kth Gaussian with a non-zero probability. The level of belief in the prior model is given by the hyperparameter τ. Lower values of τ correspond to more aggressive adaptations (higher belief in new data) while higher values correspond to less aggressive adaptation (higher belief in the previous model). In preliminar experiments, different values for τ were evaluated and the best results were obtained with $\tau = 10$. We use this value in all our experiments.

2.3 Adaptation Schemes

In [5], the native model was obtained adapting the GMM base model using the data from the native speakers and, analogously, the non-native model was obtained adapting the GMM base model using the data from the non-native speakers. We call this training scheme "parallel" (Fig. 3b), where we also consider the option where no base model is available and both models are trained from scratch. We propose an alternative scheme which we call "sequential" (Fig. 3a) in which the non-native model is obtained adapting the native model to non-native

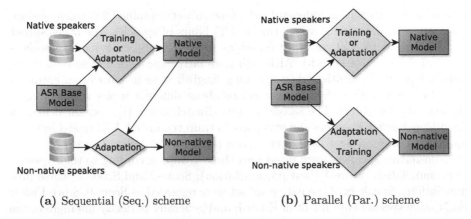

(a) Sequential (Seq.) scheme   (b) Parallel (Par.) scheme

Fig. 3. Schemes to define native and non-native models with and without using an ASR base model. The "Training" option is used for the no base model (None) approach and the "Adaptation" option is used together with the ASR base model in the adaptation (Matched, Mismatched and AdaptedToMatched) approaches

speakers. Given the three approaches to obtain the ASR based model (Fig. 2) plus the no-base-model option, and the two adaptation schemes (Fig. 3), eight possibilities to obtain the native and non-native models are defined.

2.4   LLR Scoring

Pronunciation scores are computed using the native and non-native models (Fig. 1). Log-likelihoods from the most likely path obtained by forced alignment are given at frame level (i.e. every 10 ms). In this work, phone-level log-likelihoods are obtained by averaging the frame-level log-likelihoods. The average is used because we assume that all phones should have, a priori, the same influence, regardless of their length. Finally, speaker-level scores are computed as the average of phone-level log-likelihoods over all the speech available for the speaker in the conversation. This average implicitly assumes that all phones contribute equally to pronunciation quality perception, which is not necessarily the case. Taking the importance of each phone into account when computing the speaker-level score is part of our future work. The speaker-level log-likelihoods for the native and non-native models are finally subtracted to obtain the LLR.

3   Experimental Setup

Two corpora were used for this work, both of them comprised by telephone conversations collected in the USA. The first one (Fisher, [4]) was used to obtain the native and non-native models as well as for testing and only two subsets were used. Although some speakers participated in more than one conversation, we tested each conversation independently. One subset contained 299 conversation-sides uttered by native speakers (around 25 hours of speech). The other subset was comprised by 249 conversations-sides uttered by Spanish native speakers (around 21 hours of speech). Although non-native speakers had some mispronunciations, their abilities when speaking English were in most cases excellent since they were able to hold conversations about different topics with strangers through the telephone. The second corpus (Switchboard, [1]) contained mainly American English speakers and was used to train the initial ASR model in those approaches using a separate larger corpus (around 518 hours of speech).

Non-native speakers were rated into three groups according to their quality of pronunciation: Score-1 (best pronunciation), Score-2 and Score-3 (worse pronunciation). Speakers of the native subset were regarded as Score-0. Since Fisher non-native speakers are fluent in English and generally perfectly intelligible, the scores were assigned based on the perceived accentedness (pronunciation differences with respect to native speakers) rather than on fluency or intelligibility. Around 30% of the speakers in each class were separated in order to obtain a held-out set for a final evaluation of the system. The speakers in this held-out set were selected in order to maximize the number of conversations left for development. Tables 1 and 2 show the number of conversations in each group.

Table 1. Conversation-sides for development and held-out sets per Score class

	0	1	2	3
Development	234	120	40	51
Held-out	65	24	6	8

Table 2. Speakers for development and held-out sets per Score class

	0	1	2	3
Development	200	46	16	20
Held-out	65	24	6	8

Cross-validation with 20 folds was used to generate different train and test sets in the development phase. Many speakers in the four classes were engaged in more than one conversation. In order to avoid optimistic results, the definition of the held-out and cross validation sets was carried out at speaker level.

We evaluated the use of three different sets to create the non-native models: a set composed only of Score-3 speakers, a set with both Score-2 and Score-3 and a set with all non-native speakers. The best results were obtained using Score-3 speakers only or both Score-2 and Score-3. For the following experiments we use only Score-3 speakers to create the non-native model.

3.1 ASR System Characteristics

The senone-based HMM-GMM ASR models in this work were created using the Switchboard recipe of the Kaldi toolkit [10]. The features used were MFCCs, computed in 25 ms time windows every 10 ms. Monophone ASR models were trained in a first phase and a triphone model trained in a second phase limiting the number of senones and number of gaussians to 3200 and 30000 respectively.

Finally, a second triphone model was trained to obtain the final model limiting the number of senones and number of gaussians to 4000 and 70000 respectively.

3.2   Performance Measures

In order to compare different parameters in the system, receiver operating characteristic (ROC) curves were used to measure the performance of a binary classifier for the Score-0 and Score-3 samples. The area under the ROC curve (AUC) was used as performance metric and 95% confidence intervals were computed using the bootstrap method ([9]). One thousand random samplings of the speakers were created and, for each sample, the corresponding scores used to compute an AUC. The confidence interval was given by the 2.5 and 97.5 percentiles in the distribution of the obtained AUCs. In a final phase, all speakers were used to evaluate the performance of the best model. Normalized histograms of the distributions of the four speaker classes were generated and Pearson correlation computed between the labels (0, 1, 2, 3) and the score values.

4   Results

The conversation sides uttered by native and non-native speakers in the Fisher corpus had on average 295 seconds of speech. In order to simulate smaller amounts of data available for training or adaptation, smaller regions of each conversation sides were used including 20, 40, 80 and 160 s per conversation-side. Figure 4 shows the AUCs for each approach as a function of this duration.

The figure shows that when the base model is trained with mismatched data, the sequential modeling approach is significantly superior to the parallel approach, specially when smaller amounts of data are available for adaptation. This implies that it is better to address the mismatch due to acoustic conditions first, by adapting the mismatched model, which was trained with mostly native speakers, to the matched native speakers, obtaining a native model that is acoustically matched to the test conditions. Adapting this model to the non-native population is then easier (less change is required in the parameters) than adapting the original mismatched model, which is mismatched to the non-native speakers both acoustically and in terms of pronunciation.

The sequential scheme is also better than the parallel one when the mismatched model is adapted to the full matched data and when no base model is used, though the difference between the two adaptation methods is much smaller in these cases than when using the mismatched base model. This is probably because there is less acoustic mismatch to make up for in these two cases, giving less advantage to the sequential approach.

When the base model is trained with all the matched data, the best adaptation method is the parallel one, with the sequential one being significantly worse than all other methods. In this case, there is no acoustic mismatch to compensate for, hence, the advantages described above for the sequential method no longer hold. It is then sufficient to adapt the base model directly to the two populations of speakers, which were already well represented in the base model.

Overall, Fig. 4 shows that the best approaches are those based on the sequential adaptation method with base models trained with the mismatched data (adapted or not to the matched data) or without a base model. In fact, the advantage from using a base model is quite limited, even when a very small amount of matched data is available. This is particularly surprising because the models that are obtained by adaptation to a base model trained with the large mismatched data are significantly better than those that do not rely on this additional data in terms of word error rate (WER). For example, the mismatched model adapted to 40 s per conversation of the matched native speakers gives a WER of 43.78 on the native held-out speakers, while the native model trained directly to 40 s per conversation of the matched native speakers gives a WER of 62.19. This means that the model that uses the mismatched data as a base model for adaptation is significantly better for ASR. Yet, this difference does not carry over to the pronunciation scoring task. We hypothesize that this is due to the nature of the LLR, where only the differences between models influence the score. Hence, even in models trained with very sparse data (only about 0.5 h of non-native data and 2 h of native data for the 40 s per conversation case), the LLR is a robust measure of the pronunciation quality, despite the fact that the models are significantly worse for ASR than those trained using a robust base model trained on a much larger amount of data.

Figure 5 shows two selected approaches along with the corresponding confidence intervals. Although both of them have similar patterns when more data is available, when only 20 seconds of speech per conversation are available the confidence interval is narrower and higher for the Mismatched approach showing some advantage for this approach in a scenario of extreme data scarcity.

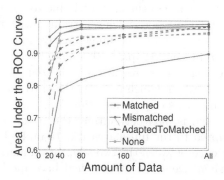

Fig. 4. AUC values for the eight different approaches. Solid lines correspond to the sequential approach, dashed lines correspond to the parallel approach for each base model

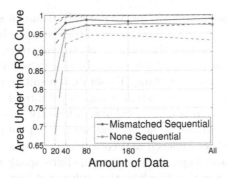

Fig. 5. AUC confidence intervals for two approaches. Solid lines correspond to the AUC (as in Fig. 4), dashed lines correspond to confidence intervals limits

4.1 Multiclass Classification Results

The best approach from the previous section (the Mismatched Sequential models adapted to all available matched data) was finally evaluated on all speaker classes and normalized distribution histograms for the development set are presented in Fig. 6. In spite of adapting models using only Score-0 and Score-3 instances, the scores given for the other two classes show the expected pattern with better pronunciation classes with lower scores and worse pronunciation classes with higher scores. The Pearson correlation on the development set was 0.74.

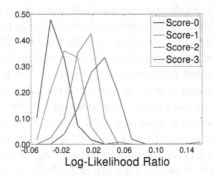

Fig. 6. Normalized distribution histogram with all classes using development set

In order to confirm that the development choices did not result in models overfitting the development data, we evaluated a model adapted to all the development data on the held-out set. The Pearson correlation on the held-out set was 0.81, which implies that the obtained models generalize quite well to unseen speakers. Furthermore, these results are comparable to those reported in previous works using datasets with relatively unclean speech, as is the case of the Fisher dataset. Hönig et al. [8] used read web-collected data using headsets and reported a correlation of 0.57 using around 10 min of speech per speaker. Cucchiarini et al. [7] reported a correlation of 0.75 on speech read over the telephone and 0.5 when evaluating the answers of students on an exam with around 1 min of speech per speaker in both cases. In our case, we use an average of 5 min of speech per speaker in testing. To obtain a result comparable to those in Cucchiarini's work, we run our system using only 1 min of speech per speaker, which gave us a correlation of 0.37, a value significantly lower than the one they obtained. However, it should be noted that we used spontaneous speech while Cucchiarini et al. used read speech and considered not only advanced speakers, as in our work, but also beginner and intermediate speakers, which are much easier to separate from native speakers than advanced learners.

5   Conclusion

We study a pronunciation scoring system based on the log-likelihood ratio between an ASR model trained with native speakers and an ASR model trained with non-native speakers. We compared results using different approaches for generating the native and non-native models using two sets of data: a large corpus acoustically mismatched to the test data, and a smaller acoustically-matched corpus. Different ways of using these sets for training and adapting the ASR models were explored.

The best results were produced when the native model was obtained by adapting an ASR model previously trained on the large mismatched corpus to matched data from native speakers, and the non-native model was obtained by adapting this native model to the matched data from non-native speakers. Nevertheless, we show that the advantage of using a large mismatched corpus for training a base model to which to adapt is quite limited. This is despite the fact that the model obtained by adaptation to the mismatched model is significantly better than the one trained from scratch in terms of WER. It appears that the LLR used for pronunciation scoring is quite robust, allowing us to train models with very sparse data without large degradations in performance with respect to generating the model by adaptation to a robust base model. This indicates that we should not rely on our intuitions built from our experience on ASR to decide how to train models for pronunciation scoring. Rather, we should revisit decisions made about the models. This might include, as in this work, the best way to use available data, as well as other issues like the choice of features, the size of the models, and so on. These are issues we plan to explore in future work.

Acknowledgments. Work partially supported by ANPCYT PICT 2014-1713.

References

1. Godfrey, J.J., Holliman, E.C., McDaniel, J.: SWITCHBOARD: telephone speech corpus for research and development. In: Proceedings of ICASSP. IEEE, San Francisco (1992)

2. Gauvain, J.-L., Lee, C.-H.: Maximum a posteriori estimation for multivariate Gaussian mixture observations of Markov chains. IEEE Trans. Speech Audio Process. **2**, 291–298 (1994)
3. Ronen, O., Neumeyer, L., Franco, H.: Automatic detection of mispronunciation for language instruction. In: Proceedings of EUROSPEECH, Rhodes (1997)
4. Cieri, C., Miller, D., Walker, K.: The fisher corpus: a resource for the next generations of speech-to-text. In: LREC, Lisbon (2004)
5. Franco, H., Ferrer, L., Bratt, H.: Adaptive and discriminative modeling for improved mispronunciation detection. In: Proceedings of ICASSP. IEEE, Florence (2014)
6. Robertson, S., Munteanu, C., Penn, G.: Pronunciation error detection for new language learners. In: Proceedings of Interspeech, San Francisco (2016)
7. Cucchiarini, C., Strik, H., Binnenpoorte, D., Boves, L.: Pronunciation evaluation in read and spontaneous speech: a comparison between human ratings and automatic scores. In: Proceedings of the New Sounds. Citeseer (2000)
8. Hönig, F., Batliner, A., Nöth, E.: Automatic assessment of non-native prosody annotation, modelling and evaluation. In: Proceedings of ISADEPT (2012)
9. Efron, B.: Bootstrap methods: another look at the Jackknife. Ann. Stat. **7**, 1–26 (1979)
10. Povey, D., Ghoshal, A., Boulianne, G., Burget, L., Glembek, O., Goel, N., Hannemann, M., Motlicek, P., Qian, Y., Schwarz, P., Silovsky, J., Stemmer, G., Vesely, K.: IEEE 2011 Workshop on Automatic Speech Recognition and Understanding (2011)

An Algorithm for Detection of Breath Sounds in Spontaneous Speech with Application to Speaker Recognition

Sri Harsha Dumpala[1(✉)] and K.N.R.K. Raju Alluri[2]

[1] TCS Innovation Labs, Mumbai, India
d.harsha@tcs.com
[2] International Institute of Information Technology, Hyderabad, India
raju.alluri@research.iiit.ac.in

Abstract. Automatic detection and demarcation of non-speech sounds in speech is critical for developing sophisticated human-machine interaction systems. The main objective of this study is to develop acoustic features capturing the production differences between speech and breath sounds in terms of both, excitation source and vocal tract system based characteristics. Using these features, a rule-based algorithm is proposed for automatic detection of breath sounds in spontaneous speech. The proposed algorithm outperforms the previous methods for detection of breath sounds in spontaneous speech. Further, the importance of breath detection for speaker recognition is analyzed by considering an i-vector-based speaker recognition system. Experimental results show that the detection of breath sounds, prior to i-vector extraction, is essential to nullify the effect of breath sounds occurring in test samples on speaker recognition, which otherwise will degrade the performance of i-vector-based speaker recognition systems.

Keywords: Non-speech sounds · Breath sounds · Excitation source · Vocal tract system · i-Vector · Speaker recognition

1 Introduction

In natural conversations, non-speech sounds occur very frequently along with regular speech (sounds). Though, speech and non-speech sounds are produced by the human speech production system, non-speech sounds may not carry any linguistic information like speech but will provide important cues about the emotional and physical state of the speaker. Non-speech sounds include vocalizations such as breath, laughter, cough, etc., [1–4]. Effective detection and classification of these sounds is necessary for applications such as speech and speaker recognition, emotion classification and emotive speech synthesis, etc.

Breath is one such non-speech sound which occurs very frequently in natural conversations including high quality recordings of singers and professional narrators [5]. Breath sounds are produced by pushing air out of the lungs through

© Springer International Publishing AG 2017
A. Karpov et al. (Eds.): SPECOM 2017, LNAI 10458, pp. 98–108, 2017.
DOI: 10.1007/978-3-319-66429-3_9

the vocal tract system with no strong constriction [6]. Generally, there is no presence of significant glottal activity during the production of breath sounds making them unvoiced [5]. Breath sounds are generally produced by speakers when under stress or strain, and also to signify pause or punctuation in conversations [7,8]. Detection of audible breath sounds is useful for enhancing the quality of audio recordings and to specify the instants of pause and punctuation in both read and spontaneous speech [5,7,9,10]. Breath sound detection is also found to be useful for cognitive analysis of speech and to improve the performance of speech and speaker recognition systems [6,11,12].

Owing to their importance in speech-based applications, different approaches were proposed for breath detection [5,7,9]. Template matching based methods were mainly considered for detection of breath sounds in audio signals [5,7]. In template matching based approach, breath templates were generated using spectral features such as mel frequency cepstral coefficients (MFCCs) and discrete wavelet transform coefficients. These templates were then considered for searching in the audio signals using dynamic time warping algorithm. Other methods such as usage of hidden Markov models trained with spectral features were also proposed for detection of breath sounds in singing recordings [9]. Most of the previous methods were developed for processing recordings of high quality collected from singers and professional narrators in a controlled environment [7,9]. These methods were found to be very sensitive, and may not be directly adapted for processing spontaneous speech [11]. Only a few studies have considered detection of breath sounds in spontaneous speech [7]. But the performance of these methods is low, emphasizing the need for further analysis to detect breath sounds. Furthermore, in most studies, only spectral features were considered for analysis but not excitation source based features, which might provide complementary information to discriminate breath sounds from speech (particularly, voiced speech sounds).

The main contributions of this paper are (a) to analyze both, excitation source and vocal tract system based characteristics of breath sounds in comparison to speech, (b) to propose a rule-based algorithm, using acoustic features capturing the excitation source and vocal tract system based variations between breath and speech, for automatic detection of breath sounds in spontaneous speech and (c) to illustrate the importance of breath detection on the performance of an i-vector-based speaker recognition system. The paper is organized as follows. Section 2 explains the database used for analysis. Section 3 provides the analysis of the breath sound. Algorithm proposed for breath detection is given in Sect. 4. Performance evaluation of the proposed algorithm is discussed in Sect. 5. Analysis of the effect of breath detection on speaker recognition is given in Sect. 6. Summary along with conclusions are given in Sect. 7.

2   Database

The Buckeye corpus of conversational speech which contains several hours of spontaneous speech recordings is considered for this study [13]. This database consists of speech data collected from 40 speakers (20 male and 20 female) in the form of informal interactions between the speaker and an interviewer. These recordings contain several occurrences of various non-speech sounds such as breath, laughter, cough, etc. These non-speech sounds were tagged as "VOCNOISE" in the database. We (a group of 3 persons) have manually listened to all the "VOCNOISE" segments, and have segregated the breath sounds for use in this study. A subset of 40 speech utterances collected from 6 speakers (3 male and 3 female) containing 30 breath sound segments is considered for analysis. A separate test set of 500 speech utterances consisting of 405 breath segments collected from 30 speakers (15 male and 15 female), not considered for analysis, is considered to evaluate the performance of the proposed algorithm. In the test set, some utterances do not contain even a single breath segment while some utterances consists of more than one breath segment.

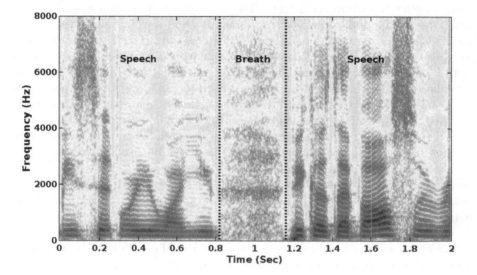

Fig. 1. Spectrogram of a speech signal with breath sound (*marked as Breath*), *whose bounds are denoted by vertical dotted lines*

3   Analysis of Breath Sounds

The excitation source and vocal tract system based characteristics of breath sounds are analyzed to define the feature set for breath detection. Generally, most of the breath sounds are unvoiced [5], signifying the absence of significant glottal activity during their production. This can also be observed from the spectrogram (shown in Fig. 1), where the overall spectral energy is very low in breath regions (see between 0.8 sec–1.2 sec, marked as breath), particularly in the frequency range of 0 Hz–1000 Hz, compared to voiced speech regions (see between 1.2 sec–1.6 sec in Fig. 1). This characteristic of breath sounds is captured using the excitation source based features i.e., zero frequency filtered signal energy (α), and strength of excitation at epochs (β). α values are computed as the energy of the zero frequency filtered (ZFF) signal using a window of length 2 msec centered at epoch locations, and the β values are computed as the slope of the ZFF signal around epoch locations (more details in [14,15]). The ZFF signal and the epoch locations are extracted directly from the speech signal using the zero frequency filtering method [16]. It can be observed from Fig. 2(a) and (b), respectively, that the α and β values are very low in breath segments compared to speech segments (particularly in voiced regions). Hence, these features can be used to distinguish breath sounds from voiced speech sounds.

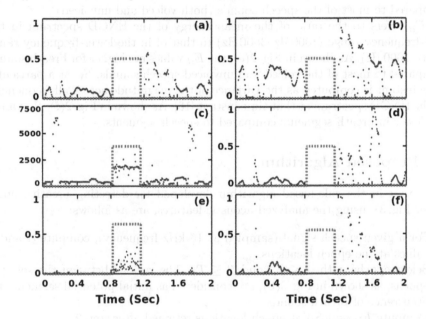

Fig. 2. Figure shows the features considered for breath sound detection. The features are (a) α, (b) β (c) F_D values in frequency (Hz), (d) S_D, (e) E_R, (f) S_V. Segments highlighted with red (dotted) line represents breath sounds as per ground truth (Color figure online)

It can be observed from the spectrogram (Fig. 1) that the breath segments has a higher concentration of spectral energy in the mid-frequency range (1000 Hz–3500 Hz) followed by lower-frequency range (0 Hz–1000 Hz) and then by higher-frequency range (3500 Hz–8000 Hz) [5]. In case of speech, the spectral energy is concentrated relatively more in the lower frequency range for voiced sounds (see between 1.2 sec–1.6 sec, and between 0.2 sec–0.8 sec in Fig. 1), and in the higher frequency range for unvoiced sounds (see between 0 sec and 0.2 sec, and at 1.8 sec in Fig. 1). These spectral variations between breath and speech sounds are captured using features extracted from the Hilbert envelope of the numerator group delay (HNGD) spectrum obtained using the zero time windowing method [17]. The spectral features considered for this analysis are dominant resonance frequency (F_D), dominant resonance strength (S_D), mid-to-low frequency energy ratio (E_R) and spectral variance (S_V).

F_D refers to the frequency of the dominant peaks in the HNGD spectrum, and S_D is measured as the magnitude of the HNGD spectrum at F_D. In this work, F_D and S_D values are obtained at epoch locations as explained in [14]. It can be observed from Fig. 2(c) that the F_D values are in the lower and mid frequency ranges for breath sounds, whereas most of the F_D values are in the higher and mid frequency ranges for voiced and unvoiced speech sounds, respectively. It can be observed from Fig. 2(d) that the S_D values are very low in breath segments compared to most of the speech sounds (both voiced and unvoiced).

E_R refers to the ratio of the mean energy of the HNGD spectrum in the mid-frequency range (1000 Hz–3500 Hz) to that of in the lower-frequency range (0 Hz–1000 Hz). As shown in Fig. 2(e), the E_R values are higher for breath sounds compared to most of the voiced and unvoiced speech sounds. S_V at a particular time instant is computed as the variance of the magnitude across all frequencies in the HNGD spectrum at that time instant [15]. As shown in Fig. 2(f), S_V values are lower in breath segments compared to speech segments.

4   Proposed Algorithm

The steps in the rule-based algorithm developed for detecting breath sounds (refer Fig. 3), using the analyzed acoustic features, are as follows:

1. For a given speech signal (sampled at 16 kHz frequency), compute α and β values at the epoch locations.
2. Select epochs with $\alpha \leq T_\alpha$ and $\beta \leq T_\beta$. The regions between the selected epochs, as shown in Fig. 3(b), are considered as initial potential segments for occurrence of breath sounds.
3. Compute F_D and S_D at epoch locations retained after step 2.
4. Select regions between epochs with F_D within the range $T_{F_{min}} \leq F_D \leq T_{F_{max}}$, and that of S_D within the range $T_{S_{min}} \leq S_D \leq T_{S_{max}}$ as in Fig. 3(c).
5. For the segments retained after Step 4, Compute E_R and S_V for every 1 msec using a window length of 2 msec.
6. Thresholds used for E_R and S_V are T_R and T_V, respectively. Select segments with E_R values above the threshold and S_V values below the threshold as shown in Fig. 3(d).
7. For the segments retained after Step 6, combine segments separated by less than 20 msec to form a single segment. Then, eliminate segments with duration less than 30 msec to obtain the final segments, considered as breath sounds, as shown in Fig. 3(d).

In the algorithm, T_α, T_β, T_E and T_V refer to the thresholds used for the features α, β, E_R and S_V, respectively. $T_{F_{min}}, T_{F_{max}}, T_{S_{min}}$ and $T_{S_{max}}$ refer to the lower and upper thresholds used for the features F_D and F_S, respectively.

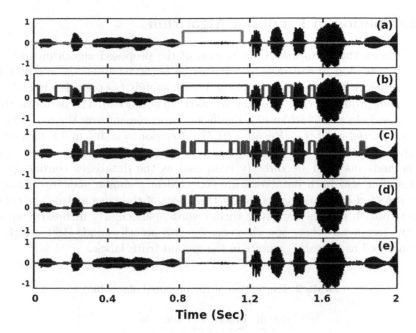

Fig. 3. Figure illustrates the steps in the proposed breath detection algorithm. (a) Speech signal marked with breath regions as in ground truth (red line), (b) speech signal marked with potential breath segments detected (blue line) using (b) α and β i.e., D_1, (c) F_D and S_D combined with D_1 i.e., D_2, (d) E_R and S_V combined with D_2 i.e., D_3, respectively. (e) Final breath regions (blue line) as detected by the algorithm. (Color figure online)

Thresholds T_α and T_β are chosen such that no breath segments are eliminated at the preliminary level, even at the cost of few false alarms. Further, thresholds $T_E, T_V, T_{F_{min}}, T_{F_{max}}, T_{S_{min}}$ and $T_{S_{max}}$ are chosen such that the initially detected false detections are eliminated apart from refining the detected breath sound boundaries as shown in Fig. 3. Thresholds used in the algorithm (as shown in Table 1) for experiments are selected based on the empirical analysis of the 40 speech utterances (containing 30 breath segments) considered for analysis.

Table 1. Thresholds used for features

Features	T_α	T_β	$T_{F_{min}}$	$T_{F_{max}}$	$T_{S_{min}}$	$T_{S_{max}}$	T_E	T_V
Thresholds	0.015	0.03	50	2800	0.0001	0.012	6×10^{-5}	1.3×10^{-4}

5 Evaluation of Proposed Algorithm

Table 2 shows the performance evaluation of the proposed algorithm in terms of recall, precision and F-measure. It can be observed from Table 2 that the proposed algorithm detects most of the breath sounds (as precision is high i.e., 97.29%) but produces a few false alarms (as recall is 78.17%). The performance of the proposed algorithm achieved a significant improvement over the performance metrics reported in [7] (i.e., Recall = 94.7%, Precision = 40.0% and F-measure = 56.1%), which is also tested on spontaneous speech. The performance of the two methods may not be directly compared as the databases considered are different, but still both databases are collected in a similar scenario. Analysis of the detected breath segments show that most of the false alarms are caused by short breath sounds occurring within words, particularly in breathy speech segments (segments where speech co-occurs with breath sounds [18]), which are not annotated as "breath" sounds in the ground truth labels.

Table 2. Evaluation of the proposed algorithm

Recall	Precision	F-measure
97.29	78.17	86.69

6 Breath Detection for Speaker Recognition

In this Section, the importance of detecting breath sounds in spontaneous speech is illustrated by considering the task of speaker recognition. The effect of breath sounds, occurring in spontaneous speech, on the performance of an i-vector-based speaker recognition system is analyzed, where the enrollment i-vectors for each speaker are obtained by considering only neutral speech of the speaker. Further, the speaker recognition performance is evaluated by including the proposed breath detection module (BDM) in the front-end of the speaker recognition system. The complete approach followed for analysis is depicted in Fig. 4. It can be observed from Fig. 4 that the test sample is passed through the BDM (used to detect the breath sounds in the test sample) prior to voice activity detection (VAD) and extraction of i-vectors from the test sample. The regions in the test sample detected as breath sounds by the BDM are eliminated, and then VAD and i-vector extraction is performed on this modified test sample (test sample obtained after removing breath regions).

As shown in Fig. 4, the test sample consists of both, speech and breath sounds produced by the same speaker. BDM uses the algorithm proposed in Sect. 4 to detect breath sounds in the test sample, and eliminate them. VAD, used to remove silence and low signal-to-noise ratio regions, is performed using Voicebox toolkit [19]. State-of-the-art GMM-UBM-based (Gaussian mixture model with universal background model) i-vector framework provided by the Voice biometry standardization (VBS) is used for the speaker recognition system considered

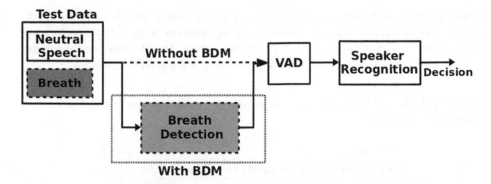

Fig. 4. Block diagram of the proposed speaker recognition system

in this analysis [20]. In VBS, the gender-independent 2048-component universal background model (UBM) was trained using NIST SRE 2004 − 2008 data ($\approx$ 1156.03 hours of data) and the total variability space 'T' of 600-dimension was trained using Fisher English (Part 1 and 2), NIST SRE 2004−2008, Switchboard (Phase 2, Phase 3, cellular part 1 and cellular part 2), which totals to $\approx$ 9010.23 hours of data. Further, the linear discriminant analysis (LDA) matrix of 200-dimensions and the within-class covariance matrix of 200-dimensions, which are used in the post-processing of the i-vectors, were also trained using the same data used for training the T matrix.

The test i-vectors (obtained from test samples) are scored against the speaker-specific enrollment i-vectors using probabilistic linear discriminant analysis (PLDA), and the resulting scores are used to evaluate the overall system performance. The system performance is evaluated in terms of equal error rate (EER).

Standard databases such as NIST SRE, which are used in speaker recognition experiments do not provide transcriptions, especially for non-speech sounds such as breath, which are required for this analysis. Hence, for the speaker recognition experiments in this analysis, we considered 32 speakers (16 male and 16 female) from the Buckeye corpus, whose audio recordings have significant presence of breath sounds. A total of 50 utterances (each of 2.5 sec to 3 sec in duration, containing only neutral speech) per speaker are considered to extract the enrollment i-vector for each speaker. To test this speaker recognition system, 10 utterances (each of 2.5 sec to 3 sec in duration) per speaker, containing both neutral speech and breath sounds produced by speaker, are considered. The amount of breath sound was about 20% to 30% (in duration) in the considered test utterances. Further, the performance of the system is also evaluated by considering 20 utterances (containing only neutral speech) per speaker, which are used to obtain the baseline performance of the speaker recognition system.

For the speaker recognition experiments, all utterances (both train and test) are down-sampled to 8 kHz, and the frames retained after VAD are represented using MFCCs. 60-dimensional MFCC vectors (first 19 static coefficients along with the 0th coefficient, and their corresponding delta and delta-delta coefficients) are extracted using 25 msec Hamming window with a 10 msec forward shift. Prior to computation of delta and delta-delta, the 20-dimensional feature vectors are mean and variance normalized using a 2 sec sliding window.

Table 3. EER (in %) obtained for the speaker recognition system trained on neutral speech of the speakers

Test case	EER (in %)
Only Neutral (without BDM) i.e., Baseline	2.62
Only Neutral (with BDM)	2.68
Neutral + Breath (without BDM)	5.36
Neutral + Breath (with BDM)	3.29

6.1 Results

The EER values obtained for the speaker recognition system, with and without the breath detection module, are provided in Table 3. As shown in Table 3, there is a significant degradation in performance (EER = 5.36%) compared to the baseline performance (EER = 2.62%), when the test samples containing breath sounds are provided directly to the speaker recognition system (without including the breath detection module). When the breath detection module is included in the front-end of the speaker recognition system, a relative improvement of about 38% in terms of EER (EER improved to 3.29% from 5.36%). This improvement in performance of the speaker recognition system obtained by including BDM highlights the importance of breath sound detection for speaker recognition. A slight degradation in performance of the system with BDM when tested with utterances containing both neutral speech and breath sounds (EER of 3.29%) compared to the baseline performance (EER = 2.62%) is observed. This may be due to the influence of the breath sounds on subsequent speech resulting in breathy speech segments, which are also found to degrade the performance of speaker recognition systems trained on neutral speech [21]. It can also be observed that the inclusion of BDM in the front-end of the speaker recognition system have no (little) effect on the performance of the system, when only neutral speech is provided as input to the system (EER = 2.68% with BDM, and EER = 2.62% without BDM).

7 Summary and Conclusions

In this paper, a rule-based algorithm, using acoustic features representing excitation source and vocal tract system based differences between speech and breath sounds, is proposed for detection of breath sounds in spontaneous speech. The proposed algorithm outperforms the previous algorithms proposed for detection of breath sounds in spontaneous speech, and is found to detect most of the breath sounds in spontaneous speech. Further, the significance of detecting breath sounds is illustrated for the task of i-vector-based speaker recognition. Experimental results show that the performance of the speaker recognition system (trained on neutral speech of the speakers) degrades when breath sounds occur during the testing phase. It is also experimentally shown that the inclusion of the breath detection module in the front-end of the speaker recognition system will compensate for the effect of breath sounds on the performance of an i-vector-based speaker recognition system.

Acknowledgments. The authors would like to thank Dr. Sunil Kumar Kopparapu, of TCS Innovation Labs - Mumbai, for providing his critical comments and suggestions which helped improve the content of this paper.

References

1. Lei, B., Rahman, S.A., Song, I.: Content-based classification of breath sound with enhanced features. Neurocomputing **141**, 139–147 (2014)
2. Dumpala, S.H., Sridaran, K.V., Gangashetty, S.V., Yegnanarayana, B.: Analysis of laughter and speech-laugh signals using excitation source information. In: ICASSP, pp. 975–979 (2014)
3. Drugman, T., Urbain, J., Dutoit, T.: Assessment of audio features for automatic cough detection. In: EUSIPCO, pp. 1289–1293 (2011)
4. Dumpala, S.H., Gangamohan, P., Gangashetty, S.V., Yegnanarayana, B.: Use of vowels in discriminating speech-laugh from laughter and neutral speech. In: Interspeech, pp. 1437–1441 (2016)
5. Ruinskiy, D., Lavner, Y.: An effective algorithm for automatic detection and exact demarcation of breath sounds in speech and song signals. IEEE Trans. Audio Speech Lang. Process. **15**(3), 838–850 (2007)
6. Zelasko, P., Jadczyk, T., Zilko, B.: HMM-based breath and filled pauses elimination in ASR. In: SIGMAP, pp. 255–260 (2014)
7. Igras, M., Zilko, B.: Wavelet method for breath detection in audio signals. In: ICME, pp. 1–6 (2013)
8. Godin, K.W., Hansen, J.H.: Physical task stress and speaker variability in voice quality. EURASIP J. Audio Speech Music Proc. **1**, 1–13 (2015)
9. Nakano, T., Ogata, J., Goto, M., Hiraga, Y.: Analysis and automatic detection of breath sounds in unaccompanied singing voice. In: ICMPC, pp. 387–390 (2008)
10. Igras, M., Zilko, B.: Different types of pauses as a source of biometry. In: Models and Analysis of Vocal Emissions for Biomedical Applications, pp. 197–200 (2013)
11. Rapcan, V., D'Arcy, S., Reilly, R.B.: Automatic breath sound detection and removal for cognitive studies of speech and language. In: ISSC, pp. 1–6 (2009)
12. Janicki, A.: On the impact of non-speech sounds on speaker recognition. In: Sojka, P., Horák, A., Kopeček, I., Pala, K. (eds.) TSD 2012. LNCS, vol. 7499, pp. 566–572. Springer, Heidelberg (2012). doi:10.1007/978-3-642-32790-2_69
13. Pitt, M.A., Dilley, L., Johnson, K., Kiesling, S., Raymond, W., Hume, E., Fosler-Lussier, E.: Buckeye Corpus of Conversational Speech (2nd release). Department of Psychology, Ohio State University (Distributor), Columbus, OH (2007)
14. Dumpala, S.H., Nellore, B.T., Nevali, R.R., Gangashetty, S.V., Yegnanarayana, B.: Robust features for sonorant segmentation in continuous speech. In: Interspeech, pp. 1987–1991 (2015)

15. Dumpala, S.H., Nellore, B.T., Nevali, R.R., Gangashetty, S.V., Yegnanarayana, B.: Robust vowel landmark detection using epoch-based features. In: Interspeech, pp. 160–164 (2016)
16. Murty, K.S.R., Yegnanarayana, B.: Epoch extraction from speech signals. IEEE Trans. Audio Speech Lang. Process. **16**, 1602–1613 (2008)
17. Yegnanarayana, B., Dhananjaya, N.G.: Spectro-temporal analysis of speech signals using zero-time windowing and group delay function. Speech Commun. **55**(6), 782–795 (2013)
18. Hirose, H.: Investigating the physiology of laryngeal structures. In: The Handbook of Phonetic Sciences, Cambridge, pp. 116–136 (1995)
19. Brookes, M., et al.: Voicebox: Speech processing toolbox for Matlab (2011). www.ee.ic.ac.uk/hp/staff/dmb/voicebox/voicebox.html
20. Voice Biometry Standardization (VBS) (2015). http://voicebiometry.org/
21. Dumpala, S.H., Kopparapu, S.K.: Improved speaker recognition system for stressed speech using deep neural networks. In: IJCNN, pp. 1257–1264 (2017)

An Alternative Approach to Exploring a Video

Fahim A. Salim[1(✉)], Fasih Haider[1], Owen Conlan[1], and Saturnino Luz[2]

[1] ADAPT Centre, Trinity College Dublin, Dublin, Ireland
{salimf,haiderf,owen.conlan}@scss.tcd.ie
[2] IPHSI, University of Edinburgh, Edinburgh, UK
S.Luz@ed.ac.uk

Abstract. Exploring the content of a video is typically inefficient due to the linear streamed nature of its media. Video may be seen as a combination of a set of features, the visual track, the audio track and transcription of the spoken words, etc. These features may be viewed as a set of temporally bounded parallel modalities. It is our contention that together these modalities and derived features have the potential to be presented individually or in discrete combination, to allow deeper and more effective content exploration within different parts of a video. This paper presents a novel system for videos' exploration and reports a recent user study conducted to learn usage patterns by offering video content as an alternative representation. The learned usage patterns may be utilized to build a template driven representation engine that uses the features to offer a multimodal synopsis of video that may lead to more efficient exploration of video content.

Keywords: Multimedia analysis · Video representation

1 Introduction

Content consumption is increasingly becoming video oriented. Due to its linear nature as media, it might take longer to evaluate the context of a video than a textual document [13]. It is because, different modalities within a video are tightly bonded together. It is our contention that exploring a video can be made more efficient by representing it in a multimodal and configurable manner, i.e. breaking the tight bond between the parallel modalities can open up new opportunities to explore a video.

By multimodality, we mean that videos are composed of a set of features, namely the moving video track, the audio track and other derived features, such as transcriptions of the spoken word. Together these modalities can give an effective way of communicating information. The content value of these modalities as a whole far exceeds their values separately i.e. the whole exceeds the sum of its part. Richness both in terms of modalities and the amount of available video content create a challenge. Videos can vary in length as some videos could be several hours in length. It is very difficult if not impossible for users to fully view every piece of video, which could be useful or important to them.

© Springer International Publishing AG 2017
A. Karpov et al. (Eds.): SPECOM 2017, LNAI 10458, pp. 109–118, 2017.
DOI: 10.1007/978-3-319-66429-3_10

Thus there is a need for more effective means to explore video content, to enable the user to find the desired content as quickly and conveniently as possible. While there has been a lot of progress in this area, current technology is still limited in this regard. It is still quite cumbersome to quickly get the gist of all the available content in order to consume only the desired. Current commercial offerings do not fully harness the multimodal potential of video content.

Currently researchers, approach video exploration by enhancing video selection capability from a large collection, either by listing search query results based on indexing of multimodal attributes [17,28] or by listing video recommendations [27]. But once a short list of videos is identified or even when users have a single video to begin with, the process of getting the desired information within the video or assessing if the video is useful or not, is still quite cumbersome. To solve that problem researchers have proposed different techniques, e.g. video navigation [25], hyper videos [18] or video summarization [8]. However, as it will be elaborated in Sect. 2, current approaches while providing useful and interesting outcomes, are still quite limited in empowering users to get the desired content within a video effectively. Thus there is a need to look at video content differently.

It is our aim to devise an approach which opens up new opportunities to explore a video by breaking the tight bond between the different modalities of a video through feature extraction. The proposed approach will utilize a template driven representation engine to represent the video as a multimedia web page. In order to streamline the design of the template engine, a user study was conducted by utilizing a novel system prototype developed to learn the usage pattern of participants. It involved extracting multimodal features from TED presentation videos and representing them to 29 users.

This paper reports the results of the user study. Multimodal features were extracted automatically using different tools and represented to users in order to enable them to explore video effectively. The usage patterns are not only useful for designing our proposed representation engine, but they also give new insights regarding user preference while exploring the content of an informational video. A novel aspect of the current study compared to [9,20] is, that all of the features extracted and shown to users were automatically extracted using already available tools. Therefore any lessons learned from the study can be readily applied to video content exploration tools.

2   State of the Art

Current techniques allow users to explore the content within a video either by providing the ability to search for something particular or by giving an overall synopsis of a video i.e. video summarization. It would not be unfair to say that in video summarization, importance is usually attributed to visual features [2,5]. However multimodal features are also getting considerable attention due to the added value they bring in terms of identifying important segments [8,12] both in produced videos and in recordings of natural interaction where the interplay among multiple modalities is often core to understanding the content [3,4].

Searching for a piece of information within video assets is still text based as far as commercial offerings (such as YouTube, etc.) are concerned. However, researchers have worked a great deal on multimodal methods to extract information from videos. In [10] authors use face recognition along with name tags to find footage of certain people in videos, while [19] use text recognition techniques to see if there is any textual information appearing in videos. [17] facilitate searching for relevant sections in baseball videos based on metadata attributes, while [25] facilitate navigation and searching within a video through visualizing low-level features and frame surrogates. In order to enhance the efficiency of search within video and [7] uses ontologies. [28] extends this idea of semantic-based search by using linked data to provide a time-based video index, which allows search within the video content. [22] devise a framework for retrieving information using multimedia queries. Another interesting example of multimodal video search is [29], in this work authors devise a cross-media retrieval approach to search for video by giving audio samples and vice versa.

As described above, current approaches to searching within video utilize the multimodal features of video in their processing but underutilized the potential of multimodal features in the representation. With the use of key-frames and other textual information, such as keywords, these approaches allow the user to search a particular item and to jump to a particular position in the video, but they lack the ability to provide an overall synopsis. Video summarization techniques provide the overall synopsis of the video, but the ability to get something particular is limited by the overall visual focus of the representation. It is our contention that exploration can be made more efficient by combining both the ability to search for specific information in a video and a synopsis of its different segments. It can by achieved by representing the original video, using combinations of multimodal features in a configurable manner.

3   Proposed Approach

This research hypothesizes that multimodal features extracted from parallel modalities of video content can be presented to viewers to enhance their exploration experience. To validate this, the proposed approach extracts multimodal features from parallel modalities along with their temporal information and stores them in a repository. To offer multimodal synopsis for exploration, the approach aims to utilize a template-based representation engine, which represents the modalities of the video by presenting the extracted features in a configurable manner. In this work, we focused on TED-style presentation videos.

TED-Style Presentation Videos: Because of their general and storytelling nature, TED talks appeal to a wider and more diverse audience and therefore are an ideal candidate for our research. While our experiment is performed on TED videos, it is our assumption that the approach will be extendable to other content types such as life-logging videos, product launches and video messages, etc. Due to its information seeking focus, the proposed approach is not expected to be effective for video type such as movies, songs or entertainment oriented videos.

3.1   Prototype Design

The objective is to enable users to explore the content of video efficiently in a multimodal manner. To achieve this, we have to divide the video into different segments and provide the user ability to explore each segment using multimodal features of their choice.

Video Segmentation: A video can be segmented in many ways utilizing different modalities (Sect. 2). The choice of modalities is often domain dependent (Sect. 2). For the current study, we segmented the video utilizing the textual modality i.e. transcript of TED video was first split into sentences using StanfordNLP toolkit [15] and was fed into text segmentation algorithm C99 [6] to get segments for the video. Once segments are identified, to facilitate exploration, they can be represented to users in different ways. Users can not only choose which segments they want to explore but also what extracted features or their combination they would use to explore a chosen segment.

A representation is composed of features extracted from the different modalities of the video. A particular representation of a segment can have different capabilities in terms of its consumption potential. Some extracted features, expose content within the segment deeply which require more time for a user to consume, while others expose much less information but are quicker to consume. For the experiment, a prototype was developed for users to consume the segments for their choice using the extracted features of their choice to facilitate their video exploration.

Prototype Details: Figure 1 shows a screen shot of the prototype showed to the study participants. The prototype was built using HTML5 and JavaScript and designed to work with both traditional and touchscreen interfaces. Figure 1 shows the representation of the TED talk by Thomas Piketty [21], C99 algorithm [6] divided the transcript of this video in 10 segments. Figure 1 shows the first four segments; the users can swipe or scroll to the right to see the rest of the segments. Highlighted in yellow are the segments where the term users searched for occurred. Each segment has five tabs, and each tab contains a rendering of extracted features. Following is a description of each tab.

Fig. 1. Screen shot of video representation, showing four out of ten segments

Visual: The Visual tab shows the key frames of a segment. A custom tool was developed using openCV to detect camera shot changes. From those scene changes, one frame from each shot was selected. From those selected frames, frames with and without a face were identified using Haar cascade [14]. Speakers often use visual aids, such as presentation slides in a TED presentation. The heuristic was that shot without a face after a shot with a face might contain some images of visual aid used by the presenter which could contain useful information. Users can tap or click on the frame to see all the selected frames to get a visual synopsis of a particular segment.

Summary: The Summary tab shows the automatic text summary generated from the transcript of the segment. An online summarization tool for generating text summaries [1] was utilized. *Terms:* The Terms Tab shows the word cloud generated from the transcript of the segment. We used the tool TagCrowd [26] for the word cloud generation. *NE:* The Named Entity tab shows the list of extracted named entities from the transcript of the segment. This prototype used the Named Entity Recognizer tool by [23]. *Video:* Video tab shows the video snippet of a segment. The text in transcript comes with timestamps. Once the segmenter segmented the text, timestamps were used to determine the start and end time of a particular segment and its video snippet was offered to users to watch.

4 Experiment

Exploratory Search Task: The study is based on a simulated task scenario [11]. 29 users (21 male and 8 females) were asked to perform an exploratory search task to explore a video using the prototype (Sect. 3.1). Exploratory search is defined as a complex search task in which the user has to retrieve some facts first, which enable further search queries solving the overall search problem. Often the user is not sure about his/her search goal and sometimes, he/she is not very familiar with the topic of the search [16,28].

Users were asked to perform an exploratory search query. For this study, the query was pre-selected to be "Income inequality in the United States". The result of their query was a TED video. But instead of watching the video, users explored the video using our custom representation (Sect. 3.1). Each user performed the query twice i.e. each user explored two TED talks using the prototype one by one. It was left to the user's discretion to choose the combination of segments and tabs they thought sufficient to have the overall synopsis of the video in regards to the query.

4.1 Feedback Capturing

While consuming the representation, users were encouraged to think out loud to describe their actions, while their interaction with the representation was recorded via screen capturing and audio recording. By analyzing their recordings, we identified the potential benefits as perceived by users in this alternative form of video consumption.

User Satisfaction Questionnaire: After the experiment, users were asked to complete a questionnaire to provide their feedback on the different aspects of the representation. The questionnaire contained 10 questions containing 5 points Likert scale(5 being strong agreement). First 3 were regarding the ease of use with the prototype. Question 4 to 6 were regarding the segmentation of video while question 7 to 10 were about user's perception of efficiency in consuming the video by the representation compared to watching the video.

User Interactions with Tabs: Both audio recording and screen capture footage were analyzed and annotated manually by the researchers. To record the feedback, following scheme was used. The heuristic was, the more users select a particular tab for a segment, the more interested they are in consuming the information using that particular feature rendering. Therefore, each interaction with tabs was noted down e.g. when a user chose to view "Terms" of a particular segment, it is counted as a user interaction with the representation.

Think Aloud: We employed a think aloud protocol [24] approach to elicit and analyze user feedback. In order to learn exploration pattern, in analyzing the recorded data, the following procedure was followed. By encouraging users to think out loud, it was intended to record their thought process in exploring the content of the represented video. We were interested in user comments on the effectiveness of different features in terms of efficiency and usability for exploring the video. Feedback like "the speaker is talking about the 70 s here" is not as important as "I find this summary more useful than the last one" or "I find short summaries useful" etc. Feedback like the latter two examples was noted down.

5   Statistical Analysis

Figure 2 shows the average score given to each question by participants. As it can be seen, users liked the representation in general, as the lowest average score is 3.5 out of 5. Female participants gave higher scores to the representation compared to their male counterparts but it is not statistical significance ($p > 0.05$ obtained using Kruskal-Wallis analysis). It can be seen in Fig. 2 that while the overall ease of use and perceived efficiency was scored quite positively by the users, their satisfaction with the segmentation is lower than the rest as question 4 to 6 have lower average score than the rest.

We performed Pearson Correlation Test with user interactions with tabs (Sect. 4.1) with the hypothesis that there is no relationship between the usage of tabs (where usage of tabs is defined as number of clicks on tabs) while using the proposed system. From the results depicted in Fig. 3, we can see that the usage of the tabs is correlated with each other, and this correlation is statistically significant ($p < 0.05$) in 4 out of 10 cases. For example, usage of 'Sum tab' is correlated with usage of 'NE tab' and this correlation ($r = 0.57$) is statistical significance($p < 0.05$).

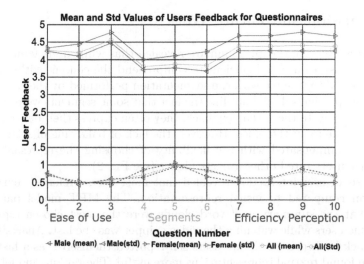

Fig. 2. Mean and standard deviation values of feedback by 29 users

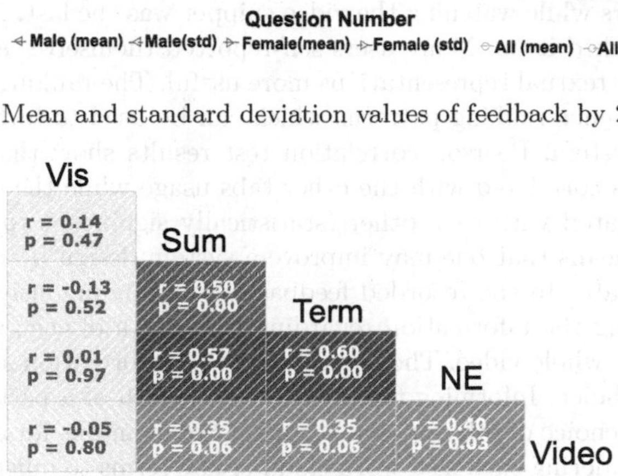

Fig. 3. Pearson correlation between usage of tabs (representation)

We rank the tabs for each user by counting the number of times a user clicked on a tab. Sometimes the users have the same number of click for two tabs. To rank in that case, we calculate an aggregated response from other users who have a different number of clicks for those tabs. This response is calculated, how many users rank one of two tabs as higher/lower than other tab. In case the most users rank a tab ($t1$) higher than other tab ($t2$) then the tab ($t1$) is assigned a higher rank than the other tab ($t2$). We have a ranked data based on user clicks. As we know that there are in total 5 tabs and number of possible permutation elements are 120. Let's say tabs are (visual, summary, term, NE, video) then the most chosen ranking is (4, 1, 2, 3, 5) that is chosen by 6 users. We employed the Mallows-Bradley-Terry (MBT) model to calculate the estimated parameter for the ranked data. The parameters are as follow (0.11071, 0.46184, 0.26687, 0.09943, 0.06115). Based on the parameters, the estimated order of ranking is (3,1,2,4,5) it means that users prefer the most is the summary tab, then term tab, then visual tab, then NE tab and the last one is the video tab.

6 Discussion and Future Work

Statistical analysis of the questionnaire revealed that while users found the representation easy to use and efficient to comprehend the content within a video. They did not always agree with the segmentation performed by the chosen algorithm. They particularly did not like the fact that some segments were either too short or too long. In the verbal feedback, they often express their desire for more balanced segments of the video. However, the lack of balancing of segmentation length was compensated with the flexibility of choosing the representation of their choice users rated other aspects higher (see Fig. 2).

Analysis of user interaction revealed that most users preferred textual representation compared to visual representation. The MBT model parameters showed that the summary and word clouds were the most chosen representations by the users while watching the video snippet was the last. Analysis of verbal feedback backed it up. Many users self-reported themselves as a fast reader and hence found textual representations more useful. The ranking model (MBT) gives user preference ranking patterns which can be used to further streamline the design of system. Pearson correlation test results show that the usage of visual tab is less correlated with the other tabs usage while the other four tabs usage are correlated with each other (statistically significant ($p < 0.05$) 4 our of 6 cases). It means that one may improve a system design by not eliminating less correlated tabs. In the recorded feedback users unanimously reported that they were missing the information regarding the length of each segment versus the length of the whole video. They considered this information as an important factor in their choice. Informing them about the length of a particular segment influenced their choice of tabs for that segment. For example, for a long segment, they prefer a rendering such as a word cloud of key terms to quickly get the info while for a shorter segment they might read the summary or watch the video snippet.

Time versus Depth Decisions: One subject analyzed the verbal and observational (Sect. 4.1) feedback of the users using grounded theory [24]. While the details of our use of this method go beyond the scope of this paper, we briefly summarize the results here. The analysis revealed an overall tendency of users to make time versus depth decisions. Different renderings (tabs) (Sect. 3.1) have different capabilities in terms of efficiency and effectiveness. Consider the rendering like word cloud of key terms. It is very efficient to consume as it can be glanced very quickly to get an idea of what a segment might be about, compared to a textual summary which would require more time to read but would give a deeper synopsis of the segment. While watching the video snippet of a particular segment would be the most effective way to consume a segment. However, it may also be the most time-consuming. Users not only chose certain tabs because of the length of the segment, but they also chose them according to their personal preferences. Users who self-reported themselves to be detail oriented opted for more detail oriented tabs such as video snippets etc. while others opted more for word clouds. It shows the personalization potential of the representation.

Future Work: Our aim is to reduce the number of choices for the user while exploring the video by multimodal representation. Based on the results of the user study we have learned some usage patterns. We aim to utilize these usage patterns to develop some representation templates for video exploration. Those templates will be used to develop representation engine which will offer an automatically generated multimodal synopsis of video to the user for efficient exploration. As seen in Fig. 2 some user did not like the segmentation of the video using the current technique. We will also experiment using different segmentation techniques by utilizing semantic uplifting of the topics discussed in the video. Although current experiment was performed as a query based search scenario, we believe that our proposed approach for video's exploration can be applied to other scenarios. For example, where the user has to consume content within video recordings such as a quick synopsis of meeting recorded by a smart conferencing system or getting a key point in a technical tutorial video.

Acknowledgement. This research is supported by Science Foundation Ireland through the CNGL Programme (Grant 12/CE/I2267) in the ADAPT Centre at School of Computer Science and Statistics, Trinity College Dublin, Ireland.

References

1. autosummarizer.com (2016). http://autosummarizer.com/
2. Belo, L., Caetano, C., do Patrocínio, Z., Guimarães, S.J.: Summarizing video sequence using a graph-based hierarchical approach. Neurocomputing **173**, 1001–1016 (2016)
3. Bouamrane, M.M., King, D., Luz, S., Masoodian, M.: A framework for collaborative writing with recording and post-meeting retrieval capabilities. IEEE Distrib. Syst. Online, 1–6 (2004)
4. Bouamrane, M.M., Luz, S.: An analytical evaluation of search by content and interaction patterns on multimodal meeting records. Multimedia Syst. **13**(2), 89–103 (2007)
5. Chen, F., De Vleeschouwer, C., Cavallaro, A.: Resource allocation for personalized video summarization. IEEE Trans. Multimedia **16**(2), 455–469 (2014)
6. Choi, F.Y.Y.: Advances in domain independent linear text segmentation. In: Proceedings of NAACL 2000, Stroudsburg, PA, USA, pp. 26–33 (2000)
7. Dong, A., Li, H.: Ontology-driven annotation and access of presentation video data. Estudios de Economía Aplicada (2008)
8. Evangelopoulos, G., Zlatintsi, A., Potamianos, A., Maragos, P., Rapantzikos, K., Skoumas, G., Avrithis, Y.: Multimodal saliency and fusion for movie summarization based on aural, visual, and textual attention. IEEE Trans. Multimedia **15**(7), 1553–1568 (2013)
9. Gravier, G., Ragot, M., Amsaleg, L., Bois, R., Jadi, G., Jamet, É., Monceaux, L., Sébillot, P.: Shaping-up multimedia analytics: needs and expectations of media professionals. In: Tian, Q., Sebe, N., Qi, G.-J., Huet, B., Hong, R., Liu, X. (eds.) MMM 2016, Part II. LNCS, vol. 9517, pp. 303–314. Springer, Cham (2016). doi:10.1007/978-3-319-27674-8_27. https://hal.inria.fr/hal-01214829

10. Haesen, M., Meskens, J., Luyten, K., Coninx, K., Becker, J., Tuytelaars, T., Poulisse, G., Pham, T., Moens, M.: Finding a needle in a haystack: an interactive video archive explorer for professional video searchers. Multimedia Tools Appl. **63**(2), 331–356 (2011)
11. Halvey, M., Vallet, D., Hannah, D., Jose, J.M.: Supporting exploratory video retrieval tasks with grouping and recommendation. Inf. Process. Manag. **50**(6), 876–898 (2014)
12. Hosseini, M.S., Eftekhari-Moghadam, A.M.: Fuzzy rule-based reasoning approach for event detection and annotation of broadcast soccer video. Appl. Soft Comput. **13**(2), 846–866 (2013)
13. Lei, P., Sun, C., Lin, S., Huang, T.: Effect of metacognitive strategies and verbal-imagery cognitive style on biology-based video search and learning performance. Comput. Educ. **87**, 326–339 (2015)
14. Lienhart, R., Kuranov, A., Pisarevsky, V.: Empirical analysis of detection cascades of boosted classifiers for rapid object detection. In: Michaelis, B., Krell, G. (eds.) DAGM 2003. LNCS, vol. 2781, pp. 297–304. Springer, Heidelberg (2003). doi:10. 1007/978-3-540-45243-0_39
15. Manning, C., Surdeanu, M., Bauer, J., Finkel, J., Bethard, S., McClosky, D.: The stanford CoreNLP natural language processing toolkit. In: ACL System Demos, pp. 55–60 (2014)
16. Marchionini, G.: Exploratory search: from finding to understanding. Commun. ACM **49**(4), 41–46 (2006)
17. Matejka, J., Grossman, T., Fitzmaurice, G.: Video lens: rapid playback and exploration of large video collections and associated metadata. In: Proceedings of UIST 2014, pp. 541–550 (2014)
18. Mujacic, S., Debevc, M., Kosec, P., Bloice, M., Holzinger, A.: Modeling, design, development and evaluation of a hypervideo presentation for digital systems teaching and learning. Multimedia Tools Appl. **58**(2), 435–452 (2012)
19. Nautiyal, A., Kenny, E., Dawson-Howe, K.: Video adaptation for the creation of advanced intelligent content for conferences. In: Irish Machine Vision and Image Processing Conference, pp. 122–127 (2014)
20. Pavel, A., Reed, C., orn Hartmann, B., Agrawala, M.: Video digests: a browsable, skimmable format for informational lecture videos. In: Symposium on User Interface Software and Technology, USA, pp. 573–582 (2014)
21. Piketty, T.: New thoughts on capital in the twenty-first century (2014)
22. Rafailidis, D., Manolopoulou, S., Daras, P.: A unified framework for multimodal retrieval. Pattern Recogn. **46**(12), 3358–3370 (2013)
23. Ratinov, L., Roth, D.: Design challenges and misconceptions in named entity recognition. In: Proceedings of the CoNLL 2009, pp. 147–155. ACL, Stroudsburg (2009)
24. Rogers, Y.: HCI Theory: Classical, Modern, and Contemporary, vol. 5. Morgan & Claypool Publishers, San Francisco (2012)
25. Schoeffmann, K., Taschwer, M., Boeszoermenyi, L.: The video explorer a tool for navigation and searching within a single video based on fast content analysis. In: Proceedings of the ACM Conference on Multimedia Systems, pp. 247–258 (2010)
26. Steinbock, D.: (2016). http://tagcrowd.com/
27. Tan, S., Bu, J., Qin, X., Chen, C., Cai, D.: Cross domain recommendation based on multi-type media fusion. Neurocomputing **127**, 124–134 (2014)
28. Waitelonis, J., Sack, H.: Towards exploratory video search using linked data. Multimedia Tools Appl. **59**(2), 645–672 (2012)
29. Zhang, H., Liu, Y., Ma, Z.: Fusing inherent and external knowledge with nonlinear learning for cross-media retrieval. Neurocomputing **119**, 10–16 (2013)

An Analysis of the RNN-Based
Spoken Term Detection Training

Jan Švec[1(✉)], Luboš Šmídl[2], and Josef V. Psutka[2]

[1] SpeechTech, s.r.o, Plzeň, Czech Republic
jan.svec@speechtech.cz
[2] Department of Cybernetics, University of West Bohemia, Plzeň, Czech Republic
{smidl,psutka_j}@kky.zcu.cz

Abstract. This paper studies the training process of the recurrent neural networks used in the spoken term detection (STD) task. The method used in the paper employ two jointly trained Siamese networks using unsupervised data. The grapheme representation of a searched term and the phoneme realization of a putative hit are projected into the pronunciation embedding space using such networks. The score is estimated as relative distance of these embeddings. The paper studies the influence of different loss functions, amount of unsupervised data and the meta-parameters on the performance of the STD system.

Keywords: Spoken term detection · Recurrent neural networks · Siamese neural networks

1 Introduction

A spoken term detection (STD) task is currently one of the most studied applications of the speech recognition. It is partly due to the IARPA supported Babel research programme. Moreover STD is applicable in many other domains such as analysis of conversations in call-centres or searching through the large spoken archives.

In this paper, we will cope with a term relevance score estimation in the STD task. The term relevance score is a confidence assigned by the STD system to a putative hit so that the resulting list of hits could be filtered using a predetermined threshold. We adopt the evaluation approach from the Babel programme which uses the actual term weighted value (ATWV) metric to score the resulting system. The ATWV metric was thoroughly studied in [17]. Its value is heavily sensitive to the following phenomenons:

- *Score normalizations* – i.e. all scores generated by a STD must be on the same scale and a particular threshold must produce a false positives and false negatives with similar probabilities for all searched terms.
- *Sensitivity to less frequent terms* – because the resulting ATWV value is computed as an arithmetic average of ATWV values for all searched terms, the weights are the same for each searched term regardless its absolute number of occurrences in the reference.

© Springer International Publishing AG 2017
A. Karpov et al. (Eds.): SPECOM 2017, LNAI 10458, pp. 119–129, 2017.
DOI: 10.1007/978-3-319-66429-3_11

– *Out-of-vocabulary (OOV) terms* – this is a specific case of a less frequent term. Due to the nature of ATWV (arithmetic average of per-term TWV values) the OOV terms have the same weight as e.g. frequent in-vocabulary (IV) terms and therefore it is important to have the possibility to search for OOV terms, either by using sub-word units [13] or proxy words [1].

The state-of-the-art methods tackle with all these phenomenons, examples are the query length normalization method [8], sum-to-one normalization [9] or the regression-based normalization [7]. The presented method uses the machine-learning based approach which employs recurrent neural networks to estimate the score of putative hits based on the pre-indexed sub-word units and the grapheme representation of the searched term.

The work was inspired by the work of Kamper et al. [5] for the query-by-example search. They used the Siamese convolutional neural networks trained to distinguish between similar and different examples of the searched audio sequence. He et al. [4] further generalized this approach to include the multi-view aspect, where the searched phrase was represented as character sequences. Subsequently, the bidirectional long-short term memory (LSTM) Siamese models were jointly trained to extract pronunciation embeddings from the corresponding audio and character sequences. The work [4] is focused on the word discrimination task and does not solve the problem of determining the list of putative hits. The work of Naaman et al. [10] used Siamese RNNs to automatically learn a similarity function between two pronunciations.

Our approach described in [16] uses the jointly trained RNN models to determine the *pronunciation embeddings*. We project the input grapheme sequence of the searched term into the space of pronunciation embeddings using the grapheme RNN. Similarly, we use the phoneme recognizer to obtain the sub-word index and to construct the list of putative hits. Then, for each putative hit, the corresponding phoneme confusion network (phoneme sausage) was projected using the phoneme RNN into the space of pronunciation embeddings. The score of the putative is then estimated as the relative distance of the reference and putative pronunciation embeddings. We use the margin-based hinge loss to express the relative distance of the two embeddings compared to other pairs [5].

The paper extends the work [16], it studies the influence of the amount of training data needed to train the RNNs and justifies other design decisions. It is organized as follows: Sect. 2 recapitulates the theoretical background of the Siamese network architecture, Sect. 3 shows the application of Siamese RNNs to the STD task, Sect. 4 describes the experimental framework used in the work, Sect. 5 discusses the experimental results and finally Sect. 6 concludes the paper.

2   A Siamese Network Architecture

The Siamese architecture of neural networks is beneficial in tasks, where the goal is to compute similarity of two input samples. In this case, it is not necessary to train the network in fully supervised manner. It is sufficient to train the network with samples labelled as *the same* or *the different*. In the original application

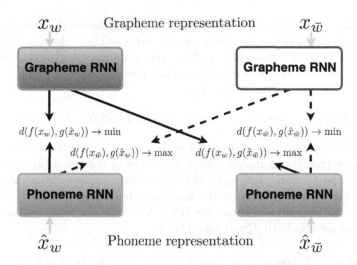

Fig. 1. Illustration of the loss function. Excluding the white node results in the original Siamese loss (Eq. 3), including it represents the symmetrized loss (Eq. 4)

of Siamese architecture to the query-by-example task [15], each training sample consisted of the triplet (x_a, x_s, x_d), where x_a is a reference input for word w (an anchor), x_s is an input containing different realisation of the *same* word w (a positive example) and x_d is an input for a word *different* from w (a negative example). During the network training, the RNN is applied to x_a and produces an output embedding y_a. The same network could be applied to x_s to obtain y_s and x_d to obtain y_d. The goal of network training is to minimize the "relative distance" between output embeddings y_a and y_s and maximize the "relative distance" between y_a and y_d. This could be formulated as minimizing the hinge loss [5] in the form:

$$l(y_a, y_s, y_d) = \max\{0, m + d(y_a, y_s) - d(y_a, y_d)\} \qquad (1)$$

where $d(y_1, y_2)$ is a distance function computing relative distance of y_1 and y_2. The meta-parameter m represents the margin between positive and negative examples. The Kamper et al. in [5] propose to use the distance function based on cosine similarity:

$$d(y_1, y_2) = 1 - \cos(y_1, y_2) = 1 - \frac{y_1 \cdot y_2}{||y_1|| \cdot ||y_2||} \qquad (2)$$

The training process is only lightly supervised, it requires just the correct sample pairs. Common stochastic gradient descent (SGD) algorithms could be used to optimize RNN parameters (Fig. 1).

Previous applications of Siamese networks suppose, that all inputs (the anchor, the positive and the negative example) are from the same domain, e.g. the sequences of MFCC coefficients in the query-by-example task [5]. For the use as scoring algorithm, we changed this paradigm. The output embeddings are computed from two different representations of the same word w – the grapheme sequence x_w and the phoneme confusion network $\hat{x}_w$. Then, the first RNN $f(x_w)$ computes the output embedding y_w from the graphemes and the second RNN $g(\hat{x}_w)$ computes the output embedding from the phonemes $\hat{y}_w$ of the word w. The loss has the same structure as Eq. 1:

$$l(w, \bar{w}) = \max\{0, m + d(f(x_w), g(\hat{x}_w)) - d(f(x_w), g(\hat{x}_{\bar{w}})\} \tag{3}$$

where $\hat{x}_{\bar{w}}$ is a phoneme confusion network of word $\bar{w}$ which is different from word w. Note that the grapheme RNN $f(\cdot)$ occur in the equation only once for each w, but the phoneme RNN $g(\cdot)$ obtains gradient updates from two different words – w and $\hat{w}$ – and therefore the learning rate of phoneme RNN is twice as large as the learning rate of grapheme RNN. We could therefore symmetrize the hinge loss to include both $f(x_w)$ and $f(x_{\bar{w}})$:

$$l(w, \bar{w}) = \frac{1}{2} \cdot \; (\max\{0, m + d(f(x_w), g(\hat{x}_w)) - d(f(x_w), g(\hat{x}_{\bar{w}})\} \tag{4}$$
$$+ \max\{0, m + d(f(x_{\bar{w}}), g(\hat{x}_{\bar{w}})) - d(f(x_{\bar{w}}), g(\hat{x}_w))\})$$

The symmetrized criterion is an arithmetic average of two instances of Eq. 3, one for x_w selected as the anchor and one for $x_{\bar{w}}$. The idea is not new, the extensions of the basic same-different loss function were studied in [4] and the findings were similar to the results presented in this paper. The RNN networks could use gated-recurrent units (GRU) or long-short term memory units (LSTM).

3   RNN-based Spoken Term Detection

To apply the approach of Siamese neural networks in the spoken term detection task, it is necessary to solve two subtasks: (1) Given a query term (input as sequence of characters) determine the set of putative hits using a pre-indexed sub-word units. (2) For each putative hit (occurrence candidate) compute the associated term relevance score.

3.1   Term Occurrence Candidates

In current implementation, the algorithm to determine the list of putative hits is very similar to the algorithm used in [13]. The only difference is that the original term relevance estimation is replaced with the RNN-based counterpart. The algorithm is built around the sub-word index where the sub-word units are triplets of consecutive phonemes. These triplets are extracted from the phoneme lattice generated by a phoneme recognizer.

In the search phase, the searched term is first transcribed into a sequence of phonemes using grapheme-to-phoneme mapping. Then, this sequence is converted into a sequence of overlapping phoneme triplets and these triplets are looked up in the index. The found triplets are then sorted according to the time of the occurrence and clustered so that the clusters are separated by at least

0.3 s. Then, each such cluster is declared as a putative hit. It must be noted that this part of the RNN-based STD still relies on the explicit grapheme-to-phoneme mapping. Elimination of the grapheme-to-phoneme mapping is a subject of further research.

3.2   Term Relevance Estimation

The goal of the relevance score estimation is to assign a relevance score to some segment of the input audio (represented by corresponding part of the phoneme sausage $\hat{x}_w$) given a searched term w (represented by grapheme sequence x_w).

The training data for the neural network consists of a set of pairs $(x_w, \hat{x}_w)$ extracted from the input data that were recognized in the unsupervised fashion. The x_w is the recognized word and $\hat{x}_w$ the corresponding phoneme sausage. We use the word x_w only if its word confidence is higher than a threshold. During training the Siamese neural network, first the pair of two different words $(w, \bar{w})$ must be sampled from the training data. To model the variations in pronunciation of words, the corresponding phoneme sausages $\hat{x}_w$ and $\hat{x}_{\bar{w}}$ are sampled from the training set of pairs. Then, the neural network is trained to optimize the criterion given by Eq. 4 using $(x_w, \hat{x}_w, x_{\bar{w}}, \hat{x}_{\bar{w}})$ as the input data.

Both the grapheme-to-embedding mapping $f(\cdot)$ and phoneme-to-embedding mapping $g(\cdot)$ is implemented in a straightforward way as a one layer bidirectional RNN with one maxout layer [3]. The graphemes are represented as one-hot vectors and grapheme embedding layer is used to represent them in a continuous space. To project the segments of phoneme sausages into the continuous space we used another RNN as a trainable feature extractor (for detail, see [16]).

Finally, the relevance score is estimated as a cosine similarity of the pronunciation embedding $f(x)$ obtained from the graphemes of the query x and the pronunciation embedding $g(\hat{x})$ computed from the phoneme sausage of the occurrence candidate $\hat{x}$, formally as $\cos(f(x), g(\hat{x}))$.

4   Experimental Framework

The presented method was evaluated on the data from a USC-SFI MALACH archive in two languages – English [14] and Czech [12]. The archive for each language was recognized using the word- and phoneme-level recognizers. For experiments with unsupervised learning, we used different amount of data up the unsupervised data length. The number of $(x_w, \hat{x}_w)$ pairs extracted for the full unsupervised data and the number of distinct words are summarized in Table 1. The unsupervised training data were generated using large vocabulary speech recognizer (LVCSR) with vocabulary size of quarter of millions for each language.

The RNNs trained in the experiments had constant structure and number of neurons: grapheme and phoneme embedding width, number of recurrent units and number of maxout neurons were 256, the width of the posterior embedding was 32. During training, we generated 100k quadruplets $(x_w, \hat{x}_w, x_{\bar{w}}, \hat{x}_{\bar{w}})$ for each

Table 1. Statistics of datasets

	English		Czech	
LVCSR vocabulary	243,699		252,082	
Unsupervised data length [hours]	2,037		997	
Number of $(x_w, \hat{x}_w)$ pairs	277 k		672k	
#distinct words w	21 k		83 k	
	Dev	Test	Dev	Test
LVCSR WER	24.10	19.66	23.98	19.11
#searched terms	628	607	2825	2621
Dataset length [hours]	11.1	11.3	20.4	19.4

training epoch. If not specified in a given experiment, the network parameters were trained using 30 epochs of the ADAM optimization [6]. We used dropout probability 0.2 and the default margin width $m = 0.5$ (metaparameter of Eq. 4).

4.1   LVCSR Speech Recognition

We followed a typical Kaldi [5] training recipe for a deep neural network (DNN) acoustic model training. This recipe supports layer-wise RBM pre-training, stochastic gradient descent training supported by GPUs and sequence-discriminative training optimizing sMBR criterion. We applied the standard 6 layers topology (5 hidden layers, each with 2048 neurons) with a softmax layer. The output dimension was equal to the number of context-dependent states (4521 for English, 4557 for Czech). We used features based on standard 12-dimensional Cepstral Mean Normalized (CMN) PLP coefficients with first and second derivatives. In total, the English acoustic model was trained from 217 h and the Czech from 84 h of signal. We used our in-house real-time decoder both for the word- and phoneme recognition with trigram word- and 5-gram phoneme language model.

4.2   Evaluation Metrics

To evaluate the experiments, we used mainly the development set (Table 1). The list of searched terms was generated automatically, a term set for development data was generally different from a term set for testing data. We used a set of all words in the transcription and then we filtered it to satisfy the conditions: (1) Each term has more than three phonemes, because the method for generating putative hits cannot search for shorter phoneme sequences; (2) The phonetic transcription of the term differs at least in two phonemes from any other phoneme subsequence in any other transcription.

We report ATWV and MTWV values, the difference is that MTWV uses an oracle threshold estimated on the reference data [2]. The ATWV/MTWV values were computed using Kaldi tools [11,17]. The ATWV values were reported on test data using MTWV oracle thresholds on development data. To analyse the RNN-based term relevance estimation, only the phoneme-based search was performed without the use of LVCSR lattices.

5 Results

The experiments conducted in this paper were prepared to give a deeper insight in the behavior of the Siamese RNNs in the STD task. We wanted to clarify the following questions:

- Is there any difference between the symmetrized and the original Siamese loss (Eq. 3 vs. Eq. 4) and between GRU and LSTM RNN units?
- Does the training loss value correlate with the ATWV of the STD system?
- How much unsupervised data do we need to train the system?
- How does the performance of the trained system depend on the value of hinge loss margin m (Eq. 4)?

5.1 Comparison of Different Training Approaches

In this experiment, we trained three different RNN systems, the GRU-based with symmetric loss (Eq. 4), GRU-based with asymmetric loss (Eq. 3) and

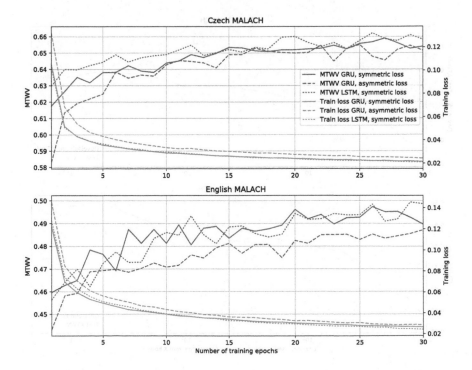

Fig. 2. Comparison of different training approaches

LSTM-based with symmetric loss. We recorded the loss values during training. After each epoch, we also ran the STD search and evaluated the MTWV metric to obtain the dependency of the system's performance on the number of training epochs. The resulting learning curves are shown on Fig. 2.

The training with symmetric loss function finishes with lower values than the training with asymmetric loss. Also the system performance expressed as MTWV values is lower for the asymmetric loss, especially for English data where the phonetics is much more complicated in comparison with Czech data. The oscillations of MTWV during the first half of the training are interesting and are probably caused by the symmetrized loss. It could be further examined if lowering the learning rate will eliminate this behavior. The learning curves also show no clear preference between GRU and LSTM. In the following experiments, we used the GRU since they have a lower number of parameters (3 M vs. 3.7 M).

5.2   Amount of UnsuperVised Training Data

Another question not answered in [16] is how much training data is sufficient to an unsupervised training method described above. For this experiment we gradually increased the number of training data and for each such subset, we trained the GRU RNN from scratch. Each subsequent subset contained all data of the previous smaller subset, i.e. subset generated from 20 h contained also the subset

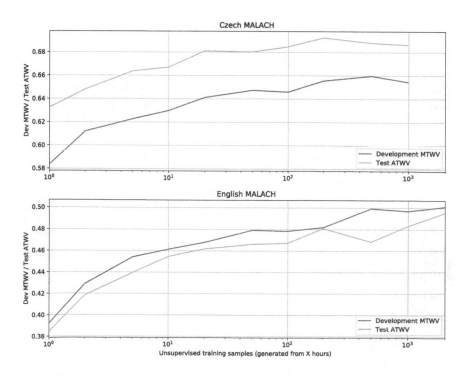

Fig. 3. Amount of unsupervised training data (x-axis is log-scaled)

generated from 10 h etc. We used at most the whole available archive, see Table 1. In this experiment we evaluated the MTWV on development data and also the ATWV on test data with the decision threshold estimated on development data.

The dependency of ATWV/MTWV on the amount of unsupervised training data is shown on Fig. 3. The most important observation is that the procedure of estimating the optimal decision threshold on development data is not affected by the amount of training data, i.e. the relative offset between development MTWV and test ATWV is almost constant.

If we accept the decrease in MTWV of 0.02, we could train the STD term relevance estimation for English on 200 h and for Czech on only 20 h. The difference is again caused by the relative complex phonetics of English (especially in the Holocaust testimonies contained in MALACH archive) compared to Czech. Both curves do not clearly show any saturation, it would be interesting to use even more training data to see the ATWV limits.

5.3   Effect of Hinge Loss Margin m

In the last set of experiments, we gradually changed the value of hinge loss margin m used to train the RNNs. The values of MTWV as a function of margin values m are depicted on Fig. 4. Although the margin value m seems to be important for the resulting STD system, by using the tolerance of MTWV decrease 0.01 from

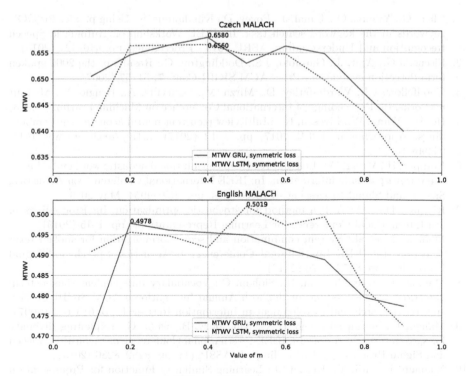

Fig. 4. Effect of hinge loss margin m

the highest value, we could select the margin from a relatively broad interval between 0.2 and 0.7. Only the extreme values below 0.2 and above 0.7 cause substantial changes in the system's performance. That is the reason, why we used the default value $m = 0.5$ in other experiments. Another important fact is that GRU and LSTM units behave similar with only slightly different peak MTWV values.

6   Conclusion

In this paper, we studied the training process of Siamese neural networks based on recurrent units for the STD task. The learnings curves as the functions of the amount of unsupervised training data and the number of training epochs were described. Also the influence of the Siamese loss function and type of recurrent units (GRU/LSTM) was studied. We also experimented with different values of the hinge loss margin. All experiments are thoroughly described in Sect. 5.

Acknowledgments. This research was supported by the Technology Agency of the Czech Republic, project No. TE01020197.

References

1. Chen, G., Yilmaz, O., Trmal, J., Povey, D., Khudanpur, S.: Using proxies for OOV keywords in the keyword search task. In: IEEE Workshop on Automatic Speech Recognition and Understanding, ASRU 2013 - Proceedings, pp. 416–421 (2013)
2. Fiscus, J.G., Ajot, J., Garofolo, J.S., Doddington, G.: Results of the 2006 spoken term detection evaluation. Proc. ACM SIGIR Conf. **7**, 51–57 (2007)
3. Goodfellow, I.J., Warde-farley, D., Mirza, M., Courville, A., Bengio, Y.: Maxout networks. In: Proceedings of International Conference on Machine Learning (2013)
4. He, W., Wang, W., Livescu, K.: Multi-view recurrent neural acoustic word embeddings. Appearing in ICLR 2017, pp. 1–12 (2017). http://arxiv.org/abs/1611.04496v2
5. Kamper, H., Wang, W., Livescu, K.: Deep convolutional acoustic word embeddings using word-pair side information. In: IEEE International Conference on Acoustics, Speech and Signal Processing - Proceedings, pp. 4950–4954, May 2016
6. Kingma, D.P.: ADAM: a method for stochastic optimization. In: Proceedings of 3rd International Conference for Learning Representations, pp. 1–15 (2015)
7. Mamou, J., et al.: System combination and score normalization for spoken term detection. In: IEEE International Conference on Acoustics, Speech and Signal Processing, pp. 8272–8276 (2013)
8. Mamou, J., Ramabhadran, B., Siohan, O.: Vocabulary independent spoken term detection. In: Proceedings of the 30th Annual International ACM SIGIR Conference on Research and Development in Information Retrieval, pp. 615–622 (2007)
9. Mangu, L., Soltau, H., Kuo, H.K., Kingsbury, B., Saon, G.: Exploiting diversity for spoken term detection. In: IEEE International Conference on Acoustics, Speech and Signal Processing - Proceedings, ICASSP, (1), pp. 8282–8286 (2013)
10. Naaman, E., Adi, Y., Keshet, J.: Learning Similarity Function for Pronunciation Variations (2017). http://arxiv.org/abs/1703.09817

11. Povey, D., Ghoshal, A., Goel, N., Hannemann, M., Qian, Y., Schwarz, P., Stemmer, G.: The Kaldi speech recognition toolkit. In: IEEE 2011 Workshop on Automatic Speech Recognition and Understanding. IEEE, Big Island, Hawaii (2011)
12. Psutka, J., Radová, V., Ircing, P., Matoušek, J., Müller, L.: USC-SFI MALACH Interviews and Transcripts Czech LDC2014S04 (2014). https://catalog.ldc.upenn.edu/LDC2014S04
13. Psutka, J., Švec, J., Psutka, J.V., Vaněk, J., Pražák, A., Šmídl, L., Ircing, P.: System for fast lexical and phonetic spoken term detection in a Czech cultural heritage archive. EURASIP J. Audio Speech Music Process. (1), 10 (2011)
14. Ramabhadran, B., Gustman, S., Byrne, W., Hajič, J., Oard, D., Olsson, J.S., Picheny, M., Psutka, J.: USC-SFI MALACH Interviews and Transcripts English LDC2012S05 (2012). https://catalog.ldc.upenn.edu/LDC2012s05
15. Settle, S., Livescu, K.: Discriminative acoustic word embeddings: recurrent neural network-based approaches. In: IEEE Workshop on Spoken Language Technology (SLT), pp. 503–510 (2016)
16. Švec, J., Psutka, J.V., Šmídl, L., Trmal, J.: A relevance score estimation for spoken term detection based on RNN-generated pronunciation embeddings. In: Proceedings of Interspeech (2017). (to appear)
17. Wegmann, S., Faria, A., Janin, A., Riedhammer, K., Morgan, N.: The TAO of ATWV: probing the mysteries of keyword search performance. In: IEEE Workshop on Automatic Speech Recognition and Understanding, pp. 192–197 (2013)

Analysis of Interaction Parameter Levels in Interaction Quality Modelling for Human-Human Conversation

Anastasiia Spirina[1]($\boxtimes$), Olesia Vaskovskaia[2], Tatiana Karaseva[2],
Alina Skorokhod[2], Iana Polonskaia[2], and Maxim Sidorov[1]

[1] Institute of Communications Engineering, University of Ulm, Ulm, Germany
{anastasiia.spirina,maxim.sidorov}@uni-ulm.de
[2] Reshetnev Siberian State University of Science and Technology,
Krasnoyarsk, Russia
{olesia.vaskovskaia,tatiana.karaseva,alina.skorokhod,
iana.polonskaia}@sibsau.ru

Abstract. Estimation of the dialogue quality, especially the quality of interaction, is an essential part for improving the quality of spoken dialogue systems (SDSs) or call centres. The Interaction Quality (IQ) metric is one of such approaches. Originally, it was designed for SDSs to estimate an ongoing human-computer spoken interaction (HCSI). Due to a similarity between task-oriented human-human conversation (HHC) and HCSI, this approach was adapted to HHC. As for HCSI, for HHC the IQ model is based on features from three interaction parameter levels: an exchange, a window, and a dialogue level. We determine the significance of different levels for IQ modelling for HHC. Moreover, for the window level we try to find an optimal window size. Our study was aimed to simplify the IQ model for HHC, as well as to find differences and similarities between IQ models for HHC and HCSI.

Keywords: Human-human interaction · Task-oriented dialogues · Performance

1 Introduction

One of the ways for improving SDSs is to use some indicators, which may assess the quality of interaction in HCSI. The IQ metric can be considered as a such indicator, which may reflect the problematic situations during an ongoing interaction. This expert-based approach was proposed in [1,2]. Due to a resemblance between task-oriented HHC and HCSI, this metric may be used for further service improvement in call centres [3].

As for HCSI, the IQ model for HHC is based on features from the following parameter levels: the exchange, the window, and the dialogue level [2,4]. In contrast to approximately 50 features for IQ modelling for HCSI, the IQ model for HHC is relied on more than 1200 features, which have been extracted from an agent's/ customer's/ overlapping speech and a dialogue itself [4].

© Springer International Publishing AG 2017
A. Karpov et al. (Eds.): SPECOM 2017, LNAI 10458, pp. 130–140, 2017.
DOI: 10.1007/978-3-319-66429-3_12

To study a contribution of each level for IQ modelling for HHC, we have performed computations using several classification algorithms on different data sets, which include features from the different combinations of the interaction parameter levels. As a result, this study could help to reduce the computational complexity for modelling IQ by reducing the number of required features. Besides, an optimal window size (for window level) remains an open question. To find an answer, we have conducted some computations varying the window size. All achieved results may be useful in designing the most accurate IQ model. In turn, it can lead to understanding similarities and differences between HHC and HCSI and makes SDSs more human-like.

The remainder of this paper is structured as follows: significant related work on an analysis of parameter levels for IQ modelling for HCSI is given in Sect. 2. An overview of corpus, which was used for conducting all computations, is provided in Sect. 3. Thereafter, a description of the formulated classification problems and applied classification algorithms is states in Sect. 4. Section 5 presents the achieved results, which are then discussed in Sect. 6. Finally, we summarise the results and outline future work in Sect. 7.

2   Related Work

The IQ metric is a modification of the concept of User/Customer Satisfaction (CS), which is widely used in the field of call centres and SDSs. The idea of IQ was introduced in [1,2]. In contrast to CS, which is mostly manually assessed at the end of the calls, the IQ metric allows to evaluate SDS performance at any point during an ongoing interaction. As it was mentioned before, the IQ model for HCSI is based on 53 features [5], which are described in [2,6]. All features belong to one of the levels: the exchange, the window, and the dialogue. The first of them consists of information about the current system-user-exchange. The next one includes the features from the n last exchanges. The last one describes the complete dialogue up to the current exchange [2].

An analysis of the levels' contribution to the overall performance of IQ modelling is presented in [5]. The results of the analysis showed that in terms of Unweighted Average Recall (UAR) [7], Cohen's Kappa [8] linearly weighted [9], and Spearman's Rho [10] the best result was obtained using all features (from the all parameter levels) [5]. But nevertheless, the study revealed an important role of the window level features in the overall performance. Concerning the question about the window size: although the main computations were performed with the window size of 3, according to [5], the best performance was achieved for a windows size of 9.

3   Corpus Description

All experiments for our study have been performed based on the spoken corpus [4], which consists of 53 task-oriented dialogues between employees and customers. In particular, this corpus contains dialogues between 4 employees and

53 customers. Subsequently, after the manual diarization almost 1,800 speech fragments were obtained, which then were split into 1,165 agent-customer-exchanges. Each exchange consists of agent's, customer's turn and possible overlaps.

Each exchange is described by more than 1,200 features, which belong to the different interaction parameter levels: the exchange, window, and dialogue levels [4]. The features from the exchange level include acoustic attributes, extracted by *OpenSMILE* [11] (a feature vector contains 384 attributes [12], which were used in Interspeech 2009 Emotion Challenge) for agent/customer speech and overlaps, information about the duration of speech and pauses (between exchanges and between turns), manually annotated emotions and others.

In turn, the features from the two remaining levels describe the information about:

- exchange itself (the total/mean duration, statistical information about who speaks first in an exchange),
- agent's/customer's speech (the total/mean duration and percentage of duration),
- pauses (duration/percentage of duration between turns, the total duration between exchanges),
- overlaps (the total/mean number of the fragments, the total/mean duration, and percentage of duration).

The window level covers in this corpus the three last exchanges with respect to the current exchange.

3.1 Interaction Quality

Each exchange in the corpus was accompanied with two IQ score labels, which are based on the different IQ-labeling guidelines. The rules for both annotation approaches were presented in [3].

It was done due to a drawback of the first approach which is based on an absolute scale and is similar to the IQ score annotation guideline for HCSI [6]. Thereby this scale consists of five classes (1-bad, 2-poor, 3-fair, 4-good, 5-excellent). According to the annotation guideline [6] all dialogues should start with the IQ score "5". In call centres there are a number of reasons why a dialogue can not start with the IQ label "5": the long waiting time or customer claims against a company with the customer aggressive behaviour due to which IQ initially can not be good. Also the use of this approach for HHC can lead to possible loss of information in the modelling process, because an agent can increase a customer loyalty that may lead to IQ improvements (the IQ score can be more than "5"). Such an example is presented in Fig. 1.

As we mentioned above, the first approach, which we will denote as *IQ1*, is based on the scale which consists of five classes, but not all classes are presented in the corpus: there are only classes with the IQ scores "3", "4", "5".

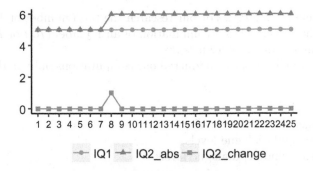

Fig. 1. IQ scores (ordinate) during the dialoge (the number of the exchange - abscissa) according to the different approaches: *IQ1* - the first approach, *IQ2_change* - the second approach with the scale of changes, and *IQ2_abs* - the second approach with the transformed absolute scale

Moreover, the number of observations with the high IQ score "5" is 96.39% of all exchanges, the smallest class (the IQ score "3") covers only four observations.

The second annotation approach, in contrast to the first, is based on a scale of changes which then is transformed into an absolute scale with the assumption that all dialogues start with the IQ score "5" (as for *IQ1*). The scale of changes is represented by the following scores: "-2", "-1", "0", "1", "2", "1_abs" (the last score is in the absolute scale). Thus, for the second approach, which we will specify as *IQ2*, we have received the following scores: "6", "5", "4", "3". Similar to the first approach, the classes are also unbalanced: the most frequent class "5" occurs in 88.24% of all samples, while the second biggest class "6" comprises 8.24% of all data. Regarding to the smallest class "3", it also contains four exchanges, as for the first approach.

3.2 Emotions

Each agent/customer speech fragment was manually annotated using three different emotion sets, which were chosen from [13] and adapted for our study. The first of them (*em1*) covers such emotion categories as: angry, sad, neutral, and happy. The following set *em2* was derived from *em1* by adding such categories as: disgust/irritation and boredom. The third emotion set *em3* consists of anger, sadness, disgust/irritation, neutral, surprise, and happiness.

For better understanding of the required emotion sets complexity for IQ modelling, the sets *em{1,2,3}* were subdivided into neutral and other emotions (denote them as *em{1,2,3}2*) and into negative, neutral, and positive emotions (*em{1,2,3}3*).

4 Experimental Setup

The IQ estimation task can be represented as a classification problem with the classes corresponding to the IQ scores. In our case there are three classes for

IQ1 and four classes for *IQ2*. For our research the total number of different sets is eighteen, where each set is a combination of an IQ label (*IQ1* or *IQ2*) and an emotion set (nine sets). Denote it tasks.

In contrast to [5], we have conducted our computations only on the following sets:

- the exchange level,
- the exchange and window levels,
- the exchange and dialogue levels,
- the exchange, window, dialogue levels.

We can not completely remove the features from the exchange level, because the features from the window and dialogue levels do not contain enough information to describe the interaction in HHC. In contrast to the experiments in [5], where the window size were changed from 1 to 20, to find an optimal window size we have varied it from 1 to 10.

For our study we have relied on the following classification algorithms, which are implementedin in *Rapidminer*[1] and *WEKA* [14]: Kernel Naive Bayes classifier (NBK) [15], *k*-Nearest Neighbours algorithm (*k*NN) [16], L2 Regularised Logistic Regression (LR) [17], Support Vector Machines [18,19] trained by Sequential Minimal Optimisation (SVM) [20].

To obtain statistically reliable results we have carried out 10-fold cross-validation. Thus, all data were split on the training and testing sets, where we have introduced one more inner 10-fold cross-validation on the training sets. This inner 10-fold cross-validation have been accomplished for the grid parameter optimisation of the classification algorithms, where F_1-score [21] was maximized.

Regarding dimensionality reduction we have employed a data transformation technique Principal Component Analysis (PCA) [22] with the fixed cumulative variance value 0.99, what allowed to reduce the number of features approximately by factor of 2.5 (approx. from 1200 to 470). What is more, the data were preprocessed using statistical normalization for each column (attribute values). As a result, the mean of each column is equal to 0 and the variance is equal to 1. Moreover, for all non-numeric features we have performed dummy coding, which is commonly used to transform non-numeric attributes into numeric type.

5   Results

To assess the obtained results we have relied on such classification performance measures as accuracy, Unweighted Average Recall [7], F_1-score. All these performance measures are macro-average (they were averaged over ten computations on different train-test splits). However, F_1-score is the main performance measure for this study, that is why we provide results almost only for this performance measure.

The results for the different combinations of the interaction parameter levels are depicted in Fig. 2. The results presented in Figs. 2 and 3 were achieved with the *k*NN algorithm.

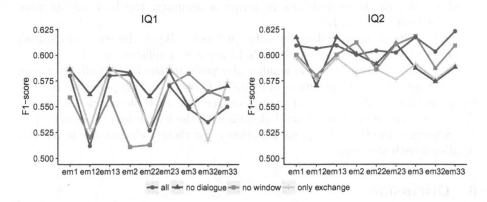

Fig. 2. *k*NN performance in F_1-score for different combinations of the parameter levels

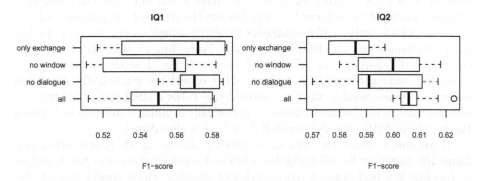

Fig. 3. Box plots for *k*NN performance in F_1-score for different combinations of the parameter level among all emotion sets

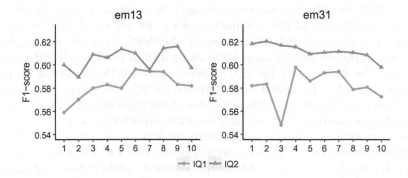

Fig. 4. *k*NN performance in F_1-score for tasks with *em13* and *em31* for the different window size on abscissa

Regarding to the evaluations in terms of accuracy, the best results were obtained with kNN and LR.

The results of IQ modelling for different types of IQ on the sets including all parameter levels (exchange, window, dialogue) were published in [23].

Pertaining the results of the window size problem, the best results were also achieved with the kNN algorithm in terms of F_1-score. In this paper we provide results for tasks with *em13* and *em31* sets (see Fig. 4). It should be mentioned that in the corpus there are four dialogues with the length less (or equal) than 10 exchanges (length: 5, 8, 9, and 10). Hence, for these dialogues the maximum possible length was used.

6   Discussion

Using the one-way analysis of variance (one-way ANOVA) [24] and the Tukey's honest significant difference (HSD) test [25] with the default settings, implemented in R programming language[1], we have found out that the differences between means of the achieved results (within the study of the parameter levels importance) are statistically significant for *IQ2* through all classification performance measures and all classification tasks. Regarding to *IQ1*, the statistically significant differences were determined only in terms of accuracy for all tasks, excepting *em31* and *em33*. To find out what results are statistically significant differ from other results, we have applied the Tukey's HSD test. This test has revealed that in all the cases there are statistically significant differences between the results of NBK (the worst results) and other algorithms.

If we speak about the results in general, almost in all classification performance measures for all tasks the obtained results outperform the baselines (a baseline is a performance metric value of classifier which always predicts the majority class). However, for some algorithms the results do not outperform the baseline in terms of accuracy, which is 0.964 for *IQ1* and 0.882 for *IQ2*.

It is noteworthy that the best results in terms of F_1-score were achieved in all the cases with kNN algorithm. Regarding to the results in terms of accuracy, not only kNN, but also LR has outperformed the other algorithms. To define a statistical significance of the obtained results (with kNN and LR) in terms of accuracy in comparison with the baseline, the Student's t-test [26] was employed. In the case of *IQ2* for all tasks and for both algorithms p-value is less than 0.007. Regarding the kNN model for *IQ1* p-value exceeds 0.15. It should be noted that concerning the LR-based model results for *IQ1*, for some tasks p-values outperform 0.05. The results, where p-value of the Student's t-test for LR-based *IQ1* model is more than 0.05, are marked with asterisk sign in Table 1.

Hence, from the results presented above for *IQ1* we have concluded that the statistically significant results have been achieved with LR, but not for all tasks. In turn, for all classification problems the obtained results in terms of accuracy statistically significantly outperform the baseline for both algorithms, namely

---

[1] http://rapidminer.com/
[1] http://r-project.org/

Table 1. Accuracy for the classification algorithms based on the different combinations of the parameter levels for *IQ1*

Algorithm	Emotion sets								
	em1	em12	em13	em2	em22	em23	em3	em32	em33
	exchange + window + dialogue levels								
*k*NN	0.968	0.96	0.968	0.962	0.962	0.961	0.966	0.963	0.966
LR	**0.97**	**0.97**	**0.97**	**0.973**	**0.969***	**0.973**	**0.97***	**0.967***	**0.973**
	exchange + window levels								
*k*NN	**0.970**	**0.964**	**0.970**	0.965	0.964	0.969	0.968	**0.967**	0.965
LR	0.969	0.963*	0.969	**0.972**	**0.966***	**0.971**	**0.970**	0.966*	**0.971**
	exchange + dialogue levels								
*k*NN	0.965	0.960	0.965	0.957	0.961	0.965	0.964	0.961	0.967
LR	**0.970**	**0.967***	**0.970**	**0.971**	**0.967***	**0.972**	**0.971**	**0.967***	**0.971**
	exchange								
*k*NN	0.967	0.964	0.967	0.968	0.965	**0.966**	0.964	0.962	0.965
LR	**0.969**	**0.967***	**0.969**	**0.969***	**0.966***	**0.966***	**0.970***	**0.966***	**0.972**

*k*NN and LR for *IQ2*. Furthermore, we have performed statistical significance tests to the results which have been obtained with *k*NN algorithm among all combinations of the interaction parameter levels. The one-way ANOVA test has revealed that there are no any statistically significant differences between the results.

From Fig. 3 for *IQ2* we can conclude that the most consistently high results were achieved using the features from all interaction parameter levels. In turn, the use of only exchange level has led to the worst results. It is similar to the results, obtained for HCSI [5]. But in contrast to *IQ2*, for *IQ1* the use of only two levels (the exchange and window levels) has shown the most stable results in Fig. 3 among all sets. Concerning to *IQ1* the obtained results have contradiction with the results obtained in [5].

In addition to the analysis of the impact of the different interaction parameter levels on the overall performance, we have performed the experiments with the different window size to understand its influence on the estimation performance. Thus, for the experiments we have varied the window size from 1 (no window) upto 10. The best results in all the cases were achieved on the *k*NN-based model. On Fig. 4 we have depicted the results obtained on tasks with *em13* and *em31*. As we can see for the different IQ approaches and tasks the better results were reached with the different window size values. So, for the task with *em13* they are 6 and 9 for *IQ1* and *IQ2*, respectively, while for the task with *em31*: 4 and 2, correspondingly. According to the results gained in [5] for HCSI, the best result was achieved with the window size of 9. As authors in [5] suggested, it can be a system dependent parameter which "related to the minimum number of system-user-exchange necessary to perform a successful dialogue" [5]. Experiments presented in this paper for HHC showed that the window size can be a corpus-dependent parameter.

7   Conclusions and Future Work

In this work, we have analysed the different aspects of interaction parameter levels for IQ modelling in HHC. We have performed experiments for two different IQ approaches: *IQ1* and its modification *IQ2*. According to the results of our study, we have concluded that the most consistently high results for *IQ1* were achieved without using features from the dialogue level, while for the second approach it was done with utilizing all levels together. Also, it should be mentioned for *IQ2* that the consistently low results were obtained based only on the features from the exchange level. Concerning the optimal window size, we could not find a unique value for all tasks. It looks like a corpus-dependent parameter.

Besides, during the research we have found out that the obtained results for *IQ2* are almost similar to the results from [5]. But nevertheless, through the results for *IQ1* we have become some contradictions with the results for HCSI [5]. On the one hand, it means that the IQ models for HHC and HCSI are similar and do not depend on the feature set (the corpora for IQ modelling for HCSI and HHC have different features). But on the other hand, it may mean that the results are corpus dependent. That is why the further research in this field with different corpora is important.

As a future direction we plan to extend the list of classification algorithms for predicting an IQ score. Taking into account a rather high dimensionality of the feature space, other dimensionality reduction methods might be helpful. Moreover, the techniques for unbalanced data should be performed.

Acknowledgments. The work presented in this paper was partially supported by the DAAD (German Academic Exchange Service), the Ministry of Education and Science of Russian Federation within project 28.697.2016/2.2, and the Transregional Collaborative Research Centre SFB/TRR 62 "Companion-Technology for Cognitive Technical Systems" which is funded by the German Research Foundation (DFG).

References

1. Schmitt, A., Schatz, B., Minker, W.: Modeling and predicting quality in spoken human-computer interaction. In: Proceedings of the SIGDIAL 2011 Conference, Association for Computational Linguistics, pp. 173–184 (2011)
2. Schmitt, A., Ultes, S., Minker, W.: A parameterized and annotated corpus of the CMU lets go bus information system. In: International Conference on Language Resources and Evaluation (LREC), pp. 3369–3373 (2012)
3. Spirina, A., Sidorov, M., Sergienko, R., Schmitt, A.: First experiments on interaction quality modelling for human-human conversation. In: Proceedings of the 13th International Conference on Informatics in Control, Automation and Robotics (ICINCO), vol. 2, pp. 374–380 (2016)

4. Spirina, A.V., Sidorov, M.Y., Sergienko, R.B., Semenkin, E.S., Minker, W.: Human-human task-oriented conversations corpus for interaction quality modelling. Vestnik SibSAU **17**(1), 84–90 (2016)
5. Ultes, S., Schmitt, A., Minker, W.: Analysis of temporal features for interaction quality estimation. In: Jokinen, K., Wilcock, G. (eds.) Dialogues with Social Robots. LNEE, vol. 999, pp. 367–379. Springer, Singapore (2017). doi:10.1007/978-981-10-2585-3_30
6. Schmitt, A., Ultes, S.: Interaction quality: assessing the quality of ongoing spoken dialog interaction by experts and how it relates to user satisfaction. Speech Commun. **74**, 12–36 (2015)
7. Rosenberg, A.: Classifying skewed data: importance to optimize average recall. In: Proceedings of INTERSPEECH 2012, pp. 2242–2245 (2012)
8. Cohen, J.: A coefficient of agreement for nominal scales. Educ. Psychol. Measur. **20**, 37–46 (1960)
9. Cohen, J.: Weighted kappa: nominal scale agreement provision for scaled disagreement or partial credit. Psychol. Bull. **70**(4), 213–220 (1968)
10. Spearman, C.: The proof and measurement of association between two things. Am. J. Psychol. **15**(1), 72–101 (1904)
11. Eyben, F., Weninger, F., Gross, F., Schuller, B.: Recent developments in opensmile, the munich open-source multimedia feature extractor. In: Proceedings of ACM Multimedia (MM), pp. 835–838 (2013)
12. Schuller, B., Steidl, S., Batliner, A.: The interspeech 2009 emotion challenge. In: Proceedings of INTERSPEECH 2009, pp. 312–315 (2009)
13. Sidorov, M., Brester, C., Schmitt, A.: Contemporary stochastic feature selection algorithms for speech-based emotion recognition. In: Proceedings of INTERSPEECH 2015, pp. 2699–2703 (2015)
14. Hall, M., Frank, E., Holmes, G., Pfahringer, B., Reutmann, P., Witten, I.H.: The weka data mining software: an update. SIGKDD Explor. **11**(1) (2009)
15. John, G.H., Langley, P.: Estimating continuous distribution in bayesian classifiers. In: Eleventh Conference on Uncertainty in Artificial Intelligence, pp. 338–345 (1995)
16. Witten, I.H., Frank, E., Hall, M.A.: Data mining: practical machine learning tools and techniques. Morgan Kaufmann, USA (2011)
17. le Cessie, S., Houwelingen, J.C.: Ridge estimators in logistic regression. Appl. Stat. **41**(1), 191–201 (1992)
18. Cristianini, N., Shawe-Taylor, J.: An Introduction to Support Vector Machines and Other Kernel-based Learning Methods. Cambridge University Press (200)
19. Vapnik, V.N.: The Nature of Statistical Learning Theory. Springer, New York (1995)
20. Platt, J.: Fast training of support vector machines using sequential minimal optimization. Adv. Kernel Methods Support Vector Learn. **3** (1999)
21. Goutte, C., Gaussier, E.: A probabilistic interpretation of precision, recall and f-score, with implication for evaluation. Advances in Information Retrieval, pp. 345–359 (2005)
22. Abdi, H., Williams, L.: Principal component analysis. WIREs Comput. Stat. **2**, 433–459 (2010)
23. Spirina, A., Vaskovskaia, O., Sidorov, M., Schmitt, A.: Interaction quality as a human-human task-oriented conversation performance. In: Proceedings of the 18th International Conference on Speech and Computer (SPECOM 2016), pp. 403–410 (2016)

24. Bailey, R.A.: Design of Comparative Experiments. Cambridge University Press (2008)
25. Kennedy, J.J., Bush, A.J.: An Introduction to the Design and Analysis of Experiments in Behavioural Research. University Press of America (1985)
26. Fay, M.P., Proschan, M.A.: Wilcoxon-mann-whitney or t-test? on assumptions for hypothesis tests and multiple interpretations of decision rules. Stat. Surv. **4**, 1–39 (2010)

Annotation Error Detection:
Anomaly Detection vs. Classification

Jindřich Matoušek[1,2]([✉]) and Daniel Tihelka[2]

[1] Department of Cybernetics, University of West Bohemia, Pilsen, Czech Republic
jmatouse@kky.zcu.cz
[2] Faculty of Applied Sciences, New Technology for the Information Society (NTIS),
University of West Bohemia, Pilsen, Czech Republic
dtihelka@ntis.zcu.cz

Abstract. We compare two approaches to automatic detection of annotation errors in single-speaker read-speech corpora used for speech synthesis: anomaly- and classification-based detection. Both approaches principally differ in that the classification-based approach needs to use both correctly annotated and misannotated words for training. On the other hand, the anomaly-based detection approach needs only the correctly annotated words for training (plus a few misannotated words for validation). We show that both approaches lead to statistically comparable results when all available misannotated words are utilized during detector/classifier development. However, when a smaller number of misannotated words are used, the anomaly detection framework clearly outperforms the classification-based approach. A final listening test showed the effectiveness of the annotation error detection for improving the quality of synthetic speech.

Keywords: Annotation error detection · Anomaly detection · Classification · Speech synthesis

1 Introduction

Word-level annotation of speech data is still one of the most important processes for many speech-processing tasks. In particular, concatenative speech synthesis methods including popular unit selection assume the word-level (textual) annotation to be correct, i.e. that textual annotation literally matches the corresponding speech signal. Such an assumption could hardly be guaranteed for corpus-based speech synthesis in which large speech corpora are typically exploited. Manual annotation of the corpora is time-consuming and costly, but, given the large amount of data, still not errorless process [6]. Automatic or semi-automatic annotation approaches could be a solution but they are still far from perfect, see, e.g. [1,12,15]. Let us note that any mismatch between speech data and its annotation may inherently result in audible glitches in synthetic speech [11].

As shown in our previous work [8], word-level annotation errors in read-speech corpora for text-to-speech (TTS) synthesis could be detected automatically using anomaly detection techniques. In this paper, we compare the anomaly

© Springer International Publishing AG 2017
A. Karpov et al. (Eds.): SPECOM 2017, LNAI 10458, pp. 141–151, 2017.
DOI: 10.1007/978-3-319-66429-3_13

detection with a "classical" classification approach. The data used in our experiments are described in Sect. 2. In Sects. 3 and 4 the anomaly- and classification-based approaches to annotation error detection are presented. The comparison of both approaches is discussed in Sect. 5. The effectiveness of the proposed annotation error detection framework for improving the quality of synthetic speech is discussed in Sect. 6. Conclusions are drawn in Sect. 7.

2   Experimental Data

We used a Czech read-speech corpus of a single-speaker male voice, recorded for the purposes of unit-selection speech synthesis [5]. The voice talent was instructed to speak in a "news-broadcasting style" and to avoid any spontaneous expressions. The full corpus consisted of 12242 utterances (approx. 18.5 h of speech) segmented to phone-like units using HMM-based forced alignment (carried out by the HTK toolkit [16]) with acoustic models trained on the speaker's data [7]. From this corpus we selected $N_n = 1124$ words which were annotated correctly (hereafter denoted as *correctly annotated words*), and $N_a = 273$ words (213 of them being different), which contained some annotation error (*misannotated words*). The decision whether the annotation was correct or not was made by a human expert who analyzed the phonetic alignment.

Various word-level feature sets were proposed to describe the annotated words [8]. The sets incorporated various acoustic, spectral, phonetic, positional, durational, and other features. To emphasize anomalies in the feature values, histograms and deviations from their expected values were also used. More details about the feature sets can be found in [8].

3   Anomaly-Based Annotation Error Detection

The problem of the automatic detection of misannotated words could be viewed as a problem of *anomaly detection* (also called *novelty detection, one-class classification,* or *outlier detection*), an *unsupervised detection technique* under the assumption that the vast majority of the examples in the unlabeled data set are normal. By just providing the "normal" training data (the correctly annotated words in our case), an algorithm creates a representational model of this data. If newly encountered data is too different from this model, it is labeled as "anomalous" (i.e. misannotated words in our case) [2]. This could be perceived as an advantage over a standard classification approach in which substantial number of both "negative" (correctly annotated) and "positive" (misannotated) examples is needed. Nevertheless, if some misannotated words are given in the anomaly detection framework, they can be used to tune the detector and to evaluate its performance.

For the purposes of the comparison with a classification-based approach (described further in Sect. 4), Grubbs' test (GT) based anomaly detector (ADET) both with the optimal hand-crafted set of features (ADET*) [10] and with a set of features reduced by the *singular value decomposition* technique

(ADET$^{(\text{dim})}$) was used [10]. The reason for choosing the GT-based detector was that it statistically outperformed other detectors when evaluated over multiple development/evaluation data splits [10]. It also performed well on both reduced and all feature sets and also showed a consistent performance on data sets with a lower number of misannotated words [9].

For the purposes of the development of an anomaly detection model (i.e., for anomaly model training and selection), correctly annotated words were divided into training and validation examples using 10-fold cross validation with 60% of the correctly annotated words used for training and 20% used for validation in each cross-validation fold. The remaining 20% of the correctly annotated words were held out for the final evaluation of the model. As for the misannotated words, 50% of them were used in cross validation when selecting the best model parameters (i.e., for the validation of an anomaly detection model), and the remaining 50% were used for the final evaluation.

The standard training procedure was utilized to train the ADET model. The model *hyper-parameters*, n (the number of features detected as outlying) and α (significance level) [10], were optimized during *model selection*, i.e. by selecting their values that yielded the best results (in terms of $F1$ score, see Sect. 5) applying a grid search over relevant values of the parameters with 10-fold cross validation. In the case of GT, the parameter n was varied in the interval $[1, \min(30, N_f)]$ (with N_f being the total number of features), and the parameter α was searched in the range $[0.01, 0.05]$.

The training and evaluation is shown in Fig. 1a and could be summarized in the following steps:

1. Correctly annotated words were split into development/evaluation partitions (with the development data being further split into training and validation parts). The ratio of development/evaluation partitions was 80/20.
2. Misannotated words were split into validation/evaluation partitions in a 50/50 ratio.
3. Correctly annotated words used for the development were split into training/validation partitions using 10-fold cross validation with 60% of the original correctly annotated words used for training and 20% used for validation in each cross-validation fold. The training data was standardized to have zero mean and unity variance.
4. A detector was trained and its hyper-parameters were optimized using a grid search and the 10-fold cross validation scheme.
5. The best detector with the best hyper-parameters was re-trained on all correctly annotated words available for the development.
6. The same standardization method as for the training data was applied to the evaluation data.
7. The performance of the resulting anomaly detector was evaluated on the evaluation data set with the metrics described in Sect. 5.

The *Scikit-learn* toolkit [13] was employed in our experiments.

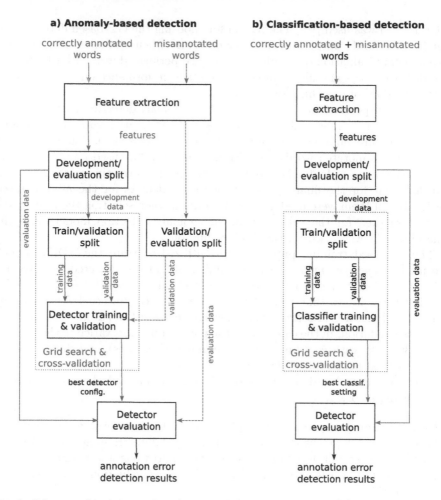

Fig. 1. Schemes of training and evaluation of the anomaly-based (a) and classification-based (b) annotation error detection

4 Classification-Based Annotation Error Detection

The problem of annotation error detection can also be viewed as a *two-class classification problem*: whether a word is misannotated or not. Being a *supervised learning model*, the main difference from the anomaly detector is that misannotated words must be used both during the training and the validation of a classifier.

For the classification experiment, the development data described in Sect. 2 (both correctly annotated and misannotated words) were split into training and validation sets using stratified 10-fold cross-validation. Stratified splits were used to keep the class proportions the same across all of the folds, which is important for maintaining a representative subset of our data set. To enable a correct comparison with the anomaly-detection approach, the evaluation data for the classification experiment were kept the same as for the anomaly-detection approach. The training and evaluation is illustrated in Fig. 1b and could be summarized in the following steps:

1. 50% of misannotated words and 20% of correctly annotated words were left for evaluation (the same examples as in the case of anomaly detection, see Sect. 3).
2. Remaining examples (both correctly annotated and misannotated words) were used for the development of a classifier.
3. Stratified 10-fold cross-validation scheme with 80% of examples (standardized to have zero mean and unity variance) used for training and 20% of examples used for validation in each fold together with a grid search to find optimal hyper-parameters of the classifier was employed to train the classifier.
4. The same standardization method as for the training data was applied to the evaluation data.
5. The performance of the resulting classifier was evaluated on the evaluation data set with the metrics described in Sect. 5.

We used *support vector machine* (SVM) classifier with Gaussian *radial basis function* (RBF) kernel which have proven to be successful in various classification tasks. The SVM classifier was trained using a similar scheme as the one used to train an anomaly detector in Sect. 3 with the exception that both correctly annotated and misannotated words were used during training in this case. The hyper-parameters of the SVM RBF classifier, the penalty parameter C of the error term and the kernel parameter γ, were optimized using a grid search over relevant values of the hyper-parameters ($C \in [2^{-5}, 2^{15}]$, $\gamma \in [2^{-15}, 2^3]$) [3] with the 10-fold cross-validation.

As for the features, we used *recursive feature elimination* [4] with cross-validation (RFECV) technique to select optimal features. Given an external estimator that assigns weights to features (support vector machine with linear kernel was used in our case), features whose weights are the smallest are pruned from the feature set. The procedure is recursively repeated until the desired number of features is reached. To find the optimal number of features, 5-fold cross-validation was employed—in our case, the optimal number of features was 81. Such a classifier is hereinafter referred to as $\text{CLF}^{(\text{dim})}$. For comparison, we also used all features (denoted as $\text{CLF}^{(\text{all})}$).

5   Results

Due to the unbalanced number of correctly annotated and misannotated words, $F1$ *score* was used to evaluate the performance of the annotation error detection models

$$F1 = \frac{2 * P * R}{P + R}, \quad P = \frac{t_p}{p_p}, \quad R = \frac{t_p}{a_p} \qquad (1)$$

where P is *precision*, the ability of a model not to detect as misannotated a word that is annotated correctly, R is *recall*, the ability of a model to detect all misannotated words, t_p means "true positives" (i.e., the number of words correctly detected as misannotated), p_p stands for "predicted positives" (i.e., the number of all words detected as misannotated), and a_p means "actual positives" (i.e., the number of actual misannotated words). $F1$ score was also used to optimize parameters during the model selection process. McNemar's test [8,14] was employed to interpret statistical significance of the obtained results.

Table 1. Comparison of classification (CLF) and anomaly-detection (ADET) based approaches to annotation error detection on the evaluation data set. $\text{CLF}^{(\text{dim})}$ and $\text{ADET}^{(\text{dim})}$ stand for the models with reduced feature sets, $\text{CLF}^{(\text{all})}$ denotes the classifier with all features employed, and ADET* denotes the anomaly-detector with optimal hand-crafted features [10]. Random detection (RAND) generating predictions by respecting the distribution of misannotated words in our development data set was also included in the comparison

Model ID	$P[\%]$	$R[\%]$	$F1[\%]$	MCC
$\text{CLF}^{(\text{dim})}$	97.20	75.91	85.25	0.7927
$\text{CLF}^{(\text{all})}$	**98.04**	72.99	83.68	0.7774
$\text{ADET}^{(\text{dim})}$	92.50	81.02	86.38	0.7935
ADET*	86.62	**89.78**	**88.17**	**0.8079**
RAND	36.96	12.41	18.58	−0.0070

The comparison of the detection accuracy of both the anomaly-detection based and classification-based approaches is provided in Table 1. As can be seen, similar results were achieved. The differences in detection accuracies were not proved to be statistically significant (McNemar's test, $\alpha = 0.05$). This is a good finding because, unlike the classification-based detection, we do not need any misannotated words to train an anomaly-based detector (with the exception of several misannotated words used for validation but the number of misannotated words could be kept very low [9]); thus, the process of training data collection should be easier. The similar detection accuracy also suggests that there is no benefit in explicit training and modeling of misannotated words. We assume that this is caused by a variety of annotation errors.

Moreover, as can be seen in Fig. 2, the classification approach is more sensitive to the number of misannotated words used during the classifier's development. As already shown in [9], a significantly lower number of misannotated words could be used to develop an anomaly detector with statistically the same performance as when all misannotated words are used (in the case of the GT detector, 27 misannotated words could be used during validation without any drop in detection performance). On the other hand, using fewer than 75 misannotated words to develop a classifier results in a statistically significant drop in detection performance when compared to an anomaly detector developed with

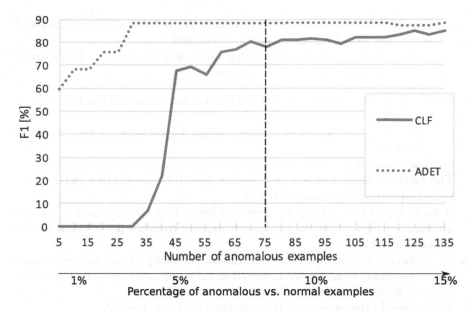

Fig. 2. The influence of the number of misannotated words used during classifier (CLF) and anomaly-detector (ADET) development on detection accuracy on the evaluation data set. The vertical dashed line indicates the number of misannotated words for which the results are statistically significant

the same low number of misannotated words (McNemar's test, $\alpha = 0.05$). On top of that, after the number of misannotated words falls below 30, the classifier fails to detect any misannotated word.

6   Listening Test Based Evaluation

Although the methods compared in this paper could be used for the detection of annotation errors in virtually any corpus, we focused on read-speech corpora typically utilized for speech synthesis. Therefore, we carried out a final listening test to show the effectiveness of the proposed method for improving the quality of synthetic speech.

For the listening test based evaluation, Grubbs' test based anomaly detector with the optimal set of features (GT*), as being the one outperforming the other detectors, was used to detect annotation errors in the original speech corpus designed for unit-selection speech synthesis. The annotation errors detected by the GT-based detector were then revised by an annotator who checked whether the detected words were really annotation errors or not. For the purposes of the listening test based evaluation, however, only the part of the speech corpus corresponding to the evaluation sets was processed [10]. The real annotation errors were corrected but the falsely detected words were left unchanged. Using this scenario, the annotation process accompanying the development of a new voice could be reduced only to the correction of words detected as misannotated. As a result, a corrected speech corpus was obtained.

Consequently, a speech synthesis experiment was carried out. The steps of the experiment can be summarized as follows:

1. The following two versions of the Czech unit-selection speech-synthesis system [5] were built:
   (a) One system (S1) was built from the original speech corpus with the annotation errors.
   (b) The other system (S2) was built from the corrected speech corpus.
   The systems differed only in the source speech corpora; other parts of the text-to-speech system were identical.
2. A large number of utterances were synthesized by the system S1, and the utterances which contained any speech segment from a word detected as misannotated were stored.
3. 60 utterances were selected so as to contain both major (multiple consecutive speech segments from a word detected as misannotated) and minor (just one segment from a misannotated word) errors.
4. The selected utterances were then synthesized by system S2.

A listening test was then carried out to compare the selected utterances synthesized by both S1 and S2 systems. The aim of the test was to show whether it is worth detecting and fixing annotation errors with respect to the quality of the resulting (unit-selection based) synthetic speech. 37 listeners (7 of them being experts in speech synthesis) participated in the listening test. All of them were native speakers of Czech aged 25 to 50 and had no hearing impairments. A listener listened to a pair of synthetic utterances synthesized from the same text (with one utterance synthesized by the S1 system and the other by the S2 system). The listener was asked to answer two queries:

1. The first query (Q1) aimed at the intelligibility of the synthetic utterance. Each listener was given a correct textual word-level transcript of the utterance and he/she had to indicate whether the synthetic utterances literally correspond to the transcript. Since Q1 expresses the essential requirement for a TTS system to work properly, it was prioritized further in the evaluation.
2. The second query (Q2) focused on the overall acoustic (and prosodic) quality of the synthetic utterances. This was realized as a three-point preference listening test in which the listener was instructed to compare the two synthetic versions of each utterance regardless of the utterance text. The three-point evaluation consisted in selecting from the following choices:
   - "the synthetic sample A sounds better than the synthetic sample B",
   - "the synthetic sample A sounds worse than the synthetic sample B",
   - "both synthetic samples sound the same".

All listeners evaluated the same 60 pairs of utterances. The order of S1- and S2-generated utterances was set at random in each pair. The listening test was organized over the web and the listeners were instructed to use head-phones.

In order to obtain a single measurement of the improvement provided by the proposed anomaly-based annotation error detection, we combined answers to both queries (Q1+Q2) in the following way and in the following order:

1. If the synthetic utterance A corresponded to the given transcript and the synthetic utterance B did not, A was evaluated as better than B. The result of the comparison in Q2 was not taken into account in this case.
2. Likewise, if the synthetic utterance B corresponded to the given transcript and the synthetic utterance A did not, B was evaluated as better than A. Again, Q2 comparison was ignored.
3. Whether or not both utterances corresponded to the transcript, the result of the comparison in Q2 was used to evaluate the utterances.

The results of this evaluation are shown in the row "Combination (Q1+Q2)" of Table 2. As can be seen, there was a clear preference for speech synthesis based on the speech corpus with the corrected annotation (S2).

Table 2. Comparison of synthetic speech synthesized by the system based on the original speech corpus with annotation errors (S1) and by the system based on the corrected speech corpus (S2). The preferences for each comparison are in percentage. "S2 > S1" stands for "S2-generated synthetic utterance is better than S1-generated synthetic utterance", "S2 < S1" stands for "S2 is worse than S1", and "S2 = S1" means that "both systems generated comparable synthetic utterances"

	S2 > S1	S2 < S1	S2 = S1
Intelligibility (Q1)	**62.07**	0.32	37.30
Acoust. quality (Q2)	**41.49**	9.32	**49.19**
Combination (Q1+Q2)	**71.17**	6.22	22.61

Looking at the other observed phenomena separately, the row "Intelligibility (Q1)" in Table 2 shows the intelligibility results (related to the Q1 queries), and the row "Acoust. quality" in Table 2 shows the results of the comparison in terms of overall acoustic (and prosodic) quality regardless of whether or not the synthetic speech corresponded to the given transcript (related to the Q2 queries). As for the intelligibility, a preference for the synthetic speech based on the corrected speech corpus was evident again. Also, in the case of the comparison of the acoustic quality, listeners either tended to prefer the corrected speech corpus or they assessed both synthetic versions as sounding the same.

7 Conclusions

We compared anomaly-based detection and classification-based approaches to detect word-level annotation errors in a speech corpus intended for unit-selection speech synthesis. The classification approach differs mainly in that it needs mis-annotated words also for training (and not only for validation as in the case of anomaly detection). We showed that both approaches led to statistically comparable results when all the available misannotated words were utilized during detector/classifier development. However, when a lower number of misannotated words were used, the anomaly detection framework clearly outperformed the classification-based approach.

Regarding the impact of annotation error detection framework on the quality of synthetic speech synthesized by a unit-selection speech-synthesis system, a preference listening test was carried out. The results of the listening test confirmed the effectiveness of the proposed annotation error detection for improving the quality of synthetic speech. It was shown that annotation errors are worth detecting in speech corpora designed for unit-selection-based speech synthesis.

Acknowledgments. This research was supported by the Czech Science Foundation (GA CR), project No. GA16-04420S. The access to the MetaCentrum clusters provided under the programme LM2015042 is highly appreciated.

References

1. Boeffard, O., Charonnat, L., Maguer, S.L., Lolive, D., Vidal, G.: Towards fully automatic annotation of audiobooks for TTS. In: Language Resources and Evaluation Conference, Istanbul, Turkey, pp. 975–980 (2012)
2. Chandola, V., Banerjee, A., Kumar, V.: Anomaly detection: a survey. ACM Comput. Surv. **41**(3), 1–58 (2009)
3. Chang, C.C., Lin, C.J.: LIBSVM: a library for support vector machines. ACM Trans. Intell. Syst. Technol. **2**(3), 27:1–27:27 (2011)
4. Guyon, I., Weston, J., Barnhill, S., Vapnik, V.: Gene selection for cancer classification using support vector machines. Mach. Learn. **46**(1/3), 389–422 (2002)
5. Kala, J., Matoušek, J.: Very fast unit selection using Viterbi search with zero-concatenation-cost chains. In: IEEE International Conference on Acoustics Speech and Signal Processing, Florence, Italy, pp. 2569–2573 (2014)
6. Matoušek, J., Romportl, J.: Recording and annotation of speech corpus for czech unit selection speech synthesis. In: Matoušek, V., Mautner, P. (eds.) TSD 2007. LNCS, vol. 4629, pp. 326–333. Springer, Heidelberg (2007). doi:10.1007/978-3-540-74628-7_43
7. Matoušek, J., Romportl, J.: Automatic pitch-synchronous phonetic segmentation. In: INTERSPEECH, Brisbane, Australia, pp. 1626–1629 (2008)
8. Matoušek, J., Tihelka, D.: Anomaly-based annotation errors detection in TTS corpora. In: INTERSPEECH, Dresden, Germany, pp. 314–318 (2015)
9. Matoušek, J., Tihelka, D.: On the influence of the number of anomalous and normal examples in anomaly-based annotation errors detection. In: Sojka, P., Horák, A., Kopeček, I., Pala, K. (eds.) TSD 2016. LNCS, vol. 9924, pp. 326–334. Springer, Cham (2016). doi:10.1007/978-3-319-45510-5_37
10. Matoušek, J., Tihelka, D.: Anomaly-based annotation error detection in speech-synthesis corpora. Comput. Speech Lang. **46**, 1–35 (2017)

11. Matoušek, J., Tihelka, D., Šmídl, L.: On the impact of annotation errors on unit-selection speech synthesis. In: Sojka, P., Horák, A., Kopeček, I., Pala, K. (eds.) TSD 2012. LNCS, vol. 7499, pp. 456–463. Springer, Heidelberg (2012). doi:10.1007/978-3-642-32790-2_55

12. Meinedo, H., Neto, J.: Automatic speech annotation and transcription in a broadcast news task. In: ISCA Workshop on Multilingual Spoken Document Retrieval, Hong Kong, pp. 95–100 (2003)

13. Pedregosa, F., Varoquaux, G., Gramfort, A., Thirion, V.M.B., Grisel, O., Blondel, M., Prettenhofer, P., Weiss, R., Dubourg, V., Vanderplas, J., Passos, A., Cournapeau, D., Brucher, M., Perror, M., Duchesnay, É.: Scikit-learn: machine learning in Python. J. Mach. Learn. Res. **12**, 2825–2830 (2011)

14. Salzberg, S.: On comparing classifiers: pitfalls to avoid and a recommended approach. Data Min. Knowl. Disc. **328**, 317–328 (1997)

15. Tachibana, R., Nagano, T., Kurata, G., Nishimura, M., Babaguchi, N.: Preliminary experiments toward automatic generation of new TTS voices from recorded speech alone. In: INTERSPEECH, Antwerp, Belgium, pp. 1917–1920 (2007)

16. Young, S., Evermann, G., Gales, M.J.F., Hain, T., Kershaw, D., Liu, X., Moore, G., Odell, J., Ollason, D., Povey, D., Valtchev, V., Woodland, P.: HTK Book (for HTK Version 3.4). Cambridge University, Cambridge (2006)

Are You Addressing Me? Multimodal Addressee Detection in Human-Human-Computer Conversations

Oleg Akhtiamov[1,2(✉)], Dmitrii Ubskii[2], Evgeniia Feldina[2],
Aleksei Pugachev[2,3], Alexey Karpov[2,3], and Wolfgang Minker[1]

[1] Ulm University, Ulm, Germany
oakhtiamov@gmail.com, wolfgang.minker@uni-ulm.de
[2] ITMO University, St. Petersburg, Russia
ubskydm@yandex.ru, feldina@speechpro.com,
terixoid@gmail.com, karpov_a@mail.ru
[3] SPIIRAS, St. Petersburg, Russia

Abstract. The goal of addressee detection is to answer the question 'Are you addressing me?' In order to participate in multiparty conversations, a spoken dialogue system is supposed to determine whether a user is addressing the system or another human. The present paper describes three levels of speech and text analysis (acoustical, lexical, and syntactical) for multimodal addressee detection and reveals the connection between them and the classification performance for different categories of speech. We propose several classification models and compare their performance with the results of the original research performed by the authors of the Smart Video Corpus which we use in our computations. Our most effective meta-classifier working with acoustical, syntactical, and lexical features provides an unweighted average recall equal to 0.917, showing a nine percent advantage over the best baseline model, though the baseline classifier additionally uses head orientation data. We also propose an LSTM neural network for text classification which replaces the lexical and the syntactical classifier by a single model reaching the same performance as the most effective meta-classifier does, despite the fact that this meta-model additionally analyses acoustical data.

Keywords: Off-Talk · Speaking style · Text classification · Long Short-Term memory · Data fusion · Multimodal interaction · Spoken dialogue system

1 Introduction

Spoken dialogue systems (SDSs) have become significantly more complex and flexible over recent years and are now capable of solving a wide range of tasks. The requirements for SDSs depend on a particular application area; e.g., personal assistants in smartphones are meant to interact with a single user – the owner. Theoretically, the interaction between a user and such a system may be considered as a pure human-computer (H-C) dialogue. However, there is the possibility that the user is solving a cooperative task that requires some interaction with other people nearby, e.g.,

© Springer International Publishing AG 2017
A. Karpov et al. (Eds.): SPECOM 2017, LNAI 10458, pp. 152–161, 2017.
DOI: 10.1007/978-3-319-66429-3_14

interlocutors may be negotiating how they will spend this evening, asking the system to show information about cafes or cinema and discussing alternatives. In this case, the system deals with a multiparty conversation which may include human-addressed utterances as well as machine-addressed ones, leading to the problem of addressee detection (AD) in human-human-computer (H-H-C) conversations [1]. Solving this problem, the system is supposed to determine whether it is being addressed or not in order to decide how to process the input utterance: respond or ignore.

Traditionally, user interfaces have been engineered to avoid addressee ambiguity by using a push-to-talk button, key words, or by assuming that all potential input utterances are system-addressed and rejecting those which cause a failure-to-recognize or a failure-to-interpret [2, 3]. Such straightforward approaches are no longer applicable, since modern SDSs support essentially unlimited spoken input. Therefore, more sophisticated classification methods are required for AD.

The present paper is a continuation of our previous study on text-based AD [4] and includes three main contributions. The first contribution is an attempt to extract as much useful information from audio signal as possible. Relying on other modalities, e.g., on visual information, is not reasonable in certain applications in which users have no visual contact with the object they are talking to, e.g., while driving a car. The second contribution is to define the connection between different levels of speech and text analysis and the classification performance for different categories of speech. The third contribution is to update the results of an existing study. We analyse the Smart Video Corpus (SVC) and compare our results on AD with the results obtained by the authors of the corpus. In their original research, the term "Off-Talk detection" is used instead of AD [5].

2 Related Work

There exist several studies investigating the separate roles of acoustical [6], textual [7], and visual [8] information towards the AD problem. It was determined that people combine prosodic, lexical, and gaze cues to specify desirable addressees [1]. Other works report that the way users talk to an SDS essentially depends on the overall system performance [5] and how people see the system (as a human-like robot or as an information kiosk) [9]. Modern SDSs are still far from perfection, and users tend to change their normal manner of speech and talk to the system as if they were talking to a child [10], making it easier to understand, and, therefore, prosodic information plays a significant role in AD. The fact that prosodic features use no lexical, context, or speaker information makes prosody a universal modality for applications nowadays [6]. Simultaneously with future SDS improvement, prosodic features will become less representative, and future systems will thus rely more on textual and gaze information. It was shown that addressee and response selection in multiparty conversations between humans can be successfully performed by analysing lexical content and conversational context with recurrent neural networks [11].

The following features are representative for AD in existing SDSs (according to their relative contribution in descending order): acoustical, automatic speech recognition (recognized text and recognition confidence), dialogue state, gaze direction, and beamforming [1].

3 Experimental Data

The SVC data (part of the Smart Web Project) has been collected within large-scaled Wizard-of-Oz experiments and models the H-H-C conversation in German between two users and a multimodal SDS. The corpus includes queries in the context of a visit to a Football World Cup stadium in 2006. A user was carrying a mobile phone, asking questions of certain categories (transport, sights, sport statistics, and also open-domain questions) and discussing the obtained information with another human whose speech is not presented in the corpus. The data comprises 3.5 h of audio and video, 99 dialogues (one unique speaker per dialogue), 2193 automatically segmented utterances with manual transcripts, and 25 073 words in total. The manual labelling of addressees was carried out for each word; four word classes were specified: On-Talk (NOT) – computer-addressed speech, 11 556 words, read Off-Talk (ROT) – reading information aloud from the system display, 3 222 words, paraphrased Off-Talk (POT) – retelling the information obtained from the system in arbitrary form, 4 674 words, and spontaneous Off-Talk (SOT) – other human-addressed speech (including self-talk), 5 621 words. The video data was captured with the frontal camera of the mobile phone. The manual labelling of video is frame-based (7.5 frames per second), two classes were specified: On-View – a user is looking at the camera (79% of the corpus duration), and Off-View – a user is not looking at the camera or out of view of the camera. No requirements regarding Off-Talk were given to obtain a realistic H-H-C interaction.

In our research, features are extracted at the utterance level for all the implemented models except an LSTM neural network in contrast to the original study in which the authors analysed word-level features initially. An utterance label is calculated as the mode of word labels in the current utterance. After performing the word-to-utterance label transformation, we obtain 1087 NOT, 474 SOT, 323 POT and 309 ROT utterances which may look as follows: < NOT >: "When was Berlin founded? Can you tell me that?" < ROT >: "Berlin was founded in 1237." < POT >: "Oh, it's quite old. The system reports that the foundation year is 1237." < SOT >: "Cool! I didn't know that." We consider a two-class task only (On-Talk vs. the three Off-Talk classes), since it is equivalent to the AD problem. Experiments with a four-class task may be found in the original paper [5]. After merging the three Off-Talk classes into one and performing the word-to-utterance label transformation, we obtain 1078 On-Talk and 1115 Off-Talk utterances.

4 Classification

4.1 Speech Analysis

The underlying idea of using acoustical information for AD is the fact that people make their speech louder, more rhythmical, and easier to understand in general once they start talking to an SDS. There is no standard feature set for acoustical AD. Several research groups analysed different sets [1, 5], and therefore, we decided to use a highly redundant paralinguistic attribute set to perform feature selection afterwards. We extract 6373 acoustical attributes for each utterance by applying the openSMILE toolkit and the feature configuration of the INTERSPEECH 2013 Computational Paralinguistics Challenge (ComParE) [12]. After that, we calculate the coefficients of the normal vector of a linear Support Vector Machine (SVM) for each fold and set them as attribute weights. We sort the attributes according to their weights and carry out recursive feature elimination removing the 50 attributes with the lowest weights per step. As a classifier, we apply a liner SVM implemented in RapidMiner Studio 7.3 [13]. It turned out that the optimal number of attributes was approximately 1000 in each fold, therefore, it was decided to use the first 1000 attributes with the highest weights. The selected features are speaker-dependent, however, they are much less sensitive to a specific domain in comparison with lexical attributes.

4.2 Text Analysis

The text obtained with automatic speech recognition (ASR) allows us to carry out syntactical and lexical analysis. In this paper, most text-based computations are performed by using manual transcripts (it is assumed that our recognizer has word recognition accuracy close to 100%). We also test our system in conjunction with a state-of-the-art recognizer (Google Cloud Speech API) with word recognition accuracy of around 80% and analyse three additional ASR-based features besides text: recognition confidence, number of recognized words and utterance length. The underlying idea is that computer-addressed speech matches the ASR pattern better than human-addressed speech does. For these three attributes, we apply the same classifier as for the acoustical features.

We carry out two stages of text analysis. The first stage is syntactical analysis which allows us to determine differences in the structure of human- and computer-addressed sentences. The main idea is that the syntax of machine-addressed speech possesses more structured patterns in comparison with the syntax of human-addressed speech. As a representation of syntactical structure, we apply part-of-speech (POS) n-gram. Firstly, we perform POS tagging by using spaCy 1.8 [14] and obtain utterances in which each word is replaced by one of 15 universal POS tags. After that, we extract uni- bi-, tri-, tetra-, and pentagrams and weight them by using the following term weighting methods: Inverse Document Frequency (IDF), Gain Ratio (GR), Confident Weights (CW), Second Moment of a Term (TM2), Relevance Frequency (RF), Term Relevance Ratio (TRR), and Novel Term Weighting (NTW) [15]. The obtained syntactical attributes are language-dependent, however, they are much less sensitive to a specific domain in comparison with lexical features. We apply three classification algorithms which demonstrated high performance for other text classification tasks [15]: k Nearest Neighbours (KNN) [16], Fast Large Margin (Liner SVM-based classifier – SVM-FLM) [17], and Rocchio classifier (Centroid classifier) [18]. The first two classifiers were implemented in RapidMiner Studio 7.3, the third one was developed in C++.

The second stage of text analysis is lexical analysis which allows us to determine typical lexical units for each class. In other words, this kind of analysis shows *what* has been said, while acoustical and syntactical analysis indicate *how* it has been said. We perform the same procedure of text classification as it was shown for syntactical analysis with a single distinction: we deal with real words instead of POS tags. Firstly, we apply two linguistic filters implemented in tm (R package for text mining): stemming and stop-word filtering. Then, we extract uni-, bi-, and trigrams, weight them by using the seven term weighting methods and apply the three classification algorithms mentioned above.

4.3 Data Fusion

In order to get benefits from all the levels of speech and text analysis, we carry out data fusion. Combining the ASR additional information and the acoustical attributes, we perform feature-level fusion, while a meta-classifier based on a linear SVM is applied for various combinations of the acoustical, syntactical and lexical models. As input features, each meta-classifier receives the classification confidence scores of the models included in it. In order to train meta-models, we split each training set into two sets in a proportion of eight to two. The first set is used for training single models, and the second one provides unique information for training the corresponding meta-model. In the original research, a linear discriminant classifier was applied for single models as well as at the meta-level [19].

4.4 LSTM Neural Network for Text Classification

Taking into account the initial word-based labelling for text, an application of deep neural networks seems to be natural for our task. The study [7] describes several applications of a recurrent (RNN), a Long Short-Term Memory (LSTM), and a feed-forward net for a text-based addressee detection task. The LSTM model demonstrated the highest performance for long utterances with a length of 10 words and more. The average utterance length for the SVC data is 11 words, therefore, it was decided to apply such a model for our task as well.

LSTM nets allow us to resolve three problems of text-based addressee detection which were impossible to solve by using classical machine learning models. One of them is the problem of mixed word labels during the utterance-based classification. This problem arises due to segmentation errors at the stage of automatic utterance detection and means that one utterance may contain words with various labels. Our multimodal classifier works at the utterance level, therefore, it may miss some important information regarding how word labels change within the utterance. LSTM nets can easily track these changes, since sequence prediction is one of the tasks they are designed for. Another problem is the necessity of additional pre-processing before applying classical machine learning models that leads to an information loss. The lexical and the syntactical text representation may be combined into one taking into account the semantical meaning of words. The third problem is the limited context coverage of *n*-grams [7]. An *n*-gram-based language model fails to determine the relations between words standing far from each other within one sentence. Due to Long Short-Term Memory, LSTM networks find such relations without any difficulties.

As input features for our LSTM net, we use word embedding vectors extracted by using a pretrained word2vec model for German which is a part of spaCy 1.8 [14]. The underlying word2vec method is GloVe [20] representing each word as a vector of 300 real values. After feature extraction, an utterance may be processed as a sequence of words (time steps). In order to simplify the model architecture, we design it for sequences of a fixed length. Each sequence is aligned to the length of the longest utterance in the corpus by using null padding and masking to inform the net that empty time steps should be ignored. Padded sequences are feed to the net implemented by using Keras 2.0 [21] with the following architecture: the first layer consists of 30 default LSTM cells, the next layer is the output one and includes two neurons with the softmax activation function. For each utterance, the net is supposed to return a sequence of word labels. For weight optimization, the RMSprop algorithm is applied with a learning rate of 0.01. The entire model is trained for 20 epochs with a batch size of 128.

During the training process, we noticed that the net was very sensitive to null vectors which appeared in the case of an unknown word. Their occurrence affects LSTM nets even more than classical n-gram representations, since the absence of one word leads to information losses only in the three neighbouring word combinations in the case of a trigram model, while the same fact causes the wrong recognition of the following subsequence in the case of an LSTM model [7]. Two word categories have this problem: proper names and long German compounds. To resolve the problem, we apply dictionary search to split compounds into several single words which are known to the word2vec model. Unknown proper names are replaced by popular names.

5 Experimental Results

For statistical analysis, we carry out leave-one-group-out cross validation splitting the entire corpus into 14 folds (7 speakers for each and one more speaker to the fold with the least number of utterances) so that the proportion of classes remains equal in each fold. All statistical comparisons are drawn by using a t-test with a confidential probability of 0.95. Unweighted average recall has been chosen as the main performance criterion in order to make a correct comparison with the original research.

An average performance value and a standard deviation are calculated for each model and depicted in Fig. 1. The ASR additional information (ASR info) and the acoustical attributes (ac) demonstrate a significant dependence on speakers and also show the lowest performance of 0.668 and 0.822 respectively which becomes significantly higher up to 0.828 after their feature-level fusion. The most effective models for syntactical and lexical analysis include POS tagging + trigrams + RF term weighting + SVM-FLM classifier and stemming + unigrams + RF term weighting + SVM-FLM classifier respectively. There is no significant difference between the acoustical and the syntactical model (synt) which demonstrates a performance of 0.836. Stemming (lex s) reduces the dimensionality of the text classification task by 20% (the average dictionary size falls from 1381 to 1108) keeping the AD performance at the level of the lexical model without linguistic filtering (lex) which demonstrates the highest result among single classifiers of 0.911, while stop-word filtering (lex f) significantly decreases the performance to 0.883.

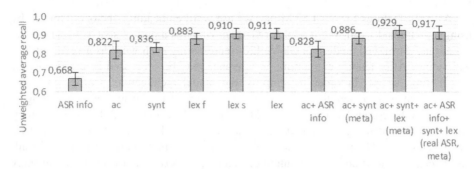

Fig. 1. Classification performance of different models

The most effective meta-classifier analysing the information at all three levels reaches a performance of 0.929 and demonstrates a statistically significant advantage over the other models. The performance of another meta-classifier working with acoustical and syntactical information is significantly lower and equal to 0.886. However, the main advantage of this meta-model is domain-independence and a higher degree of universality in comparison with the most effective meta-model involving lexical analysis.

There is no significant difference between the most effective meta-classifier using the textual information obtained from the manual transcripts and the analogical meta-model working with the real ASR and showing a performance of 0.917.

We tried to reproduce the original experiment [5] as precisely as possible. Four speakers which had technical problems were excluded, then we randomly split the remaining speakers into a training (58 speakers) and a test set (37 speakers) until we obtained approximately the same number of utterances in the respective sets as they were in the original research. Table 1 demonstrates that all the proposed models outperform the corresponding baselines analysing related groups of features, particularly, our most effective meta-classifier reaches a performance of 0.917 showing almost a nine percent advantage over the best baseline classifier, though this baseline model additionally uses head orientation data.

Table 1. Comparison with the results of the original research

	Baseline	Proposed
Acoustical	0.766	0.800
Syntactical	0.760	0.830
Acoustical + Syntactical(meta)	0.808	0.857
Best	**0.845**	**0.917**

We carry out the same experiment for the LSTM-based text classifier. The model receives a sequence of word embedding vectors and returns a sequence of word labels, however, we need an utterance-based prediction to perform a correct comparison with the other classifiers. Therefore, we carry out the word-to-utterance label transformation described above and calculate unweighted average recall. Using the same training and test sets, we train the model 10 times in order to estimate the influence of the initial weight distribution and calculate an average performance score. Using only text, the LSTM net demonstrates an average performance of 0.918 that is comparable with the result of the most effective multimodal meta-classifier.

6 Discussion

The obtained meta-model analysing acoustical and syntactical features may be theoretically applied in various domains, since it uses the attributes containing no lexical information. The most effective meta-classifier considers also lexical content. The text-based models are less speaker-dependent in comparison with the acoustical model but also language-dependent (syntactical model) and even domain-dependent (lexical model). The lexical models demonstrate the highest results among single models for the particular domain. The following groups of lexical terms have the highest RF weights and are therefore considered to be important: question words and polite requests for On-Talk, pronouns (particularly, second person), indirect speech, colloquial words and interjections for Off-Talk. Lexical AD is not sensitive to various word forms, since stemming does not influence the classification performance, while stop-word filtering decreases the performance removing some important terms, e.g., pronouns.

Solving the two-class task and comparing the classification performance for separate categories of speech in Fig. 2, we see that the text-based classifiers have the strongest confusion between NOT and SOT and significant confusion between NOT and POT that leads us to the conclusion that the more spontaneous the speech is, the worse the text-based models work. The acoustical and the ASR-info-based classifier possess the strongest confusion between NOT and ROT and significant confusion between NOT and POT, meaning that the more limited the speech is, the worse results these models demonstrate.

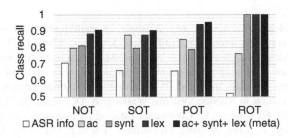

Fig. 2. Classification performance for different categories of speech

7 Conclusions and Future Work

The meta-fusion of several classical machine learning models working with different modalities in combination with a lot of data pre-processing is able to demonstrate effective results for the AD problem. However, the classification performance of the LSTM-based text classifier in conjunction with the pretrained word2vec model is almost the same as the performance of the most effective multimodal meta-classifier.

We are planning to integrate head orientation data into the present research to perform a more complete comparison with the baseline [5]. Let us imagine that our system has a camera near the display. We assume that if a user is not looking at the camera or out of view of the camera, then his or her speech is not addressed to the system at that moment. Our classifier is thus supposed to distinguish On-View from any other frames. A video-based prediction is not enough for accurate AD, however, it is able to increase the overall AD performance within a meta-model [1, 5]. We expect the confusion between NOT and POT and between NOT and SOT (except self-talk) to be lower, since people tend to look at the object they are talking to [22]. It is evident, though, that the confusion between NOT and ROT will not change significantly.

It is necessary to keep in mind that the more advanced the SDS turns out to be, the more naturally users behave, and the less it should rely on acoustical information while detecting addressees. Text and dialogue state will remain reliable, and therefore, we are planning to focus on conversational context-based AD for multiparty SDSs in our future work [11].

Acknowledgements. This research is partially supported by DAAD together with the Ministry of Education and Science of the Russian Federation within Michail Lomonosov Program (project No. 8.704.2016/DAAD), by RFBR (project No. 16-37-60100), by the Government of the Russian Federation (grant No. 074-U01), and by the Transregional Collaborative Research Centre SFB/TRR 62 "Companion-Technology for Cognitive Technical Systems" which is funded by the German Research Foundation (DFG).

References

1. Tsai, T.J., Stolcke, A., Slaney, M.: A study of multimodal addressee detection in human-human-computer interaction. IEEE Trans. Multimed. **17**(9), 1550–1561 (2015)
2. Dowding, J., Alena, R., Clancey, W.J., Sierhuis, M., Graham, J.: Are you talking to me? Dialogue systems supporting mixed teams of humans and robots. In: Proceedings of AAAI Fall Symposium Aurally Informed Performance: Integrating Machine Listening and Auditory Presentation in Robotic Systems, Washington, DC, USA, pp. 22–27 (2006)
3. Paek, T., Horvitz, E., Ringger, E.: Continuous listening for unconstrained spoken dialog. In: Yuan, B., Huang, T., Tang, X. (eds). Proceedings of ICSLP, vol. 1, pp. 138–141 (2000)
4. Akhtiamov, O., Sergienko, R., Minker, W.: An approach to Off-Talk detection based on text classification within an automatic spoken dialogue system. In: Proceedings of ICINCO, Lisbon, Portugal, vol. 2, pp. 288–293 (2016)
5. Batliner, A., Hacker, C., Noeth, E.: To talk or not to talk with a computer. J. Multimodal User Interfaces **2**(3), 171–186 (2008)

6. Shriberg, E., Stolcke, A., Ravuri, S.: Addressee detection for dialog systems using temporal and spectral dimensions of speaking style. In: Proceedings of Interspeech, pp. 2559–2563 (2013)
7. Ravuri, S., Stolcke, A.: Recurrent neural network and LSTM models for lexical utterance classification. In: Proceedings of Interspeech, pp. 135–139 (2015)
8. Johansson, M., Skantze, G., Gustafson, J.: Head pose patterns in multiparty human-robot team-building interactions. In: Proceedings of ICSR, Bristol, UK, pp. 351–360 (2013)
9. Lee, M.K., Kiesler, S., Forlizzi, J.: Receptionist or information kiosk: how do people talk with a robot? In: Proceedings of ACM Conference on Computer Supported Cooperative Work, pp. 31–40 (2010)
10. Schuller, B., et al.: The INTERSPEECH 2017 computational paralinguistics challenge: addressee, cold & snoring. In: Proceedings of Interspeech, Stockholm, Sweden (2017)
11. Ouchi, H., Tsuboi, Y.: Addressee and response selection for multi-party conversation. In: Proceedings of EMNLP, Austin, Texas, pp. 2133–2143 (2016)
12. Schuller, B., et al.: The INTERSPEECH 2013 computational paralinguistics challenge: social signals, conflict, emotion, autism. In: Proceedings of Interspeech, Lyon, France (2013)
13. Ben-Hur, A., Weston, J.: A User's Guide to Support Vector Machines. Data Mining Techniques for the Life Sciences, pp. 223–239. Humana Press (2010)
14. spaCy library. https://github.com/explosion/spaCy
15. Sergienko, R., Shan, M., Minker, W.: A comparative study of text preprocessing approaches for topic detection of user utterances. In: Proceedings of LREC, Portorož, Slovenia, pp. 1826–1831 (2016)
16. Zhou, Y., Li, Y., Xia, S.: An improved KNN text classification algorithm based on clustering. J. Comput. 4(3), 230–237 (2009)
17. Fan, R.E., Chang, K.W., Hsieh, C.J., Wang, X.R., Lin, C.J.: Liblinear: a library for large linear classification. J. Mach. Learn. Res. 9, 1871–1874 (2008)
18. Joachims, T.: A probabilistic analysis of the Rocchio algorithm with TFIDF for text categorization. No. CMU-CS, pp. 96–118, Carnegie-Mellon University, Pittsburgh, PA, Department of Computer Science (1996)
19. Klecka, W.: Discriminant Analysis, 9th edn. Sage Publications Inc., Beverly Hills (1988)
20. Pennington, J., Socher, R., Manning, C.: GloVe: Global vectors for word representation. In: Proceedings of EMNLP, Doha, Qatar, vol. 14, pp. 1532–1543 (2014)
21. Keras library. https://github.com/fchollet/keras
22. Maglio, P.P., Matlock, T., Campbell, C.S., Zhai, S., Smith, B.A.: Gaze and speech in attentive user interfaces. In: Tan, T., Shi, Y., Gao, W. (eds.) ICMI 2000. LNCS, vol. 1948, pp. 1–7. Springer, Heidelberg (2000). doi:10.1007/3-540-40063-X_1

Assessing Spoken Dialog Services from the End-User Perspective: Usability and Experience

Otilia Kocsis[1(✉)], Basilis Kladis[2], Anastasios Tsopanoglou[2], and Nikos Fakotakis[1]

[1] Department of Electrical and Computer Engineering,
University of Patras, Patras, Greece
`okocsis@bok.gr, fakotaki@upatras.gr`
[2] SingularLogic AE, Athens, Greece
`{bkladis,atsopanoglou}@singularlogic.eu`

Abstract. Assessment of usability and user experience of spoken dialog services is a rather complex task, which remains difficult to achieve with real end-users. In this work a three-fold evaluation approach is introduced, which supports reliable assessment of usability and user experience. The approach combines interaction log data based assessment (at dialog, task and node level) with an optimized questionnaire-based end-users evaluation and a controlled stress test performed by an IVR system. The 3-fold evaluation approach was used for the assessment of usability and user experience of the pilot deployment of a voice banking systems. The proposed assessment approach provides sufficient evidence for the business informed decision-making with respect to perceived user quality of the interaction and offered services and allows for investigation of potential improvement areas.

Keywords: Spoken dialog service · System usability · User experience · Perceived interaction quality

1 Introduction

The economic constraints of the last decade resulted in a large-scale adoption of Interactive Voice Response (IVR) systems as cost-efficient replacements of call-centres and support services. In many cases, the replacement is only partial, providing automated service for certain business cases which can be easier served by machines, or only for certain tasks to shorten the time a human operator needs to handle a call. From the interaction point of view, the traditional IVR systems used to employ voice output (pre-recorded messages) and Dual-Tone Multi-Frequency Signalling (DTMF) tones input via the phone keypad. Such IVRs are considered a cheap automation option, as the technology is currently a built-in feature of most telephony switches [1]. While easy to configure and cheap, these IVRs are offering very limited capabilities when compared to increasingly sophisticated speech and language processing features of emerging IVRs, implementing Spoken Dialog Services (SDSs). SDSs are currently used in many domains, including timetable information services (e.g. train, ferry,

© Springer International Publishing AG 2017
A. Karpov et al. (Eds.): SPECOM 2017, LNAI 10458, pp. 162–170, 2017.
DOI: 10.1007/978-3-319-66429-3_15

cinema), order management for personal use (e.g. food) or business-to-business services (e.g. wholesale orders), tourist services (e.g. car rental, hotel booking), smart interactive environments (e.g. in-car, smart house command and control, serious games), and other customer support services (e.g. banking) [2–4]. The interactive functionality supported by such systems is highly variable, depending on the complexity of business scenarios implemented and on the selected dialog management strategy [5, 6]. Furthermore, the end-user perceived quality of the delivered services is highly affected by many other factors, such as: (i) technical specifications of the speech recognition and understanding engine; (ii) technology used for system messages generation; (iii) quality of back-end support services (e.g. database server response); (iv) error handling and recovery strategies implemented. As such, the assessment of usability of and user experience with SDSs remains a complex task, making it difficult to decide which system is best even when pilot implementations are based on the same business scenarios and are using the same dialog management strategy.

Interaction parameters, established at dialogue and task level, are usually automatically collected by SDSs in order to provide performance insights of the individual modules and of the system as a whole [7]. However, such parameters alone do not quantify the interaction quality from the user's point of view and existing frameworks for interactive system usability assessment [8] are usually too generic, thus must be adapted to the specific system evaluation task. The SUXES evaluation procedure suggests differentiating between user expectations, experience and opinion when evaluating user interaction experience with speech-based and multimodal interaction systems [9], but does not accounts contextual usability factors encountered in real-life usage of SDSs (e.g. environmental noise). While real-life usage of dialog systems can reach thousands of calls per day, the questionnaire-based evaluation techniques are usually limited to only a small sample of users, which are not always statistically representative for the actual user population. Crowdsourcing technology has been used to recruit large groups of test users, but it remains biased, as one user usually makes many calls and it is not clear to what degree the test users represent the actual user population [10]. While questionnaire-based evaluation is important in establishing interaction quality from user's point of view, user sample and test scenarios selection must be optimized to best represent actual user population and usage scenarios.

In this work we introduce a 3-fold evaluation approach which supports reliable assessment of usability and user experience, for informed business decision-making in SDSs selection, especially when implementation technical details are unknown. In a first step, interaction log data (automatically collected interaction parameters and user speech records) are annotated and processed to establish key performance parameters (KPIs) at dialog, task and node level. The results of the first step are used to guide an optimized questionnaire-based end-users evaluation along with a controlled stress test performed by an IVR system. The 3-fold evaluation approach was used for the assessment of usability and user experience of the pilot deployment of a voice banking systems.

2 Methods

In this section the details of the 3-fold evaluation approach are presented. In Sect. 2.1 the KPIs established at dialog, task and node level, along with the annotation procedure of the interaction logs from real end-users is presented. Section 2.2 provides details on the procedure followed to implement the questionnaire-based assessment of end-user experience. In Sect. 2.3 the implementation details of the IVR application used to perform the controlled stress test of the voice banking system are presented.

2.1 Interaction Logs Based Assessment

The interaction logs from real end-users (bank clients) were recorded during an usual working day, in a pilot running in parallel with the bank's call centre system, by randomly routing ~10% of the calls to the SDS. A total of 1024 calls were recorded and annotated, from which 159 calls were removed due to extremely high noise conditions, extremely low voice intensity levels or user's hang-up for reasons unrelated to the performance of the system (e.g. answering another phone call, speaking to another person, etc.). For the audio transcription and semantic annotation a dedicated software was used (a screenshot of the interface is shown in Fig. 1). The remaining 865 calls were used for further analysis to establish task and node frequencies, and a set of KPIs defined as follows.

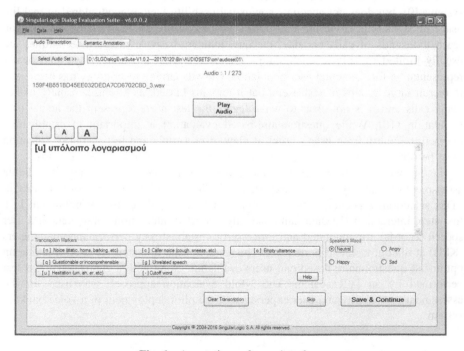

Fig. 1. Annotation software interface

Node Recognition Confidence (NRC), with a range between 0 and 100, was automatically recorded by the voice banking system.

Node Recognition Rate (NRR), with a range between 0 and 5 for node recognition, was estimated by the annotators by comparing the word-level recognition (automatically recorded) with the actual user speech.

Node Understanding Rate (NUR), with discrete values 0 or 1 for node understanding, was estimated by the annotators comparing the interpretation results (filled slots) to the actual user speech.

Node Iteration Rate (NIR), recorded automatically by the system as the total iterations needed to fill the slots of a node.

Node Speaker Mood (NSM), estimated by the annotator as Neutral, Angry, Happy, Sad.

Task Understanding Rate (TUR), with discrete values 0 or 1 for task understanding, established by the annotators, based on the correct understanding of user intention by filling all necessary slots.

Task Completion Rate (TCR), with discrete values 0 or 1 for task completion, established by the annotators, based on the successful completion of a task.

Dialog Completion Rate (DCR), with discrete values 0 or 1 dialog completion, established by the annotators, by assessing either the user received the correct service before ending the call or being routed to human operator. In the latter case, either it was routed to the correct operator was assessed.

Dialog Mean Duration (DMD), was automatically calculated from the start and end timestamps of the interaction log.

2.2   Questionnaire-Based User Experience

The questionnaire developed for system usability assessment for the second step of the evaluation, included:

(1) One section dedicated to gather demographic user data: gender, age group, education level, employment information, overall technology usage level, and previous experience with IVRs. A total of 32 users were recruited for the questionnaire-based assessment, of which 60% were male and 40% were female. The age distribution covered all age groups and all education levels, with sample distribution being guided by the corresponding distributions of actual end-users (derived from the interaction logs analysis).

(2) A second section dedicated to guide the user through the test process, including the selected scenarios to be test, the target they should try to achieve for each scenario, but avoiding to indicate specific wording usage or step-by-step indications. Each user was handled 3 scenarios, which were selected according to the task frequency established by the analysis of real users annotated interaction logs.

(3) The third section was dedicated to collect the feedback from the user after the completion of all 3 scenarios. In a first subsection, the usability of the voice banking system was assessed with a 5-level Likert scale (5 points – excellent, 4 points – good, 3 points – acceptable, 2 points – poor, 1 point – very poor) with respect to: system understanding capability, system guidance appropriateness,

system response to requests, provided information quality, speed, perceived efficiency, and perceived quality of system speaker. In a second subsection, the opinion of the users was further explored through multiple-answer questions or agree-disagree statements, with respect to various facets of the SDS assessed, including their intention and preference to use the system in the future. In the last section, the users provided an overall mark for the system, between 0 and 10, along with their freely-expressed positive and negative comments.

2.3 Controlled Stress Test

The third step of the overall assessment was dedicated to test the system for a series of important scenarios (ranked by usage frequency and business-driven) for various controlled environmental conditions. A dedicated application was implemented to place outgoing calls using another IVR, and provide timed answers to the tested pilot voice banking system. Each call was testing a different scenario or other context condition (e.g. level of noise, type of noise), including:

- credit card number recognition: 10 visa and 10 MasterCard numbers were considered, as these are the most frequent card types emitted by the specific bank;
- 6 different wordings (the most frequently encountered in the annotation of real-users interactions) for the same task was tested for 15 tasks;
- 5 tasks were tested in varying noise conditions, by adding 5 different noises (road, metro, in-car engine noise, dogs, and music) with 3 levels.

3 Results

The voice banking system tested in this work, was based on an architecture implementing 18 banking business scenarios (e.g. account balance, change card pin, activate POS, etc.) through 33 user-initiated or system-initiated tasks. In the annotated interaction log files, a total of 165 different nodes were encountered, including clarification or confirmation nodes.

3.1 Interaction Logs Based Assessment Results

At dialog level, the system achieved a DCR of 97% and a DMD of 61.36 s, for the 865 calls considered for the analysis.

At task level, the average TUR achieved was 92% for the total of 1288 tasks encountered in the valid calls. The variability between tasks was high, ranging from as low as 42% and as high as 100%, demonstrating that insufficient attention was given during implementation to certain business scenarios. Although the overall task understanding is high, the achieved TCR is 87%, with a range between 39% and 100%.

At node level, it is observed that although the number of implemented nodes is rather large, their frequency is largely unbalanced. As expected, the node corresponding to the first question of the system has the highest frequency (26%), followed by a frequency of 2 to 4% of ~15 nodes related to card and bank account tasks, while the vast majority of the nodes had very small frequencies. With respect to NRC, the overall distribution of all nodes recognition per confidence intervals is presented in Fig. 2.

When assessing the NRC for specific nodes, the distribution changes, such as in the case of the nodes corresponding to the first question of the system (see Fig. 3) where the percentage of low NRC is much higher, while in the case of the node corresponding to the card expiration date the frequency of nodes with high NRC is much increased (see Fig. 4).

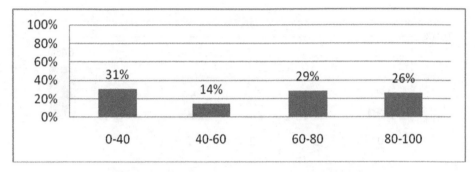

Fig. 2. Distribution of all nodes per NRC achieved

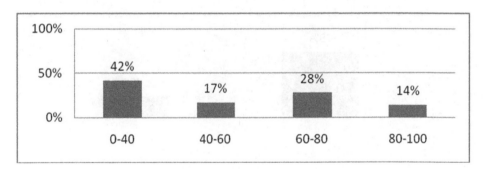

Fig. 3. Distribution of nodes per NRC intervals achieved

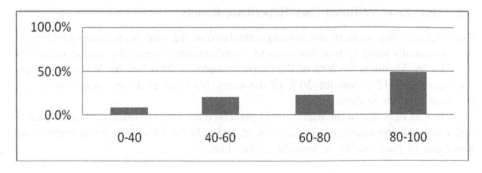

Fig. 4. Distribution of nodes per NRC intervals achieved

The achieved NRR for all nodes are presented in Fig. 5 and show a good word-level recognition capability of the system, as the user input was very well recognized in 64% of the cases. Furthermore, the input of the user was correctly interpreted, even when not very well recognized, as the NUR reaches an average of 75% for all nodes (see Fig. 6) excluding confirmations ones (YES/NO questions).

With respect to NIR, a total of 86% of the nodes was passed with one iteration, ~8% of the nodes requested an additional repeat, and 6% were repeated 3 and 4 times for the dialogue to move on.

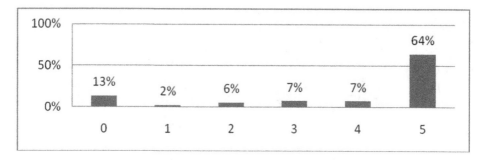

Fig. 5. NRR distribution

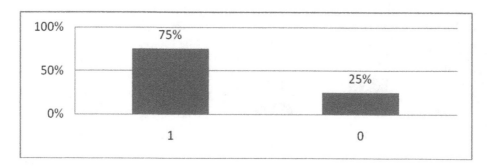

Fig. 6. NUR distribution

3.2 Questionnaire-Based User Experience Results

The total usability score of the system, calculated as the total points corresponding to the individually rated system functions (e.g. understanding capability, speed, etc.), was between 26–35 points for 20% of the users, between 16–25 points for 50% of the users and between 5–15 points for 30% of the users. No users evaluated with less than 5 points in total the system.

The vast majority of the users (96%) perceived the voice banking system's speaker and voice as being appropriate and pleasant, and only 4% found it as being unpleasant, annoying, of poor quality or sounding robot-like.

A larger percentage of users (57%) indicated their positive intention in future use of the system compared to those who opted for not or rather not using in the future the system.

With respect to the user perceived overall performance of the system, $\sim 44\%$ considered they system is of average quality, marking it with the grade of 6 or 7, 30% considered the system provided poor quality services (marks < 5), and only 26% perceived the offered services as of good-excellent quality (see Fig. 7).

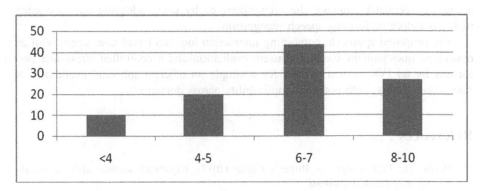

Fig. 7. Distribution of overall user perceived quality of services

3.3 Controlled Stress Test Results

The average NRC of the system for the credit card number recognition node was high, with over 75% of the cases achieving recognition confidence between 80 and 100%, and the remaining 25% of the cases achieving recognition confidence between 60 and 80%. As a result, the NUR for the credit card number recognition node was very high, with only 1 wrong understanding for the 20 tested numbers.

With respect to the NRR, 55% of the 90 phrase variations were recognized with very good accuracy, while the NUR reached 76% of nodes with correct understanding.

The varying nose tests indicated that at L1, although the NRR was decreased, the NUR remained similar to that of no noise conditions. L2 and L3 of noise resulted in a higher decrease of the NRR, which was also visible in the NUR results.

4   Discussion and Conclusion

The 3-fold assessment approach for the usability of the voice banking system provided sufficient evidence for the business informed decision-making with respect to perceived user quality of the interaction and offered services, and at the same time allowed for investigation of potential improvement areas. Enhancement of SDSs with real-time user modelling and adaptation components has the potential to increase perceived user quality, even in the case that very simple user models are considered, based on characteristics such as age group, gender and emotional speech [11]. One of the missing features noticed by annotators were the navigation commands, such as providing help to the user in cases of specific expected input, allowing him to go back, allowing to listen again to certain question/information or to go directly to human operator when unsatisfied with the quality of the service.

The controlled stress test results indicate that the tested voice banking system could benefit of a denoising pre-processing step, which although has reached very good results with noise-adapted schemes [2], it is not currently adopted at large by commercial system developers. As shown in Sect. 3.3, noise variance can result in extremely poor performance of systems, thus it should be considered by IVR implementers either by adequately training the recognizers or by using adequate pre-processing methods before performing speech recognition.

The proposed approach, combining interaction log data based assessment with an optimized questionnaire-based end-users evaluation and a controlled stress test performed by an IVR system, allows for a simple an efficient spherical evaluation of interaction quality, with potential applicability across domains.

References

1. Harris, D.: IVR Systems – Buyer's Guide (2017). http://www.softwareadvice.com/call-center/ivr-system-comparison/
2. Mporas, I., Kocsis, O., Ganchev, T., Fakotakis, N.: Robust speech interaction in motorcycle environment. Expert Syst. Appl. **37**(3), 1827–1835 (2010)
3. Diewald, S., Moller, A., Roalter, L., Kranz, M.: Mobile device integration and interaction in the automotive domain. In: Proceedings of AutomotiveUI 2011 (2012)
4. Strauss, P.M., Minker, W.: Proactive Spoken Dialogue Interaction in Multi-Party Environments. Springer Science + Business Media, New York (2010)
5. Kocsis, O., Kladis, B.: Entrance manager application: alternative ways for event handling at the front door of a smart house. In: Janse, M.D. (ed.) Amigo Project Workshop Proceedings, pp. 47–48 (2008)
6. Almeida, N., Silva, S., Teixeira, A.: Design and development of speech interaction: a methodology. In: Kurosu, M. (ed.) HCI 2014. LNCS, vol. 8511, pp. 370–381. Springer, Cham (2014). doi:10.1007/978-3-319-07230-2_36
7. Moller, S.: Evaluating interaction with spoken dialogue telephone services. Chapter in Recent Trends in Discourse and Dialogue **39**, 69–100 (2008)
8. Bangor, A., Kortum, P.T., Miller, J.T.: An empirical evaluation of system usability scale. Int. J. Human-Comput. Inter. **24**(6), 574–594 (2008) doi:10.1080/10447310802205776
9. Turunen, M., Hakulinen, J., Melto, A., Heimonen, T., Laivo, T., Hella, J.: SUXES – User experience evaluation method for spoken and multimodal interaction. In: Proceedings of INTERSPEECH 2009, pp. 2567–2570 (2009)
10. Jurcicek, F., Keizer, S., Gasic, M., Mairesse, F., Thomson, B., Yu, K., Young, S.: Real user evaluation of spoken dialogue systems using Amazon Mechanic Turk. In: Proceedings of INTERSPEECH 2011 (2011)
11. Metze, F., Englert, R., Bub, U., Burkhardt, F., Stegmann, J.: Getting closer: tailored human-computer speech dialog. Univ. Access Inf. Soc. **8**, 97–108 (2009), doi:10.1007/s10209-008-0133-0

Audio-Replay Attack Detection Countermeasures

Galina Lavrentyeva[1](✉), Sergey Novoselov[1,2], Egor Malykh[1],
Alexander Kozlov[2], Oleg Kudashev[1,2], and Vadim Shchemelinin[1]

[1] ITMO University, St. Petersburg, Russia
{lavrentyeva,novoselov,malykh,kudashev,shchemelinin}@speechpro.com
[2] STC-innovations Ltd., St. Petersburg, Russia
kozlov-a@speechpro.com

Abstract. This paper presents the Speech Technology Center (STC) replay attack detection systems proposed for Automatic Speaker Verification Spoofing and Countermeasures Challenge 2017. In this study we focused on comparison of different spoofing detection approaches. These were GMM based methods, high level features extraction with simple classifier and deep learning frameworks. Experiments performed on the development and evaluation parts of the challenge dataset demonstrated stable efficiency of deep learning approaches in case of changing acoustic conditions. At the same time SVM classifier with high level features provided a substantial input in the efficiency of the resulting STC systems according to the fusion systems results.

Keywords: Spoofing · Anti-spoofing · Speaker recognition · Replay attack detection · ASVspoof

1 Introduction

In recent years, due to increasing security concerns in all aspects of our daily lives, the need for convenient and non-intrusive authentication methods has grown. Automatic speaker verification (ASV) offers a low-cost and reliable solution for identification problem when voice services are provided. It is already used in social security entitlement, immigration control and election management. Speaker recognition systems are widely used in customer identification during call to a call center, Internet-banking systems and other fields of e-commerce. However, despite the fact that it has reached the point of mass market adoption this technology is acknowledged to be vulnerable to spoofing attacks [1,2].

According to the [3] ASV spoofing are classified into direct and indirect attacks according to the stage they are applied to. Indirect ones attack inner modules (feature extraction module, voice models, classification results). In opposite, direct attacks use the recording stage or transmission level and is focused on the substitution of the input data. Since speaker verification is mostly used in automatic systems without face-to-face contact, direct attacks are more

© Springer International Publishing AG 2017
A. Karpov et al. (Eds.): SPECOM 2017, LNAI 10458, pp. 171–181, 2017.
DOI: 10.1007/978-3-319-66429-3_16

likely to be used by criminals due to implementation simplicity. The most well-known spoofing attacks are impersonation, replay attack (RA), voice conversion (VC) attack and text-to-speech (TTS) attack [4,5].

Unlike other spoofing types, impersonation does not leave any traces of the recording, playback devices or signal processing, as it is genuine speech. It can be detected by reliable speaker verification system [5]. TTS and VC detection methods were the topic of Automatic Speaker Verification Spoofing (ASVspoof) 2015 Challenge [6]. Results of ASVspoof 2015 confirmed the great potential in detection of VC and TTS. Compared to these spoofing types RA is much more simpler as it does not require specific audio signal processing knowledges. In RA fraudster uses pre-recorded speech samples of the target speaker that can be easily prepared via low-cost recording devices or smartphones. Due to this RA is the most available and therefore critical spoofing technique.

For today there is a small number of studies addressed to the RA detection. The most part of solutions presented for text-dependent ASV are based on the comparison of the test utterance with the stored utterance recorded during the registration. Vulnerability of text-independent ASV to RA was considered in [4,7]. These papers show the serious increase in false acceptance rate of ASV system in case of RA presence. RA detection methods for text-independent case are mostly based on additional noise detection, specific for acoustic conditions.

The ASVspoof Challenge conducted in 2017 was aimed to promote the development of RA countermeasures reliable to both known and unknown conditions [8] which can vary greatly. ASVspoof 2017 was focused on a standalone RA detection task for text-dependent case considered without ASV system and any pre-recorded enroll data.

In this paper we described Speech Technology Center (STC) RA detection systems proposed for ASVspoof 2017. Here we investigated and compared different approaches for spoofing detection. These were Gaussian Mixture Model (GMM) based systems, systems based on high level features with simple classifier and deep learning approaches.

2   Automatic Speaker Verification Spoofing Detection Challenge 2017

ASVspoof Challenge was organized in order to assess the potential to detect RA "in the wild", specifically in varying acoustic conditions. For this purpose the spoofing database was collected using text-dependent RedDots data [9]. RedDots corpus was replayed and recaptured in heterogeneous acoustic environment (open lab space, balcony, etc.). For spoofing trials 15 different playback and 16 recording devices were used, including smartphones and high-quality speakers. The original RedDots records were used as genuine speech trials. This dataset was divided into training, development and evaluation parts. The evaluation part contained no information about spoofing trials, devices and recording conditions. Spoofing trials from evaluation part were prepared with the use of devices that were not used in the recording process of the training or development data. In this way they presented previously unforeseen spoofing attacks.

3   GMM Approach

Authors of [10] insist that spoofing detection methods should be more focused on the feature engineering rather than on models complication. They proposed the system based on constant Q transform cepstral coefficients (CQCC) and simple GMM. This approach showed impressive results on the ASVspoof 2015 dataset and achieved the 72% improvement over the best system participated in the challenge. That is why the reference implementation of this system was provided as a Baseline system by organisers of ASVspoof 2017.

3.1   Baseline

Constant Q transform (CQT) is widely used in music signal processing. By using geometrically spaced frequency bins it overcomes the lack of frequency resolution at lower frequencies and time resolution at higher frequencies that can be produced by Fourier transform with regular space frequency bins. Figure 1 demonstrates the example of CQT spectrum. CQCC estimated according to the scheme in Fig. 2 were used as input features in the Baseline system.

In the Back-End the Baseline system used standard 2-class GMM classifier. 512-component models were trained with an expectation-maximisation (EM) algorithm with random initialisation for genuine and spoofed speech, respectively. For each utterance the log-likelihood score was obtained from GMM models and the final score was computed as the log-likelihood ratio: $\Lambda(X) = \log L(X|\theta_g) - \log L(X|\theta_s)$, where X is a sequence of test utterance feature vectors, L denotes the likelihood function, and θ_g and θ_s represent the GMM for genuine and spoofed speech.

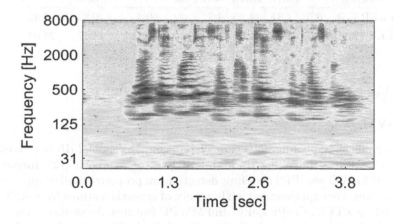

Fig. 1. Log power magnitude CQT spectrum

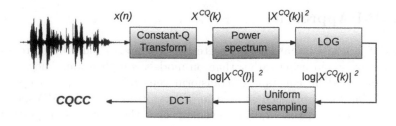

Fig. 2. CQCC features extraction

3.2 Baseline Modifications

The first modifications we tried were normalization techniques for acoustic features. We considered mean and variance normalization on the log power spectrum (mvn) and cepstral coefficients (cmvn) in different combinations. We have also tried acoustic features that were effective for VC and TTS detection. These were Mel Wavelet Packet Coefficients (MWPC), based on applying the multiresolution wavelet transform and phase-based features CosPhasePC [11].

Experiments results obtained on the development part (Table 1) confirm the efficiency of normalization for CQCC based systems. Systems with other Front-End features did not outperform these results.

Table 1. Experimental results for GMM-based systems obtained on the train and development parts of ASVspoof 2017 database (EER %)

Features	CQCC				MWPC	MWPC	CosPhasePC
Normalization	-	mvn	cmvn	mvn+cmvn	-	cmvn	-
train EER (%)	0.03	1.81	1.25	1.1	0.4	0.23	0.43
dev EER (%)	10.35	8.74	11.86	9.85	8.81	19.17	24.64

4 I-Vector Based System

4.1 $SVM_{i\text{-}vector}$

The most efficient spoofing detection systems on ASVspoof 2015 were based on high level features modelling by standard i-vector approach [12]. Inspired by its success for VC ans TTS spoofing detection we proposed similar approach for RA detection. We experimented with variety of acoustic features from ASVspoof 2015, such as MFCC, CosPhasePC and MWPC features. According to our observations the best system was the system based on the Linear Prediction Cepstral Coefficients (LPCC).

78 LPCC coefficients were obtained using the Hanning window function with a 0.128 s window size and a 0.016 s step for FFT power spectrum estimation [13]. I-vectors of the Total Variability space were extracted from the

whole speaker utterances. Here we used the 128-component Gaussian mixture model of the described features for diagonal covariance UBM (Universal Background Model), and the dimension of the T-matrix was 200. After centering and length-normalization i-vectors were used as an input for a linear kernel SVM classifier. For SVM training the efficient LIBLINEAR [14] library was used.

4.2 Phrase-Dependent System

During our investigations we suggested that phrase-dependent system can perform a higher accuracy than text-independent system. We compared i-vector based system with the similar systems trained for several different phrases independently. Our experiments presented in Table 2 showed reduction in spoofing detection in comparison with the common systems trained on the whole training dataset. This effect can be explained by the insufficient size of the training data in a phrase-dependent case which leads to fast overfitting.

Table 2. Experimental results for the i-vector based system obtained on the train and development parts of ASVspoof 2017 database (EER %)

UBM	Phrase-dependent	Common	Common	Common
T-matrix	Phrase-dependent	Phrase-dependent	Common	Common
SVM	Phrase-dependent	Phrase-dependent	Phrase-dependent	Common
train EER (%)	0.398	0.133	0.401	1.459
dev EER (%)	11.702	12.368	11.447	9.95

5 Deep Learning Approaches

Deep learning approaches have already achieved remarkable performance in many classification and recognition tasks. The success of CNN in video classification [15], image classification [16,17], face recognition [18] prompts to apply such approaches for ASV anti-spoofing tasks. The idea of employing CNN for spoofing detection is not new and was used in face spoofing detection [19,20].

Several experimental results confirm the efficiency of CNN based approaches for synthetic speech detection. For example in [21] authors demonstrated high efficiency of deep neural network (DNN), CNN and recurrent neural network (RNN) architectures for VC and TTS spoofing detection on the base of ASVspoof 2015 dataset. They also proposed a stacked CNN+RNN architecture and demonstrated its state-of-the-art performance. It is particularly important to note that CNN architecture showed similar to CNN+RNN results and their fusion outperformed the best individual system twice in terms of detection quality.

In [22] temporal CNN architectures were proposed for VC and TTS detection. This approach also achieved notable results on the ASVspoof 2015 corpora.

In this section we describe several systems based on CNN frameworks for RA spoofing detection. Such problem can be reduced to the detection of local spectral artifacts presented in the reproduced replay attack that distinguish it from the genuine speech. For this purpose the CNN was used as a robust feature extractor from the input signal representation in a time-frequency domain.

5.1 Unified Shape Time-Frequency Features

In our research we chose 2 types of features based on spectrum estimation of the utterance. To prepare CNN input acoustic features we used the normalized log power magnitude spectrum obtained via:

- constant Q transform (CQT) [10]
- Fast Fourier Transform (FFT)
- Discrete wavelet Transform (DWT), obtained by Daubechies wavelets db4

Special attention should be paid here to the fact that CNN input data should have a unified form. We considered two techniques for obtaining a unified time-frequency (T-F) shape of features. First one truncates the spectrum along the time axis with a fixed size. During this procedure short files are extended by repeating their contents if necessary to match the required length. The other technique uses a sliding window approach with a fixed window size.

5.2 Deep Learning Architectures

It is known from image processing that the choice of convolutional neural network architecture is a critical task and greatly affects learning result. In this research we investigated several deep neural network architectures, demonstrated the best results in RA detection.

Inception CNN Based System $ICNN_{CQT}^{SW}$: The first proposed neural network architecture was CNN with inception modules (ICNN) ([23]). The proposed architecture was the reduced version of GoogLeNet and contained 3 inception modules. Inception module acts as multiple convolution filter inputs, that are processed on the same input in parallel. It also does pooling at the same time. All resulting feature maps are then concatenated before going to the next layer. This allows the model to pick the best convolutions and take advantages of multi-level feature extraction by recovering both local feature via smaller convolutions and high abstracted features with larger convolutions.

The ICNN was applied for high level feature extraction from the log power magnitude CQT spectrum. The last fully-connected (FC) layer with softmax activation function was used to discriminate between genuine and spoofing classes during the training process. And a low-dimensional high-level audio representation was extracted from the penultimate FC layer.

To obtain unified time-frequency representation of the audio-signal we used sliding window technique with $864 \times 200 \times 1$ window size and 90% overlapping. For ICNN input we applied mean variance normalization.

Since in this space of high level features genuine and replay spoofing classes are well separated, it was enough to use the simplest one-component models for each class distribution modelling. We used the standard 2-class GMM classifier (1 GMM for genuine speech and 1 for spoofed speech) trained on the training part of the ASVspoof 2017 database with EM algorithm. The score for an input signal was computed as the loglikelihood ratio. In this scenario we extracted high-level features independently for each sliding window and all high-level features corresponding to one utterance were used to estimate GMM likelihood. However, it should be mentioned that such deep neural approach can be used for End-To-End solution without additional classifier.

Light CNN. The second CNN we explored was the reduced version of the LCNN proposed in [24] with a smaller number of filters in each layer. LCNN consisted of 5 convolution layers, 4 Network in Network (NIN) layers [25], 10 Max-Feature-Map layers, 4 max-pooling layers and 2 fully connected layers [26]. The proposed LCNN used Max-Feature-Map activation function that allows to reduce CNN architecture. In contrast to commonly used Rectified Linear Unit function that suppresses a neuron by a threshold (or bias), MFM suppresses a neuron by a competitive relationship. In this way being applied in particular MFM selects more informative features. Each convolution layer was a combination of two independent convolutional parts calculated for layer's input. MFM activation function was used then to calculate element-wise maximum of these parts. Max-Pooling layers with kernel of size 2×2 and stride of size 2×2 were used for time and frequency dimensions reduction. Described CNN was used to obtain high-level audio features similar to the ICNN based system and simple GMM classifier was used at the evaluation stage.

We proposed a number of systems based on LCNN high-level features extractor with different acoustic features. $LCNN_{CQT}$ used truncated features obtained from the normalized CQT spectrograms with $864 \times 400 \times 1$ size. Additionally we explored FFT based features instead of CQT: $LCNN_{FFT}$ system used truncated features of size $864 \times 400 \times 1$ and $LCNN_{FFT}^{SW}$ was based on the sliding window features extraction with $864 \times 200 \times 1$ window and 90% overlapping along time axis. Alternative system $LCNN_{DWT}^{SW}$ was based on DWT implementation with sliding window of $256 \times 200 \times 1$ size and 83.4% overlapping.

Stacking CNN and RNN. We also probed the combined CNN+RNN architecture from [21] for RA spoofing detection. In this stacked architecture CNN was used as a feature extractor and RNN modeled the long-term dependencies of a speech sequence. Both CNN and RNN were optimized jointly through the back-propagation algorithm. In this implementation CNN+RNN was used as End-to-End solution.

CNN was a reduced version of LCNN, but unlike the previous systems max-pooling was applied with the stride 2 along the frequency axis to compress frequency information and stride 1 along the time axis to save time dimensionality.

The RNN part consists of two gated recurrent units [27] forming the bidirectional gated recurrent unit (BGRU). The first GRU was responsible for the forward pass, while the second GRU performed the backward pass. The last output vectors of both forward and backward passes were taken further to obtain two 16-dimensional vectors. Such BGRU unit was applied to each channel of CNN's output resulting in $16 \times 2 \times 8$ tensor. Weights were shared between each channel's unit to prevent overfitting. The flattened output of RNN was used as an input to the fully-connected layers with MFM activations resulting in probability of the utterance being spoofed.

System based on this architecture, $CNN_{FFT}+RNN$, used truncated features extracted from log magnitude power FFT spectrum. But due to the limited computational resources we reduced the input data dimension to $256 \times 400 \times 1$.

Alternatively we used CNN+RNN architecture for $CNN_{\Delta EEMD}+RNN$ system based on the ensemble empirical mode decomposition (EEMD) features. These features were obtained with the use of libEEMD library [28] as follows:

1. Let S_o be the FFT spectrogram of the original signal $x(t)$
2. Get the first empirical mode $c_1(t)$ of the signal $x(t)$ using the EEMD with ensemble size of 50 and noise strength equals to $0.1\sqrt{\mathrm{Var}(x(t))}$
3. Compute S_r as the FFT spectrogram of the signal $c_1(t)$
4. $S_\Delta = |S_o - S_r|$

6   Evaluation Results and Discussion

The experimental results of all described individual systems on development and evaluation parts of ASVspoof 2017 corpus are presented in Table 3.

The best result for development and evaluation sets was demonstrated by LCNN system with FFT truncated features. Similar system with CQT features showed poor stability on the evaluation set. This is explained by the poor robustness of CQT features, which is also approved by results of the baseline system.

The sliding window technique demonstrated worse results compared to the truncated approach on the evaluation set. A possible reason for this is that using spectrograms of the whole utterances (in most cases) as CNN input leads to more accurate text-dependent deep model.

Our CNN+RNN combination also performed worse RA detection quality than single LCNN. We explain performance degradation by the reduced frequency resolution in the spectrum estimation.

Summarizing all results of our individual systems we prepared two solutions that use fusion of individual systems on the score level with Bosaris toolkit [29]. Our primary system used fusion of $LCNN_{FFT}$, SVM_{i-vect} and $CNN_{FFT}+RNN$ systems scores. And our contrastive system combined SVM_{i-vec}, $ICNN_{CQT}^{SW}$, $LCNN_{FFT}$, $LCNN_{FFT}^{SW}$, $LCNN_{DWT}^{SW}$, $CNN_{FFT}+RNN$ and $CNN_{\Delta EEMD}+RNN$ systems.

Table 3. Evaluation results

Individual system	EER (%)	
	Dev set	Eval set
Baseline	10.35	30.6
Baseline$_{MVN+CMVN}$	9.85	17.31
SVM$_{i-vec}$	9.80	12.54
ICNN$_{CQT}^{SW}$	10.74	15.11
LCNN$_{FFT}$	**4.53**	**7.37**
LCNN$_{FFT}^{SW}$	5.25	11.81
LCNN$_{CQT}$	4.80	16.54
LCNN$_{DWT}$	8.71	16.08
CNN$_{FFT}$ + RNN	7.51	10.69
CNN$_{\Delta EEMD}$ + RNN	9.94	18.90
Fusion system		
Primary: LCNN$_{FFT}$, SVM$_{i-vec}$, CNN$_{FFT}$+RNN	**3.95**	**6.73**
Contrastive: SVM$_{i-vec}$, ICNN$_{CQT}^{SW}$, LCNN$_{FFT}$, LCNN$_{FFT}^{SW}$, LCNN$_{DWT}^{SW}$, CNN$_{FFT}$+RNN, CNN$_{\Delta EEMD}$+RNN	2.77	7.56

Comparing two fusion systems on the development and evaluation parts we can see that complicated fusion of 7 systems have less performance than simpler fusion of three systems which are completely different in architectures, features and presumably detect different artifacts. Despite the noticeable quality reduction for some individual systems on the eval part, the difference in 1% of EER for fusion systems is explained by the impressive result of LCNN$_{FFT}$. According to Bosaris fusion model, this system has the biggest weight in both fusion solutions. However, we suppose that complex system will better detect RA spoofing with more various conditions.

7   Conlusions

In this paper we explored the applicability of several different approaches for replay attack spoofing detection. We investigated state-of-the-art methods from VC and TTS spoofing detection and deep learning approaches. Our experiments conducted on the ASVspoof 2017 dataset confirmed high efficiency of deep learning frameworks for spoofing detection "in the wild". EER of the best individual CNN system was 7.34%. At the same time SVM classifier with high level features provides a substantial input into the efficiency of the resulting STC systems according to the fusion systems results. Our primary system based on systems score fusion provided 6.73% EER on the evaluation set.

Acknowledgements. This work was financially supported by the Ministry of Education and Science of the Russian Federation, Contract 14.578.21.0126 (ID RFMEFI57815X0126).

References

1. Marcel, S., Nixon, M.S., Li, S.Z. (eds.): Handbook of Biometric Anti-Spoofing. ACVPR. Springer, London (2014)
2. Shchemelinin, V., Simonchik, K.: Study of voice verification system tolerance to spoofing attacks using a text-to-speech system. Instrum. Eng. **57**(2), 84–88 (2014). in Russian
3. Faundez-Zanuy, M., Hagmller, M., Kubin, G.: Speaker verification security improvement by means of speech watermarking. Speech Commun. **48**(12), 1608–1619 (2006)
4. Villalba, J., Lleida, E.: Speaker verification performance degradation against spoofing and tampering attacks. In: FALA 2010, pp. 131–134 (2010)
5. Wu, Z., Evans, N., Kinnunen, T., Yamagishi, J., Alegre, F., Li, H.: Spoofing and countermeasures for speaker verification: a survey. Speech Commun. **66**, 130–153 (2015)
6. Wu, Z., Kinnunen, T., Evans, N., Yamagishi, J., Hanilçi, C., Sahidullah, M., Sizov, A.: ASVspoof 2015: the first automatic speaker verification spoofing and countermeasures challenge. Training **10**(15), 3750 (2015)
7. Villalba, J., Lleida, E.: Preventing replay attacks on speaker verification systems. In: IEEE International Carnahan Conference on Security Technology, ICCST 2011, pp. 284–291. IEEE (2011)
8. Kinnunen, T., Sahidullah, M., Delgado, H., Todisco, M., Evans, N., Yamagishi, J., Lee, K.A.: The ASVspoof 2017 challenge: assessing the limits of replay spoofing attack detection. In: Interspeech 2017 (2017, submitted)
9. Lee, K.A., Larcher, A., Wang, G., Kenny, P., Brmmer, N., van Leeuwen, D.A., Aronowitz, H., Kockmann, M., Vaquero, C., Ma, B., Li, H., Stafylakis, T., Alam, M.J., Swart, A., Perez, J.: The reddots data collection for speaker recognition. In: INTERSPEECH, ISCA, pp. 2996–3000 (2015)
10. Todisco, M., Delgado, H., Evans, N.: A new feature for automatic speaker verification antispoofing: constant Q cepstral coefficients. In: Processings of Odyssey (2016)
11. Novoselov, S., Kozlov, A., Lavrentyeva, G., Simonchik, K., Shchemelinin, V.: STC anti-spoofing systems for the ASVspoof 2015 challenge. In: 2016 IEEE International Conference on Acoustics, Speech and Signal Processing (ICASSP) (2016)
12. Li, M., Zhang, X., Yan, Y., Narayanan, S.: Speaker verification using sparse representations on total variability i-vectors. In: Processings of INTERSPEECH (2011)
13. P., D., Ellis, W.: PLP and RASTA (and MFCC, and inversion) in Matlab (2005)
14. Wu, T., Wang, C.C., Yu, H.F.: Liblinear library. http://www.csie.ntu.edu.tw/cjlin/liblinear
15. Karpathy, A., Toderici, G., Shetty, S., Leung, T., Sukthankar, R., Fei-Fei, L.: Largescale video classification with convolutional neural networks. In: Proceedings of the IEEE Conference on CVPR 2014, pp. 1725–1732 (2014)
16. Bengio, Y., Courville, A., Vincent, P.: Representation learning: a review and new perspectives. IEEE Trans. Pattern Anal. Mach. Intell. **35**(8), 1798–1828 (2013)

17. Krizhevsky, A., Sutskever, I., Hinton, G.E.: ImageNet classification with deep convolutional neural networks. In: Advances in Neural Information Processing Systems, pp. 1097–1105 (2012)
18. Taigman, Y., Yang, M., Ranzato, M., Wolf, L.: Deepface: closing the gap to human level performance in face verification. In: Proceedings of the IEEE Conference on Computer Vision and Pattern Recognition, pp. 1701–1708 (2014)
19. Galbally, J., Marcel, S., Fierrez, J.: Biometric antispoofing methods: a survey in face recognition. IEEE Access **2**, 1530–1552 (2014)
20. Yang, J., Lei, Z., Li, S.Z.: Learn convolutional neural network for face anti-spoofing. arXiv preprint arXiv:1408.5601 (2014)
21. Zhang, C., Yu, C., Hansen, J.H.L.: An investigation of deep learning frameworks for speaker verification anti-spoofing. IEEE J. Sel. Top. Sign. Process. **4**(99), 684–694 (2011)
22. Tian, X., Xiao, X., Siong, C.E., Li, H.: Spoofing speech detection using temporal convolutional neural network. In: 2016 Asia-Pacific Signal and Information Processing Association Annual Summit and Conference (APSIPA) (2016)
23. Szegedy, C., Liu, W., Jia, Y., Sermanet, P., Reed, S., Anguelov, D., Erhan, D., Vanhoucke, V., Rabinovich, A.: Going deeper with convolutions. In: Computer Vision and Pattern Recognition (2015)
24. X., X.W., He, R., Sun, Z., Tan, T.: A light CNN for deep face representation with noisy labels. IEE J. Sel. Top. Sign. Process. (2015)
25. Lin, M., Chen, Q., Yan, S.: Network in network. CoRR abs/1312.4400 (2013)
26. Lavrentyeva, G., Novoselov, S., Malykh, E., Kozlov, A., Kudashev, O., Shchemelinin, V.: Audio replay attack detection with deep learning frameworks. In: Interspeech-2017 (2017, submitted)
27. Chung, J., Gülçehre, Ç., Cho, K., Bengio, Y.: Empirical evaluation of gated recurrent neural networks on sequence modeling. CoRR abs/1412.3555 (2014)
28. Luukko, P., Helske, J., Rsnen, E.: libeemd library. https://bitbucket.org/luukko/libeemd
29. Brmmer, N., de Villiers, E.: Bosaris toolkit. https://sites.google.com/site/bosaristoolkit

Automatic Estimation of Presentation Skills Using Speech, Slides and Gestures

Abualsoud Hanani$^{(\boxtimes)}$, Mohammad Al-Amleh, Waseem Bazbus,
and Saleem Salameh

Birzeit University, Birzeit, Palestine
ahanani@birzeit.edu

Abstract. This paper proposes an automatic system which uses multimodal techniques for automatically estimating oral presentation skills. It is based on a set of features from three sources; audio, gesture and power-point slides. Machine learning techniques are used to classify each presentation into two classes (high vs. low) and into three classes; low, average, and high-quality presentation. Around 448 Multimodal recordings of the MLA'14 dataset were used for training and evaluating three different 2-class and 3-class classifiers. Classifiers were evaluated for each feature type independently and for all features combined together. The best accuracy of the 2-class systems is 90.1% achieved by SVM trained on audio features and 75% for 3-class systems achieved by random forest trained on slides features. Combining three feature types into one vector improves all systems accuracy by around 5%.

Keywords: Presentation skills · Audio features · Gesture · Slides features · Multi-Modality

1 Introduction

Performing a good presentation in front of a crowd is an essential skill that every successful and professional person should master. This is one of the student outcomes most undergraduate programs aim to develop in their study journey and after that in their work life. Throughout courses, people obtain such skill and nourish it. But what remains an issue is judging how well a person is performing or how better he/she has become since last time. Watching presentations is both time consuming and harder than it seems for evaluators to judge and provide feedback. Without feedback none can get better. In most cases, presenters do not receive objective feedback after their presentations since this requires tremendous amount of effort and time from the evaluators. Usually, presentation performance assessment is done by focusing on multi-modality, speech cues, gesture and slides. Speech cues include way of speaking, volume, intonation, speaking rate, etc. whereas, gesture cues include facial expressions, eye contact, head poses, hand gesture and body posture.

Most of the current rubrics for presentation performance assessment rely on both verbal and non-verbal aspects, and it is mainly done by humans. Doing this process automatically and providing instants feedback is highly desirable.

© Springer International Publishing AG 2017
A. Karpov et al. (Eds.): SPECOM 2017, LNAI 10458, pp. 182–191, 2017.
DOI: 10.1007/978-3-319-66429-3_17

In this work, we are proposing an automatic system which uses multi-modality, namely speech, gesture and slides content and formatting, for presentation performance assessment. Most of the previous studies in this field used one or two modalities, and to our knowledge, this is the first work which combines cues from three modalities for assessing presentation performance.

2 Previous Work

In [1] prosodic audio features and personality assessment provided by humans were used (each alone and combined) to classify speakers as professional and non-professional (2-classes). The audio features they used are: pitch, energy, first and second formants, length of voiced and unvoiced segments and their respective statistics (minimum, maximum, mean and entropy of feature variation). In personality assessment by humans, the score for each audio clip is the average of 10 judges' assessment (the BFI-10 questionnaire). They obtained an accuracy of 87.2%, 75.5% and 90.0% when they used prosodic features, personality assessments and when prosodic features and personality assessments were combined together, respectively.

The liveliness of a voice is defined as the degree to which a voice varies in intonation, rhythm and loudness [2]. In [2], the Pitch Dynamism Quotient (PDQ) was used to analyze the liveliness of speech and it was hypothesized that monotonous speech has PDQ values around 0.10 and lively speech has PDQ values around 0.25. In [3], "high-dimensional acoustic feature extractions" approach was employed to develop a system to assess the oral presentations skills of pre-service principals. Their approach incorporates multimodal behavioral data (audio and video) to classify pre-service principal's presentations into low and high presentations.

In [4], The level of the cognitive load that a person is experiencing was classified to low, moderate and high cognitive load based on some speech features, namely, articulation rate, pause rate and pause duration.

In [5], features extracted form audio and slides were used to classify students' performance in presentations into two classes, high and low. From audio, they used some prosodic features namely, Minimum Pitch value (MINP), Maximum pitch value (MAXP), Average Pitch value (AVGP) and Pitch Standard Deviation value (STDP). They used also the speech rate, articulation rate and The Average Syllable duration. For slides, they used the total number of images, minimum and maximum font size, maximum number of different font sizes per slide, total number of words, total number of chart and total number of tables. Also, they processed each slide as a gray JPGE image to calculate its entropy and they computed the following features: maximum entropy value, minimum entropy value, average of entropy values and standard deviation of entropy values. It is worth mentioning that we will use the dataset that they used in their work and to build on what they have done.

Many researchers tried to automate the way in which presentation slides are assessed. They have chosen numbers as their reference starting with simple count of images or tables inside a presentation slide and ending with whether a footer exists at the bottom of the slide or not. According to Seongchan Kim et al. in [6], with the huge increase in PowerPoint slides count and their hosting sites, an efficient way to estimate the quality of slides without any human intervention is required [6]. They extracted a set of useful features from slides.

Gestures and body movements can alter how people conceptualize abstract concepts [7] and even their sense of their own dominance [8]. Despite the fact that gestures are a substantial aspect in a presentation, studies do not seem to give it much attention. However, there is some research done that uses gestures to predict the emotions of the speakers. This is helpful for our work in terms of how to capture and use gestures information for presentation assessment.

Burgoon et al. [9] proposed an approach for analyzing cues from multiple body regions for the automated identification of emotions displayed in videos, focusing on hands and arms movement, facial pleasantness and head movement. This work does not have clear results. All what they conclude is that "this research has already shown great promise and is setting the stage for real-world relevance". In addition, S. Kopf et al. in [10] developed a software tool using Microsoft's Kinect and captured gestures, eye-contact, movement, speech, and the speed of slide changes to provide real time feedback for presentation skills. Speaker movement and body gestures were detected well while not all spoken words and slide changes could be recognized.

3 Dataset

3.1 MLA'14 Data Set

In all of reported experiments in this paper, we have used a dataset that was collected by international Multimodal Learning Analytics workshop and challenges (MLA 2014) which seeks to answer questions like how multimodal techniques can help the assessment of presentation skills? And how to integrate between individual performance (audio, video and posture) and the quality of the slides used, in determining how good a presentation is.

This dataset is composed of 448 multimodal recordings on 86 oral presentations of undergraduate students' groups. Each group consists of a varied number of students (1–6). It is important to note that each PowerPoint file is shared for each students' group, where, audio and gestures are recorded for each student individually.

Human coded information about the quality of the presentation was included, six aspects was taken into consideration in determining the quality of presentation. The coding process was done by four individuals, taking the average as the final rate for each criteria. The human coding was recorded with a rubric that measured: speech organization, volume and voice quality, use of language, slides presentation quality, body language and level of confidence during the presentation. Table 1 shows all evaluation criteria used to assess the quality of the presentation. The score goes from 1 (low) to 4 (high). The students of each group were evaluated individually using these metrics. The evaluation of the metrics related to the slides was the same for all group members.

Table 1. Evaluation criteria used for scoring the student oral presentations

Metric	Description
Speech organization	Structure and connection of ideas
Volume/voice	Presents relevant information with good pronunciation
	Maintains an adequate voice volume for the audience
Language	Language used in presentation according to audience
Slides presentation	Grammar
	Readability
	Impact of the visual design of the presentation
Body language	Posture and Body language
	Eye contact
Confidence during the presentation	Self-confidence and enthusiasm

As shown in Table 1, there are three classification aspects human experts used in the presentations evaluation; one is related to the voice of the presenter, one is related to the slides of the presentation and one is related to the gestures and body language of the presenter. In order to build an automatic system for presentation evaluation, this system should consider features extracted from these three aspects; voice, slides and gestures. To do so, we built three sub-systems, each uses one of these features, i.e. one system uses features extracted from voice, one uses features extracted from slides and one uses features extracted from gestures.

3.2 Two-Class Labeling

For building voice based system, the dataset was divided into two classes; high performance (average voice-related scores > 2.5) and low performance (average voice-related scores $\leq$ 2.5). By applying this criteria, 331 audio files were labeled as high performance and 117 were labeled as low performance. Similarly, the dataset was re-divided into two classes (High and Low), but this time, according to the average rate of the slides-related evaluation criteria, and one time according to the gestures based scores for the gesture based system. By Appling this criteria, 45 PowerPoint files were labeled as class 'High' and 41 files as class 'Low'. Similarly, 231 Kinect csv files were labeled as class 'High' and 217 as class 'Low'.

3.3 Three-Class Labeling

To have more details of the presentation quality, all students in the dataset were re-divided into three classes; High (rating range 1–2), Average (rating range 2–3) and Low (rating greater than 3) for our three sub-systems. Table 2 shows the number of data files of each class after applying the above criteria, for each sub-system.

Table 2. Three-class data division

Model	Class	No. of instances
Audio	High	195
	Average	191
	Low	62
Slides	High	32
	Average	26
	Low	28
Gesture	High	102
	Average	246
	Low	100

4 Feature Extraction

4.1 Audio Features

To build an automatic assessment system based on voice, audio recordings were used to extract representative features from speech signal. The following subsections describe the audio features used in our experiments.

- *Short frame energy:* Speech signal is divided into 50% overlapped 20 ms frames. Each frame is multiplied by Hamming window and then the energy, in decibel, is calculated for each frame and used as an audio feature for our system.
- *Short frame Zero-Crossing Rate (ZCR):* After subtracting average (dc) of speech signal from each sample, the number of zero-axis crossings is calculated for each short frame. These counts are then divided by the total number of zero-crossings of the whole utterance.
- *Mel Frequency Cepstral Coefficients (MFCCs):* MFCC features are the most commonly used in the speech processing applications. They represent the general shape of power spectrum for each frame with low dimensional feature vectors (typically 12). More details about MFCC technique can be found in [11]. The first 12 MFCCs of each frame are appended to the audio feature vectors of our audio-based system.
- *Short frame pitch:* Pitch refers to the fundamental frequency of the voiced speech. Pitch is an important feature that contains speaker-specific information. It is a property of vocal folds in the larynx and is independent of vocal tract. A single pitch value is determined from every windowed frame of speech. There is a number of algorithms for estimating pitch form speech signal. Among these, one of the most popular algorithms is the Robust Algorithm for Pitch Tracking (RAPT) proposed by Talkin [12]. This algorithm was used to extract pitch for use in all experiments reported in this paper.
- *Formant Frequencies:* The general shape of the vocal tract is characterized by the first few formant frequencies. *Praat* toolkit [13] was used to estimate the first three formants and their gains and appended to the acoustic feature vectors.

- *Speaking rate:* Speaking rate has been used as a feature in numerous speech processing applications. In this work, speaking rate was estimated from the number of syllables divided by the total duration in seconds of each participant presentation.
- *Articulation Rate:* The number of syllables divided by the speaking time.
- *The Average Syllable duration:* The ratio of the speaking time over the number of syllables. The number of syllables in each audio recording is found by counting the detected syllables nuclei using Praat script by Nivja de Jong [14].
- *Pauses:* There are two types of pauses; presence of silent intervals (empty pauses) and vocalizations (filled pauses) which do not have a lexical meaning. Usually, non-confident presenters need time for selecting proper words and making meaningful sentences while speaking. These times are longer than the natural pauses confident presenters usually make while they are speaking. Therefore, the length and number of occurrences of pauses may carry a useful information about the presenter skills. A simple algorithm based on the short frame energy and zero-crossing rates has been developed for estimating length and number of occurrences of pauses in each utterance. Frames with low energy and high zero-crossing are usually resemble pauses, whereas, frames with high energy and relatively low zero crossings resemble speech frames. If a number of successive pause frames exceeds a practically specified threshold, they are considered as a pause. So, if it exceeds certain duration time or if it is repeated many times while talking, this may indicate that the presenter has a low presentation skills.
- *Rhythm Patterns (RP), Statistical Spectrum Descriptor (SSD) and Rhythm Histogram (RH):* Rhythm Patterns are features sets derived from content-based analysis of audio, particularly music, and reflect the rhythmical structure in the audio recording. According to the occurrence of beats or other rhythmic variation of energy on a specific critical band, statistical measures (e.g. mean, median, variance, skewness, kurtosis, min- and max-value) are able to describe the audio content. The Rhythm Histogram features are a descriptor for general Rhythmic in an audio segment. Contrary to the RP and SSD, information is not stored per critical band. Rather, the magnitudes of each modulation frequency bin of all critical bands are summed up, to form a histogram of "rhythmic energy" per modulation frequency. 1440 RP features, 1500 RH and 168 SSD are computed using open-source Musical Information Retrieval toolkit[1].

4.2 Slides Features

Each students group has one PowerPoint presentation file. Therefore, unlike audio and gesture features, features extracted from slides are the same for each group member.

A macro was created to automatically compute a set of features from each slide of the presentation files to be used for presentation assessment, as shown in Table 3.

---

[1] http://www.ifs.tuwien.ac.at/mir/downloads.html.

Table 3. Set of features extracted from slides

Slide features	
Words count per slide	Unique font mean per slide
Total number of images per slide	Entropy of a slide
Font sizes per slide	Delta Entropy of two consecutive slides
Unique font sizes per slide	Word to image ratio per slide
Minimum font size per slide	Mean font per slide
Maximum font size per slide	Font difference per slide

4.3 Gesture Features

In the dataset, each student has a Kinect recording (csv format) which includes XYZ coordinates of 20 joint body positions in a rate of 120 frames per second. We extracted a set of features from Kinect motion traces for each presenter, as shown in Table 4 below.

Table 4. Gesture features extracted from Kinect csv files

Gesture feature	
Position of the 20 points of the skeleton	Contraction index
Position of the 7 points related to the head, shoulders and arms	Energy and power
Speed of movement	Overall activity
Acceleration of the movement	Shape of movement
Fluency and smoothness	

5 Experiments and Results

5.1 Experiments Setup

In all reported experiments in this paper, 10-fold cross validation technique was used for training and validation of each system. In order to investigate the usefulness of each feature type (audio, slides and gesture) for estimating presentation skills, we conducted one experiment for each feature type alone and then combined all together. As mentioned earlier, presentation skill of each participant in the dataset was classified into two classes (high vs. low), one time, and into three classes (high, average and low) another time. This classification was done based on the human ratings. Therefore, for each feature type, there are two classification experiments, one with two classes and one with three classes. In all experiments, three different classifiers implemented in Weka toolkit were used, namely, Support Vector Machines (SVM), Simple Logistic (SL) and Random Forest (RF).

The above mentioned audio features are computed for each audio file and concatenated together to form feature vectors of a dimension 3140 (energy, ZCR, 12 MFCCs, pitch, 6 formant frequencies with their gains, speaking rate, articulation rate, average Syllable duration, average pauses length, number of pauses, 1440 Rhythm Patterns, 168 Statistical Spectrum Descriptor and 1500 Rhythm Histogram features).

5.2 Results

For each experiment, accuracy, precision, recall, F-measure and ROC area were used as evaluation measures. The results of the three classifiers when trained and tested on audio features, slides features and gesture features are presented in Table 5 (two-class) and Table 6 (three-class).

Table 5. Two-class (high vs low) experiments results of the three systems

System	Classifier	Accuracy	Precision	Recall	F-Measure	ROC Area
Audio	SVM	**0.901**	**0.901**	**0.901**	**0.903**	**0.909**
	Simple logistic	0.869	0.872	0.869	0.87	0.907
	Random forest	0.809	0.804	0.809	0.802	0.894
Slides	SVM	0.701	0.69	0.701	0.69	0.646
	Simple logistic	0.694	0.68	0.694	0.677	0.739
	Random forest	**0.83**	**0.829**	**0.83**	**0.829**	**0.908**
Gesture	SVM	0.635	**0.694**	0.305	0.421	0.602
	Simple logistic	**0.714**	0.689	**0.632**	**0.618**	**0.704**
	Random forest	0.668	0.612	0.598	0.586	0.653
Combined	SVM	**0.953**	**0.952**	**0.951**	**0.952**	**0.919**
	Simple logistic	0.912	0.906	0.911	0.911	0.914
	Random forest	0.871	0.864	0.866	0.861	0.903

Table 6. Three-class (high, average, low) experiments results of the three systems

System	Classifier	Accuracy	Precision	Recall	F-Measure	ROC Area
Audio	SVM	**0.675**	**0.667**	**0.675**	**0.67**	**0.784**
	Simple logistic	0.559	0.56	0.559	0.56	0.692
	Random forest	0.492	0.506	0.492	0.495	0.653
Slides	SVM	0.465	0.457	0.465	0.449	0.587
	Simple logistic	0.475	0.468	0.475	0.467	0.647
	Random forest	**0.753**	**0.752**	**0.753**	**0.752**	**0.902**
Gesture	SVM	0.383	0.352	0.346	0.343	0.497
	Simple logistic	**0.433**	**0.428**	**0.429**	**0.432**	**0.551**
	Random forest	0.381	0.371	0.368	0.364	0.489
Combined	SVM	0.722	0.714	0.721	0.693	0.825
	Simple logistic	0.653	0.635	0.646	0.623	0.782
	Random forest	**0.812**	**0.817**	**0.812**	**0.813**	**0.911**

As expected, treating presentation skills estimation as a two-class problem gives better results than a three-class problem for all systems and all classifiers. All of the systems which use audio features outperform the systems that use slides and gesture features. As shown from the results, SVM system outperforms RF and SL when using audio features with an accuracy of 90.1% and 67.5% for 2-class and 3-class experiments, respectively. Random forest worked the best for the slides features, with accuracies of 83.0% and 75.3% for 2-class and 3-class experiments, respectively. Simple logistic classifier worked the best for the body language features (gesture) with accuracies of 66.8% and 43.3% for 2-class and 3-class respectively.

Combining the three feature types into one feature vector, then train and evaluate the three classifiers on the resulting vectors, improves all systems accuracy by around 5%. Combining three systems by fusing their output scores is considered in the future work.

6 Conclusion

In this paper, we presented a comprehensive framework for automatically estimating presentation skills by extracting features from presenter voice, slides and body language. MLA'14 dataset was used for training and testing (10-fold cross validation) in all of reported experiments. Presentation skills prediction was treated as a 2-class and 3-class classification problems. In each case, three different classifiers were built on audio features, slides features and gesture features, independently. SVM worked the best for the audio features, whereas, Random forest and simple logistic worked better for the slides features and gesture features respectively.

The best accuracy of the 2-class systems is 90.1% achieved by SVM trained on audio features, and 75% for 3-class systems achieved by Random forest classifier. Combining three feature types into one vector improves all systems accuracy by around 5%.

References

1. Mohammadi, G., Vinciarelli, A.: Humans as feature extractors: combining prosody and personality perception for improved speaking style recognition. In: Proceedings of the IEEE International Conference on Systems, Man and Cybernetics, Anchorage, Alaska, USA, 9–12 October 2011, pp. 363–366 (2011)
2. Hincks, R..: Processing the prosody of oral presentations. In: InSTIL/ICALL Symposium (2004)
3. Shan-Wen, H., Sun, H.C., Hsieh, M.C., Tsai, M.H., Lin, H.C., Lee, C.C.: A multimodal approach for automatic assessment of school principals' oral presentation during pre-service training program. In: Sixteenth Annual Conference of the International Speech Communication Association (2015)
4. Gorovoy, K., Tung, J., Poupart, P.: Automatic speech feature extraction for cognitive load classification. In: Conference of the Canadian Medical and Biological Engineering Society (CMBEC) (2010)
5. Luzardo, G., Guaman B., Chiluiza, K., Castells, J., Ochoa, X.: Estimation of presentations skills based on slides and audio features. In: Proceedings of the 2014 ACM Workshop on Multimodal Learning Analytics Workshop and Grand Challenge, MLA 2014, pp. 37–44. ACM, New York (2014)
6. Kim, S., Jung, W., Han, K., Lee, J.-G., Yi, Mun Y.: Quality-based automatic classification for presentation slides. In: Rijke, M., Kenter, T., Vries, A.P., Zhai, C., Jong, F., Radinsky, K., Hofmann, K. (eds.) ECIR 2014. LNCS, vol. 8416, pp. 638–643. Springer, Cham (2014). doi:10.1007/978-3-319-06028-6_69
7. Jamalian, B., Tversky, T.: Gestures alter thinking about time. In: Proceedings of the 34th Annual Conference of the Cognitive Science Society (CogSci) (2012)

8. Carney, A.J.C., Dana, R., Yap, A.J.: Power posing: brief nonverbal displays affect neuroendocrine levels and risk tolerance. Psychol. Sci. **21**(10), 1363–1368 (2010)
9. Burgoon, J.K., Jensen, M.L., Meservy, T.O., Kruse, J., Nunamaker, J.F.: Augmenting human identification of emotional states in video. In: Intelligence Analysis Conference, McClean, VA (2005)
10. Kopf, S., Guthier, B., Rietsche, R., Effelsberg, W., Schon, D.: A real-time feedback system for presentation skills. In: MLA 2014, Mannheim, Germany, pp. 1633–1640 (2015)
11. Fang, Z., Zhang, G., Song, Z.: Comparison of different implementations of MFCC. J. Comput. Sci. Technol. **16**(6), 582–589 (2001)
12. Talkin, D.: A robust algorithm for pitch tracking (RAPT). In: Kleijn, W., Paliwal, K. (eds.) Speech Coding and Synthesis, pp. 495–518. Elsevier, New York (1995)
13. Paul, B., David, W.: PRAAT: doing phonetics by computer [Computer program]. Version 6.0.26. http://www.praat.org/. Accessed 2 Mar 2017
14. Jong, D., Nivja, H., Wempe, T.: Praat script to detect syllable nuclei and measure speech rate automatically. Behav. Res. Methods **41**(2), 385–390 (2009)

Automatic Phonetic Transcription for Russian: Speech Variability Modeling

Vera Evdokimova$^{(\boxtimes)}$, Pavel Skrelin, and Tatiana Chukaeva

Saint Petersburg State University, 7/9 Universitetskaya nab.,
St. Petersburg 199034, Russia
{postmaster,skrelin,chukaeva}@phonetics.pu.ru
http://www.phonetics.spbu.ru

Abstract. At the moment more advanced approaches to phonetic transcription are required for different speech technology tasks such as TTS or ASR. All subtle differences in phonetic characteristics of sound sequences inside the words and in the word boundaries need more accurate and variable transcription rules. Moreover, there is a need to take into account not only the normal rules of phonetic transcription. it is important to include the information about speech variability in regional and social dialects, popular speech and colloquial variants of the high frequency lexis. In this paper a reliable method for automatic phonetic transcription of Russian text is presented. The system is used for making not only an ideal transcription for the Russian text but also takes into account the complex processes of sound change and variation within the Russian standard pronunciation. Our transcribing system is reliable and could be used not only for the TTS systems but also in ASR tasks that require more flexible approach to phonetic transcription of the text.

Keywords: Automatic phonetic transcription · Russian · Phonetics · Speech processing · Speech transcription · Speech variability modeling

1   Introduction

For the last 30 years various large speech corpora have been developed through the world [1]. Well-known examples are TIMIT [2], Switchboard [3], Verbmobil [4], the Spoken Dutch Corpus [5] and the Corpus of Spontaneous Japanese [6]. At the moment a number of medium and large size Russian speech corpora are available. The largest published corpus of the Russian speech is ORD (One Day of Speech) corpus that is still under development [7]. It contains more than 1000 h of everyday speech. It has partial annotation and transcription. However, this corpus is not publicly available. The most annotated publicly available corpus nowadays is PrACS-Russ (Prosodically Annotated Corpus of Spoken Russian) that contains over 4 h of monologue speech [8]. It is available as part of Russian National Corpus [9]. The corpora containing well-annotated high-quality recordings are not publicly available. One of them is Corpus of Professionally Read Speech (CORPRES) contains over 30 h of speech recorded in a professional studio [10].

© Springer International Publishing AG 2017
A. Karpov et al. (Eds.): SPECOM 2017, LNAI 10458, pp. 192–199, 2017.
DOI: 10.1007/978-3-319-66429-3_18

The corpus of monologues RuSpeech contains about 50 h of transcribed recordings produced by 220 speakers [11]. CoRuSS (Corpus of Russian Spontaneous Speech) is designed as a publicly available resource containing high-quality recordings of spontaneous speech with detailed prosodic transcription [12]. The recordings include dialogues between native Russian speakers, with a part of it - at least 14 h of speech from 60 speakers - annotated by expert linguists at lexical and prosodic levels.

One of the main reasons that provide the usability of large speech corpora is the availability and accuracy of annotations. For example, the TIMIT corpus is very popular for the phonetic and speech technology studies because of the very accurate phonetic transcriptions. The broad phonetic transcriptions are often used and sometimes even required for different tasks such as lexical pronunciation variation modelling for automatic speech recognition, unit selection for speech synthesis [10,11,13], automatic pronunciation training and assessment in Computer Assisted Language Learning [14] and general research on pronunciation variation [15]. Contemporary speech corpora are usually provided with a broad phonetic transcription of at least part of their material. In addition, time and money permitting, contemporary speech corpora are at least partially enriched with broad phonetic transcription with the help of expert phoneticians in order to ensure a more accurate representation of the material. The employment of experts is known to be exceedingly time-consuming and expensive when they have to transcribe speech from scratch. That is why, it is common practice to provide people with an example transcription they have to verify on the basis of their own perception of the speech signal [1].

Among the numerous approaches to providing text-to-speech transcription, the simplest is to use a small set of letter-to-sound rules to guess the pronunciation of any word. Each rule specifies a phonetic correspondence of sounds and letters. In some cases the letter's context is used to determine which rule should be applied. However, any language has great variation in the pronunciation. The transcription made for the TTS systems usually have one ideal variant for the text. It could be predicted and changed according to the acoustic and phonetic quality of the sounds, speaker characteristics and so on. In the speech recognition tasks it is more important to have the correct information not only about the phonemes but also about the exact acoustic characteristics and their variation. Those characteristics that can be predicted by the context beforehand. The grapheme-to-phoneme transcriber can use a dictionary-lookup approach but it tells nothing about the sound changes between the words and phrase boundaries. Therefore the rules of transcribing should use all the knowledge about the context variations of the sounds in the standard pronunciation, the phonetic changes and their frequencies of occurency in speech.

In this paper we present a reliable method for automatic phonetic transcription of Russian text into phonetic symbols. The system was used for modelling phonetic transcription for the Speech Corpus of spontaneous speech CoRuSS for Russian Language [12].

This paper is organised as follows. In Sect. 2, we introduce the automatic transcriber design and main principles. Section 3 sketches the problems of rules extensions. Section 4 presents the inclusion of the speech variability rules. In Sect. 5 we formulate our conclusions.

2   Design of the Automatic Phonetic Transcriber

The program was developed in java jdk 1.8. Each rule specifies a phonetic correspondence of phonetic symbols to letters. The letter's context is used to determine which rule should be applied. We implemented these processes as context-dependent rule modelling both within-word and cross-word contexts in which phones could be deleted, inserted or substituted with other phones.

The set of phonological and phonetic rules that differs according to conditions has been based on the phonetic knowledge obtained in experimental study of the great amount of the Russian speech corpora since the beginning of the previous century. There are 6 vowel phonemes and 36 consonant phonemes in the Russian literary speech [16–18]. The transcriber has been developed following the principles proposed by S. Stepanova [19] and K. Shalonova [20,21]. Besides, the coarticulation and sound change processes for Russian standard language (as for any other language) constantly modify. In order to include all the variation we decided to work not with separate letter-to-phoneme assosiations but use the characteristics of sound classes and the processes of assimilation, dissimilation, insertion or deletion of sounds. It gives us opportunity to model different allophone variations that are not usually provided by other phonetic transcription systems. Besides, all the exclusion are taken into account.

For example, the Russian phoneme "č" has no voiced pair in the system. Among the allophones of "č" there are voiced and unvoiced variants. Therefore it is important for the transcriber to model correctly the exact variant which should be used in the transcription using the preceding and following letters.

The quality of the vowel phonemes in Russian varies according to the word stress, position in a phrase and the quality of the neighboring sounds consonants before and after the vowel. For the correct result the transcriber needs information about the place of the word stress. It could process the words with primary and secondary stress. The signs for these are "1" for primary word stress and "0" for secondary stress. The numbers should be put after the vowel in the orthographic text. Our transcriber does not include the automatic stress detection in the orthographic text.

There are more than 200 rules for the vowel transformations that include all this information. Also the exclusions are taken into account for vowel transformation by inserting them into the rules (Fig. 1).

The consonant variation depends upon the quality of the neighboring sounds. There are different kinds of consonant assimilation in Russian which is usually regressive one. The consonants became similar or different in the palatalization, voiced/unvoiced characteristic, place of articulation, manner of articulation. The consonant insertions and deletion processes are also taken into account.

There more than 200 rules for consonant transformation including the consonant special sequences inside words (Fig. 2).

The resulting rule set comprised phonological and phonetic rules describing progressive and regressive voice assimilation, palatalisation and more specific rules modelling pronunciation variation in high-frequency words. We tried to take into account all the possible modifications and sound change that can happen within the word and on the word borders. Besides, the transcriber processes the pause signs and modifies the resulted transcription according to the place of the pause in the text and the pause type. There are several types of pauses: the end of phrase, the inhale sign, the sudden speech hesitation etc. According to the sound type the transcriber decides if the last consonant should be voiced or unvoiced for noise consonants (Fig. 3).

The processes in the word boundaries in the connected speech and the sound transformations in the end of the phrase are also included in the program. If the processed text has the phrase boundary markers and information about the pauses, speech breaks and intakes of breath it will process them automatically and decide about the phonetic quality of the sounds in the borders according to the Russian pronunciation (Figs. 4 and 5).

```
JA_JA_6_1_2('я', "ja", Arrays.asList(
                Condition.accented,
                Condition.firstInTheWord, // 1
                Condition.group1, // 5
                Condition.lastInTheWord, // 2
                Condition.afterPause,
                Condition.beforePause
```

Fig. 1. Example of the grapheme-to phoneme rules for vowels

```
//consonant changes:
        ConsonantChanger.put("б", "b");
        ConsonantChanger.put("в", "v");
        ConsonantChanger.put("г", "g");
        ConsonantChanger.put("д", "d");
```

Fig. 2. Example of the grapheme-to phoneme rules for consonants

```
consonantTerminalChainRules.add(new
ConsonantTerminalRuleBuilder("č'", 'т', 'ч').build());
```

Fig. 3. Example of the grapheme-to phoneme rules for consonants sequencies

а [11b]я2 сего1дня / в [10]обе1д / 9 / [10]ду1маю / сх* сх* моро1женного ка1к-то не [11]хоте1лось е1сть / потому1 что2 на [+]у1лице тако1й [11]дуба1к / что2 не до2 [02]моро1женного / 9 / ду1маю пойду1 куплю1 в [11]Не1тто / себе1 э1ти [02]ола1душкино / они2 ж та1м со [11]ски1дочкой / 9 / [02]во1:т / 9 / э- / [+]дошла1 зна1чит до [11]Не1тто / а та1м тепе1рь вме1сто [11]Не1тто / [04]ди1кси

Fig. 4. Example of the Russian orthographic text for processing. '1' is put after vowels to show the primary stress, '2' is written after the vowels to show the secondary stress. The intonation markers are also included in the orthographic text. They show the intonation phrase borders and type of intonation

key: a65 value: a [11b]ja8 s'ivo0dn'i / v [10]ab'e0t / 9 / [10]du0maju / sx* sx* maro0žin:ava ka0k-ta n'i [11]xat'e0las' je0s't' / patamu0 što8 na [+]u0l'iсɨ tako0j [11]duba0k / što8 n'i do8 [02]maro0žin:ava / 9 / du0maju pajdu0 kupl'u0 v [11]n'e0t:a / s'ib'e0 e0t'i [02]ala0dušk'ina / an'i8 š ta0m sa [11]sk'i0dač'kaj / 9 / [02]vo0:t / 9 / э- / [+]dašla0 zna0č'id da [11]n'e0t:a / a ta0m t'ip'e0r' vm'e0sta [11]n'e0t:a / [04]d'i0ks'i

Fig. 5. Example of transcription. '0' is put after vowels to show the primary stress, '8' is written after the vowels to show the secondary stress

3 Rules Extensions and Refinements

At first we aimed at approximating transcription that were made with a limited rules and symbol set. Then we included the rules for pronunciation exclusions from the dictionary. The transcriber was developed to make transcriptions for the corpus *CoRuSS* [12] containing 30 h of high quality recorded spontaneous Russian speech. The recordings consist of dialogues between two speakers, monologues (speakers self-presentations) and reading of a short phonetically balanced text. Since the corpus is labeled for a wide range of linguistic-phonetic and prosodic information, it provides basis for empirical studies of various spontaneous speech phenomena. Besides, it allows comparing those phenomena with the ones we observe in prepared read speech. The corpus has orthographic and prosodic annotation for the part of the material. The orthographic decoding of the recording was made using no capital letters or punctuation marks; the only exception was a question mark to denote question phrases. Each word was written using standard spelling no matter whether it was pronounced in a proper way, mispronounced, or produced in a contracted form. Orthographic annotation also contained information about lexical stress: strong (primary) stress was marked with 1 after the vowel. Symbol 2 was used for vowels carrying secondary or weak stress, for vowels /o/, /e/ with no qualitative reduction. The Russian grapheme 'ё' in this corpus was never replaced by 'e'.

The transcriber was properly tested manually. At first different texts from the CoRuSS corpus [12] were processed and checked by expert phoneticians. The manually verified phonetic transcriptions were required to tune the transcription procedures and to evaluate their performance. We took into account very special cases of Russian pronunciation that occur in the connected speech and cannot be known from the orthographic dictionary containing only word transcriptions.

In order to ensure the applicability of the transcription procedures in contexts we optimised our procedures with limited resources and minimal human effort using the statistics of the sound change in standard pronunciation from the real speech corpus CORPRES. Further additions and refinements to the rules could reduce the error rate still further.

4 Modeling Speech Variation

The resulting transcription were updated using the results of the manual real speech segmentation and labelling that was made by expert phoneticians for the CORPRES speech corpus [10]. The material contains two types of transcription: manual phonetic transcription (the sounds actually pronounced by the speakers) and the level of rule-based phonetic transcription (automatically generated by another text transcriber for TTS and partially corrected by the experts). The ideal transcription in the CORPRES corpus did not contain phonetic variants within pronunciation standard.

We counted the occurrence rate of different phonetic sequences in the same contexts for ideal transcriptions in CORPRES corpus and improved the rules using several variants of transcription or the most frequent one.

For example in Russian the word /pagul'a0j/ has different variants of phonetic transcriptions that could be met in standard pronunciation (Fig. 6):

[pəgul'a0i] - that variant was met 0 times in corpus (the dictionary standard).
[pogul'ai] - that variant was met 3 times in corpus.
[pugul'ai] - that variant was met 5 times in corpus.

v naš [11]v'e0k / 9 / dva0c:at' [10]p'e0rvɨj / e0ta [10]vazmo0žna / to0 jis't' 9 a0= [10]pr'idu0mal / n'e0skal'ka [11]**var'ia0ntaf (vɨr'ia0ntaf (8), ver'ea0ntaf (3))** / ad'i0n ɨs [11]**var'ia0ntaf (vɨr'ia0ntaf (8), ver'ea0ntaf (3))** / e0ta apt'a0g'ivat' 9 ɘ- šɨn* / [+]nu0 / abr'e0zak ɘ- šɨ0nɨ aftamab'i0l'naj vakru0k [11]stvala0 /

Fig. 6. Example of transcription including the results of speech variability from the CORPRES. '0' is put after vowels to show the primary stress, '8' is written after the vowels to show the secondary stress

The example shows the variants of standard pronunciation and their frequency of occurrence in the phonetic transcription.

5   Conclusions

The results have shown that our transcriber is reliable and it could be used for the speech technology tasks that require the phonetic transcriptions of the text for speech segmentation, text-to-speech systems, and automatic speech recognition systems.

The transcriber could be adapted to the speaker as long as we know his/her speech peculiarities.

The automatic transcription can serve as an example for the human transcribers.

The ASR system and speech alignment system can be provided by a precise phonetic transcription if it has the text that has to be recognised.

Acknowledgments. The authors would like to thank the Saint Petersburg State University. This work has been carried out in the framework of SPbSU project n. 31.37.353.2015.

References

1. Van Bael, Ch., Boves, L., van den Heuvel, H., Strik, H.: Automatic transcription of large corpora. Comput. Speech Lang. **21**, 652–668 (2007)
2. TIMIT, Acoustic-Phonetic Continuous Speech Corpus. National Institute of Standards and Technology Speech Disc 1-1.1, NTIS Order No. PB91-505065 (1990)
3. Godfrey, J., Holliman, E., McDaniel, J.: SWITCHBOARD: telephone speech corpus for research and development. In: Proceedings of the IEEE International Conference on Acoustics, Speech and Signal Processing (ICASSP), San Francisco, USA, pp. 737–740 (1992)
4. Hess, W., Kohler, K.J., Tillman, H.-G.: The Phondat-Verbmobil speech corpus. In: Proceedings of Eurospeech, Madrid, Spain, pp. 863–866 (1995)
5. Oostdijk, N.: The design of the spoken Dutch corpus. In: Peters, P., Collins, P., Smith, A. (eds.) New Frontiers of Corpus Research, pp. 105–112. Rodopi, Amsterdam (2002)
6. Maekawa, K.: Corpus of spontaneous Japanese: its design and evaluation. In: Proceedings of the ISCA/IEEE Workshop on Spontaneous Speech Processing and Recognition (SSPR), Tokyo, Japan (2003)
7. Bogdanova-Beglarian, N., Martynenko, G., Sherstinova, T.: The "One Day of Speech" corpus: phonetic and syntactic studies of everyday spoken Russian. In: Ronzhin, A., Potapova, R., Fakotakis, N. (eds.) SPECOM 2015. LNCS, vol. 9319, pp. 429–437. Springer, Cham (2015). doi:10.1007/978-3-319-23132-7_53
8. Kibrik, A., et al. (eds.): Rasskazy o snovidenijakh. Korpusnoe issledovanie ustnogo russkogo diskursa. Jazyki slavyanskoj kultury (2009)
9. Apresjan, J., Boguslavsky, I., Iomdin, B., Iomdin, L., Sannikov, A., Sizov, V.: A syntactically and semantically tagged corpus of Russian: state of the art and prospects 1. In: Proceedings of the 5th International Conference on Language Resources and Evaluation, LREC 2006, pp. 1378–1381 (2006)
10. Skrelin, P., Volskaya, N., Kocharov, D., Evgrafova, K., Glotova, O., Evdokimova, V.: CORPRES: corpus of Russian professionally read speech. In: Sojka, P., Horák, A., Kopeček, I., Pala, K. (eds.) TSD 2010. LNCS, vol. 6231, pp. 392–399. Springer, Heidelberg (2010). doi:10.1007/978-3-642-15760-8_50

11. Krivnova, O.: Russkij rechevoj korpus ruspeech. In: Proceedings of the VII International Scientific Conference Fonetika Segodnia, pp. 54–56 (2013)
12. Kachkovskaia, T., Kocharov, D., Skrelin, P., Volskaya, N.: CoRuSS a new prosodically annotated corpus of Russian spontaneous speech. In: Proceedings of the 10th International Conference on Language Resources and Evaluation (LREC 2016), Portoro, Slovenia (2016)
13. Mizutani, T., Kagoshima, T.: Concatenative speech synthesis based on the plural unit selection and fusion method. IEICE Trans. Inf. Syst. **E88–D**(11), 2565–2572 (2005)
14. Neri, A., Cucchiarini, C., Strik, H.: Selecting segmental errors in non-native Dutch for optimal pronunciation training. Int. Rev. Appl. Linguist. **44**(4), 357–404 (2006)
15. Riley, M., Byrne, W., Finke, M., Khudanpur, S., Ljolje, A., McDonough, J., Nock, H., Saraclar, M., Wooters, C., Zavaliagkos, G.: Stochastic pronunciation modelling from hand-labelled phonetic corpora. Speech Commun. **29**, 209–224 (1999)
16. Avanesov, R.: Russian Standard Pronunciation [Russkoe literaturnoe proiznoshenie]. Prosveschenije (1984)
17. Bondarko, L.V.: Phonetics of Russian modern language, SPbSU (1998). (in Russian)
18. Kodzasov, S.V., Krivnova, O.F.: General Phonetics, Moscow (2001)
19. Stepanova, S.B.: The phonetic properties of Russian speech: realisation and transcription. Ph.D. dissertation. Leningrad (1988)
20. Shalonova, K.: Flexible transcriber for Russian continuous speech. In: 2nd International Conference on Speech and Computer, SPECOM, pp. 171–175 (1997)
21. Shalonova, K.B.: Automatic modelling of regional pronunciation variation for Russian. In: Matousek, V., Mautner, P., Ocelíková, J., Sojka, P. (eds.) TSD 1999. LNCS, vol. 1692, pp. 329–332. Springer, Heidelberg (1999). doi:10.1007/3-540-48239-3_60

Automatic Smoker Detection from Telephone Speech Signals

Amir Hossein Poorjam[1(✉)], Soheila Hesaraki[2], Saeid Safavi[3],
Hugo van Hamme[4], and Mohamad Hasan Bahari[4]

[1] Audio Analysis Lab, AD:MT, Aalborg University, Aalborg, Denmark
ahp@create.aau.dk
[2] Department of Electrical Engineering, Faculty of Engineering,
Ferdowsi University of Mashhad, Mashhad, Iran
soheila.hesaraki@alumni.um.ac.ir
[3] ECE Division, Information Engineering and Processing Architectures Group,
School of Engineering and Technology, University of Hertfordshire, Hatfield, UK
s.safavi@herts.ac.uk
[4] Center for Processing Speech and Images (PSI), KU Leuven, Leuven, Belgium
hugo.vanhamme@kuleuven.be, mohamadhasan.bahari@esat.kuleuven.be

Abstract. This paper proposes an automatic smoking habit detection from spontaneous telephone speech signals. In this method, each utterance is modeled using i-vector and non-negative factor analysis (NFA) frameworks, which yield low-dimensional representation of utterances by applying factor analysis on Gaussian mixture model means and weights respectively. Each framework is evaluated using different classification algorithms to detect the smoker speakers. Finally, score-level fusion of the i-vector-based and the NFA-based recognizers is considered to improve the classification accuracy. The proposed method is evaluated on telephone speech signals of speakers whose smoking habits are known drawn from the National Institute of Standards and Technology (NIST) 2008 and 2010 Speaker Recognition Evaluation databases. Experimental results over 1194 utterances show the effectiveness of the proposed approach for the automatic smoking habit detection task.

Keywords: Smoker detection · i-Vector · Non-negative factor analysis · Score fusion · Logistic regression

1 Introduction

Speech signals carry speaker's important information such as age, gender, body size, language, accent and emotional/psychological state [1–5]. Automatic identification of speaker characteristics has a wide range of commercial, medical and forensic applications such as interactive voice response systems, service customization, natural human-machine interaction, recognizing the type of pathology of the speakers, and directing the forensic investigation process. In this research, we focus on speaker's smoking habit detection, which is an ingredient

© Springer International Publishing AG 2017
A. Karpov et al. (Eds.): SPECOM 2017, LNAI 10458, pp. 200–210, 2017.
DOI: 10.1007/978-3-319-66429-3_19

of speaker profiling systems and behavioral informatics. The effect of smoking habits also on different speech analysis systems such as speaker gender detection, age estimation, intoxication-level recognition and emotional state identification shows the importance of an automatic smoking habits detection system and motivates the analysis of the smoking habit effects of speech signals. Experimental studies show that many acoustic features of the speech signal such as fundamental frequency, jitter and shimmer are influenced by cigarette smoking [6,7]. Although experimental studies reveal the effect of smoking on different acoustic characteristics of speech, the relation of these acoustic cues with speaker smoking habits is usually complex and affected by many other factors such as speaker age, gender, emotional condition and drinking habits [3]. Furthermore, technical factors such as speech duration, recording device and channel conditions also influence the estimation accuracy and make smoking habit detection very challenging for both humans and machines.

In this paper, we propose an automatic smoker detection from the telephone speech signals. To our knowledge, this is the first work on this condition and thus the result of no baseline system is reported in this paper. However, we adopt and apply state-of-the-art techniques developed within speaker and language recognition fields.

Modeling speech recordings with Gaussian mixture model (GMM) mean supervectors is considered as an effective approach to convert variable duration signals into fixed dimensional vectors to be used as features in support vector machines (SVM) [8]. This technique has been successfully applied to different speech processing tasks such as speaker's age estimation [9]. While effective, GMM mean supervectors are of a high dimensionality resulting in high computational cost and difficulty in obtaining a robust model in the context of limited data. Consequently, dimension reduction through PCA-based methods has been found to improve performance in age estimation from GMM mean supervectors [9]. In the field of speaker and language recognition, recent advances using i-vector framework [10], which provide a compact representation of an utterance in the form of a low-dimensional feature vector, have considerably increased the classification accuracy [10,11]. I-vectors successfully replaced GMM mean supervectors in speaker age estimation too [12]. We have recently introduced a new framework for adaptation and decomposition of GMM weights based on a factor analysis similar to that of the i-vector framework [13]. In this method, namely non-negative factor analysis (NFA), the applied factor analysis is constrained such that the adapted GMM weights are non-negative and sum to unity. This method, which yields new low-dimensional utterance representation approach, was applied to speaker and language/dialect recognition successfully [13,14]. In this paper, we propose a hybrid architecture of NFA and i-vector frameworks for smoker habit detection. This architecture consists of two subsystems based on i-vectors and NFA vectors and score-level fusion of i-vector-based and NFA-based recognizers is considered to improve the classification accuracy. The performance of the proposed method is evaluated on a spontaneous telephone speech signals of National Institute of Standards and Technology (NIST) 2008 and 2010

Speaker Recognition Evaluation (SRE) databases. Experimental results confirm the effectiveness of the proposed approach.

2   System Description

2.1   Problem Formulation

In the smoking habit estimation problem, we are given a set of training data $D = \{\boldsymbol{\nu}_i, y_i\}_{i=1}^N$, where $\boldsymbol{\nu}_i \in \mathbb{R}^d$ denotes the ith utterance and y_i denotes the corresponding smoking habits. The goal is to approximate a classifier function g, such that for an utterance of an unseen speaker, $\boldsymbol{\nu}_{\text{tst}}$, the probability of the estimated output classified in the correct class get maximum. That is, the estimated label, $\hat{y} = g(\boldsymbol{\nu}_{\text{tst}})$, is as close as the true label.

2.2   Utterance Modeling

First, we convert variable-duration speech signals into fixed-dimensional vectors, which is performed by fitting a GMM to acoustic features extracted from each speech signal. The parameters of the obtained GMMs characterize the corresponding utterance. Due to lack of data, fitting a separate GMM for a short utterance can not be performed accurately, specially in the case of GMMs with a high number of Gaussians. Therefore, parametric utterance adaptation methods are usually applied to adapt a universal background model (UBM) to characteristics of utterances in training and testing databases. In this paper, i-vector framework for adapting UBM means and NFA framework for adapting UBM weights are applied.

Universal Background Model and Adaptation: Consider a UBM with the following likelihood function of data $\mathcal{X} = \{\mathbf{x}_1, \ldots, \mathbf{x}_t, \ldots, \mathbf{x}_\tau\}$.

$$p(\mathbf{x}_t | \lambda) = \sum_{c=1}^{C} b_c p(\mathbf{x}_t | \boldsymbol{\mu}_c, \boldsymbol{\Sigma}_c)$$
$$\lambda = \{b_c, \boldsymbol{\mu}_c, \boldsymbol{\Sigma}_c\}, \ c = 1, \ldots C, \tag{1}$$

where $\mathbf{x}_t$ is the acoustic vector at time t, b_c is the mixture weight for the cth mixture component, $p(\mathbf{x}_t | \boldsymbol{\mu}_c, \boldsymbol{\Sigma}_c)$ is a Gaussian probability density function with mean $\boldsymbol{\mu}_c$ and covariance matrix $\boldsymbol{\Sigma}_c$, and C is the total number of Gaussians in the mixture. The parameters of the UBM $-\lambda-$ are estimated on a large amount of training data from smoking and non-smoking speakers.

i-vector Framework: One effective method for speaker age estimation involves adapting UBM means to the speech characteristics of the utterance. Then the adapted GMM means are extracted and concatenated to form Gaussain mean supervectors. This method have been shown to provide a good level of performance [9]. Recent progress in this field, however, has found an alternate method of modeling the class dependent GMM mean supervectors that provides superior recognition performance [3]. This technique referred to as total variability modeling [10], assumes the GMM mean supervector, $\mathbf{M}$, can be decomposed as:

$$\mathbf{M} = \mathbf{u} + \mathbf{Tv}, \tag{2}$$

where $\mathbf{u}$ is the mean supervector of the UBM, $\mathbf{T}$ spans a low-dimensional subspace (400 dimensions in this work) and $\mathbf{v}$ are the factors that best describe the utterance-dependent mean offset $\mathbf{Tv}$. The vector $\mathbf{v}$ is treated as a latent variable with the standard normal prior and i-vector is its maximum-a-posteriori (MAP) point estimate. The subspace matrix $\mathbf{T}$ is estimated via maximum likelihood in a large training dataset. An efficient procedure for training $\mathbf{T}$ and for MAP adaptation of i-vectors can be found in [15]. In the total variability modeling approach, i-vectors are the low-dimensional representation of an audio recording that can be used for classification and estimation purposes.

The NFA Framework: The NFA is a new framework for adaptation and decomposition of GMM weights based on a constrained factor analysis [14]. This new low-dimensional utterance representation approach was applied to speaker and language/dialect recognition tasks successfully [13,14]. The basic assumption of this method is that for a given utterance, the adapted GMM weight supervector can be decomposed as:

$$\mathbf{w} = \mathbf{b} + \mathbf{Lr}, \tag{3}$$

where $\mathbf{b}$ is the UBM weight supervector (2048 dimensional vector in this paper). $\mathbf{L}$ is a matrix of dimension $C \times \rho$ spanning a low-dimensional subspace. $\mathbf{r}$ is a low-dimensional vector that best describes the utterance-dependent weight offset $\mathbf{Lr}$. In this framework, neither subspace matrix $\mathbf{L}$ nor subspace vector $\mathbf{r}$ are constrained to be non-negative. However, unlike the i-vector framework, the applied factor analysis for estimating the subspace matrix $\mathbf{L}$ and the subspace vector $\mathbf{r}$ is constrained such that the adapted GMM weights are non-negative and sum up to one. The procedure of calculating $\mathbf{L}$ and $\mathbf{r}$ involves a two-stage algorithm similar to EM. In the first stage, $\mathbf{L}$ is assumed to be known, and we try to update $\mathbf{r}$. Similarly in the second stage, $\mathbf{r}$ is assumed to be known and we try to update $\mathbf{L}$. The subspace matrix $\mathbf{L}$ is estimated over a large training dataset and is used to extract a subspace vector $\mathbf{r}$ for each utterance in train and test datasets. The obtained subspace vectors representing the utterances in train and test datasets are used to estimate the smoking habits of speakers in this paper.

2.3   Classifiers

Logistic Regression (LR): Logistic regression (LR) is a widely used classification method [16], which assumes that

$$y_i \sim Bernoulli(f(\boldsymbol{\theta}^\top \boldsymbol{\nu}_i + \theta_0)) \tag{4}$$

where $^\top$ represents a transpose, y_is are independent, $\boldsymbol{\theta}$ is a vector with the same dimension of $\boldsymbol{\nu}$, θ_0 is a constant and $f(\cdot)$ is a logistic function and defined as:

$$f(\cdot) = \frac{1}{1 + e^{-(\cdot)}} \tag{5}$$

The output of the logistic function, is a value between zero and one. In the problem of smoker detection, we intend to model the probability of a smoker speaker given his/her speech. That is, $P(Smoker|\boldsymbol{\nu}_i) = f(\boldsymbol{\theta}^\top \boldsymbol{\nu}_i + \theta_0)$, where $\boldsymbol{\nu}_i$ is the feature vector corresponding to the ith utterance. Vector $\boldsymbol{\theta}$ and constant θ_0 are the model parameters, which are found through the maximum likelihood estimation (MLE).

Naive Bayesian Classifier (NBC): Bayesian classifiers are probabilistic classifiers working based on Bayes' theorem and the maximum posteriori hypothesis. They predict class membership probabilities, i.e., the probability that a given test sample belongs to a particular class. The Naive Bayesian classifier (NBC) is a special case of Bayesian classifiers, which assumes class conditional independence to decrease the computational cost and training data requirement [17]. In this paper, class distributions are assumed to be Gaussian.

Gaussian Scoring (GS): This classification approach, labeled as GS in this paper, assumes that each category has a Gaussian distribution and full covariance matrix is shared across all categories [18]. In this method, GS score of the test vector $\boldsymbol{\nu}_{\text{test}}$ for the lth class is calculated as:

$$s_l = \boldsymbol{\nu}_{\text{test}}^\top \boldsymbol{\Psi}^{-1} \bar{\boldsymbol{\nu}}_l - \frac{1}{2} \bar{\boldsymbol{\nu}}_l^\top \boldsymbol{\Psi}^{-1} \bar{\boldsymbol{\nu}}_l, \tag{6}$$

where $\bar{\boldsymbol{\nu}}_l$ is the mean of the vectors for the lth class in the training dataset and $\boldsymbol{\Psi}$ is the common covariance matrix shared across all categories.

Von-Mises-Fisher Scoring (VMF): This classification approach, labeled as VMF in this paper, works based on simplified VMF distribution [19]. In this method, VMF score of the test vector $\boldsymbol{\nu}_{\text{test}}$ for the lth class is calculated as:

$$s_l = \boldsymbol{\nu}_{\text{test}}^\top \bar{\boldsymbol{\nu}}_l, \tag{7}$$

2.4   Training and Testing

The proposed smoking habit detection approach is depicted in Fig. 1. During the training phase, each utterance is mapped onto a high dimensional vector using one of the mentioned utterance modeling approaches described in Sect. 2.2. The obtained vectors of the training set are then used as features with their corresponding smoking habit labels to train a classifier. During the testing phase, the utterance modeling approaches are applied to extract high dimensional vectors from an unseen test utterance and the smoking habit is recognized using the trained classifier.

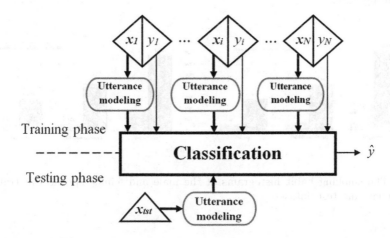

Fig. 1. Block-diagram of the proposed smoker detection approach in training and testing phases

3   Experimental Setup

3.1   Database

The National Institute for Standard and Technology (NIST) have held annual or biannual speaker recognition evaluations (SRE) for the past two decades. With each SRE, a large corpus of telephone (and more recently microphone) conversations are released along with an evaluation protocol. These conversations typically last 5 min and originate from a large number of participants for whom additional meta data is recorded including age, height, language and smoking habits. The NIST databases were chosen for this work due to the large number of speakers and because the total variability subspace requires a considerable amount of development data for training. The development data set used to train the total variability subspace and UBM includes more than 30,000 speech recordings and is sourced from the NIST 2004–2006 SRE databases, LDC releases of Switchboard 2 phase III and Switchboard Cellular (parts 1 and 2). For the purpose of smoker detection, telephone recordings from the common protocols of the recent NIST 2008 and 2010 SRE databases are used. Speakers of NIST 2008 and 2010 SRE databases are divided into three disjoint parts such that 60%, 20% and 20% of all speakers are used for training, development and testing, respectively. The smoking habits histogram of male and female utterances (there might be multiple utterances from each speaker) of training, development and testing databases are depicted in Fig. 2. As depicted in the figure, the problem is dealing with an unbalanced datasets which can make the problem of classification more difficult. The effect of unbalancing in the database can be slightly alleviated by considering the distribution of each class of the training set into consideration during the training phase.

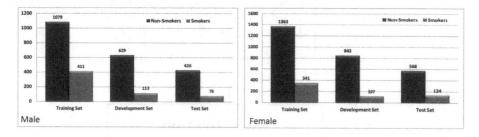

Fig. 2. The smoking habit histograms of the male and female speakers in training, development and test datasets

3.2 Performance Metric

Two performance metrics, namely minimum log-likelihood-ratio cost $C_{llr,min}$ and area under the receiver operating characteristic curve are considered. In this section, the applied performance measure methods are described briefly.

Log-Likelihood Ratio Cost: Log-Likelihood Ratio Cost ($C_{llr,min}$) is a performance measure for classifiers with soft, probabilistic decisions output in the form of log-likelihood-ratios. This performance measure is an application-independent since it is independent of the prior distribution of the classes [20]. $C_{llr,min}$ represents the minimum possible C_{llr} which can be achieved for an optimally calibrated system [20]. In this study, in order to calculate $C_{llr,min}$, the FoCal Multiclass Toolkit [21] is utilized.

Area Under the ROC Curve (AURC): Receiver operating characteristic (ROC) curve is a widely used approach to measure the efficiency of classifiers. In a ROC curve the true positive rate (sensitivity) is plotted versus the false positive rate (1-specificity) for different operating points. Each point on the ROC curve represents a sensitivity/specificity pair corresponding to a particular decision threshold. A classifier with perfect discrimination has a ROC curve that passes through the upper left corner (100% sensitivity, 100% specificity). Therefore the closer the ROC curve is to the upper left corner, the higher the overall accuracy of the test [22]. Therefore, classifiers can be evaluated by comparing their area under the ROC curves (AURCs). The AURC takes a value between 0 and 1. This value for a perfect classifier is 1, and for a useless classifier, which its posterior is equal to its prior, is 0.5.

4   Results and Discussion

This section presents the results of the proposed smoking habit detection approach. The acoustic feature consists of 20 Mel-frequency cepstrum coefficients (MFCCs) [23] including energy appended with their first and second order derivatives, forming a 60 dimensional acoustic feature vector. This type of feature is very common in state-of-the-art i-vector based speaker and language recognition systems [24]. To have more reliable features, Wiener filtering, speech activity detection [25] and feature warping [26] have been considered in front-end processing. The obtained $C_{\text{llr,min}}$ and AURC of applying different classifiers over the i-vector based and the NFA based classifiers are reported in Table 1.

Table 1. The $C_{\text{llr,min}}$ and AURC of applying different classifiers over the i-vector and NFA frameworks

Utterance modeling	$C_{\text{llr,min}}$					AURC				
	LR	VMF	GS	NN	NBC	LR	VMF	GS	NN	NBC
i-vector	0.86	0.90	0.98	0.90	0.93	0.74	0.51	0.56	0.70	0.66
NFA-vector	0.90	0.91	0.97	0.93	0.98	0.68	0.65	0.59	0.66	0.56

We can observe that LR yields more accurate results compared to other applied classifiers. Thus, this classifier is used in the rest of experiments in this paper. It is also shown that i-vector framework, which works based on Gaussian means, is more accurate than NFA framework working based on Gaussian weights. Different studies show that GMM weights, which entail a lower dimension compared to Gaussian mean supervectors, carry less, yet complimentary, information to GMM means [5, 27]. For example, Zang et al. applied GMM weight adaptation in conjunction with mean adaptation for a large vocabulary speech recognition system to improve the word error rate [27]. In [5], a feature-level fusion of i-vectors, GMM mean supervectors, and GMM weight supervectors is applied to improve the accuracy of accent recognition. To enhance the smoking habit detection accuracy we apply a score-level fusion of the i-vector and the NFA classifiers. The fusion is performed by training a logistic regression on the outputs of the classifiers using the development data. The $C_{\text{llr,min}}$ and AURC of obtained results after fusion are 0.845 and 0.754, respectively. The relative improvements of $C_{\text{llr,min}}$ obtained by the proposed fusion scheme compared to

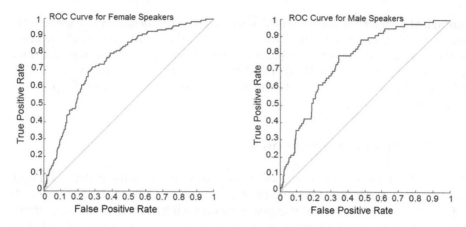

Fig. 3. The ROC curve of the proposed method for female and male speakers

the i-vector and the NFA frameworks are 1.8% and 6.5%, respectively. The relative improvements of AURC after fusion compared to the i-vector-based and the NFA-based systems are 1.9% and 11%, respectively. The ROC curves of the proposed fusion for male and female speakers are illustrated in Fig. 3.

5   Conclusions

In this paper, we proposed a new approach for automatic smoking habit detection from telephone speech signals. In this method, utterances were modeled using the i-vector and the NFA frameworks, which are based on the factor analysis on GMM means and weights, respectively. Then, several classifier were employed to discriminate smokers and non-smokers. To improve the performance, the score-level fusion of the i-vector-based and the NFA-based systems was considered. The proposed method was evaluated on telephone speech signals of NIST 2008 and 2010 SRE databases. Experimental results over 1194 utterances demonstrated the effectiveness of the proposed approach in automatic smoker detection.

References

1. Poorjam, A.H., Bahari, M.H., van Hamme, H.: A novel approach to speaker weight estimation using a fusion of the i-vector and NFA frameworks. J. Electr. Syst. Signals **3**(1), 47–55 (2017)
2. Poorjam, A.H., Bahari, M.H., van Hamme, H.: Multitask speaker profiling for estimating age, height, weight and smoking habits from spontaneous telephone speech signals. In: Proceedings of International Conference on Computer and Knowledge Engineering, pp. 7–12 (2014)
3. Bahari, M.H., van Hamme, H.: Speaker age estimation using hidden Markov model weight supervectors. In: Proceedings of 11th International Conference on Information Science, Signal Processing and their Applications (2012)

4. Poorjam, A.H., Bahari, M.H., Vasilakakis, V., van Hamme, H.: Height estimation from speech signals using i-vectors and least-squares support vector regression. In: Proceedings of International Conference on Telecommunications and Signal Processing (2015)
5. Bahari, M.H., Saeidi, R., van Hamme, H., van Leeuwen, D.: Accent recognition using i-vector, gaussian mean supervector and gaussian posterior probability supervector for spontaneous telephone speech proceedings. In: Proceedings of ICASSP, pp. 7344–7348 (2013)
6. Sorensen, D., Yoshiyuki, H.: Cigarette smoking and voice fundamental frequency. J. Commun. Disord. **15**(2), 135–44 (1982)
7. Gonzalez, J., Carpi, A.: Early effects of smoking on the voice: a multidimensional study. Med. Sci. Monit. **10**(12), 49–56 (2004)
8. Campbell, W., Sturim, D., Reynolds, D.: Support vector machines using GMM supervectors for speaker verification. IEEE Signal Process. Lett. **13**(5), 308–311 (2006)
9. Dobry, G., Hecht, R.M., Avigal, M., Zigel, Y.: Supervector dimension reduction for efficient speaker age estimation based on the acoustic speech signal. IEEE Trans. Audio Speech Lang. Process. **19**(7), 75–85 (2011)
10. Dehak, N., Kenny, P., Dehak, D., Dumouchel, P., Ouellet, P.: Front-end factor analysis for speaker verification. IEEE Trans. Audio Speech Lang. Process. **19**(4), 788–798 (2011)
11. Poorjam, A.H., Saeidi, R., Kinnunen, T., Hautamäki, V.: Incorporating uncertainty as a quality measure in i-vector based language recognition. In: Proceedings of Odyssey, pp. 74–80 (2016)
12. Bahari, M.H., McLaren, M., van Hamme, H., van Leeuwen, D.A.: Age estimation from telephone Speech using i-vectors. In: Proceedings of Interspeech (2012)
13. Bahari, M.H., Dehak, N., van Hamme, H., Burget, L., Ali, A.M., Glass, J.: Nonnegative factor analysis of Gaussian mixture model weight adaptation for language and dialect recognition. IEEE/ACM Trans. Audio Speech Lang. Process. **22**(7), 1117–1129 (2014)
14. Bahari, M.H., Dehak, N., van Hamme, H.: Gaussian mixture model weight supervector decomposition and adaptation. Technical report. Computer Science and Artificial Intelligence Laboratory (CSAIL) of MIT (2013)
15. Kenny, P., Ouellet, P., Dehak, N., Gupta, V., Dumouchel, P.: A study of interspeaker variability in speaker verification. IEEE Trans. Audio Speech Lang. Process. **16**(5), 980–88 (2008)
16. Bishop, C.M.: Pattern Recognition and Machine Learning. Springer, New York (2006)
17. Yager, R.: An extension of the naive Bayesian classifier. Inf. Sci. **176**(5), 577–588 (2006)
18. Martinez, D., Plchot, O., Burget, L., Glembek, O., Matejka, P.: Language recognition in i-vectors space. In: Proceedings of Interspeech, pp. 861–864 (2011)
19. Singer, E., Torres-Carrasquillo, P., Reynolds, D., McCree, A., Richardson, F., Dehak, N., Sturim, D.: The mitll NIST LRE 2011 language recognition system. In: Proceedings of Odyssey, pp. 209–215 (2012)
20. Brummer, N., van Leeuwen, D.A.: On calibration of language recognition scores. In: Proceedings of Odyssey (2006)
21. Brummer, N.: FoCal multi-class: toolkit for evaluation, fusion and calibration of multi-class recognition scores (2007)
22. Zweig, M., Campbell, G.: Receiver-operating characteristic (ROC) plots: a fundamental evaluation tool in clinical medicine. Clin. Chem. **39**, 561–577 (1993)

23. Deller, J.R., Hansen, J.H.L., Proakis, J.G.: Discrete-Time Processing of Speech Signals, 2nd edn. IEEE Press, New York (2000)
24. Lee, K.A., et al.: The 2015 NIST language recognition evaluation : the shared view of I2R, Fantastic4 and SingaMS. In: Proceedings of Interspeech, pp. 3211–3215 (2016)
25. McLaren, M., van Leeuwen, D.: A simple and effective speech activity detection algorithm for telephone and microphone speech. In: Proceedings of NIST SRE Workshop
26. Pelecanos, J., Sridharan, S.: Feature warping for robust speaker verification. In: Proceedings of Odyssey, pp. 213–218 (2001)
27. Zhang, X., Demuynck, K., van Hamme, H.: Rapid speaker adaptation in latent speaker space with non-negative matrix factorization. Speech Commun. **55**, 893–908 (2013)

Bimodal Anti-Spoofing System
for Mobile Security

Eugene Luckyanets[1,2], Aleksandr Melnikov[1(✉)], Oleg Kudashev[3],
Sergey Novoselov[1], and Galina Lavrentyeva[1]

[1] ITMO University, St. Petersburg, Russia
{lukyanets,melnikov-a,novoselov,lavrentyeva}@speechpro.com
[2] Speech Technology Center Ltd., St. Petersburg, Russia
[3] STC-innovations Ltd., St. Petersburg, Russia
kudashev@speechpro.com

Abstract. Multi-modal biometric verification systems are in active development and show impressive performance nowadays. However, such systems need additional protection from spoofing attacks. In our paper we present full pipeline of anti-spoofing method (based on our previous work) for bimodal audiovisual verification system. This method allows to evaluate parameters of quality for a sequence of face images during a verification process. Based on this parameters it's decided whether the data is suitable for processing by the standard method (fiducial points based audiovisual liveness detection, FALD). If the quality of data is not sufficient, then our system switches to a new algorithm (svm-based audiovisual liveness detection, SALD), which provides less protection quality, but is able to operate when FALD is unsuitable. To improve the quality of the FALD algorithm we have collected the special dataset. This dataset allows to get better reliability of the algorithm for searching of fiducial points on the user's face image. Tests show that developed system can significantly improve the quality of anti-spoofing protection versus our previous work.

Keywords: Bimodal · Liveness detection · Anti-Spoofing · Voice features · Facial features

1 Introduction

In context of increasing advance of biometric security systems the importance of their spoofing attacks reflection is very high. In this paper we are continuing the work from our previous work [1]. Here two biometric modalities are considered: face and voice. Such systems are susceptible to spoofing attacks that involve user photo or video. There are a large number of works devoted to the detection of such spoofing attacks [2]. It uses a variety of methods: frequency and texture based [3–6], variable focusing based [7,8], movement of the eyes based [9], optical flow based [10–12], blinking based [13], 3D face shape based [14,15], binary classification based [16,17], scenic clues based [18,19], lip movement based [20,21], context based [22].

© Springer International Publishing AG 2017
A. Karpov et al. (Eds.): SPECOM 2017, LNAI 10458, pp. 211–220, 2017.
DOI: 10.1007/978-3-319-66429-3_20

Development of voice verification systems vulnerability to spoofing attacks has greatly increased recently. A lot of works [23–26] examine effects of voice synthesis and voice conversion to speaker recognition performance as well as propose countermeasures to these attacks [27–29].

There are a few works devoted to the bimodal liveness detection. In paper [20] authors determine lip region and mouth fiducial points via color segmentation. MFCC features are extracted from the speech signal. The resulting audiovisual features are classified using GMM. Method requires model parameters optimization for each individual user.

Research of [30] present algorithm that finds the degree of synchronization between the audio and image recordings of a human speaker. However anti-spoofing is out of scope of this paper and authors were not provided tests of described algorithm in sense of ability to determine face spoofing attacks.

In [31] authors combine mouth fiducial points with PCA eigenlips features. Authors of [32] describe the bimodal system for user verification. The similar approach is described in [33].

Here we develop a new anti-spoofing system based on markup of voice signal and lips movements described in our previous work [1]. The main difference from previous work is that we automatically detect and handle cases when FALD algorithm can't provide good results. We create new SALD algorithm, which provides less protection quality, but is able to operate when FALD is unsuitable.

The remainder of this paper is organized as follows. Section 2 shortly describes FALD algorithm. Overall anti-spoofing system is described in Sect. 3. Finally, our results are presented in Sect. 4.

2 Audio-Visual Liveness Detection

In our previous work [1] a bimodal liveness detector based on audio-visual synchronization estimation was proposed. For this task we considered passphrases containing 5 English digits without repetition, that are generated dynamically at the time of user verification. This section provides a brief overview of proposed liveness detector algorithm as well as its main drawbacks.

2.1 Algorithm Overview

Audio-visual synchronization estimation algorithm consists of three steps:

- Audio segmentation
- Visual features extraction
- Visual features classification

A workflow of proposed algorithm is presented on Fig. 1.

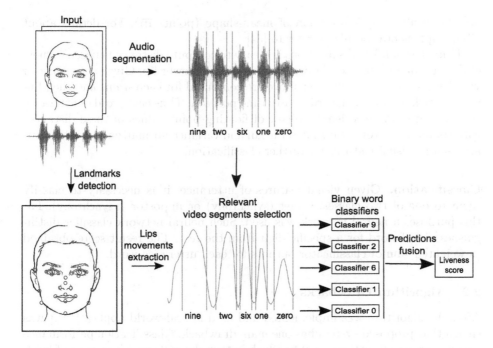

Fig. 1. Algorithm workflow

Audio Segmentation. The audio segmentation task consists of automatic determination of time position of pronounced phrase words. We used Hidden Markov Models (HMM) to solve this task. Each word of the target phrase was represented as a sequence of hidden states. Each state had 0.04 sec. average length and was defined by single diagonal Gaussian. The 12 first MFCC without energy were used for signal parametrization. Also we used two additional hidden states, "pause" and "mean speech", to represent audio segments which are not a part of the target phrase. The Viterbi algorithm was used to decode and define words hidden states time positions.

Visual Features. For visual modeling of words it is useful to parameterize the lips shape. A method based on Constrained Local Model (CLM) is used for anthropometric face points detection (landmark detection). CLM mainly consists of three components: points distribution model (PDM), Patch Experts (PE) and algorithm for PDM parameters fitting. PDM describes non-rigid shape variations and global rigid transformation. After parameters of PDM are estimated it's possible to compute location $\mathbf{x} = [x_i, y_i]$ of each facial landmark:

$$\mathbf{x} = sR(\overline{\mathbf{m}} + \Phi q) + t,$$

where s, R and t terms are rigid parameters responsible for global shape scaling, rotation and translation accordingly and a set of non-rigid parameters q which are responsible for deformation of mean-shape (points $\overline{m}$). For details about CLM implementation please refer to [34].

Using face landmarks positions it is easy to compute distance between corners of the mouth and distance between the upper and lower lip. Given a sequence of video frames, distances defined above are computed for each frame and then linear interpolated for each words states time position. Thus each word of utterance is represented by fixed-length vector of floating point values of these distances corresponding to word states. After mean and variance normalization such vector are used as visual features for further classification.

Classification. Given visual features of utterance, it is necessary to classify them to one of two classes: target (synchrony) or impostor (asynchrony). For this purposes a neural network was used. Such neural network classifier distinguishes visual word for a specific digit from the rest. The result score obtained as weighted sum of classificator outputs for each utterance word.

2.2   Algorithm Drawbacks

After the algorithm was implemented and used in real-world application it was shown that proposed system has one main drawback. Classification performance depends on visual features quality which in turn depends on correctness of landmarks detection. For most cases CLM works well, but for some persons the false reject rate (FRR) can reach 80%. This issue is caused by differences in train and real-world usage conditions. Particularly, next conditions are different:

- **Skin color.** CLM Patch Experts was trained mostly on white-skinned persons and it leads to mismatch on dark-skinned users.
- **The presence of facial hair.** Because the CLM was trained mostly on clean-shaven persons, the presence of facial hair leads to dramatical performance reduction. In this case mouth landmarks are shifted to mustache.

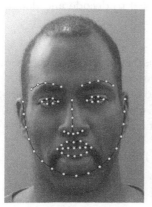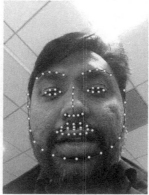

Fig. 2. CLM drawbacks examples

- **Camera distance.** In our application we used frontal camera of mobile device to record video. It leads to the effect of "fish eye" and corresponding face shape deformation.

The most illustrative cases of CLM drawbacks are presented on Fig. 2.
In these cases it is necessary to use an alternative algorithm, SALD.

3 System Description

3.1 SVM-based Visual Liveness Detection

In case when FALD can't work, it is necessary to use another method. We try to estimate lips movements by alternative algorithm when CLM fails to localize fiducial points. As can be seen from the title, SALD method is based on SVM classifier. This classifier estimates openness of the mouth. HOG descriptors (Fig. 3) are used as input features for SVM classifier.

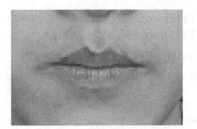
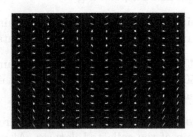

Fig. 3. HOG features for mouth image

First, it is required to estimate right position of the mouth. This step is needed because sometimes CLM strongly fails at fiducial points detection (Fig. 4).

CLM points are used as mouth initial position. Then we select the most probable position of the mouth near the initial one using Viola-Jones cascade mouth detector. This technique allows to reduce search area for cascade detector and improve detection speed.

Next step is to train SVM classifier for binary classification problem: whether the mouth closed or not. This classifier allows us to determine the degree of openness of the mouth. Then openness is passed to neural network classifiers like in FALD algorithm.

This workaround has significantly higher error rate than FALD (section 4), but it provides better result than FALD on complicated sessions like on Fig. 4.

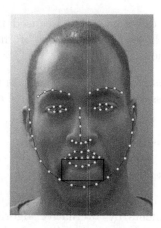

Fig. 4. Bad fiducial points localization and mouth detector result

3.2 CLM Improving

To minimize mismatch between training and real-world conditions (see Sect. 2.2) we have collected special training dataset. This dataset consists of

- 1450 facial photos from frontal camera of mobile device;
- 750 internet images which contains facial photos of dark-skined and/or bearded persons.

To adapt CLM model to the required properties we have performed manual markup of the collected dataset. Also we have prepared additional test dataset composed of 400 facial photos of dark-skined and bearded persons from frontal camera of mobile device. Previous CLM model provides gross error at mouth region on more than 30% of mentioned test dataset. New CLM trained on our dataset reduces number of such gross errors more than twice. CLM training process includes Patch Experts parameters update as well as PDM mean-shape re-estimation. Also we adapt sigmas of PDM model for better flexibility at the mouth area. These steps provides better accuracy of the facial landmarks detection on the target conditions.

3.3 Overall System Description

Complete liveness detection system consists of two parts: real-time part and post-processing part. During real-time part algorithm acquires images from camera. For each frame, several quality parameters of the face image are estimated:

- Face position (face must be in the center of image)
- Face orientation (face must have frontal pose)
- Face sharpness (image must be sharp enough)
- Landmarks likelihood in mouth area (CLM likelihoods are used to decide which algorithm should be used)

- Jerky movements (jerky face movements are not allowed)
- Grayscale density (image must be color)
- Openness of the mouth (estimated by CLM and SVM-based algorithms)

Based on these characteristics, we may reject the current session recording.

Result: Liveness score
for *images in session* **do**
    landmarks ← detect(image) ;   `/* detect landmarks */`
    quality ← estimateQuality(landmarks, image) ;   `/* quality of the`
    `face image and landmarks localization */`
    if *quality is poor* **then**
        | break, reject this session ;
    CLMopenness(i) ← get(landmarks) ;   `/* obtained by CLM */`
    SVMopenness(i) ← get(landmarks, image) ;   `/* obtained by SVM`
    `classifier */`
end
if *quality is enough for FALD algorithm* **then**
    | livenessScore ← FALD(CLMopenness) ;
else
    | livenessScore ← SALD(SVMopenness) ;
end

Algorithm 1. Overall system schema

After the whole session is processed we need to make a decision which algorithm should be used. This decision is based mainly on CLM likelihood values in mouth area. If likelihood is low, then we are likely to misjudge the position of the mouth, so SALD algorithm is used. Full system schema is shown at algorithm 1.

4   Results

In this section we present experimental results produced for GRID corpus dataset [35]. This dataset consists of 34 speakers, 1000 sessions for each. However, one speaker has no video sessions, so we did not use them. Digits from 'zero' to 'nine' were chosen from dataset to evaluate algorithm. Dataset was split into train and test parts by speakers. In order to increase train dataset size we chose only one speaker for testing at each time. So, we provide 33 train-test cycles with 32 speakers for training and 1 for testing. All results were averaged to obtain final EER result.

In Table 1 EER results for different passphrase lengths obtained by concatenation of several speaker sessions are shown. It can be seen that EER decreases with increased number of digits in passphrase.

In Table 2 distribution of session from GRID dataset over algorithms is shown. It can be seen that 16% of sessions have insufficient quality for FALD algorithm. Error of the SALD algorithm is approximately twice as high than FALD error.

Table 1. EER results for system on digits, %

Num. of digits	2	3	4	5
Res. from [1]	12.37	8.29	5.82	4.38
New system	10.24	6.69	4.31	3.51

Table 2. Dataset distribution via FALD and SALD algorithms

Algorithm	Part of dataset	5 digits EER on this part, %
FALD	84%	3.02
SALD	16%	6.23

Our implementation of the algorithm allows to achieve necessary performance and use proposed system on modern smartphones with hi-end chipsets in real-time.

5   Conclusion

In this paper we have introduced the improved system for liveness detection. Schema of the algorithm is robust for cases when CLM detector fails to locate landmarks on the face properly. Error reduction on GRID dataset is shown.

Acknowledgements. This work was financially supported by the Ministry of Education and Science of the Russian Federation, Contract 14.578.21.0189 (ID RFMEFI57816X0189).

References

1. Melnikov, A., Akhunzyanov, R., Kudashev, O., Luckyanets, E.: Audiovisual liveness detection. In: Murino, V., Puppo, E. (eds.) ICIAP 2015. LNCS, vol. 9280, pp. 643–652. Springer, Cham (2015). doi:10.1007/978-3-319-23234-8_59
2. Chakraborty, S., Das, D.: An overview of face liveness detection. arXiv preprint arXiv:1405.2227 (2014)
3. Das, D., Chakraborty, S.: Face liveness detection based on frequency and microtexture analysis. In: 2014 International Conference on Advances in Engineering and Technology Research (ICAETR), pp. 1–4. IEEE (2014)
4. Maatta, J., Hadid, A., Pietikainen, M.: Face spoofing detection from single images using micro-texture analysis. In: 2011 International Joint Conference on Biometrics (IJCB), pp. 1–7. IEEE (2011)
5. Määttä, J., Hadid, A., Pietikäinen, M.: Face spoofing detection from single images using texture and local shape analysis. IET biometrics 1(1), 3–10 (2012)
6. Kim, G., Eum, S., Suhr, J.K., Kim, D.I., Park, K.R., Kim, J.: Face liveness detection based on texture and frequency analyses. In: 2012 5th IAPR International Conference on Biometrics (ICB), pp. 67–72. IEEE (2012)

7. Yang, L.: Face liveness detection by focusing on frontal faces and image backgrounds. In: 2014 International Conference on Wavelet Analysis and Pattern Recognition (ICWAPR), pp. 93–97. IEEE (2014)
8. Kim, S., Yu, S., Kim, K., Ban, Y., Lee, S.: Face liveness detection using variable focusing. In: 2013 International Conference on Biometrics (ICB), pp. 1–6. IEEE (2013)
9. Ali, A., Deravi, F., Hoque, S.: Liveness detection using gaze collinearity. In: 2012 Third International Conference on Emerging Security Technologies (EST), pp. 62–65. IEEE (2012)
10. Bao, W., Li, H., Li, N., Jiang, W.: A liveness detection method for face recognition based on optical flow field. In: International Conference on Image Analysis and Signal Processing, IASP 2009, pp. 233–236. IEEE (2009)
11. Kollreider, K., Fronthaler, H., Bigun, J.: Evaluating liveness by face images and the structure tensor. In: Fourth IEEE Workshop on Automatic Identification Advanced Technologies 2005, pp. 75–80. IEEE (2005)
12. Kollreider, K., Fronthaler, H., Bigun, J.: Non-intrusive liveness detection by face images. Image Vis. Comput. **27**(3), 233–244 (2009)
13. Sun, L., Pan, G., Wu, Z., Lao, S.: Blinking-based live face detection using conditional random fields. In: Lee, S.-W., Li, S.Z. (eds.) ICB 2007. LNCS, vol. 4642, pp. 252–260. Springer, Heidelberg (2007). doi:10.1007/978-3-540-74549-5_27
14. Lagorio, A., Tistarelli, M., Cadoni, M., Fookes, C., Sridharan, S.: Liveness detection based on 3D face shape analysis. In: 2013 International Workshop on Biometrics and Forensics (IWBF), pp. 1–4. IEEE (2013)
15. Wang, T., Yang, J., Lei, Z., Liao, S., Li, S.Z.: Face liveness detection using 3D structure recovered from a single camera. In: 2013 International Conference on Biometrics (ICB), pp. 1–6. IEEE (2013)
16. Tan, X., Li, Y., Liu, J., Jiang, L.: Face liveness detection from a single image with sparse low rank bilinear discriminative model. In: Daniilidis, K., Maragos, P., Paragios, N. (eds.) ECCV 2010. LNCS, vol. 6316, pp. 504–517. Springer, Heidelberg (2010). doi:10.1007/978-3-642-15567-3_37
17. Peixoto, B., Michelassi, C., Rocha, A.: Face liveness detection under bad illumination conditions. In: 2011 18th IEEE International Conference on Image Processing (ICIP), pp. 3557–3560. IEEE (2011)
18. Yan, J., Zhang, Z., Lei, Z., Yi, D., Li, S.Z.: Face liveness detection by exploring multiple scenic clues. In: 2012 12th International Conference on Control Automation Robotics & Vision (ICARCV), pp. 188–193. IEEE (2012)
19. Pan, G., Sun, L., Wu, Z., Wang, Y.: Monocular camera-based face liveness detection by combining eyeblink and scene context. Telecommun. Syst. **47**(3–4), 215–225 (2011)
20. Chetty, G., Wagner, M.: Automated lip feature extraction for liveness verification in audio-video authentication. In: Proceedings of Image and Vision Computing, pp. 17–22 (2004)
21. Kollreider, K., Fronthaler, H., Faraj, M.I., Bigun, J.: Real-time face detection and motion analysis with application in "liveness" assessment. IEEE Trans. Inf. Forensics Secur. **2**(3), 548–558 (2007)
22. Komulainen, J., Hadid, A., Pietikainen, M.: Context based face anti-spoofing. In: 2013 IEEE Sixth International Conference on Biometrics: Theory, Applications and Systems (BTAS), pp. 1–8. IEEE (2013)

23. Shchemelinin, V., Topchina, M., Simonchik, K.: Vulnerability of voice verification systems to spoofing attacks by TTS voices based on automatically labeled telephone speech. In: Ronzhin, A., Potapova, R., Delic, V. (eds.) SPECOM 2014. LNCS (LNAI), vol. 8773, pp. 475–481. Springer, Cham (2014). doi:10.1007/978-3-319-11581-8_59

24. Kinnunen, T., Wu, Z.Z., Lee, K.A., Sedlak, F., Chng, E.S., Li, H.: Vulnerability of speaker verification systems against voice conversion spoofing attacks: the case of telephone speech. In: 2012 IEEE International Conference on Acoustics, Speech and Signal Processing (ICASSP), pp. 4401–4404, March 2012

25. Novoselov, S., Pekhovsky, T., Shulipa, A., Sholokhov, A.: Text-dependent GMM-JFA system for password based speaker verification. In: 2014 IEEE International Conference on Acoustics, Speech and Signal Processing (ICASSP), pp. 729–737. IEEE (2014)

26. Shchemelinin, V., Simonchik, K.: Study of voice verification system tolerance to spoofing attacks using a text-to-speech system. J. Instrum. Eng. **57**(2), 84–88 (2014) (in Russian). ITMO University

27. Marcel, S., Nixon, M.S., Li, S.Z.: Handbook of Biometric Anti-Spoofing. Springer, London (2014)

28. Wu, Z., Evans, N., Kinnunen, T., Yamagishi, J., Alegre, F., Li, H.: Spoofing and countermeasures for speaker verification: A survey. Speech Commun. **66**, 130–153 (2015)

29. Novoselov, S., Kozlov, A., Lavrentyeva, G., Simonchik, K., Shchemelinin, V.: STC anti-spoofing systems for the asvspoof 2015 challenge. In: 2016 IEEE International Conference on Acoustics, Speech and Signal Processing (ICASSP), pp. 5475–5479. IEEE (2016)

30. Slaney, M., Covell, M.: Facesync: A linear operator for measuring synchronization of video facial images and audio tracks. In: NIPS, pp. 814–820 (2000)

31. Chetty, G., Wagner, M.: Multi-level liveness verification for face-voice biometric authentication. In: 2006 Biometrics Symposium: Special Session on Research at the Biometric Consortium Conference, pp. 1–6. IEEE (2006)

32. Çetingül, H.E., Erzin, E., Yemez, Y., Tekalp, A.M.: Multimodal speaker/speech recognition using lip motion, lip texture and audio. Signal Process. **86**(12), 3549–3558 (2006)

33. Dean, D., Sridharan, S.: Dynamic visual features for audio-visual speaker verification. Comput. Speech Lang. **24**(2), 136–149 (2010)

34. Baltrusaitis, T., Robinson, P., Morency, L.: 3d constrained local model for rigid and non-rigid facial tracking. In: 2012 IEEE Conference on Computer Vision and Pattern Recognition (CVPR), pp. 2610–2617. IEEE (2012)

35. Cooke, M., Barker, J., Cunningham, S., Shao, X.: An audio-visual corpus for speech perception and automatic speech recognition. J. Acoust. Soc. Am. **120**(5), 2421–2424 (2006)

Canadian English Word Stress:
A Corpora-Based Study of National Identity
in a Multilingual Community

Tatiana Shevchenko[✉] and Daria Pozdeeva[✉]

Moscow State Linguistic University,
38 Ostozhenka St., Moscow 119034, Russian Federation
tatashevchenko@mail.ru, da_pozdeeva@mail.ru

Abstract. Canadian English (CE) word stress, apart from sharing stress patterns with either the American or the British norms, reveals nationally specific rhythm-based features. The evidence was collected by working through the English Pronouncing Dictionary (EPD) and the Canadian Oxford Dictionary (COD). The next step was comparing frequencies of words with varying stress patterns in three national written and spoken speech corpora: the British National Corpus (BNC), the Corpus of Contemporary American English (COCA) and the Corpus of Canadian English (CCE). The words under analysis displayed nearly identical frequencies in the three sources; 89 most frequent polysyllabic words were selected for online express-survey. Canadian subjects (30) representing the diversity of CE linguistic identities (anglophones, francophones, allophones) which affected their decisions on word stress locations demonstrated their preferences for either the Canadian, the British or the American stress patterns, accordingly. The viability of the Canadian stress patterns was supported by the data from two more Canadian natural speech corpora: International Dialects of English Archive (IDEA) and Voices of the International Corpus of English (VOICE). Acoustic and perceptual analyses based on production and perception processing performed by native (anglophone) CE speakers demonstrated the significance of secondary stress in CE stress patterns.

Keywords: Canadian English · Word stress · Speech corpora · National identity-Multilingual community

1 Introduction

Canadian English (CE), according to contemporary linguistic sources, remains "one of the least empirically documented major varieties of English. Frequently depicted as a composite of British and American English speech patterns owing to the formative influence of these varieties on its development, it is now viewed as an autonomous national variety engaged in its own trajectory of evolution" [24].

The pronunciation base of CE is described as showing convergence on the American norms, while the British component is more clearly manifested in vocabulary and spelling practices [6, 7, 29]. However, the growth of a distinct Canadian identity in

© Springer International Publishing AG 2017
A. Karpov et al. (Eds.): SPECOM 2017, LNAI 10458, pp. 221–232, 2017.
DOI: 10.1007/978-3-319-66429-3_21

pronunciation can be evidenced by at least two uniquely CE features in vowels: Canadian Raising, i.e. the pronunciation of /ai/ and /aw/ with a raised central onset before voiceless consonants in *bite, out*, and also Canadian Vowel Shift which was triggered by *cot/caught* merging [3].

In the current study we will show another CE feature in pronunciation which, although it is not unique in its origin, might be a diagnostic feature of CE identity due to its distribution and relative frequency. The feature is concerned with the phenomenon of word stress, an area insufficiently explored in a CE distinctive aspect, to say the least of it, in comparison with what has been found about stress patterning in many world languages. The English language stress is classified as quantity-sensitive, edge-sensitive, bounded, with a tendency for a trochaic rhythm [18, 20, 21]. Most of the rules apply to nouns only, in which case the stress is termed *lexical stress* [8, 11, 12]. The differences between stress patterns in British and American varieties of English based on pronunciation dictionaries cover around 1.7% of the total amount of words, or 2.4% of the polysyllabic words registered in the 18th ed. of the English Pronouncing Dictionary (EPD) by D. Jones (around 80 000 words) [2, 5]. Word stress appears to be the least variable part of English phonology [3, 5, 23]. Stress convergence in contact languages is considered as a possibility for CE and First Nations languages of Canada [28].

Starting from the prevalent assumption about the conflicting norms of American impact and the British legacy in CE pronunciation, we will first have a look at American/British differences in word stress, and then see if they are reflected in CE norm and usage. Our *hypothesis* is that CE word stress, apart from sharing stress patterns common with either the American or the British norm, may reveal nationally specific features of a rhythmic nature.

The study of phonetic variation in CE ought to consider the CE speakers' attitudes to other varieties of English, American and British ones, in particular. Charles Boberg reported on the opinion survey among students "all around Canada", in which 80 percent of the respondents chose to emphasize the distinctness rather than the similarity of CE and American English; British English came on top as 'more correct' and "nice-sounding" [34, 35]. The data suggest that a sense of identity is quite acute there, with American influence tempered in reality by attitudinal obstacles.

Another prevalent (and controversial) assumption is concerned with linguistic homogeneity of middle class urban population in Canada. Here we have to introduce the socio-demographic dimension which presents Canada as a multicultural country, with two official languages and diversity of others promoted by language policy [19, 25]. The population of Canada is divided into three large groups by reported mother tongues: English-speaking (58%), French-speaking (22%), other languages (20%), including First Nations languages. The most widely-spread immigrant languages are those of the Romance group (Spanish, Portuguese, Italian), of the Indo-Iranian group (Punjabi, Hindi), and dialects of the Chinese language (Cantonese, Mandarin). The diversity of languages that coexist on the territory of Canada form a unique linguistic situation which affects the CE variety of the language. The heterogeneous character of the CE linguistic landscape is obvious.

The *goal* of the current multidimensional study is to explore CE distinctness in stress patterns occurrence based on the norms codified in the pronunciation dictionaries; on the frequency of words with varying stress patterns based on national corpora; on the cognitive representations in the minds of CE speakers with diverse linguistic backgrounds based on express survey; and on the actual stress patterns usage based on national sound corpora. The phonetic reality of the extracted stress patterns is further tested by perceptual and acoustic analyses.

2 Methodology

Corpora-based analysis proceeded in a number of steps:

Comparison of stress patterns norms codified in pronunciation dictionaries: EPD [23], COD [1].

Comparison of frequencies of the words with varying stress patterns based on BNC [4], COCA [10] and CCE [9] corpora; selection of a body of most frequent words for further analysis.

Express-survey (online questionnaire) of 30 Canadian subjects with diverse linguistic backgrounds and complex national identities: Anglophone (English is the first language), Francophone (balanced bilingual, self-reported as mother tongue is French/English), Allophone (speakers of other languages, English is the second language; the term is borrowed from [27]). The differences in linguistic background affected their decisions on stress locations in the 89 selected most frequent polysyllabic English words. The online survey was created and shared via Google Forms; it included an instruction for participants, a personal-data form (age, country of the origin, mother tongue, other languages the participant can speak), and the list of words divided into syllables. The participants (random choice, volunteers) were instructed to mark the location of primary and secondary (if any) stresses.

Auditory (perceptual) analysis. The sound corpora of CE authentic recorded speech were investigated with the purpose of testing the viability of previously established CE stress patterns. In other words, we wanted to see if the non-primary stresses were present in actual speech, in the speech signal, not only in the minds of the speakers. The original set of 89 words turned into a short list of 35 words (64 tokens) found in the corpora. The narrow corpus of 64 tokens was composed of 39 tokens (25 words) from the prepared public speeches in VOICE [30] and 25 tokens (10 words) from the unprepared speech (interviews) in IDEA [22]. 22 CE speakers (12 men and 10 women) were found to use the stress patterns with secondary stresses.

Another set of participants (10 Anglophone, all native speakers of CE with no special training) volunteered to be labelers of 64 tokens cut out from the Canadian natural speech sound corpora, VOICE and IDEA, sampling prepared and unprepared talks, spoken by 22 CE speakers. The instruction to labelers included a few examples for practising stress marking as primary or secondary. The list of words was arranged in the order the words appeared in the spoken material to avoid marking similar words by analogy. The list of isolated words was followed by the list of the same words in the context (sentences). Thus each token was first presented and annotated in isolation and then in the context of the sentence. The time interval between the words for taking a decision on stress placement was 3 s. The primary and the secondary (if any) stresses were annotated by hand, the lists of words and their contexts were scanned and sent to the researchers by email.

Acoustic analysis of the narrow CE sound corpus which consisted of the 64 samples annotated by native speakers of CE was aimed at looking at the prosodic (pitch, duration, intensity) nature of secondary stresses, as distinct from primary stresses. In search of nationally-specific prosodic cues to syllable prominence the following measurements were taken for each syllable: F0max, F0min in fundamental frequency, Intmax, Intmin in intensity, and Tsyll in duration. Acoustic measurements were computed by PRAAT (Boersma and Weenik, v.6.0.14). Dispersion was statistically tested by one-way ANOVA.

3   Results

3.1   Stress Patterns Norms Codified in Pronunciation Dictionaries

Comparison of pronunciations of polysyllabic words, namely their stress patterns, in British and American variants according to the EPD, 18th ed. [23] reflected in previous research [5] yielded a list of 1390 words. Checking the data on Br/Am word stress differences, item by item, in the Canadian Oxford Dictionary (COD) provided evidence for the variability of Canadian stress patterns. The initial list of 1390 polysyllabic words can be grouped according to COD as follows:

1. fall together with American stress patterns 22.8%
2. fall together with British stress pattern 20.1%
3. are different from both 13.7%
4. are not transcribed in COD 20.7%
5. are not included in COD 22.7%

The data testifies to a slight dominance of American stress patterns (22.8%) over the British ones (20.1%), as well as the presence of specifically Canadian stress patterns (13.7%) characterized by secondary stress occurrence. Regrettably, quite a few words are not transcribed in COD for lack of space, as the editors explained (in personal correspondence). Another group of words is not included into COD on account of their low frequency, as previous research suggested (geographical names, proper names, recent loan words) [5].

By looking closer at the nature of differences in the words which possess varying stress patterns in the three national dictionaries we found that specific CE patterns constitute one fourth (25.5%) of the total amount of words (750) for which COD supplied transcription. The most salient features to characterize the CE word stress are:

(a) differences in *primary stress* location in relation to either the British (65.8%) or the American variant (45.8%);
(b) differences in either the presence or location of *secondary stress* (73.7%) which is the major CE differentiating feature.

3.2   Frequency of Words with Varying Stress Patterns in National Speech Corpora

In order to establish frequencies of words with varying stress patterns in the three national corpora (BNC, COCA, CCE) and select the most frequent ones, the original body of selected 1390 items were checked for their frequency.

Given the different number of words in the three sources, the frequencies were calculated per 1 million words. The basic results consist in the following: (1) Stress-different words are less frequent than words with common stress patterns. (2) The frequencies of stress-different words are nearly identical in the three national corpora. (3) The list of selected polysyllabic words amounts to 89 most frequent, at 50 tokens per 1 million, in the three national corpora. The selected set was grouped according to the number of syllables: two-syllable words (58.4%), three-syllable words (27%), four-syllable words (4.5%), five-syllable words (6.8%), six-syllable words (2.2%), seven-syllable words (1.1%).

3.3   Express-Survey Data

This stage of the analysis involved an express-survey (online questionnaire created and shared via Google Forms) of 30 Canadian subjects' preferences for the location of stress, both primary and secondary, in the 89 most frequent polysyllabic English words. According to the self-reported personal data the participants (30) were grouped as follows:

1. Anglophones (16 participants, English is the first language).
2. Francophones (5 participants, balanced bilinguals, mother tongue French/English).
3. Allophones (9 participants, speakers of other languages, English is the second language).

The results of the express-survey demonstrate the choice of stress patterns depending on the linguistic background of the speakers. They reveal stress patterns associated with certain words in the mental representations of CE speakers' lexicon. The diversity of linguistic experience and education norms affected the most frequent stress pattern found in two-syllable, three-syllable, four-syllable and five-syllable words. We will comment on the patterns which scored highest for a particular group of population. For the Anglophone group the typical CE patterns with secondary stresses are most common in the first three types of word structure (Figs. 1, 2 and 3).

The most amazing pattern on the Anglophone preferences list is the stress pattern in a two-syllable word with a primary stress on the first syllable and a secondary stress on the second syllable: *ballet, detail, fragment*. The frequency of this pattern (65.4%) is impressive (Fig. 1, Pattern 3). The stress pattern in a three-syllable word also contains a post-tonic (placed after the primary stress) secondary stress, and it is close to a half of the cases (45.8%): *contractor, gasoline, partisan* (Fig. 2, Pattern 3). The pre-tonic (preceding the primary stress) secondary stress in a four-syllable word, with a lower percentage (25%), still follows the CE way of adding a secondary stress alternating with the primary one: *electronic* (Fig. 3, Pattern 4).

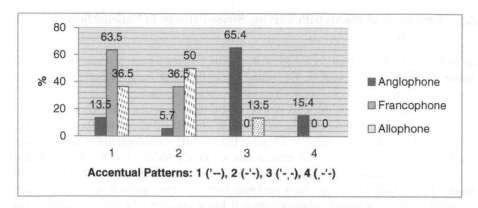

Fig. 1. Two-syllable accentual patterns

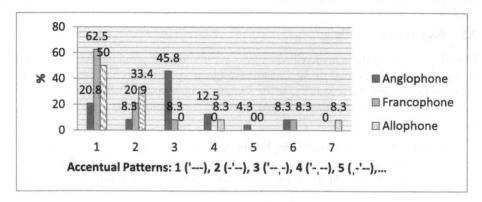

Fig. 2. Three-syllable accentual patterns

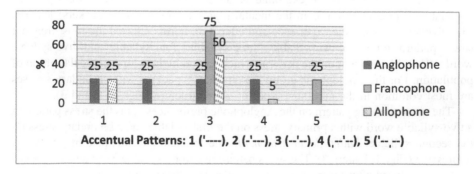

Fig. 3. Four-syllable accentual patterns

Canadian bilingual Francophones demonstrate a different tendency: they tend to choose only a single primary stress for the initial syllable in two- and three-syllable words: *address, dictate*; *Amsterdam, composite* (Fig. 1, Pattern 1; Fig. 2, Pattern 1), which corresponds with the typical British variants. They also tend to ignore secondary stresses in long four-syllable words: *predecessor* (Fig. 3, Pattern 3) and five-syllable words: *disciplinary* (Fig. 4, Patterns 1, 2, 3, 5), which will be against the rules of English stress placement in any national variant.

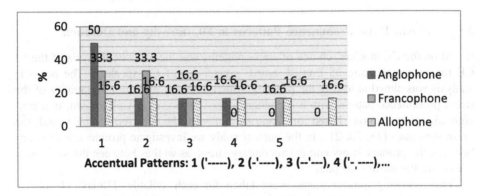

Fig. 4. Five-syllable accentual patterns

The responses of the Allophone group participants do not coincide with any of the two main groups of Canadian speakers. The location of the primary stress on the second syllable in two-syllable and three-syllable words corresponds with the American variant of English stress placement: *debut, dictate, garage*; *adulthood* (Fig. 1, Patterns 1, 2; Fig. 2, Patterns 1, 2). The four-syllable pattern is close to the Francophone group variant: *mathematics* (Fig. 3, Pattern 3), while the five-syllable cases are equally distributed: *laboratory* (Fig. 4). The overall impression is definitely in favour of the American stress patterns.

By way of summing up the results at this stage we may conclude that the most common stress pattern of a polysyllabic word with a secondary stress, first established as a CE distinctive feature and as a national norm in COD, was also chosen by the Anglophone majority of the respondents. The Francophone participants marked the stresses according to the British patterns, and the Allophones bore more resemblance to the American patterns. Noteworthy is the fact that Francophone and Allophone respondents avoid the CE identifying feature of secondary stress location. We will discuss the possible reasons for their choices in the Conclusions and Discussion section.

3.4   Auditory Analysis

The labelers, 10 CE speakers for whom English is L1, volunteered to annotate the 64 tokens of English words extracted from natural CE speech corpora, from both prepared (VOICE) and unprepared (IDEA) speech samples. The samples were presented as a recording of the words first in isolation and then in context, with 3 s. intervals between the words. The coincidence level of stress patterns for isolated words and the same words presented in context was very high: 98%. The labelers' agreement on the stress pattern choice was 69%.

The results of the labelers' marking gave support to the presence of secondary stresses, both in the post-tonic and pre-tonic positions, with the former position dominating. The total of 40.8% of CE tokens were marked as possessing a secondary stress, a feature not found in other varieties of English in such proportions.

3.5   Acoustic Data: Prominence Patterns in F0, Intensity and Duration

Based on the CE labelers' choice of stress patterns was the acoustic analysis of the 64 CE tokens representing 35 English words spoken by 21 CE speakers. The acoustic analysis was aimed at testing the prosodic (pitch, intensity and duration) reality of the stress prominence pattern with a secondary stress. Stress, as is well known, is a syntagmatic phenomenon, based on contrast between the stressed syllable and the unstressed ones [18, 20, 21]. In the current study we investigate prominence relations between the primary stress and the secondary stress, as well as between the secondary stress and the unstressed one.

The following measurements were taken for each syllable: F0max, F0 min in fundamental frequency, Int max, Int min in intensity, and Tsyll in duration. Acoustic measurements were computed by PRAAT (Boersma and Weenik, v.6.0.14). Dispersion was statistically tested by one-way ANOVA.

By looking at F0 max parameter we find that in female speech the primary/secondary contrast is non-significant ($p = .530$), while secondary/unstressed distinction is significant ($p = .027$) (Fig. 5). In male speech neither distinction proved to be significant. Intensity parameter did not supply any significant distinctions either (Fig. 6).

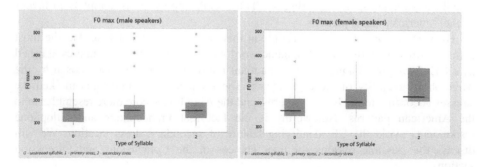

Fig. 5. F0 max (male and female speakers)

Prosodic prominence data on duration was particularly informative in both gender groups: in female speech secondary/unstressed distinction is significant at $p = .015$, while in male speech both primary/unstressed ($p = .001$) and secondary/unstressed distinctions ($p = .029$) are significant (Fig. 7).

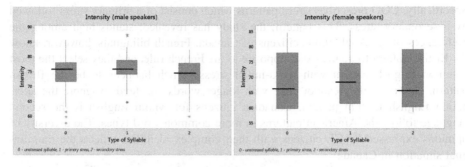

Fig. 6. Intensity (male and female speakers)

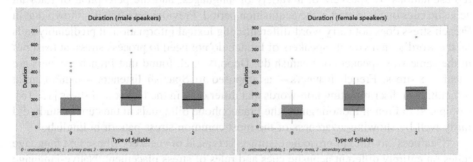

Fig. 7. Duration (male and female speakers)

Thus it was found that secondary stress prominence was invariably supported by duration which provides for the stress pattern with a secondary stress. In addition to that women's speech is marked by higher pitch (F0 max) to provide for greater prominence of secondary stress in running speech. None of the speakers made significant enough distinction between the primary and the secondary stresses (*accents* in the flow of speech). Alternating stress patterns that bring out either the initial or the second syllable into a primary position in a two-syllable word like *detail, defence, research* suggest that these stress locations are competing in modern English, as EPD data on American and British English showed [23]; CE is no exception.

4   Conclusions and Discussion

Although English word stress system is assumed to be less susceptible to change than other parts of English phonology, the present corpora-based study has found enough evidence to demonstrate its variance. Given the lack of data on specific CE word stress, we felt there was a pressing need for well-documented research in the area.

Comparisons made across national pronunciation dictionaries suggest that there is a unique combination of American, British and specific Canadian English features in the codified CE stress norm; the latter constitute one fourth of the total amount of patterns.

Specifically, COD prescribes stress patterns which consist of a primary stress followed by a secondary stress. This pattern, the study has revealed, stands high among the preferences of the Anglophone citizens of Canada. French bilinguals, however, know the British pattern to be the exact opposite to the French rule, and they select the most common English pattern with word-initial stress, which happens to be the British pattern. However, they cannot cope with longer words and tend to ignore the alternating English rhythm pattern. Canadian citizens for whom English is the second language follow the American patterns in more common word types. The diversity of opinions expressed by CE citizens with their complex identities reflects the multilingual situation in Canada.

To account for stress divergence we could make reference to cross-linguistic studies of stress "deafness" in French, for instance, to prove that stress is encoded in lexical representations by speakers of a variety of languages, and the perception of relevant acoustic cues ought to start at the acquisition period. Previous research has shown that in French stress does not carry word-differentiating lexical information: it predictably falls on the word's final vowel. Speakers of French do not need to process stress, at least not in the same way speakers of Spanish do. Dupoux et al. found that French listeners are "deaf" to stress. French listeners – as opposed to Spanish listeners – exhibit great difficulties in discriminating non-words that differ only in the location of stress [15, 16]. Compared to French monolinguals, the Francophone bilinguals in the current study did fairly well by showing awareness of the most common stress pattern in English.

"Deafness" to foreign prosodic contrasts is typical of speakers whose first language relies on entirely different acoustic cues and rules of stress placement. Native-language listening procedures are applied to foreign-language input. French listeners are known to apply syllabic segmentation to English, while Japanese listeners apply moraic segmentation to English, French and Spanish [8]. Native listeners of English, according to laboratory research data, employ a 'metrical segmentation strategy' which exploits the fact that around 90% of content words in connected English speech are either monosyllabic or bear lexical stress on their first syllable: listeners work on the assumption that each stressed syllable marks the onset of a new word [12]. There is also evidence that information from two syllables is more effective than information from one syllable [8], the condition which was facilitating for the recognition of stress patterns in the present study. Both perception and production of English stress patterns appear to be affected by the first language habits. Bilinguals, however, are reported to demonstrate monolingual nature of speech segmentation [14]. Balanced Francophone bilingualism, as our results suggest, is still more complex in perception and output.

Anglophone majority was the source of more data on selected most frequent words in the Canadian corpus which was found to be nearly identical with the British and the American core of most frequent words. In Canadian sound corpora only 22 speakers actually used the words we were after, yielding 64 tokens of 35 words in their prepared and unprepared talks. 40% of the words were pronounced with the stress patterns that included a secondary stress, as the untrained CE labelers annotated them. The specific CE preference for the pattern was viable.

The results of the acoustic analysis, although preliminary at the present stage of the research, may be considered symptomatic. The secondary stress was made acoustically prominent from the unstressed ones due to at least one prosodic cue in naturally produced connected speech. The basic prosodic cue which enhanced the secondary stress turned out to be duration, not pitch which had been ranked highest in most American and British studies. Higher pitch values were observed in the female realizations only on account of their wider pitch range.

The distinction between the primary and the secondary (non-primary) stresses proved to be non-significant, as the statistic analysis indicated.

Another specific feature consisted in the distribution of the pattern: not only rhythm-based post-tonic position was secured for a secondary stress in polysyllabic three-syllable and four-syllable words but two-syllable words were also marked by Canadian speakers with that feature. In actual speech the two positions, the initial and the final one in a two-syllable word, could be made more prominent, with the primary and the secondary stresses being in trading relations.

Typical CE stress patterns with a secondary stress in polysyllabic words may not be impeding speech intelligibility in the way previous laboratory experiments found for the two-syllable stress misplacements [17], but they do possess a potential for CE national identification.

References

1. Barber, K. (ed.): Canadian Oxford Dictionary, 2nd edn. Oxford University Press, Toronto (2004)
2. Berg, T.: Stress variation in British and American English. World Englishes 18(2), 123–143 (1999)
3. Boberg, Ch.: The English Language in Canada. Status, History and Comparative Analysis. McGill University, Montreal (2010)
4. British National Corpus. http://www.natcorp.ox.ac.uk/. Accessed 05 Dec 2015
5. Buraya, E.A.: Accentuation in British and American Englishes: convergence or divergence? Phonetics and phonology of discourse. Vestnik MSLU 1(580), 23–41 (2010)
6. Chambers, J.K.: English: Canadian varieties. In: Edwards, J. (ed.) Language in Canada, pp. 252–272. Cambridge University Press, Cambridge (1998)
7. Clarke, S.: Nooz or nyooz?: The complex construction of Canadian identity. Can. J. Linguist. 51, 225–246 (2006)
8. Cooper, N., Cutler, A., Wales, R.: Constraints of lexical stress on lexical access in English: evidence from native and non-native listeners. Lang. Speech 45(3), 207–228 (2002)
9. Corpus of Canadian English: http://corpus.byu.edu/can/. Accessed 12 Dec 2015
10. Corpus of Contemporary American English: http://corpus.byu.edu/coca/. Accessed 05 Dec 2015
11. Cutler, A.: Lexical stress in English pronunciation. In: Reed, M., Levis, J.M. (eds.) The Handbook of English Pronunciation, pp. 106–124. Wiley Blackwell, Chichester (2015)
12. Cutler, A.: Native listening. The flexibility dimension. Dutch J. Appl. Linguist. 1(2), 169–188 (2012)
13. Cutler, A., Carter, D.M.: The predominance of strong initial syllables in the English vocabulary. Comput. Speech Lang. 2, 133–142 (1987)
14. Cutler, A., Mehler, J., Norris, D., Segui, J.: The monolingual nature of speech segmentation by bilinguals. Cogn. Psychol. 24, 381–410 (1992)
15. Dupoux, E., Pallier, C., Sebastian, N., Mehler, J.: A distressing deafness in French? J. Mem. Lang. 36, 406–421 (1997)

16. Dupoux, E., Peperkamp, S.: Fossil markers of language development: phonological 'deafnesses' in adult speech processing. In: Durand, J., Laks, B. (eds.) Phonetics, Phonology and Cognition, pp. 168–190. Oxford University Press, Oxford (2004)
17. Field, J.: Intelligibility and the listener: the role of lexical stress. TESOL Q. **39**(3), 399–424 (2005)
18. Fox, A.: Prosodic Features and Prosodic Structure. The Phonology of Suprasegmentals. Oxford University Press, Oxford (2007)
19. Hayday, M.: Bilingual today, united tomorrow: official languages in education and Canadian Federalism. McGill-Queen's University Press, Montreal (2005)
20. van der Hulst, H. (ed.): Word Stress: Theoretical and Typological Issues. Cambridge University Press, Cambridge (2014)
21. van der Hulst, H.: Brackets and grid marks, or theories of primary accent and rhythm. In: Raimy, E., Cairns, C. (eds.) Contemporary Views on Architecture and Representations in Phonological Theory, pp. 225–245. MIT Press, Cambridge (2009)
22. International Dialects of English Archive. http://www.dialectsarchive.com/canada. Accessed 17 Oct 2015
23. Jones, D.: English Pronouncing Dictionary. Roach, P., Setter, J., Esling J. (eds.). 18th edn. Cambridge University Press, Cambridge (2011)
24. Levey, S.: The Englishes of Canada. In: Kirkpatrick, A. (ed.) The Routledge Handbook of World Englishes, pp. 113–131. Routledge Taylor and Francis Group, London and New York (2012)
25. Linguistic Characteristics of Canadians: http://www12.statcan.ca/census-recensement/2011/as-sa/98-314-x/98-314-x2011001-eng.cfm. Accessed 18 Jan 2017
26. McQueen, J.M., Cutler, A.: Cognitive processes in speech perception. In: Hardcastle, W.J., Laver, J., Gibbon, F.E. (eds.) The Handbook of Phonetic Sciences, 2nd edn, pp. 489–520. Wiley-Blackwell, Chichester, U.K. (2013)
27. Parkin, A., Mendelsohn, M.: A New Canada: An Identity Shaped by Diversity. The CRIC Papers. Centre for Research and Information on Canada, Montreal (2003)
28. Rice, K.: Convergence of prominence systems? In: van der Hulst, H. (ed.) Word Stress: Theoretical and Typological Issues, pp. 194–227. Cambridge University Press, Cambridge (2014)
29. Schneider, E.W.: English in North America. In: Kachru, B.B., Kachru, Y., Nelson, C.L. (eds.) The Handbook of World Englishes, pp. 58–73. Wiley-Blackwell, Chichester (2009)
30. Voices of the International Corpus of English (VOICE) CANADA Dataverse. https://dataverse.library.ualberta.ca/dvn/dv/VOICE. Accessed 07 Aug 2016

Classification of Formal and Informal Dialogues Based on Turn-Taking and Intonation Using Deep Neural Networks

István Szekrényes[1][✉] and György Kovács[2,3]

[1] University of Debrecen, Debrecen, Hungary
szekrenyes.istvan@arts.unideb.hu
[2] MTA Research Institute for Linguistics, Budapest, Hungary
gykovacs@inf.u-szeged.hu
[3] MTA-SZTE Research Group on Artificial Intelligence, Szeged, Hungary

Abstract. Here, we introduce a classification method for distinguishing between formal and informal dialogues using feature sets based on prosodic data. One such feature set is the raw fundamental frequency values paired with speaker information (i.e. turn-taking). The other feature set we examine is the prosodic labels extracted from the raw F0 values via the ProsoTool algorithm, which is also complemented by turn-taking. We evaluated the two feature sets by comparing the accuracy scores our classification method got, which uses them to classify dialogue-excerpts taken from the HuComTech corpus. With the ProsoTool features we achieved an average accuracy score of 85.2%, which meant a relative error rate reduction of 24% compared to the accuracy scores attained using F0 features. Regardless of the feature set applied, however, our method yields better accuracy scores than those got by human listeners, who only managed to distinguish between formal and informal dialogue to an accuracy level of 56.5%.

Keywords: Turn-taking · Intonation · HuComTech · ProsoTool · Deep neural networks

1 Introduction

In the area of speech processing, spontaneous speech can be characterised in various ways. Many previous studies focused on the correlations of formal, measurable features and the underlying communicative or linguistic phenomena such as speech acts [15], topic structure [16,21] and some paralinguistically relevant properties like age, gender and expressed emotions of the speakers [17]. Beyond the theoretical questions, the main practical challenge of these studies is how we can make the *content* – which is readily accessible for humans – machine-readable (detectable or predictable) based on physically measurable acoustic parameters.

The principle of our study is to characterise the situational context of dialogues by making a binary decision about the origin of topic units using

© Springer International Publishing AG 2017
A. Karpov et al. (Eds.): SPECOM 2017, LNAI 10458, pp. 233–243, 2017.
DOI: 10.1007/978-3-319-66429-3_22

neural nets and two kinds of dataset, namely formal and informal conversations taken from the HuComTech corpus [10]. Our assumption was that the different sequences of turn-taking (including overlapping speech and silence) and – based on the contextualizing function of prosody [7] – intonation movements described with normalised, discrete categories can provide sufficient information for a fairly successful classification of dialogue types. Following the approach of a previous study [11], the preprocessed annotation labels of turn-taking and intonation were used as training material instead of direct acoustic measurements, but for the sake of comparison, an experiment was also performed with the raw F0 data.

2   Research Material

The HuComTech multimodal corpus was designed within the framework of the HuComTech project [10] and used to analyse the underlying structure of human–human communication [9]. The corpus contains 50 h of spontaneous speech in Hungarian recorded from 111 native speakers between the ages of 19 and 30. The speakers were asked to participate in a simulated job interview, and an informal conversation, discussing such topics as their happiest/saddest memories, friendship and jokes. Both scenarios were performed spontaneously and were directed by the same agent. Although it was only a simulation, the speakers were more polite and careful in their speech production during the job interview, than during the subsequent informal conversation. Because of the agent's directive role and the resulting unmotivated topic shifts, the two scenarios are very similar (making the classification more complicated), but based on the above-mentioned differences in behaviour and conversation topics, we were able to divide them into categorically different (formal and informal) subsets.

2.1   Annotation of Turn-Taking

In the HuComTech corpus, the speech of participants was transcribed manually in two separate annotation tiers, then the transcriptions were automatically converted to a simplified, acoustic representation of turn-taking that was divided into four levels: isolated speech segments of the *agent* and the *speaker*, segments of *overlapping speech*, and *silences*. As Fig. 1 shows, the verbal interaction can be characterised by various patterns of consecutive events, using just these four categories of segmentation. In the absence of the original, manually created transcription, speaker diarisation algorithms are also available [8] to perform the task by means of automatic methods.

Information concerning the average occurrence (per minute) and average duration (in seconds) of various segments is displayed in Table 1. As can be seen, utterances of the agent are more frequent in the informal conversations than in the formal job interviews. This might be due to the fact that unlike in the job interviews, where the role of the agent was mostly limited to posing the initial questions and providing feedback to the interviewee (speaker), in the informal scenario the agent is more active and involved in the conversation.

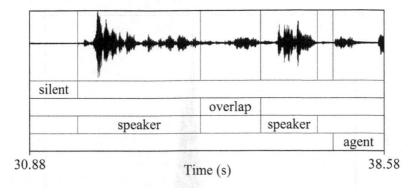

Fig. 1. Annotation of turn-taking. A sample taken from the HuComTech corpus

Table 1. Average occurrences (per minute) and durations (in seconds) of speech segments (agent, speaker, overlapping speech) and silences

	Subset	Speaker	Agent	Overlap	Silence
Occurrence	Formal	9.25	5.59	2.48	10.43
	Informal	9.88	8.52	6.32	8.99
Duration	Formal	4.77 s	3.02 s	0.53 s	0.77 s
	Informal	3.09 s	2.55 s	0.76 s	0.67 s

In Table 1, we can see a more significant difference regarding the frequency of overlapping speech. On average, overlapping speech is approximately 2.5 times more frequent in the informal conversations than it is in the formal job interviews. Although a higher frequency of overlapping speech would be expected with the increased activity of the agent, the increase in the frequency of overlapping speech is much bigger than the increase in the frequency of agent utterances. This means that the increased overlap in speech is probably a good indicator of the difference in the speaker behaviour in the two scenarios.

2.2 Annotation of Intonation

The annotation of intonation was performed by a rule-based algorithm called *ProsoTool*, which was implemented in the scripting language of the Praat speech processing program [1]. The development was inspired by the work of Piet Mertens [14] using similar objectives along with the psychoacoustic model of tonal perception. The main principle of ProsoTool was to transform the series of raw F0 values into smoothed, perceptually relevant, stylised trends of pitch modulation which can be classified as discrete contours of the evolving intonation structure. The script has a preprocessing module to isolate the voices of every speaker using the acoustic representation of turn-taking. Based on the F0 distribution, the algorithm divides the individual vocal range of speakers into five levels (see Fig. 2), which were treated as normalised categories to locate the

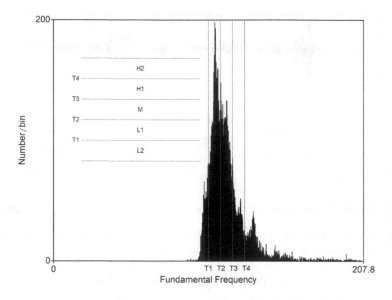

Fig. 2. Calculating individual pitch ranges of the speaker based on the F0 distribution: $L_2 < L_1 < M < H_1 < H_2$

relative position of the resulting intonation trends. In Fig. 3, the final output can be seen with the segmented and labeled F0 plots using five possible categories of intonation contour (*rise, fall, ascending, descending* and *level*), depending on the amplitude and the duration of the modulation. Further details on the method

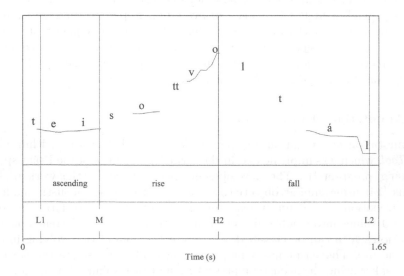

Fig. 3. Output for a Hungarian yes-no question: "Te is ott voltál? [Were you there, too?]"

are described in [18]. The same algorithm is available at the official website[1] of the e-magyar project under the name of *emPros* (in accordance with the naming guideline of the project).

3   Methodology

3.1   Representation of Data

Preparation and Conversion. As a first preprocessing step, the annotations of conversations were divided into smaller units of dialogue topics. Some filtering criteria were also applied, namely pieces without any topic (e.g. the very beginning of conversations) or appreciable topic elaboration (when the total duration is less than 30 s) were excluded from the analysis. The annotation of turn-taking was converted to a sequential representation without any information on timing, but keeping the original order and marking the duration of each segment. In the case of ProsoTool's output, it was supplemented with the sequence of intonation trends describing the duration, the contour and the relative height of each trend (e.g. agent, 0.34, rise, M, H2). Unvoiced speech segments were also included to preserve the structure of turn-taking. In the third experiment, F0 values were measured everywhere using the default settings of the Praat "To Pitch..." function [1]. This resulted in sequences of 10-millisecond-long frames containing speaker information and the measured fundamental frequency in Hertz.

Feature Extraction. The last step for converting our data into a format suitable for machine learning was feature extraction. Here, various different data types had to be handled, such as categorical data (speaker information and the F0 contour category), ordinal data (F0 level), and numerical data (the duration for each segment and raw F0 measurements). Categorical data was handled by 1 of N dummy coding (N being the number of categories), where silence was not considered as an independent category, but a lack of categorical information. It meant that turn-taking for example was coded as three binary features, corresponding to the three possible categories of speakers (speaker, agent, and overlapping speech), while all three binary features having the value of zero signified silence. The same method was used to encode the contour of the fundamental frequency (coding it as six binary features - corresponding to the five contour-types, and unvoiced intervals), as well as the ordinal data (also coded as six binary features). The only transformation applied on the numerical data was a standardisation to a zero mean and unit variance.

Train/Development/Test Partitioning. To create separate sets to train our models, to tune the corresponding hyper-parameters, and also to evaluate the models trained, the speakers (and also the dialogue excerpts associated with the speakers) were partitioned into a train, development and test set. This partitioning

---

[1] http://e-magyar.hu/en/speechmodules/empros.

was used in our auditory experiments as well, but this also meant that the potential size of the test set was limited by the workload we could realistically expect to be taken on by the volunteers in our experiments. In the end, similar to our earlier study on the HuComTech corpus [11], the partitioning was carried out with a 75/10/15 ratio. Thus from the 111 speakers, 17 were selected for the test set, 11 were selected for the development set, and the remaining 83 speakers were put into the train set. Both the test set and the development set were separated from the full set in such a way that they represented it as closely as possible. Meaning that from our candidate sets, we selected those whose parameters most closely resembled the full set. These parameters were the ratio of female/male speakers, the mean and deviation of the speakers' age, and the mean and deviation of formal and informal dialogue lengths. We also required that the number of formal and informal dialogues be equal in both the development set and the test set. This requirement helped to remove any unambiguity of the evaluation. And more importantly, the relative frequencies of informal and formal dialogues (the former slightly outnumbering the latter) in the full set of suitable dialogue-candidates of the HuComTech corpus did not necessarily reflect the real-life relative frequencies of such dialogues. As a consequence of our requirements, the partitioning resulted in a train set of 1058 dialogues, a development set of 136 dialogues, and a test set of 216 dialogues.

3.2   Machine Learning

Not only were there slightly more informal dialogues in the HuComTech corpus among dialogues suitable for our experiments, but they were also approximately twice as long on average as their formal counterparts. We did not expect that this would be representative of formal and informal dialogues in general. Moreover, we sought to ensure that the classification should work regardless of the length of the dialogue, and regardless of whether the full dialogue was available for the classifier or not. For this, we decided to use a method that could not make use of the information of dialogue length. We applied a similar method to that used by Gosztolya [4] in the classification of laughter. For each segment with its context of a given size, a neural net estimated the probability of the given segment having been derived from an informal/formal dialogue, after which the classification was carried out based on the average of the resulting probability values.

Probabilistic Sampling. The difference between the average length of formal and informal dialogues also means that even though the number of formal and informal dialogues is roughly the same, at the segmental level there is a significant imbalance in the class distribution. This may cause a bias towards the more common (informal) class, and result in a worse classification performance of the rarer (formal) class [12]. One possible way of overcoming this problem is to omit entire informal dialogues, or just use smaller pieces of certain informal dialogues. This, however, would lead to the loss of important training data [2]. We might also try adding extra samples from the more rare class, or with the lack of extra examples, simulate this by using the same sample n times. In the probabilistic sampling method this can be achieved by first selecting a class at random, and then drawing a random sample from the selected class [20]. The first step can be viewed as sampling from a multinomial distribution, given that each class has a probability $P(c_i)$ [6]. That is,

$$P(c_i) = \lambda(1/N) + (1 - \lambda)Prior(c_i) \qquad (1 \leq i, j \leq N; \lambda \in [0, 1]), \qquad (1)$$

where N is the number of classes, and λ controls the uniformity of the distribution. Here, $\lambda = 0$ leads to the original distribution, while $\lambda = 1$ (a setting also referred to as "uniform class sampling" [20]) leads to a uniform distribution. In the second step, we take a random sample from the selected class.

Deep Rectifier Neural Nets. Here, probability estimates for segments are provided by deep rectifier neural nets (DRNs). These are artificial neural nets that contain more than one hidden layer with neurons using the rectifier activation function ($rectifier(x) = max(0, x)$) instead of the traditional sigmoid function. As this architecture not only leads to more sparse neural nets, but also alleviates the problem of vanishing gradients even with multiple layers, it has gained popularity in recent years, not just in speech technology [5, 13, 19], but elsewhere as well [3, 6, 11]. The neural nets applied here had three hidden layers each containing 250 neurons, and an output layer containing two neurons, with a softmax nonlinearity. The training of the neural net was performed using the train set, while the development set was applied in the learn-rate scheduler, using Unweighted Average Recall (UAR) for validation.

4 Results and Discussion

4.1 Experiments Using Speaker Information

In this study, one of our aims was to discover what classification accuracy could be attained using raw F0 measurements, and using information derived from these measurements with the ProsoTool algorithm. To make our feature sets more useful, both F0 measurements and ProsoTool labels were supplemented with turn-taking information (i.e. information on whether the current measurements correspond to an utterance of the speaker, the agent, both, or neither – if a measurement is taken during a period of silence). This raises the question of just how useful this information is in itself for classification purposes. We examined this question in our first set of experiments. Here, for each context size from 0 to 10 we trained three independent neural nets for $\lambda \in [0, 1]$. Figure 4 shows the average accuracy scores we got using the classifier with different neural nets. For each context size, the accuracy score of the best performing λ setting is shown. As can be seen in the figure, we achieved the best accuracy scores on the development set, when using 4-4 neighbours to estimate the probability values corresponding to a given segment. With this setting, using $\lambda = 0.9$, we obtained

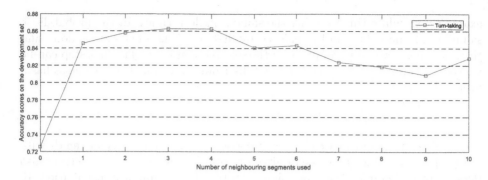

Fig. 4. Dialogue level accuracy scores got on the development set as a function of neighbouring segments used (the average of three independently trained classifiers)

an accuracy score of 81.5% on the test set. This tells us that a reasonable classification performance can be achieved by just using turn-taking information as features.

4.2 Experiments Using Intonation

The same set of experiments was repeated using the feature set derived directly from the raw F0 data, as well as using the feature set derived from the output of ProsoTool algorithm. Figure 5 shows some results got from these experiments on the development set. As in the F0 feature set, one segment represents a much smaller context (10 ms); hence when using this filter set, more neighbouring segments were utilised in estimating the probability values of a segment derived from an informal/formal dialogue. Figure 5 shows that we get the best results using the raw F0 features, with a context of 400-400 neighbouring segments, while in the case of ProsoTool features, 7-7 neighbouring segments were used to obtain the best accuracy scores.

Table 2 shows the average accuracy scores got using the raw F0 and the ProsoTool feature sets, along with the average accuracy scores obtained using just the turn-taking information. As can be seen, utilising the F0 feature set (containing both the turn-taking information and the raw F0 measurements) not only failed to increase the accuracy scores compared to those obtained using just the turn-taking information, but even led to a slightly lower performance. This might seem counterintuitive, but the way the turn-taking information is represented within the F0 feature set (speaker information is given for every 10 ms along with the fundamental frequency measurements), might be the reason it proved to be less efficient for the classifier. We also see that using the features from the ProsoTool algorithm did increase the performance of the classifier, leading to a relative error rate reduction of more than 24% compared to the accuracy scores got using the raw F0 feature set, and a relative error rate reduction of 20% compared to the classifier using just turn-taking information.

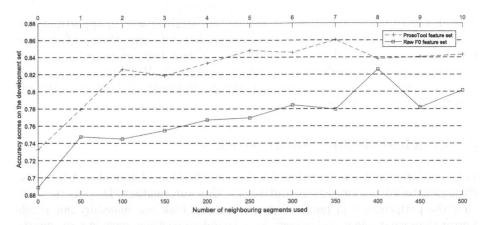

Fig. 5. Dialogue level accuracy scores got on the development set as a function of neighbouring segments used (the average of three independently trained classifiers)

Table 2. Accuracy scores attained on the development set and test set using different feature sets (reported scores are the average of three independently trained classifiers)

Feature set	λ	No. of neighbouring segments used	Accuracy Development	Test
Raw F0	1.0	400	82.6%	80.4%
Turn-taking	0.9	4	86.3%	81.5%
ProsoTool	1.0	7	86.0%	85.2%

To facilitate a comparison with the auditory experiments (see below), we created a classification based on the majority vote of the classifiers using the ProsoTool features. This resulted in an improved accuracy score of 85.6%.

4.3   Auditory Experiments

Along with our machine learning experiments, an auditory experiment was devised to test the classification capability of human listeners based on the same information that was given to our automatic classification method, namely intonation and turn-taking. Hence, in this experiment, the original audio recordings (taken from the test set) were regenerated and presented as stereo channels (agent and speaker) of sine waves with varying frequency to represent only the intonation of communicative partners. The subjects had to listen to these samples through a Web-based interface and decide whether the dialogue was "formal" or "informal". Participants also had the chance to mark a dialogue as undecidable if they were unable to make a decision. The test set of 216 recordings was divided into three parts and three decisions were made about each recording by three different subjects. The final decision for each recording was made by a majority vote, resulting in an accuracy score of 56,5%. It should be mentioned here that the only training the human listeners received was an opportunity to familiarise themselves with the Web-based interface. Of course their performance could have been better if they had undergone a short training period where the correct answer was revealed after their decision made. However, as the aim of the experiment here was to determine their performance without any external assistance, this was not done.

5   Conclusions and Future Work

Here, we presented an algorithm for the classification of formal and informal dialogues based on intonation and turn-taking information. Despite the fact that the performance of human listeners on this task was generally not much better than what one would expect from a random decision, with our automatic classification method we achieved good accuracy scores. Furthermore, our results seem to confirm the utility of ProsoTool, as we achieved our best accuracy scores using the features provided by this algorithm.

In the future we would like to extend the dataset with the annotation of other prosodic features of speech rate and intensity using the upcoming, new modules of ProsoTool. And as the HuComTech is a multimodally annotated corpus, information from other modalities (such as facial expressions or deixis) could also be incorporated into the dataset. Besides this, it would be a good idea to examine more sophisticated methods for the aggregation of probability values. Here, this aggregation was carried out by a simple averaging, but it is not strictly necessary that every part of the dialogue should have the same importance regarding the final decision. We also intend to investigate different neural net architectures for this task, like Long-Short Term Memory (LSTM) neural networks and other recurrent networks.

Acknowledgments. The research reported in the paper was conducted with the support of the Hungarian Scientific Research Fund (OTKA) grant #K116938 and #K116402.

References

1. Boersma, P., Weenink, D.: PRAAT: doing phonetics by computer [computer program]. version 6.0.22 (2016). http://www.praat.org/. Accessed 15 Nov 2016
2. Domingos, P.: A few useful things to know about machine learning. Commun. ACM **55**(10), 78–87 (2012)
3. Glorot, X., Bordes, A., Bengio, Y.: Deep sparse rectifier neural networks. In: Proceedings of AISTATS, pp. 315–323 (2011)
4. Gosztolya, G., Beke, A., Neuberger, T., Tóth, L.: Laughter classification using deep rectifier neural networks with a minimal feature subset. Arch. Acoust. **41**(4), 669–682 (2016)
5. Grósz, T., Busa-Fekete, R., Gosztolya, G., Tóth, L.: Assessing the degree of nativeness and Parkinson's condition using Gaussian processes and deep rectifier neural networks. In: Proceedings of Interspeech, pp. 1339–1343 (2015)

6. Grósz, T., Nagy, I.: Document classification with deep rectifier neural networks and probabilistic sampling. In: Proceedings of TSD, pp. 108–115 (2014)
7. House, J.: Prosody and context selection: a procedural approach. In: Barth-Weingarten, D., Dehé, N., Wichmann, A. (eds.) Where Prosody Meets Pragmatics, pp. 129–142. Emerald (2009)
8. Huijbregts, M.: Segmentation, diarization and speech transcription: surprise data unraveled. Ph.D. thesis, University of Twente (2008)
9. Hunyadi, L.: Multimodal human-computer interaction technologies. Theoretical modeling and application in speech processing. Argumentum **7**, 240–260 (2011)
10. Hunyadi, L., Váradi, T., Szekrényes, I.: Language technology tools and resources for the analysis of multimodal communication. In: Proceedings of LT4DH, pp. 117–124. University of Tübingen, Tübingen (2016)
11. Kovács, G., Grósz, T., Váradi, T.: Topical unit classification using deep neural nets and probabilistic sampling. In: Proceedings of CogInfoCom, pp. 199–204 (2016)
12. Lawrence, S., Burns, I., Back, A., Tsoi, A.C., Giles, C.L.: Neural network classification and prior class probabilities. In: Orr, G.B., Müller, K.-R. (eds.) Neural Networks: Tricks of the Trade. LNCS, vol. 1524, pp. 299–313. Springer, Heidelberg (1998). doi:10.1007/3-540-49430-8_15
13. Maas, A.L., Hannun, A.Y., Ng, A.Y.: Rectifier nonlinearities improve neural network acoustic models. In: Proceedings of ICML, vol. 30 (2013)
14. Mertens, P.: The prosogram: semi-automatic transcription of prosody based on a tonal perception model. In: Proceedings of Speech Prosody (2004)
15. Mushin, I., Stirling, L., Fletcher, J., Wales, R.: Identifying prosodic indicators of dialogue structure: some methodological and theoretical considerations. In: Proceedings of SIGdial, pp. 36–45. Association for Computational Linguistics (2000)
16. Nakajima, S., Allen, J.F.: A study on prosody and discourse structure in cooperative dialogues. Technical report, Rochester, NY, USA (1993)
17. Schuller, B., Steidl, S., Batliner, A., Burkhardt, F., Devillers, L., Müller, C., Narayanan, S.: Paralinguistics in speech and language-state-of-the-art and the challenge. Comput. Speech Lang. **27**(1), 4–39 (2013)
18. Szekrényes, I.: ProsoTool, a method for automatic annotation of fundamental frequency. In: Proceedings of CogInfoCom, pp. 291–296 (2015)
19. Tóth, L.: Phone recognition with deep sparse rectifier neural networks. In: Proceedings of ICASSP, pp. 6985–6989 (2013)
20. Tóth, L., Kocsor, A.: Training HMM/ANN hybrid speech recognizers by probabilistic sampling. In: Proceedings of ICANN, pp. 597–603 (2005)
21. Zellers, M.: Prosodic variation for topic shift and other functions in local contrasts in conversation. Phonetica **69**(4), 231–253 (2013)

Clustering Target Speaker on a Set of Telephone Dialogs

Andrey Shulipa[1]([✉]), Aleksey Sholohov[1], and Yuri Matveev[1,2]

[1] ITMO University, Saint Petersburg, Russia
{shulipa,sholohov,matveev}@speechpro.com
[2] STC-innovations Ltd., Saint Petersburg, Russia
http://en.ifmo.ru/
http://speechpro.com/

Abstract. The ability of the speaker's voice model to reproduce detailed parameterization of individual speech features is an important property for its use in solving different biometric problems. In general case one of the main reasons of performance degradation in voice biometric systems is the voice variability that occurs when speaker's state (emotional, physiological, etc.) or channel conditions are changing. Therefore, accurate modeling of the intra-speaker voice variability leads to a more accurate voice model. This can be achieved by collecting multiple speech samples of the same speaker recorded in diverse conditions to create so-called multi-session model. We consider the case when speech data is represented by dialogues recorded in a single channel. This setup raises the problem of grouping the segments of a target speaker from the set of dialogues. We propose a clustering algorithm to solve this problem, which is based on the probabilistic linear discriminant analysis (PLDA). Our experiments demonstrate effectiveness of the proposed approach compared to solutions based on exhaustive search.

Keywords: Speaker recognition · Voice model · Clusterization

1 Introduction

Voice biometrics is an advanced biometric technology that is widely used in different areas, such as forensics [1,2], fraud detection [3] and secure financial transactions [4]. It can be also applied for structuring speech data by collecting the speech segments or utterances of the same speakers. This task is called target speaker clustering. It is important for speaker recognition on summed channel speech data and multi-session enrollment.

The target speaker clustering task mainly occurs in the speaker recognition field in cases of multi-session voice models implementation. It is also used in database storage optimization for systematization and structuring speech data. Different approaches of diarization and clustering are known to resolve this problem [5–7,16]. These approaches based on joint factor analysis (JFA) [8] demonstrate high performance in speaker labeling of the speech data. In recent years

© Springer International Publishing AG 2017
A. Karpov et al. (Eds.): SPECOM 2017, LNAI 10458, pp. 244–252, 2017.
DOI: 10.1007/978-3-319-66429-3_23

i-vector representation of the voice models has dominated in the speaker recognition technology [9,10,17]. Probabilistic linear discriminant analysis (PLDA) is a probabilistic extension of linear discriminant analysis (LDA) and is closely related to JFA [10,11,18,19]. PLDA performed on the i-vectors yields state-of-the-art speaker recognition results and provides a probabilistic interpretation. Results obtained in [12] confirm the effectiveness of this approach for clustering the target speaker involved in multiple summed channel enrolling conversations. Authors of this study applied a probability perspective to specify log likelihood as an objective function, which allows to define a combination of i-vectors belonging to the target speaker. As shown in [12], the best results of clustering in terms of the low error rate are obtained due to using the log likelihood objective functions. The application of this approach leads to the best clustering results but requires considerable computational costs. Since one correct combination needs to be found among all possible combinations (in case of dialogs, 2^R combinations, R - number of conversations).

In this study we investigate the target speaker clustering problem under conditions similar to those ones described in [12]. We consider the set of dialogue conversations in the telephone channel as an input speech data. The speech segments of the target speaker have to be found among non-target ones and combined in the cluster. It is assumed that all non target speakers in the set of conversations for multi-session enrollment are different. In this paper, we develop the PLDA clustering approach presented in [12]. Instead of searching through all combinations, we propose an iterative decision procedure that allows to define the labels of the target speaker speech segments without the performance loss and excessive computational costs.

The clustering algorithm proposed in this paper is generative and has the following properties:

- It doesn't use mutual comparisons between speech segments, that is why there is no need in knowledge about the threshold parameters.
- The probabilistic model takes into account a priori information about the structure of a given speech data, which allows to produce the decision much easier.

The paper is organized as follows. In Sect. 2 we give a general information about i-vector representation of the speech utterances and PLDA modeling. The description of the problem formulation, a reference approach and the proposed decision procedure for the target speaker clustering task are presented in Sect. 3. Section 4 describes experimental setup and results. Finally, we give the conclusion in Sect. 5.

2 Preliminary Information

In this section, a brief overview of the i-vector PLDA framework utilized in our investigation is given.

2.1   The I-vector Presentation

The i-vector is an effective representation of speech utterances which includes voice biometric characteristics of a speaker and inter session variability. It is supposed that a GMM supervector $\boldsymbol{\mu}$ (stacked means of the Gaussian mixture model), corresponding to an utterance is modeled as:

$$\boldsymbol{\mu} = \bar{\boldsymbol{\mu}} + \mathbf{T}\boldsymbol{\omega} \tag{1}$$

where $\boldsymbol{\omega}$ is a random vector called as an i-vector that follows standard normal distribution, $\mathbf{T}$ is a basis for the total variability space of a much lower dimension (typically 400–600) than the supervector space, $\bar{\boldsymbol{\mu}}$ is a Universal Background Model (UBM) supervector.

2.2   PLDA Modeling

In recent years, the PLDA is successfully used in speaker recognition to specify a generative model of the i-vector presentation. Accordingly, the PLDA it is assumed that an i-vector can be modeled as:

$$\mathbf{x} = \mathbf{m} + \mathbf{V}\mathbf{y} + \boldsymbol{\epsilon} \tag{2}$$

where $\mathbf{m}$ is a mean of i-vectors, $\mathbf{y}$ denotes speaker dependent latent variable with standard normal prior and residual noise $\boldsymbol{\epsilon}$ is normally distributed with a zero mean and precision $\boldsymbol{\Lambda}$. The expectation-maximization (EM) algorithm is used to estimate the parameters of the PLDA model $(\mathbf{V}, \boldsymbol{\Lambda})$ as presented in [11]. The trained PLDA model on the development set can be used for speaker recognition or speaker clustering. The use of marginal log likelihood given by the PLDA model allows to obtain the decision of the clustering problem in terms of maximum probability.

3   Target Speaker Clustering

3.1   Problem Formulation

In this study it is assumed that the collection of enrolling conversations for target speakers has a certain structure. Each conversation from the set contains speech of the target and non-target speaker. All non target speakers are different between these conversations. To obtain speaker-dependent speech segments the conversations are processed by the speaker diarization system. Then these segments are transformed into i-vectors which are used in the target speaker clustering procedure. For a collection of N enrolling conversations the corresponding D dimensional i-vectors can be denoted by $\mathbf{X} = \{\mathbf{x}_{n,k} \in \mathbb{R}^D, n = 1..N, k = 1..2\}$. Where k is the index that enumerates i-vectors $\mathbf{x}_{n,k}$ belonging to the speech segments on the n-th conversation. To resolve the problem it is required to find the binary sequence $\mathbf{z} = \{z_1, z_2, ..., z_N\} \in \{0,1\}^N$ which defines the speech segments of the target speaker on the set of the enrolling conversations. If the target speaker is found on the speech segment $\mathbf{x}_{n,1}$ then the binary index $z_n = 0$ otherwise $z_n = 1$.

3.2 Reference Approach

We consider the reference approach presented in [12]. This approach is based on the probabilistic perspective that uses the PLDA generative model and demonstrates the best results in the target speaker clustering. The methods proposed in [12] use two objective functions to find the binary sequence $\mathbf{z}$ that indexes speech segments of the target speaker. The optimal solution $\hat{\mathbf{z}}$ is found by maximizing an objective function with respect to all possible binary sequences:

$$\hat{\mathbf{z}} = \arg \max_{\mathbf{z}} F(\mathbf{z}, \mathbf{X}) \tag{3}$$

The first method based on the log likelihood takes into account only i-vectors of the same speaker and can be calculated as presented in [10]. In this case, the objective function has a following form:

$$F_{like}(\mathbf{z}, \mathbf{X}|M) = \int \prod_{n=1}^{N} P(\mathbf{x}_{n,z_n}|\mathbf{y}) P(\mathbf{y}) d\mathbf{y} \tag{4}$$

where M is a PLDA model, $\mathbf{z}$ is an N dimensional binary sequence, $\mathbf{X}$ is a set of i-vectors.

The second method is related to the previous one but additionally considers non-target speaker speech segments in the objective function. It allows to use information about all speech segments belonging both the target and non-target speakers. So Eq. (4) can be modified as follows:

$$F_{\overline{like}}(\mathbf{z}, \mathbf{X}|M) = F_{like} + \int \prod_{n=1}^{N} P(\mathbf{x}_{n,\bar{z}_n}|\mathbf{y}_n) P(\mathbf{y}_n) d\mathbf{y}_n \tag{5}$$

where $\bar{\mathbf{z}}$ is an N dimensional binary sequence to choose i-vectors of the non-target speakers from the input set $\mathbf{X}$. It is clearly that $\mathbf{z}$ and $\bar{\mathbf{z}}$ binary sequences satisfy the following condition $z_n \oplus \bar{z}_n = 1$, $n = 1...N$, $\oplus$ is an exclusive OR operator. Conditional probabilities and prior distributions in Eqs. (4) and (5) are defined according to the PLDA model as follows:

$$\mathbf{x}|\mathbf{y} \sim \mathcal{N}(\mathbf{x}|\mathbf{m} + \mathbf{V}\mathbf{y}, \mathbf{\Lambda}), \quad \mathbf{y} \sim \mathcal{N}(\mathbf{y}|\mathbf{0}, \mathbf{I}) \tag{6}$$

3.3 Proposed Scheme

In our investigation we propose the solution of the target speaker clustering problem based on i-vector representation and PLDA modeling. Unlike [12] we do not perform exhaustive search on all possible binary sequences. We propose an iterative procedure that gives an approximate solution for the problem by using the variational Bayes approach [13].

The experimental set consists of conversations which include speech segments of two speakers. There are both target and non-target speakers in all conversations. Given a recording n, a binary index of the target speaker z_n and two

i-vectors $\mathbf{x}_{n,1}$ $\mathbf{x}_{n,2}$ of speech segments belonging to the speakers, the joint density using PLDA modeling can be written as:

$$P(\mathbf{X}, \mathbf{y}, \mathbf{y}_1 ... \mathbf{y}_n, \mathbf{z}) = \prod_{n=1}^{N} [P(\mathbf{x}_{n,1}|\mathbf{y}_n)P(\mathbf{x}_{n,2}|\mathbf{y}))]^{z_n} [P(\mathbf{x}_{n,2}|\mathbf{y})P(\mathbf{x}_{n,1}|\mathbf{y}_n))]^{1-z_n}$$
$$\times P(\mathbf{y}_n)P(\mathbf{y})P(z_n)$$

$$(7)$$

where the speaker dependent factors of the target and non-target speakers are denoted by $\mathbf{y}$ and $\mathbf{y}_n$ respectively. A prior distribution for z_n is a Bernoulli distribution that has a form $z \sim \pi^z (1-\pi)^{1-z}$. We supposed $\pi = 0.5$, since prior probabilities of the target speaker on two speech segments are equal to each other. In order to reduce an excessive number of unknown variables and simplify the calculations, the non-target speaker factors $\mathbf{y}_n$ can be omitted from Eq. (7) by using marginalization. Thus, we obtain a new form of the probabilistic model that can be presented as follows:

$$P_n(\mathbf{X}, \mathbf{y}, \mathbf{z}) = \prod_{n=1}^{N} [P(\mathbf{x}_{n,1})P(\mathbf{x}_{n,2}|\mathbf{y})]^{z_n} [P(\mathbf{x}_{n,1}|\mathbf{y})P(\mathbf{x}_{n,2})]^{1-z_n}$$
$$\times P(\mathbf{y})P(z_n)$$

$$(8)$$

where the marginal probability density function of $\mathbf{x}$ is obtained from the Gaussian distribution $\mathbf{x} \sim \mathcal{N}(\mathbf{x}|\mathbf{m}, \mathbf{V}\mathbf{V}^{\mathbf{T}} + \mathbf{\Lambda}^{-1})$. Graphical representation of the probabilistic conditional dependencies for our clustering model before and after marginalization is shown in Fig. 1.

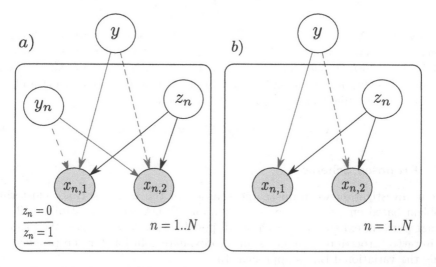

Fig. 1. Probabilistic graphical models for our clustering model: (a) complete latent variables presentation, (b) after marginalization on the local speaker factors

It is computationally intractable to evaluate the latent variables $\mathbf{y}$ and z_n using the maximum likelihood condition. We used variational Bayes estimation to estimate parameters of the posterior distributions of the latent variables $\mathbf{y}$ and z_n. It can be done on the set of observed variables $\mathbf{x}_{n,1}$ and $\mathbf{x}_{n,2}$ by maximizing a lower bound [13] instead of the marginal likelihood. In a general case the marginal likelihood $P(\mathbf{X})$ and a lower bound $\mathcal{L}$ on visible $\mathbf{X}$ and latent ψ variables satisfy inequality:

$$\ln P(\mathbf{X}) \geq \mathcal{L} = \mathbb{E}_{q(\psi)}[\ln P(\mathbf{X}, \psi)/q(\psi)] \tag{9}$$

where $q(\psi)$ - approximating distribution defined on ψ. If $q(\psi)$ exactly coincides with posterior distribution $p(\psi|\mathbf{X})$ then the inequality (9) becomes an equality as shown in [13]. We need to find the approximating distribution $q(\mathbf{y}, \mathbf{z})$ that satisfies condition $\arg\max_{q(\mathbf{y},\mathbf{z})} \mathcal{L}(q(\mathbf{y}, \mathbf{z}))$. In our case, $\mathcal{L}$ is a lower bound that can be expressed as:

$$\mathcal{L} = \mathbb{E}_{q(\mathbf{y},\mathbf{z})}\left[\sum_{n=1}^{N} \log P(\mathbf{x}_{n,1}, \mathbf{x}_{n,2}, \mathbf{y}, z_n)\right] - \mathbb{E}_{q(\mathbf{y},\mathbf{z})}[q(\mathbf{y}, \mathbf{z})] \tag{10}$$

We assume a distribution for $q(\mathbf{y}, \mathbf{z})$ to be factorized over all hidden variables $q(\mathbf{y}, \mathbf{z}) = q(\mathbf{y}) \prod_{n=1}^{N} q(z_n)$. It allows to suppose that posterior and prior distributions have an identical form: $q(\mathbf{y}) = \mathcal{N}(\mathbf{y}|\mathbf{m}_\mathbf{y}, \Lambda_\mathbf{y})$ and $q(z_n) = \theta_n^{z_n}(1 - \theta_n)^{1-z_n}$. The $q(.)$ that maximize the low bound (10) are:

$$\log q(\mathbf{y}) = \mathbb{E}_{q(\mathbf{z})}\left[\sum_{n=1}^{N} \log P(\mathbf{x}_{n,1}, \mathbf{x}_{n,2}, \mathbf{y}, z_n)\right] + const$$

$$\log q(\mathbf{z}) = \mathbb{E}_{q(\mathbf{y})}\left[\sum_{n=1}^{N} \log P(\mathbf{x}_{n,1}, \mathbf{x}_{n,2}, \mathbf{y}, z_n)\right] + const \tag{11}$$

By taking into account $\mathbf{x}'_{n,1(2)} = \mathbf{x}_{n,1(2)} - \mathbf{m}$ and $\Lambda_y = N\mathbf{V}^T\Lambda\mathbf{V} + \mathbf{I}$, the update equations we obtain using variational inference are provided as follows:

$$\mathbf{m}_\mathbf{y} = \Lambda_\mathbf{y}^{-1}\mathbf{V}^\mathbf{T}\Lambda \sum_{n=1}^{N} ([1 - \theta_n]\mathbf{x}'_{n,1} + \theta_n\mathbf{x}'_{n,2})$$

$$\alpha_n = \log(P(\mathbf{x}_{n,1})P(\mathbf{x}_{n,2}|\mathbf{y})) - \log(P(\mathbf{x}_{n,2})P(\mathbf{x}_{n,1}|\mathbf{y})), \quad n = 1...N \tag{12}$$

$$\langle z_n \rangle = \frac{1}{1 + \exp(-\alpha_n)}$$

Finally, elements of a $\mathbf{z}$ binary sequence can be sampled from the Bernoulli distribution as $z_n \sim \theta_n^{z_n}(1 - \theta_n)^{1-z_n}$, where $\theta_n = \langle z_n \rangle$.

4   Experimental Setup

4.1   System Configuration

In our experiments we used the clustering system based on a text independent speaker recognition system that represents utterances as i-vectors in a low dimension space. To extract features from the speech signal we used 20 ms analysis windows with a 10 ms shifting step by calculating 13 MFCC parameters. Then we combined the parameters with their first and second derivatives to form a 39-dimensional feature vector. Voice activity detection is performed by using speech energy based on the algorithm as described in [14]. Finally, a gender independent UBM of 2048 components was applied. The UBM was trained on the NIST SRE-2004, 2005, 2006, Switchboard II and Switchboard Cellular 1, 2 databases. In this paper, we used a gender-independent 600-dimensional i-vector space which was trained on the same data as the UBM. Modeling of i-vectors distribution was performed by using PLDA. We trained the parameters of the PLDA model by the maximum likelihood criteria. We used two gender-dependent PLDA models and a gender-independent PLDA model that were trained on the telephone speech data in English. The number of speakers for training the gender-dependent PLDA models was 1616 and 2269 for male and female, respectively. The dimension of the latent space was set to 500 in these PLDA models.

4.2 Evaluation Database

We experimented with the speech database provided by the National Institute of Standard and Technology (NIST). All evaluation speech data in our experiments were from telephone conversations in English. To evaluate the performance of our clustering system we conducted experiments using the data drawn from the 8conv training condition of the NIST SRE 2010. There are eight two-channel telephone conversations involving the target speaker on their sides [15] in this training condition. The total duration of the each conversation is approximately five minutes. The number of the target speakers to be clustered is 115 and 152 for male and female, respectively.

4.3 Results

We investigated approaches for the target speaker clustering based on PLDA. In this section, we compare performance of the proposed clustering procedure with approaches using objective functions that are described in Sect. 3.2. To estimate clustering performance we counted the false clustered speech segments of the target speaker. The evaluation set contained 115 * 8 and 152 * 8 male and female speech segments. Since we focused on the clustering problem, we considered two channel speech data to avoid using the speaker diarization. The next focus of our investigation is the mismatched environment conditions between the train and test data. It occurs in realistic scenarios when we do not have a prior information about the test conditions. In our experiments, we investigated the dependence of the clustering performance on gender conditions of PLDA training and target speaker clustering.

The results of our experiments are presented in Table 1. As can be seen from the table, the proposed approach demonstrates similar performance for matched training and testing conditions.

Table 1. Counts of false clustered speech segments under different approaches

Gender condition	F_{like}	$F_{\overline{like}}$	Proposed
Male PLDA			
Male	2	1	1
Female	208	6	132
Female PLDA			
Male	71	0	12
Female	15	3	11
Mix PLDA			
Male	5	1	2
Female	8	3	11

In the case of mismatched conditions the performance may degrade significantly (especially male PLDA training and female clustering). It should be noted that approach based on the $F_{\overline{like}}$ objective function demonstrates the best results but requires more computations than the proposed procedure. It can be noted that the gender independent PLDA model (mixPLDA) is the most preferable among other ones when it is not known a priori knowledge about gender in the test.

It is interesting that applicability of our algorithm can be extended to polylogue conversations. In this case instead of the Bernoulli distribution it is necessary to apply a multinomial distribution $\mathbf{z_n} \sim \prod_{n=1}^{N} \theta_{n,k}^{z_{n,k}}$, where $\mathbf{z_n}$ is a K dimensional binary random variable in which a particular element is equal to 1 and all other elements are equal to 0, K is a number of speakers on the n-th polylogue.

5 Conclusion

In this paper we present the target speaker clustering method based on PLDA. We compare our clustering procedure with existing approaches which use two kinds of the objective functions. The objective functions are based on likelihoods that can be obtained from the PLDA model. Experimental results demonstrate effectiveness of our approach in clustering performance and reducing computational cost.

Acknowledgements. This work was financially supported by the Ministry of Education and Science of the Russian Federation, Contract 14.578.21.0126 (ID RFMEFI57815X0126).

References

1. Jain, A.K., Ross, A., Prabhakar, S.: An Introduction to biometric recognition. IEEE Trans. Circuits Syst. Video Technol. **14**(1), 4–20 (2004)
2. Batchelor, J., Lee, D., Banks, D., Crosby, D., Moore, K., Kuhn, S., Rodriguez, T., Stephens, A.: Investigative Report. Florida Department of Law Enforcement (2012)
3. Averbouch, D., Kahn, J.: Fraud targets the contact center: What now? Speech Technology Magazine, November 2013
4. SESTEK, the rise of voice biometrics as a key security solution. Speech Technology Magazine (2013)
5. Kenny, P., Reynolds, D., Castaldo, F.: Diarization of telephone conversations using factor analysis. Sel. Top. Sign. Process. **4**(6), 1059–1070 (2010)
6. Kenny, P.: Bayesian analysis of speaker diarization with eigenvoice priors. CRIM, Montreal, Technical report (2008)
7. Zheng, R., Zhang, C., Zhang, S., Xu, B.: Variational bayes based i-vector for speaker diarization of telephone conversations. In: IEEE International Conference Acoustics, Speech and Signal Processing (2014)
8. Kenny, P.: Joint factor analysis of speaker and session variability: Theory and algorithms. Technical report CRIM-06/08-13 (2005). http://www.crim.ca/perso/patrick.kenny
9. Dehak, N., Kenny, P., Dehak, R., Dumouchel, P., Ouellet, P.: Front-end factor analysis for speaker verification. IEEE Trans. Audio Speech Lang. Process. **19**(4), 788–798 (2011)
10. Kenny, P.: Bayesian speaker verification with heavy tailed priors. In: Speaker and Language Recognition Workshop. IEEE, Odyssey (2010)
11. Prince, S.J., Elder, J.H.: Probabilistic linear discriminant analysis for inferences about identity. In: Proceeding of ICCV, pp. 1–8. IEEE (2007)
12. Zhang, S., Zhang, C., Zheng, R., Xu, B.: An investigation of summed-channel speaker recognition with multi-session enrollment. In: International Conference on Acoustics, Speech and Signal Processing (ICASSP), pp. 1640–1644 (2014)
13. Bishop, C.M.: Pattern Recognition and Machine Learning. Springer, New York (2006)
14. Kozlov, A., et al.: SVID speaker recognition system for NIST SRE 2012. In: Speech and Computer: 15th International Conference (SPECOM), pp. 278–285 (2013)
15. NIST SRE 2010 Evaluation Plan. http://www.itl.nist.gov/iad/mig//tests/sre/2010/NIST_SRE10_evalplan.r6.pdf
16. Sholokhov, A., Pekhovsky, T., Kudashev, O., Shulipa, A., Kinnunen, T.: Bayesian analysis of similarity matrices for speaker diarization. In: International Conference on Acoustics, Speech and Signal Processing (ICASSP), pp. 106–110 (2014)
17. Novoselov, S., Pekhovsky, T., Simonchik, K., Shulipa, A.: RBM-PLDA subsystem for the NIST i-vector challenge. In: Annual Conference of the International Speech Communication Association, pp. 378–382 (2014)
18. Novoselov, S., Pekhovsky, T., Shulipa, A., Kudashev, O.: Plda-based system for text-prompted password speaker verification. In: International Conference on Advance Video- and Signal-based Surveillance (AVSS), pp. 1–5 (2015)
19. Pekhovsky, T., Sizov, A.: Comparison of various mixtures of Gaussian PLDA-models in the problem of text-independent speaker verification. J. Instrum. Eng. **56**(2), 51–61 (2013)

Cognitive Entropy in the Perceptual-Auditory Evaluation of Emotional Modal States of Foreign Language Communication Partner

Rodmonga Potapova[1](✉) and Vsevolod Potapov[2]

[1] Institute of Applied and Mathematical Linguistics,
Moscow State Linguistic University, Ostzhenka 38, Moscow 119034, Russia
rkpotapova@yandex.ru
[2] Faculty of Philology, Lomonosov Moscow State University,
GSP-1, Leninskie Gory, Moscow 119991, Russia
volikpotapov@gmail.com

Abstract. The paper deals with the phenomenon of perceptual-auditory divergence in the evaluation of the foreign language communication partner's emotional-modal state. The problem of "human – human" interaction (vice versa "man – machine") is characterized by a very complex phenomenon associated with the communication "native language – foreign language" taking into account the idiosyncrasy of speech production and speech perception. The idiosyncrasy can be determined from the positions of the individual mixing of various types of below-specified information (e.g., biological, psychological, social, cognitive, etc.). All these factors affect the process of recognizing the communication partner's emotional-modal state. Therefore, one can assume that the idiosyncratic features of the perceiver (in this case, the listener) affect, in turn, the evaluation of the emotional-modal state, primarily that of a foreign language communication partner. In our pilot study special emphasis is laid on this problem considered on the basis of Russian-German and German-Russian matches. The obtained data suggest a new model of perceptual-auditory processing of verbal stimuli including such components as perceptual-auditory idiosyncrasy and auditory-perceptual cognitive entropy.

Keywords: Emotional-modal state · Divergence · Foreign language incentive · Perceptual-auditory evaluation · Spoken language communication · Iidiosyncrasy · Cognitive entropy

1 Introduction

In the communication process it is important not only to understand the communication partner's verbal content, but (to a greater degree) also to recognize their emotional-modal state. An additional difficulty is found in searching a solution of a similar problem in the case of communication with foreign language and foreign-culture partner. The complexity of solving this problem is escalated in distant mediated communication (for example, mobile communications, social-network communication on the Internet, Voice over IP (VoIP), Skype, WhatsApp, Viber, Google Hangouts, etc.).

© Springer International Publishing AG 2017
A. Karpov et al. (Eds.): SPECOM 2017, LNAI 10458, pp. 253–261, 2017.
DOI: 10.1007/978-3-319-66429-3_24

In the course of the study a hypothesis was formulated that in the communication act not only the principle of speech signal generation idiosyncrasy (stimulus) is implemented, but also the principle of signal auditory perception (reaction) idiosyncrasy.

2 Theoretical Background of the Research

It is known that a common unified theory of emotions does not exist. In particular, P.V. Simonov's need-information theory is widespread [22: 320–328]. According to this theory, the emergence of emotions is determined by certain needs and evaluation of the possibility to satisfy and meet these needs, which are formally expressed as follows:

$$\pm E = f[-N(I_r - I_a)],$$

where E is the emotion intensity and its sign; N is needs degree; $I_r - I_a$ is an evaluation of the possibility to satisfy this need considering of the available experience; I_r is information of the means objectively required to satisfy the need; I_a is information of the means available to a person.

According to this theory, if there is an excess of information on the possibility to satisfy the need, then a positive emotion emerges; if there is a lack of information, then a negative emotion is produced. It is believed that the variety of emotions is determined by the variety of needs. This view coincides with the concept of deprivation [4], which is developing successfully nowadays and provides the possibility to "outreach" the solution of problems found in studying the nature of destructive actions, aggression and terror reflected on a significant scale in the information and communication media (e.g., in the social-network discourse) [21].

The classification is based on binary principle: every key set includes some subsets (e.g. situational subsets). Division may be, for example, into primary and situational subsets. Primary subsets include unsatisfied needs correlated with search of the target object. Situational emotions emerge as a result of evaluations made for steps of behavior and encourage either action in the same direction or modification of the behavior [24, 25]. Emotions are also divided by the nature of actions including overcoming, protection, and attack [23]. Emotions can be the result of two or more overlapping emotions.

To describe emotions W. Wundt [26] identified three features:

- Hedonic tone or emotion sign (positive–negative),
- Readiness for action (relaxation–tension),
- Activation level (tranquility–excitement).

H. Schlossberg developed Wundt's theory and introduced a feature including the opposition "acceptance-rejection" [5: 40].

In addition to the above approaches to the analysis of emotions worthy of mention is the concept that takes into account the ratio of an emotion and an event. In this case, anticipatory (before the event associated with the achievement/failure to reach the target) and summative (after the event associated with the achievement/failure to reach the target) emotions are distinguished. A significant factor is the orientation of emotions: to or away from oneself. The primary function of emotions is the body mobilization for rapid reaction to the situation in most appropriate manner [3].

The above points of view relate primarily to interpretation of the concept of "emotion". As for the emotional-modal state, the linguistic literature considers three aspects of modality: subjective, objective and secondary [8]. The subjective modality includes evaluative attitude of the speaker to the degree of cognition of these objective relations [6]: for example, doubt, certainty/uncertainty, presupposability. In other words, the subjective modality is understood as the modality of credibility degree.

Thus, the subjective modality expresses the speaker's attitude to the verbal and non-verbal behavior of the percipient: emotional-expressive attitude, self-evaluation, evaluation derived from features of the content, etc. (e.g., confidence, diffidence, belief, presupposability, etc.).

As in the classification of emotions, all emotional-modal states (EMSs) are distributed in the following basic types: positive/negative; subjective/objective; primary/secondary; single-factor (uniform)/multifactor (mixed); strong/weak.

In our opinion, for any EMS classification, first of all, an evaluative criterion is common: evaluative; communicative-evaluative; situationally evaluative; socio-evaluative; ethnocultural-evaluative one.

3 Auditory Idiosyncratic Classification Features

Speech features that characterize the speaker and their psychophysiological features (idiosyncratic features) contain, as a rule, various types of information: verbal content (information-communicative content of the message); paraverbal content (pronunciation features of speech production "woven" into the prosodic and spectral-temporal substance of sound matter of any utterance); non-verbal content (facial expressions, gestures, proxemics, etc.); extraverbal content (gender, age, place of birth, places of long-term residence, upbringing, education, social status, situation, hairstyle, clothes, etc.).

The following classification of idiosyncratic information contained in the speech signal is proposed [1, 2, 7, 9, 10, 14, 15, 19]:

- Biological: anatomical, physiological, physical, psycho-emotional, psychomental, gender, age, sexual-genetic.
- Psychological: mental characteristic of the person as a single integrated functional system of behavior and activity regulation (consciousness, attention, memory).
- Sociobiological: sociobehavioral (signs indicating belonging to a certain group of people (for example, ethnic, cultural, regional and social one)).
- Socio-humanitarian: evolutionary-genetic, ethnic, interethnic, cultural-historical, general psychological, differential-psychological, psychogenetic.
- Multifactor: intellectual, verbal, cognitive, factor-analytical.

In describing the speaker's "profile" by voice and speech (i.e., for example, individual attributes in forensics), three types of norms are distinguished: universal, group and idiosyncratic ones. The special role belongs to the voice information decoded at the level of auditory perception as follows [13, 14, 16, 17]:

- description that relates to the speaker's profile and their place in the perceiver's real existence;
- associative correlation with the speaker's name;
- speaker's psychophysical, psychophysiological and psychopathological forms (general constitution, face, gestures, manner of walking, etc.);
- speaker's voice, manner of phonation, articulation, coarticulation with regard to speech manner ("trophotropica" – "ergotropica") determined by distinct (acoustic, perceptual) features.

Speech features of the speaker are divided into controlled (external) and uncontrolled (internal) ones. Some experts mention potentially controlled features. The degree of control depends on two factors:

- speaker's ability to use auditory and proprioceptive feedback forms in the process of articulation program implementation;
- speaker's perceptual ability to use auditory forms of information to detect sound differences [2, 7].

Both of the above factors are part of the "control skills" concept. Factors beyond any control are conditioned by speaker's organic-genetic features: the structure of the speech apparatus including the length of the vocal tract, sizes of their tongue, soft palate, throat, jaw and mouth cavity; form (configuration) of the laryngeal tract and nasal cavity. This also may include so-called structural defects (e.g., presence of cleft in the hard palate ("cleft palate"), missing teeth, etc.) [7].

Controlled factors are not related ("derived") with organic-genetic constraints and include changes in the voice dynamics and all potentially controllable muscle articulatory gestures that characterize the manipulation components of the voice quality.

Uncontrolled features are considered as permanent and at the same time non-permanent organic basis for the speaker's features based on their anatomy and physiology and correlated with the invariant-norm of the physical state characteristic for the speaker's voice features.

Permanence and non-permanence of uncontrolled features is related to the differentiation of long-term and short-term features (the principle of identifying short-term uncontrolled features is speech production with sore throat, after running, fast ascent up the stairs, etc.). The short-term features cannot include, for example, features of voice break (puberty). Both controlled and uncontrolled features can be grouped on the basis of intraspeaker and interspeaker similarities and differences [9, 14]. Information on the speaker is hidden in the speech signal that relates to their anatomical features and muscular voice samples stored at the neuronal level that correlate, for example, with the speaker's constitution.

In addition to these special features, the study of emotions and emotional-modal states by voice and speech is especially complex, in particular, the problem of their perceptual-auditory identification [12, 13, 16–19].

4 Method, Experimental Results

In the preliminary research devoted to the study of emotions involving various groups of subjects (actors, subjects in a state of hypnosis and subjects with manic-depressive disorders (**n = 540**)), it was concluded that a fundamental distinction between "emotion" and "emotional-modal state" is needed, which allows classification of peoples' emotive behavior considering the following [14]:

- basic, so-called primal unconscious emotions (e.g., anger, rage and fear/fear as unconscious or conscious reaction of neurons to stimuli of any kind, in particular, to danger (with active and passive (stupor) forms)/horror, joy, admiration);
- unconscious and conscious reactions to stimuli forming complex social emotional and cognitive systems correlated with the concept of "feeling" (e.g., love, hate, happiness, etc.);
- complementary emotional-modal states, reflecting a subjective self-estimate of a person, their communication partner, the current situation, reality, etc. (e.g., confidence, diffidence, doubt, indifference, contentment, compassion, credulity, depression, hopelessness, anxiety, dissatisfaction, satisfaction, disgust, contempt, shame, resentment, malice, etc.) [17–21].

This concept provides a comprehensive description and analysis of the multifaceted role that speech parameters play regarding basic (so-called primal) emotions, the latter, social emotions (feelings) and concrete situated emotional-modal states [11].

The results of the longitudinal experiment conducted in Russia and Germany for ten years with the different authentic materials (TV Talk-Shows of Russia and Germany; volume of 227 h) and for three years with authentic Skype dialogues (volume of 120 h) provided for evaluation of emotionally charged Russian and German speech by listeners native Russian and native German speakers without visual imagery (studies with visual imageries have also been carried out) revealed that auditory perception of the same emotional-modal stimuli is evaluated by representatives of the above-mentioned cultural and verbal communities in different ways [15–17].

The data used in this paper derive from two sources. The first source of data comes from the investigation on the basis of Russian Television Talk-Shows and the second source of data was Russian Skype dialogues. 120 native listeners of Russian (60 females, 60 males) were selected from the student population of Moscow State Linguistic University (Russia) and 120 native listeners of German (60 females, 60 males) from University Halle-Wittenberg (Germany) were used for this experiment.

The discursive presentation of focusing on different emotional-modal states regarding speech communication in Russian dialogues and polylogues on the bases of Talk-Shows and later Skype communication gave possibility to define peculiarities of perceptual-auditory divergence regarding evaluation of the foreign language emotional-modal state interpretation.

The task of Russian and German experiment participants was to listen every speech fragment without visual channel, time limitation and to answer all questions of a special questionnaire. The data base of emotional-modal states included positive and negative lexemes (n = 55) (e.g. neutral, natural, wistful worry, depressed, disappointed, aggressive, joyful etc.)

Listeners were requested to analyse the audio fragments and instructed to determine prosodic features of speech samples (pitch, speech rate, timbre, dynamics).

It was found out that the auditory-perceptual evaluation of emotional-modal state of foreign-language and foreign-culture communicants by their speech features is significantly different from innate and genetically structured neuro-emotional mechanisms of perceptual-auditory evaluation of the emotional-modal behavior of native speakers. During the experiments we also were able to establish statistically reliable specifics of the German-Russian and Russian-German speech tactics and speech strategies used in the decision-making process to evaluate the emotional-modal state of foreign language and foreign-culture partners in communication.

The data of the perceptual-auditory analysis of recognition of emotions and emotional-modal states were subjected to the subsequent statistical processing using signed rank tests with two-sided alternative hypothesis H0 with a 5% significance value, as well as to two-factor analysis of variance, which allowed to obtain reliable and significant differences.

In the experiments on the perceptual auditory evaluation of the emotional-modal states of foreign-language and foreign-culture communicants special questionnaires were developed including such parameters as the melodic range with a certain gradation system; melodic register and its change stages; voice pitch; voice tone dynamics, tone with inclusion of a number of varied forms; dynamic and temporal features of speech production, etc.

Studying the same material with the inclusion of verbalics (parameters were separated as a special research provided knowledge of the languages) and non-verbalics (e.g. facial expressions, gestures, etc.) accompanying communication act.

Key findings related to the auditory evaluation of the verbal representations of foreign-language and foreign-culture communicants' EMSs can be reduced to the following.

The majority of German listeners perceive emotional-modal state of the Russian speech as "neutral" (66%), as "agitated" (27%) and as "aggressive" (7%); for speakers of Russian listeners it is typical to some extent to perceive emotional-modal state of German speaking communicants also as "neutral" (40%). Other emotional-modal states are evaluated with a high degree of variability. However, the same Russian speech stimuli-utterances evaluated by German listeners as "agitated" are, in most cases, perceived by Russian speaking subjects as "joyful" (27%). The evaluation "aggressive" falls into one connotative-emotional zone with the inclusion of other states, such as "agitated", "joyful", etc. (33%). The most significant is the presence of divergence in evaluating emotional-modal states "agitated" for German speaking subjects and "joyful" for Russian speakers [15].

All participants listeners (Russian and German native speakers) completed special questionnaires during the longitudinal experiment. Average results are presented in Fig. 1.

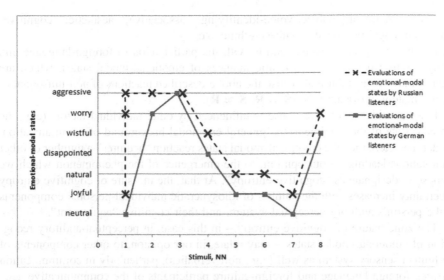

Fig. 1. Divergence in the perceptual auditory evaluation of emotional modal states of foreign language communication partners (data differ significantly (p – value <5%))

Comparing the prosodic means used by the listeners to evaluate emotional-modal states also revealed a number of divergent features:

- perceptual auditory evaluation by Russian listeners of emotional-modal states of German speaking subjects is based on evaluation of the perceived voice timbre (73%), melodic variation (20%) and temporal features (7%);
- perceptual auditory evaluation by German listeners of emotional-modal of Russian speaking subjects is based on the use of melodic features (60%), temporal features (20%), volume levels (13%), pausation features (7%).

5   Conclusion

The obtained results show primarily the functioning of the language categoriality mechanism with regard to foreign language stimulus auditory perception in the communication process that imposes specific restrictions on the interpretation of the results, in this case on the auditory analysis of foreign language spoken material.

Thus, idiosyncrasy on the example of spoken language communication can be of two types: not only at the level of speech production, as it is commonly believed, but also at the speech perception level. Regarding dialogic communication (in this case with regard to emotional-modal states reaction of the listener to spoken stimuli of the speaker due to the divergence process), reactions to stimuli can be of two main types: non-unisonant (S ≠ R) and approximately unisonant (S ≈ R). For foreign-language communicants the degree of non-unisonant perceptual auditory reactions increases.

It should be emphasized that perceptual-auditory idiosyncrasy, in our view, is compounded by the fact that it includes such components of the hearing, as physiological;

musical; emotional; subject-voice-identifying; associative; aesthetic; cognitive-individual; cognitive-social; cognitive-ethnic, etc.

During the speech communication with the participation of foreign-language and foreign-culture partners, idiosyncratic nuances of emotional-modal states, which are stimuli, may cause and usually cause the above-described reactions of non-unisonant or approximately unisonant type ($S \neq R$, $S \approx R$).

If we consider that the response is influenced by other individual factors (e.g., the physical state of the percipient, the general emotional background of communication, gender, age etc.), then the emotional-modal states reaction "acquires" a number of other connotations leading, in our opinion, to the emergence of the phenomenon which we propose to designate as "cognitive entropy". At that, the measure of cognitive entropy uncertainty increases with the number of idiosyncratic individual-personal components of the person's auditory perceptual-system, and their cognitive "equipment".

The zone nature of cognitive entropy – in this case, in perceptual-auditory recognition of emotional-modal states – may relate, in our opinion, to other components of the human sensory system as well (e.g., non-verbalics), particularly in communication between foreign-language and foreign-culture participants of the communicative act.

The next stage of this research will include: (a) perceptual visual, (b) perceptual visual and perceptual auditory evaluation and analysis of emotional-modal state of non-verbal stimuli by native and non-native subjects without analysis of verbal speech signals.

Cross-language comparison of these data sets will give us the opportunity to define facts of divergences between reactions on the same emotional-modal stimuli and the peculiarities of the cognitive entropy regarding cognitive reactions on the same stimuli by aural and visual channels for native and non-native subjects. The data obtained and expected to be obtained in the future stages of the research may prove useful for fine-tuning voice and multimodal biometric analysis systems with regard to different languages possessing of different predominant distinctive parameters correlating to emotional-modal states and speaker-specific features in real communication, including both language- and culture-dependent phenomena.

Acknowledgements. This research is supported by Russian Science Foundation, Project №14-18-01059.

References

1. Abercrombie, D.: Elements of General Phonetics. University Press, Edinburgh (1967)
2. Brown, R.: Auditory speaker recongition. In: Forum Phoneticum, Bd. 38. Helmut Buske Verlag, Hamburg (1987)
3. Ekman, P.: Basic emotions. In: Dalgleish, T., Power, M. (eds.) Handbook of Cognition and Emotion. John Wiley and Sons, Ltd., Sussex (1999)
4. Gurr, T.R.: Why Men Rebel. Princeton University Press, Princeton (1970)
5. Isard, C.E.: Human Emotions. Plenum Press, New York (1977)
6. Krivonosov, A.T.: Modal particle as a signal of subjective modal significance in the German spoken language. In: Structural Features of Spoken Language and Development of Conversational Skills, Irkutsk, pp. 132–147 (1964). (in Russian)
7. Laver, J.: Voice quality and indexical information. Br. J. Disord. Commun. 3, 43–54 (1968)

8. Lomtev, T.P.: Sentence and Its Grammatical Categories. MSU, Moscow (1972). (in Russian)
9. Potapova, R.K.: Subject-oriented perception of foreign language speech. Issues Linguist. **2**, 46–64 (2005). (in Russian)
10. Potapova, R.K.: Speech: Communication, Information, Cybernetics, 4th edn. Publ. House "Radio i svyaz'", Moscow (2010). (in Russian)
11. Potapova, R.: From deprivation to aggression: verbal and non-verbal social network communication. In: Materials of the VI International Conference "Global Science and Innovation", vol. I, Chicago, pp. 129–137, 18–19 November 2015
12. Potapova, R., Komalova, L.: Auditory-perceptual recognition of the emotional state of aggression. In: Ronzhin, A., Potapova, R., Fakotakis, N. (eds.) SPECOM 2015. LNCS (LNAI), vol. 9319, pp. 89–95. Springer, Cham (2015). doi:10.1007/978-3-319-23132-7_11
13. Potapova, R.K., Potapov, V.V.: Auditory Perception of Speech by Non-Native Speakers. The Phonetician, CL-78, pp. 6–12 (1998)
14. Potapova, R.K., Potapov, V.V.: Language, Speech, Personality. Yazyki slavyanskoj kul'tury, Moscow (2006). (in Russian)
15. Potapova, R.K., Potapov, V.V.: Perception of emotional behavior of foreign-language and foreign-culture communicants. In: Phonetics and Non-phonetics. On Sandro Kodzasov's 70th anniversary, pp. 602–617. Yazyki slavyanskikh kul'tur, Moscow (2008). (in Russian)
16. Potapova, R.K., Potapov, V.V.: Kommunikative Sprechtaetigkeit: Russland und Deutschland im Vergleich. Boehlau Verlag, Koeln (2011)
17. Potapova, R., Potapov, V.: Auditory and visual recognition of emotional behaviour of foreign language subjects (by native and non-native speakers). In: Železný, M., Habernal, I., Ronzhin, A. (eds.) SPECOM 2013. LNCS(LNAI), vol. 8113, pp. 62–69. Springer, Cham (2013). doi:10.1007/978-3-319-01931-4_9
18. Potapova, R., Potapov, V.: Associative mechanism of Foreign spoken language perception (forensic phonetic aspect). In: Ronzhin, A., Potapova, R., Delic, V. (eds.) SPECOM 2014. LNCS(LNAI), vol. 8773, pp. 113–122. Springer, Cham (2014). doi:10.1007/978-3-319-11581-8_14
19. Potapova, R., Potapov, V.: Cognitive mechanism of semantic content decoding of spoken discourse in noise. In: Ronzhin, A., Potapova, R., Fakotakis, N. (eds.) SPECOM 2015. LNCS(LNAI), vol. 9319, pp. 153–160. Springer, Cham (2015). doi:10.1007/978-3-319-23132-7_19
20. Potapova, R., Potapov, V.: On individual polyinformativity of speech and voice regarding speakers auditive attribution (forensic phonetic aspect). In: Ronzhin, A., Potapova, R., Németh, G. (eds.) SPECOM 2016. LNCS(LNAI), vol. 9811, pp. 507–514. Springer, Cham (2016). doi:10.1007/978-3-319-43958-7_61
21. Potapova, R., Potapov, V.: Polybasic attribution of social network discourse. In: Ronzhin, A., Potapova, R., Németh, G. (eds.) SPECOM 2016. LNCS(LNAI), vol. 9811, pp. 539–546. Springer, Cham (2016). doi:10.1007/978-3-319-43958-7_65
22. Simonov, P.V.: Brain mechanisms of emotions. J. High. Nerv. Activ. **47**(2), 320–328 (1997). (in Russian)
23. Simonov, P.V.: Emotional Brain. Nauka, Moscow (1981). (in Russian)
24. Vilyunas, V.K.: Psychology of Emotional Phenomena. MSU Publ. House, Moscow (1976). (in Russian)
25. Vilyunas, V.K.: Psychological Mechanisms of Person's Motivation. MSU Publ. House, Moscow (1990). (in Russian)
26. Wundt, W.: Grundriss der Psychologie. W. Engelman, Leipzig (1896)

Correlation Normalization of Syllables and Comparative Evaluation of Pronunciation Quality in Speech Rehabilitation

Evgeny Kostyuchenko[1]($\boxtimes$), Roman Meshcheryakov[1], Dariya Ignatieva[1],
Alexander Pyatkov[1], Evgeny Choynzonov[1,2], and Lidiya Balatskaya[1,2]

[1] Tomsk State University of Control Systems and Radioelectronics,
Lenina Street 40, 634050 Tomsk, Russia
key@keva.tusur.ru, mrv@tusur.ru
[2] Tomsk Cancer Research Institute, Kooperativniy Avenue 5, 634050 Tomsk, Russia
nii@oncology.tomsk.ru
http://www.tusur.ru
http://www.oncology.tomsk.ru/

Abstract. The paper considers the solution of aligning syllables in time problem. This kind of normalization allows to compare different implementations of the same syllable. This allows us to talk about a comparative evaluation of the syllables pronunciation quality in the event that one of the syllables is a reference implementation. If a patient's record before the operative treatment of oral cancer is used as such a syllable, a comparative assessment of the quality of pronunciation of syllables in the process of speech rehabilitation can be made. In the process of normalization, an approach aimed at maximizing the correlation between individual fragments of the syllable is applied. Then, as a measure of similarity between the reference and the estimated syllable, the correlation coefficient is used. The work demonstrates the validity of such a decision based on the processing of records from healthy people and patients before and after surgical treatment. The results of this work allow us to approach the implementation of an automated software system for assessing the quality of pronunciation of syllables and proceed to implement its working prototype.

Keywords: Time normalization · Correlation · Cancer of the oral cavity and oropharynx · Speech quality criteria

1 Introduction

This paper discuss the speech rehabilitation of patients after surgical treatment of cancer of the oral cavity and oropharynx. Process of rehabilitation can be accelerated using biological feedback, but this requires the automated estimation of pronunciation quality. The relevance of this problem is confirmed by the higher incidence of these diseases. In 2014 in Russia the incidence of cancer of the

© Springer International Publishing AG 2017
A. Karpov et al. (Eds.): SPECOM 2017, LNAI 10458, pp. 262–271, 2017.
DOI: 10.1007/978-3-319-66429-3_25

oral cavity and pharynx was 5.6 per 100 thousand (diagnostic of new affected). The prevalence (total count of affected) −36.5 per 100 thousand. Thus, each year near 13,000 new cancers with oropharyngeal localization are diagnosed in the country, and the total number of patients suffering from this disease is estimated at over 53,000 people [1,2]. The partial or complete surgical removal of the tongue or some other organs of speech production is one of the main problems in the treatment. After this patients have need in speech learning. But we should to estimate the quality of the patient's speech for solving of this problem. Current rehabilitation use only subjective evaluation of speech quality. In previous studies we have proposed a method based on the use of GOST R-50840-95 "Speech transmission over various communication channels. Techniques for measurements of speech quality, intelligibility and voice identification" [3]. In the [4], an objective approach to measurement of the syllables pronunciation quality was created. But for its implementation, syllables should be normalized by time. This paper presents solution of this problem, which is last step before creation of the first version of automated prototype for speech quality estimation during the process of speech rehabilitation.

2 Description of the Procedure for the Comparative Evaluation of the Syllables Pronunciation Quality

2.1 Algorithm of the Comparative Evaluation of the Syllables Pronunciation Quality

Let us consider the integrated sequence of actions at a comparative estimation of syllables pronunciation quality.

1. Working with the reference signal
   (a) Recording of the speech signal −3 syllables with problem phonemes, for 5 repetitions of each, then - according to the table of syllables with the phonemes most affected by the change, 90 phonemes by 1 utterance, totaling 105 syllables per session. A list of phonemes that are most affected by changes after tongue surgery ([s], [t], [k] and their soft implementations) was compiled based on early research stages detailed in [5]. It corresponds to the previously obtained classical results presented in [6].
   (b) Direct detection of pronounced syllables in the recorded signal. This stage in the software will have to be implemented in real time by stream processing of the incoming signal. This is necessary for the automatic presentation of the syllables to the patient for utterance. Syllables are presented on 2 channels: visual - the syllable is recorded using the notation of the Russian alphabet - and audial - the syllable is played back in the headphones to eliminate possible variations of utterances. The use of syllable transcription to solve this problem does not seem to be practical, since not all patients have the skills to correctly read it. The implementation of this stage is simplified due to the wellknown range of the duration of the spoken syllables and pauses, which helps to effectively eliminate possible

errors in the voice activity detector. Certainly, impossible use automated correction of errors related with possible inaccuracies or extraneous noise (for example, coughing), it is possible only to manually correct them by returning to the previous syllable. It is impossible to exclude a person from the execution of this stage and this does not allow us to speak about the complete automaticity of the approach (on the other hand, there is a sufficiently high degree of automation with control over the recorded information).

(c) Recording the detected syllables as separate files on the disk for subsequent processing. Additionally, a continuous audio file is also saved for identification and elimination of possible problems in the operation of the algorithm.

(d) Time normalization of three groups with identical syllables (three groups of five records). For normalization, the correlation approach is used, which detail is presented in Sect. 4 of this article.

(e) The correlation criterion of received realizations proximity is calculated. It is calculated as the average of the values of the linear correlation coefficient for each group. For 5 realizations of the syllable, 20 values of the correlation coefficient can be calculated (taking into account the specifics of the procedure for time normalization, it is not strictly symmetric, although the variation is small). This value is taken as the reference for further evaluation of the quality of phonemes.

(f) The allocation of problematic phonemes from the remaining records and steps (d) and (e) for the problem phonemes is carried out. This stage seems more problematic due to the need to detect the boundaries of phonemes and possible accumulation of errors at various stages of processing. The task is facilitated by the fact that it is precisely known which syllable was pronounced and which phoneme is to be allocated.

2. Working with the estimated signal
   (a) Steps (a)-(d) are performed, but already for the estimated signal, which is a record after the operation.

   (b) The correlation criterion of the proximity between previous syllable records and records after the operations is calculated. It is found as the average of the values of the linear correlation coefficient for each group of syllables. For 5 realizations of the syllable, 50 values of the correlation coefficient can be calculated ($2 \cdot 25$, it is not strictly symmetric, taking into account the specific procedure of the time normalization, although the variation is small). Then the ratio of this mean to the mean value found for the reference signals is calculated. The closer this value is to 1, the higher the quality of the pronunciation of the syllable is.

   (c) A similar procedure is performed for pairs of other syllables before and after the operation. The average correlation value between groups of syllables containing problematic phonemes and not containing them is considered. The ratio of these means is calculated. The closer this value is to 1, the higher the quality of the pronunciation of the syllable is.

(d) The allocation of problematic phonemes from the remaining records is carried out and stages (d) and (e) for the same problem phonemes are conducted. A similar comparison procedure is performed for various implementations of individual phonemes and a comparative criterion for the quality of phoneme pronunciation is determined.

The obtained estimates can be used independently or as part of a complex criterion of pronunciation quality as separate components along with others developed earlier [4].

2.2   Implemented Modules of the Algorithm

In previous research studies, variants for obtaining estimates of syllables pronunciation quality based on Fourier spectra [4,7] have been realized. In addition, the applicability of other characteristics such as linear prediction coefficients [8], mfcc [9], autocorrelation function [10] has been revealed. As algorithms for voice activity detection algorithms G.729 Voice Activity Detection [11], and [12] for the detection of individual syllables within the records obtained in the previous stages of using earlier version of the complex are used. The main drawback of this version is the high degree of user involvement and the subjectivity of the evaluations, which does not allow to speak about the possibility of its exploitation beyond the scope of research. However, its use has made it possible to compile a database of sound recordings that are used in this work.

In addition, based on the results of this work, prototypes (d)-(e) for the reference signal and (a)-(c) for the estimated signal are realized. Due to their implementation, the problem of the need for manual time-based normalization, which was used in the testing of the previous criteria [4], was partially solved. This allows us to talk about the possibility of developing prototype software for comparative assessments of the syllables pronunciation quality. On the other hand, there remains the possibility for its further fundamental improvement due to the allocation of individual phonemes and their separate comparison [13].

3   Approaches to Detecting of Speech Signals

Consider more detail used approaches to solving the problem of the detection of speech signals, to show which of the speech signal characteristics are already allocated and are used for further processing. The G.729 Voice Activity Detection algorithm uses the following characteristics:

1. A spectral distortion.
2. An energy difference.
3. A low-band energy difference.
4. A zero-crossing difference.

A detailed description of the algorithm can be found in [11].

The second algorithm is based on applying only two of these characteristics:

1. An energy difference
2. A zero-crossing difference

Detailed description of the algorithm can be found in [12].

Comparison of algorithms reveals that due to adaptation at work on long signals during stream processing the first algorithm makes it possible to receive the best results and it will be used in the final implementation. However, with the correct selection of parameters based on the results of testing for individual syllables (short recordings), the second algorithm makes it possible to achieve results that are at least not the worst. When using the G.729 Voice Activity Detection algorithm in the absence of significant areas of silence for adaptation (which is typical for the records of individual syllables), some problems were revealed, which manifested in the fact that almost the whole signal was marked as speech (including silence). This, in turn, led to problems with normalization by time. That is why the second algorithm was used to process the already existing records of individual syllables, which allowed achieving better results.

4   Time Normalization of the Speech Signal

For normalization by time, an approach based on maximizing the correlation between individual fragments of the signals was realized [14]. This algorithm can be represented as a step-by-step sequence as follows:

1. Bringing the first signal to the reference length t.
2. Select the number of subintervals for nomalization - n.
3. Search the end for the i-th subinterval of the second signal, providing the maximum correlation with the i-th fixed interval of the first signal.
4. Bringing the found i-th subinterval to the length of the i-th sub-interval of the first signal, adding it to the end of the final normalized second signal.
5. Repeat steps 3 and 4 for i = 1..n-1.
6. Bringing the last remaining n-th subinterval to the length of the n-th sub-interval of the first signal, adding it to the end of the final normalized second signal.

In the process of the implementation of the algorithm, the following values were used: the standard duration of the syllable is $t = 1$ second (has nothing to do with the actual duration, specifies the number of points in the normalized signals), the number of subintervals of the partition $n = 10$. A more detailed justification of these (or other) values choice and their impact on the result will be carried out in the future. At this moment, these values make it possible to obtain the values of pronunciation quality criteria, albeit not optimal in the accuracy of the normalization.

Examples of three normalized signals are presented in Fig. 1.

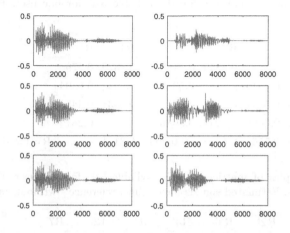

Fig. 1. Examples of three normalized signal pairs

5   Testing the Implemented Approach for the Comparative Evaluation of the Syllables Pronunciation Quality

5.1   Comparative Analysis for Healthy Speakers

The recording of syllables containing problematic phonemes with and without the use of the tongue was carried out by healthy speakers. This approach made it possible to obtain missing materials at this stage, since multiple record of the same syllable was not used in the previous stages of work. A single recording did not allow us to calculate the correlation for signal before the operation for comparison with correlation after surgery. At the first stage the proposed approach made it possible to obtain this estimate and draw conclusions about the applicability of such solution. The values of the correlation coefficient between time-normalized signals, and, to be more precise, their mean value acted as such criterion. In this case, attention should be paid to the fact that, unlike directly the correlation coefficient having the commutativity property, the proposed criterion does not possess this property, since the signal pairs normalized by the first and second signals, respectively, will differ from each other. In accordance with this, we obtain the matrix $n \times n$ without the main diagonal, filled with values of the correlation coefficients, where n is the number of reference signals. When evaluating the quality, we perform the same operation for the signal pairs with and without the use of language. The same thing again, swap the signals, we get 2 matrices $n \times m$, where m is the number of estimated signals. Examples of matrices for the syllable [sit] for one user are presented in Tables 1, 2 and 3, in 1 - pair reference - reference signals, in 2 - pair reference - estimated signals, in 3 - pair estimated - reference signals. Estimated signals have a line, reference - without. $m = n = 5$.

Table 1. Examples of matrices for the syllable [sit] for one user. Pair reference - reference signals. n = 5

-	R1	R2	R3	R4	R5	
R1	-	0.6849	0.5186	0.7326	0.579	
R2	0.6416	-	0.5388	0.6542	0.6304	
R3	0.5147	0.6539	-	0.5331	0.4456	
R4	0.6696	0.3247	0.3986	-	0.2819	
R5	0.5768	0.64	00 0.2982	0.3151	-	R = 0.5316

Table 2. Examples of matrices for the syllable [sit] for one user. Pair reference - estimated signals. Estimated signals have a line, reference - without. m = 7, n = 5

-	R1'	R2'	R3'	R4'	R5'	R6'	R7'	
R1	0.2967	0.4878	0.2461	0.1792	0.1795	0.1416	0.2409	
R2	0.1913	0.312	0.2062	0.1809	0.1051	0.0835	0.1042	
R3	0.0763	0.2078	0.0887	0.1115	0.1195	0.2254	0.1305	
R4	0.1891	0.4461	0.2428	0.3695	0.2842	0.1618	0.1960	
R5	0.1105	0.5822	0.1569	0.1633	0.3033	0.1226	0.1280	R1' = 0.2106

Table 3. Examples of matrices for the syllable [sit] for one user. Pair estimated - reference signals. Estimated signals have a line, reference - without. m = 7, n = 5

-	R1'	R2'	R3'	R4'	R5'	R6'	R7'	
R1'	0.2487	0.6067	0.0766	0.5811	0.1497	0.0684	0.0823	
R2'	0.0843	0.2712	0.1223	0.4191	0.0507	0.0279	0.0662	
R3'	0.0746	0.109	0.1084	0.0774	0.0191	0.0284	0.0375	
R4'	0.179	0.3511	0.246	0.2585	0.1595	0.0512	0.3222	
R5'	0.2273	0.1126	0.3309	0.2559	0.0537	0.0344	0.0827	R2' = 0.1707

The average values of the correlation coefficients R and R' and they ratio a = R'/R, which is essentially the criterion of the syllables pronunciation quality for four speakers, are shown in Table 4. The average value of the quality criterion a, that estimate the pronunciation of a syllable with a problematic phoneme without using a tongue is also presented.

Table 4. The average values of the correlation coefficients R and R' and they ratio a = R'/R for four speakers

	U1	U2	U3	U4	
R	0.5316	0.2973	0.3605	0.4216	
R'	0.1906	0.1943	0.2700	0.2182	
a	0.3586	0.6535	0.7490	0.5176	a = 0.5697

Based on the obtained values, we can say about the revealing of explicit differences between signals with and without the use of tongue, and on the applicability of the proposed criterion a for evaluating the comparative syllables pronunciation quality.

5.2 Comparison of Real Patients Speech Signals Before and After Surgery

Due to the lack of multiple entries of one syllable before the operation from one patient (it seemed inadvisable before this stage), it is not possible to make a similar comparison according to the available data from real patients. However, in this case, it is possible to measure the correlation for a group of syllables containing the phonemes most susceptible to change (R') and for a group of syllables that do not contain them and evaluated by the expert as being said qualitatively (R"). This average correlation coefficients values and their ratio for four users is presented in Table 5. It was based on 20 syllables before surgery and 20 after.

Table 5. Average correlation coefficients values and their ratio for four users

	U1	U2	U3	U4	
R"	0.3193	0.2630	0.3712	0.3318	
R'	0.2114	0.2262	0.1823	0.1632	
a	0.6621	0.8601	0.4911	0.4919	a = 0.6263

Analyzing the results obtained, we can preliminarily talk about the applicability of the proposed approach to real records, since the obtained value significantly differs from 1. However, to confirm this fact more accurately, it will be necessary to make a comparison similar to that described in paragraph 5.1. This is due to the fact that the version about comparability of the obtained values for different syllables (with and without problem phonemes) seems plausible, but not proven.

6 Conclusion

The presented work discusses the approach to the automated comparative estimation of syllables pronunciation quality. The applicability of the correlation normalization by time for syllables and the correlation criterion for comparison estimating the syllables pronunciation quality are shown. This fact is confirmed for signals received from healthy speakers (with and without the use of tongue), as well as on the signals of real speakers (with a modification of the estimation technique for single pairs of syllables). The modification consisted of comparing the syllables containing phonemes prone to change and qualitatively pronounced syllables without them. At the next stage, it is planned to develop a single prototype of a software package that implements an automated comparative assessment of the quality of phoneme pronunciation. This prototype will be used in the implementation of a software package that will shorten the term and verbal rehabilitation of patients after surgical treatment of oral cancer, and it will be based on biofeedback.

Acknowledgments. The study was performed by a grant from the Russian Science Foundation (project 16-15-00038).

References

1. Kaprin, A.D., Starinskiy, V.V., Petrova, G.V.: Status of cancer care the population of Russia in 2014. MNIOI name of P.A. Herzen, Moscow, 236 p. (2015)
2. Kaprin, A.D., Starinskiy, V.V., Petrova, G.V.: Malignancies in Russia in 2014 (Morbidity and mortality). MNIOI name of P.A. Herzen, Moscow, 250 p. (2015)
3. Standard GOST R 50840–95 Voice over paths of communication. Methods for assessing the quality, legibility and recognition. Publishing Standards, Moscow, 234 p. (1995)
4. Kostyuchenko, E., Roman, M., Ignatieva, D., Pyatkov, A., Choynzonov, E., Balatskaya, L.: Evaluation of the speech quality during rehabilitation after surgical treatment of the cancer of oral cavity and oropharynx based on a comparison of the fourier spectra. In: Ronzhin, A., Potapova, R., Németh, G. (eds.) SPECOM 2016. LNCS, vol. 9811, pp. 287–295. Springer, Cham (2016). doi:10.1007/978-3-319-43958-7_34
5. Balatskaya, L.N., Choinzonov, E.L., Chizevskaya, S.Y., Kostyuchenko, E.U., Meshcheryakov, R.V.: Software for assessing voice quality in rehabilitation of patients after surgical treatment of cancer of oral cavity, oropharynx and upper jaw. In: Železný, M., Habernal, I., Ronzhin, A. (eds.) SPECOM 2013. LNCS, vol. 8113, pp. 294–301. Springer, Cham (2013). doi:10.1007/978-3-319-01931-4_39
6. Kostyuchenko, E.Y., Mescheryakov, R.V., Balatskaya, L.N., Choynzonov, E.L.: Structure and database of software for speech quality and intelligibility assessment in the process of rehabilitation after surgery in the treatment of cancers of the oral cavity and oropharynx, maxillofacial area. In: Proceedings of SPIIRAN, vol. 32, pp. 116–124 (2014)
7. MedFind. Oncology. Plastic surgery in the surgical treatment of tumors of the face, jaws, http://medfind.ru/modules/sections/index.php?op=viewarticle&artid=324
8. Sergienko, A.B.: Digital Signal Processing. Peter, St. Petersburg, 751 p. (2006)
9. Benesty, J., Sondhi, M.M., Huang, Y. (eds.): Springer Handbook of Speech Processing, 1176 p. Springer, Heidelberg (2008)
10. Rabiner, L.R., Schafer, R.W.: Introduction to Digital Speech Processing. Foundations and Trends in Signal Processing, 194 p. (2007)
11. Shuyin, Z., Ying, G., Buhong, W.: Auto-correlation property of speech and its application in voice activity detection. In: First International Workshop on Education Technology and Computer Science, ETCS 2009, pp. 265–268 (2009)
12. ITU-T Recommendation G.729. Coding of speech at 8 kbit/s using conjugate-structure algebraic-code-excited linear prediction (CS-ACELP) (2012)

13. Atal, B., Rabiner, L.: A pattern recognition approach to voiced-unvoiced-silence classification with applications to speech recognition. IEEE Trans. ASSP **ASSP-24**, 201–212 (1976)
14. Ronzhin, A.L., Karpov, A.A.: Russian voice interface. Pattern Recognit. Image Anal. **17**(2), 321–336 (2007)
15. Chu, W., Alwan, A.: A correlation-maximization denoising filter used as an enhancement frontend for noise robust bird call classification. In: Proceedings of Interspeech 2009, pp. 2831–2834 (2009)

CRF-Based Phrase Boundary Detection Trained on Large-Scale TTS Speech Corpora

Markéta Jůzová[✉]

Department of Cybernetics and New Technologies for the Information Society,
Faculty of Applied Sciences, University of West Bohemia, Pilsen, Czech Republic
juzova@kky.zcu.cz

Abstract. The paper compares different approaches in the phrase boundary detection issue, based on the data gained from speech corpora recorded for the purpose of the text-to-speech (TTS) system. It is showed that conditional random fields model can outperform basic deterministic and classification-based algorithms both in speaker-dependent and speaker independent phrasing. The results on manually annotated sentences with phrase breaks are presented here as well.

Keywords: Phrasing · Classification · Conditional random fields · Speech corpora

1 Introduction

The term *phrasing* is used to describe the tendency of grouping words within a sentence when speaking [15]. And it should be emphasized, that the phasing is both style and speaker specific [17], and thus there is not only one correct sequence of break/non-break placements for almost all sentences.

The phrasing issue is closely related to the syntax structure of the sentence and also to the positions of sentence punctuation, especially commas [15,23]. In Czech texts, the commas are much more frequent compared e.g. to English texts, so it is a good indicator for the phrase boundary detection. However, phrasing based only on commas can produce extremely long phrases, for example in the case of a long compound sentence containing several simple sentences joined with a coordinate conjunction (e.g. *a*, EN: *and*) where no comma is written in Czech.

The main role of phrasing consists in logical division of a thoughts flow and contributes to the intelligibility and naturalness. The phrase break insertion in speech (often accompanied with a pause) also relates to human physical limitations since people need to take a breath when talking. Although the TTS systems do not need to breathe, frequent phrase breaks with pauses and appropriate phrase-ending prosody influence positively the overall quality of the synthesized samples. Long sentences are, when synthesized, unnatural and also much more demanding on listeners' attention. In addition, there may be a higher probability of a disturbing speech artefact appearance.

© Springer International Publishing AG 2017
A. Karpov et al. (Eds.): SPECOM 2017, LNAI 10458, pp. 272–281, 2017.
DOI: 10.1007/978-3-319-66429-3_26

The current version of the TTS system *ARTIC* [12], developed at the author's department, implements only a simple punctuation-based rule-driven deterministic algorithm for the phrase boundary detection suffering from the problems mentioned above. This paper is the extension of the former study [6]. Different approaches are used to test the phrase boundary detection, including a technique based on *conditional random fields* (CRF) [8], being a sequence modeling framework well suited for sequential data flows – which the phrasing really is. As described in [23,24], the phrase break in a read sentence is inserted in specified intervals and it also depends on the neighbouring boundaries. Phrases contains usually only a few words (as follows from the histograms of phrase lengths for English in the aforementioned publications). This leads to the usage of *Hidden Markov Models* (HMM) [22,24], CRF models [10] and different neural networks for phrase boundary detection task, as they can take the positions of other boundaries into consideration.

In addition, to confirm the fact that, similarly to English, the phrase lengths usually range between 3 and 6 words [23] in Czech speech data, one of the large speech Czech corpora [13], recorded for the purposes of TTS systems and containing about 10,000 sentences, was explored – the pauses detected in the segmentation process were considered to be phrase breaks, as well as the commas in the text (see Sect. 2.2). The histogram of phrase and sentence lengths is shown in Fig. 1. The other speech corpora used the experiments described in following sections evince similar tendencies.

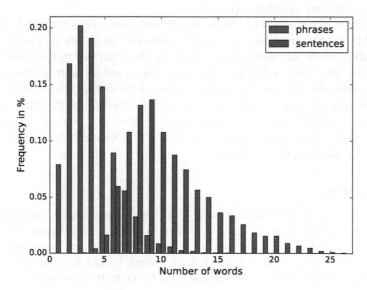

Fig. 1. A histogram of phrase and sentence lengths in the Czech speech corpus (marked as *corpus1* in Sect. 3.1)

2   Phrasing as a Classification Problem

The main goal of this paper is to test different approaches on the task of phrase boundary detection from text. As the phrasing model is supposed to be used on the input sentences of the TTS system, all the features must be easily extracted from the text. In addition, the detected phrase breaks should be consistent with the phrasing speaker's style of the TTS voice used, which might lead to more natural synthesized outputs – the system would copy the speaker's manners.

2.1   Source Data

The classification problem needs a sufficient amount of data for training. To obtain enough data to train a classifier used to detect phrase boundaries, it would take a lot of time and manual work to prepare that – moreover, these annotations should be gained from more annotators since people differ in phrase breaks insertions [18]. To avoid this, the data for classification training were prepared in a different way – the author utilizes large speech corpora recorded for the purposes of the TTS system [13], as did e.g. the authors of [10,16,20]. The data were extracted automatically, which brings a great advantage – since no manually annotated breaks are required, the process of data gaining can be easily and quickly applied on another speech corpus. Moreover, a single speech corpus, containing in the case of TTS system *ARTIC* about 10,000 sentences, represents a sufficient amount of data needed for training a phrase model which will be, in addition, speaker-dependent.

In addition, the corpora had been already automatically segmented on phones level [9,11] for the purposes of speech synthesis, and thus they also contain special units *breath* and *pause* which indicate the positions in the speech where the speaker has made a break. And since the speakers were professionals or semi-professionals, the speech breaks (pauses/breaths) are expected to occure in reasonable positions of read sentences. More detailed investigation of pauses in corpora showed that not all pauses were related to a comma, which means that the information about a pause (or a breath) presense in speech can help to improve the phrasing of a sentence.

2.2   Features

Now, let us describe the phrasing issue as a 2-class classification problem. Every sentence of N words $w_0, w_1, \ldots, w_{N-1}$, taken from the speech corpora mentioned, with Czech morphological tags $t_0, t_1, \ldots, t_{N-1}$ (determined using our n-gram tagger) can be represented as follows, with speech breaks b_i set to 1 if the word w_i was followed by a breath or a pause, and b_i set to 0 otherwise:[1]

words+tags	(w_0,t_0)	(w_1,t_1)	(w_2,t_2)	...		(w_{N-1},t_{N-1})
speech breaks	b_0	b_1	b_2	...	b_{N-2}	
juncture	j_0	j_1	j_2	...	j_{N-2}	

---

[1] The term 'juncture' was adopted from [23] and refers to required phrase breaks.

Contrary e.g. to [16], where only speech pauses were considered to be phrase boundaries, it was decided to consider both commas and speech pauses/breaths to be phrase breaks in this study. First, making a phrase boundary at a punctuation seems to be reasonable in Czech, and second, extra speech pauses, which do not correspond to any comma, represent a "value added" and, hopefully, ensure more accurate phrasing compared to the phrasing just at commas. To formally summarize, the true "gold data" answers were extracted from the speech corpus based on the following rules:

- $j_i = 1$ if w_i is followed by a comma,
- $j_i = 1$ if $b_i = 1$,
- $j_i = 0$ otherwise.

Inspired by other classification-based approaches to phrase boundary detection, e.g. [3,22], the following feature set was used for every juncture j_i:

- word w_i,
- word w_i has or has not a comma,
- following word w_{i+1},
- morphological tag t_i of the word w_i,
- morphological tag t_{i+1} of the word w_{i+1},
- bigram $t_i + t_{i+1}$,
- trigram $t_{i-1} + t_i + t_{i+1}$,
- sentence lenght N,
- position of the word w_i in the sentence $\frac{i}{N}$,
- distance from the preceding word followed by a comma $i - i_{LC}$
  ($i_{LC} \leq i$; $i_{LC} = 0$ if none of words $w_0 \ldots w_{i-1}$ has a comma),
- distance to the next word followed by a comma $i_{NC} - i$
  ($i_{NC} \geq i$; $i_{NC} = N - 1$ if none of words $w_{i+1} \ldots w_{N-1}$ has a comma).

3 Phrase Boundary Detection Experiments

The presented paper compares the results on speaker-dependent and speaker-independent phrasing of several deterministic (rule-based) and non-derministic approaches. Besides two representatives of simple classification-based method, used e.g. in [3,14] and also in the author's former study [6], the *CRF* model (used for sequential training e.g. in [8,10]) is tested, since the positions of phrase boundaries depend on other neighbourring boundaries (as mentioned in Sect. 1).
    The complete list of all tested algorithms is stated below:

- *NoBreaks* – does not set any phrase boundary,
- *Comma* – sets the boundary after every comma (this algorithm is performed in the current version of the TTS system *ARTIC* [12]),
- *CommaAnd* – sets the boundary after every comma and before every *a* (EN: *and*) conjunction (this one should, in theory, improve the phrasing of compound sentences compared to previous),
- *LogReg* – Logistic Regression classifier

- *SVC-lin* – Support Vector Machines with *linear* kernel
- *CRF* – Conditional Random Fields

Note that no cross-validation results for classifier's parameters are presented in this paper since they were a part of the previous study in [6], and the parameters were set according to the best results shown in the aforementioned paper. Also no other rule-based deterministic algorithms were used (using e.g. more conjunctions) as it was proved that they considerably decreased the *precision* value. The listed classifiers *LogReg* and *SVC-lin* were chosen as providing better results compared to the other classification-based approaches tested in [6].

3.1 Speaker-Dependent Phrasing

As mentioned in Sect. 1 and showed e.g. in [17], the phrasing of read sentences highly depends on the particular speaker. Therefore, the experiments were, at first, performed on each speech corpus independently. As usual, 80% of available data were always used for training and 20% for testing. It is actually a speaker-dependent phrasing issue. The results for 6 different corpora (each containing 10,000 sentences) and all phrasing approaches defined above are presented in Table 1 using 4 standard evaluation measures – *accuracy* (A), *precision* (P), *recall* (R) and *F1-score* (*F1*).

The results clearly show that the classification-based approaches significantly outperformed the deterministic algorithms in *F1-score* and *recall* – it means that more "real" phrase boundaries are detected, which results in finer phrasing and prevents from the creation of very long phrases. Furthermore, the results of *CRF* are even better then *LogReg* and *SVC-lin* classifiers for all corpora, which points out the advantage of this method used on the phrasing issue. Moreover, the *CRF* model is characterized by higher *precision* value (contrary to *LogReg* and *SVC-lin*), and thus fewer "false alarms" (i.e. nonsense boundary placements) are detected, which is more important for this task than the lower number of missed boundaries (related to lower *recall* value).

The numbers in Table 1 also show that the results differ across the corpora used. The reasons for the different success rates is probably the consistency (or inconsistency) of the phrasing style of particular speakers, and also the different frequency of pauses in their speech – e.g. the speakers who recorded the *corpus2* and *corpus4* made almost all pauses at comma punctuation and not many others. And it should be emphasized that not all "false alarms" and "miss-detections" are true errors [6,20] since the "gold data" were extracted automatically from speech corpora, and thus they represent only one of possible breaks/non-breaks sequences. Manual check also revealed that the pauses sometimes appeared from another reason than a phrase boundary – there were caused by an inappropriate reading of the sentence (some pauses appeared before long difficult words and some other were caused by a lack of breath before the sentence end which should not be considered to be phrase boundaries).

Table 1. Speaker-dependent phrase boundary detection for all 6 Czech speech corpora
– classifiers comparison (*nan* values are caused by 0/0 divisions)

	Classifier	A	P	R	F1		Classifier	A	P	R	F1
corpus1	*NoBreaks*	0.830	*nan*	0.000	*nan*	corpus4	*NoBreaks*	0.830	*nan*	0.000	*nan*
	Comma	0.954	1.000	0.743	0.852		*Comma*	0.990	1.000	0.938	0.968
	CommaAnd	0.965	0.956	0.838	0.893		*CommaAnd*	0.975	0.889	0.955	0.921
	LogReg	0.972	0.870	0.960	0.912		*LogReg*	0.991	0.947	0.995	0.970
	SVC-lin	0.971	0.873	0.954	0.912		*SVC-lin*	0.991	0.947	0.991	0.969
	CRF	0.973	0.895	0.944	**0.919**		*CRF*	0.991	0.949	0.994	**0.971**
corpus2	*NoBreaks*	0.847	*nan*	0.000	*nan*	corpus5	*NoBreaks*	0.882	*nan*	0.000	*nan*
	Comma	0.993	1.000	0.954	0.976		*Comma*	0.967	1.000	0.801	0.889
	CommaAnd	0.974	0.886	0.962	0.922		*CommaAnd*	0.958	0.902	0.838	0.868
	LogReg	0.994	0.959	1.000	0.979		*LogReg*	0.972	0.860	0.960	0.907
	SVC-lin	0.994	0.964	0.997	0.980		*SVC-lin*	0.972	0.862	0.957	0.907
	CRF	0.995	0.965	0.999	**0.982**		*CRF*	0.973	0.880	0.947	**0.912**
corpus3	*NoBreaks*	0.761	*nan*	0.000	*nan*	corpus6	*NoBreaks*	0.838	*nan*	0.000	*nan*
	Comma	0.893	1.000	0.541	0.703		*Comma*	0.966	1.000	0.794	0.885
	CommaAnd	0.884	0.899	0.568	0.696		*CommaAnd*	0.954	0.883	0.828	0.855
	LogReg	0.892	0.650	0.867	0.743		*LogReg*	0.968	0.809	0.989	0.890
	SVC-lin	0.892	0.658	0.855	0.744		*SVC-lin*	0.967	0.818	0.974	0.889
	CRF	0.895	0.700	0.835	**0.762**		*CRF*	0.968	0.834	0.956	**0.891**

3.2   Speaker-Independent Phrasing

The results in the previous section show that all three classification-based approaches, especially *CRF*, outperform the baseline algorithms in phrase boundary detection from text, when used in a speaker-dependent mode. However, the utilization of phrasing in TTS systems often requires generalization since there are many synthetic voices built upon a small corpora, e.g. those from voice conservation process of people facing voice loss due to fatal diseases [4,5,7]. The speakers who have recorded these voices were unprofessionals with speaking problems and the recorded data are rather (sometimes even very) inconsistent. As those (small) corpora can not be used for training, a general phrasing model may be better to be used.

In order to that, all 6 Czech large available speech corpora used in Sect. 3.1 were joined and the same experiment was performed on that. Table 2 shows the results of all deterministic and classification-based approaches when using 80 % of randomly selected sentences from the joined corpus for training and the remaining 20 % for testing, and the corpora were approximately equally covered by the testing and training data.

Again, the CRF model provides better results on testing data compared to other approaches. And *McNemar tests* [21] proved that these results are statistically significant at the significance level $\alpha = 0.01$ compared to *LogReg'* results, and *LogReg* is significantly better than *SVC-lin* at the same signicifance level. The increasing and decreasing trends of the evaluation measures evinces similar course across the tested approaches as in speaker-dependent phrasing.

Table 2. Speaker-independent phrase boundary detection (trained and tested on the joined corpus) – classifiers comparison

Classifier	A	P	R	F1
NoBreaks	0.826	*nan*	0.000	*nan*
Comma	0.959	1.000	0.767	0.868
CommaAnd	0.951	0.906	0.803	0.851
LogReg	0.960	0.813	0.953	0.877
SVC-lin	0.959	0.809	0.946	0.872
CRF	0.963	0.829	0.953	**0.887**

3.3 Speaker-Independent Phrasing Tested on Manual Annotated Data

Up to now, a part of the data gained from speech corpora was used for testing. Nevertheless, these data could contain some miss-placed pauses (as mentioned in Sect. 3.1) and also the speaking styles of the speakers have a great impact on the resulting phrasing since the tested approaches learn to imitate that.

To test the trained models on different, "real" data, the author decided to collect a small amount of sentences manually annotated with phrase boundaries. And since the phrasing problem is ambiguous and particular phrasing depends a lot on the speaker or the annotator, two annotators were invited to provide the manual boundary detection. The annotators were marking phrase boundaries in 20 sentences, the *annotator1* marked 65 boundaries and *annotator2* 71 boundaries, while they agreed on 58 of them. The inter-annotator agreement was calculated using *Cohen's kappa* [1] which is, for the particular set of sentences, equal to 0.83. This number is surprisingly quite high (compared to results on inter-annotator agreement presented in [19]), but it could be caused by a small number of annotated sentences.

The results of phrase boundary detection on manually-annotated testing data are shown in Table 3. Since the annotators differ in several detected boundaries, the results are presented both for all boundaries marked by at least one of the annotators (*all boundaries* column in Table 3) and for boundaries where the annotators agreed (*agreed boundaries*; boundaries detected only by one annotator were considered to be a non-break). Note that all the models for phrasing were trained on the whole joined speech corpus created from all available Czech TTS voices. In both cases, the *recall* values of all approaches are low, which means that not all phrase boundaries were detected, but, on the other hand, the precision value is quite high and so only a few "false alarms" occurred.

Similarly to the experiments presented in Sects. 3.1 and 3.2, the *CRF* model outperformed both classification-based approaches and simple deterministic algorithms, namely in *accuracy*, *recall* and *F1-score*. The *precision* values are equal or close to 1.000 for *Comma*, since the phrasing at commas does not make many "false alarms" in Czech. It can be seen from the table that the results are

Table 3. Speaker-independent phrase boundary detection – classifiers comparison on manually annotated data

All boundaries					Agreed boundaries				
Classifier	A	P	R	F1	Classifier	A	P	R	F1
NoBreaks	0.840	nan	0.000	nan	NoBreaks	0.879	nan	0.000	nan
Comma	0.897	1.000	0.359	0.528	Comma	0.940	0.964	0.466	0.628
CommaAnd	0.907	0.870	0.483	0.621	CommaAnd	0.940	0.805	0.611	0.695
LogReg	0.909	0.905	0.487	0.633	LogReg	0.944	0.881	0.627	0.733
SVC-lin	0.907	0.902	0.474	0.622	SVC-lin	0.942	0.878	0.610	0.720
CRF	0.924	0.956	0.551	**0.699**	CRF	0.951	0.889	0.678	**0.769**

much lower compared to the results on testing data extracted from the same joined speech corpus as the training data (presented in Table 2) – maybe due to different annotation style of the addressed annotators when compared to the speaking style of the professional speakers who recorded the corpora used.

It is also good to emphasize that the *precision* of *CRF*, when applied at *all boundaries* data, is very high, thus, there are hardly any nonsense detected boundaries. And this fact is very crucial for the phrasing problem, since the most important is not to make a phrase boundary at completely wrong position in the sentence.

4 Conclusion

The presented paper showed that the speech corpora data could be used for training of different phrasing models, which prevents from time-consuming manual phrase breaks annotations and enables to extract a large amount of data easily and quickly from different corpora. Using this data, it was proved that the *CRF* model can outperform the other tested classifiers and its results are even better compared to the simple rule-based algorithm based on punctuation (which has been used in our TTS system ARTIC up to now).

The results presented in Sect. 3.1 show that it is possible to train a speaker-dependent phrasing model which, when used on the same speech corpus as used for the training, is in consistency with the phrasing style of the particular speaker. However, a generalized phrasing model might be better to be used for "small" TTS voices, and thus the experiment on speaker-independent model training was performed in Sect. 3.2. The results of the model used in a speaker-independent mode clearly prove the advantages of *CRF* sequence model compared to other approaches.

The results obtained on a small number of manually annotated sentences also confirm the presented conclusion concerning the *CRF* being the best choice. The high *precision* values ensure that almost no "false alarms", representing nonsense phrase boundaries in this issue, are detected – and it is exactly what is expected from a good phrasing model. Furthermore, although the *recall* values are not very high on manually annotated breaks, these computed by *CRF* are, again, higher compared to the deterministic *Comma* algorithm – *CRF* detects more true phrase boundaries, which should, hopefully, lead to the improvement of naturalness and intelligibility of synthesized sentences if the trained model was implemented in the TTS system.

In any case, the contribution to the overall quality of speech synthesis produced by the TTS system extended with the proposed trained *CRF* phrasing models, both speaker-dependent and speaker-independent, is planned to be verified by large-scale listening tests [2,25] before releasing this modification into the publicly available version of the system.

Acknowledgement. This research was supported by Ministry of Education, Youth and Sports of the Czech Republic, project No. LO1506, and by the grant of the University of West Bohemia, project No. SGS-2016-039.

References

1. Cohen, J.: A coefficient of agreement for nominal scales. Educ. Psychol. Meas. **20**(1), 37 (1960)
2. Grůber, M., Matoušek, J.: Listening-test-based annotation of communicative functions for expressive speech synthesis. In: Sojka, P., Horák, A., Kopeček, I., Pala, K. (eds.) TSD 2010. LNCS, vol. 6231, pp. 283–290. Springer, Heidelberg (2010). doi:10.1007/978-3-642-15760-8_36
3. Hirschberg, J., Prieto, P.: Training intonational phrasing rules automatically for English and Spanish text-to-speech. Speech Communication **18**(3), 281–290 (1996)
4. Jůzová, M., Romportl, J., Tihelka, D.: Speech corpus preparation for voice banking of laryngectomised patients. In: Král, P., Matoušek, V. (eds.) TSD 2015. LNCS, vol. 9302, pp. 282–290. Springer, Cham (2015). doi:10.1007/978-3-319-24033-6_32
5. Jůzová, M., Tihelka, D., Matoušek, J.: Designing high-coverage multi-level text corpus for non-professional-voice conservation. In: Ronzhin, A., Potapova, R., Németh, G. (eds.) SPECOM 2016. LNCS (LNAI), vol. 9811, pp. 207–215. Springer, Cham (2016). doi:10.1007/978-3-319-43958-7_24
6. Jůzová, M.: Prosodic phrase boundary classification based on Czech speech corpora. In: Text, Speech and Dialogue. LNCS. Springer, Berlin, Heidelberg (2017)
7. Jůzová, M., Tihelka, D., Matoušek, J., Hanzlíček, Z.: Voice conservation and TTS system for people facing total laryngectomy. In: Proceedings of Interspeech 2017 (2017)
8. Lafferty, J.D., McCallum, A., Pereira, F.C.N.: Conditional random fields: probabilistic models for segmenting and labeling sequence data. In: Proceedings of 18th ICML 2001, pp. 282–289. Morgan Kaufmann Publishers Inc. (2001)
9. Legát, M., Matoušek, J., Tihelka, D.: A robust multi-phase pitch-mark detection algorithm. In: Proceedings of Interspeech 2007, pp. 1641–1644 (2007)
10. Louw, A., Moodley, A.: Speaker specific phrase break modeling with conditional random fields for text-to-speech. In: Proceedings of PRASA-RobMech 2016, pp. 1–6 (2016)
11. Matoušek, J., Romportl, J.: Automatic pitch-synchronous phonetic segmentation. In: Proceedings of Interspeech 2008. pp. 1626–1629. ISCA (2008)

12. Matoušek, J., Tihelka, D., Romportl, J.: Current state of Czech text-to-speech system ARTIC. In: Sojka, P., Kopeček, I., Pala, K. (eds.) TSD 2006. LNCS, vol. 4188, pp. 439–446. Springer, Heidelberg (2006). doi:10.1007/11846406_55
13. Matoušek, J., Romportl, J.: Recording and annotation of speech corpus for Czech unit selection speech synthesis. In: Matoušek, V., Mautner, P. (eds.) TSD 2007. LNCS, vol. 4629, pp. 326–333. Springer, Heidelberg (2007). doi:10.1007/978-3-540-74628-7_43
14. Mishra, T., Jun Kim, Y., Bangalore, S.: Intonational phrase break prediction for text-to-speech synthesis using dependency relations. In: Proceedings of ICASSP 2015, pp. 4919–4923 (2015)
15. Palková, Z.: Rytmická výstavba prozaického textu. Studia ČSAV; čis. 13/1974, Academia (1974)
16. Parlikar, A., Black, A.W.: Data-driven phrasing for speech synthesis in low-resource languages. In: Proceedings of ICASSP 2012, pp. 4013–4016 (2012)
17. Prahallad, K., Raghavendra, E.V., Black, A.W.: Learning speaker-specific phrase breaks for text-to-speech systems. In: Proceedings of SSW 2010, Kyoto, Japan, September 22–24, 2010. pp. 162–166 (2010)
18. Romportl, J.: Statistical evaluation of prosodic phrases in the Czech language. In: Proceedings of the Speech Prosody 2008, pp. 755–758. Editora RG/CNPq, Campinas (2008)
19. Romportl, J.: Automatic prosodic phrase annotation in a corpus for speech synthesis. In: Proceedings of Speech Prosody 2010. University of Illionois, Chicago (2010)
20. Romportl, J., Matoušek, J.: Several aspects of machine-driven phrasing in text-to-speech systems. Prague Bull. Math. Linguist. 95, 51–61 (2011)
21. Salzberg, S.L.: On comparing classifiers: pitfalls to avoid and a recommended approach. Data Min. Knowl. Disc. 1(3), 317–328 (1997)
22. Sun, X., Applebaum, T.H.: Intonational phrase break prediction using decision tree and n-gram model. In: Proceedings of Eurospeech 2001, pp. 3–7 (2001)
23. Taylor, P.: Text-to-Speech Synthesis, 1st edn. Cambridge University Press, New York, NY, USA (2009)
24. Taylor, P., Black, A.W.: Assigning phrase breaks from part-of-speech sequences. Comput. Speech Lang. 12(2), 99–117 (1998)
25. Tihelka, D., Grůber, M., Hanzlíček, Z.: Robust methodology for TTS enhancement evaluation. In: Habernal, I., Matoušek, V. (eds.) TSD 2013. LNCS, vol. 8082, pp. 442–449. Springer, Heidelberg (2013). doi:10.1007/978-3-642-40585-3_56

Deep Recurrent Neural Networks in Speech Synthesis Using a Continuous Vocoder

Mohammed Salah Al-Radhi[1(✉)], Tamás Gábor Csapó[1,2],
and Géza Németh[1]

[1] Department of Telecommunication and Media Informatics,
Budapest University of Technology and Economics, Budapest, Hungary
{malradhi, csapot, nemeth}@tmit.bme.hu
[2] MTA-ELTE Lendület Lingual Articulation Research Group,
Budapest, Hungary

Abstract. In our earlier work in statistical parametric speech synthesis, we proposed a vocoder using continuous F0 in combination with Maximum Voiced Frequency (MVF), which was successfully used with a feed-forward deep neural network (DNN). The advantage of a continuous vocoder in this scenario is that vocoder parameters are simpler to model than traditional vocoders with discontinuous F0. However, DNNs have a lack of sequence modeling which might degrade the quality of synthesized speech. In order to avoid this problem, we propose the use of sequence-to-sequence modeling with recurrent neural networks (RNNs). In this paper, four neural network architectures (long short-term memory (LSTM), bidirectional LSTM (BLSTM), gated recurrent network (GRU), and standard RNN) are investigated and applied using this continuous vocoder to model F0, MVF, and Mel-Generalized Cepstrum (MGC) for more natural sounding speech synthesis. Experimental results from objective and subjective evaluations have shown that the proposed framework converges faster and gives state-of-the-art speech synthesis performance while outperforming the conventional feed-forward DNN.

Keywords: Deep learning · LSTM · BLSTM · GRU · RNN

1 Introduction

Statistical parametric speech synthesis (SPSS) based text-to-speech (TTS) systems have steadily advanced in terms of naturalness during the last two decades. Even though the quality of synthetic speech is still unsatisfying, the benefits of flexibility, robustness, and control denote that SPSS stays as an attractive proposition. One of the most important factors that degrade the naturalness of the synthesized speech is known as the limited capabilities of the acoustic model which captures the complex and nonlinear relationship between linguistic and acoustic features [1]. Although there have been many attempts to create a more accurate acoustic model for SPSS (such as [2]), the hidden Markov model (HMM) has been the most popular attempt for a long time [3]. Even though this model can enhance accuracy and synthesis performance, it usually increases the amount of computational complexity with higher number of model parameters [4].

© Springer International Publishing AG 2017
A. Karpov et al. (Eds.): SPECOM 2017, LNAI 10458, pp. 282–291, 2017.
DOI: 10.1007/978-3-319-66429-3_27

Recently, deep learning algorithms have shown their ability to extract high-level, complex abstractions and data representations from large volumes of supervised and unsupervised data [5], and achieve significant improvements in various machine learning areas. Neural approaches have been also used in SPSS as deep feed-forward neural networks (DNNs) with more than one layer of hidden units between its input and output layers. By mapping directly linguistic features to vocoder parameters, DNNs can be viewed as a replacement for the decision tree used in HMM-TTS systems [6]. DNNs have also other advantages, including the ability to model high-dimensional acoustic parameters [7], and the availability of multi-task learning [8]. However, Zen, et al. [9] comprehensively listed the limitations of the conventional DNN-based acoustic modeling for speech synthesis, e.g. its lack of ability to predict variances, unimodal nature of its objective function, and the sequential nature of speech is ignored because it assumes that each frame is sampled independently. In other words, the mapping is performed frame by frame without considering contextual constraints between statics and deltas during training.

To overcome these problems, recurrent neural networks (inserting cyclical connections in feed-forward DNNs) have proven to have an advantage in modeling sequences whose activation at each time is dependent on that of the previous time to shape prediction output. Although it is difficult to train RNNs to capture long term dependencies [10], successful approaches were used to reduce the negative impacts of this limitation. It was suggested in [11] to store information over long or short time intervals to include contextual constraints called as a long short-term memory (LSTM). In [12] a bidirectional LSTM based RNN was employed in which there is a feedback to retain previous states. In [13], gated recurrent unit (GRU) based RNN was proposed to adaptively capture dependencies of different time scales. In this paper, four variants of neural networks are investigated in the speech synthesis scenario and implemented using a continuous vocoder.

In our earlier work, we proposed a computationally feasible residual-based vocoder [14], using a continuous F0 model [15], and Maximum Voiced Frequency (MVF) [16]. In this method, the voiced excitation consisting of pitch synchronous PCA residual frames is low-pass filtered and the unvoiced part is high-pass filtered according to the MVF contour as a cutoff frequency. The approach was especially successful for modelling speech sounds with mixed excitation. However, we noted that the unvoiced sounds are sometimes poor due to the combination of continuous F0 and MVF. In [17], we removed the post-processing step in the estimation of the MVF parameter and thus successfully modelled the unvoiced sounds with our continuous vocoder, which was integrated into a HMM-TTS system. In [18], we successfully modelled all vocoder parameters (continuous F0, MVF, and MGC) with feed-forward DNNs. The goal of this paper is to extend modeling of our continuous vocoder parameters using RNN, LSTM, BLSTM, and GRU models. Besides, noise components in voiced sounds are parameterized and modeled to meet the requirements of high sound quality.

The rest of this paper is structured as follows: Sect. 2 describes the novel methods we used for speech synthesis. Then, experimental conditions are showed in Sect. 3. Evaluation and discussion are presented in Sect. 4. Finally, Sect. 5 concludes the contributions of this paper.

2   Methodology

2.1   Continuous Vocoder

For the current RNN-TTS experiments, the improved version of our continuous vocoder was used [17]. During the analysis phase, F0 is calculated on the input waveforms by the open-source implementation[1] of a simple continuous pitch tracker [15]. In regions of creaky voice and in case of unvoiced sounds or silences, this pitch tracker interpolates F0 based on a linear dynamic system and Kalman smoothing. Next, MVF is calculated from the speech signal using the MVF_Toolkit[2], resulting in the MVF parameter [16]. In the next step 60-order Mel-Generalized Cepstral analysis (MGC) [19] is performed on the speech signal with alpha = 0.58 and gamma = 0. In all steps, 5 ms frame shift is used. The results are the F0cont, MVF and the MGC parameter streams. Finally, we perform Principal Component Analysis (PCA) on the pitch synchronous residuals [14].

During the synthesis phase, voiced excitation is composed of PCA residuals overlap-added pitch synchronously, depending on the continuous F0. After that, this voiced excitation is lowpass filtered frame by frame at the frequency given by the MVF parameter. In the frequencies higher than the actual value of MVF, white noise is used. Voiced and unvoiced excitation is added together. Finally, an MGLSA filter is used to synthesize speech [20].

2.1.1   Improved Version of Continuous Vocoder

In the standard continuous vocoder, there is a lack of voiced components in higher frequencies. However, it was shown that in natural speech, the high-frequency noise component is time-aligned with the pitch periods. For this reason, in a recent study, we applied several time envelopes to shape the high-frequency noise excitation component [21]. From the several envelopes investigated, the True envelope was found to be the best. Therefore, this will be used in the current study.

The True Envelope (TE) algorithm starts with estimating the cepstrum and updating it in such a way that the original spectrum signal and the current cepstral representation is maximized [22]. To have an efficient real time implementation, [23] proposed a concept of a discrete cepstrum which consists of a least mean square approximation, and [24] added a regularization technique that aims to improve the smoothness of the envelope. Here, the procedure for estimating the TE is shown in Fig. 1 in which the cepstrum can be calculated as the inverse Fourier transform of the log magnitude spectrum of the voiced frame. Moreover, TE with weighting factor will bring us a unique time envelope which makes the convergence closer to natural speech. In practice, the weight factor which was found to be the most successful is 10.

---

[1] https://github.com/idiap/ssp.

[2] http://tcts.fpms.ac.be/ ~ drugman/files/MVF.zip.

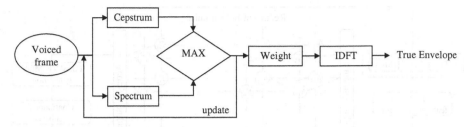

Fig. 1. Procedures for estimating the true envelope

2.2 Acoustic Modeling

Figure 2 conceptually illustrates the main components of the continuous vocoder when applied in RNN-based training. Textual and phonetic parameters are first converted to a sequence of linguistic features as input, and neural networks are employed to predict acoustic features as output for synthesizing speech. Because standard RNNs with sigmoid activation function suffer from both vanishing gradients and exploding [10], our goal is to present and evaluate the performance of recently proposed recurrent units on sequence modeling for improved training of the continuous vocoder parameters.

2.2.1 Feedforward DNN (Baseline)

DNNs have become increasingly a common method for deep learning to achieve state-of-the-art performance in real-world tasks [6, 8]. Simply, the input is used to predict the output with multiple layers of hidden units, each of which performs a non-linear function of the previous layer's representation, and a linear activation function is used at the output layer. In this paper, we use our baseline model [18] as a DNN with feed-forward multilayer perceptron architecture. We applied a hyperbolic tangent activation function whose outputs lie in the range (−1 to 1) which can yield lower error rates and faster convergence than a logistic sigmoid function (0 to 1).

2.2.2 Recurrent NN

A more popular and effective acoustic model architecture is a version of the recurrent neural networks (RNNs) which can process sequences of inputs and produces sequences of outputs [13]. In particular, the RNN model is different from the DNN the following way: the RNN operates not only on inputs (like the DNN) but also on network internal states that are updated as a function of the entire input history. In this case, the recurrent connections are able to map and remember information in the acoustic sequence, which is important for speech signal processing to enhance prediction outputs.

2.2.3 Long Short-Term Memory

As originally proposed in and recently used for speech synthesis [25], long short-term memory networks (LSTM) are a class of recurrent networks composed of units with a particular structure to cope better with the vanishing gradient problems during training and maintain potential long-distance dependencies [11]. This makes LSTM applicable to learn from history in order to classify, process and predict time series. Unlike the conventional recurrent unit which overwrites its content at each time step, LSTM have

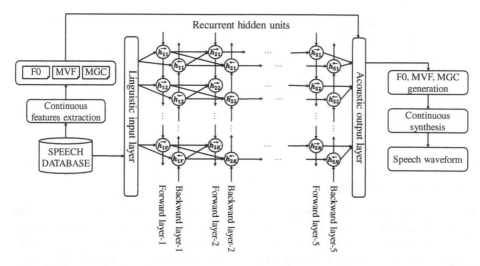

Fig. 2. A general schematic diagram of the proposed method based on recurrent networks

a special memory cell with self-connections in the recurrent hidden layer to maintain its states over time, and three gating units (input, forget, and output gates) which are used to control the information flows in and out of the layer as well as when to forget and recollect previous states.

2.2.4 Bidirectional LSTM

In a unidirectional RNN (URNN) only contextual information from past time instances are taken into account, whereas a bidirectional RNN (BRNN) can access past and future contexts by processing data in both directions [26]. BRNN can do this by separating hidden layers into forward state sequence and backward state sequence. Combining BRNN with LSTM gives a bidirectional-LSTM (BLSTM) which can access long range context in both input directions, and can be defined generally as in [12].

2.2.5 Gated Recurrent Unit

A slightly more simplified variation of the LSTM, the gated recurrent unit (GRU) architecture was recently defined and found to achieve a better performance than LSTM in some cases [13]. GRU has two gating units (update and reset gates) to modulate the flow of data inside the unit but without having separate memory cells. The update gate supports the GRU to capture long term dependencies like that of the forget gate in LSTM. Moreover, because an output gate is not used in GRU, the total size of GRU parameters is less than that of LSTM, which allow that GRU networks converge faster and avoid overfitting.

3 Experimental Conditions

3.1 Data

To measure the performance of the obtained model, the US English female (SLT) speaker was chosen for the experiment from the CMU-ARCTIC database [27], which consists of 1132 sentences. 90% of the sentences were used for training and the rest was used for testing.

3.2 Network Topology and Training Settings

Neural network models used in this research were implemented in the Merlin open source speech toolkit[3] [25]. For simplicity, the same architecture is used in both duration and acoustic models. Weights and biases were prepared with small nonzero values, and optimized with stochastic gradient descent to minimize the mean squared error between its predictions and acoustic features of the training set. The Speech Signal Processing Toolkit [28] was used to apply the spectral enhancement. Delta and delta-delta features were calculated for all the features. The input linguistic features have min-max normalization, while output acoustic features have mean-variance normalization. In general, the design configuration of current neural network model is similar to those we have given in [18]. The training procedures were conducted on a high performance NVidia Titan X GPU.

We trained a baseline DNN and four different recurrent neural network architectures, each having either LSTM, BLSTM, GRU, or RNN. Each model has fairly the same number of parameters, because the objective of these experiments is to compare all four units equally in order to find out the best unit to model our continuous vocoder. The systems we implemented are as follows:

- **DNN:** This system is our baseline approach [18] which uses 6 feed-forward hidden layers; each one has 1024 hyperbolic tangent units.
- **LSTM:** 4 feed-forward hidden lower layers of 1024 hyperbolic tangent units each, followed by a single LSTM hidden top layer with 512 units. This recurrent output layer makes smooth transitions between sequential frames while the 4 bottom feed-forward layers intended to act as feature extraction layers.
- **BLSTM:** Similar to the LSTM, but replacing the LSTM top layer with a BLSTM layer of 512 units.
- **GRU:** Similar to the LSTM architecture, but replacing the top hidden layer with a GRU layer of 512 units.
- **RNN:** Similar to the LSTM architecture, but replacing the top hidden layer with a RNN layer of 512 units.

---

[3] https://github.com/CSTR-Edinburgh/merlin.

4 Evaluation and Discussion

In order to achieve our goals and to verify the effectiveness of the proposed method, objective and subjective evaluations were carried out. We conducted two kinds of experimental evaluations. In the first evaluation, we experimentally modeled our continuous vocoder parameters in deep recurrent neural networks by systems given in Sect. 3, and objectively verified. In the second evaluation, we tested them using a subjective listening experiment.

4.1 Objective Evaluation

To get an objective picture of how these four RNN systems evaluate against the DNN baseline using the continuous vocoder, the performance of these systems is evaluated by calculating the overall validation error (as mean square error between valid and train values per each iteration) for every training model. The test results for the baseline DNN and the proposed recurrent networks are listed in Table 1. It is confirmed that all parameters generated by the proposed systems presented smaller prediction errors than those generated by the baseline system. More specifically, the BLSTM model can achieve the best results and outperforms other network topologies.

Table 1. The objective experimental results for the synthesized speech signal using continuous vocoder

Systems	Training validation error
DNN (baseline)	1.54
RNN	1.53
LSTM	1.53
BLSTM	1.52
GRU	1.53

4.2 Subjective Evaluation

In order to evaluate the perceptual quality of the proposed systems, we conducted a web-based MUSHRA (MUlti-Stimulus test with Hidden Reference and Anchor) listening test [29]. We compared natural sentences with the synthesized sentences from the baseline (DNN), proposed (RNN and BLSTM), and a benchmark system. From the four proposed systems, we only included RNN and BLSTM, because in informal listening we perceived only minor differences between the four variants of the sentences. The benchmark type was the re-synthesis of the sentences with a standard pulse-noise excitation vocoder. In the test, the listeners had to rate the naturalness of each stimulus relative to the reference (which was the natural sentence), from 0 (highly unnatural) to 100 (highly natural). The utterances were presented in a randomized order.

11 participants (7 males, 4 females) with a mean age of 35 years, mostly with engineering background were asked to conduct the online listening test. We evaluated twelve sentences. On average, the test took 11 min to fill. The MUSHRA scores for all the systems are showed in Fig. 3. According to the results, both recurrent networks

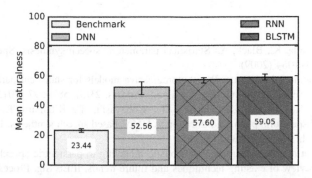

Fig. 3. Results of the MUSHRA listening test for the naturalness question. Error bars show the bootstrapped 95% confidence intervals. The score for the reference (natural speech) is not included

outperformed the DNN system (Mann-Whitney-Wilcoxon ranksum test, $p < 0.05$). It is also found that the BLSTM system reached the best naturalness scores in the listening test, consistent with objective errors reported above. However, the difference between RNN and BLSTM is not statistically significant.

5 Conclusion

The goal of the work reported in this paper was to apply a Continuous vocoder in recurrent neural network based speech synthesis to enhance the modeling of acoustic features extracted from speech data. We have implemented four deep recurrent architectures: LSTM, BLSTM, GRU, and RNN. Our evaluation focused on the task of sequence modeling which was ignored in the conventional DNN. From both objective and subjective evaluation metrics, experimental results demonstrated that our proposed RNN models can improve the naturalness of the speech synthesized significantly over our DNN baseline. These experimental results showed the potential of the recurrent networks based approaches for SPSS. In particular, the BLSTM network achieves better performance than others.

For future work, the authors plan to investigate other recurrent network architectures to train and refine our continuous parameters. In addition, we will try to implement firstly a mixture density recurrent network and then combining this with BLSTM-RNN based TTS.

Acknowledgements. The research was partly supported by the VUK (AAL-2014-1-183) and the EUREKA/DANSPLAT projects. The Titan X GPU used for this research was donated by NVIDIA Corporation. We would like to thank the subjects for participating in the listening test.

References

1. Zen, H., Tokuda, K., Black, A.: Statistical parameteric speech synthesis. Speech Commun. **51**(11), 1039–1064 (2009)
2. Zen, H., Shannon, M., Byrne, W.: Autoregressive models for statistical parametric speech synthesis. IEEE Trans. Acoust. Speech Lang. Process. **21**(3), 587–597 (2013)
3. Yoshimura, T., Tokuda, K., Masuko, T., Kobayashi, T., Kitamura T.: Simultaneous modeling of spectrum, pitch, and duration in HMM based speech synthesis. In: Proceedings of Eurospeech, pp. 2347–2350 (1999)
4. Ling, Z.H., et al.: Deep learning for acoustic modeling in parametric speech generation: a systematic review of existing techniques and future trends. IEEE Sig. Process. Mag. **32**(3), 35–52 (2015)
5. Najafabadi, M., Villanustre, F., Khoshgoftaar, T., Seliya, N., Wald, R., Muharemagic, E.: Deep learning applications and challenges in big data analytics. J. Big Data **2**(1), 1–21 (2015)
6. Zen, H., Senior, A., Schuster, M.: Statistical parametric speech synthesis using deep neural networks. In: Proceedings of ICASSP, pp. 7962–7966 (2013)
7. Valentini-Botinhao, C., Wu, Z., and King, S.: Towards minimum perceptual error training for DNN-based speech synthesis. In: Interspeech, pp. 869–873 (2015)
8. Wu, Z., Valentini-Botinhao, C., Watts, O., and King, S.: Deep neural networks employing multi-task learning and stacked bottleneck features for speech synthesis. In: ICASSP, pp. 4460–4464 (2015)
9. Zen, H., Senior, A.: Deep mixture density networks for acoustic modeling in statistical parametric speech synthesis. In: ICASSP, pp. 3844–3848 (2014)
10. Bengio, Y., Simard, P., Frasconi, P.: Learning long-term dependencies with gradient descent is difficult. IEEE Trans. Neural Networks **5**(2), 157–166 (1994)
11. Hochreiter, S., Schmidhuber, J.: Long short-term memory. Neural Comput. **9**(8), 1735–1780 (1997)
12. Fan, Y., Qian Y., Xie F., Soong, F.K.: TTS synthesis with bidirectional LSTM based recurrent neural networks. In: Interspeech, pp. 1964–1968 (2014)
13. Chung, J., Gulcehre, C., Cho, K., Bengio, Y.: Empirical evaluation of gated recurrent neural networks on sequence modeling arXiv preprint: 1412.3555 (2014)
14. Csapó, T.G., Németh, G, and Cernak M.: Residual-based excitation with continuous F0 modeling in HMM-based speech synthesis. In: 3rd International Conference on Statistical Language and Speech Processing, SLSP 2015, vol. 9449, pp. 27–38 (2015)
15. Garner, P.N., Cernak, M., Motlicek, P.: A simple continuous pitch estimation algorithm. IEEE Sig. Process. Lett. **20**(1), 102–105 (2013)
16. Drugman, T., Stylianou, Y.: Maximum voiced frequency estimation: exploiting amplitude and phase spectra. IEEE Sig. Process. Lett. **21**(10), 1230–1234 (2014)
17. Csapó, T.G., Németh, G., Cernak, M., Garner, P.N.: Modeling unvoiced sounds in statistical parametric speech synthesis with a continuous vocoder. In: EUSIPCO, Budapest (2016)
18. Al-Radhi, M.S., Csapó T.G., and Németh, G.: Continuous vocoder in deep neural network based speech synthesis. In: Preparation (2017)
19. Tokuda, K., Kobayashi, T., Masuko, T., Imai, S.: Mel-generalized cepstral analysis – a unified approach to speech spectral estimation. In: Proceedings of ICSLP, pp. 1043–1046 (1994)
20. Imai, S., Sumita, K., Furuichi, C.: Mel log spectrum approximation (MLSA) filter for speech synthesis. Electron. Commun. Jpn. (Part I: Commun.) **66**(2), 10–18 (1983)

21. Al-Radhi, M.S., Csapó, T.G., Németh, G.: Time-domain envelope modulating the noise component of excitation in a continuous residual-based vocoder for statistical parametric speech synthesis. In: Interspeech (2017)
22. Robel, A., Villavicencio, F., Rodet, X.: On cepstral and all-pole based spectral envelope modeling with unknown model order. Pattern Recogn. Lett. **28**(11), 1343–1350 (2007)
23. Galas, T., Rodet, X.: An improved cepstral method for deconvolution of source-filter systems with discrete spectra. In: Proceedings of the ICMC, pp. 82–84 (1990)
24. Cappe, O., Moulines, E.: Regularization techniques for discrete cepstrum estimation. IEEE Sig. Process. **3**(4), 100–103 (1996)
25. Wu, Z., Watts, O., King, S.: Merlin: an open source neural network speech synthesis system. In: Proceedings of the 9th ISCA Speech Synthesis Workshop, Sunnyvale, USA (2016)
26. Schuster, M., Paliwal, K.: Bidirectional recurrent neural networks. IEEE Trans. on Signal Processing **45**(11), 2673–2681 (1997)
27. Kominek, J., Black, W.: CMU ARCTIC databases for speech synthesis. Language Technologies Institute (2003). http://festvox.org/cmu_arctic/
28. Imai, S., Kobayashi, T., Tokuda, K., Masuko, T., Koishida, K., Sako, S., Zen, H.: Speech signal processing toolkit (SPTK) (2016)
29. ITU-R Recommendation BS.1534. Method for the subjective assessment of intermediate audio quality (2001)

Design of Online Echo Canceller in Duplex Mode

Andrey Barabanov[✉] and Evgenij Vikulov

Saint Petersburg State University,
Universitetskaya Nab., 7/9, Saint Petersburg, Russia
Andrey.Barabanov@gmail.com, jenyav94@gmail.com

Abstract. A new online echo canceller system was developed that perfectly works in the duplex mode and shows a good performance in the conventional half-duplex mode. The near speech signal is not corrupted in the duplex mode by the linear compensation procedures but degrades significantly by nonlinear suppression. The conventional linear compensation system is based on the LMS adaptation or its modifications that do not provide a necessary high accuracy of a big number of the impulse response coefficients. We have implemented the LS method for online estimation of the full impulse response using the superfast Schur algorithm for Toeplitz matrix inversion. Implementation details are important. They include numerical accuracy, initialization, update criteria, packet control. Good results of an echo compensation are shown on the data from the Matlab Audio System Toolbox.

Keywords: Echo canceller · Numerical methods · LMS estimates · Superfast Schur algorithm

1 Introduction

The standard approach of the acoustic echo cancellation system design is based on the least mean square algorithm (LMS) [1–3] and it's modifications. It is a gradient type algorithm of estimation of the echo impulse response. This sequence can be long and the convergence speed and accuracy appeared to be critical. They essentially depend on the step of the numerical procedure. The normalized least mean square algorithm (NLMS) determines the maximum value of this step.

The class of the affine projection (AP) algorithms has faster convergence rate, especially for speech signals [4]. Similarly to the NLMS algorithm AP contains the step-size parameter. But the weight vector update in the AP algorithms is made by expanded data, by multiple, most recent input vectors. This increases the convergence rate.

Another approach of adaptive-filtering algorithms for convergence acceleration is presented by the class of the subband adaptive filtering (SAF) algorithms [5–10]. In adaptive filtering in subbands, the input signal and the system output signal are split into adjacent frequency subbands by analysis filter banks. Then each subband signal is subsampled and the adaptive filtering algorithm is applied. The subsampling leads to a greater computational efficiency than the

© Springer International Publishing AG 2017
A. Karpov et al. (Eds.): SPECOM 2017, LNAI 10458, pp. 292–301, 2017.
DOI: 10.1007/978-3-319-66429-3_28

conventional full-band scheme. Also processing in separate subbands provides better convergence speed than the LMS algorithm, since in each subband the adaptation step size can be matched to the energy of the input signal in that band. The early SAF algorithms suffer from structural problem, such as aliasing and band-edge effects, because of the subsampling. Solutions to this problem have been proposed, including spectral gaps between subbands, oversampling of the filter banks, and adaptive cross-terms between the subbands. Today SAF has a lot of modifications, such as NSAF algorithm, which was presented in [9]. It improves the convergence speed but has almost the same computational complexity as the NLMS algorithm. Also the set-membership NSAF algorithm proposed in [4] which achieves fast convergence, low steady-state misalignment and reduced computational complexity simultaneously.

A nonlinear system identification method for echo cancellation was presented in [11]. Adaptation of the system was made using the Normalized Least Mean Square algorithm. Algorithm combined the adaptive linear, Volterra and power filters. Nonlinear models with adaptive Volterra kernels were implemented in [12] using a new updating technique for unknown feedback paths identification of a nonlinear echo reverberation system. A combination of adaptive linear, Volterra and power filters was used and compared in [12] for Echo Return Loss Enhancement in the second-order Volterra filter Normalized Least-Mean-Square algorithm for kernel adaptation. The implemented system gives a superior convergence speed.

The concept of stereophonic acoustic echo suppression (SAES) method without preprocessing in a open-loop teleconferencing systems was proposed in [13] where the Wiener filter in the short-time Fourier transform (STFT) domain is used. Algorithm estimates the echo spectra from the stereo signals using two weighting functions. The spectral modification technique originally proposed for noise reduction is adopted to remove the echo from the microphone signal.

A framework for the echo canceller design of full-duplex communication systems was presented in [14] for the case of discrete multi-tone (DMT) modulation system in an arbitrary mixed domain. This is achieved by introducing a generic decomposition of the Toeplitz data matrix at the transmitter in terms of arbitrary unitary matrices. It is shown that this canceller has a faster convergence rate than other cancellers with similar complexity and is more robust.

The well known lack of the open audio communication systems like Skype or Web RTC is their failure in the full duplex mode. In fact, they support the half-duplex mode only. This means the following. If two persons talk and at each time instant only one or nobody is speaking (half-duplex) then communication does not meet problems. But if they speak simultaneously then the system decides which voice will be transmitted. One of the speakers "captures" the channel. His voice is transmitted normally but the voice of his partner will be blocked. This situation can be lasted until pause of the transmitted speech signal, and after that the talkers can change the roles. Everybody can verify this effect by putting a talk experiment as it is described in [15]. We have done it and our simultaneous talk together failed as it was expected.

The reason of the duplex failure is the strong nonlinear echo suppression after the standard linear compensation.

Let (x_t) be the far signal which is received from the network and goes to the loudspeaker. Let $h = (h_k)_{k=0}^{L-1}$ be the echo impulse response and (z_t) be the sound signal of a speaker near the computer. Then the microphone receives the signal

$$y_t = z_t + y_t^e + n_t, \qquad y_t^e = \sum_{k=0}^{L-1} h_k x_{t-k}$$

where y_t^e is echo, n_t is the noise. Both signals x_t and y_t are known. If $\widehat{h} = (\widehat{h}_k)_{k=0}^{L-1}$ is the estimate of the echo impulse response then the result of the linear echo canceller is

$$z_t^\ell = y_t - \widehat{y}_t^e, \qquad \widehat{y}_t^e = \sum_{k=0}^{L-1} \widehat{h}_k x_{t-k}.$$

The echo compensation error is $\delta_t = y_t^e - \widehat{y}_t^e$.

With a fixed $\widehat{h}$ there is no difference in accuracy $|\delta_t|$ between the full duplex and half-duplex mode (with $z_t = 0$).

If linear compensation does not provide necessary level of residual echo then further nonlinear suppression of the signal z_t^ℓ is implemented in the frequency domain. The details can be found, for instance, in the description of the Web RTC echo canceller system [16]. The duplex mode is actually rejected at this step. Thus, the crucial condition for the duplex audio communication is the high performance of the linear echo compensation.

2   Estimation of the Echo Impulse Response

Assume a time interval $t \in [1, T]$ is chosen where there is no near speech, $z_t = 0$. For any time instant t denote the current estimate of the echo impulse response by $\widehat{h}_t = (\widehat{h}_{k,t})_{k=0}^{L-1}$. The current output error is

$$\delta_t = y_t - \sum_{k=0}^{L-1} \widehat{h}_{k,t} x_{t-k}, \qquad 1 \leq t \leq T.$$

In accordance with the standard LMS method the update procedure is

$$\widehat{h}_{k,t+1} = \widehat{h}_{k,t} + \alpha \delta_t x_{t-k}, \qquad 0 \leq k \leq L-1, \qquad 1 \leq t \leq T.$$

where the step $\alpha > 0$ is the important parameter of the algorithm.

The main problem of this simple estimator is a very slow convergence. The estimator quickly answers to any change of the reverberation conditions. But it takes too many steps to obtain perfect accuracy of coefficients $\widehat{h}_{k,t} \approx h_k$. The reason is a high dimension of the estimated array and the actual independence of its components. An example of the echo impulse response measured to a high accuracy in a small room is shown in Fig. 1.

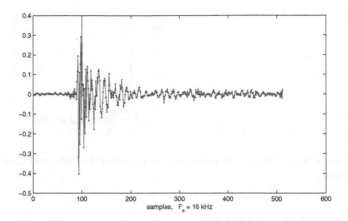

Fig. 1. An example of the real echo impulse response. The sample rate is 16 kHz

We propose an another procedure of the impulse response estimation based on the global LS.

Define the cost function

$$J(\widehat{h}) = \frac{1}{T} \sum_{t=1}^{T} \left| y_t - \sum_{k=0}^{L-1} \widehat{h}_k x_{t-k} \right|^2 \rightarrow \min_{\widehat{h}}$$

The main problem of this approach is the numerical inversion of the square matrix of a big dimension in real time:

$$\widehat{h}_{\mathrm{opt}} = R^{-1} Y$$

where $R = (R_{i,j})_{i,j=0}^{L-1}$, $Y = (Y_i)_{i=0}^{L-1}$,

$$R_{i,j} = \sum_{t=1}^{T} x_{t-i} x_{t-j}, \qquad Y_i = \sum_{t=1}^{T} x_{t-i} y_t.$$

The matrix R is symmetric and Toeplitz. We have implemented the superfast Schur algorithm for its inversion [17]. A benefit of this approach is a direct and exact calculation of a full impulse response at once.

In our room test experiments the echo impulse response updates 5–10 times per second in average. The estimates obtained from completely different input data appeared to be similar. Figure 2 shows the estimates of the impulse response during 3 s and the standard deviations of each coefficient. Accuracy of the LS estimator is much better than accuracy of any gradient procedure. No convergence problem occurs, the problems move to algorithm details and implementation.

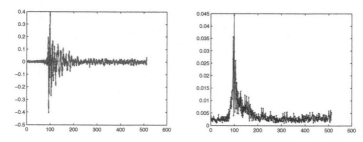

Fig. 2. Estimates of the impulse response obtained during 3 s (left) and their standard deviations (right)

3   Implementation Details

The impulse response estimation procedure ignores time intervals with a near speech. Hence, it must detect time intervals with the far speech only for the impulse response estimation. This is done by the value of the function $J(\widehat{h})$ with the current estimate $\widehat{h}$ which is small when there is no near speech signal and the estimate $\widehat{h}$ is sufficiently good.

The matrix R and the vector Y are calculated online before the decision about the near speech is made. Since their elements are convolutions this does not take many resources.

An initialization procedure is a special task. At the beginning no estimate $\widehat{h}$ is available and a detection of the first interval without near speech is made separately.

Any estimate of an impulse response is constructed by a far speech signal on some time interval. The spectral content of the signal reflects an accuracy of the estimate. Therefore, a number of the last successful estimates are averaged. An new estimate $\widehat{h}_{\mathrm{opt}}$ is determined to be successful by the value of the same cost function $J(\widehat{h}_{\mathrm{opt}})$. If reverberation conditions essentially change then the estimates become unsuccessful and the initialization procedure starts.

An accuracy of both the estimate $\widehat{h}$ and the cost function $J(\widehat{h})$ is very important for a correct work of the system. It is well known that the superfast Schur algorithm may be numerically unstable. We implement a regularization with the 3% increase of the diagonal element of the inverted Toeplitz matrix. This does not degrade significantly an estimate but prevents a singularity. The advanced methods of a regularization are based on the preconditioning [19, 20].

A synchronization of the stream (x_t) that is sent to the loudspeaker and the stream (y_t) received by the microphone is crucial at the stage of the impulse response estimation. This requires a very accurate interaction with the buffers of the loudspeaker and the microphone. If an overflow or an underflow appears then it is detected and delays are corrected.

Finally, the developed AEC system contains both linear and nonlinear compensation parts. The nonlinear processing is based on a slight suppression by smoothed residuals in the frequency domain. The nonlinear part is optional and is expected to be adaptive in the future since the linear compensation is strong.

4   Evaluation

The input data for the test described on this Section were taken from the Matlab Audio System Toolbox [18].

The far speech signal and the near speech signal are shown in Fig. 3. Obviously, there is a full duplex in the end of the talk. There are also a couple of pauses.

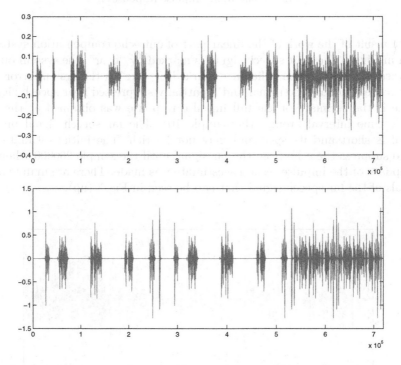

Fig. 3. Far speech (up) and near speech (bottom) signals. Time is graduated in samples. The sample rate is 16 kHz

The echo impulse response is fixed in the Toolbox [18] and is shown in Fig. 4. The microphone input is a sum of the near speech signal and the filtered far speech signal. It is shown in Fig. 5. The task of the AEC system is a suppression of the part of this signal which is the filtered far speech signal.

This microphone input signal was processed by our echo canceller system. First, the nonlinear part was switched off and the linear compensation was working only.

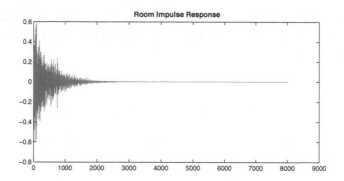

Fig. 4. The room impulse response

The result of the work of the linear part of our echo compensation system is shown in Fig. 6. The near speech signal is marked by "near", the system output is marked by "out". Their difference marked by "err" is the system error that includes the residual echo signal and a partially suppressed near speech signal.

The initial estimate of the full impulse response was obtained at the first suitable time interval around the sample 10^4. The far speech signal on this interval is short and its spectrum may not be rich. The initial estimate was used to suppress the echo from the far signal until the sample 260000 when the first update of the impulse response estimate was made. There are many voiced intervals of the far speech signal that can be seen in Fig. 3 (up).

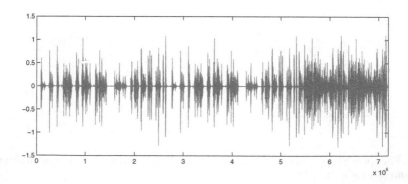

Fig. 5. The microphone input

Totally 8 updates of the full impulse response were made. The last one was obtained on the interval [501120, 506088] samples. The estimates were averaged.

The near speech signal is not corrupted because it the linear compensation algorithm is completely not sensitive to them.

The last part of the sample 520000 is the full duplex conversation. The near speech signal did not change as it should be. The error is equal exactly to the residual echo. It is relatively small with respect to the speech intelligibility.

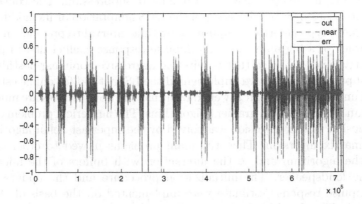

Fig. 6. Result of the linear compensation. Near speech ("near"), EC output ("out"), their difference("err")

The result of the work of the full echo compensation system including the nonlinear part is shown in Fig. 7. The near speech signal is marked by "near", the system output is marked by "out", and their difference is marked by "err". As it was expected a compensation of the far signal in pauses is better but the near speech signal is partially corrupted especially in the duplex mode.

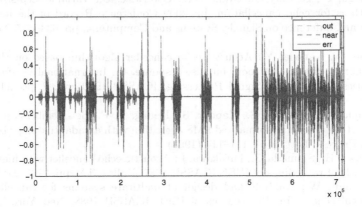

Fig. 7. Result of the nonlinear compensation. Near speech ("near"), EC output ("out"), their difference("err")

5   Conclusion

The conventional echo canceller systems do not work properly in the duplex mode but in the half-duplex only. Duplex is not corrupted by the linear compensation procedures but it is very sensitive to nonlinear suppression. The conventional linear compensation system is based on the LMS adaptation or its modifications. These gradient type algorithm require a long time interval to provide a necessary high accuracy of a big number of the impulse response coefficients. In practice, the accuracy is not achieved that requires an aggressive nonlinear postfilter with a strong suppression. We have implemented the LS method for online estimation of the full impulse response. It is well known that the LS estimates are much more precise than estimates from gradient algorithms. The numerical problem of a very high dimension matrix inversion was solved by the superfast Schur algorithm for Toeplitz matrix inversion. Then the main problems moved to other sensitive parts of the algorithm and to the interaction with buffers of the microphone and of the loudspeaker. The initialization procedure and the update criteria for the impulse response estimate were implemented on the basis of the same LS approach. The developed echo canceller has shown good performance in the standard half-duplex mode and it perfectly works in the duplex mode.

In the future, the spectral content of the input signal should be taken into account to obtain a uniform spectral accuracy of the reverberation transfer function during averaging particular estimates.

References

1. Haykin, S.S.: Adaptive Filter Theory, 4th edn. Prentice-Hall, Upper Saddle River (2002)
2. Paleologu, C., Benesty, J., Grant, S.L., Osterwise, C.: Variable step-size NLMS algorithms for echo cancellation. In: 2009 Conference Record of the forty-third Asilomar Conference on Signals, Systems and Computers., pp. 633–637, November 2009
3. Makino, S., Kaneda, Y.: Acoustic echo canceller algorithm based on the variation characteristics of a room impulse response. In: International Conference on Acoustics, Speech, and Signal Processing, ICASSP 1990, vol. 2, pp. 1133–1136 (1990)
4. Gollamudi, S., Nagaraj, S., Kapoor, S., Huang, Y.-F.: Set-membership filtering and a set-membership normalized LMS algorithm with an adaptive step size. IEEE Signal Process. Lett. 5(5), 111–114 (1998)
5. Yasukawa, H., Shimada, S., Furukawa, I.: Acoustic echo canceller with high speech quality. In: Proceedings of IEEE ICASSP 1987, Dallas, TX, pp. 2125–2128 (1987)
6. Kellermann, W.: Analysis and design of multirate systems for cancellation of acoustical echoes. In: Proceedings of IEEE ICASSP 1988, New York, NY, pp. 2570–2573 (1988)
7. Gilloire, A., Vetterli, M.: Adaptive filtering in subbands. In: Proceedings of IEEE ICASSP 1988, New York, NY, pp. 1572–1575 (1988)
8. Gilloire, A., Vetterli, M.: Adaptive filtering in subbands with critical sampling: analysis, experiments, and application to acoustic echo cancellation. IEEE Trans. Signal Process. 40(8), 1862–1875 (1992)

9. Lee, K.A., Gan, W.S.: Improving convergence of the NLMS algorithm using constrained subband updates. IEEE Signal Process. Lett. **11**(9), 736–739 (2004)
10. Zheng, Z., Liu, Z., Zhao, H., Yu, Y., Lu, L.: Robust set-membership normalized subband adaptive filtering algorithms and their application to acoustic echo cancellation. IEEE Trans. Circ. Syst., pp. 1–14 (2017)
11. Contan, C., Topa, M., Kirei, B., Homana, I.: Nonlinear acoustic system identification using a combination of volterra and power filters. In: IEEE 10th International Symposium on Signals, Circuits and Systems (ISSCS), pp. 1–4 (2011)
12. Contan, C., Zeller, M., Kellermann, W., Topa, M.: Excitation-dependent stepsize control of adaptive volterra filters for acoustic echo cancellation. In: 20th European Signal Processing Conference-EUSIPCO (2012)
13. Yang, F., Wu, M., Yang, J.: Stereophonic acoustic echo suppression based on wiener filter in the short-time fourier transform domain. IEEE Signal Process. Lett. **19**(4), 227–230 (2012)
14. Ehtiati, N., Champagne, B.: A general framework for mixed-domain echo cancellation in discrete multitone systems. IEEE Trans. Commun. **61**(2), 769–780 (2013)
15. https://appr.tc
16. Cromium, https://chromium.googlesource.com/external/webrtc
17. Ammar, G.S., Gragg, W.B.: Numerical experience with a superfast real Toeplitz solver. Linear Algebra Appl. **121**, 185–206 (1989)
18. Mathworks Corporation, https://www.mathworks.com/help/audio/examples/acoustic-echo-cancellation-aec.html
19. Tudisco, F., Fiore, C.D., Tyrtyshnikov, E.E.: Optimal rank matrix algebras preconditioners. Linear Algebra Appl. **438**, 405–427 (2013)
20. Zamarashkin, N.L., Oseledets, I.V., Tyrtyshnikov, E.E.: Approximation of Teoplitz matrices by sums of circulants and small-rank matrices. Doklady Math. **73**(1), 100–101 (2006)

Detection of Stance and Sentiment Modifiers in Political Blogs

Maria Skeppstedt[1]([⊠]), Vasiliki Simaki[1,2], Carita Paradis[2],
and Andreas Kerren[1]

[1] Department of Computer Science, Linnaeus University, Växjö, Sweden
{maria.skeppstedt,vasiliki.simaki,andreas.kerren}@lnu.se
[2] Centre for Languages and Literature, Lund University, Lund, Sweden
carita.paradis@englund.lu.se

Abstract. The automatic detection of seven types of modifiers was studied: *Certainty, Uncertainty, Hypotheticality, Prediction, Recommendation, Concession/Contrast* and *Source*. A classifier aimed at detecting local cue words that signal the categories was the most successful method for five of the categories. For *Prediction* and *Hypotheticality*, however, better results were obtained with a classifier trained on tokens and bigrams present in the entire sentence. Unsupervised cluster features were shown useful for the categories *Source* and *Uncertainty*, when a subset of the training data available was used. However, when all of the 2,095 sentences that had been actively selected and manually annotated were used as training data, the cluster features had a very limited effect. Some of the classification errors made by the models would be possible to avoid by extending the training data set, while other features and feature representations, as well as the incorporation of pragmatic knowledge, would be required for other error types.

Keywords: Stance modifiers · Sentiment modifiers · Active learning · Unsupervised features · Sesource-aware natural language processing

1 Introduction

Stance detection and sentiment analysis are typically modelled as binary classification tasks within the field of natural language processing. That is, authors express stance by positioning themselves as *for* or *against* a given target or topic, or sentiment by giving a *positive* or *negative* opinion [11]. It has, however, been argued that this simple, binary model does not capture the full complexity of the language used for expressing stance and opinions [6]. Instead, authors employ a wide range of modifiers in their opinionated language. The *first aim* of this study is to investigate the automatic detection of seven types of such modifiers.

Many classification tasks within natural language processing rely on a large set of manually annotated training samples. However, in the cases when large training sets are not available, resource-aware methods must instead be relied upon. Active learning is one such resource-aware method that has previously

© Springer International Publishing AG 2017
A. Karpov et al. (Eds.): SPECOM 2017, LNAI 10458, pp. 302–311, 2017.
DOI: 10.1007/978-3-319-66429-3_29

been shown successful for detecting language modifiers. The method is built on the idea to reduce the number of training samples required by actively selecting useful samples. Using a previously applied active learning approach as a baseline, the *second aim* of this study is to investigate two methods with a potential to improve this approach: (i) to provide annotations with a higher granularity and (ii) to incorporate machine learning features derived in an unsupervised fashion.[1]

2   Background

Based on previous research [6], we study seven types of possible ways in which the categories *positive/negative* sentiment or stance *for/against* can be modified.

Certainty and *Uncertainty* are epistemic modifiers, which in the context of sentiment and stance taking might also give information about the strength with which an opinion is expressed. The following three evaluations would all be classified as positive: "The arguments are irrefutable and readers will definitely enjoy the trip back in time", "The arguments are accurate and readers will enjoy the trip back in time", and "The arguments seem accurate and readers might enjoy the trip back in time". Still, given their different values on the *Certainty/Neutral/Uncertainty* scale, they all convey a slightly different message.

The modifiers *Hypotheticality*, *Recommendation* and *Prediction* indicate that an expression is not necessarily true at the moment at which it is expressed. For instance, the *Hypotheticality* in "If it had been less complicated, it would have been good" makes it into an expression of negative sentiment, despite containing "good". "A good film should never be too complicated" could, on the surface, be a positive or neutral expression. However, since it is a *Recommendation*, it is likely to rather have been primed by a negative opinion. Finally, "Her next film will be the best ever made", expresses positive sentiment without any indications of uncertainty, but since it is a *Prediction*, the author is likely to be less certain of this opinion, than had it been about a film that already had been made.

That an expression contains *Concession/Contrast* typically indicates that opinions of different polarities are expressed, e.g., "I enjoyed reading this book, but parts of it were boring". The occurrence of a contrast affects the overall opinion conveyed, i.e., the overall opinion is not likely to be unequivocally positive or negative. Finally, if an expression contains a statement of its *Source*, this also modifies how an opinion should be interpreted. That is, the existence of a source indicates that the opinion expressed is not necessarily the opinion of the author, e.g., "According to the guide book, this is the best restaurant in town".

We are only aware of one previous study in which resource-aware approaches have been applied for detecting stance and sentiment modifiers [14]. By simulating active learning, that study showed that active sampling outperformed random sampling of training data for categories that closely resemble *Uncertainty*, *Hypotheticality* and *Concession/Contrast*. We therefore here apply the

[1] We are very grateful to the Swedish Research Council (framework grant "the Digitized Society – Past, Present, and Future" with No. 2012-5659), to Tom Sköld for data annotation and to Kostiantyn Kucher for annotation tool construction.

same successful active learning method as our baseline method. In contrast to the previous study, we do not simulate active learning, but use it as the real sampling method for creating our training corpus. We also apply the method to a wider range of modifier categories than in the previous study, and we evaluate the effect of extending the method with additional resource-aware techniques.

3   Method

The baseline active learning method was compared to two extensions (i) to add more granular annotations and (ii) to use features from unlabelled data. A previously constructed gold standard corpus, in which the seven categories studied here had been (doubly) annotated [6] was used as evaluation data. This gold standard corpus consisted of opinionated texts in the form of political blogs on the topic of Brexit. The same procedure that had been used for creating this gold standard corpus was applied to create a large pool of data to use in the process of active selection of the training samples that were annotated in the present study. That is, documents from URL:s that started with the word *blog* and that contained expressions related to Brexit were downloaded. Boilerplate text, non-English text and HTML code were then removed using jusText, and the text was segmented into sentences with the standard sentence segmentation technique included in NLTK [2]. It was also ensured that no duplicates from the gold standard were included in the pool of unlabelled data. The annotation of the actively selected sentences was performed with an annotation tool [9] specifically designed for this task. Sentences selected for annotation were presented to the annotator, who classified them according to the seven modifying categories included in the study. Annotation was conducted on the basis of a sentence, with respect to whether the sentence included a modifier (one or more) or not. One sentence at a time, without context, was presented for annotation. The annotator could also mark a sentence as irrelevant if it was a result of a pre-processing error (e.g., boiler plate texts or incomplete sentences). All annotations were performed in an entirely topic-independent fashion. That is, a sentence was, for instance, classified as *Uncertain* if it contained uncertainty in general, regardless of whether this uncertainty was targeted towards a statement related to Brexit.

The active sampling of training data was performed according to the active learning method that had previously been shown successful for modifiers [14]. That is, the training samples that were estimated to be most useful for a support vector machine classifier were actively selected for annotation from the pool of unlabelled data. The estimation was based on the standard method of selecting the unlabelled sample closest to the separating hyperplane of the classifier [16]. The Scikit-learn [12] SVC class with a linear kernel was used for implementing the data selection. A separate binary SVM model was trained for each of the seven categories, using unigrams and bigrams as features and the same classifier settings that had previously been shown successful for detecting modifiers [14]. A previously constructed vocabulary with 20 terms signalling each of the modifying categories studied was used for creating the seed set required to start the active learning process. Three corpus sentences containing each one of these vocabulary terms were selected from the pool of unlabelled data to form a seed set. The annotator first annotated the sentences in the seed set. Thereafter, active learning was applied to select the five most useful unlabelled sentences for each one of the seven categories. These sentences were then manually annotated, and, thereafter, the models were retrained, also including these newly annotated sentences. This process was then repeated, until 2,095 actively selected sentences had been annotated to form the training set. Results achieved when evaluating the SVM classifier on the gold standard corpus were used as the baseline results.

3.1   Adding Annotations with a Higher Granularity

We hypothesised that the categories studied are mainly expressed by local cue words, and that it would therefore not be optimal to model the task as the text classification task based on sentence-level occurrences of unigrams and bigrams that was used in the training data selection process. Instead, we hypothesised that the task would be more suitable to model as a chunk detection task, with the aim of detecting chunks that function as cue words for the categories studied. A second round of annotation was therefore performed on the training data, in which annotations on a more granular level were provided, on a token-level instead of on a sentence-level. That is, the tokens signalling the modifying categories were marked, using the Brat annotation tool [15].

A classifier was, thereafter, trained to detect tokens/chunks signalling the modifying category in question. For evaluation, the detected chunks were, however, transformed back to a text classification format, in order to match the format of the sentence-level annotations of the gold standard. That is, if the classifier marked a token/text chunk as signalling a modifier category, the sentence containing the token/chunk was classified as belonging to that category. As classifier, Scikit-learn's LogisticRegression classifier was used. The choice was based on an external requirement to provide classifications with easily interpretable confidence estimates, which would not be provided by, e.g., an SVM or a rule/lexicon-based classifier. The token to be classified, as well as the two tokens immediately preceding and the one following it were used as features. To limit the dimensionality of the feature vectors created, a minimum of three occurrences in the training data was required for a neighbouring token to be included as a feature, while a minimum of three occurrences in the entire pool of unlabelled data was required for the current token. A suitable value for the logistic regression regularisation parameter was determined by 30-fold cross-validation on the training data.

Similar to previous studies [10], information derived from a large, unlabelled corpus was also incorporated as features. This was achieved by applying the Gensim library [13], through which semantic vectors in the form of word embeddings from an out-of-the-box word2vec model trained on Google news[2] are provided.

---

[2] https://code.google.com/archive/p/word2vec/.

Semantic vectors corresponding to the words in the training corpus were clustered using dbscan clustering [5], and each of the n clusters created were given a unique representation in the form of a *cluster representation vector* of length n. That is, all vector elements were set to 0, except the one element that represented the cluster, which was set to 1. The cluster information was incorporated in the feature representation for a token by (i) determining which cluster was closest to the semantic vector that corresponds to the token (measured through the Euclidean distance between the semantic vector and the cluster centroids), and (ii) concatenating the *cluster representation vector* of this cluster to the feature representation for the token. A maximum Euclidean distance of 0.8 between two semantic vectors in the same cluster was allowed when performing the dbscan clustering. This distance was determined by manually inspecting the semantic coherence in a subset of created clusters, for different distances.

4   Results and Discussion

Models using the three methods investigated were trained on two versions of the training corpus, after 1,525 actively selected sentences had been annotated and after 2,095 actively selected sentences had been annotated. F-scores obtained when evaluating these models against the gold standard are presented in Table 1, and precision and recall are presented in Fig. 1.

The hypothesis that a chunk detection model would be most suitable seems to hold for five of the categories. For *Hypotheticality* and *Prediction*, however, the sentence-level classifiers performed better. The general trend (with the exception of *Certainty*) was that the baseline method resulted in a better recall, while better precision was shown by the other two methods investigated. When only 1,525 training data samples were used, the cluster features had (i) a relatively large positive effect on the *Source* category and (ii) a small positive effect on the *Uncertainty* category. The effects of incorporating cluster features were, however, very limited when all data available was used.

Regardless of which method was used, only the results for the best-performing classifier, *Concession/Contrast*, were close to the annotator agreement. Results for the best performing chunk-level models were, therefore, analysed to identify frequent reasons for false negatives, i.e., when the classifier failed to detect the category in question, and false positives, i.e., sentences incorrectly classified as belonging to the category in question. Table 2 lists typical challenges to the classifiers (referred to as Ex. 1.1–16.5 in the following paragraphs).

In sentences annotated according to the category *Uncertainty*, there were eight frequently used words, including "think", "should" and "would" that caused classification problems (Ex. 1.1–8.2). These words occurred in 76%/75%/59% of the true positives/false negatives/false positives, respectively. Whether these words function as cues for uncertainty can, sometimes, be determined by the words in their context. As many of the examples illustrate, however, pragmatic knowledge is often required to determine what they indicate, i.e., knowledge that is not possible to capture without using vast resources of annotated data. Some of these words were also frequently used in sentences classified

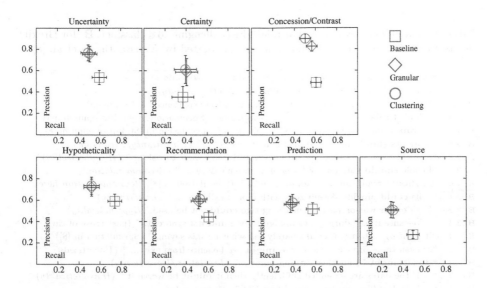

Fig. 1. Precision and recall when using a training set of 2,095 sentences. The error bars show the 95% confidence interval for the results [3, pp. 91–92, 94–96]

Table 1. F-scores for the three methods investigated, when using 1,525 sentences and 2,095 sentences to train the classifiers, respectively. Best results for each data size are shown in bold. F-scores for the intra-annotator agreement are provided with a relatively low confidence (as they were calculated on half of the gold standard corpus) and no point estimates are, therefore, given. Instead, confidence intervals (95%) were computed with a bootstrap resampling approach [7], using the 2.5/97.5 percentiles of 10,000 bootstrapping folds. *Category frequency* is the percentage of sentences that contain the category in question (in the gold standard/after 1,525 training sentences had been annotated/after 2,095 training sentences had been annotated)

	F-score 1,525 training instances			F-score 2,095 training instances			F-score intra-annotator	Category frequency
	Baseline	Granular	Cluster	Baseline	Granular	Cluster	(Min – Max)	(%)
Uncertainty	0.53	0.59	**0.63**	0.56	**0.61**	0.60	0.74 – 0.87	10/14/14
Certainty	0.29	0.50	**0.52**	0.36	**0.48**	0.48	0.55 – 0.78	4/7/6
Conc./Contrast	0.52	**0.66**	0.65	0.54	**0.67**	0.65	0.71 – 0.81	17/21/20
Hypotheticality	**0.65**	0.60	0.59	**0.66**	0.60	0.61	0.72 – 0.86	8/13/13
Recommend	0.48	**0.60**	0.57	0.51	0.55	**0.57**	0.72 – 0.85	10/14/13
Prediction	**0.50**	0.44	0.48	**0.54**	0.44	0.46	0.73 – 0.84	12/14/15
Source	0.35	0.34	**0.42**	0.35	0.37	**0.39**	0.66 – 0.79	14/14/17
	F-score, previous studies							
Speculation	0.92	(10-fold cross validation on 17,263 sentences [4])						
Speculation	0.89	(500 actively selected sentences [14])						
Conc./Contrast	0.56	(500 actively selected sentences [14])						
Hypotheticality	0.73	(500 actively selected sentences [14])						

(Speculation corresponds to *Uncertainty* ∪ *Hypotheticality*)

Table 2. Examples of sentences that might be challenging to a classifier. **B** (for **B**rexit) means annotated in this study and *K* means annotated by *K*onstantinova et al. [8]

		Sentences containing difficult expressions (and their classifications)
B	1.1	"I **think** you are from a well to do family ..." (*Uncertainty*)
B	1.2	"I **think** it's a slap in the face to anyone who has experienced ..." (opinion)
K	1.3	"I don't **think** it's too bad for a cordless phone." (Speculation in [8], but opinion here)
K	1.4	"I **think** it makes the phone look less modern." (Speculation in [8], but opinion here)
B	2.1	"... events **should** make it difficult for Camerlot ..." (*Uncertainty/Prediction*)
B	2.2	"**Should** they not win a constituency vote I don't want to risk ... " (*Hypotheticality*)
B	2.3	"People **should** vote on the basis of a citizen's duty ... " (*Recommendation*)
K	2.4	"P. **should** really consider adding this ... " (Speculation in [8], *Recommendation* here)
B	3.1	"This **could** provide Washington with more flexibility ... " (*Uncertainty*)
B	3.2	"If an officer was on parade such language **could** not be used. (*Hypotheticality*)
B	3.3	"... because it was during a campaign they **could** not ignore it. " (past tense of can)
K	3.4	"It went by so fast you **could** barely tell what he was saying." (Speculation in [8])
B	4.1	"... even these pro - EU industries **might** see benefits from exit ... " (*Uncertainty*)
B	4.2	"Brexit **might** be another turning point ..." (*Prediction/Uncertainty*)
B	4.3	"... If the dates are extended sufficiently then it **might** be worth it." (*Hypotheticality*)
B	5.1	"... it looked like Iain Gray **would** be FM." (*Uncertainty*)
B	5.2	"... more integrated capital markets **would** tie things together better." (*Hypotheticality*)
B	6.1	"Be that as it **may**, we finally did join the European Union in January 1973."
B	6.2	"Granted, his party **may** commit regicide in the process." (*Uncertainty*)
B	7.1	" ... being elected **seems** to be about reconciling the unreconcilable. (*Source*)
B	7.2	" ... international cooperation **seems** to have lost its way ... " (*Uncertainty*)
B	8.1	"In this fall he **appeared** to hurt his leg ... (*Source*)
B	8.2	"Capitalism doesn't **appear** to work without someone losing out." (*Uncertainty*)
B	9.1	"It is **vanishingly unlikely** ... "/"It is **inconceivable** that ..." (*Certainty*)
B	10.1	"I asked a man **if** he knew the way." (indirect question)
B	10.2	"There will be no going back **if** we decide to leave" (*Hypotheticality*)
B	10.3	"There'd be no residue of benefit – **even if** that were possible." (*Hypotheticality*)
B	10.4	"I listen carefully to what is being said **even if** I don't agree." (*Conc./Contrast*)
B	11.1	"The referendum has triggered the eurogroups **need** for additional safeguards"
B	11.2	"What we actually **need** is a manifesto that provides detail" (*Recommendation*)
B	12.1	"I can't **see** him winning by putting his foot in his mouth." (*Prediction*)
B	12.2	"I could **see** that many of the trees in his orchard bore the scars ..." (*Source*)
B	13.1	"**But** it is not the funding side of Greek banks that is the real problem." (no contrast)
		Sentences containing antithesis without a contrast marker
B	14.1	"Public schools in Barcelona teach in Catalan, not Spanish." (*Conc./Contrast*)
B	14.2	"Germany has not searched our mails as have the British." (*Conc./Contrast*)
B	14.3	"... any other author, alive or deceased" (*Conc./Contrast*)
B	14.4	"Having heavily lost the referendum, their vote soared to over 49% ..." (*Conc./Contrast*)
		Sentences categorised as *Source* (the source in italics and the marker in bold)
B	15.1	"*Nigel Farage*, the 'Saviour of British Sovereignty', whilst knowing this, **insists** that .."
B	15.2	"*Statistics* also **show**, that despite or because of the NHS, no one gets out of here alive!"
B	15.3	"Most *opinion polls* have Ukip, which has 11 MEPs .."
		Sentences using a number of isolated markers to express *Prediction* (markers in bold)
B	16.1	"... the **possibility** that the Government's policies **could harm growth** ..."
B	16.2	"The situation is **moving** too fast now for a controllable **outcome**."
B	16.3	"Greece **may** experience rapidly **accelerating** inflation."
B	16.4	"I **think** the early **2020s** are the **best bet**."
B	16.5	"I don't **think** this **can last**."

into *Hypotheticality* ("could", "would", "should" or "might" occurred in 89% of the false negatives and 66% of the false positives for *Hypotheticality*). This might have caused additional difficulties for the classifiers, and might be the reason why the baseline classifier, which used cues from the entire sentence, outperformed the chunk-based one for the category *Hypotheticality*. Many previous studies (for instance [4,8,14], but not [17]) have (i) grouped *Hypotheticality* and *Uncertainty* into one category, and (ii) treated, e.g., "think"/"should"/"could" as markers for *Uncertainty* regardless of the pragmatics (Ex. 1.3/1.4/2.4/3.4), which might explain why lower results were achieved here than in previous studies (Table 1).

For the category *Certainty*, 24% of the false negatives included either one of the words "clear" or "sure", and there were also other expressions, for which it is dependent on the context whether they signal *Certainty*, e.g., "of course". The classifier, however, also failed to detect many evident cues for *Certainty*, e.g., "definitely" and some (but not all) modified uncertainty cues, e.g., "without doubt" and "too plausible". There were also confusions between *Certainty* and *Uncertainty*, for cases that might be equally challenging for a human (Ex. 9.1).

For 13% of the false negatives for *Concession/Contrast*, an expression of contrast started the sentence. This might be explained by that contrast markers often start a sentence without signalling contrast (Ex. 13.1). The expressions "even if", "yet", "and then" caused another 10% of the false negatives (Ex. 10.3, 10.4), while 20% contained more univocal contrast markers, e.g., "compared with". Most false negatives did, however, not contain an explicit contrast marker, but expressed *antithesis* [1], e.g., by applying negations or antonyms (Ex. 14.1–14.4). These constructions are impossible to detect by the models applied here, but more complex approaches would be required, e.g., approaches built on external semantic resources that model semantic relations between words.

For *Source*, 17% of the false negatives and 26% of the false positives contained versions of the ambiguous expressions "appear", "seem" or "see" (Ex. 7.1–8.2). 75% of the remaining false negatives contained a clear cue that indicated the existence of a source, e.g., "show" or "insists" (Ex. 15.1,15.2). In only a few cases was the source mentioned without a marker (Ex. 15.3). There was, however, a large variation in what cues were used, which might explain the low results. Sometimes there was also a distance of many tokens between the cue and the actual source (Ex. 15.1), which indicates that information from a parser might be useful for constructing features for this category. As the source of information often consists of names, the output from a named entity recogniser might also be useful. Among false positives, there were many examples where the model had learnt to detect typical cues for a source, but had not learnt in which contexts it functions as a cue for *Source*. For instance, "report" in "The IMF is leaking a report ...". This indicates that more training data, which would allow more examples of context, would be required in order to improve the *Source*-classifier.

Modifiers expressed by someone else than the author were not counted as belonging to that modifying category. E.g., "The US suspect Iran of ..." should not be classified as *Uncertainty*, since the uncertainty is expressed by someone else than the author. This was a general source of false positives, which shows the need for a high-performing *Source*-classifier for improving the other classifiers.

The model learnt for *Recommendation* did not reflect the complexity with which the category was expressed. 79% of the true positives and 61% of the false positives contained versions of "should"/"must"/"need"/"have to" (Ex. 2.3, 11.1–11.2). These expressions were, however, only present in 30% of the false negatives. Among the rest of the false negatives, around half contained specific expressions that mark recommendation, e.g., "let's", "I urge" and "I suggest", while the rest were recommendations expressed by an imperative verb, e.g., "Stop using it" and "Count me out". Using the same features and a larger training data set might lead to that more of the recommendation-specific expressions will be detected. Features that include part-of-speech tagging might, however, be required for detecting recommendations expressed by an imperative verb.

The model learnt for *Prediction* seems to be even less complex, with 86% of the true positives and 56% of false positives that contained versions of "will"/"going to". There is, however, a potential for a large complexity of a good model, since the same frequency among false negatives was 33%, and there was a large variety in how predictions were expressed. Contrary to the other categories that were typically expressed by isolated chunks in the sentence, *Prediction* was often expressed using several different cues that would all be required for the reader (and thereby the model) to understand that the sentence contained a prediction. This difference (Ex. 16.1–16.5) is likely to be the reason why the sentence-level baseline classifier outperformed the chunk-based one for *Prediction*.

Future work includes an incorporation of some of the types of features suggested here, as well as a further expansion of the training data. It would also be possible to combine the two approaches evaluated here, by applying the output of a chunk-based classifier as features for training the sentence-level classifier.

5   Conclusion

We hypothesised that stance and sentiment modifiers are mainly expressed by local cue words, and that detection of such modifiers therefore is most suitable to model as a chunk detection task, with the aim of detecting these cue words. This hypothesis held true for five of the categories studied, but for *Prediction* and *Hypotheticality*, better results were obtained with a sentence-level classifier trained on tokens and bigrams present in the entire sentence. Cluster features derived in an unsupervised fashion were useful for the categories *Source* and *Uncertainty* when a subset of the training data available was used. When all data available (2,095 actively selected sentences) was used, however, the effects of incorporating cluster features were very limited. The analysis showed that some types of classifier errors might be avoided by providing more training data, and thereby more examples of cue words and contexts that could determine whether potential cue words signal the categories investigated. For other types of errors, however, other features and feature representations than the ones used here might be required. Yet other types of errors would only be possible to avoid by taking on the difficult task of incorporating pragmatic knowledge.

References

1. Azar, M.: Argumentative text as rhetorical structure: an application of rhetorical structure theory. Argumentation **13**(1), 97–114 (1999)
2. Bird, S.: NLTK: the natural language toolkit. In: Proceedings of the Workshop on Effective Tools and Methodologies for Teaching NLP and Computational Linguistics. Association for Computational Linguistics, Stroudsburg, PA, USA (2002)
3. Campbell, M.J., Machin, D., Walters, S.J.: Medical Statistics : A Textbook for the Health Sciences, 4th edn. Wiley, Chichester (2007)
4. Cruz, N.P., Taboada, M., Mitkov, R.: A machine-learning approach to negation and speculation detection for sentiment analysis. J. Assoc. Inf. Sci. Technol. **67**(9), 526–558 (2015)
5. Ester, M., Kriegel, H.P., Sander, J., Xu, X.: A density-based algorithm for discovering clusters in large spatial databases with noise. In: Proceedings of the International Conference on Knowledge Discovery and Data Mining, pp. 226–231. AAAI Press (1996)
6. Forthcoming: Annotating speaker stance in discourse: the Brexit Blog Corpus (2017)
7. Kaplan, D.: Resampling stats in MATLAB. http://www.macalester.edu/~kaplan/Resampling/. Accessed 1999
8. Konstantinova, N., de Sousa, S.C., Cruz, N.P., Maña, M.J., Taboada, M., Mitkov, R.: A review corpus annotated for negation, speculation and their scope. In: Proceedings of the Conference on Language Resources and Evaluation, pp. 3190–3195. European Language Resources Association, Paris, France (2012)
9. Kucher, K., Kerren, A., Paradis, C., Sahlgren, M.: Visual analysis of text annotations for stance classification with ALVA. In: EuroVis 2016 - Posters, pp. 49–51. The Eurographics Association, Geneva, Switzerland (2016)
10. Miller, S., Guinness, J., Zamanian, A.: Name tagging with word clusters and discriminative training. In: Proceedings of NAACL HLT, pp. 337–342. Association for Computational Linguistics, Stroudsburg, PA, USA (2004)
11. Mohammad, S.M., Sobhani, P., Kiritchenko, S.: Stance and sentiment in tweets. arXiv preprint arXiv:1605.01655 (2016)
12. Pedregosa, F., Varoquaux, G., Gramfort, A., Michel, V., Thirion, B., Grisel, O., Blondel, M., Prettenhofer, P., Weiss, R., Dubourg, V., Vanderplas, J., Passos, A., Cournapeau, D., Brucher, M., Perrot, M., Duchesnay, E.: Scikit-learn: machine learning in Python. J. Mach. Learn. Res. **12**, 2825–2830 (2011)
13. Řehůřek, R., Sojka, P.: Software framework for topic modelling with large corpora. In: Proceedings of Workshop on New Challenges for NLP Frameworks, pp. 45–50. European Language Resources Association, Paris, France, May 2010
14. Skeppstedt, M., Sahlgren, M., Paradis, C., Kerren, A.: Active learning for detection of stance components. In: Proceedings of the PEOPLES Workshop, pp. 50–59. Association for Computational Linguistics, Stroudsburg, PA, USA, December 2016
15. Stenetorp, P., Pyysalo, S., Topic, G., Ohta, T., Ananiadou, S., Tsujii, J.: BRAT: a web-based tool for NLP-assisted text annotation. In: Proceedings of EACL, pp. 102–107. Association for Computational Linguistics, Stroudsburg, PA, USA (2012)
16. Tong, S., Koller, D.: Support vector machine active learning with applications to text classification. J. Mach. Learn. Res. **2**, 45–66 (2002)
17. Velupillai, S.: Shades of Certainty - Annotation and Classification of Swedish Medical Records. Doctoral thesis, Department of Computer and Systems Sciences, Stockholm University, Stockholm, Sweden, April 2012

Digits to Words Converter for Slavic Languages in Systems of Automatic Speech Recognition

Josef Chaloupka$^{(\boxtimes)}$

Technical University of Liberec, 461 17 Liberec, Czech Republic
josef.chaloupka@tul.cz
https://www.ite.tul.cz/speechlabe/

Abstract. In this paper, a system for digits to words conversion for almost all Slavic languages is proposed. This system was developed for improvement of text corpora which we are using for building of a lexicon or for training of language models and acoustic models in the task of Large Vocabulary Continuous Speech Recognition (LVCSR). Strings of digits, some other special characters (%, €, $, ...) or abbreviations of physical units (km, m, cm, kg, l, °C, etc.) occur very often in our text corpora. It is in about 5% cases. The strings of digits or special characters are usually omitted if a lexicon is being built or if the language model is being trained. The task of digits to words conversion in non-inflected languages (e.g. English) is solved by relatively simple conversion or lookup table. The problem is more complex in inflected Slavic languages. The string of digits can be converted into several different word combinations. It depends on the context and resulting words are inflected by gender or cases. The main goal of this research was to find the rules (patterns) for conversion of string of digits into words for Slavic languages. The second goal was to unify this patterns over Slavic languages and to integrate them to the universal system for digits to words conversion.

Keywords: Digits to words converter · LVCSR · Text processing

1 Introduction

Systems of automatic processing, recognition and synthesis of audio speech signal are practically used in many research areas at the present (2017) [1,2]. They are mainly systems for voice dictation to PC, voice controlled PC tools, voice-interactive dialogue systems, automatic broadcast programs transcription systems, text-to-speech synthesis systems, etc. There has been noticeable progress also while recognizing the speech of inflected languages, where the form or ending of some words changes because of nouns' declination, verbs' conjugation and adjectives' or adverbs' escalation. Slavic languages belong among these inflectional languages and they are used approximately by 293 millions people worldwide. Because of inflection much bigger lexicons have to be used during recognition of continuous speech than in uninflected languages (e.g. English).

© Springer International Publishing AG 2017
A. Karpov et al. (Eds.): SPECOM 2017, LNAI 10458, pp. 312–321, 2017.
DOI: 10.1007/978-3-319-66429-3_30

Also the speech models are much more extensive and therefore more difficult as for computational complexity.

In our laboratory of computer speech processing we have developed systems for automatic large vocabulary continuous speech recognition (LVCSR) that work in real time with lexicons containing more than 500 000 words [3]. These systems we originally developed for the Czech language (CZ) [4]. During the last ten years they were however adapted for Slovak (SK) [5], Polish (PL) [6], Russian (RU), Belorussian (BY), Ukrainian (UA), Serbian (RS), Croatian (HR), Slovenian (SL), Bulgarian (BG) and Macedonian languages (MK) [7]. For each language, there was created a Language Model (LM), lexicon and hybrid Acoustic Model (AM) based on triphones. Triphones are presented by combination of Hidden Markov Models (HMM) and Deep Neural Networks (DNN) [8]. A higher Word Recognition Rate (WRR) was achieved with HMM-DNN models during all our Automatic Speech Recognition (ASR) experiments than while using traditional models HMM-GMM (Gaussian Mixture Models). Average WRR in task of Voice Dictation to PC is higher than 98% and it is about 86% in task of broadcast programs transcription for all mentioned Slavic Languages.

To train a LM and create a lexicon, huge text corpora is necessary. We have used mainly internet resources from major newspapers to adapt our LVCSR system to a new Slavic language. However there is a problem with numbers that appear in text as strings of digits and not as strings of words. The second more-less similar problem is if we would like to train or to adapt new AM from audio database. Speech in audio signals is manually or semi-automatically transcribed into text by human annotators. The numbers occur again as strings of digits very often in text part of the audio databases.

A large number of Digits-to-Words converter tools exist e.g. for English at present but almost non for Slavic languages. The main problem is that there isn't any clear way how to create them. The task to create a Digit-to-Words converter tool for Slavic languages isn't unambiguous because Slavic languages are inflected according to case or gender and text forms of numbers can get many different inflected forms. A few studies exist but they aren't mostly described in English literature or it is relatively hard to find them. As the case may be these studies cannot be easily practically realized. Moreover these strings of digits can often be accompanied by abbreviations (mostly of physical units) and their pronunciation (transcription) depends on the previous number or the transcription of digits to words can depend on another word, e.g. the name of a month.

The first goal of this work was to create a tool for digits to words conversion. This tool should be able to translate strings of digits (and possible abbreviations) into text word form. In case that the transcription is not clear, the tool should not transcribe the text. The second goal was to create a generator for word strings and related abbreviations, alternatively also the names of months that exist (with possible alternatives and their probabilities). This generator should be used especially to train the language model - for example randomly generated decimal numbers and randomly generated main or minor patterns (if there are more possibilities). Both tools (systems) should be universally used for any Slavic language.

2   Patterns for Digits to Words Converter

Study of rules how to convert digits to words had to be made in the beginning of this research work. String of digits can be translated as cardinal, ordinal or decimal number. These strings can be part of a date. The converter was designed also for translation of abbreviations of physical units or special characters which are pre-connected with strings of digits. The translation of abbreviations or special characters depends on previous number. The study was performed for all examined Slavic languages. Universal patterns for conversion were searched in this study.

2.1   Cardinal Number Patterns

A string of digits is converted as a cardinal number if it does not contain character dot and if name of month, special character or abbreviations does not follow this string. The words for numbers 1 and 2 (or 3, 4 in SK) are inflected by gender in almost all Slavic languages. The converter does not translate these numbers because it is a very difficult task and we cannot solve this task at present. Numbers from 3 (5) to 20 are translated by XML–translation table (XMLtab). It isn't a good idea to generate numbers from 11 to 19 as units (1–9) plus 'teen' because there exist several exceptions in different Slavic languages.

Numbers from 21 to 99 are generated from connection words for Units (U) and Decades (D). There exist several patterns how to make it in Slavic languages, see Table 1. There are only main patterns, other (minor) patterns are used in several Slavic languages, e.g. U_&_D in CZ. Words for decades (20, 30, ...) and hundreds (100, 200, 300, ...) are again saved in XMLtab. There exist again several exceptions here therefore decades and hundreds are not generated.

Table 1. Cardinal number patterns for numbers 21–99

Language	Example	Pattern
CZ	dvacet pět	D _ U
SK	dvadsatpäť	DU
PL	dwadzieścia pięć	D _ U
RU	двадцать пять	D _ U
BY	дваццаць пяць	D _ U
UA	двадцять п'ять	D _ U
HR	dvadeset i pet	D _ & _ U
RS	двадесет и пет	D _ & _ U
SL	petindvajset	U&D
BG	двайсет и пет	D _ & _ U
MK	дваесет и пет	D _ & _ U

The conversion of numbers higher than 999 is once again specific. Being gendered, all the higher scale names (thousands, millions, milliards, ...) follow the declension rules in different Slavic languages. They are most often 3 word forms of higher scale names (HSN). First is for one HSN, second from two to four HSN and third for more than four HSN, see example in Table 2. BG and MK have only two word forms (as in English) – one HSN and more than one HSN. The reason is that BG and MK have relatively simple declension rules and they don't have cases. Word forms are saved in XMLtab. The same word is saved for second and third word form in case of BG and MK.

Table 2. Example of three (CZ) and two word forms (BG)

Digits	Words - CZ	Words - BG
1000000	jeden milion	един милион
2000000	dva miliony	два милиона
3000000	tři miliony	три милиона
4000000	čtyři miliony	четири милиона
5000000	pět milionů	пет милиона

The interesting thing is that two different large-number naming systems are used for different Slavic languages. They are long and short scale systems. Every new word-term higher than million is one million times larger than the previous term in long scale system and every new word-term higher than million is one thousand times larger than the previous term in short scale system. The long scale system is used in CZ, SK, PL, HR, RS and the short scale system in RU, UA, BY, BG and MK. There is one exception in the Slavic short scale system: The word for billion is replaced by word milliard.

2.2 Decimal Number Patterns

The string of digits is converted as decimal number if it contains character dot or comma (decimal separator) inside a string. The string is separated into two parts (Integer (I) and Fractional (F)) according to decimal separator. These two strings are translated as cardinal numbers and they are connected with a word depending on Slavic language, see Table 4. The words comma (c), and (&) or 'whole' (w) are used in different Slavic languages.

Table 3. Word 'whole' in decimal numbers - SK

Digits	Words
0,5	nula celých päť desátin
1,5	jedna celá päť desátin
2,5–4,5	dve, tri, Štyri celé pět desetin
5,5	päť celých päť desátin

The word 'whole' is inflected according to previous integer part, see Table 3. There exist several exceptions in different Slavic languages therefore different word forms are saved in XMLtab for I–numbers (0, 1, 2, 3, 4 and more than 4).

The name of the last digit's place value (DN) can be used in decimal number conversion in several Slavic languages (e.g. tenths, hundredths, thousandths, ten-thousandths, hundred-thousandth, millionth). DN can be again inflected depending on resulting decimal number and different word forms are in XMLtab. Reading of decimal number, where integer part is zero, is specific in some Slavic languages, see example in Table 5. Third pattern is the most common in the CZ.

Table 4. Decimal number patterns - example for 8.25

Language	Example	Pattern
CZ	osm celých dvacet pět setin	I_w_F(DN)
SK	osem celých dvadsaťpäť stotín	I_w_F(DN)
PL	osiem i dwadzieścia pięć setnych	I_&_F(DN)
RU	восемь целых двадцать пять сотых	I_w_F(DN)
BY	восем і дваццаць пяць сотых	I_&_F(DN)
UA	вісім цілих і двадцять п'ять сотих	I_w_&_F(DN)
HR	osam zarez dvadeset i pet	I_c_F
RS	осам зарез двадесет и пет	I_c_F
SL	osem celih petindvajset stotite	I_w_F(DN)
BG	осем цяло и двайсет и пет стотни	I_w_&_F(DN)
MK	осум запирка дваесет и пет	I_c_F

Table 5. Different patterns for 0.25 - CZ

No.	Pattern	Words	English translation
1	I_w_F(DN)	nula celá dvacet pět setin	zero point twenty five hundredths
2	I_w_F	nula celá dvacet pět	zero point twenty five
3	F(DN)	dvacet pět setin	twenty five hundredths

2.3 Ordinal Number Patterns

The string of digits can be an ordinal number if the last character is dot or if it precedes or follows other ordinal number (it can be date expression) or it precedes name of a month. There exist two patterns for string of digits to word conversion for different Slavic languages.

All words are Ordinal (AO) numbers or only Last word is Ordinal number (LO), see Table 6. Combination of digit(s) and abbreviation is used in some Slavic languages, e.g. in RU - 1- й (первый - first). This isn't solved in our converter but it is solved by a look-up table in our other text pre-processing tool.

Table 6. Ordinal number patterns - example for 48

Language	Example	Pattern
CZ	čtyřicátý osmý	AO
SK	štyridsiatyôsmy	AO
PL	czterdzieści ósmy	AO
RU	сорок восьмой	LO
BY	сорак восьмы	LO
UA	всорок восьмий	LO
HR	četrdeset i osmi	LO
RS	четрдесет и осми	LO
SL	osmiinštirideset	LO
BG	четиридесет и осми	LO
MK	четириесет и осми	LO

2.4 Date Expression

The date can occur in the text in form of strings of digits (e.g. 14. 4. 2017) or as combination of string of digits with the name of month (e.g. CZ: 14. dubna 2017 or RU: 1 апреля 2017 года). We solve separately day together with month and year. Latin-derived names (in SK, RU, RS, SL, BG and MK) or older Slavic names (in CZ, PL, UA, BY and HR) are used as names of months in Slavic languages.

String of digits, which represented day or month, are always ordinal numbers in all Slavic languages and the ordinal numbers are inflected by case. Day is an ordinal number in genitive and month is ordinal number in nominative in CZ and SK. Both day and month are ordinals number in nominative in PL and both are genitive in HR.

Name of month instead of string of digits is more common in date expression in all other Slavic languages. The string of digits is detected as year if:

1. The name of the month precedes the string of digits.
2. Two short strings of digits precede the string of digits.
3. Word 'year' or its abbreviation precedes or follows the string of digits. The year expression is cardinal number in CZ, SK and SL or it is an ordinal number in all other mentioned Slavic languages.

2.5 Abbreviation to Words Conversion

Some special characters or mainly abbreviations of physical units which follow cardinal or decimal number are translated in our conversion system. There are integrated following special characters: '%' percent, ' €' euro, '$' dollar, and abbreviations of physical units: 'mm' millimeter, 'cm' centimeter, 'm' meter, 'dm' decimeter, 'km' kilometer, 'km/h' kilometer per hour, 'm/h' meter per hour, 'km/s' kilometer per second, 'km/h' kilometer per hour, 'm/s' meter per

Table 7. Example of three (CZ) and two word forms (BG)

Digits + Abbrev.	Words - CZ	Words - BG
1 km. (км)	jeden kilometr	един километър
2 km. (км)	dva kilometry	два километра
3 km. (км)	tři kilometry	три километра
4 km. (км)	čtyři kilometry	четири километра
5 km. (км)	pět kilometrů	пет километра

second, 'm/h' meter per hour, 'g' gram, 'dg(dkg)' decagram, 'kg' kilogram, 'ml' milliliter, 'cl' centiliter, 'l' liter, '°C' degree Celsius.

There exist three or two word forms for transcription of abbreviations or special characters into words, see Table 7. The word form depends on previous number. First word form is for previous cardinal number one, second for previous cardinal numbers from two to four and third form for previous cardinal numbers higher than four or if the previous number is decimal.

3   Digits to Words Converter - System Overview

Designed system for digits to words conversion is relatively complex, see Fig. 1. The input to the system is string of text, conversion patterns (described above) for selected Slavic language and XML script where translation table for cardinal, ordinal or decimal numbers, date and abbreviations is saved. The input text string is tokenized to short strings (words, strings of digits, abbreviations, etc.). In the first step, it is investigated if single short string (ShS) contains character dot ('.'). The system decides that ShS is decimal number if ShS contains dot, all other characters are digits and last character isn't dot. The string of digits is separated to fractional and integer part according to dot. These two parts are translated as cardinal numbers and they are connected with word(s) which expresses separator – decimal mark ('whole', 'comma', etc.). A name of last digit place is added to the end of resulting word string if it is usual in the particular Slavic language. The subsystem for conversion of abbreviation is used if abbreviations follow the decimal number. Third word form of abbreviation is used always in such case, see Sect. 2.5.

The ShS is ordinal number if it contains dot as last character and all other characters are digits. This step is valid only for Slavic languages where ordinal numbers are written as strings of digits with dot in the end. It is specified in the set of patterns. The ordinal number is determined as part of date if name of month follows the ordinal number or if some other ordinal number follows the first ordinal number.

The ShS is assessed afterwards if any dot character doesn't exist in it and all characters are digits. A problem is that string of digits can be translated into several different word combinations. It depends on the context:

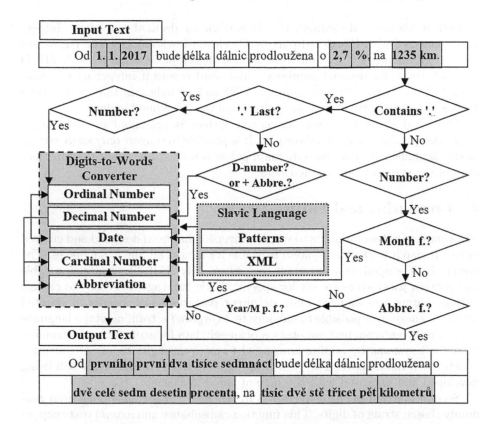

Fig. 1. The principle of digits to words converter

1. It could be part of date if the name of month follows.
2. It is verbal expression of year if word 'year' or its abbreviation precedes or follows the string of digits or if name of month precedes the string of digits. The string of digits is converted as cardinal or decimal number depending on Slavic language and selected (year) pattern.
3. The subsystem for abbreviation conversion is used if abbreviation of physical unit or some special character follows the string of digits. The string of digits is converted as cardinal number and abbreviation (or special character) is converted to word form according to (abbreviation) pattern.
4. The string of digits is translated as cardinal number if all previously mentioned cases don't occurr.

Typical adjustment of main patterns for digits to words conversion system in e.g. CZ is:

D_U, GD 2, AO, L_w_F, DN Yes, ZERO Yes, Year 11 CN

where D_U: pattern for cardinal numbers – first Decades, second Units, connected by space. GD 2: digits 1 and 2 are not transcribed. AO: pattern for ordinal numbers – All Ordinal. Lw_F: pattern for decimal numbers – Integer part connected with Fractional part by Czech word 'whole'. DN Yes: parameter for decimal numbers – the name of the last digit's place value is used. ZERO Yes: parameter for decimal numbers – first word is zero if Integer part is zero. Year 11 CN: year is cardinal number (CN) and 11 indicates that years above 1000 and below 2000 are read as multiples of the word one hundred.

Simplified digits to words conversion system is presented on web pages: http://kvap.tul.cz/slavic_symbols.php. It is possible to convert only short strings in this simplified system and only main patterns are used here but the functionality of the system is maintained here.

4   Conclusion and Future Work

The complex system for digits to words conversion has been designed and created in this research work. This system is usable for almost all Slavic languages. The system is developed as a universal tool where only XML-like conversion table and pattern parameters are set for specific Slavic language. It is easy to change pattern parameters and set main or minor patterns which occurs in selected Slavic language. It is possible to enhance text corpora for training of the language model and to enhance text annotation of speech data for acoustic model training in LVCSR systems by adding translated forms from digits to words converter which is described above. The system for digits to words conversion is still being developed and improved with the help of native speakers.

Second function of the converter is to generate words connections from randomly chosen string of digits. This function can enhance and extend text corpora but it is necessary to find a probability of frequency occurrence of main and minor patterns firstly. We plan to investigate this probability for every single Slavic language from our audio databases in the near feature.

Acknowledgments. The research was supported by the Technology Agency of the Czech Republic in project no. TA04010199.

References

1. Zhang, Y., Pezeshki, M., Brakel, P., Zhang, S., Laurent, C., Bengio, Y., Courville, A.: Towards end-to-end speech recognition with deep convolutional neural networks. In: Proceedings of the Annual Conference of the International Speech Communication Association, INTERSPEECH 2016, pp. 410–414 (2016). ISSN: 2308–457X
2. Deng, L., Li, J., Huang, J.-T., Yao, K., Yu, D., Seide, F., Seltzer, M., Acero, A.: Recent advances in deep learning for speech research at Microsoft. In: IEEE International Conference on Acoustics, Speech and Signal Processing - ICASSP 2013, pp. 8604–8608 (2013). ISBN: 978-147990356-6
3. Nouza, J., Blavka, K., Zdansky, J., Cerva, P., Silovsky, J., Bohac, M., Chaloupka, J., Kucharova, M., Seps, L.: Large-scale processing, indexing and search system for Czech audio-visual cultural heritage archives. In: 2012 IEEE 14th International Workshop on Multimedia Signal Processing, MMSP 2012, pp. 337–342 (2012). ISBN: 978-146734572-9

4. Nouza, J., Zdansky, J., David, P., Cerva, P., Kolorenc, J., Nejedlova, D.: Fully automated system for Czech spoken broadcast transcription with very large (300K+) lexicon. In: Interspeech 2005, Lisboa, Portugal, pp. 1681–1684 (2005). ISSN: 1018-4074

5. Nouza, J., Silovsky, J., Zdansky, J., Cerva, P., Kroul, M., Chaloupka, J.: Czech-to-Slovak adapted broadcast news transcription system. In: Proceedings of the 9th Annual Conference of the International Speech Communication Association, (Interspeech 2008), pp. 2683–2686, 22–26 September, Brisbane, Australia (2008). ISSN: 1990-9772

6. Nouza, J., Cerva, P., Safarik, R.: Cross-lingual adaptation of broadcast transcription system to polish language using public data sources. In: 7th Language and Technology Conference: Human Language Technologies as a Challenge for Computer Science and Linguistics, Poland, pp. 181–185 (2015). ISBN: 978-83-932640-8-7

7. Nouza, J., Safarik, R., Cerva, P.: ASR for south slavic languages developed in almost automated way. In: Proceedings of the 17th Annual Conference of the International Speech Communication Association (INTERSPEECH 2016), San Francisco, USA, pp. 3868–3872 (2016). doi:10.21437/Interspeech.2016-747, Scopus EID: 2-s2.0-84994385032, ISSN: 2308-457X

8. Dahl, G.E., Sainath, T.N., Hinton, G.E.: Improving deep neural networks for LVCSR using rectified linear units and dropout. In: IEEE International Conference on Acoustics, Speech and Signal Processing - Proceedings, ICASSP 2013, pp. 8609–8613 (2013). ISBN: 978-147990356-6

Discriminating Speakers by Their Voices — A Fusion Based Approach

Halim Sayoud$^{(\boxtimes)}$, Siham Ouamour, and Zohra Hamadache

Electronics and Computer Engineering Faculty,
USTHB University, Bab Ezzouar, Algeria
{halim.sayoud,siham.ouamour}@uni.de,
zohra.hamadache@yahoo.fr

Abstract. The task of Speaker Discrimination (SD) consists in checking whether two speech segments belong to the same speaker or not. In this research field, it is often difficult to decide what could be the best classifier in terms of accuracy and robustness. For that purpose, we have implemented 9 classifiers: Support Vector Machines, Linear Discriminant Analysis, Multi-Layer Perceptron, Generalized Linear Model, Self Organizing Map, Adaboost, Second Order Statistical Measures, Linear Regression and Gaussian Mixture Models. Furthermore, a new fusion approach is proposed and experimented in speaker discrimination. Several experiments of speaker discrimination were conducted on Hub4 Broadcast-News with relatively short segments. The obtained results have shown that the best classifier is the SVM and that the proposed fusion approach is quite interesting since it provided the best performances at all.

Keywords: Speaker discrimination · Speaker identification · Discriminative classification · Fusion

1 Introduction

Speaker discrimination consists in checking whether two different pronunciations (speech signals) are uttered by the same speaker or by two different speakers [1]. This research domain has several applications such as automatic speaker verification [2], speech segmentation [3] or speaker based clustering (Meignier, 2002). All these tasks can be performed either by generative classifiers or by discriminative ones.

However, existing approaches are not robust enough in noisy environment or in telephonic speech. Any new model must therefore improve the reliability of existing discriminative systems, without altering their architectures.

To address the above issue, we implemented 9 different classifiers and applied a PCA reduction with these different classifiers. Furthermore, a new relativistic characteristic is proposed: we called it "Relativistic Speaker Characteristic" [4]. Basically, the introduction of the relative notion in speaker modelization allows getting a flexible relative speaker template, more suitable for the task of speaker discrimination in difficult environments. Moreover, to further intensify the feature reduction, a PCA reduction is applied to reduce again the RSC feature. For that purpose, several speaker discrimination experiments are conducted on a subset of Broadcast-News dataset.

© Springer International Publishing AG 2017
A. Karpov et al. (Eds.): SPECOM 2017, LNAI 10458, pp. 322–331, 2017.
DOI: 10.1007/978-3-319-66429-3_31

The overall structure of this paper is organized as follows: In Sect. 2, we describe some related works and explain the motivation of this investigation. Section 3 defines the nine used classifiers. Section 4 describes the RSC notion employed for the task of speaker discrimination and feature reduction. Experiments of speaker discrimination are presented in Sect. 5 and finally a general conclusion is presented at the end of this manuscript.

2   Some Related Works of Feature Reduction in Speaker Recognition

Speaker discrimination is the ability to check whether two utterances come from the same speaker or from different speakers, but in a broader sense, speaker recognition is the task of recognizing the true speaker of a given speech signal. Hence, in this section, we will shortly quote some recent works of speaker recognition using feture reduction (such as PCA for instance).

In 2008, Li et al. [5] proposed a novel hierarchical speaker verification method based on PCA and Kernel Fisher Discriminant (KFD) classifier. Later on, Zhao et al. [6] presented a new method which takes full advantage of both vector quantization and PCA. Also in 2009, Jayakurnar et al. [7] presented an effective and robust method for speaker identification based on discrete stationary wavelet transform (DSWT) and principal component analysis techniques. Ingeniously, Zhou et al. [8] proposed a method to reduce feature dimension based on Canonical Correlation Analysis (CCA) and PCA. In the same period, Mehra et al. [9] presented a detailed comparative analysis for speaker identification by using lip features, PCA, and neural network classifiers: it was a multimodal feature combination. Then, Xiao-chun et al. [10] proposed a text-independent (TI) speaker identification method that suppresses the phonetic information by a subspace method: a Probabilistic Principle Component Analysis (PPCA) is utilized to construct these subspaces. Recently, Jing et al. [11] introduced a new method of extracting mixed characteristic parameters using PCA techniques. This speaker recognition approach is based on the performance of the PCA on the Linear Prediction Cepstral Coefficients (LPCC) and Mel Frequency Cepstral Coefficients (MFCC). All of these works (or at least most of them) used the principal component analysis to reduce the feature space dimensionality without altering the recognition performances.

In this investigation, we not only propose a completely different feature reduction technique (i.e. relativistic approach), but we also combine it with PCA reduction to further enhance both the memory size and recognition precision. Moreover, we evaluate our relativistic approach efficiency in real environment (Broadcast News), with 9 different classifiers and with 2 new fusion techniques.

3 Description of the Classifiers and Classification Process

The choice of the optimal classifier is crucial before any application of pattern recognition that is why we have decided to implement 9 classifiers and evaluate them in the same experimental conditions.

The different classification methods are described in the following sub-sections. However, since we are limited by the pages number of the article, we will only give the general definitions of the different classifiers; the details could be found in the cited references.

3.1 LDA: Linear Discriminant Analysis

Linear discriminant analysis (LDA) is a method used in statistics, pattern recognition and machine learning to find a linear combination of features which characterizes or separates two or more classes of objects or events.

Consider a set of observations $\vec{x}$ (also called features, attributes, variables or measurements) for each sample of an object or event with known class y. This set of samples is called the training set. The classification problem is then to find a good predictor for the class y of any sample of the same distribution (not necessarily from the training set) given only an observation $\vec{x}$ [12].

3.2 AdaBoost: Adaptive Boosting

AdaBoost, short for "Adaptive Boosting", is a machine learning meta-algorithm. It can be used in conjunction with many other types of learning algorithms to improve their performance [13]. The output of the other learning algorithms ('weak learners') is combined into a weighted sum that represents the final output of the boosted classifier. AdaBoost is adaptive in the sense that subsequent weak learners are tweaked in favor of those instances misclassified by previous classifiers.

AdaBoost refers to a particular method of training a boosted classifier. A boost classifier is a classifier in the form

$$F_T(x) = \sum_{t=1}^{T} f_1(x). \tag{1}$$

3.3 SVM: Support Vector Machines

The basic SVM takes a set of input data and predicts, for each given input, which of two possible classes forms the output, making it a non-probabilistic binary linear classifier. A SVM model is a representation of the examples as points in space, mapped so that the examples of the separate categories are divided by a clear gap that is as wide as possible. New examples are then mapped into that same space and predicted to belong to a category based on which side of the gap they fall on [14]. The SMO algorithm is used to speed up the training of the SVM [15].

3.4   MLP: Multi Layer Perceptron

MLP is a feed-forward neural network classifier that uses the errors of the output to train the neural network: it is the "training step" [16].

MLP is organized in layers, one input layer of distribution points, one or more hidden layers of artificial neurons (nodes) and one output layer of artificial neurons (nodes).

3.5   LR: Linear Regression

Linear regression is the oldest and most widely used predictive model. The method of minimizing the sum of the squared errors to fit a straight line to a set of data points was published by Legendre in 1805 and by Gauss in 1809. Linear regression models are often fitted using the least squares approach, but they may also be fitted in other ways, such as by minimizing the "lack of fit" in some other norms (*as with least absolute deviations regression*), or by minimizing a penalized version of the least squares loss function as in ridge regression [17, 18].

3.6   GLM: Generalized Linear Model

In statistics, the Generalized Linear Model or GLM [19] is widely utilized. It is a flexible generalization of ordinary linear regression that allows for response variables that have error distribution models other than a normal distribution. The GLM generalizes linear regression by allowing the linear model to be related to the response variable via a link function and by allowing the magnitude of the variance of each measurement to be a function of its predicted value.

3.7   SOM: Self Organizing Map

A self-organizing map (SOM) is a type of artificial neural network that is trained using unsupervised learning to produce a low-dimensional, discretized representation of the input space of the training samples, called a map. Self-organizing maps are different from other artificial neural networks in the sense that they use a neighborhood function to preserve the topological properties of the input space.

This makes SOMs useful for visualizing low-dimensional views of high-dimensional data. The model was first described as an artificial neural network by Kohonen, and is sometimes called a Kohonen map. A Self-organizing Map is a data visualization technique developed by Kohonen in the early 1980's [20, 21].

3.8   SOSM: Second Order Statistical Measure

We recall bellow the most important properties of this approach [4].

Let $\{x_t\}_{1 \leq t \leq M}$ be a sequence of M vectors resulting from the P-dimensional acoustic analysis of a speech signal uttered by speaker x. These vectors are summarized by the mean vector $\bar{x}$ and the covariance matrix X.

Similarly, for a speech signal uttered by speaker y, a sequence of N vectors $\{y_t\}_{1 \leq t \leq N}$ can be extracted. These vectors are summarized by the mean vector $\bar{y}$ and the covariance matrix Y.

The Gaussian likelihood based measure µG is defined by:

$$\mu_G(x,y) = \frac{1}{P}\left[-\log\left(\frac{\det(Y)}{\det(X)}\right) + tr(YX^{-1}) + (\bar{y} - \bar{x})^T X^{-1}(\bar{y} - \bar{x})\right] - 1, \qquad (2)$$

we have:

$$Arg\max_{x} \overline{G}x(y_1^N) = Arg\min_{x} \mu_G(x,y). \qquad (3)$$

3.9   GMM: Gaussian Mixture Model

A Gaussian Mixture Model (GMM) is a parametric probability density function represented as a weighted sum of Gaussian component densities [22, 23]. GMMs are commonly used as a parametric model of the probability distribution of continuous measurements or features in a biometric system, such as vocal spectral features in a speaker recognition system. GMM parameters are estimated from training data using the iterative Expectation-*Maximization* algorithm or *Maximum A Posteriori* estimation from a well-trained prior model.

A Gaussian mixture model is a weighted sum of M component Gaussian densities as given by the equation,

$$p\left(\frac{X}{\lambda}\right) = \sum_{i=1}^{M} \omega_i g(X/\mu_i, \Sigma_i), \qquad (4)$$

where x is a D-dimensional continuous-valued data vector, wi, i = 1,..., M, are the mixture weights, and g(x|µi,_i), i = 1,..., M, are the component Gaussian densities. Each component density is a D-variate Gaussian function of the form,

$$g(X/\mu_i, \Sigma_i) = \frac{1}{(2\pi)^{D/2}|\Sigma_i|^{1/2}} exp\left\{-\frac{1}{2}(X - \mu_i)'\sum_i^{-1}(X - \mu_i)\right\}, \qquad (5)$$

with mean vector µi and covariance matrix $\sum_i$. The complete Gaussian mixture model is parameterized by the mean vectors, covariance matrices and mixture weights from all component densities.

3.10   PCA Feature Reduction

PCA provides an interesting way to reduce a complex data set to a lower dimension to reveal the sometimes hidden, simplified dynamics that often underlie it [24, 25]. PCA is mathematically defined as an orthogonal linear transformation that transforms the data to a new coordinate system such that the greatest variance by some projection of the data comes to lie on the first coordinate (i.e. the first principal component), the second greatest variance on the second coordinate, and so on.

In our investigation, PCA has been intensively used to further reduce the dimensionality of the features of our relative characteristic RSC.

4 New Fusion Approach

The fusion in the broad sense can be performed at different hierarchical levels or processing stages. A very commonly encountered taxonomy of data fusion is given by the following three-stage hierarchy [18, 26–28]: Feature level, Score (matching) level and Decision level.

In our case, we have proposed a new fusion technique, based on a dynamic scheme (Fig. 1): we call it "Dynamic Score-Based Fusion" or DSBF.

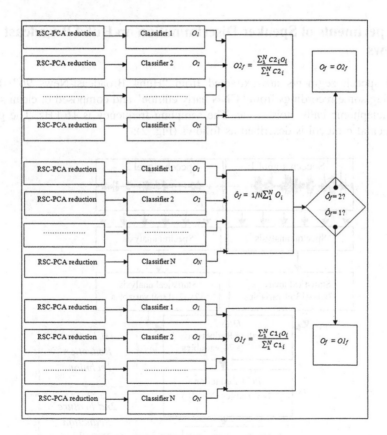

Fig. 1. Principle of the Dynamic Fusion

In this new method, an estimation of the DSB score is first computed (as we can see in Fig. 2), and then, according to the retrieved score (1 or 2), a new fusion is performed thanks to $O1_f$ formula if the estimated score is equal to 1 or thanks to $O2_f$ formula if the estimated score is equal to 2 (see Fig. 1). Note that there are only two possible decisions: 1 if the two speech segments belong to different speakers and 2 if they come from the same speaker. Consequently, if the speakers seem to be different (case 1), the dynamic method proposes the use of the $O1_f$ formula, which gives more importance to some specific classifiers that are more appropriate for inter-variability discrimination. On the other hand, if the speakers appear to be the same (case 2), the proposed method will use the $O2_f$ formula, which gives more importance to some specific classifiers that are more appropriate for intra-variability discrimination. Mathematically speaking, this dynamic process consists in tuning the weighting coefficients $C1_i$ and $C2_i$.

In this new approach, an estimation of the discrimination decision $\hat{O}_f$ is evaluated first, and then a comparison test is performed (see Fig. 1).

5 Experiments of Speaker Discrimination on Hub4 Broadcast News

Several speech segments are extracted from "Hub4 Broadcast-News 96" dataset, containing some recordings from "CNN early edition" and composed of clean speech, music, telephonic calls, noises, etc. The sampling frequency is 16 kHz. The general experimental protocol is described as follows (Fig. 2):

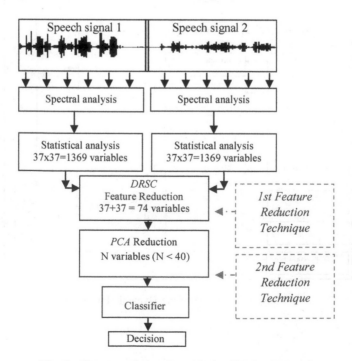

Fig. 2. The general experimental classification protocol

The different results obtained during these experiments are summarized in Table 1.

Table 1. Scores of good speaker discrimination in %

Method	Accuracy
SOMap	80.51
SOSM-muGc	82.56
Adaboost	84.62
MLP	85.64
GMM	87.18
LDA	89.23
Lin regress	89.74
GLM regress	90.26
SVM	91.28
Dynamic fusion	93.33

We can see that the 4 last classifiers, namely: LDA, Linear regression, GLM regression and SVM are the most accurate classifiers with a score about 90% of good classification.

The SVM is the best classifier at all by providing a score of 91.28% of good classification.

The 3 classifiers located in the middle, namely: Adaboost, MLP and GMM are relatively less accurate with a score of about 85%. Although those 3 classifiers are known to be quite robust, the lack of training data makes them not very efficient. Also, as explained in a previous section, although the GMMs are known to be very efficient in speaker identification, their performances in discrimination are not so convincing.

Finally, for the 2 remaining classifiers, namely: SOM and SOSM, the performances noticed during the discrimination experiments, show that those classifiers are not very suitable for the task of speaker discrimination, since the score of good classification is about only 81%. However, one must note that the SOSM approach remains quite interesting since it doesn't require any training (i.e. it is a distance measure). Moreover, in the present experiments, no PCA reduction was applied for the SOSM (i.e. not possible technically). That is, if we observe the results of speaker discrimination without PCA, we do notice that the SVM and SOSM provide the best performances.

Finally, the third observation we can make is that the proposed fusion technique has efficiently improved the classification performances, where the discrimination accuracy has reached the score of 93.33% of good classification, which is considered as absolutely the best score obtained during all the experiments.

6 Discussion

In this new research work, nine different classifiers were employed for the task of speaker discrimination: Linear Discriminant Analysis, Adaboost, Support Vector Machines, Multi-Layer Perceptron, Linear Regression, Generalized Linear Model, Self Organizing Map, Second Order Statistical Measures and Gaussian Mixture Models.

Moreover, a new technique of fusion is proposed and applied between the different classifiers, and the experiments have shown that this fusion has further improved the performances.

This investigation has allowed comparing the performances of the different classifiers on the same experimental conditions. Hence, the best score, about 91.3%, was reached by using the SVM classifier, followed by the GLM regression, Linear regression, LDA etc.

Furthermore the proposed fusion approach has appreciably enhanced the score of speaker discrimination with an accuracy of 93.33%. This score is considered as absolutely the best score obtained during this investigation.

In perspectives we think to apply this approach in text processing and especially for the task of author discrimination.

References

1. Rose, P.: Forensic speaker discrimination with australian english vowel acoustics. In: ICPhS XVI Saarbrücken, pp. 6–10 (2007)
2. Matrouf, D., Bonastre, J.F.: Accurate Log-Likelihood Ratio Estimation By Using Test Statistical Model For Speaker Verification. In: The Speaker and Language Recognition Workshop (2006)
3. Meignier, S., et al.: Step-by-step and integrated approaches in broadcast news speaker diarization. Comput. Speech Lang. **20**, 303–330 (2006)
4. Ouamour, S., Guerti, M., Sayoud, H.: A New Relativistic Vision in Speaker Discrimination. Can. Acoust. J. **36**(4), 24–34 (2008)
5. Li, M., Xing, Y., Luo, R.: Hierarchical Speaker Verification Based on PCA and Kernel Fisher Discriminant. In: Fourth International Conference on Natural Computation, pp. 152–156 (2008)
6. Zhao, Z.D., Zhang, J., Tian, J.F., Lou, Y.Y.: An effective identification method for speaker recognition based on PCA and double VQ. In: Proceedings of the Eighth International Conference on Machine Learning and Cybernetics, Baoding, pp. 1686–1689 (2009)
7. Jayakurnar, A., Vimal, K.V.R., Babu Anto, P.: Text dependent speaker recognition using discrete stationary wavelet transform and PCA. In: International Conference on the Current Trends in Information Technology (CTIT), pp. 1–4 (2009)
8. Zhou, Y., Zhang, X., Wang, J., Gong, Y.: Research on speaker feature dimension reduction based on CCA and PCA. In: International Conference on Wireless Communications and Signal Processing (WCSP), pp. 1–4 (2010)
9. Mehra, A., Kumawat, M., Ranjan, R.: Expert system for speaker identification using lip features with PCA. In: 2nd International Workshop on Intelligent Systems and Applications (ISA), pp. 1–4 (2010)

10. Xiao-Chun, L., Jun-Xun, Y.: A text-independent speaker recognition system based on probabilistic principle component analysis. In: 2012 3rd International Conference on System Science, Engineering Design and Manufacturing Informatization, pp. 255–260 (2012)
11. Jing, X., Ma, J., Zhao, J., Yang, H.: Speaker recognition based on principal component analysis of LPCC and MFCC, pp. 403–408. IEEE (2014)
12. Venables, W.N., Ripley, B.D.: Modern Applied Statistics with S-PLUS, 4th edn. Springer, New York (2002)
13. Ruihi, W..: AdaBoost for feature selection, classification and its relation with SVM, a review. In: International Conference on Solid State Devices and Materials Science, 1–2, April 2012, vol. 25, pp. 800–807. Physics Procedia, Macao (2012)
14. Witten, I.H., Frank, E., Trigg, L., Hall, M., Holmes, G., Cunningham, S.J.: Weka: practical machine learning tools and techniques with Java implementations. In Kasabov, N., Ko, K. (eds.) Proceedings of the ICONIP/ANZIIS/ANNES 1999 Workshop on Emerging Knowledge Engineering and Connectionist-Based Information Systems, pp. 192–196 (1999)
15. Keerthi, S.S., Shevade, S.K., Bhattacharyya, C., Murthy, K.R.K.: Improvements to platt's SMO algorithm for SVM classifier design. Neural Comput. **13**, 637–649 (2001)
16. Sayoud, H.: Automatic speaker recognition–Connexionnist approach. PhD thesis, USTHB University, Algiers (2003)
17. Wikipedia, "Linear regression", From Wikipedia, the free encyclopedia. The web page was last modified on 28 March (2013), http://en.wikipedia.org/wiki/Linear_regression
18. Huang, X., Pan, W.: Linear regression and two-class classification with gene expression data. Bioinformatics **19**(16), 2072–2078 (2003)
19. Wang, X., Fan, J.: Variable selection for multivariate generalized linear models. J. Appl. Stat. **41**(2) (2014)
20. Kohonen, T.: The self-organizing map. Proc. IEEE **78**(9), 1464–1480 (1990). doi:10.1109/5. 58325
21. Tambouratzis, G., Hairetakis, G., Markantonatou, S., Carayannis, G.: Applying the SOM model to text classification according to register and stylistic content. Int. J. Neural Syst. **13** (1), 1–11 (2003)
22. McLachlan, G.J., Peel, D., Bean, R.W.: Modelling high-dimensional data by mixtures of factor analyzers. Comput. Stat. Data Anal. **41**(3–4), 379–388 (2003)
23. Přibil, J., Přibilová, A., Matoušek, J.: GMM classification of text-to-speech synthesis: identification of original speaker's voice. In: Sojka, P., Horák, A., Kopeček, I., Pala, K. (eds.) TSD 2014. LNCS, vol. 8655, pp. 365–373. Springer, Cham (2014). doi:10.1007/978-3-319-10816-2_44
24. Shlens, J.: A Tutorial on Principal Component Analysis–Derivation, Discussion and Singular Value Decomposition. Version number 1 (2003), www.cs.princeton.edu/picasso/mats/PCA-Tutorial-Intuition_jp.pdf
25. Shayegan, M.A., Aghabozorgi, S.: A new dataset size reduction approach for PCA-based classification in OCR application. Math. Prob. Eng. **2014**, 14 (2014), http://dx.doi.org/10. 1155/2014/537428
26. Dasarathy, B.V.: Decision fusion. In: Proceedings of IEEE Computer Society Press, Los Alamitos, CA (1994)
27. Verlinde, P.: Contribution à la vérification multimodale d'identité en utilisant la fusion de decisions. PhD thesis, Ecole Nationale Supérieure des Télécommunications, Paris, France, 17 September (1999)
28. Jain, A.K., Ross, A., Prabhakar, S.: An Introduction to Biometric Recognition. J. IEEE Trans. Circ. Syst. Video Technol. **14**(1), 4–20 (2004)

Emotional Poetry Generation

Aitzol Astigarraga$^{(\boxtimes)}$, José María Martínez-Otzeta, Igor Rodriguez,
Basilio Sierra, and Elena Lazkano

Department of Computer Science and Artificial Intelligence,
University of the Basque Country UPV/EHU, Donostia-San Sebastian,
20018 Lejona, Spain
{aitzol.astigarraga,josemaria.martinezo,igor.rodriguez,
b.sierra,e.lazkano}@ehu.eus
http://www.sc.ehu.es/ccwrobot

Abstract. In this article we describe a new system for the automatic creation of poetry in Basque that not only generates novel poems, but also creates them conveying a certain attitude or state of mind. A poem is a text structured according to predefined formal rules, whose parts are semantically related and with an intended message, aiming to elicit an emotional response. The proposed system receives as an input the topic of the poem and the affective state (positive, neutral or negative) and tries to give as output a novel poem that: (1) satisfies formal constraints of rhyme and metric, (2) shows coherent content related to the given topic, and (3) expresses them through the predetermined mood. Although the presented system creates poems in Basque, it is highly modular and easily extendable to new languages.

Keywords: Poetry generation · Sentiment analysis · Basque language · Affective computing

1 Introduction

Writing poetry requires both creativity to construct a meaningful message and lyrical skills to produce rhyme patterns and follow metrical constraints. Furthermore, oral poetry, poetry constructed without the aid of writing [1], implies that a work has to be composed and performed at the moment, with no prior preparation. Nowadays many improvisational oral practices exists around the world, such as Serbo-Croatian guslars [1], freestyle rap [2] and Basque *bertsolaritza*. It is obvious that improvising novel poems under challenging formal constraints, transmitting an intended message and all that at once, in front of an audience requires both high technical skills and creativity.

That is exactly our main goal: to develop a system that is able to generate Basque poetry under the constraints of *bertsolaritza*, a form of oral and improvised poetry.

Basque, *euskara*, is the language of the inhabitants of the Basque Country. And *bertsolaritza*, Basque improvised contest poetry, is one of the manifestations

© Springer International Publishing AG 2017
A. Karpov et al. (Eds.): SPECOM 2017, LNAI 10458, pp. 332–342, 2017.
DOI: 10.1007/978-3-319-66429-3_32

of traditional Basque culture that is still very much alive. In the book The Art of Bertsolaritza [3], it is described as a sung, rhymed and metered discourse. The *bertsolari* performs without the help of any musical instrument; but the *bertsolari*'s discourse is always sung.

The Basque *bertso* follows strict constraints on meter and rhyme. In the case of a metric structure of verses known as *Zortziko Txikia*, the poem is composed of 4 verses, called *puntuak*. Each verse has 13 syllables and must rhyme with others.

Rhyme is the formal quid of the *bertso*; without the rhyme there is no *bertso*. If we rhyme (although its quality may not be the best), we are creating a *bertso*. If the two rhymed words in the same verse turn out to be the same, the *bertsolari* is considered to have committed a *poto*. It is simply the act of repeating a rhyming word but is undoubtedly the most penalized mistake both for a judging panel and for the public.

Although technical aspect of a *bertso* are highly demanding, the quality of the *bertso* is reflected in its force of reasoning and in its poetical-rhetorical value [4].

Our proposed system, based on a corpus-based poetry generation approach, uses two methods to construct poems according to given constraints on rhyme, meter, semantic similarity and sentiment. Thus, the system can be asked to view a topic (e.g. *spring*)from a particular affective stance (eg. *negative*). In doing so, the goal is to not only convey a message in a form of a poem but also to respond to an affective target and/or to create an affective response in the audience. That is, creating a poem in an intentional way.

The rest of the paper is organized as follows: in Sect. 2 related work is surveyed, while Sect. 3 is devoted to present the developed tools and resources. The proposed verse-maker module is presented in Sect. 4, and results are drawn in 5. Finally the conclusions are summarized in Sect. 6.

2   Related Work

Computational modeling for poetry generation has become a topic in the artificial intelligence community in the last years. Before the computer science community took an interest in the area, people with a background closer to humanities made early efforts in systematic generation of poetry. We could mention works related to generating variations over a predetermined set of verses [5], or to select a template to produce poems from it [6].

According to Gervás [7], nowadays two main strategies can be outlined in the field of computer generation of poetry: corpus-based approach and composition from scratch.

In the corpus-based approach the computer is used to harvest and reuse text already formatted into poem-like structure of lines. This approach can be formulated as an information retrieval task, where the objective is to extract and select existing lines to compose new poems. Many computer-based systems rely nowadays in this method. Most relevant include PoeTryMe [8], the poetry generation platform used for Portuguese; an approach using text mining methods, morphological analysis, and morphological synthesis to produce poetry in Finnish presented in [9]; constraint programming for poetry composition explored in [10]; WASP [11,12], a Spanish verse-generation system developed following the generate-and-test strategy; and [13], in which an approach of poetry generation based in POS-tag is presented. This corpus-based procedure is also adopted in our previous works [14,15] where two methods to ensure internal coherence of poems were presented.

On the other hand, the composition from scratch approach relies on building a stream of text from scratch, character by character or word by word, and establishing a distribution of the resulting text into poem lines by some additional procedure. An example of this procedure is the evolutionary system presented by Manurung in [16]. Poetry generation in Chinese language based on recurrent neural networks has also been analyzed in [17,18].

A popular -and rather simple- method to generate text from scratch is the N-gram model, which is the simplest Markov model. N-grams assign probabilities to sequences of words and the generated model can be used to stochastically generate sequences of words based on the generated distributions [19,20]. An N-gram probability is the conditional probability of a word given the previous N-1 words. Markov chains have been widely used as the basis of poetry generation systems as they provide a clear ans simple way to model some syntactic and semantic characteristics of language [21]. Popular and recent examples of N-gram poem generators are [7,22,23]. But text poetry hold non-local properties such as rhyme and metric that cannot be modeled by an ordinary N-gram model. Therefore, the above mentioned methods need additional procedures for distributing the resulting text into poem lines with metrical and rhyming constraints.

Poetry tries to convey messages and to evoke emotions in an aesthetic way. The sentiment conveyed in a text is a line of research within the Natural Language Processing (NLP) area that has drawn a lot of interest recently. The goal of text sentiment analysis is to extract the affective information or writer's attitude from the source text [24]. Basically the sentiments may be considered within the polarity classification (positive, negative or neutral) [25].

The computational methods for sentiment analysis are usually based either on machine learning techniques such as naive Bayes classifiers trained on labeled dataset, or use lists of words associated with the emotional value (positive-negative evaluation or sentiment score values). A survey of current techniques is presented in [26].

It is a challenging task for a system intended to interact with people, to combine in a single system the above reviewed automatic poetry generation and sentiment analysis capabilities. That is, the development of a system not only capable of creating meaningful poems, but also of creating them with emotional personality.

An overview of works that incorporate emotional affects in creation process must include Full face poetry system [27], a corpus based poetry generator that creates poems according to days mood estimated from the news of the day.

Another example would be the Stereotrope system [28] which generates emotional and witty metaphors for given topic based on corpus analysis. An interesting approach is also described in [29], in which a system capable of expressing feelings in the form of a poem is presented. The emotional state is extracted from text. Finally, MASTER [30] is a computer-aided tool for poetry generation. In this approach, a society of agents with initial moods and words influences each other to create the final poem.

Our approach also tries to combine both approaches: detecting specific emotions and transmitting them through the poem.

3   Resources

Several linguistic tools and resources have been developed and used in the verse-maker project.

3.1   Corpora

It has been shown already that the use of human generated corpora (oral or text) is of common use in computational poetry. It has the advantage of avoiding the generation of text that is un-interpretable. However, it may be interpreted as plagiarism. Hence, we have chosen initially to work with phrases mined from a newpaper alongside sentences extracted from the work of well-known *bertsolaris*. The later reflects the desire to maintain the language-model of the *bertsolaritza*, and the former tends to increase quality while not appropriating text intended for poems.

- **Mixed-corpus:** 18913 lines and 94314 words, of which them 21411 are unique. This corpus is a compilation of sentences mined from Basque newspaper Egunkaria[1] (85%) alongside poetry sung in *bertsolari* contests by different performers[2] (15%).

3.2   Text Applications

- **Rhyme search:** Finding words that rhyme with a given word is an essential task that the verse-generation system must perform. Basque rhyme schemes are mainly consonant. The widely consulted rhyming dictionary *Hiztegi Errimatua* [31] contains a number of documented phonological alternations that are acceptable as off-rhymes. These alternations have been implemented using regular expressions.
- **Syllable counter:** Counts the number of syllables present in the given text. For the syllabification itself, the approach describing the principal elements of Basque language structure [32] has been implemented.

---

[1] https://en.wikipedia.org/wiki/Egunkaria.
[2] http://bdb.bertsozale.eus/en.

- **Similarity measure:** The main purpose of this module is to measure the semantic relationship between pairs of words and sentences. The module computes for each pair of words/sentences a score that evaluates how similar they are. Latent Semantic Analysis (LSA) method [33,34] has been implemented to capture the semantic relatedness. This semantic model has been generated with news mined from Egunkaria, a Basque-language newspaper.
- **Sentiment analysis:** To extract the sentiment evaluation, we use the EliXa tool, a supervised Sentiment Analysis system [35]. It estimates the negative, neutral and positive sentiment values in short texts. The polarity classification is addressed by means of a multiclass SVM algorithm which includes lexical based features such as the polarity values obtained from domain and open polarity lexicons.

4   Verse-Maker Module

The aforementioned modules have been integrated into a verse-maker architecture for automatic poem generation. In the basic scenario, a topic and a sentiment to be expressed (positive, negative or neutral) is given by the user and the system then aims to give as output a novel poem that satisfies the formal constraints, conveys a predetermined sentiment and also shows coherent content related to the given topic.

For our particular challenge, the selected stanza will be *Zortziko Txikia*, a poem consisting of four lines, each 13 syllables long and all of them sharing a common rhyme.

The general problem of poem generation can be split up into two subproblems: the generation of content and the combination of fragments into the final poem.

4.1   Sentence Generator

The Sentence Generator module is used to compose meaningful and metrically correct natural language sentences. Two corpus-based methods are used towards this end:

- **Harvesting a corpus to retrieve sentences that fulfill the constraints.** The basics of this method is to extract sentences from the corpus that meet rhyme and metric constraints. All the sentences created in this way will come from the corpus *verbatim*. This approach is useful as a way to test the corpus potential to bring meaningful poems without further processing and, therefore, as a benchmarking for other approaches.
- **Generating sentences from scratch using an N-gram model.** Starting from the rhyming word, the verse is built backwards using the selected N-gram model; extending at each step the sequence of words with new ones that have a non-zero probability of appearing after the last word. When this approach is used, it is assured that the final sentence is different from the existing ones in the original corpus.

4.2 Poem Generator

This module organizes sentences such that they suit a target template of a poetic form (*Zortziko Txikia*). After that, according to some heuristics, sentences are selected to form the final poem. The following criteria is used to select candidate sentences:

- **Semantic similarity with respect to the given theme.** It is measured according to the cosine distance of the sentence and the theme when both are represented as vectors in the space generated by a LSA model.
- **Sentiment value of the text.** It is assured that the sentiment conveyed by the poem is the desired one. Currently we demand that all the verses in the poem share the same sentiment, but it could be possible to easily adapt the system to evaluate the poem as a whole, or analyze it by chunks and tolerate some percentage of them to differ.
- **Rhyme.** The sentences that are part of a poem have to comply with some rhyming constraints, that have to be enforced.

The overall architecture, depicted in Fig. 1, is modular and provides a high level of customization, depending on the needs of the user.

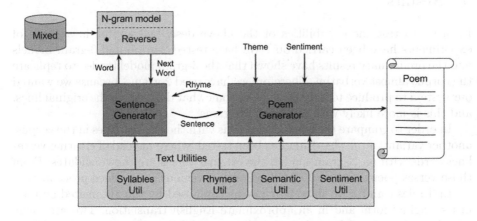

Fig. 1. System architecture

The procedure to create a poem involves prompting the user for a *theme*, a *sentiment* to be expressed, a *metric* and a background *corpus*. This is captured by the Algorithm 1.

With this process it is possible that in some step no valid sentence is found (in case of rarely occurring bigrams) or that a combinatorial explosion occurs (in the case of bigger corpus or longer number of syllables). In our case the latter situation is prevented imposing a maximum number of generated sentences. If the former problem arises, the system keeps trying another last words till the list is exhausted. An additional check ensures that no solution copies *verbatim* lines in the original corpus. In our experiments always a minimum of five poems have been generated.

Data: topic, sentiment, corpus, numPoems
Result: poems related to the topic with conveying sentiment

wordList ← ExtractSentenceEndingWords(corpus);
simList ← OrderBySimilarity(wordList, topic);
while *not generated numPoems* **do**
    rhymeBase ← pop(simList);
    createBertso(rhymeBase);
end
Procedure createBertso(*rhymeBase*)
    rhymeList ← getRhymes(rhymeBase);
    while *bertso not generated* **do**
        if *NgramGenerate(rhymeList) has sentiment* **then**
            add line to bertso;
        end
    end
    return ;

Algorithm 1. General procedure for *bertso* generation

5 Results

In order to test the capabilities of the above described approach, a series of experiments have been carried out. We have tested 2-gram and 3-gram models and the preliminary results have shown that the 3-gram model tended to replicate the corpus almost verbatim. Therefore we have used 2-grams, because we wanted our system to produce tentative solutions somewhat different to the original lines, and this is more likely with low order N-grams.

In order to compare the generated poems with the original lines in the corpus, another variant of the algorithm has been tested, where instead of creating verses backwards with an N-gram model, the original verses are the candidates. From those verses poems are created following the previously explained procedure.

In Tables 1 and 2 we show four poems composed by the automated system, in its original form and in an approximate English translation. Two are made with sentences mined from the original corpus and the other two produced from scratch with the 2-gram model. Some general conclusions can be drawn:

- The emotional affect of the poems can be clearly appreciated.
- The generated poems are related to the subject. This relationship is not only appreciated through the repetition of the key word or theme, but also through the incursion in the poem of words semantically similar to the theme (e.g. with the theme *music*, the terms *tone*, *classic*, *concert* and *public* appear).
- With respect to the content generator methods, corpus-harvesting and N-gram model, the corpus-harvesting method ensures the internal coherence of the sentences (since it extracts entire phrases from the corpus) but, on the other hand, creates more rigid poems. It can be seen sentences related to everyday news (due to the influence of the corpus used) that are hardly related to the proposed theme.

Table 1. Two poems created by the system with the theme 'music' and with lines from the original corpus. On the left with negative sentiment and on the right with positive sentiment

Basque	Gutxien ezagutzen zen musikaria hak bertsotan aurkeztu zuen jaialdia haiengandik aldendu hori nire nahia Bolibarko Txikito puntista ohia	Basque	Atzo eskaini zuten lehen kontzertua eta bertsolariok antza talentua Gorrotxategirena dugu sonatua proposizioaren bigarren puntua
English	The least known of the musicians he introduced the festival improvising verses get away from them, that's my goal Txikito de Bolivar, ex pelotari	English	Yesterday they offered the first concert and the bertsolaris, it seems to be, talent Gorrotxategi is well known the second point of the proposition

Table 2. Two poems created by the system with the theme 'music' and with lines created from scratch with 2-grams. On the left with negative sentiment and on the right with positive sentiment

Basque	Ez har ta ez det lortu nahi dute tonua klasiko bat da ta ez dezu zuk lekua eta beste bat izan zen denen patua jo ta orain ezin da bere sekretua	Basque	Zaintzen nahiko lan daukat emanaldiekin eta libre izan nahi dut entzuleekin zorion gehiago gaur ez gaude ezberdin nere musika ez al duzu zuk atsegin
English	Don't pick up, I haven't got their tone It's a classic and you have no room and the destiny of all was another and now also you can not your secret	English	I've enough taking care of myself in concerts and I want to be free with the listeners more happiness, today we are not different Don't you like my music?

- The N-gram method is more flexible, malleable, and seems to get closer to the given topic. But, the toll to be paid is that flexibility is sometimes translated into unintelligible phrases.

6   Conclusions and Further Work

In this paper we have presented an automated system to generate poetry in Basque language. The proposed method not only generates novel poems, but also creates them conveying a certain attitude or state of mind. The system receives as an input the topic of the poem and the affective state (positive, neutral or negative) and tries to give as output a novel poem that satisfies formal constraints of rhyme and metric, shows coherent content related to the given topic and expresses them through the predetermined mood.

Two methods has been tested for creating content: on the one hand composing verses from scratch and putting together phrases already made by the other. The performed experiments have served as a basis for better insight of the proposed methods as well as to mark the way and future lines of work. We are already working on further enhancements to each of the processes involved, including:

1. We are trying to test another ways to assert the sentiment of a whole poem. That is, capturing the general sentiment conveying of the poem, instead of calculating it line by line. The main message of a *bertso* goes always at the end. Therefore, perhaps we could only take into account the sentiment of the last line, leaving free the sentiment of the others.
2. Exploring new models to measure the semantic coherence of the poem. We are currently experimenting with a word embedding approach to measure semantic similarity between sentences.
3. Implementing improved methods to generate phrases for templates and working with other corpora. To generate the Markov chain, the use of other bigger or more diverse corpus would also be interesting.
4. Improving the performance of the algorithm to create verses in real-time (as real *bertsolaris* do) and use it in live performances.

Acknowledgments. This paper has been supported by the Spanish Ministerio de Eco-nomía y Competitividad, contract TIN2015-64395-R (MINECO/FEDER, UE), as well as by the Basque Government, contract IT900-16.

References

1. Lord, A.B., Mitchell, S.A., Nagy, G.: The Singer of Tales. Harvard Studies in Comparative Literature, vol. 24. Harvard University Press (2000)
2. Pihel, E.: A furified freestyle: Homer and hip hop. Oral Tradition **11**(2), 249–269 (1996)
3. Garzia Garmendia, J., Sarasua, J., Egaña, A.: The art of bertsolaritza: Improvised basque verse singing (2001)
4. Egaña, A.: Oral tradition **22** (2007)
5. Queneau, R.: 100.000.000.000.000 de poemes. Gallimard Series. Schoenhof's Foreign Books (1961)
6. Oulipo, A.: Atlas de Litterature Potentielle. Collection Idees, Gallimard (1981)
7. Gervás, P.: Constrained creation of poetic forms during theme-driven exploration of a domain defined by an n-gram model. Connection Sci. **28**(2), 111–130 (2016)
8. Oliveira, H.G., Cardoso, A.: Poetry generation with PoeTryMe. In: Besold, T.R., Schorlemmer, M., Smaill, A. (eds.) Computational Creativity Research: Towards Creative Machines. ATM, vol. 7, pp. 243–266. Atlantis Press, Paris (2015). doi:10.2991/978-94-6239-085-0_12
9. Toivanen, J., Toivonen, H., Valitutti, A., Gross, O., et al.: Corpus-based generation of content and form in poetry. In: Proceedings of the Third International Conference on Computational Creativity, Dublin, Ireland, pp. 175–179 (2012)
10. Toivanen, J.M., Järvisalo, M., Toivonen, H., et al.: Harnessing constraint programming for poetry composition. In: Proceedings of the Fourth International Conference on Computational Creativity, Sydney, Australia, pp. 160–167 (2013)
11. Gervás, P.: WASP: evaluation of different strategies for the automatic generation of Spanish verse. In: Proceedings of the AISB-2000 Symposium on Creative & Cultural Aspects of AI, Birmingham, United Kingdom, pp. 93–100 (2000)
12. Gervás, P.: Engineering linguistic creativity: Bird flight and jet planes. In: Proceedings of the NAACL HLT 2010 Second Workshop on Computational Approaches to Linguistic Creativity, Association for Computational Linguistics, pp. 23–30 (2010)

13. Agirrezabal, M., Arrieta, B., Astigarraga, A., Hulden, M.: Pos-tag based poetry generation with wordnet. In: ENLG 2013 - Proceedings of the 14th European Workshop on Natural Language Generation, 8–9 August, 2013, Sofia, Bulgaria, pp. 162–166 (2013)
14. Astigarraga, A., Jauregi, E., Lazkano, E., Agirrezabal, M.: Textual coherence in a verse-maker robot. In: Hippe, Z.S., Kulikowski, J.L., Mroczek, T., Wtorek, J. (eds.) Human-Computer Systems Interaction: Backgrounds and Applications 3. AISC, vol. 300, pp. 275–287. Springer, Cham (2014). doi:10.1007/978-3-319-08491-6_23
15. Astigarraga, A., Agirrezabal, M., Lazkano, E., Jauregi, E., Sierra, B.: Bertsobot: the first minstrel robot. In: 2013 The 6th International Conference on Human System Interaction (HSI), pp. 129–136. IEEE (2013)
16. Manurung, H.: An evolutionary algorithm approach to poetry generation. PhD thesis, University of Edinburgh. College of Science and Engineering. School of Informatics (2004)
17. Zhang, X., Lapata, M.: Chinese poetry generation with recurrent neural networks. In: Proceedings of the 2014 Conference on Empirical Methods in Natural Language Processing, EMNLP, 25–29, 2014, Doha, Qatar, A Meeting of SIGDAT, a Special Interest Group of the ACL, pp. 670–680, October 2014
18. Yan, R.: i, poet: automatic poetry composition through recurrent neural networks with iterative polishing schema. In: Proceedings of the Twenty-Fifth International Joint Conference on Artificial Intelligence (IJCAI 2016), New York, United States, pp. 2238–2244 (2016)
19. Jurafsky, D., James, H.: Speech and language processing an introduction to natural language processing, computational linguistics, and speech (2000)
20. Manning, C.D., Schütze, H., et al.: Foundations of statistical natural language processing. MIT Press (1999)
21. Langkilde, I., Knight, K.: Generation that exploits corpus-based statistical knowledge. In: Proceedings of the 36th Annual Meeting of the Association for Computational Linguistics and 17th International Conference on Computational Linguistics, vol. 1. Association for Computational Linguistics, pp. 704–710 (1998)
22. Barbieri, G., Pachet, F., Roy, P., Esposti, M.D.: Markov constraints for generating lyrics with style. In: Proceedings of the 20th European Conference on Artificial Intelligence, pp. 115–120. IOS Press (2012)
23. Das, A., Gambäck, B.: Poetic machine: Computational creativity for automatic poetry generation in bengali. In: 5th International Conference on Computational Creativity, ICCC, pp. 230–238 (2014)
24. Pang, B., Lee, L., et al.: Opinion mining and sentiment analysis. Found. Trends® Inf. Retrieval 2(1–2), 1–135 (2008)
25. Wilson, T., Wiebe, J., Hoffmann, P.: Recognizing contextual polarity in phrase-level sentiment analysis. In: Proceedings of the Conference on Human Language Technology and Empirical Methods in Natural Language Processing, HLT 2005, Stroudsburg, PA, USA, pp. 347–354. Association for Computational Linguistics (2005)
26. Ravi, K., Ravi, V.: A survey on opinion mining and sentiment analysis: tasks, approaches and applications. Knowl.-Based Syst. 89, 14–46 (2015)
27. Colton, S., Goodwin, J., Veale, T.: Full face poetry generation. In: Proceedings of the Third International Conference on Computational Creativity, pp. 95–102 (2012)
28. Veale, T.: Less rhyme, more reason: Knowledge-based poetry generation with feeling, insight and wit. In: Proceedings of the International Conference on Computational Creativity, pp. 152–159 (2013)

29. Misztal, J., Indurkhya, B.: Poetry generation system with an emotional personality. In: Proceedings of the 5th International Conference on Computational Creativity, pp. 72–81 (2014)
30. Kirke, A., Miranda, E.: Emotional and multi-agent systems in computer-aided writing and poetry. In: Proceedings of the Artificial Intelligence and Poetry Symposium, pp. 17–22 (2013)
31. Amuriza, X.: Hiztegi Errimatua. Lanku (1981)
32. Jauregi, O.: Euskal testuetako silaba egituren maiztasuna diakronikoki. Anuario del Seminario de Filología Vasca "Julio de Urquijo" 37(1), 393–410 (2013)
33. Deerwester, S., Dumais, S.T., Furnas, G.W., Landauer, T.K., Harshman, R.: Indexing by latent semantic analysis. J. Am. Soc. Inf. Sci. 41(6), 391–407 (1990)
34. Zelaia, A., Arregi, O., Sierra, B.: Combining singular value decomposition and a multi-classifier: a new approach to support coreference resolution. Eng. Appl. AI 46, 279–286 (2015)
35. San Vicente, I., Saralegi, X., Agerri, R., Sebastián, D.S.: EliXa: a modular and flexible ABSA platform. In: Proceedings of the 9th International Workshop on Semantic Evaluation (SemEval 2015), pp. 748–752 (2015)

End-to-End Large Vocabulary Speech Recognition for the Serbian Language

Branislav Popović[1,2(✉)], Edvin Pakoci[1,2], and Darko Pekar[1,2]

[1] Department for Power Electronic and Telecommunication Engineering,
Faculty of Technical Sciences, University of Novi Sad,
Trg Dositeja Obradovića 6, 21000 Novi Sad, Serbia
bpopovic@uns.ac.rs
[2] AlfaNum Speech Technologies,
Bulevar Vojvode Stepe 40, 21000 Novi Sad, Serbia

Abstract. This paper presents the results of a large vocabulary speech recognition for the Serbian language, developed by using Eesen end-to-end framework. Eesen involves training a single deep recurrent neural network, containing a number of bidirectional long short-term memory layers, modeling the connection between the speech and a set of context-independent lexicon units. This approach reduces the amount of expert knowledge needed in order to develop other competitive speech recognition systems. The training is based on a connectionist temporal classification, while decoding allows the usage of weighted finite-state transducers. This provides much faster and more efficient decoding in comparison to other similar systems. A corpus of approximately 215 h of audio data (about 171 h of speech and 44 h of silence, or 243 male and 239 female speakers) was employed for the training (about 90%) and testing (about 10%) purposes. On a set of more than 120000 words, the word error rate of 14.68% and the character error rate of 3.68% is achieved.

Keywords: Eesen · End-to-end · LSTM · Speech recognition · Serbian

1 Introduction

Serbian is a highly inflected language. A large number of parameters have to be set according to some previous expert knowledge. A number of different architectures have been examined in the last few years, and most of them were based on Kaldi speech recognition toolkit [1].

The results for the HMM-GMM system and a trigram-based language model, on a test vocabulary of more than 14000 words, are presented in [2]. Other than preparing the transcriptions, a number of different settings had to be optimized, e.g. the topology of the HMM states, selected type of features, training recipe, the number of regression tree leaves and the number of Gaussians per each stage. A number of different training configurations have also been examined, including various training stages, such as training of monophone models, progressive step-by-step training of triphone models, another triphone pass using linear discriminant analysis and maximum likelihood linear transform, maximum mutual information and boosted maximum mutual information

© Springer International Publishing AG 2017
A. Karpov et al. (Eds.): SPECOM 2017, LNAI 10458, pp. 343–352, 2017.
DOI: 10.1007/978-3-319-66429-3_33

[3] on top of the previous stage, minimum phone error [4], speaker adaptive training [5], as well as various combinations of the above mentioned transforms. More than 200 clustering questions have been created according to the acoustic similarity between the phones and the expert knowledge. Different phonetic segmentation (alignment) procedures have been examined in [6].

A deep neural network (DNN) based continuous speech recognition system is presented in [7]. Stacked restricted Boltzmann machines, trained in a greedy layer-wise fashion, were used to initialize the DNNs. Individual frames were classified into triphone-states according to the cross-entropy criterion. However, the described procedure was built upon the previous HMM-GMM framework.

Unlike previously described systems, Eesen [8] is an end-to-end framework that discards most of the above mentioned elements, such as HMM-GMM state topologies, decision tree questions and other complicated features. On the other hand, it provides highly efficient and a reasonably accurate decoding procedure, based on weighted finite-state transducers (WFSTs) [9], and allows parallel GPU training using the connectionist temporal classification (CTC) as the objective function [10].

In Sect. 2, experimental setup, including training and decoding particularities, are discussed. In Sect. 3, the database used for the experiments is thoroughly described. In Sect. 4, experimental results are presented. Conclusions and the directions for future research are presented in Sect. 5.

2 Experimental Setup

2.1 Training

Training of acoustic models in Eesen presumes learning a single deep bidirectional recurrent neural network (RNN) in a sequence-to-sequence manner, over pairs of speech and context-independent label sequences (phonemes or characters) [8]. The alignments between speech frames representing an utterance $X = (x_1, \ldots, x_T)$ and a label sequence $Z = (Z_1, \ldots Z_U), U \leq T, Z_u \in \{1, \ldots K\}$, K is the number of unique labels (blanks are denoted as 0), are inferred using the connectionist temporal classification (CTC) objective function [10]. The RNNs are trained using back-propagation through time for 3 or 4 (see Sect. 4) bidirectional long short-term memory layers (LSTM). Each LSTM unit represents a memory block storing temporal states of the network. The structure of the LSTM units is illustrated in [8].

The training was conducted using a single CUDA GPU (GeForce GTX 980). 40-dimensional filterbank features together with 3 additional features representing pitch (optional) with their first and second-order derivatives, normalized via mean subtraction and variance normalization per speaker are used in the experiments. Therefore, 120 or 129-dimensional feature vectors were used as inputs of the RNNs. Each LSTM layer (both the forward and the backward sublayers) contains 320 or 1024 memory cells (considering the number of layers and the number of memory cells, 4 different configurations were examined, 3/320, 3/1024, 4/320 and 4/1024).

Eesen allows multiple utterances to be processed in parallel in order to speed up the computation, by replacing matrix-vector multiplication over single frames with matrix-matrix multiplication over multiple frames. Each utterance is padded to the length of the longest utterance in the group, but those frames are of course excluded from gradients computation. Utterances from the training set are sorted by length. In order to prevent running out of GPU memory, the number of frames to be processed in parallel has to be limited. The maximum number of training samples could be determined based on the number of parallel sequences and the number of parallel frames, whatever is reached first. The number of sequences in the experiments presented in Sect. 4 ranged between 128 and 256, and the number of frames was set in a range from 20000 to 40000, which depends on the RNN structure, in order to achieve the optimal usage of GPU capacity, i.e., the maximum available acceleration.

The learning rate was set to 0.00004. The proposed rate decreases after the accuracy improvement falls below 0.5, by half at each subsequent epoch. The training terminates as soon as the accuracy improvement falls below 0.1 between any 2 successive epochs. Other values (0.001, 0.0001 and 0.00001) and other learning rate parameters were also explored. However, the value 0.001 lead to the explosion of gradients, 0.0001 was too unstable, leading to unexpected jumps in accuracy between consecutive epochs, and therefore providing suboptimal solution, while 0.00001 converged extremely slowly. Therefore, the value 0.00004 was used as a starting value for all the experiments presented in Sect. 4.

2.2 Decoding

In order to decode CTC-trained models, Eesen employs a generalized decoding method based on weighted finite-state transducers (WFSTs) [9]. Individual components, i.e., CTC labels (T), lexicon (L) and language model (G), are encoded into a single search graph, following the expression

$$TLG = T \circ min(det(L \circ G)) \tag{1}$$

TLG provides the mapping between a sequence of CTC labels and a sequence of words (min denotes minimization, det denotes determinization and $\circ$ denotes composition). This allows highly efficient search using the OpenFst library [11] or other highly-optimized FST libraries.

A grammar WFST is composed from a set of permissible word sequences, given in a form of an ARPA language model. Trigram language models are used in this paper for the purpose of the experiments. The Kneser-Ney smoothing method [12] is applied in order to calculate the probability distribution of n-grams. The probabilities are pruned according to the minimum entropy increase criterion (10^{-7} and 10^{-6}) to reduce the size of a language model. The optimal performance in terms of the recognition accuracy was achieved by using a pruning threshold of 10^{-7}. Therefore, this value was used for all the experiments presented in Sect. 4. The final language model contains 121197 unigrams, 1279389 bigrams and 357721 trigrams. It was built based on the training corpus described in Sect. 3 and the additional 442000 sentences from the Serbian journalistic corpus (this corpus contains newspaper articles, books, etc.).

A lexicon WFST defines the mapping between sequences of words and sequences of lexicon units. It contains words from both training and testing sets (there are no out-of-vocabulary words) and the additional words from the Serbian journalistic corpus, together with their pronunciations. Two sets of lexicon units have been employed. The first one (labeled as "phn" in Table 2) contains a set of 77 lexicon units, including silence, damaged versions of all the phones (denoting all noised, shortened, or otherwise damaged phones), as well as stressed versions of all the vowels in the database. This is a standard set of phones that was previously used in Kaldi. However, bearing in mind that Eesen does not provide any mechanism that would allow tying of acoustical states according to some expert knowledge (e.g., tying of A, A_d, A_s and A_{sd} into A, s is for stressed, d is for damaged, tying of vowels, etc.), the second set (labeled as "gph" in Table 2) contains 31 lexicon units, including silence and 30 phonemes from the Serbian alphabet. Serbian orthography is largely phonemic. Therefore, the second set could also be observed as the set of graphemes (the Cyrillic and Latin letters are treated the same), plus the silence.

A token WFST provides the mapping from a sequence of frame-level CTC labels (allows occurrences of the blank label, as well as repetitions of non-blank labels) into a single lexicon unit. The final RNN layer is a softmax layer containing $K + 1$ nodes, corresponding to $K + 1$ labels (including the additional blank label), $K \in \{77, 31\}$. Finally, the acoustic model scores are scaled by a factor $f \in \{0.5, 0.6, 0.7, 0.8, 0.9, 1.0\}$, that corresponds to the acoustic model weight (ACWT) from 5 to 10, given Sect. 4.

3   Data Preparation

The database used for the experiments presented in Sect. 4 represents a combination of two different data sets. The first one is a set of audio books (AB). It contains a list of longer and more complex utterances, e.g. "*Glas joj je bio isti kao i pre šesnaest godina kad smo se poslednji put videle, bio je čist, zvonak, veseo, čak senzacionalan na svoj način.*"/ "Her voice was the same as sixteen years ago when we met for the last time, it was clear, resonant, cheerful, even sensational in its own way". The second one is a set of utterances recorded by using different mobile phone devices (MOB). It contains a list of somewhat less complicated utterances, such as user commands, inputs or queries, e.g. "*Trebala bi mi informacija o vremenu dolaska voza iz Ciriha.*"/ "I need an information about the time of arrival of the train from Zurich.", but also "*Milano važi za centar mode i dizajna, i jedan od središta svetske mode.*"/ "Milano is considered as a center of fashion and design, and one of the world fashion capitals.". Database duration (per segments) is presented in Table 1.

Table 1. Database duration (per segments)

Set	Train		Test		Total	
	Duration	Num. spk.	Duration	Num. spk.	Duration	Num. spk.
AB	139 h 15 m	69 M, 54 F	14 h 48 m	5 M, 4 F	154 h 3 m	74 M, 58 F
MOB	57 h 45 m	161 M, 172 F	3 h 12 m	8 M, 9 F	60 h 57 m	169 M, 181 F

The second set was added not only to increase the total amount of training and testing data, but also to improve the recognition accuracy in voice assistant applications. 95% of the training data was used for the actual training, while another 5% was used for the cross-validation (as a development set).

4 Experimental Results

In Table 2, the results are presented in terms of the word error rate (WER) and character error rate (CER, reflecting the number of inserted, deleted or substituted characters) for the network with 3 or 4 layers and 320 or 1024 memory cells per each LSTM forward and backward sublayer. For the configurations 1 to 4, the filterbank features (120-dimensional feature vectors) were employed in combination with the standard dictionary (77 lexicon units, including silence, damaged versions of all the phones, and the stressed versions of all the vowels in the database). WER for the configurations with 320 memory cells was generally better than the WER for the configurations with 1024 memory cells. These results were expected, bearing in mind that Essen is an end-to-end framework which does not take expert knowledge into account. Therefore, it was harder for the system to infer such a large number of parameters.

Table 2. The results in terms of WER and CER

#	Num. layers	Cell dim.	Lexicon	Features	ACWT	WER [%]	CER [%]	Ins.	Del.	Sub.
1	3	320	phn	fbank	8	16.41	5.58	2532	4587	18922
2		1024			6	20.93	11.09	2566	6073	24568
3	4	320			7	16.96	7.00	2295	4761	19849
4		1024			7	17.56	7.52	2493	4667	20693
5	3	320	gph	fbank	8	15.08	3.80	2148	5199	16585
6				fbank + pitch	9	16.26	4.13	2377	5546	17871
7	4			fbank	9	15.23	3.82	2367	4915	16878
8				fbank + pitch	9	14.73	3.69	2374	4810	16183

For the configurations 5 to 8, 320 memory cells per each LSTM layer were employed, based on the previous results. In order to reduce the number of substitutions, instead of the standard dictionary with 77 lexicon units, the set of 31 lexicon units, including silence and 30 phonemes, i.e. graphemes from the Serbian alphabet, was employed. In the case of configurations 6 and 8, 3 additional features representing pitch with their first and second order derivatives were added to the set of 40 filterbank features with their derivatives, finally giving 129-dimensional feature vectors. The best configuration was the one with 4 LSTM layers and 129-dimensional feature vectors, i.e. the configuration number 8. The number of substitutions was reduced by several thousand instances (the total number of words in the test set was 158653).

In Table 3, more detailed results are given for the configuration number 8. Different blank scale values {1.0, 0.75, 0.5, 0.25} were explored, which further reduced the number of substitutions and insertions, probably by giving larger probability to the word endings, allowing the system to recognize the real word. The best WER (14.68%) was achieved for the blank scale value 0.75. It was much better than the baseline HMM-GMM configuration (WER 18.5%), but worse than nnet2 configuration implemented in Kaldi (WER 12.01%, note that Kaldi allows the usage of expert knowledge [1]). The configuration with 4 bidirectional LSTM layers and 320 memory cells was also the best one reported in [8].

Table 3. The results for the best configuration (#8) and different blank scale values

Blank scale	WER [%]	CER [%]	Ins.	Del.	Sub.
1.00	14.73	3.69	2374	4810	16183
0.75	14.68	3.68	2237	4959	16101
0.50	14.76	3.71	2076	5256	16084
0.25	15.15	3.84	1893	5876	16260

In Fig. 1, the list of top 20 insertions is presented in the graph form for the configuration number 8 and the blank scale value 0.75. Short, single syllable words, such as proposals, particles and conjunctions, recognized instead of noise or falsely recognized in-between words constitute a very significant portion of the total number of insertions.

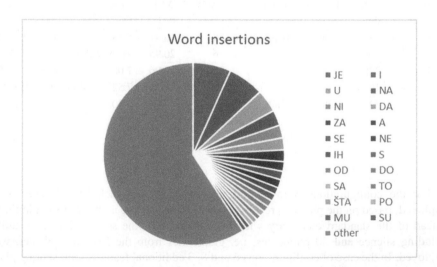

Fig. 1. Top 20 insertions chart for the configuration number 8 (blank scale 0.75)

In Fig. 2, the list of top 20 deletions is presented in the same manner. Again, short words and vowels, badly pronounced or poorly covered by the language model contribute significantly to the total number of deletions (top 20 deletions given in Fig. 2 constitute more than 50% of all the deletions in the system).

In Fig. 3, the list of top 20 substitutions is presented. The number of substitutions per each pair of words is given in the figure. Other than short words, most of the substitutions are produced by different gender or plural identifiers, inappropriate case, missing prefixes or suffixes, etc. Most of those cases could be successfully corrected by providing a more suitable language model.

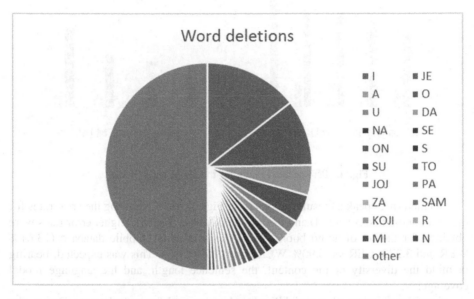

Fig. 2. Top 20 deletions chart for the configuration number 8 (blank scale 0.75)

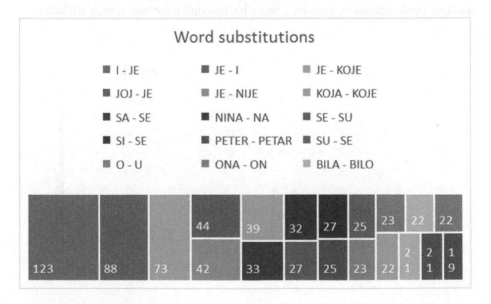

Fig. 3. Top 20 substitutions for the configuration number 8 (blank scale 0.75)

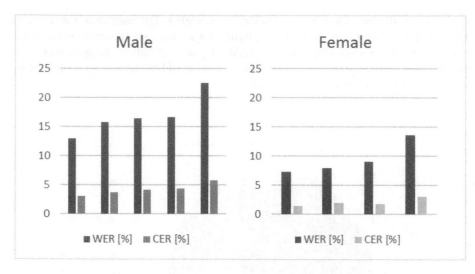

Fig. 4. Per-speaker results for the set of audio books

Detailed (per-speaker) results are given in Figs. 4 and 5, showing the error rates for the set of audio books (Fig. 4) and the mobile database (Fig. 5). Higher error rates were obtained for the set of audio books, in comparison to the mobile database (13.61% WER and 3.27% CER vs. 3.90% WER and 0.95% CER). This was expected, bearing in mind the diversity of the content, the sentence length, and the language model coverage.

Significant inter-speaker variability can be observed for both datasets. Due to the random selection of the test sets, female speakers usually perform better than male speakers (male utterances contained more background noise and speech artifacts).

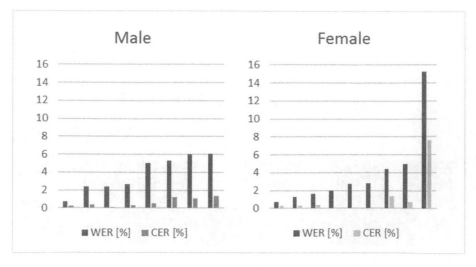

Fig. 5. Per-speaker results for the mobile database

5   Conclusion

According to the results presented in the previous sections, Eesen provides a reasonably accurate and highly efficient alternative for the automatic speech recognition in the case of Serbian. The best system configuration was achieved for the network with 4 LSTM layers and 320 memory cells per each LSTM forward and backward layer. Limited set of lexicon units provided higher accuracy in comparison to the previously used "standard" set of units, due to the high number of substitutions. Tonal characteristics of the language (Serbian vowels can be distinguished by their tone and length) captured inside the additional features helped reducing the word error rate by an additional percentage. Although the best system WER was relatively high - 14.68%, the character error rate was only 3.68%. This parameter is important, bearing in mind that the number of substitutions was highly influenced by the language infectivity and the obvious lack of the proper language model. On the other hand, short words and noises highly contributed to the total number of insertions and deletions.

In the future, other LSTM configurations will be explored. Tonal characteristics of the language will be additionally exploited, by using the morphological dictionary for the Serbian language and the part-of-speech tagging (accentuation of the lexicon the corpus, phoneme types - shorter/ longer, opened/ closed, etc.). Wider context for feature extraction will also be explored in order to detect the endings and the beginnings of a sentence (border phonemes have somewhat different acoustics). In order to reduce the need for greater database, (wider) class n-grams instead of the ordinary trigrams will be examined.

Acknowledgments. The work described in this paper was supported in part by the Ministry of Education, Science and Technological Development of the Republic of Serbia, within the project "Development of Dialogue Systems for Serbian and Other South Slavic Languages", EUREKA project DANSPLAT, "A Platform for the Applications of Speech Technologies on Smartphones for the Languages of the Danube Region", id E! 9944, and the Provincial Secretariat for Higher Education and Scientific Research, within the project "Central Audio-Library of the University of Novi Sad", No. 114-451-2570/2016-02.

References

1. Povey, D., Ghoshal, A., Boulianne, G., Burget, L., Glembek, O., Goel, N., Hannemann, M., Motlíček, P., Qian, Y., Schwarz, P., Silovský, J., Stemmer, G., Veselý, K.: The Kaldi speech recognition toolkit. In: IEEE Workshop on Automatic Speech Recognition and Understanding (ASRU), pp. 1–4. IEEE Signal Processing Society (2011)
2. Popović, B., Pakoci, E., Ostrogonac, S., Pekar, D.: Large vocabulary continuous speech recognition for Serbian using the Kaldi toolkit. In: 10th Digital Speech and Image Processing, DOGS, pp. 31–34. Novi Sad, Serbia (2014)
3. Povey, D., Kanevsky, D., Kingsbury, B., Ramabhadran, B., Saon, G., Visweswariah, K.: Boosted MMI for model and feature-space discriminative training. In: 33rd International Conference on Acoustics, Speech and Signal Processing, ICASSP, Las Vegas, pp. 4057–4060 (2008)

4. Povey, D., Woodland, P.C.: Minimum phone error and I-smoothing for improved discriminative training. In: 27th International Conference on Acoustics, Speech and Signal Processing ICASSP, Orlando, pp. I-105–I-108 (2002)
5. Povey, D., Kuo, H-K.J., Soltau, H.: Fast speaker adaptive training for speech recognition. In: 9th Annual Conference of the International Speech Communication Association, INTER-SPEECH, Brisbane, pp. 1245–1248 (2008)
6. Pakoci, E., Popović, B., Jakovljević, N., Pekar, D., Yassa, F.: A phonetic segmentation procedure based on hidden markov models. In: Ronzhin, A., Potapova, R., Németh, G. (eds.) SPECOM 2016. LNCS, vol. 9811, pp. 67–74. Springer, Cham (2016). doi:10.1007/978-3-319-43958-7_7
7. Popović, B., Ostrogonac, S., Pakoci, E., Jakovljević, N., Delić, V.: Deep neural network based continuous speech recognition for serbian using the Kaldi toolkit. In: Ronzhin, A., Potapova, R., Fakotakis, N. (eds.) SPECOM 2015. LNCS, vol. 9319, pp. 186–192. Springer, Cham (2015). doi:10.1007/978-3-319-23132-7_23
8. Miao, Y., Gowayyed, M., Metze, F.: EESEN: End-to-end speech recognition using deep RNN models and WFST-based decoding. In: Automatic Speech Recognition and Understanding Workshop, ASRU 2015, arXiv:1507.08240 (2015)
9. Mohri, M., Pereira, F., Riley, M.: Weighted finite-state transducers in speech recognition. Comput. Speech Lang. 16(1), 69–88 (2002)
10. Graves, A., Fernández, S., Gomez, F., Schmidhuber, J.: Connectionist temporal classification: labelling unsegmented sequence data with recurrent neural networks. In: 23rd International Conference on Machine Learning, pp. 369–376. ACM (2006)
11. Allauzen, C., Riley, M., Schalkwyk, J., Skut, W., Mohri, M.: OpenFst: a general and efficient weighted finite-state transducer library. In: Holub, J., Žďárek, J. (eds.) CIAA 2007. LNCS, vol. 4783, pp. 11–23. Springer, Heidelberg (2007). doi:10.1007/978-3-540-76336-9_3
12. Kneser, R., Ney, H.: Improved backing-off for M-gram language modeling. In: 20th International Conference on Acoustics, Speech and Signal Processing, ICASSP, Detroit, pp. 181–184 (1995)

Examining the Impact of Feature Selection
on Sentiment Analysis for the Greek Language

Nikolaos Spatiotis[1], Michael Paraskevas[1,3], Isidoros Perikos[1,3,4(✉)],
and Iosif Mporas[2]

[1] Computer and Informatics Engineering Department,
Technological Educational Institute of Western Greece, Missolonghi, Greece
{mparask, perikos}@cti.gr
[2] School of Engineering and Technology,
University of Hertfordshire, Hatfield, UK
[3] Computer Technology Institute and Press "Diophantus", Patras, Greece
[4] Computer Engineering and Informatics Department,
University of Patras, Patras, Greece

Abstract. Sentiment analysis identifies the attitude that a person has towards a
service, a topic or an event and it is very useful for companies which receive
many written opinions. Research studies have shown that the determination of
sentiment in written text can be accurately determined through text and part of
speech features. In this paper, we present an approach to recognize opinions in
Greek language and we examine the impact of feature selection on the analysis
of opinions and the performance of the classifiers. We analyze a large number of
feedback and comments from teachers towards e-learning, life-long courses that
have attended with the aim to specify their opinions. A number of text-based and
part of speech based features from textual data are extracted and a generic
approach to analyze text and determine opinion is presented. Evaluation results
indicate that the approach illustrated is accurate in specifying opinions in Greek
text and also sheds light on the effect that various features have on the classification performance.

Keywords: Sentiment analysis · Feature selection · Text mining · Machine
learning

1 Introduction

In recent years, sentiment analysis is becoming an emerging topic mainly due to the
vast amount of people opinions and user generated comment on the web [4]. In order to
identify and extract opinion and subjective information in text, natural language processing methods, text analytics and machine learning approaches are widely used [5,
15, 18]. An important stage in sentiment analysis concerns the extraction and the
utilization of appropriate and meaningful features that will be indicative and assistive in
the classification process.

Sentiment analysis methods are applied mainly on three different levels:
document/text level, sentence level and entity/feature level [8]. Document/text level
considers the whole document a basic information unit and expresses a specific

© Springer International Publishing AG 2017
A. Karpov et al. (Eds.): SPECOM 2017, LNAI 10458, pp. 353–361, 2017.
DOI: 10.1007/978-3-319-66429-3_34

sentiment for a product-service. In sentence-level, each sentence is considered to express a different opinion or emotion without being influenced by the content of adjacent sentences. So, sentences are identified as positive, negative or neutral. The entity and feature level, aims to classify the sentiment with respect to the specific aspects. The issue of extracting and classifying opinions from text can roughly be divided in two main approaches, namely the machine learning and the lexicon-based [9]. The first approach considers opinion mining as a text classification problem using machine learning algorithms for classification and syntactic and/or linguistic features. The second approach relies on opinion lexicons using the prior polarity of words or phrases.

According to the degree of human intervention in the learning process, the machine learning approach is divided into two major categories: supervised and unsupervised. Pang and Lee have made extensive research regarding sentiment analysis and opinion mining, In one of them [11], they proposed an approach to classify movie reviews in two classes, positive and negative. They experimented with features like unigrams, bigrams, term frequency, term presence and position, and parts-of speech. In a following approach, they [10] suggested to remove objective sentences by extracting subjective ones. They proposed a text-categorization technique that is able to identify subjective content using minimum cut. Regarding unsupervised methods, the researchers presented the classification of reviews as recommended (thumbs up) or not recommended (thumbs down) [17]. This categorization of reviews based on adjectives and adverbs, which were contained in words, phrases and proposals and parts of speech, determined the emotional orientation of each review. With the assistance of two given seed words, i.e., "poor" and "excellent", the algorithm calculated the emotional load of the candidate word for semantic orientation. The algorithm depended on patterns of two constant words where first word is an adverb or adjective used for orientation and the second word is used to represent the context. On the other hand the lexicon-based approaches can be distinguished into two main categories: the dictionary-based and the corpus-based. In corpus-based approaches, Hatzivassiloglou and McKeown [7] proposed an algorithm to determine the polarity of adjectives. They hypothesize that pairs of conjoined adjectives by "and" have the same polarity, while those separated by "but" have opposite orientation.

A difficulty that supervised machine learning approaches have to address concerns the high formal dimensionally of the feature space [2]. Since text feature space is vast, it is highly desirable to reduce it by selecting proper and meaningful features without however, sacrificing the performance of the classification process [3]. Feature selection, refers to the stage of selecting a subset of the features available for describing the data before applying a learning algorithm and is a common technique for addressing the challenges rising from the high dimensionality of the data [6].

Implementing sentiment analysis for Greek language is a quite challenging task. What is more, there are few available tools for the analysis of Greek text and also resources and annotated corpora for Greek language are limited. In this paper, we present an approach to recognize opinions in Greek language and we examine the impact of feature selection on the analysis of opinions. In our work, feature ranking and successive selection of features is performed in order to improve the accuracy of sentiment classification on Greek text. The data used in the work concern the teachers' reviews towards lifelong learning courses that they attended and which were conducted by the Greek School Network. The reviews were used to train machine learning algorithms and their performance was studied under various feature selection approaches and on different number of features. A number of text-based and part-of speech based features from textual data are extracted and a generic approach to analyze text and determined opinion in is presented.

The rest of the paper is organized as follows: Sect. 2 presents the research design and the methodology. Section 3 describes the experimental study conducted and the results collected. Finally, conclusions and directions for future work are presented in Sect. 4.

2 Research Design and Methodology

2.1 Data and Features Description

In our paper, we present a multi-level sentiment analysis of Greek texts conducted by various machine learning algorithms and examine their performance under different number of features. The data used in our work, are set of reviews of teachers that participated in lifelong learning courses which were conducted by the Greek School Network [13]. More specifically, the reviews were made by over 2600 of teachers who participated in e-Learning courses on computer science [19] which were offered through teleconference services [14] and the teachers expressed their opinions and experiences by answering multiple choice and open-ended questions [1]. The dataset of teachers opinions, initially were manually annotated by experts on a five level scale (1–5). In the annotation process, "1" was used to denote a very negative opinion towards the learning process, while "5" was used to express a very positive opinion respectively. We follow an entity and feature- level approach, reviews that bear multiple meanings, were divided into concrete parts according to the content carrying and their opinion was assessed on the 1 to 5 polarity scale. Example reviews along with the corresponding annotation are illustrated in Fig. 1.

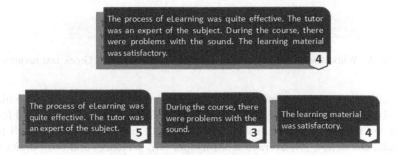

Fig. 1. Example of an opinion evaluation and classification in a class label

After that, a corpus of 11.156 annotated reviews was created and it is used to train machine learning algorithms. The average length of the reviews was 10.4 words. In the dataset, 133 reviews were annotated by the experts with score 1, and they belonged to

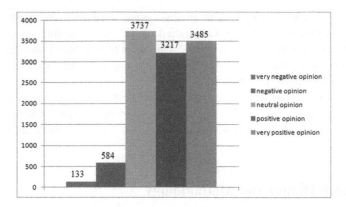

Fig. 2. Distribution of the annotated reviews

the very negative opinion class, 584 reviews were annotated with score 2 and belonged to the negative opinion class, 3737 with score 3 in the neutral opinion class, 3217 with score 4 in the positive opinion class and 3485 were annotated with score 5 and belonged to the very positive opinion class. In Fig. 2, the rate of the annotated reviews is illustrated.

In the context of our work, a supervised machine learning approach was followed and the workflow is illustrated in the next figure (Fig. 3).

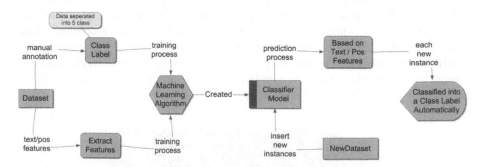

Fig. 3. Workflow of the methodology for the classification of Greek text reviews

Initially, the reviews are analyzed and two types of features are extracted, which are the text-based and the Part of Speech (POS) based. Specifically, the text-based features concern the number of (i) characters, (ii) words, (iii) capital letters, (iv) small letters, (v) special characters, (vi) average word length, (vii) sentences and (viii) digits which appear in a review. On the other hand the POS based features concern the number of (i) nouns, (ii) adjectives, (iii) verbs, (iv) proper nouns, (v) articles, (vi) pronouns, (vii) adverbs, (viii) prepositions and (ix) interjections. POS based features are extracted with the use of POS tagger of Xerox [12], a wide used tool for the morphosyntactic analysis of text which also supports Greek language. Furthermore, we extract

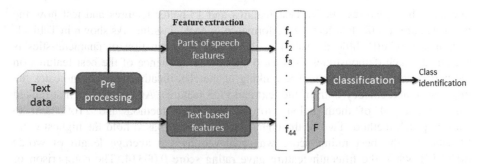

Fig. 4. Feature extraction process

additional features such as the number of (i) punctuations, (ii) verb tenses, (iii) foreign words (Fig. 4).

2.2 Sentiment Identification Methodology

The recognition of the opinion is performed in two stages. Firstly, machine learning algorithms are trained with a large number of instances that are characterized from the text/POS based features and the class. The classification algorithms are trained using a large plurality of data. In the second stage (prediction), the classifiers have the ability to classify new reviews represented as feature vectors in the appropriate class. For the classification stage, a number of machine learning algorithms were investigated. In particular, we experimented with multilayer perceptron neural network (MLP), decision tree namely C4.5 algorithm (J48), lazy algorithm (IBK) and SVM classifier based on the RBF kernel. The experiments of the sentiment classification models were conducted using the WEKA toolkit. This provides implementations of state-of-the-art data mining and machine learning algorithms. It contains modules for data preprocessing, classification, clustering and association rule extraction. We examined the performance and the reliability of classifiers according to different feature sets specified by Relief feature selection algorithm, which is heuristics-independent, noise-tolerant algorithm. Our dataset was processed by the ReliefF algorithm, implemented using the WEKA machine learning toolkit, and feature ranking scores were estimated. The feature ranking results are presented in Table 1.

3 Experimental Results

For the performance of above algorithms, we used the 10-fold cross validation approach. The dataset was divided into ten folds by random selection and then for each of the folds, the classifier model was trained on the nine instances and tested on the control fold. In previous approach, we examined the performance of classifiers training them with all text and POS features [16]. The sum of features was 43, where 14 of them were text-based feature and 29 of them were part-of-speech features. The aim of the study was to examine the performance of each classifier based on different feature sets like the 5-best features, the 10-best features and 15-better features and test how the n-best features is able to affect the performance of each classifier. As shown in Table 1, after using ReliefF, little deviation in the degree of fluctuation of characteristics is presented which demonstrates the lack of significant influence of the best features on the performance of classifiers. The ranking of the classification features indicates the importance and efficacy both of the text and POS features. Among the 15 first ranked characteristics, 4 of them belong to the text-based method and 11of them to part-of-speech method. Two of the characteristics of text-based hold the highest rank. Specifically, the best rating score was achieved by the average length of words (0.00917), while the fifteenth feature gave rating score 0.00314. The comparison of scores demonstrates our above finding, little typical deviation between first and fifteenth ranked feature as a result little influence on the performance of classifiers.

Table 1. ReliefF ranking scores for the top-15 features

	ReliefF score	Feature description	Feature class
1	0.00917	# average length of words	Text based
2	0.00860	# maximum length of words	Text based
3	0.00765	# number of nouns in a review	Part of speech
4	0.00730	# total number of possessive pronouns in a review	Part of speech
5	0.00687	# total number of adjectives in a review	Part of speech
6	0.00630	# total number of subjective in a review	Part of speech
7	0.00557	# total number of words contains refusal	Text based
8	0.00517	# total number of articles in a review	Part of speech
9	0.00486	# total number of pronouns in a review	Part of speech
10	0.00462	# total number of adjectives in a review	Part of speech
11	0.00406	# total number of verbs in active voice	Part of speech
12	0.00333	# total number of letters in a review	Text based
13	0.00318	# total number of verbs in a review	Part of speech
14	0.00316	# total number of preposition in a review	Part of speech
15	0.00314	# total number of small letters in a review	Text based

Series of experiments were conducted in order to determine whether a feature selection approach would produce the same, or better improvements. For each feature, we computed its information gain and then selected the N features with the highest scores. In a parallel set of experiments, we reduced the size of the feature set, and then selected the best N features using information gain. Table 2 and Fig. 5 show the results of the experiments for the J48, IBK, MLP and RBFkernel classifiers.

Table 2. Correct classified instances for different set of features

Algorithms	5-best features	10-best features	15-best features	All features
J48	**54 .2%**	**56%**	**56.1%**	**56.9%**
IBK	50.7%	53.9%	55.3%	54.9%
MLP	48.3%	51.3%	53.8%	53.7%
RBFkernel	45.1%	43.7%	43.9%	45.7%

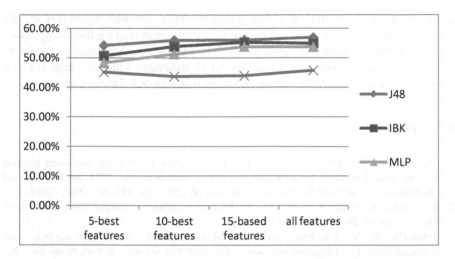

Fig. 5. Accuracy of classification algorithms under different sets of features

As illustrated in the table, lower accuracy appears when the algorithms are trained with small sets of features. In contrast, the highest performance is achieved when the algorithms are trained with the best-15 or more features. Specifically the performance of J48, IBK and MLP is increased approximately 3% when the classifiers use the 10-best features compared to their performance when trained with the 5-best features.

It was also observed that when the 15-best features were used, the performance of these three classifiers was improved. Namely, the performance of J48 was only slightly increased by 0.1%, the performance of IBK was increased by 1.4% and the accuracy of MLP was improved by 2.5% compared to 10-best features. IBK and MLP achieved the best of their performance on the set of 15-best features. In addition, results indicate that among all the classifiers, J48 algorithm achieved the best performance for each set of features, 5-best, 10-best, 15-best and all 44 features achieving the best accuracy 56.9% for the set of all features. On the other hand, RBFkernel had the best score for the set of all feature and was very close with the set of 5-best features, while for the middle number of characteristics had decreased performance.

4   Concussions and Future Work

The vast amount of user generated content necessitates accurate methods to analyze and specify opinions and attitudes. In this work we examine the impact of feature selection in sentiment analysis of Greek comments. A number of text-based and part of speech based features are extracted from textual data and a generic approach to analyze text and determined opinion is presented. The evaluation results indicate that the approach has very good performance in specifying opinions in Greek text and also sheds light on the effect that various features have on the classification performance.

There are various directions for future work. A main direction concerns the utilization of aspect based methods to specify user opinions towards specific aspects they address. Moreover, in future work we intend to apply this with techniques for the analysis of different types of textual data in Greek language ranging from blogs, news articles and different customer opinions on sites. Finally, another direction for future work concerns the examination of additional classification schemas, deep learning approaches and also the study of techniques for handling imbalanced data.

References

1. Angelopoulos, P., Paraskevas, M., Perikos, I., Zarouchas, T.: A highly motivated blended learning model oriented to computer engineering educators. In: 2014 9th International Conference on Computer Science and Education (ICCSE), pp. 457–461. IEEE (2014)
2. Baccianella, S., Esuli, A., Sebastiani, F.: Feature selection for ordinal text classification. Neural Comput. **26**(3), 557–591 (2014)
3. Bolón-Canedo, V., Sánchez-Maroño, N., Alonso-Betanzos, A.: Recent advances and emerging challenges of feature selection in the context of big data. Knowl.-Based Syst. **86**, 33–45 (2015)
4. Cambria, E., Schuller, B., Xia, Y., Havasi, C.: New avenues in opinion mining and sentiment analysis. IEEE Intell. Syst. **2**, 15–21 (2013)
5. Cercel, D.C., Trăuşan, Ş.: Research challenges in opinion mining from a natural language processing perspective. Univ. Politehnica Bucharest Sci. Bull. Ser. C-Electr. Eng. Comput. Sci. **78**(3), 157–168 (2016)
6. Dasgupta, A., Drineas, P., Harb, B., Josifovski, V., Mahoney, M.W.: Feature selection methods for text classification. In: Proceedings of the 13th ACM SIGKDD International Conference on Knowledge Discovery and Data Mining, pp. 230–239. ACM (2007)
7. Hatzivassiloglou, V., McKeown, K.R.: Predicting the semantic orientation of adjectives. In: Proceedings of the Eighth Conference on European Chapter of the Association for Computational Linguistics EACL 1997, pp. 174–181. Association for Computational Linguistics, Stroudsburg (1997)
8. Liu, B.: Sentiment Analysis and Opinion Mining. Synthesis Lectures on Human Language Technologies. Morgan & Claypool Publishers (2012)
9. Medhat, W., Hassan, A., Korashy, H.: Sentiment analysis algorithms and applications: a survey. Ain Shams Eng. J. **5**(4), 1093–1113 (2014)
10. Pang, B., Lee, L.: A sentimental education: sentiment analysis using subjectivity summarization based on minimum cuts. In: Proceedings of the 42nd Annual Meeting on Association for Computational Linguistics, ACL 2004. Association for Computational Linguistics, Stroudsburg, PA, USA (2004)
11. Pang, B., Lee, L., Vaithyanathan, S.: Thumbs up?: sentiment classification using machine learning techniques. In: Proceedings of the ACL-02 Conference on Empirical Methods in Natural Language Processing, EMNLP 2002, vol. 10, pp. 79–86. Association for Computational Linguistics, Stroudsburg (2002)
12. https://open.xerox.com/Services/fst-nlp-tools/Consume/Part%20of%20Speech%20Tagging%20(Standard)-178
13. Paraskevas, M., Zarouchas, T., Angelopoulos, P., Perikos, I.: Formulating an adaptable e-training framework to computer science educators. Int. J. Continuing Eng. Educ. Life Long Learn. **25**(2), 151–173 (2015)
14. Perikos, I., Gkamas, V., Zarouchas, T., Paraskevas, M.: Educational capabilities of a novel teleconference service integrated into the Greek school community. In: Proceedings of the 20th Pan-Hellenic Conference on Informatics. ACM (2016)

15. Perikos, I., Hatzilygeroudis, I.: Recognizing emotions in text using ensemble of classifiers. Eng. Appl. Artif. Intell. **51**, 191–201 (2016)
16. Spatiotis, N., Mporas, I., Paraskevas, M., Perikos, I.: Sentiment Analysis for the Greek Language. In: Proceedings of the 20th Pan-Hellenic Conference on Informatics. ACM (2016)
17. Turney, P.D.: Thumbs up or thumbs down?: semantic orientation applied to unsupervised classification of reviews. In: Proceedings of the 40th Annual Meeting on Association for Computational Linguistics, ACL 2002, pp. 417–424. Association for Computational Linguistics, Stroudsburg (2002)
18. Yi, J., Nasukawa, T., Bunescu, R., Niblack, W.: Sentiment analyzer: extracting sentiments about a given topic using natural language processing techniques. In: Third IEEE International Conference on Data Mining, 2003, ICDM 2003, pp. 427–434. IEEE (2003)
19. Zarouchas, T., Perikos, I., Paraskevas, M., Pegiazis, T.: A hybrid training framework oriented to computer engineering educators. In: Proceedings of the 19th Panhellenic Conference on Informatics, pp. 33–37. ACM (2015)

Experimenting with Hybrid TDNN/HMM Acoustic Models for Russian Speech Recognition

Irina Kipyatkova[1,2]($\boxtimes$)

[1] St. Petersburg Institute for Informatics and Automation of the Russian Academy of Sciences (SPIIRAS), St. Petersburg, Russia
kipyatkova@iias.spb.su
[2] St. Petersburg State University of Aerospace Instrumentation (SUAI), St. Petersburg, Russia

Abstract. In this paper, we study an application of time delay neural networks (TDNNs) in acoustic modeling for large vocabulary continuous Russian speech recognition. We created TDNNs with various numbers of hidden layers and units in the hidden layers with p-norm nonlinearity. Training of acoustic models was carried out on our own Russian speech corpus containing phonetically balanced phrases. Duration of the speech corpus is more than 30 h. Testing of TDNN-based acoustic models was performed in the very large vocabulary continuous Russian speech recognition task. Conducted experiments showed that TDNN models outperformed baseline deep neural network models in terms of the word error rate.

Keywords: Time delay neural networks · Acoustic models · Automatic speech recognition · Russian speech

1 Introduction

In recent years, artificial neural networks (NNs) have become very popular in automatic speech recognition (ASR). Developers of ASR system use NNs for both acoustic and language modeling. For acoustic modeling, NNs are often combined with Hidden Markov Models (HMMs) [1]. In many scientific papers (for example, [2]) it was shown that hybrid NN/HMM acoustic models allow increasing speech recognition accuracy with HMMs supporting long-term dependencies and deep NN (DNN) providing discriminative training. In a hybrid NN/HMM system, the NN is trained to predict a-posteriori probabilities of each context-dependent state with given acoustic observations. During decoding the output probabilities are divided by the prior probability of each state forming a "pseudo-likelihood" that is used in place of the state emission probabilities in the HMM [1].

Different types of NNs are used for acoustic modeling: feed-forward deep neural networks (DNNs), convolutional neural networks (CNN), deep belief networks (DBN), time delay neural networks (TDNN), Long Short-Term Memory (LSTM) [3].

© Springer International Publishing AG 2017
A. Karpov et al. (Eds.): SPECOM 2017, LNAI 10458, pp. 362–369, 2017.
DOI: 10.1007/978-3-319-66429-3_35

Investigations on combination of NNs and HMMs started at the end of the 1980s [1]. Recently, the number of such investigations increases with increasing computation capabilities of computers [4]. For example, context-dependent DNNs/HMMs (CD-DNN-HMMs) are described in [5]. CNN for acoustic modeling was used in [6]. In that paper, context adaptive DNNs for acoustic models based on CNNs are researched. Context adaptation showed up to 6% improvement over a baseline CNN model. DNNs and CNNs with feedback connection was explored in [7], where the input features were augmented with the features obtained from the output of the last hidden layer and it improved the performance of speech recognition. The usage of LSTM in a hybrid DNN/HMM system was presented in [8]. LSTM allowed the authors to reduce word error rate (WER) comparing to the DNN-based system. TDNN-based acoustic models were presented in [9], where introduction of time delays allowed obtaining relative WER reduction of 2.6%. There are a few researches on application of DNNs in Russian speech recognition systems. Samples of Russian speech recognition systems with DNN-based acoustic models are presented in [10–12].

In this paper, we study and compare DNNs and TDNNs for acoustic modeling in Russian ASR. The paper is organized as follows: in Sect. 2 we give a description of DNN-based acoustic models, in Sect. 3 we present our language model and vocabulary, Sect. 4 describes our training and testing speech corpora, experiments on speech recognition using DNN-based acoustic models are presented in Sect. 5.

2 Acoustic Modeling with DNNs

2.1 Hybrid DNN/HMM Acoustic Models

We have tried two types of NNs for acoustic modeling: feed-forward DNN and TDNN. Acoustic models were trained using the open-source Kaldi toolkit [13]. Mel-frequency cepstral coefficients (MFCCs) were used as input to the NNs. For speaker adaptation, 100-dimensional i-Vector [14] was appended to the 40-dimensional MFCC input.

We used Dan's implementation [15] of DNN training realized in Kaldi and experimented with DNNs having p-norm activation function [16]. The output was a softmax layer with the dimension equal to the number of context-dependent states (1609 in our case). We created DNNs with diverse number of hidden layers: from 3 till 5. For the p-norm DNNs, there is no parameter of hidden layer dimension; instead, there are two other parameters: (1) p-norm output dimension and (2) p-norm input dimension. The input dimension needs to be an exact integer multiple of the output dimension; normally a ratio of 5 or 10 is used [16]. We have tried p-norm DNNs with input/output dimensions of 1000/100 and 2000/200 respectively. The system was trained for 15 epochs with the learning rate varying from 0.02 to 0.004 and then for 5 epochs with a constant final learning rate (0.004). Our hybrid DNN/HMM system is described in [12] in more detail.

2.2   Time-Delay Neural Network-Based Acoustic Models

TDNN is a feed-forward DNN with nodes modified by the introduction of time delays [17]. An example of a node with delays is presented in Fig. 1, where $U_1...U_J$ are inputs of the node; each of J inputs is multiplied by a corresponding weight w; $D_1...D_N$ are time delays; F is an activation function [18]. Thereby, a short-term memory is integrated in the NN.

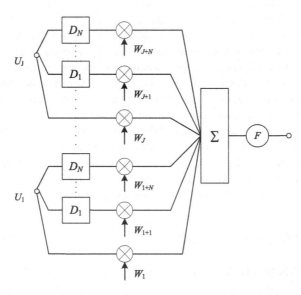

Fig. 1. An example of neural network's node with time delays [18]

TDNNs are efficient for modeling temporal dynamics in speech allowing capturing long term dependencies between acoustic events. In [9], a subsampling technique for TDNN was proposed, which speeds up training and makes training time comparable to the standard feed-forward DNN training. According to this technique, hidden activations are computed only on a few time steps instead of computing at all time steps. In this approach, instead of splicing together neighboring temporal windows of frames at each layer, it is proposed to splice together no more than two frames.

We created TDNNs with diverse number of hidden layers, different temporal contexts and splice indexes. p-norm non-linearity was also used for hidden layers. An example of the architecture for TDNN with time context $[-7, 4]$ (the interval consists of integer numbers corresponding to the time steps) using sub-sampling is presented in Fig. 2. The input layer splices together frames at a context $\{-1, 0, 1\}$ (or we can write it more compact as $[-1, 1]$). For the hidden layer, the sub-sampling $\{-2, 1\}$ is performed; it means that the input at the current frame minus 2 and the current frame plus 1 are spliced together. Then at 2nd hidden layer, the sub-sampling $\{-4, 2\}$ is applied.

For TDNN training we also used Kaldi toolkit. Parameters of several created TDNNs are summarized in Table 1.

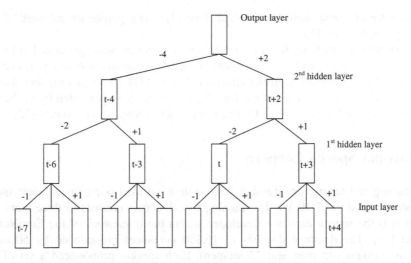

Fig. 2. An example of TDNN architecture with sub-sampling for network context [−7, 4]

Table 1. Parameters of created TDNNs

Model	Network context	Layerwise context					
		1	2	3	4	5	6
TDNN1	[−7, 4]	[−1, 1]	{−2, 1}	{−4, 2}	{0}	–	–
TDNN2	[−8, 8]	[−2, 2]	{−1, 1}	{−2, 2}	{−3, 3}	{0}	–
TDNN3	[−13, 10]	[−2, 2]	{−1, 2}	{−3, 4}	{−7, 2}	{0}	–
TDNN4	[−15, 11]	[−2, 2]	{−2, 1}	{−4, 3}	{−7, 5}	{0}	–
TDNN5	[−15, 15]	[−2, 2]	{−1, 1}	{−2, 2}	{−3, 3}	{−7, 7}	{0}
TDNN6	[−18, 15]	[−2, 2]	{−1, 1}	{−2, 2}	{−4, 3}	{−9, 7}	{0}
TDNN7	[−13, 13]	[−2, 2]	{−1, 1}	{−2, 2}	{−3, 3}	{−5, 5}	{0}

3 Language Model and Pronunciation Vocabulary

For the language model creation, we collected and automatically processed a Russian text corpus consisting of a number of Russian on-line newspapers. The procedure of preliminary text processing and normalization is described in [19]. At first, the texts were divided into sentences. Then, a text written in any brackets was deleted, and sentences consisting of less than six words were also removed. Uppercase letters were replaced by the lowercase ones, if a word started with an uppercase letter. If a whole word was written by the uppercase letters, then such change was made, when this word was in the vocabulary only. The size of the corpus after text normalization is over 350M words, and it has above 1M unique word-forms.

For the statistical text analysis, we used SRI Language Modeling Toolkit (SRILM) [20]. During language model creation, we used the Kneser-Ney discounting method, and did not apply any n-gram cutoff. We created various 3-gram language models with different vocabulary sizes, and in our recent experiments the best speech recognition results were obtained with 150K vocabulary [21]. The perplexity measure of this language model was 553.

Phonetic transcriptions for the vocabulary word-forms were generated automatically. At first, stress vowels in word-forms were defined using a dictionary, which was a fusion of two different morphological databases: AOT (www.aot.ru) and Starling (http://starling.rinet.ru/morpho.php). Then transcriptions were generated by application of transcription rules to the list of word-forms with denoted stress vowels [22].

4   Russian Speech Corpora

For training and testing the Russian ASR system we used our own different speech corpora recorded in SPIIRAS. The training speech corpus consists of three parts. The first part is the speech database developed within the framework of the EuroNounce project [23]. The database consists of 16,350 utterances pronounced by 50 native Russian speakers (25 men and 25 women). Each speaker pronounced a set of 327 phonetically rich and meaningful phrases and texts. The second part of the corpus consists of recordings of other 55 native Russian speakers. Each speaker pronounced 105 phrases: 50 phrases were taken from the Appendix G to the Russian State Standard P 50840–95 [24] (these phrases were different for each speaker), and 55 common phrases were taken from a phonetically representative text, presented in [25]. The third part is an audio part of the audio-visual speech corpus HAVRUS [26]. 20 native Russian speakers (10 male and 10 female speakers) with no language or hearing problems participated in the recordings. Each of them pronounced 200 Russian phrases: (a) 130 phrases for training are two phonetically rich texts common for all speakers, and (b) 70 phrases for testing are different for every speaker: 20 phrases were commands for the MIDAS information kiosk [27] and 50 phrases are 7-digits telephone numbers (connected digits). The total duration of the entire speech data is more than 30 h.

To test the system we used another speech dataset consisting of 500 phrases pronounced by 5 native Russian speakers (3 male and 2 female speakers) [19]. The phrases were taken from the materials of one Russian on-line newspaper (Fontanka.ru) that was not presented in the training speech and text data.

The recording of speech data was carried out with the help of two professional condenser microphones Oktava MK-012. The speech data were collected in clean acoustic conditions, with 44.1 kHz sampling rate, 16 bit per sample. The signal-to-noise ratio (SNR) was about 35 dB. For the recognition experiments, all the audio data were down-sampled to 16 kHz. Each phrase was stored in a separate wav file. Also a text file containing orthographical representation (transcription) of utterances was provided.

5   Results of Experiments on LVCSR for Russian

Firstly, we have made experiments on Russian speech recognition using the DNN-based acoustic models. The speech recognition results obtained with p-norm DNNs are presented in Table 2. The obtained results show that the number of layers

Table 2. WERs obtained with *p*-norm DNN/HMM models (%)

Number of hidden layers	Input/output dimension	
	1000/100	2000/200
3	23.48	25.09
4	21.63	23.86
5	20.82	22.58
6	21.52	25.07

has only slight influence on speech recognition results. The best result (WER = 20.82%) was obtained, when the DNN had 5 hidden layers and input/output dimension of 1000/100. Increasing the number of hidden layers and units led to increasing the WER, it can be caused by the limited amount of the training data and overtraining.

Then, we have made experiments with TDNN acoustic models. Table 3 presents obtained results.

Table 3. WERs with *p*-norm DNN/HMM models (%)

Model	Input/output dimension	
	1000/100	2000/200
TDNN1	20.64	21.03
TDNN2	**19.04**	20.26
TDNN3	19.06	20.73
TDNN4	20.56	21.61
TDNN5	20.84	21.50
TDNN6	21.76	21.54
TDNN7	19.89	20.43

The lowest WER was 19.04% and it was achieved by the TDNN with 5 hidden layers and time context [−8, 8] (TDNN2). The usage of the models with larger temporal time led to increasing of WER that also can be caused by overtraining.

6 Conclusions and Future Work

We have studied hybrid TDNN/HMM acoustic models for large vocabulary continuous Russian speech recognition. We created several TDNNs with diverse number of hidden layers, different temporal contexts and splice indexes. The experiments on continuous Russian speech recognition with the very large vocabulary showed that TDNN allows decreasing WER with respect to the DNN-based acoustic models. We have obtained the relative WER reduction of 9% comparing to the best DNN/HMM acoustic model. In further research, we plan to investigate other types of DNNs, such as CNN, LSTM, and bidirectional LSTM for acoustic modeling, to try deep learning software tools (for example, CNTK) for training of NNs, and to apply NN-based Russian language model [28] for lattice rescoring.

Acknowledgments. This research is partially supported by the Council for Grants of the President of the Russian Federation (project No. MK-1000.2017.8) and by the Russian Foundation for Basic Research (project No. 15–07–04322).

References

1. Yu, D., Deng, L.: Automatic Speech Recognition. A Deep Learning Approach. Springer, London (2015)
2. Hinton, G., Deng, L., Yu, D., Dahl, G., Mohamed, A., Jaitly, N., Senior, A., Vanhoucke, V., Nguyen, P., Sainath, T., Kingsbury, B.: Deep neural networks for acoustic modeling in speech recognition: the shared views of four research groups. IEEE Sign. Process. Mag. **29**(6), 82–97 (2012)
3. Kipyatkova I., Karpov, A.: Variants of deep artificial neural networks for speech recognition systems. In: SPIIRAS Proceedings, vol. **6**(49), pp. 80–103 (2016). (in Russian) doi:http://dx.doi.org/10.15622/sp.49.5
4. Deng, L.: Deep learning: from speech recognition to language and multimodal processing. APSIPA Trans. Sign. Inf. Process. **5**, 1–15 (2016)
5. Seide, F., Li, G., Yu, D.: Conversational speech transcription using context-dependent deep neural networks. In: INTERSPEECH 2011, pp. 437– 440 (2011)
6. Delcroix, M., Kinoshita, K., Ogawa, A., Yoshioka, T., Tran, D., Nakatani, T.: Context adaptive neural network for rapid adaptation of deep CNN based acoustic models. In: INTERSPEECH 2016, pp. 1573–1577 (2016)
7. Tran, D.T., Delcroix, M., Ogawa, A., Huemmer, C., Nakatani, T.: Feedback connection for deep neural network-based acoustic modeling. In: IEEE International Conference on Acoustics, Speech, and Signal Processing (ICASSP 2017), pp. 5240–5244 (2017)
8. Geiger, J.T., Zhang, Z., Weninger, F., Schuller, B., Rigoll, G.: Robust speech recognition using long short-term memory recurrent neural networks for hybrid acoustic modelling. In: INTERSPEECH 2014, pp. 631–635 (2014)
9. Peddini, V., Povey, D., Khundanpur, S.: A time delay neural network architecture for efficient modeling of long temporal contexts. In: INTERSPEECH 2015, pp. 3214–3218 (2015)
10. Tomashenko, N., Khokhlov, Y.: Speaker adaptation of context dependent deep neural networks based on MAP-adaptation and GMM-derived feature processing. In: INTERSPEECH 2014, pp. 2997–3001 (2014)
11. Prudnikov, A., Medennikov, I., Mendelev, V., Korenevsky, M., Khokhlov, Y.: Improving acoustic models for Russian spontaneous speech recognition. In: Ronzhin, A., Potapova, R., Fakotakis, N. (eds.) SPECOM 2015. LNCS(LNAI), vol. 9319, pp. 234–242. Springer, Cham (2015). doi:10.1007/978-3-319-23132-7_29
12. Kipyatkova, I., Karpov, A.: DNN-based acoustic modeling for Russian speech recognition using kaldi. In: Ronzhin, A., Potapova, R., Németh, G. (eds.) SPECOM 2016. LNCS, vol. 9811, pp. 246–253. Springer, Cham (2016). doi:10.1007/978-3-319-43958-7_29
13. Povey, D., et al.: The Kaldi speech recognition toolkit. In: IEEE Workshop on Automatic Speech Recognition and Understanding ASRU (2011)

14. Saon, G., Soltau, H., Nahamoo, D., Picheny, M.: Speaker adaptation of neural network acoustic models using i-Vectors. In: IEEE Automatic Speech Recognition and Understanding Workshop (ASRU), pp. 55–59 (2013)

15. Povey, D., Zhang, X., Khudanpur, S.: Parallel training of DNNs with natural gradient and parameter averaging (2014). Preprint: arXiv:1410.7455, http://arxiv.org/pdf/1410.7455v8.pdf

16. Zhang X., Trmal J., Povey D., Khudanpur S.: Improving deep neural network acoustic models using generalized maxout networks. In: IEEE International Conference on Acoustics, Speech and Signal Processing (ICASSP), pp. 215–219 (2014)

17. Gapochkin, A.V.: Neural networks in speech recognition systems. Sci. Time 1(1), 29–36 (2014). (in Russian)

18. Waibel, A., Hanazawa, T., Hinton, G., Shikano, K., Lang, K.: Phoneme recognition using time-delay neural networks. IEEE Trans. Acoust. Speech Sign. Process. 37(3), 328–339 (1989)

19. Karpov, A., Markov, K., Kipyatkova, I., Vazhenina, D., Ronzhin, A.: Large vocabulary Russian speech recognition using syntactico-statistical language modeling. Speech Commun. 56, 213–228 (2014)

20. Stolcke, A., Zheng, J., Wang, W., Abrash, V.: SRILM at sixteen: update and outlook. In: Proceedings of IEEE Automatic Speech Recognition and Understanding Workshop ASRU 2011 (2011)

21. Kipyatkova, I., Karpov, A.: Lexicon size and language model order optimization for Russian LVCSR. In: Železný, M., Habernal, I., Ronzhin, A. (eds.) SPECOM 2013. LNCS (LNAI), vol. 8113, pp. 219–226. Springer, Cham (2013). doi:10.1007/978-3-319-01931-4_29

22. Kipyatkova, I., Karpov, A., Verkhodanova, V., Zelezny, M.: Modeling of pronunciation, language and nonverbal units at conversational russian speech recognition. Int. J. Comput. Sci. Appl. 10(1), 11–30 (2013)

23. Jokisch, O., Wagner, A., Sabo, R., Jaeckel, R., Cylwik, N., Rusko, M., Ronzhin A., Hoffmann, R.: Multilingual speech data collection for the assessment of pronunciation and prosody in a language learning system. In: Proceedings of SPECOM 2009, pp. 515–520 (2009)

24. State Standard P 50840–95. Speech transmission by communication paths. Evaluation methods of quality, intelligibility and recognizability, p. 230. Standartov Publ., Moscow (1996). (in Russian)

25. Stepanova, S.B.: Phonetic features of Russian speech: realization and transcription, Ph.D. thesis (1988). (in Russian)

26. Verkhodanova, V., Ronzhin, A., Kipyatkova, I., Ivanko, D., Karpov, A., Železný, M.: HAVRUS corpus: high-speed recordings of audio-visual Russian speech. In: Ronzhin, A., Potapova, R., Németh, G. (eds.) SPECOM 2016. LNCS, vol. 9811, pp. 338–345. Springer, Cham (2016). doi:10.1007/978-3-319-43958-7_40

27. Karpov, A.A., Ronzhin, A.L.: Information enquiry kiosk with multimodal user interface. Pattern Recogn. Image Anal. 19(3), 546–558 (2009)

28. Kipyatkova, I., Karpov, A.: A study of neural network Russian language models for automatic continuous speech recognition systems. Autom. Remote Control 78(5), 858–867 (2017). Springer

Exploring Multiparty Casual Talk for Social Human-Machine Dialogue

Emer Gilmartin$^{(\boxtimes)}$, Benjamin R. Cowan, Carl Vogel, and Nick Campbell

Trinity College, Dublin, Ireland
{gilmare,vogel,nick}@tcd.ie, benjamin.cowan@ucd.ie

Abstract. Much talk between humans is casual and multiparty. It facilitates social bonding and mutual co-presence rather than strictly being used to exchange information in order to complete well-defined practical tasks. Artificial partners that are capable of participating as a speaker or listener in such talk would be useful for companionship, educational, and social contexts. However, such applications require dialogue structure beyond simple question/answer routines. While there is body of theory on multiparty casual talk, there is a lack of work quantifying such phenomena. This is critical if we are to manage and generate human machine multiparty casual talk. We outline the current knowledge on the structure of casual talk, describe our investigations in this domain, summarise our findings on timing, laughter, and disfluency in this domain, and discuss how they can inform the design and implementation of truly social machine dialogue partners.

Keywords: Speech interfaces · Dialogue modelling · Casual social talk

1 Introduction

Human talk is a fundamentally social activity, and casual conversation is inevitable whenever humans gather together. It forms a fundamental part of human communication. With the growth of interest in the development of avatars and robots as social companions, it is important to understand the nature of such talk in situations where there is more than one conversational actor so as to endow machines with the ability to converse appropriately in such contexts. Currently, much of the speech interface research is focused on task based dialogue interactions. Early dialogue system researchers recognised the complexity of dealing with social talk [1], and initial prototypes concentrated on practical tasks such as travel bookings and the logistics of moving boxcars of oranges. In these tasks, the lexical content of utterances was enough to drive successful completion of the task. Task-based systems have proven invaluable in many practical domains. However the desire to develop more social companions (be it robot or avatar based) in a number of domains such as healthcare and education means that social talk must become a significant strand of research and the nature of dialogue as a multi-party activity needs to be addressed. We argue that the field

© Springer International Publishing AG 2017
A. Karpov et al. (Eds.): SPECOM 2017, LNAI 10458, pp. 370–378, 2017.
DOI: 10.1007/978-3-319-66429-3_36

now needs to move towards understanding and incorporating casual multiparty conversation so as to create more natural dialogue interactions between machine and human partners. In this paper we highlight work in the area of social talk and summarise recent research conducted by the authors in this domain.

2 What Is Social Talk?

Social talk, rather than following Gricean maxims of efficient communication of information, seems rather to be based on avoidance of silence and engagement in unthreatening but entertaining verbal display and interaction [32]. In casual talk, all participants can contribute at any time, unlike the more restricted roles found in more formal situations [14,34]. Rather than following a question and answer format of the type which drives task based dialogues, casual conversation has been described as occurring in stages - chat and chunk [17]. In chat phases, participants contribute utterances more or less equally with many questions and short comments. Chat is often used to 'break the ice' among strangers involved in casual talk [28]. Chat phases are also interspersed with chunk phases – longer contributions from one participant – often in the form of narrative anecdotes and recounts, opinion or discussion. The 'ownership' of chunks seems to pass around the participants in the talk, with chat linking one chunk to the next [17]. The structure of casual conversation has also been described as a more detailed sequence of structural elements or phases [33]. These phases include opening and closing Greeting, Address, Leavetaking and Goodbye sequences. The main content of the conversation is described as a sequence of Approach and Centring stages, similar to chat and chunk, with added subtypes for the Approach phases depending on social distance between participants. Approach phases can be indirect - dealing with topics such as the weather, or direct - involving more personal subject matter. Figure 1 shows a schematic of the phases described by Ventola, while Fig. 2 shows examples drawn from our data of typical chat and chunk phases in a 5-party conversation.

The design of more social speech interfaces and companion applications depends on knowledge of the type of talk being modelled. Below we outline our work in this area, focussing on corpus analysis to determine the characteristics of longer form multiparty casual talk.

3 Corpora Used for Casual Conversation Research

Relevant corpora of human interaction are essential to understanding different genres of spoken dialogue. Interestingly, the design of systems and the production of corpora has often followed the path taken in the development of pragmatic theories of talk. Early task-based systems were based on a literal view of speech as transmission of text. Many of the multimodal corpora and indeed several earlier audio corpora created in laboratory and 'real-world' conditions have been collections of performances of the same spoken task by different subjects, or of interactions specific to particular domains where lexical content was fundamental

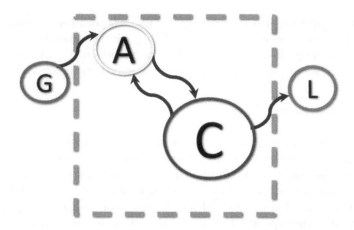

Fig. 1. The phases of casual talk described by Ventola - greeting, approach, centre, and leavetaking. Note that approach and centre phases may freely recur

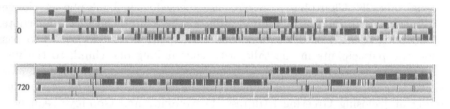

Fig. 2. Examples of chat (top) and chunk (bottom) phases in two stretches from a 5-party conversation in the D64 corpus. each row denotes the activity of one speaker across 120 s. Speech is green, and laughter is yellow on a grey background (silence). The chat frame, taken at the beginning of the conversation, can be seen to involve shorter contributions from all participants with frequent laughter. The chunk frame shows longer single speaker stretches (Color figure online)

to acheivment of a practical goal - such corpora include collections of information gap activities such as the HCRC MapTask corpus of dyadic information gap task-based conversations [3]. Other corpora have focussed on collecting recordings of real or staged meetings, such as the ICSI and AMI multiparty meeting corpora [25, 29], or recordings of particular genres of interaction, such as televised political interviews [6]. All of these corpora have contributed greatly to understanding of different facets of spoken interaction such as timing, turntaking, and dialogue architecture. However, the speech in these resources, while spontaneous and conversational, cannot be considered casual talk, and the results obtained from their analysis may not transfer to casual conversation.

In terms of non-task interaction, there have been audio collections made of casual talk, including telephonic corpora such as SWITCHBOARD [22] and the ESP-C collection of Japanese telephone conversations [13], and corpora comprising recordings of face-to-face talk as in the Santa Barbara Corpus [15], and sections of the ICE corpora [23] and of the British National Corpus [8]. These corpora are audio only and thus cannot be used to inform research on facial expression, gestural or postural research. The Gothenburg Corpus of recordings of different types of human activity contains both audio and video recordings including casual or small talk [2], leading a trend toward multimodal recordings which can be used to study more aspects of conversation.

Increasing interest in social talk among dialogue system designers has resulted in systems which engage users in 'chat' similar to the smalltalk described at the margins of more serious practical talk in the pragmatics literature [7,36]. In the recent years, researchers have started to produce corpora of mostly dyadic 'first encounters' where strangers were recorded engaged in casual conversation for periods of 5 to 20 min or so [4,16,31]. These corpora have appeared in several languages including Swedish, Danish, Finnish, and English. These corpora are very valuable for the study of dyadic interaction, particularly at the opening and early stages of interaction. For a fuller review of available corpora and the challenges of genre in conversation, see [18]. However, pragmatic work has described the substance of longer casual conversation beyond these first encounters, and it is this area which interests us, informing the design of systems which can take the user into a longitudinal series of conversations beyond the first chat phases.

We focus on multiparty casual conversation, and have created a dataset of six informal conversations with three to five participants, each around an hour long. The conversations were drawn from three multimodal corpora, d64, DANS, and TableTalk [12,24,30], to allow for comparison of our results from analysis of the audio data with results of video analysis at a later date. Recordings of this type are not easily found with those corpora being the most popular for such work. Our data was manually segmented and transcribed using Praat [9] and Elan [35]. Details of the dataset can be seen in Table 1, and further details of the annotation process can be found in [20]. In the next section, we give an overview of recent work on this dataset.

Table 1. Source corpora and details for the conversations used in dataset

Corpus	Participants	Gender	Duration (s)
D64	5	2F/3M	4164
DANS	3	1F/2M	4672
DANS	4	1F/3M	4378
DANS	3	2F/1M	3004
TableTalk	4	2F/2M	2072
TableTalk	5	3F/2M	4740

In each of the corpora used, participants were recorded in casual conversation in a living room setting or around a table, with no instructions on topic of type of conversation to be carried out - participants were also clearly informed that they could speak or stay silent as the mood took them.

4   Overview of Recent Work

Our analysis of social talk focuses on a number of dimensions; chat and chunk duration, laughter distribution, disfluency distribution, and the patterning of utterances by different speakers in different phases, as these elements are largely independent of the lexical content of the conversations, and have been analysed in meeting corpora [5,11,27]. Thus, our analyses of casual multiparty talk can be contrasted with existing analyses of task-based multiparty talk. Timing information in multiparty meeting corpora, in particular, has been shown to be amenable to stochastic modelling of the distribution of talk and laughter [26], which is a longer term goal of the work described here.

4.1   Chat and Chunk Duration and Chat Positioning

From our analysis of data from the corpora highlighted we have found that the distributions of durations of chat and chunk phases are different, with chat phases durations varying more while chunk durations have a more consistent clustering around the mean. Chat phase durations (Mean = 28 s) tend to be shorter than chunk durations (Mean = 34 s). These findings are not speaker specific in our preliminary experiments and seem to indicate a natural limit for the time one speaker should dominate a conversation. The dimensions of chat and chunk durations observed would indicate that social talk should 'dose' or package information to fit chat and chunk segments of roughly these lengths. In particular, the tendency towards chunks of around half a minute could help in the design of narrative or education-delivering speech applications, by allowing designers to partition content optimally.

We also observed more chat at conversation beginnings, with chat predominating for the first 8–10 min of conversations. Although our sample size is small, this observation conforms to descriptions of casual talk in the literature, and reflects the structure of 'first encounter' recordings. However, as the conversation develops, chunks start to occur much more frequently, and the structure is an alternation of single-speaker chunks interleaved with shorter chat segments. While the initial extended chat segments can be used to model 'getting to know you' sessions, and will therefore be useful for familiarisation with a digital companion, it is clear that we need to model the chunk heavy central segments of conversation if we want to create systems which form a longer-term dialogic relationship with users.

4.2   Laughter and Disfluency Distribution

We have also been investigating the frequency and distribution of laughter and disfluencies in multiparty casual talk. Early experiments showed that laughter, and particularly shared laughter, appears more common in social talk than in meeting data, and that laughter happens more around topic endings/topic changes [10,19]. This is consistent with our current work on chat and chunk phases, as we are seeing that laughter is more common in chat phases – which provide a 'buffer' between single speaker and topic chunks. In the current dataset we have found that laughter accounts for approximately 10% of vocal time in chat phases while it only accounts for 4% of chunk phases. For disfluencies, a pilot study has shown differences in the occurrence and distribution of disfluency types for chunk owners in chunks and all other speakers [21]. In the chunk modality one speaker holds the floor for an extended period and this behaviour is different to that of all other speakers in chunks, to that of all speakers in chat, and indeed to that of the chunk owner when in somebody else's chunk.

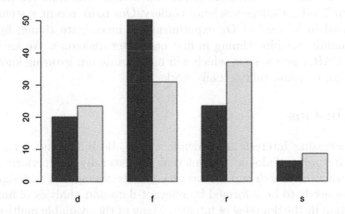

Fig. 3. Distribution of disfluency types (deletion, filled pause, repetition, substitution) in chunk owner versus all other speech. Frequencies are shown proportionally in percentages with grey denoting chunk owner speech.

Figure 3 shows the distribution of disfluency types (deletion, filled pause, repetition, substitution) in two modalities – where the speaker is the? owner? of a chunk versus all other speech. It can be seen that filled pauses are proportionally less frequent in chunk owner speech than in general speech – 31% vs 50%, while repetition is proportionately more common in chunk owner speech – 37% vs 23%. In view of the very small sample of speakers, we checked the distributions for each speaker, although the proportions varied. For individual speakers, in all cases, filled pauses were also proportionally lower in chunk owner speech versus other speech, and repetitions were also proportionally higher in chunk owner speech for each speaker.

4.3   Speaker Contribution

We are studying the patterning of speaker contributions in both phases, particularly the length of gap or overlap in the vicinity of speaker and phase changes. We are performing prosodic analysis of the utterance final pitch movements in different contexts, and believe the results of this work will provide information helpful in developing more finegrained 'endpointing' systems to determine *when* the system should speak; with knowledge of how turntaking occurs in different phases of talk we can work towards providing systems with turntaking behaviour appropriate to the current conversational phase.

5   Systems Developed for Casual Talk

Based on our analysis we have built a number of prototype 'first encounter' systems whose purpose is to chat engagingly with users. The HERME robot, based on casual talk structure, successfully chatted with several hundred members of the public in Trinity College's Science Gallery. Our more recent system, CARA, has been used in Wizard of Oz experiments to investigate timing by humans versus automatic machine timing in first encounter dialogues. We are currently developing CARA as a system which will incorporate our growing knowledge of how longer form casual talk actually works.

6   Conclusions

There is increasing interest in academic circles, business, and from the general public in spoken dialogue systems that act naturally and perform functions beyond information search and narrow task-based exchanges. The design of these new systems needs to be informed by relevant data and analysis of human spoken interaction in the domains of interest. Many of the available multiparty data are based on meetings or first encounters. While first encounters are very relevant to the design of human machine first encounters, there is a lack of data on longer human conversations. We hope that the encouraging results of our analysis of casual social talk will help make the case for the creation and analysis of corpora of longer social dialogues. We believe that the exponential growth in speech technology and companion systems means that data and scientific investigation around this type of talk is urgently needed so as to design more effective automated dialogue partners.

Acknowledgements. This work is supported by the European Coordinated Research on Long-term Challenges in Information and Communication Sciences and Technologies ERA-NET (CHISTERA) JOKER project, JOKe and Empathy of a Robot/ECA: Towards social and affective relations with a robot, and by the Speech Communication Lab, Trinity College Dublin, and by Science Foundation Ireland funding for ADAPT (13/RC/2106) at Trinity College Dublin.

References

1. Allen, J., Byron, D., Dzikovska, M., Ferguson, G., Galescu, L., Stent, A.: An architecture for a generic dialogue shell. Nat. Lang. Eng. **6**(3&4), 213–228 (2000)
2. Allwood, J., Björnberg, M., Grönqvist, L., Ahlsén, E., Ottesjö, C.: The spoken language corpus at the department of linguistics, Göteborg University. In: FQS-Forum Qualitative Social Research, vol. 1 (2000). http://www.ling.gu.se/~jens/publications/bfiles/B45.pdf

3. Anderson, A., Bader, M., Bard, E., Boyle, E., Doherty, G., Garrod, S., Isard, S., Kowtko, J., McAllister, J., Miller, J., et al.: The HCRC map task corpus. Lang. Speech **34**(4), 351–366 (1991)
4. Aubrey, A.J., Marshall, D., Rosin, P.L., Vandeventer, J., Cunningham, D.W., Wallraven, C.: Cardiff conversation database (CCDb): a database of natural dyadic conversations. In: 2013 IEEE Conference on Computer Vision and Pattern Recognition Workshops (CVPRW), pp. 277–282, June 2013
5. Baron, D., Shriberg, E., Stolcke, A.: Automatic punctuation and disfluency detection in multi-party meetings using prosodic and lexical cues. Channels **20**(61), 41 (2002)
6. Beattie, G.: Talk: an Analysis of Speech and Non-verbal Behaviour in Conversation. Open University Press, Milton Keynes (1983)
7. Bickmore, T., Cassell, J.: Social dialogue with embodied conversational agents. In: van Kuppevelt, J., Dybkjaer, L., Bernsen, N. (eds.) Advances in Natural Multimodal Dialogue Systems, pp. 23–54. Kluwer, New York (2005)
8. BNC-Consortium: British national corpus (2000). URL http://www.hcu.ox.ac.uk/BNC
9. Boersma, P., Weenink, D.: Praat: doing phonetics by computer [Computer program], Version 5.1. 44 (2010)
10. Bonin, F., Campbell, N., Vogel, C.: Laughter and topic changes: temporal distribution and information flow. In: 2012 IEEE 3rd International Conference on Cognitive Infocommunications (CogInfoCom), pp. 53–58 (2012)
11. Bonin, F., Campbell, N., Vogel, C.: Temporal distribution of laughter in conversation. In: Proceedings of the Third Interdisciplinary Workshop on Laughter and other Non-Verbal Vocalization in Speech, pp. 25–26 (2012)
12. Campbell, N.: Multimodal processing of discourse information, the effect of synchrony. In: Second International Symposium on Universal Communication, ISUC 2008, pp. 12–15 (2008)
13. Campbell, N.: Approaches to conversational speech rhythm: speech activity in two-person telephone dialogues. In: Proceedings of XVIth International Congress of the Phonetic Sciences, Saarbrucken, Germany, pp. 343–348 (2007). http://www.icphs2007.de/conference/Papers/1775/1775.pdf
14. Cheepen, C.: The Predictability of Informal Conversation. Pinter, London (1988)
15. DuBois, J.W., Chafe, W.L., Meyer, C., Thompson, S.A.: Santa Barbara corpus of spoken american english. Linguistic Data Consortium, CD-ROM, Philadelphia (2000)
16. Edlund, J., Beskow, J., Elenius, K., Hellmer, K., Strömbergsson, S., House, D.: Spontal: a swedish spontaneous dialogue corpus of audio, video and motion capture. In: LREC (2010)
17. Eggins, S., Slade, D.: Analysing Casual Conversation. Equinox Publishing Ltd., Sheffield (2004)
18. Gilmartin, E., Bonin, F., Cerrato, L., Vogel, C., Campbell, N.: What's the game and who's got the ball? genre in spoken interaction. In: 2015 AAAI Spring Symposium Series (2015)
19. Gilmartin, E., Bonin, F., Vogel, C., Campbell, N.: Laugher and topic transition in multiparty conversation. In: Proceedings of the SIGDIAL 2013 Conference, pp. 304–308. Association for Computational Linguistics, Metz, August 2013
20. Gilmartin, E., Campbell, N.: Capturing chat: annotation and tools for multiparty casual conversation. In: Proceedings of the Tenth International Conference on Language Resources and Evaluation (LREC 2016) (2016)

21. Gilmartin, E., Vogel, C., Campbell, N.: Disfluency in multiparty social talk. In: Proceedings of DISS 2015, Edinburgh (2015)
22. Godfrey, J.J., Holliman, E.C., McDaniel, J.: SWITCHBOARD: telephone speech corpus for research and development. In: 1992 IEEE International Conference on Acoustics, Speech, and Signal Processing, ICASSP-92, vol. 1, pp. 517–520 (1992)
23. Greenbaum, S.: ICE: the international corpus of english. Engl. Today **28**(7.4), 3–7 (1991)
24. Hennig, S., Chellali, R., Campbell, N.: The D-ANS corpus: the Dublin-Autonomous Nervous System corpus of biosignal and multimodal recordings of conversational speech. Reykjavik, Iceland (2014)
25. Janin, A., Baron, D., Edwards, J., Ellis, D., Gelbart, D., Morgan, N., Peskin, B., Pfau, T., Shriberg, E., Stolcke, A.: The ICSI meeting corpus. In: 2003 IEEE International Conference on Acoustics, Speech, and Signal Processing, Proceedings, ICASSP 2003, vol. 1, pp. I-364 (2003)
26. Laskowski, K.: Predicting, detecting and explaining the occurrence of vocal activity in multi-party conversation. Ph.D. thesis, Carnegie Mellon University (2011)
27. Laskowski, K., Burger, S.: Analysis of the occurrence of laughter in meetings. In: INTERSPEECH, pp. 1258–1261 (2007)
28. Laver, J.: Communicative functions of phatic communion. In: Organization of Behavior in Face-to-Face Interaction, pp. 215–238 (1975)
29. McCowan, I., Carletta, J., Kraaij, W., Ashby, S., Bourban, S., Flynn, M., Guillemot, M., Hain, T., Kadlec, J., Karaiskos, V.: The AMI meeting corpus. In: Proceedings of the 5th International Conference on Methods and Techniques in Behavioral Research. vol. 88 (2005)
30. Oertel, C., Cummins, F., Edlund, J., Wagner, P., Campbell, N.: D64: a corpus of richly recorded conversational interaction. J. Multimodal User Interfaces **7**, 1–10 (2010)
31. Paggio, P., Allwood, J., Ahlsén, E., Jokinen, K.: The NOMCO multimodal Nordic resource-goals and characteristics (2010). http://bada.hb.se/handle/2320/7400
32. Schneider, K.P.: Small Talk: Analysing Phatic Discourse, vol. 1. Hitzeroth, Marburg (1988)
33. Ventola, E.: The structure of casual conversation in English. J. Pragmatics **3**(3), 267–298 (1979)
34. Wilson, J.: On the Boundaries of Conversation, vol. 10. Pergamon Press, Pergamon (1989)
35. Wittenburg, P., Brugman, H., Russel, A., Klassmann, A., Sloetjes, H.: Elan: a professional framework for multimodality research. In: Proceedings of LREC, vol. 2006 (2006)
36. Yu, Z., Xu, Z., Black, A.W., Rudnicky, A.: Strategy and policy learning for non-task-oriented conversational systems. In: Proceedings of the 17th Annual Meeting of the Special Interest Group on Discourse and Dialogue (2016)

First Experiments to Detect Anomaly Using Personality Traits vs. Prosodic Features

Cedric Fayet[1,2], Arnaud Delhay[1,2]([✉]), Damien Lolive[1,2],
and Pierre-François Marteau[1,3]

[1] IRISA - EXPRESSION Team, Lannion and Vannes, France
{cedric.fayet,arnaud.delhay,damien.lolive,
pierre-francois.marteau}@irisa.fr
[2] Université de Rennes 1, Lannion, France
[3] Université de Bretagne Sud, Vannes, France

Abstract. This paper presents the design of an anomaly detector based on three different sets of features, one corresponding to some prosodic descriptors and two extracted from Big Five traits. Big Five traits correspond to a simple but efficient representation of a human personality. They are extracted from a manual annotation while prosodic features are extracted directly from the speech signal. We evaluate two different anomaly detection methods: One-Class SVM (OC-SVM) and iForest, each one combined with a threshold classification to decide the "normality" of a sample. The different combinations of models and feature sets are evaluated on the SSPNET-Personality corpus which has already been used in several experiments, including a previous work on separating two types of personality profiles in a supervised way. In this work, we propose the above mentioned unsupervised methods, and discuss their performance, to detect particular audio-clips produced by a speaker with an abnormal personality. Results show that using automatically extracted prosodic features competes with the Big Five traits. In our case, OC-SVM seems to get better results than iForest.

Keywords: Anomaly detection · Isolation Forest · Isolation Tree · One Class – Support Vector Machine · Threshold classification · Social signal · Big Five · Prosody · SSPNET-Personality

1 Introduction

According to Chandola *et al.* [6], "an anomaly is defined as a pattern that does not conform to an expected normal behavior". The main objective of any anomaly detection system is to identify abnormal states from normal state distributions. The feature sets that describe these states are related to the nature of the input data (continuous, categorical, spatial, or spatio-temporal data), but also to the nature of the anomalies that we aim to track (point-wise, contextual or collective anomalies). Finally, to choose an adequate anomaly detection model,

© Springer International Publishing AG 2017
A. Karpov et al. (Eds.): SPECOM 2017, LNAI 10458, pp. 379–388, 2017.
DOI: 10.1007/978-3-319-66429-3_37

we also need to consider the desired output (score or label) and the availability of labeled data (supervised or unsupervised techniques).

In the literature, anomaly detection techniques are applied to intrusion detection [3], fraud detection [1], sensor network [15], monitoring flight safety [12], *etc.* As far as we know, the use of anomaly detection with the speech signal is more focused on speech pathology or disorder [2], or on the deduction of another type of pathology or disease (e.g. cancer) [7]. The speech signal is also used for detecting stress or depression [10,20], that could be seen as an anomaly detection in the way that it can be considered as an abnormal mental state.

Handling audio, video or biological signal to infer social information such as personality is part of a field called *Personality Computing* [21].

The Big Five model has been proposed to describe the speaker personality through the five following personality traits: openness, conscientiousness, extraversion, agreeableness and neuroticism [11]. Different tests with adaptation to a local context have been conducted on different languages and cultures, and the big five model seems to be generalizable to them [8,9]. SSPNET-Personality corpus was built to experiment the prediction of the big five scale over audio features [14]. It is composed of French audio clips extracted from the "Radio Suisse Romande". These clips are records of professional (journalists) and guest speakers.

In [19], Schuller *et al.* offers a good overview of the different systems using this corpus. A lot of experiments have already been conducted on this corpus and most of them try to predict the value of the big five scales using different audio representations. In addition, some experiments done by Mohammadi and Vinciarelli [14] suggest that the big five representation could be a good predictor of the role of a speaker. The authors propose a supervised SVM method that learns to recognize if a speaker is a professional one or a guest. The feature set used in this work is the psychological evaluation of a sample given by annotators using Big five traits. Their predictor reaches an accuracy of about 75%.

The purpose of our work is to compare the use of the big five features to the use of prosodic features to design a personality predictor able to separate professional speakers from non-professional guests. To this end, we consider a professional speaker as belonging to a normal personality class and a guest to an abnormal one. Contrary to [14], we propose to work in the unsupervised anomaly detection framework and we propose to evaluate two unsupervised strategies. Three sets of features are evaluated. Results show that prosodic features perform well and are less costly compared to manually annotated Big Five traits, even if those last features may provide better detection accuracy.

The remainder of the paper is structured as follows. The proposed anomaly detection method is described in Sect. 2. In Sect. 3, the feature sets that we compare are detailed before describing the experimental setup in Sect. 4. Finally, the results are presented and discussed in Sect. 5.

2   Method

This work aims at determining if a sample is normal (professional speaker) or abnormal (guest speaker) based on a train set containing only normal audio clips.

Each audio clip is described by a feature vector summarizing the time evolution of the features as described in Sect. 3.

In this section, we describe the two methods that we have used to perform the anomaly detection: an Isolation Forest approach (referred to as iForest in the paper) and a One-Class Support Vector Machine approach (referred to as OC-SVM in the paper). The OC-SVM has been used to ensure a comparison baseline with the SVM method used in [14].

2.1 Isolation Forest (iForest)

Isolation Forest is an ensemble learning method designed to detect anomaly. The particularity of this method is that it explicitly isolates anomalies rather than learns a model for normal instances [13]. The main assumption behind iForest is that a normal sample is hard to isolate from other samples, and on the contrary, an anomaly is more easily isolated from other samples. iForest is composed of T iTrees, each one built on a random selection of ψ samples drawn from the training set. From this subset of samples, an iTree is constructed by a random recursive partitioning, until all the samples are isolated or until a stop criterion is reached (a depth limit for example). The partitioning is realized by the random selection of an attribute (feature) and the random choice of a pivot value in the range of the selected attribute. For an iTree, the sample score is computed as the path length between the leaf node containing the sample and the root node of the tree.

Let x be a sample, n the number of samples on which the iTrees are built. Let f be the iForest, with $f = \{t_1, t_2, ...t_T\}$. Let $h(t, x)$ be the number of edges of the t iTree between the root and the leaf which contains (or isolates) x. Let $c(n)$ be the average path length of unsuccessful search in a Binary Search Tree. $c(n)$ estimates the average path length of an iTree.

The anomaly score s of an instance x estimated with the f iForest is given Eq. 1.

$$s(\mathbf{x}, \mathbf{f}, \mathbf{n}) = 2^{-\frac{\sum_{k=1}^{T} h(\mathbf{f_k}, \mathbf{x})}{T * c(\mathbf{n})}} \tag{1}$$

2.2 One-Class SVM (OC-SVM)

In short, a SVM classifier learns a boundary which maximizes the margin between classes. This well-known approach has been shown to be very effective on many classification problems. OC-SVM is an adaptation of SVM to the one-class problem. After transforming the feature space via a kernel, OC-SVM considers as a starting point, all the available data as member of a single class $C_{inliers}$ and the origin in the space defined by the nonlinear kernel as the only member of a class $C_{outliers}$ [18].

During the training, the hyper-parameter ν corresponds to a penalizing term which represents a trade-off between inliers and outliers. With the SVM approaches, the choice of the kernel is important to improve the results. The most widely used kernels are linear (inner product), polynomial, RBF and sigmoid. Related to the kernel used (RBF, polynomial, sigmoid) we have to determine its parametric coefficients. For instance, one can take the sigmoid kernel given in Eq. 2.

$$k(\mathbf{x}, \mathbf{y}) = \tanh(\gamma \mathbf{x}^T \mathbf{y} + c_0) \tag{2}$$

where $\mathbf{x}$ and $\mathbf{y}$ are input vectors and γ (slope) and c_0 (intercept) are parametric values related to the kernel.

We choose to use the distance between a new sample and the learned boundary as an anomaly score, instead of directly deciding which class the samples belong to. We then use a classification threshold based on this anomaly score to decide if a sample is normal or abnormal. This two steps strategy introduces some adjustable fuzziness around the boundary.

3   Materials

The experiments are conducted over the SSPNET-Personality Corpus [14]. The corpus contains 640 audio clips divided into 307 audio clips of professional speakers and 333 audio clips of guests in French language. The duration of each audio clip is about 10 s, based on the assumption that it takes short time to get an opinion about others personality.

3.1   Big Five Features

For each sample, 11 non-native French speakers evaluate the BFI-10 Questionnaire [17] from which a score is computed for each Big Five's scale. Consequently, 11 evaluations of the big five features are available. For our experiment, we consider two sets of features based on the big five model:

- *BigFive5*: for each sample and for each Big Five scale, we compute the mean of the 11 evaluations which leads to 5 features.
- *BigFive55*: for each sample, we concatenate the 11 evaluations given for each sample which leads to 55 features.

The purpose of this last set of features is to verify if the information contained in several distinct annotations is complementary or can simply be aggregated in a lower dimension feature vector, as in *BigFive5* feature vector. The main drawback of these two feature sets is that they are the result of manual annotation, which is furthermore difficult to predict from the speech signal only.

3.2   Prosodic Features

Prosodic features are commonly used to capture affect cues in a speech signal. Contrary to the Big Five traits, a large number of prosodic features are much easier to extract automatically from the speech signal. In this study, we adopt the 6 dimensional prosodic feature set as described in [14]. Using the PRAAT software [4], we extract the pitch, the first two formants, the energy and the duration of voiced/unvoiced segments with a sliding analysis window size of 40 ms with a step of 10 ms. From these low-level features, resulting from the extraction, we derive the final features that summarize their time evolution by computing mean, maximum, minimum and entropy values for each of the 6 features. Consequently, the final *Prosodic* feature set is composed with 24 features for each audio clip.

3.3 Pre-processing

Normalizing the features is an important preprocessing step before using the OC-SVM approach. Features that do not share the same range of values and the same variations could affect the quality of the OC-SVM model. Therefore this step is really important in the case of *Prosodic* features, which are composed of different types of features. We choose to perform a standardization (zero mean and unit variance) on all types of features.

4 Experimental Setup

The different experiments described in this section are carried out by following the same procedure and use python 3.5 and scikit-learn [16]. From the corpus, we build three sets (train, test, and validation sets), as described below. To increase the statistical confidence of our results, we run each experiment 60 times by distributing randomly the samples on the three sets. For each experiment, we compute the mean and the standard-deviation divided by the mean of the different runs. The data is thus split into three folds as follows:

- Train set: 207 clips of professional speakers and a variation from 0 to 103 guest clips.
- Test set: 50 clips of professional speakers and 50 clips of guests.
- Validation set: 50 clips of professional speakers and a variation from 0 to 50 of guest clips.

4.1 Hyper-parameters Tuning

According to the available data, since 207 samples are available in the training set, we need to be careful about the number of parameters in our model to avoid over-fitting.

In the case of the OC-SVM approach, after testing different types of kernel in our experiments, we have chosen to present the results with the sigmoid kernel which gives the best results (on the train data). With the sigmoid kernel, we need to determine three hyper-parameters ν, γ and c_0. For the rest of the paper, we choose to fix c_0 at 0. Without considering the fuzzy boundary, the OC-SVM gives a first classification of the sample. By using it, we compute a classification score [5] which can be used to evaluate the classification quality and consecutively the

Table 1. Hyper-parameters chosen for each AD

	iForest		OC-SVM	
	T	ψ	γ	ν
BigFive5	17	0.29	0.016	0.7
BigFive55	77	0.31	0.007	0.6
Prosodic	59	0.26	0.009	0.57

quality of the hyper-parameters. An exhaustive grid search is used to determine the values of the two hyper-parameters. For ν, we considered a range between 0.001 and 1 with a step of 0.025. For γ, the range is between 0.0001 and 1 with a step of 0.0001. The classification score is used to elect the best couple of hyper-parameters.

In the case of the iForest approach, we need to find two hyper-parameters: ψ (sub-sampling size given as a percentage of the available data) and t (number of sub-estimators *i.e* iTrees). When using an iForest, each sample is associated to an anomaly score. We consider 10 percents of the samples as abnormal samples, those with the highest probability to be abnormal. With this assumption, we can use a classification score as we did previously, and then, use an exhaustive grid search to get the two hyper-parameters. The range for ψ is between 0.1 and 0.9 with a step of 0.01, and for t between 10 and 200 with a step of 10.

For each set of features, we considered a training set with all the available normal samples to determine the hyper-parameters (Table 1) with respect to the aforementioned methods.

4.2   Experiments

To compare the different sets of features according to the chosen approach, we carry out the following steps: for each set of values (*BigFive5*, *BigFive55*, *Prosodic*), we test each anomaly detection model after tuning hyper-parameters as explained before (Sect. 4.1). Then, we compare the different models by using a ROC (Receiver Operating Characteristic) curve. It means that for a given FPR (False Positive Rate), we search the associated TPR (True Positive Rate). This sampled association is obtained by testing a range of possible threshold values. The ROC curve gives an information about the detector quality as a function of the threshold value.

The second step consists in estimating the robustness of each detector to a degradation of the training set. In this purpose, we introduce a certain percentage of abnormal samples into the training set (0% to 50%). We keep the different hyper-parameter values unchanged.

The last step consists in observing anomaly scores obtained for the different sets of features with both approaches. Considering the hyper-parameters obtained previously, we train the predictor with all the available normal samples. Then, we compute anomaly scores for normal and abnormal samples separately.

Table 2. Mean area under ROC curve (ROC-AUC score) and standard deviations, for the two approaches combined with the three feature sets

	BigFive5	BigFive55	Prosodic
OC-SVM	0.857 ± 0.030	0.918 ± 0.024	0.876 ± 0.036
iForest	0.762 ± 0.031	0.890 ± 0.032	0.801 ± 0.037

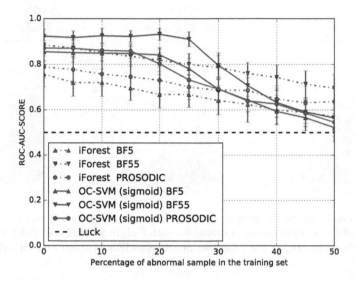

Fig. 1. Models Robustness to the introduction of abnormal samples in the training set

5   Results

Our first experiment step (Table 2) consists in evaluating the quality of each feature set. With our data, the *BigFive55* feature vector, regardless of the method used, performs better than the others. If we consider the OC-SVM approach, the *Prosodic* and *BigFive5* feature vectors get comparable results. For the iForest approach, *BigFive5* feature vector achieves a worst performance than the others. Moreover, the *BigFive5* feature vector has the lowest results for both methods, thus showing that the aggregation of the individual annotations induces a significant information loss.

Our second experiment step (Fig. 1) consists in evaluating the quality of each AD model when the training set is degraded, *i.e.* by including a certain percentage of abnormal samples in it. The results show that the iForest and OC-SVM approaches have different responses to degradation. The OC-SVM approaches have a degradation in two steps: before a certain percentage of contamination, they are robust to degradation and after this limit their scores decrease down to around 0.5 (random detector) for 50% of degradation. The iForest approaches have a kind of linear degradation along the degradation axis. For the OC-SVM

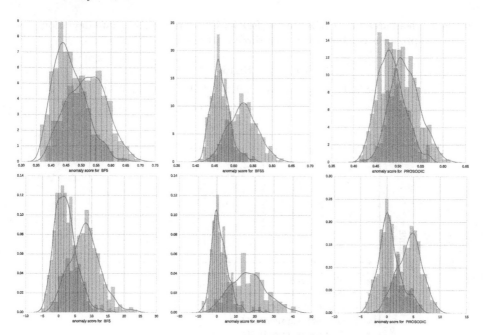

Fig. 2. Anomaly scores for normal samples (blue curve, left curve) and for abnormal samples (red curve, right curve) obtained for each feature set BigFive5 (left), BigFive55 (middle), Prosodic (right) with the two approaches iForest (top) and OC-SVM (bottom)

approach, the *BigFive55* feature vector seems to keep stable results for approximately 25 percents of degradation. The other two feature vectors start to have a decrease of their quality for less than 15 percent of degradation. For the iForest approach, the *Prosodic* feature vector seems to be more robust to degradation than the *BigFive5*. In any case, the *BigFive55* feature vector gives a more robust separation between normal and abnormal samples.

In our final experiment step (Fig. 2), we analyze the anomaly score obtained for all the available samples in the corpus. We draw one curve for normal samples and another one for abnormal samples. For both approaches, the intersection area between abnormal and normal curves is greater for *BigFive5* than for *Prosodic*, and greater for *Prosodic* than for *BigFive55*. By comparing the curves for *BigFive5* and *BigFive55* with both approaches, we notice that the distributions of anomaly scores for abnormal and normal samples are more different for *BigFive55* than for *BigFive5*. Indeed, by aggregating the annotators of *BigFive55* to get *BigFive5*, we diminish the ability to discriminate between normal and abnormal samples. It is noticeable that the iForest achieves a lower performance than the OC-SVM. It suggests that, in our context, modeling the normality class is better than considering anomalies as isolated points.

6   Conclusion

The main objective of this paper was to compare the use of prosodic cues and the Big Five annotation traits as feature sets for anomaly detection. We have conducted some experiments with the SSPNET-Personality Corpus using professional speakers as normal samples and guest as abnormal samples. This choice was motivated by Mohammadi *et al.* work [14] that demonstrates the effectiveness of using the Big Five features to train a supervised classifier able to separate these two categories of speakers. We built three sets of features (*BigFive5*, *BigFive55* and *Prosodic*) based on the speech signal and a psychological evaluation (Big Five model) available on the data set. We have used two different unsupervised machine learning methods (iForest, OC-SVM) to build our anomaly predictors. Based on the results, the good performance of the *BigFive55* feature set compared to the *Prosodic* feature set indicates that features based on psychological information can bring more information than audio features only. However, the prosodic features are easy to extract from the speech signal and thus seem to be the best compromise between ease of extraction and performance. The better results obtained with OC-SVM compared to iForest seem to indicate that an anomaly in our context is more related to learning a single specific cluster in the data than searching for samples which are really different from the others. A natural follow-up is to test other feature sets: for instance one can increase the number of features to reach a size similar to the *BigFive55* feature vector. Finally, conducting these experiments on other audio corpora, or trying to generalize our results on multimedia data are part of our future work.

Acknowledgments. This research has been financially supported by the French Ministry of Defense - Direction Générale pour l'Armement and the région Bretagne (ARED) under the MAVOFA project.

References

1. Abdallah, A., Maarof, M.A., Zainal, A.: Fraud detection system: a survey. J. Netw. Comput. Appl. **68**, 90–113 (2016)
2. Alonso, J.B., Díaz-de María, F., Travieso, C.M., Ferrer, M.A.: Using nonlinear features for voice disorder detection. In: ISCA Tutorial and Research Workshop (ITRW) on Non-linear Speech Processing (2005)
3. Axelsson, S.: Intrusion detection systems: A survey and taxonomy, Technical report. Chalmers University of Technology, Göteborg, Sweden (2000)
4. Boersma, P., Weenink, D.: Praat: doing phonetics by computer, http://www.praat.org/
5. Caliski, T., Harabasz, J.: A dendrite method for cluster analysis. Commun. Stat.-Theory Methods **3**(1), 1–27 (1974)
6. Chandola, V., Banerjee, A., Kumar, V.: Anomaly detection: a survey. ACM Comput. Surv. (CSUR) **41**(3), 15 (2009)

7. Clapham, R.P., van der Molen, L., van Son, R.J.J.H., van den Brekel, M.W.M., Hilgers, F.J.M.: NKI-CCRT corpus - speech intelligibility before and after advanced head and neck cancer treated with concomitant chemoradiotherapy. In: Proceedings of the 8th International Conference on Language Resources and Evaluation (LREC) (2012)

8. Goldberg, L.R.: Language and individual differences: the search for universals in personality lexicons. Rev. Pers. Soc. Psychol. **2**(1), 141–165 (1981)

9. Gurven, M., von Rueden, C., Massenkoff, M., Kaplan, H., Lero Vie, M.: How universal is the big five? testing the five-factor model of personality variation among forager farmers in the bolivian amazon. J. Pers. Soc. Psychol. **104**(2), 354–370 (2013)

10. He, L., Lech, M., Maddage, N.C., Allen, N.: Stress detection using speech spectrograms and sigma-pi neuron units. In: Fifth International Conference on Natural Computation, ICNC 2009. vol. 2, pp. 260–264. IEEE (2009)

11. John, O.P., Srivastava, S.: The big five trait taxonomy: history, measurement, and theoretical perspectives, vol. 2, pp. 102–138. Guilford (1999)

12. Li, L., Gariel, M., Hansman, R.J., Palacios, R.: Anomaly detection in onboard-recorded flight data using cluster analysis. In: IEEE/AIAA 30th Digital Avionics Systems Conference, p. 4A4-1–4A4-11. IEEE (2011)

13. Liu, F.T., Ting, K.M., Zhou, Z.H.: Isolation forest. In: Eighth IEEE International Conference on Data Mining, pp. 413–422 (2008)

14. Mohammadi, G., Vinciarelli, A.: Automatic personality perception: prediction of trait attribution based on prosodic features. IEEE Trans. Affect. Comput. **3**(3), 273–284 (2012)

15. Park, K., Lin, Y., Metsis, V., Le, Z., Makedon, F.: Abnormal human behavioral pattern detection in assisted living environments. In: Proceedings of the 3rd International Conference on PErvasive Technologies Related to Assistive Environments, p. 9 (2010)

16. Pedregosa, F., Varoquaux, G., Gramfort, A., Michel, V., Thirion, B., Grisel, O., Blondel, M., Prettenhofer, P., Weiss, R., Dubourg, V., Vanderplas, J., Passos, A., Cournapeau, D., Brucher, M., Perrot, M., Duchesnay, E.: Scikit-learn: machine learning in python. J. Mach. Learn. Res. **12**, 2825–2830 (2011)

17. Rammstedt, B., John, O.P.: Measuring personality in one minute or less: a 10-item short version of the big five inventory in english and german. J. Res. Pers. **41**(1), 203–212 (2007)

18. Schölkopf, B., Platt, J.C., Shawe-Taylor, J., Smola, A.J., Williamson, R.C.: Estimating the support of a high-dimensional distribution. Neural Comput. **13**(7), 1443–1471 (2001)

19. Schuller, B., Steidl, S., Batliner, A., Nth, E., Vinciarelli, A., Burkhardt, F., van Son, R., Weninger, F., Eyben, F., Bocklet, T., Mohammadi, G., Weiss, B.: A survey on perceived speaker traits: Personality, likability, pathology, and the first challenge. Comput. Speech Lang. **29**(1), 100–131 (2015)

20. Valstar, M., Gratch, J., Schuller, B., Ringeval, F., Lalanne, D., Torres Torres, M., Scherer, S., Stratou, G., Cowie, R., Pantic, M.: AVEC 2016: Depression, mood, and emotion recognition workshop and challenge. In: Proceedings of the 6th International Workshop on Audio/Visual Emotion Challenge, pp. 3–10. ACM (2016)

21. Vinciarelli, A., Mohammadi, G.: A survey of personality computing. IEEE Trans. Affect. Comput. **5**(3), 273–291 (2014)

Fusion of a Novel Volterra-Wiener Filter Based Nonlinear Residual Phase and MFCC for Speaker Verification

Purvi Agrawal[1](✉) and Hemant A. Patil[2]

[1] Indian Institute of Science, Bengaluru, Karnataka, India
purvi_agrawal@ee.iisc.ernet.in
[2] Dhirubhai Ambani Institute of Information and Communication Technology,
Gandhinagar, Gujarat, India
hemant_patil@daiict.ac.in

Abstract. This paper investigates the complementary nature of the speaker-specific information present in the Volterra-Wiener filter residual (VWFR) phase of speech signal in comparison with the information present in conventional Mel Frequency Cepstral Coefficients (MFCC) and Teager Energy Operator (TEO) phase. The feature set is derived from residual phase extracted from the output of *nonlinear* filter designed using Volterra-Weiner series exploiting *higher order* linear as well as non-linear relationships hidden in the sequence of samples of speech signal. The proposed feature set is being used to conduct Speaker Verification (SV) experiments on NIST SRE *2002* database using state-of-the-art GMM-UBM system. The score-level fusion of proposed feature set with MFCC gives an EER of *6.05%* as compared to EER of *8.9%* with MFCC alone. EER of *8.83%* is obtained for TEO phase in fusion with MFCC, indicating that residual phase from proposed nonlinear filtering approach contain complementary speaker-specific information.

Keywords: Volterra-Wiener filter residual (VWFR) · Volterra-Weiner series · Nonlinear filter · GMM-UBM · MFCC · TEO phase

1   Introduction

The speech production mechanism is assumed to be a *linear* system according to the acoustic theory of speech production. Speech analysis and speech synthesis finds effective application of Linear Prediction (LP) analysis [1]. The frequency response of the time-varying vocal tract area function is indeed captured implicitly by the LP analysis. Hence, speech production process can be modeled approximately as linear system with a major source of excitation to vocal tract system as airflow through the glottis, and hence the speaker-specific features are either termed as source or system features. Based on the characteristics one tries to capture, most commonly being used vocal tract (i.e., acoustic system) features are linear prediction cepstral coefficients (LPCC) and Mel frequency cepstral coefficients (MFCC) [2].

© Springer International Publishing AG 2017
A. Karpov et al. (Eds.): SPECOM 2017, LNAI 10458, pp. 389–397, 2017.
DOI: 10.1007/978-3-319-66429-3_38

Significant efforts have been made for improved speaker recognition performance, by exploiting the excitation source-related features. However, a landmark work on Linear Prediction (LP) residual [3] demonstrated that the excitation source component of speech contains speaker-specific information captured by the higher-order relations *hidden* in the sequence of speech samples. In [4], LP residual phase was introduced for speaker recognition defined by the cosine of the instantaneous phase function of the analytic signal (derived from the LP residual of the speech signal). This work exploits regions around Glottal Closure Instants (GCIs) for extracting residual phase features, (which are known to convey speaker-specific source information due to high signal-to-noise ratio (SNR) regions because of impulse-like excitation). Recently, Teager Energy Operator (TEO) phase (i.e., cosine of the instantaneous phase function of the *analytic* signal derived from the TEO profile of the speech signal) has been proposed for speaker recognition task [5–7]. It also exploits the regions around GCIs for extracting TEO phase features because of significantly high SNR at GCIs. This research work was basically motivated by the landmark work presented in [8].

The present paper is an extension of work reported in [5,6]. In particular, the application of TEO in [5,6] tries to capture the lower-order nonlinear relations (relation present among adjacent speech samples), while studies have shown the presence of speaker-specific information present in the higher-order relations (such as relations present among the *distant* speech samples) [4,8]. In this paper, we have used nonlinear filter designed using Volterra-Weiner-Korenberg series [9] such that its residual phase captures the higher-order relations hidden in the sequence of speech samples. Results are reported on *330* speakers of standard and statistically meaningful NIST SRE *2002* database [10]. In addition, for feature extraction around GCIs, we have used recently developed Zero Frequency Resonator (ZFR) method [11] to detect GCI and state-of-the-art Gaussian Mixture Model-Universal Background Model (GMM-UBM)-based SV system [12].

The rest of the paper is organized as follows: Sect. 2 describes the nonlinear filtering approach in detail, the generalization of Teager's algorithm and its usefulness from speech analysis perspective. Section 3 explains the extraction of proposed Volterra-Wiener filter residual (VWFR) phase features for SV task. Section 4 gives the details of experimental setup with results obtained on standard NIST SRE *2002* database. Section 5 concludes the paper along with future research directions.

2 Nonlinear Filtering Approach

This section presents the effectiveness of capturing higher-order relations hidden in the sequence of samples of speech signal through nonlinear filter residual approach. The nonlinear filtering method discussed is based on exploiting relation between TEO [7] and the Volterra-Wiener-Korenberg (VWK) series approximation [9].

2.1   Teager Energy Operator (TEO)

Airflow propagation in the vocal tract is assumed to be linear planar wave according to linear speech production model. However, the airflow is *separate* and concomitant vortices are distributed throughout the vocal tract [13,14]. Thus, the nonlinear *vortex-flow* interactions have been proved to be the true source of sound production. A nonlinear model has been suggested based on the energy of airflow by using a nonlinear energy-tracking TEO for signal analysis with the supporting observation that hearing is the process of detecting energy embedded in various subbands of speech spectrum [7,14]. TEO for discrete-time signal s(n) is defined as [7]:

$$\psi_d\{s(n)\} = TEO\{s(n)\} = s^2(n) - s(n+1)s(n-1) = \psi(n) \tag{1}$$

In [5], it has been observed that TEO profile gives high energy pulses around GCIs for a speech segment, similar to the LP residual profile [4]. Studies reported in [5] have used instantaneous phase of the analytic signal derived from TEO profile with the help of Hilbert transform, shown in Fig. 1 (primarily motivated by the landmark work on LP residual phase for speaker recognition task [4,8]). The analytic signal corresponding to TEO profile is given by

$$\psi_a(n) = \psi(n) + j\psi_h(n); \qquad \Psi_a(e^{j\omega}) = 0; \qquad -\pi \leq \omega < 0, \tag{2}$$

$$\psi_h(n) = F^{-1}[\Psi_h(e^{j\omega})], \qquad \Psi_a(e^{j\omega}) = \Psi(e^{j\omega}) + j\Psi_h(e^{j\omega}), \tag{3}$$

where $\psi_h(n)$ is the Hilbert transform of TEO profile $\psi(n)$, $F^{-1}\{\cdot\}$ indicates the inverse Fourier transform and $\Psi_a(e^{j\omega})$ is the discrete-time Fourier transform (DTFT) of $\psi_a(n)$. The magnitude of the analytic signal, i.e., Hilbert envelope (HE), $h_e(n)$ is given by $h_e(n) = |\psi_a(n)|$, and the cosine of the instantaneous phase of the analytic signal $\psi_a(n)$ is called as TEO phase (denoted by $\theta_\psi(n)$) given by [5]

$$\theta_\psi(n) = cos[\theta(n)] = \frac{Re[\psi_a(n)]}{h_e(n)} \tag{4}$$

In Fig. 1(b), *bumps* observed between the TEO pulses indicate the presence of *nonlinearities* associated with the speech production [15]. If the speech production mechanism (which can be modeled as *convolution* of excitation source with impulse response of vocal tract; which in turn is a cascade of several 2nd order digital resonators each corresponding to a particular formant and having impulse response as damped sinusoid) would have been *linear*, then the TEO profile would have been exponentially decaying signal [5]. The presence of bumps within every GCI gives the evidence of associated nonlinearity in speech production mechanism.

2.2   A Generalization of Teager Algorithm-Volterra-Weiner (VW) Series

A generalization of the Weinerstrass-Stone theorem states that the set of Volterra functionals is *complete* (i.e., every Cauchy sequence converges to a *limit point* which belongs to the same *function* space). It implies that every continuous functional of a signal $s(t)$ can be approximated as a sum of a finite number of Volterra functions in $s(t)$ with arbitrary precision [16,17]. In order to perform the nonlinear prediction (NLP) of speech, consider a system with input data series $s(n)$ and the output $y(n)$, $n = 1, 2, \cdots, N$, with sampling interval τ. A power series expansion may be used to describe the system as [9]:

$$y(n) = \sum_{p=0}^{\infty} c_p s^p(n) \tag{5}$$

Equation (5) can be extended and used to represent a nonlinear system with k memory terms, extension being termed as the Volterra-Wiener (VW) series expansion. Studies have shown that for a dynamical system, the Volterra series can be transformed into a closed-loop in which the output $y(n)$ feeds back as a delayed input (i.e., $s(n) \equiv y(n)$). Therefore, we analyze the above time series by using a discrete VW series of degree d and predictor memory k to calculate the predicted time series, $\hat{y}(n)$ given by:

$$\hat{y}(n) = g_0 + g_1 y(n-1) + g_2 y(n-2) + \cdots + g_k y(n-k) + g_{k+1} y^2(n-1)$$
$$+ g_{k+2} y(n-1) \times y(n-2) + \cdots + g_{M-1} y^d(n-k), \tag{6}$$

with a total dimension $M = (k+d)!/(k!d!)$ [9]. Thus, the *predictor memory* k and the *degree d* of nonlinearity parameterizes the model. The coefficients $g_m s$ in (6) are termed as kernel values and are estimated through Korenbergs fast algorithm using Gram-Schmidt procedure from linear and nonlinear autocorrelation of the data-series itself [9].

The Teager Energy Operator (TEO) as a Volterra system. The discrete version of Teagers algorithm is a Volterra-Wiener filter defined by [18]:

$$\hat{y}[n] = s[n]s[n] - s[n-1]s[n+1], \tag{7}$$

which contains two non-zero kernel values and thus, will capture lower-order nonlinear relations only.

Volterra-Wiener filter residual (VWFR). Therefore, in the light of above discussion, for the NLP model, nonlinear prediction error which may be termed as Volterra-Wiener filter residual (VWFR), viz., e_{VWFR} is given by [17]

$$e_{VWFR}(n) = s(n) - \hat{y}(n). \tag{8}$$

Figure 2(b) shows the VWFR profile of the speech signal (shown in Fig. 2(a)). The vocal tract contribution may get removed from the speech signal during its inverse filtering and the resultant signal is known as NLP residual or VWFR (Table 1).

Hence, it can be observed that TEO captures the lower-order nonlinear relations hidden in the sequence of speech signal whereas proposed VWFR tries to capture the higher-order both linear and nonlinear relations hidden in sequence

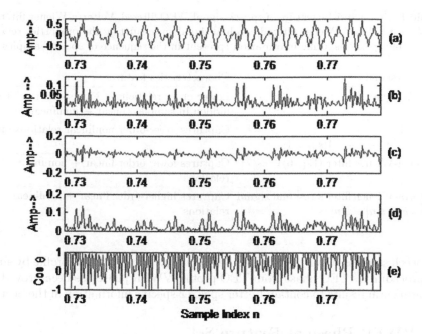

Fig. 1. (a) Voiced speech segment, (b) its TEO profile, (c) Hilbert transform, (d) Hilbert envelope and (e) TEO Phase (After [5]). Bumps can be observed in (b)

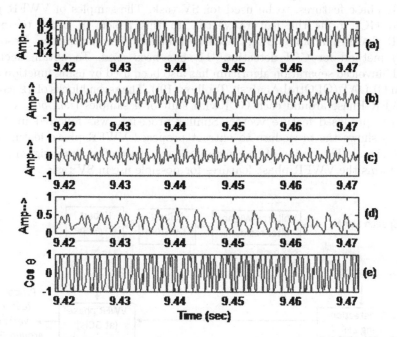

Fig. 2. (a) Voiced speech segment, (b) its VWFR profile (for d = 2, k = 5), (c) Hilbert transform, (d) Hilbert envelope and (e) VWFR Phase

Table 1. Characteristic feature of speech signal, TEO filtered, Volterra-Wiener filtered, and hence Volterra-Wiener filtered residual signal encapsulating the properties related to possible speaker-specific information (present in the sequence of speech samples)

Type of signal	Characteristics features
Speech signal $s[n]$	Lower-order relations + higher-order relations hidden in samples (linear + nonlinear)
TEO filter $\hat{y}[n] = s^2[n] - s[n+1]s[n-1]$	Captures lower-order nonlinear relations only
Volterra-Wiener filter (Eq. (6))	Captures lower-order linear + nonlinear relations
Volterra-Wiener filter's residual signal $e_{VWFR} = s[n] - \hat{y}[n]$	Captures higher-order linear + nonlinear relations

of speech samples. VWFR phase has been computed from VWFR profile by similar procedure as TEO phase from TEO profile. VWFR phase has been proved by experimental results to contain better speaker-specific information in the Sect. 4.

3   VWFR Phase as Feature Set

In this Section, the algorithm has been discussed for extraction of proposed VWFR phase features, to be used for SV task. The samples of VWFR phase around GCI forms the feature vector. In this paper, in order to extract VWFR features around GCI, recently proposed Zero-Frequency Resonator (ZFR) method for GCI detection [11] has been used. To obtain accuracy, voiced/unvoiced separation algorithm has also been used by using function available in GLOAT (GLOttal Analysis Toolbox [19]). The seven blocks of *12* samples of VWFR Phase around each GCI with shift of *6* samples (i.e., *50%* overlap) form the proposed feature vector. Similar procedure was followed in [5,6,8]. Figure 3 shows the procedure to extract proposed VWFR phase features of a speech signal. The cosine of the instantaneous phase of analytic signal around GCIs forms the VWFR phase features for possible use in SV task.

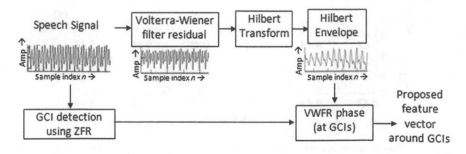

Fig. 3. Block diagram for extraction of VWFR phase features

4   Experimental Results

In this paper, the experiments for the SV system have been conducted on NIST SRE *2002* database with *139* male and *191* female speakers' utterances used for training the GMM-UBM system [10,12]. The modeling has been done with $M=256$ component Gaussian models. In first stage of training, a GMM-UBM system consisting of model parameters, a gender-independent UBM is constructed from collection of non-target speakers' feature vector. In the second stage of training, feature vectors are extracted from target speakers' utterances, which in turn, are used to maximum a-posteriori (MAP) - adapt only the mean vectors of the GMM-UBM to form speaker-dependent models [12]. During testing, the log-likelihood ratio, also termed as *score*, is calculated and the claimant speaker is accepted if score is greater than a decision threshold.

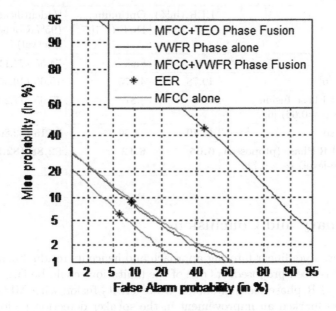

Fig. 4. Detection Error Tradeoff (DET) curve

The testing is done for *3654* utterances, each being tested with *11* claimants, where the true or genuine speaker may or may not be present and rest being impostors, respectively. The performance of the SV system is estimated using VWFR phase features, MFCC feature vectors and their score-level fusion. The results are compared with the performance of TEO phase [6]. The Detection Error Tradeoff (DET) curve for the three feature sets are shown in Fig. 4 [20]. The score-level fusion of MFCC with VWFR phase is done as follows:

$$S_{fusion} = \alpha S_{MFCC} + (1 - \alpha)S_{VWFRphase}; \quad 0 \leq \alpha \leq 1, \tag{9}$$

where α is the weight of fusion. In addition, S_{MFCC}, $S_{VWFRphase}$ and S_{fusion} are the score for MFCC, proposed VWFR phase and their score-level fusion, respectively. The values of $C_{miss} = 1$, $C_{false} = 1$ and $P_{target} = 0.5$ have been used to compute optimum Detection Cost Function (DCF) [20].

Figure 4 illustrates that the speaker detection performance of the GMM-UBM SV system has got improved by 2.78% reduction in EER, i.e., from '8.83% EER of MFCC-TEO Phase fusion to 6.05% EER of proposed MFCC-VWFR Phase which indicates that proposed VWFR phase features carry *complementary* speaker-specific information (Table 2).

Table 2. % EER, optimum DCF and *95%* confidence interval (shown in brackets) for SV system trained using GMM-UBM system for MFCC, TEO phase, VWFR phase and their score-level fusion with MFCC on NIST SRE-*2002* database, respectively

Feature set	EER (in%)	Optimum DCF (x 10^{-2})	%Identification Rate (95% Confidence interval)
MFCC [6]	8.90	8.65	74.55 (74.11–74.98)
TEO Phase [6]	49.78	49.75	10.66 (10.35–10.96)
MFCC-TEO Phase fusion (score-level)(α =0.66) [6]	8.83	8.87	77.65 (77.23–78.06)
VWFR Phase	44.79	44.56	33.15 (32.86–33.79)
MFCC-VWFR Phase (proposed) fusion (score-level) (α =0.71)	**6.05**	**6.12**	**82.88 (82.50–83.25)**

5   Summary and Conclusions

In this paper, a nonlinear filtering approach and hence its residual phase feature extraction has been proposed. Its one of the limitations could be larger absolute EER for VWFR phase features alone. However, its fusion with MFCC feature at score-level marked an improvement in the speaker detection performance of the overall system. In future, further analysis of SV system based on combining evidences of other relevant *source* and *system* features will be explored. In addition, robustness of proposed feature will be evaluated under signal degradation conditions.

References

1. Markhoul, J.: Linear prediction: a tutorial review. Proc. IEEE **63**(4), 561–580 (1975)
2. Furui, S.: Cepstral analysis technique for automatic speaker verification. IEEE Trans. Acoust. Speech Signal Process. **29**(2), 254–272 (1981)

3. Prasanna, S., Gupta, C.S., Yegnanarayana, B.: Extraction of speaker-specific excitation from linear prediction residual of speech. Speech Commun. **48**(10), 1243–1261 (2006)
4. Murty, K., Prasanna, S., Yegnanarayana, B.: Speaker-specific information from residual phase. In: International Conference on Signal Processing and Communications (SPCOM), IISc Bangalore India, pp. 516–519 (2004)
5. Patil, H., Parhi, K.: Development of TEO phase for speaker recognition. In: International Conference on Signal Processing and Communications (SPCOM), IISc Bangalore, India, pp. 1–5 (2010)
6. Agrawal, P., Patil, H.: Fusion of TEO phase with MFCC features for speaker verification. In: Proceedings 2nd International Conference on Perception and Machine Intelligence (PerMIn), C-DAC Kolkata, India, pp. 161–166 (2015)
7. Kaiser, J.: On a simple algorithm to calculate the energy of a signal. In: Proceedings of International Conference on Acoustic, Speech and Signal Processing (ICASSP), Albuquerque New Mexico, USA, vol. 1, pp. 381–384 (1990)
8. Murty, K., Yegnanarayana, B.: Combining evidences from residual phase and MFCC features for speaker recognition. IEEE Sig. Process. Lett. **13**(1), 52–55 (2006)
9. Korenberg, M.: Indentifying nonlinear difference equation and functional expansion representation: the fast orthogonal algorithm. Ann. Biomed. Eng. **16**(1), 123–142 (1988)
10. NIST: The NIST Year 2002 Speaker Recognition Evaluation Plan. www.nist.gov/spcech/tests/spk/2002/. Last Accessed 25 Mar 2015
11. Murty, K., Yegnanarayana, B.: Epoch extraction from speech signals. IEEE Trans. Audio Speech Lang. Process. **16**(8), 1602–1613 (2008)
12. Reynolds, D., Quatieri, T., Dunn, R.: Speaker verification using adapted Gaussian mixture models. Digital Sig. Process. **10**(1), 19–41 (2000)
13. Teager, H.M.: Some observations on oral airflow during phonation. IEEE Trans. Acoust. Speech Sig. Process. **28**(5), 599–601 (1980)
14. Teager, H.M., Teager, S.M.: Evidence for nonlinear sound production mechanisms in the vocal tract. In: Hardcastle, W.J., Marchal, A. (eds.) Speech Production and Speech Modelling. NATO ASI Series (Series D: Behavioural and Social Sciences), vol. 55, pp. 241–261. Springer, Dordrecht (1990). doi:10.1007/978-94-009-2037-8_10
15. Quatieri, T.: Discrete-Time Speech Signal Processing. Prentice-Hall, Upper Saddle River (2002)
16. Sicuranza, V., Mathews, G.: Polynomial Signal Processing. Wiley, New York (2000)
17. Patil, H., Patel, T.: Nonlinear prediction of speech signal using Volterra-Wiener series, pp. 1687–1691. INTERSPEECH, Lyon, France (2013)
18. Moorel, M., Bernstein, R., Mitra, S.: A generalization of the Teager algorithm. In: Proceedings of IEEE Workshop on Nonlinear Signal Processing, September 1997
19. Drugman, T.: GLOAT (GLOttal Analysis Toolbox). http://tcts.fpms.ac.be/drugman/Toolbox/. Last Accessed 25 Mar 2015
20. Martin, A., Doddington, G., Kamm, T., Ordowski, M., Przybocki, M.: The DET curve in assessment of detection task performance. In: Proceedings of European Conference on Speech Processing Technology, Rhodes, Greece, pp. 1895–1898 (1997)

Hesitations in Spontaneous Speech: Acoustic Analysis and Detection

Vasilisa Verkhodanova[(✉)], Vladimir Shapranov, and Irina Kipyatkova

SPIIRAS, St. Petersburg, Russia
{verkhodanova,kipyatkova}@iias.spb.su, equidamoid@gmail.com

Abstract. Spontaneous speech is different from any other type of speech in many ways, with speech disfluencies being the prominent feature. These phenomena both play an important role in communication, and also cause problems for automatic speech processing. In this study we present the results of acoustic analysis of the most frequent disfluencies - voiced hesitations (filled pauses and lengthenings) across different speaking styles in spontaneous Russian speech, as well as results of experiments on their detection using SVM classifier on a joint Russian and English spontaneous speech corpus. Results of acoustic analysis showed significant differences in fundamental frequency and energy distribution ratios of hesitations and their contexts across speaking styles in Russian: comparing to the dialogues, in monologues speakers exhibit more prosodic cues for the adjacent context and hesitations. Experiments on detection of voiced hesitations on a mixed language and style corpus with SVM resulted in achieving F1–score = 0.48 (With F1–score = 0.55 for only Russian data).

Keywords: Speech disfluencies · Hesitations · Filled pauses · Lengthenings · Speech processing · Support vector machines

1 Introduction

Speech disfluencies are common in spontaneous speech: hesitations, self-repairs, repetitions, deletions, substitutions, insertions, etc. In the literature there are two main perspectives to describe speech disfluencies: (a) as speech errors, disrupting fluent speech, and (b) as fluent linguistic devices used to manage speech [17,18]. Speech disfluencies may be critical for successful turn-taking or may express the speaker's thinking process of formulating the upcoming utterance fragment [6,20]. Disfluencies also play a major role in speech structuring [5] and may be used to introduce new information [3] or serve as cues to the complexity of upcoming phrases for native and non-native listeners [34].

Disfluencies occur very often in the everyday speech. About 6 per 100 words are disfluent in conversational speech in American English [25]. In Japanese, fillers alone consist of about 6% of the total words in presentations [34]. Evidence on speech disfluencies differs across languages, genres, and speakers, however, on average there are several disfluencies per 100 syllables, filled pauses and

© Springer International Publishing AG 2017
A. Karpov et al. (Eds.): SPECOM 2017, LNAI 10458, pp. 398–406, 2017.
DOI: 10.1007/978-3-319-66429-3_39

lengthenings (later on jointly referred as FPs) being the most frequently ocurring disfluency type [19]. According to [29] in the conversational Switchboard database [10], about 39.7% of the all disfluencies contain a filled pause. In the corpus of Portuguese lectures LECTRA filled pauses are the most frequent disfluency type in the corpus: they correspond to 1.8% of all the words and to 22.9% of all disfluency types [15]. In Russian speech, FPs occur at a rate of about 4 times per 100 words and approximately at the same rate inside clauses and at the discourse boundaries [14].

FPs have universal as well as linguistic and genre specific features. They are represented mainly by vocalizations with rare cases of prolonged consonants (which was shown to be a peculiarity of Armenian hesitation phenomena [13]). Due to the articulatory economy FPs are pronounced with minimal movements of the articulatory organs, thus they are phonetically different from other lexical items [28]. However, it was also shown that phonological system of the language may influence the quality of FPs vocalizations [9]. Even universal characteristics of FPs, such as lengthenings being accompanied by creaky voice, may operate differently in different languages: e.g. in Finnish it was proposed that creaky voice may indicate turn-transitional locations [20], which is not the case for English [26].

However, disfluencies are one of the factors that makes the spontaneous speech processing challenging [22]. Disfluencies have an impact on automatic speech recognition results, they can occur at any point of spontaneous speech as well as can be easily confused with functional words, thus leading to misrecognition or incorrect classification of adjacent words, what results in fragment-like structures. Therefore, handling speech disfluencies is crucial for the development of robust speech recognition and transcription systems.

2 Related Work

During last years, there has been a great deal of research devoted to speech disfluencies. Disfluencies have been shown to characterize social and emotional behavior [24]. They also have been used to draw inferences about processing difficulties: e.g. comparison of children with specific language impairment and children with normal language development [30].

However, speech disfluencies have received more attention in the field of speech processing due to speech recognition tasks. And within works on automatic disfluency detection filled pauses are likely to be the most studied type of disfluency [16, 21].

It has been shown that along with the duration, prominent characteristic of FPs is a gradual fall of fundamental frequency (F0) [21]: FPs tend to be low in F0 and display a gradual, roughly linear F0 fall. In [27] it was shown that for fair detection of FPs these two characteristics and distance to a pause are enough. In [32] authors used duration and statistical characteristics of F0, first three formants and energy for the experiments based on gradient decent optimizing parameters for maximization of F1–score; achieved result was F1–score = 0.46.

In [16] authors focused on detection of filled pauses basing on acoustic and prosodic features as well as on some lexical features. Experiments with several machine learning methods on a speech corpus of university lectures in European Portuguese Lectra showed best results for Classification and Regression Trees algorithm. Further experiments on filled pauses detection in European Portuguese using prosodic and lexical features showed best results when using J48, corresponding to about 61% F-measure [15].

In [23] authors presented a method for filled pauses detection using an SVM classifier, applying a Gaussian filter to infer temporal context information and performing a morphological opening to filter false alarms. For the feature set authors used the same as was proposed for [12], extracted with the openSMILE toolkit [8]. Experiments were carried out on the LAST MINUTE corpus of naturalistic multimodal recordings of 133 German speaking subjects in a so called Wizard-of-Oz (WoZ) experiment. The obtained results were recall of 70%, precision of 55%, and AUC of 0.94.

3   Material

The material we have used in this study consists of the several parts. The part with Russian speech is represented by dialogues and monologues, collected in different conditions and in different periods of time.

The corpus of task-based dialogues collected at SPIIRAS in St. Petersburg in the end of 2012 - beginning of 2013 [31] consists of 18 dialogues from 1.5 to 5 min, where people in pairs fulfilled map and appointment tasks. Recording was performed in the sound isolated room. Participants were students: 6 women and 6 men from 17 to 23 years old with technical and humanitarian specialization. The recorded speech is informal, unrehearsed and is the result of direct dialogue communication, what makes it extremely close to the spontaneous conversational speech. Recordings were annotated manually into different types of disfluencies, the quantity of FPs is 492 phenomena (222 filled pauses and 270 lengthenings). In addition to this corpus, we used task-based dialogues collected at the same time that were not part of the previous corpus since these recordings are unbalanced by gender and specialization. This part is represented by 39 dialogues between students: 24 men and 2 women speakers with technical background. The length of this part is 1.8 h, with 211 filled pauses and 201 sound lengthenings (total 412 FPs).

The monologues part is represented by three subcorpora. First is Russian casual conversations from Multi-Language Audio Database [35]. This database consists of approximately 30 h of sometimes low quality, varied and noisy speech in each of three languages, English, Mandarin Chinese, and Russian. Recordings were collected from public web sites, such as http://youtube.com. All recordings have been orthographically transcribed at the sentence/phrase level by human listeners. The Russian part of this database consists of 300 recordings of 158 speakers (approximately 35 h). The casual conversations part consists of 91 recordings (10.3 h) of 53 speakers [35]. From this Russian part we have taken the random 6 recordings of casual conversations (3 female speakers and 3 male speakers) that were manually annotated into FPs. The quantity of annotated phenomena is 284 (188 filled pauses and 96 sound lengthenings).

Second is the corpus of scientific reports from seminar on analysis of conversational speech held at SPIIRAS in 2011. Recordings of reports of 6 people (3 female and 3 male speakers) were manually annotated into speech disfluencies. Since speakers didn't base their reports on a written text, these recordings are semi-spontaneous speech and contain considerable amount of speech disfluencies. 951 FPs were manually annotated: 741 filled pauses and 210 lengthenings.

Third is the the records from the appendix No5 to the phonetic journal "Bulletin of the Phonetic Fund" belonging to the Department of Phonetics of Saint-Petersburg University [1]. The 12 recorded reports concerned different scientific topics (linguistics, logic, psychology, etc.). They were all recorded in 70 s–80 s in Moscow except one that was recorded in Prague. All speakers (6 men and 6 women) were native Russian speakers, and were recorded while presenting on conferences and seminars. The quantity of manually annotated FPs is 285 (225 filled pauses and 60 lengthenings).

In total, the Russian data set we used is about 4.5 h and comprises 2214 hesitations.

In addition to Russian material we included several recordings of English spontaneous speech to make our corpus more quality and situation diverse for the experiments on automatic detection and classification. This part is represented by 6 dialogues approximately 6 min each from SwitchBoard corpus [10] and 2 dialogues approximately 20 min each from SantaBarbara corpus [7]. Total duration of English dialogues recordings is about 1 h. The quantity of manually annotated FPs in SwitchBoard part is 113 (67 filled pauses and 46 lengthenings) and 87 FPs (59 filled pauses and 28 lengthenings) in SantaBarbara part. Distribution of FP duration over the whole mixed corpus is shown on Fig. 1. The duration of a single FP lies between 6 ms and 2.3 s, the average duration is 380 ms.

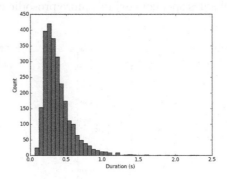

Fig. 1. The distribution of FPs duration

4   Acoustic Analysis Across Speaking Styles

There are many studies on acoustic features of FPs, with all authors agreeing on long duration and gradual fall of fundamental frequency [14,21,25,28]. However, there is not much on differences of acoustical features of FPs in different speaking styles or comparison between languages. In [17] authors showed that distribution of disfluency types is different for different speaking styles, as well as strategies of prosodic contrast markings for disfluencies vary across different speaking styles. Dialogues are more dynamic than reports or lectures, they have more sentence-like units with fewer words and the information is delivered faster [17]. For different measurements and comparisons (such as speech rate, duration of sentences and disfluent sequences, average number of words, syllables and phones within fluent and disfluent sequences, etc.) between map-task dialogues and university lectures in European Portuguese see [17].

Following them, we have checked if there are any acoustic/prosodic variability in the context of only FPs across different speaking styles in Russian. Pitch and energy are two important sources of prosodic information that can be extracted directly from the speech signal. Thus, we have compared fundamental frequency and energy for the following pairs: preceding context and FPs, following context and FPs. For dialogues we used annotated words as the context. For monologues the context was found around the hesitation by checking presence of fundamental frequency in a window of 400 ms.

Our findings showed that there are statistically significant differences between distribution ratios of fundamental frequency in FPs and their context (both precededing and following) in monologues and dialogues (see Figs. 2 and 3). As for energy, the significant difference has been found for the ratios of FPs and their following context in monologues and dialogues (Fig. 4).

These findings comply with [17]: the highest pitch reset from disfluency to the repair region for European Portuguese was found for filled pauses. It is also matches the overall trend for different disfluencies found for the European Portuguese [17]: in monologues speakers exhibit more prosodic cues for the adjacent

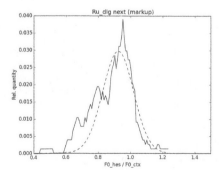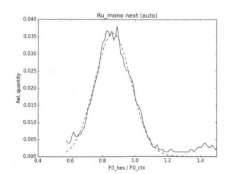

Fig. 2. Fundamental frequency differences between FPs and their following context for dialogues and for monologues in Russian

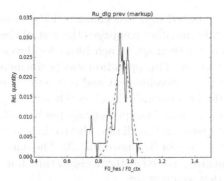
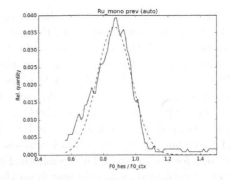

Fig. 3. Fundamental frequencys differences between FPs and their preceding context for dialogues and for monologues in Russian

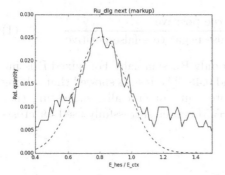
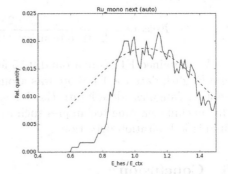

Fig. 4. Energy differences between FPs and their following context for dialogues and for monologues in Russian

context and FPs than in dialogues, whereas in dialogues there are less obvious differences in ratios. However, the energy distribution in our material is in agreement with the overall trend of monologues exhibiting more explicit strategies of prosodic context marking, what was not the case in [17]. This result is possibly due to the fact that we calculated not the mean fundamental frequency and energy but distribution estimation to account for the possible noises.

5   Experiments on Detection

This study is continuation of [33], where we followed [23], basing our experiments on support vector machine (SVM) classifier. The scikit-learn Python library [2] implementation of SVM with polynomial kernel was used, it enables the probability estimates by means of C-Support Vector Classification, the implementation is build upon libsvm [4]. Features were extracted with the openSMILE toolkit [8] on the frame-level basis (25 ms window, 10 ms shift), the whole feature set being based on the set used for the INTERSPEECH 2013 Social Signals Sub-Challenge [12]. This resulted in 162 values per frame.

For the experiments, data has been separated into two classes: "FPs" and "Other". First one consists of FPs only, while the other comprises the rest of the frames. Each 10th file was selected for train set, then again each 10th - for development set, and the rest was used as the test set. This operation was performed 10 times producing 10 different triplets of train, development and test sets. The train set was then downsampled to avoid the bias towards the class "Other" [23].

As the post-processing step the Gaussian filter and morphological opening [11, 23] were applied, since it improving both precision and recall rates due to the usage of contextual information, which was also the case for Russian data [33]. The parameters for Gaussian and morphological opening, as well as the decision threshold were determined using grid search on the development set.

We performed experiments on both only Russian data and mixed Russian and English data. For the results evaluation we used the F1–score, the harmonic mean of precision and recall:

$$F_1\text{score} = \frac{2 \cdot \text{true positive}}{2 \cdot \text{true positive} + \text{false negative} + \text{false positive}} \tag{1}$$

We obtained F1–score around 0.55 for only Russian data. For mixed Russian and English data the F1–score was around 0.48. The results showed that adding another language deteriorate the F1–score, but not crucially, suggesting that the machine learning techniques such as SVM can be successfully used for cross-linguistic hesitation detection.

6 Conclusion

In this paper we presented the results of acoustic analysis of voiced hesitations and their context across monologues and dialogues in Russian, confirming that there are differences in fundamental frequency and energy distribution across speaking styles in Russian. Comparing to the dialogues, in monologues speakers exhibit more prosodic cues for the adjacent context and FPs. Whereas in dialogues there are less obvious differences in hesitations and their context ratios. We have also reported results of the experiments on detection of voiced hesitations on a mixed language and style corpus with SVM, achieving F1–score = 0.48 (With F1–score = 0.55 for only Russian data). Future research will tackle both the impact of speaking styles and different languages in automatic hesitation detection.

Acknowledgments. This research is supported by the grant of Russian Foundation for Basic Research (project No. 15-06-04465) and by the Council for Grants of the President of the Russian Federation (projects No. MK-1000.2017.8).

References

1. Department of Phonetics of Saint Petersburg University. http://phonetics.spbu.ru/
2. Scikit-Learn: Machine learning in Python. http://scikit-learn.org
3. Allwood, J., Nivre, J., Ahlsén, E.: Speech management on the non-written life of speech. Nordic J. Linguist. **13**(1), 3–48 (1990)
4. Chang, C.C., Lin, C.J.: LIBSVM: a library for support vector machines. ACM Trans. Intell. Syst. Technol. (TIST) **2**, 1–27 (2011). http://www.csie.ntu.edu.tw/cjlin/libsvm
5. Clark, H.H., Tree, J.E.F.: Using uh and um in spontaneous speaking. Cognition **84**(1), 73–111 (2002)
6. Clark, H.: Using Language. Cambridge University Press, Cambridge (1996)
7. Du Bois, J.W., Chafe, W.L., Meyer, C., Thompson, S.A., Martey, N.: Santa Barbara Corpus of Spoken American English, Linguistic Data Consortium. Philadelphia (2000–2005)
8. Eyben, F., Wöllmer, M., Schuller, B.: OpenSMILE: the Munich versatile and fast open-source audio feature extractor. In: Proceeding of 18th ACM International Conference on Multimedia, pp. 1459–1462. ACM (2010)
9. Giannini, A.: Hesitation phenomena in spontaneous Italian. In: Proceeding of 15th International Congress of Phonetic Sciences, Barcelona, Spain, pp. 2653–2656 (2003)
10. Godfrey, J.J., Holliman, E.C., McDaniel, J.: SwitchBoard: telephone speech corpus for research and development. In: Proceeding of International Conference on Acoustics, Speech, and Signal Processing (ICASSP-1992), vol. 1, pp. 517–520. IEEE (1992)
11. Heijmans, H.J.: Mathematical morphology: a modern approach in image processing based on algebra and geometry. SIAM Rev. **37**(1), 1–36 (1995)
12. INTERSPEECH: Computational Paralinguistic Challenge (2013). http://emotion-research.net/sigs/speech-sig/is13-compare
13. Khurshudian, V.: Hesitation in typologically different languages: an experimental study. In: Proceeding of International Conference on Computational Linguistics Dialogue, pp. 497–501 (2005)
14. Kibrik, A., Podlesskaya, V. (eds.): Rasskazy o Snovideniyah: Korpusnoye Issledovaniye Ustnogo Russkogo Diskursa [Night dream stories: Corpus study of Russian discourse]. Litres (2014)
15. Medeiros, H., Batista, F., Moniz, H., Trancoso, I., Meinedo, H.: Experiments on automatic detection of filled pauses using prosodic features. Actas de Inforum **2013**, 335–345 (2013)
16. Medeiros, H., Moniz, H., Batista, F., Trancoso, I., Nunes, L., et al.: Disfluency detection based on prosodic features for university lectures. In: Proceeding of INTERSPEECH 2013, Lyon, France, pp. 2629–2633 (2013)
17. Moniz, H., Batista, F., Mata, A.I., Trancoso, I.: Speaking style effects in the production of disfluencies. Speech Commun. **65**, 20–35 (2014)
18. O'Connel, D.C., Kowal, S.: Communicating with One Another: Toward a Psychology of Spontaneous Spoken Discourse. Cognition and Language: A Series in Psycholinguistics. Springer Science & Business Media, New York (2009). doi:10.1007/978-0-387-77632-3
19. O'Connell, D., Kowal, S.: The history of research on the filled pause as evidence of the written language bias in linguistics. J. Psycholinguist. Res. **33**(6), 459–474 (2004)

20. Ogden, R.: Turn-holding, turn-yielding and laryngeal activity in finnish talk-in-interaction. J. Int. Phonetics Assoc. **31**(1), 139–52 (2001)
21. O'Shaughnessy, D.: Recognition of hesitations in spontaneous speech. In: Proceeding of International Conference on Acoustics, Speech, and Signal Processing, (ICASSP-1992), vol. 1, pp. 521–524. IEEE (1992)
22. Ostendorf, M., Shriberg, E., Stolcke, A.: Human language technology: opportunities and challenges. Technical report, DTIC Document (2005)
23. Prylipko, D., Egorow, O., Siegert, I., Wendemuth, A.: Application of image processing methods to filled pauses detection from spontaneous speech. In: Proceeding of INTERSPEECH 2014, Singapore, pp. 1816–1820. ISCA (2014)
24. Ranganath, R., Jurafsky, D., McFarland, D.A.: Detecting friendly, flirtatious, awkward, and assertive speech in speed-dates. Comput. Speech Lang. **27**(1), 89–115 (2013)
25. Shriberg, E.: Preliminaries to a theory of speech disfluencies. Ph.D. thesis, University of California at Berkeley (1994)
26. Shriberg, E.: To 'Errrr' is human: ecology and acoustics of speech disfluencies. J. Int. Phonetic Assoc. **31**(1), 153–169 (2001)
27. Shriberg, E., Bates, R.A., Stolcke, A.: A prosody only decision-tree model for disfluency detection. In: Proceeding of the Eurospeech 1997, 5th European Conference on Speech Communication and Technology, Rhodes, Greece, pp. 2383–2386 (1997)
28. Stepanova, S.: Some features of filled hesitation pauses in spontaneous Russian. In: Proceeding of 16th International Congress of Phonetic Sciences, Saarbrucken, Germany, vol. 16, pp. 1325–1328 (2007)
29. Stolcke, A., Shriberg, E., Bates, R.A., Ostendorf, M., Hakkani, D., Plauche, M., Tür, G., Lu, Y.: Automatic detection of sentence boundaries and disfluencies based on recognized words. In: ICSLP (1998)
30. Thordardottir, E.T., Weismer, S.E.: Content mazes and filled pauses in narrative language samples of children with specific language impairment. Brain Cogn. **48**(2–3), 587–592 (2001)
31. Verkhodanova, V., Shapranov, V.: Automatic detection of filled pauses and lengthenings in the spontaneous Russian speech. In: Proceeding of 7th International Conference Speech Prosody, pp. 1110–1114 (2014)
32. Verkhodanova, V., Shapranov, V.: Multi-factor method for detection of filled pauses and lengthenings in Russian spontaneous speech. In: Ronzhin, A., Potapova, R., Fakotakis, N. (eds.) SPECOM 2015. LNCS (LNAI), vol. 9319, pp. 285–292. Springer, Cham (2015). doi:10.1007/978-3-319-23132-7_35
33. Verkhodanova, V., Shapranov, V.: Detecting filled pauses and lengthenings in Russian spontaneous speech using SVM. In: Ronzhin, A., Potapova, R., Németh, G. (eds.) SPECOM 2016. LNCS (LNAI), vol. 9811, pp. 224–231. Springer, Cham (2016). doi:10.1007/978-3-319-43958-7_26
34. Watanabe, M., Hirose, K., Den, Y., Minematsu, N.: Filled pauses as cues to the complexity of upcoming phrases for native and non-native listeners. Speech Commun. **50**(2), 81–94 (2008)
35. Zahorian, S.A., Wu, J., Karnjanadecha, M., Vootkur, C.S., Wong, B., Hwang, A., Tokhtamyshev, E.: Open-source multi-language audio database for spoken language processing applications. In: Proceeding of INTERSPEECH 2011, Florence, Italy, pp. 1493–1496 (2011)

Human as Acmeologic Entity in Social Network Discourse (Multidimensional Approach)

Rodmonga Potapova[1](✉) and Vsevolod Potapov[2]

[1] Institute of Applied and Mathematical Linguistics,
Moscow State Linguistic University, Ostozhenka 38, Moscow 119034, Russia
rkpotapova@yandex.ru
[2] Faculty of Philology, Lomonosov Moscow State University,
GSP-1, Leninskie Gory, Moscow 119991, Russia
volikpotapov@gmail.com

Abstract. The main aim of the project is to study development of the acmeological approach to modeling the characteristics of the speech activity of communicants in the social network discourse (SND), taking into account the degree
of "maturation" of the destructive features of the personality considering the fact
that formerly some material was used, which includes features of the personality
structure for the "subjects" based on samples of their written and spoken speech
in the electronic media environment for the purpose of constructing an acmeological matrix that will enable experimental "measurement" of the acmeological
difference in the potentials of an individual. Scientific novelty and significance of
this research are determined by the modern social network situation with regard
to a lot of negative information communication utterances.

Keywords: Acmeology · Destructive dynamics · Cognitive image
diagnostics · Speech activity · Social-network discourse

1 Introduction

It is widely known that speech (spoken language and written language) contains
speaker-specific information that includes personal deprivation features with regard to
intellectual, social, economic, confessional, political, geopolitical etc. factors. This
article considers for the first time the role of the investigation of author profiling and
personality attribution on the basis of acmeologic entity analysis. The motivation of
this research was an attempt to analyze all personal features (verbal, paraverbal and
non-verbal) of communicants in the Internet, focusing on social network discourse
(SND). The fundamental conception of this approach was acmeology regarding, first of
all, the negative dynamics of personal attributes of "electronic" communicants.

Acmeology is a science the main task of which is to study the potential of the full
development of the human personality considered as a subject of any activity (intellectual, social, spiritual, etc.). Acmeological identity of a human is one of the basic
concepts of acmeology, which relate both to positive and negative person identity. In
the first case, one can talk about a person who aspires to positive solutions of various

© Springer International Publishing AG 2017
A. Karpov et al. (Eds.): SPECOM 2017, LNAI 10458, pp. 407–416, 2017.
DOI: 10.1007/978-3-319-66429-3_40

problems, and in the second case about a person whose actions are aimed at achievement of his/her goals, even if there is a conflict with the social macro- and micro-environment. In acmeology, as a rule, one talks only about the positive qualities of a person that have reached their heights in positive personality dynamics [1–4, 6, 7, 17]. We propose, for the purpose of a comprehensive analysis of the individual's attributes, to extend this definition to negative dynamics as well.

It is a novel and not observed field. Given the inclusion of deprivation factors into the model of the personality functioning in the virtual space, it is logical to assume that the attributes of a person ("portrait") can be fuller not only from the positions of the positive, but also from the positions of the negative, which has developed as a consequence of deprivation [8, 9].

The acmeological concept of individuality is currently considered taking into account the following factors:

- personality identity factor as a result of its purely individual formation on the basis of ontogenetic development, where the properties of the individual, personality and subject of activity are focused.
- factor of the personality identity formation under the influence of the surrounding society with the inclusion of energy, information and field exchange of meanings and values;
- factor of the spiritual and practical activities of a person associated with joint actions within the micro- and macro-community;
- factor of the formation of individual acmeological identity of the human, that is, individual identity in the highest degree of its development with a positive or negative self-assessment.

When analyzing the emotional-modal behavior of a person in conditions of interpersonal, socio-economic, interethnic, confessional, political and geopolitical deprivation, including value expectations and value capabilities, the analysis of the personal, individual "portrait" of communicants participating in the social-network discourse becomes especially important [10–16].

2   Approaches to Research, Material, Method

The research is based on the mental, moral and ethical development of the subjects in terms of social network discourse. The proposed acmeological approach to the study of attributes, that is, individual "portraits" of participants in the social-network discourse will later selectively identify and determine the following:

- degree of depth (taking into account the positive or negative) of "immersion" into the development of one or another idea explicated by the author in the process of virtual communication;
- degree of dynamics of the individual and personal evaluation in time.

To solve this problem, it is proposed to develop a method for constructing acmeological matrices, which will allow for a multidimensional study of the structure of personality features based on the speech discourse product.

The acmeological matrix shall include various features that the subject (author of the text (in our study – a fragment of the discourse)) assign to described personalities, objects, events, processes, phenomena, etc. N texts (fragments of the text) of a certain participant of the social-network discourse shall be included in this analysis.

In the course of the analysis, various types of links between the nominations of personalities, objects, events, processes, phenomena, etc. should be pointed out:

* strong, medium, weak;
* positive, negative, neutral;
* unilateral, bilateral, multilateral;
* conscious, unconscious;
* repeating, non-repeating;
* semantically explicable, semantically not explicable (allusions, indirect speech acts, etc.);
* synsemantic, autosemantic;
* monothematic, polythematic;
* informationally saturated (high contextual), information-unsaturated (low contextual);
* provoking debates (specific actions, acts of destructive nature), not provoking debates (specific actions, deeds of destructive nature).

Thus, using the method of establishing the acmeological identity of a person used, for example, in psychology, valeology, pedagogy, in our study, for the first time it is proposed to develop a special method for constructing an acmeological matrix with a number of new re-interpreted positions and further corrective additions, taking into account the verbal characteristics of the analyzed material and tasks, among which the task of building an individual social and virtual "portrait" of communicants plays a special role.

When constructing an acmeological matrix of a particular person using verbal and paraverbal data, it is suggested to rely on information about the main ways of "personality personalization":

* personality and his/her relationship with particular members of community ("intimate, close, distant", etc.);
* personality and his/her attitude to the temporary factor (by "yesterday – today – tomorrow" type);
* personality and his/her understanding of the social distance "me and the power";
* personality and his/her existential status ("I'm in a team", "I'm outside the team", "I'm on my own");
* personality and his/her attitude to the abrupt change of social paradigms ("change of power", "change of goals", etc.);
* personality and his/her idea of their values (material, spiritual, aesthetic ones, etc.).

The conflict between the above features of the personality's personalization and the degree of the aim attainability causes an effect of deprivation, which in ontogenesis generates a negative dynamics in the development of the personality and can lead to an acmeological peak of a negative nature with the resulting most manifested consequences (destructive actions, terror, etc.). The development of the method of acmeological description of the personality in a negative way has a direct relation to the cognitive approach based on the theory of imprinting, which are an integral part of a person's individuality.

For the first time in solving the problems posed in the study, we propose a method for constructing an acmeological matrix based on verbal and paraverbal characteristics of the verbal and paraverbal product of the personality reflecting the relationship between a certain degree of frustration and the effect of deprivation.

As a result, we expect to obtain individual attributes of a person analyzed and the possibility of establishing the presence or absence of deprivation of a certain type. Further research will allow establishing groups of deprived individuals, that is, an integrative picture correlated with the task of establishing a typology of verbal and paraverbal determinants of the emotional-modal behavior of communicants under conditions of the multi-factor deprivation regarding electronic media sources, social networks and IP Internet telephony. In the future, the simulation will be carried out taking into account individual acmeological matrices correlated with individual features of the acmeological dynamics with reference to each analyzed person. An individual acmeological matrix pattern is presented below (Table 1):

Table 1. Individual acmeological matrix as the personality attribution of acmeological dynamics (on the basis of annotated database analysis)

№№ of texts (text fragments)	Text analysis criteria													
	Temporality			Intertextuality		Distance with regard to the power			Individualism / community spirit		Masculinity / Femininity		Reaction to an abrupt change of events		
	Past	present	Future	with precedence	without precedence	close	medium	distant	individualism ("me")	community spirit ("we")	Masculinity	Femininity	negative	positive	Neutral

A representative annotated corpus of Russian electronic media discourse has been created. The corpus includes samples of written and spoken monologues, dialogues, and macropolylogues classified with respect to their form, content, function, influence types, emotional and modal colouring etc. One excerpt from the corpus with all types of annotation is provided here as an example (Table 2). Each item of the annotated corpus includes the headline, name of the resource, a link to the SND fragment, date of "publication", main topic of the verbal item, number of communicants, type of communication (monologue, dialogue, polylogue), gender and approximate age of communicants, their social and economic status and nationality, communication means (verbalics, paraverbalics, non-verbalics).

The existing annotated linguistic data corpus (created during the previous year of the research) was significantly expanded to include new subcorpora representing socioeconomic and ecological topic areas. The written language part of the corpus comprises 40 Mb of social network communication sample texts (which makes about 7 million tokens) by at least 4000 authors. The spoken language corpus (including both

Table 2. An example from annotated corpus of Russian electronic media discourse

Назв-ание кли-па	Описа-ние	Ин-фор-мант	Роль	Ин-тер-вал	Невер-бальное поведе-ние	Ма-нера гово-рения	Просодические средства переда-чи эмоционального и эмоцио-нально-модального состояния-росодия	Способ заполне-ния пауз	Использу-емая лексика	Эмо-ция/ЭС
Ми-тинг	Группа моло-дежи проте-стует против собра-ния неофа-шистов в Санкт-Петер-бурге, в гости-нице «Хо-лидей Инн» нака-нуне дня победы.	1м	участ-ник ми-тинга	0:00:05 - 0:00:16	Поворот головы (не смотрит в камеру, отводит взгляд), поджима-ет правый угол рта.	напря-жен-ная	средний мелодический регистр; узкий мелодический диапазон; преобладание форм мелодической завершенности; средний темп; стабильно-постоянный темп; постоянный ритм; узкий диапазон изменения громкости; равномерная громкость в пределах высказывания; средняя частотность пауз; средняя длительность пауз; преоб-ладание незаполненных пауз;	"ааа"	сходка; я против этого	недо-вольство
		2м	участ-ник ми-тинга	0:00:16 - 0:00:55	Дергает левым углом рта, усмешка	нена-пря-жен-ная	низкий мелодический регистр; узкий мелодический диапазон; преобладание форм мелодической завершенности; замедленный темп; стабильно-постоянный темп; постоянный ритм; узкий диапазон изменения громкости; равномерная громкость в пределах высказыва-ния; средняя частотность пауз; средняя длительность пауз; преоб-ладание заполненных пауз; карта-вость	"ааа", "ммм", как бы	ну, в общем заклей-менных у себя на родине людей; планы по пере-устройству человече-ства	недо-воль-ство, с ухмыл-кой
	Показан митинг моло-дежи и вмеша-тель-ство в него поли-цей-ских.	3м	участ-ник ми-тинга	0:03:04 - 0:03:35	Поворот головы от камеры, «кривит» род (губы сжаты, углы опущены вниз)	напря-жен-ная	низкий мелодический регистр; узкий мелодический диапазон; преобладание форм мелодической завершенности; умеренно-средний темп; стабильно-постоянный темп; постоянный ритм; узкий диапазон изменения громкости; равномерная громкость в пределах высказыва-ния; средняя частотность пауз; средняя длительность пауз; преоб-ладание незаполненных пауз	"аам"	теперь с этой историей покончено; нога моя и моих товарищей сюда больше никогда не ступит	неприязнь, брезгли-вость
		1ж	участ-ник ми-тинга	0:03:35 - 0:04:33	-	напря-жен-ная	монотонность, средний мелодический регистр; узкий мелодический диапа-зон; преобладание форм мелодической завершенности; умеренно-средний, стабильно-постоянный темп; постоян-ный ритм; узкий диапазон изменения громкости; равномерная громкость в пределах высказывания; равномерная паузация; средняя частотность пауз; средняя длительность пауз; преобла-дание незаполненных пауз; "резкий" тембральный оттенок	"эээ", как бы, ну	нацист-ский форум; у меня возникло очень сильное негодова-ние по этому поводу; пример подмены понятий	неприязнь

audio and video recordings representing multimodal communication) contains 50 h of speech by at least 300 speakers. The size of the spoken language corpus is 35 GB.

All the data collected are classified according to their predominant topic areas mapping to respective predominant types of deprivations. The topic areas include politics, geopolitics, ecology, economy, interethnic and interreligious conflicts, and interpersonal relationships.

On the basis of the results of lexical-semantic, perceptual auditory and acoustic types of analysis an inventory of verbal (for written and spoken discourse) and par-averbal (for spoken discourse) descriptors was defined characterizing various types of deprivations with respect to their correlation with different axiological categories (such as prosperity, power, influence, social standing, personal fulfillment, security, economic competition, political and geopolitical ambitions, authoritarian orientation). Groups of features were developed allowing for partial automatization of the analysis of the language corpus. Lists of lexical markers corresponding to the abovementioned features were defined. Various speech acts were classified in accordance with the defined feature groups.

At this stage, a model was developed for searching the negative acmeological component characterizing the dynamics of speech behavior of the SND communicants. The principle of cognitive dissonance (according to L. Festinger [5]) is significantly manifested in the individual negative acmeological model (based on the material of our observations with reference to the social-network discourse), when SND users knowing of the indecency of any judgments (for example, in terms of "outrages") violate all laws of ethics and act verbally (in the format of a locutionary act) against the common sense and established ethical norms well-known in the given community (Fig. 1).

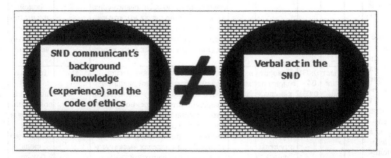

Fig. 1. The model (No. 1) of cognitive dissonance implemented in the SND in the presence of a deprivation factor regarding individual negative acmeological dynamics in case the user's background knowledge and verbal means of a specific communicative act do not match

The development of each of the deprivation constituents in time can be accompanied by such complementary verbal determinants of human speech behavior as aggression, hostility, resentment, etc., without any indication of consensus and compromise. The formation of the acmeological attributes of an individual (at least by the SND data) is directly related to the subject on which the memory of the Internet user is focused: on the past (for example, nostalgia), the present (surrounding reality) or the future (vision in time dynamics), see Figs. 2, 3, 4 and 5.

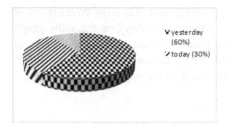

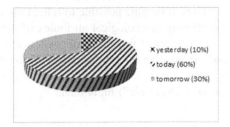

Fig. 2. The case of "orientation to the past" (for example, nostalgia for the past)

Fig. 3. The case of "orientation to the present" (for example, criticism of current events)

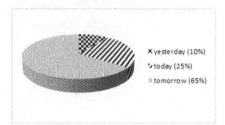

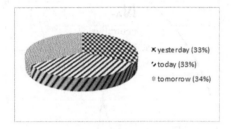

Fig. 4. The case of "orientation to the future" (for example, an optimistic perspective of development for certain events)

Fig. 5. The case of "disorientation in responses to external stimuli" (for example, depression, disappointment, indifference to all events discussed in the SND)

Further in the course of the study, it was necessary to establish a functional relationship between the two variables, their ratio on the graph of the functional dependence based on two abscissae (according to the Cartesian system): (a) for negative acmeological dynamics; and (b) for positive acmeological dynamics (Fig. 6). The dynamics can be recorded: (a) for individual SND users, (b) for groups of SND users; as applied to the time quantization, taking into account days of a week, weeks of a month, months of a year, etc.

It is proposed to introduce two abscissae (from 0 to N: for N_{A+} and N_{A-}) and two ordinates (from 0 to N: for N_{A0} at N_{A+} and N_{A-}) for constructing the dynamics of the acmeological matrix $DA\mp$, where

A− is negative acmeological dynamics;
A + is positive acmeological dynamics;
N_{A-} is neutral dynamics with A−;
N_{A+} is neutral dynamics with A +.

This approach made it possible to obtain two hemispheres (semi-spheres), each containing: a) a negative acmeological curve with A− (along the abscissa) and a neutral curve with A− (along the ordinate), and b) a positive curve with A + (along the abscissa) and a neutral curve with A + (along the ordinate).

Thus, it became possible to reflect the change (dynamics) of two (or three) types of establishing acmeological attributes of the "electronic personality" on the same graph of the combined functional dependence: the negative in combination with the neutral and the positive in combination with the neutral, which makes it possible to establish the presence or absence of the deprivation component in the cognitive portrait of the virtual ("electronic") individual.

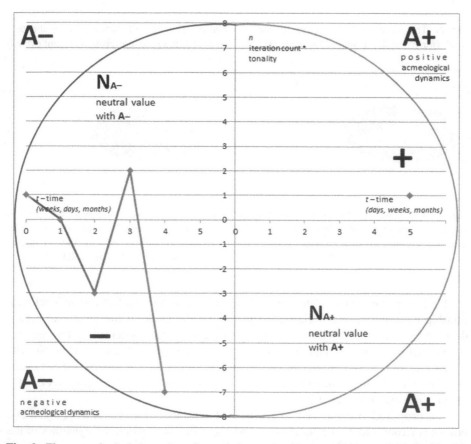

Fig. 6. The acmeological dynamics of a varied type (positive/negative/neutral) depicted with two hemispheres: a hemisphere (on the left), which includes values of negative acmeological dynamics and neutral indicators that make up the negative acmeological dynamics, and a hemisphere (on the right) including values of positive acmeological dynamics and neutral indicators that make up the positive acmeological dynamics

The above functional relationship between the negative acmeological dynamics of the "electronic personality's" deprivation state (DA–) and his/her verbal (V), par-averbal (PV) and nonverbal (NV) content in the SND can be expressed by the following formula:

$D_{A-}(t) = f(n(V(t), PV(t), NV(t)), t)$, where $D_{A-}(t)$ is the dynamics of negative acmeological attributes of the individual; V(t) are values of the verbal content in time; PV(t) are values of the paraverbal content in time (prosody, etc.); NV(t) are values of the non-verbal content in time (facial expressions, gestures, etc.).

Using the proposed approach, depending on the problem solved in the course of the study, it is possible to distinguish:

- only verbal one-component means (V(t)) of transmitting a negative attitude of the individual to events, personalities, objects, etc. considered in time;
- two-component mixed verbal (V(t)) and paraverbal (PV(t)) means of the same negative modality considered in time;
- three-component mixed verbal, paraverbal and non-verbal means (V(t)/PV(t)/NV (t)) of the negative acmeological attributes of the "electronic" individual considered in time.

3 Conclusion

The proposed model of qualitative and quantitative evaluation of the acmeological attributes of the "electronic" individual on the material generated during the study conducted within the framework of this project appears to be unique and promising and can be used in the development of a software product which helps establish individual and group specificities for achieving the acmeological peak (particularly of a negative nature) to solve the main task of the study.

The acmeological method is very perspective in forensic linguistics and phonetic too in the domain of personality identification and attribution. The acmeological features can be not SND-user-specific, but can characterize a group of SND users by determining users' intellectual, social, material, spiritual, aesthetic etc. parameters.

This approach to acmeological analysis can be realized, first of all, with regard to legal communication in international community in a range of national and international semiotic, sociolinguistic, psychological, philosophical, sociopolitical, institutional etc. contexts [18, 19].

Acknowledgment. This research is supported by Russian Science Foundation. Project No.14-18-01059.

References

1. Ananiev, B.G.: Human as a Subject of Cognition. Leningrad State University Press, Leningrad (1989). (in Russian)
2. Anisimov, O.S.: Professionalism in training and education. In: Derkach, A.A. (ed.). Foundation of General and Applied Acmeology, pp. 205–219. RAGS, Moskva (1995) (in Russian)
3. Bogdanov, E.N., Zazykin, V.G.: Introduction to Acmeology. University Press, Kaluga, Kaluga State Ped (2000). (in Russian)

4. Bransky, V.P., Pozharsky, S.D.: Social synergetics and acmeology. Theory of self-organization of individual and of society. Polytekhnika, Sankt Petersburg (2001) (in Russian)
5. Festinger, L.: Cognitive dissonance. Sci. Am. **207**(4), 93–107 (1962)
6. Il'in, V.V., Pozharsky, C.D. Philosophy and Acmeology. Polytechnika, Sankt Petersburg (2003) (in Russian)
7. Polanyi, M.: Personal Knowledge: Towards a Post-Critical Philosophy. Taylor & Francis, London (2005)
8. Potapova, R.: From deprivation to aggression verbal and non verbal social network communication. In: Global Science and Innovation: Materials of the VI International Scientific Conference. Chicago, 18–19 November 2015, Chicago (USA). Accent Graphics Communications Publishing Office, 2015, vol. 1, pp. 129–137 (2015)
9. Potapova, R.K.: Deprivation as a basic mechanism of human verbal and paraverbal behavior (Regarding social network communication). In: Potapova, R.K. (ed.). Speech Communication in Information Space, pp. 17–36. Lenand Press, Moskva (2017) (in Russian)
10. Potapova, R.K., Potapov, V.V.: Language, Speech, Personality. Languages of the Slavic Cultures Press, Moskva (2006). (in Russian)
11. Potapova, R.K., Potapov, V.V.: Speech Communication: From Sound to Utterance. Languages of the Slavic Cultures Press, Moskva (2012). (in Russian)
12. Potapova, R., Potapov, V.: Auditory and visual recognition of emotional behaviour of foreign language subjects (by native and non-native speakers). In: Železný, M., Habernal, I., Ronzhin, A. (eds.) SPECOM 2013. LNCS, vol. 8113, pp. 62–69. Springer, Cham (2013). doi:10.1007/978-3-319-01931-4_9
13. Potapova, R., Potapov, V.: Associative mechanism of foreign spoken language perception (Forensic Phonetic Aspect). In: Ronzhin, A., Potapova, R., Delic, V. (eds.) SPECOM 2014. LNCS, vol. 8773, pp. 113–122. Springer, Cham (2014). doi:10.1007/978-3-319-11581-8_14
14. Potapova, R., Potapov, V.: Cognitive mechanism of semantic content decoding of spoken discourse in noise. In: Ronzhin, A., Potapova, R., Fakotakis, N. (eds.) SPECOM 2015. LNCS, vol. 9319, pp. 153–160. Springer, Cham (2015). doi:10.1007/978-3-319-23132-7_19
15. Potapova, R., Potapov, V.: On individual polyinformativity of speech and voice regarding speakers auditive attribution (forensic phonetic aspect). In: Ronzhin, A., Potapova, R., Németh, G. (eds.) SPECOM 2016. LNCS, vol. 9811, pp. 507–514. Springer, Cham (2016). doi:10.1007/978-3-319-43958-7_61
16. Potapova, R., Potapov, V.: Polybasic attribution of social network discourse. In: Ronzhin, A., Potapova, R., Németh, G. (eds.) SPECOM 2016. LNCS, vol. 9811, pp. 539–546. Springer, Cham (2016). doi:10.1007/978-3-319-43958-7_65
17. Tartakovsky, M.: Acmeology. Panorama Press, Moskva (1992). (in Russian)
18. Vijay, K.B., Hafner, C.A., Lindsey, M., Wagner, A. (eds.): Transparency, Power, and Control: Perspectives on Legal Communication. Ashgate, Farnham (2012)
19. Wagner, A., Brockman, J.M. (eds.): Prospects of Legal Semiotics. Springer, London (2010)

Improved Speaker Adaptation by Combining I-vector and fMLLR with Deep Bottleneck Networks

Thai Son Nguyen[✉], Kevin Kilgour, Matthias Sperber, and Alex Waibel

Institute for Anthropomatics and Robotics,
Karlsruhe Institute of Technology, Karlsruhe, Germany
thai.nguyen@kit.edu

Abstract. This paper investigates how deep bottleneck neural networks can be used to combine the benefits of both i-vectors and speaker-adaptive feature transformations. We show how a GMM-based speech recognizer can be greatly improved by applying feature-space maximum likelihood linear regression (fMLLR) transformation to outputs of a deep bottleneck neural network trained on a concatenation of regular Mel filterbank features and speaker i-vectors. The addition of the i-vectors reduces word error rate of the GMM system by 3–7% compared to an identical system without i-vectors. We also examine Deep Neural Network (DNN) systems trained on various combinations of i-vectors, fMLLR-transformed bottleneck features and other feature space transformations. The best approach results speaker-adapted DNNs which showed 15–19% relative improvement over a strong speaker-independent DNN baseline.

Keywords: DNN · fMLLR · I-vector · Bottleneck extraction

1 Introduction

In statistical speech recognition, speaker adaptation techniques can fall into two categories: Model adaptation involves modifying the parameters of the acoustic model to fit the actual speech data from a target speaker. Maximum Likelihood Linear Regression (MLLR) [5] and Maximum A Posteriori (MAP) [7] are the powerful model adaptation techniques that improve Gaussian Mixture Models (GMMs). However, there is no similar technique for Deep Neural Network (DNN) models which have become prominent in recent years. Due to their many large hidden layers, DNNs have a significantly higher number of parameters. It is therefore hard to adapt DNNs with only a small amount of data. Several studies [11,19] have shown that DNN models have greater invariance to speaker variations resulting in model adaptation being less effective than for GMMs. Further, model adaptation usually results in new models for individual speakers, significantly increasing complexity and required storage space.

Unlike model adaptation, feature adaptation techniques use regular acoustic features and adaptation data to provide new features which better fit the trained

© Springer International Publishing AG 2017
A. Karpov et al. (Eds.): SPECOM 2017, LNAI 10458, pp. 417–426, 2017.
DOI: 10.1007/978-3-319-66429-3_41

acoustic model, thus improving recognition accuracy without the need to change the model. Feature adaptation is attractive for dealing with the limitations of model adaptation, especially for DNNs. Feature-space MLLR (fMLLR) [5] is a well-known adaptation technique which makes better inputs for GMMs. However, providing good fMLLR features for DNNs is challenging: Due to the huge difference between DNN and GMM models, fMLLR features which are optimized for GMMs are not guaranteed to be better for DNNs than other regular features. Recently, identity vectors (i-vectors) for speaker representation have been introduced [3], and have been successfully used in speaker verification and speaker recognition. Further research [18,20] proved that i-vectors can be used in conjunction with regular features to improve DNN performance.

In this paper we examine how i-vectors and fMLLR transformations can be combined in order to improve both GMM and DNN systems. In particular we analyse speaker-adaptive bottleneck features (SA-BNF), where log scale Mel filterbank (FBANK) features are concatenated with i-vectors to form their input features and investigate how both speaker-adaptive bottleneck features and speaker-independent bottleneck features can be further transformed and augmented before being used as DNN or GMM input features.

The paper is organized as follows: Sect. 2 reviews speaker adaptation using fMLLR and i-vector techniques. In Sect. 3, the hierarchical combination of fMLLR and i-vectors is presented. The experiments and results are explained in Sects. 4 and 5. In Sect. 6, we conclude and discuss future work.

2 Speaker Adaptation Using fMLLR and I-vector

fMLLR is a commonly used adaptation technique for ASR systems. When a small amount of adaptation data for an individual speaker is available, fMLLR can be applied with a trained GMM to employ an affine transformation which transforms acoustic features for speaker normalization. The transformed features are well-known to be better inputs for the GMM system. [16] showed DNN systems can also be improved when using fMLLR features. In their study, the best input features for DNN system are obtained using a sequence of transformations including Linear Discriminate Analysis (LDA), global Semi-tied covariance (STC) and fMLLR. The authors presented 3% absolute improvement of the proposed DNN over a very good adapted GMM. In [14], the authors proposed to estimate fMLLR transforms using simple target models (STM) and combine with FBANK features to improve DNN performance.

I-vectors describes a speaker's identity and are successfully used in speaker verification and speaker recognition tasks. This powerful technique is also useful for speech recognition since i-vectors encapsulate the speaker relevant information in a low-dimensional representation. Applied to speech recognition, [18,20] augment regular acoustic features with i-vectors as a speaker adaptation for their DNNs. Both works showed that i-vectors possibly provide additional information allowing for an improving recognition performance. Saon et al. presented 10% relative improvement on 300 h of Switchboard data, while Senior et al. just showed

4% relative improvement on 1700 h of Google Voice data. [12] introduced speaker adaptive training for DNN (SAT-DNN) which learns an adaptation neural network to convert i-vectors to speaker-specific linear feature shifts. The original features (e.g. MFCC) are then speaker-normalized by adding theses shifts. Their SAT-DNN model achieved 13.5% relative improvement on 118 h of TED talks. In [1] i-vectors are incorporated with a bottleneck extraction architecture to improve low-resource ASR systems.

Recently, Tan et al. [22] have investigated to use i-vectors at different layers of a Long Short-Term Memory Recurrent Neural Network (LSTM-RNN) to normalise speaker variability. They reduced word error rates by 6.5% relative when using FMLLR features which are transformed from MFCC with LDA and STC. Tomashenko et al. [23] proposed to use bottleneck features for GMM-derived feature extraction and combine with fMLLR features to be DNN input.

In terms of speaker adaptation, fMLLR tries to remove speaker variability while i-vector provides more speaker information. Both techniques help to improve feature processing in different ways. The aforementioned study [18] also proposed to simply augment their fMLLR features with i-vectors to further improve their recognition results. Our study is motivated by that paper and investigates how to best combine fMLLR and i-vectors.

3   Combining I-vector and fMLLR

Deep bottleneck network (DBNF) has been shown to extract effective speaker-independent bottleneck features (SI-BNF) to both GMM and DNN models. In this study, we use DBNF to perform several combinations of i-vector and fMLLR adaptations. These combinations yield improved speaker-adapted features for GMMs and DNNs. An overview of our proposed feature extraction process is shown in Fig. 1. We propose to use i-vectors as additional features to a DBNF for extracting speaker-adapted bottleneck features, then perform fMLLR and other linear transformations before feeding them to GMM systems. To build speaker-adapted features for DNNs, we combine i-vectors and fMLLR features that are estimated on top of the bottleneck features.

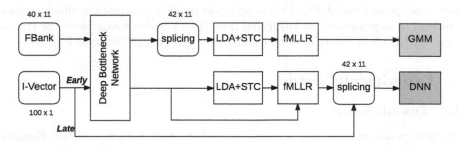

Fig. 1. Hierarchical combination of bottleneck, fMLLR and i-vector features for either early or late combinations

In Sects. 3.1 and 3.3 we discuss two different approaches of integrating i-vectors. Section 3.2 explains how fMLLR and other transformations can be used in our feature extraction pipeline.

3.1   Early I-vectors

Having a similar architecture to DNNs, DBNFs are also capable of modeling high-dimensional correlated input features. We investigate the ability of incorporating acoustic features and i-vectors to train DBNFs. In our approach, regular acoustic features (e.g. FBANK) are spliced for 11 consecutive frames and then concatenated with i-vector features to be fed into DBNFs. After the training, we are able to build speaker-adapted bottleneck neural networks which can extract speaker-adapted bottleneck features (SA-BNF).

3.2   fMLLR

LDA can be used to extract the most useful features for the classification from many consecutive acoustic frames while STC transformation is applied to decorrelate the input features. These techniques are popularly adopted to transform Mel-frequency cepstral coefficients (MFCC) [16] or bottleneck features [8, 25] to become effective input for GMM models. Then, fMLLR transformation is further estimated and applied to make the acoustic data of individual speakers more accurately modeled by the trained GMMs. We also perform these transformations on top of SA-BNF to build speaker-adapted features for the GMMs. However, to keep the same temporal context of frames fed into the DNNs (i.e., wider context reduces the classification performance), we do not use LDA for feature-dimensionality reduction from concatenated features. Instead, we propose to either estimate fMLLR transformation directly on SI-BNF or SA-BNF without using LDA and STC transformations, or use them without applying context-window. So that, we can later splice 11 frames of fMLLR features as the input to the DNNs.

3.3   Late I-vectors

After applying fMLLR transformation, new transformed features are supposed to have less speaker variability. Providing again speaker information with i-vectors can lead to improvement as suggested from [18]. We also concatenate the transformed SI-BNF or SA-BNF with i-vectors for different DNN input features.

4   Experimental Setup

4.1   Overall Setup

In the experiments, we used a big training dataset of 460 h from 12000 English talks. This dataset includes the TED-LIUM [17], Quaero [21] and Broadcast News [9] corpora. We used the tst2013 and the tst2014 sets from the IWSLT evaluation campaign [2] which sequentially contains 27 and 15 talks.

The DBNFs were constructed with 5 hidden layers containing 2000 units, followed by a 42 units bottleneck layer and the final classification layer, using input as 11 stacked frames of 40-dimensional mel scale filterbank coefficients with or without concatenating i-vector features. All the DNN models also share the same architecture which has 6 hidden layers with 2000 units per layer. The input of the DNNs is 11 stacked frames of 42-dimensional transformed SI-BNF or SA-BNF, with or without combining i-vector features. We used sigmoid activation for hidden layers and soft-max for output layer.

DNN and DBNF systems were trained using cross-entropy loss function to predict 8000 context-dependent states. The same training method is applied for all DNNs and DBNFs, which includes pre-training with denoising auto-encoders and followed by fine-tuning with back-propagation. We used an exponential schedule for all of the trainings. The GMM models were trained using incremental splitting of Gaussians (MAS) [10] and followed by optimal space training (OFS) (a variant of STC [6]) if LDA features are used.

The systems were decoded using Janus Recognition Toolkit (JRTK) [4] with the Cantab 4-gram language model [24] from more than 150k words.

4.2 I-vector Extraction

To extract i-vectors, a full universal background model (UBM) with 2048 mixtures was trained on the training dataset using 20 Mel-frequency cepstral coefficients with delta and delta-delta features appended. The total variability matrices were estimated for extracting 100-dimensional i-vector which was observed to give the optimal recognition performance in [18,20]. The UBM model training and i-vector extraction were performed by using the sre08 module from the Kaldi toolkit [15].

4.3 fMLLR Estimation

The GMMs trained with SI-BNF and SA-BNF were used to compute fMLLR transformations. The process of fMLLR estimation were performed as the traditional approach. During the training, we used the adaptation data of the same speaker and the reference transcriptions to do the alignment, while the same GMMs were used as first-pass systems to generate transcriptions in the testing.

5 Experimental Results

5.1 Baseline Systems

In our experiments, we used a DNN system with FBANK features as the speaker independent baseline (SI-DNN). This is a strong baseline since DNNs training with mel scale filterbank is known to outperform other regular features [13]. The other baseline is a speaker-adapted DNN (SA-DNN) using i-vectors. This baseline is similar to the speaker-adapted DNNs presented in [20] except our

Table 1. Word error rate of baseline systems

Baseline	tst2013 (tst2014)
SI-DNN	16.2 (12.9)
SA-DNN	**15.1 (12.4)**

i-vectors are extracted for speaker-level instead of utterance-level. The results of the baselines on two test sets are shown in Table 1. In our setup, we are able to reproduce the improvement when using i-vector adaptation for DNN systems in both the test sets. The improvement is not large as reported in [18], but is comparable to [20] since we used a similar baseline setup.

5.2   Results from GMM Systems

Table 2 presents the results of our evaluated GMM systems. The first three columns show the possible techniques applied to make inputs to the GMMs. The techniques include *Early I-vector* for extracting speaker-adapted bottleneck features, followed by splicing and *LDA+STC* transformations, and *fMLLR* transformation at the last step. The last column presents word error rates (WER) on the both test sets.

By using discriminative bottleneck features, the GMM systems can achieve good recognition performance which is close to the DNN baseline. This also explains the smaller gains of applying *LDA+STC* and *fMLLR* transformations than performing on regular acoustic features such as MFCC. However, these techniques have still been effective when producing constant improvements over different test sets.

The results of the GMMs using SA-BNF are consistently better than using SI-BNF with identical constructions. The regular bottleneck GMM (with full transformation techniques) is 3–7% less effective than the adapted bottleneck GMM. This shows that DBNF can explore the adapted input with the addition of i-vectors to provide better discriminative features.

Table 2. Comparison of word error rate for GMM systems using context-window of 462 bottleneck features

Early I-vector	Splice+LDA+STC	fMLLR	tst2013 (tst2014)
✗	✗	✗	16.7 (13.1)
✗	✓	✗	15.9 (12.5)
✗	✓	✓	15.4 (12.3)
✓	✗	✗	15.7 (12.7)
✓	✓	✗	14.9 (12.4)
✓	✓	✓	**14.4 (11.9)**

In Table 3, we present the performance of different GMMs that were used to estimate fMLLR features for DNN systems. Without using context-window of bottleneck features, the combination of *LDA+STC* transformations shows less effective. However, using *fMLLR* and *Early I-vector* still presents achievable improvements.

It is worth noting that while the trained GMM systems have good performance, the best speaker-adapted GMM is even better than SA-DNN baseline. This indicates that feeding their input features to DNNs may improve systems due to the better capacity of DNNs in classification task.

Table 3. Comparison of word error rate for GMM systems using 42 bottleneck features

Early I-vector	LDA+STC	fMLLR	tst2013 (tst2014)
✗	✓	✗	16.5 (12.9)
✗	✗	✓	16.1 (12.5)
✗	✓	✓	15.8 (12.3)
✓	✓	✗	15.5 (12.7)
✓	✗	✓	15.0 (12.0)
✓	✓	✓	15.1 (12.2)

5.3 Results from DNN Systems

In Table 4, we compare the results of the examined DNNs using transformed SI-BNF with or without the addition of *Late I-vector*. Again, the last column shows the results in word error rates, while the other columns indicates the usage of our proposed adaptation techniques.

Table 4. Comparison of word error rate for DNN systems

LDA+STC	fMLLR	Late I-vector	tst2013 (tst2014)
✗	✗	✗	15.3 (12.4)
✓	✗	✗	15.4 (12.5)
✗	✓	✗	14.5 (11.8)
✓	✓	✗	14.8 (12.1)
✗	✗	✓	14.1 (11.5)
✓	✗	✓	14.8 (12.7)
✗	✓	✓	**13.1 (11.1)**
✓	✓	✓	13.7 (11.3)

Interestingly, *LDA+STC* transformations which usually produce better input to GMM modeling show a negative effect when applying to DNN inputs. However, performing *fMLLR* and *Late I-vector* adaptations on bottleneck features individually show effectiveness. When concatenating fMLLR transformed features with i-vectors, we found the best features combination. The best DNN system with *fMLLR* and *Late I-vector* gives 15–19% relative improvement over SI-DNN baseline and 11–13% over SA-DNN baseline.

Since SA-BNF features have been effective to GMM modeling, we also investigate to see if the DNNs can be also benefited from it. Table 5 compares the DNNs with SA-BNF against SI-BNF. Using *fMLLR* transformation on top of SA-BNF can improve the performance up to 8% relative. We could not however achieve further improvement with the DNNs by *Late I-vector* together with *Early I-vector* and *fMLLR*. That may be due to either fMLLR transformation not being able to completely remove speaker variability, or our used DNN architecture not being able to exploit this combined structure.

Table 5. Comparison of DNN systems with SA-BNF against SI-BNF

Early I-vector	fMLLR	Late I-vector	tst2013 (tst2014)
✗	✗	✗	15.3 (12.4)
✓	✗	✗	14.6 (12.6)
✗	✓	✗	14.8 (12.1)
✓	✓	✗	14.1 (11.5)
✗	✓	✓	13.1 (11.1)
✓	✓	✓	13.7 (11.2)

6 Conclusion and Future Work

We have presented an effective way of combining deep bottleneck network with i-vectors and fMLLR to produce speaker-adapted features for ASR systems. In our experiments, a GMM system with speaker-adapted bottleneck features outperforms a regular bottleneck GMM system with 3–7% relative improvement, while a DNN system even achieves higher improvements of 15–19% over a strong DNN baseline. Since the used deep bottlenecks network is open to modeling a variety of different input features, the replacement of *Late I-vector* or *Late I-vector* with other speaker codes, or FBANK with other single or multiple regular features can be done without changing the feature extraction pipeline. A further study can go in this direction to better explore speaker-adapted bottlenecks features.

References

1. Cardinal, P., Dehak, N., Zhang, Y., Glass, J.: Speaker adaptation using the i-vector technique for bottleneck features. In: Proceedings of Interspeech, vol. 2015 (2015)
2. Cettolo, M., Niehues, J., Stüker, S., Bentivogli, L., Frederico, M.: Report on the 10th iwslt evaluation campaign. In: The International Workshop on Spoken Language Translation (IWSLT) (2013)
3. Dehak, N., Kenny, P.J., Dehak, R., Dumouchel, P., Ouellet, P.: Front-end factor analysis for speaker verification. IEEE Trans. Audio Speech Lang. Process. **19**(4), 788–798 (2011)
4. Finke, M., Geutner, P., Hild, H., Kemp, T., Ries, K., Westphal, M.: The Karlsruhe VERBMOBIL speech recognition engine. In: Proceedings of ICASSP (1997)
5. Gales, M.J.: Maximum likelihood linear transformations for HMM-based speech recognition. Comput. Speech Lang. **12**(2), 75–98 (1998)
6. Gales, M.J.: Semi-tied covariance matrices for hidden markov models. IEEE Trans. Speech Audio Process. **7**(3), 272–281 (1999)
7. Gauvain, J.L., Lee, C.H.: Maximum a posteriori estimation for multivariate Gaussian mixture observations of Markov chains. IEEE Trans. Speech Audio Process. **2**(2), 291–298 (1994)
8. Gehring, J., Miao, Y., Metze, F., Waibel, A.: Extracting deep bottleneck features using stacked auto-encoders. In: 2013 IEEE International Conference on Acoustics, Speech and Signal Processing, pp. 3377–3381 (2013)
9. Graff, D.: The 1996 broadcast news speech and language-model corpus. In: Proceedings of the DARPA Workshop on Spoken Language Technology (1997)
10. Kaukoranta, T., Franti, P., Nevalainen, O.: A new iterative algorithm for VQ codebook generation. In: Proceedings of the 1998 International Conference on Image Processing, ICIP 1998, vol. 2, pp. 589–593 (1998)
11. Liao, H.: Speaker adaptation of context dependent deep neural networks. In: 2013 IEEE International Conference on Acoustics, Speech and Signal Processing, pp. 7947–7951. IEEE (2013)
12. Miao, Y., Zhang, H., Metze, F.: Speaker adaptive training of deep neural network acoustic models using i-vectors. IEEE/ACM Trans. Audio Speech Lang. Process. **23**(11), 1938–1949 (2015)
13. Mohamed, A.R., Hinton, G., Penn, G.: Understanding how deep belief networks perform acoustic modelling. In: 2012 IEEE International Conference on Acoustics, Speech and Signal Processing (ICASSP), pp. 4273–4276 (2012)
14. Parthasarathi, S.H.K., Hoffmeister, B., Matsoukas, S., Mandal, A., Strom, N., Garimella, S.: fMLLR based feature-space speaker adaptation of DNN acoustic models. In: Proceedings of Interspeech, vol. 2015 (2015)
15. Povey, D., Ghoshal, A., Boulianne, G., Burget, L., Glembek, O., Goel, N., Hannemann, M., Motlicek, P., Qian, Y., Schwarz, P., et al.: The Kaldi speech recognition toolkit. In: IEEE 2011 Workshop on Automatic Speech Recognition and Understanding, No. EPFL-CONF-192584 (2011)
16. Rath, P.S., Povey, D., Veselý, K., Černocký, J.: Improved feature processing for deep neural networks. In: Proceedings of Interspeech 2013, vol. 8, pp. 109–113 (2013)
17. Rousseau, A., Deléglise, P., Estève, Y.: Enhancing the TED-LIUM corpus with selected data for language modeling and more TED talks. In: LREC (2014)
18. Saon, G., Soltau, H., Nahamoo, D., Picheny, M.: Speaker adaptation of neural network acoustic models using i-vectors. In: ASRU, pp. 55–59 (2013)

19. Seide, F., Li, G., Chen, X., Yu, D.: Feature engineering in context-dependent deep neural networks for conversational speech transcription. In: 2011 IEEE Workshop on Automatic Speech Recognition and Understanding (ASRU), pp. 24–29. IEEE (2011)
20. Senior, A., Lopez-Moreno, I.: Improving DNN speaker independence with i-vector inputs. In: 2014 IEEE International Conference on Acoustics, Speech and Signal Processing (ICASSP) (2014)
21. Stüker, S., Kilgour, K., Kraft, F.: Quaero 2010 speech-to-text evaluation systems. In: Nagel, W., Kröner, D., Resch, M. (eds.) High Performance Computing in Science and Engineering 2011, pp. 607–618. Springer, Heidelberg (2012). doi:10.1007/978-3-642-23869-7_44
22. Tan, T., Qian, Y., Yu, D., Kundu, S., Lu, L., Sim, K.C., Xiao, X., Zhang, Y.: Speaker-aware training of LSTM-RNNS for acoustic modelling. In: 2016 IEEE International Conference on Acoustics, Speech and Signal Processing (ICASSP), pp. 5280–5284. IEEE (2016)
23. Tomashenko, N., Khokhlov, Y., Esteve, Y.: On the use of gaussian mixture model framework to improve speaker adaptation of deep neural network acoustic models. In: Proceedings of INTERSPEECH (2016)
24. Williams, W., Prasad, N., Mrva, D., Ash, T., Robinson, T.: Scaling recurrent neural network language models. In: 2015 IEEE International Conference on Acoustics, Speech and Signal Processing (ICASSP), pp. 5391–5395 (2015)
25. Yu, D., Seltzer, M.L.: Improved bottleneck features using pretrained deep neural networks. In: Interspeech, vol. 237, p. 240 (2011)

Improving of LVCSR for Causal Czech Using Publicly Available Language Resources

Petr Mizera[✉] and Petr Pollak

Faculty of Electrical Engineering, Czech Technical University in Prague,
K13131, Technicka 2, 166 27 Praha 6, Czech Republic
{mizera,pollak}@fel.cvut.cz
http://www.fel.cvut.cz
http://noel.feld.cvut.cz/speechlab

Abstract. The paper presents the design of Czech casual speech recognition which is a part of the wider research focused on understanding very informal speaking styles. The study was carried out using the NCCCz corpus and the contributions of optimized acoustic and language models as well as pronunciation lexicon optimization were analyzed. Special attention was paid to the impact of publicly available corpora suitable for language model (LM) creation. Our final DNN-HMM system achieved in the task of casual speech recognition WER of 30–60% depending on LM used. The results of recognition for other speaking styles are presented as well for the comparison purposes. The system was built using KALDI toolkit and created recipes are available for the research community.

Keywords: Speech recognition · LVCSR · Spontaneous speech · Casual speech · Czech · NCCCz · KALDI

1 Introduction

Nowadays, Large Vocabulary Continuous Speech Recognition (LVCSR) is very well developed for all major world languages as well as for the majority of other languages, spoken mostly by smaller amount of native speakers. The main research in the field of automatic speech recognition (ASR) is focused on the development of systems for low resources languages and improvements to the existing systems deployed under adverse conditions [1,2]. The recognition of spontaneous speech is a typical example of an ASR system intended for real-life environments. It represents a very challenging task, mainly because the accuracy of spontaneous speech recognition is still rather low in comparison with generally high accuracy of standard LVCSR systems [3–7]. Spontaneous or colloquial speech recognition deals with problems similar across all languages, the most typical ones being: strong variability in the pronunciation (mainly strong pronunciation reduction), changes in word morphology, free word order in the sentence, sentence breaks, etc. [8,9].

Many authors have presented solutions for the above mentioned tasks and achieved results different for various languages, speaking styles, or recording

© Springer International Publishing AG 2017
A. Karpov et al. (Eds.): SPECOM 2017, LNAI 10458, pp. 427–437, 2017.
DOI: 10.1007/978-3-319-66429-3_42

conditions, e.g. the authors in [10] worked with transcriptions of oral interviews of survivors and witnesses of the Holocaust and they reported 39.60% Word Error Rate (WER) for English and 39.40% for Czech. However, when the level of speech spontaneity is higher, typically for very informal speaking style, the accuracy of speech recognition falls. Authors in [3] worked with the recordings of telephone conversations and reported 48% WER for the Czech language. Similarly in [6], authors presented results around 31–56% WER for the case of very informal speech recognition task.

The purpose of this paper is to present the results of very informal speech recognition performed on Nijmegen Corpus of Casual Czech (NCCCz) using the current state-of-the-art setup of LVCSR and publicly available language resources. It is a part of the research focused on understanding very informal speaking styles. The paper is organized as follows. In Sect. 2, we summarize the current state-of-the art of Czech LVCSR and we describe our approach applied to Czech casual speech recognition. Section 3 describes the setup of our experiments realized on casual speech data from NCCCz. In Sect. 4, the results of particular experiments are discussed in the context of other results obtained also for other speaking styles. The paper is concluded with the summary of achieved results and the information about the availability of used tools and recipes is presented.

2   Casual Speech Recognition for Czech

Due to the intensive studies of several research groups in the Czech Republic during last decades, available LVCSR systems for Czech language reach results similar to other languages spoken by a significantly higher number of native speakers. Concerning spontaneous speech recognition, several systems were presented e.g. in [3,6,9] or [7] and achieved accuracy is significantly lower then for LVCSR working under standard conditions.

Casual speech is defined as a way of talking used within a conversation among close people. Our investigation of casual speech recognition is done for the Czech language and it is based on exploiting the data from the Nijmegen Corpus of Casual Czech (NCCCz) [11] which consists of 30 h of spontaneous conversations of 60 speakers (30 males and 30 females recorded always in groups of 3 speakers of the same gender). The amount of available data is huge, since every group of three speakers was conversing for approximately 90 min. Also the recording procedure of NCCCz (the same one as used for the collection of similar Dutch, French, or Spanish corpora [12]) and the first analysis presented in [11] guarantee that NCCCZ contains highly casual speech. A lot of pronunciation reduction, extremely fast speed of talking, free grammar, word cutting, sentence restarts, etc. can be observed within speech data in NCCCz. Consequently, the recognition results using LVCSR with standard setup failed significantly [13].

2.1   LVCSR Architecture

The solution for improving the accuracy of casual speech recognition for Czech language is based on LVCSR based on Hidden Markov Models (HMM) and

Deep Neural Networks (DNN). Especially, the DNN-HMM based approach has been recently shown to increase the performance of LVCSR systems significantly [14, 15]. Encouraged by these results, we compared both the conventional GMM-HMM system and the modern DNN-HMM hybrid approach. For both architectures, we used a rather standard training procedure without any special modifications related to the spontaneous speech because the conversations available in NCCCz were recorded in the quiet environment.

2.2 Front-End Processing

As basic features, the Mel-frequency cepstral coefficients (MFCC) with the standard setup are used in our system. Standardly, pre-emphasis with the coefficient of 0.97 is applied, short-time frame has the length of 25 ms and is moved with the step of 10 ms. Mel-filter bank contains 30 bands in the frequency range 100–7940 Hz and 12 cepstral coefficients with additional $c[0]$ are computed. Cepstral mean normalization (CMN) over the speaker is applied and these features with delta and delta-delta parameters are used for the creation of initial acoustic models.

In the next steps only static and normalized MFCC features are extended with the both-side context of 5 frames to a higher dimension vector which is then reduced and decorrelated by LDA+MLLT transforms. This target feature vector of the size 40 is further speaker-adapted using feature-space Maximum Likelihood Linear Regression (fMLLR) and these features are used in designed LVCSR with GMM-HMM architecture as standard setup used nowadays in modern advanced LVCSR systems.

System based on DNN-HMM hybrid architecture works with above described features used for GMM-HMM system but for the purpose of an application at the input of DNN mean and variance normalization (MVN) is applied and further both-side context of 5 frames is used again. We obtain 440 dimension vector which is directly applied to the input of DNN. Illustrative block scheme of feature extraction procedure is in Fig. 1.

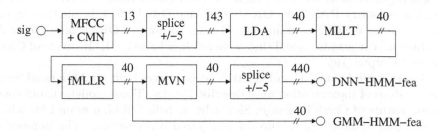

Fig. 1. Feature extraction used in GMM-HMM and DNN-HMM LVCSR

2.3   Acoustic Modeling

Acoustic models are also built using standardly used approach in modern ASR systems. The set of 45 Czech phones expanded to the context-dependent crossword triphones is used. Concerning *GMM-HMM approach*, the basic conventional GMM-HMM system is created first using the above mentioned LDA+MLLT features. It is followed by feature-space maximum likelihood linear regression (fMLLR) per each speaker (speaker adaptive training - SAT). Next iteration is based on UBM (Universal Background Model) in the combination with SGMM (Subspace GMM) and the system is finally retrained discriminatively using bMMI.

Concerning *DNN-HMM hybrid approach*, DNN topology consisted of input layer with 440 units (the context of 5 frames with 40 dimensional fMLLR features with MVN) followed by 6 hidden layers with 2048 neurons per layer and the sigmoid activation function. The process of building of DNN-HMM system started with the initialization of hidden layers of used network by Restricted Boltzmann Machines (RBMs) and then the output layer was added. The process continued by the frame cross-entropy training and ending with sMBR sequence-discriminative training.

Both AMs were trained using the utterances from SPEECON database [16] and CZKCC (private database of car speech).

2.4   Language Models for Casual Czech

Concerning language modeling, we work with standard n-gram-based statistical language models (LMs). According to the preliminary assumptions and also on the basis of experimental evaluations, Witten-Bell discounting was used for the smoothing of created LMs. This procedure is rather standard, the significant problem which had to be solved was in the choice of suitable resource for coverage casual nature of speech which should have been recognized.

We have analyzed the suitability of five general LMs collected from three different publicly available resources, i.e. from Czech National Corpus (CNC) [17], Google n-grams distributed by Linguistic Data Consortium (WEB1T) [18], and from the corpora ORAL 2006, ORAL 2008, and ORAL 2013. While the corpora CNC same as WEB1T contain general text, corpora of ORAL family contain spontaneous conversations and they were produced also by the Institute of Czech National Corpus [19].

General LMs from CNC and WEB1T corpora were built for 340 k word forms and the steps of their creation were described in [18]. These models should cover general nature of Czech language. Similarly, we built ORAL n-gram LMs which should cover spontaneous nature of recognized conversations. The number of word forms obtained from spontaneous conversations was 162 k for ORAL corpus and 29 k for NCCCz which maent a contribution of 73 k specific words from ORAL and 9 k words from NCCCz approximately.

Finally, to cover the maximum vocabulary for our task we have also created LMs from NCCCz, first, from defined training part of NCCCz containing the transcription of 60% utterances per each recorded session which were not used the for the evaluations later. It represents slightly more realistic scenario as the content of recognized utterances has not been seen before. Second, we created also for comparison purposes optimum LM for causal speech from all available NCCCz transcriptions.

2.5   Modeling of Pronunciation Variation

Finally, the modeling of pronunciation variation in casual speech (mainly its reduction) was taken into account. We apply particular rules, some of them known from other works, e.g. [9] or [20], others obtained on the basis of results of realized psycholinguistic study of pronunciation reduction in NCCCz [21]. In the end, we have used approximately 6700 additional pronunciation variants. The illustrative examples of several rules are

"v[sSzZ]→[sSzZ]" - e.g. *"vždyt', vstát"* (*"but, to stand up"*),
"[td]J → [cJ\J]" - e.g. *"letní"* ("adj. *summer"*),
"cons_1-t-cons_2 → cons_1-cons_2" - e.g. *"jestli"* (*"if"*),
"js → s" - e.g. *"jsem"* (*"I am"*),
"j[eai] → [eai]" - e.g. *"jestli, jinam"* (*"if, elsewhere"*),
"zj → z" - e.g. *"zjistíš"* (*"You will find"*),
"t-S → t_S" - e.g. *"většina"* (*"majority"*),
"nsk → nt_sk" - e.g. *"čínský"* (*"Chinesse"*),
"vZd → vd" - e.g. *"vždycky"* (*"always"*).

3   Experimental Part

Within the experimental part of this study, the behavior of designed systems on the principal task of spontaneous and casual speech recognition was analyzed. For the comparison purposes the results obtained for standard read speech recognition are also presented in the paper.

3.1   Used Speech Corpora

Experiments were performed on utterances from the following Czech databases: SPEECON (Czech database from SPEECON family which contains mainly standard read speech), CtuTest (private database of read journal sentences of various topics), CzLecDSP (recording of technical lectures from the field of DSP, these data have spontaneous nature but they are more formal [22]), and finally with NCCCz with strongly informal (casual) utterances. For the training of AMs also CZKCCC database was used (car-speech data). The following particular setups were used:

- *TA1 - read speech recognition*
    (a) read sentences, phonetically rich (SPEECON database),
    (b) journal sentences (CtuTest database),

– *TA2 - spontaneous speech recognition* recordings of lectures (CzLecDSP database),
– *TA3 - casual speech recognition*
recordings of highly informal conversations (NCCCz database).

Signals from all used databases were available at 16 kHz sampling frequency in 16-bit PCM format and final amounts of data in particular train and test subsets are summarized in Table 1.

Table 1. Evaluation data subsets for training and testing

Training subsets				Testing subsets			
Database	Speakers	Utterances	Hours	Database	Speakers	Utterances	Hours
SPEECON	225	60877	53.6	SPEECON	24	699	1.1
CZKCC	302	12771	20.6	CtuTest	40	577	1.1
NCCCz	40	10975	21.0	CzLecDSP	8	1417	1.7
Total	567	84623	95.2	NCCCz	20	890	1.1

3.2   Used Tools

Designed LVCSR systems were built using KALDI toolkit [23], while SRILM toolkit was used for the creation of particular LMs. The process of feature extraction was performed by our internal tool *CtuCopy* [24]. In comparison to *compute-mfcc-feats* available in KALDI, *CtuCopy* enables to extract features as MFCC, PLP, DCT-TRAP, and also to apply frequency-domain noise reduction, various cepstral normalizations. Recently, the compatibility with KALDI tools has been also added [25]. All recipes created for described experiments with Czech casual speech recognition using KALDI toolkit are publicly available under APACHE 2.0 license in "Download" section at "http://noel.feld.cvut.cz/speechlab".

3.3   Results and Discussion

The achieved results for previously established recognition tasks are presented from the following points of view: the *optimization of acoustic modeling*, the impact of *language modeling* and *pronunciation variation*.

I. The impact of AM
The first results describe the quality of used AM, i.e. from basic GMM-HMM approach to the best AM based on DNN-HMM architecture. General bigram LM from CNC with 340 k words was used for all these experiments with results in Table 2. Particular acronyms represent the following systems:

- "tri2" - triphone GMM-HMM with LDA+MLLT features,
- "tri3" - triphone GMM-HMM with LDA+MLLT followed by SAT,
- "SGMM" - subspace GMM,

- "bMMI" - discriminatively trained models,
- "DNN" - DNN-HMM system.

Achieved results show that our target DNN-HMM LVCSR system works with the accuracy comparable to the current state-of-the art, i.e. 15.2% of WER for standard read speech. For spontaneous speech we received WER of 37.4% for the transcription of lectures (i.e. with slightly more formal speaking style) and 72.0% for very informal speech from NCCCz.

Table 2. WERs of LVCSR in the phase of AM optimization

Tasks	tri2	tri3	SGMM	bMMI	DNN
TA1a	29.8	23.4	22.2	21.8	21.1
TA1b	24.0	17.0	15.9	15.3	15.2
TA2	49.9	41.3	39.9	38.0	37.4
TA3	82.5	76.1	74.9	74.2	72.0

II. The impact of LM

The results shown in Table 3 present the influence on used various LMs in analyzed tasks. The first part summarizes the results of recognition for all speaking styles using general CNC and WEB1T LMs where the strong decrease for the case of casual speech is clearly shown. The second part of Table 3 presents the results for TA3 task (casual speech) and LMs from ORAL a NCCCz (transcribed spontaneous speech corpora). The reduction of out-of-vocabulary (OOV) confirmed better modeling of casual speech and led to results around 60–70% WER. An exceptional case is LM *NCCCzAll* created from all available data including the test set so that it had OOV of 0%. We present these results for this non-realistic situation as a limit case which can be achieved using ideal setup.

The next experiments were focused on minimization OOV and WER in the TA3 task by merging of various bigram LMs. The results for merged LMs with uniform interpolation weight are summarized in Table 4. Using various merged LMs reduced the level of OOV significantly but the WER decreased just a little as the setup of the interpolation weights (λ) was not optimal. Therefore, we optimized the value of λ for particular LMs and the best result was obtained with the following setup: 0.2 weight for ORAL LM, 0.15 for CNC 0.15 for WEB1T and 0.5 for NCCCz achieving WER about 59.7%. The final investigation was based on merging various LMs with the NCCCz-based LM. The contributions of various interpolation weights λ to the final WER are summarized in Table 5. The best results were achieved for the setup with $\lambda = 0.75$.

In the end, the combination of all LMs brought an improvement in target OOV but the decrease of WER was smaller. The results proved that general LMs (CNC and WEB1T) did not contain proper information describing the causal speech in NCCCz, however, LMs ORAL corpus covered casual speech

Table 3. WERs of LVCSR with various 2-gram a 3-gram LMs on particular tasks

Tasks	LM	OOV	PPL	2-gram	3-gram
TA1a	CNC	1.6	3572	21.1	21.8
TA1b	CNC	1.8	2034	15.2	14.7
TA2	CNC	4.8	2937	37.4	37.2
TA3	CNC	4.6	2065	72.0	72.2
	WEB1T	4.5	4427	68.9	-
TA3	ORAL06	6.5	389	67.1	66.4
	ORAL08	6.7	445	66.8	66.3
	ORAL13	4.7	475	66.1	65.4
	ORALall	4.0	426	63.6	62.5
	NCCCz60	7.2	248	61.4	61.2
	NCCCzAll	*0*	*69*	*41.3*	*28.4*

Table 4. DNN-HMM casual speech recognition (TA3) with merged bigram LMs

Bigram LMs	OOV	WER
CNC+WEB1T	4.3	69.8
CNC+WEB1T+ORALall	2.8	64.7
CNC+WEB1T+ORALall+NCCCz60	1.5	61.2

Table 5. DNN-HMM with various weights of NCCCz in merged LMs on TA3 task

LMs	OOV	NCCCz weight λ				
		0.0	0.25	0.50	0.75	1
CNK340+NCCCz60	2.2	72.0	62.8	60.8	59.4	61.4
ORALall+NCCCz60	2.5	63.6	60.9	59.8	58.9	61.4
WEB1T+NCCCz60	2.1	68.9	62.3	60.6	60.0	61.4

very similarly as LM created directly from NCCCz, of course, except the case when used LM NCCCzAll was created also using the test data.

III. The impact of pronunciation reduction

The final results describe the achieved WER for three approaches of pronunciation modeling in casual speech. Firstly, we used automatically generated pronunciation for all words in analyzed LMs (which is used always for any new word not present in a available dictionary). Secondly, we used approved canonic pronunciation of all words from NCCCz which was created by manual checks by two independent experts. Thirdly, the dictionary with the additional pronunciation variants with phone reductions on the basis of rules described in Sect. 2 was used and obtained results are in Table 6. According to the assumptions, the

Table 6. Impact of pronunciation variation in DNN-HMM system

LM	Lexicon	WER
0.25 ORALall + 0.75 NCCCz60	Automatic	59.8
	Canonic checked	58.9
	Reduction variants	58.4

recognition accuracy has improved for the most proper case taking into account the reduced pronunciation, however, its decrease was only about 1.4%

4 Conclusions

In this paper, we described an optimization of DNN-HMM based LVCSR for casual speech recognition in Czech and its performance on speech from the Nijmegen Corpus of Casual Speech (NCCCz). Achieved results proved possible usage of these systems for casual speech recognition, however, the results are significantly worse than for the recognition of more formal speech. It was also demonstrated that publicly available corpora ORAL with transcriptions of spontaneous conversations commonly with available corpora of formal Czech can be used for the creation of basic LMs for the task of casual speech recognition.

Concerning obtained results, the best setup of DNN-HMM system with merged language model and pronunciation variation modeling achieved 58.4% WER, which is comparable to results of other authors. The built system was also tested on other spontaneous data (lecture recordings which were slightly more formal) where it achieved better WER of 37.2%, similarly in the task of formal read speech recognition where WER of 14.7% was achieved. The observed margin between the casual and formal speech recognition illustrated the challenge for the research in the field of more informal speech recognition.

Finally, created KALDI recipes for the recognition of Czech casual speech from NCCCz are publicly available in the Download section at the WEB-page "http://noel.feld.cvut.cz/speechlab". These scripts can be easily modified especially for the data from the family of Nijmegen casual speech corpora and SPEECON databases for other languages.

Acknowledgments. The research described in this paper was supported by internal CTU grant SGS17/183/OHK3/3T/13 "Special Applications of Signal Processing".

References

1. Cui, J., Ramabhadran, B., Cui, X., Rosenberg, A., Kingsbury, B., Sethy, A.: Recent improvements in neural network acoustic modeling for LVCSR in low resource languages. In: Proceedings of Interspeech 2014: 15th Annual Conference of the International Speech Communication Association, Singapore (2014)

2. Seltzer, L.M., Dong, Y., Yongqiang, W.: An investigation of deep neural networks for noise robust speech recognition. In: IEEE International Conference on Acoustics, Speech and Signal Processing, ICASSP 2013, Vancouver, Canada (2013)
3. Korvas, M., Plátek, O., Dušek, O., Žilka, L., Jurčíček, F.: Free English and Czech telephone speech corpus shared under the CC-BY-SA 3.0 license. In: Proceedings of LREC 2014: 9th International Conference on Language Resources and Evaluation, Reykjavik, Iceland, pp. 365–370 (2014)
4. Barras, C., Lamel, L., Gauvain, J.L.: Automatic transcription of compressed broadcast audio. In: Proceedings of the IEEE International Conference on Acoustics, Speech, and Signal Processing, Salt Lake City, USA, pp. 265–268 (2001)
5. Nouza, J., Ždánský, J., Červa, P.: System for automatic collection, annotation and indexing of Czech broadcast speech with full-text search. In: Proceedings of 15th IEEE MELECON Conference, La Valleta, Malta, pp. 202–205 (2010)
6. Nouza, J., Blavka, K., Bohac, M., Cerva, P., Málek, J.: System for producing subtitles to internet audio-visual documents. In: 38th International Conference on Telecommunications and Signal Processing, TSP 2015, Prague, Czech Republic, pp. 1–5, 9–11 July 2015
7. Psutka, J., Psutka, J., Ircing, P., Hoidekr, J.: Recognition of spontaneously pronounced TV ice-hockey commentary. In: Proceedings of ISCA & IEEE Workshop on Spontaneous Speech Processing and Recognition, Tokyo, pp. 83–86 (2003)
8. Lehr, M., Gorman, K., Shafran, I.: Discriminative pronunciation modeling for dialectal speech recognition. In: Proceedings of Interspeech 2014, Singapore, pp. 1458–1462 (2014)
9. Nouza, J., Silovský, J.: Adpating lexical and language models for transcription of highly spontaneous spoken Czech. In: Proceedings of Text, Speech, and Dialogue, LNAI, vol. 6231, Brno, Czech Republic, pp. 377–384 (2010)
10. Byrne, W., et al.: Automatic recognition of spontaneous speech for access to multilingual oral history archives. IEEE Trans. Speech Audio Process. 12(4), 420–435 (2004)
11. Ernestus, M., Kočková-Amortová, L., Pollák, P.: The Nijmegen corpus of casual Czech. In: Proceedings of LREC 2014: 9th International Conference on Language Resources and Evaluation, Reykjavik, Iceland, pp. 365–370 (2014)
12. Torreira, F., Adda-Decker, M., Ernestus, M.: The Nijmegen corpus of casual French. Speech Commun. 52, 201–221 (2010)
13. Prochazka, V., Pollak, P.: Conversational speech from Nijmegen corpus of casual Czech by general ASR language models. In: Production and Comprehension of Conversational Speech, pp. 34–35 (2011)
14. Hinton, G., Deng, L., Yu, D., Dahl, G., Mohamed, A., Jaitly, N., Senior, A., Vanhoucke, V., Nguyen, P., Sainath, T., Kingsbury, B.: Deep neural networks for acoustic modeling in speech recognition: the shared views of four research groups. IEEE Sig. Process. Mag. 29(6), 82–97 (2012)
15. Vesely, K., Karafiat, M., Grezl, F.: Convolutive bottleneck network features for lVCSR. In: 2011 IEEE Workshop on Automatic Speech Recognition and Understanding (ASRU), December 2011
16. Pollak, P., Cernocky, J.: Czech SPEECON adult database. Technical report (2004)
17. Institute of the Czech National Corpus: SYN2006PUB corpus (2006). http://ucnk.ff.cuni.cz/english/syn2006pub.php
18. Prochazka, V., Pollak, P., Zdansky, J., Nouza, J.: Performance of Czech speech recognition with language models created from public resources. Radioengineering 20, 1002–1008 (2011)

19. Institute of the Czech National Corpus: Corpus oral 2006 and oral 2008 and oral 2013, Institute of the Czech National Corpus FF UK. http://www.korpus.cz

20. Schuppler, B., Adda-Decker, M., Morales-Cordovilla, J.A.: Pronunciation variation in read and conversational Austrian German. In: Proceedings of Interspeech 2014, Singapore (2014)

21. Kolman, A., Pollak, P.: Speech reduction in Czech. In: Proceedings of LabPhone 14, The 14th Conference on Laboratory Phonology, Tokyo, Japan (2014)

22. Rajnoha, J., Pollák, P.: Czech spontaneous speech collection and annotation: the database of technical lectures. In: Esposito, A., Vích, R. (eds.) Cross-Modal Analysis of Speech, Gestures, Gaze and Facial Expressions. LNCS, vol. 5641, pp. 377–385. Springer, Heidelberg (2009). doi:10.1007/978-3-642-03320-9_35

23. Povey, D., et al.: The Kaldi speech recognition toolkit. In: Proceedings of ASRU 2011, IEEE 2011 Workshop on Automatic Speech Recognition and Understanding (2011)

24. Fousek, P., Pollak, P.: Efficient and reliable measurement and simulation of noisy speech background. In: Proceedings of EUROSPEECH 2003, 8-th European Conference on Speech Communication and Technology, Geneve, Switzerland (2003)

25. Borsky, M., Mizera, P., Pollak, P.: Noise and channel normalized cepstral features for far-speech recognition. In: Proceedings of SPECOM 2013, The 15th International Conference on Speech and Computer, Pilsen, Czech Republic (2013)

Improving Performance of Speaker Identification Systems Using Score Level Fusion of Two Modes of Operation

Saeid Safavi[✉] and Iosif Mporas

School of Engineering and Technology, University of Hertfordshire College,
Lane Campus, Hatfield, Hertfordshire AL10 8PE, UK
{s.safavi,i.mporas}@herts.ac.uk

Abstract. In this paper we present a score level fusion methodology for improving the performance of closed-set speaker identification. The fusion is performed on scores which are extracted from GMM-UBM text-dependent and text-independent speaker identification engines. The experimental results indicated that the score level fusion improves the speaker identification performance compared with the best performing single operation mode of speaker identification.

Keywords: Speaker identification · Fusion · Machine · Learning

1 Introduction

Speaker identification uses voice as a unique characteristic to identify a person's identify. This task is also classified into closed and open set speaker identification. In the closed set speaker identification task, an unknown utterance will be assigned to the known speaker reference template with the highest level of similarity. So the initial assumption is that the unknown utterance is from one of the given set of speakers and system makes a forced decision by choosing the best matching speaker from the speaker database. In the open-set speaker identification reference template for an unknown speaker may not exist, therefore, when the highest matching score is lower than a pre-set threshold. Speaker identification task can be further divided into text-dependent and text-independent task [1, 2]. Unlike text-independent speaker verification system [3–6], which is a process of verifying the identity without constraint on the speech content, text-dependent speaker verification requires the speaker pronouncing pre-determined pass-phrase [7–9]. These pass-phrases may be unique (chosen by user or system), or prompted by the system.

The concurrent technology in speaker identification is based on short-time speech signal analysis followed by machine learning based modeling. The most commonly used features for speaker recognition are the Mel frequency cepstral coefficients (MFCCs) [10, 11]. In terms of speaker modeling, the Gaussian Mixture Models (GMMs) introduced in the mid-1990s [12] is widely considered to be a benchmark for modern text-independent Speaker Recognition. GMM technology has proved to perform well using universal background models (UBMs) trained from a large number of

© Springer International Publishing AG 2017
A. Karpov et al. (Eds.): SPECOM 2017, LNAI 10458, pp. 438–444, 2017.
DOI: 10.1007/978-3-319-66429-3_43

background speakers and maximum a-posteriori (MAP) adaptation or means-only adaptation of the UBM to speaker specific data. Discriminative approaches, such as support vector machines (SVMs) have also successfully been used in the task of speaker recognition [13]. As a stand-alone method as well as in combination with GMMs by concatenating the means of the Gaussian components of the GMMs to super-vectors and applying discriminative classification on them [13]. The recently developed paradigm of i-vector extraction [14, 22] provides an elegant way to obtain a low dimensional fixed length representation of a speech utterance that preserves the speaker-specific information. A Factor Analysis (FA) model is used to learn a low-dimensional subspace from a large collection of data. A speech utterance is then projected into this subspace and its coordinates vector is denoted as i-vector [14]. Although in specific setups subspace methods have proved to outperform probabilistic models, the GMM-UBM approach in general offers more stable results, especially when not enough training and development data are available. For this reason, in the present evaluation we relied in this technology.

In this work, we present a methodology for fusing the speaker identification scores produced by two different modes of operation, namely the text-dependent and the text-independent. The exploitation of the advantages of each of the two modes of operation is achieved using a machine learning based scheme for fusion, in order to get a final speaker identification decision.

The rest of the article is organized as follows. Section 2 presents the proposed fusion methodology for combining prompted text-dependent and text-independent speaker verification modes. Section 3 describes our experimental setup and Sect. 4 presents and analyses the experimental results. Finally Sect. 5 draws the conclusions of this work.

2   Fusion of Speaker Identification Operation Modes

Different modes of operation in speaker identification can offer complementary information about the identity of a speaker. We present a machine learning based methodology for speaker identification which fuses the information and extends the selection of the speaker from simple maximum selection to data-driven model based selection.

The user is providing the system with one voice response to a prompted text-independent message and one voice response to a prompted text-dependent message. Each of the two inputs is processed by mode-specific models and for each mode a score vector against each speaker model is estimated. The two score vectors are fused by a machine learning algorithm in order to make a final identification decision. The proposed methodology for score fusion based speaker identification is illustrated in Fig. 1.

Let us denote as X the input test utterance after pre-processing and parameterization. A number of speaker models, N, is used in order to estimate not only scores for the text-dependent input, $S^{TD} \in \mathbb{R}^N$, but also scores for the text-independent input, $S^{TI} \in \mathbb{R}^N$. Instead of selecting the maximum (or minimum) score per mode, we con-

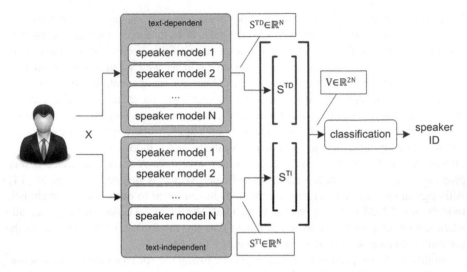

Fig. 1. Block diagram of the proposed methodology for fusion of prompted text-dependent and text-independent modes of speaker identification operation

catenate the estimated scores into a single feature vector, $V \in \mathbb{R}^{2N}$, which is then used as input to a fusion classifier as:

$$d = f(V), \tag{1}$$

where f denotes the fusion classification model and d is the decision, i.e. the detected speaker identity.

We deem the fusion classification model will capture the underlying information between the scores of the text-dependent and text-independent mode of operation, as well as between the scores of the speaker-specific models.

3 Experimental Setup

The experimental setup for evaluating the fusion methodology described in Sect. 2 is presented here. Specifically, we describe the dataset used in the evaluation, the setup of the single-mode speaker identification engines and the setup of the fusion stage.

3.1 Speech Corpus

In this evaluation RSR2015 speech corpus [9] is used. RSR2015 consists of recordings from 300 speakers (157 males, 143 females). For each speaker, there are 3 enrollment sessions of 73 utterances each and 6 verification sessions of 73 utterances each. In total there are 657 utterances distributed in 9 sessions per speaker. The sampling frequency of the speech recordings is 16 kHz and the speech samples are stored with analysis equal to 16 bits per sample.

In addition to RSR2015, we used TIMIT [15] for training a universal background model. TIMIT consists of recordings of 630 speakers, sampled at 16 kHz with resolution analysis equal to 16 bits per sample.

3.2 Single-Mode Speaker Identification Engines

Each of the two single-mode speaker identification engines, i.e. the text-dependent and the text-independent ones, were based on the well-known GMM-UBM technique [13]. Each voice input was initially pre-processed and parameterized. During pre-processing an energy-based speech activity detector was applied to retain the speech only parts. The speech input was frame blocked using a time shifting Hamming window of 20 ms length with10 ms overlap between successive frames. For each frame the first 19 Mel frequency cepstral coefficients (MFCCs) were estimated, which were further expanded to their first and second derivatives, thus resulting to a feature vector of length equal to 57. In order to reduce the effect of handset mismatch and make the features more robust relative spectra (RASTA) [16] and cepstral mean and variance normalization (CMVN) processing were applied to the MFCC features.

The universal background model (UBM) was built by a mixture of 128 Gaussian distributions and was trained using all utterances from 630 speakers in TIMIT. For each of the speakers of the RSR2015 database we applied MAP adaptation (means only adaptation) on the UBM model, using the speaker-specific enrollment.

3.3 Setup for the Score Level Fusion of Speaker Identification Modes

This research provides a tentative set of results on the recent RSR2015 corpus intended for benchmarking different modes of automatic speaker identification and their fusion. In particular, training and trial lists (definition of speaker pairs) are designed to simulate system evaluation of two different configurations concerning speech content, (a) text-prompted phrases and (b) text-independent engines. The first protocol refers to a scenario whereby a system prompts a randomly selected phrase out of a close subset of pass-phrases. The second scenario is essentially a text-independent scenario with arbitrary enrollment and test phrases. Each single mode biometric engine is evaluated for the two different circumstances, (a) and (b), respectively.

To assess the performance for the two protocols, different enrollment and trial lists were designed. The experiments are conducted on a subset of male section of recently released RSR2015 dataset. For both protocols, 43 identical speakers are used. In the protocol (a), speakers are enrolled with 15 different pass-phrases. For each speaker, the 15 pass-phrases are sentences 01 to 05 taken from session 04, 06 to 10 from session 01 and 11 to 15 from session 07. One out of the 15 sentences used in the enrollment is randomly selected and prompted during testing.

For protocol (b), the enrollment is done in a similar way as in protocol (a). But the test data is exclusively different from the enrollment data. Here, the remaining 15 sentences (from 16 to 30) are used in testing.

The identification scores produced by the text-dependent and the text-independent speaker identification engines were concatenated into 2-dimensional feature vectors as described in Sect. 2.

For the classification stage, each pair of text-dependent and text-independent scores was processed by a classification model, implemented by several machine learning algorithms for classification. Specifically, the following algorithms were used: (I) support vector machines (SVM) [17] using the sequential minimal optimization implementation, (II) multilayer perceptron neural networks (MLP) [18], (III) C4.5 decision trees (C4.5) [19]. For the implementation of these machine learning algorithms for classification we used the WEKA toolkit [20, 21].

4 Experimental Results

The proposed fusion methodology for speaker identification presented in Sect. 2 was evaluated based on the experimental setup described in Sect. 3. For all evaluations a 5-folds cross validation protocol were applied. The performance of the proposed methodology was evaluated in terms of identification rate.

Operation mode (a) offers an identification rate equals to approximately 87%, while operation mode (b) offers an identification rate of nearly 74%. However, since operation mode (a) is sensitive to replay attacks, text independent operation is widely used in real-life identification applications. In order to exploit the high identification rate of operation mode (a), while retaining the robustness of operation mode (b) we further examined the score level fusion of these operation modes (as described in Sect. 2).

The experimental results for the single-mode text-dependent and text-independent speaker identification engines as well as their fusion using several classification algorithms is tabulated in Table 1.

Table 1. Speaker identification, in terms of percentages correctly identified speakers, for single mode of operation and their fusion

Single mode	Identification rate (%)	Fusion	Identification rate (%)
Text-independent (b)	73.93	C4.5	76.05
Text-dependent (a)	**86.77**	SVM	90.88
		MLP	**96.86**

As can be seen in Table 1, the best performing single mode operation is text-dependent (a). This is in agreement with the literature and is owed to the fact that the acoustic model's parameters are more precisely fit to the acoustic characteristics of the target speaker for known utterance, as in the protocol of text-dependent.

As shown in Table 1, the fusion of the two modes of operation using different types of classification algorithm outperformed both single modes and in case of C4.5 decision trees only operation mode (b). The best performance has been achieved by fusion of scores using MLP, which offered absolute improvement of 10.09% compare to the best performing single mode speaker identification system, text-dependent (a). This is due to the fact that the fusion methodology is able to exploit the complementary underlying information from each single mode of speaker identification and thus lead to an overall more robust identification performance.

5   Conclusions

Speaker identification accuracy when using clean speech is in general high, especially in text-dependent scenario. However, such scenario is vulnerable to the replay attacks. In this paper we presented a fusion approach, which combines the two common single operation modes of speaker identification, i.e. the prompted text-dependent and text-independent. The speaker identification scores produced by each mode of operation are used as an input to fusion algorithm. Our experimental results using the proposed fusion approach indicated an absolute improvement of 10.09% in terms of identification rate comparing to the best performing single mode of operation (text-dependent). We deem the proposed fusion approach is not only improving the performance of identification process but also improve the robustness against replay attacks.

Acknowledgement. This work was partially supported by the H2020 OCTAVE Project entitled "Objective Control for TAlker VErification" funded by the EC with Grand Agreement number 647850.

The authors would like to thank Dr Md Sahidullah, Dr Nicholas Evans and Dr Tomi Kinnunen for their support in this work.

References

1. Campbell Jr., J.P.: Speaker recognition: a tutorial. Proc. IEEE **85**(9), 1437–1462 (1997)
2. Bimbot, F., et al.: A tutorial on text-independent speaker verification. EURASIP J. Appl. Signal Process. **1**, 430–451 (2004)
3. Reynolds, D.A., Quatieri, T.F., Dunn, R.B.: Speaker verification using adapted gaussian mixture models. Digital Signal Proc. **10**(1–3), 19–41 (2000), ISSN 1051–2004
4. Safavi, S., Hanani, A., Russell, M., Jancovic, P., Carey, M.J.: Contrasting the effects of different frequency bands on speaker and accent identification. IEEE Signal Process. Lett. **19**(12), 829–832 (2012)
5. Safavi, S., Najafian, M., Hanani, A., Russell, M., Jancovic, P., Carey, M.: Speaker recognition for children's speech. In: INTERSPEECH, pp. 1836–1839 (2012)
6. Safavi, S.: Speaker characterization using adult and children's speech. Ph. D. dissertation, University of Birmingham (2015)
7. Safavi, S., Gan, H., Mporas, I., Sotudeh, R.: Fraud detection in voice-based identity authentication applications and services. In: Proceedings of ICDM (2016)
8. Hébert, M., Sondhi, M., Huang, Y.: Text-Dependent Speaker Recognition. Handbook of Speech Processing, pp. 743–762. Springer, Heidelberg (2008)
9. Larcher, A., Lee, K.A., Ma, B., Li, H.: Text-dependent speaker verification: classifiers, databases and RSR2015. Speech Commun. **60**, 56–77 (2014), ISSN 0167–6393, http://dx.doi.org/10.1016/j.specom.2014.03.001
10. Davis, S., Mermelstein, P.: Comparison of parametric representations for monosyllabic word recognition in continuously spoken sentences. IEEE Trans. Acoust. Speech Signal Process. **28**(4), 357–366 (1980)
11. Furui, S.: Cepstral analysis technique for automatic speaker verification. IEEE Trans. Acoust. Speech Signal Process. **29**(2), 254–272 (1981)
12. Reynolds, D.A., Rose, R.C.: Robust text-independent speaker identification using Gaussian mixture speaker models. IEEE Trans. Speech Audio Process. **3**(1), 72–83 (1995)

13. Campbell, W.M., Sturim, D.E., Reynolds, D.A.: Support vector machines using GMM supervectors for speaker verification. IEEE Signal Process. Lett. **13**(5), 308–311 (2006)
14. Dehak, N., Kenny, P., Dehak, R., Dumouchel, P., Ouellet, P.: Front-end factor analysis for speaker verification. IEEE Trans. Audio Speech Lang. Process. **19**(4), 788–798 (2010)
15. Campbell J.P., Reynolds, D.A.: Corpora for the evaluation of speaker recognition systems. In Proceedings of ICASSP 1999, vol. 2, pp. 829–832 (1999)
16. Hermansky, H., Morgan, N.: RASTA processing of speech. IEEE Trans. Speech Audio Process. **2**(4), 578–589 (1994)
17. Schölkopf, B., Burges, CJ.: Advances in Kernel Methods: Support Vector Learning. MIT press (1999)
18. Pal, S.K., Mitra, S.: Multilayer perceptron, fuzzy sets, and classification. IEEE Trans. Neural Netw. **3**(5), 683–697 (1992)
19. Quinlan, J.R.: Improved use of continuous attributes in c4.5. J. Artif. Intell. Res. **4**, 77–90 (1996)
20. Witten, I.H., Frank, E., Hall, M.A.: Data Mining: Practical Machine Learning Tools and Techniques, 3rd edn. Morgan Kaufmann, San Francisco (2011)
21. Najafian, M., Safavi, S., Weber, P., Russell, M.: Identification of British English regional accent using fusion of i-vector and multi accent phonotactic systems. In: Proceedings of the ODYSSEY, pp. 132–139 (2016)
22. Safavi, S., Russell, M., Jancovic, P.: Identification of age-group from children's speech by computers and humans. In: INTERSPEECH, pp. 243–247 (2014)

Improving Speech-Based Emotion Recognition by Using Psychoacoustic Modeling and Analysis-by-Synthesis

Ingo Siegert[1(✉)], Alicia Flores Lotz[1], Olga Egorow[1], and Andreas Wendemuth[1,2]

[1] Cognitive Systems Group, Institute of Information and Communication Engineering, Otto von Guericke University, 39016 Magdeburg, Germany
ingo.siegert@ovgu.de
[2] Center for Behavioral Brain Sciences, 39118 Magdeburg, Germany

Abstract. Most technical communication systems use speech compression codecs to save transmission bandwidth. A lot of development was made to guarantee a high speech intelligibility resulting in different compression techniques: Analysis-by-Synthesis, psychoacoustic modeling and a hybrid mode of both. Our first assumption is that the hybrid mode improves the speech intelligibility. But, enabling a natural spoken conversation also requires affective, namely emotional, information, contained in spoken language, to be intelligibly transmitted. Usually, compression methods are avoided for emotion recognition problems, as it is feared that compression degrades the acoustic characteristics needed for an accurate recognition [1]. By contrast, in our second assumption we state that the combination of psychoacoustic modeling and Analysis-by-Synthesis codecs could actually improve speech-based emotion recognition by removing certain parts of the acoustic signal that are considered "unnecessary", while still containing the full emotional information. To test both assumptions, we conducted an ITU-recommended POLQA measuring as well as several emotion recognition experiments employing two different datasets to verify the generality of this assumption. We compared our results on the hybrid mode with Analysis-by-Synthesis-only and psychoacoustic modeling-only codecs. The hybrid mode does not show remarkable differences regarding the speech intelligibility, but it outperforms all other compression settings in the multi-class emotion recognition experiments and achieves even an ∼3.3% absolute higher performance than the uncompressed samples.

Keywords: Automatic emotion recognition · Speech compression · Intelligibility of affective speech

1 Introduction

Human-computer interaction recently received increased attention while the dissemination of technical systems is growing. In this context, one main research

© Springer International Publishing AG 2017
A. Karpov et al. (Eds.): SPECOM 2017, LNAI 10458, pp. 445–455, 2017.
DOI: 10.1007/978-3-319-66429-3_44

goal is to enable a natural (human-like) spoken conversation with technical systems [2]. Therefore, besides the pure content, also the affective information transmitted by spoken language has to be evaluated, as it contains further information needed to successfully accomplish the conversation. Up to date approaches for an automatic speech-based affect recognition utilize high-quality mostly uncompressed speech [30], although speech compression techniques have shown a significant impact on acoustic characteristics [5, 22]. This issue gains more importance, since the analyses started to use natural emotions [24, 28] and go "in the wild" [6], often interpreted as using data from non-laboratory conditions having noises, echoes etc. In our understanding "in the wild" conditions have more consequences and investigations in this field should also incorporate transmission techniques as needed for mobile applications.

For signal transmission, speech compression is heavily used within modern (mobile) systems. Compression allows to reduce the transmission bandwidth, while retaining the speech intelligibility [1]. For acoustic signals, two different compression approaches have been developed. One approach, psychoacoustic modeling (PsyMo), is mainly used for transparent music compression aiming to simultaneously reduce the file size and preserve all audible acoustic information. The other approach, Analysis-by-Synthesis (AbS), is used for real-time speech conversation aiming to work with limited bandwidth and to obtain an acceptable speech intelligibility also for very low bitrates. Several codecs have been developed implementing both approaches separately and offering various computational and intelligibility improvements [20]. The Opus codec, standardized in 2012, additionally offers a hybrid mode combining both approaches, aiming to further improve the speech intelligibility at low bitrates. But, as compression approaches do not incorporate the retention of affective information during compression it is still unclear how they behave in the context of emotional speech.

We hypothesize that Opus's hybrid mode outperforms the AbS and the PhyMo modes/codecs in terms of both, speech intelligibility for emotional speech as well as automatic emotion recognition performance. The explanation for this hypothesis is that the hybrid mode, in contrast to the pure AbS mode, enriches the synthesized signal with further characteristics represented by a psychoacoustic model. To prove this assumption, we conducted speech intelligibility assessments utilizing Perceptual Objective Listening Quality Assessment (POLQA) and state-of-the-art speech-based emotion classification experiments. To this avail, we used two well-known benchmark corpora and compared Opus's hybrid mode with its AbS and PsyMo mode. To exclude possible side-effects caused by the bitrate, we also employed an AbS-only codec (AMR-WB) and a PsyMo-only codec (MP3).

The remainder of the paper is structured as follows: Sect. 2 presents related research. In Sect. 3 the used codecs are described and in Sect. 4 the utilized datasets are presented. Section 5 introduces the experimental design and methods. Our results are then presented in Sect. 6. Finally, Sect. 7 concludes the paper and presents an outlook.

2   Related Research

Several intelligibility tests are reported in the literature for the Opus codec. In [20], all three modes of Opus are evaluated by subjective listening tests and compared to three well-known AbS codecs. The authors stated that Opus is a good alternative, and especially the hybrid mode was experienced with excellent voice quality. Another study summarized the various listening tests conducted with Opus in comparison to several speech and audio codecs [11]. They concluded that Opus performs better at higher bitrates, especially for wider bandwidths.

Unfortunately, all of these studies utilized read speech or music samples without taking into account emotional variations in speech. Only a few studies analyzed speech intelligibility and recognisability of emotional speech. They concluded that Mean Opinion Score (MOS-LQO) values of emotional samples are significantly lower than for clean and neutral speech or music [16] but that the recognisability is not correlated to the intelligibility assessment [23]. But these studies either focused only on Opus's PsyMo mode or investigated other codecs.

Regardless of all the efforts made so far to preserve the speech intelligibility of compressed speech, the effects of speech compression on speech-based emotion recognition have only been rarely addressed. The authors of [29] analyzed the effect of an AbS codec (FR GSM 06.10) on the detection of acted negative emotions for voiced and unvoiced frames sampled from the emoDB database. They noticed a decreased recognition performance in comparison to the uncompressed samples. Also the authors of [1] used the voiced frames of all seven types of emotions of emoDB. As codecs they also concentrated on AbS codecs (AMR-NB, AMR-WB, and AMR-WB+) and could confirm the general expectation that, in most cases, lower bitrates imply lower accuracies for emotion recognition. The authors of [9] utilized the same database and emotion samples but with a broader selection of AbS codecs as well as Opus. For some codecs, including Opus, an improvement was observed for voiced segments, but for unvoiced segments always a decreased performance was observed. In [17], all samples of emoDB were coded using codecs of both techniques. The recognition performance of both, a state-of-the-art automatic recognition system and human labeling as well as spectral error and the speech intelligibility was analyzed. Again, the recognition worked best on uncompressed samples, but there are indications that lower bitrates not always imply lower emotion recognition performance.

3   Description of Utilized Codecs

This study focuses on the Opus codec and its three different operation modes. For comparison purposes, a pure AbS (AMR-WB) and a pure PsyMo codec (MP3) was used. As reference format the standard Waveform Audio File (WAV) [12] is used. Table 2 gives an overview on the chosen codecs and selected bitrates.

Opus is an open source lossy audio codec standardized by the IETF [26] and can be used for both speech and music signals, as it has a very short coding latency (default 26.5 ms) and variable bitrates in the range of 6 to 510 kbit/s. It is a hybrid codec combined from the speech-oriented SILK and a full-bandwidth CELT [27]. SILK is based on Linear predictive coding (LPC) with an optional Long-Term Prediction filter to model speech signals. CELT uses, as most music codecs, a modified discrete cosine transform. Opus uses three different operating modes, dependent on sampling frequency, bitrate and acoustic characteristics of the analyzed sample: SILK, hybrid and CELT. We secured that Opus uses the desired mode by checking the range file which indicates the mode for each frame. Only bitrates where all frames are encoded with the desired mode were used.

Adaptive Multirate Wideband (AMR-WB), described in the ITU-T Recommendation G722.2 [14], was developed by 3GPP and ETSI for 3G systems [14] and uses an AbS compression algorithm. Based on algebraic Code-excited Linear Prediction on the pre-processed and down-sampled signal, the LPC parameters together with algebraic codebook parameters describing the excitation are transmitted for decoding. To reconstruct the speech signal a synthesis based on these parameters is performed. The AMR-WB codec operates with bitrates from 6.6 to 23.85 kbit/s.

MPEG-1/MPEG-2 Audio Layer III (MP3) is a popular lossy audio codec, developed by Fraunhofer Institute and released in 1993 [3]. MP3 uses perceptual coding for audio compression: certain parts of the original sound signal, considered to be beyond the auditory resolution ability, are discarded. Afterwards, the remaining information is stored in an efficient manner using Huffman-coding. The bitrates range from 8 to 320 kbit/s.

4   Datasets

To verify our assumption that Opus's hybrid mode improves both speech intelligibility and automatic emotion recognition performance, we used two prominent benchmark corpora, DES and emoDB [21]. Both feature emotion categories and comprise different languages, and sampling rates, see Table 1 and the following database descriptions. Due to the lack of suitable emotional speech databases in terms of having both, a sample-bandwidth above 14 kHz and a category based annotation, we decided to use emoDB and applied an upsampling beforehand[1]. Selected bitrates for each codec regarding the two datasets are given in Table 2.

The **Danish Emotional Speech (DES)** corpus is a studio-recorded database containing perceptually selected acted emotions of Danish sentences, words and chunks spoken by four professional actors (two female) in five emotional states: anger, happiness, neutral, sadness, and surprise [7].

The **Berlin Emotional Speech Database (emoDB)** is a studio-recorded corpus, for which ten (five female) professional actors spoke ten German sentences with emotionally neutral content in seven emotion states: anger, boredom,

---

[1] We upsampled emoDB from 16 kHz to 20 kHz. Hence, also the bitrate increased from 256 kbit/s to 320 kbit/s. This does not add missing information in the high frequency range but forces Opus to use the hybrid mode, as this mode is only available for super-wideband and fullband signals.

Table 1. Differing properties of DES and emoDB. Both have fixed content with acted emotions recorded in a studio environment.

	Bitrate [kbit/s]	Sample rate [kHz]	Language	Speaker	# Classes	# Samples
DES	320	20	Danish	4 (2f)	5	419
emoDB	320 (256)[1]	20 (16)[1]	German	10 (5f)	7	494

Table 2. Selected audio codecs and used bitrates. Codecs using AbS , PsyMo or a hybrid mode are highlighted accordingly.

Codec	Bitrates [kbit/s]		
MP3	16.00	20.00	24.00
AMR-WB	15.85	19.85	23.85
Opus (emoDB)	16.00	19.00	24.00
Opus (DES)	16.00	20.00	24.00

disgust, fear, joy, neutral, and sadness. The final phrases entering the corpus were selected using a perception test [4]. To be able to use the hybrid mode of Opus, an upsampling to 20 kHz was conducted.

5   Experimental Design

5.1   Mean Opinion Score

To measure the speech intelligibility, a POLQA with regard to the ITU-T recommendation P.863 is carried out using SwissQual's SQuadAnalyzer. POLQA is an objective method to predict the overall listening speech quality as perceived by humans in an ITU-T P.800 Absolute Category Rating listening-only test, [13,15] without performing these human listening tests. We decided against human perceptions tests, as these tests are quite time consuming. We utilized POLQA in super-wideband mode. The prediction algorithm reaches a saturation level at a certain MOS-LQO value, which is 4.75 for super wide-band (SWB) samples. We reported mean and standard deviation of the MOS-LQO values for each codec and bitrate per dataset. For the interpretation of the values, given in Table 3, we used the evaluation scheme of [18]. The author analyzed quality of Experience Models for high-definition VoIP signals. The evaluation scheme was obtained from a series of subjective auditory tests, enabling the derivation of a ratio between the objective PESQ and the subjective MOS-LQO assessments.

5.2   Recognition Experiments

To analyze the automatic emotion recognition performance, we conducted state-of-the-art experiments comparable to [17]. For feature extraction, we used the

Table 3. Interpretation values for MOS-LQO according to [18].

Interpretation	MOS-LQO
Maximum for SWB codec	4.75
Very Good	4.64
Good	4.35
Fair	3.28
Moderate	2.01
Bad	1.04

"emobase" feature set provided by openSMILE [8]. It comprises 988 features derived from 19 functionals calculated for 54 Low-Level-Descriptor (LLDs) and has been successfully used for various classification experiments (cf. [19,25]). Afterwards, we normalized the values to eliminate differences between the data samples by using standardization [31]. As recognition system, a Support Vector Machine (SVM) with linear kernel and a cost factor of 1 was utilized with WEKA [10]. This setup has been proven to generally achieve high recognition performances. As validation scheme, we applied a Leave-One-Speaker-Out (LOSO) validation. As performance measure, the Unweighted Average Recall (UAR) was calculated for each validation step over all emotion classes available for one speaker. Finally, the mean and standard deviation of the UAR was reported over all speakers.

6   Results

6.1   Mean Opinion Score

In Fig. 1, it can be seen that only Opus' AbS and hybrid mode achieves MOS-LQO values above or near good values (>4.35). Values for Opus's PsyMo mode are in the upper range of the fair sector (4.05) and how an overall tendency to decrease. This can be attributed to the low bitrate of 24 kbit/s, driving the PsyMo modeling to its limit. For AMR-WB fair values, slightly rising with increasing bitrates are achieved (3.71–3.80). For AMW-WB, this can be explained by the highly optimized codec, designed to work with low bitrates. MP3 at 16 and 20 kbits/s achieves just moderate values. But the distinct improvement from 20 to 24 kbit/s for MP3 illustrates that MP3 is optimized for higher bitrates. Comparing the bitrate and the speech intelligibility for AMR-WB and MP3, a direct connection is present: higher bitrates achieve higher MOS-LQO values. In contrast, the uncompressed samples of the databases achieve very good (emoDB) or just marginally below very good MOS-LQO-values (~4.64) for DES.

The remarkable best MOS-LQO values for all bitrates are achieved by Opus. Its AbS mode and PsyMo mode significantly outperform the corresponding intelligibility results on both datasets using AMR-WB and MP3. But no significant

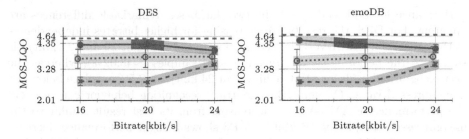

Fig. 1. Mean and standard deviation of the MOS-LQO values for the different codecs, AMR-WB $(\cdots\mathbf{o}\cdots)$, MP3 $(\text{-}\ast\text{-})$, and Opus $(\text{---}\bullet\text{---})$, with different bitrates for both datasets. The mean MOS-LQO of the uncompressed WAV-samples is marked as horizontal line $(\text{-}\text{-}\text{-})$. The utilized compression technique is highlighted according to Table 2.

differences between Opus's hybrid mode and its AbS mode could be observed. For DES, the hybrid mode of Opus outperforms the AbS mode just by 0.036, which is within the standard deviation. For emoDB the AbS mode outperforms the hybrid mode by 0.14. This can be caused by the upsampling of emoDB, which influences the MOS-LQO calculation. But for both datasets, the best MOS-LQO values of the compressed samples are still below the speech intelligibility values of the uncompressed dataset. Our first assumption that Opus's hybrid mode increases the speech intelligibility can neither be approved nor disproved.

6.2 Automatic Recognition Results

The results of our multi-class emotion recognition experiments are depicted in Fig. 2. Analyzing the recognition results per codec, it is apparent that AMR-WB, optimized for lower bitrates, significantly outperforms MP3 for 16 and 20 kbit/s for both databases. These results reflect the calculated speech intelligibility, which was also better for AMR-WB. But, comparing the recognition

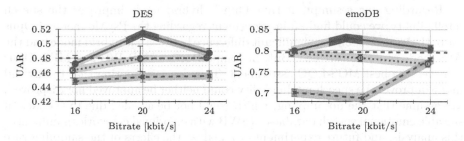

Fig. 2. Mean and standard deviation of the UAR for the different codecs, AMR-WB $(\cdots\mathbf{o}\cdots)$, MP3 $(\text{-}\ast\text{-})$, and Opus $(\text{---}\bullet\text{---})$, with different bitrates for both datasets. The mean UAR of the uncompressed WAV-samples is marked as horizontal line $(\text{-}\text{-}\text{-})$. The utilized compression technique is highlighted according to Table 2.

performance for both codecs on the two databases, remarkable differences are apparent. For DES, the results are increasing for higher bitrates independently of the codecs. On AMR-WB the recognition performance at 20 and 24 kbit/s is similar to the performance for uncompressed samples (~48.02%), whereas the best recognition result for MP3, achieved at 24 kbit/s, is 2.5% absolute below the uncompressed value. On emoDB, a contrary recognition behavior can be seen: the performance of AMR-WB is decreasing from its best result similar to the uncompressed samples at 16 kbit/s. MP3 shows a slight performance decrease from 16 to 20 kbit/s and a distinct performance increase towards 24 kbit/s outperforming AMR-WB. But also on emoDB, MP3's best result is still 1.6% absolute below the performance on the uncompressed samples.

The recognition performance of Opus outperforms the performance of AMR-WB and MP3 for all bitrates. Although in some cases, AMR-WB with 16 kBit/s on DES as well as AMR-WB and MP3 with 24 kbit/s on emoDB, Opus' performance is just slightly better. Furthermore, the hybrid mode achieves the best result, which is even significantly higher than the recognition results on the uncompressed samples. The UAR rises from 48.02% for uncompressed samples to 51.47% for DES and from 79.61% to 82.95% for emoDB, compared to uncompressed samples. Thus, our second assumption that Opus's hybrid mode increases the performance of speech-based emotion recognition is confirmed.

7   Conclusion and Future Work

Our hypotheses for this investigation were that Opus's hybrid mode achieves both, a better speech intelligibility and a better emotion recognition performance than its AbS or PsyMo mode. We furthermore tested Opus against an AbS-only codec (AMR-WB) and a PsyMo-only codec (MP3).

To prove our assumptions, we utilized two well-known benchmark corpora, DES and emoDB comprising different languages and types of emotions. We conducted instrumental quality assessment using POLQA as well as speech-based emotion recognition experiments utilizing openSMILE for feature extraction and WEKA's SVM implementation for training and testing.

Regarding our assumption that Opus's hybrid mode improves the speech intelligibility, we could find an improvement regarding the PsyMo mode of Opus for both databases, but no significant difference between the hybrid mode and the AbS mode could be revealed. But, in comparison to AMR-WB and MP3, Opus achieved the best MOS-LQO assessment. Thus, our assumption that the hybrid mode improves the speech intelligibility could neither be approved nor disproved. We assume that the upsampling, which could not be avoided due to the lack of suitable emotional speech databases (SWB with emotional categories), influences this analysis, and future experiments to analyze the effects of the sampling rate have to be conducted.

In the multi-class emotion recognition experiments, we achieved a significant performance increase (3.34%–3.45% absolute) for Opus's hybrid mode for both datasets, DES and emoDB. Thus, our assumption that the hybrid mode leads to an increased recognition performance is approved. The identification of the affective acoustic characteristics that are preserved due to the combination of AbS and PsyMo is part of ongoing investigations.

Our findings imply that for emotion recognition, it is best to opt for the hybrid mode of the Opus codec – if the bandwidth and bitrate can be parameterized to match it. In future experiments, we want to investigate which acoustic characteristics are responsible for the significant recognition improvement and whether this behavior can be generalized to other emotional databases with different types of emotions and content. Furthermore, we want to investigate, if this can be generally applied for the "affective enhancing" of speech signals.

The open question here is how to deal with samples of lower bandwidth, where the hybrid mode is not directly applicable.

Acknowledgments. The authors thank for continued support by the SFB/TRR 62 "Companion-Technology for Cognitive Technical Systems" (www.sfb-trr-62.de) funded by the German Research Foundation (DFG). This work has further been sponsored by the Federal Ministry of Education and Research in the program Zwanzig20 – Partnership for Innovation as part of the research alliance 3Dsensation (www.3d-sensation.de). We would further like to thank SwissQual AG (a Rhode & Schwarz company), in particular Jens Berger, for supplying the POLQA testbed.

References

1. Albahri, A., Lech, M., Cheng, E.: Effect of speech compression on the automatic recognition of emotions. IJSPS **4**(1), 55–61 (2016)
2. Biundo, S., Wendemuth, A.: Companion-technology for cognitive technical systems. KI - Künstliche Intelligenz **30**(1), 71–75 (2016)
3. Brandenburg, K.: MP3 and AAC explained. In: 17th AES International Conference: High-Quality Audio Coding, Florence, Italy, September 1999
4. Burkhardt, F., Paeschke, A., Rolfes, M., Sendlmeier, W., Weiss, B.: A database of German emotional speech. In: Proceedings of the INTERSPEECH-2005, pp. 1517–1520, Lisbon, Portugal (2005)
5. Byrne, C., Foulkes, P.: The 'mobile phone effect' on vowel formants. Int. J. Speech Lang. Law **11**(1), 83–102 (2004)
6. Dhall, A., Goecke, R., Gedeon, T., Sebe, N.: Emotion recognition in the wild. J. Multimodal User Interfaces **10**, 95–97 (2016)
7. Engberg, I.S., Hansen, A.V.: Documentation of the danish emotional speech database (DES), Tech. rep. Aalborg University, Denmark (1996)
8. Eyben, F., Wöllmer, M., Schuller, B.: openSMILE - the munich versatile and fast open-source audio feature extractor. In: Proceedings of the ACM MM-2010, Firenze, Italy (2010)
9. García, N., Vásquez-Correa, J.C., Arias-Londoño, J.D., Várgas-Bonilla, J.F., Orozco-Arroyave, J.R.: Automatic emotion recognition in compressed speech using acoustic and non-linear features. In: Proceedings of STSIVA 2016, pp. 1–7 (2015)
10. Hall, M., Frank, E., Holmes, G., Pfahringer, B., Reutemann, P., Witten, I.H.: The weka data mining software: an update. SIGKDD Explor. Newsl. **11**(1), 10–18 (2009)

11. Hoene, C., Valin, J.M., Vos, K., Skoglund, J.: Summary of Opus listening test results draft-valin-codec-results-03. Internet-draft, IETF (2013)
12. IBM Corporation and Microsoft Corporation: Multimedia programming interface and data specifications 1.0. Tech. rep., August 1991
13. ITU-T: Methods for subjective determination of transmission quality. REC P.800 (1996), https://www.itu.int/rec/T-REC-P.800-199608-I/en
14. ITU-T: Wideband Coding of Speech at around 16 kbit/s using adaptive multi-rate wideband (AMR-WB). REC G.722.2 (2003), https://www.itu.int/rec/T-REC-G.722.2-200307-I/en
15. ITU-T: Methods for objective and subjective assessment of speech quality (POLQA): Perceptual Objective Listening Quality Assessment. REC P.863, September 2014, http://www.itu.int/rec/T-REC-P.863-201409-I/en
16. Jokisch, O., Maruschke, M., Meszaros, M., Iaroshenko, V.: Audio and speech quality survey of the opus codec in web real-time communication. In: Elektronische Sprachsignalverarbeitung 2016, vol. 81, Leipzig, Germany, pp. 254–262 (2016)
17. Lotz, A.F., Siegert, I., Maruschke, M., Wendemuth, A.: Audio compression and its impact on emotion recognition in affective computing. In: Elektronische Sprachsignalverarbeitung 2017, vol. 86, Saarbrücken, Germany, pp. 1–8 (2017)
18. Paulsen, S.: QoS/QoE-Modelle für den Dienst Voice over IP (VoIP). Ph.D. thesis, Universität Hamburg (2015)
19. Pfister, T., Robinson, P.: Speech emotion classification and public speaking skill assessment. In: Salah, A.A., Gevers, T., Sebe, N., Vinciarelli, A. (eds.) HBU 2010. LNCS, vol. 6219, pp. 151–162. Springer, Heidelberg (2010). doi:10.1007/978-3-642-14715-9_15
20. Rämö, A., Toukomaa, H.: Voice quality characterization of IETF opus codec. In: Proceedings of the INTERSPEECH-2011, pp. 2541–2544, Florence, Italy (2011)
21. Schuller, B., Vlasenko, B., Eyben, F., Rigoll, G., Wendemuth, A.: Acoustic emotion recognition: a benchmark comparison of performances. In: Proceedings of the IEEE ASRU-2009, Merano, Italy, pp. 552–557 (2009)
22. Siegert, I., Lotz, A.F., l. Duong, L., Wendemuth, A.: Measuring the impact of audio compression on the spectral quality of speech data. In: Elektronische Sprachsignalverarbeitung 2016, vol. 81, pp. 229–236. Leipzig, Germany (2016)
23. Siegert, I., Lotz, A.F., Maruschke, M., Jokisch, O., Wendemuth, A.: Emotion intelligibility within codec-compressed and reduced bandwith speech. In: ITG-Fb. 267: Speech Communication : 12. ITG-Fachtagung Sprachkommunikation 5–7. Oktober 2016 in Paderborn, pp. 215–219. VDE Verlag (2016)
24. Steininger, S., Schiel, F., Dioubina, O., Raubold, S.: Development of user-state conventions for the multimodal corpus in smartkom. In: Workshop on Multimodal Resources and Multimodal Systems Evaluation, Las Palmas, pp. 33–37 (2002)
25. Tickle, A., Raghu, S., Elshaw, M.: Emotional recognition from the speech signal for a virtual education agent. J. Phys.: Conf. Ser., vol. 450, p. 012053 (2013)
26. Valin, J.M., Vos, K., Terriberry, T.: Definition of the opus audio codec. RFC 6716, http://tools.ietf.org/html/rfc6716
27. Valin, J.M., Maxwell, G., Terriberry, T.B., Vos, K.: The opus codec. In: 135th AES International Convention, New York, USA, October 2013
28. Ververidis, D., Kotropoulos, C.: Emotional speech recognition: resources, features, and methods. Speech Commun. **48**, 1162–1181 (2006)
29. Vásquez-Correa, J.C., García, N., Vargas-Bonilla, J.F., Orozco-Arroyave, J.R., Arias-Londoño, J.D., Quintero, M.O.L.: Evaluation of wavelet measures on automatic detection of emotion in noisy and telephony speech signals. In: International Carnahan Conference on Security Technology, pp. 1–6 (2014)

30. Zeng, Z., Pantic, M., Roisman, G.I., Huang, T.S.: A survey of affect recognition methods: audio, visual, and spontaneous expressions. IEEE Trans. Pattern Anal. Mach. Intell. **31**, 39–58 (2009)

31. Zhang, Z., Weninger, F., Wöllmer, M., Schuller, B.: Unsupervised learning in cross-corpus acoustic emotion recognition. In: Proceedings of the IEEE ASRU-2011, Waikoloa, USA, pp. 523–528 (2011)

In Search of Sentence Boundaries
in Spontaneous Speech

Natalia Bogdanova-Beglarian[✉]

Saint Petersburg State University,
7/9 Universitetskaya Nab, St. Petersburg 199034, Russia
n.bogdanova@spbu.ru

Abstract. Oral text is certainly discrete. It is built of "small bricks", units of not only lexical but also the higher syntactical level. Common syntagmatic pauses, hesitative pauses such as physical (unfilled ones including breaks of clauses), sound pauses (*e-e, m-m*), and verbal (*vot, kak eto, nu, znachit* etc.) are markers of this discreetness. However, that reveals neither syntagma nor sentence as a unit to describe a syntactic structure of an oral text. Any type of pauses may occur in any place of an audio sequence. Thus, the search of sentences in spontaneous speech is quite complicated. In order to obtain such units a methodic of coercive punctuation that was used for marking the spontaneous monologues from the collection of oral texts named «Balanced Annotated Textotec» could be offered. The testee (philology experts) were asked to mark ends of the sentences by putting a period in the transcripts where neither pauses nor punctuation had been marked. The testee could only rely on the syntactic structure of the text and the connection between words and predicate centers. Involving more than twenty experts in an experiment provides more statistically accurate results. In this work we describe the results of our experiment and discuss further perspectives how those results can be used for automatic search of sentence boundaries in spontaneous speech.

Keywords: Speech corpus · Spontaneous monologue · Phrase boundary · Syntagma · Sentence · Discreetness of the oral text

1   Introduction

The oral speech has attracted acute attention of linguists of various fields and has provided a rich data for examination, research and conclusions. But at the same time it has appeared quite challenging to convert to the text form, to describe and to process and annotate automatically. One of the challenges is finding units of the spoken discourse on different levels – phonetic, morpheme, lexical, morphological and syntactical [1], particularly clause boundaries and markers. The current paper discusses means of describing the oral monologue and introduces a methodic of coercive punctuation, that was used for marking the spontaneous monologues from the collection of oral texts, named "Balanced Annotated Textotec" (corpus SAT) [2, 3]. It is important to notice that as a material for the investigation is used the spontaneous monologue, which has not been before an object of the oral speech researchers' attention. The majority of works

© Springer International Publishing AG 2017
A. Karpov et al. (Eds.): SPECOM 2017, LNAI 10458, pp. 456–463, 2017.
DOI: 10.1007/978-3-319-66429-3_45

[4–6] concentrated on a dialogue that do not raise the problem of sentence boundaries in general, or this problem is solved simply as a sentence matches to a remark.

2 Syntactical Units of Oral Spontaneous Text

It was discovered long ago by oral discourse students that it is impossible to describe such a text in the usual terms of *sentence*. Different minimal units for the analysis of syntax have been proposed. For example, W. Chafe's *syntagma* [7]; V. I. Podlesskaya and A. A. Kibrik's *elementary discourse unit* (EDU) [8]; S. V. Andreeva's *constitutive syntactical unit* (CSU) [9, 10]; N. S. Philippova's *structural syntactical unit* (SSU) [2, 11]. Although many of the approaches are valid, a full syntactical account for the text srill requires a unit correlating with the traditional sentence, for a variety of speech competence level (SCL) diagnostic features are based on sentence characteristics (simple – complex, one-member – two-member, types of one-member, parenthetical clauses, etc.) [12]. Average sentence length is a bright feature: the longer it is the higher the SCL. The very dividedness of a text would be sociolinguistically significant [13].

Dividing spontaneous text by intonation has also given no satisfactory result, because, as a research has found, intonational and syntactical fragmentation correlate in less than 54% of cases [14] (the research was carried out under the author's supervision). An endeavour to divide the text into *syntagmas* by instrumental and hearing analysis has demonstrated the same 50/50 effectiveness [15]. That is why in this investigation the search of sentence boundaries was realized not with the hearing analysis (audio, perceptive analysis), but using the experimental punctuating.

One of the last attempts at finding a useable unit was the idea of *structural syntactical unit* (SSU), which is a predicate with linked words [11] (the research was carried out under the author's supervision). Dividing the text into such complexes (notional sections), unlike sentences, usually causes no difficulty. But though it's a good way to avoid major difficulties of syntactical division and describe the structure it doesn't resolve the questions that arise when we are trying to interpret some pieces of the monologues, and that are caused by their spontaneous nature.

In order to preserve sentence as the main unit of analysis the *expert punctuating* experimental method can be used, in which way the SAT corpus was annotated.

3 Methodology of Data Collection

The SAT corpus is a collection of monologues having been collected in the Saint Petersburg State University for 25 years and known as a module of the Sound Corpus of the Russian Language [3, 16, 17]. The SAT is collected using the method introduced by the author (N. V. Bogdanova-Beglaryan) that implies an exact experimental procedure. The corpus was from the very beginning balanced sociologically, psychologically and linguistically.

That the corpus is *linguistically balanced* means that all the monologues fit into one of the *communicative scenarios*: *reading* and *retelling* (a narrative and a non-narrative text); *description of a picture* (narrative and non-narrative); *free narration on a given topic*.

Sociolinguistic balance means account of the speakers' social characteristics such as gender, age, profession, professional or not professional attitude towards speech, level of speech competence, etc.

Psycholinguistic balance means that psychological characteristics are taken into account, first of all extroversion/introversion (the differentiation is based on the G. Eysenck's psychological test).

Presently the corpus contains monologues collected from five professional groups (medical; law; computer, professionals; philologists, teachers of Russian as a foreign language; and philosophy lecturers), several blocks consisting of student's monologues (philologists and not), and four blocks of foreigner's interfered speech: Americans, the Chinese, the French and the Dutch. Sum total is about 800 texts and 50 h of audio recordings [3].

All audio recordings were transcribed, phonetically annotated (intonation and paralinguistic data) and, partially, syntactically (experimental punctuating), as well as provided with information about the type of communicative situation (speech scenario), social and psychological characteristics of the speakers.

4   Expert Punctuating Method

The punctuating experiment goes as follows. The monologues are transcribed in the orthographic form without any punctuation marks ("finding the stop" is the goal of the experiment) or intonational division. Such "mute" texts are offered to 20 experts for placing full stops. The testees have only the syntactical structure of the monologue, bonds between the words and the predicates, as much as they are apparent in a material represented this way, to rely on. Having no less than 20 philologists as testees to some extent ensures statistical value of the result. A period put by no less than 60% of the testees (no less than 12 out of 20 periods must coincide; one may speak about "hard-and-fast rule zones", if use T. M. Nikolayeva's term [18, 19]) is considered the true boundary between the sentences. This method has been used in spontaneous monologue studies for a rather long time, but it's very application that spots the many problems of such division.

4.1   Problem Zones on Sentence Boundaries. Coordinating and Asyndetic Connection

The most problematic (and interesting to study) are those zones of the text that were punctuated by 10 or 11 testees (50–55% was called the "free choice zone" by T. M. Nikolayeva [18, 19]). By the conditions of the experiment these periods are neither recognized as boundaries nor taken into account, although it is highly possible that the text could be divided in those places, hence they are noteworthy. For example, it may be predicates bonded with coordinate conjunctions or without any (the number of periods put by experts in the respective place is in the brackets; periods that occurred less than 10 times were left unmarked):

- *vam neobhodimo otdoxnut' (11) // sjezdite v gory / pokatajtes' na lyzhax / u vas vs'o projd'ot (20)*;
- *i dejstvitel'no kogda nastroenie horoshee / vs'o ladits'a / vs'o vokrug chudesno / i solnce svetit jarche / i pticy pojut horosho / i na dushe radostno i vs'o kazhets'a udasts'a (11) // i dazhe te mechty kotorye kazalos' by sovsem / nereal'ny oni ob'azatel'no ispoln'ats'a (20).*

Such constructions may be interpreted either as a unite conjunctionless complex sentence or as a sequence of independent clauses. The choice in this case is determined solely by the expert's will and does not depend on the sentence structure itself (see: [20]). The punctuating method strictly applied gives no reliable solution here.

4.2   Problematic Zones on Sentence Boundaries. Discourse Markers Between Sentences

Another kind of difficult situations are those where the boundary is filled with a meaningless word (discourse marker), forming a hesitation pause – *vot, znachit, nu vot,* and such (hereafter we are going to call the units by the word *vot* for convenience). A. A. Stepikhov called the position "a kind of a "buffer zone" between two clauses", equally likely to be ascribed to either the left or the right structural unit [14]. Meaningful components, most often circumstantial modifiers, might happen is such zones:

- *i vdrug slyshysh' rychanie medved'a / gde-to tam **vot** / **vot** / **vot** / **vot** / **vot** i ne znaesh' / to li bezhat' / to li hvatat' bol'shushchij / neskol'ko belyh gribov (17)*;
- *i on nachal katat's'a val'at' po polu // katat's'a i val'at's'a po polu // **nu vot** (11) nu on znachit byl gr'aznyj / ryzhyj*;
- *sobirajut vsem selom // ot mala do velika / to jest' sobirajuts'a i devushki molodye / i uzhe zhenshchiny / kak govorit's'a i / samye razlichnye i s kosami na golove (11) / **nu vot** (4) muzhyki / m-m s... / mal'chishki / nu i zdes' konechno i domashnie zhyvotnye / sobaki / tozhe sdes' priv'azannye k derevu prisutstvujut (10) // **pri etom** (8) dl'a togo chtoby sobrat's'a i chtoby eto bylo / a-a / udobnee / m-m ispol'zujut shalashy / zaranee zagotovlennye (18)*;
- *nashli cheloveka i pon'ali chelovek ne mog peshkom daleko-to ujti / znachit gde-to ne tak daleko / i zhyljo (9) **mozhet byt'** (7) / eto spaslo i / novos'olkovskih muzhykov.*

The experts feel the boundary very well and, as a rule, place a period in it, but – differently. Three variations can occur: a full-stop after *vot* (it comes to be the last in the sentence), a full-stop before *vot* (it "opens" a new sentence) and two full-stops around *vot* (it forms its own syntactical unit). It's probable that a testee would choose any of the variants, but it also might happen that none of the three possibilities is fulfilled full 12 times. In other words, an evident sentence boundary if left unmarked according to the experimental requirements. It seems that naming the word *vot* the boundary between the sentences, considering only the amount of periods around it, regardless of where they are placed, would be a reasonable solution. Yet it will eliminate a considerable amount of one-word indivisible sentences, into which class *vot* can be sorted out and which are altogether peculiar to oral spontaneous speech.

4.3   Other Problematic Zones of Spoken Text

There are other challenges to stating boundaries between sentences in a spontaneous text – say, qualification of broken or inconsistent clauses, repeats and self-corrections that are inherent to oral speech:

- *i hoteli oni vy... / oni tol'ko znali chto on byl jarko-ryzhego cveta (12)*;
- *nu sushchestvuet eshcho r'ad ochen' / bolee / pro prirodu mne konechno slozhno ochen' / m-m ochen' slozhnyx / primet (13) // naprimer kogda tam gorizont / chto-to / sluchaets'a tam / jesli oblaka / vysoko v nebe to mozhet byt' / s....v... veter / nu vs'o takoe (13)*;
- *na etoj kartinke priroda v obshchem-to / ne raduet glaz men'a // potomu chto ona kakaja-to ochen' / temno i sumrachno v lesu // net cvetov / kotorye ja l'ubl'u (18) // ne ochen' zhyzneradostnaja takaja kartinka (18)*.

It is such difficulties of syntactical division that make students of oral speech abandon the term "sentence". In addition to the units mentioned above we note the term *utterance*, maintained by A. A. Stepikhov. The author sees utterance as a "a speech sequence as it was perceived by experts during linguistic (punctuating. – *N. B.–B.*) experiment, that is <...> a reflection of the speech in the testees' minds" [14], p. 11. This approach indeed follows the tradition of oral speech studies, although it doesn't resolve the problems of dividing the speech into any kind of structural units.

5   Prospects of Linguistic Account on Spoken Monologue Based on "Sentence", Elicited with the Punctuating Experiment

Many interesting data about the spoken monologue syntax were collected using the expert punctuating method with the SAT material.

5.1   To What Extent an Oral Text Can Be Divided into "Sentences"

An analysis of medical worker's texts from the SAT revealed that the very divisibility into sentences during the experiment can be a feature of a speech competence level (SCL) or a type of text. The higher the SCL, the more full-stops coincide and the less the dispersion (the difference between the minimal and the maximal number of "sentences" in a text) in the experts' responses. In other words better divisibility corresponds with the high SCL, and bad divisibility – with the low SCL (assuming that difficulties with dividing a spontaneous text into "sentences" is itself a feature of unprepared speech) (see Table 1).

The table shows that this factor has an equally strong correlation both with the speech competence level and the type of monologue: easier division (which is the higher number) marks not only the high SCL texts, but also retellings as the most given text-oriented and the least spontaneous in our data (comp. the figures in bold). All narrative monologues turned out to be marked in this matter to the same extent

Table 1. Factors contributing to difficulty of division of different types of monologues (in %)

Monologue type		Speech competence level of speakers	
		High SCL	Low SCL
Retelling	Narrative text	90,8	84,2
	Non-narrative text	89,7	81,1
	Total	**90,2**	**82,6**
Description	Narrative picture	86,6	79,3
	Non-narrative picture	84,7	72,7
	Total	**85,7**	**76,0**
Free narration		**77,4**	**74,8**

(narrative text retellings and narrative picture descriptions): they demonstrate a better divisibility than the respective non-narrative monologues [2].

5.2   Average "Sentence" Length in Words and Text Length in "Sentences"

Both features show a clear correlation with the speech competence level: the higher the SCL, the longer and larger in number are the "sentences". For instance, texts of medical workers with the low SCL count in average 13.2 words per 'sentence'; in text of the high SCL it is 16.8. Also, the higher the SCL, the more extensive the monologues (from the overall 511 'sentences' in the low SCL monologues to 894 in the high) [2].

5.3   More About Syntactical Peculiarities of Oral Monologues

Another feature bonded to the SCL appeared to be *syntactical construction ("sentence") diversity*. It turned out that diversity of structure (impersonal, compound, infinitive) and also the number of clauses in a 'sentence' agrees with the high SCL [2].

6   Conclusions

All said above convincingly demonstrates, on one hand, that syntactical (just as any other, it seems) account of the oral spontaneous monologue, and, subsequently, creating a *speech grammar book* offers a significant challenge to scholars, but, on the other hand, that there is a broad spectrum of possibilities to overcome the difficulties and reach the goal. The punctuating experiment allows to find a "sentence" in the spontaneous monologue structure and carry out a full syntactic analysis.

References

1. Bogdanova, N.V.: Basic concepts of speech and language (search of units description of spontaneous speech). In: The MAPRYAL Conference. Innovation in Studies of Russian Language, Literature and Culture. Proceedings, Hungary, Plovdiv, vol. I, pp. 189–194 (2007) (In Russian)
2. Bogdanova-Beglarian, N.V. (ed.): Speech Corpus as a Base for Analysis of Russian Speech. Collective Monograph. Part 1. Reading. Retelling. Description, 532 p. Philological Faculty of SPb State Univ. Publ., St. Petersburg (2013) (In Russian)
3. Bogdanova-Beglarian, N.V., Sherstinova. T.J., Zajdes, K.D.: Corpus «balanced annotated textotec»: methodology multi-level analysis of the russian monologue speech. In: Kocharov, D.A., Skrelin, P.A. (eds.) Analysis of Conversational Russian Speech Proceedings of the 7th Interdisciplinary Seminar, pp. 8–13. Polytekhnica-print, St. Petersburg (2017) (In Russian)
4. Zemskaja, E.A. (ed.): Russian Conversational Speech, 485 p. Nauka, Moscow (1973) (In Russian)
5. Sirotinina, O.B.: Modern Conversational Speech and Its Peculiarities, 144 p. Prosveshchenie, Moscow (1974) (In Russian)
6. Lapteva, O.A.: Russian Conversational Syntax, 397 p. Nauka, Moscow (1976) (In Russian)
7. Chafe, W.: Integration and involvement in speaking, writing, and oral literature. In: Tannen, D. (ed.) Spoken and Written Language: Exploring Orality and Literacy, pp. 35–54. Ablex, Norwood (1982)
8. Podlesskaya, V.I., Kibrik, A.A.: Disfluency correction in spontaneous speech: a corpus study. In: Computational Linguistics and Intellectual Technologies: Proceedings of the International Conference, Dialog 2005, [Electronic Resource] (2005). http://www.dialog-21.ru/media/2416/podlesskaya-kibrik.pdf. (In Russian)
9. Andreeva. S.V.: Elementary Constructive-Syntactic Units of Spoken Language and Their Communicative Potential. Author's Abstract of Ph.D. Thesis. 49 p. Saratov (2005) (In Russian)
10. Andreeva. S.V.: Speech Units of Spoken Russian Language: System, Area Use, Functions. In: Sirotinina, O.B. (ed.) 192 p. Moscow (2006) (In Russian)
11. Filippova, N.S.: Principles of Oral Descriptive Discourse (a Case Study of Russian Spontaneous Speech). Ph.D. Thesis (typing), 220 p. St. Petersburg (2010) (In Russian)
12. Bogdanova, N.V.: On the syntactic correlates of the differentiation of levels of speech culture. In: Zhivoe slovo v russkoj rechi Prikamja [The Living Word in the Russian Language of Kama Region], pp. 92–100. Perm. State Univ. Publ., Perm (1993) (In Russian)
13. Bogdanova, N.V., Brodt, I.S.: Divisibility of oral different types monologues. In: Remneva, M.L. (ed.) Problems of Russian Linguistics, Iss. XI. Aspects of speech study. The Collection for the Elena Andreevna Bryzgunova's Anniversary, pp. 95–97. Moscow State Univ. Publ., Moscow (2004) (In Russian)
14. Stepikhov, A.A.: The Correlation of Syntactic and Intonational Discreteness of Spontaneous Monologue. Ph.D. Thesis (typing), 197 p. St. Petersburg (2005) (In Russian)
15. Vol'skaya, N.B., Stepanova, S.B.: Some problems of syntagmatic divisibility of a spontaneous text. In: XXX International Philological Conference. Phonetics Panel. Part 1, vol. 10, pp. 16–24. Philological Faculty of SPbGU Publ., St. Petersburg (2005) (In Russian)
16. Bogdanova, N.V., Brodt, I.S., Kukanova, V.V., Pavlova, O.V., Sapunova, E.M., Filippova, N.S.: The corpus of spoken russian: design principles and approaches to data analysis. In: Kibrik, A.E. (ed.) Computational Linguistics and Intelligent Technologies: Proceedings of the International Conference, Dialog 2008, pp. 57–61. Russian State Human. Univ. Publ., Moscow (2008) (In Russian)

17. Bogdanova, N.V.: The corpus of spoken russian: new receipts and the first results of research. In: Kibrik, A.E. (ed.) Computational Linguistics and Intelligent Technologies: Proceedings of the International Conference, Dialog 2010, pp. 35–40. Russian State Human. Univ. Publ., Moscow (2010) (In Russian)

18. Nikolaeva, T.M.: Semantic division of the text and its individual variants. In: Semiotics and Text Structure, pp. 71–79. Warszawa (1973) (In Russian)

19. Nikolaeva, T.M.: Text linguistics: present state and perspectives. In: New in Foreign Linguistics. Iss. VIII, pp. 5–39. Progress, Moscow (1978) (In Russian)

20. Stepikhov, A.: Sociolinguistic factors in text-based sentence boundary detection. In: Ronzhin, A., Potapova, R., Fakotakis, N. (eds.) Speech and Computer. 17th International Conference, SPECOM 2015, Athens, Greece, 20–24 September 2015, Proceedings, pp. 372–380. Athens (2015)

Investigating Acoustic Correlates of Broad and Narrow Focus Perception by Japanese Learners of English

Gábor Pintér[1]([⊠]), Oliver Jokisch[2], and Shinobu Mizuguchi[3]

[1] Linguwerk GmbH, Dresden, Germany
gabor.pinter@linguwerk.de
[2] Leipzig University of Telecommunications (HfTL), Leipzig, Germany
jokisch@hftl.de
[3] Kobe University, Kobe, Japan
mizuguti@kobe-u.ac.jp

Abstract. This work is an addition to the relatively short line of research concerning second language prosody perception. Using a prominence marking experiment, the study demonstrates that Japanese learners of English can perceptually discriminate between different focus scopes. Perceptual score profiles imply that narrowly focused words are identified and discriminated relatively easily, while differentiation of different scopes of broad focus presents a greater challenge. An analysis of a range of acoustic cues indicates that perceptual scores correlate most strongly with F0-based features. While this result is in contradiction with previous research results, it is shown that the divergence is attributable to the particular acoustic characteristics of the stimulus.

Keywords: Prosody perception · Narrow versus broad focus · Japanese learners of English · L2 acquisition

1 Introduction

The term *focus* generally refers to the part of the sentence that introduces *novel* information to the discourse [5,7]. Although novel information can usually be easily identified based on semantic or pragmatic context, languages often provide extra information about the focus in the form of synthetic (e.g., word order), morphological (e.g., particles), or prosodic cues. Breen et al. [3] demonstrated that native speakers of English tend to mark focus prosodically, using greater intensity, longer duration, and higher mean and maximum F0. In a range of experiments Jennifer Cole and her colleagues discovered that prosodic prominence is consistently detected in natural speech by non-trained native listeners [4,8,10]. In co-operation with Cole, Pintér and his colleagues [12,13] revealed that Japanese speakers of English can also detect prosodic prominence in natural speech to a certain level, but with much less consistency than native speakers. A research study by Yamane et al. [14] seems to contradict these findings claiming

© Springer International Publishing AG 2017
A. Karpov et al. (Eds.): SPECOM 2017, LNAI 10458, pp. 464–472, 2017.
DOI: 10.1007/978-3-319-66429-3_46

that focus perception of Japanese speakers closely approximates that of native speakers of English.

As Pinter & Kihara [11] and Miziguchi et al. [9] point out, these seemingly contradicting findings about L2 prominence perception are both maintainable, if differences in focus types are taken into consideration. Novel information in an utterance can range from a single word to a whole sentence (cf. *thetic* sentences by Kuroda [6]). *Narrow focus* refers to cases when a single word receives focus; the term *broad focus* encompasses cases with focus scopes being broader than a single word (see Halliday 1967 [5]). As for prosodic marking, it is believed that cue intensity is inversely proportional to focus scope [1,3]. The broader the focus scopes are, the less prominent acoustic cues they carry. Since the stimuli in Yamane's research consisted of narrowly focused elements, they presented perceptually salient, easily identifiable targets—even for foreign learners of English. The natural utterances in experiments in the other set of experiments were, however, dominated by sentences with broad focus. The less consistent performance of L2 listeners in this case, can be explained by the less salient acoustic marking of broad focus types. Findings in [9,11] confirm the validity of this hypothesis.

The goal of this article is to re-analyze data presented in [11] and provide a more thorough analysis that statistically confirms that L2 listeners are capable of perceptually distinguishing focus types within and across categories of narrow and broad foci. The perceptual findings are augmented with an acoustic analysis demonstrating that prominence ratings show the greatest correlation—contrary to previous findings—with pitch-based cues. This result, however, is believed to be affected by the acoustically skewed stimuli, which was collected from a single native speaker. While this interpretation prevents generalizations about L2 prominence perception, it demonstrates aptly how acoustic characteristics of the input can influence perceptual strategies, and calls for more careful selection and more thorough analysis of stimuli in prosody perception studies.

2   Experiment Materials and Design

The prosody perception experiment reported in this article follows the design outlined in Bishop (2012) [2], with some modification. The experiment was carried out in August 2015, at Kobe University.

2.1   Participants

Twenty-two Japanese undergraduate students of Kobe University participated in the experiment. Their English proficiency was not assessed for this research, but most of them were at high-intermediate level, with the average of 641 points at the TOEIC-IP test—out of the possible 990.

2.2   Stimuli

The audio stimuli for the experiment were extracted from controlled mini-dialogues with a native adult female speaker of North-American English, Southern Californian dialect. The single question-and-answer type of dialogues were

Table 1. Stimuli sentences with different focus scopes: s1–s4

(s1) Verb Phrase	Q:	*What did you do yesterday?*
	A:	I [saw a bad film]$_{VP}$ yesterday
(s2) Object	Q:	*What did you see yesterday?*
	A:	I saw [a bad film]$_{NP}$ yesterday
(s3) Modifier	Q:	*What film did you see yesterday?*
	A:	I saw a [bad]$_{Adj}$ film yesterday
(s4) Adjunct	Q:	*When did you see a bad film?*
	A:	I saw a bad film [yesterday]$_{Adjunct}$.

designed in a way that the questions elicited answers with four different focus scopes: *verb phrase* (s1), *object noun phrase* (s2), *modifier* (s3), and *adjunct* (s4) scopes. The different focus scopes are represented by square brackets in Table 1.

The same dialogue pattern was used with 5 different sentences (see Table 2). The recordings took place in a quiet room using a Tascam DF-5 audio recorder. The response parts from the mini-dialogues were extracted and saved into separate audio files in 44.1 kHz, mono, PCM format. The stimuli set consisted of 4 (focus types) × 5 (sentence types) = 20 utterances.

Table 2. Stimuli sentences types

	SUBJECT	VERB		MODIFIER	OBJECT	ADJUNCT
(a)	I	saw	a	bad	film	yesterday
(b)		bought		pink	hat	
(c)		found		large	book	
(d)		made		sweet	cake	
(e)		learned		mean	trick	

2.3 Experiment Design

The response parts from the mini-dialogues were printed on a sheet of paper and handed out to participants as response sheets. The audio stimuli were presented to them over a classroom loudspeaker in a previously fixed, randomized order. One sentence from the stimuli set was used for practice; otherwise, each stimuli was presented only once, with sufficient time between them to mark responses

Table 3. Sample response with prominence marks over some words

2   5

I   saw   a bad   film   yesterday

at a slow pace. The participants were asked to mark the level of strength of the most *prominent* words in the sentences on a scale of 1 to 5 (see Table 3).

The participants were encouraged to evaluate only those words that they felt were prominent. This is a deviation from Bishop's experiment in which all target words had to be scored.

2.4   Results

Each sentence received at least 1, at most 4, on average 1.89 prominence scores from each participant. There were 22 (participants) × 4 (focus conditions) × 5 (sentence types) × 5 (words per sentence) = 2200 data points collected, 62.2% of which did not receive a score mark (see Fig. 1). Intermediate marks of 1s and 2s were relatively rare.

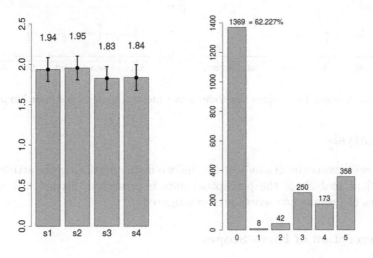

Fig. 1. Responses: (a) average mark per sentence; (b) score distribution

Figure 2 summarizes the responses over sentence constituents in the 4 different focus conditions. Each sub-plot in the figure summarizes responses over all participants and all of the 5 sentence variants. It is apparent from the figures that narrowly focused words (i.e., s3: modifier, s4: adjunct) were perceived as most salient. Also, these narrow focus peaks stood out more prominently from their context than broadly focused elements in s1 and s2. The perceptual peaks in broad focus conditions were lower and less contrastive. Interestingly, the s1 focus condition with the broadest scope elicited higher scores than the narrower NP focus s2. A one-tailed, paired Wilcoxon test confirmed that the sentence objects in s1 condition got higher scores than in s2 ($p =< 0.01$). This result is contrary to our expectations, since utterances with wider focus scopes (here: s1) are reported to be acoustically less prominent and consequently also expected to be perceptually less salient.

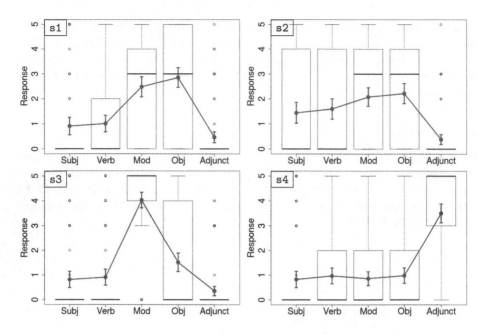

Fig. 2. Averaged responses per focus type: mean responses laid over boxplots

3   Analysis

The following two subsections address the two main questions of the article. First, a statistical analysis of the perceptual data is presented. Second, the acoustic correlates of prominence scores are investigated.

3.1   Perception of Focus Scopes

Table 4 represents p-values from pairwise, two-tailed Wilcoxon tests iterating over each pair of focus conditions and each sentence constituent. The figures justify the preliminary observation in the previous section: narrow focus conditions s3 and s4 are clearly different from broad focus utterances and from each other. Differences over the narrowly focused adjunct and modifier can separate s3 and s4 conditions from broad focus cases of s1 and s2, and from each other. Positioned between the modifier and the adjunct, objects also seem to play an important role in differentiating narrow and broad focus types. Differences between the two broad focus conditions (s1 and s2) are the least salient. Although differences between s1 and s2 over sentence subjects and verbs were statistically significant, the levels of significance ($p < 0.05$) are remarkably smaller than in the cases involving narrow foci ($p < 0.0001$).

These observations confirm the hypothesis that Japanese speakers of English can relatively easily identify narrowly focused words, while their perception of different broad focus types are less reliable, but still bears statistical significance. This finding is compatible with [9,11].

Table 4. *P*-values from paired Wilcoxon tests

Subj	s2	s3	s4	Verb	s2	s3	s4
s1	*0.041	0.598	0.670	s1	*0.017	0.671	0.883
s2		*0.025	*0.013	s2		**0.003	*0.017
s3			0.987	s3			0.908

Mod	s2	s3	s4	Obj	s2	s3	s4
s1	0.125	****	****	s1	0.010	****	****
s2		****	****	s2		**0.004	****
s3			****	s3			*0.011

Adjunct	s2	s3	s4
s1	0.381	0.637	****
s2		0.868	****
s3			****

3.2 Acoustic Correlates of Prosodic Focus

For each stimuli a word and phoneme level label transcription was created and aligned manually with the audio. Acoustic measures were taken only for the stressed vowels in the words, so measurements for article 'a' and the last two syllables of 'yesterday' were excluded from the data set. A Praat script was used to extract vowel timestamps, F0 and RMS measurements from the audio.

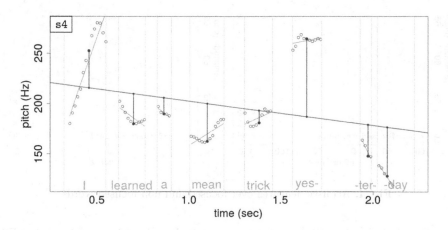

Fig. 3. Distance from overall F0 trend (`F0 dist`) and micro-intonation slope (`F0 msl`)

F0-based measurements included: F0 minimum, median, maximum values, and a special feature (`F0 dist`) that was calculated by taking the median distance of vowels from the general F0 trend in the utterance (see Fig. 3). The F0 tendency was calculated as a regression line fitted against F0 values over the vowels. Micro-intonation slopes (`F0 msl`), that is local F0 trends were also calculated over each vowel. Amplitude measures involved mean and maximum values over vowels. Vowel durations were z-score normalized at utterance level (`dur`).

Two types of correlation estimates, Kendall's tau and Pearson's rho, were used to test the relation between acoustic features and perceptual scores. Kendall correlation appears in numerous previous prosody perception studies, but Pearson is more robust against skewed data. As shown in Table 5, in both correlation types F0 based features produced the strongest correlation estimates. Amplitude came second, duration third. All of the correlations were statistically significant.

Table 5. Kendall's and Pearson's correlation of scores to acoustic features

FEATURE	τ	ρ	FEATURE	τ	ρ
F0 dist	0.330	0.451	ΔF0	0.303	0.391
F0 max	0.328	0.432	Amp max	0.298	0.375
OME	0.327	0.431	Amp mean	0.278	0.344
F0	0.322	0.430	F0 min	0.264	0.338
ΔF0 dist	0.309	0.391	F0 msl	0.207	0.262
ΔOME	0.305	0.374	dur	0.176	0.290

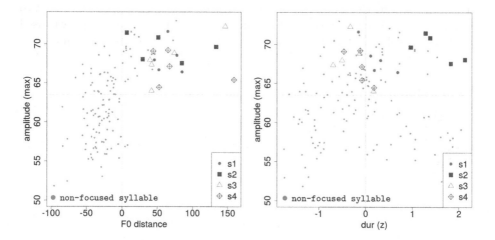

Fig. 4. Acoustic features over focused and non-focused words

Since Japanese is a pitch-accent language, it should not be surprising that F0-based features were the strongest correlates of perceived prosodic prominence. However, this result is in contrast with previous studies [9,12], which found vowel duration to be the strongest correlate of prosodic prominence perception in L2. Duration may be a reliable acoustic cue for prominence; however, there is always a possibility that a speaker prefers other means of prosody marking. Figure 4 displays the distribution of acoustic features over stressed and unstressed words—provided by a single speaker. It can be seen that prominence is cued most prominently along dimensions of F0 and intensity. All focused words are in the upper right quarter of the amplitude versus F0 distance plot. The subplot on the right shows that durational cues do not add much to the separation of focused and non-focused elements. These results imply that the high correlation scores for F0 based cues in perception is motivated by the acoustic characteristics of the audio stimuli.

4   Conclusion

The purpose of this study was twofold. First, it aimed to prove that Japanese speakers of English perceive various narrow and broad focus type utterances differently. Re-analyzing the results of a prosody labeling experiment from [11], this study confirmed that Japanese listeners perceive and discriminate narrow focus types relatively easily, while being less consistent with broad focus types.

This finding not only explains the seemingly contradictory findings of previous L2 prosody research, but also implies that studies investigating focus need to carefully consider the scope of focus they refer to.

The other goal of the study was to investigate the acoustic correlates of focus perception. F0-based features (e.g., F0 dist, F0 max, F0) were found to correlate the strongest with prosody scores. This result diverges from findings of previous research, but due to limitation in the size of the audio set, the discrepancy does not allow for far-fetching conclusions. Nevertheless, it highlights a potential problem in perceptual studies: perceptual profiles of responses are affected by acoustic characteristics of the stimuli. If the stimuli is acoustically skewed, the listeners can learn these characteristics, just like adapting in perception to an L2 dialect, and the responses eventually reflect the characteristics of the input stimuli, and not necessarily the listeners original preferences for acoustic cues.

References

1. Baumann, S., Grice, M., Steindamm, S.: Prosodic marking of focus domains: Categorical or gradient? In: Proceedings of 3rd International Conference on Speech Prosody 2006, pp. 301–304. TUDpress, Dresden (2006)
2. Bishop, J.: Information structural expectations in the perception of prosodic prominence. Prosody Mean. 239–269 (2012)
3. Breen, M., Fedorenko, E., Wagner, M., Gibson, E.: Acoustic correlates of information structure. Lang. Cogn. Process. 25, 1044–1098 (2010)
4. Cole, J., Mo, Y.S., Baek, S.: The role of syntactic structure in guiding prosody perception with ordinary listeners and everyday speech. Lang. Cogn. Process. 7–19, 1141–1177 (2010)
5. Halliday, M.: Notes on transitivity and theme in English Part II. J. Linguist. 3, 199–244 (1967)
6. Kuroda, S.Y.: The categorical and the thetic judgment. Found. Lang. 9, 153–185 (1972)
7. Lambrecht, K.: Information Structure and Sentence Form: Topic, Focus, and the Mental Representations of Discourse. Cambridge University Press, Cambridge (1994)

8. Mahrt, T., Huang, J.T., Mo, Y., Cole, J., Hasegawa-Johnson, M., Fleck, M.: Feature sets for the automatic detection of prosodic prominence (2011)
9. Mizuguchi, S., Pintér, G. Tateishi, K.: Natural speech perception cues by Japanese learners of English. In: Proceedings of Pacific Second Language Research Forum (PacSLRF) 2016, Tokyo, pp. 151–156 (2017)
10. Mo, Y., Cole, J., Lee, E.K.: Naïve listeners' prominence and boundary perception. In: Proceedings of Speech Prosody, Campinas, Brazil, pp. 735–738 (2008)
11. Pintér, G., Kihara, E.: Broad and narrow focus perception in Japanese learners of english before and after a short-term study tour. Bull. Sch. Lang. Commun. Kobe Univ. **12**, 30–39 (2016)
12. Pintér, G., Mizuguchi, S., Tateishi, K.: Perception of prosodic prominence and boundaries by L1 and L2 speakers of English. In: Proceedings of Interspeech 2014, Singapore, pp. 544–547 (2014)
13. Pintér, G., Mizuguchi, S., Yamato, K.: Boundary and prominence perception by Japanese learners of English: A preliminary study. Phonol. Stud. **17**, 59–66 (2014)
14. Yamane, N., Yoshimura, N., Fujimori, A.: Prosodic transfer from Japanese to English: Pitch in focus marking. Phonol. Stud. **19**, 97–105 (2016)

Language Adaptive Multilingual CTC Speech Recognition

Markus Müller[1,2]([✉]), Sebastian Stüker[1,2], and Alex Waibel[1,2,3]

[1] Institute for Anthropomatics and Robotics, Karlsruhe, Germany
m.mueller@kit.edu
[2] Karlsruhe Institute of Technology, Karlsruhe, Germany
[3] Language Technology Institute, Carnegie Mellon University, Pittsburgh, PA, USA
http://isl.anthropomatik.kit.edu

Abstract. Recently, it has been demonstrated that speech recognition systems are able to achieve human parity. While much research is done for resource-rich languages like English, there exists a long tail of languages for which no speech recognition systems do yet exist. The major obstacle in building systems for new languages is the lack of available resources. In the past, several methods have been proposed to build systems in low-resource conditions by using data from additional source languages during training. While it has been shown that DNN/HMM hybrid setups trained in low-resource conditions benefit from additional data, we are proposing a similar technique using sequence based neural network acoustic models with Connectionist Temporal Classification (CTC) loss function. We demonstrate that setups with multilingual phone sets benefit from the addition of Language Feature Vectors (LFVs).

Keywords: Speech recognition · Low-resource · Multilingual training · Connectionist temporal classification

1 Introduction

In recent years, the use of artificial neural networks (ANNs) has lead to dramatic improvements in the field of automatic speech recognition (ASR), lately achieving human parity [27,42]. ANNs are being used as part of the pre-processing pipeline, e.g., for dimensionality reduction [13], or as part of the acoustic model in DNN/HMM hybrid systems. Latest developments include sequence based ANN based setups with Connectionist Temporal Classification (CTC) [9] loss function. Such systems do not require certain types of resources traditional model do, like time-aligned labels, HMMs and cluster trees. Popular network topologies to use in such setups are bi-directional Long-Short Term Memory (LSTM) networks [14].

While proposed back in 2006, this method has gained popularity quite recently, due to the availability of increased computing power that enabled using large amounts of training data. One of the main advantages of CTC based systems over conventional speech recognition systems is that they are able to

© Springer International Publishing AG 2017
A. Karpov et al. (Eds.): SPECOM 2017, LNAI 10458, pp. 473–482, 2017.
DOI: 10.1007/978-3-319-66429-3_47

capture temporal dependencies by themselves. While HMM based systems use context-dependent states to mitigate the error made by the Markov assumption (the current state only depends upon the previous state), CTC based systems learn to model context implicitly by the use of Recurrent Neural Networks (RNNs).

But CTC based models are more sensitive to the amount of available training data. This is especially problematic if only a limited amount of data is available during training. In this work, we are proposing a method for adding data from additional source languages. Similar to methods proposed for DNN/HMM based systems, we use data from multiple languages during training. To train our setup truly multilingual, we use a global phone set combining the phone sets of all source languages. In addition, we demonstrate that the recognition performance can be improved by the addition of Language Feature Vectors (LFVs) [23]. By applying this proposed method, multilingual systems outperform monolingual systems trained on the target language only.

This paper is organized as follows: In the next Section, we provide an overview of related work in the field. We describe our approach in Sect. 3, followed by the description of the experimental setup in Sect. 4. Section 5 contains the results and we conclude this paper in Sect. 6, where we also provide an outlook to future work.

2   Related Work

2.1   GMM Based Multi- and Crosslingual Systems

Prior to using neural networks as part of speech recognition systems, the use of GMM/HMM based systems was common. The problem of training systems multi- and crosslingually has been addressed in the past to handle data sparsity [32,41]. Techniques for adapting the cluster tree were proposed [33], but methods for crosslingual adaptation exist as well [36].

2.2   Multilingual DBNFs

Building DNN-based systems in low resource conditions is challenging, especially because DNNs are a data-driven method with many parameters to be trained. Hence, a large amount of data is required for the model to generalize. Several methods have been proposed to use data from additional source languages. The first step is to pre-train models unsupervised, which is language independent [38]. For fine-tuning, several approaches exist to incorporate multilingual data. One possibility is to share the hidden layers between languages, but use language specific output layers [8,12,29,39]. Instead of having independent output layers, block softmax can also be applied [11]. By partitioning the output layer or using language specific output layers, the systems use separate phone sets for each language instead of a global phone set. In general, training DNNs using data from multiple languages in parallel can be considered as a form of multi-task learning [5,22].

2.3   Neural Network Adaptation

A common method to adapt neural networks to different speakers is the use of i-Vectors [28] or Bottleneck Speaker Vectors (BSVs) [15]. By using such vectors, speaker adaptive neural networks [21] can be built. These low dimensional vectors encode speaker peculiarities which enable the network to adapt to different speaker characteristics. These methods demonstrate that neural networks benefit from additional input modalities.

Similar to BSVs, we have shown that feature augmentation can also be used to adapt ANNs to different languages when trained multilingually. Providing the language identity information using one-hot encoding leads to improvements [25], but does not provide any language characteristics to the network. Language Feature Vectors (LFVs) [23,24] have shown to encode such language peculiarities, even if the LFV net was not trained on the target language.

2.4   CTC Based Systems

While originally proposed in 2006 [9], CTC-based systems are becoming more popular these days. Systems can be trained using either phones or graphemes as labels, or jointly together [6]. Recently, a setup being trained directly on words has been proposed [34]. The notion of multi-task learning can also be applied to CTC-based setups [16,18,26].

3   Language Adaptive Multilingual CTC

We aimed at training our setup multilingually, opting for using phones over characters. By merging pronunciation dictionaries from multiple languages, we created a global phone set. While there are many approaches of training CTC systems directly on characters and omitting the pronunciation dictionary, we used phones as targets in this first approach because characters or groups of characters are pronounced very differently between languages, e.g., "*th*" in English or "*sch*" in German. Being language independent, phones are always pronounced in the same way, but eventually with a language specific twang. This might introduce classification errors as the network might have difficulties identifying the correct phone independent of the language. Another issue might have been language dependent phone contexts. While HMM-based systems in general suffer in performance when using a multilingual phone set, special techniques have been proposed to adapt the set of context-dependent states (see Sect. 2.1). CTC-based systems potentially do not suffer as much from this problem because all phone contexts are learned implicitly by the network. In order to compensate for language dependent peculiarities, we used LFVs which have shown to improve the performance of multilingual HMM-based systems.

We based our setup on Baidu's Deepspeech 2 architecture [4]. The network topology is shown in Fig. 1. The input features were first processed by 2 2D convolution layers. Convolutional Neural Networks (CNNs) are based on the idea of Time-delay Neural Networks (TDNNs) [40]. By applying 2D convolution on the spectrogram, these 2D TDNN layers learn filters to extract features in both the frequency and time dimension. We added LFVs to the output of the convolution layers as input to the bi-directional LSTM [14] layers by appending them to the feature vector. The output layer was a fully connected feed-forward layer with softmax activations. In a series of experiments, we evaluated different hidden layer sizes and different amounts of hidden layers to determine the optimal hyper parameter configuration.

During decoding / testing, we did not apply any advanced techniques like WFST decoding [20] or incorporated an external language model. Instead, we used a naive argmax decoding and computed the label error rate (LER), which is similar to the phone error rate (PER), but also accounts for incorrect word separations.

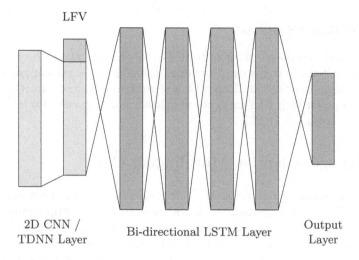

Fig. 1. Network layout, based on Deepspeech2 configuration. LFVs are being added after final convolution layer

4   Experimental Setup

We based our experiments on the Euronews corpus [10]. It features TV broadcast news recordings from 10 languages. For each language, 70 h of data is available, as shown in Table 1. We filtered utterances being shorter than 1 s and removed utterances with long phonetic transcripts, because the CUDA implementation supported a maximum label length of 639 symbols[1]. We used only half of the available data per language (approx. 35 h) to simulate a resource-constraint task and set aside 10% for testing. We trained systems for both English and German, as well as a system trained jointly on data from both languages.

---

[1] see: https://github.com/baidu-research/warp-ctc, accessed 2017-04-13.

Table 1. Overview Euronews Corpus

Language	Audio data	# Recordings
Arabic	72.1 h	4,342
English	72.8 h	4,511
French	68.1 h	4,434
German	73.2 h	4,436
Italian	77.2 h	4,464
Polish	70.8 h	4,576
Portuguese	68.3 h	4,456
Russian	72.2 h	4,418
Spanish	70.5 h	4,231
Turkish	70.4 h	4,385
Total	715.6 h	44,253

We used MaryTTS [30] to create pronunciations for words contained in the transcriptions. MaryTTS supports multiple languages, with each language having their own set of symbols representing phones. While most of the symbols represent the same phones across languages, we manually mapped symbols which did not match to ensure same phones shared the same symbol. For matching the symbols, we used the definitions of articulatory features embedded in MaryTTS' language definition files. This allowed us to derive a global phone set. Additionally, MaryTTS used special marks to indicate long vowels. As preliminary experiments indicated, the network had difficulties distinguishing between short and long instances of the same vowel. Hence, we discarded marks indicating long vowels. The phone count after and prior to mapping is shown in Table 2. Merging the sound inventory of both languages resulted on a set of 56 phones.

Table 2. Size of different phone sets

Language	Phone set	Size
English	MaryTTS	42
	Mapped	39
German	MaryTTS	59
	Mapped	48
Combined	Merged	56

To extract acoustic input features, we used the Janus Recognition Toolkit (JRTk) [3], which features the IBIS single-pass decoder [35]. We used our standard pre-processing pipeline consisting of 40 dimensional log Mel scaled coefficients, as well as 14 dimensional tonal features (FFV [17] and pitch [31]).

Adding tonal features even for non-tonal languages has shown improvements [19]. We extracted the features using a window size of 32ms and a frame shift of 10ms. To train the networks, we used PyTorch [1], which provided Python bindings to Torch [7], as well as warp-ctc [2] for computing the CTC loss during network training. The networks were trained using stochastic gradient descent (SGD) with Nesterov momentum [37], a learning rate of 0.0003 and momentum of 0.9. Mini-batch updates with a batch size of 20 and batch normalization were used. Annealing was applied to the learning rate every epoch with a value of 1.1. To prevent gradients from exploding, a max norm constraint of 400 was enforced. During the first epoch, the network was trained with utterances sorted ascending by length.

5   Results

In this section, we first present monolingual results as baseline, followed by the evaluation of different hyper parameter configurations. We then combine data from multiple languages to train a multilingual system and also evaluate adding LFVs to our setup.

5.1   Baseline

As baseline experiment, we trained monolingual systems on English and German using 4 LSTM layers with 400 neurons each. We evaluated the mapping of phones from MaryTTS to actual phone targets of our system. Table 3 shows the results. Using the original phone set from MaryTTS does result in the highest LER, for both English and German.

Table 3. Monolingual results on test set showing the label error rate (LER)

System	Phone Set	LER
English	MaryTTS	20.4%
English	Mapped	**19.0%**
German	MaryTTS	16.0%
German	Mapped	**15.5%**

5.2   Multilingual Experiments

Next, we trained networks multilingually and also evaluated different network hyper parameters. While we kept the configuration of the 2 2D CNN / TDNN layers identical, we varied the parameters of the LSTM layers. For reference, we also included corresponding results of a monolingual system trained on English. As shown in Table 4, we observed gains from increasing the layer size. But we could not increase the size of the LSTM layers beyond 1,000 neurons per layer because of limitations in GPU memory. Adding an additional layer did not improve the LER.

Table 4. Multilingual results showing the label error rate (LER) for different network configurations

LSTM layer size	# LSTM layers	LER ML	LER EN
350	5	19.6%	–
400	4	20.0%	19.0%
400	5	19.6%	–
600	4	17.3%	–
800	4	16.9%	17.8%
800	5	17.0%	–
1000	**4**	**16.3%**	**17.7%**

5.3   Language Adaptive Networks

Based on the best network configuration (1,000 nodes per layers, 4 LSTM layers), we added LFVs after the CNN / TDNN layers and evaluated the performance of the network for both English and German, as well as multilingually. The results are shown in Table 5. Adding LFVs lowered the LER in all cases. After 7 epochs, the gain over the baseline was bigger on English (8% rel.), compared to German (6% rel.). Training the nets for 70 epochs results in a slight decrease in performance multilingual over monolingual.

Table 5. Multilingual results showing the label error rate (LER)

System	Monolingual	Multilingual	LFV	LER (7 ep.)	**LER (70 ep.)**
English	x	–	–	17.7%	13.1%
	–	x	–	18.7%	14.8%
	–	x	x	**16.4%**	**13.5%**
German	x	–	–	14.6%	10.8%
	–	x	–	14.0%	11.8%
	–	x	x	**13.8%**	**11.0%**
Combined	–	x	–	16.3%	12.9%
	–	x	x	**15.7%**	**12.4%**

6   Conclusion

We have presented a method for training CTC based speech recognition systems multilingually. By using LFVs in addition to acoustic input features, we could improve the recognition performance of our multilingual systems. Future work includes the evaluation of additional language combinations and different mixtures of training data. We also intent to use additional adaptation methods like i-Vectors to adapt the networks to different speakers, as well as to further optimize the network architecture and the training process.

References

1. PyTorch. http://pytorch.org. Accessed 13 Apr 2017
2. warp-ctc. https://github.com/baidu-research/warp-ctc. Accessed 13 Apr 2017
3. Woszczyna, M., et al.: JANUS 93: towards spontaneous speech translation. In: International Conference on Acoustics, Speech, and Signal Processing 1994, Adelaide, Australia (1994)
4. Amodei, D., Anubhai, R., Battenberg, E., Case, C., Casper, J., Catanzaro, B., Chen, J., Chrzanowski, M., Coates, A., Diamos, G., et al.: Deep speech 2: end-to-end speech recognition in english and mandarin. arXiv preprint (2015). arXiv:1512.02595
5. Caruana, R.: Multitask learning. Mach. Learn. **28**(1), 41–75 (1997)
6. Chen, D., Mak, B., Leung, C.C., Sivadas, S.: Joint acoustic modeling of triphones and trigraphemes by multi-task learning deep neural networks for low-resource speech recognition. In: 2014 IEEE International Conference on Acoustics, Speech and Signal Processing (ICASSP), pp. 5592–5596. IEEE (2014)
7. Collobert, R., Kavukcuoglu, K., Farabet, C.: Torch7: a Matlab-like environment for machine learning. In: BigLearn, NIPS Workshop (2011)
8. Ghoshal, A., Swietojanski, P., Renals, S.: Multilingual training of deep-neural networks. In: Proceedings of the ICASSP, Vancouver, Canada (2013)
9. Graves, A., Fernández, S., Gomez, F., Schmidhuber, J.: Connectionist temporal classification: labelling unsegmented sequence data with recurrent neural networks. In: Proceedings of the 23rd International Conference On Machine Learning, pp. 369–376. ACM (2006)
10. Gretter, R.: Euronews: a multilingual benchmark for ASR and LID. In: Fifteenth Annual Conference of the International Speech Communication Association (2014)
11. Grézl, F., Karafiát, M., Vesely, K.: Adaptation of multilingual stacked bottle-neck neural network structure for new language. In: 2014 IEEE International Conference on Acoustics, Speech and Signal Processing (ICASSP), pp. 7654–7658. IEEE (2014)
12. Heigold, G., Vanhoucke, V., Senior, A., Nguyen, P., Ranzato, M., Devin, M., Dean, J.: Multilingual acoustic models using distributed deep neural networks. In: Proceedings of the ICASSP, Vancouver, Canada, May 2013
13. Hinton, G.E., Osindero, S., Teh, Y.W.: A fast learning algorithm for deep belief nets. Neural Comput. **18**(7), 1527–1554 (2006)
14. Hochreiter, S., Schmidhuber, J.: Long short-term memory. Neural Comput. **9**(8), 1735–1780 (1997)
15. Huang, H., Sim, K.C.: An investigation of augmenting speaker representations to improve speaker normalisation for DNN-based speech recognition. In: ICASSP, pp. 4610–4613. IEEE (2015)
16. Kim, S., Hori, T., Watanabe, S.: Joint ctc-attention based end-to-end speech recognition using multi-task learning. arXiv preprint (2016). arXiv:1609.06773
17. Laskowski, K., Heldner, M., Edlund, J.: The fundamental frequency variation spectrum. In: Proceedings of the 21st Swedish Phonetics Conference (Fonetik 2008), pp. 29–32, Gothenburg, Sweden, June 2008

18. Lu, L., Kong, L., Dyer, C., Smith, N.A.: Multi-task learning with ctc and segmental crf for speech recognition. arXiv preprint (2017). arXiv:1702.06378
19. Metze, F., Sheikh, Z., Waibel, A., Gehring, J., Kilgour, K., Nguyen, Q.B., Nguyen, V.H., et al.: Models of Tone for tonal and non-tonal languages. In: 2013 IEEE Workshop on Automatic Speech Recognition and Understanding (ASRU), pp. 261–266. IEEE (2013)
20. Miao, Y., Gowayyed, M., Metze, F.: EESEN: end-to-end speech recognition using deep RNN models and WFST-based decoding. In: 2015 IEEE Workshop on Automatic Speech Recognition and Understanding (ASRU), pp. 167–174. IEEE (2015)
21. Miao, Y., Zhang, H., Metze, F.: Towards speaker adaptive training of deep neural network acoustic models (2014)
22. Mohan, A., Rose, R.: Multi-lingual speech recognition with low-rank multi-task deep neural networks. In: 2015 IEEE International Conference on Acoustics, Speech and Signal Processing (ICASSP), pp. 4994–4998. IEEE (2015)
23. Müller, M., Stüker, S., Waibel, A.: Language Adaptive DNNs for improved low resource speech recognition. In: Interspeech (2016)
24. Müller, M., Stüker, S., Waibel, A.: Language feature vectors for resource constraint speech recognition. In: ITG Symposium, Proceedings of Speech Communication, vol. 12. VDE (2016)
25. Müller, M., Waibel, A.: Using language adaptive deep neural networks for improved multilingual speech recognition. In: IWSLT (2015)
26. Sak, H., Rao, K.: Multi-accent speech recognition with hierarchical grapheme based models (2017)
27. Saon, G., Kurata, G., Sercu, T., Audhkhasi, K., Thomas, S., Dimitriadis, D., Cui, X., Ramabhadran, B., Picheny, M., Lim, L.L., et al.: English conversational telephone speech recognition by humans and machines. arXiv preprint (2017). arXiv:1703.02136
28. Saon, G., Soltau, H., Nahamoo, D., Picheny, M.: Speaker adaptation of neural network acoustic models using i-Vectors. In: ASRU, pp. 55–59. IEEE (2013)
29. Scanzio, S., Laface, P., Fissore, L., Gemello, R., Mana, F.: On the use of a multilingual neural network front-end. In: Proceedings of the Interspeech, pp. 2711–2714 (2008)
30. Schröder, M., Trouvain, J.: The German text-to-speech synthesis system MARY: a tool for research, development and teaching. Int. J. Speech Technol. 6(4), 365–377 (2003)
31. Schubert, K.: Grundfrequenzverfolgung und deren Anwendung in der Spracherkennung. Master's thesis, Universität Karlsruhe (TH), Germany (1999) (in German)
32. Schultz, T., Waibel, A.: Fast bootstrapping of lvcsr systems with multilingual phoneme sets. In: Eurospeech (1997)
33. Schultz, T., Waibel, A.: Language-independent and language-adaptive acoustic modeling for speech recognition. Speech Commun. 35(1), 31–51 (2001)
34. Soltau, H., Liao, H., Sak, H.: Neural speech recognizer: acoustic-to-word lstm model for large vocabulary speech recognition. arXiv preprint (2016). arXiv:1610.09975
35. Soltau, H., Metze, F., Fugen, C., Waibel, A.: A One-pass decoder based on polymorphic linguistic context assignment. In: IEEE Workshop on Automatic Speech Recognition and Understanding, ASRU 2001, pp. 214–217. IEEE (2001)
36. Stüker, S.: Acoustic modelling for under-resourced languages. Ph.D. thesis, Karlsruhe University, Dissertation (2009)
37. Sutskever, I., Martens, J., Dahl, G., Hinton, G.: On the importance of initialization and momentum in deep learning. In: Proceedings of the 30th International Conference on Machine Learning (ICML-2013), pp. 1139–1147 (2013)

38. Swietojanski, P., Ghoshal, A., Renals, S.: Unsupervised cross-lingual knowledge transfer in DNN-based LVCSR. In: SLT, pp. 246–251. IEEE (2012)
39. Vesely, K., Karafiat, M., Grezl, F., Janda, M., Egorova, E.: The language-independent bottleneck features. In: Proceedings of the Spoken Language Technology Workshop (SLT), pp. 336–341. IEEE (2012)
40. Waibel, A., Hanazawa, T., Hinton, G., Shikano, K.: Phoneme recognition using time-delay neural networks. In: ATR Interpreting Telephony Research Laboratories, 30 October 1987
41. Wheatley, B., Kondo, K., Anderson, W., Muthusamy, Y.: An evaluation of cross-language adaptation for rapid hmm development in a new language. In: 1994 IEEE International Conference on Acoustics, Speech, and Signal Processing, ICASSP-1994, vol. 1, pp. I-237. IEEE (1994)
42. Xiong, W., Droppo, J., Huang, X., Seide, F., Seltzer, M., Stolcke, A., Yu, D., Zweig, G.: Achieving human parity in conversational speech recognition. arXiv preprint (2016). arXiv:1610.05256

Language Model Optimization for a Deep Neural Network Based Speech Recognition System for Serbian

Edvin Pakoci[1(✉)], Branislav Popović[1], and Darko Pekar[2]

[1] Faculty of Technical Sciences, Department for Power,
Electronic and Telecommunication Engineering, University of Novi Sad,
Trg Dositeja Obradovića 6, Novi Sad, Serbia
edvin.pakoci@uns.ac.rs
[2] AlfaNum Speech Technologies, Bulevar Vojvode Stepe 40, Novi Sad, Serbia

Abstract. This paper presents the results obtained using several variants of trigram language models in a large vocabulary continuous speech recognition (LVCSR) system for the Serbian language, based on the deep neural network (DNN) framework implemented within the Kaldi speech recognition toolkit. This training approach allows parallelization using several threads on either multiple GPUs or multiple CPUs, and provides a natural-gradient modification to the stochastic gradient descent (SGD) optimization method. Acoustic models are trained over a fixed number of training epochs with parameter averaging in the end. This paper discusses recognition using different language models trained with Kneser-Ney or Good-Turing smoothing methods, as well as several pruning parameter values. The results on a test set containing more than 120000 words and different utterance types are explored and compared to the referent results with GMM-HMM speaker-adapted models for the same speech database. Online and offline recognition results are compared to each other as well. Finally, the effect of additional discriminative training using a language model prior to the DNN stage is explored.

Keywords: Deep neural networks · Kaldi · Serbian · Language modeling · MMI

1 Introduction

Several architectures have been examined for speech recognition on large vocabularies for Serbian in the last years. The newer ones were all based on the widely used open source Kaldi toolkit. Acoustic model training for Serbian involves a few specifics – specially designed phone topologies and context dependency questions for regression tree creation for HMM state tying, input feature selection, model and tree complexity, training type and more.

Some of the previously designed systems are described in [1] and [2]. They are trained on a smaller speech database consisting of telephone recordings (with poorer spectral content) of specific type, such as personal advertisements and similar. Therefore, they are more fit for usage on smaller vocabularies – such as ones they were

© Springer International Publishing AG 2017
A. Karpov et al. (Eds.): SPECOM 2017, LNAI 10458, pp. 483–492, 2017.
DOI: 10.1007/978-3-319-66429-3_48

tested on (around 14000 words). In this paper, a larger speech database with more variability is utilized to train a much more robust system.

Kaldi recipes allow for different types of pre-DNN training stages to provide good input alignments for DNNs. These include context-dependent triphone GMM-HMM model training, speaker adaptive training (SAT) [3], maximum mutual information (MMI) discriminative training [4], minimum phone error (MPE) discriminative training [5], and many more. Several DNN training procedures exist as well, like the one described in [2], based on stacked restricted Boltzman machines and the cross-entropy classification criterion, or the one in this paper, based on modified SGD optimization and parameter averaging. Like already mentioned, these procedures require an input GMM-HMM framework and per-frame alignments. There are other types of DNN training, but those are not the topic of this paper. Here, the optimal language model for the given procedure is chosen, based on several parameters.

In the following section, the used LVCSR speech database for Serbian is described in more detail. Section 3 explains language modeling, parameters and their optimization. Section 4 describes the performed training and experimental setups for different language models, while in the next section the results are presented and discussed. Finally, the last section is about conclusions and future research directions.

2   Speech Database for LVCSR for Serbian

Two different speech databases for Serbian were used for training and testing of DNN acoustic models. The first and larger one is a part of the database described in detail in [6]. It consists of audio books in Serbian, mostly read by professional speakers in studio environment, as well as several other freely available audio books. The quality of speech data is generally high, with only a small amount of background noises and a very high percentage of correctly pronounced words and phones. All the materials were manually reviewed during preparation, before any training. This part of the database accounts for around 154 h of data, out of which approximately 129 h is pure speech, and the rest (25 h) is made of silence segments. The data is divided into more than 87000 separate utterances, which are quite long – with around 15 words each on average. There are 21 identified male speakers and 27 identified female speakers, as well as 10–15 different unidentified speakers (in total, overlaps are possible). The narrative functional style naturally dominates here.

The second part of the database consists of more domain-oriented utterances recorded on mobile phones. These are mostly shorter sentences (around 4–5 words on average), and include various utterance types such as commands (for tasks on the mobile device), questions, spellings, numbers, proper nouns (names, cities, etc.), as well as regular declarative sentences. This set makes up around 61 h of total audio material, out of which 42 h is speech, and 19 h is silence. It has 170 male and 181 female speakers. Each one of them recorded a set of all mentioned utterance types. There are around 74000 utterances in this set. Recording quality is usually good, but certain speakers had a significant amount of background noise as well.

Both database parts are sampled at 16 kHz, 16 bits per sample, mono PCM. The described composition of the speech database is chosen so that acoustic models can be well trained on both regular, carefully pronounced utterances (like in audio books) and more spontaneous and more specific, domain-based speech (like in the so-called mobile database). They were tested on both of these types of speech.

Around 10% of the diverse audio book set was extracted randomly to create the test set (5 male speakers, 4 female speakers, 15 h, 9000 utterances, 140000 words), as well as around 5% of the more-uniform mobile database (3 h, 8 male speakers, 9 female speakers, 4000 utterances, 20000 words).

3 Language Modeling

Language modeling is, alongside acoustic modeling, the other very important part of automatic speech recognition (ASR), especially on larger vocabularies. For experiments presented in this paper, all language models (LMs) were trained on a Serbian textual corpus consisting of the training transcriptions – which by themselves contain around 1.5 million words, out of which just about 121000 different ones – supplemented by a part of the Serbian journalistic textual corpus for better estimation of probabilities. This part accounted for around 60% of the LM-training database, and included around 442000 additional sentences mostly from newspaper articles and similar sources, but used in such a way that it did not supply additional words, so all the final LMs still consist of around 121000 words (this may have affected the number of bigrams and trigrams taken into account, but we did not want to raise the vocabulary size higher than it already was). All language models are trigram-based and created using the SRILM toolkit [7]. What was varied was the smoothing method, as well as pruning. For smoothing, either the Kneser-Ney method [8] was used, or the Good-Turing method [9]. As for pruning, the pruning parameter value was chosen between 10^{-6}, 10^{-7} or no pruning. The test set was not included in LM training to simulate real situations, where a speaker may utter something that the system does not support, no matter the given situation or domain of interest. The pronunciation dictionary contained all the used words, of course, with possible multiple pronunciations for each word. Total number of unigrams, bigrams and trigrams for mentioned LMs are shown in Table 1, and respective perplexity values on the used test set in Table 2.

Table 1. Number of certain entries in used language models

Pruning 10^{-6}			Pruning 10^{-7}			No pruning		
Unigrams	Bigrams	Trigrams	Unigrams	Bigrams	Trigrams	Unigrams	Bigrams	Trigrams
121 k	205 k	63 k	121 k	1.3 M	358 k	121 k	2.3 M	843 k

Table 2. Perplexity of used language models on the test set

Pruning 10^{-6}		Pruning 10^{-7}		No pruning	
Kneser-Ney	Good-Turing	Kneser-Ney	Good-Turing	Kneser-Ney	Good-Turing
1124.2	1226.4	768.8	1080.2	–	1043.8

4   Training and Experimental Setup

Several trainings and tests were performed. All the DNN trainings were run on a single GPU (NVIDIA Tesla K40C). Up to the DNN stage, one training variant directly performed fMLLR speaker adaptive training on top of triphones (obtained by the so-called "tri2a" stage), and the other one first performed boosted maximum mutual information (bMMI) [10] based discriminative training on top of triphones (to provide even better input alignments for SAT), then SAT, and finally bMMI again on top of SAT to produce final alignments. The language model used for the extra discriminative training stages was either an unigram LM with probabilities calculated using the training set transcriptions, or the trigram LM which was also used for decoding.

The following DNN training itself was performed using the "nnet2" Kaldi recipe originally developed by Dan Povey [11], over 8 epochs, with 6 hidden layers and an architecture for efficient modeling of long temporal contexts [12], while keeping most of other parameters at their default values (see more in depth training description in referenced papers). Finally, for decoding, for each given LM, 4 variants were performed – online decoding with i-vectors (per speaker, i.e., with carrying information forward from previous utterances of the same speaker), online decoding per utterance, (without carrying forward speaker information), offline decoding (per speaker, but computing i-vectors when all available speaker data is acquired), and offline decoding per utterance (looking to the end of each utterance while computing i-vectors).

As mentioned before, to find the optimal LM configuration, the smoothing method and the pruning parameter value were varied. The following tests were performed – LM with Kneser-Ney smoothing with pruning parameter 10^{-6} versus pruning parameter 10^{-7}, and LM with Good-Turing smoothing with pruning parameter 10^{-7} versus no pruning at all. These tests were mutually compared to determine the optimal LM configuration out of the ones we had at hand. Afterwards, the optimal LM was used for the training variant with added bMMI steps. All the results are presented below.

5   Results and Discussion

First, let us mention the baseline results (GMM-HMM SAT system). Considering the previously described training variants, there are 3 results here – without additional discriminative training, with additional bMMI training based on a unigram LM, and same based on the optimal trigram LM, after it has been chosen (this test was obviously performed last). These results are shown in Fig. 1. As seen there, pure triphone (GMM-HMM) models give a word error rate (WER) of 27.13%, SAT without bMMI improves that to 21.82%, and SAT after bMMI to a slightly better 21.48% (trigram LM) or 21.6% (unigram LM). Final pre-DNN models – which are estimated using bMMI after SAT – lower the WER down to 18.45% (unigram LM) or 19.2% (trigram LM). The error rate here flips, as unigrams give better results than trigrams, most likely because the unigram probabilities were tied directly to the training set, and no additional corpus. Also, these results are with fMLLR transformations calculated per each utterance instead of per speaker (because those are consistently better).

Now let us take a look at DNN decoding results with language models using Kneser-Ney smoothing. The more strict pruning value of 10^{-6} results in a WER of 13.99% for offline decoding per utterance. Meanwhile, offline decoding per speaker gives a slightly worse WER of 14.48%, while online decoding gives 14.22% per speaker, and 14.56% per utterance. The last result can be called WER for true online decoding, as it simulates a real interaction (speaker utters one sentence at a time, e.g. using a microphone). This result is important for ASR systems in practice, as most of the time online decoding is required to satisfy the recognition speed requirements (as it is helpful to start the recognition before the speaker completed the utterance). However, the best result is 13.99% and it will be used for further comparison – other results tend to follow a similar pattern anyway. Results with the more relaxed pruning parameter 10^{-7} are the following: the best result 12.36% for offline decoding per utterance and 12.88% per speaker, while online decoding results in WER of 12.62% per speaker, and 12.91% per utterance. All the results for LMs with Kneser-Ney smoothing are given in Fig. 2. The stricter pruning parameter seems to be a bit too strict, as the more relaxed one provides significantly better results (12% relative improvement).

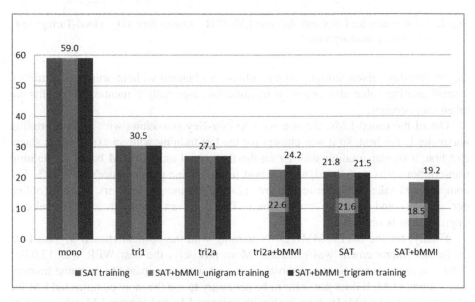

Fig. 1. WER results for pre-DNN training stages

For Good-Turing smoothing tests, pruning parameter value of 10^{-7} was compared to no pruning at all. Results are also given within Fig. 2, and they are as follows. With pruning, WER of 13.59% is obtained for offline per-utterance decoding. Other results are slightly worse, similarly like in Kneser-Ney tests. On the other hand, no pruning produces WER of 13.33% as the best result. Therefore, no pruning gives just slightly better results, but at the cost of using more disk space (about twice as much just for the so-called "grammar FST", or "G FST"), a bit more time and disk space for decoding preparation (mostly "HCLG FST" graph creation and storing), as well as slightly

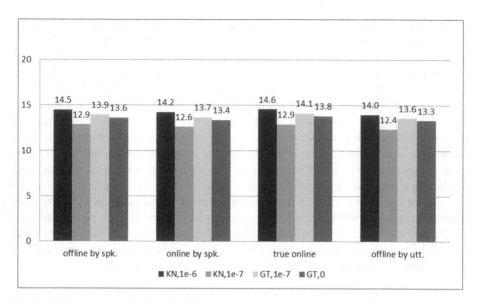

Fig. 2. WER results for DNN with different LMs (KN – Kneser-Ney, GT – Good-Turing; 1e-6, 1e-7, 0 – pruning parameter values)

slower decoding. Even though better results were obtained without pruning (naturally), a small pruning value also proves to be quite fair, especially if mentioned benefits are taken into account.

Out of the tested LMs, the one with Kneser-Ney smoothing with a small pruning parameter is the best, so it was chosen for the last training with an extra bMMI stage. But first, a similar training with an on-the-fly created unigram LM based on training transcriptions was performed, and the best result (offline per utterance) is 12.01%. For completeness sake, the other results are: 12.48% (offline per speaker), 12.18% (online per speaker) and 12.61% (true online). Therefore, an approximately 3% relative improvement is obtained.

Finally, for the SAT+bMMI+DNN training with the optimal chosen trigram LM, no further improvement was obtained. More precisely, the best WER was 12.04%. Others were also very close and mostly just a bit worse compared to the same training with unigram LM. It does not seem to be necessary to use the more complicated LM for MMI training. The bMMI stage, both with unigram LM and trigram LM, takes a lot of additional time, but only once during training, so it is still justified to use it for the additional improvement. All mentioned results can be seen in Fig. 3.

In Figs. 4 and 5 the best configuration is analysed in more detail. Besides WER, the character error rate (CER) is shown, as well as a breakdown for genders and test database parts (audio books and mobile set). The CER value is especially interesting, because Serbian is a highly inflective language, meaning that small changes in words are used to express different grammatical categories, like tense, case, number and gender.

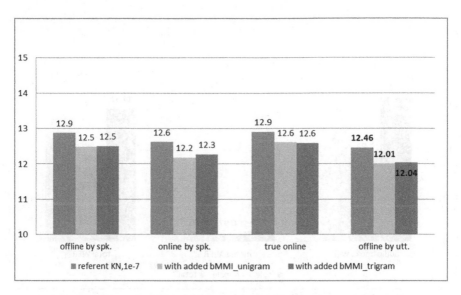

Fig. 3. Effects of additional bMMI training before DNN on WER results

The really low obtained value for CER – 3.11%, especially on such a vocabulary as the given one (over 120000 words), means that the trained acoustic models are actually really good, and assuming the usage of this training configuration (including phone topology, etc.), it means that better suited LMs are probably the path to further improvement of accuracies for more specific tasks, as most errors are on only 1–2 characters of the whole word (e.g. the wrong case or tense was recognized). Other numerous word errors include splitting one word into two or more parts – here, all characters are recognized well, yet the word error is counted (even more than once). Another proposed ASR system estimation metric for highly inflective languages is inflectional WER (IWER) which assigns a lower-than-one weight to "weak" substitutions, where the lemma of the recognized word-form is correct [13]. Using a weight of 0.5, best IWER of 10.76% is obtained, with a lot of other small recognition errors still persisting. Looking at different test sets, the larger set – audio books – holds the most errors (13.54% WER, 3.45% CER), which is expected, as those sentences are long and not task-specific (basically very random), which generally makes them harder to be consistently recognized well. On the other hand, errors on the mobile test set are very rare – the WER of 1.05% is more than excellent, and CER of 0.44% is even better. This database is task-oriented, with a lot of repeating phrases, but it still includes a lot of variability, and the results are just another proof of the quality of trained acoustic models. As for gender, results on the female parts of the test database are a lot better on audio books, and a bit better on the mobile set, but that is due to random selection of the test set – for audio books, male utterances happened to be longer and more problematic (more background noise and speech artifacts in selected speakers).

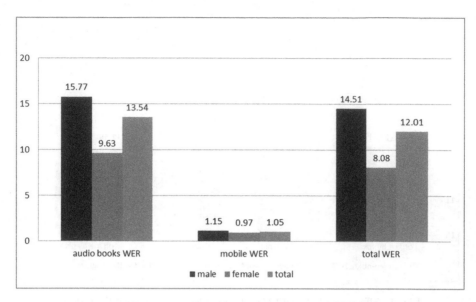

Fig. 4. WER results breakdown for test database types and genders

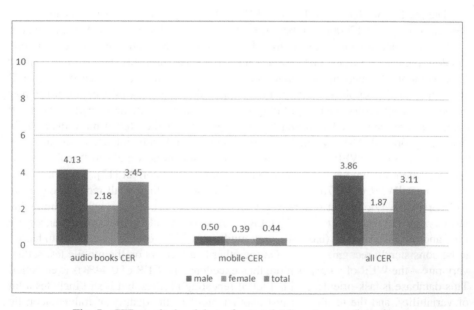

Fig. 5. CER results breakdown for test database types and genders

Finally, in Table 3 a list of several words that were substituted, inserted and deleted the most is given. It can be seen again that the main problems are very short words that occur often in Serbian (related to insertion and deletion) and the high language inflectivity (related to substitution).

Table 3. Lists of most substituted, inserted and deleted words during recognition

#Substitutions (From → To)	#Insertions	#Deletions
je → i	i	je
i → je	na	i
je → koje	u	u
bilo → bila	je	a
koja → koje	da	da
joj → je	ni	on
koje → koji	sa	na
sa → se	mu	o
koju → koji	od	ona
su → se	ne	se
ili → i	po	joj
Nina → na	a	me
samo → sam	s	su
revolucija → revolucije	ih	pa

6   Conclusion

In this paper, a DNN-based LVCSR system for Serbian in described, and an optimal language model is chosen based on several configuration parameters. It was shown that a LM trained with Kneser-Ney smoothing and a small pruning value works very well for a vocabulary of over 120000 words. Discriminative training step with on-the-fly created unigram-based LM can be added to regular SAT training to provide better input alignments for the DNN training stage, which leads to further improvements in final WER. Results on a more specific task-oriented database are excellent, but for more general purposes a better suited LM can be used (trained on a different type of textual corpus), even though the results are already good. Further research will include training on more specific models of certain phones, i.e., creation of different models for different variations of pitch, accent, duration and other phone-related features in Serbian for vowels, as well as inclusion of different language models, such as class n-grams, which might amplify the good acoustic modeling with better language modeling as well, by preventing recognition errors like seen in these experiments (e.g. wrong case). Taking wider contexts into consideration during feature extraction will be tested as well.

Acknowledgments.   . The work described in this paper was supported in part by the Ministry of Education, Science and Technological Development of the Republic of Serbia, within the project "Development of Dialogue Systems for Serbian and Other South Slavic Languages", EUREKA project DANSPLAT, "A Platform for the Applications of Speech Technologies on Smartphones for the Languages of the Danube Region", ID E! 9944, and the Provincial Secretariat for Higher Education and Scientific Research, within the project "Central Audio-Library of the University of Novi Sad", No. 114-451-2570/2016-02.

References

1. Popović, B., Pakoci, E., Ostrogonac, S., Pekar, D.: Large vocabulary continuous speech recognition for Serbian using the Kaldi toolkit. In: Proceedings of the 10th Conference on Digital Speech and Image Processing, DOGS, Novi Sad, pp. 31–34 (2014)
2. Popović, B., Ostrogonac, S., Pakoci, E., Jakovljević, N., Delić, V.: Deep neural network based continuous speech recognition for Serbian using the Kaldi toolkit. In: Ronzhin, A., Potapova, R., Fakotakis, N. (eds.) SPECOM 2015, LNCS, vol. 9319, pp. 186–192. Springer, Cham (2015)
3. Povey, D., Kuo, H.-K.J., Soltau, H.: Fast speaker adaptive training for speech recognition. In: Proceedings of the 9th Annual Conference of the International Speech Communication Association, INTERSPEECH, Brisbane, pp. 1245–1248 (2008)
4. Povey, D.: Discriminative training for large vocabulary speech recognition. Ph.D. thesis, University, Engineering Department, Cambridge (2003)
5. Povey, D., Woodland, P.C.: Minimum phone error and I-smoothing for improved discriminative training. In: Proceedings of the 27th International Conference on Acoustics, Speech and Signal Processing, ICASSP, Orlando, pp. I-105–I-108 (2002)
6. Suzić, S., Ostrogonac, S., Pakoci, E., Bojanić, M.: Building a speech repository for a Serbian LVCSR system. Telfor J. 6(2), 109–114 (2014). Paunović, Đ., Milić, L. (Eds.) Telecommunications Society, Belgrade
7. Stolcke, A., Zheng, J., Wang, W., Abrash, V.: SRILM at sixteen: update and outlook. In: IEEE Workshop on Automatic Speech Recognition and Understanding, ASRU, Waikoloa, p. 5 (2011)
8. Kneser, R., Ney, H.: Improved backing-off for M-gram language modeling. In: Proceedings of the 20th International Conference on Acoustics, Speech and Signal Processing, ICASSP, Detroit, pp. 181–184 (1995)
9. Gale, W.A., Sampson, G.: Good-Turing smoothing without tears. J. Quant. Linguist. 2(3), 217–237 (1995). Köhler, R. (Ed.) Swets & Zeitlinger, Lisse
10. Povey, D., Kanevsky, D., Kingsbury, B., Ramabhadran, B., Saon, G., Visweswariah, K.: Boosted MMI for model and feature-space discriminative training. In: Proceedings of the 33rd International Conference on Acoustics, Speech and Signal Processing, ICASSP, Las Vegas, pp. 4057–4060 (2008)
11. Povey, D., Zhang, X., Khudanpur, S.: Parallel training of DNNs with natural gradient and parameter averaging. In: Proceedings of the 3rd International Conference on Learning Representations Workshop, ICLR, San Diego (2015)
12. Peddinti, V., Povey, D., Khudanpur, S.: A time delay neural network architecture for efficient modeling of long temporal contexts. In: Proceedings of the 14th Annual Conference of the International Speech Communication Association, INTERSPEECH, Dresden, pp. 2–6 (2015)
13. Bhanuprasad, K., Svenson, D.: Errgrams – a way to improving ASR for highly inflective Dravidian languages. In: Proceedings of the 3rd International Joint Conference on Natural Language Processing, IJCNLP, Hyderabad, pp. 805–810 (2008)

Lexico-Semantical Indices of "Deprivation – Aggression" Modality Correlation in Social Network Discourse

Rodmonga Potapova and Liliya Komalova[✉]

Institute of Applied and Mathematical Linguistics,
Moscow State Linguistic University, Moscow, Russia
{RKPotapova, GenuinePR}@yandex.ru

Abstract. The article analyzes the social network discourse (SND) with elements of speech aggression actualized by communicants, whose emotional state is caused by various deprivation factors. The analysis of 398 statements from men and women revealed the frequency use of these statements the stylistic modality of which relates to the aggressive type, while actualizing topics in the speech communication associated with facts of social-cognitive deprivation. The dominant type of speech activity in the analyzed SNDs is an aggressive speech response of the SND-communicant (SND-addressee) to the speech provocation of another communicant (SND-sender). Previously it was revealed that, as a rule, a major role is played by the gender factor: compared to women, men feel more at ease in using statements of the aggressive type, both for speech provocation and for aggressive speech response.

Keywords: Quasi-spontaneous written speech · Aggressive speech provocation · Aggressive speech response · Russian language · Social-cognitive deprivation · Gender

1 Introduction

Traditionally, the concept of "deprivation" refers to the area of study of macro-level social processes (see, e.g. [1, 4, 7, 9, 14, 26, 28]): biologists consider deprivation as a factor of disorganization and adaptation of a living organism; economists are interested in finding a deprivation threshold that enables to keep society on the level of sustainable development; sociologists focus on deprivation factors that promote social changes and protest movements; political scientists are interested in the effect of deprivation on political processes, etc. In this work, we rely on Gurr's concept, in which, by analyzing the social and psychological acts of destructiveness that encourage individuals to political violence, the author develops the concept of "relative deprivation" [8]. According to this concept, relative deprivation is felt by an individual as a result of perception and is characterized by a divergence between value expectations and value capabilities of the perceiving subject (individual, group, mass). "Value expectations are goods and living conditions, which, as people believe, they can rightfully claim. Value capabilities are goods and conditions that people, in their

© Springer International Publishing AG 2017
A. Karpov et al. (Eds.): SPECOM 2017, LNAI 10458, pp. 493–502, 2017.
DOI: 10.1007/978-3-319-66429-3_49

opinion, could achieve and hold" [8]. Relative deprivation (RD) is the judgment that one or one's group is worse off compared to some standard accompanied by feelings of anger and resentment [27]. The above mentioned concept was first developed in respect to the speech activity in "dialogue – polylogue format" in general and in social network discourse on the informational and communicational network of the Internet, in particular, by R.K. Potapova [17][1].

The negative effects of deprivation are described in various studies. For example, the effects of living under long-term bombardment in Israel revealed that "students from a low socioeconomic status (SES) and girls presented more negative symptoms than high SES students and boys, while concomitantly exhibiting greater posttraumatic growth" [29]. Many authors investigate negative outcomes correlated with deprivation experienced in childhood. Galán Ch.A. et al. mention, that "efforts to identify and test mediating mechanisms by which neighborhood deprivation confers increased risk for behavioral problems have predominantly focused on peer relationships and community-level social processes. Less attention has been dedicated to potential cognitive mediators of this relationship, such as aggressive response generation, which refers to the tendency to generate aggressive solutions to ambiguous social stimuli with negative outcomes" [5]. Cummings E.M. and colleagues are sure, that "politically-motivated community violence has distinctive effects on children's externalizing and internalizing problems through the mechanism of increasing children's emotional insecurity about community" [2]. Other authors indicate that "social capital deprivation in the form of peer pressure and verbal victimization and anti-social capital deprivation in the form of delinquent friends, bullying perpetration, verbal perpetration, and physical perpetration are significantly associated with an increased likelihood of engaging in negative bystander behavior" [3]. The studies clearly indicate that one of the possible forms of response to various conditions of deprivation in real life is aggression including speech aggression [6, 10–13, 15, 16, 19, 25].

The deprivation being the object of study in linguistics, traditionally includes sensory (visual, auditory, tactile) and emotional types of deprivation. At the same time, "social and cognitive types of deprivation associated with the external factors of the social environment and society in the whole, playing an important role in the development of a full-fledged individual, as well as conditioning the periods of social unrest, economic crises and revolutionary changes are often not covered" [12].

While in the case of short-term effects of deprivation factors there are constructive ways to respond to external stimuli, the long-term deprivation leads to such negative consequences as feelings of anxiety, undue fear, depression and associated cognitive disorders, as well as existential problems of personality, acceptance of illegitimate patterns of behavior. Thus, long-term inability to cope with the difficulties (frustration) and deprivation leads to a decrease in the total activity of an individual and the formation of a negative view on the world – the attitude that surrounding reality is a priori hostile [10]. Another way of coping with emotional and psychological stress caused by deprivation is immersion into a virtual reality.

---

[1] See the concept details in [15, 16, 18].

2 Method and Procedure

The purpose of this study is to determine the features of the destructive speech behavior of the message sender, whose speech production is affected by deprivation factors (external information blockade of the country, domestic policy coup d'etat, economic crisis, general social instability) and provokes emotional and psychological stress and "infects" other communication participants (Russian-speaking users of the social network "VKontakte") with aggressive attitudes.

The analyzed speech material, Internet-communication of social network users (polylogues, topics of which are included in the semantic field "aggression") should be considered within the social network discourse concept (by R.K. Potapova). According to this concept, social network discourse (SND) is a "special electronic macropolylogue considered as the result of a combination of spoken and written versions of a particular language" [18]. In [15–19] the following characteristics distinguishing social network discourse were revealed: irreversibility; situationality; dynamics; violation of social relationships hierarchy (democratism/pseudodemocratism); combinatorics of monochronosity and polychronicity due to the high speed (tempo) of information dissemination; combinatorics of statements of low context and high context cultures representatives; increased interpersonal space; topics diversity; casual conditionality; manipulation of the recipient's consciousness; emotional-modal saturation [15–19].

The studied SND-polylogues were selected for analysis by continuous sampling from the author database[2] "Russian-language agressogen discourse of social networks (including specific annotation parameters)©" [23]. The topic of these SNDs was the discussion of political and geopolitical events.

The SND-participants (the total number of statements[3] n = 398) were 103 males and 31 females. In those SNDs the participants communicated in Russian, very rarely using remarks in other languages. Changing the language code was caused probably by the participant's (communicant's) desire to dramatically change the discussion subtopic, to draw attention to their statements and clearly divide the group into "us" and "them".

In creating the speech profile of each SND-communicants the following indicators of his/her speech activity were considered: the total number of statements of all SND-communicants; the total number of statements of each SND-communicant; the number of statements of each SND-communicant, which served as a speech provocation for an aggressive speech response from other communicant(s); stylistic modality of provoking statements; the number of statements implementing an aggressive speech response of other SND-communicants to provocative statement of each SND-communicant; the number of statements of each SND-communicant implementing an aggressive speech response of this particular SND-communicant to provoking statements of other communicants; stylistic modality of statements in aggressive speech responses.

---

[2] More on the principles of database on semantic field "aggression" formation and development of annotated corpuses on this subject, see in [20–22, 24].

[3] One statement equals to one publication of a particular SND-communicant.

The provoking statements and the statements in form of aggressive speech responses included in the analysis represented semantic component within the semantic field "aggression". The SND-communicant's gender also was taken into account. The speech activity of each individual communicant in the social network discourse is evidenced by the ratio of their statements to the total number of statements from all SND-communicants. The speech profile of SND-communicant was formed on the base of semantic indicators of general speech activity of each communicant, their provocative speech activity, their responsive aggressive speech activity, the ratio of provoking and responsive aggressive speech activities of this particular communicant, and the indicator of speech aggression for each SND-communicant.

3   Results and Discussion

Communicants identifying themselves from the position of the Russian linguaculture tended to a more open position in the analyzed SNDs, they formulated their opinions more confidently and in a more civil manner as compared to the representatives of other linguacultures. This can be explained primarily by the fact that the social network "VKontakte" is a Russian resource that gives its participants the right to identify themselves with the "host party".

Tables 1, 2, 3 and 4 and Fig. 1 show the results obtained during the analysis of SND-communicants' speech activity from a gender perspective.

Table 1. Quantitative indicators of the analyzed SNDs (in %)

Analyzed statements, total	Statements with positive and neutral semantic content	Statements of aggressive type	
		49.5 of these	
		Statements provoking speech aggression	Aggressive speech responses
100	50.5	13.1	36.4

The analyzed SND-content can be described as an aggressive type of communication: the sum of the statements provoking speech aggression and the statements in the form of aggressive speech responses in the structure of the analyzed SNDs comes to 49.5% (Table 1). The dominant type of aggressive speech activity in the analyzed SNDs is aggressive speech responses to speech provocation from another communicant (36.4%).

Despite the fact that the number of female communicants is considerably less than the number of male communicants (Table 2), women in the analyzed SNDs are more active regarding their speech activity (3.65). The index of their speech activity exceeds the speech activity index of male communicants (2.77), which affects the increase in the index of the total group (2.97).

From Table 3 it can be seen that within the aggressive speech activity of the SND-communicants, a group of provocative statements and a group of aggressive

Table 2. Speech activity of SND-communicants from a gender perspective

	Number of communicants	Number of communicants' statements	Speech activity index of SND-communicants
Total	134	398	2.97
Males	103	285	2.77
Females	31	113	3.65

Table 3. Aggressive speech activity of the SND-communicants from a gender perspective (in %)

	Provoking statements	Aggressive speech responses	Statements of aggressive type
Total	26.4	**73.6**	100
Males	24.5	**75.5**	100
Females	30.2	**69.8**	100

speech responses can be distinguished. Both for men (75.5%) and women (69.8%) the main type of the aggressive speech activity is aggressive speech responses.

Any statement in the social network discourse is implicitly addressed to all communicants. Because of this publicity it is not always possible to determine exactly to whom the specific sender directs a provocative statement, but it is possible to keep track of the communicants who respond to the speech provocation in different forms including the form of speech aggression.

According to the preliminary findings (Table 4), in the analyzed SNDs women tend to speech activity provoking speech aggression (0.30) more than men; while compared to women, men are tend more to speech provocations and are more likely to respond to provocations in the form of speech aggression (0.48). According to the index of speech aggression in the analyzed SNDs women (0.74) can be ranged in a group of more proagressive communicants in comparison with men (0.73), although the differences in these indices are negligible.

The index of aggressive stimuli triggered (the ratio of the normalized number of statements provoking speech aggression and the normalized number of statements in the form of aggressive speech responses to this speech provocation) for the analyzed

Table 4. Profile of the SND-communicants' speech aggressiveness from a gender perspective

	Index of provoking speech activity	Index of responsive aggressive speech activity	Index of speech aggression	Index of aggressive stimuli triggered
Midpoint	0.26	0.46	0.72	1.06
Males	0.24	**0.48**	0.73	**1.12**
Females	**0.30**	0.43	**0.74**	0.88
Difference (M–F)	0.06 (23%)	0.05 (10.9%)	0.01 (1.4%)	0.24 (22.6%)

SNDs is 1.06, that means that there is one aggressive speech response per one provocative statement in average. In the analyzed SNDs men's provoking statements (1.12) are more productive (have more feedbacks in form of aggressive speech responses) compared to provoking statements made by women (0.88). The consistency and reliability of the obtained data is planned to be tested for larger samples.

The responsive aggressive speech is more likely to be aimed at the "provocateur" of the same gender as the sender (Fig. 1): men are more likely to manifest speech aggression in response to speech provocation from male communicants; and women, respectively to speech provocation from female communicants.

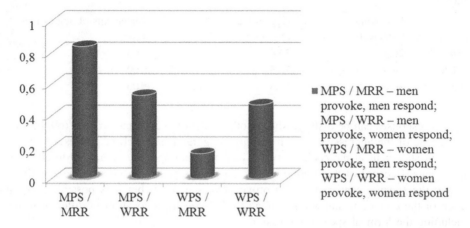

■ MPS / MRR – men provoke, men respond;
MPS / WRR – men provoke, women respond;
WPS / MRR – women provoke, men respond;
WPS / WRR – women provoke, women respond

Fig. 1. Correlation between provocative speech activity and responsive aggressive speech activity of communicants in the analyzed SNDs from a gender perspective

The qualitative analysis of the SND semantics allowed classification of aggressive statements regarding their negative modal stylistic coloring (Figs. 2 and 3).

The analysis of the statements in the SNDs revealed that the most frequent statements with negative stylistic modality provoking aggressive speech responses are the statements expressing and perceived by the communicants as some form of accusation, insult, causticity[4] (Fig. 2). As compared to women men use more diverse stylistically negatively charged statements. The range of women's statements provoking speech aggression, unlike men's ones, misses statements perceived as mockery. In men's speech there are no statements perceived as provocative questions and negations. There is no menace and sneering in the statements provoking aggressive speech response.

The analysis of the aggressive speech responses revealed that the most frequent statements of responsive speech aggression with negative stylistic modality are those expressing and perceived by communicants as an insult, causticity and accusation (Fig. 3). As compared to men, women implement responsive speech aggression even less diversely, also in women's speech there are no statements in response to

---

[4] See details in [10].

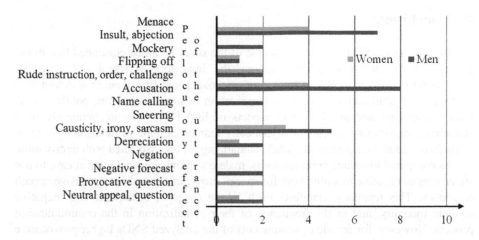

Fig. 2. Stylistic modality of statements *provoking* aggressive speech responses

speech provocations that are perceived as a mockery, flipping off, sneering and negative forecast. There is no name calling, depreciation, provocative questioning in the analyzed aggressive speech responses.

When comparing statements of various negative modalities of the provocative type and aggressive speech responses (Figs. 2 and 3) it was revealed that in the analyzed SNDs menace and sneering do not belong to provocative statements, and name calling, communicant depreciation and provocative questions do not belong to aggressive speech responses.

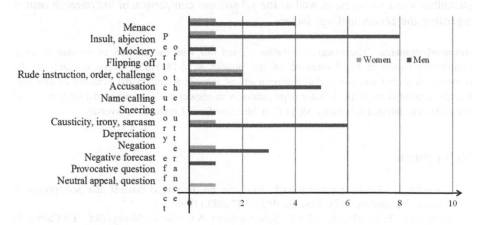

Fig. 3. Stylistic modality of statements expressing aggressive speech *responses*

4 Conclusions

On the basis of data obtained in the course of the study it can be concluded that in the process of speech communication among the indicators of social and cognitive deprivation in written speech of individuals, whose actual life situation is determined by long-term multi-factor deprivation (deprivation in social, economic, political, cognitive, emotional and psychological aspects of life) [17] there are frequently used statements transmitting a negative stylistically marked attitude of defamatory content towards the addressee (recipient), while actualizing topics associated with deprivation.

As compared to female communicants, male communicants feel more at ease to use statements of negative modality both for speech provocations and for aggressive speech responses. This tendency manifests itself in the range of statements with negative stylistic modality, and in the frequency of their actualization in the communication process. However, for female communicants of the analyzed SNDs higher provocative speech activity is typical. It should be noted that for provoking speech aggression and aggressive speech responses men and women use similar types of statements with negative stylistic modalities. Statements most frequently used in SNDs are those expressing and perceived as insult, accusation and causticity.

5 Prospects of Investigation

Further development of the research is deemed in the study of the correlation, on the one hand, of the deprivation factor and, on the other hand, the speech behavior of an aggressive type in social network discourses involving representatives of various linguacultures and societies, as well as the subsequent comparison of the research results regarding the gender and age factors.

Acknowledgments. The research is being carried out with the support of Russian Science Foundation (RSF) in the framework of the project №14-18-01059 "Basic research of the typology of verbal and paraverbal determinants of emotional and modal behavior of communicants in conditions of multi-factor deprivation (with respect to electronic media sources, social networks and Internet telephony Skype)" at Moscow State Linguistic University.

References

1. Canache, D.: Looking out my back door: the neighborhood context and perceptions of relative deprivation. Polit. Res. Q. **49**(3), 547–583 (1996)
2. Cummings, E.M., Merrilees, Ch.E., Schermerhorn, A.C., Goeke-Morey, M.C., Ed Cairns, P. Sh.: Longitudinal pathways between political violence and child adjustment: the role of emotional security about the community in Northern Ireland. J. Abnorm. Child Psychol. **39**(2), 213–224 (2011). doi:10.1007/s10802-010-9457-3
3. Evans, C.B.R., Smokowski, P.R.: Negative bystander behavior in bullying dynamics: assessing the impact of social capital deprivation and anti-social capital. Child Psychiatry Hum. Dev. **47**, 1–16 (2016). doi:10.1007/s10578-016-0657-0

4. Field, T.: Violence and touch deprivation in adolescents. Adolescence **31**(148), 735–749 (2002)
5. Galán, Ch.A., Shaw, D.S., Dishion, Th.J., Wilson, M.N.: Neighborhood deprivation during early childhood and conduct problems in middle childhood: Mediation by aggressive response generation. J. Abnorm. Child Psychol., 1–12 (2016) doi:10.1007/s10802-016-0209-x
6. Gordeev, D.: Detecting state of aggression in sentences using CNN. In: Ronzhin, A., Potapova, R., Németh, G. (eds.) SPECOM 2016. LNCS, vol. 9811, pp. 240–245. Springer, Cham (2016). doi:10.1007/978-3-319-43958-7_28
7. Grant, P.R., Brown, R.: From ethnocentrism to collective protest: responses to relative deprivation and threats to social identity. Soc. Psychol. Q. **58**(3), 195–237 (1995)
8. Gurr, T.R.: Why men rebel. Piter, Saint-Petersburg (2005). (in Russian)
9. Heldt, B.: Domestic politics, absolute deprivation, and use of armed force in interstate territorial disputes, 1950-1990. J. Conflict Resolut. **43**(4), 451–478 (1999)
10. Komalova, L.R.: Aggressogen Discourse: The Multilingual Aggression Verbalization Typology. Sputnik+, Moscow (2017). (in Russian)
11. Komalova, L.R.: Interpersonal communication: From conflict to consensus. INION RAS, Moscow (2016). (in Russian)
12. Komalova, L.R.: Verbalization of aggression as a fruit of social-cognitive deprivation. J. Psycholinguistics **4**(30), 103–115 (2016). http://iling-ran.ru/library/voprosy/30.pdf. (in Russian)
13. Komalova, L.R.: Verbalization of aggression in speech communication of social network users. In: 4th Conference-School Language Issues: Young Scientists' Perspective, pp. 115–126. Kanzler, Moscow (2016). http://iling-ran.ru/library/sborniki/problemy_jazyka_4.pdf. (in Russian)
14. Pereira, M., Negrão, M., Soares, I., Mesman, J.: Predicting harsh discipline in at-risk mothers: the moderating effect of socioeconomic deprivation severity. J. Child Fam. Stud. **24**(3), 725–733 (2015)
15. Potapova, R.K.: Deprivation as basic a mechanism of verbal and paraverbal behavior of a human being (on basics of social network communication). In: Speech communication in information space, pp. 17–36. Lenand, Moscow (2017). (in Russian)
16. Potapova, R.: From deprivation to aggression: verbal and non-verbal social network communication. In: VIth International Scientific Conference "Global Science and Innovation", Chicago, pp. 129–137 (2015)
17. Potapova, R.K.: Scientific research project "Basic research of the typology of verbal and paraverbal determinants of emotional and modal behavior of communicants in conditions of multi-factor deprivation (with respect to electronic media sources, social networks and Internet telephony Skype)", grant № 14-18-01059, Moscow (2014-2016). (in Russian)
18. Potapova, R.K.: Social network discourse as the object of interdisciplinary research. In: 2nd International Scientific Conference "Discourse as the Social Activity: Priorities and Perspectives", Rema, Moscow, pp. 20–22 (2014). (in Russian)
19. Potapova, R.K. (ed.): Speech Communication in Information Space. Lenand, Moscow (2017). (in Russian)
20. Potapova, R.K., Komalova, L.R.: Database of Russian texts containing items of the semantic field "aggression". Vestnik of Moscow State Linguistic University **19**(705), 112–121 (2014). http://www.vestnik-mslu.ru/Vest-2014/Vest-19z.pdf. (in Russian)
21. Potapova, R., Komalova, L.: Lingua-cognitive survey of the semantic field "aggression" in multicultural communication: typed text. In: Železný, M., Habernal, I., Ronzhin, A. (eds.) SPECOM 2013. LNCS(LNAI), vol. 8113, pp. 227–232. Springer, Cham (2013). doi:10.1007/978-3-319-01931-4_30

22. Potapova, R., Komalova, L.: On principles of annotated databases of the semantic field "aggression". In: Ronzhin, A., Potapova, R., Delic, V. (eds.) SPECOM 2014. LNCS(LNAI), vol. 8773, pp. 322–328. Springer, Cham (2014). doi:10.1007/978-3-319-11581-8_40

23. Potapova, R.K., Komalova, L.R.: Russian aggressive-gen discourse of social network (with the special parameters of annotation©. Database, 28 Mb., 277 000 word forms, 208 polylogues (2015). (in Russian)

24. Potapova, R.K., Komalova, L.R.: Verbal structure of communicative act of aggression: thematic explanatory dictionary, edn. 1. INION RAS, Moscow (2015). (in Russian)

25. Potapova, R., Potapov, V.: Auditory and visual recognition of emotional behaviour of foreign language subjects (by native and non-native speakers). In: Železný, M., Habernal, I., Ronzhin, A. (eds.) SPECOM 2013. LNCS(LNAI), vol. 8113, pp. 62–69. Springer, Cham (2013). doi:10.1007/978-3-319-01931-4_9

26. Sen, Ja., Pal, D.P.: Changes in relative deprivation and social well-being. Int. J. Soc. Econ. **40**(6), 528–536 (2013)

27. Smith, H.J., Pettigrew, Th.F.: Advances in relative deprivation theory and research. Soc. Justice Res. **28**(1), 1–6 (2015) doi:10.1007/s11211-014-0231-5

28. van den Bos, K., van Veldhuizen, T.S., Au, Al.K.S.: Counter cross-cultural priming and relative deprivation: the role of individualism-collectivism. Soc. Justice Res. **28**(1), 52–75 (2015)

29. Yablon, Ya.B., Pagorek-Eshel, Ha.I.Sh.: Positive and negative effects of long-term bombardment among Israeli adolescents: the role of gender and social environment. Child Adolesc. Soc. Work J. **28**(3), 189–202 (2011) doi:10.1007/s10560-011-0227-z

Linguistic Features and Sociolinguistic Variability in Everyday Spoken Russian

Natalia Bogdanova-Beglarian, Tatiana Sherstinova[(✉)],
Olga Blinova, and Gregory Martynenko

Saint Petersburg State University,
11 Universitetskaya nab., St. Petersburg 199034, Russia
{n.bogdanova, t.sherstinova, o.blinova,
g.martynenko}@spbu.ru

Abstract. The paper reviews the results of the project aimed at describing everyday Russian language and analyzing the special characteristics of its usage by different social groups. The presented study was made on the material of 125,000 words annotated subcorpus of the ORD corpus, which contains speech fragments of 256 people representing different gender, age, professional and status groups. The linguistic features from different linguistic levels, which could be considered as diagnostic for different social groups, have been analyzed. It turned out that in terms of sociolinguistic variability all features under investigation may be divided into three categories: (1) the diagnostic features, which display statistically significant differences between certain social groups; (2) the linguistic features, which could be considered as common for all sociolects and referring to some permanent, universal properties of everyday language; and (3) the potentially diagnostic features, which have shown some quantitative difference between the considered groups, but the extent of this difference does not allow to regard them as statistically significant at the moment. The last group of features is the most extensive and requires additional studies on a larger amount of speech data.

Keywords: Russian speech corpus · Everyday speech · Sociolinguistics · Social groups · Multilevel linguistic analysis · Diagnostic features · Phonetics · Vocabulary · Morphology · Syntax

1 Introduction

The paper reviews the results of the project aimed at describing everyday Russian language and analyzing the special characteristics of its usage by different social groups. Speech of the major social groups of modern Russian city (age-, gender-, professional-related etc.) was analyzed on phonetic, lexical, morphological and syntactic levels in regard to social information about the speakers [1].

The research data were taken from the most representative Russian everyday speech corpus known as "One Day of Speech" (the ORD corpus), collected by using the long-term speech monitoring method. This implies that everything a volunteer-respondent says through the day is saved on a recorder that is literally hanging on his/her neck [2]. The first recordings were made in Saint Petersburg in 2007.

© Springer International Publishing AG 2017
A. Karpov et al. (Eds.): SPECOM 2017, LNAI 10458, pp. 503–511, 2017.
DOI: 10.1007/978-3-319-66429-3_50

In the framework of the project referred to here, the significant extension of the ORD corpus was achieved (as compared to data as at early 2014) [3]. Nowadays the corpus contains more than 1250 h of audio recordings, collected from 128 respondents and more than 1000 of their interlocutors, representing different social groups (sociolects) of the modern Russian city. The recordings relate to 2800 macroepisodes of speech communication [4]. Text transcripts are made for about 15% of audio files, and there are 1M words in transcripts.

Earlier, several preliminary sociolinguistic studies were conducted on the ORD data (see, for example [5–7]. In this paper, we will describe the results of the research made on the material of 125,000 words annotated subcorpus of the ORD corpus.

2   The Research Methodology

First of all, let us introduce the list of sociolects, which are recognized in the ORD database.

2.1   The Social Groups Under Investigation

Sociological data on the respondents recorded for the corpus are taken from the Sociological questionnaire for the volunteers and their main interlocutors [3]. Only a part of these data was involved in the current research, in which the linguistic features of the following 20 social groups were investigated [1]:

   I. **Gender groups:**
   1   MUZ – men;
   2   ZEN – women.
  II. **Age groups:**
   3   A1 – youth group (18–30 years old);
   4   A2 – middle-aged group (31–54 years old);
   5   A3 – senior group (55 + years old).
 III. **Status Groups:**
   6   UCH – students;
   7   SPEC – employees and specialists;
   8   RUK – executive employees or senior officials;
   9   BUS – businessmen and private entrepreneurs;
  10   NOR – non-working or retired people.
  IV. **Professional groups:**
  11   RAB – blue-collar workers;
  12   ENG – engineers;
  13   SIL – men of arms and other power forces;
  14   EST – representatives of natural sciences;
  15   HUM – representatives of the humanities;
  16   OBR – workers of education;
  17   CO – representatives of the service sector;
  18   IT – IT specialists and programmers;

19 OF – office employees;
20 TVOR – creative professionals.

Obviously, each respondent (or interlocutor) can be referred to one category from the 1st or 2nd group, and to no less than one category from the 3rd and the 4th groups.

2.2 The Annotated Subcorpus of 100 Macroepisodes

An exploratory subcorpus, consisting of 100 communicative macroepisodes, and containing speech of 100 respondents, who are representatives of the above-mentioned 20 social groups, was compiled. Besides speech of 100 respondents balanced from sociolinguistic point of view, the subcorpus contains additionally that of their 156 interlocutors. It is necessary to recognize that it was impossible to balance interlocutors sociologically, and hence this has resulted in some disproportion between the number of people representing certain social groups. This is particularly noticeable in relation to professional and status groups, which – being consisted of a larger number of subgroups than gender or age groups – are inevitably represented in the subcorpus by fewer respondents.

The absolute majority of macroepisodes in the annotated subcorpus refer to private, non-working settings. It was made intentionally to facilitate comparison between sociolects and individual respondents. We tried to select macroepisodes of about the same duration, however, the number of words for each sociolect that finally was found in the subcorpus differs (and sometimes to a considerable degree) (see Table 1). Total amount of words in the research subcorpus equals to 125,437 words.

Table 1. The number of words for different social groups in the subcorpus

N	I. Gender groups:	Words	N	IV. Professional groups:	Words
1*	MUZ (men)	47,135	11	RAB (blue-collar workers)	3,516
2*	ZEN (women)	78,302	12	ENG (engineers)	8,987
	II. Age groups:		13	SIL (men of arms)	7,067
3*	A1 (youth group)	46,328	14	EST (natural sciences)	9,552
4*	A2 (middle-aged)	51,431	15*	HUM (humanities)	14,465
5*	A3 (seniors)	23,475	16*	OBR (education)	12,512
	A0 (kids)	4,203	17*	CO (service sector)	18,744
	III. Status Groups:		18	IT (IT specialists)	4,048
6*	UCH (students)	13,689	19*	OF (office employees)	15,161
7*	SPEC (specialists)	68,960	20	TVOR (creative professionals)	6,940
8	RUK (executive employees)	5,958			
9	BUS (businessmen)	10,531			
10	NOR (non-working)	7,635		**In total**	**125,437**

Since for each parameter under study, referring to different linguistic levels, different sample sizes are required in order to obtain reliable results, it was necessary to find a compromise that would satisfy most of these parameters. In this research, a threshold value of 10,000 words was chosen as the minimum sample size. From this point of view, not all social groups are presented in the subcorpus in sufficient numbers. Here, we consider that only sociolects marked in Table 1 by asterisks have enough data for reliable conclusions.

Table 1 shows that the compiled subcorpus is sufficient enough for studying gender and age variation. Besides speech of adults, some amount of children's speech was provided by kids-interlocutors, though its research was not initially planned. As regards status and professional variation, only some of these groups have enough data and therefore substantial grounds for quantitative analysis. Thus, the largest number of words in subcorpus is provided by the group of employees and specialists. The sets of words exceeding 10,000 was also obtained by the student group, as well as by four professional groups (listed in decreasing order): (1) representatives of the service sector; (2) office employees; (3) representatives of the humanities; and (4) workers of education.

Probably, the prone to "wordiness" may be also considered as a factor distinguishing different social groups. Thus, it was already noticed that men in general speak less than women (see, in particular, [8]). Our data shows that seniors speak less than young and middle-aged people, and some professional groups of people (e.g., blue-collar workers, IT specialists, soldiers, policemen, and even creative professionals) on the average speak less than people from other professional groups. However, this hypothesis should be tested on the larger volumes of spoken data.

2.3 Linguistic Annotation of the Subcorpus

The annotation of the exploratory subcorpus on different linguistic levels has been carried out. The annotation of speech material has been made on the phonetic, lexical, morphological and syntactic levels in the following aspects (linguistic features) [7]:

On phonetic level: (1) the distribution of phonemes; (2) the distribution of allophones; (3) speech rate; (4) intonation characteristics (the dynamics of pitch frequency); (5) the usage of reduced forms.

On lexical level: (1) functional activity of lexical units, which was obtained from the frequency word lists; (2) stylistically marked words, professional words, slang words, neologisms, individual derivational forms, etc.; (3) the index of lexical diversity (the lexical richness); (4) pragmatic markers and pragmatemes.

On morphological level: (1) the distribution of parts of speech; (2) occasional grammatical forms; (3) agrammatical and deviant forms, the phenomenon of a language game; (4) "complicated" forms and pragmatically marked forms.

On syntactic level: (1) linear structures of verb phrases; (2) the amount of the left- and right-branching verb phrases; (3) nonprojective syntactic structures; (4) linear structures of noun phrases; (5) cases of parcellation, ellipsis, incomplete utterances, and self-correction.

As it was already mentioned, the volume of the annotated speech subcorpus has 125,437 words on lexical and morphological levels. There are 13,200 structures annotated on syntactic level, and 172,000 allophones were analyzed on phonetic level.

The frequency of each linguistic feature was measured for subcorpus in general and for the individual social groups, and the comparison of sociolects was made by means of the standard statistical criteria (Student's t-test, Chi-squared test, etc.).

3 Linguistic Features and Sociolinguistic Variability

It turned out that in terms of sociolinguistic variability all analyzed linguistic features fall into three following categories: (1) the diagnostic features, which Display Statistically Significant Differences between Certain social groups; (2) the linguistic features, which could be considered as common for all sociolects and referring to some permanent, universal properties of everyday language; and (3) the potentially diagnostic features, which have shown some quantitative difference between the considered groups, but the extent of this difference does not allow to regard them as statistically significant at the moment.

3.1 Diagnostic Features, which Display Statistically Significant Differences between Certain Social Groups

There is a limited number of diagnostic features which have shown statistically significant differences between social groups under consideration. Most of these features were already described in earlier papers by both Russian and Western scientists, see e.g. [9–13]. In particular, they are the following:

The diagnostic features **on phonetic level** are rather predictable:

- speech rate is diagnostic for different age groups (the average speech rate slows down with age) [5];
- average pitch frequency usually distinguishes male and female voices (135 Hz (SD = 43 Hz) vs. 228 Hz (SD = 60 Hz) on the average).

On lexical level, the diagnostic features seen in our data are as follows:

- the use of neologisms tends to decrease with age;
- obscene language is much more common for male speech than for the female one [8]. The use of lexical hedges and intensifiers is different in male and female speech;
- the use of professional words in everyday conversations is much more common for speech of natural-science specialties compared to that of specialists in humanities.

No significant diagnostic features were revealed on morphological and syntactic levels in the framework of this project. Probably, it may mean that from grammatical point of view spoken Russian is homogeneous, despite its spontaneity and its seemingly irregularities. However, the potentially diagnostic features (see below Sect. 3.3) should be taken into account and further investigated.

3.2   Universal Features, which Seem to Be Common for All Social Groups

The project revealed the set of linguistic parameters in respect of which all sociolects behave roughly the same. It looks like that these parameters reflect some permanent, universal properties of everyday Russian. They are the following:

On phonetic level:

- the distributions of high frequency allophones and phonemes are similar for all sociolects. In speech of all social groups, the phonemes /a/ (18%), /i/ (9%), /t/ (6%), /o/ (5%), /u/ (4%), /n/ (4%), /j/ (3,8%), /e/ (3,6%), and /k/ (3,4%), are the most frequent. These results are the same with those obtained from the ORD data earlier [7]. As for allophones, the most frequent sounds for all social groups are the following: stressed [a0] (6,7%), [t] (6%), stressed [o0] (5,4%), 1st pre-stressed [a1] (5,3%), post-stressed [a4] (4.4%), and [n] (4,4%).

On lexical level:

- high frequency of discourse markers and other fillers is observed in private conversations of all social groups. For example, "nu" (2,84%), "vot" (2,13%), etc.

On morphological level:

- the distribution of parts of speech seems to be rather universal for spoken Russian as a whole. Here, the most frequent are verbs (17%), nouns (15%), personal pronouns (14%), particles including discourse markers (13%), and conjunctions (9%). The similar distribution is observed in speech of all social groups.

On syntactic level:

- the most frequent syntactic structures of utterances are the simplest ones for all sociolects. They are the following: (1) D – an isolated discourse marker (3–4%), (2) {D} – a group of discourse markers (2%), (3) V – a verb (appr. 1,9%), (4) S – a noun (appr. 2%), and 5) SV – noun + verb (1%).
- left-branching verb phrases prevail in spoken Russian [14].

3.3   The Potentially Diagnostic Features

The majority of the investigated linguistic features fall into the category of "potentially diagnostic parameters", because they have shown some quantitative difference between the considered groups, but the extent of this difference does not allow to regard them as statistically significant at the moment. This is the most extensive group of linguistic features. They are, inter alia, the following:

- the use of reduced forms;
- the use of pragmatic markers/pragmatemes [15];
- other lexical features of professional and status groups [1];
- the percentage of grammatical mistakes;

- the use of a language game;
- the syntactic irregularities of speech [1].

With regard to these parameters, it is necessary to conduct additional studies on a larger amount of speech data. Intrapersonal variation should be also taken into consideration [16].

4 Conclusion

In the presented research, the linguistic features were analyzed at different linguistic levels, which could be considered as diagnostic for different social groups. They are the following: (1) the distribution of phonemes; (2) the distribution of allophones; (3) speech rate; (4) the dynamics of pitch frequency; (5) the usage of reduced forms; (6) functional activity of lexical units; (7) stylistically marked words, professional words, slang words, neologisms, individual derivational forms, etc.; (8) lexical diversity; (9) pragmatic markers and pragmatemes; (10) the distribution of parts of speech; (11) occasional grammatical forms; agrammatical and deviant forms, the phenomenon of a language game; (12) "complicated" forms and pragmatically marked forms; (13) linear structures of verb phrases; (14) the amount of the left- and right-branching verb phrases; (15) nonprojective syntactic structures; (16) linear structures of noun phrases; and (17) cases of parcellation, ellipsis, incomplete utterances, and self-correction.

It turned out that in terms of sociolinguistic variability these linguistic features may be divided into three categories: (1) the diagnostic features, which display statistically significant differences between certain social groups (in particular, speech rate, average speech frequency, obscene language, the use of neologisms, professional words, etc.); (2) the linguistic features, which could be considered as common for all sociolects and referring to some permanent, universal properties of everyday language (the distributions of frequent allophones and phonemes; the distribution of parts of speech; the high share of discourse markers; the prevailing of left-branching verb phrases; etc.); and (3) the potentially diagnostic features, which have shown some quantitative difference between the considered groups, but the extent of this difference does not allow to regard them as statistically significant at the moment (in particular, the use of reduced forms, pragmatic markers/pragmatemes, the percentage of grammatical mistakes, the syntactic irregularities of speech, etc.). The last group of features is the most extensive and requires additional studies on a larger amount of speech data.

However, the research revealed that in many aspects (primarily prosodic, lexical and syntactic) the variability of colloquial language is very high, including that inside sociolects. This factor significantly increases the data volume requirements. Therefore, for making a statistically reliable conclusion on social variation of language and proving the developed hypotheses it is necessary to study a more representational amount of spoken material.

Furthermore, it is necessary to study how previously unconsidered sociological factors (such as education, social background, place of birth and history of residence, etc.) influence everyday speech. It is also important to estimate the influence that the psychological constitution brings on the entropy of speech characteristics in social groups.

Another major conclusion is that a speaker's language characteristics can significantly change in different communicative settings. The most significant factors in this aspect are the social role in a scenario (the same person may play various roles in different scenarios: for example, son/daughter, parent, friend, colleague, superior/subordinate) and social integrity of interlocutors (cf. men's vs. women's talk). These factors are also need to be examined.

Acknowledgements. The presented research was supported by the Russian Science Foundation, project No. 14–18–02070 "Everyday Russian Language in Different Social Groups".

References

1. Bogdanova-Beglarjan, N.V., Sherstinova, T.J., Baeva, E.M., Blinova, O.V., Martynenko, G.J., Ermolova, O.B., Ryko, A.I.: Russian everyday language in different social groups. Commun. Stud. **2**(8), 81–92 (2016)
2. Asinovsky, A., Bogdanova, N., Rusakova, M., Ryko, A., Stepanova, S., Sherstinova, T.: The ORD speech corpus of Russian everyday communication "One Speaker's Day": creation principles and annotation. In: Matoušek, V., Mautner, P. (eds.) TSD 2009. LNCS, vol. 5729, pp. 250–257. Springer, Heidelberg (2009). doi:10.1007/978-3-642-04208-9_36
3. Bogdanova-Beglarian, N., Sherstinova, T., Blinova, O., Ermolova, O., Baeva, E., Martynenko, G., Ryko, A.: Sociolinguistic extension of the ORD corpus of Russian everyday speech. In: Ronzhin, A., Potapova, R., Németh, G. (eds.) SPECOM 2016. LNCS, vol. 9811, pp. 659–666. Springer, Cham (2016). doi:10.1007/978-3-319-43958-7_80
4. Sherstinova, T.: Macro episodes of Russian everyday oral communication: towards pragmatic annotation of the ORD speech corpus. In: Ronzhin, A., Potapova, R., Fakotakis, N. (eds.) 17th International Conference on Speech and Computer, SPECOM-2015, Athens, Greece, 20–24 September 2015, Proceedings, pp. 268–276 (2015)
5. Stepanova, S.: Speech rate as reflection of speaker's social characteristics. In: Thielemann, N., Kosta, P. (eds.), Approaches to Slavic Interaction. Dialogue Studies, 20, pp. 117–129. John Benjamins Publishing Company, Amsterdam/Philadelphia (2013)
6. Bogdanova-Beglarian, N., Martynenko, G., Sherstinova, T.: The "One Day of Speech" corpus: phonetic and syntactic studies of everyday spoken Russian. In: Ronzhin, A., Potapova, R., Fakotakis, N. (eds.) SPECOM 2015. LNCS, vol. 9319, pp. 429–437. Springer, Cham (2015). doi:10.1007/978-3-319-23132-7_53
7. Bogdanova-Beglarian, N., Sherstinova, T., Blinova, O., Martynenko, G.: An exploratory study on sociolinguistic variation of Russian everyday speech. In: Ronzhin, A., Potapova, R., Németh, G. (eds.) SPECOM 2016. LNCS, vol. 9811, pp. 100–107. Springer, Cham (2016). doi:10.1007/978-3-319-43958-7_11
8. Sherstinova, T.: The most frequent words in everyday spoken Russian (in the gender dimension and depending on communication settings). Komp'juternaja Lingvistika i Intellektual'nye Tehnologii, Proc. of the Int. Scient. Conference "Dialogue", **15**(22), 616–631 (2016)
9. Kendall, T.: Speech Rate, Pause and Sociolinguistic Variation. Studies in Corpus Sociophonetics. Palgrave Macmillan UK, Basingstoke (2013)
10. Cheshire, J.: Sex and gender in variationist research. In: Chambers, J.K., Trudgill, P., Schilling-Estes, N. (Ed.). The Handbook of Language Variation and Change. Blackwell, Malden, Oxford (2004)

11. Krysin, L.P., (ed.): Modern Russian: actual processes at the turn of the XX–XXI centuries. Languages of Slavic Cultures (2008)
12. Eckert, P., Rickford, J.R. (eds.): Style and Sociolinguistic Variation, vol. 14(2), pp. 302–304. Cambridge University Press, Cambridge (2004)
13. Holmes, J., Meyerhoff, M. (eds.): The Handbook of Language and Gender. Blackwell, Oxford (2003)
14. Martynenko, G.: Syntax of live spontaneous speech: the symmetry of linear orders. In: Zakharov, V.P., Mitrofanova, O.A., Khokhlova, M.V. (eds.) Proceedings of the International Conference "Corpus linguistics-2015", pp. 371–378 (2015)
15. Bogdanova-Beglarian, N.V.: Pragmatic items functions in Russian everyday speech of different social groups. Perm University Herald. Russian Foreign Philol. 2(34), 38–49 (2016)
16. Potapova, R.K., Potapov, V.V.: Language, Speech, Personality. Languages of Slavic Cultures (2006). (In Russian)

Medical Speech Recognition: Reaching Parity with Humans

Erik Edwards, Wael Salloum, Greg P. Finley, James Fone, Greg Cardiff,
Mark Miller, and David Suendermann-Oeft[✉]

EMR.AI Inc., San Francisco, CA, USA
david@emr.ai
http://emr.ai

Abstract. We present a speech recognition system for the medical
domain whose architecture is based on a state-of-the-art stack trained
on over 270 h of medical speech data and 30 million tokens of text from
clinical episodes. Despite the acoustic challenges and linguistic complexity of the domain, we were able to reduce the system's word error rate
to below 16% in a realistic clinical use case. To further benchmark our
system, we determined the human word error rate on a corpus covering
a wide variety of speakers, working with multiple medical transcriptionists, and found that our speech recognition system performs on a par
with humans.

Keywords: Medical speech recognition · Human word error rate · Parity

1 Introduction

There are several unique challenges in medical-domain automatic speech recognition (ASR). Acoustically, there is often significant background noise during medical dictations, for example, ranging from sirens to office noises to competing talkers and background conversations. This is a challenge not only because of the
lower signal-to-noise ratio, but also because of the diversity of acoustic environments and noise sources which may affect a given recording. This is different than,
say, a system designed to work with car noise or other known noise sources. Second, a large number of microphones and dictation devices are used, e.g. Dicta-
phone, SpeechMike, Digital Voice Recorders, or regular telephone handsets, many
of which use special lossy codecs of varying sound quality. Also, the speakers do
not maintain any consistent distance or orientation to the microphone, such that
even a single utterance can vary widely in quality and absolute volume.

Speech in medical dictations differs from normal (conversational) speech in
several ways, although the presence and magnitude of these differences varies
from one recording to another. Thus, dictations are often spoken very rapidly,
but other files are found with slower speech and lengthy hesitations. Many voiced
hesitations are also present, as are repeated words and restarted sentences. Sentences often lack clear juncture, boundaries, or formatting commands. Even item-
ized lists are sometimes spoken in rapid succession that is unrevealing of boundaries. One often gets the impression that the speech is spoken without a sense

© Springer International Publishing AG 2017
A. Karpov et al. (Eds.): SPECOM 2017, LNAI 10458, pp. 512–524, 2017.
DOI: 10.1007/978-3-319-66429-3_51

of a human listener, or even the intention of being understood, but rather only for required cataloging purposes. On the other hand, some dictations are spoken with excellent quality by certain physicians or their professional assistants.

Finally, and perhaps most importantly, is the challenge of highly complex, domain-specific medical terminology, including thousands of drug names. This presents a significant out-of-vocabulary challenge and is perhaps why most existing medical ASR work has only taken on a single domain (usually radiology).

Although medical-domain ASR has been reported in some form since the 1980s [1–3], all work prior to 1999 used single-word as opposed to continuous ASR, with a single early exception for German [4]. Early works on continuous medical ASR [5–7] immediately recognized the importance of including medical domain-specific terminology in the statistical language model. However, the physicians (usually radiologists) were themselves enlisted to provide manual corrections to update the ASR lexicon. Only gradually in the 21st century have a handful of studies begun to use non-physician transcriptions for language model training. Most reports come from the single domain of radiology (e.g. [8,9]), although a smaller number of restricted-domain systems have been reported elsewhere (dermatology: [10]; temporomandibular disorder: [11]). We are developing language model methodology that scales to larger volumes of data from multiple subspecialties.

We found 45 studies since 1999 that assess the quality of medical ASR, e.g. those covered in reviews by Hodgson et al. [12] and Hammana et al. [13]. Among the few publications on speech recognition on medical corpora reporting results in terms of Word Error Rate (WER) is the work by [14,15] on clinical question answering. The latter focuses on spontaneously spoken medical questions and reports 29.3% for the SRI Decipher system and 37.3% for Nuance Dragon, Medical version. Both systems were adapted to the specific study domain by language model adaptation. Nuance Dragon also underwent profile training to enhance performance. Luu et al. [16] covers nursing handover and reports a WER of 24.6%. Paats et al. [17] and Alumäe [18] both cover radiology reports in Estonian and report WERs of 18.4% and 13.7%, respectively.

We found ten studies since 1999 that compare ASR quality with human transcription (HT) in healthcare. All 10 report more errors with ASR than HT, often substantially more [12,19–21]. Where categorized, serious errors were also greater with ASR than HT. For example du Toit et al. [22] report 9.6% of ASR'd and 2.3% of HT'd charts having 'clinically significant' errors, and Basma et al. [23] conclude that 'major' errors were 8 times more likely with ASR than HT.

We report here on our current progress in developing a medical ASR system whose initial version was discussed in [24]. As indicated in the abstract, our system approaches human WER in the medical transcription domain covered by the corpus described in Sect. 2. Details on how we determined human transcription performance on this corpus are provided in Sect. 3. Reaching performance parity in this work was not due to novelty in one particular part of the ASR methodology, but rather to the accumulation of advances in all stages of the ASR training and decoding. Therefore, this paper presents an overview of our system with commentary on each of the stages in Sect. 4. Results are being discussed in Sect. 5 followed by conclusion and future outlook in Sect. 6.

2 Corpus of Medical Dictation

The studies described in this paper were carried out using a massive collection of English dictated out-patient reports covering a variety of different medical specializations. To perform the experiments whose details are provided in the sections following, three different types of corpora were required:

- The first corpus, (**M1**), contains both audio recordings and textual transcriptions of a small number of prototypical speakers covering the whole spectrum of difficulty levels of clinical dictation. We selected a total of nine speakers reaching from excellent, almost professional speakers dictating in clean office conditions, providing grammatically accurate sentences and punctuation commands, all the way to ones who dictated in an extreme rush, mumbling with no natural pauses, flat intonation, and extreme background noise and reverberation.
- The second corpus, (**M2**), features a random sample of audio and transcriptions of over 200 speakers in a hospital network representing the natural distribution of users in an operational scenario.
- The third corpus, (**M30**), consists of dictations of over 30 thousand outpatient letters used to build the language model for the clinical speech recognizer.

Detailed statistics of these corpora are provided in Table 1.

Table 1. Corpus statistics

		M1	M2	M30
Train	Episodes	1 818	4 574	33 684
	Speakers	9	233	
	Duration/h	67	204	
	Tokens	620 926	1 629 469	29 846 087
	Types	9 872	20 203	68 369
	Singletons	3 451 (35%)	5 968 (30%)	15 613 (23%)
Test	Episodes	30	88	500
	Speakers	6	60	
	Duration/h	1.0	3.7	
	Tokens	10 077	28 696	138 792

3   Human Baseline Performance

Multiple methods to determine human baseline performance on transcription tasks of differing complexity have been discussed in literature. [25] had several expert transcribers transcribe long spontaneous utterances of English language learners and compared their transcriptions with respect to word error rate. In a second phase, transcribers were allowed to choose preferred transcriptions from the set of available ones and correct them, and in a third phase, a gold standard transcription was picked by majority vote among all transcribers. Human word error rates varied between 20.5% in Phase 1 and 5.1% in Phase 3. More recently, [26] used a two-pass transcription approach comparing a first draft transcription with a second pass corrected version of another listener. Resulting human word error rates were reported on two standard research corpora, 5.9% on Switchboard and 11.3% on CallHome. [27] also measured the human error rate on these standard corpora by coupling three junior transcribers with a senior listener who performed error correction. The best resulting error rates were 5.1% on Switchboard and 6.8% on CallHome. Especially the discrepancy of the reported results on CallHome indicates that the measurement of human baseline performance on speech recognition is not a straightforward task.

In the present work, we followed a similar approach to these recent publications in that we compared a single pass transcription with one that went through multiple rounds of quality improvements. These rounds included: First draft of the medical report, quality assurance of the report to the level that it could be delivered as out-patient letter, and, finally, assuring that transcription guidelines were properly followed, e.g. that every uttered word is spelled out. The transcribers used in this study were professionally trained medical transcriptionists embedded in a private crowd [28], as described in further detail in [29].

In order to cover the full spectrum of difficulty levels of human and automatic transcription, we chose the M1 test set for this study. It contains a variety of different recording and speaking conditions, and has a size of over ten thousand tokens to reliably test for statistical significance of performance differences. The human word error rate achieved for this set following the above described methodology was 17.4%.

4   Acoustic and Language Model Training

At the time of decoding, the ASR system requires a language model (LM) and an acoustic model (AM). The former represents N-gram statistics of words, obtained from text processing. The latter represents a mapping from an audio file to phonology, which provides the link to the LM via the lexicon. The lexicon is an a priori mapping from words to phonological representation (pronunciations). The AM training proceeds in three global stages (Fig. 1): (a) feature extraction; (b) alignments; (c) DNN training. During decoding, only (a) and (c) are used; i.e., the features are extracted from test data, and the final DNN model provides the nonlinear mapping to phonology. The linguistic probabilities are represented by

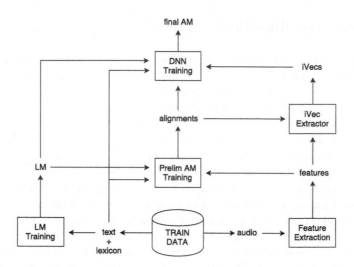

Fig. 1. Overview of acoustic model (AM) training for ASR. The deep neural network (DNN) training takes LM input, alignments (between phonemes and features timeline), and iVectors (iVecs) that are extracted from the audio features

finite-state transducers (FSTs) [30,31], which are implemented e.g. in Sphinx-4 [32], the OpenFST library [33,34], and Kaldi [35].

(a) Feature extraction. This stage transforms the raw acoustic waveform, $w(n)$, sampled at 8–48 kHz, into a multivariate time-series of C features, sampled at 100 Hz frame rate. As it turns out, the raw waveform in medical dictations presents with widely-varying dynamic range. Some recording systems use spectral subtraction [36] or other speech enhancement [37], which can result in sections of near-absolute silence in some audio files; other sections include strong background noises (e.g. sirens) and loud speech; and a typical medical-dictation audio file includes more variability in speech volume and orientation w.r.t. the microphone than typical in standard speech corpora. Therefore, we have carefully considered waveform root-mean-square (RMS) normalization, power-normalization of the spectrogram, and mean/variance normalization of the final features. First, contiguous sections of near-silence (below 0.1% of max level) are clipped out (Fig. 2). Second, the RMS (squared signal smoothed with 200-ms time-constant) is normalized such that all audio files are scaled to a common 70 dB sound-pressure level in units of pressure (Pascals), where 70 dB is chosen as the typical normal-to-loud conversational range [38]. Whereas perceptual loudness correlates to recent amplitude maxima [39], the use of maxima for amplitude normalization is unstable, as extrema are always subject to greater statistical variation. We chose the RMS 90-percentile for each audio file as the normalization point, which we found to be more homogeneous across files. Third, we considered three methods of power-normalization following the short-term Fourier transform (STFT) log compression (standard), the nonlinear power-normalization (PN) method of Kim and Stern [40,41], and their simple

PN (sPN) method, which is first-order running-mean normalization. Preliminary results indicate PN as the preferred method, but these studies are ongoing
and all results reported here use traditional log compression. Finally, the feature
time-series are subjected to per-utterance mean and variance normalization (z-
score method of Fig. 2), or per-speaker mean and variance normalization, as in
[35]. We are currently exploring the options shown in Fig. 2 with very promising results, but all results presented in this paper use traditional mel-frequency
cepstral coefficients (MFCCs) [42] utilizing the following options: 25-ms Hamming window, mel-frequency scale [43], no spectral transformations by PLP [44]
or MVDR [45,46], log compression, cepstral coefficients (CCs), and the typical "lifter" (cepstral-domain weighting) used in speech processing (as given by
Juang et al. [47]). For DNN training, we use 40-dim MFCCs, as suggested by the
study of Rath et al. [48], but for alignments we use 13-dim MFCCs with deltas
and delta-deltas.

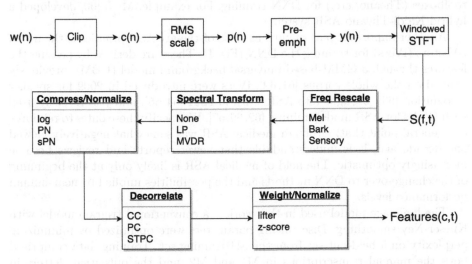

Fig. 2. Overview of acoustic feature extraction for a single utterance. The raw sampled
waveform, $w(n)$, corresponding to a single wav file, is clipped of silent sections, and
then RMS scaled into units of pressure in Pascals, $p(n)$. This is subjected to standard
1st-order pre-emphasis, before the windowed STFT. Note that n indexes samples at 8
to 48 kHz, whereas t indexes frames at 100 Hz. The subsequent stages are listed with
options as described in the text

(b) Alignments. Transcribed medical dictations provide the correct word
sequences for training, but no temporal information. Alignment to the audio
file requires learning a model to map from acoustic features to phonological
sequences, along with the lexicon to map from phonology to words. Several
toolboxes can be used to obtain alignments, for example Praat [49], HTK [50],
Julius [51], Kaldi [35], or RASR [52]. We do not conceive of alignment as a
generic pipeline which is run on the data set at large. Rather, a best alignment can be obtained for each utterance and retained in the database, with

each potentially derived from independent sources. The results reported here are based on triphone models [53], implementing a pipeline of speaker-independent Gaussian mixture models (GMMs) and linear discriminant analysis + maximum-likelihood linear transformation (LDA+MLLT), followed by speaker-adaptive training (SAT) using LDA+MLLT and feature-space maximum-likelihood linear regression (fMLLR).

(c) Deep neural network (DNN) training. Although artificial neural networks have been attempted since the late 1980s in ASR [54], and steadily advanced over the ensuing decades [55,56], they have only become the most widely used state-of-the-art method in ASR in the last five years, joining other fields in the deep learning revolution. For example, the initial publication of the Kaldi toolkit [35] does not mention DNNs, and the recent theses of Plátek [57] and Gil [58] use Kaldi for ASR, but no DNNs. Kaldi introduced two DNN methods circa 2013 [48,59], which we explored along with several other general machine learning toolboxes (Theano, etc.) for DNN training. For example, Miao [60] developed a hybrid Kaldi-Theano ASR system.

Another important part of current state-of-the-art ASR practice is the use of i-Vectors (iVecs) for training the DNN (Fig. 1). These are derived by passing the features through a GMM-based universal background model (UBM), previously trained on the whole corpus [61,62]. iVecs were introduced in 2009 for speaker recognition [63], brought into ASR work in 2011 [64,65], and just recently used with DNNs for ASR model training [62,66,67]. We specify these dates to reinforce our general point that: although medical ASR was somewhat negatively viewed one decade ago, it is understandable that newer reports and reviews become increasingly optimistic. The field of medical ASR is likely only at the beginning of the change-over to DNN methods and the possibilities implied by near-human performance levels.

The language model used in this work is a conventional trigram model with Kneser-Ney smoothing. Discounting parameters were optimized by minimizing perplexity on a held-out set from the M1 training set. Training data comprised both the manual transcriptions in M1 and M2, and the outpatient letters in M30. The latter differ from transcriptions in that they contain case distinctions, formatting, punctuations, and numerals that are either absent or spelled out in transcriptions—e.g., a spoken 'colon' in transcriptions versus ':' in letters, 'twenty-three' in transcriptions versus '23' in letters. Prior to LM training, we processed M30 to remove formatting and spell out those characters and numerals that are typically spelled out in transcriptions.

Investigations into more sophisticated language modeling techniques are currently carried out, examples of which are given in Sect. 6. They will be subject to a future review publication.

5   Experimental Results and Discussion

As indicated in Sect. 2, in this study, we carried out two major experiments. The first one was dedicated to comparing human transcription performance on medical dictation to the performance of our speech recognition system on a range of difficulty levels. The second one was to investigate how the presented speech recognition system performs on a comprehensive selection of speakers, following the distribution in a realistic clinical use case. In the following, we will present and discuss results of these two experiments.

5.1   Comparing Human and ASR Performance

We trained the recognition models according to the pipeline described in Sect. 4 using all available speech data (M1 and M2 training sets) for the acoustic model and the transcriptions of the very same data for the language model. For evaluation, we used the M1 test set as motivated in Sect. 2. Table 2 shows the results of this experiment and compares them to the human baseline performance established in Sect. 3. The achieved performance of our speech recognizer in this task was 18.3% WER which is less than one percentage point higher than the human baseline. To test whether this performance difference is of statistical significance, we carried out a two-proportion z-test. The resulting p-value is 0.10 which suggests that the difference observed in this experiment was *not* statistically significant at the $p < 0.05$ level, despite the rather large test set comprising over ten thousand tokens. While increasing the size of the test set will eventually reveal which of the two, human or machine, outperforms the other, this experiment shows that the accuracy of the speech recognizer we constructed is only marginally different from that of a professional medical transcriptionist, and is, hence, reaching parity.

Table 2. Comparing human and ASR performance

	Errors	Tokens	WER
ASR	1 850	10 115	18.3%
Human baseline	1 760	10 115	17.4%

5.2   ASR Performance in a Realistic Clinical Use Case

For the second experiment, we used the same acoustic model as before, trained on the M1 and M2 training sets, i.e. a total of 271 h of speech. In order to prepare for a deployment in a realistic clinical use case, we substantially increased the size of the language model training corpus by including another 30 million tokens of medical reports (the training set of M30). This time, the experiment was carried out on the M2 test set which matches the target distribution in a realistic clinical setting. The results are shown in Table 3. The error rate, 15.4% is statistically significantly lower than that reported in the first experiment and establishes a strong baseline performance for a realistic clinical use case.

Table 3. ASR Performance in a Realistic Clinical Use Case

Errors	Tokens	WER
4 413	28 696	15.4%

6 Conclusion and Future Directions

We have shown that a carefully tuned state-of-the-art speech recognizer, whose acoustic and language models were trained on moderate size speech and language corpora covering speech and relevant report samples of a set of over 270 physicians, is able to perform on a par with professional human medical transcribers. The human performance was measured in a single pass scenario, i.e., with no additional quality assurance or automated assistance (apart from a spell checker). Following previous work on measuring and optimizing human performance, e.g., in multi-pass or quality control scenarios, indicates that the human word error rate can be further improved. However, as it stands, the presented speech recognizer could be capable of serving as an automated first-pass transcriptionist. Furthermore, the authors are currently working on a number of enhancements to the speech recognizer which should result in substantial further improvements to the error rate, including

- optimizing the feature extraction configuration—the graph in Fig. 2 shows our feature extraction pipeline and the diverse algorithms which we can choose from
- optimizing speaker clustering—we have seen significant performance gains by splitting speakers into specific speaker groups by certain criteria (e.g. region, gender, native language); our goal is to find the optimal split to optimize overall word error rate
- unsupervised acoustic model adaptation—making use of tens of thousands of hours untranscribed speech
- enhancing the language model by (a) adding substantially more data (several million episodes), (b) using sophisticated interpolation techniques, and (c) rescoring with RNN-based, skip, or class language models.

References

1. Leeming, B., Porter, D., Jackson, J., Bleich, H., Simon, M.: Computerized radiologic reporting with voice data-entry. Radiology **138**(3), 585–588 (1981)
2. Akers, G.: Using your voice: speech recognition technology in medicine and surgery. Clin. Plast. Surg. **13**(3), 509–511 (1986)
3. Matumoto, T., Iinuma, T., Tateno, Y., Ikehira, H., Yamasaki, Y., Fukuhisa, K., Tsunemoto, H., Shishido, F., Kubo, Y., Inamura, K.: Automatic radiologic reporting system using speech recognition. Med. Prog. Technol. **12**(3–4), 243–257 (1987)
4. Steinbiss, V., Ney, H., Essen, U., Tran, B.H., Aubert, X., Dugast, C., Kneser, R., Meier, H.G., Oerder, M., Haeb-Umbach, R., Geller, D., Höllerbauer, W., Bartosik, H.: Continuous speech dictation from theory to practice. Speech Commun. **17**(1–2), 19–38 (1995)

5. Hundt, W., Stark, O., Scharnberg, B., Hold, M., Kohz, P., Lienemann, A., Bonél, H., Reiser, M.: Speech processing in radiology. Eur. Radiol. **9**(7), 1451–1456 (1999)
6. Zafar, A., Overhage, J., McDonald, C.: Continuous speech recognition for clinicians. J. Am. Med. Inf. Assoc. **6**(3), 195–204 (1999)
7. Devine, E., Gaehde, S., Curtis, A.: Comparative evaluation of three continuous speech recognition software packages in the generation of medical reports. J. Am. Med. Inf. Assoc. **7**(5), 462–468 (2000)
8. Paulett, J., Langlotz, C.: Improving language models for radiology speech recognition. J. Biomed. Inf. **42**(1), 53–58 (2009)
9. Hawkins, C., Hall, S., Hardin, J., Salisbury, S., Towbin, A.: Prepopulated radiology report templates: a prospective analysis of error rate and turnaround time. J. Digit Imaging **25**(4), 504–511 (2012)
10. Smith, K.: A discrete speech recognition system for dermatology: 8 years of daily experience in a medical dermatology office. Semin. Cutan. Med. Surg. **21**(3), 205–208 (2002)
11. Hippmann, R., Dostálová, T., Zvárová, J., Nagy, M., Seydlová, M., Hanzlícek, P., Kriz, P., Smídl, L., Trmal, J.: Voice-supported electronic health record for temporomandibular joint disorders. Methods Inf. Med. **49**(2), 168–172 (2010)
12. Hodgson, T., Coiera, E.: Risks and benefits of speech recognition for clinical documentation: a systematic review. J. Am. Med. Inf. Assoc. **23**(e1), e169–e179 (2016)
13. Hammana, I., Lepanto, L., Poder, T., Bellemare, C., Ly, M.S.: Speech recognition in the radiology department: a systematic review. HIM. J. **44**(2), 4–10 (2015)
14. Cao, Y.G., Liu, F., Simpson, P., Anticau, L., Bennett, A., Cimino, J., Ely, J., Yu, H.: Askhermes: an online question answering system for complex clinical questions. J. Biomed. Inf. **44**(2), 277–288 (2011)
15. Liu, F., Tur, G., Hakkani-Tür, D., Yu, H.: Towards spoken clinical-question answering: evaluating and adapting automatic speech-recognition systems for spoken clinical questions. J. Am. Med. Inf. Assoc. **18**(5), 625–630 (2011)
16. Luu, T., Phan, R., Davey, R., Hanlen, L., Chetty, G.: Automatic clinical speech recognition for CLEF 2015 ehealth challenge. Working notes report/paper, University of Canberra (2015)
17. Paats, A., Alumäe, T., Meister, E., Fridolin, I.: Evaluation of automatic speech recognition prototype for estonian language in radiology domain: a pilot study. In: Mindedal, H., Persson, M. (eds.) 16th Nordic-Baltic Conference on Biomedical Engineering. IFMBE Proceedings, vol. 48, pp. 96–99. Springer, Cham (2015). doi:10.1007/978-3-319-12967-9_26
18. Alumäe, T.: Full-duplex speech-to-text system for Estonian. In: Proceedings of the Baltic HLT, Kaunas, Lithuania, pp. 3–10. IOS Press (2014)
19. du Toit, J., Hattingh, R., Pitcher, R.: The accuracy of radiology speech recognition reports in a multilingual south african teaching hospital. BMC Med. Imaging **15**(8), 1 (2015)
20. Strahan, R., Schneider-Kolsky, M.: Voice recognition versus transcriptionist: error rates and productivity in MRI reporting. J. Med. Imaging Radiat. Oncol. **54**(5), 411–414 (2010)
21. Zick, R., Olsen, J.: Voice recognition software versus a traditional transcription service for physician charting in the ed. Am. J. Emerg. Med. **19**(4), 295–298 (2001)
22. DuToit, J., Hattingh, R., Pitcher, R.: The accuracy of radiology speech recognition reports in a multilingual South African teaching hospital. BMC Med. Imaging **15**(8), 1–5 (2015)

23. Basma, S., Lord, B., Jacks, L., Rizk, M., Scaranelo, A.: Error rates in breast imaging reports: comparison of automatic speech recognition and dictation transcription. AJR Am. J. Roentgenol. **197**(4), 923–927 (2011)
24. Suendermann-Oeft, D., Ghaffarzadegan, S., Edwards, E., Salloum, W., Miller, M.: A system for automated extraction of clinical standard codes in spoken medical reports. In: Proceedings of Workshop SLT, San Diego, CA. IEEE (2016)
25. Zechner, K.: What did they actually say? Agreement and disagreement among transcribers of non-native spontaneous speech responses in an English proficiency test. In: Proceedings of SLaTE, Warwickshire, UK, pp. 25–28. ISCA (2009)
26. Xiong, W., Droppo, J., Huang, X., Seide, F., Seltzer, M., Stolcke, A., Yu, D., Zweig, G.: Achieving human parity in conversational speech recognition, pp. 1–13 (2017). arXiv:1610.05256
27. Saon, G., Kurata, G., Sercu, T., Audhkhasi, K., Thomas, S., Dimitriadis, D., Cui, X., Ramabhadran, B., Picheny, M., Lim, L.L., Roomi, B., Hall, P.: English conversational telephone speech recognition by humans and machines, pp. 1–7 (2017). arXiv:1703.02136
28. Suendermann, D., Pieraccini, R.: Crowdsourcing for industrial spoken dialog systems. In: Eskénazi, M., Levow, G.A., Meng, H., Parent, G., Suendermann, D. (eds.) Crowdsourcing for Speech Processing, pp. 280–302. J. Wiley, Chichester (2013)
29. Salloum, W., Edwards, E., Ghaffarzadegan, S., Suendermann-Oeft, D., Miller, M.: Crowdsourced continuous improvement of medical speech recognition. In: Proceedings of AAAI Workshop Crowdsourcing, San Francisco, CA. AAAI (2017)
30. Glass, J., Hazen, T., Hetherington, I.: Real-time telephone-based speech recognition in the Jupiter domain. In: Proceedings of ICASSP, vol. 1, pp. 61–64. IEEE (1999)
31. Mohri, M., Pereira, F., Riley, M.: Weighted finite-state transducers in speech recognition. Comput. Speech Lang. **16**(1), 69–88 (2002)
32. Walker, W., Lamere, P., Kwok, P., Raj, B., Singh, R., Gouvêa, E., Wolf, P., Woelfel, J.: Sphinx-4: a flexible open source framework for speech recognition. Technical report SMLI TR2004-0811, Sun Microsystems, Inc. (2004)
33. Allauzen, C., Riley, M., Schalkwyk, J., Skut, W., Mohri, M.: OpenFst: a general and efficient weighted finite-state transducer library. In: Holub, J., Žd'árek, J. (eds.) CIAA 2007. LNCS, vol. 4783, pp. 11–23. Springer, Heidelberg (2007). doi:10.1007/978-3-540-76336-9_3
34. Gorman, K.: Openfst library (2016). http://openfst.org
35. Povey, D., Boulianne, G., Burget, L., Glembek, O., Goel, N., Hannemann, M., Motlícek, P., Qian, Y., Schwarz, P., Silovsky, J.: The kaldi speech recognition toolkit. In: Proceedings of Workshop ASRU, 4 p. IEEE (2011)
36. Boll, S.: Suppression of acoustic noise in speech using spectral subtraction. IEEE Trans. Acoust. **27**(2), 113–120 (1979)
37. Hermus, K., Wambacq, P., Van Hamme, H.: A review of signal subspace speech enhancement and its application to noise robust speech recognition. EURASIP J. Adv. Signal Process. **2007**(45821), 1–15 (2007)
38. Zwicker, E., Feldtkeller, R.: Das Ohr als Nachrichtenempfänger, 2nd edn. Monographien der elektrischen Nachrichtentechnik; Bd. 19. Hirzel, Stuttgart (1967)
39. Fastl, H., Zwicker, E.: Psychoacoustics: Facts and Models, 3rd edn. Springer, Berlin (2007)
40. Kim, C., Stern, R.: Power-normalized cepstral coefficients (PNCC) for robust speech recognition. In: Proceedings of ICASSP, pp. 4101–4104. IEEE (2012)

41. Kim, C., Stern, R.: Power-normalized cepstral coefficients (PNCC) for robust speech recognition. IEEE/ACM Trans. Audio Speech Lang. Process. **24**(7), 1315–1329 (2016)
42. Imai, S.: Cepstral analysis synthesis on the mel frequency scale. In: Proceedings of ICASSP, vol. 8, pp. 93–96. IEEE (1983)
43. Stevens, S., Volkmann, J.: The relation of pitch to frequency: a revised scale. Am. J. Psychol. **53**(3), 329–353 (1940)
44. Hermansky, H.: An efficient speaker-independent automatic speech recognition by simulation of some properties of human auditory perception. In: Proceedings of ICASSP, vol. 12, pp. 1159–1162. IEEE (1987)
45. Murthi, M., Rao, B.: Minimum variance distortionless response (MVDR) modeling of voiced speech. In: Proceedings of ICASSP, vol. 3, pp. 1687–1690. IEEE (1997)
46. Yapanel, U., Dharanipragada, S., Hansen, J.: Perceptual mvdr-based cepstral coefficients (PMCCS) for high accuracy speech recognition. In: Proceedings of EUROSPEECH, pp. 1829–1832. ISCA (2003)
47. Juang, B.H., Rabiner, L., Wilpon, J.: On the use of bandpass liftering in speech recognition. IEEE Trans. Acoust. **35**(7), 947–954 (1987)
48. Rath, S., Povey, D., Veselý, K., Cernocký, J.: Improved feature processing for deep neural networks. In: Proceedings of INTERSPEECH, pp. 109–113. ISCA (2013)
49. Boersma, P., van Heuven, V.: Praat, a system for doing phonetics by computer. Glot. Int. **5**(9/10), 341–345 (2002)
50. Young, S., Evermann, G., Gales, M., Hain, T., Kershaw, D., Liu, X., Moore, G., Odell, J., Ollason, D., Povey, D., Valtchev, V., Woodland, P.: The HTK book (for HTK version 3.4). Book HTK Version 3.4, Cambridge University Engineering Department, March 2009
51. Lee, A.: The Julius Book. Nagoya Institute of Technology, May 2010
52. Rybach, D., Hahn, S., Lehnen, P., Nolden, D., Sundermeyer, M., Tüske, Z., Wiesler, S., Schlüter, R., Ney, H.: RASR - the RWTH Aachen University open source speech recognition toolkit. In: Proceedings of ASRU Workshop, IEEE (2011)
53. Gaida, C., Lange, P., Petrick, R., Proba, P., Malatawy, A., Suendermann-Oeft, D.: Comparing open-source speech recognition toolkits. Technical report, DHBW, October 2014
54. Lippmann, R.: Review of neural networks for speech recognition. Neural Comput. **1**(1), 1–38 (1989)
55. Bourlard, H., Morgan, N., Renals, S.: Neural nets and hidden markov models: review and generalizations. Speech Commun. **11**(2–3), 237–246 (1992)
56. Hinton, G., Deng, L., Yu, D., Dahl, G., Mohamed, A.R., Jaitly, N., Senior, A., Vanhoucke, V., Nguyen, P., Sainath, T., Kingsbury, B.: Deep neural networks for acoustic modeling in speech recognition: the shared views of four research groups. IEEE Signal Process. Mag. **29**(6), 82–97 (2006)
57. Plátek, O.: Speech recognition using Kaldi. Masters thesis, Charles University (2014)
58. Gil, V.: Automatic speech recognition with Kaldi toolkit. Doctoral thesis, University Politècnica de Catalunya (2016)
59. Zhang, X., Trmal, J., Povey, D., Khudanpur, S.: Improving deep neural network acoustic models using generalized maxout networks. In: Proceedings of ICASSP, pp. 215–219. IEEE (2014)
60. Miao, Y.: Kaldi + pdnn: building dnn-based ASR systems with kaldi and PDNN, 4 p. (2014). arXiv:1401.6984
61. Povey, D., Chu, S., Varadarajan, B.: Universal background model based speech recognition. In: Proceedings of ICASSP, pp. 4561–4564. IEEE (2008)

62. Snyder, D., Garcia-Romero, D., Povey, D.: Time delay deep neural network-based universal background models for speaker recognition. In: Proceedings of Workshop ASRU, pp. 92–97. IEEE (2015)
63. Dehak, N., Dehak, R., Kenny, P., Brümmer, N., Ouellet, P., Dumouchel, P.: Support vector machines versus fast scoring in the low-dimensional total variability space for speaker verification. In: Proceedings of INTERSPEECH, pp. 1559–1562. ISCA (2009)
64. Zhang, Y., Yan, Z.J., Huo, Q.: A new i-vector approach and its application to irrelevant variability normalization based acoustic model training. In: Proceedings of Workshop MLSP, pp. 1–6. IEEE (2011)
65. Karafiát, M., Burget, L., Matejka, P., Glembek, O., Cernocký, J.: ivector-based discriminative adaptation for automatic speech recognition. In: Proceedings of Workshop ASRU. IEEE (2011)
66. Senior, A., Lopez-Moreno, I.: Improving DNN speaker independence with i-vector inputs. In: Proceedings of ICASSP, pp. 225–229. IEEE (2014)
67. Peddinti, V., Chen, G., Manohar, V., Ko, T., Povey, D., Khudanpur, S.: Jhu aspire system: robust LVCSR with TDNNS, ivector adaptation and RNN-LMS. In: Proceedings of Workshop on ASRU, pp. 539–546. IEEE (2015)

Microphone Array Post-filter in Frequency Domain for Speech Recognition Using Short-Time Log-Spectral Amplitude Estimator and Spectral Harmonic/Noise Classifier

Sergey Salishev[1]($\boxtimes$), Ilya Klotchkov[2], and Andrey Barabanov[1]

[1] Saint Petersburg State University, Saint Petersburg, Russia
{s.salischev,a.barabanov}@spbu.ru
[2] Intel Labs, Intel Corporation, Santa Clara, CA 95054-1549, USA
ilya.v.klotchkov@intel.com

Abstract. We propose a novel computationally efficient real-time microphone array speech enhancement postfilter with a small delay that takes into account features of speech signal and recognition algorithms. The algorithm is efficient for small microphone arrays. The filter is based on applying a binary classification model to the Log Short-Term Spectral Amplitude (Log-STSA). The proposed algorithm allows substantial improvement of recognition accuracy with minor increase in complexity compared to Wiener post-filter and lower complexity compared to existing voice model based approaches. Objective tests using dual microphone array, ETSI binaural noise database, TIDIGITS database, and CMU Sphinx 4 speech recognizer demonstrate overall 41% Error Rate reduction for SNR from 15 dB to 0 dB. Subjective evaluation also demonstrates substantial noise reduction and intelligibility improvement without musical noise artifacts common for Wiener and Spectral Subtraction based methods. Testing with SiSEC10 four microphone linear equispaced array database shows that recognition accuracy is improved with increased base and/or number of microphones in array.

Keywords: Beamforming · Postfilter · Noise reduction · Speech recognition

1 Introduction

Using multiple microphones for speech recognition is a common technique in consumer electronics, wearables etc. The problem is extensively studied by hosting regular machine learning challenges and benchmarks e.g. CHiME [4]. Most of the proposed solutions which demonstrate noticeable improvement in recognition accuracy are based on deep learning and other high complexity techniques which are not suitable for low-power devices without Internet connectivity.

We were particularly interested in improving speech recognition word error rate (WER) in small-vocabulary voice command task for low-power wearable

© Springer International Publishing AG 2017
A. Karpov et al. (Eds.): SPECOM 2017, LNAI 10458, pp. 525–534, 2017.
DOI: 10.1007/978-3-319-66429-3_52

devices. The basic beamformer algorithm is delay-and-sum. Many works are aimed to improve the directivity of a beamformer such as a generalized sidelobe canceler (GSC) [6]. This approach works well for point sources of interference but does not suppress reverberant noise, as it arrives from all directions.

Reverberant noise causes major degradation of recognition accuracy in practical applications. The common technique for reverberant noise suppression is SNR driven adaptive filtering by multiplication with real-valued filters in frequency domain called postfilters. This includes families of spectral subtraction, Wiener, Log-STSA optimal, etc. filters, which differ by the gain function and the SNR estimation method. In this approach microphone array is used mainly for SNR estimation. Postfilters can be combined with directivity improvement techniques such as a superdirective beamformer [12].

Zelinski [17] proposes a time domain postfilter for the microphone array based on Wiener filter. The postfilter provides substantial noise reduction for the spatially uncorrelated e.g. thermal noise.

In many applications the noise in the microphones is characterized by noise signals of equal power at all locations, propagating with equal probability in all directions. This spatially isotropic or diffuse noise is studied by McCowan et al. [11] who generalize the Zelinski's results. Typical filtering techniques due to inaccuracies in estimated SNR exhibit musical-noise artifacts as they over-suppress low-magnitude spectral components of noise unmasking noise spectral peaks. For single microphone noise suppression these artifacts were studied by Plapous et al. [13]. To prevent this, the common engineering practice is to limit attenuation by some margin [15].

The Wiener filter provides MSE optimal estimate of time domain signal for Gaussian processes while most of speech recognizers use Mel-frequency cepstrum coefficients (MFCC) as primary features of speech. The set of logarithms of the short time spectral amplitudes (Log-STSA) defines the main part of the MFCC for a voiced speech signal. Ephraim and Malah [5] propose an optimal estimator of Log-STSA for Gaussian processes. It provides weaker attenuation than Wiener (Lefkimmiatis MSE) and McCowan Wiener filters for the same method of estimating SNR. Log-STSA (Ephraim Malah $\gamma = \infty$) behaves in log domain similarly to Spectral Subtraction.

Lefkimmiatis and Maragos [9] notice that the Zelinsky and the McCowan filters are not actually postfilters but prefilters, as they overestimate noise ignoring attenuation by the beamformer. They propose a family of true postfilters. During evaluation we have noticed that despite inadequate statistical model Wiener prefilter provides better recognition accuracy compared to to Log-STSA prefilter, Wiener postfilter and Log-STSA postfilter, due to stronger attenuation which is caused by lower filter gain and overestimation of noise.

All the above methods are generic and do not account for properties of human voice. We empirically measured mean Log-STSA optimal filter gain for TIDIG-ITS database [10] corrupted by a synthetically added white noise with SNR measured at the input of the beamformer. TIDIGITS was selected as an example of a small-vocabulary dataset for local real-time speech recognition on a low-power device. Figure 1 shows gains for different methods, Lefkimmiatis gains are shown for 2 microphone setup. SNR on the figure X-axis is shown on the output of the beamformer according to Lefkimmiatis.

The resulting gain function is significantly lower than that of the McCowan filter in high-to-medium SNR range and constant for low SNR. Also the optimal filter gain strongly depends on overall SNR (i.e. speech loudness) which suggests that the multiplicative model is inaccurate, and better noise suppression model accounting for speech signal properties is possible.

Yoshioka and Nakatani [16] propose an off-line postfilter using GMM based statistical model of speech and demonstrate substantial improvement of speech recognition compared to McCowan at the cost of substantial complexity increase and off-line usage. Raj and Stern [14] propose a binary classification based noise suppression for speech recognition. Their approach requires substantial modification of the recognizer and cannot be used for speech enhancement for listening.

We propose a novel simple real-time microphone array speech enhancement postfilter with a small delay that takes into account features of speech signal and recognition algorithms. The algorithm is efficient for small microphone arrays. The filter is based on applying binary classification model to the Log Short-Term Spectral Amplitude. The algorithm uses gain function accounting for expected speech loudness model, which prevents musical noise while keeping high attenuation in loud noise. The proposed algorithm allows substantial improvement of recognition accuracy with minor increase in complexity compared to Wiener postfilter and lower complexity compared to existing voice model based approaches. In practice the complexity is comparable to a typical MFCC based ASR frontend.

The algorithm output can be restored to time domain for listening by combining it with phases of beamformer output. Our implementation uses simple delay-and-sum rule. Similarily to other postfilters the proposed approach can be combined with various beamformer directivity improvement techniques.

Objective tests using dual microphone array, TIDIGITS with synthetically added noises from ETSI binaural noise database [1], and CMU Sphinx 4 [8] speech recognizer with supplied TIDIGITS recipe demonstrate overall 41% error rate reduction for SNR from 15 dB to 0 dB. Listening also demonstrate substantial reduction of musical noise artifacts common to Wiener and Spectral Subtraction based methods. Testing with SiSEC10 four microphone linear equispaced array database [2] (distance between adjacent microphones is 8.6 cm) shows that recognition accuracy is improved with increased base and/or number of microphones in array.

2   Gains and Noises

The McCowan filter without attenuation limit produces musical noises in the frequency bands with low SNR, which causes substantial degradation of ASR recognition performance compared to the beamformer output without a postfilter. The transfer function of the Wiener filter is $W(f) = \xi/(1 + \xi)$ where $\xi = \xi(f) = E|S|^2/E|V|^2$ is calculated by the spectrum of the speech signal $S(f)$

and the spectrum of the noise $V(f)$. Here and further E stands for the expectation. $E|S|^2$ and $E|V|^2$ are the signal and noise PSD. The on-line filter contains a random variable $\widehat{\xi}$ as an estimate of the ideal value of ξ. Assume the SNR ξ is small on a wide frequency band. Then the main part of the spectrum of the measured signal in this band is the noise V and it is suppressed by the ideal Wiener filter. The estimate $\widehat{\xi}$ is expected to be close to ξ in average. Therefore output of the on-line filter is also essentially small in average. But both $\widehat{\xi}$ and $|V|$ are random and they may have common frequency peaks which become isolated spectral peaks of the filter output. The spectral peaks are perceived as musical noises [13].

To prevent the well-known effect of musical noises, the ideal Wiener filter is usually corrected so that $W(f)$ is bounded from below by a fixed threshold $\varepsilon > 0$. If ε is relatively big then a big noise is not attenuated when ξ is small. Thus, a choice of ε is a trade-off between musical noises and noise attenuation [15].

We empirically measured mean Log-STSA optimal filter gain for speech as a function of ξ. We synthetically added the white noise to the TIDIGITS database [10] with SNR level set at the input of the beamformer. At the sample rate of 16 kHz for half-overlapped frames of the length of 20 ms the following values are calculated: $S(f)$, $V(f)$, $\xi(f) = |S(f)|^2/|V(f)|^2$ and the log-optimal gain $G(f) = \log|S(f)| - \log|(S(f) + V(f))|$. Then for any fixed ξ_0 the gains $G(f)$ with $\xi(f) = \xi_0$ are averaged over all frames and over all frequencies f in the speech band from 200 Hz to 4800 Hz. The averaged optimal gain in the logarithmic scale is shown in Fig. 2 by the dashed lines for several values of the input SNR values. The averaged gain G as a function of ξ for any postfilter can be calculated directly in a similar way. Figure 2 shows gains of spectral subtraction, Log-STSA, Wiener (Lefkimmiatis MSE) filter [9] for 2 microphone setup and the McCowan filter [11]. ξ on the figure X-axis is shown on the output of the beamformer according to Lefkimmiatis.

The resulting optimal gain functions are significantly lower than that of the McCowan filter in high-to-medium ξ range and constant for low ξ. Also the optimal filter gain strongly depends on overall SNR (i.e. speech loudness) which suggests that the multiplicative model depending only on ξ is inaccurate, and better noise suppression model accounting for speech signal properties is possible.

The musical noise appear in the frequency bands with small ξ. Since the speech signal is less than the noise in these bands, a small comfort noise can be added to the filter output that can mask the spectral peaks after the Wiener filter and neglect the musical noises which is a common engineering practice [15]. In the next algorithm, separation of "small" and "big" values of ξ leads to a simple classifier that can be considered as a soft decision in the trade-off between musical noises and noise attenuation. Then the classifier is followed by the Bayes rule for the gain estimation.

3 Algorithm Description

Assume a beam is fixed and steering has been implemented if needed. Voice and noises are uncorrelated and voice is not reverberated. Noise is assumed to be

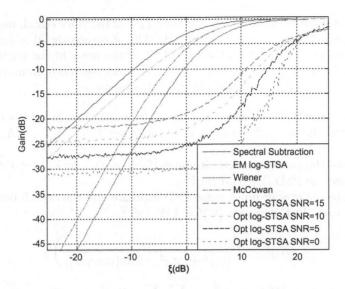

Fig. 1. Averaged gains for various postfilters as a function of the instantaneous frequency-by-frequency SNR

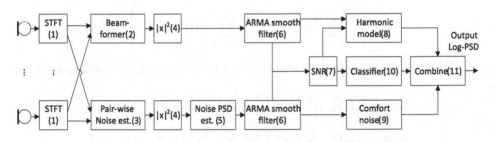

Fig. 2. Algorithm diagram

isotropic with spatial correlation in the frequency domain Γ_{ij} between the microphones i and j. Γ_{ij} is estimated from observations. For a spherically isotropic acoustic field and free standing microphones $\Gamma_{ij}(f) = \mathrm{sinc}((2\pi f d_{ij})/c)$, $\mathrm{sinc}(x) = \sin(x)/x$, here f is a frequency, d_{ij} is the distance between microphones, and c is the sound speed. For embedded microphones the diffraction on the device should also be accounted for. Let n be the number of microphones in the array.

Assume t is a time instant when a frame of input samples is formed. The speech signal and the noises also form the frames of the same size. The FFT is calculated for all these frames. Fix a frequency bin f from the basis of FFT.

Consider the following model of the spectra in each frequency bin f:

$$X_i = h_i S + N_i, \qquad E(SN_i) = 0,$$
$$E(N_i N_i) = |N|^2, \qquad E(N_i N_j) = \Gamma_{ij}|N|^2, \quad i \neq j,$$

where i is the microphone number, S is the STFT of the voice signal, the complex number h_i represents the phase/amplitude shift of speech signal of microphone i in the frequency bin f, N_i is the the STFT of the noise in the microphone i. The f is omitted, as frequency bins are modeled independently from each other.

The algorithm (Fig. 2) consists of the following steps:

1. Calculate the STFT frames $\{X_i\}$ for each beamformer input $i = 1..n$.
2. Calculate the the filter-and-sum beamformer $Y = \sum_{i=1}^{n} w_i X_i$, $w_i = (nh_i)^{-1}$.
3. Calculate the pairwise noise estimates $V_{ij} = w_i X_i - w_j X_j$, $i < j$.
4. Calculate the PSD $|Y|^2$ and $|V_{ij}|^2$.
5. Calculate the overall input noise PSD estimate and the overall beamformer output noise PSD estimate $|V|^2 = E|Y - S|^2$,

$$|N_{ij}|^2 = \left(\frac{|V_{ij}|^2}{|w_i|^2 + |w_j|^2 - 2Re(w_i w_j)\Gamma_{ij}} \right),$$

$$|N|^2 = \frac{2}{(n-1)n} \sum_{i=1}^{n-1} \sum_{j=i+1}^{n} |N_{ij}|^2,$$

$$|V|^2 = \left(\sum_{i=1}^{n} |w_i|^2 + 2 \sum_{i=1}^{n-1} \sum_{j=i+1}^{n} Re(w_i w_j)\Gamma_{ij} \right) |N|^2.$$

6. Calculate the smoothed values of $|\widetilde{Y}|^2$ and $|\widetilde{V}|^2$ with 1 frame looking ahead:

$$|\widetilde{Y}_t|^2 = 0.9|\widetilde{Y}_{t-1}|^2 + 0.1 \left(\frac{1}{2}|Y_t|^2 + \frac{1}{4}(|Y_{t-1}|^2 + |Y_{t+1}|^2) \right),$$

$$|\widetilde{V}_t|^2 = 0.9|\widetilde{V}_{t-1}|^2 + 0.1 \left(\frac{1}{2}|V_t|^2 + \frac{1}{4}(|V_{t-1}|^2 + |V_{t+1}|^2) \right).$$

7. Calculate the Wiener filter gain and the SNR

$$G = \max(\varepsilon, \frac{|\widetilde{Y}|^2 - |\widetilde{V}|^2)}{|\widetilde{Y}|^2}, \quad \xi = (G^{-1} - 1)^{-1}.$$

8. Calculate the optimal estimate for log-spectral power of harmonic voice components, integral summand can be removed for simplification with minor negative impact on final result

$$M_H = \ln|Y|^2 + 2\ln G + \int_{\xi}^{\infty} \frac{e^{-x}}{x} dx.$$

9. Calculate the comfort noise model, here σ_0^2 is the expected variance of the breath noise, which is dependent on the expected loudness of voice.

$$M_N = \alpha \ln|V|^2 + (1-\alpha) \ln \sigma_0^2.$$

10. Calculate the signal/noise classifier $P_H(\xi) = \left(1 + e^{-(\beta_0 + \beta_1 \ln \xi)}\right)^{-1}$.

11. Calculate the output Log-PSD $\ln |S|^2 = P_H(\xi)(M_H - M_N) + M_N$.

Steps 1–5 and 7 correspond to the Lefkimmiatis MSE [9] filter. The amplitude estimator in step 8 is derived from Ephraim and Malah [5] with $\gamma = \infty$. Similarly to Aleinik [3] to save computations and memory the smoothing in step 6 is performed on nominator and denominator of gain estimate instead of individual correlations.

The algorithm parameters $\alpha, \beta_0, \beta_1, \sigma_0^2$ are optimized for best recognition accuracy by coordinate gradient descent beforehand using a representative database of speech and noise samples. For this purpose we used 100 male and 100 female sentences from TIDIGITS train data corrupted with random segments of ETSI noise data.

4   Evaluation

For the evaluation we used CMU Sphinx 4 [8] ASR with supplied TIDIGITS recipe on TIDIGITS database with baseline WER accuracy is 99.6%. We used McCowan [11] as a baseline, as our preliminary experiments showed, that other post-filters with higher gains provide lower recognition accuracy. Noise was synthetically added to the clean speech signal. The signal was corrupted by random segments of each environment noise with SNR from 0 to 15 dB, using the mean multiplier between channels. SNR was calculated only on segments of speech with active voice, pauses were ignored. Noise was filtered using high-pass filter at 150 Hz. We used ETSI binaural noise database [1]. Noise coherence for binaural noise was estimated as for spherical isotropic noise with increased microphone base, same as Kamkar-Parsi et al. [7]. The effective microphone base used was 36 cm. Recognition accuracy is shown in Table 1. For comparison we used our own implementation of McCowan postfilter denoted MC in the table.

The algorithm substantially improves the recognition accuracy over McCowan post-filter with overall 10% absolute improvement, which is especially noticeable on non-stationary noises such as babble noise. At the same time complexity of the proposed algorithm is almost the same as that of McCowan.

To better understand the reason of improvement we calculated mean Log-STSA model to Ground Truth ratio (Fig. 3). For an ideal model it should be 1 (0 dB). As expected for the proposed algorithm it is closer to 1 than McCowan. The plateau on the McCowan ratio plot is due to attenuation limit at 13 dB SNR at beamformer output. It should be noticed that it is possible to choose model parameters providing overall ratio closer to 1. But the recognition accuracy for such parameters is slightly worse than for recognition wise optimal parameters. This observation suggests that Log-STSA metric does not fully correspond to recognition accuracy.

To evaluate the algorithm operations with more than 2 microphones we used 4 microphone linearly spaced array noise database SiSEC10 [2]. The distance between adjacent microphones is 8.6 cm. The coherence function was calculated for spherical isotropic noise based on the array geometry. Results for different microphones sets are shown in Table 2. We can conclude that larger base and more microphones increases recognition accuracy.

To validate our results we used commercially available Car Voice Control ASR toolkit with embedded single microphone noise suppression. We observed noticeable improvement over one channel recognition on non-stationary noises such as babble but very small or no improvement on stationary noises such as Aircraft with even 0.5% absolute degradation on Car noise at SNR 0 dB. Overall recognition accuracy in stationary noises was also substantially better than that of Sphinx 4. This suggests that the proposed noise suppression model can be improved for stationary noises. It also should be noted that recognition-wise optimal parameters for the second ASR were slightly different from Sphinx 4 parameters and σ_0^2 was substantially higher. This suggests that some of the model parameters describe not the fundamental parameters of speech signal but internal parameters of the ASR.

Table 1. Sphinx 4 recognition accuracy for different NR methods on TIDIGITS with ETSI binaural noise. W/O - single channel, BF - delay-and-sum beamformer, MC - McCowan postfilter

Noise	SNR 0				SNR 5				SNR 10				SNR 15			
	W/O	BF	MC	New	W/O	BF	MC	New	W/O	BF	MC	New	W/O	BF	MC	New
Aircraft	3.7	9.7	47.1	73.4	23.7	35.1	78.3	90.3	61.3	69.2	91.8	95.6	87.5	88.9	95.6	98
Bus	15	21.1	53.6	74.9	43	50.7	79.4	89.6	74.2	78.2	91.5	95.5	91.6	91.7	96.1	97.5
Cafe	16.1	19.1	44.2	64.8	38.1	43.1	68.9	82.1	66.7	69.8	86.3	91.7	87.2	87.7	93.8	95.9
Car	43.9	39.7	75	88.2	75	70.6	90.4	95.3	91.7	88.5	95.6	97.7	97.2	95.3	97.6	98.5
K-garten	21.5	26.6	50.7	70.5	47.9	52.5	75.1	85.6	75.9	77.3	89.3	93.5	91.4	90.7	95.5	97
Outside	7.3	13.3	33.1	60.9	26.2	36.7	65.9	81	58.2	67.9	85.7	91.4	83.8	87.7	94.4	96
Pub	9.2	10.1	36	61.2	27.3	28	68.8	84	61.3	59.6	87	92.6	86.7	83.5	94.6	96.9
Shop	12.2	17.5	38	57	34.9	43.3	64.7	77.3	66.7	71.3	82.2	89.1	87	87.7	92.1	94.9
Soccer	46.6	49.5	62	77	72.3	72.9	81.3	88.7	88	87.3	91.9	95	95.6	94.7	96.6	97.3
Station	7.3	11.8	29.4	55.5	19.9	27.7	59.8	78.4	42.7	54.9	82.5	89.8	72.5	79.8	93.1	95.6
Train	16.6	20.3	41.8	64.5	47.4	50.6	73	84.4	78.9	78.7	89.1	93.9	93.5	92	95.3	97.3
MEAN	18.1	21.7	46.4	68	41.4	46.5	73.2	85.2	69.6	73	88.4	93.3	88.5	89.1	95	96.8

Table 2. Sphinx 4 recognition accuracy for different microphone configurations on TIDIGITS with SiSEC10 4 microphone noise

Noise	SNR 0			SNR 5			SNR 10			SNR 15		
	M2,3	M1,4	M1–4	M2,3	M1,4	M1–4	M2,3	Mic1,4	M1–4	M2,3	M1,4	M1–4
Cafe	63.8	67.2	73.1	83.0	84.9	88.5	93.4	94.1	95.2	96.6	96.9	97.3
Square	48.7	55.1	62.8	74.8	76.9	82.4	87.6	89.5	92.2	94.8	95.2	96.5
Subway	56.0	64.9	71.4	78.4	83.4	86.8	91.3	92.1	93.9	95.7	96.6	97
MEAN	56.2	62.4	69.1	78.7	81.7	85.9	90.8	91.9	93.8	95.7	96.2	96.9

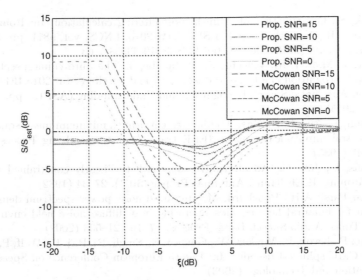

Fig. 3. Model To Ground Truth Ratio for McCowan and New NR for various global SNR (TIDIGITS, ETSI binaural, 2 mic. Beamformer)

5 Conclusions

A new speech enhancement algorithm was proposed that is based on a simple classifier by statistics of the frequency-by frequency SNR versus the filter gain. The proposed algorithm demonstrates good noise suppression in different environments. The algorithm complexity is small compared to typical wideband beamformer design and dominated by STFFT for each input channel.

Minor degradation in recognition accuracy on car noise with 0 dB SNR using commercial Car Voice Control Toolkit suggests the signal model can be improved for stationary noises. The expected voice loudness and noise field coherency are the external parameters of the model. It would be natural to estimate them from the observed signal. The classifier currently takes into account only the data in one frequency bin, more complex classifier using data from other frequency bins may be beneficial. These are the topics of further research.

Acknowledgements. The work was supported by Saint-Petersburg State University, grants 6.37.349.2015 and 6.38.230.2015.

References

1. ETSI EG 202 396–1 speech and multimedia transmission quality (STQ); part 1: Background noise simulation technique and background noise database, March 2009
2. Source separation in the presence of real-world background noise: Test database for 2 channels case (2010). http://www.irisa.fr/metiss/SiSEC10/noise/SiSEC2010_diffuse_noise_2ch.html. Accessed 27 May 2017

3. Aleinik, S.: Optimization of Zelinski post-filtering calculation. In: Ronzhin, A., Potapova, R., Németh, G. (eds.) SPECOM 2016. LNCS, vol. 9811, pp. 523–530. Springer, Cham (2016). doi:10.1007/978-3-319-43958-7_63

4. Barker, J., Marxer, R., Vincent, E., Watanabe, S.: The third chimespeech separation and recognition challenge: dataset, task and baselines. In: 2015 IEEE Workshop on Automatic Speech Recognition and Understanding (ASRU), pp. 504–511. IEEE (2015)

5. Ephraim, Y., Malah, D.: Speech enhancement using a minimum mean-square error log-spectral amplitude estimator. IEEE Trans. Acoust. Speech Sig. Process. **33**(2), 443–445 (1985)

6. Griffiths, L., Jim, C.: An alternative approach to linearly constrained adaptive beamforming. IEEE Trans. Antennas Propag. **30**(1), 27–34 (1982)

7. Kamkar-Parsi, A.H., Bouchard, M.: Improved noise power spectrum density estimation for binaural hearing aids operating in a diffuse noise field environment. IEEE Trans. Audio Speech Lang. Process. **17**(4), 521–533 (2009)

8. Lamere, P., Kwok, P., Walker, W., Gouvea, E., Singh, R., Raj, B., Wolf, P.: Design of the CMU sphinx-4 decoder. In: Eighth European Conference on Speech Communication and Technology (2003)

9. Lefkimmiatis, S., Maragos, P.: A generalized estimation approach for linear and nonlinear microphone array post-filters. Speech Commun. **49**(7), 657–666 (2007)

10. Leonard, R.G., Doddington, G.: Tidigits. Linguistic Data Consortium, Philadelphia (1993)

11. McCowan, I.A., Bourlard, H.: Microphone array post-filter based on noise field coherence. IEEE Trans. Speech Audio Process. **11**(6), 709–716 (2003)

12. McCowan, I.A., Marro, C., Mauuary, L.: Robust speech recognition using near-field superdirective beamforming with post-filtering. In: 2000 IEEE International Conference on Acoustics, Speech, and Signal Processing, ICASSP 2000, Proceedings, vol. 3, pp. 1723–1726. IEEE (2000)

13. Plapous, C., Marro, C., Scalart, P.: Improved signal-to-noise ratio estimation for speech enhancement. IEEE Trans. Audio Speech Lang. Process. **14**(6), 2098–2108 (2006)

14. Raj, B., Stern, R.M.: Missing-feature approaches in speech recognition. IEEE Sig. Process. Mag. **22**(5), 101–116 (2005)

15. Schmidt, G.: Lecture notes in pattern recognition: noise suppression (2016). http://dss.kirat-online.de/images/teaching/lectures/pattern_recognition/slides/pattern_recognition_02_noise_suppression.pdf. Accessed 27 May 2017

16. Yoshioka, T., Nakatani, T.: A microphone array system integrating beamforming, feature enhancement, and spectral mask-based noise estimation. In: 2011 Joint Workshop on Hands-free Speech Communication and Microphone Arrays (HSCMA), pp. 219–224. IEEE (2011)

17. Zelinski, R.: A microphone array with adaptive post-filtering for noise reduction in reverberant rooms. In: 1988 International Conference on Acoustics, Speech, and Signal Processing, ICASSP-1988, pp. 2578–2581. IEEE (1988)

Multimodal Keyword Search for Multilingual and Mixlingual Speech Corpus

Abhimanyu Popli[1,2]($\boxtimes$) and Arun Kumar[1]

[1] Centre for Applied Research in Electronics,
Indian Institute of Technology Delhi, Hauz Khas, New Delhi, India
{crz108049,arunkm}@care.iitd.ac.in
[2] Centre for Development of Telematics, Mandi Road, Mehrauli, New Delhi, India
apopli@cdot.in

Abstract. A novel framework for searching keywords in multilingual and mixlingual speech corpus is proposed. This framework is capable of searching spoken as well as text queries. The capability of spoken search enables it to search out-of-vocabulary (OOV) words. The capability of searching text queries enables it to perform semantic search. An advanced application of searching keyword translations in mixlingual speech corpus is also possible within posteriorgram framework with this system. It is shown that the performance of text queries is comparable or better than the performance of spoken queries if the language of the keyword is included in the training languages. Also, a technique for combining information from text and spoken queries is proposed which further enhances the search performance. This system is based on multiple posteriorgrams based on articulatory classes trained with multiple languages.

Keywords: Keyword search · Spoken term detection · Multilingual posteriorgrams · Mixlingual search

1 Introduction

Two types of frameworks have dominated the research area of keyword search in speech corpus.

Posteriorgram based algorithms aim at aligning posteriorgrams of spoken queries to the posteriorgrams of speech corpus by Dynamic Time Warping (DTW). Gaussian posteriorgrams [7,14] and phonemic posteriorgrams [5,6] are widely used for representing spoken queries and evaluation speech. This framework is useful for developing Query-by-Example Spoken Term Detection (QbE-STD) for languages which have less resources. It also enables a language independent audio search. However, it has some major limitations. Only spoken queries can be searched with this algorithm. The user would like to detect similar meaning words of the query for most of the applications. Moreover, the performance of query search in case of posteriorgram based methods is dependent on detecting proper boundaries of the spoken query. The performance of the search also

© Springer International Publishing AG 2017
A. Karpov et al. (Eds.): SPECOM 2017, LNAI 10458, pp. 535–545, 2017.
DOI: 10.1007/978-3-319-66429-3_53

depends on the quality of the spoken query [13]. It has been shown that multiple instances of independent pronunciations can enhance performance but it might be inconvenient for the user to speak the same query multiple times. Speaking the queries in noisy background may affect the performance of the spoken query search. One limitation of phonemic posteriorgrams is that their performance is language dependent.

The second class of algorithms is based on acoustic keyword search and lattice search based methods [8,11]. A large volume of transcribed speech data is required to train HMMs in an LVCSR (Large Vocabulary Continuous Speech Recognition System). Lattices of speech can be generated by HMMs. Lattices can be used for searching sub-word sequences but sub-word units like phonemes and syllables are language dependent. Therefore, the use of this system is limited to a single language (training language) only. However, the speech corpus which is to be searched may contain multiple languages. For example, the news corpus in linguistically diverse regions like Indian subcontinent consists of multiple languages. The proper nouns (names of local places and people) are pronounced with phonemes of the regional language while the news may be in English or vice versa. Therefore any useful keyword spotting system should represent a larger set of phonemes.

The limitations mentioned above can be addressed by posteriorgrams based on articulatory features. The posteriorgrams used in this work are similar to low dimensional articulatory motivated (LDAM) posteriorgrams [9]. Some alterations were made in the LDAM mapping given in [9] so that joint training with data from multiple languages can be done [10]. A detailed study was carried out to show that the posteriorgrams generated from the jointly trained MLPs can represent multilingual phonemes uniquely [10]. The LDAM posteriorgrams were applied to spoken query based system only.

One of the key contributions to the present work is a text query search algorithm based on articulatory classes (LDAM framework). Some of the issues associated with spoken queries mentioned above e.g. improper boundaries, noisy environment and pronunciation variations are not relevant in a text query search. The novelty of the present approach is that text queries of multiple languages can be searched in a mix-lingual speech corpus which is not possible in lattice based approaches. Text query based search is integrated into posteriorgram based spoken query search without affecting its performance. A combined query mode (combination of text and spoken queries) is also presented in this work. This multimodal framework (consisting of spoken, text and combined query modes) will have far reaching implications discussed in the later part of this work.

Results are reported for 4 Indian languages in this work. Only two of them are used for training. English and Bangla data is used for joint training of Multi Layer Perceptrons (MLPs). The details of training are given in Sects. 2 and 3. English belongs to Indo-European group of languages. The languages Hindi and Bangla belong to Indo-Aryan group which is a branch of the Indo-European languages. Telugu belongs to the Dravidian group. Indian languages are chosen for this work but this work may be applicable to many languages across the world.

Rest of the paper is organized as follows: A brief review of LDAM mapping is given in Sect. 2. The data and its usage is described in Sect. 3. Three modes of query generation are explained in Sect. 4. The experiments are described along with the results in the same section. Conclusions are presented in Sect. 5. Implications of this work are listed in Sect. 6.

2   LDAM Posteriorgrams and DTW Framework

Phonemes are mapped to LDAM classes as shown in Table 1. The procedure of arriving at this mapping is described in [9,10]. The key design principle behind this arrangement is that large number of multilingual phonemes should have a unique representation with this mapping. The class name *vow* refers to vowel-like phonemes, while *cpos* and *cman* refer to the position of articulation and manner of articulation of consonants. These three classes correspond to the three MLPs which are trained independently. These MLPs are used to generate three posteriorgrams from acoustic feature vectors (MFCC, delta and delta-delta coefficients of total dimension 39). The elements of the *vow*, *cpos* and *cman* posteriorgrams correspond to the probabilities of subclasses listed in Table 1. The vowels which differ only in duration e.g. /ih/ and /iy/ are clubbed in the same subclass. Other vowels are assigned one subclass each.

Table 1. LDAM classes, subclasses and dimensions of the LDAM posteriorgrams

MLP/ Class	Constituent subclasses (label)	Dimension
vow	front upper (fup), front bottom (fbo), back bottom (bbo), back middle (bmi), back upper (bup), phoneme /ey/ (fey), phoneme /eh/ (feh), schwa vowel (cen), phoneme /w/ (www) , phoneme /v/ (vvv), lateral (lll), rhotics (rrr), aspiration (asp), approximant (apx), diphthong /ay/ (day), diphthong /aw/ (daw), diphthong (doy), not-a-vowel (nvo), silence (sil)	19
cpos	velar stops (vel), retroflex stops (ret), palatal stops (pal), palatal fricatives (pfr), dental stops (den), dental fricatives (dfr), labial stops (lab), labiodental fricatives (ldn), glottal (glo), silence (sil), rej (reject all vowels)	10
cman	vowel-like (vol), voiced stops (vos), unvoiced stops (unv), voiced fricatives (vof), unvoiced fricatives (unf) ,nasals (nas), silence(sil)	7

The version of DTW used in this work is similar to the one in [5]. Several measures can be used to compute the cost of traversing a point in the DTW matrix. The symmetric KL distance between two posterior vectors $\mathbf{x}$ and $\mathbf{y}$ is defined in eqn. 1. The Symmetric KL distance will be referred to as KL distance in this work.

$$kl_{sym}(\mathbf{x}||\mathbf{y}) = \sum_i \left[x^i log\left(\frac{x^i}{y^i}\right) + y^i log\left(\frac{y^i}{x^i}\right) \right] \tag{1}$$

The Dot product measure between two posteriorgrams $\mathbf{x}$ and $\mathbf{y}$ is defined as:

$$dot(\mathbf{x}||\mathbf{y}) = - \log(\mathbf{x} \cdot \mathbf{y}) \tag{2}$$

KL distance is known to be useful in speech processing applications for determining distance between two distributions [1]. Spoken query search involves computation of distance between two posterior vectors (belonging to evaluation speech and keyword speech) which represent two distributions. KL distance seems appropriate for this task. The relevance of Dot product measure is explained in Sect. 5 with the help of results.

3   MLP Training and Data Used in This Work

5,000 time aligned sentences of WSJ0 [3] corpus (English Data) and 7,000 time aligned sentences from Shruti corpus [2] (Bangla data) are used to train pre-initialized *vow*, *cpos* and *cman* MLPs. The MLPs used for initialization are trained with 30,000 sentences of WSJ0 corpus (English data). The English and Bangla phonemic MLPs used in this work (Sect. 4.1) are trained with 30000 English and 7000 Bangla sentences respectively.

The queries and test utterances for English and Bangla are taken from WSJ1 [4] and Shruti corpus [2] respectively. It is ensured that the training data, the test utterances and the queries are taken from disjoint portions of the corpus. The queries and test utterances for Telugu and Hindi are also picked from disjoint portions of databases of these languages. The number of queries and test utterances used in these languages are given in Table 2. It may be noted that trainable speech corpus of all these languages is not available in public domain.

Table 2. Data used for Spoken Term Detection

Hindi	Bangla	Telugu	English
15 queries	29 queries	25 queries	36 queries
789 utterances	2000 utterances	2400 utterances	3000 utterances

4   Modes of Query Generation

The schema of multi-modal keyword search is shown in Fig. 1.

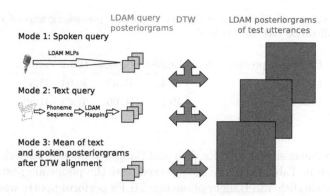

Fig. 1. Three modes of Keyword Search

Three modes of queries viz. spoken queries, text queries and combined queries are shown in Fig. 1. LDAM posteriorgrams for the three modes of queries are generated by the algorithms described in the following subsections. The LDAM posteriorgrams of test utterances are generated by LDAM MLPs for all three modes of queries. DTW is used to match LDAM posteriorgrams of queries and test utterances in all the cases as shown in Fig. 1.

The results of keyword search are presented in average P@N (percentage) for all the languages. Other evaluation measures like ATWV are not used since development data is not available in these languages. P@N is the proportion of hits in the top N utterances returned by the system.

4.1 Spoken Queries

In this mode, posteriorgrams of spoken queries are generated by LDAM MLPs (like posteriorgrams of test utterances). The boundaries of spoken queries are chosen manually by analysing the phonemic transcription generated by posteriorgrams of the sentences containing queries. Dynamic Time Warping (DTW) is used to rank the test utterances. The result of spoken query search is shown in Table 3. It may be noted that KL distance scores are better than Dot product measure scores for spoken queries.

Table 3. Spoken query search results for different languages in LDAM framework

Languages	English	Bangla	Hindi	Telugu
Dot product measure	61.35	42.11	49.06	33.98
KL distance	71.97	51.89	64.36	42.19

Table 4. Results with the state-of-the-art phonemic posteriorgrams of English and Bangla (KL distance used for DTW)

Phonemic posteriorgram	English	Bangla	Hindi	Telugu
English	78.46	45.33	48.04	35.33
Bangla	40.18	56.06	57.62	31.89

Results are also shown with English and Bangla phonemic posteriorgrams for each language in Table 4. It may be observed that the phonemic posteriorgrams generated by English and Bangla phonemic MLPs perform poorly when used for other languages. Jointly trained LDAM posteriorgrams are better if the language of test utterances is not known priori.

4.2   Text Queries

The following steps are implemented for converting text queries to LDAM posteriorgrams:

1. Text queries are first mapped to phoneme sequences. This mapping is done as per the dictionary used in corresponding language datasets in case of English and Bangla. In case of Hindi and Telugu, words are already represented in terms of phonemes in the datasets. In case of Hindi, *schwa deletion rule* was applied while converting text queries into phonemic sequences. This rule says that a schwa vowel is deleted in the pronunciation of words if it is preceded by a consonant and it is succeeded by a consonant that is further followed by a vowel [12]. It is noted that this rule significantly improves the performance of query search.
2. The phonemes are mapped to three LDAM subclasses initially as shown for the word 'business' in Fig. 2. The abbreviations of the subclasses are given in Table 1. For English and Bangla, the phoneme to LDAM mapping is kept exactly same as the phoneme to LDAM mapping used in training of LDAM MLPs. As mentioned earlier all Hindi and Telugu phonemes can also be uniquely represented by this mapping.
3. The three LDAM subclasses for each phoneme are then expanded into 36 dimensional posteriorgrams (Fig. 2) in the following manner. Three matrices consisting of zeros corresponding to LDAM posteriorgrams are generated. The zeros are replaced with ones in the indices of the present subclasses in the LDAM posteriorgrams. Instead of zeros, small positive random numbers are found useful for representing probabilities of the absent subclasses. This is because metrics like symmetric KL distance involve log function. The probabilities of all subclasses are smoothed by mean filters of length l_{filt} along time frames of all subclasses of the posteriorgram. It is ensured that the three LDAM posteriorgrams sum up to 1 by normalization.

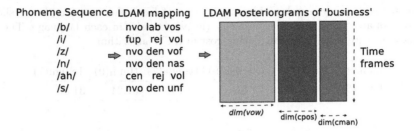

Fig. 2. Posteriorgram generation for the text keyword 'business'

The length of each phoneme (in terms of the number of frames) in the posteriorgrams can be either fixed for all phonemes or it can be phoneme-specific. We have experimented with both these configurations as explained below. Let the number of phonemes in the text queries be denoted by n.

Fixed Phoneme Length. In this case the phoneme length is fixed. Let us denote it as l_{fix}. Therefore, dimensions of query posteriorgrams are $(n \times l_{fix}) \times (dim(vow) + dim(cpos) + dim(cman))$. The fixed phoneme length l_{fix} is varied from 5 to 11 in case of English to determine the optimum fixed length query. The queries thus generated are used for Spoken Term Detection. The results are shown in Table 5 for both the KL distance and the Dot product measure.

Table 5. Text query search results for English. Each phoneme has a fixed frame length l_{fix}

l_{filt}	KL distance				Dot product measure			
	l_{fix}				l_{fix}			
	5	7	9	11	5	7	9	11
3	54.18	67.55	62.74	56.26	57.82	71.42	71.73	68.20
5	54.29	67.87	62.76	56.26	58.47	70.95	71.61	68.69
7	54.51	67.71	62.91	56.08	58.54	71.34	71.53	68.19

The observations are:

(a) The values 7 and 9 for l_{fix} yield best results.
(b) The Dot product measure performs much better than KL distance.
(c) The mean filter length l_{filt} does not have any impact on the performance of query search.

It was observed that the best l_{fix} in case of different languages are different. This observation may be explained by the hypothesis that phoneme durations are language-dependent. We assume that the language of the queries is known

Table 6. Text query search results in the case of fixed phoneme length are shown. The results are shown with the best l_{fix} (in parenthesis) in each language. The Dot product measure is used for calculating cost in DTW algorithm

Language (best l_{fix})	English(9)	Bangla(7)	Hindi(9)	Telugu(7)
P@N(%)	71.61	62.10	61.24	31.36

priori. Therefore, P@N scores in case of fixed phoneme length are presented with optimum l_{fix} values for all the languages in Table 6. Since l_{filt} does not affect the performance of text query search, it is randomly set to 5 for all experiments involving text queries.

Variable Phoneme Length. In this case, the phoneme specific length l_{ph} of each phoneme is determined from the training databases of English and Bangla. The most commonly occurring phoneme length is extracted for each phoneme by computing histogram of lengths of that phoneme. The minimum of the phoneme lengths is used if the phoneme is common in the two languages. The phoneme lengths from two languages are mostly similar with some exceptions. In case the duration of the common phonemes is more than 3 frames, different phoneme lengths are used for Bangla and English queries. In the case of variable phoneme length, dimensions of posteriorgram are $(\sum_{i=1}^{n} l_{ph}(i)) \times (dim(vow) + dim(cpos) + dim(cman))$, where $l_{ph}(i)$ is the length of the ith phoneme in a query of n phonemes.

Table 7. Text query search results in the case of phoneme specific length. Dot product measure is used for calculating cost in DTW algorithm

Language	English	Bangla	Hindi	Telugu
P@N	73.07	61.17	53.24	31.32

Although the scores obtained by this method (Table 7) are close to the scores in the best score performances in fixed phoneme length method, there are some shortcomings of this method. First, the phonemes may have different lengths in different queries due to co-articulation. Second, the lengths of common phonemes may be different in different languages. These issues are addressed in the next mode of query generation.

4.3   Combination of the Text Queries and the Spoken Queries

The technique presented here does not require the user to utter a query for improving performance. The user may first use a text query to search the speech corpus. Any spoken version of the query may be chosen by the user from the results returned from the system. To simulate experiments with this method, we have utilized the spoken queries from Sect. 4.1. The text queries corresponding to the best fixed length l_{fix} are chosen for all the languages for the experiment reported here. Posteriorgrams generated by text queries are aligned with the posteriorgrams of sentences containing spoken queries. The aligned frames of posteriorgrams of spoken and text queries are averaged to get new queries referred to as combined queries in this work. The P@N scores of combined queries are presented in Table 8. It may be noted that KL distance scores are better than Dot product measure scores.

Table 8. Combined query search results for Indian languages in LDAM framework

Languages	English	Bangla	Hindi	Telugu
Dot product measure	66.73	53.67	57.62	37.41
KL distance	80.78	56.48	65.55	46.34

5 Discussion and Conclusion

The P@N scores of the spoken queries, the text queries and the combined queries are presented in Table 9. The results are shown for the better measure (among Dot product measure and KL distance) for computing DTW cost for each mode.

Table 9. Comparison of different modes of query generation for Indian languages in LDAM framework

Query mode	DTW cost measure	English	Bangla	Hindi	Telugu
Spoken	KL distance	71.97	51.89	64.36	42.19
Text	Dot product measure	71.61	62.10	61.24	31.32
Combined	KL distance	80.78	56.48	65.55	46.34

Following conclusions can be drawn from the results:

1. The Dot product measure is better than the KL distance for text queries. The KL distance works better for spoken queries and combined queries. This is expected since probabilities in text queries are *impulsive* whereas the probabilities in spoken queries are more distributed. The problem of text query search boils down to sampling the probabilities of ideal subclasses in the evaluation speech. The ideal subclasses for a keyword are known a priori from text query posteriorgram. The results indicate that Dot product measure is better suited for sampling the probabilities of ideal subclasses.

2. The LDAM posteriorgrams perform better than the phonemic posteriorgrams (considered to be the state-of-the-art) for spoken query search if the language of evaluation speech is different than training speech (Sect. 4.1).
3. Since we are not aware of any state-of-the-art text query search system in multilingual posteriorgrams, the results of text queries are compared with spoken queries in the LDAM system in Table 9. Surprisingly, text queries perform much better than spoken queries in case of Bangla. In English the scores are similar. Text queries perform slightly worse than spoken queries in case of Hindi. The system is not trained with Hindi but it is trained with Bangla which belongs to the same language family. Text queries perform worse than spoken queries in Telugu probably because the LDAM posteriorgrams are not trained with any Dravidian language.
4. Combined queries perform better than spoken queries for all the languages. They are also better than text queries except Bangla language. Text posteriorgrams represent ideal phoneme sequence of a text query. The results imply that increasing the probability of the ideal articulatory subclasses in spoken query posteriorgrams increases the performance of query search.

6   Implications

There are several implications of this work in multilingual scenario:

1. To the best of our knowledge, this is the first study on searching text queries in the posteriorgrams of multilingual speech. This will enable a search of translations of the text queries in a mixlingual speech corpus. For example, if a user wants to search 'tree', the text 'tree' can be mapped to the text query 'पेड़' by an English to Hindi dictionary. Phoneme sequence of 'tree' as well as its translation 'पेड़' (phoneme sequence : /p/ /ey/ /dxz/) can be searched. This is possible because LDAM posteriorgrams uniquely represent phonemes of English as well as Hindi phonemes like /dxz/ (rhotic version of /d/).
2. Out-of-vocabulary words can either be searched by spoken or by text queries. Here it is worthwhile to mention that there is a one-to-one grapheme to phoneme mapping in most of the Indian languages. Therefore, text queries can be directly converted from text written in regional scripts to phoneme sequences without using any word to phoneme dictionary.
3. Mispronunciations can often be modelled by rules in case of non-native speakers, e.g., /sh/ is often pronounced as /s/ by Indian speakers. These mispronunciations can be accommodated by generating different text queries for different pronunciations. This provision is not possible with systems taking only spoken queries.
4. The present framework also enables fusion of text and spoken queries which leads to better results in majority of the languages.

Acknowledgment. The authors would like to thank Dr. K. Samudravijaya (TIFR) and Dr. S. Lata (MEITY) for providing Hindi data and Dr. Suryakanth V. Gangashetty (IIIT, Hyderabad) for providing Telugu data. The first author would like to thank his managers Mr. Shiv Narayan, Mr. Biren Karmakar and Mr. Vipin Tyagi, Executive Director, CDOT, New Delhi for their permission to carry out this research.

References

1. Aradilla, G., Bourlard, H., Magimai.-Doss, M.: Using KL-based acoustic models in a large vocabulary recognition task. Idiap-RR Idiap-RR-14-2008. IDIAP (2008)
2. Das, B., Mandal, S., Mitra, P.: Bengali speech corpus for continuous automatic speech recognition system. In: 2011 International Conference on Speech Database and Assessments (Oriental COCOSDA), pp. 51–55 (2011)
3. Garofolo, J.: Csr-i (wsj0) complete ldc93s6a (1993)
4. Garofolo, J.: Csr-ii (wsj1) complete ldc94s13a (1994)
5. Gupta, V., Ajmera, J., Kumar, A., Verma, A.: A language independent approach to audio search. In: Proceedings of INTERSPEECH, pp. 1125–1128. ISCA (2011)
6. Hazen, T., Shen, W., White, C.: Query-by-example spoken term detection using phonetic posteriorgram templates. In: Proceedings of ASRU, pp. 421–426 (2009)
7. Mantena, G., Prahallad, K.: Use of articulatory bottle-neck features for query-by-example spoken term detection in low resource scenarios. In: Proceedings of ICASSP, pp. 7128–7132 (2014)
8. Motlicek, P., Valente, F., Szoke, I.: Improving acoustic based keyword spotting using lvcsr lattices. In: 2012 IEEE International Conference on Acoustics, Speech and Signal Processing (ICASSP), pp. 4413–4416 (2012)
9. Popli, A., Kumar, A.: Query-by-example spoken term detection using low dimensional posteriorgrams motivated by articulatory classes. In: 2015 IEEE 17th International Workshop on Multimedia Signal Processing (MMSP), pp. 1–6 (2015)
10. Popli, A., Kumar, A.: Multilingual query-by-example spoken term detection in indian languages. Submitted to a Journal (2017)
11. Thambiratnam, K., Sridharan, S.: Dynamic match phone-lattice searches for very fast and accurate unrestricted vocabulary keyword spotting. In: Proceedings of ICASSP, vol. 1, pp. 465–468 (2005)
12. Wikipedia: Schwa deletion in indo-aryan languages - wikipedia, the free encyclopedia (2017)
13. Xu, J., Zhang, G., Yan, Y.: Effective utilization of multiple examples in query-by-example spoken term detection. In: 2016 IEEE International Conference on Acoustics, Speech and Signal Processing (ICASSP), pp. 5440–5444 (2016)
14. Zhang, Y., Glass, J.: Unsupervised spoken keyword spotting via segmental DTW on gaussian posteriorgrams. In: Proceedings of ASRU, pp. 398–403 (2009)

Neural Network Doc2vec in Automated Sentiment Analysis for Short Informal Texts

Natalia Maslova[1(✉)] and Vsevolod Potapov[2]

[1] Institute of Applied and Mathematical Linguistics,
Moscow State Linguistic University, Ostozhenka 38, Moscow 119034, Russia
natalia.maslova277@gmail.com
[2] Faculty of Philology, Lomonosov Moscow State University,
GSP-1, Leninskie Gori, Moscow 119991, Russia
volikpotapov@gmail.com

Abstract. The article covers approaches to automated sentiment analysis task. Under the supervised learning method a new program was created with the help of Doc2vec – a module of Gensim that is one of Python's libraries. The program specialization is short informal texts of ecology domain which are parts of macropolylogues in social network discourse.

Keywords: Automated sentiment analysis · Social network discourse · Deprivation · Supervised learning · Word embeddings · Russian

1 Introduction

The automated sentiment classification task is very relevant for opinion mining. Sentiment analysis is rapidly developing nowadays. Researchers need new instruments to put automated text processing on a large scale. There are such methods developed by now as: (a) rules- and lexicon-based analysis, (b) supervised learning, (c) unsupervised learning.

Lexicon-based sentiment classification is very popular at present. It forms the basis of many massmedia monitoring systems which work upon positive and negative lists of words – tonality dictionaries. The machine calculates representatives of which group prevail. Lexicon-based analysis is usually rules-based: n-grams are processed in a different way, syntagmatic boundaries marked with punctuation characters are taken into account as well as diminutives, augmentatives and negation. Beyond that a variation of this method was developed according to which words play different role in text sentiment formation (graph-theoretical models for Norwegian [2], for Russian [19]). Such algorithms construct text graphs, rank nodes and compute word weights based on the sentiment dictionary and the word rank. The mentioned method found its practical application in online Russian media monitoring systems such as Integrum[1], Mediaology[2], IQBuzz[3], SemanticForce[4], PalitrumLab[5] (for a review of the latter system see [12]).

---

[1] www.integrum.ru/.
[2] www.mlg.ru/.
[3] www.iqbuzz.pro/.
[4] www.semanticforce.net/.
[5] www.palitrumlab.ru/.

© Springer International Publishing AG 2017
A. Karpov et al. (Eds.): SPECOM 2017, LNAI 10458, pp. 546–554, 2017.
DOI: 10.1007/978-3-319-66429-3_54

Nevertheless, lexicon-based sentiment analysis has its own weaknesses. First, a word gets its expressive meaning only when it becomes a part of an utterance [1, 20]. Before this moment, while the word is only a part of the language system it cannot have an expressive meaning even if it belongs to the emotive lexicon. Second, this method gets stuck with polysemy, homonymy and idioms. Third, it ignores nonce words which occur quite often in unofficial texts. Then, such systems are very vulnerable to errors and misprints (though Thelwall et co. [18] made a smart effort to work it around). Last, sentiment dictionary creation involves a lot of human resources, deep linguistic work. That is why other algorithms of media monitoring should be developed.

POS-labelling and word recognition were confronted with a lot of pitfalls such as polysemy, homonymy, idioms and their modifications, word coinage. A new step was made in big text data processing with the creation of neural network modules (also known as word embeddings or neural language models) Word2vec and Doc2vec by T. Mikolov [9]. These modules were developed on the basis of R. Rehurek's library Gensim [15]. No labels, minimum preprocessing, a big scale of analyzed data – these are the advantages of neural networks. Word2vec models work fine on micro-texts such as posts on Tweeter [10, 17]. However, the results are not so encouraging on longer texts due to the word order ignorance. Word2vec is an example of a popular bag-of-words method [16].

Baroni et al. compare the new method with the classic distribution semantic models, or context-predicting with context-counting models, and gets empirical demonstration of the former's excellence [3]. Levy and Goldberg used dependency-based contexts "as an alternative to the linear bag-of-words approach". With the help of parsing technologies they derived contexts based on the syntactic relations the word participates in [8]. Because of the sentiment analysis popularity a lot of forums are created to discuss this problem, for example [5, 21]. The program code described there got development in our software solution.

Social network discourse (SND) has been under the spotlight of internet linguistics since the end of the XX-th century [4]. For example, [7] suggested the term "massive polylogue" under which "a multilingual and global comment thread following some video" was meant. We make use of Potapova's SND definition: "It is a special electronic macropolylogue, considering the relevant categories of its form, content and functional weight" [12]. The mentioned categories include the following:

(1) The passport of the utterance (URL, data and time, the trigger article and its data, the author of the utterance);
(2) The form type of SND ("distant, indirect, real-time (on-line) and put off-time (off-line), single-vector – polyvector, monochronic – polychronic");
(3) The function type of SND ("monothematic – polythematic, high contextual – low contextual, action- or polemic-provoking – not action- or polemic-provoking");
(4) The content type of SND ("informative with the sender's point of view, influencing, containing certain verbal means which can produce influence on recipient of the message, provoking with a certain aim to commit specific actions (particularly destructive, realized according to the "stimulus → pragmatic reaction in a form of specific destructive action" scheme), recipient's consciousness manipulation, aimed at a limited target group of users – aimed at an infinite number of users");

The SND parameter system has been applied to the written as well as spoken Russian language [13].

It is the linguistic manifestation of human deprivation that stands in the current research's spotlight. The problem of deprivation study is broader than aggression analysis as aggression is an instance (though a frequent one) of deprivation manifestation. The notion was introduced into the sociology by T. R. Gurr [6]: it "is the discrepancy between what people think they deserve, and what they actually think they can get". Meanwhile R. K. Potapova [12] was first to pronounce its influence on "speech production and speech perception of written and spoken language". Its role in speech behavior lays in the following. The subsystems of human beings (such as biological, physiological, sociopsychological, biomechanical, anthropophonical, cognitological and cogitological subsystems) get into deprivated condition under internal and external factors. They react to external stimuli and these reactions serve as stimuli for the system of verbal, extraverbal and paraverbal behavior. That is, they influence "speech production and speech perception of written and spoken language" [12].

2   Methods

Under our scrutiny was Russian ecology-focused social network discourse. Its main feature is informality which leads to high level of word coinage and colloquial grammar. This makes lexicon- and rules-based method of sentiment classification ineffective. Besides, the macropolylogue (Potapova's term, [11]) discourse structure makes users to write short utterances as if creating a big shared text. Due to this fact unsupervised learning cannot work either. Thus, the empiric material characteristics dictate conditions on our research instrument.

The empiric material was online discussions of Russian ecologic problems. Being a preliminary project, the sample is rather small (about 1,5 thousand utterances, each containing 1-5 sentences). Our goal is to test the innovative classification algorithm while the sample enlargement is the task of future research. Each utterance was described according to Potapova's SND parameters system [11]. Thus was formed the annotated database. The Doc2vec model constructs word- and utterance-vectors which are put into a SGD-classifier. Each word has the same word-vector in different texts of the database while the utterance-vectors are unique. The annotated database is divided into the training and testing subsets at the ratio 4:1. The model builds word-vectors for the training subset and then tries them on the testing subset. In such manner supervised learning is implemented. As one can see, neural networks are not attached to words' dictionary definitions that is why neither homonymy nor polysemy problems arise.

The main difference of the developed product is the ability to maintain not only binary classification (positive – negative) but also several levels of classification. This allows to investigate the influence of Potapova's SND parameters system [11] on the classification accuracy. For example, the deprivation type role is under examination (see further for the term elaboration). On the training stage each utterance gets a label of either positive or negative tonality according to the annotated database. Then the same utterance gets another label of either private or stratified deprivation type. The vectors are built and applied to the testing subset. After that the classification accuracy is counted and the results are visualized with the help of a confusion matrix. The classification was run this way with every SND system parameter on the same empiric material and the resulting accuracies were compared.

In this research Potapova's SND parameter system is amplified with another content type of SND, namely, deprivation type. We declare that there are two types of deprivation: private and stratifying. **Private deprivation** arises when a person sees the cause of their problem in their own abilities/disabilities, action/inaction etc. **Stratifying deprivation** exists if a person believes that the cause of their problem lies in the society structure or some social circumstances – in other words, because of the place that person has in the society. An example of private deprivation happens when someone can be dissatisfied with their salary because their neighbor has a similar job and earns more. If a person is dissatisfied with their salary because (to the best of their knowledge) everyone of this profession has inadequate salary in this region – then we meet a case of stratifying deprivation. This SND parameter is significant for sentiment classification task because it has a pronounced impact on human verbal behavior. A person suffering stratifying deprivation is very likely not only to share their feelings with others but also to try to organize (or participate in) collective actions aimed at the settlement of the problem. This implies a distinguishing type of discourse with certain vocabulary and syntactic structures.

3 Experiments

As was written above, neural networks can process colossal amounts of texts without misprints and error corrections usual for lexicon- and rules-based methods. No doubt, one need an annotated database to run supervised learning first. But as far as the word vectors are built unannotated data can be processed in disregard for size. The text volume growth stimulates classification accuracy though the dependency is not linear what is demonstrated on Fig. 1.

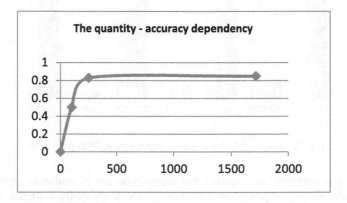

Fig. 1. The influence of utterances number upon classification quality

Two different classifiers were compared: logistic regression and k mean. The best result (98%) was achieved with logistic regression. On the other hand, k mean neighbors could not surpass 70%. Furthermore, the first classifier works better for negative utterances of stratifying deprivation (SD) while the other one – for utterances of private deprivation (PD). As we are more interested in stratifying deprivation the logistic regression classifier was chosen for this research. The confusion matrix was applied for visualization of classifiers efficiency (for illustration see Table 1) because its representation of rightly and wrongly classified cases is the most clear.

Table 1. The comparison of two classifiers

Logistic regression, %				k mean, %		
	Class 1	Class 2	Class 3	Class 1	Class 2	Class 3
Pos.	**25**	75	0	**25**	75	0
Neg. PD	0	**0**	100	43	**43**	14
SD	2	1	**98**	16	14	**70**

In the manner described in the previous section the classification was run with every SND system parameter on the same empiric material and the resulting accuracies were compared. As the parameters are grouped in a binary opposition, one half of them is called active parameters while the other – inactive. The analysis shows that the parameters have different influence on sentiment classification accuracy. Figure 2 shows cases of classification which were successful under active parameters. Correspondingly, Fig. 3 shows cases of classification which were effective under inactive parameters. There are two of them with most promising results: monochronic/ polychronic (91%), private/stratifying deprivation (92%).

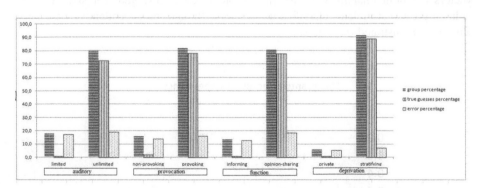

Fig. 2. Successful classification under active SND parameters

The best parameters for negative test recognition are monothematic/polythematic and private/stratifying deprivation. This fact serves as a validity evidence of deprivation type emphasizing. The confusion matrix for the deprivation type classification is shown below (Fig. 4). Table 2 gives precision, recall and F-measure for the best parameters (not the classifier in whole).

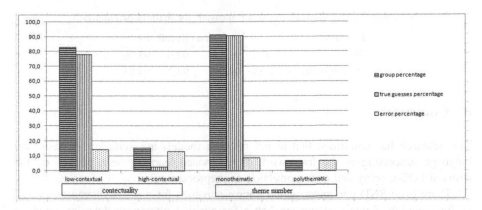

Fig. 3. Successful classification under inactive SND parameters

These results can be compared to the F-measure for negative sentences achieved by Thelwall [18] – 72,8%, in [10] 88,93, in [17] – 86,58. On the other hand, it should be admitted that there are groups that are poorly recognized by our classifier. This makes the classifier whole accuracy not so satisfying (54%).

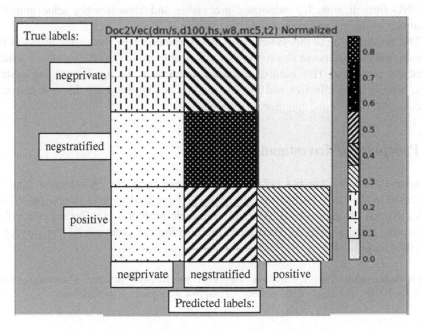

Fig. 4. Confusion matrix for deprivation type classification

Table 2. Precision, Recall and F-measure for optimal parameters

Parameter	Precision	Recall	F1
Stratified deprivation	96,85	92,67	95,96
Monothematic discourse	99,09	91,29	94,83

4 Conclusion

This research has confirmed that neural network models are quite advantageous for language processing in the framework of supervised learning because they do not demand POS-tagging and error correction as preprocessing.

There is no SND parameter which improves results for positive utterances as well as for negative. Some of them are better for positive utterances detection (such as auditory and provocative) and the others – for negative (contextuality, functions, monothematic, deprivation type). However, this experiment showed that word embeddings are suitable for sentiment classification of flexional languages, for example, Russian.

The SND parameter system elaborated by Potapova [11–14] makes a profound step in the social network discourse study. It reflects such key characteristics of SND as the contents (*what* is said), form (*how* it is said) and function (*why* it is said). This enables the SND formalization for automated processing and harnesses the achievements of semantics, stylistics and pragmatics.

The amplification of this system with the deprivation type parameter allows to filter a certain kind of discourse due to the fact that people try to find the collective solution to society problems. This kind of discourse is relevant for opinion mining systems. Thus, a new, more effective and flexible method is suggested for this task instead of lexicon- and rules-based monitoring systems.

5 Prospects of Investigation

As neural networks are not bound to dictionaries they are crossdomain (that was confirmed in [15–21]). Further investigation can be related with various domains, such as discussions of confessional, political, economic problems etc. Besides, the volume of empiric material will be increased. Methodological concepts of the project are described in [11–14].

Acknowledgement. This research is supported by Russian Science Foundation, Project № 14-18-01059. The head of the project – Potapova Rodmonga Kondratjevna.

References

1. Bahtin, M.M.: Aesthetics of Word Creation. Iskusstvo, Moscow (1979). (in Russian)
2. Bai, A., Engelstad, P., Hammer, H., Yazidi, A.: Building sentiment Lexicons applying graph theory on information from three Norwegian thesauruses. In: Amine, A., Bellatreche, L., Elberrichi, Z., Neuhold, E., Wrembel, R. (eds.) Computer Science and Its Application: 5th IFIP TC 5 International Conference, CIIA 2015, pp. 205–216, Saida, Algeria (2015), https://folk.uio.no/paalee/publications/2014-nik.pdf
3. Baroni, M., Dinu, G., Kruszewski, G.: Don't count, predict! A Systematic Comparison of context-counting vs. context-predicting semantic vectors. In: Proceedings of the 52nd Annual Meeting of the Association for Computational Linguistics (Short Papers), pp. 238–247, Baltimore, Maryland, USA (2014)
4. Crystal, D.: Language and the Internet. University of Wales, Bangor (2004)
5. Czerny, M.: Modern methods for sentiment analysis, https://districtdatalabs.silvrback.com/modern-methods-for-sentiment-analysis#disqus_thread
6. Gurr, T.R.: Why Men Rebel. Princeton University Press, Princeton (1970)
7. Isosaevi, J., Lehti, L., Laippala, V., Luotolahti, M.: Linguistic analysis of online conflicts: a case study of flaming in the Smokahontas comment thread on YouTube (2016), http://widerscreen.fi/numerot/2016-1-2/linguistic-anaead-on-youtube/
8. Levy, O., Goldberg, Y.: Dependency-based word embeddings. In: Proceedings of th 52nd Annual Meeting of the Association for Computational Linguistics (Short Papers), pp. 302–308, Baltimore, Maryland, USA (2014)
9. Mikolov, T., Le, Q.: Distributed representations of sentences and documents. In: Proceedings of the 31st International Conference on Machine Learning, Beijing, China (2014), https://cs.stanford.edu/~quocle/paragraph_vector.pdf
10. Mohammad, S.M., Kiritchenko, S., Zhu, X.: NRC-Canada: building the state-of-the-art in sentiment analysis of tweets. In: Second Joint Conference on Lexical and Computational Semantics (*SEM), vol. 2, Seventh International Workshop on Semantic Evaluation (SemEval 2013), pp. 321–327, Atlanta, Georgia (2013)
11. Potapova, R.K.: Social-network discourse in the spotlight of cross-disciplinary studies. In: Proceedings of the 2nd International Scientific Conference Discourse as a Social-Network Activity: Priorities and Perspectives, pp. 20–32, MSLU, Moscow (2014) (in Russian)
12. Potapova, R.K.: From deprivation to aggression: verbal and non-verbal social network communication. In: 6th International Scientific Conference on Global Science and Innovation, pp. 129–137. Accent Graphics Communications Publishing Office, Chicago (2015)
13. Potapova, R., Potapov, V.: On individual polyinformativity of speech and voice regarding speakers auditive attribution (forensic phonetic aspect). In: Ronzhin, A., Potapova, R., Németh, G. (eds.) SPECOM 2016. LNCS, vol. 9811, pp. 507–514. Springer, Cham (2016). doi:10.1007/978-3-319-43958-7_61
14. Potapova, R.K.: Deprivation as the basic algorithm of verbal and paraverbal human behavior (on the material of social-network communication). In: Verbal Communication in the Infospace. Lenand, Moscow (2017) (in Russian)
15. Rehurek, R., Sojka, P.: Software framework for topic modelling with large corpora. In: Proceedings of the LREC 2010 Workshop on New Challenges for NLP Frameworks, ELRA, pp. 45–50 (2010). https://github.com/RaRe-Technologies/gensim#citing-gensim
16. Sadeghian, A., Sharafat, A.: Bag of Words Meets Bag of Popcorn (2015). https://www.kaggle.com/c/word2vec-nlp-tutorial

17. Tang, D., Wei, F., Yang, N., Zhou, M., Liu, T., Qin, B.: Learning sentiment-specific word embedding for twitter sentiment classification. In: Proceeding of the 52th Annual Meeting of the Association for Computational Linguistics, ACL, pp. 1155–1166 (2014). http://anthology.aclweb.org/P/P14/P14-1146.pdf
18. Thelwall, M., Buckley, K., Paltoglou, G., Cai, D., Kappas, A.: Sentiment strength detection in short informal text. J. Am. Soc. Inform. Sci. Technol. **61**(12), 2544–2558 (2010)
19. Ustalov, D.A.: Term extraction from Russian texts via graph models. In: Graphs Theory and Applications, pp. 62–69 (2012) (in Russian)
20. Volf, E.M.: The Functional Semantics of assessment. Editorial, Moscow (2002) (in Russian)
21. Word Embeddings for Fun and Profit: Document classification with Gensim, https://github.com/RaRe-Technologies/movie-plots-by-genre/blob/5a2d9157f9bf1bf908794051597b7851333dcfca/ipynb_with_output/Document%20classification%20with%20word%20embeddings%20tutorial%20-%20with%20output.ipynb#L1403

Neural Network Speaker Descriptor in Speaker Diarization of Telephone Speech

Zbyněk Zajíc[1]([✉]), Jan Zelinka[1,2], and Luděk Müller[1,2]

[1] Faculty of Applied Sciences, NTIS - New Technologies for the Information Society, University of West Bohemia, Univerzitní 8, 306 14 Plzeň, Czech Republic
{zzajic,muller}@ntis.zcu.cz
[2] Department of Cybernetics, Faculty of Applied Sciences, University of West Bohemia, Univerzitní 8, 306 14 Plzeň, Czech Republic
zelinka@kky.zcu.cz
http://www.zcu.cz

Abstract. In this paper, we have been investigating an approach to a speaker representation for a diarization system that clusters short telephone conversation segments (produced by the same speaker). The proposed approach applies a neural-network-based descriptor that replaces a usual i-vector descriptor in the state-of-the-art diarization systems. The comparison of these two techniques was done on the English part of the CallHome corpus. The final results indicate the superiority of the i-vector's approach although our proposed descriptor brings an additive information. Thus, the combined descriptor represents a speaker in a segment for diarization purpose with lower diarization error (almost 20% relative improvement compared with only i-vector application).

Keywords: Neural network · Speaker diarization · i-Vector

1 Introduction

For a majority of speech processing tasks is convenient to work with a signal containing only one voice. In the real world, this condition is very difficult to fulfill. So, the Speaker Diarization (SD) system is necessary to determining "Who spoke when" without any prior information about the number of speakers and their identities. The process of diarization divides an input signal and merges these segments into clusters corresponding to individual speakers [23,24]. Another approach (not used in this paper) combines the segmentation and the clustering step [6,28].

The main problem in SD is how to describe the segments of the signal for subsequent clustering. Ideally, each segment consists of only one speaker. In recent years, i-vector approach has gained popularity in the Speaker Verification (SV) task [4,8] as well as in SD [9,35].

For many years, Neural Networks (NNs) have been successfully used in the field of speech recognition generally [7], and nowadays NNs are used extensively

© Springer International Publishing AG 2017
A. Karpov et al. (Eds.): SPECOM 2017, LNAI 10458, pp. 555–563, 2017.
DOI: 10.1007/978-3-319-66429-3_55

also in SD systems: in the segmentation task [13,15] or in the clustering process [14,20]. In paper [25], NNs are adopted to replace unsupervised Universal Background Model (UBM) for an accumulation of statistics in the i-vector generation process.

In this paper, we propose the NN-based descriptor as a representation of a speaker in an acoustics data segment. Similar approaches using NN were adopted to the representation of the speaker for the SD task in [30,31], where the NN is used for replacing the Mel Frequency Cepstral Coefficients (MFCCs) features or very recently in [2], where the triplet loss paradigm was used for training the NN descriptor with extremely short speech turn. This speaker representation must be closer to the representations of the segments containing a speech of the same speaker than to the other segments. In the spontaneous conversation, the continuous speech of one speaker (one segment) could by very short, i.e. much less than ten seconds [35]. Our proposed NN-based descriptor creates his own features and accumulates the statistics from very short speech segments (appearing in the telephone speech diarization task).

2   Diarization System

Our SD system consists of four modules (see Fig. 1). These are described in detail in the following subsections.

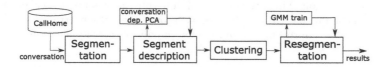

Fig. 1. The schema of the diarization system

2.1   Segmentation

The input conversation (audio signal) is divided into short segments. The duration of the segments should be long enough to represent the contained speaker and simultaneously to avoid the risk of a speaker change being present within the segment, as may happen in longer segments. Usually, the Speaker Change Detection (SCD) that allows obtaining segments with only one speaker is applied for this purpose [1,23]. However, in a spontaneous telephone conversation containing obstacles as very short speaker turns and frequent overlapping speech, diarization systems often omit the SCD process and use a simple constant length window segmentation of speech [24,26]. This two principles of segmentation (constant length window and SCD based on GLR distances or Convolutional NN) is compared in our papers [15,32]. The results of both these approaches are very similar. Thus, only the segmentation with constant window length is applied in this work.

2.2 Segment Description

After a recording is segmented, a speaker representation is computed for each segment. For this purpose, the i-vectors representation of the speaker in the acoustics data borrowed from SV is used in recent SD systems [24,35]. The i-vector representation can handle relatively short speaker utterances. For each conversation segment the supervector of statistics is accumulated [33] and subsequently, the i-vector is extracted from this supervector. For the i-vector extraction, the Factor Analysis (FA) approach [17,18] (or extended Joint Factor Analysis (JFA) [16] to handle more sessions of each speaker) is used for dimensionality reduction of the supervector of statistics. In Sect. 3 our proposed approach to segment description based on NN is described.

When segment representation computation works perfectly, a representation is closer to the segments which contain the same voice than to the segments which contain some other voice, i.e. the representation makes clusters. But the low amount of speaker's data in the segments disturbes this presumption. Because of the differences among all conversations (and the similarity inside one conversation), we also compute a conversation dependent Principal Component Analysis (PCA) transformation, which further reduces the dimensionality of the i-vector. The dimension of the PCA latent space is dependent on the parameter p, the ratio of eigenvalue mass [27].

2.3 Clustering and Resegmentation

The segments representations are clustered in order to determine which segments are produced by the same speaker. Since the homogeneity of one segment can not be ensured, it is convenient to refine the final diarization by resegmentation based on a smaller unit then segments. The system iteratively performs the resegmentation applying a Gaussian Mixture Model (GMM) representation of each cluster and redistributing of the whole conversation frame by frame according to the likelihood of the GMMs.

3 Neural Network Descriptor

In order to verificate the speaker or to resolve another similar task such as our main problem, special statistics that describe relevant speaker are computed from a recording. A recurrent NN could be employed to compute such statistics. But, because a recurrent NN training has some issues (especially it has high computation demands), a standard feed-forward NN was used. A similar system for SV task was introduced in our paper [34].

Naturally, a standard feed-forward NN gives exactly the same number of vectors as it has on its input. To compute one single vector of speaker statistics, an average of all vectors was computed. All parts of a recording are not equally relevant. In particular, parts where is no activity of speakers vocal tract are certainly not relevant at all. Furthermore, for one speaker statistics are relevant another parts than for another speaker statistics. Therefore, instead of a simple average, a weighted average where each statistic has own series of weights was computed. The weights could be computed as means of separated NNs. But in this case, some information could be surely computed redundantly. To prevent this redundancy, one single NN with two output layers was trained instead training of two separated NN.

Our speaker descriptor computes the square of the euclidian distance between two vectors of speaker statistics (i.e. results of the weighted average) and then a sigmoid function is applied. The resultant metric range is obviously in the interval between zero and one. In the training process, an inclination of the sigmoid function was fixed. Only a bias have been trained by means of backpropagation in the same way as all other parameters.

No part of the descriptor is trained separately. Naturally, targets in the training process were ones (for matching pairs of recordings) and zeros (otherwise). The used criterion was modified mean square error. The modification lies in different weights for different types of errors. The criterion ε is given by the following equation

$$\varepsilon = \sum_i w_i (y_i - t_i)^2, \tag{1}$$

where y_i denotes i-th output, t_i denotes i-th target, $w_i = 100$ when $t_i = 1$ and $y_i < 0.5$ or $t_i = 0$ and $y_i > 0.5$. Otherwise, $w_i = 1$. This approach emphasizes errors which lead to a classification error.

As we found in our preliminary experiments, using weighted average brings one serious risk. This risk is a collapse of training algorithm. In such collapse, weights choose only one or very small number of feature vectors to compute statistics. These statistics are nearly irrelevant then. To prevent the training process from these collapsing, two systems with tied parameters were trained. The first one with the plain averaging and the second with the weighted averaging. The first one has been deviating the second one from collapsing. A schema of the resultant speaker descriptor is displayed in Fig. 2.

The mentioned NN computes the speaker statistics from features vectors. The standard feature extraction methods such as Linear/Mel Frequency Cepstral Coefficients (LFCCs/MFCCs) might lose a lot of information about speaker identity. Hence, another NN-based feature extraction method was applied. An input of an NN for feature extraction is the absolute spectrum that is very close to the raw signal. The layers used in the described NN-based feature extraction method were not trained to make an LFCCs approximator, but all layers in the whole system for speaker description were randomly initialized and trained simultaneously after the initialization. For testing purposes, only one part of the trained NN was used. The output y is considered to by the vector describing the speaker used in SD system.

The delta and the delta-delta coefficient computation is likely beneficial. However, mean or even variance normalization could be inappropriate in the case of speaker verification. Thus, the original features were not replaced with a normalization but were joined together with delta and delta-delta coefficients, mean

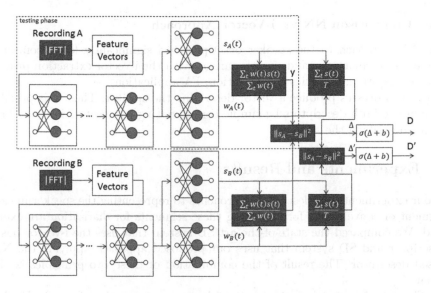

Fig. 2. The neural-network-based speaker verification system. After the feature extraction, the statistics (**y**) are accumulated and in the case of the training process two different decisions (D and D') about the similarity between recording A and B are made. For the testing purpose, only **y** is used as a speaker descriptor (speaker vector)

normalization (MN), variance normalization (VN) with new delta and delta-delta coefficients into a new larger feature vector. Moreover, splicing that makes long-temporal-feature vectors was applied. The resultant number of features is too high. Hence, the last fully connected layer was applied to reduce the feature dimension. The NN-based feature vector computation is shown in Fig. 3.

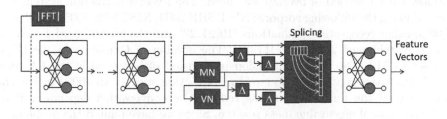

Fig. 3. The neural-network-based feature vectors extraction

The difference between our approach and the one introduced in [2,10] lies in the fact that we using these DNN features instead of precomputed MFCCs. Meanwhile in [30,31], the DNN features are used with MFCCs as a stream in an GMM/HMM diarization model.

3.1   Comparison NN vs. i-Vector Approach

The NN approach to the speaker descriptor has significantly lower computational and memory demands in comparison with the i-vector extraction process (parametrization, statistics accumulation, FA application).

Both processes produce a vector describing the speaker. Thus, it is possible to combine both descriptors by simple concatenating two vectors into one final vector describing the speaker.

4   Experiments and Results

In our experiment, two described approaches to representing the speaker in each segment of conversation for clustering these segments for diarisation are examined. We compared the state-of-the-art SD system that uses the i-vector based descriptor and SD system that uses our proposed approach applying the NN-based descriptor. The result of the combination of these two principles is also given.

The experiment was carried out on telephone conversations from the English part of CallHome corpus [3] (two channels have been mixed into one), where only two speaker conversations were selected (so the clustering can be limited to two clusters), this is 77 conversation each with about 10 min duration in a single telephone channel sampled at 8 kHz.

The SD system that is the same as in our papers [15,32] uses the feature extraction based on Linear Frequency Cepstral Coefficients (LFCCs), Hamming window of length 25 ms with 10 ms shift of the window. There are 25 triangular filter banks that are spread linearly across the frequency spectrum and 20 LFCCs were extracted. Added delta coefficients extend the feature vector to a 40-dimensional feature vector. Instead of the voice activity detector, the reference annotation about missed speech was used. For segmentation, only 2-second window with 1-second of overlap was used. The i-vector extraction system was trained using the following corpora: NIST SRE 2004, NIST SRE 2005, NIST SRE 2006 speaker recognition evaluations [19,21,22] and the Switchboard 1 Release 2 and Switchboard 2 Phase 3 [11,12]. The number of Gaussians in the UBM was set to 512. The latent dimension (dimension of i-vectors) in the FA total variability space matrix in the i-vector extraction was set to 400. Finally, the dimension of the final i-vector was reduced by conversation dependent PCA with the ratio of eigenvalue mass $p = 0.5$. Since we have limited the problem to conversations with only two speakers, we applied for segments clustering only K-means algorithm with cosine distance.

For the NN training, the NIST-04,05,06 corpora were used and all recordings were cut up to 2-seconds long pieces. All pieces with too low energy (i.e. pieces which included a significant amount of silence) were excluded from the training process. The dimension of the NN input is 128, hidden layers have 1024 neurones and the dimension of the NN output is 64. The dimension of the feature vector is 40. Training process was implemented utilizing The Theano toolbox [29] that allows complicated gradient propagations and a GPU usage with almost no effort.

For evaluation of our approach, the Diarization Error Rate (DER) was used as described by NIST in the RT evaluations [5], with 250 ms tolerance around the reference boundaries. DER combines all types of error (missed speech, mislabeled non-speech, incorrect speaker cluster). In our experiments, a correct information about the silence from the reference annotation were used and so our results represent only the error in speaker cluster. The comparison of the examined systems is shown in Table 1. The experimental results of the two approaches to the speaker description indicate that the proposed approach using the NN-based descriptor brings some new information about the speaker in the short segment in addition to the i-vector. The result of the NN-based approach do not overcome the result of the i-vector descriptor, but the combination gets significant improvement in DER.

Table 1. DER [%] for SD system with the i-vector speaker representation, the NN speaker representation and the combination of these two representations

Descriptor	DER [%]
i-vector	9.59
NN	11.20
i-vector + NN	7.72

5 Conclusions

In this work, our goal was to propose and investigate a novel technique to represent speaker information available in the short segment (of the conversation provided to the diarisation system) for further clustering. The NN were trained to gain a small vector (the essence of the speaker) from the short acoustics data presented to the net. The final vector representation must be as similar as possible to the representations of another segment containing a speech of the same speaker and most diverse to the others. This method of the speaker description was compared with the i-vector descriptor and both methods were tested in the speaker diarization system. The test results of these two approaches show that the i-vector approach leaded to a better performance, but the NN brings new useful information about the speaker that i-vector approach did not obtain. Hence, the combination of both these descriptors outperforms i-vector approach.

Acknowledgments. This research was supported by the Ministry of Culture Czech Republic, project No. DG16P02B048.

References

1. Adami, A.G., Kajarekar, S.S., Hermansky, H.: A new speaker change detection method for two-speaker segmentation. In: ICASSP, vol. 4, pp. 3908–3911 (2002)
2. Bredin, H.: TristouNet: triplet loss for speaker turn embedding. In: ICASSP, New Orleans, pp. 5430–5434 (2017)
3. Canavan, A., Graff, D., Zipperlen, G.: CALLHOME American English speech, LDC97S42. In: LDC Catalog. Linguistic Data Consortium, Philadelphia (1997)
4. Dehak, N., Kenny, P.J., Dehak, R., Dumouchel, P., Ouellet, P.: Front-end factor analysis for speaker verification. IEEE Trans. Audio Speech Lang. Process. **19**(4), 788–798 (2011)
5. Fiscus, J.G., Radde, N., Garofolo, J.S., Le, A., Ajot, J., Laprun, C.: The rich transcription 2006 spring meeting recognition evaluation. Mach. Learn. Multimodal Interact. **4299**, 309–322 (2006)
6. Fredouille, C., Bozonnet, S., Evans, N.: The LIA-EURECOM RT 2009 Speaker Diarization System. In: NIST Rich Transcription Workshop (RT09), Melbourne, USA (2009)
7. Furui, S., Itoh, D.: Neural-network-based HMM adaptation for noisy speech. In: ICASSP, Salt Lake City, pp. 365–368 (2001)
8. Garcia-Romero, D., Espy-Wilson, C.Y.: Analysis of i-Vector length normalization in speaker recognition systems. In: Interspeech, Florence, pp. 249–252 (2011)
9. Garcia-Romero, D., McCree, A., Shum, S., Brummer, N., Vaquero, C.: Unsupervised domain adaptation for i-Vector speaker recognition. In: Odyssey - Speaker and Language Recognition Workshop, Joensuu, pp. 260–264 (2014)
10. Garcia-Romero, D., Snyder, D., Sell, G., Povey, D., McCree, A.: Speaker diarization using deep neural network embedings. In: ICASSP, New Orleans, pp. 4930–4934 (2017)
11. Graff, D., Miller, D., Walker, K.: Switchboard-2 phase III audio. In: LDC Catalog. Linguistic Data Consortium, Philadelphia (1999)
12. Graff, D., Walker, K., Canavan, A.: Switchboard-2 phase II, LDC99S79. In: LDC Catalog. Linguistic Data Consortium, Philadelphia (2002)
13. Gupta, V.: Speaker change point detection using deep neural nets. In: ICASSP, Brisbane, pp. 4420–4424 (2015)
14. Hershey, J.R., Chen, Z., Roux, J.L., Watanabe, S.: Deep clustering: discriminative embeddings for segmentation and separation. In: ICASSP, Shanghai, pp. 31–35 (2016)
15. Hrúz, M., Zajíc, Z.: Convolutional neural network for speaker change detection in telephone speaker Diarization system. In: ICASSP, New Orleans, pp. 4945–4949 (2017)
16. Kenny, P.: Joint factor analysis of speaker and session variability: theory and algorithms. Technical report, Centre de Recherche Informatique de Montreal (2006)
17. Kenny, P., Dumouchel, P.: Experiments in speaker verification using factor analysis likelihood ratios. In: Odyssey - Speaker and Language Recognition Workshop, Toledo, pp. 219–226 (2004)
18. Machlica, L., Zajíc, Z.: Factor analysis and nuisance attribute projection revisited. In: Interspeech, Portland, pp. 1570–1573 (2012)
19. Martin, A., Przybocki, M.: 2004 NIST speaker recognition evaluation, LDC 2006 S44. In: LDC Catalog. Linguistic Data Consortium, Philadelphia (2011)
20. Milner, R., Hain, T.: DNN-based speaker clustering for speaker Diarisation. In: Interspeech, San Francisco, 08 September 2012, pp. 2185–2189 (2016)

21. NIST Multimodal Information Group: 2005 NIST Speaker Recognition Evaluation Training Data, LDC2011S01. In: LDC Catalog. Linguistic Data Consortium, Philadelphia (2011)
22. NIST Multimodal Information Group: 2006 NIST Speaker Recognition Evaluation Training Set, LDC2011S09. In: LDC Catalog (2011)
23. Rouvier, M., Dupuy, G., Gay, P., Khoury, E., Merlin, T., Meignier, S.: An open-source state-of-the-art toolbox for broadcast news Diarization. In: Interspeech, Lyon, p. 5 (2013)
24. Sell, G., Garcia-Romero, D.: Speaker Diarization with PLDA i-Vector scoring and unsupervised calibration. In: IEEE Spoken Language Technology Workshop, South Lake Tahoe, pp. 413–417 (2014)
25. Sell, G., Garcia-Romero, D., Mccree, A.: Speaker Diarization with i-Vectors from DNN senone posteriors. In: Interspeech, Dresden, pp. 3096–3099 (2015)
26. Senoussaoui, M., Kenny, P., Stafylakis, T., Dumouchel, P.: A study of the Cosine distance-based mean shift for telephone speech diarization. Audio, Speech Lang. Process. **22**(1), 217–227 (2014)
27. Shum, S., Dehak, N., Chuangsuwanich, E., Reynolds, D., Glass, J.: Exploiting intra-conversation variability for speaker diarization. In: Interspeech, Florence, pp. 945–948 (2011)
28. Shum, S.H., Dehak, N., Dehak, R., Glass, J.R.: Unsupervised methods for speaker diarization: an integrated and iterative approach. Audio, Speech Lang. Process. **21**(10), 2015–2028 (2013)
29. Theano Development Team: Theano: A Python Framework for Fast Computation of Mathematical Expressions. arXiv e-prints abs/1605.0 (2016)
30. Wang, R., Gu, M., Li, L., Xu, M., Zheng, T.F.: Speaker segmentation using deep speaker vectors for fast speaker change scenarios. In: ICASSP, New Orleans, pp. 5420–5424 (2017)
31. Yells, S.H., Stolcke, A., Slaney, M.: Artificial neural network features for speaker diarization. In: Proceedings of IEEE Spoken Language Technology Workshop, pp. 402–406. IEEE (2014)
32. Zajíc, Z., Kunešová, M., Radová, V.: Investigation of segmentation in i-vector based speaker diarization of telephone speech. In: Ronzhin, A., Potapova, R., Németh, G. (eds.) SPECOM 2016. LNCS, vol. 9811, pp. 411–418. Springer, Cham (2016). doi:10.1007/978-3-319-43958-7_49
33. Zajíc, Z., Machlica, L., Müller, L.: Initialization of fMLLR with sufficient statistics from similar speakers. In: Habernal, I., Matoušek, V. (eds.) TSD 2011. LNCS, vol. 6836, pp. 187–194. Springer, Heidelberg (2011). doi:10.1007/978-3-642-23538-2_24
34. Zelinka, J., Vaněk, J., Müller, L.: Neural-network-based spectrum processing for speech recognition and speaker verification. In: Statistical Language and Speech Processing, Budapest, vol. 9449, pp. 288–299 (2015)
35. Zhu, W., Pelecanos, J.: Online speaker Diarization using adapted i-Vector transforms. In: ICASSP, Shanghai, pp. 5045–5049 (2016)

Novel Linear Prediction Temporal Phase Based Features for Speaker Recognition

Ami Gandhi[1]([⊠]) and Hemant A. Patil[2]

[1] Infinium Solutionz Pvt Ltd, Ahmedabad, India
ami.gandhi@infiniumsolutionz.com
[2] Dhirubhai Ambani Institute of Information Communication and Technology,
Gandhinagar, India
hemant_patil@daiict.ac.in

Abstract. This paper proposes novel features based on linear prediction of temporal phase (LPTP) for speaker recognition task. The proposed LPTC feature vector represents Discrete Cosine Transform (DCT) (for energy compaction and decorrelation) coefficients of LP spectrum derived from temporal phase of speech signal. The results are shown on standard NIST 2002 SRE and GMM-UBM (Gaussian Mixture Modeling-Universal Background Modeling) approach. A recently proposed supervised score-level fusion method is used for combining evidences of Mel Frequency Cepstral Coefficients (MFCC) and proposed feature set. Performance of proposed feature set is compared with state-of-the-art MFCC features. It is evident from the results that proposed features gives *4%* improvement in % identification rate and *2%* decrement in % EER than that of standard MFCC alone. In addition, when the supervised score-level fusion is used, identification rate improves *8%* and EER is decreased by *2%* indicating that proposed feature captures *complimentary* information than MFCC alone.

Keywords: Linear prediction (LP) spectrum · Temporal phase · Speaker recognition · Score-level fusion

1 Introduction

Speaker recognition is a biometric system used to define a person's identity from their speech data [1]. Application of the speaker recognition system includes security and verification services, banking, forensics etc. In order to implement effective speaker recognition system, it is necessary to capture speaker-specific information from the speech signal. Various types of features are proposed to extract the information from speech signal. Features are divided mainly in four types *viz.* *(i) short-time spectral features* like MFCC (Mel Frequency Cepstral Coefficients) [2], LPCC (Linear Prediction Cepstral Coefficients) [3] and CFCC (Cochlear Filter Cepstral Coefficients) [4]. These features are easy to extract and very short amount of data is required to extract the features from it. Therefore, short-time spectral features are most commonly used in many speaker recognition systems. *(ii) voice source features* derived from Glottal Closure Instants (GCIs) or epoch locations to represents the source characteristics from

© Springer International Publishing AG 2017
A. Karpov et al. (Eds.): SPECOM 2017, LNAI 10458, pp. 564–571, 2017.
DOI: 10.1007/978-3-319-66429-3_56

speech signal. *(iii) spectro-temporal and prosodic features*, which are derived from rhythm, pitch, duration and other segmental or superasegmental-level information. These features are extracted from much longer duration segment to characterize the speaking style of speaker. *(iv) high-level features* are derived from phonetic, semantics and lexical part of speech signal. These features requires very complex front-end for computing the features from the speech signal [1].

Because of simplicity of extraction and good efficiency, short-time features are most commonly used. From short segments of speech signal, most features are extracted using magnitude spectrum of speech signal. However, phase spectrum is also having equal importance in perception of speech signal. The importance of phase in speech signal is briefly described in [5]. Several approaches are developed to extract the features through phase of speech signal. In [6], modified group delay function is calculated from speech signal for speaker recognition task. However, an assumption of minimum-phase nature of speech signal is made, which limits the results. Feature extraction from analytic phase of speech signal is reported in [7] for speaker recognition. Features from LP residual phase are combined with MFCC in [8] for improved speaker recognition system. Features from TEO phase is combined with MFCC for speaker verification task in [9].

In [10], features based on temporal phase are extracted. Temporal phase of speech signal is modeled with all pass modeling and can be used to extract feature known as All Pass Cepstral Coefficients (APCC) which are then used for speaker verification task. Epoch locations are extracted from APCC in [11], which gives an idea of ability of temporal phase for capturing source-based information. In [12], LPC of temporal phase is used for building the speaker recognition system. This paper gives further modification on the features proposed in [12].

Rest of the paper is organized as follows: Sect. 2 presents details of proposed feature extraction algorithm and effectiveness of proposed feature extraction method. Section 3 gives details about experimental setup and results. Finally, Sect. 4 concludes the paper along with future research directions.

2   Linear Prediction of Temporal Phase (LPTP) Features

Figure 1 shows the basic block diagram for proposed Linear Prediction of Temporal Phase (LPTP)-based feature extraction algorithm.

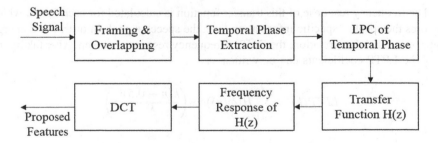

Fig. 1. Basic block diagram for extracting LPTP feature set

Feature extraction component in any speaker recognition system is the main building block. The efficiency of the entire system mostly dependent upon the effectiveness of speaker-specific feature extracted from speech signal. To extract the temporal phase from speech signal, it is necessary to know the Fourier representation of speech signal $x[n]$. In a Fourier-domain:

$$X(j\omega) = \sum_{n=-\infty}^{\infty} x[n]e^{-j\omega n}. \tag{1}$$

Magnitude and phase representation can be written from Eq. (1) as:

$$X(j\omega) = |X(j\omega)|e^{j\angle|X(j\omega)|}. \tag{2}$$

Temporal phase now can be given as magnitude suppressed phase spectrum, which can be written as:

$$y[n] = \text{IFT}\left\{\frac{X(j\omega)}{|X(j\omega)|}\right\}. \tag{3}$$

Note that, the above equation is valid only for $|X(j\omega)| \neq 0$. This temporal phase is totally different from Fourier phase and it represents the value of phase with respect to time. Temporal phase is free from phase unwrapping problem unlike Fourier phase [11]. Thus, it requires less complex computations.

To extract the LPTP features, speech signal is first divided into *25* ms duration segment with *10* ms overlap. This is because non-stationary nature of speech signals. The temporal phase of speech signal is then calculated using Eq. (3) for each segment. As represented in Fig. 1, the Linear Prediction Coefficients is extracted from each this temporal phase. In earlier research, the LPC of temporal phase is taken into account as a feature vector. Database used in this experiment contains the sampling frequency of *8000* Hz, LPC of 12-dimensions are calculated from temporal phase. These LPC coefficients can be written as $\{a_1, a_2, \ldots a_{12}\}$. from these coefficients, transfer function $H(z)$ for all-pole model can be written as:

$$H(z) = \frac{1}{1 - a_1 z^{-1} - a_2 z^{-2} - a_3 z^{-3} - \ldots a_{12} z^{-12}}. \tag{4}$$

The frequency response of this transfer function is calculated for each frame, which captures the speaker-specific information from the speech signal. In order to do energy compaction and decorrelation, the DCT of frequency response is taken. After taking the DCT the LPTP coefficients can be written as:

$$LPTP(k) = \sum_{n=1}^{N} H(\omega(n))cos\left(\frac{k(n-0.5)}{N}\pi\right). \tag{5}$$

Here, N is number of DCT coefficients and $H(\omega)$ is the frequency response of $H(z)$. From Eq. (5), *12*-D feature vectors of LPTP are calculated which then can be given as input of modeling system.

Figure 2 shows the effectiveness of proposed feature set for capturing speaker-specific information. From Fig. 2(b) and (c), it can be seen that frequency response of T-Phase LPC for two different speakers gives different characteristics (indicated by doted curves) and that is captured through proposed feature.

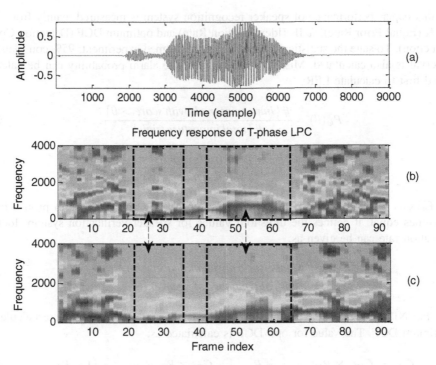

Fig. 2. (a) Original speech signal, (b) frequency response of T-Phase LPC for word "zero" of *speaker 1*, (c) frequency response of T-Phase LPC for word "zero" of *speaker 2*

3 Experimental Results

3.1 Experimental Setup

Speaker recognition system is built using NIST 2002 SRE cellular database with one speaker detection test conditions [12]. It contains *330* training speech segments, each of 2 min duration and *3564* test segments with *15* to *45* s duration. *12*-D feature vectors for each training and test segments are calculated and feature vectors of training data are given to the input of modeling algorithm. Standard adaptive Gaussian Mixture Modeling- Universal Background Modeling (GMM-UBM) is used to model each train speaker [13]. UBM is developed using feature vectors of all training data. The training mean vectors are adapted from UBM using MAP (Maximum a Priory) adaptation.

Finally, log-likelihood ratio is calculated and true and false scores are computed for each trial. Each test segment is tested against *11* different training models out of which only one model is genuine. Some cases may contain none of genuine training model. Total *39204* trials are performed, out of which *2977* are genuine and *36227* are imposter trials.

3.2   Performance Measures

In this paper, performance of speaker recognition system is measured mainly from % EER (Equal Error Rate), % IR (Identification Rate) and optimum DCF (Detection Cost Function). To state the statistical importance of performed experiment, *95%* confidence interval is also calculated. Miss probability and false alarm probability can be calculated first to calculate EER:

$$P_{fa}(\theta) = \frac{\#\{Imposture\ trials\ with\ score > \theta\}}{\#\{total\ imposture\ trials\}}, \tag{6}$$

$$P_{miss(\theta)} = \frac{\#\{genuine\ trials\ with\ scores \leq \theta\}}{\#\{total\ genuine\ trials\}}. \tag{7}$$

% EER is given from the point where miss probability and false alarm probability becomes equal. It defines the threshold values for speaker verification system. Identification rate can be given as:

$$\% \ IR = \frac{\#Number\ of\ truly\ identified\ speakers}{\#Total\ number\ of\ speakers} \times 100. \tag{8}$$

For NIST 2002 SRE, $C_{miss} = 10$, $C_{fa} = 1$ and $P_{target} = 0.01$ are taken to calculate optimum DCF. The value for opt. DCF is calculated as:

$$C_{Det} = C_{Miss} \times P_{Miss|Target} \times P_{Target} + C_{FA} \times P_{FA|NonTarget} \times (1 - P_{Target}). \tag{9}$$

95% confidence interval gives statistical significance of experimental results [15]. It defines the range where the accuracy of experiment is likely to come most probably. The smaller range of confidence interval gives more better and accurate results of identification rate. The range of interval can be given as [P + IR, P − IR], where P can be written as:

$$P = 1.96\sqrt{\frac{IR(100 - IR)}{N(Total\ Number\ of\ Trials)}}. \tag{10}$$

3.3   Results

Table 1 shows the experimental results obtained from LPTP and MFCC features. In addition, it shows result of T-phase features which are derived recently from LPC of temporal speech and reported in [12]. It can be seen from the Table 1 that % IR for LPTP is very low compared to MFCC individually, however, when proposed LPTP feature set is fused with MFCC, the identification rate increases by 4%. Furthermore, 95% confidence interval deviation is much lesser in fused feature set. Table 1 also shows the effectiveness of proposed LPTP features over T-Phase feature proposed in [12] with % IR and % EER.

Table 1. Effectiveness of LPTP features for NIST 2002 SRE database

Feature set	% IR	95% conf. interval	% EER	Opt. DCF
T-Phase [12]	56.16	(55.67–56.65)	39.74	0.1000
Proposed LPTP	58.45	(57.96–58.93)	21.93	0.0893
MFCC	72.62	(72.18–73.06)	17.77	0.0683
MFCC + T-Phase [12]	76.18	(75.76–76.60)	16.09	0.0627
MFCC + LPTP*	**76.28**	**(75.86–76.70)**	**15.89**	**0.0652**
MFCC + LPTP#	**80.82**	**(80.43–81.20)**	17.33	0.0753

* With linear opinion pool method

Here, the fusion of feature is done with generalized score-level fusion given by:

$$\lambda_{fused} = \alpha\lambda_{MFCC} + (1 - \alpha)\lambda_{LPTP}. \tag{11}$$

The value of α is taken as 0.7, which gives maximum results. Though, this gives more weights to MFCC features, proposed LPTP features also captures speaker-specific information from speech signal which MFCC cannot capture. Thus, fusion gives better result than standard MFCC alone. Result from the Table 1 shows that fusion done with supervised score-level fusion method gives 8% more identification accuracy than that of MFCC feature alone. However, it does not decrease the % EER and optimum DCF value, but significant improvement over % identification rate improves the recognition ability of speaker recognition system.

Figure 3 shows Detection Error Tradeoff (DET) curve for all three performed experiments [16]. It can be seen from the graph as well as from Table 1 that. % EER of MFCC is 17.77, whereas fusion gives EER of 15.89 which is 2% lesser than that of MFCC alone. This shows the effectiveness of proposed LPTP feature over standard MFCC features. Optimum DCF values are also reported and that also gives results specifying the more efficiency of fused features. 95% confidence interval is also reported and it gives lesser deviation for fusion of MFCC and LPTP than MFCC alone. It can be seen that the range of 95% confidence interval is very small, which gives statistical significance of experimental results. Results also report that the proposed fusion gives more % IR and less % EER than fusion of MFCC and T-Phase feature set.

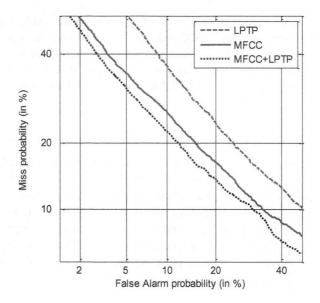

Fig. 3. DET curve comparing results for LPTP and MFCC features for NIST 2002 database

4 Summary and Conclusions

The speaker recognition studies represented in this paper gives effectiveness of proposed LPTP features over standard MFCC. It can be concluded from this study that proposed LPTP features are able to capture speaker-specific characteristics which is complementary to the MFCC and hence combining evidences of MFCC and LPTP gives more efficient speaker recognition system. Score-level fusion of MFCC and LPTP features gives more better results than fusion of MFCC and T-Phase features in terms of both % IR and % EER. It can be also observed from this study that LPC of temporal phase is more effective than LPC of speech and thus shows the effectiveness of temporal phase to capture speaker-specific information. Future research of this work will be directed toward robustness evaluation of proposed LPTP feature set under various noise or signal degradation conditions. Various score normalization technique such as Z-norm and T-norm will be explored for much better performance.

References

1. Kinnunen, T., Li, H.: An overview of text-independent speaker recognition: from features to supervectors. Speech Commun. **52**(1), 12–40 (2010)
2. Davis, S.B., Mermelstein, P.: Comparison of parametric representations for monosyllabic word recognition in continuously spoken sentences. IEEE Trans. Acoust. Speech Sig. Process. ASSP **28**, 357–366 (1980)
3. Makhoul, J.: Linear prediction: a tutorial review. Proc. IEEE **63**(4), 561–580 (1975)

4. Li, Q., Huang, Y.: Robust speaker identification using an auditory based feature. In: Proceedings of IEEE International Conference on Acoustics, Speech and Signal Process (ICASSP), Dallas, Texas, pp. 4514–4517 (2010)
5. Shi, G., Shanechi, M.M., Aarabi, P.: On the importance of phase in human speech recognition. Symp. IEEE Trans. Audio, Speech Lang. process. **14**, 1867–1874 (2006)
6. Hegde, R.M., Murthy, H.A., Rao, G.V.R.: Application of the modified group delay function to speaker identification and discrimination. In: Proceedings of IEEE International Conference on Acoustics, Speech, and Signal Process (ICASSP), Montreal, Canada, pp. 517–520 (2004)
7. Vijayan, K., Kumar, V., Murthy, K.S.R: Feature extraction from analytic phase of speech signal. In: Proceedings of INTERSPEECH, Singapore, pp. 1658–1662 (2014)
8. Murty, K.S.R., Yegnanarayana, B.: Combining evidence from residual phase and MFCC features for speaker recognition. IEEE Sig. Process. Lett. **13**, 52–56 (2006)
9. Agrawal, P., Patil, H.A.: Fusion of TEO phase with MFCC features for speaker recognition. In: Proceedings of the 2nd International Conference on Perception and Machine Intelligence (PerMin), pp. 161–166 (2015)
10. Vijayan, K., Kumar, V., Murty, K.S.R.: Allpass modelling of Fourier phase for speaker verication. In: Proceedings of ODYSSEY: The Speaker and Language Recognition Workshop, Joensuu, Finland, pp. 112–117 (2014)
11. Vijayan K., Murthy, K.S.R.: Epoch Extraction From Allpass residual of speech signals. In: IEEE International Conference on Acoustics, Speech and Signal Processing, pp. 1493–1497 (2014)
12. NIST 2002 Speaker Recognition Evaluation. http://www.nist.gov/speech/tests/spk/2002/. Last Accessed 20 Apr 2017
13. Reynolds, D.A., Quatieri, T.F., Dunn, R.B.: Speaker verification using adapted Gaussian mixture models. Digit. Signal Proc. **10**, 19–41 (2000)
14. MSR identity toolkit, Microsoft research (2013). http://research.microsoft.com/. Last Accessed 28 Mar 2017
15. Pelaez-Moreno, C., Gallardo-Antolin, A., Diaz-de-Maria, F.: Recognizing voice over IP: a robust front-end for speech recognition on the world wide web. IEEE Trans. Multimedia **3** (2), 209–218 (2001)
16. Martin, A., Doddington, G., Kamm, T., Ordowski, M.: The DET curve in assessment of detection task performance. In: European Conference on Speech Processing Technology, Rhodes, Greece, pp. 1895–1898 (1997)
17. Mike Brookes: VOICEBOX: Speech Processing Toolbox for MATLAB (2014). http://www.ee.ic.ac.uk/hp/staff/dmb/voicebox/voicebox.html. Last Accessed 2 Apr 2017

Novel Phase Encoded Mel Cepstral Features for Speaker Verification

Apeksha J. Naik$^{(\boxtimes)}$, Rishabh Tak, and Hemant A. Patil

Dhirubhai Ambani Institute of Information
and Communication Technology (DA-IICT), Gandhinagar, Gujarat, India
apekshajnaik26@gmail.com,
{rishabh_tak,hemant_patil}@daiict.ac.in

Abstract. In this paper, we propose novel phase encoded Mel cepstral coefficients (PEMCC) features for Automatic Speaker Verification (ASV) task. This is motivated by recently proposed phase encoding scheme that uses causal delta dominance condition (CDD). In particular, we got on an average of 80% reduction in log-spectral distortion (LSD) for reconstruction error compared to its magnitude spectrum counterpart, using CDD scheme. This result indicates that phase encoded magnitude spectrum is having better reconstruction capability. The experiments of proposed PEMCC features are carried out on standard statistically meaningful NIST 2002 SRE database and the performance is compared with baseline MFCC features. Furthermore, score-level fusion of MFCC+PEMCC features gave better results for GMM-UBM-based system, i-vector probabilistic linear discriminant analysis (PLDA)-based system and i-vector Cosine Distance Scoring (CDS)-based system over MFCC and PEMCC features alone. This illustrates, the proposed PEMCC features capture complementary speaker-specific information.

Keywords: Speaker verification · Causal delta dominance · Phase encoding · i-Vector · Cosine distance scoring · Probiblistic linear discriminant analysis

1 Introduction

Automatic Speaker Verification (ASV) is a task in which machine is used to verify a speaker's claimed identity from his or her speech sample [3]. Every speaker is having some unique characteristic traits in his or her voice and these characteristic traits are known as features. These features play very important role in Automatic Speaker Verification (ASV). Now-a-days most of the ASV systems use features extracted from magnitude spectrum of speech signal such as mel frequency cepstral coefficients (MFCC), linear prediction cepstral coefficients (LPCC). However, both magnitude and phase spectra characteristics are important for speaker verification. Recently, Shenoy et al. have proposed the idea of exact phase retrieval in principal shift-invariant spaces [12,13]. They have identified a class of continuous-time signals that are neither causal nor minimum

© Springer International Publishing AG 2017
A. Karpov et al. (Eds.): SPECOM 2017, LNAI 10458, pp. 572–581, 2017.
DOI: 10.1007/978-3-319-66429-3_57

phase and yet guarantee the retrieval of exact phase. In [11], a new technique to encode a phase of a signal in magnitude spectrogram by satisfying the condition of delta dominance was proposed. Motivated by this phase encoding technique, we proposed novel phase-based features called as Phase Encoded Mel Cepstral Coefficients (PEMCC) that can be used to verify a claimed speaker's identity from a speech signal.

In [10], we have proposed these features for the classification of natural *vs.* Spoofed speech in the context of speaker verification problem, i.e.,as a possible countermeasure for voice biometric attacks. In particular, we got very encouraging results using proposed PEMCC features and its score-level fusion with state-of-the-art MFCC features (approximately 14.54% reduction in EER w.r.t MFCC alone). This encouraging results motivated us to investigate possible discrimination capability of proposed features for actual ASV task. Hence, in this paper, we attempt suitability of these novel countermeasures as features in generic ASV system on statistically meaningful NIST SRE 2002 corpus [6]. In our earlier work, GMM-based classifier was used in spoofed speech detection task. In this paper, we have explored the effectiveness of proposed feature set on three ASV systems: classical GMM-UBM-based ASV system, state-of-the-art i-vector-based ASV system with CDS and PLDA as classifier. Performance evaluation of PEMCC features is done on NIST SRE 2002 database [6] for all three ASV systems and the results were compared with the baseline MFCC features.

The rest of the paper is organized as follows: Sect. 2 describes phase-encoded speech spectrogram. Section 3 presents the details of PEMCC feature extraction scheme. Section 4 describes briefly the speaker verification system. The experiments and results are presented in Sect. 5. Finally, Sect. 6 concludes the paper.

2   Phase-Encoded Speech Spectrogram

Fourier transform (FT)-based phase information is important to generate an intelligible speech. In general, the speech signal is a mixed phase [8]. Hence, if the speech signal is reconstructed using only from the magnitude spectrum, only the minimum-phase component of the speech signal can be recovered [7]. Since the magnitude spectrum does not contain phase information, phase spectrum does not contain magnitude information of the signal, magnitude and phase spectra are independent functions [4]. A minimum-phase system that has its poles and zeros inside the unit circle, can be completely specified by either magnitude or phase spectrum. In a very recent study [11], an algorithm is developed for new class of signals known as Causal Delta Dominant (CDD) signal, which can be reconstructed back from its magnitude spectrum alone. An interesting aspect of this work is that, there are no constraints on the signal, i.e., it is not necessary for signal to be minimum-phase or need not to have rational system function . To make the signal CDD, a Kronecker impulse delta of right amplitude is added at the origin of the signal, i.e., at $s(0)$ This condition of CDD allows encoding the phase in spectrogram, which is known as *phase encoded spectrogram* [11]. Figure 1 shows the block diagram of phase encoded spectrogram and the capability of signal reconstruction. Consider a causal finite-length sequence, $\{s[n]\}_{n\in[1,N]}$, by adding a Kronecker impulse of amplitude β to $s[n]$, and we get,

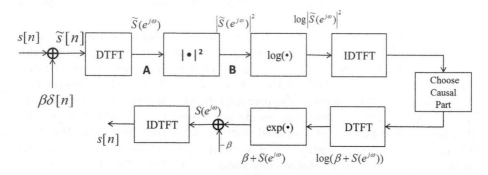

Fig. 1. Block diagram of phase encoded spectrogram and signal reconstruction. After [11]

$$\tilde{s}[n] = s[n] + \beta\delta[n]. \tag{1}$$

Discrete-Time Fourier Transform (DTFT) of causal sequence is

$$S(e^{j\omega}) = \sum_{n=1}^{N} s[n]e^{-j\omega n}, \tag{2}$$

which is a 2π-periodic function in ω i.e., $S(e^{j(\omega+2\pi)}) = S(e^{j\omega})$. As in Eq. (1), a sequence $\tilde{s}[n] = \beta\,\delta[n] + s[n]$ is reconstructed, which differs from $s[n]$ only at the origin $n = 0$. Thus, the DTFT of $\tilde{s}[n]$ can be given as:

$$\tilde{S}(e^{j\omega}) = \sum_{n=0}^{N} \tilde{s}[n]e^{-j\omega n} = \beta + S(e^{j\omega}), \tag{3}$$

It is observed from Eq. (3), that a DC-shift is introduced across all the frequencies in the STFT spectrum of the signal $s[n]$, where β is positive real-valued constant. Applying logarithm on both sides of Eq. (3) gives,

$$\log|\tilde{S}(e^{j\omega})|^2 = \log\tilde{S}(e^{j\omega}) + \log\tilde{S}^\star(e^{j\omega})$$
$$= \log(\beta + S(e^{j\omega})) + \log(\beta + S^\star(e^{j\omega})). \tag{4}$$

The first term in the R.H.S of the Eq. (4) is given by:

$$\log(\beta + S(e^{j\omega})) = \log(\beta) + \log(1 + \frac{1}{\beta}S(e^{j\omega})), \tag{5}$$

Here, we consider $\beta > |S(e^{j\omega})|$. Therefore, using Taylor series:

$$\log(1 + \frac{1}{\beta}S(e^{j\omega})) = \sum_{m=1}^{\infty} \frac{(-1)^{m-1}}{m}\frac{S^m(e^{j\omega})}{\beta^m}. \tag{6}$$

Larger the value of β, faster is the decay of terms in the expansion [11]. Since $s[n]$ is the causal signal, convolution of $s[n]$ with itself will also be causal. Hence, $\log(\beta + S(e^{j\omega}))$ is the DTFT of a causal sequence. Similarly, for the second term of Eq. (4), $\log(\beta + S^\star(e^{j\omega}))$ will be DTFT of anti-causal sequence. Therefore, the inverse DTFT of $\log|\tilde{S}(e^{j\omega})|^2$ is the cepstrum that contains two components, namely, causal sequence and anti-causal sequence. If we retain only with the causal part of the cepstrum, we can reconstruct the signal [11]. Hence, we have seen that by adding a Kronecker impulse of sufficient strength, phase encoding is possible in the magnitude spectrum and we can get back our signal using (phase encoded) magnitude spectrum only. Using this concept, we propose PEMCC features discussed in next Section.

3   Proposed PEMCC Feature Set

To use the phase-encoded approach for speech-related applications, it is necessary to derive a set of features. It is possible that feature extraction can be done from point B in Fig. 1, which is a representation of the phase-encoded spectrogram. However, the dynamic range of phase-encoded spectrogram is not suitable for feature extraction. Therefore, to use the concept of phase-encoded spectrogram as features, we propose following modifications shown in Fig. 2.

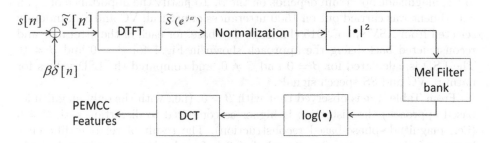

Fig. 2. Block diagram of proposed PEMCC feature extraction scheme. After [10]

As shown in Fig. 2, a Kronecker impulse delta of β amplitude at the origin in each frame of a signal. Next, we take DTFT of every frame and apply the normalization on each FFT-bins. Then, calculate the power spectrum of frames. This identifies which frequencies are present in the frames. Mel filterbank is applied to the power spectra, which gives the total energy present in each subband filter. Once we have the subband energies, we take the logarithm followed by Discrete Cosine Transform (DCT) of log-energies to get the proposed PEMCC feature set. There is a practical issue that, we cannot calculate the DTFT of a signal. However, we can compute the DFT, which is the sampled version of DTFT [11]. We set number of FFT-bins as total number of samples per frame. The proposed algorithm to extract PEMCC feature from the speech signal is given in Algorithm 1.

3.1   Choice of β

For phase encoding, we are adding a Kronecker impulse, such that the amplitude of the signal at $n = 0$ should be greater than the absolute sum of all amplitudes points except at the origin. We segment the speech signal and reconstructed every frame using approach given in Fig. 1. Thus, each frame has its own β value that is given by Eq. (7). Here β_i gives value of β for i^{th} frame. Instead of this, we have calculated the β as per Eq. (8).

$$\beta_i = k \sum_{n=1}^{N} |s_i[n]|, k >> 1, \tag{7}$$

$$\beta = k \sum_{n=1}^{N} |s[n]|, k >> 1, \tag{8}$$

where $s[n]$ is the speech signal. In general, the l^1-norm of a frame of a speech signal is always less than l^1-norm of entire utterance. Hence, instead of defining the β for every frame, we have taken only one β value for all the speech frames. Experimentally, we have found that Log Spectral Distortion (LSD) for both the β are almost the same. Hence, to reduce the time computation and complexity, we have used Eq. (8) for our proposed method. The key idea of encoding phase in the magnitude spectrum depends on the β. To justify the importance of β, an experiment was carried out on 1500 utterances of natural, VC and SS randomly selected from ASV spoof 2015 challenge database, for each of the utterance and reconstructed back using the approach shown in Fig. 1 for $\beta = 0$ and $\beta \neq 0$. The LSD is calculated for $\beta = 0$ and $\beta \neq 0$, and compared the LSD values for natural, VC and SS speech signals.

From Table 1, it is observed that with $\beta = 0$, (i.e., with the only magnitude-based approach) the distortion is higher as compared to distortion with $\beta \neq 0$ (i.e., magnitude-phase-based reconstruction). The result of relative difference between LSD values for $\beta = 0$ and $\beta \neq 0$ is found to be approximately 80%. Thus, it indicates encoding of phase in the magnitude spectrum captures better reconstruction capability (i.e., synthesis) of the speech pattern.

Table 1. Mean LSD values of 1500 utterances for various β values from ASVspoof 2015 database1

Speakers	$\beta = 0$	$\beta \neq 0$	Relative difference (%)
Natural	1.97	0.39	80.11
VC	2.04	0.36	82.36
SS	2.10	0.39	81.23

Algorithm 1 Proposed PEMCC Feature Extraction Algorithm

1: Take a speech signal $s[n]$.
2: Apply framing on the signal, let $(s_t)_{t\epsilon[1,T]}$ is the tth frame with 20 ms window size and 10 ms window shift.
3: Add Kronecker impulse delta of β amplitude to each speech frame at the origin, $\tilde{s}_t[n] = s_t[n] + \beta\delta[n]$.
4: Take DFT of each frame, such as $\tilde{S}_t^i(e^{j\omega}) = \beta + S_t^i(e^{j\omega})$, where $S_t^i(e^{j\omega})$ indicates i^{th} FFT-bin, $\forall$ $t\epsilon[1,T]$.
5: Perform the normalization on each FFT-bin.

$$Y_t^i(e^{j\omega}) = \frac{\tilde{S}_t^i(e^{j\omega}) - mean(\tilde{S}_t^i(e^{j\omega}))}{std(\tilde{S}_t^i(e^{j\omega}))}$$

6: Perform absolute squaring that results in power spectra.
7: Apply Mel filterbank on power spectra.
8: Apply DCT on Mel spectrum and retain first few coefficients of PEMCC.

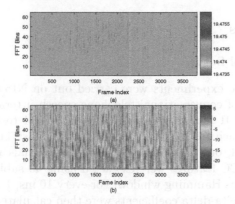

Fig. 3. Effect of normalization on power spectrum (a) without normalization, (b) with normalization

The important aspect of Figs. 1 and 2 is the normalization block between points A and B. It is observed in Fig. 3 that the dynamic range of power spectrum is better after using normalization as compared to without normalization. However, with normalization, formants and harmonics are more visible as compared to without normalization as shown in Fig. 3(b). Hence, normalization increases the energy variations. Features was extracted on both normalized and without normalized and found that performance of normalized features were much effective.

4 Speaker Verification System

The classical method in ASV is the Gaussian mixture model-Universal background model (GMM-UBM) [9]. In this method, speaker models are adapted from the UBM using maximum a-posteriori (MAP) adaptation. The disadvantage of this method is, it is very slow during verification of target *vs.* test trials and it fails to capture the channel variability information. Combination of support vector machine (SVM) with GMM was also a successful method for ASV [1]. Mean vectors of the adapted GMM are concatenated to form a GMM supervector, which are then modeled by the SVM classifier. The advantage of this method is that it combines the effectiveness of adapted GMM model and discriminating capability of SVM. Most recent state-of-the-art method in speaker verification is i-vector-based system that uses cosine distance scoring (CDS) [2] and probabilistic linear discriminant analysis (PLDA) [5] as a pattern classifier. This method captures both speaker and channel variability effectively in low-dimensional subspace (Total variability space) [2]. i-vector effectively summarizes utterance that is nothing but low-dimensional representation of GMM supervector. In this paper, we extracted i-vectors from MFCC as well as PEMCC features. Then, these i-vectors are used as features for PLDA and CDS classifier.

5   Experiments

5.1   Experimental Setup

In this paper, all the experiments were carried out on NIST 2002 SRE database [2]. It consists of conversational telephone speech utterances of about 139 male speakers and 191 female speakers. There are 3564 test utterances, each of 1 min duration. Each test segment is evaluated against 11 different hypothesized speaker model, out of which 2977 are genuine trials whereas 36227 are impostor trials. MFCC features were extracted using 40 subband filters in Mel filterbank and a 25-ms Hamming window. For every 10 ms, 13 MFCCs were calculated. Delta and delta-delta coefficients were then calculated to produce a 39-dimensional feature vector. PEMCC features were extracted using the procedure described in Sect. 3, which resulted in 13 static coefficients. Then delta and delta-delta coefficients were appended to produce a 39-dimensional PEMCC feature vector. The feature vectors obtained from the development data was then used to train 256 as well as 512 Gaussian mixture component gender-independent UBM, 400-dimensional T-matrix and 200-dimensional PLDA models. These trained models are used to calculate the scores in terms of log-likelihood ratio (LLR) for GMM-UBM-based ASV system and i-vector-PLDA-based ASV system. On the other hand, scores are directly calculated using cosine kernel in i-vector-CDS-based ASV system given the UBM and Total variability matrix (T). In practice, the MSR Identity Toolbox [3] was used to implement the ASV systems.

5.2   Experimental Results

The performance of ASV system is given in terms of equal error rate (EER) and Detection error trade-off (DET) curve. Table 2 shows the performance of the three different ASV systems. The results obtained for the proposed PEMCC

Table 2. Equal Error Rates (%) for GMM-UBM system, i-vector-PLDA system and i-vector-CDS system on NIST SRE 2002 database

Gaussian components	Feature set	GMM-UBM EER (%)	i-vector PLDA EER (%)	CDS EER (%)
256	**MFCC**	18.6021	14.9971	14.7017
	PEMCC	19.9866	18.3742	16.6312
	MFCC+PEMCC	**17.1585**	**13.1559**	**13.4028**
		($\alpha = 0.58$)	($\alpha = 0.5$)	($\alpha = 0.5$)
512	**MFCC**	17.6967	14.3769	14.3567
	PEMCC	18.8781	18.4414	17.1985
	MFCC+PEMCC	**16.8626**	**13.2348**	**13.3692**
		($\alpha = 0.8$)	($\alpha = 0.53$)	($\alpha = 0.53$)

features are comparable with the baseline MFCC features for all the three ASV systems. These results clearly show the speaker-specific nature of the proposed PEMCC features.

The results also show that our proposed PEMCC features perform better with i-vector-based systems over GMM-UBM-based system. Our proposed features encode the phase information in it, which motivated us to find the possibility of presence of complementary speaker-related information in MFCC and PEMCC. For exploring this, we have done the score-level fusion. The results obtained for score-level fusion is better in terms of EER (%) than obtained with individual features. This clearly shows the presence of complementary information in MFCC and PEMCC features. The relative performance improvement of ASV systems after score-level fusion is 20–25% in i-vector-based system over GMM-UBM-based system, 5–8% improvement over MFCC features alone and 10–14% improvement over PEMCC features alone. Figures 4(a), (b) and 5(a) shows the DET curves for i-vector PLDA-based, i-vector CDS-based and GMM-UBM-based systems, respectively, for 512 Gaussian components. DET curves for MFCC+PEMCC fusion are moving towards origin, which shows the improvement in performance as compared to the baseline MFCC features. Figure 4(b) shows the DET curves for the comparison of GMM-UBM-based system, i-vector PLDA-based system and i-vector CDS-based system. It clearly shows that two state-of-the-art systems perform better than the GMM-UBM-based system.

Figure 6 shows the effect of score level fusion weight (α) for different ASV systems, namely, i-vector PLDA-based system, i-vector CDS-based system, GMM-UBM-based system. Score-level fusion of MFCC+PEMCC works better for i-vector-based system over GMM-UBM-based system using optimum value of $\alpha (0 \leq \alpha \leq 1)$.

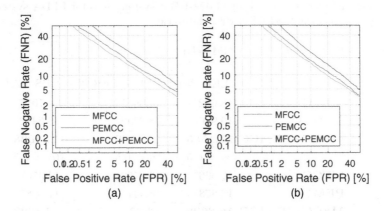

Fig. 4. DET curves for NIST SRE 2002 database for (a) i-vector PLDA-based system, (b) i-vector CDS-based system

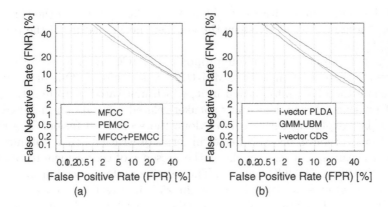

Fig. 5. DET curves for NIST SRE 2002 database for (a)GMM-UBM-based system, (b)comparison of GMM-UBM-based and i-vector-based system

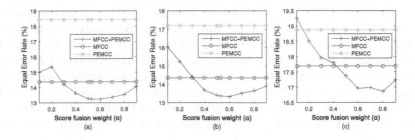

Fig. 6. Effect of fusion weight in different ASV systems (a) i-vector PLDA system, (b) i-vector CDS system and (c) GMM-UBM system

6   Summary and Conclusions

In this paper, we proposed a novel PEMCC feature set that exploit the contribution of encoded phase for speaker verification task. Performance evaluation of proposed feature set was carried out on standard NIST SRE 2002 database. Performance of PEMCC features found to be comparable with the baseline MFCC feature set. The i-vector CDS-based ASV system found to be the best among all three system when MFCC and PEMCC features were used alone. The score-level fusion of magnitude and phase based-features show lower EER as compared to the individual feature set. The complementary information is observed on an almost equal contribution of magnitude and phase-based features. This is observed for GMM-UBM-based ASV system, i-vector CDS-based ASV system and i-vector PLDA-based ASV system.

References

1. Campbell, W.M., Sturim, D.E., Reynolds, D.A.: Support vector machines using gmm supervectors for speaker verification. IEEE Signal Process. Lett. **13**(5), 308–311 (2006)
2. Dehak, N., Kenny, P.J., Dehak, R., Dumouchel, P., Ouellet, P.: Front-end factor analysis for speaker verification. IEEE Trans. Audio Speech Lang. Process. **19**(4), 788–798 (2011)
3. Hansen, J.H., Hasan, T.: Speaker recognition by machines and humans: a tutorial review. IEEE Signal Process. Mag. **32**(6), 74–99 (2015)
4. Hayes, M., Lim, J., Oppenheim, A.: Signal reconstruction from phase or magnitude. IEEE Trans. Acoust. Speech Signal Process. **28**(6), 672–680 (1980)
5. Kenny, P.: Bayesian speaker verification with heavy-tailed priors. In: Speaker Odyssey. p. 14 (2010)
6. Martin, A., Przybocki, M.: The NIST year 2002 speaker recognition evaluation plan (2001)
7. Oppenheim, A.V., Schafer, R.W.: Discrete-Time Signal Processing, 2nd edn. Pearson Education, India (1999)
8. Quatieri, T.F.: Discrete-Time Speech Signal Processing: Principles and Practice. Pearson Education, India (2006)
9. Reynolds, D.A., Quatieri, T.F., Dunn, R.B.: Speaker verification using adapted gaussian mixture models. Digit. Signal Proc. **10**(1–3), 19–41 (2000)
10. Tak, R., Kamble, M.R., Patil, H.A.: Analysis-by-synthesis approach for phase encoded Mel cepstral features to detect spoofed speech. In: Submited for possible publication in INTERSPEECH (2017)
11. Seelamantula, C.S.: Phase-encoded speech spectrograms. In: INTERSPEECH, San Francisco, USA, pp. 1775–1779 (2016)
12. Shenoy, B.A., Mulleti, S., Seelamantula, C.S.: Exact phase retrieval in principal shift-invariant spaces. IEEE Trans. Signal Process. **64**(2), 406–416 (2016)
13. Shenoy, B.A., Seelamantula, C.S.: Exact phase retrieval for a class of 2-D parametric signals. IEEE Trans. Signal Process. **63**(1), 90–103 (2015)

On a Way to the Computer Aided Speech Intonation Training

Boris Lobanov[(⊠)], Yelena Karnevskaya, and Vladimir Zhitko

The United Institute of Informatics Problems of National Academy
of Sciences of Belarus, Minsk, Belarus
lobanov@newman.bas-net.by, lobbormef@gmail.com,
zhitko.vladimir@gmail.com

Abstract. Presented in the paper is a software system designed to train learners
in producing a variety of recurring intonation patterns of speech. The system is
based on comparing the melodic (tonal) portraits of a reference phrase and a
phrase spoken by the learner and involves active learner-system interaction.
Since parametric representation of intonation features of the speech signal faces
fundamental difficulties, the paper intends to show how these difficulties can be
overcome. The main algorithms used in the training system proposed for analyzing and comparing intonation features are considered. A set of reference
sentences is given which represents the basic intonation patterns of English
speech and their main varieties. The system's interface is presented and the
results of the system operation are illustrated.

Keywords: Speech intonation · Melodic/tonal portrait · Intonation analysis ·
Computer system for teaching · Intonation training

1 Introduction

Intonation plays a significant role in speech communication. It shows the general aim of
an utterance and points out its information centre (nucleus) as well as giving prominence
to the nonnuclear semantically relevant elements and deaccenting those lacking in
novelty or semantic weight; it splits an utterance into phrases (clauses) and
intonation-units (groups), each presenting a syntactically organized parcel of information, and integrates these parts into an utterance, distinguishing thereby between more
and less closely connected 'chunks' of the speech flow. Intonation is widely recognized
as an important aspect of speech that provides both linguistic and socio-cultural information. Therefore, prosodic aspects of speech should be explicitly introduced to language learners to help them communicate effectively in a foreign language.

A current linguistic idea is that a foreign accent is more evident and stable in
intonation than in segmental sounds. A foreign accent in intonation emerges mainly as
a result of prosodic interference, an inevitable 'by-product' of bilingualism and, particularly, under the influence of the prosodic patterns of the learner's native language
on those of the target language. Considering the variety of functions of intonation in
speech and its potential socio-cultural effects, deviations in this area can lead to serious
semantic losses in communication. It is a well-known fact that it is incorrect intonation

© Springer International Publishing AG 2017
A. Karpov et al. (Eds.): SPECOM 2017, LNAI 10458, pp. 582–592, 2017.
DOI: 10.1007/978-3-319-66429-3_58

that is often the cause of the wrong impression a non-native language speaker might produce [1]. Native speakers of American English, e.g., made the following observation concerning the Russian accent in English: "Ask an average American what they think about the Russian accent, and the answer will be as follows: *"Russians don't sound very friendly. I feel like they don't like me at all. I am not sure whether it comes from their language or from their culture?"* (See also: https://www.youtube.com/ watch?v=e0MZW3AbzxI)." One of the reasons many Russian speakers of English sound unfriendly is the so called "flat" tone associated in American English with the above mentioned negative connotations. Obviously, many Russian speakers fail to capture the language-specific phonetic-phonological features of American/British English intonation and, moreover, are unaware of the drastic socio-cultural effects of the deviations from the prosodic form of an utterance. Helping nonnative learners eliminate such errors presupposes ensuring their familiarity and acquisition of the prosodic patterns of the foreign language being studied.

Accuracy of reproducing the foreign intonation patterns in the process of speaking as well as adequacy of identifying the patterns on the level of perception present considerable difficulty for the learners, particularly related to their ability to control their performance and perception (especially for those who have no ear for music). The linguaphone courses and equipment available at present provide only "a hearing" feedback for intonation accuracy control, which is obviously insufficient.

The present paper is concerned with the progress achieved in developing a computer trainer providing an additional *visual* feedback as well as a *quantitative assessment* of the learners' intonation accuracy in the foreign language teaching process.

In the course of creating the speech intonation training systems we faced a number of difficulties connected with the necessity of solving a number of technical problems, namely:

1. *An adequate comparison of the pattern signal and a spoken one which is usually characterized by a non-linear time deformation and its beginning and end are not known beforehand.*
   The solution of this problem has become possible thanks to the application of the modified method of a **continuous dynamic time warping** (CDTW) of two signals, developed by the author earlier [2]. The use of this method ensures automatic recognition of the end and beginning of a phrase being uttered simultaneously with its comparison with the pattern phrase.
2. *Automatic segmentation of the signal being analyzed into areas for which the notion of F0 is relevant as far as the formation of the tonal contour of the phrase is concerned (the segments of vowels and most of the sonorants).*
   This problem is being solved by means of a non-linear transfer of segment markers from the preliminarily marked pattern-phrase onto the phrase being uttered with the help of the author's earlier suggested technology of cloning the prosodic characteristics of speech [3].
3. *Precise calculation of F0 of the pattern speech signal and of that produced by the learner within a very wide voice range {30–1000 Hz}, for male and female voices pooled.*

The task is solved by using the traditional methods of singling F0 out of a speech signal. Seeking a solution to the given problem has been the subject matter of a large number of publications (see e.g. [4]).

4. *Automatic interpolation of current values F0 on the segments for which measuring F0 is invalid, i.e. on most of the consonants.*

This task is solved by using well-known interpolation mathematical formulas determining the way of finding intermediate values on the basis of an available discrete set of given values.

5. *An adequate calculation of a similarity measure between the pattern signal and the uttered one under the condition of their differences in duration and F0 voice-ranges.*

This task is solved by using a representation of an intonation curve in the form of a unified melodic portrait (UMP) described below in the next section of the paper. Calculation of the similarity measure of two UMPs is carried out with the help of traditional formulas either by means of calculating a samples correlation coefficient or through determining the vector distance between the curves.

In dealing with these problems, we relied on the results of earlier research in the field of developing automatic intonation assessment systems for computer aided language learning [5–8] as well as the results of our earlier research in the area of speech intonation analysis and synthesis [9–11].

2 Intonation Stylization Model and Acoustic Database

The present work is a follow up study to the previously introduced model of universal melodic portraits (UMP) of accentual units (AU) for the representation of phrase intonations in text-to-speech synthesis [9]. According to this model, a phrase is represented by one or more AUs (Accent Unit is often referred to as Accent Group). Each unit, in turn, can be composed of one or more words. In the latter case, only one word bears full stress while the other words carry partial stress. Each AU consists of *pre-nucleus* (all phonemes preceding the main stressed vowel), *nucleus* (the main stressed vowel) and *post-nucleus* (all phonemes following the main stressed vowel).

The UMP model assumes that typological features of an AU pitch movement for a particular type of intonation do not depend either on the number or quality of segments in the phonemic content of the pre-nucleus, nucleus or post-nucleus, or on the fundamental frequency range specific for a given speaker. The model allows of representing the intonation constructions of a given language as a set of melodic patterns in normalized space {*Time – Frequency*}. Time normalization is performed by bringing pre-nucleus, nucleus and post-nucleus elements of AU to standard time lengths. This sort of normalization levels out the differences in melodic contours caused by the number of words and phonemes in an AU.

For fundamental frequency normalization $F_{0\ min}$ and $F_{0\ max}$ are determined within the ensemble of melodic contours produced by a certain speaker. This sort of normalization cancels out the differences of melodic contours caused by the speaker's voice register and range.

The normalization is calculated by the formula:

$$F_0^N = (F_0 - F_{0\,min}) / (F_{0\,max} - F_{0\,min}). \tag{1}$$

We note that the value:

$$R = [(F0\,max/F0\,min)] - 1 \tag{2}$$

expressed in an octave scale, can be used to estimate the range of the F0 change (*wide-medium-narrow*).

In certain cases it may be beneficial to use statistical normalization instead of (1):

$$F_0^N = (F_0 - M) / \zeta, \tag{3}$$

where M is mathematical expectation, ζ is standard deviation. Note that M can be interpreted as a register and ζ – as a range of the speaker's voice.

Therefore, the normalized space for UMP may be presented as a rectangle with axes (T_N, F_0^N) as schematically shown in Fig. 1, while the interval [0–1/3] on the abscess T_N is a pre-nucleus, [1/3 – 2/3] is a nucleus, and [2/3 – 1] is a post- nucleus. The intervals on the ordinate F_0^N: [0–1/3] – low level, [1/3 – 2/3] – mid-level, [2/3 – 1] – high level.

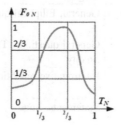

Fig. 1. The UMP model

UMP representation focuses on the peculiarities of the shape of the F0 curve on the nucleus with less attention to the quantitative and qualitative composition of the pre- and post-nucleus. Within the framework of the UMP it is possible to describe the melodic curve minutely, using well-known terms, such as:

- *"low-medium-high"* – for the pitch level;
- *"falling-level-rising"* – for the direction of the pitch change;
- *"wide-medium-narrow"* – for the range of the pitch change.

In [10] the positive experience of creating melodic portraits of complex narrative sentences of Russian speech with the use of the PAE model and UMP is described, and in [11] it was shown that the representation of intonation in the form of UMP allows to reveal the characteristic differences when comparing melodic portraits of English and Russian phrases of dialogue speech.

3 Acoustic Database

The developed prototype of the system is realized in 2 variants for implementation in multimedia course-books for advanced learners of English [12] and Russian [13] intonation. Application of this system makes it possible for the students not only to listen to phrases pronounced with standard intonation but also observe the model F0(t) и A0(t) curves on display, reproduce these phrases, compare their F0(t) и A0(t) curves with the original ones and obtain a numerical evaluation of their similarity. Used as models are male-and-female-spoken sample phrases from the above-mentioned multimedia course-books.

In practice of teaching English intonation 10 tonal patterns are used which represent the pitch varieties of the four basic types of pitch change in English (see: Table 1). The principle of selecting the varieties is both structural and functional: on the one hand - perceptible discrimination and identification, and, on the other hand - a tendency towards association with a particular modal-pragmatic type of utterance (statements, general questions, requests, implications, apologies, etc.). In Table 1 the [+] sign indicates the position of the nuclear vowel of the phrase.

Table 1. The basic types of English tonal patterns

Type of tone pattern	N°	Pitch varieties	Types of utterances. Common usage.	Typical examples
Rising	1	Mid Wide	General, Elliptical questions, Tags	Is it di + fficult?
	2	Low Wide	General questions, Tags, Non finality	Can I speak to Ma + ry?
	3	High Narrow	Interrogative repetitions	Na + tive?
	4	Low Narrow	Statements, Tags	Ye + sterday.
Falling	5	High Wide	Statements, Imperatives, Special questions	Li + sten to me, please!
	6	Mid Wide	Statements, Imperatives, Tags, Special questions	Whe + re is she?
	7	Low Narrow	Statements, Imperatives, Tags	It's in the So + uth.
Falling-Rising	8	Undivided	Imperatives, Questions, Statements, Non-finality, Conversational formulas	They are re + ady.
	9	Divided		No + t no + w.
Rising-Falling	10	Undivided	Statements, Special questions	It's wo + nderful.

The acoustic signals realizing each of the given phrases are marked for the boundaries of each of the vowels contained as well as for indicating the functional status of the vowel: pre-nucleus, nucleus, post-nucleus of an accentual unit. In the database used, there are 4 to 5 commonly used samples for each of the *10 tonal patterns* of the phrases, as well as several samples of conversational speech and a piece of narrative prose. In addition to the most commonly used samples, the database includes examples of different *types of utterances* (see Table 1) for each of the 10 tonal patterns, read by a professional British English speaker.

As far as computer training is concerned, we proceed from the model of *intonation patterns* (IP) by Elena Bryzgunova [14], which is widely used in teaching Russian speech intonation. This model includes seven patterns: IP1 (the falling tone), IP2 (the falling tone with some prosodic emphasis), IP3 (the rising tone with a subsequent fall), IP4 (the falling-rising tone). IP5 (combination of the rising, level and falling tones), IP6 (combination of the rising and level tones), IP7 (combination of the rising tone with a glottal stop).

In the database used, there are 5 samples of common *types of utterances* for each *intonation pattern* as well as several samples of conversational speech and a piece of narrative prose.

4   Block Diagram of the Intonation Training System

Figure 2 contains a block diagram illustrating a sequence of algorithms for the analysis and evaluation of speech intonation within the computer system developed. The main goal of the system is to provide a student with a compact and easily interpretable pitch image of the results obtained in the course of analyzing the pitch and energy contours of the phrases carrying different intonation patterns. The system will also provide an auditory, visual and numerical evaluation of a student's performance in the intonation of a foreign language.

Block 1 contains the database of sample phrases (teacher's phrases) with different intonation patterns, compiled from multimedia course-books (see, e.g. [12] for the English language, or [13] – for Russian). Every sample phrase is preliminarily marked for the perceptible prosodic phrase boundaries and the location of its nucleus (Fig. 3).

Depending on the concrete goal of intonation training, the student selects the sample phrase needed, listens to it and pronounces it. The student's phrase is recorded on the buffer in block 2.

In block 3, the signals from both the sample and the student-spoken phrase are spectrum analyzed and compared using the algorithm of continuous dynamic time warping (CDTW). This is accompanied by the transfer of prosodic marks and labeling of a pronounced phrase (Fig. 3).

In block 4, prosodic phrase parameters, such as the fundamental frequency of the tone F0 and energy of the signal A0 are calculated. These parameters are further interpolated on the non-vocal areas, median-smoothed and normalized (Fig. 4).

In block 5, an estimation and comparison of F0 trajectories first in real time space (Figs. 5 and 7) and then in normalized UMP-space (Figs. 6 and 8) are produced.

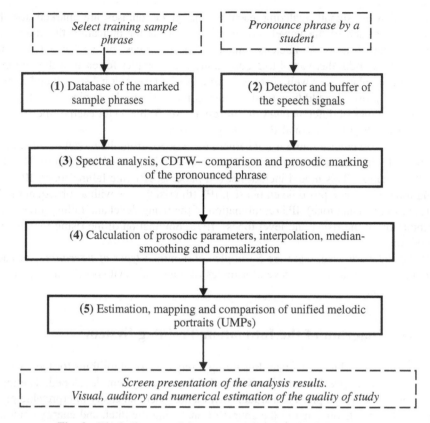

Fig. 2. Block diagram of the computer intonation training system

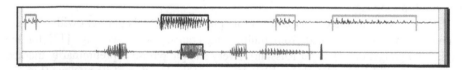

Fig. 3. Illustration of speech signals marking: the phrase *"It's Saturday"* pronounced by the teacher (above) and by a learner (below)

At the top of Figs. 5, 6, 7 and 8, numerical estimates are presented as a percentage of the proximity of the teacher's and student's phrases: for the F0 shape of curves – (Ps) curves and for their ranges – (Pr). The measure of proximity is defined as the vector distance between them.

On the left side of Figs. 6 and 8, light and dark columns are shown. They expresses the values R in an octave scale calculated by using Formula (2). Value R is used to show the difference range of F0 change between the teacher's and student's phrases.

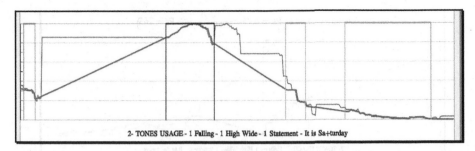

Fig. 4. Illustration of F0 trajectory processing for the teacher's phrase *"It's Saturday"*: original (*light curve line*) and interpolated, median-smoothed and normalized (*dark curve line*) tracks

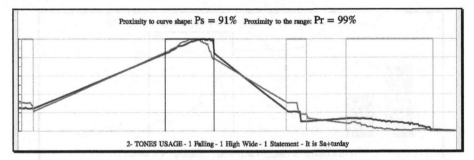

Fig. 5. Illustration of F0 curve comparison in real time space between the teacher's (*light curve line*) and a student's (*dark curve line*) phrase *"It's Saturday"* **(correct pronunciation)**

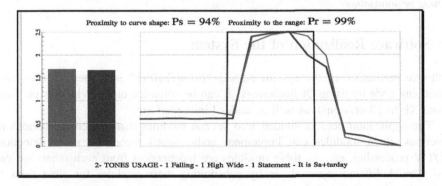

Fig. 6. Illustration of F0 range and curve comparison in UMP-space between the teacher's (*left column, light curve line*) and a student's (*right column, dark curve line*) phrase *"It's Saturday"* **(correct pronunciation)**

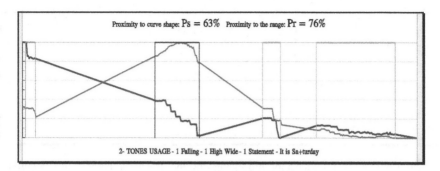

Fig. 7. Illustration of F0 curve comparison in real time space between the teacher's (*light curve line*) and a student's (*dark curve line*) phrase *"It's Saturday"* (***wrong pronunciation***)

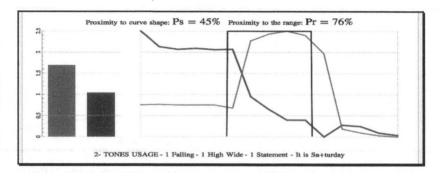

Fig. 8. Illustration of F0 range and curve comparison in UMP-space between the teacher's (*left column, light curve line*) and a student's (*right column, dark curve line*) phrase *"It's Saturday"* (***wrong pronunciation***)

5   Software Realization of the System

Software realization of the system named ***"IntonTrainer"*** is written on C++ programming code by using Qt framework. It can be compiled under Windows platform (from XP to 10 versions), as well as under Linux platform.

The application core is divided into several modules that implement standalone functions. Such modules can implement audio signal recording, voice detection, CDTW processing, etc. As these modules are independent from each other, we can easily build different applications by substituting these modules for other ones or integrating them in external systems.

For building the main user interface a built-in web engine is used. The user interface is built on html5, css3 and js (ReactJs js frame-work). The "Developer mode" user interface is built on standard Qt forms.

The main user interface is independent from the application core and can be modified or even replaced by another one. The use of html/css/js standard allows an easy change of application front-end for different purposes. For the interaction with application core there exist a number of special links formats processed by application core. Such links can open different applications dialogues (like settings, developer mode and so on), process input audio signals and play audio files.

Thus we can easily build in different training systems by replacing the front-end and training data files.

The starting page of the User Interface is shown in Fig. 9.

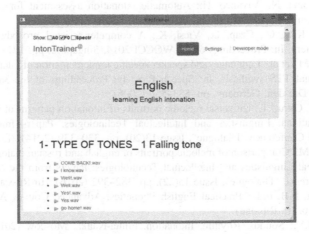

Fig. 9. Starting page of the user interface

6   Conclusions

At present, using the IntonTrainer system, experiments are conducted to learn by students the intonation of Russian and English. Preliminary results indicate a significant effectiveness of its use.

To date, there are demo versions of the "IntonTrainer" system, focused on learning the intonation of Russian and English. For those who want to test the system, a site https://intontrainer.by/ is open.

A working version of the prototype system will be demonstrated to the conference participants.

References

1. Chun, D.M.: The neglected role of intonation in communicative competence and proficiency. Mod. Lang. J. **72**, 295–303 (1988)
2. Lobanov, B.M., Levkovskaya, T.V.: Continuous speech recognizer for aircraft application. In: Proceedings of the 2nd International Workshop "Speech and Computer" – SPECOM 1997 - Cluj-Napoca, pp. 97–102 (1997)
3. Lobanov, B.M., Tsirulnik, L.I., Sizonov, O.N.: «IntoClonator» – computer system of cloning prosodic characteristics of speech. In: Proceedings of the International Conference "Dialogue 2008", Moscow, pp. 330–338 (2008). (In Russian)

 4. Shimamura, T., Kobayashi, H.: Weighted autocorrelation for pitch extraction of noisy speech. IEEE Trans. Speech Audio Process. **9**, 727–730 (2001)
 5. Anne Bonneau, Vincent Colotte.: Automatic Feedback for L2 Prosody Learning. In: Speech and Language Technologies, pp. 55–70 (2011)
 6. Xu, Y.: ProsodyPro — a tool for large-scale systematic prosody analysis. In: Proceedings of the TRASP 2013, Aix-en-Provence, France, pp. 7–10 (2013)
 7. Arias, J., Yoma, N., Vivanco, H.: Automatic intonation assessment for computer aided language learning. Speech Commun. **52**, 254–267 (2010)
 8. Sztahó, D., Kiss, G., Czap, L., Vicsi, K.: A computer-assisted prosody pronunciation teaching system. In: Proceedings of the WOCCI 2014, Singapore, pp. 121–124 (2014)
 9. Lobanov, B.M., et al.: Language- and speaker specific implementation of intonation contours in multilingual TTS synthesis. In: Speech Prosody: Proceedings of the 3rd International Conference, Dresden, Germany, pp. 553–556 (2006)
10. Lobanov, B., Okrut, T.: Universal melodic portraits of intonation patterns of russian speech. In: Computational Linguistics and Intellectual Technologies: Papers from the Annual International Conference "Dialogue", Issue 13(20), pp. 330–339 (2014). (In Russian)
11. Lobanov, B.M.: Comparison of melodic portraits of english and russian dialogic phrases. In: Computational Linguistics and Intellectual Technologies: Papers from the Annual International Conference "Dialogue", Issue 15(22), pp. 382–392 (2016). (In Russian)
12. Karnevskaya, E.B. (ed.): Practical English Phonetics. Advanced Course. Aversev, Minsk (2016). 409 p. (In Russian)
13. Odintsova, I.V.: Sounds. Rhythm. Intonation. Flinta-Nauka, Moscow (2011). 378 p. (In Russian)
14. Bryzgunova, E.A.: Sounds and Intonation of Russian Speech. Nauka, Moscow (1968). 267 p. (In Russian)

On Residual CNN in Text-Dependent Speaker Verification Task

Egor Malykh[1]([✉]), Sergey Novoselov[1,2], and Oleg Kudashev[1,2]

[1] ITMO University, St. Petersburg, Russia
[2] STC-innovations Ltd., St. Petersburg, Russia
{malykh,novoselov,kudashev}@speechpro.com

Abstract. Deep learning approaches are still not very common in the speaker verification field. We investigate the possibility of using deep residual convolutional neural network with spectrograms as an input features in the text-dependent speaker verification task. Despite the fact that we were not able to surpass the baseline system in quality, we achieved a quite good results for such a new approach getting an 5.23% ERR on the RSR2015 evaluation part. Fusion of the baseline and proposed systems outperformed the best individual system by 18% relatively.

Keywords: Speaker verification · Residual learning · CNN · FFT

1 Introduction

I-vector systems are well-known for being state-of-the-art solutions to the text-independent speaker verification task [1–3,21]. Recently, the solution of this task has increasingly been considered from the perspective of deep learning approaches. For instance, ASR deep neural network (DNN) model [3,22] divides the acoustic space into senone classes and discriminates the speakers in this space using the classic total variability (TV) model [1]. In such phonetic discriminative DNN based systems two main approaches can be distinguished. The first is to use DNN posteriors to calculate Baum-Welch statistics, and the second is to use the bottleneck features in combination with speaker specific features (MFCC) for training the full TV-UBM system. The second approach is considered the most robust to varying conditions [4].

As demonstrated by recent publications [6,8–10,23,24], substantial success of the state-of-the-art text-dependent verification systems is mainly due to the progress in text-independent speaker recognition task. Thus, the success of the phonetic discriminative DNN in such a task leads to attempts to use similar approach in text-dependent systems [5,11,16].

In parallel, there are several studies on the use of Deep-Learning approaches aiming to create an end-to-end solutions for discriminating speakers directly in a text-dependent task [13,14]. Such approaches are easily applicable when the duration of the considered utterances is small, since they can be fed as an input of a deep architecture entirely, for example as a spectrogram.

© Springer International Publishing AG 2017
A. Karpov et al. (Eds.): SPECOM 2017, LNAI 10458, pp. 593–601, 2017.
DOI: 10.1007/978-3-319-66429-3_59

A speaker discriminative approach is the most natural way for speaker verification. [12] describes a DNN for extracting a small speaker footprint which can be used to discriminate between speakers.

In this paper we investigate the deep residual CNN [15] for direct speaker discrimination. Unlike [14] we focus on the use of spectrograms instead of MFCC as the input features and deep but light residual architecture instead of VGG-like network as the mapping.

2   Baseline

A standard i-vector system is used as the baseline in our experiments. The i-vector system models a speech utterance as a low dimensional vector of channel- and speaker-dependent factors using total variability approach, as follows:

$$s = \mu + Tw,$$

where s is the mean supervector, μ is the mean supervector of an Universal Background Model (UBM), T is a low rank matrix and w is the i-vector estimated using the Factor Analysis method [1].

We used implementation of the back-end from [16]. All i-vectors are length normalized and further regularized using the phrase-dependent Within-class Covariance Normalization (WCCN). A simple cosine distance scoring is used followed by phrase-dependent s-norm score normalization [10].

19 Mel-Frequency Cepstral Coefficients (MFCC) + log energy is used as the baseline features. They are normalized by mean and variance and augmented with Δ and $\Delta\Delta$. For this system we did not apply voice activity detection.

3   CNN

3.1   Features

We use the normalized log power magnitude spectrum obtained via Fast Fourier Transform (FFT) as the input acoustic features for this system. Spectrograms are extracted with the following parameters: window size is 256, step size is 64 and Blackman window function is used. Example of such spectrogram is shown in Fig. 1.

The length of the spectrogram along the frequency axis is fixed, but the length along the time axis varies depending on the utterance. However, CNN requires a constant-size image as the input. In order to satisfy this requirement we use the following technique. Images longer than 800 pixels wide are cropped. Images shorter than 800 pixels wide are complimented to the right by their own copy. Such cropping and padding technique is illustrated in Fig. 2.

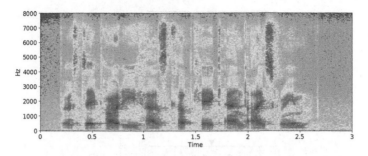

Fig. 1. Log power magnitude spectrum of an utterance corresponding to the phrase "Birthday parties have cupcakes and ice cream"

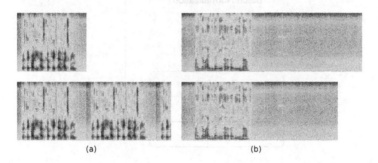

Fig. 2. Spectrogram preprocessing for short (a) and long (b) utterances

3.2   Residual Architecture

Spectrograms, being two-dimensional tensors, can be considered as images and can be processed by methods used for image processing. Currently, the best convolutional architecture for solving image processing tasks is a Residual CNN [15]. Residual architecture is described in [15,20] as a stack of several residual units. Residual unit is a mapping

$$x_{l+1} = x_l + \mathcal{F}(x_l, \mathcal{W}_l),$$

where x_l and x_{l+1} are the unit's input and output. $\mathcal{F}$ consists of two 3×3 convolutions with weights $\mathcal{W}_l$. Additive "shortcut connection" allows the network to satisfy the basic property: adding more layers does not lead to a degradation of the network. Thus, it becomes possible to train very deep networks with a size of 152 or more layers, as shown in the [15]. For this study, a network with 18 layers from [15] with modifications from [20] was used. Network architecture is shown in Table 1. The structure of basic residual block is presented in Fig. 3.

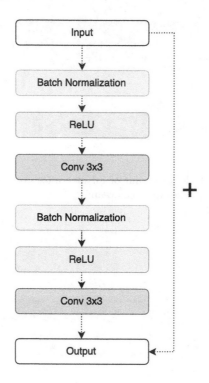

Fig. 3. Residual block

4   Experimental Setup

4.1   RSR2015 Corpus

In our experiments we use the RSR2015 database [7]. The RSR2015 provides data for three main use-case verification scenarios:

- **unique pass-phrase:** each client pronounces the same pass-phrase,
- **user-dependent pass-phrase:** each client pronounces his or her own pass-phrase,
- **prompted text:** each client pronounces a sentence prompted by the system.

In this paper, our focus is on the first use-case where each speaker pronounces a particular sentence. The RSR2015 database contains audio recordings from 300 speakers (143 female and 157 male). There are 9 sessions for each of the participants. Each session consists of 30 short sentences. The database is collected in the office environment using six different portable recording devices (four smartphones and two tablets). Each speaker was recorded using three random different devices out of the six.

The database is randomly split into three non-overlapping groups of speakers, one for background training, one for development stage and one for evaluation

Table 1. Residual CNN architecture

Layer	Kernel/stride	Output	#parameters
Input	–	$257 \times 800 \times 1$	0
Conv+BN+ReLU	$7 \times 7/2 \times 2$	$129 \times 400 \times 64$	3.2K
Maximum pooling	$3 \times 3/2 \times 2$	$65 \times 200 \times 64$	0
Residual block	$3 \times 3/1 \times 1$ $3 \times 3/1 \times 1$	$65 \times 200 \times 64$	74.1K
Residual block	$3 \times 3/1 \times 1$ $3 \times 3/1 \times 1$	$65 \times 200 \times 64$	74.1K
Residual block	$3 \times 3/2 \times 2$ $3 \times 3/1 \times 1$	$33 \times 100 \times 128$	230.1K
Residual block	$3 \times 3/1 \times 1$ $3 \times 3/1 \times 1$	$33 \times 100 \times 128$	296.2K
Residual block	$3 \times 3/2 \times 2$ $3 \times 3/1 \times 1$	$17 \times 50 \times 256$	919.8K
Residual block	$3 \times 3/1 \times 1$ $3 \times 3/1 \times 1$	$17 \times 50 \times 256$	1 182.2K
Residual block	$3 \times 3/2 \times 2$ $3 \times 3/1 \times 1$	$9 \times 25 \times 512$	3 674.7K
Residual block	$3 \times 3/1 \times 1$ $3 \times 3/1 \times 1$	$9 \times 25 \times 512$	4 723.7K
Average pooling	–	512	0
SoftMax	–	97	50K
Total			11 228.0K

stage. The number of male/female speakers is balanced for each group: 50/47 in the background set, 50/47 in the development set and 57/49 in the evaluation set.

We use the background set only for training our speaker verification systems. The development set is used to estimate calibration and fusion parameters. All test trials are performed on the evaluation set.

We focuse only on the scenario where the speaker pronounces correct passphrase. All experiments are conducted according to the part 1 protocols of the RSR2015 database. We consider pooled male and female trials for system performance measure.

Extended training set which contains the background and development sets is used in additional experiment.

4.2   Baseline

Parameters of WCCN matrix and i-vector extractor are estimated using the background subset of the RSR2015 corpus only. As described in [16], we use the following representation of the WCCN matrix:

$$\overline{W} = W + \frac{1}{2}E,$$

where E is the unit matrix of appropriate dimensionality. This trick helps to prevent an overfitting despite the small number of speakers in the background subset.

4.3   CNN

CNN is implemented using the Keras framework [17] on top of the TensorFlow [18] backend. ADAM optimizer [19] with learning rate set at 10^{-4} is used for training

Network is trained to discriminate between all speakers in training set using the softmax layer and categorical cross-entropy loss function. In the evaluation phase an output from the 512-dimensional (same as i-vector) penultimate layer is used as the embedding corresponding to the input utterance.

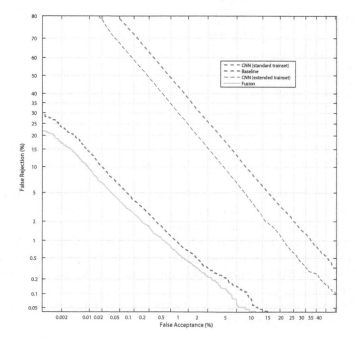

Fig. 4. DET curves for the RSR2015 evaluation part

5 Results and Discussion

The result of our research is presented in Table 2 in terms of the Equal Error Rate (EER) and the minimum detection cost function (minDCF) with $P_{tar} = 10^{-3}$. Baseline system demonstrated a very good result with an EER of less than 1% which is comparable with the result from [16]. Deep CNN system achieved an EER of 6.02%. Fusion of this two systems shows 18% relative improvement over the baseline system which is the evidence of the fact that classic i-vector systems and deep learning systems results in decorrelated embeddings and thus can be used together.

Relatively poor performance of the system under investigation can be explained by the small size of the training set (97 speakers). Such conditions leads to overfitting of discriminative model. The hypothesis is that the deep residual CNN requires much more data for training and expanding training set will lead to a significant increase in accuracy. Experiments on the extended training set (194 speakers) sustains it resulting in an 5.23% EER. We hope that deep learning approaches will be able to outperform the i-vector based systems in the future.

Figure 5 illustrates the projection of CNN embeddings of the 9 randomly chosen speakers on two principal axis using the Principal Component Analysis. DET-curves of the all considered methods are shown in Fig. 4.

Table 2. Evaluation results in terms of EER [%] and minDCF

System	EER	minDCF
Baseline	0.79	0.23
Deep CNN	6.02	0.94
Deep CNN (ext)	5.23	0.92
Fusion	**0.64**	**0.18**

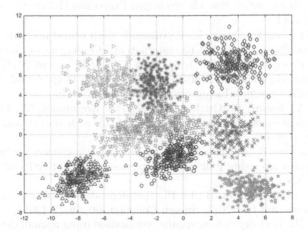

Fig. 5. Projection of embeddings to two main principal axis for 9 speakers

6   Conclusion

In this paper, we presented studies of deep residual CNN architecture in the task of text-dependent verification. Raw normalized spectrograms of speech signals is used as the input features. Experiments conducted on Part 1 of the RSR2015 database showed that despite the small amount of training data, it is possible to train a deep speaker embeddings extractor, which makes it possible to separate the speaker classes fairly well. Best achieved result of the individual system is an 5.23% EER.

We also showed that increasing the amount of training data leads to the expected strengthening of the extractor and improvement of the results. Our future work will be focused on the improving the quality of deep CNN based systems and bringing them to the level of baseline i-vector systems. It can be noted already that fusion of the deep CNN and i-vector extractors gives a good performance gain of 18% relative improvement.

Acknowledgements. This work was financially supported by the Ministry of Education and Science of the Russian Federation, contract 14.578.21.0126 (ID RFMEFI57815X0126).

References

1. Dehak, N., Kenny, P.J., Dehak, R., Dumouchel, P., Ouellet, P.: Front-end factor analysis for speaker verification. IEEE Trans. Audio Speech Lang. Process. **19**(4), 788–798 (2011)
2. Kenny, P., Ouellet, P., Dehak, N., Gupta, V., Dumouchel, P.: A study of inter-speaker variability in speaker verification. IEEE Trans. Audio Speech Lang. Process. **16**(5), 980–988 (2008)
3. Lei, Y., Scheffer, N., Ferrer, L., McLaren, M.: A novel scheme for speaker recognition using a phonetically-aware deep neural network. In: 2014 IEEE International Conference on Acoustics, Speech and Signal Processing (ICASSP), pp. 1695–1699. IEEE, May 2014
4. McLaren, M., Lei, Y., Ferrer, L.: Advances in deep neural network approaches to speaker recognition. In: 2015 IEEE International Conference on Acoustics, Speech and Signal Processing (ICASSP), pp. 4814–4818. IEEE, April 2015
5. Bhattacharya, G., Alam, J., Stafylakis, T., Kenny, P.: Deep Neural Network based Text-Dependent Speaker Recognition: Preliminary Results
6. Stafylakis, T., Kenny, P., Ouellet, P., Perez, J., Kockmann, M., Dumouchel, P.: Text-dependent speaker recognition using PLDA with uncertainty propagation. Matrix 500, 1 (2013)
7. Larcher, A., Lee, K. A., Ma, B., Li, H.: RSR2015: database for text-dependent speaker verification using multiple pass-phrases. In: INTERSPEECH, pp. 1580–1583, September 2012
8. Larcher, A., Lee, K.A., Ma, B., Li, H.: Text-dependent speaker verification: classifiers, databases and RSR2015. Speech Commun. **60**, 56–77 (2014)
9. Aronowitz, H.: Text dependent speaker verification using a small development set. In: Odyssey 2012-The Speaker and Language Recognition Workshop (2012)

10. Novoselov, S., Pekhovsky, T., Shulipa, A., Sholokhov, A.: Text-dependent GMM-JFA system for password based speaker verification. In: 2014 IEEE International Conference on Acoustics, Speech and Signal Processing (ICASSP), pp. 729–737. IEEE, May 2014
11. Matějka, P., Glembek, O., Novotný, O., Plchot, O., Grézl, F., Burget, L., Cernocký, J.H.: Analysis of DNN approaches to speaker identification. In: 2016 IEEE International Conference on Acoustics, Speech and Signal Processing (ICASSP), pp. 5100–5104. IEEE, March 2016
12. Variani, E., Lei, X., McDermott, E., Moreno, I.L., Gonzalez-Dominguez, J.: Deep neural networks for small footprint text-dependent speaker verification. In: 2014 IEEE International Conference on Acoustics, Speech and Signal Processing (ICASSP), pp. 4052–4056. IEEE, May 2014
13. Heigold, G., Moreno, I., Bengio, S., Shazeer, N.: End-to-end text-dependent speaker verification. In: 2016 IEEE International Conference on Acoustics, Speech and Signal Processing (ICASSP), pp. 5115–5119. IEEE, March 2016
14. Zhang, S.X., Chen, Z., Zhao, Y., Li, J., Gong, Y.: End-to-End attention based text-dependent speaker verification. In: 2016 IEEE Spoken Language Technology Workshop (SLT), pp. 171–178. IEEE, December 2016
15. He, K., Zhang, X., Ren, S., Sun, J.: Deep residual learning for image recognition. In: Proceedings of the IEEE Conference on Computer Vision and Pattern Recognition, pp. 770–778 (2016)
16. Zeinali, H., Burget, L., Sameti, H., Glembek, O., Plchot, O.: Deep neural networks and hidden markov models in i-vector-based text-dependent speaker verification. In: Odyssey-The Speaker and Language Recognition Workshop, June 2016
17. Chollet, F.: Keras (2015). http://keras.io
18. Abadi, M., Agarwal, A., Barham, P., Brevdo, E., Chen, Z., Citro, C., Ghemawat, S., et al.: Tensorflow: Large-scale machine learning on heterogeneous distributed systems (2016). arXiv preprint: arXiv:1603.04467
19. Kingma, D., Ba, J.: Adam: a method for stochastic optimization, arXiv preprint: arXiv:1412.6980
20. He, K., Zhang, X., Ren, S., Sun, J.: Identity mappings in deep residual networks. In: Leibe, B., Matas, J., Sebe, N., Welling, M. (eds.) ECCV 2016, Part IV. LNCS, vol. 9908, pp. 630–645. Springer, Cham (2016). doi:10.1007/978-3-319-46493-0_38
21. Novoselov, S., Pekhovsky, T., Kudashev, O., Mendelev, V., Prudnikov, A.: Non-linear PLDA for i-vector speaker verification. In: Proceedings of the Annual Conference of the International Speech Communication Association, INTERSPEECH, pp. 214–218 (2015)
22. Kudashev, O., Novoselov, S., Pekhovsky, T., Simonchik, K., Lavrentyeva, G.: Usage of DNN in Speaker recognition: advantages and problems. In: Cheng, L., Liu, Q., Ronzhin, A. (eds.) ISNN 2016. LNCS, vol. 9719, pp. 82–91. Springer, Cham (2016). doi:10.1007/978-3-319-40663-3_10
23. Novoselov, S., Pekhovsky, T., Shulipa, A., Kudashev, O.: PLDA-based system for text-prompted password speaker verification. In: 2015 12th IEEE International Conference on Advanced Video and Signal Based Surveillance (AVSS), pp. 1–5. IEEE, August 2015
24. Novoselov, S., Sukhmel, V., Sholokhov, A., Pekhovsky, T.: Employment of DTW-based HMM-GMM multi-session training in textdependent speaker verification. J. Instrum. Eng. 57(2), 77–84 (2014). (in Russian)

Perception and Acoustic Features of Speech of Children with Autism Spectrum Disorders

Elena Lyakso$^{(\boxtimes)}$, Olga Frolova, and Aleksey Grigorev

Saint Petersburg State University, Saint Petersburg, Russia
lyakso@gmail.com

Abstract. The goal of our study is to reveal verbal and non-verbal information in speech features of children with autism spectrum disorders (ASD). 30 children with ASD aged 5–14 years and 160 typically developing (TD) coevals were participants in the study. ASD participants were divided into groups according to the presence of development reversals (ASD-1) and developmental risk diagnosed at the birth (ASD-2). The listeners (n = 220 adults) recognized the word's meaning, correspondence of the repetition word's meaning and intonation contour to the sample, age, and gender of ASD child's speech with less probability vs. TD children. Perception data are confirmed by acoustic features. We found significant differences in pitch values, vowels formants frequency and energy between ASD groups and between ASD and TD in spontaneous speech and repetition words. Pitch values of stress vowels were significantly higher in spontaneous speech vs. repetition words for ASD-1 children, ASD-2, and TD children aged 7–12 years. Pitch values in the spontaneous speech of the ASD-1 were higher than in the ASD-2 children. The coarticulation effect was shown for ASD and TD repetition words. Age dynamic of ASD children acoustic features indicated mastering of clear articulation.

Keywords: Acoustic features · Children · Typically developing · Autism spectrum disorders · Repetition speech · Spontaneous speech · Speech perception

1 Introduction

The study of speech of child with autism spectrum disorders (ASD) includes two main problems. On the one hand, disruption of ASD child's communication makes it difficult to obtain speech material [1], on the other, the acoustic features widely used for speech analysis of typically developing (TD) children [2] do not completely reflect the specificity of ASD child speech. ASD is associated with differences in prosody production from monotonous machine-like to variable, exaggerated [3] and abnormal speech spectrum [4]. In some works, the differences between ASD and TD children in average spectra [4], formant frequencies and their energy [5] were revealed. We assume that some of the noted features of ASD child speech are associated with recording situations, language environment, methods of teaching. In our pilot study [5] we indicated clearer articulation and lower pitch values of repetition words vs. words in spontaneous speech in ASD children. At present we use repetition task as model for ASD children speech research. The purpose of our study is to reveal verbal and non-verbal information in speech features of ASD children.

© Springer International Publishing AG 2017
A. Karpov et al. (Eds.): SPECOM 2017, LNAI 10458, pp. 602–612, 2017.
DOI: 10.1007/978-3-319-66429-3_60

2 Method

2.1 Data Collection

Participants in the study were 30 children with ASD (F84 according to ICD-10), biologically aged 5–14 years, mental aged 4–7 years and 160 TD coevals (control). For this study the ASD participants were divided into groups according to developmental features: presence of development reversals at the age 1.5–3.0 years (first group – ASD-1) and developmental risk diagnosed at the infant birth (second group – ASD-2). For these children, the ASD is a symptom of neurological diseases associated with brain damage. The ASD groups don't differ significantly on the base of Child Autism Rating Scale [6] scores and psychophysiological tests on the stage divided child into groups. Places of recording were at home, in the laboratory, kindergarten and school. The situations of speech recording were the play with the standard set of toys, dialogues with parents (for ASD child) and the experimenter, word repetition after experimenter. The recordings were made by the "Marantz PMD222" recorder with a "SENNHEIZER e835S" external microphone.

2.2 Data Analysis

Two types of experimental methods of speech analysis were performed: perceptual (by listeners) and spectrographic.

The aim of the perceptual study is the review of listeners' (Russian native speakers, adults) recognition of the correspondence of the word repeated by the child to the sample by the meaning and intonation contour, child age and gender on the base of speech samples. The test sequences included words from spontaneous speech (n = 4 tests, for 21 samples of ASD test, and for 30 samples of TD test) and repetition words (n = 14 tests, "adult sample – child response" for 35 samples). Repetition tests contained the words with stress vowels /a/, /i/, and /u/. We used two types of test sequences: the first type (tests 1, 3) included words with minimum coarticulation effect for stress vowels; the second type (tests 2, 4) – words with maximum coarticulation effect. The test sequences were presented to listeners (n = 220, age – 18–46, 23.7 ± 6.8y) for perceptual analysis. The factor of the adult's experience of interaction with children (at the household level) was not significant, so all data are presented together.

A special experiment included the listening of two tests (ASD and TD with minimum coarticulation effect) for the group of adults (programmer students). For this control group of listeners (n = 12, age – 24.4 ± 12.6 y; 21–44 y) the phonemic hearing, hearing thresholds, and lateral asymmetry profile were determined. This information was needed to determine individual characteristics of an adult (gender, age, experience with children, hearing, phonemic hearing, the leading hemisphere by ear), which have the greatest impact on their recognition of the speech of children with ASD.

Spectrographic analysis of speech was carried out in the Cool Edit (Syntril. Soft. Corp. USA) sound editor. We analyzed and compared pitch values, max and min values of pitch, pitch range, formants frequency (F1, F2, F3), energy and duration for vowels and stationary part of vowels. The same parameters were compared using the Mann-Whitney U criterion in /a/, /i/ and /u/ after the following consonants: /k/ and /d/

for /a/, /b/ and /g/ for /u/, and /t'/ for /i/. Formant triangles were plotted for vowels with apexes corresponding to the vowels /a/, /u/, and /i/ in F1, F2 coordinates and their areas were compared. Vowel formant triangle areas were calculated [7]. The values of the amplitudes (energy) of pitch and the first three formants of vowels by the dynamic spectrogram were determined. The normalized values of formants amplitude concerning to the amplitude of the pitch (E0/En, where E0 is the amplitude of pitch, En is the amplitude of Fn, (n = 1, 2, 3) were calculated [5]. The intonation contour correspondence in "adult sample – child response" was analyzed in Praat program v.6.20.

All procedures were approved by the Health and Human Research Ethics Committee (HHS, IRB 00003875, St. Petersburg State University) and written informed consent was obtained from parents of the child participant.

3   Result

3.1   Perceptual Data

Word's meaning and intonation contour: Comparative data showed that the majority of listeners (range 0.75–1.0) recognized the meaning of 67% of words of 5–7 years old TD children, 73% of words of TD children aged 7–12 years, 43% of the words of ASD-1 children and 40% of words of ASD-2 children in the test sequences containing the words from spontaneous speech. For those TD children, gender was associated F $(6,734) = 19.333$ p < 0.000, $R^2 = 0.1359$ with F0 values (Beta = 0.2163) and E2/E0 (Beta = -0.6819); age correlated $F(6,737) = 95.256$, p < 0.000, $R^2 = 0.4368$ with F1 values (Beta = -0.2122), F0 values (Beta = -0.1132), and E2/E0 (Beta = 0.1394) – Multiple Regression analysis.

Determining the correspondence of the intonation contour of the child's repeated word to the sample caused greater difficulty for the listeners than determining the meaning of the word. The meaning of TD child words in all tests was recognized by listeners better than intonation contour (Fig. 1A, B).

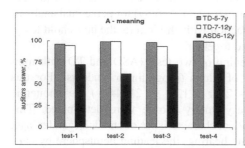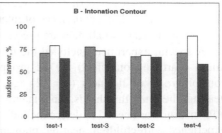

Fig. 1. Correspondence of the word repeated by the child to the sample by the meaning (A) and intonation contour (B)

The coarticulation context (tests 1, 3 and tests 2, 4) doesn't have influence on the recognition of the word's meaning and intonation contour. The exception is the data of test 2 for the correspondence of the word meaning recognition of ASD child (61.8%) vs. the words from test 1 (72.2%), test 3 (72.7%), and test 4 (72.2%).

Gender and age: The second task for listeners in repetition tests was to recognize the child age and gender. In the TD tests the speech of boys and girls is presented equally. Adults identified correctly the gender of the TD children. Exclusion was the test of TD children aged 7–12 years in which 11% of the speech samples belonging to girls were attributed to boys. In the tests of ASD children the number of samples of the speech of boys is greater than that of girls, but listeners indicate a greater number of speech patterns as belonging to girls (Fig. 2A).

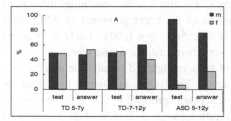 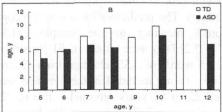

Fig. 2. A – Percentages of boy's and girl's speech samples in test sequences and perceived by listeners as male and female. B – Age of TD children and ASD children recognized by listeners. Horizontal axis – child's real age, vertical axis – age of the child indicated by the listeners

The age of TD children was determined by adults almost correctly, listeners recognized age of ASD children as below the real age (Fig. 2B). These data are confirmed by the results of the control perceptual experiment (Table 1). Two tests were presented to the listeners, each test contained repetition speech of 5–12 years old TD and ASD children.

Table 1. The boy's and girl's speech samples in control tests sequences and perceived by listeners as male and female, percentages

Analysis	Test – (ASD + TD – 1)				Test – (ASD + TD – 2)			
	TD		ASD		TD		ASD	
	m	f	m	f	m	f	m	f
Test	50	50	89	11	50	50	78	22
Answer	52	48	87	13	55	45	83	17

Child age was associated with average pitch values $F(4,272) = 4.077$ $p < 0.000$ (Beta = -0.5712, $R^2 = 0.043$) – Multiple Regression analysis. The predictors for child gender $F(5,271) = 11.2$, $p < 0.0000$ were pitch values (Beta = 0.3081, $R^2 = 0.1712$, $p < 0.000$), values of F1 (Beta = -0.2087, $p < 0.0004$), F2 (Beta = -0.2573, $p < 0.0011$), F3 (Beta = 0.1920, $p < 0.02$).

The result of the special experiment showed that listeners hearing thresholds (the left ear) influenced on the recognition of the correspondence of word meaning of ASD child to the sample $F(4,7) = 2.3752$, $p < 0.1499$ (Beta $= 0.732$ $R^2 = 0.5758$ – Multiple Regression analysis). Correlations (Spearman $p < 0.5$) between the adult's phonemic hearing (the repetition of triples of the syllables) and the recognition of the correspondence of the intonation contour of ASD child words to the sample ($r = 0.673$, $p < 0.5$), the child age determination ($r = 0.632$, $p < 0.5$) were revealed. The listeners' experience of interaction with children influenced ($r = 0.657$, $p < 0.5$) the determination of TD children age. The results of this perceptual experiment correspond to data obtained by other listeners.

The larger amount of control listeners (75–100%) attributed the words of TD children to the category of corresponding by word meaning (95.8%) and intonation contour (70.7%) than words of ASD children (75% and 62.6% - meaning, intonation contour). The predictors for listeners recognition of the correspondence of ASD child word's meaning to the sample $F(1,33) = 9.1548$ $p < 0.004$ (Beta $= -0.4660$ $R^2 = 0.21717$) were values of F1 for stress vowels /a/, /i/, /u/ in the words.

15 words of ASD children from different tests recognized by all listeners (probability 1.0) are included in the new test sequence. This test was listened by 20 adults aged 22 to 81 years (group-1 – n = 6, 22–28 years, group-2 – n = 7, 37–64 years, group-3 – n = 7, 71–81 years). The best recognition (range 0.75–1.0) of the meaning of the words of children listening to the second age group was found, compared with the third one $F(1,12) = 10.348$ $p < 0.007$ (Beta $= -0.6804$, $R^2 = 0.4182$ – Multiple Regression analysis). Adult gender and experience of interaction with children did not have an influence on the recognition of the meaning of ASD child words.

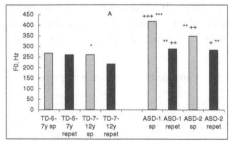 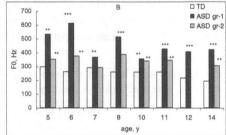

Fig. 3. Pitch values (median) of stress vowels from word for 5–7 years old TD children, TD children 7–12 years, ASD-1 and ASD-2 children (A); pitch values of vowels from words for TD children (white), ASD-1 (black), ASD-2 (gray) in spontaneous speech (B). $*$ – $p < 0.05$, ++**– $p < 0.01$, *** – $p < 0.001$ Mann-Whitney test; differences between: *** ASD-1 sp vs. ASD-1 rep.; ** ASD-2 sp. vs. ASD-2 rep.; ** ASD-1 rep vs. ASD-2 sp; * ASD-2 rep. vs. ASD-1 rep.; * TD 7-12 sp. vs. TD rep.; +++ ASD-1 sp. vs. TD (sp. & rep.); ++ ASD-2 sp., rep. vs. TD (sp. & rep); + ASD-2 rep vs. TD (sp.& rep)

3.2   Acoustic Features of TD vs. ASD Spontaneous vs. Repetition Child Speech

Pitch values of stress vowels were significantly higher in spontaneous speech vs. repetition words for ASD-1 children ($p < 0.001$ Mann-Whitney test), ASD-2 ($p < 0.01$), and TD children aged 7–12 years ($p < 0.05$). Pitch values in the spontaneous speech of the ASD-1 were higher ($p < 0.001$) than in the ASD-2 children (Fig. 3A).

Table 2. Correlation between acoustical features of child speech and child gender, and age, Multiple Regression analysis

Type of speech	Statistical data, Multiple regression analysis		
	Gender	Age	Group (for ASD child)
TD 7-12y spont	$F_{(1,118)} = 10.380$, $p < 0.001$; $R^2 = 0.0809$: F0 max (Beta = 0.2843)	$F_{(6,113)} = 8.6781$ $p < 0.000$, $R^2 = 0.3154$: F3 (Beta = -0.4873); E2/E0 (Beta = -0.3224); E1/E0 (Beta = 0.2013).	
TD 7-12y repet	$F_{(5,94)} = 5.2242$, $R^2 = 0.2175$: F1 (Beta = -0.3065, $p < 0.003$); F3 (Beta = 0.2656, $p < 0.006$)	$F_{(4,95)} = 4.5471$, $R^2 = 0.1669$: F0 (Beta = -0.4044 $p < 0.008$); F2 (Beta = -0.2368, $p < 0.02$)	
ASD spont	$F_{(6,43)} = 10.7$; $R^2 = 0.5983$ $p < 0.000$: F0 (Beta = -0.5895); Vowel duration (Beta = 0.4494)	$F_{(2,48)} = 15.593$; $R^2 = 0.3685$ E0 (Beta = -0.700, $p < 0.000$)	$F_{(5,45)} = 11.947$, $p < 0.000$, $R^2 = 0.5703$: Vowel duration (Beta = 0.4011); F0 (Beta = -0.5720)
ASD repet (test)	$F_{(1,111)} = 5.7635$ $p < 0.01$; Vowel duration - (Beta = 0.2222, $R^2 = 0.04936$); $F_{(2,110)} = 4.003$ $p < 0.02$ F2 (Beta = 0.1910, $R^2 = 0.06784$)	$F_{(4.103)} = 6.2155$ $p < 0.0001$; $R^2 = 0.1944$: F0 (Beta = -0.2872); $F_{(3,107)} = 5.9867$ $p < 0.000$, $R^2 = 0.1437$: F1 (Beta = -0.2317); F3 (Beta = -0.2197); $F_{(2,111)} = 4.7826$ $p < 0.01$ $R^2 = 0.0793$: E2/E0 (Beta = -0.3128); E1/E0 (Beta = 0.4191)	$F_{(1,109)} = 5.2872$ $p < 0.02$; $R^2 = 0.0463$: Vowel duration – (Beta = 0.2151); $F_{(1,110)} = 5.683$, $p < 0.01$ $R^2 = 0.0593$: F0 (Beta = -0.2437); $F_{(1,112)} = 5.7625$ $p < 0.01$; $R^2 = 0.048$: F2 (Beta = 0.2212)

** Coarticulation effect was revealed for values of F2 ($p < 0.01$ – Mann-Whitney U test) of stress vowels /a/ in words.

The differences (p < 0.01) between TD 7–12 years-old boys and girls on the base of pitch values of stress vowels in spontaneous speech were revealed. The pitch in spontaneous speech represented by the ages of all children has high values in ASD-1 and ASD-2 children (Fig. 3B). The first two formant frequencies (acoustic keys for vowel recognition) are less correlated with the individual characteristics of the child (gender and age) than their energy (Table 2).

This finding allows comparing data from different types of child speech without individual age and gender. The formant triangles of vowels for the spontaneous speech differ from the ones for the repetition words (Fig. 4A, B). The largest square of formant triangles for the repetition words vs. spontaneous speech were showed (Fig. 4E). The shifts in the values of the first two formants of vowels, leading to displacement of the formant triangles into the higher-frequency area, were seen for the vowels of ASD-1 children vs. ASD-2 peers in spontaneous speech (Fig. 4A); ASD-2 vs. ASD-1 in the repetition words (Fig. 4B). The words with the vowels with maximum coarticulation effect occupy the large area on the two-coordinate plot (Fig. 4D), the formant triangles

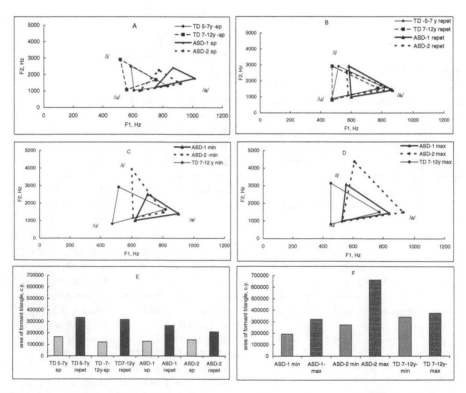

Fig. 4. The vowels formant triangles with apexes /a/, /u/, /i/ for spontaneous words (A), repetition words from tests (B); repetition words with min. coarticulation effect for vowels (C), and repetition words with max coarticulation effect for vowels (D). Areas of vowels formant triangles for repetition and spontaneous speech (E), and for repetition words with min and max coarticulation effect for vowels (F) in conventional units. Horizontal axis values are F1, Hz, vertical axis values are F2, Hz (A, B, C, D)

of these vowels have a larger square (Fig. 4F) than those of the vowels with minimal coarticulation effect (Fig. 4C, F).

We found the specific features of the dynamic spectrum of the stress vowels from the ASD child words. The energy of the third formant higher (p < 0.001) of ASD child vs. TD child. This characteristic more expressed in spontaneous speech vs. repetition words.

3.3   Acoustic Features of the Repetition Words: Longitudinal Data

To confirm the assumption about the clearer articulation in the repetition words and its positive dynamic in the learning, the acoustic characteristics of stress vowels in the words repeated by five children twice at the interval of one year were compared. The significant differences between vowel's pitch values and values of three formant frequencies from the same word repetition by every child twice per year were shown (Table 3).

Table 3. Differences between correspondence features of vowels from the same word repetition by child twice per year, Mann-Whitney U test

Child	CARS [1, 2]	Vowel	F0 average	F0 st.	F1	F2	F3
1	3,5	/a/	0.000		0.002	0.002	0.000
		/u/	0.01	0.01	0.02	0.001	0.000
2	1	/a/	0.01	0.000	0.000	0.02	0.000
		/u/	0.002	0.000	0.000	0.01	0.000
		/i/			0.000		0.004
3	0,5*	/a/	0.000	0.000			0.001
		/u/	0.001	0.005	0.01	0.001	0.000
		/i/				0.01	
4	6**	/a/			0.000	0.000	0.000
		/u/		0.04	0.009		0.000
		/i/	0.02	0.02	0.02		
5	1	/a/			0.003	0.01	0.01
		/u/			0.02		0.2

[CARS1, CARS 2] – the difference in points between the first and second testing of the child, numerals indicated the significance level. *, ** – data are presented in Fig. 5

The coarticulation effect for words with the stressed vowel /i/ is absent. Significant effect (p < 0.002) for the stressed vowel /a/ on the values of F0, for the words with the stressed vowel /u/ on the values of F0 (p < 0.01) and values of F3 (p < 0.006) were revealed. All children accurately repeated a larger number of words by their meaning (p < 0.01) and intonation (p < 0.01) in the second time of repetition. The energy of the third formant for vowels from repetition words with the minimum and maximum coarticulation effect differs between the first and second testing (for max. & min. coarticulation effect). The Fig. 5 presents data for severely autistic child 4 according CARS score with maximal developmental progress (Fig. 5A) and for mildly autistic child 3 with minimal developmental progress (Fig. 5B).

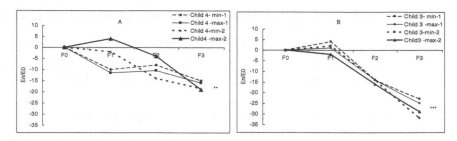

Fig. 5. The distribution of the first three formant amplitudes normalized to the amplitude of the pitch for vowels /a/ in repetition words for two children (A, B). Vertical axis – En/E0 (normalized amplitude), horizontal axis – F0 and formants (F1, F2, F3). Min and max coarticulation effect; 1 – first testing, 2 – second. **– $p < 0.01$, *** – $p < 0.001$ Mann-Whitney U test

4 Discussion

The ability of adults to recognize gender, age, meaning of words, the correspondence of the word's meaning and intonation contour of the child's repeated word to the sample with less determination of ASD child was shown. Perception data are confirmed by acoustic features. We found significant differences in pitch values, vowel formant frequency and energy between ASD groups and between ASD and TD in spontaneous speech and repetition words.

Adults detected the age of children with ASD lower than the actual age that correlated with higher pitch values of ASD children. The association between child age and pitch values was shown in studies [7, 8]. Data on specific non-developmental phonetic and phonological errors of 5–13 year olds with ASD [9] confirm our results on worse word meaning recognition of ASD children vs. TD children. The meaning of the words of TD children was recognized by listeners better than intonation contour. We revealed the ASD child's skills to repeat intonation contour. It was surprising because for emotional speech of our participants with ASD the correlation between emotional state and intonation contour specific for TD children [10] was not revealed [11]. Our data are confirmed by the study of prosodic patterns imitation by ASD children and TD children using more complex task in PEPS-C program [12].

Higher pitch values were described in some studies for the spontaneous speech of ASD children [3]. In our work high pitch values were shown for spontaneous speech and repetition words. Repetition task leads to decrease of pitch values and clear articulation that corresponds with spectral characteristics of ASD children. Repetition task is relevant for ASD children; it is based on the developmental specificity of speech – echolalia [1]. Correct repetition needs the motor program for articulation mastering and using verbal memory that allows use this task for speech training. According to the opinion [13], echolalia can be used for communication in speech-language intervention. The repetition task is one of the ways to obtain a speech material from children with ASD for our future studies including speech corpora for automatic recognition. The finding of our work is the revealing of spectral features, the coarticulation effect and longitudinal data for speech of ASD children.

5 Conclusions

On the base of perceptual experiment the recognition of ASD and TD child age and gender, meaning of words and correspondence of the word's meaning and intonation contour of the child's repeated word to the sample with less recognition of ASD child was revealed. We found significant differences in pitch values, vowel formant frequency and energy between ASD groups and between ASD and TD in spontaneous speech and repetition words. Pitch values of stress vowels were significantly higher in spontaneous speech vs. repetition words for ASD and TD children, in the spontaneous speech of the ASD-1 vs. ASD-2 children. The coarticulation effect was shown for ASD and TD repetition words. Age dynamic of ASD children acoustic features indicated mastering of clear articulation.

Acknowledgements. This study is financially supported by the Russian Foundation for Basic Research (projects 15-06-07852a, 16-06-00024a) and Russian Foundation for Humanitarian Studies (project 17-06-0053a).

References

1. Kanner, L.: Autistic disturbances of affective contact. Nerv. Child. **2**, 217–250 (1943)
2. Vorperian, H., Kent, R.D.: Vowel acoustic space development: a synthesis of acoustic and anatomic data. J. Speech Lang. Hear. Res. **50**(6), 1510–1545 (2007). doi:10.1044/1092-4388 (2007/104)
3. Fusaroli, R., Lambrechts, A., Bang, D., Bowler, D.M., Gaigg, S.B.: Is voice a marker for Autism spectrum disorder? A systematic review and meta-analysis. Autism Res. **10**(3), 384–407 (2017). doi:10.1002/aur.1678
4. Bonneh, Y.S., Levanov, Y., Dean-Pardo, O., Lossos, L., Adini, Y.: Abnormal speech spectrum and increased pitch variability in young autistic children. Front. Hum. Neurosci. **4** (237), 1–7 (2011). doi:10.3389/fnhum.2010.00237
5. Lyakso, E., Frolova, O., Grigorev, A.: A comparison of acoustic features of speech of typically developing children and children with autism spectrum disorders. In: Ronzhin, A., Potapova, R., Németh, G. (eds.) SPECOM 2016. LNCS, vol. 9811, pp. 43–50. Springer, Cham (2016). doi:10.1007/978-3-319-43958-7_4
6. Schopler, E., Reichler, R.J., DeVellis, R.F., Daly, K.: Toward objective classification of childhood autism: childhood autism rating scale (CARS). J. Autism Dev. Disord. **10**(1), 91–103 (1980)
7. Lyakso, E.E., Grigor'ev, A.S.: Dynamics of the duration and frequency characteristics of vowels during the first seven years of life in children. Neurosci. Behav. Physiol. **45**(5), 558–567 (2015). doi:10.1007/s11055-015-0110-z
8. Lee, S., Potamianos, A., Narayanan, S.: Acoustics of children's speech: developmental changes of temporal and spectral parameters. J. Acoust. Soc. Am. **105**(3), 1445–1468 (1999)
9. Cleland, J., Gibbon, F.E., Peppé, S.J., O'Hare, A., Rutherford, M.: Phonetic and phonological errors in children with high functioning autism and Asperger syndrome. Int. J. Speech Lang. Pathol. **12**(1), 69–76 (2010)

10. Lyakso, E., Frolova, O., Dmitrieva, E., Grigorev, A., Kaya, H., Salah, A.A., Karpov, A.: EmoChildRu: emotional child Russian speech corpus. In: Ronzhin, A., Potapova, R., Fakotakis, N. (eds.) SPECOM 2015. LNCS, vol. 9319, pp. 144–152. Springer, Cham (2015). doi:10.1007/978-3-319-23132-7_18
11. Lyakso, E., Frolova, O., Grigorev, A., Sokolova, V., Yarotsaja, K.: Reflection of the emotional state in verbal and nonverbal behavioral of normally developing children and children with autism spectrum disorders. In: Proceeding of the 17th European Conference on Developmental Psychology, 2015, pp. 93–98. Medimond Publishing Company (2016). S908C0327
12. Diehl, J.J., Paul, Rh.: Acoustic differences in the imitation of prosodic patterns in children with autism spectrum disorders. Res. Autism Spectr. Disord. 6(1), 123–134 (2012). doi:10.1016/j.rasd.2011.03.012
13. Saad, A.G., Goldfeld, M.: Echolalia in the language development of autistic individuals: a bibliographical review. Pro. Fono. 21(3), 255–260 (2009). doi:10.1590/S0104-56872009000300013

Phase Analysis and Labeling Strategies in a CNN-Based Speaker Change Detection System

Marek Hrúz[✉] and Petr Salajka

Faculty of Applied Sciences, NTIS - New Technologies for the Information Society,
University of West Bohemia in Pilsen,
Univerzitní 22, 306 14 Pilsen, Czech Republic
{mhruz,salajka}@ntis.zcu.cz

Abstract. In this paper we analyze different labeling strategies and their impact on speaker change detection rates. We explore binary, linear fuzzy, quadratic and Gaussian labeling functions. We come to the conclusion that the labeling function is very important and the linear variant outperforms the rest. We also add phase information from the spectrum to the input of our convolutional neural network. Experiments show that even though the phase is informative its benefit is negligible and may be omitted. In the experiments we use a coverage-purity measure which is independent on tolerance parameters.

Keywords: Convolutional neural network · Speaker change detection · Spectrogram · Labeling · Phase · Coverage-purity measure

1 Introduction

Speaker change detection (SCD) is a relevant task in many applications. It can be beneficial for the process of speaker diarization [1], speaker identification [2], voice activity detection, multimodal processing of audio-visual data [3], etc. A speaker change is an instance in time when the source of the speech signal changes. In general, we might be interested in changes of sources of any audio signal. For example when we are trying to learn features describing a person's voice we might want to know when a background noise such as music is present and when not. In this paper we present a general approach of speaker change detection by the means of Convolutional Neural Network (CNN) that depends on the labeling strategy and thus can be suitable for more tasks. We present different labeling functions and their impact on SCD. In our previous papers [1,4] we used the logarithm of magnitude of a spectrogram of speech as input for the CNN. In this paper we present experiments with added information about the phase of the spectrogram. In theory the added information should benefit the detection process. Also instead of using a DET curve for evaluating our results we use the approach of coverage and purity [2] which is not dependent on a tolerance parameter.

© Springer International Publishing AG 2017
A. Karpov et al. (Eds.): SPECOM 2017, LNAI 10458, pp. 613–622, 2017.
DOI: 10.1007/978-3-319-66429-3_61

2   Previous Work

This work is an extension of our previous papers [1,4] in which we used CNN for SCD. The CNN is given a logarithm of the magnitude of the spectrogram of a 1.4 s audio segment and outputs a value in the interval $\langle 0, 1 \rangle$. The value represents the probability of speaker change in the middle of the analyzed window. In the first experiments we realized that the reference annotations of speech segments from human annotators are imprecise and cannot be used reliably as they are. The imprecisions cause confusions during the training process and the CNN is unable to minimize the loss as desired. We modeled the imprecision with a tolerance labeling which we denoted as binary labeling. It has the form

$$L^B(t) = \begin{cases} 1, & \text{if } \min_i \left(|t - s_i|\right) \leq \tau \\ 0, & \text{otherwise} \end{cases}, \tag{1}$$

where s_i are the annotated speaker change time instances and τ is the tolerance factor. The tolerance factor models the uncertainty of the labeling. It should be however less than the length of the audio segment that the CNN sees. In our case the tolerance factor was chosen to be $\tau = 0.6$.

We then saw that although this labeling strategy is beneficial for the detection process it can be also confusing for the CNN. This is due to the conflicting nature of the labeling. Some spectrograms even though very similar in appearance are sometimes labeled as 0 and sometimes as 1. It mostly happens at the edge of the tolerance. We found out that relaxing the labeling function in a linear way helps a lot and the network is able to regress to these values better. We named this labeling the fuzzy labeling, see Fig. 1. The formula for the labeling function is

$$L^F(t) = \max \left(0, 1 - \frac{\min_i \left(|t - s_i|\right)}{\tau} \right). \tag{2}$$

With this setup we were able to achieve much better results. They are summarized in Table 1. We also provide Equal Error Rate (EER) for a system based on Bayesian Information Criterion (BIC). In our previous experiments [4] we found out the best setting for BIC was to use window size of 0.7 s (BIC-0.7 in Table 1). To compute the EER we used a tolerance of ±0.2 s.

Table 1. EER values for different systems

System	BIC-0.7	CNN-binary	CNN-fuzzy
EER	0.3229	0.2482	0.1747

The CNN proved to be a suitable model for SCD from the magnitude of spectrogram data. Since the fuzzy labeling had such an impact on the detection rate, we want to test other labeling functions and compare their experimental results.

3   Convolutional Neural Network

In this paper we use the same architecture and learning processes of the CNN as in our previous works. The CNN consists of three triplets of layers and two fully connected layers. Each triplet of layers is a convolutional layer with ReLU activation function, followed by a max pooling layer [5] and normalized by a batch normalization layer [6]. The last two layers are fully connected with 4000 neurons and 1 output neuron both with sigmoidal activation functions. The architecture is summarized in Table 2.

Table 2. Summary of the architecture of the CNN

Layer	Kernels	Size	Shift
Convolution	50	16×8	2×2
Max pooling		2×2	2×2
Batch Norm			
Convolution	200	4×4	1×1
Max pooling		2×2	2×2
Batch Norm			
Convolution	300	3×3	1×1
Max pooling		2×2	2×2
Batch Norm			
Fully Connected	4000		
Fully Connected	1		

3.1   Training of the CNN

For the training of the CNN we use the binary cross-entropy loss

$$\text{loss}(\omega) = -\frac{1}{N} \sum_{n=1}^{N} \left[y_n \log \hat{y}_n + (1 - y_n) \log(1 - \hat{y}_n) \right], \tag{3}$$

where y_n is the desired output, $\hat{y}_n$ is the output of the CNN, and ω are the parameters of the net - weights and biases. The desired output is a number between $\langle 0, 1 \rangle$ given by the labeling function $L(t)$. The criterion is minimized

$$\omega^* = \arg \min_{\omega} [\text{loss}(\omega)], \tag{4}$$

with the Stochastic Gradient Descent (SGD) on mini-batches of data. The batch size was set to 64. We used the Nesterov momentum [7] in the gradient updates, which has been shown to yield good results [8]. Similar to [5] we use momentum of 0.9, weight decay of 0.0005, and learning rate of 0.01.

4   Data

For the training and testing purposes we used a fraction of telephone conversation data from CallHome [9] corpus. The data are sampled at 8 kHz and are in English. We consider only the conversations where two speakers are present. For all experiments the data are split into 35 conversations for training which is 5 h and 48 min and the remaining 77 conversations for testing which is 11 h and 20 min. The CNN uses 1.4 s long windows of the audio signal. The original input is the logarithm of the magnitude of the spectrogram of the speech. The spectrogram was computed on overlapping Hamming windows and for each window 512 frequencies were computed. We utilize only half of the frequencies since the spectrum is symmetrical. Thus the input is a matrix with 256 rows (frequencies) and 134 columns (number of overlapping windows in 1.4 s).

4.1   Phase Information

The phase of the spectrum is omitted in our original experiments. Since there exist reports [10] that indicate that the phase of the spectrum is important in speaker identification tasks we wanted to analyze its impact on SCD. In general, the spectrum is computed as a Fourier transform of the input signal which yields results in complex numbers. When the magnitude of the spectrum is computed the phase is not reflected at all. Geometrically speaking, when we imagine the complex numbers as vectors in a 2D plane, the magnitude is the length of the vector and the phase is the angle between the real x-axis and the vector. It is computed as

$$\theta = \arctan \frac{Im(x)}{Re(x)}, \tag{5}$$

where θ is the phase, $Im(x)$ is the imaginary part of a complex number x and $Re(x)$ is the real part. When computing the phase of the spectrogram there is a problem with the arctan function which outputs the angle in interval $\langle -\pi, \pi \rangle$. When presented to other algorithms which rely on the numerical representations such as CNNs this can result in problems. The most notable one is when we are computing angle differences. Consider two angles $\alpha = \pi - \epsilon$ and $\beta = -\pi + \epsilon$, where ϵ is a small number. Intuitively the angles are very close (in this case 2ϵ) but when computed numerically as an absolute difference then the result will be $|\alpha - \beta| = |\pi - \epsilon + \pi - \epsilon| = 2\pi - 2\epsilon$. That is why the angle directly cannot be successfully used. There are some approaches that try to handle this issue, for example group delay or phase delay. However, these approaches are also not ideal for representing the phase for a CNN.

We chose three representations of the phase information as an input for the CNN. The first approach P_1 is the most direct one. We represent the complex spectrogram as a 2-channel data stream in the form of a matrix $2 \times 256 \times 134$. In the first channel there is the real part of a complex number and in the second channel there is the imaginary part. In this case the filters in the first convolutional layer also become 2-channeled. Thus, the channels are handled as dependent signals. The second approach P_2 adds the phase information to the already present magnitude information. The phase is represented as the cosine and sine components of the complex number. This enables to compute the phase difference as euclidean distance which might be more suitable data representation for the neural network than the original angle θ. The input matrix becomes 3-channeled. In the first channel there is the magnitude and in the second and third channel there is the cosine and sine component respectively. The third approach P_3 of phase representation is a modification of the second one, where we put the logarithm of the magnitude into the first channel.

4.2   Labeling of Data

The base for the computation of the labeling functions are the annotations created by humans. The annotations are a binary signal in time, where zero indicates no speaker change and one indicates a speaker change. We can represent this annotations as a set of time points $\{s_i\}_{i=1}^{N}$ where N is the total number of speaker changes for the given audio. We design two new non linear labeling functions to test against the linear fuzzy labeling function. The first one is the quadratic form of the linear fuzzy labeling function.

$$L^Q(t) = \max(0, 1 - \frac{\min_i (|t - s_i|)^2}{\tau^2}).$$

(6)

The second one is a Gaussian form

$$L^G(t) = \exp\left(-\frac{\min_i (|t - s_i|)^2}{2\sigma^2}\right),$$

(7)

where

$$\sigma^2 = \frac{-\tau^2}{2\log(\epsilon)},$$

(8)

and ϵ is a small constant which represent the desired output of the function $L^G(t)$ at the tolerance distance τ from the nearest annotation s_i. In our case $\epsilon = 0.09$. The labeling functions can be seen in Fig. 1.

5   Experiment

We want to find experimentally the best combination of labeling and phase representation. For each combination we train a different CNN. The individual networks have the same architecture except the first layer which is dependent on the size of the input. The number of filters stays the same but they have different number of channels. The training data from which different phase representations are calculated is the same for each CNN and they are tested on the same set of data. The training and testing data are two disjoint sets. The CNNs are trained

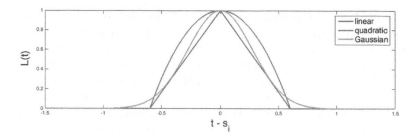

Fig. 1. Different labeling functions. The functions represent the target values for the CNN. On the x-axis is the distance from the nearest speaker change

for the same amount of iterations, which is approximately 13 epochs. The hyperparameters of the training are fixed. The CNNs output a probability of speaker change in the given time. We detect local peaks in this signal and then use a threshold to generate the segments. We measure the coverage and purity of the CNN generated segmentations against the reference annotations. The larger the values of both coverage an purity the better results we have achieved. A perfect result has both coverage and purity equal to one. We compute it for different thresholds. Given R the set of reference speech segments, and H the set of hypothesized segments, coverage is:

$$\text{coverage}(R, H) = \frac{\sum_{r \in R} \max_{h \in H} |r \cap h|}{\sum_{r \in R} |r|}, \tag{9}$$

where $|s|$ is the duration of segment s and $r \cap h$ is the intersection of segments r and h. A segment is a time interval between two subsequent speaker changes. Purity is the dual metric where the roles of R and H are interchanged. Oversegmentation (i.e. detecting too many speaker changes) would result in high purity but low coverage, while missing lots of speaker changes would decrease purity, which is critical for subsequent speech turn agglomerative clustering [2].

Coverage-purity curve is created by connecting the coverage-purity points. These points are obtained by varying the value of the threshold used to detect the speaker change instances. Regularly distributed thresholds produced highly irregularly distributed coverage-purity points. Because of that we decided to use a simple threshold choosing algorithm to produce more regularly distributed coverage-purity points. We assume that the threshold is limited as $t \in \langle 0, 1 \rangle$. First, we compute points for thresholds $t = 0$ and $t = 1$. Then, the following algorithm can be repeated until the required quality of the curve is obtained. We find two neighboring points, p_0 and p_1, with the largest euclidean distance $d = |p_1 - p_0|$ in the coverage-purity space. We do not know the true projection $t \to (c, p)$. Therefore, using a linear approximation the threshold for the new point will be $t = (t_{p_0} + t_{p_1})/2$. At first, the approximation looks raw, but as the count of points increases, it results in a smooth curve. The process is visualized in Fig. 2.

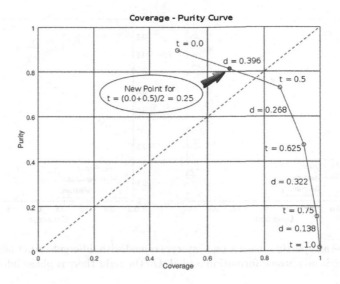

Fig. 2. Visualization of the choosing of the new threshold for the coverage-purity curve approximation

First we tested the impact of labeling on the CNN trained from the original input of logarithm of magnitude of the spectrogram (see Fig. 3 on the left) and from the phase input represented by real and imaginary parts of the spectrum - P_1 (see Fig. 3 on the right).

In Table 3 we show the performance of the systems in the means of equal coverage and purity and their respective thresholds. It turns out that the non linear versions of labeling perform notably worse than their linear counterpart. This is the case in both scenarios with and without the phase information. This leads to a conclusion that in this format of SCD the labeling function is very important. The linear version of labeling (denoted as fuzzy) is better by a margin. Also the thresholds resulting in equal coverage-purity are closer to 0.5 as expected.

Table 3. C-P equal values for different systems

Labeling	Linear	Quadratic	Gaussian
C-P	0.8	0.745	0.741
threshold	0.4	0.19	0.19
C-P phase	0.79	0.73	0.73
threshold	0.51	0.12	0.18

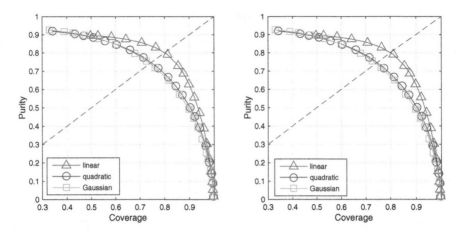

Fig. 3. Coverage-purity measure on systems trained with different target labellings. On the left there is no phase information added. On the right there is phase information P_1

In the next experiment we want to investigate the impact of phase information on the detection process. As mentioned before we represent the phase in three ways. The first way denoted P_1 is representing the complex spectrogram as a 2-channel matrix. The second approach P_2 uses magnitude and the cosine and sine components of the complex number resulting into 3-channel matrix. The last approach P_3 is used to investigates the importance of logarithm applied to the magnitude of the spectrogram in the first channel. We use the fuzzy labeling function L^F as the target.

Table 4. C-P equal values for different phase representations

Phase	None	P_2	P_3
C-P	0.8	0.802	0.803
threshold	0.4	0.45	0.36

As can be seen in Fig. 4 and Table 4 the phase information gives a slightly better results. The improvement is negligible and it seems that the CNN cannot benefit from the phase information. The logarithm of the magnitude also improves the results but again not significantly. It may be concluded that in this setup the phase information is not crucial for the SCD.

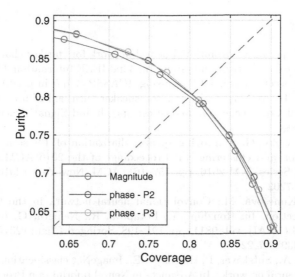

Fig. 4. Coverage-purity measure on systems trained with only magnitude data and magnitude-phase data represented as P_1 and P_2. The target is the linear fuzzy labeling function L^F

6 Conclusion

In this paper we have investigated different labeling functions and their impact on the CNN-based SCD. We also incorporated the phase information from the spectrogram into the input of the CNN-based SCD system and evaluated its added value. We have found out that the linear fuzzy labeling function outperforms other forms of labeling significantly. Also the threshold used for generating the speaker change instances is closer to 0.5 leaving more room for fine tuning the system depending on the usage of the SCD. When a lower threshold is selected we obtain good purity and a higher threshold results in higher coverage.

The experiments with the phase information showed that even though there is a slight improvement in the coverage-purity curve, one has to weight the impact. The load of the CNN rises, more memory is needed to store the weights of the CNN and the input. The threshold generating equal coverage-purity for the phase information represented as P_2 is closest to 0.5. The experiments with the phase also showed that the representation of the phase is important. P_2 and P_3 representations outperformed the P_1 representation. This is highly dependent on the type of network we used. Other approaches that do not use convolutional layers may benefit from other representations.

Acknowledgment. This research was supported by the Grand Agency of the Czech Republic, project No. P103/12/G084. We would also like to thank the grant of the University of West Bohemia, project No. SGS-2016-039. Access to computing and storage facilities owned by parties and projects contributing to the National Grid Infrastructure MetaCentrum, provided under the programme "Projects of Large Research, Development, and Innovations Infrastructures" (CESNET LM2015042), is greatly appreciated.

References

1. Hrúz, M., Zajíc, Z.: Convolutional neural network for speaker change detection in telephone speaker diarization system. In: 42nd IEEE International Conferecnce on Acoustics, Speech and Signal Processing, ICASSP (2017, in press)
2. Bredin, H.: TristouNet: triplet loss for speaker turn embedding. In: 42nd IEEE International Conferecnce on Acoustics, Speech and Signal Processing, ICASSP (2017, in press)
3. Bredin, H., Gelly, G.: Improving speaker diarization of TV series using talking-face detection and clustering. In: Proceedings of the 2016 ACM on Multimedia Conference, Series, MM 2016, pp. 157–161. ACM, New York (2016). doi:10.1145/2964284.2967202
4. Hrúz, M., Kunešová, M.: Convolutional neural network in the task of speaker change detection. In: Ronzhin, A., Potapova, R., Németh, G. (eds.) SPECOM 2016. LNCS (LNAI), vol. 9811, pp. 191–198. Springer, Cham (2016). doi:10.1007/978-3-319-43958-7_22
5. Krizhevsky, A., Sutskever, I., Hinton, G.E.: ImageNet classification with deep convolutional neural networks. In Advances in Neural Information Processing Systems, pp. 1106–1114 (2012)
6. Ioffe, S., Szegedy, C.: Batch normalization: accelerating deep network training by reducing internal covariate shift. CoRR, abs/1502.03167 (2015)
7. Nesterov, Y.: A method of solving a convex programming problem with convergence rate O (1/k2). Soviet Math. Doklady **27**(2), 372–376 (1983)
8. Sutskever, I., Martens, J., Dahl, G., Hinton, G.: On the importance of initialization and momentum in deep learning. In Proceedings of the 30th International Conference on International Conference on Machine Learning, ICML 2013, vol. 28, pp. 1139–1147 (2013)
9. Canavan, A., Graff, D., Zipperlen, G.: CALLHOME American English Speech LDC97S42. Linguistic Data Consortium, DVD, Philadelphia (1997)
10. Oo, Z., Kawakami, Y., Wang, L., Nakagawa, S., Xiao, X., Iwahashi, M.: DNN-based amplitude and phase feature enhancement for noise robust speaker identification. In: INTERSPEECH 2016, 17th Annual Conference of the International Speech Communication Association, San Francisco, CA, USA, 8–12 September 2016, pp. 2204–2208 (2016)

Preparing Audio Recordings of Everyday Speech for Prosody Research: The Case of the ORD Corpus

Tatiana Sherstinova[(✉)]

Saint Petersburg State University,
Universitetskaya nab. 11, St. Petersburg 199034, Russia
t.sherstinova@spbu.ru

Abstract. Studying prosody is important for understanding many linguistic, pragmatic, and discourse phenomena, as well as for solution of many applied tasks (in particular, in speech technologies). Prosody of everyday speech is extremely diverse, demonstrating high interpersonal and intrapersonal variations. Furthermore, natural everyday speech produces a multitude of effects which are hardly possible to obtain in speech laboratories. Because of this fact, it is very important to create resources containing representative collections of everyday speech data. The ORD corpus is a large resource aimed at studying everyday Russian speech. The paper describes the main stages of speech processing in the ORD corpus starting from segmentation of original files into macroepisodes and up to compiling prosody information into the database. This prosody database will be further used for building empirical prosody models.

Keywords: Russian · Everyday speech · Phonetics · Prosody · Duration · Pitch · Sociolinguistics · Communication settings · Pragmatics · Speech corpus

1 The ORD Corpus and Its Data

Studying prosody is important for understanding many linguistic, pragmatic, and discourse phenomena [1–8, etc.], as well as for solution of many applied tasks (in particular, in speech technologies) [9–13]. Prosody of everyday speech is extremely diverse, demonstrating high interpersonal and intrapersonal variations. At the same time prosody may be considered to be central in the interpretation of everyday spoken language [14], as it can completely change the meaning of utterances.

Natural everyday speech produces a multitude of effects which are hardly possible to obtain in speech laboratories [15]. Because of this fact, it is very important to create resources containing representative collections of everyday speech data.

The ORD corpus is a large resource aimed at studying everyday Russian speech. For collecting speech data for the ORD corpus the methodology of longitudinal recordings is used [16–18], for which the participants-volunteers have to spend a whole day with turned-on voice recorders that record all their audible communications. This methodology can be compared with a daily cardio monitoring, which is widely practiced in medicine.

© Springer International Publishing AG 2017
A. Karpov et al. (Eds.): SPECOM 2017, LNAI 10458, pp. 623–631, 2017.
DOI: 10.1007/978-3-319-66429-3_62

The ORD corpus was started in 2007 [19]. Recently it was expanded significantly due to the support of the Russian Science Foundation in the framework of the project 'Everyday Russian Language in Different Social Groups' [20]. Nowadays, the corpus contains more than 1250 h of recordings which refer to about 2800 communicative episodes. Those are the recordings of 128 respondents and more than 1000 of their interlocutors, representing different social strata and different gender, age and professional groups of residents of a big Russian city.

The recordings were made in St. Petersburg, Russia in 2007–2016. Speech was recorded in diverse communication settings: the recordings were made at home, in the offices, outdoors, in service centers, in universities and colleges, in coffee bars and restaurants, in transport, in shops, in parks, etc. [19]. Text transcripts are made for 480 communicative episodes (17% audio recordings of corpus) and number 1 million of word usages [21].

All ORD recordings are supplied by sociological information concerning more than 1000 people recorded for the corpus. It allows to make search queries for speech of people with diverse social characteristics.

The ORD collection provides valuable research data for many other interdisciplinary studies like anthropological linguistics, behavioral and communication studies, studies in pragmatics, discourse analysis, psycholinguistics, and forensic phonetics.

Since ORD recordings are not "laboratory speech", only a part of gathered audio data is suitable for phonetic and prosody research. On average, there is only about 1/10 of all macroepisodes, the quality of which allows to conduct phonetic analysis of speech. The paper describes the main stages of speech processing in the ORD corpus: segmentation into macroepisodes, audio conversion, transcribing, segmentation onto words and syllables, obtaining prosody information and its implementation into the database.

2   The Main Stages of Speech Processing in the ORD Corpus

2.1   Segmentation into Macroepisodes

First of all, having received 8–14 h of recordings from each respondent, we are faced with the task to segment it into fragments, which are homogeneous in terms of communication settings (united by setting/scene of communication, social roles of participants and their general activity). We call such fragments "macroepisodes" [22].

Before segmentation, all files are subjected to audio conversion to the format adopted in the corpus: PCM, 22050 Hz, 16 bit, mono. The original recordings are kept in the archive.

The task of segmentation of audio recordings into macroepisodes is performed manually by linguists, who listen all gathered files, defining at the same time the boundaries between episodes. Further, the researchers save each macroepisode into a separate file, make a standardized description for each file in the database, and cut out all "pauses" (i.e., segments not containing speech which are longer than 5 min) from each audio file.

The methodology of macroepisode annotation was described in [22]. Thus, each macroepisode gets both verbal and standardized descriptions in three aspects: (1) Where does the situation take place? (2) What are the participants doing? (3) Who is (are) the main interlocutor(s). In addition, a concise description of the episode may be given in an auxiliary database field called *SceneName*. The duration of each file is indicated in the database, too.

The phonetic quality of each macroepisode is evaluated and measured in a 4-grade scale: 1 – the best quality, suitable for precise phonetic/prosody analysis, 2 – rather good quality, which is partially suitable for phonetic analysis, 3 – noisy recordings of intermediate and low quality, which are not suitable for phonetic analysis but are suitable enough for other aspects of research, and 4 – unintelligible conversations or remarks in extreme noise, which could not be understood without noise reduction techniques [23].

At this stage, macroepisodes, which are to be transcribed, are selected with a priority indication of their ranks in the database. When choosing files for transcribing, phonetic quality is usually considered, however, it is not the only factor that is taken into account (the other important causes may be linguistic, pragmatic or discourse peculiarities of the recorded data, as well as anthropological issues).

2.2   Speech Transcribing and Primarily Annotation

Selected macroepisodes are further subjected to transcribing and primarily multilevel annotation both of which are made in ELAN [24]. The main principles for transcribing and annotating are described in [19].

Besides speech transcripts and the correspondent anonymized codes of speakers, primarily annotation contains the following information: (1) voice quality (e.g., hoarse, whisper, scanning, irritated, imitating, ironical, dramatic, etc.); (2) non-language audio events (dog barking, squeak of a door, phone ring, etc.); and (3) "miniepisodes", which are minor communicational units homogeneous either by the topic of conversation or by its main pragmatic task [25]. Other linguistic, pragmatic or discourse comments are to be written on layers *FraseComment* and *Notes*.

Here, it should be mentioned that in the first transcripts of the corpus, there was only one level reserved for speech transcription in the annotation template. The multiple cases of overlapping speech were marked by special symbols # and @ in linearized transcript [ibid.]. This form of transcript is convenient enough for further linguistic annotation, however it does not reflect the audio reality in fragments with overlapping speech.

Because of that fact, since 2014 we practice multilevel speech transcribing similar to that used in Conversational Analysis, when each participant of the recorded conversation has his own level for transcription. In order to maintain compatibility with previous transcripts of the corpus, currently we practice both versions of transcribing: being initially made in a linear form, speech transcription is later converted into its multilevel variant.

Transcripts are made manually by linguists in ELAN, each transcript being then checked and approved by two or three experts. After that, the files are subjected to automatic processing.

2.3   Automatic Processing of Transcripts

Further, all annotation files are processed by means of *Corrector* software utility, specially developed for the ORD corpus. It was designed to automatically fix possible technical drawbacks in transcripts (e.g., to remove extra spaces), and to reveal possible mismatch between the levels of speech and speakers that may occur in cases of overlapping speech. Such a situation is often encountered in everyday conversations, making it very difficult to analyze speech. In cases where such discrepancies were detected, manual expert correction of the corresponding fragments is made followed by another launch of *Corrector* utility. This is a necessary step for further processing of annotation files.

After that, annotation files are processed by another ORD utility – *Eafer* program – with the help of which the linear one-level transcript is converted into several layers, each of which referring to one participant of the conversation. This approach allows to separate speech from different speakers, no matter how many people are participating in the conversation and to which social groups they belong.

At the next stage, the boundaries of annotation boxes are to be manually adjusted on fragments with overlapping speech. This procedure is made directly in ELAN. After that, the annotation files are ready for phonetic transcribing and segmentation.

2.4   Phonetic Transcribing and Segmentation

Phonetic transcribing of ORD transcripts is made automatically with the use of software specially designed for this purpose by Speech Technology Center [26].

The following set of allophones is used:
[a0], [a1], [a2], [a4], [o0], [o1], [o4], [e0], [e1], [y0], [y1], [y4], [u0], [u1], [u4], [i0], [i1], [i4], [b], [b'], [p], [p'], [d], [d'], [t], [t'], [g], [g'], [k], [k'], [c], [ch], [v], [v'], [f], [f'], [z], [z'], [s], [s'], [zh], [sh], [sc], [h], [h'], [m], [m'], [n], [n'], [l], [l'], [r], [r'], [j].

The numbers after vowels have the following meanings: 0 – stressed, 1 – pre-stressed, 4 – post-stressed. For /a/, in addition, the second pre-stressed position [a2] is distinguished.

For transcribing, the software uses the typical algorithm of conversion of text into sequence of allophones. Besides, it can distinguish different variants of word pronunciation, which are described in the Lexicon of exceptions.

For example, for the frequent Russian word "*sejchas*" ("*now*"), the transcription based on standard rules will be [s'i1jcha0s], but this full form rarely occurs in spontaneous speech. Instead, two other variants are usually used: [s'i1cha0s] and [sca0s]. Because of that, all non-standard forms should be listed in the Lexicon. When a program comes across any word from this list, its decision on its pronunciation is based on statistical variability of each variant which is calculated on the base of comparison of audio data from the corresponding wave segment with the variants described in the Lexicon.

The other important function of this software is to segment audio file into words and allophones. Actually, it means to define segment boundaries on these two levels. Technologically, the algorithm is also based on the usage of statistical probabilities [27], which takes into account three following aspects: acoustic data, speech transcript, and the Lexicon.

The program has two files as input: (1) audio file, and (2) ELAN-annotation file with the level of speech transcript, on which each utterance is referred to correspondent time segment. The result of the program is the updated ELAN-annotation file, which has two additional levels – for words and allophone segments (see Fig. 1).

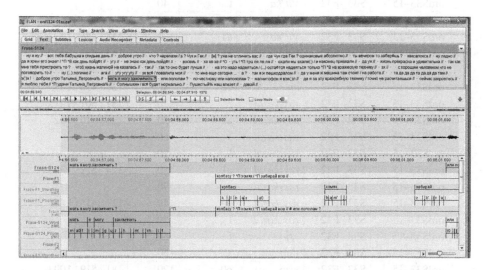

Fig. 1. Multilevel speech annotation in ELAN with its segmentation into words and allophones

The efficiency of this software depends to a large extent on the phonetic quality of the recorded signal. Thus, low level of recording, background noise or overlapping speech significantly worsen the results. As for the accuracy of segment boundaries, it is typically better on neutral speech fragments rather than on emotional speech, which is frequently characterized by a significant prolongation of sounds, unforeseen by the model, and therefore requiring expert correction. Generally, the use of this software allows to significantly reduce the labor costs for manual speech segmentation.

2.5 Duration, Pitch, and Intensity

The information on the duration of speech segments is easily obtained from segmentation data.

Recently, the new version of the utility described in the previous section has been developed by Speech Technology Center. Beside graphic interface, it has got new facilities allowing to automatically get the information concerning the mean values of F0, F1 and F2 measured in Hz.

Therefore, two prosody parameters – allophone duration and its average pitch – may be easily calculated for any allophone and further exported into the database.

For illustrative purposes, the example of such information for one phrase – *Vit'ka mne rasskazal vsjo pro jelektronnye sigarety [Vitka told me everything about electronic cigarettes]* – is presented in Table 1.

Table 1. The fragment of the table ALLOPHONES from the ORD Database

Macro-episode	SC	Phrase	Word	Allophone	Dur (ms)	F0	F1	F2
ordS33–15	S33	F32	*Vit'ka*	v'	70	122	384	1693
ordS33–15	S33	F32	*Vit'ka*	i0	140	185	446	1614
ordS33–15	S33	F32	*Vit'ka*	t'	40			
ordS33–15	S33	F32	*Vit'ka*	k	70			
ordS33–15	S33	F32	*Vit'ka*	a4	30	158	446	1401
ordS33–15	S33	F32	*mne*	m	40	145	443	1522
ordS33–15	S33	F32	*mne*	n'	60	139	458	1755
ordS33–15	S33	F32	*mne*	e0	40	137	493	1579
ordS33–15	S33	F32	*rasskazal*	r	50	131	501	1415
ordS33–15	S33	F32	*rasskazal*	a2	30	128	510	1321
ordS33–15	S33	F32	*rasskazal*	s	60			
ordS33–15	S33	F32	*rasskazal*	k	80			
ordS33–15	S33	F32	*rasskazal*	a1	50	124	512	1308
ordS33–15	S33	F32	*rasskazal*	z	90			
ordS33–15	S33	F32	*rasskazal*	a0	40	117	515	1443
ordS33–15	S33	F32	*rasskazal*	l	70			
ordS33–15	S33	F32	*vsjo*	f	60			
ordS33–15	S33	F32	*vsjo*	s'	160			
ordS33–15	S33	F32	*vsjo*	o0	120	181	519	1093
ordS33–15	S33	F32	*pro*	p	100			
ordS33–15	S33	F32	*pro*	r	50	117	435	1314
ordS33–15	S33	F32	*pro*	a2	30	117	454	1435
ordS33–15	S33	F32	*jelektronnye*	y1	30	113	448	1687
ordS33–15	S33	F32	*jelektronnye*	l'	70	109	387	1621
ordS33–15	S33	F32	*jelektronnye*	i1	30	107	415	1584
ordS33–15	S33	F32	*jelektronnye*	k	40			
ordS33–15	S33	F32	*jelektronnye*	t	70			
ordS33–15	S33	F32	*jelektronnye*	r	60	117	471	1168
ordS33–15	S33	F32	*jelektronnye*	o0	80	119	473	1069
ordS33–15	S33	F32	*jelektronnye*	n	60	120	323	1115
ordS33–15	S33	F32	*jelektronnye*	y4	45	117	404	1273
ordS33–15	S33	F32	*jelektronnye*	i4	45	111	472	1462
ordS33–15	S33	F32	*sigarety*	s'	110			
ordS33–15	S33	F32	*sigarety*	i1	30			
ordS33–15	S33	F32	*sigarety*	g	77			
ordS33–15	S33	F32	*sigarety*	a1	83	97	558	1652
ordS33–15	S33	F32	*sigarety*	r'	60	91	436	1772
ordS33–15	S33	F32	*sigarety*	e0	80	83	439	1744
ordS33–15	S33	F32	*sigarety*	t	120			
ordS33–15	S33	F32	*sigarety*	a4	110			

In particular, it contains data referring to (1) macroepisode (i.e., sound file), which is a link to the information on communication settings; (2) speaker's code (SC), which is a link to sociolinguistic information about speakers; (3) the phrase itself; (4) word; (5) allophone; (6) correspondent boundaries (not shown in Table 1); (7) allophone duration; (8) average pitch; (9) average F1; and (10) average F2.

As for the detailed dynamics of pitch and the intensity, they may be analyzed in Praat [28] after exporting annotation data from ELAN to TextGrid.

3   Conclusion

It this concise review, we have described the main points of preparation of the ORD audio data to prosody research. In the result of such processing, the prosodic data are accumulated in the corpus database, where they can be linked with other relevant information (linguistic, pragmatic and discourse). Therefore, it will be possible to analyze speech with specified parameters (e.g., recorded in a specific place, under specific circumstances, by a speaker of specific characteristics, etc.). The compiled prosody database will be further used for building empirical prosody models. Besides, it seems particularly perspective to combine prosody information with pragmatic annotation of speech acts [29].

Acknowledgements. The creation of the ORD speech corpus was supported by several grants: Russian Foundation for Humanities projects No. 07–04–94515e/Ya (Speech Corpus of Russian Everyday Communication "One Speaker's Day") and No. 12–04–12017 (Information System of Communication Scenarios of Russian Spontaneous Speech), the Russian Ministry of Education project "Sound Form of Russian Grammar System in Communicative and Informational Approach". Significant extension of the corpus and the software development was achieved in the framework the project "Everyday Russian Language in Different Social Groups" supported by the Russian Science Foundation, project No. 14–18–02070.

References

1. Couper-Kuhlen, E.: English Speech Rhythm: Form and Function in Everyday Verbal Interaction. John Benjamins Publications, Amsterdam (1993)
2. Couper-Kuhlen, E., Selting, M. (eds.): Prosody in conversation: Interactional studies. Cambridge University Press, Cambridge (1996)
3. Wells, B., Macfarlane, S.: Prosody as an interactional resource: turn-projection and overlap. Lang. Speech **41**, 265–294 (1998)
4. Klatt, D.H.: Linguistic uses of segmental duration in English: acoustic and perceptual evidence. J. Acoust. Soc. Am. **59**, 1208–1221 (1976)
5. Kello, C.T.: Patterns of timing in the acquisition, perception, and production of speech. J. Phonetics **31**(3–4), 619–626 (2003)
6. Campbell, N.: Timing in speech. A Multi-Level Process. In: Horne, M. (ed.) Prosody: Theory and Experiment, pp. 281–334. Kluwer Academic Publishers (2000)
7. O'Connell, D.C.: Communicating with One Another: Toward a Psychology of Spontaneous Spoken Discourse. Springer New York, New York (2008)

8. Barth-Weingarten, D., Reber, E., Selting, M.: Prosody in interaction. John Benjamins, Amsterdam, Philadelphia (2010)
9. Benesty, J., Sondhi, M., Huang, Y. (eds.): Handbook of Speech Processing, Springer (2008)
10. Harrington, J.: The Phonetic Analysis of Speech Corpora. Wiley-Blackwell, Chichester (2010)
11. Huang, X., Acero, A., Hon, H.-W.: Spoken Language Processing: A Guide to Theory, Algorithm, and System Development. Pearson Prentice Hall, Englewood Cliffs (2001)
12. Jurafsky, D., Martin, J.H.: Speech and Language Processing: An Introduction to Natural Language Processing, Computational Linguistics, and Speech Recognition. Pearson Prentice Hall, Englewood Cliffs (2008)
13. Potapova, R.K., Potapov, V.V., Lebedeva, N.N., Agibalova. T.V.: Interdisciplinarity in the study of speech polyinformativity. Languages of Slavic Culture (2015)
14. Wennerstrom, A.K.: The Music of Everyday Speech: Prosody and discourse analysis. Oxford University Press, New York (2001)
15. Cummins, F.: Probing the dynamics of speech production. In: Sudhoff, S. et al. (ed.) Methods in Empirical Prosody Research. Language, Context and Cognition. W. De Gruyter, Berlin–New York, pp. 211–228 (2006)
16. Sibata, T.: Sociolinguistics in Japanese contexts. In: Kunihiro, T., Inoue, F., Long, D. (eds.) Mouton de Gruyter. Berlin-New York (1999)
17. Campbell, N.: Speech & expression; the value of a longitudinal corpus. LREC **2004**, 183–186 (2004)
18. Burnard, L. (ed.): Reference guide for the British National Corpus (XML edition). Published for the British National Corpus Consortium by Oxford University Computing Services (2007). http://www.natcorp.ox.ac.uk/docs/URG/. Accessed 2 June 2017
19. Asinovsky, A., Bogdanova, N., Rusakova, M., Ryko, A., Stepanova, S., Sherstinova, T.: The ORD speech corpus of Russian everyday communication "One Speaker's Day": creation principles and annotation. In: Matoušek, V., Mautner, P. (eds.) TSD 2009. LNCS, vol. 5729, pp. 250–257. Springer, Heidelberg (2009). doi:10.1007/978-3-642-04208-9_36
20. Bogdanova-Beglarian, N., Sherstinova, T., Blinova, O., Ermolova, O., Baeva, E., Martynenko, G., Ryko, A.: Sociolinguistic extension of the ORD corpus of Russian everyday speech. In: Ronzhin, A., Potapova, R., Németh, G. (eds.) SPECOM 2016. LNCS, vol. 9811, pp. 659–666. Springer, Cham (2016). doi:10.1007/978-3-319-43958-7_80
21. Bogdanova-Beglarian, N., Sherstinova, T., Blinova, O., Ermolova, O., Baeva, E., Martynenko, G., Ryko, A.: Everyday Russian language in different social groups. Commun. Res. **2**(8), 81–92 (2016)
22. Sherstinova, T.: Macro episodes of Russian everyday oral communication: towards pragmatic annotation of the ORD speech corpus. In: Ronzhin, A., Potapova, R., Fakotakis, N. (eds.) SPECOM 2015. LNCS, vol. 9319, pp. 268–276. Springer, Cham (2015). doi:10.1007/978-3-319-23132-7_33
23. Sherstinova, T.: The structure of the ORD speech corpus of Russian everyday communication. In: Matoušek, V., Mautner, P. (eds.) TSD 2009. LNCS, vol. 5729, pp. 258–265. Springer, Heidelberg (2009). doi:10.1007/978-3-642-04208-9_37
24. Hellwig, B., Van Uytvanck, D., Hulsbosch, M., et al.: ELAN – Linguistic Annotator. Version 5.0.0-alfa [in:]. http://www.mpi.nl/corpus/html/elan/. Accessed 28 Mar 2017
25. Sherstinova, T.: Pragmaticheskoe annotirovanie konnunicativnykh jedinic v korpuse ORD: mikroepisody i rechevye akty (Approaches to Pragmatic Annotation in the ORD Corpus: Microepisodes and Speech Acts). In: Proceedings of the International Conference on "Corpus linguistics-2015", pp. 436–446 (2015)
26. Speech Technology Center. http://speechpro.com

27. Prodan, A., Chistikov, P., Talanov, A.: The system of preparation of a new voice for the speech synthesis system "VITALVOICE". Komp'juternaja lingvistika i intellektual'nye tehnologii 9(16), 394–399 (2010)
28. Praat: Doing Phonetics by computer. http://www.praat.org
29. Sherstinova, T.: Speech acts annotation of everyday conversations in the ORD corpus of spoken Russian. In: Ronzhin, A., Potapova, R., Németh, G. (eds.) Speech and Computer (SPECOM 2016). LNAI. Springer, Switzerland (2016)

Recognizing Emotionally Coloured Dialogue Speech Using Speaker-Adapted DNN-CNN Bottleneck Features

Kohei Mukaihara, Sakriani Sakti$^{(\boxtimes)}$, and Satoshi Nakamura

Graduate School of Information Science,
Nara Institute of Science and Technology, Ikoma, Japan
{mukaihara.kohei.me4,ssakti,s-nakamura}@is.naist.jp

Abstract. Emotionally coloured speech recognition is a key technology toward achieving human-like spoken dialog systems. However, despite rapid progress in automatic speech recognition (ASR) and emotion research, much less work has examined ASR systems that recognize the verbal content of emotionally coloured speech. Approaches that exist in emotional speech recognition mostly involve adapting standard ASR models to include information about prosody and emotion. In this study, instead of adapting a model to handle emotional speech, we focus on feature transformation methods to solve the mismatch and improve the ASR performance. In this way, we can train the model with emotionally coloured speech without any explicit emotional annotation. We investigate the use of two different deep bottleneck network structures: deep neural networks (DNNs) and convolutional neural networks (CNNs). We hypothesize that the trained bottleneck features may be able to extract essential information that represents the verbal content while abstracting away from superficial differences caused by emotional variance. We also try various combinations of these two bottleneck features with feature-space speaker adaptation. Experiments using Japanese and English emotional speech data reveal that both varieties of bottleneck features and feature-space speaker adaptation successfully improve the emotional speech recognition performance.

Keywords: Emotional speech recognition · Feature transformation · Deep bottleneck features

1 Introduction

Human communication is naturally coloured by emotion. Developing a natural spoken dialogue system that mimics human interaction requires a speech-oriented interface that can handle the various emotions often found in conversations. Researchers have been working on ASR technology for decades. ASR approaches have progressed from a simple machine that responds to a small set of sounds to more sophisticated systems that recognize conversational speech.

© Springer International Publishing AG 2017
A. Karpov et al. (Eds.): SPECOM 2017, LNAI 10458, pp. 632–641, 2017.
DOI: 10.1007/978-3-319-66429-3_63

On the other hand, research on emotion recognition from text or speech has also recently gained considerable interest [17]. Numerous official emotion recognition challenges [17–19] have been held, improving the features and classifiers that capture the traits of spoken emotion. However, despite rapid progress in ASR and emotion research, much less work has examined ASR systems that recognize the verbal content of emotionally coloured speech [3].

Previous studies [10,12,23] reported that emotion largely changes acoustic realization, including pitch range, speech rate, voice quality, etc. As a result of this mismatch from neutral speech models, performing such emotion-affected speech recognition tasks is not trivial, and several studies have shown that recognition rates are in fact quite low [3]. Approaches in emotional speech recognition generally adapt models that include information about prosody and emotion. Athanaselis et al. improved recognition rates by including emotional sentences in their model, including emotionally coloured dictionaries and language models [2,3]. Polzin et al. also modified the training process to include acoustic pronunciation variations in emotional speech [14]. Schuler et al. handled the problems by constructing two separate systems, emotion recognition and acoustic model adaptation [16], and constructed a standard neutral acoustic model that is adapted to each variety of emotional speech. Although these existing approaches show significant advantages, they also require deep knowledge of and data regarding every possible emotion that must be covered by the models.

In this study, we take a different direction. Instead of modifying the models to handle various types of emotional speech, we focus on lightweight feature transformation methods to solve the mismatch and improve the ASR performance with our standard ASR models without modification. In this way, we can train the model with emotionally coloured speech without any explicit emotional annotation. We propose using bottleneck features trained by DNNs and CNNs and hypothesize that bottleneck features, which greatly reduce the dimensions of the input speech, might be able to extract the essential information that represents the verbal content while abstracting away from the differences that result from the speech's emotional colouring. We also try various combinations of the two bottleneck features with feature-space speaker adaptation. Although bottleneck features have been widely used in the ASR community, to the best of our knowledge, ours is the first attempt to investigate the optimum combination of DNN-CNN bottleneck features and feature-space adaptation for emotionally coloured dialogue speech in Japanese and English.

2   Proposed Methods

This section describes our proposed feature transformation methods for emotional speech recognition based on DNN-CNN bottleneck features in combination with feature-space speaker adaptation.

2.1   DNN-Based Bottleneck Features

Figure 1 illustrates the DNN bottleneck architecture. Bottleneck features are simply vectors that consist of activations at a bottleneck layer, which has fewer hidden units than the other hidden layers in the network. These bottleneck features represent a nonlinear transformation and a dimensionality reduction of the acoustic input.

In this paper, we use a stack of denoising auto-encoders (SDAE) [21] for generative pre-training in a layer-wise, unsupervised manner. After pre-training is completed, fine-tuning connects the whole network, including both the bottleneck and final classification layers, and then the network is trained in a supervised manner to predict a phonetic target or HMM-states. After the training is completed, the layers after the bottleneck features are discarded, and the network is used to generate features that are input to a GMM-HMM model. The generated bottleneck features are called DBNF.

2.2   CNN-Based Bottleneck Features

Figure 2 illustrates an alternative to the standard DNN-based bottleneck features that use a CNN framework[1] with a bottleneck hidden layer. Using convolution and pooling, CNNs have spatial-temporal connectivity and local translation invariance for the given input and also allow weight sharing, which reduces the number of free parameters and improves the generalization ability.

For architecture that is compatible with the proposed DNN-based bottleneck features, in this study, we slightly modify the fully connected hidden layers to include one bottleneck hidden layer with relatively few hidden units compared to the other hidden layers in the fully connected parts. The CNN is trained as usual without pre-training. Similarly to DNNs, after the training is completed, the layers after the bottleneck features are discarded, and the network is used to generate bottleneck features for the GMM-HMM model. The generated bottleneck features are called CBNF.

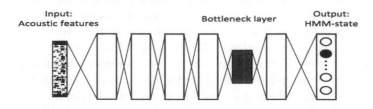

Fig. 1. DNN architecture with bottleneck hidden layer

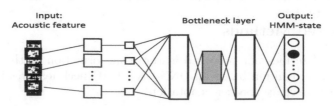

Fig. 2. CNN architecture with bottleneck hidden layer

---

[1] This framework was originally called a time-delay neural network [22] in speech recognition.

2.3   Bottleneck Feature Combination

Because the DNN-based and CNN-based bottleneck features are expected to capture different information about input acoustic signals, we also propose methods that combine them in two ways: (1) stack combination and (2) parallel combination.

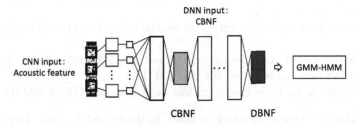

Fig. 3. Stack combination of CNN-DNN bottleneck features

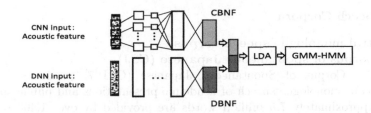

Fig. 4. Parallel combination of CNN-DNN bottleneck features

Stack combination. We first combine these transformations one-after-another in a stacked manner. Since CNN commonly uses two-dimensional input and DNN uses one-dimensional input, we constructed DNN bottleneck features on top of the CNN bottleneck features (Fig. 3). Here, the bottleneck features provided by the CNN framework are not directly fed to the GMM-HMM model, but instead they are used as input for the DNN. Then the output of the DNN bottleneck features is used for learning the GMM-HMM model. Both the CNN and DNN bottleneck features are trained sequentially.

Parallel combination. Figure 4 illustrates the proposed parallel combination of the CNN-DNN bottleneck features. Here, they are trained entirely independently. The bottleneck features that are output from the CNN and DNN are then combined into one large feature vector. To allow for a fair comparison with the other proposed bottleneck features, LDA is used to project these large feature vectors into smaller dimensions, and then these features are provided to the GMM-HMM model.

To further improve robustness against emotion variations from different speakers, we also combined the DNN-CNN bottleneck features with feature-space maximum likelihood linear regression (fMLLR) [4] for speaker adaptation and investigated various possible combinations such as DBNF+fMLLR, CBNF+fMLLR, stack combination DBNF-CBNF with fMLLR, and parallel combination DBNF-CBNF with fMLLR.

3   Experimental Conditions

We conducted the overall model training procedure as follows:

- Train the standard GMM-HMM model on neutral speech.
- Train the DNN and CNN bottleneck feature transforms on neutral and emotionally coloured speech.
- Run the bottleneck feature extractor on the neutral and emotionally coloured speech.
- Retrain the GMM parameters on the extracted bottleneck features, while keeping the same parameters for the HMMs.
- Use the system for speech recognition as in standard GMM-HMMs.

The experiments were performed in both Japanese and English. Details about the data and the system set-up are described in the following sections.

3.1   Speech Corpora

1. **Neutral monologue speech corpus**
   - **Corpus of spontaneous Japanese (CSJ)**
     The Corpus of Spontaneous Japanese (CSJ)[7] consists of spontaneous monologue speech of academic presentations and public speaking. Approximately 7.5 million words are provided by over 1,400 speakers. The training part contains about 490k utterances (518 hours of speech). The speech format is mono-channel with 16-kHz sampling frequency and 16-bit quantization.
   - **English Wall Street Journal (WSJ)**
     The Wall Street Journal (WSJ) corpus [11] is a large, well-known vocabulary, a speaker-independent continuous speech corpus for native American English. Here, we trained models on the SI-84 (WSJ0) training material that consists of about 40k utterances (16-kHz sampling frequency and 16-bit quantization).
2. **Emotionally coloured dialogue speech corpus**
   - **Online gaming voice chat (OGVC)**
     The OGVC corpus [1] consists of both spontaneous and acted speech for emotional research. Spontaneous emotional speech data were recorded by two or three online game players through a voice chat system, resulting in six dialogs and 9,114 utterances. Emotions are manually annotated based on the perceptual emotion categories of Plutchik's model [13], including acceptance (ACC), anger (ANG), anticipation (ANT), disgust (DIS), fear (FEA), joy (JOY), sadness (SAD), and surprise (SUR). In addition, four professional actors (two males, two females) uttered 17 dialog sequences extracted from the transcriptions of the spontaneous dialogs with various emotional strengths: calm (level 0), weak (level 1), medium (level 2), and strong (level 3). There are approximately 664 utterances per actor, resulting in 2656 acted utterances. In this study, since the effect of various

emotions and emotion levels are important factors to explore, we used only the acted speech parts. For eight emotion types and four emotion levels, we have 32 different test sets with 40 utterances in each test set.

- **Sustained emotionally coloured machine-human interaction using nonverbal expression (SEMAINE)**
  The SEMAINE material [8] was developed specifically to address the task of achieving emotion-rich interaction with an automatic agent, called a sensitive artificial listener, (SAL). Each user interacts with four characters in a Wizard-of-Oz framework: constantly angry Spike, happy Poppy, gloomy Obadiah, and sensible Prudence. Emotional annotation involved full ratings with intervals of 0.02 s for five dimensions: valence, activation, power, anticipation, and intensity. In this preliminary study, to limit mitigating factors regarding the emotional content and acoustic realization, the speech data from the user side were not used at the moment. So only conversations derived from the SAL automatic agent were used with 1520 speech utterances for training and 467 speech utterances for the test set.

3.2 Emotionally Coloured Speech Recognition Set-Up

We constructed a speech recognition system with Kaldi [15], a free open-source toolkit. The front-end provides 39-dimensional MFCCs every 10 ms with a width of 25 ms. To incorporate the temporal structures and dependencies, 11 adjacent (center, 5 left, and 5 right) MFCC frames were stacked into one single super vector, which was projected down to an optimal 40 dimensions by applying LDA. After that, the resulting features were further de-correlated using a maximum likelihood linear transformation (MLLT) [6], which is also known as a global semi-tied covariance (STC) [5] transform. Here, speaker adaptive training was also performed using a fMLLR [4] transform that was estimated per speaker.

Standard GMM-HMM acoustic models were trained on the above provided features. Japanese speech recognition was trained with the CSJ corpus, and the English speech recognition system was trained with the WSJ corpus. All models are context-dependent, and cross-word triphones with a standard three-state left-to-right HMM topology were derived from 39 Japanese and English phonemes. A pronunciation dictionary was constructed with CSJ and WSJ pronunciation dictionaries for Japanese and English, respectively. We built trigram language models with the SRILM toolkit [20].

To train the DNN- and CNN-based feature transformations, we used the Kaldi-PDNN toolkit [9]. Japanese DNNs and CNNs were trained with the OGVC corpus, while English DNNs and CNNs were trained with the SEMAINE corpus. The number of nodes in the input layer depends on the dimension size of the speech feature input. Specific to CNN, the input is two-dimensional. The number of nodes in the output layer equals the number of HMM phone states in the GMM-HMM model. The total number of hidden layers is six, in which the standard hidden layer consists of 1024 nodes, and the bottleneck hidden layer (at the 5th position) consists of 42 nodes. The CNN has two convolutional-pooling layers with three fully connected hidden layers on top (including a bottleneck hidden layer in the middle). All other parameters used the default set in Kaldi-PDNN.

4 Experimental Evaluation

First, we discuss recognition on emotionally coloured speech in Japanese. Table 1 shows the average word error rate (WER) on the Japanese OGVC in eight emotion types (ACC, ANG, ANT, DIS, FEA, JOY, SAD, and SUR) plus neutral (NEU), and Fig. 5 illustrates the WER average on the Japanese OGVC in four emotion levels (calm, weak, medium, and strong).

Table 1. WER(%) on Japanese OGVC for all emotion types

	MFCC	LDA	LDA+ fMLLR	DBNF	DBNF+ fMLLR	CBNF	CBNF+ fMLLR	StackComb	ParComb	ParComb+ fMLLR
NEU	12.36	12.29	10.15	11.29	10.07	11.69	11.93	16.60	8.94	7.15
ACC	23.33	25.08	16.83	15.40	14.29	18.73	20.95	17.78	12.86	9.36
ANG	24.02	24.51	16.79	20.34	12.26	20.10	15.69	18.13	11.40	7.48
ANT	15.14	16.88	9.91	16.56	10.13	18.52	13.07	22.98	11.55	10.24
DIS	21.89	27.11	27.11	35.74	22.29	30.32	27.71	28.92	16.87	18.88
FEA	37.34	42.62	31.43	26.79	22.78	25.95	27.43	36.08	26.58	20.89
JOY	23.87	20.12	13.52	17.27	8.11	21.77	17.87	29.13	15.31	13.06
SAD	27.08	27.20	24.27	30.27	17.53	31.50	25.37	28.18	18.38	12.38
SUR	58.43	56.74	33.71	31.27	22.09	38.39	35.77	43.82	28.84	23.22
Avr	**27.05**	**28.06**	**20.41**	**22.77**	**15.50**	**24.11**	**21.75**	**26.84**	**16.74**	**13.62**

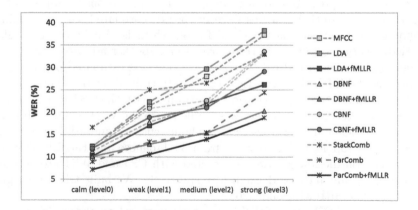

Fig. 5. WER(%) on Japanese OGVC for all emotion levels

Looking at the aggregate results of the DBNF and CBNF bottleneck features, both DBNF and CBNF proved advantageous for ASR in comparison with MFCC and LDA baseline, demonstrating that bottleneck features indeed allow for abstraction away of the variance caused by emotionally coloured speech. On average, the ASR performance with DBNF is still better than the performance with CBNF, but CBNF did outperform DBNF in some emotions, such as disgust and fear, motivating our feature combination methods.

In the bottleneck feature combination, the stacked feature combination method did not provide improvements, perhaps because in the feature extraction process, CBNF removes some useful information that might be captured more effectively by DBNF. Since DBNF probably wasn't able to perform any further extraction, it could not improve the recognition performance. By combining them in a parallel manner, we got significant improvement.

Utilizing bottleneck features with feature-space speaker adaptation, such as DBNF+fMLLR, CBNF+fMLLR, stack combination DBNF-CBNF with fMLLR, and parallel combination DBNF-CBNF with fMLLR, also provided advantages to ASR. The best proposed method is the parallel combination of bottleneck features with feature-space speaker adaptation, which allows for a large improvement of a 6.78% WER absolute over the LDA-fMLLR feature transformation baseline.

Looking at the effect of emotion levels, we confirmed that the expected results are more difficult to recognize when the speech has higher emotion levels. Scrutinizing the emotion-by-emotion results, the most difficult-to-recognize variety is speech coloured with fear or surprise, where the MFCC baseline achieved WERs of 37.34% and 58.43%, and the LDA-fMLLR baseline achieved WERs of 31.43% and 33.71%. This indicates that emotions with a higher pitch, a faster speech rate, and short durations are the most difficult to handle. The DBNF-CBNF parallel combination with speaker-dependent feature-space adaptation reduced the fear and surprise WERs to 20.89% and 23.22%. Furthermore, anger, sadness, and joy/happiness emotions with slightly faster or slightly lower speech rate and moderate duration provided moderate difficulties to the recognizer. The LDA-fMLLR baseline achieved WERs of 16.79%, 24.27%, and 13.52%, while the proposed parallel DBNF-CBNF plus fMLLR combination reduced the WERs to 7.48%, 12.38%, and 13.06% for anger, sadness, and joy/happiness, respectively.

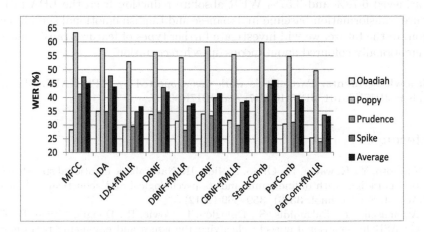

Fig. 6. Summary of WER(%) on English emotional speech SEMAINE

Next, we confirmed that the improvements afforded by our method are carried over to English speech recognition on emotionally coloured speech. Figure 6 illustrates the WER average on the English SEMAINE in four emotion types (angry Spike, happy Poppy, gloomy Obadiah, and sensible Prudence). The results reveal that even with different languages and different neutral speech styles (used to train the standard ASR), the results have the same tendency. The best system was also achieved using a parallel combination of bottleneck features with feature-space adaptation, providing a 3.57% absolute WER from the LDA-fMLLR feature transformation baseline.

Comparing emotion-by-emotion across two languages, joy/happy in Japanese acted speech seems to provide similar moderate difficulties with anger and sad, but in conversational English speech, happy seems difficult to handle. This might be due to additional non-verbal laughter during the speech, complicating recognition of the verbal content. Nevertheless, the proposed approach still reduced the absolute joy/happy WER by 3.33% from the LDA-fMLLR feature transformation baseline.

5   Conclusion

We proposed DNN or CNN bottleneck features as a way to abstract away from the variability due to emotion coloured speech as well as methods to combine multiple types of features to further improve robustness. The results reveal that both single DBNF and CBNF provide advantages for recognizing the verbal content of emotionally coloured speech. The DBNF and CBNF combination in a parallel manner also provided significant improvement. The best system performed a parallel combination of bottleneck features with feature-space speaker adaptation to handle both emotion and speaker variability. With this set-up, we achieved 6.78% and 3.57% WER absolute reduction from the LDA-fMLLR feature transformation baseline in Japanese and English emotional speech recognition. In the future, we will investigate further types of feature transformations for emotionally coloured spontaneous speech recognition.

Acknowledgements. Part of this work was supported by JSPS KAKENHI Grant Numbers JP17H06101, JP17H00747, and JP17K00237.

References

1. Arimoto, Y., Kawatsu, H., Ohno, S., Iida, H.: Naturalistic emotional speech collection paradigm with online game and its psychological and acoustical assessment. Acoust. Sci. Technol. **33**(6), 359–369 (2012)
2. Athanaselis, T., Bakamidis, S., Dologlou, I., Cowie, R., Douglas-Cowie, E., Cox, C.: ASR for emotional speech: clarifying the issues and enhancing performance. Neural Netw. **18**(4), 437–444 (2005)
3. Athanaselis, T., Bakamidis, S., Dologlou, I.: Recognizing verbal content of emotionally coloured speech. In: Proceedings of EUSIPCO, Florence, Italy (2006)

4. Gales, M.: Maximum likelihood linear transformations for HMM-based speech recognition. Comput. Speech Lang. **12**(2), 75–98 (1998)
5. Gales, M.: Semi-tied covariance matrices for hidden Markov models. IEEE Trans. Speech Audio Process. **7**(3), 272–281 (1999)
6. Gopinath, R.: Maximum likelihood modeling with Gaussian distributions for classification. In: Proceedings of ICASSP, pp. 661–664 (1998)
7. Maekawa, K., Koiso, H., Furui, S., Isahara, H.: Spontaneous speech corpus of Japanese. In: Proceedings of LREC, Athens, Greece, pp. 947–952 (2000)
8. McKeown, G., Valstar, M., Cowie, R., Pantic, M., Schroder, M.: The SEMAINE database: annotated multimodal records of emotionally coloured conversations between a person and a limited agent. IEEE Trans. Affect. Comput. **3**(1), 5–17 (2012)
9. Miao, Y.: Kaldi+PDNN: building DNN-based ASR systems with Kaldi and PDNN. arXiv:1401.6984 (2014)
10. Murray, I., Arnott, L.: Toward the simulation of emotion in synthetic speech: a review of the listerature on human vocal emotion. J. Acoust. Soc. Am. **93**(2), 1097–1108 (1993)
11. Paul, D., Baker, J.: The design for the Wall Street Journal-based CSR corpus. In: Proceedings of DARPA Speech and Language Workshop, San Mateo, USA (1992)
12. Picard, R.: Affective Computing. MIT Press, Cambridge (1997)
13. Plutchik, R.: A general psychoevolutionary theory of emotion. In: Theories of emotion. Academic Press (1980)
14. Polzin, S., Waibel, A.: Pronunciation variations in emotional speech. In: Proceedings of ESCA, pp. 103–108 (1998)
15. Povey, D., Ghoshal, A., Boulianne, G., Burget, L., Glembek, O., Goel, N., Hannemann, M., Moticek, P., Qian, Y., Schwarz, P., Silovsky, J., Stemmer, G., Vesely, K.: The Kaldi speech recognition toolkit. In: Proceedings of ASRU, Hawaii, USA (2011)
16. Schuller, B., Stadermann, J., Rigoll, G.: Affect-robust speech recognition by dynamic emotional adaptation. In: Proceedings of Speech Prosody (2006)
17. Schuller, B., Steidl, S., Batliner, A.: The INTERSPEECH 2009 emotion challenge. In: Proceedings of INTERSPEECH, Brighton, United Kingdom, pp. 312–315 (2009)
18. Schuller, B., Steidl, S., Burkhardt, F., Devillers, L., Muller, C., Narayanan, S.: The INTERSPEECH 2010 paralinguistic challenge. In: Proceedings of INTERSPEECH, Makuhari, Japan, pp. 2794–2797 (2010)
19. Schuller, B., Valstar, M., Eyben, F., McKeown, G., Cowie, R., Pantic, M.: AVEC 2011 - the first international audio/visual emotion challenge. In: Proceedings of International Conference on Affective Computing and Intelligent Interaction (ACII), Memphis, Tennessee, pp. 415–424 (2011)
20. Stolcke, A.: SRILM - an extensible language modeling toolkit. In: Proceedings of of ICSLP, Denver, USA, pp. 901–904 (2002)
21. Vincent, P., Larochelle, H., Lajoie, I., Bengio, Y., Manzagol, P.A.: Stacked denoising autoencoders: learning useful representations in a deep network with a local denoising criterion. J. Mach. Learn. Res. **37**, 3371–3408 (2010)
22. Waibel, A., Hanazawa, T., Hinton, G., Shikano, K., Lang, K.J.: Phoneme recognition using time-delay neural networks. IEEE Trans. Acoust. Speech Signal Process. **37**(3), 328–339 (1989)
23. Williams, C., Stevens, K.: Emotion and speech: some acoustical correlates. J. Acoust. Soc. Amer **52**, 1238–1250 (1972)

Relationship Between Perception of Cuteness in Female Voices and Their Durations

Ryohei Ohno[1($\boxtimes$)], Masanori Morise[2], and Tetsuro Kitahara[1]

[1] Nihon University, Setagaya-ku, Tokyo 1568550, Japan
{ryouhei,kitahara}@kthrlab.jp
[2] University of Yamanashi, Kofu, Yamanashi 4008510, Japan
mmorise@yamanashi.ac.jp

Abstract. The cuteness of female voices is especially important in Japanese pop culture. We investigate the relationship between the perception of cuteness in female voices and the voices' duration. In our hypothesis, the perception of cuteness should become more ambiguous and unstable as the duration becomes shorter. To confirm this hypothesis, we conducted listening tests where participants listened to female voices with various durations and rated their cuteness on scale of 1 to 5. The results show: (1) the instability of cuteness perception becomes higher as the duration is lower, (2) for voices rated "4" or higher when presented fully, their ambiguity of cuteness perception increases (i.e., the ratings become close to "3 (indeterminable)") when presented shortly, and (3) for voices rated "2" or lower when presented fully, the ambiguity of cuteness perception does not increase even if the durations are short.

Keywords: Cuteness · female voice · duration

1 Introduction

The *cuteness* of female voices is important especially in Japanese pop culture. For example, in Japanese *anime* works, cute voices by female actresses often play a significant role in increasing the popularity of the work. In maid cafes— cosplay restaurants popular in Japan— the waitresses dress in maid costumes and often use characteristic voices that are usually described as cute. Such voices are also called *moe* voices where *moe* is a Japanese Internet slang meaning strong attachment to a specific object.

This work is part of a larger study, which aims to develop techniques that make it possible to synthesize cute voices on a computer. Therefore, we investigate the relationship between acoustic features and human perception of cuteness. There have been attempts to investigate the relationship between acoustic features and human perceptions or preferences [1]. Jones et al. found that men strongly preferred women's voices when the pitch is raised [2]. Liu et al. argued that men's preferences for women's voices are related to the voices' breathiness as well as the pitches [3,4]. Ferdenzi et al. claimed that there were differences of

© Springer International Publishing AG 2017
A. Karpov et al. (Eds.): SPECOM 2017, LNAI 10458, pp. 642–650, 2017.
DOI: 10.1007/978-3-319-66429-3_64

listeners' impressions when they listened to a single vowel and an actual word or sentence (such as "Bonjour") [5]. Babel et al. found that the preferences for voices have positive correlation between listeners' genders. They also found that acoustic features related to the body size contribute to predict vocal attractiveness [6]. Puts et al. argued that women are sensitive to formant dispersion that strongly affects men's preference of the female voice, and conclude that women use vocal characterstics to track their rival in mating [7]. Takano et al. investigated the relationship between acoustic features and how strongly the listeners felt *moe* in the voices [9,10]. They found that the degree of moe in voices depends on the speaker's individual characteristics rather than emotional expressions controlled by the speaker. They also reported that the degree of moe could be enhanced by making the mean F0 higher, making the standard deviation of F0 larger, and making the speech rate faster. Kawahara analyzed voices spoken by maid cafes' waitresses (maid voices) and showed that the waitresses use higher and faster voices in maid cafes than their natural voices. In particular, the temporal increase in the F0 tends to be faster than their natural voices [11,12]. Moreover Starr argued that the voice quality (e.g., breathy and creaky) is important to evaluation of characters and actresses who make use of sweet voice [8].

Here, we focus on the relationship of voice durations and cuteness perception. In other words, we focus on whether humans can perceive the cuteness of voices even if the durations are very short. If they can, then cuteness could be derived from instantaneous features (for example, F0 or spectrum at one frame). If not, cuteness is related to the temporal evolution of features. We conducted an experiment in which the participants listened to 75-ms, 150-ms, 300-ms, and 600-ms excerpts of female voices and rated their cuteness. We hypothesize that the ratings of cuteness would become ambiguous and unstable as shorter durations.

2   Method

2.1   Speech Stimulus

We used speech samples taken from the *Onichan CD* [13], which consists of 1200 voices saying *"Onichan"* (meaning "my (older) brother"). These voices are spoken under assumptions of 100 different situations by 12 female voice actresses. This CD was also used in the experiments on *moe* voices by Takano et al. [9]. For our experiments, we took voices at the situation of *"chotto tanoshii"* (meaning a little fun) because these voices had higher *moe* than those in Takano et al.'s experiment [9].

By cutting out each of these 12 voices (one voice by the 12 actresses), we prepared shortened speech stimuli. The durations are 75 ms, 150 ms, 300 ms, and 600 ms. Because we chose three different cutout positions at random, there are 36 voices (3 cutout positions × 12 actresses) for each duration. The resulting stimuli are listed in Table 1. When the stimulus was cut out, silent part was excluded in advance.

Table 1. Breakdown of voice stimulus by each actress

Duration	Cut-out position	For all actors
75 [ms]	3 patterns (random)	36
150 [ms]	3 patterns (random)	36
300 [ms]	3 patterns (random)	36
600 [ms]	3 patterns (random)	36
Full	1 pattern (no cut-out)	12
Sum		156

2.2   Participants

The participants were 14 Japanese university students (7 males and 7 females) between the age of 21 and 24 (average: 21.43, standard deviation: 0.94).

2.3   Procedure

The experiments were conducted through the following steps:

1. For the 75-ms voice stimulus,
1-1. Listen to each of them in random order.
1-2. After each listening, rate its cuteness within five seconds.
   The ratings shall be 1 (never cute), 2 (hardly cute), 3 (indeterminable), 4 (mostly cute), or 5 (definitely cute).
   The number of ratings is 108 in total (12 actresses × 3 cutout positions × 3 times).
1-3. Rest after every 54 ratings.
2. Do the same thing for 150-ms, 300-ms, and 600-ms voices.
3. Do the same thing for the full-duration voices. The number of ratings is 36 in total (12 actresses × 3 times). The participants therefore do not rest.

2.4   Method of Analysis

We hypothesize that the perception of cuteness becomes more ambiguous and unstable as the durations become shorter. The ambiguity of cuteness perception can be measured by how close the scores are to "3 (indeterminable)," and the instability can be measured as variations in scores for the same stimulus. Based on these ideas, we analyze scores as follows:

Analysis of Instability. Within-listener variations in the rating scores for the same stimulus are analyzed. If the cuteness perception requires a certain duration for heard voices, then these variations should increase according to the shortness. We therefore analyze the relationship between the durations and the ranges (i.e., the difference between the maximum and the minimum) of the scores for the same stimulus.

Analysis of Ambiguity. The ambiguity of cuteness perception is analyzed, but cuteness perception seriously depends on the listeners; they may never feel the cuteness for a certain voice even if they fully listen. Therefore, we analyze how close the average of scores are to "3" for only the voices that the same participant gave scores of "4" or "5" when he/she fully listened. If cuteness perception requires a certain duration for heard voices, then these ratios should be lower according to the shortness. We conducted similar analysis for only the voices rated as "1" or "2" when he/she fully listened.

3   Results

3.1   Instability

The ranges of the scores for the same stimulus are shown in Fig. 1. This figure shows the following:

- The participants gave the same score to the same stimulus for 46.9% of stimuli on average.
- The ranges of the scores for the same stimulus tend to become larger according to the shortness.
- However, even at 75 ms, 66.9% of the stimuli on average had ranges of 1 or smaller.

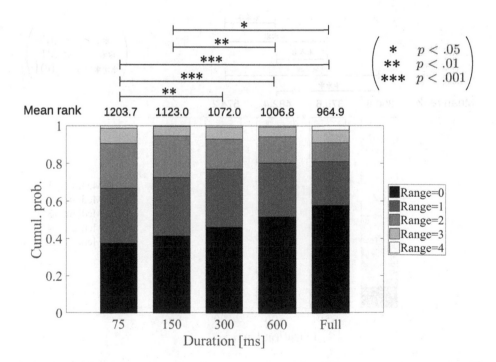

Fig. 1. Cumulative probability of ranges of scores given to the same stimulus by the same listener

We conducted statistical tests. First, we applied the Kruskal-Wallis H test (KW-test, $\alpha = .05$)—a non-parametric version of ANOVA— to confirm whether the distributions of within-listener score ranges for the five durations have significant differences between at least one pair. The sample size of each distribution except for the full duration is 504; the full duration is 168. The result ($H(df = 4) = 39.04$, $p < .001$) shows that they have significant differences between at least one pair. Next, we applied multiple comparisons using the Mann-Whitney U test (U-test, $\alpha = .05$) with the Bonferroni correction to each pair of the five distributions. The results of the multiple comparisons reveal that there are significant differences between the mean ranks of the distributions for 75 ms and 300 ms ($z = 3.53$, $p < .01$), for 75 ms and 600 ms ($z = 5.25$, $p < .001$), for 75 ms and full duration ($z = 4.33$, $p < .001$), for 150 ms and 600 ms ($z = 3.39$, $p < .01$), and for 150 ms and the full duration ($z = 3.15$, $p < .05$). Thus, the instability of cuteness perception becomes higher as the duration is shorter, although this instability is not so high.

3.2 Ambiguity

Distributions of Scores for Voices Rated Highly in the Full Duration.
We extracted the voices that each participant rated "4" or higher in the full duration and analyzed the distributions of scores that the same participant gave

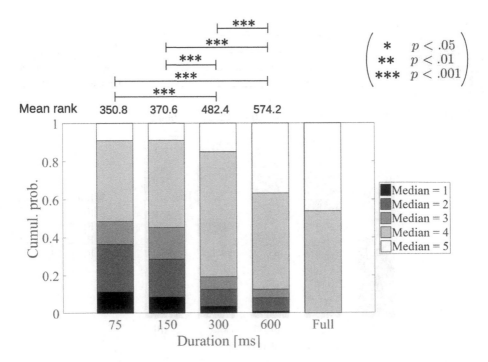

Fig. 2. Cumulative probability of median scores for voices rated highly in the full duration

to these voices when the duration decreased. These distributions are shown in Fig. 2. This figure shows the following:

- Low scores increase relatively according to the shortness even though all voices are rated at "4" or higher when presented fully.
- However, even for the duration of 75 ms, 51.4% of the stimuli on average had medians of "4" or higher.

To confirm the correlation between the central tendency of scores and the durations, we conducted statistical tests for distributions. We excluded the distribution for the full duration because this distribution is the result of excerpting the scores of "4" or higher, and accordingly, these have scores of "4" or higher only. The sample size of each distribution is 222. From the result of KW-test($\alpha = .05$), the four distributions have significant differences between at least one pair ($H(df = 3) = 128.01, p < .001$). Moreover, the results of multiple comparisons show that there are significant differences between the mean ranks of the distributions for 75 ms and 300 ms ($z = -6.12, p < .001$), for 75 ms and 600 ms ($z = -9.34, p < .001$), for 150 ms and 300 ms ($z = -5.40, p < .001$), for 150 ms and 600 ms ($z = -8.84, p < .001$) and for 300 ms and 600 ms ($z = -4.81, p < .001$).

Distributions of Scores for Voices Rated Low in the Full Duration. We extracted the voices that each participant rated "2" or lower in the full duration and analyzed the distributions of scores that the same participant gave to these voices when presented with short duration clips. These distributions are shown in Fig. 3. This figure shows the following:

- Some of the voices (e.g., 9.4% for 600 ms, 27.1% for 300 ms, 24.5% for 150 ms, 23.9% for 75 ms) were rated "3" or higher even though they all were rated "2" or lower when presented as a the full clip.
- These ratios and the durations did not show clear relationship (at least, not monotonous) unlike Fig. 2.
- 76.1% of the ratings at 75 ms were consistent with the ratings in the full duration.

Similar to the last section, we conducted statistical tests for the distributions. We excluded the distribution for the full duration because this distribution is the result of excerpting the scores of "2" or lower and accordingly only has scores of "2" or lower.

The sample size of each distribution is 159. The results of the KW-test ($\alpha = .05$) show no significant differences between any pairs of the four distributions ($H(df = 3) = 7.16, p = 0.067$).

4   Discussion

4.1   Instantaneous Acoustic Cues vs Dynamic Acoustic Cues

In previous studies, perception of cuteness (including *moe*) in female voices lies on temporal variations in acoustic features (such as F0 contour [11,12] and

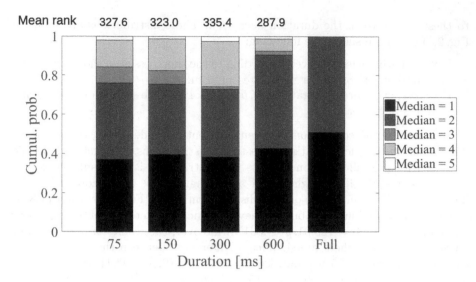

Fig. 3. Cumulative probability of median scores for voices rated low in the full duration

temporal standard deviation of F0 [9,10]). These conclusions match our findings that the cuteness perception becomes unstable when only short pieces of the voices are presented. On the other hand, 51.4% of the ratings for 75-ms voices were consistent with those for the corresponding full-duration voices are rated "4" or higher. This implies that instantaneous cues also play a significant role in cuteness perception.

4.2 Asymmetry of "Cuteness" and "Uncuteness"

Even though the ambiguity of cuteness perception increased when the participants listened to short parts of the voices that they rated highly in the full duration, this tendency was not shown for the voices that they rated low in the full duration. This difference may be derived from asymmetry of cuteness and uncuteness. In typical listening tests, we use a pair of adjectives that have opposite meaning to each other, e.g., bright and dark. However, there is no opposite word of "cute" (*kawaii*) in Japanese, so we used negative forms of this word, i.e., "never cute" and "hardly cute". This means that the ratings of "1" and "2" are not necessarily because the listeners found a negative property in the voices, but rather because they did not find any cuteness in the voices. This asymmetry might be one reason for the above-mentioned differences.

4.3 Remaining Issues

There are some important aspects that are not considered here. First, no stimuli are spontaneous utterances but rather acting utterances by voice actresses in which the cuteness might be exaggerated. According to Kawahara's study [11,12], acting voices tend to have larger temporal deviations in acoustic features. The results may therefore change if we use spontaneously uttered voices. Second, 75-ms voices and 600-ms voices have differences not only in acoustic features but also in semantics. From 600-ms voices, listeners may be able to find out that they are excerpts of voices meaning *"Onichan"* (my older brother), but this cannot happen with 75-ms clips. The attractiveness of the voices depends on the semantic content [2], so the results may change if we use non-meaningful voices such as /aeaeae/.

5   Conclusions

Here, we investigated the relationship between the perception of cuteness in female voices and the voices' durations. The results show that: (1) the score instability increases as the duration is shorter, (2) for voices rated "4" or higher when presented fully, the ambiguity of the scores was higher when the duration becomes shorter, (3) for voices rated "2" or lower when presented fully, the ambiguity of scores was not higher even if the duration was short; and (4) however, even at 75 ms, instability and ambiguity were not so high. We suspect that it is possible to perceive vocal cuteness partly and also uncuteness more correctly even if the duration is very short.

In the future, we will investigate the types of acoustic features used in judging cuteness from very short voices by calculating correlations between the participants' ratings and various acoustic features.

Acknowledgments. Part of this study received the furtherance of JSPS Grant in Aid for Scientific Research 16H05899, 17H00749 and 26240025.

References

1. Hill, A.K., Puts, D.A.: Vocal attractiveness. In: Shackelford, T.K., Weekes-Shackelford, V. (eds.) Encyclopedia of Evolutionary Psychological Science. Springer International Publishing (2016)
2. Jones, B.C., Feinberg, D.R., DeBruine, L.M., Little, A.C., Vukovic, J.: Integrating cues of social interest and voice pitch in men's preferences for women's voices. Biol. Lett. 4(2), 192–194 (2008)
3. Liu, X., Xu, Y.: What makes a female voice attractive. In: Proceedings of XVIIth ICPHS, Hong Kong, pp. 1274–1277 (2011)
4. Xu, Y., Lee, A., Wu, W.L., Liu, X., Birkholz, P.: Human vocal attractiveness as signaled by body size projection. PloS one 8(4), e62397 (2013)
5. Ferdenzi, C., Patel, S., Mehu-Blantar, I., Khidasheli, M., Sander, D., Delplanque, S.: Voice attractiveness: influence of stimulus duration and type. Behav. Res. Methods 45(2), 405–413 (2013)
6. Babel, M., McGuire, G., King, J.: Towards a more nuanced view of vocal attractiveness. PloS one 9(2), e88616 (2014)
7. Puts, D.A., Barndt, J.L., Welling, L.L., Dawood, K., Burriss, R.P.: Intrasexual competition among women: vocal femininity affects perceptions of attractiveness and flirtatiousness. Pers. Individ. Differ. 50(1), 111–115 (2011)

8. Starr, R.L.: Sweet voice: the role of voice quality in a Japanese feminine style. Lang. Soc. **44**(01), 1–34 (2015)
9. Takano, S., Takezawa, Y., Takeuti, Z., Yamada, M.: Moe voice - its' auditory evaluation, acoustic parameters and evaluation of synthesized voice. Proc. of 2014 Spring Meeting of Acoust. Soc. Jpn. 503–506 (2014)
10. Takano, S., Yamada, M.: Perception and analysis of "Moe" voice. J. Acⲅust. Soc. Am. **140**(4), 3399–3399 (2016)
11. Kawahara, S.: The phonetics of Japanese maid voice I: Apreliminary study. Phonol. Stud. **16**, 19–28 (2013)
12. Kawahara, S.: The prosodic features of the "moe" and "tsun Voices". J. Phonet. Soc. Jpn. **20**(2), 102–110 (2016)
13. Onichan CD, Cffon (record label) (2006)

Retaining Expression on De-identified Faces

Li Meng[1(✉)] and Aruna Shenoy[2]

[1] University of Hertfordshire, Hatfield AL10 9AB, UK
L.l.Meng@herts.ac.uk
[2] National Physical Laboratory, Teddington, UK
aruna.shenoy@npl.co.uk

Abstract. The extensive use of video surveillance along with advances in face recognition has ignited concerns about the privacy of the people identifiable in the recorded documents. A face de-identification algorithm, named k-Same, has been proposed by prior research and guarantees to thwart face recognition software. However, like many previous attempts in face de-identification, k-Same fails to preserve the utility such as gender and expression of the original data. To overcome this, a new algorithm is proposed here to preserve data utility as well as protect privacy. In terms of utility preservation, this new algorithm is capable of preserving not only the category of the facial expression (e.g., happy or sad) but also the intensity of the expression. This new algorithm for face de-identification possesses a great potential especially with real-world images and videos as each facial expression in real life is a continuous motion consisting of images of the same expression with various degrees of intensity.

Keywords: Privacy protection · Face de-identification · Facial expression preservation · Linear discriminant analysis · K-Anonymity

1 Introduction

Recent advances in both camera technology and computing hardware have highly facilitated the effectiveness and efficiency of image and video acquisition. This capability is now widely used in a variety of scenarios to capture images of people in target environments, either for immediate inspection or for storage and subsequent analysis/sharing [1]. These improved recording capabilities, however, has ignited concerns about the privacy of people identifiable in the scenes. The Council of Europe Convention of 1950 formally declared privacy protection as a human right. This was later embodied in the 1995 Data Protection Directive of the European Union (Directive 95/46/EC) and the 2016 General Data Protection Regulation (GDPR Regulation (EU) 2016/679). Both regulations demand the deployment of appropriate technical and organizational measures to protect private information in the course of transferring or processing such data. This legal requirement along with ethical responsibilities has restricted data sharing and utilization while various organizations may require the use of such data for research, business, academic, security and many other purposes. To comply with the regulations, de-identification has become the focus of attention by many organizations with the ultimate goal of removing all personal identifying information while protecting the utility of the data.

© Springer International Publishing AG 2017
A. Karpov et al. (Eds.): SPECOM 2017, LNAI 10458, pp. 651–661, 2017.
DOI: 10.1007/978-3-319-66429-3_65

Various methods have been proposed for the de-identification of faces in still images. These methods can be put into two categories: the ad hoc methods (such as masking, pixelation and blurring [2–4]) and the k-anonymity based methods (such as k-Same [5]). The ad hoc methods are usually simple to implement. However, these methods significantly distort the integrity of the image data. Imagine the eye area being blacked out by masking methods or the resolution of the image being sacrificed by pixelation or blurring. Even worse, ad hoc methods fail to serve their purpose as they are unable to thwart the existing face recognition software [5, 6]. To achieve privacy protection, the concept of k-anonymity was introduced by Sweeney in 2002 [7]. All k-anonymity based methods de-identify a face image by replacing it with the average of k faces from a gallery and hence achieve privacy protection by guaranteeing a recognition risk lower than $1/k$. Among the k-anonymity methods, the most widely used method is k-Same [5]. However, k-Same was not designed for preserving data utility. As a result, the de-identified version of a male face might look feminine (Fig. 1 (a)) and a neutral face might put on a smile (Fig. 1(b)). The work presented in this paper is an extension to the k-Same method. In addition to privacy protection, consideration has been taken for retaining the facial expression of the original image and the intensity of the expression.

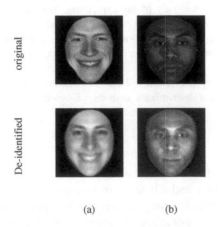

(a)   (b)

Fig. 1. Risk of losing data utility with the k-Same algorithm: (a) loss of gender and (b) loss of expression

The next section introduces the benchmark algorithms that support the method proposed in this work. Section 3 defines our method. Section 4 describes the face image database used in this work, gives an overview of the approaches used in the experiments and presents the results. Finally, the findings of this work are concluded in Sect. 5, with a discussion on the general applicability of this work and some proposals for further work.

2 Benchmark Methods

2.1 Principal Component Analysis and Face Recognition

Principal Component Analysis (PCA) is a benchmark method for the unsupervised reduction of dimensionality [8]. It has been widely used in the global approach to face recognition [9], where D-dimensional pixel-based face images are projected into a d-dimensional PCA subspace called the facespace (typically $d < <D$). The goal of PCA is to reduce the dimensionality of the face images while retaining as much as possible of the variation present in them. In face recognition, the PCA projection along with the face space are established through training a set of face images and PCA achieves its goal by projecting these training images along the directions where they vary the most. Figure 2 presents the general PCA-based training process of a face recognition system. Typically, the face space is defined based on the eigenvectors of the covariance matrix corresponding to the largest eigenvalues. The magnitude of the eigenvalues corresponds to the variance of the data along the eigenvector directions. In this work, all eigenvectors with a nonzero eigenvalue are kept to avoid losing information on data utility.

Let **H** be the training set of M face images and every image Γ_i in **H** be a $N \times 1$ vector. Perform the following steps:

1) $\bar{\Gamma} = \frac{1}{M}\sum_{i=1}^{M}\Gamma_i$
2) For each $\Gamma_i \in \mathbf{H}, \Phi_i = \Gamma_i - \bar{\Gamma}$
3) Form the matrix $\mathbf{A} = [\Phi_1,...,\Phi_M]$, then compute the covariance matrix $\mathbf{C} = \mathbf{A}\,\mathbf{A}^T$ (covariance matrix **C** characterizes the scatter of the face images in **H**)
4) Compute the eigenvalues $\lambda_1,...,\lambda_N$ of **C** such that $|\mathbf{C} - \lambda_i| = 0$ for $i = 1,...,N$
5) Sort eigenvalues in descending order, i.e. $\lambda_1 \geq \cdots \geq \lambda_N$ for $i = 1,...,N$
6) Compute the eigenvectors $\mathbf{v}_1,...,\mathbf{v}_N$ of **C** such that $\mathbf{Cv}_i = \lambda_i\mathbf{v}_i$ for $i = 1,...,N$
7) Select the top N' eigenvectors such that

$$\lambda_i \neq 0 \text{ for } i = 1,...,N'$$

8) Form the matrix $\mathbf{V} = [\mathbf{v}_1,...,\mathbf{v}_{N'}]$. Construct the eigen face space by projecting the training images to the PCA subspace defined by **V**:

$$\mathbf{facespace}_i = \mathbf{V}^T(\Gamma_i - \bar{\Gamma}) \text{ for } i = 1,...,M$$

Fig. 2. Training process of a PCA-based face recognition system

In face recognition, each PCA eigenvector is a face image. These eigenvectors are therefore named Eigenfaces. Figure 3 displays the top two and the last two Eigenfaces used in this work. The image set used for computing/training these Eigenfaces contains both neutral and smiley faces.

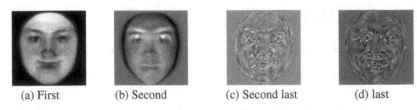

| (a) First | (b) Second | (c) Second last | (d) last |

Fig. 3. The first two and the last two Eigenfaces used in this work

PCA-based face recognition, also known as the Eigenfaces technique [9], projects a probe face image Γ into the Eigen face space using (1) and matches faces there based on the Euclidean distance:

$$\text{projected probe face: } \Omega = \mathbf{V}^T (\Gamma - \overline{\Gamma}), \tag{1}$$

2.2 Linear Discriminant Analysis and Classification of Facial Expression

Face data have multiple attributes and individual face images can be grouped into classes according to attributes such as age or gender. Although PCA is effective in terms of maximizing the scatter among individual face images, it ignores the underlying class structure. As a result, the projection axes chosen by PCA might not provide good discrimination power for classification purposes.

To this problem, Linear Discriminant Analysis (LDA) or Fisher Linear Discriminant (FLD) analysis [10, 11] seems to be the perfect solution as it maximizes the scatter between image classes while minimizing the scatter within the classes. The steps involved in the LDA process are presented in Fig. 4. With face data, $\mathbf{S}_W$ is often singular since image vectors are of large dimensionality while the size of the data set is much smaller. To alleviate this problem, typically the original face images are first projected into the PCA space to reduce dimensionality. LDA is then applied to find the most discriminative directions. In this work, $\mathbf{x}_i$ is the PCA projection of face image Γ_i. The eigenvectors obtained from LDA are called Fisherfaces. In the cases with two classes, for example our work, the corresponding eigenvalues will have only one nonzero value and therefore only the top Fisherface is kept and used for projecting data into the Fisher face space.

LDA can be used to estimate various attributes of the face, for example expression, gender, age, identity and race, etc. In this work, LDA has been used to identify the expression on a face as either 'neutral' or 'smiley' and evaluate the intensity of the expression identified. Next section presents more detail on how LDA is utilized in the proposed algorithm.

2.3 k-Same for Face de-Identification

Introduced for preserving privacy [5], k-Same is based on the k-anonymity framework of Sweeney's [7]. It guarantees that each de-identified face image could be representative of k faces and therefore limit the recognition risk of the de-identified faces to $1/k$.

1) For M $N \times 1$ samples $\{\mathbf{x}_1,...,\mathbf{x}_N\}$, C classes $\{\mathbf{X}_1,...,\mathbf{X}_C\}$, calculate the average $\boldsymbol{\mu}_i$ for each class i along with the total average $\boldsymbol{\mu}$.

2) Calculate the scatter $\mathbf{S}_i$ for each class i as

$$\mathbf{S}_i = \sum_{\mathbf{x}_k \in \mathbf{X}_i} (\mathbf{x}_k - \boldsymbol{\mu}_i)(\mathbf{x}_k - \boldsymbol{\mu}_i)^T$$

3) Calculate the within-class scatter as

$$\mathbf{S}_W = \sum_{i=1}^{C} \mathbf{S}_i$$

4) Calculate the between-class scatter as:

$$\mathbf{S}_B = \sum_{i=1}^{C} |\mathbf{X}_i|(\boldsymbol{\mu}_i - \boldsymbol{\mu})(\boldsymbol{\mu}_i - \boldsymbol{\mu})^T$$

5) Compute the matrix $\mathbf{C} = \mathbf{S}_W^{-1}\mathbf{S}_B$.

6) Compute the eigenvalues $\lambda_1,...,\lambda_N$ of $\mathbf{C}$ such that $|\mathbf{C} - \lambda_i| = 0$ for $i = 1,...,N$

7) Compute the eigenvectors (Fisherfaces) $\mathbf{v}_1,...,\mathbf{v}_N$ of $\mathbf{C}$ such that $\mathbf{C}\mathbf{v}_i = \lambda_i\mathbf{v}_i$ for $i = 1,...,N$.

Fig. 4. General procedure of LDA

In [5], Newton introduced two versions of the k-Same algorithm, namely k-Same-Pixel and k-Same-Eigen. Both versions find the k closest faces to the probe in the PCA face space, while the former returns the pixel-wise average of the k closest and the later performs the averaging in the PCA facespace. Compared to k-Same-Pixel, k-Same-Eigen brings an extra blurring effect which contributes to the reduction of ghost artifacts in the de-identified face. Considering this, this 7work follows the approach of k-Same-Eigen. For more in-depth details of the k-Same algorithm, refer to [5].

3   The New Algorithm–k-SameClass-Eigen

The k-Same algorithms ignores utility features of the face images (such as gender, age, and expression) and searches for the k closest faces merely based on the appearance. As displayed in Fig. 1, the utility information are often lost. To address this problem, consideration has been taken in this work for retaining the utility of the original face. Although this work focuses merely on facial expressions, the same principal can be applied to the preservation of other utilities of face images.

Inspired by [12], the algorithm proposed here is an extension to k-Same, where the k closest faces are selected only among the gallery faces with the same expression to the probe image. However, unlike [12] where the classification of facial expression is achieved using a support vector machine, our algorithm uses LDA. One advantage of LDA is that it is able to not only classify the expression but also evaluate the intensity of the expression. The work in [12] focused on the preservation of merely the class label of a given face image (e.g. male or female, young or old). While we aim to preserve both class label and intensity here. In this work, the LDA Fisher space is trained to classify two expression classes {neutral, smiley}. As shown in Fig. 5, the LDA projection of all the gallery neutral faces used in this work has an average of 4.2

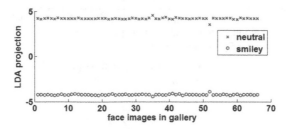

Fig. 5. LDA projection of the gallery images used in this work

with a small variance of 0.004; while the average LDA projection of the smiley faces is −4.2 with a small variance of 0.011. Results in Fig. 5 suggest that the LDA projection can be used as the classifier of facial expressions and the measure of expression intensity.

Furthermore, through changing the value of the LDA projection, fine adjustment of facial expression has been achieved in this work. As mentioned in the previous section, for a two-class problem only the top Fisherface is available for the LDA projection. Figure 6 displays the Fisherface used in this work. The number of components in the Fisherface equals the number of Eigenfaces used in our PCA projection. As the facial expression might be encoded by the last few Eigenfaces (refer to Fig. 3), all Eigenfaces with a nonzero Eigenvalue are kept in this work. As shown in Fig. 6, the Fisherface has a dominant component (the sixth component). In other words, the expression on a face is mainly determined by the value of this component. For this reason, this dominant component is named the 'expression index'. In this work, the expression on a face or the intensity of the expression is adjusted through changing the value of the expression index while keeping the value of other Fisherface components unchanged. Given a target expression intensity d, the value of the expression index $v(6)$ is changed to:

$$v(6)_{\text{new}} = d - \sum_{i=1}^{N} v(i) + v(6)_{\text{current}}. \tag{2}$$

As the algorithm proposed in this work selects the closest faces from a specific class in the gallery, we name it as k-SameClass-Eigen.

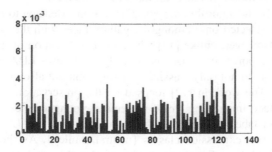

Fig. 6. The Fisherface used in this work

4   Experiments

4.1   Image Database: Binghamton

Our experiments have been carried out with the 95 × 95 gray scale images from the Binghamton database [13]. The face gallery in our experiments contains 132 Binghamton images (33 images from each of the following four classes: Female Neutral, Female Smiley, Male Neutral, and Male Smiley. All images in the gallery are used for training both the PCA and the LDA spaces.

4.2   Evaluation of Privacy

There are two types of probe image sets, 'seen' and 'unseen', with each set containing 20 images randomly selected from the Binghamton database. The 'seen' probe image set follows the closed universe model meaning that every face image in this probe set is also a member of the gallery whereas the face images in the 'unseen' probe set are taken from outside the gallery. Visual results of our k-SameClass-Eigen algorithm are displayed in Fig. 7 for k = 2, 5, 10, and 20 from left to right. Figure 7(I) displays the results for examples of seen probe faces and Fig. 7(II) displays the results for examples of unseen probe faces.

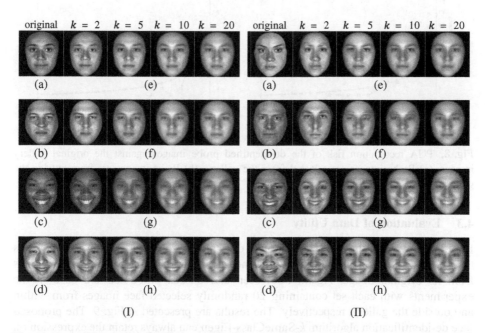

Fig. 7. Examples of (I) original seen and (II) original unseen face images as well as their de-identified faces generated by the method of k-SameClass-Eigen for k = 2, 5, 10, and 20 from left to right: (a) original female neutral, (b) original male neutral, (c) original female smiley, (d) original male smiley, and (e)–(h) de-identified results for (a)–(d)

To evaluate the privacy protection power of the proposed algorithm k-SameClass-Eigen, the de-identified probe images are matched to the original images in the gallery. The privacy protection performance is measured in terms of the average recognition risk of the de-identified face images. For the seen probe images, the recognition risk is the percentage at which a de-identified face is recognized as its own original. For the unseen probe images, it is the percentage of a de-identified face being recognised as the gallery image that is closest to the original probe. For both probe sets, close-set identification has been performed, i.e., the closest face from the gallery is always returned as the best match despite how large the closest distance is. To exam the impact of k, the level of k has been varied between 1 and 20. Figure 8(a) and (b) show the recognition risk for the de-identified seen and unseen probe faces, respectively.

In both Fig. 8(a) and (b), the recognition risk decreases with the increase of k-level and the recognition risk tends to remain lower than the theoretical maximum of $1/k$. The zig-zags presented in Fig. 8(a) and (b) are due to the relatively small size of each probe set, which can be improved by introducing more probe images. Nevertheless, the recognition risk converges to a value below $1/k$ in both Fig. 8(a) and (b) despite the fact of a small probe set.

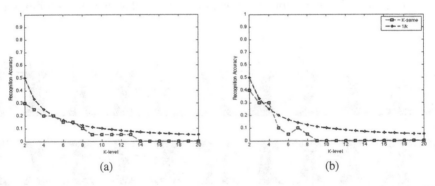

(a)   (b)

Fig. 8. PCA recognition risk of the de-identified probe images against the original gallery images. (a) Probe images are selected from the gallery. (b) Probe images are from outside the gallery

4.3   Evaluation of Data Utility

In order to evaluate the algorithm's power of retaining data utility, this work measures the rate at which the same expression is measured from a de-identified face image as from its original image. Again, both seen and unseen probe sets are used in the experiments with each set containing 20 randomly selected face images from within and outside the gallery, respectively. The results are presented in Fig. 9. The proposed face de-identification algorithm k-SameClass-Eigen can always retain the expression on a seen (or known) probe face and therefore delivers a perfect expression accuracy. For the unknown probe faces, the accurary is between 80% and 95% with an average of 86%. The lower expression accuracy with the unknown faces is due to the fact that the LDA has been trained with the known faces in the gallery and the LDA projection obtained in this way may fail to correctly classify an unknown face. When the expression on a unknown face has been incorrectly classified, the same incorrect expression with the measured expression intensity will be imposed onto the de-identified face by the *k*-SameClass-Eigen method using (2).

4.4   Evaluation of the Ability to Change Expression Intensity

In order to evaluate the algorithm's ability to adjust expression intensity and the visual quality of the result images, experiments are conducted in this work where the expression intensity on the de-identified neutral faces is continuously varied between 5 (completely neutral) and –5 (very happy). The range of the expression intensity is

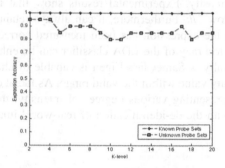

Fig. 9. Expression accuracy for both of the probe image

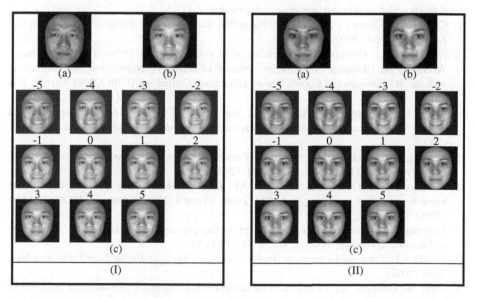

Fig. 10. Results of (I) an example male face and (II) an example female face. (a) original, (b) de-identified, and (c) mutations of (b) for various expression intensities (intensity values are given above the corresponding face image)

defined following the results of LDA training (refer to Fig. 5). Figure 10 displays the visual results for (I) an example male face and (II) an example female face, respectively. As displayed in Fig. 10, the proposed algorithm has the ability to switch between facial expressions and continuously adjust the intensity of the expression. Furthermore, the visual quality of the result images remains good across the various expression intensity values.

5   Discussion and Conclusions

A new face de-identification algorithm k-SameClass-Eigen has been proposed in this paper with a goal to preserve privacy as well as retain both the facial expression class and the expression intensity. Experimental results show that it is able to limit the recognition risk to below $1/k$. Furthermore, it can always retains the expression on a face image as long as the expression has been measured correctly by the LDA classifier. In practice, the accuracy of the LDA classifier can be enhanced by the use of a larger training set. Finally, k-SameClass-Eigen is capable of changing the expression intensity on a face to any value within the valid range. As facial expression is naturally a continuous motion presenting various degrees of intensity, the proposed algorithm has a great potential with the de-identification of real-world images and videos.

References

1. Sweeney, L.: Surveillance of Surveillances camera watch project (2005), http://dataprivacylab.org/dataprivacy/projects/camwatch
2. Crowley, J., Coutaz, J., Berard, F.: Perceptual user interfaces: things that see. Commun. ACM **43**, 54–64 (2000)
3. Neustaedter, C., Greenberg, S.: Balancing privacy and awareness in home media spaces. In: Workshop on Ubicomp Communities: Privacy as Boundary Negotiation, in Conjunction with the 5th International Conference on Ubiquitous Computing (UBICOMP), Seattle, WA (2003)
4. Boyle, M., Edwards, C., Greenberg, S.: The effects of filtered video on awareness and privacy. In: Proceedings of ACM Conference on Computer Supported Cooperative Work (2000)
5. Newton, E.M., Sweeney, L., Malin, B.: Preserving privacy by de-identifying face images. IEEE Trans. Knowl. Data Eng. **12**(2), 232–243 (2005)
6. Neustaedter, C., Greenberg, S., Boyle, M.: Blur filtration fails to preserve privacy for home-based video conferencing. ACM Trans. Comput. Human Interact. (TOCHI) **13**(1) (2006)
7. Sweeney, L.: k-Anonymity: a model for protecting privacy. Int'l J. Uncertainty, Fuzziness, and Knowledge-Based Systems, **10**(5), 557–570 (2002)
8. Jolliffe, I.T.: Principal Component Analysis, 2nd edn. Springer-Verlag New York, Inc., New York (2002)
9. Turk, M., Pentland, A.P.: Eigenfaces for recognition. J. Cognitive Neuroscience **3**(1), 71–86 (1991)

10. Belhumeur, P.N., Hespanha, J.P., Kriegman, D.J.: Eigenfaces vs. fisherfaces: recognition using class specific linear projection. IEEE Trans. Pattern Anal. Mach. Intell. **19**, 711–720 (1997)
11. Fisher, R.A.: The use of multiple measurements in taxonomic problems. Ann. Eugenics **7**(2), 179–188 (1936)
12. Gross, R., Airoldi, E., Malin, B., Sweeney, L.: Integrating utility into face de-identification. In: Workshop on Privacy-Enhanced Technologies (2005)
13. Yin, L., Wei, X., Sun, Y., Wang, J., Rosato, M.J.: A 3D facial expression database for facial behavior research. In: International Conference Automatic Face and Gesture Recognition (2006)

Semi-automatic Facial Key-Point Dataset Creation

Miroslav Hlaváč[1,2,3]($\boxtimes$), Ivan Gruber[1,2,3], Miloš Železný[1],
and Alexey Karpov[3,4]

[1] Department of Cybernetics, Faculty of Applied Sciences, UWB,
Pilsen, Czech Republic
{mhlavac,grubiv,zelezny}@kky.zcu.cz
[2] Faculty of Applied Sciences, NTIS, UWB,
Pilsen, Czech Republic
[3] ITMO University, St. Petersburg, Russia
karpov@iias.spb.su
[4] SPIIRAS, St. Petersburg, Russia

Abstract. This paper presents a semi-automatic method for creating
a large scale facial key-point dataset from a small number of annotated
images. The method consists of annotating the facial images by hand,
training Active Appearance Model (AAM) from the annotated images
and then using the AAM to annotate a large number of additional images
for the purpose of training a neural network. The images from the AAM
are then re-annotated by the neural network and used to validate the
precision of the proposed neural network detections. The neural network
architecture is presented including the training parameters.

Keywords: Key-points · Dataset · Annotation · Neural networks ·
Active appearance model · Images · Lips

1 Introduction

Key-points detection is a very important task in multiple fields like audio-visual
speech recognition, lip-reading, face identification and verification, tracking etc.
Key-points represent important features of the observed object. In the process of
speech recognition the key-points are used to measure the geometric and texture
characteristics of the speaker mouth region. The detection of facial key-points
is usually based on statistical methods of modelling the shape variations or in
recent years by the use of deep neural networks.

The process of training a neural network for key-point detection requires a
large number of data. The data are usually obtained by various forms of augmentations of a set of annotated images. The images may be annotated by hand
or by automatic methods. There are many datasets available across the scientific community [8] and for the purpose of key-point detection challenges. The
problem arises when a dataset needs to be created from a set of recorded data
without any annotations.

© Springer International Publishing AG 2017
A. Karpov et al. (Eds.): SPECOM 2017, LNAI 10458, pp. 662–668, 2017.
DOI: 10.1007/978-3-319-66429-3_66

In this article, we present a method of annotating a large number of images by manually annotating a few images and building an Active Appearance Model (AAM) [7,11] over the annotated data. The AAM is then used to create a training set of thousands of images with AAM detections as annotations. This data are then augmented by methods further discussed in the next section and used to train a neural network.

In others works [5,6], the authors create audio-visual datasets from TV shows by using elaborate pipelines and commercial tools. The key-points in those papers are detected by a simple Kanade-Lukas-Tomasi tracker [15]. This datasets are usually speaker independent and for the English language only. The use of neural networks allows for a reliable and fast simultaneous detection of multiple key-points. In [14] the authors used a cascade of convolutional networks to detect 5 face key-points in various poses.

2   Training Data Creation

The dataset was created for the purpose of speaker specific audio-visual speech recognition. Hours of video where the speaker reads a phonetically balanced set were recorded. The individual sessions were one hour long and each of them was captured under different settings to provide a various light and distance conditions. The speaker was always facing the camera and the same camera

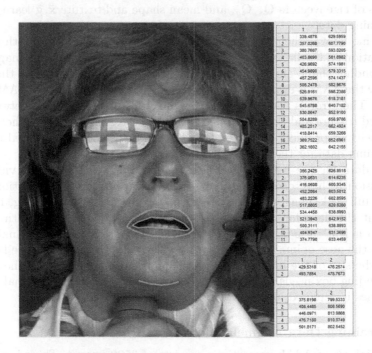

	1	2
1	339.4878	629.5959
2	357.0268	687.7790
3	380.7687	593.0205
4	403.8690	581.6982
5	426.9692	574.1981
6	454.9890	579.3315
7	487.2596	574.1437
8	508.2478	582.9676
9	526.9161	566.2386
10	539.9676	618.3181
11	545.6788	640.7182
12	530.0647	652.9100
13	504.8289	658.9786
14	485.2517	662.4924
15	418.8414	659.3266
16	389.7522	652.6961
17	362.1802	642.2155

	1	2
1	356.2425	626.0518
2	376.0631	614.6235
3	416.0608	600.9345
4	452.2084	603.5012
5	483.2226	602.8595
6	517.8895	620.8280
7	534.4458	638.8993
8	521.3943	642.9152
9	500.3111	638.8993
10	484.9347	631.3696
11	374.7798	633.4459

	1	2
1	429.5318	476.2574
2	493.7854	478.7673

	1	2
1	375.8198	799.5333
2	408.4485	808.5690
3	446.0971	813.0868
4	476.7180	810.0749
5	501.8171	802.5452

Fig. 1. Training data for AAM with annotated key-points

with automatic settings was used for Full HD recording. The image depicting one frame from a session with manually annotated key-points is shown in Fig. 1. The points are represented as a polygon to better illustrate the shape and the actual values are visible on the right side. We created a GUI application in Matlab for the purpose of annotating the data. The manual annotation can be sped up by training an AAM model from few annotated images and using it to create a preliminary fit where each point of the polygon can be manually shifted to a desired position.

The model is composed of 35 points with two indices (x, y). This gives a vector of 70 float numbers as a label for each image.

2.1 Active Appearance Model

We have trained an Active Appearance Model [7] from the set of 350 manually annotated data. The model consists of two Principal Component Analysis (PCA) over the shape and texture data and then an additional PCA to create a combined model. The basic formula for creating one instance of the model is given as follows:

$$\mathbf{x} = \bar{\mathbf{x}} + \mathbf{Q}_s \mathbf{c}, \tag{1}$$

$$\mathbf{g} = \bar{\mathbf{g}} + \mathbf{Q}_g \mathbf{c}, \tag{2}$$

where $\mathbf{x}, \mathbf{g}$ are instances of shape and texture, controlled by model parameters $\mathbf{c}$, matrices of eigenvectors $\mathbf{Q}_s, \mathbf{Q}_g$, and mean shape and texture $\bar{\mathbf{x}}, \bar{\mathbf{g}}$ learned from the training data.

The model was then used as a tracker for the recorded videos with manual initialization on the first frame. This process generated thousands of images with corresponding shape annotations made by the AAM. The quality of the shape found by the AAM is evaluated by the error [7] generated during the AAM fitting process. The error is computed as a per pixel absolute difference between the generated texture and the overlapped texture in the image. We have chosen only images with error under a selected threshold value as good fit and used them as the training data for the neural network.

The data for the network are then randomly chosen from each video and each session to have enough data representing various lighting conditions. The original full scale images were used for the purpose of AAM tracking, however we re-cut the data for the network by creating a bounding box with a fixed width to height ratio around the detected key-points. Since the original model includes the nose points with the lowest y values and the chin with the largest y values, the size of the bounding box is changing during speech and the data in the bounding box needs to be resized to a constant resolution. The final form of the images is depicted in Fig. 2.

2.2 Training Data Augmentation

The initial set of AAM annotations consists of 3500 images. These images are then augmented using Gaussian blur, additive Gaussian noise and various global

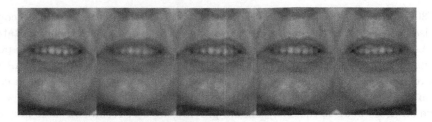

Fig. 2. Augmentations of the training data. Original image, Gaussian blur, augmentation of brightness, Gaussian noise, flip

intensities changes. The images were also horizontally flipped to produce a mirror like images. Labels for those images had to be adjusted to represent the flip by switching the corresponding indices. The augmentations are depicted in Fig. 2.

3   Network Architecture

We have tested various neural network architectures spanning from simple CNN used by Krizhevsky [10], VGGM [3], and VGG16 [12]. We then devised our own architecture for the purpose of this research based on experience with the previously mentioned networks parameters. The final architecture is depicted in Table 1.

Table 1. Parameters of deep neural network architecture used to detect mouth region key-points. All strides were set to 1. BN means batch normalization layer. Pooling is done by max-poling with kernel size 2 × 2. Dropout probability was set to 0.5

conv1	conv2	conv3	conv4	conv5	conv6	dense1	dense2	dense3
64 × 3 × 3	64 × 3 × 3	128 × 3 × 3	128 × 3 × 3	256 × 3 × 3	256 × 3 × 3	4096	4096	70
	pool 2 × 2		pool 2 × 2				drop-out	drop-out	
	BN		BN		BN	BN	BN	

The network is composed of 6 convolutional layers with kernels 3 and stride 1. After each other convolutional layer there is a max-pooling layer with kernel size 2 and stride 1, and batch normalization layer [9]. Dense1 and dense2 are regularised by drop-out [13]. All the layers besides the last use ReLU activation function, where dense3 uses linear activation to provide suitable output for regression. The network was trained by Stochastic Gradient Descent(SGD) with parameters $learning rate = 0.01, decay = 10^{-6}, momentum = 0.9$. The whole training was implemented using Keras [4] with Tensor Flow [1] back-end.

4   Experiments

Our network took 100 epochs to train. After this process the error converged to a value of 0.59. This value is a mean absolute error across all 70 values of the key-points coordinates. The error is computed on a set of development data.

300 additional images were manually annotated to provide a basis for comparison of AAM and the network performance. These images are then annotated by AAM and our network, and the results are compared in the Table 2. The performance is also evaluated on the original set of the training data for the AAM, where it should have clear advantage. Since the images were used for the creation of the model and all the perturbations for the fitting algorithm [7] were done on those images, the AAM should provide the best results on these images. However as can be seen in the first row of the table our network outperformed the AAM on the previously unseen data. It is notable to say that the accuracies are all in sub-pixel precisions. By visual analysis of the actual detections we draw a conclusion that most of the error is caused by the chin key-points where the boundary is detected accurately but the actual position of the key-points is not set by any clear markers. This causes a significant variance in the chin key-points coordinates in both AAM and our network in comparison to manual annotations where the annotator sticks to a consistent pattern.

Table 2. Accuracy of key-point detection of our NN vs. AAM. Manual annotations is a set of 300 images not used to train AAM. AAM training is the original set used to create the model

	AAM	Network
Manual annotations	0.9843	0.8412
AAM training	0.6712	0.8151

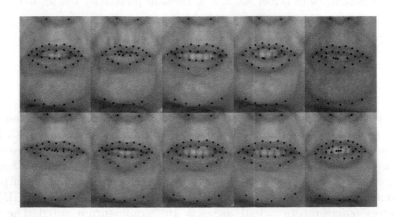

Fig. 3. Results of key-point detection by our network - top row, and AAM - bottom row. The last column shows examples of wrong detection

The results of key-point detections are also shown in Fig. 3, where in the top line are detections from our network, the bottom line contains detections from the AAM. Images of wrong detections are also included as last in the line. These images are part of test dataset which does not include the augmentations but only the real data cut from the original recordings.

5   Conclusion and Future Work

We have presented a semi-automatic method for creating large scale dataset from a small initial set of manually annotated images. The network was able to learn the distribution of the key-points and the internal relations between them to provide a tool for automatic annotation of large scale dataset. We have also showed that the network was able to outperform the AAM algorithm in previously unseen data, which was tested in a separated dataset with manual annotations. Since both methods are able to provide sub-pixel accuracy the main advantage of the network lies in its speed.

In the future we would like to include the forced aligned annotations for audio signal to create an audio visual dataset with people speaking using electrolarynx [2]. This will lead to further research in audio-visual speech recognition and synthesis for the people after laryngectomy.

Acknowledgments. This work is supported by grant of the University of West Bohemia, project No. SGS-2016-039, by Ministry of Education, Youth and Sports of Czech Republic, project No. LO1506, by Russian Foundation for Basic Research, projects No. 15-07-04415 and 16-37-60100, and by the Government of Russia, grant No. 074-U01. Computational resources were supplied by the Ministry of Education, Youth and Sports of the Czech Republic under the Projects CESNET (Project No. LM2015042) and CERIT-Scientific Cloud (Project No. LM2015085) provided within the program Projects of Large Research, Development and Innovations Infrastructures.

References

1. Abadi, M., Barham, P., Chen, J., Chen, Z., Davis, A., Dean, J., Devin, M., Ghemawat, S., Irving, G., Isard, M., et al.: TensorFlow: a system for large-scale machine learning. In: Proceedings of the 12th USENIX Symposium on Operating Systems Design and Implementation (OSDI), Savannah, Georgia, USA (2016)
2. Barney, H., Haworth, F., Dunn, H.: An experimental transistorized artificial larynx. Bell Syst. Tech. J. **38**(6), 1337–1356 (1959)
3. Chatfield, K., Simonyan, K., Vedaldi, A., Zisserman, A.: Return of the devil in the details: delving deep into convolutional nets. arXiv preprint arXiv:1405.3531 (2014)
4. Chollet, F., et al.: Keras: deep learning library for Theano and TensorFlow (2015). https://keras.io/k (2015)
5. Chung, J.S., Senior, A., Vinyals, O., Zisserman, A.: Lip reading sentences in the wild. arXiv preprint arXiv:1611.05358 (2016)
6. Chung, J., Zisserman, A.: Lip reading in the wild. In: Asian Conference on Computer Vision (2016)
7. Cootes, T.F., Taylor, C.J., et al.: Statistical models of appearance for computer vision (2004)

8. Gruber, I., Hlaváč, M., Hrúz, M., Železný, M., Karpov, A.: An analysis of visual faces datasets. In: Ronzhin, A., Rigoll, G., Meshcheryakov, R. (eds.) ICR 2016. LNCS, vol. 9812, pp. 18–26. Springer, Cham (2016). doi:10.1007/978-3-319-43955-6_3
9. Ioffe, S., Szegedy, C.: Batch normalization: accelerating deep network training by reducing internal covariate shift. arXiv preprint arXiv:1502.03167 (2015)
10. Krizhevsky, A., Sutskever, I., Hinton, G.E.: ImageNet classification with deep convolutional neural networks. In: Pereira, F., Burges, C.J.C., Bottou, L., Weinberger, K.Q. (eds.) Advances in Neural Information Processing Systems, vol. 25, pp. 1097–1105. Curran Associates Inc., Red Hook (2012)
11. Matthews, I., Baker, S.: Active appearance models revisited. Int. J. Comput. Vision 60(2), 135–164 (2004)
12. Simonyan, K., Zisserman, A.: Very deep convolutional networks for large-scale image recognition. CoRR abs/1409.1556 (2014)
13. Srivastava, N., Hinton, G.E., Krizhevsky, A., Sutskever, I., Salakhutdinov, R.: Dropout: a simple way to prevent neural networks from overfitting. J. Mach. Learn. Res. 15(1), 1929–1958 (2014)
14. Sun, Y., Wang, X., Tang, X.: Deep convolutional network cascade for facial point detection. In: Proceedings of the IEEE conference on computer vision and pattern recognition, pp. 3476–3483 (2013)
15. Tomasi, C., Kanade, T.: Selecting and tracking features for image sequence analysis. Robotics and Automation (1992)

Song Emotion Recognition Using Music Genre Information

Athanasios Koutras[✉]

Informatics and Mass Media Department,
TEI of Western Greece, 27100 Pyrgos, Greece
koutras@teiwest.gr

Abstract. Music Emotion Recognition (MER) is an important topic in music understanding, recommendation and retrieval that has gained great attention in the last years due to the constantly increasing number of people accessing digital musical content. In this paper we propose a new song emotion recognition system that takes into consideration the song's genre and we investigate the effect that genre has, on the recognition task of four basic music emotions of the valence-arousal (VA) plane: happy, angry, sad and peaceful. Experiments on a database consisting of 1100 songs from four different music genres (blues, country, pop and rock) using timbral, spectral, dynamical and chroma descriptors of the music, have shown that successful recognition of the song's genre as a pre-processing step, can improve the recognition of its emotion by a factor of 10–15%.

Keywords: Music emotion · Music genre · ICA mixture models

1 Introduction

During the last years, there has been a vast flourishing of digital music libraries making music listening accessible to almost everyone. More and more people nowadays have gained easy access to digital musical content while being on the road, or in their homes through their smart phones, tablets, smart TVs, etc. Services like Spotify, Pandora or Lastfm, offer a wealth of music content that users can browse and categorize based on their genre, ethnicity, era, emotion, etc. It is therefore a huge need to develop automated systems that will help search, organize and categorize music content and related data [1, 2].

Among the most encountered search and retrieval criteria when it comes to music information, is the music genre. This characteristic when compared with others is more easily quantified to a correct and generally agreed upon answer, and this is the main reason why it has gained better attention from researchers worldwide [3–6]. On the other hand, searching for emotions that a song carries, or keeping track of the changes in a song's mood, has also been a criterion of people in their search for the right tracks when they want to build a custom playlist depending on their state, activity they are engaged into, mood etc. But music emotion, in contrast to music genre or category is far from being easily quantified and definitely, not only one correct and generally agreed upon answer exists. This is the main reason automatic recognition of music emotion is still in early stages but is receiving a great interest in the recent years [7–9].

© Springer International Publishing AG 2017
A. Karpov et al. (Eds.): SPECOM 2017, LNAI 10458, pp. 669–679, 2017.
DOI: 10.1007/978-3-319-66429-3_67

Recognizing emotion in songs involves various disciplines that span from the signal processing area, pattern recognition and machine learning as well as auditory perception, psychology and theory of music [7, 8]. Music theory and auditory perception are used to extract features and characteristics from the songs that could best describe the emotional state of a song. Different approaches have been proposed in music emotion estimation that take into account either the whole music song, or a representative section of the song (e.g. chorus, verse), a fixed-length clip (e.g. 20–30 s duration), or a shorter segment (e.g. 1 s) depending on the application under test. In every situation, a set of features are extracted that represent mood as either a single multi-dimensional vector, or a time series of vectors that change over the space of emotions. As opposed to emotion recognition where one can extract features from a segment or successive segments of a song to track the changes of the song's mood, in the task of genre recognition, features are extracted by considering the whole song.

Although there has been a great deal of research during the last years in the area of music genre recognition, research that studies the relation (if any) between genre and emotion of songs is still very limited to our knowledge. In this paper we propose a new song emotion recognition system that takes into consideration the song's genre and we investigate the effect that genre has on the recognition of four basic music emotions: happy, angry, sad, peaceful that span over all four quadrants of the valence-arousal plane.

The structure of this paper is as follows: In the next section we present the proposed song emotion recognition system. The system consists of a feature extraction module that calculates the music genre and emotion descriptors, together with a feature selection algorithm that reduces the dimensionality of the feature descriptors and estimates the most significant ones depending on the song's genre. In the same section, we present the music genre recognition system that is based on the ICA mixture model classifier and the emotion recognition system that uses SVM classifiers. In Sect. 3 the experimental setup and results are presented, while in Sect. 4 some conclusions and remarks are given.

2 Method

In this paper we examine the role of music genre in the automatic song emotion recognition task. To this end, we propose a system that consists of two main modules: The first is used to recognize the song's genre from a list of well-known genres using ICA mixture model classifiers. The second is used to recognize the song's emotion, based on a set of different trained SVM emotion classifiers, one for each music genre. The feature set that is used in both modules consists of timbral, spectral, dynamical and chroma descriptors of music. Furthermore, we also examine whether the inclusion of an extra feature selection step, can find the most representative features that characterize each music genre effectively, reduce the dimensionality of the feature vector and finally improve the accuracy of the second module.

The overall system is shown in Fig. 1. In the next sections we present analytically the parts of the proposed emotion recognition system.

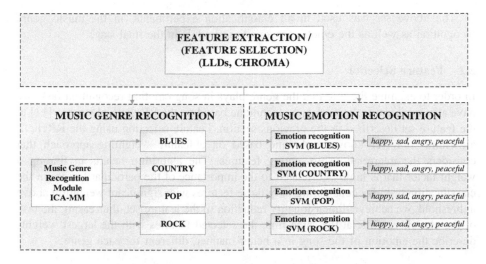

Fig. 1. The two level emotion recognition system

2.1 Feature Extraction

The purpose of the feature extraction step is to estimate the appropriate set of features that can differentiate songs according to their music genre and emotion [10]. In Music Information Retrieval (MIR), these features are discriminated mainly into two categories: (a) Low Level Descriptors (LLDs) of the timbre and the dynamics of the songs and (b) Chroma Descriptors (CHROMA) that capture the song's tonality. The total features are in most of the cases expanded by applying to them a number of statistical functionals [10].

In this paper for the music genre and emotion recognition task we have used 18 LLDs: the signal Loudness (F1), the number of Zero Crossings (F2), four spectral descriptors (F3–F6) (the roll-off point 95%, the spectrum entropy, the spectrum centroid, and the spectrum variance), and the first 12 cepstral coefficients computed at 16-band power Mel-spectrum, MFCC (F7–F18). From the second category, the 12 CHROMA descriptors are computed from the 12 Chroma features (F19–F30).

To all derived features, a temporal smoothing is applied to eliminate possible artifacts by averaging the estimated descriptors using a moving average filter with window length 3 (taking the previous, the next and the current window in the smoothing process).

All above descriptors are estimated independently from successive frames of the songs and therefore, no information of previous or next frames of the audio is included into them. In order to include the important temporal information that is present in music due to its nature, we have also included 30 delta regression coefficients as in [10]. To the above 60 descriptors in total (18 LLDs, 12 CHROMA, together with their 30 delta regression coefficients), 4 functionals are applied, which include the arithmetic mean, the standard deviation, the skewness and their kurtosis, resulting to a total set of 240 descriptors for each music excerpt.

The above set was used in all classification experiments, in the music genre recognition as well as the emotion recognition module in the final stage.

2.2   Feature Selection

In order to examine the role that the genre plays in song emotion recognition task, we have also applied a feature selection technique based on the RReliefF algorithm [11] to the feature set described in the previous section. Feature selection using the RReliefF algorithm is a well-known technique based on a feature weighting approach that considers the interrelationship among features. The algorithm results in finding a weight factor that is highly correlated to the importance of the particular feature in the classification task. By considering only those features with significant weighting above a threshold, we achieve dimensionality reduction of the feature set, thus easing the task of the classifier, while at the same time the selected features with the largest weights describe the emotion of the song in a better manner, different for each genre.

2.3   Genre Recognition Module

For song genre recognition we have used the ICA mixture model (ICA-MM) based classifier. Classification based on ICA-MM has been widely used in many situations that include but are not limited to speech recognition, image processing, biomedical signal analysis and many others, showing great performance and recognition accuracy.

An ICA-MM based classifier tries to estimate the ICA model parameters for each class in an unsupervised manner, being presented only with a number of training samples. The ICA-MM based classifier can work completely in blind as well as in semi-blind manner. In the first case, the number of different classes of the training data is completely unknown and the model estimates it together with the parameters for every class. In the second case, the ICA-MM classifier knows the number of the classes beforehand, and it only estimates the parameters for each class. In this study, the number of the different classes is known beforehand and equals to the number of the different music genre categories the songs fall into.

When a mixture model is used in classification problems [12, 13], the observed data are categorized into several mutually exclusive classes. The utilized ICA-MM, which is a generalization of the Gaussian mixture model (GMM), models each class with independent variables. The main superiority that ICA mixture model presents when compared to the GMM, is that it allows modeling of classes with non-Gaussian structure (i.e. leptokyrtic or platykyrtic) something that fits in the case of music information characterization.

Let assume that the observed data $\mathbf{X} = \{\mathbf{x}_1, \mathbf{x}_2, ..., \mathbf{x}_T\}$ (with $\mathbf{x}_i$ an N-dimensional vector) are drawn independently and are generated by a mixture density model. The likelihood of the data is given by:

$$p\left(\mathbf{X}|\Theta\right) = \prod_{t=1}^{T} p\left(\mathbf{x}_t|\Theta\right), \tag{1}$$

and the mixture density is:

$$p(\mathbf{x}_t|\Theta) = \sum_{k=1}^{K} p(\mathbf{x}_t|C_k, \theta_k)p(C_k), \tag{2}$$

where $\Theta = \{\theta_1, \theta_2, ..., \theta_K\}$ are the unknown parameters for each component density p $(\mathbf{x}|C_k, \theta_k)$. By C_k we denote the class k which is known beforehand. The data $\mathbf{x}_t$ within each class are considered to be generated by:

$$\mathbf{x}_t = \mathbf{A}_k\mathbf{s}_k + \mathbf{b}_k, \tag{3}$$

where $\mathbf{A}_k$ is a NxN scalar matrix and $\mathbf{b}_k$ is a vector containing the biases for each class. The vector $\mathbf{s}_k$ is called the source vector that generates the observed data $\mathbf{x}_t$ in each class.

In order to find the mixture models parameters $\{\mathbf{A_k}, \mathbf{b_k}\}$ for each class, we process the training data of each class separately in the following way: Let us assume we want to find the model parameters for class C_k. The observations $\mathbf{X_k}$ are fed into the ICA network, which results in the independent source data $\mathbf{s_k}$ for the class C_k:

$$\mathbf{s}_k = \mathbf{W}_k \cdot \mathbf{X}_k. \tag{4}$$

The matrix $\mathbf{W_k}$ is a scalar NxN matrix, called separating matrix. The separating matrix is learnt adaptively by [14]:

$$\Delta\mathbf{W}_k = n \cdot \left(\mathbf{I} - f(\mathbf{s}_k) \cdot \mathbf{s}_k^T\right) \cdot \mathbf{W}_k, \tag{5}$$

where the nonlinear function $f(.)$ is directly associated with the probability density function of the source data $\mathbf{s_k}$ in each class and plays an important role to the efficacy of the ICA network's performance. In our case the non-linear function was chosen to be the $tanh(.)$ function. The model parameter $\mathbf{A_k}$ is the inverse of the separating matrix $\mathbf{W_k}$ and can be calculated by $\mathbf{A_k} = \mathbf{W_k^{-1}}$.

The bias vector $\mathbf{b_k}$ is estimated as the mean value of the observations $\mathbf{X_k}$ and it's role is to allow non-zero-meaned data to be classified as well.

At the end of the learning procedure, we have estimated the K sets of parameters for our ICA-MM $\theta_k = \{\mathbf{A_k}, \mathbf{b_k}\}$. These will be used in the classification procedure, which consists of the following steps:

- First we compute the log-likelihood of the testing data for each one of the classes using:

$$\log p(\mathbf{x}_t|C_k, \theta_k) = \log p(\mathbf{s}_k) - \log(\det|\mathbf{A}_k|). \tag{6}$$

Note that in the above equation $\mathbf{s}_k$ is calculated by $\mathbf{s}_k = \mathbf{A}_k^{-1} \cdot (\mathbf{x}_t - \mathbf{b}_k)$.

- Next the probability for each class is computed given the testing vector $\mathbf{x}_t$ as:

$$p(C_k|\mathbf{x}_t, \Theta) = \frac{p(\mathbf{x}_t|Ck, \theta_k)p(C_k)}{\sum_k p(\mathbf{x}_t|Ck, \theta_k)p(C_k)}, \tag{7}$$

- Finally, the classification of the unknown data $\mathbf{x}_t$ is performed using the following decision rule based on the maximum class probability:

$$\mathbf{x}_t \in \arg\max_{C_k}(p(C_k|\mathbf{x}_t, \theta_k)). \tag{8}$$

2.4   Emotion Recognition Module

Russell and Thayer [15] proposed the Arousal – Valence model (Fig. 2) which is widely accepted and used by researchers in the field of Music Information Retrieval. The AV model consists of a 2D plane with arousal and valence on its principal axes. In the horizontal axis is the valence which describes how positive (rightmost values on the axis) or negative (leftmost values on the axis) the emotion of the song is characterized by the listener, whereas in the vertical axis is the arousal describing how exiting (upper values) or calming (lower values) a song is. Both axes range in the [−1:1] with values closer to 1 denoting higher positive and exciting emotions.

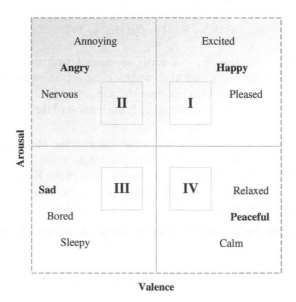

Fig. 2. The Valence – Arousal (AV) emotion plane

The AV plane can be clustered into four distinct areas – four quadrants and due to the pair values of the valence – arousal, four major categories of music emotion are constructed: (a) emotions in the first quadrant (Q1): excited, happy, pleased (b) emotions in the second quadrant (Q2): annoying, angry, nervous (c) emotions in the third quadrant (Q3): sad, bored, sleepy and finally (d) emotions in the fourth quadrant (Q4): relaxed, peaceful, calm.

Emotion recognition in this work is performed using different Support Vector Machines [16, 17] with 4 outputs (the number of the quadrant that the song's emotion lays) for every music genre category the song under test belongs to. In the case when the Feature Selection algorithm is used, the SVMs have different inputs that correspond to the outcome of the RReliefF algorithm for each music genre.

3 Experiments

For our experiments we have used songs taken from the Free Music Archive (FMA) [18]. The database consists of 1100 unique song excerpts, 30 s long, all with sampling frequency of 44100 Hz. The 30 s excerpts are extracted from random (uniform distribution) starting points for each song.

The songs are categorized in 4 different music genres: Blues, Country, Pop and Rock. All songs were annotated by human listeners aged between 23–30 years old with no professional experience in music. The songs were annotated for their arousal and separately for their valence value. The annotators were asked to mark the song's emotion, and not the emotional state they were into at the time of the experiment. As mentioned in the previous section, the proposed emotion recognition system classifies each song in one of the four quadrants of the AV plane. To test the performance of the proposed emotion recognition system, we have taken into account each song's emotion ground truth, which is estimated via subjective tests of at least 10 listeners by averaging their opinions on the valence and the arousal value in the scale of $[-1:1]$ and mark the quadrant the song's emotion falls into. In Table 1 we present the distribution of the database songs used for the testing purposes on the AV plane using four principle emotions: Happy (Q1), Angry (Q2), Sad (Q3) and Peaceful (Q4).

All songs were re-sampled to the format of 16 kHz, 16bit resolution and mono channel PCM wave files prior to their processing described in the next section.

Table 1. Number of songs in TS used in the emotion recognition task

	Blues	Country	Pop	Rock	Total
Q1	25	20	20	25	90
Q2	20	18	19	24	81
Q3	20	16	22	21	79
Q4	19	19	23	19	80
Total	84	73	84	89	**330**

4   Results

In our experiments we initially used the song database to form two subsets: the training set (TR) that contains 60% of the songs (770 songs) and the testing set (TS) containing the rest of the songs (330 songs). To be fair, when forming the subsets, we have taken into consideration that all different music genres were equally (as far as this can be accomplished) represented in both training and testing sets (Table 1).

All features described in the previous section, were extracted using the openSMILE tool [19] and were normalized using the mean – variance normalization (MVN) technique [10]. The normalized features of the songs in the training set were used in the ICA based classifier to estimate the ICA mixture model parameters for each music genre. For the music genre classification task, the songs of the testing set were classified by estimating the a-posteriori maximum class probability of the different genre ICA models given in Eq. 8.

In our genre recognition experiment, the proposed ICA-MM classifier accomplishes a recognition accuracy of 88.18% (291/330 songs). In Table 2 we present the confusion matrix of the ICA-MM classifier. It is clear that the proposed classifier works better for the Country and Pop music genres (over 89% accuracy), while achieves great performance for the remaining genres as well (88% in recognizing the Rock and 85% the Blues songs). For comparison reasons, instead of the ICA-MM, the 3rd order polynomial kernel SVM classifier was trained using the 770 songs of the training set (TR) in the same music genre task, however its accuracy on the 330 songs of the testing set (TS) was measured to be 79.69% (263/330 songs), significantly lower than that of the ICA-MM classifier. In order to find the best configuration of the SVM classifier, throughout this paper, a "grid-search" approach was used in a systematic manner with different values for the classifier parameters (C: soft margin constant, d: degree of the polynomial) followed by a cross validation to pick the best combination. The polynomial kernel was chosen as it was found to have superior performance when compared to the linear as well as the RBF kernel based SVM in all cases.

Table 2. Genre Recognition using ICA-MM classifier

	Blues	Country	Pop	Rock
Blues	**72/84**	5/84	3/84	4/84
Country	2/73	**65/73**	1/73	5/73
Pop	1/84	3/84	**75/84**	5/84
Rock	3/89	5/89	2/89	**79/89**

In our emotion recognition experiment, where *no prior knowledge* of the music genre was taken into account, a 3rd order polynomial kernel SVM recognizer (that was found to perform better compared to the linear and RBF kernels) was trained using the 240 dimensional feature vectors of the 770 songs in TR, and tested using the 330 songs in the TS. The emotion classification has reached an accuracy of 69.39% (Q1: 67.77%, Q2: 72.83%, Q3: 69.62%, Q4: 67.5%).

To examine the significance of the music genre on song emotion recognition, we have trained four different SVM classifiers, one for each different genre (Blues, Country, Pop, Rock) using songs taken from the TR set. Each classifier was trained to recognize the quadrant (thus the emotion) each song belongs to, using initially the 240 LLD and Chroma descriptors. For all four SVM classifiers, the polynomial kernel SVMs (3rd order for the Pop and Rock genre, 4th order for Blues and Country) were found to perform best.

In addition, all extracted features, were analyzed independently for each genre using the RReliefF algorithm to find the most representative ones for each music genre category. Then, the emotion of the songs in the TS was recognized, using four different SVM classifiers with inputs according to the RReliefF outcome. For all four SVM classifiers, again the polynomial kernel SVMs (3rd order for all genres) were found to perform at best.

In Table 3 we present the emotion recognition results when using all 240 features for all songs in TS by taking into account their genre classification from the previous step and using the appropriate SVM emotion classifier. The four SVM classifiers present a total recognition accuracy of 77.57% and classify correctly 256 out of 330 songs emotions. The classifiers performance is further analyzed and was found to categorize 69/90 (76.66%) songs emotion in Q1, 65/81 (80.24%) songs emotion in Q2, 60/79 (75.94%) songs emotion in Q3 and finally 62/80 (77.5%) songs emotion in quadrant Q4 in the case of the 240-dimension feature vector. The performance of the classifier is stable across the music genres or the different emotions of the song with a slight exception of the "sad" emotion (Q3).

In the same Table, we present the emotion recognition results for the songs in the TS after the application of the RReliefF feature selection algorithm. From the results, it can be seen that the proposed method works better and manages to recognize the emotion of the songs up to 85.15% (Q1: 81.11%, Q2: 83.95%, Q3: 87.34% and Q4: 88,75%), taking advantage of the information of their music genre.

Table 3. Emotion recognition results using (a) 240-dimension feature vector and (b) feature selection technique based on the RReliefF algorithm

		Q1	Q2	Q3	Q4
Q1	240 features	69/90	10/90	5/90	6/90
	RReliefF	**73/90**	9/90	3/90	5/90
Q2	240 features	8/81	65/81	4/81	4/81
	RReliefF	9/81	**68/81**	2/81	2/81
Q3	240 features	6/79	5/79	60/79	8/79
	RReliefF	1/79	3/79	**69/79**	6/79
Q4	240 features	6/80	4/80	8/80	62/80
	RReliefF	2/80	1/80	6/80	**71/80**

5 Conclusion

In this paper we have studied the effect that music genre has on the recognition of a song's emotion. We propose a song emotion recognition system that consists of two modules: A genre recognition module based on the ICA mixture model classifier and an emotion recognition module that recognizes the emotion of the song based on different genre SVM classifiers. To find the most representative descriptors for each genre, we have applied the RReliefF feature selection algorithm on a set of timbral, spectral, dynamical and chroma features and estimated different feature sets with reduced dimensionality and differences between music genres. Experiments have shown the proposed method's efficacy in the task of four basic music emotions recognition when genre is taken into account, achieving an overall recognition accuracy of 85%, greater than 15% compared to the classification accuracy when music genre is not taken into account. Further studies should examine the efficacy of the proposed method on bigger datasets with songs from different music genre categories as well as different within the same quadrants of the AV plane emotions.

References

1. Fu, Z., Lu, G., Ting, K.M., Zhang, D.: A survey of audio-based music classification and annotation. IEEE Trans. Multimedia 13(2), 303–319 (2011)
2. Tzanetakis, G., Cook, P.: Music analysis and retrieval systems for audio signals. J. Am. Soc. Inform. Sci. Technol. 55(12), 1077–1083 (2004)
3. Li, T., Ogihara, M., Li, Q.: A comparative study on content-based music genre classification. In: Proceedings of the 26th Annual International ACM SIGIR Conference on Research and Development in Information Retrieval, pp. 282–289 (2003)
4. Baniya, B.K., Ghimire, D., Lee, J.: Automatic music genre classification using timbral texture and rhythmic content features. ICACT Trans. Adv. Commun. Technol. (TACT) 3(3), 434–443 (2014)
5. Scaringella, N., Zoia, G., Mlynek, D.: Automatic genre classification of music content: a survey. IEEE Sig. Process. Mag. 23(2), 133–141 (2006)
6. Tzanetakis, G., Cook, P.: Musical genre classification of audio signals. IEEE Trans. Speech Audio Process. 10(5), 293–302 (2002)
7. Yang, Y.H., Chen, H.: Music Emotion Recognition. CRC Press, Boca Raton (2011)
8. Kim, Y.E., Schmidt, E.M., Migneco, R., Morton, BG, Richardson, P., Scott, J., Specj, J.A., Turnbull, D.: Music emotion recognition: a state of the art review. Int. Soc. Music Inf. Retrieval 255–266 (2010)
9. Koolagudi, S.G., Sreenivasa, R.K.: Emotion recognition from speech: a review. Int. J. Speech Technol. 15, 99–117 (2012)
10. Eyben, F.: Real-time Speech and Music Classification by Large Audio Feature Space Extraction. ST. Springer, Cham (2016). doi:10.1007/978-3-319-27299-3
11. Robnik-Sikinja, M., Kononenko, I.: Theoretical and empirical analysis of reliefF and rreliefF. Mach. Learn. 53, 23–69 (2003)
12. Lee, T.W., Lewicki, M.S.: Unsupervised image classification, segmentation, and enhancement using ICA mixture models. IEEE Trans. Image Process. 11(3), 270–279 (2002)

13. Lee, T.W., Lewicki, M.S., Sejnowski, T.J.: ICA mixture models for unsupervised classification of non-Gaussian classes and automatic context switching in blind signal separation. IEEE Trans. Pattern Anal. Mach. Intell. **22**(10), 1078–1089 (2000)
14. Cardoso, J.: Blind signal separation: statistical principles. IEEE Proc. **9**(10), 2009–2025 (1998)
15. Thayer, R.E.: The Biopsychology of Mood and Arousal. Oxford University Press, New York (1989)
16. Vapnik, V.: Statistical Learning Theory. Wiley, New York (1998)
17. Shen, P., Pan, Y., Shen, L.: Speech emotion recognition using support vector machine. Int. J. Smart Home **6**(2), 101–108 (2012)
18. Free Music Archive HomePage. http://freemusicarchive.org/. Last Accessed 10 Apr 2017
19. Eyben, F., Weninger, F., Gross, F., Schuller, B.: Recent developments in openSMILE, the munich open-source multimedia feature extractor. In: Proceedings of ACM Multimedia (MM), Barcelona, Spain, pp. 835–838. ACM (2013)

Spanish Corpus for Sentiment Analysis Towards Brands

María Navas-Loro[1](✉)(iD), Víctor Rodríguez-Doncel[1](iD),
Idafen Santana-Perez[1](iD), and Alberto Sánchez[2]

[1] Ontology Engineering Group, Universidad Politécnica de Madrid, Madrid, Spain
mnavas@fi.upm.es
[2] Havas Media, Madrid, Spain

Abstract. Posts published in the social media are a good source of
feedback to assess the impact of advertising campaigns. Whereas most
of the published corpora of messages in the Sentiment Analysis domain
tag posts with polarity labels, this paper presents a corpus in Spanish
language where tagging has been made using 8 predefined emotions: love-
hate, happiness-sadness, trust-fear, satisfaction-dissatisfaction. In every
post, extracted from Twitter, sentiments have been annotated towards
each specific brand under study. The corpus is published as a collection of RDF resources with links to external entities. Also a vocabulary
describing this emotion classification along with other relevant aspects
of customer's opinion is provided.

Keywords: Corpus · Sentiment analysis · NLP · Opinion mining

1 Introduction

Emotions, rather than cognitive thinking, determine our purchase decisions.
Modern marketing campaigns strive to link brands to specific emotions and
the success of these campaigns can be evaluated with more complex instruments
than the mere figures of sales. Emotions aroused by brands can be found in posts
in the social media, and computer algorithms can, to some extent, automatically
evaluate the impact of the marketing campaigns. These messages are important
per se, as a large percent of social media users (up to 70% according to Nielsen
[33]) take into account the product experience published by other users.

Even if Sentiment Analysis has progressed fast in the last few years, there is
not much research on other aspects of the message besides polarity that might
be useful for commercial companies and the image of their brands. One of the
objectives of the LPS BIGGER [25] project is to cover this gap. The intended
analysis goes deeper in more complex aspects and nuances of opinions, such as
the feelings arisen in customers by different brands or the stage in the whole
shopping process the client is in at the moment of giving their opinion. Once
combined, all these analyses result into remarkably rich information that opens
up rich potential exploitation opportunities, such as automatically personalized

© Springer International Publishing AG 2017
A. Karpov et al. (Eds.): SPECOM 2017, LNAI 10458, pp. 680–689, 2017.
DOI: 10.1007/978-3-319-66429-3_68

offering generation or immediate reactions to events related to brands. Focusing mainly on Twitter as source of opinions, at least the following four aspects (see Fig. 1) are of interest with respect to the brands:

- **Sentiment Analysis** identifies emotions towards a brand in a post beyond polarity. Several classification of human sentiments have been proposed in Psychology, such as Plutchik's [36] or Ekman's [14]; the one used in the project is based in the taxonomy stated by the latter in conjunction with those by Shaver [45] and Richins [39], distinguishing between four non-exclusive sentiments and their direct opposite: *love* and *hate*, *happiness* and *sadness*, *trust* and *fear*, and *satisfaction* and *dissatisfaction*. This new taxonomy has been proposed by industrial partners in the LPS BIGGER project as a response of an uncovered necessity of an emotion taxonomy thought specifically for marketing purposes.
- **Purchase Funnel** places the opinion within a five-staged consumer decision journey: *Awareness, Evaluation, Purchase, Postpurchase* and *Review*.
- **Marketing Mix** comprises the different marketing strategies the customers can evaluate, known as the four Ps: *product, price, promotion* and *place* [3].
- **Meaningful Brands**^{TM} is a metric proposed by Havas Media [23] that measures the value of the brand, based on the customer's wellbeing. It is divided in *marketplace* (relating the product to performance such as quality and price), *personal wellbeing* (such as self-esteem) and *collective wellbeing* (the role brands play in communities).

Given that the available corpora, identified in Sect. 2, are only of tangential interest for classifying Twitter messages related to brands, we have built a simple vocabulary and a new corpus to fill the gap: the Sentiment Analysis towards Brands (SAB). Whereas the vocabulary covers the four aspects described above, our first release covers only the brand and emotional tagging, focusing on the Sentiment Analysis aspects. This corpus is published both as an spreadsheet and as linked RDF [41], using vocabulary terms defined by well-known ontologies and mapping some of the resources with external datasets.

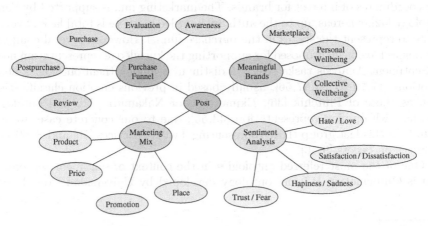

Fig. 1. The four aspects of interest for each tweet.

2 Related Work

2.1 Corpora for Sentiment Analysis

Even when most of the available corpora for Sentiment Analysis is English oriented, several Spanish corpora have also been described. Opinions in fields as different as Medicine [35] or Tourism [29] have been collected from diverse sources, such as social networks [11,26,38] or specialized opinion websites [10,29,35].

The publication style of corpora of tweets varies. Many researchers collect by themselves a set of tweets and keep it as a private corpus; others share the tweet IDs and instructions to retrieve them from Twitter, or share them preprocessed [52]. This behavior often responds to Twitter policies on text dissemination [30]. However, since Twitter periodically deletes tweets from their servers (making the text eventually irretrievable), the lifetime of a corpus with no text but only ID is randomly short, hindering its re-usability. Some of the few corpora available with text are only distributed on demand for private use, such as happens with the TASS [11] and the COST [26] corpora (see Table 1 for a review of representative corpora). In addition to this lack of appropriate public Twitter corpora, we also find that mainstream Opinion Mining annotation provides just the notion of polarity, determining if an opinion is positive or negative, sometimes expanded with intensity [11] or a rating scale [10,29,35]. The only available sentiment corpus the authors are aware of in Spanish is EmIroGeFb [38]; however, since it does not refer to brands and uses a different sentiment classification, none of the requirements for the project are fulfilled. The Spanish corpus for Sentiment Analysis towards Brands (SAB) we present covers therefore a gap in Spanish Sentiment Analysis, providing emotion tags toward brands, even if it is inevitably subordinated to Twitter policies[1].

2.2 Ontologies for Sentiment Analysis Towards Brands

Not many published ontologies are of use for supporting post classification within the coordinates of interest for brands. The marketing mix is supported by Sam's ontology [42], whereas, up to the authors' knowledge, there is total lack of vocabulary to represent the stages in the purchase funnel. However, several computer ontologies have been proposed for supporting the knowledge representation needs in Sentiment Analysis tasks. We can distinguish among them ontologies about emotions [17,19–21,34,37,56], usually based in previous emotion classifications such as those of Plutchik [36], Ekman [14] or Nakamura [32], and ontologies dealing with opinion representation [43,55]; due to our concrete case, we also include in this last group those representing Twitter services [50] and Sentiment Analysis on tweets [9,40].

One of the most referred ontologies in the context of sentiment representation is Ontoemotion [17], an ontology developed by Universidad Complutense

---

[1] The SAB corpus is available online offering only the ID of the tweets.

Table 1. Spanish Corpora available for sentiment analysis.

Corpus	Sector	Source	Annotation	Amount	Access	Text
HOPINION [8]	Tourism	TripAdvisor [51]	Rating (1-5)	17934	Registration	Yes
COST [26]	General	Twitter	Polarity (0/1)	34634	On request	Yes
COPOS [35]	Patient opinions	MasQueMedicos [27]	Rating (0-5)	743	On request	Yes
COAH [29]	Tourism	TripAdvisor	Rating (1-5)	1816	Registration	Yes
COAR [6]	Restaurants	TripAdvisor	Rating (1-5)	2202	Registration	Yes
Spanish Movie Reviews [10]	Cinema	MuchoCine [31]	Rating (1-5)	3878	Free	Yes
TASS General [11]	Personalities	Twitter	Level of agreement, polarity (P+,P,NEU,N, N+,NONE)	>68000*	On Request	Yes*
TASS Social-TV [11]	Sports	Twitter	Polarity (P,NEU,N), aspects	2773*	On Request	Yes*
TASS STOMPOL [11]	Politics	Twitter	Polarity (P,NEU,N), aspects	1284*	On Request	Yes*
SFU Spanish Corpus [46]	Several items	Ciao [5]	Rating (1-2,4-5)	400	Registration	Yes
EmIroGeFb [38]	Politics, Football, Celebrities	Facebook	Ekman emotions, gender, topic, presence of irony	1200	Free	No(IDs)

(*) As of 2015 [11]. TASS corpora change every year.

de Madrid for Emotional Voice Synthesis and later extended for its use in Italian texts [2]. In this ontology, emotions are defined in a space of three emotional dimensions (*Power*, *Activation* and *Evaluation*), having as one of the root classes the concept of *Emotion*. Also in the media context we find the Ontology of Emotional Cues [34], that models emotional cues linking them with the media properties that reveal them and classifying the different types of cues (e.g. verbal or psychological); in this ontology, the concrete emotions could both be expressed as categories or dimensions. For representing emotional responses, the EmotionsOnto ontology [19] (and its later version [48]) offers an easy integration both with FrameNet [1] and the DOLCE upper ontology [18]. Another proposal, the Emotion Ontology [21,22], represents emotions related to mental diseases, linking to other ontologies of the field but being also usable just for emotional purposes.

Finally, it must be noted that also cultural differences intervene in emotion classification. Such is the case of the Chinese ontology [56] built from the Chinese knowledge-base HowNet [13], or the one built from Japanese corpora [37] by using among others the EmotionML markup language [15] and Nakamura's emotion classification with only two binary dimensions: *Valence* (*positive* or *negative*) and *Activation* (*activated* or *deactivated*). In the case of dealing with different sentiment classifications, the high level Human Emotion Ontology (HEO) [20] covers different sentiment taxonomies and supports different dimensions, using as default *Arousal*, *Valence* and *Dominance* but admitting also other emotional spaces (such as the previously presented for Ontoemotion).

Related to opinion representation, the Marl [55] and Onyx [43] ontologies allow to represent opinions in RDF, being the former oriented to polarity and the latter to emotions. They are aligned with previous efforts and ontologies, such as WordNet-Affect [47] and linguistic linked data resources. Focusing on tweet representation, the Twitter API Rest Ontology [50] allows to represent the whole REST process but can also be used partially for expressing the opinion text and related information (such as the user and if the tweet is a retweet or not); other proposals include TwO [53] (Twitter Ontology) or SIOC [4]. Reusing some of these options we find ontologies directly dealing with Sentiment Analysis in tweets, such as EmpaTweets [40] and TweetOntoSense [9].

3   Building the Corpus

In existing corpora we find different ways to obtain tweets: some of them are built from concrete sentiment seeds, looking for polarized hashtags [28] or emoticons [26]. Even when this leads to corpora richer in actual sentiment-expressing messages, most of posts with just non-explicit emotions are lost in the process. Since the LPS BIGGER project demands a system capable of detecting also tweets with no emotions, ambiguous or without a context, we don't want to lose in our corpus this kind of messages. What we search are therefore the names of the brands we want to analyze, just imposing a constraint in the language of the tweets. Since not all the users directly refer to the brand by its official profile or the complete name of the brand, we also searched for names commonly used. The steps in the corpus building process included therefore preprocessing, and were the following:

1. Selection of the brands to analyze: we need to know the official names but also the Twitter profiles and the commonly used names for each brand in order to retrieve related tweets. The final list of analyzed brands (derived from the LPS BIGGER project) can be found in the website of the corpus.
2. Acquisition of tweets: the data collection took place between the 1st and the 7th February of 2017, having different capture processes (with different keywords searched) for each sector. The only filters used were the language ("es" for Spanish) and the brand keywords; tweets marked as retweets were not retrieved.
3. Sifting: The collected tweets were screened, searching for repeated tweets. Also messages where there was no real brand (in case the brand name was polysemous, or might appear as a part of other words) were deleted; so was done for tweets in other languages (even with the Twitter language filter, some messages in different languages managed to pass) and repeated tweets where the only difference was a URL (since Twitter automatically shortens them, the message would be in this case exactly the same).
4. Tagging: Three different people intervened in the tagging process, which consisted in determining if each message showed or not each of the emotions on the taxonomy (being possible several for the same message), or if on the

contrary it was a neutral tweet. For this task, a document explaining the criteria to follow was given to the taggers. These criteria (provided with the corpus) include for instance that a recurrent purchase should be tagged as *trust* and that *happiness* can only be inspired by an already acquired product or service; also usual combinations of emotions are explained: not finding a desired product would be for example *satisfaction* and *sadness*.

5. Transformation: treatment of the data to link it to other resources. Main ontologies and resources used, as well as a sample record, can be found in Sect. 4.

4   Spanish Corpus for Sentiment Analysis Towards Brands

The corpus comprises 4548 tagged messages, covering 7 sectors and 8 emotions; Table 2 shows percentages of appearance per sector and emotion, becoming apparent how neutral tweets (e.g. coming from community managers or news) must be also identified, since they often mention brands and usually contain emotional words that may mislead classifiers. It must be also noted how the occurrence of emotions is linked to the sector; *fear*, for instance, makes sense in BANKING but not in SPORTS or BEVERAGES.

Table 2. Column ANY shows the percentage of posts with any emotion (non neutral posts); remaining show the percentage for each emotion among these non neutral posts.

	ANY	HAT	SAD	FEA	DIS	SAT	TRU	HAP	LOV
FOOD	50.68	2.69	2.15	0	15.05	82.26	80.11	26.88	23.66
AUTOMOTIVE	7.80	0	2.33	11.63	25.58	76.74	39.53	13.95	11.63
BANKING	21.21	21.19	3.97	60.93	96.69	5.30	1.99	0	0
BEVERAGES	63.12	3.46	1.85	1.15	30.25	69.75	51.96	11.78	12.24
SPORTS	34.15	7.17	7.62	0.90	39.01	55.16	34.98	14.35	33.18
RETAIL	20.41	9.96	3.69	4.80	36.90	43.91	43.54	11.44	10.33
TELECOM	38.96	32.99	2.06	0.00	75.26	21.65	15.46	8.25	3.09
TOTAL	30.88	9.05	3.42	8.33	41.03	54.06	43.09	12.68	14.74

In order to evidence the subjectivity of emotion tagging, one of the sectors (BEVERAGES) has been completely tagged by two additional people, as it is the most expressive one in terms of expressed sentiments. We calculated the inter-annotator agreement using both the Fleiss' kappa [16] between the three taggers (all of them Spanish native speakers) for each emotion and the Cohen's kappa [7] for pairwise inter-agreement. As shown in Table 2 for BEVERAGES, several emotions appear scarcely in the corpus, being therefore statistically insignificant and leading to unrealistic kappas. Conversely, well-represented emotions such as

```
lps:826812979421257730 a sioc:Post ;
   sioc:id "826812979421257730" ;
   sioc:content "Ya me quede sin credito?? Hace 3 dias tengo
   credito nomas... Movistar y la concha de tu hermana"@es ;
   marl:describesObject lps:Movistar ;
   lps:isInPurchaseFunnel lps:postPurchase;
   lps:hasMarketingMix lps:price;
   lps:hasMeaningfulBrand lps:marketplace;
   onyx:hasEmotion lps:hate, lps:dissatisfaccion ;
   marl:hasPolarity marl:negative ;
   marl:forDomain "TELCO" .

lps:hate a onyx:Emotion ;
   rdfs:label "odio"@es, "hate"@en .

lps:dissatisfaction a onyx:Emotion ;
   rdfs:label "insatisfaccion"@es, "dissatisfaction"@en .


lps:Movistar a gr:Brand ;
   rdfs:seeAlso <http://dbpedia.org/resource/Movistar> ;
   rdfs:label "Movistar" .

lps:1-5000062703 a gr:Business ;
   rdfs:label "Telefonica de Espana, S.A.U.";
   rdfs:seeAlso <https://opencorporates.com/companies/es/82018474> ;
   owl:sameAs permid:1-5000062703 .
```

Fig. 2. Sample tagged post, and extra information on its brand and company.

dissatisfaction get Fleiss' kappa of 0.372 and average Cohen's kappa of 0.354; detailed results and extensive information on distribution in the corpus can be found with it.

Pursuing a richer representation, the dataset is published in RDF with extensive links to other datasets. Different vocabularies and ontologies have been used, such as Marl and Onyx [44], SIOC [4] or GoodRelations [24]. In addition, our own vocabulary to cover the purchase funnel and the marketing mix has been published [54]; extended information on the brands and companies, such as links to external databases like Thomson Reuters' PermID [49] or DBpedia [12], is also provided whenever possible. A sample post in RDF referring to a given brand (*Movistar*) and tagged as *hate* and *dissatisfaction* is shown in Fig. 2.

5   Conclusions and Future Work

The SAB corpus presented in this paper is the first one in Spanish containing tagged tweets related to brands. The corpus has been published not only as a spreadsheet but also as an RDF graph linked to external resources like DBpedia and Thomson Reuters's PermID. After this first publication, the corpus will be enlarged in size and tagging labels in forthcoming versions. Results of common classification algorithms and strategies will follow for each of the categories: whether a tweet bears an emotion, at which stage of the purchase funnel the Twitter user is and whether the post is related to the marketing mix or with a meaningful brands dimension. We dare to make the reasonable guess that using the information obtained from external entities (easily retrievable as the corpus is already linked) will enhance the results when comparing with the information in the bare text. This will hopefully support the publication of linked corpora, as it will evidence the advantages of using linked data for classification tasks.

Acknowledgments. This work has been partially supported by LPS-BIGGER (IDI-20141259, Ministerio de Economía y Competitividad), a research assistant grant by the Consejería de Educación, Juventud y Deporte de la Comunidad de Madrid partially founded by the European Social Fund (PEJ16/TIC/AI-1984) and a Juan de la Cierva contract.

References

1. Baker, C.F., Fillmore, C.J., Lowe, J.B.: The Berkeley FrameNet project. In: Proceedings of the COLING-ACL, vol. 1, pp. 86–90. ACL (1998)
2. Baldoni, M., Baroglio, C., et al.: ArsEmotica: emotions in the social semantic web. In: Proceedings of the 7th International Conference on Semantic Systems, pp. 171–174 (2011)
3. Borden, N.H.: The concept of the marketing mix. J. Advertising Res. **4**(2), 2–7 (1964)
4. Breslin, J.G., Decker, S., et al.: Sioc: an approach to connect web-based communities. Int. J. Web Based Communities **2**(2), 133–142 (2006)
5. Ciao, website with opinions on several topics. http://www.ciao.es/
6. Corpus COAR, with opinions about restaurants. http://sinai.ujaen.es/coar/
7. Cohen, J.: A coefficient of agreement for nominal scales. Educ. Psychol. Meas. **20**(1), 37–46 (1960)
8. Corpus HOpinion. http://clic.ub.edu/corpus/es/node/106
9. Cotfas, L.-A., Delcea, C., Roxin, I., Paun, R.: Twitter ontology-driven sentiment analysis. In: Barbucha, D., Nguyen, N.T., Batubara, J. (eds.) New Trends in Intelligent Information and Database Systems. SCI, vol. 598, pp. 131–139. Springer, Cham (2015). doi:10.1007/978-3-319-16211-9_14
10. Cruz, F.L., Troyano, J.A., et al.: Clasificación de documentos basada en la opinión: experimentos con un corpus de críticas de cine en espanol. Procesamiento Lenguaje Nat. **41**, 73–80 (2008)
11. Cumbreras, M.Á.G., Cámara, E.M., et al.: TASS 2015 - The evolution of the Spanish opinion mining systems. Procesamiento Lenguaje Nat. **56**, 33–40 (2016)
12. DBPedia website. http://dbpedia.org/
13. Dong, Z., Dong, Q., Hao, C.: Hownet and its computation of meaning. In: Proceedings of COLING 2010: Demonstrations, pp. 53–56. ACL (2010)
14. Ekman, P., Friesen, W.V., Ellsworth, P.: Emotion in the Human Face: Guidelines for Research and an Integration of Findings. Pergamon Press (1972)
15. Emotion ML. https://www.w3.org/TR/emotionml/
16. Fleiss, J.L., Cohen, J.: The equivalence of weighted kappa and the intraclass correlation coefficient as measures of reliability. Educ. Psychol. Meas. **33**(3), 613–619 (1973)
17. Francisco, V., Gervás, P., Peinado, F.: Ontological reasoning to configure emotional voice synthesis. In: Marchiori, M., Pan, J.Z., Marie, C.S. (eds.) RR 2007. LNCS, vol. 4524, pp. 88–102. Springer, Heidelberg (2007). doi:10.1007/978-3-540-72982-2_7

18. Gangemi, A., Guarino, N., Masolo, C., Oltramari, A., Schneider, L.: Sweetening ontologies with DOLCE. In: Gómez-Pérez, A., Benjamins, V.R. (eds.) EKAW 2002. LNCS, vol. 2473, pp. 166–181. Springer, Heidelberg (2002). doi:10.1007/3-540-45810-7_18

19. Gil, R., Virgili-Gomá, J., et al.: Emotions ontology for collaborative modelling and learning of emotional responses. Comput. Hum. Behav. **51**, 610–617 (2015)

20. Grassi, M.: Developing HEO human emotions ontology. In: Fierrez, J., Ortega-Garcia, J., Esposito, A., Drygajlo, A., Faundez-Zanuy, M. (eds.) BioID 2009. LNCS, vol. 5707, pp. 244–251. Springer, Heidelberg (2009). doi:10.1007/978-3-642-04391-8_32

21. Hastings, J., Ceusters, W., et al.: The emotion ontology: enabling interdisciplinary research in the affective sciences. In: International and Interdisciplinary Conference on Modeling and Using Context, pp. 119–123 (2011)

22. Hastings, J., Ceusters, W., et al.: Annotating affective neuroscience data with the emotion ontology. In: Proceedings of the Workshop Towards an Ontology of Mental Functioning at ICBO, pp. 1–5 (2012)

23. Havas Media website. http://www.havasmedia.com/

24. Hepp, M.: GoodRelations: an ontology for describing products and services offers on the web. In: Gangemi, A., Euzenat, J. (eds.) EKAW 2008. LNCS, vol. 5268, pp. 329–346. Springer, Heidelberg (2008). doi:10.1007/978-3-540-87696-0_29

25. LPS BIGGER project website. http://www.cienlpsbigger.es/

26. Martínez-Cámara, E., Martín-Valdivia, M.T., et al.: Polarity classification for Spanish tweets using the COST corpus. J. Inf. Sci. **41**(3), 263–272 (2015)

27. Masquemedicos, with opinions in the medical domain. http://masquemedicos.com

28. Mohammad, S.M., Kiritchenko, S.: Using hashtags to capture fine emotion categories from tweets. Comput. Intell. **31**(2), 301–326 (2015)

29. Molina-González, M.D., Martínez-Cámara, E., et al.: Cross-domain sentiment analysis using Spanish opinionated words. In: Métais, E., Roche, M., Teisseire, M. (eds.) NLDB 2014. LNCS, pp. 214–219. Springer, Cham (2014). doi:10.1007/978-3-319-07983-7_28

30. Montejo-Ráez, A., Díaz-Galiano, M.C., et al.: Crowd explicit sentiment analysis. Knowl. Based Syst. **69**(1), 134–139 (2014)

31. MuchoCine, Spanish website with reviews about films. www.muchocine.net

32. Nakamura, A.: Kanjo Hyogen Jiten. Tokyodo Publishing (1993)

33. Nielsen: The social media report. http://blog.nielsen.com/nielsenwire/social/2012/

34. Obrenovic, Z., Garay, N., López, J.M., Fajardo, I., Cearreta, I.: An ontology for description of emotional cues. In: Tao, J., Tan, T., Picard, R.W. (eds.) ACII 2005. LNCS, vol. 3784, pp. 505–512. Springer, Heidelberg (2005). doi:10.1007/11573548_65

35. Plaza-Del-Arco, F.M., Martín-Valdivia, M.T., et al.: COPOS: Corpus of patient opinions in Spanish. Application of sentiment analysis techniques. Procesamiento Lenguaje Nat. **57**, 83–90 (2016)

36. Plutchik, R.: The nature of emotions: Human emotions have deep evolutionary roots (2001)

37. Ptaszynski, M., Rzepka, R., et al.: A robust ontology of emotion objects. In: Proceedings of the 18th Annual Meeting of the Association for Natural Language Processing, pp. 719–722 (2012)

38. Rangel, F., Rosso, P., Reyes, A.: Emotions and irony per gender in facebook. In: Proceedings of Workshop ES3LOD, LREC-2014, pp. 1–6 (2014)

39. Richins, M.L.: Measuring emotions in the consumption experience. J. Consum. Res. **24**(2), 127–146 (1997)

40. Roberts, K., Roach, M., Johnson, J.: EmpaTweet: annotating and detecting emotions on twitter. In: Proceedings of LREC 2012, pp. 3806–3813 (2012)
41. SAB corpus website. http://sabcorpus.linkeddata.es
42. Sam, K.M., Lei, P., Chatwin, C.: Ontology development for e-marketing mix model mapping with internet consumers' decision-making styles. In: Sobh, T. (ed.) Innovations and Advanced Techniques in Computer and Information Sciences and Engineering, pp. 279–282. Springer, Dordrecht (2007). doi:10.1007/978-1-4020-6268-1_50
43. Sánchez-Rada, J.F., Iglesias, C.A.: Onyx: a linked data approach to emotion representation. Inf. Process. Manag. **52**(1), 99–114 (2016)
44. Sánchez Rada, J.F., Torres, M., et al.: A linked data approach to sentiment and emotion analysis of twitter in the financial domain. In: 2nd International Workshop on Finance and Economics on the Semantic Web (2014)
45. Shaver, P., Schwartz, J., et al.: Emotion knowledge: further exploration of a prototype approach. J. Pers. Soc. Psychol. **52**(6), 1061–1086 (1987)
46. Spanish Corpus of reviews about films. http://www.sfu.ca/~mtaboada/research/SFU_Review_Corpus.html
47. Strapparava, C., Valitutti, A.: WordNet-Affect: an affective extension of WordNet. In: Proceedings of LREC, pp. 1083–1086 (2004)
48. The Emotions & Cognition Ontology. http://rhizomik.net/html/ontologies/emotions&cognitionontology/
49. Thomson Reuter's PermID website. https://permid.org/
50. Togias, K., Kameas, A.: An ontology-based representation of the twitter REST API. In: Proceedings of the IEEE 24th ICTAI, vol. 1, pp. 998–1003 (2012)
51. Tripadvisor website, with opinions on tourism. https://www.tripadvisor.es/
52. Twitter preprocessed datasets available at the TU Eindhoven. http://www.win.tue.nl/~mpechen/projects/smm/#Datasets
53. TwO, the Twitter Ontology. https://github.com/joshhanna/Twitter-Ontology
54. Vocabulary of the SAB corpus. http://sabcorpus.linkeddata.es/vocab
55. Westerski, A., Iglesias, C.A., Rico, F.T.: Linked opinions: describing sentiments on the structured web of data. In: Proceedings of the 4th International Workshop Social Data on the Web, vol. 830 (2011)
56. Yan, J., Bracewell, D.B., et al.: The creation of a Chinese emotion ontology based on HowNet. Eng. Lett. **16**(1), 166–171 (2008)

Speech Enhancement for Speaker Recognition Using Deep Recurrent Neural Networks

Maxim Tkachenko[1(✉)], Alexander Yamshinin[1], Nikolay Lyubimov[2],
Mikhail Kotov[1], and Marina Nastasenko[3]

[1] ASM Solutions LLC, Moscow, Russia
makseq@gmail.com, lex.sapfir@gmail.com, kotov.mike@gmail.com
[2] Lomonosov Moscow State University, Moscow, Russia
lubimov.nicolas@gmail.com
[3] Master Synthesis LLC, Moscow, Russia
marina.nastasenko@gmail.com

Abstract. This paper describes the speech denoising system based on long short-term memory (LSTM) neural networks. The architecture of the presented network is designed to make speech enhancement in spectrogram magnitude domain. The audio resynthesis is performed via the inverse short-time Fourier transform by maintaining the original phase. Objective quality is assessed by root mean square error between clean and denoised audio signals on CHiME corpus and speaker verification rate by using RSR2015 corpus. Proposed system demonstrates improved results on both metrics.

Keywords: Noise suppression · Denoising · Speech restoration · LSTM · Neural networks · Speaker verification

1 Introduction

It is common that different audio channel distortions like additive noise, reverberation and background speech can reduce the performance of automatic speech and speaker recognition systems. The main reason is that these distortions introduce nonlinear bias in feature space that cannot be properly modeled on the training phase. The research on automatic noise suppression as a standalone audio processing task as well as preliminary step for recognition systems has been studied for many years. Earlier systems were dedicated to suppress stationary noises with constant spectral characteristics in time [1,2]. Modern approaches are applied to use neural networks as primary mechanism for eliminating noise from input signal. Neural networks can gain more benefits from denoisers: non-stationary impulse noises, background speech, reverberations and others can be effectively localized in both time and frequency domains and subsequently suppressed [3]. De-reverberation is an important task in automatic speech recognition (ASR) and good results are shown using deep autoencoders [4]. Recently various recurrent neural network architectures have shown to greatly boost the

© Springer International Publishing AG 2017
A. Karpov et al. (Eds.): SPECOM 2017, LNAI 10458, pp. 690–699, 2017.
DOI: 10.1007/978-3-319-66429-3_69

performance on various audio and voice processing tasks [5–7]. Recurrent neural networks (RNN) are used to handle temporal events, and their Long short-term memory (LSTM) extension increases network's memory through the gating mechanism [8]. Both RNN and LSTM units have a big nonlinear capacity and they are suitable for the dynamically processing sequences like speech and audio raw samples and features. The good speech enhancer operates like preprocessing step for the ASR and speaker verification systems and should be robust against the changes in channel conditions [9].

The main focus of this paper is that the investigation of various network architectures as well as different feature domains these nets operate on. The denoising model and network configuration are described first, then the algorithm for audio signal reconstruction is given. Finally, experimental setups and results are discussed.

2 Denoising and Signal Restoration

2.1 Model

It is supposed to deal with general noise that is assumed to be non-stationary and not necessarily additive. By using the following general notation

$$d = f(s) \tag{1}$$

where s is a clean signal, d is a noisy and corrupted signal by some non-linear transformation f, the goal of the proposed speech denoiser is to estimate its inverse $g \approx f^{-1}$. As it is unfeasible to do it analytically, artificial neural networks (NN) help to estimate this mapper in an implicit way by using gradient descent updates on stochastically generated pairs of noisy and clean audio excerpts. The loss function is given via the l_2 norm:

$$||g(d, \theta) - s||^2 \to \min_{\theta} \tag{2}$$

where θ are learned parameters of the specified neural network.

2.2 Configuration and Network Topology

For the experiments we use Keras machine learning framework due to its flexibility [10]. We have found that there are different possible topologies that could be applicable to solve the initial task. Only finally chosen graph topology is presented in this paper, and could be inspected from Fig. 1.

We have investigated the following schemes of feature extraction: raw input (1-dimensional input, sample by sample), raw frames (one short multidimensional time frame as single input), and short time FFT-based extractors: raw magnitude spectrum, logarithmic magnitude and triangular mel-scaled filter banks [11].

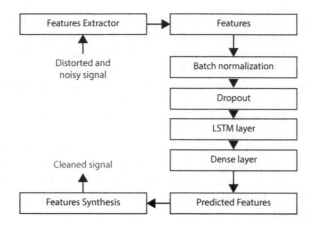

Fig. 1. RNN Denoiser Configuration

By designing hidden layers of the mapper g, several stacked topologies were investigated: fully-connected layers with ReLU activation (DNN) and recurrent hidden units: vanilla RNN and LSTM layers. Dropout regularization [12] with probability 0.75 is applied before hidden layers. The batch normalization procedure [13] has been found to be very helpful to overcome audio channel sensitivity problem.

The first layer is LSTM and it always has the same dimension as dirty features. The LSTM gives a benefit in comparison with DNN, Simple RNN because they have memory and forget gates and can reset their states themselves in a manner human brain does it [14].

The final fully connected layer above recurrent hidden layer with linear activation helps to normalize LSTM outputs and squeeze dimension to the output.

2.3   Signal Reconstruction

The target of a denoising system is to reproduce audio signal that exposes as high SNR rates as possible. It is possible to achieve by the following two steps. First, the described neural net is used to predict some output short-time signal representation p with the lowered noise level. The next steps depend on which signal representation is used to train neural enhancer. The upsampling scheme is applied to the spectrum envelope in FFT or filter banks (FBanks). The upsampling algorithm consists of reversing any non-linearities given at the preprocessing step (e.g. exponentiate logarithmic magnitude) and optionally applying some interpolation to get enhanced spectrum p_i for every input $i - th$ frequency bin. Otherwise the network's output is used as if the target feature was the raw audio. Assuming that additive noise model is adequate approximation for the general model given in (1), the pure noise signal is drawn by subtracting p_i values from incoming corrupted input d_i. Therefore, by using Wiener filtering procedure, the unwanted noise is removed for any temporal frame by attenuating corresponding time-frequency components in the input noisy signal:

$$r_i = n_i \cdot \frac{p_i}{d_i - p_i} \tag{3}$$

where r_i – restored complex spectrum at, n_i – noisy complex spectrum, p_i – predicted envelope, d_i – input magnitude spectrum. Note that phase information is preserved in output complex spectrum, and therefore it is possible to straightforwardly apply the inverse Fourier transform and use overlap-add method [15] for consecutive frames in order to get valid audible signals.

3 Experiment Setup

3.1 Denoiser Parameters

Experimental investigations have been made to find the best network parameters relative to the input/output features representation. All benchmark comparisons are reported in term of the root mean square error (RMSE) between denoised and clean signals on the separate test set. It has been found that increasing frequency bins number (i.e. FFT size) leads to lesser RMSE values, as depicted in Fig. 2. This could be explained by the fact that neural net could more effectivcly model noise signal if it is occupied the whole time-frequency bin, that is seemed to be more realistic with smaller bins. Finally the FFT size 0.064 ms with 8000 sample rate and hope is 0.008 ms have been chosen. For FBanks 52 cepstral coefficients are used.

It is crucial to remove initial signal bias to increase cross-channel robustness. The input mean and variance are estimated on the separated development set and applied to all features. Also we have experimented with different mean and

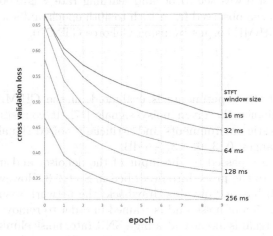

Fig. 2. Cross validation loss value wrt number of epochs for different FFT sizes

variance normalization (MVN) transformers for clean and dirty signals. It's a good idea to use MVN for each file to increase cross-channel robustness but at the same time it causes additional difficulties with model training: the network should be able to predict means and variances for each file.

Stacking multiple LSTM layers brings smearing of the spectrogram and it was decided to use only one layer but with a higher number of units starting from 1024 Fig. 3. The last dense layer output is 129 that is half plus one of the real FFT size. The feature splice was set to 5 with step 1 for a DNN-only experiment. For the recurrent nets splicing is automatically handling by the corresponding connections.

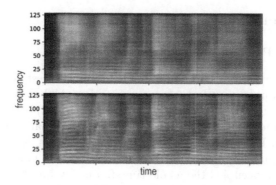

Fig. 3. Top to down: predicted spectrogram by LSTM+LSTM (very smeared) and LSTM (clear)

The Adam optimizer [16] has been used to learn neural models. It uses first-order stochastic gradient descent updates with adaptive estimates of lower-order moments. Batch size was set to 50 and learning rate was 0.001. The training convergence has been observed from 10th to 40th epoch and about 100 s elapsed per 1 epoch on CHiME corpus by using GeForce GTX970.

3.2   Dataset

The first part of the experiments is evaluated on the CHiME corpus and is devoted to re-enhance the given noisy signals [17]. It consists of audios with reverberant domestic environments and artificially noised signals within signal-to-noise (SNR) ranges: 0, 3, 6, −3, −6 dB.

Noisy signals are passed to the input of the denoiser and mapped to clean signals according to the procedure described in Sect. 2.3. However this straight-forward approach has one obvious drawback: the network assumes each input contains some portion of noise and is trained in order to remove this noise part. But if the input signal is already at a high SNR rate, noise elimination may hurt the quality. To overcome this limitation, the files with pure clean signal have also been appended to the training dataset. For the later case the network is mapped to the same clean signal and acts like an identity function. It was experimentally found that this sophisticated procedure can greatly improve results when dealing with wide noise level variations.

The second experiment has been made on the speaker verification task. For this setup the Part I male development set of the RSR2015 [18] was taken to learn a new denoiser model. To create noisy signals from the Part I male development set recipes from Idiap Research Institute Acoustic Simulator [19] were taken. A noisy signal was generated for each clean signal from the development set in three different SNR (0 dB, 3 dB, 6 dB) using randomly chosen background noises. After augmentation about 20 h of speech were obtained for denoiser training. To estimate the speaker verification system in different SNR the same procedure was applied for the Part I male evaluation set of the RSR2015.

3.3 Speaker Verification

Speaker verification system based on i-vector [20] and probabilistic linear discriminant analysis (PLDA) [21] has shown to be state-of-the methods for solving a text-independent speaker recognition problem. This system consists of the universal background model (UBM) with 512 Gaussian mixture components, 400-dimensional i-vector extractor trained on Switchboard-1 Telephone Speech Corpus (SWBD1) (about 250 h of speech) and the PLDA model pre-trained on the Part I male development set of the RSR2015 database (about 8 h of speech). 20 mel-frequency cepstral coefficients (MFCC) computed on enhanced spectrum followed by cepstral mean variance normalization (CMVN) are used as input features. The goal of the evaluations is to test how the performance drops down when the noise is mixed artificially with RSR2015 and how much gain in term of speaker identification rate (IR) could be achieved when trying to restore these noisy signals. Part I male evaluation set (about 9 h of speech) is used for testing speaker verification. All utterances are resampled to 8 kHz.

The speaker verification system is evaluated in three conditions as described in the RSR2015. In all three conditions trials are considered positive if a speaker and a phrase are the same as in enrollment. In condition 1 trial is considered as negative if a speaker is the same but a phrase is different. In condition 2 trial is considered as negative if a speaker is different but a phrase is the same. In condition 3 trial is considered as negative if a speaker and a phrase are different.

4 Results

All the results, scores and other meta information about the experiments are stored in the Testarium — research tool and experiment repository [22]. This tool provides efficient parameters grid searching: recurrent unit type, the number of the hidden units, features parameters, etc.

4.1 Denoiser

All audio restoration examples are available to listen on the website [23]. We have used RMSE between clean and restored audio signals as an objective quality metric (Table 1).

Table 1. RMSE with different denoiser parameters

Noised	0.01821
DNN 1024	
Log FFT 256	0.00831
Log FBank 52	0.00782
LSTM 1024	
FFT 256	0.00734
Log FFT 256	0.00667
Log FBank 52	0.00655
Bidirectional LSTM 1024	
Log FFT 256	0.00633

Apparently the FBank based spectrum representation is the best on the proposed metric. This effect takes place due to the more detailed spectrum in those frequency bands that contain speech signals. On the other hand, the linear frequency scale spectrum sets equal importance to all frequency bins, therefore, restoration is applied also to the high-frequency bands, which are useless because a speech signal mostly lies in low and mid frequencies. Logarithmic representations are also seemed to have a positive effect due to reduce large-scaled magnitude variations apart from linear MVN transformation.

Also the raw audio signal (without spectrum magnitude transformation) is subjected to be tested together with LSTM-based denoiser. The RMSE reaches the value 0.00950 after convergence, but subjective evaluations have exposed no denoising effect compared with FFT-based approaches. This is explained by insufficient memory capacity in recurrent units when operating on just single sample. When dealing with raw frames so that input dimensions are equal to number of samples in frame, performance grows up, but still it doesn't sound well.

Finally, it could be noticed that look-aheading nature of bidirectional LSTM is helpful to enhance non-stationary noises, but comes at the cost of increasing training time and ability to utilize denoising in online manner.

The example of denoised spectrograms are visualized in Fig. 4 for CHiME corpus.

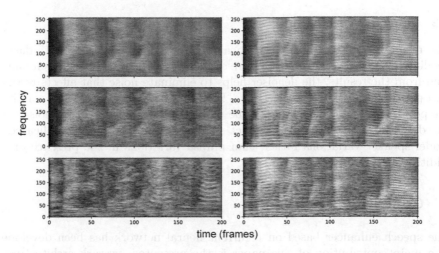

Fig. 4. Top down: denoised, clean and noisy spectrograms on 2 CHiME examples

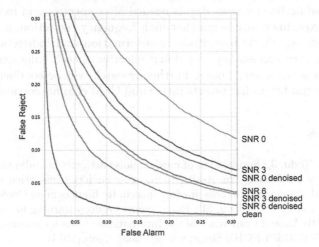

Fig. 5. False Alarm and False Rejects (FAFR) plot for RSR2015 speaker verification in condition 1

Table 2. Equal error rate (EER, %) on evaluation part of RSR2015

Signal/Condition	1	2	3
Clean	4.02	4.01	0.69
SNR 0 dB	18.63	20.17	10.20
SNR 0 dB denoised	13.89	15.62	6.41
SNR 3 dB	14.78	15.74	6.81
SNR 3 dB denoised	11.15	12.27	4.23
SNR 6 dB	11.54	12.14	4.31
SNR 6 dB denoised	8.82	9.69	2.79

4.2   Speaker Verification

The results of the text-dependent speaker verification on the RSR2015 dataset for different signals and conditions are depicted in (Table 2). Indeed, as it can be seen from the results, the denoiser helps to eliminate noise that affects recognition performance in all three settings. It's interesting that in the 2nd condition the performance drop has found to be more sensible to the additive noise compared to the 1st condition. This fact suggests that it is more complicated to model speaker variations rather than phrase variations in the presence of the additive noise.

5   Conclusions

The speech enhancer based on recurrent neural network has been developed. The main contribution of this paper is the presented network architecture is able to enhance noisy speech following end-to-end paradigm: only final overlap-and-add based audio synthesis step is needed after spectrogram reconstruction. It has been experimentally found that high frequency resolution, mel frequency bands scaling, non-linear magnitude transformation and bidirectional temporal processing are success keys for doing effective speech enhancement in the presence of non-stationary noises. Further research will be conducted on more difficult noise conditions like reverberation and GSM channel corruption (Fig. 5).

References

1. Lukin, A., Todd, J.: Suppression of musical noise artifacts in audio noise reduction by adaptive 2D filtering. In: Audio Engineering Society Convention 123 (2007)
2. Valin, J.-M.: Speex: a free codec for free speech. In: linux.conf.au Conference (2006)
3. Liu, D., Smaragdis, P., Kim, M.: Experiments on deep learning for speech denoising. In: 15th Annual Conference of the International Speech Communication Association (INTERSPEECH), Singapore, pp. 2685–2689 (2014)
4. Feng, X., Zhang, Y., Glass, J.: Speech feature denoising and dereverberation via deep autoencoders for noisy reverberant speech recognition. In: International Conference on Acoustics, Speech and Signal Processing (ICASSP), pp. 1759–1763. IEEE Press, Italy (2014)
5. Weninger, F., Erdogan, H., Watanabe, S., Vincent, E., Roux, J., Hershey, J.R., Schuller, B.: Speech enhancement with LSTM recurrent neural networks and its application to noise-robust ASR. In: 12th International Conference on Latent Variable Analysis and Signal Separation (LVA/ICA), Liberec, Czech Republic (2015)
6. Sun, L., Kang, S., Li, K., Meng, H.: Voice conversion using deep Bidirectional Long Short-Term Memory based Recurrent Neural Networks. In: International Conference on Acoustics, Speech and Signal Processing (ICASSP), Queensland, Australia (2015)
7. Mimura, M., Sakai, S., Kawahara, T.: Speech dereverberation using long short-term memory. In: 16th Annual Conference of the International Speech Communication Association (INTERSPEECH), Dresden, Germany, pp. 2435–2439 (2015)

8. Hochreiter, S., Schmidhuber, J.: Long short-term memory. Neural Comput. **9**(8), 1735–1780 (1997)
9. Xu, Y., Du, J., Da, L.-R.: A regression approach to speech enhancement based on deep neural networks. IEEE/ACM Trans. Audio Speech Lang. Process. **23**(1), 7–19 (2015). IEEE Press
10. Keras: Deep Learning library for Theano and TensorFlow. https://keras.io
11. Hinton, G., Deng, L., Dahl, G.E., Mohamed, A., Jaitly, N., Senior, A., Vanhoucke, V., Nguyen, P., Sainath, T., Kingsbury, B.: Deep neural networks for acoustic modeling in speech recognition. IEEE Sig. Process. Mag. **29**(6), 82–97 (2012). IEEE Press
12. Srivastava, N., Hinton, G.E., Krizhevsky, A., Sutskever, I., Salakhutdinov, R.R.: Dropout: a simple way to prevent neural networks from overfitting. J. Mach. Learn. Res. **15**(1), 1929–1958 (2014)
13. Ioffe, S., Szegedy, C.: Batch normalization: accelerating deep network training by reducing internal covariate shift. In: 32nd International Conference on Machine Learning (ICML), Lille, France (2015)
14. Gers, F.A., Schmidhuber, J., Cummins, F.: Learning to forget: continual prediction with LSTM. Neural Comput. **12**(10), 2451–2471 (2000)
15. Crochiere, R.: A weighted overlap-add method of short-time Fourier analysis/synthesis. IEEE Trans. Acoust. Speech Sig. Process. **ASSP–28**, 99–102 (1980)
16. Kingma, D., Ba, J.: Adam: a method for stochastic optimization. In: 3rd International Conference for Learning Representations, San Diego (2015)
17. Christensen, H., Barker, J., Ma, N., Green, P.: The CHiME corpus: a resource and a challenge for computational hearing in multisource environments. In: 11th Annual Conference of the International Speech Communication Association (INTERSPEECH), Chiba, Japan (2010)
18. Larcher, A., Lee, K.A., Ma, B., Li, H.: RSR2015: database for textdependent speaker verification using multiple pass-phrases. In: 13th Annual Conference of the International Speech Communication Association (INTERSPEECH), Portland, Oregon, USA (2012)
19. Ferras, M., Madikeri, S., Motlicek, P., Dey, S., Bourlard, H.: A large-scale open-source acoustic simulator for speaker recognition. IEEE Sig. Process. Lett. **23**(4), 527–531 (2016)
20. Dehak, N., Kenny, P., Dehak, R., Dumouchel, P., Ouellet, P.: Front-end factor analysis for speaker verification. IEEE Trans. Audio Speech Lang. Process. **19**, 788–798 (2011). IEEE Press
21. Prince, S.J., Elder, J.H.: Probabilistic linear discriminant analysis for inferences about identity. In: 11th International Conference on Computer Vision (ICCV), Rio de Janeiro, Brazil, pp. 1–8 (2007)
22. Testarium. Research tool. http://testarium.makseq.com
23. Denoising examples. http://denoiser.makseq.com

Stance Classification in Texts from Blogs on the 2016 British Referendum

Vasiliki Simaki[1,2](✉), Carita Paradis[1], and Andreas Kerren[2]

[1] Centre for Languages and Literature, Lund University, Lund, Sweden
{vasiliki.simaki,carita.paradis}@englund.lu.se
[2] Department of Computer Science, Linnaeus University, Växjö, Sweden
andreas.kerren@lnu.se

Abstract. The problem of identifying and correctly attributing speaker stance in human communication is addressed in this paper. The data set consists of political blogs dealing with the 2016 British referendum. A cognitive-functional framework is adopted with data annotated for six notional stance categories: CONTRARIETY, HYPOTHETICALITY, NECESSITY, PREDICTION, SOURCE OF KNOWLEDGE, and UNCERTAINTY. We show that these categories can be implemented in a text classification task and automatically detected. To this end, we propose a large set of lexical and syntactic linguistic features. These features were tested and classification experiments were implemented using different algorithms. We achieved accuracy of up to 30% for the six-class experiments, which is not fully satisfactory. As a second step, we calculated the pair-wise combinations of the stance categories. The CONTRARIETY and NECESSITY binary classification achieved the best results with up to 71% accuracy.

Keywords: Stance-taking · Text classification · Political blogs · BREXIT

1 Introduction

Stance is the performance by humans in communication–actions taken by speakers to express their beliefs, evaluations and attitudes towards objects, events and propositions [3,4]. The exploitation of the verbal ways in which speakers position themselves in relation to their addressees and to the information they provide are useful clues to social science studies and applications. In our case, stance in political blogs is examined and our findings are conceived to provide a contribution to opinion analysis studies. Recently, automatic identification of stance has been the subject of interest in several studies in text mining. For quite a long time, researchers have investigated beyond the identification of whether speakers express a positive or a negative opinion about a fact/event/idea, and they explore the speakers' positioning in discourse, in terms of being for or against something.

Recent studies in stance classification focus their interest on whether a speaker supports a fact/event/idea or not, but researchers mostly perform binary

© Springer International Publishing AG 2017
A. Karpov et al. (Eds.): SPECOM 2017, LNAI 10458, pp. 700–709, 2017.
DOI: 10.1007/978-3-319-66429-3_70

searches and classify texts into *pro* or *con* using these labels as stance categories. In the present paper, more refined stances based in notional categories, which are different from the ones used in most stance classification studies, are examined as classification attributes. Following research in linguistics [3], we define stance-taking in terms of language users' positioning, alignment and evaluation in communication. Our study has a dual purpose:

1. Exploiting the stance classification problem in text data extracted from political blogs regarding the 2016 British referendum.
2. Determining the efficacy of lexical and syntactic features using six novel stance classes.

In our previous work [17], we introduced a cognitive-functional stance framework highlighting ten notional stance categories, and a corpus annotated with these stances. The categories were manually attributed to utterances extracted from political blogs on the 2016 British referendum, according to the total semantic information of the utterance. In this paper, a classification methodology based on six notional stance categories is proposed. Lexical and syntactic features were extracted and classification experiments were performed in a subset of the annotated corpus. We tested the efficacy of the framework and the feature set by performing multi-class classification experiments and also binary experiments, in order to evaluate each stance pairing (15 combinations in total).

2 Related Work

Stance classification is connected to the fields of Subjective Language Identification [27], Opinion Mining and Sentiment Analysis [15,23]. The majority of these studies addresses stance-taking as a binary issue of the *pro* or *con* positioning of the speaker towards a fact/event/idea. In most cases, the data are extracted from online debates, where controversial opinions and stance-taking is observed. These data are mainly automatically annotated. In other cases, where the data are derived from social media such as Twitter, stance-taking can be retrieved through hashtags (e.g., *#NOT*, *#PRO*, *#pride*, etc.). In Table 1 we present a number of recent studies of stance classification in the order of best classification accuracy achieved during their classification experiments.

The identification of stance has also been the topic of interest in other text mining studies. Sridhar et al. [21] investigated the performance of linguistic and relational features in a subset of the Internet Argument Corpus [26]. They showed that features comprising information about complex interactions between authors and posts are important in the detection of speaker positioning. Rajadesingan and Liu [16] identified different types of stance-taking (*for* or *against* a topic) in a collection of tweets from more than 100,000 different Twitter users, using their ReLP novel framework. Kucher et al. [13] created the uVSAT tool for visual stance analysis. This tool contains multiple approaches for analysing temporal and textual data as well as exporting stance markers in order to prepare a stance-oriented training data set.

Table 1. The classification accuracy achieved in recent stance classification studies

Authors	Classification accuracy
Walker et al. [24]	88%
Faulkner [5]	82%
Hasan and Ng [9]	75.9%
Hasan and Ng [10]	75.4%
Walker et al. [24]	75%
Hasan and Ng [8]	75%
Ferreira and Vlachos [6]	73%
Anand et al. [1]	69%
Hasan and Ng [11]	69%
Mohammad et al. [14]	69%
Somasundaran and Wiebe [20]	63.93%

3   Data Description and Methodology

3.1   Data Description

As mentioned above, in our previous work [17] we designed and implemented a cognitive-functional framework about speaker stance consisting of ten core stance categories. These categories comprise the basic and distinctive stances as agreement and disagreement, certainty, prediction, hypotheticality, etc. Stance was detected in more than 76% of randomly extracted utterances from political blogs, and in many cases more than one stance category was attributed by the annotators, a fact that highlights the frequency of the stances in discourse. These stances were manually attributed to the utterances by two human experts, through an annotation process that was based on the overall meaning of the utterance by using the ALVA system [12].

The annotation process resulted in a gold standard corpus, the Brexit Blog Corpus (BBC), containing 1,682 utterances (in English, 35,492 words, 169,762 characters without spaces). In this study, an *utterance* is the chunk between full stops, question marks or exclamation marks. The size of this corpus cannot be compared to large data sets extracted from social media sources and used for text classification purposes. BBC was manually annotated according to the semantic information of each utterance, a process which is highly resource- and time-consuming. For this study, we used a subset of this corpus and excluded the less common stance categories (AGREEMENT/DISAGREEMENT, CERTAINTY, TACT/RUDENESS and VOLITION) in the BBC (about 150 utterances), in order to perform experiments on a more balanced data set, and we worked with the utterances annotated with the six stance categories as presented in Table 2.

Table 2 shows the number of the utterances attributed to each stance category, and the mean F-score of the agreement achieved between the two

Table 2. The distribution of the stance categories in our data set and the inter-annotator agreement mean score per category

Stance category	Number of utterances	Inter-annotator F-score
CONTRARIETY	352	0.78
SOURCE OF KNOWLEDGE	287	0.53
PREDICTION	252	0.57
NECESSITY	204	0.77
UNCERTAINTY	196	0.62
HYPOTHETICALITY	171	0.78
Total number of utterances	1,462	

annotators. The total size of the data set is 1,462 utterances (31,331 words; 150,190 characters). In these stance categories the agreement among the annotators when labels were attributed to the utterances, in terms of inter-annotation agreement mean F-score, varies from 0.53 to 0.78. The CONTRARIETY stance includes cases where the authors express a compromising or contrastive opinion, e.g., *He is always referred to as British, yet was born in Namibia, spent all his life in Namibia, and speaks with a Namibian 'English' accent.* In this example, the annotators detected a contrastive meaning, and the presence of *yet* supported their decision. SOURCE OF KNOWLEDGE is attributed when the authors express the origin of what they say, e.g., *As the Dutch foreign minister admitted last week, the EU was always a journey rather than a goal.* In this case, the *Dutch foreign minister* is the source providing information and knowledge about something. PREDICTION is identified in the cases where the authors make a guess/conjecture about a future (or future in the past) event, e.g., *Today is the Grexit, tomorrow is the Brexit, and the day after tomorrow it will be the Frexit.* The identification of PREDICTION is supported by the predictive meaning of the whole utterance, and by the items *tomorrow* and *will*. The NECESSITY category includes cases in which the authors express a request, recommendation, instruction or an obligation. In the following example it can be easily detected by the presence of *need*: *And at national level, we need to build support in the UK for the regulations that Cameron is seeking to remove.* Annotated utterances with the UNCERTAINTY label contain the authors' doubt as to the likelihood of what they are saying, e.g., *But I don't see how they can just mark time on the constitution for the next five years - that bird has well and truly flown.* In this example, the sequence *I don't see how* expresses the speaker's doubt about a fact/event/idea. And, finally, HYPOTHETICALITY contains utterances where the authors express a possible consequence of a condition, and it is mostly formulated with conditional clauses, e.g., *If the people vote the referendum down, then they leave the euro.*

The data are thematically related to the 2016 British referendum and, in many cases, to broader political topics, extracted from the web from June to

August of 2015. With the Gavagai API [7], the targets were detected using seed words such as *Brexit, EU referendum, etc.* The URLs from www.lobbyplanet.eu/links/eu-blog are retrieved and filtered, and the texts were split into utterances.

3.2 Methodology

In this study, we explore the efficacy of classification algorithms when novel stance categories are used and linguistic features are extracted. This is a novel approach in the field, given the fact that these stance categories are used for the first time in an automatic stance classification task. For the experiments, we composed a feature set of linguistic features predefined by researchers, as our baseline. We used a large number of lexical and syntactic features that are common in previous studies in authorship attribution [29], gender and age identification [18,19], opinion mining and sentiment analysis [15]:

- **Lexical features** can be further divided into *character-* and *word-based* features. The character-based features include the calculation of all characters, spaces, special characters, upper case characters, alphabetical characters and digit characters per utterance, the average utterance length in terms of characters, the frequency of each special character and alphabetical letter per utterance. The word-based lexical features calculate the average word length, the average utterance length in terms of words, the frequency of short words (less than four characters), the frequency of different types, of hapax legomena and hapax dislegomena.
- **Syntactic features** include the total number of punctuation symbols per utterance, the frequency of each punctuation symbol, and the frequency of the Part-of-Speech (POS) tags in the utterances.

The 78, in total, features used in the present study were normalized and extracted using the NLTK toolkit [2]. The feature set was tested with various classifiers in different searches. The main goal of this study is to evaluate the proposed stance framework, and determine whether the stance classes used here show a robust matching with the corresponding stance concepts, and whether they can be automatically identified and attributed when a baseline feature set consisted of simple features is used.

4   Experiments

In this section, we evaluate the methodology using our data set, as described in Sect. 3. For the classification stage, we relied on several machine learning algorithms, which have been discussed in the literature. We used a Bayesian classifier (BayesNet), a sequential minimal optimization (SMO) algorithm, three different logistic regression models (Logistic, SimpleLogistic, LogiBoost), a boosting algorithm combined with decision trees (AdaBoost), a multilayer perceptron neural network (MLP) algorithm, decision tree algorithms (LMT, Decision

Table 3. The results for the six-class classification experiments. The best result is highlighted in bold

Classifier	Classification accuracy
DecisionTable	26.23 %
BayesNet	25.54 %
REPTree	21.84 %
LMT	29.58 %
LogiBoost	25.13 %
MultiClassClassifier	29.17 %
MLP	20.95 %
SMO	28.90 %
SimpleLogistic	**30.00 %**
Logistic	28.42 %

Stump, RepTree), two meta-classifiers (MultiClassClassifier, MultiClassClassifierUpdateable) and a default rule-based classifier, the ZeroR. All classifiers were implemented using WEKA machine learning toolkit [28]. In order to avoid overlap between training and test subsets a 10-fold cross validation evaluation protocol was followed.

The performance results in terms of percentages of correctly classified utterances are shown in Table 3. The experimental results for our six-class problem did not prove to be satisfactory, achieving in the best case 30% of classification accuracy with the SimpleLogistic classifier. The large size of the feature set could be one of the reasons for the low classification accuracy percentages in our experiments. In a future step, methods for the dimensionality reduction of the feature set could be implemented, and more refined features related to the different stances (i.e., the most frequent items in each stance) could be added to the lexical and syntactic features. The size and nature of the data set, and the number of different classes could also be responsible for the relatively low accuracy in our experiments. It was a challenging task to perform classification experiments in a data set in which the utterances were in many cases annotated with more than one stance. In several cases (595 utterances in total), two or more stance labels are attributed to the same utterance, which means that these utterances appear in more than one position in the data. In order to carry out additional investigations on the basis of these findings, we compared the performance of the classifier for each class in terms of precision, recall and F-measure (F1), when SimpleLogistic classifier was used. These metrics, presented in Table 4, highlight the performance of the classifier during the classification task. We observed that the order of the classes that achieved the highest F1 value corresponds to the frequency order of the stance categories in the data set. This means that the more frequent a stance type is in the data set, the more correctly the classifier identifies it.

Table 4. The precision, recall, and F1 scores of the stance classes during the six-class experiments

Class	Precision	Recall	F1
CONTRARIETY	0,298	0,561	0,389
HYPOTHETICALITY	0,294	0,088	0,135
NECESSITY	0,328	0,191	0,241
PREDICTION	0,287	0,262	0,274
SOURCE OF KNOWLEDGE	0,330	0,402	0,363
UNCERTAINTY	0,118	0,031	0,049

We then reduced the number of classes used during the classification task, and we performed binary searches among all possible pairs of the six stance classes resulting in 15 binary setups. We created 15 different data subsets according to all stance categories pairings, and we tested the accuracy of the correctly classified utteranaces. In Table 5 we present the classification results starting from the best accuracy 71.17% achieved when CONTRARIETY and NECESSITY were tested with SMO, LMT and SimpleLogistic algorithms with all features.

Table 5. The classification accuracy results for each pair of stance categories

Pairs of classes	Classification accuracy	Classifier
Contrariety - Necessity	71.17%	SMO, LMT, SimpleLogistic
Hypotheticality - Source of knowledge	69.58%	MultiClassClassifierUpdateable
Contrariety - Hypotheticality	68.60%	SMO
Contrariety - Uncertainty	66%	LMT
Necessity - Source of knowledge	65.10%	MultiClassClassifier
Contrariety - Prediction	65%	SMO
Prediction - Source of knowledge	64.86%	LMT, MultiClassClassifier Updateable
Source of knowledge - Uncertainty	62.03%	SimpleLogistic, LMT
Hypotheticality - Necessity	60.8%	SimpleLogistic
Contrariety - Source of knowledge	60.59%	SimpleLogistic, SMO
Hypotheticality - Prediction	59.57%	SimpleLogistic, LMT, Ababoost, ZeroR
Necessity - Uncertainty	58.75%	SimpleLogistic
Hypotheticality - Uncertainty	58.58%	MultiClassClassifierUpdateable
Necessity - Prediction	57.67%	RepTree
Prediction - Uncertainty	56.69%	LMT

5   Discussion

The binary classification results show that multi-class classification problems cannot be solved easily, and it is difficult to achieve high classification accuracy, especially when a baseline feature set is used. As already stated in the introduction, our approach had a dual purpose and we achieved to:

- Exploit the stance classification problem in text data extracted from political blogs regarding the 2016 British referendum.
- Determine the efficacy of lexical and syntactic features using six novel stance classes.

We performed classification experiments using six new core stance categories, which puts our study a step beyond stance classification studies that use *pro* and *con* as stance labels. We showed that these stance categories (based on the BBC's annotation labels) can be applied and used as classification attributes as differences among them can be automatically identified.

An interesting finding of the binary classification experiments is that some stance pairs are more discriminative than others, achieving better classification accuracy scores. This can be explained by the fact that some stance categories are expressed in similar ways with similar constructions and they tend to co-occur in many utternaces in our data set. For example, the utterances annotated as PREDICTION are frequently co-annotated with UNCERTAINTY. As a result, this pair showed the lowest classification accuracy (56.67%) among all other stance combinations. The HYPOTHETICALITY–SOURCE OF KNOWLEDGE pair on the other hand, which achieved the second best accuracy (69.58%), does not co-occur in the data set. These two classes are expressed through different constructions. In addition, some stance classes trigger different cognitive functions, and therefore they do not seem to co-occur in discourse, as for instance the CONTRARIETY and the NECESSITY. These classes also show high inter-annotator agreement scores, a clue that proves that the utterances annotated as such are clearly different. As a result, the classifier easily distinguish them, and a higher percentage of utterances is correctly classified.

In this preliminary study of stance classification, where six novel stance categories were used, we used simple lexical and syntactic features as our baseline. These features in the cases where binary classification experiments were performed proved to be efficient. This fact highlights that differences among the various stance classes can be observed at character-, word- and sentence-level, and the refinement of this feature list can reveal interesting insights about the different stances. Based on an annotated data set, and without any refined, computationally complex or stance-focused features, we showed that basic clues such as the length of the words and the utterances, different metrics about the vocabulary richness (i.e., hapax legomena, type ratios, short words, etc.), and characteristics related to the syntactic structure of stance-annotated utterances such as punctuation and POS tag frequencies provide important information about stance differentiation in political blogs, and they deserve to be further investigated in future studies.

6   Conclusions

In this paper a stance classification framework using six novel and frequently used (in discourse) stance classes is presented. The efficacy of lexical and syntactic features for the identification of the notional stance categories were explored in a data set of annotated texts extracted from political blogs regarding the 2016 British referendum. The classification experiments showed that multi-class experiments are challenging and only binary searches outperform the multi-class ones, achieving accuracy score up to 71.17% for the CONTRARIETY–NECESSITY stance pair.

Acknowledgments. This research is part of the StaViCTA project [22], supported by the Swedish Research Council (framework grant "the Digitized Society – Past, Present, and Future", No. 2012-5659). We thank Maria Skeppstedt and Tom Sköld for the data annotation, and Kostiantyn Kucher for the implementation of the annotation tool.

References

1. Anand, P., Walker, M., Abbott, R., Tree, J.E.F., Bowmani, R., Minor, M.: Cats rule and dogs drool!: classifying stance in online debate. In: Proceedings of the 2nd Workshop on Computational Approaches to Subjectivity and Sentiment Analysis, pp. 1–9. Association for Computational Linguistics, June 2011
2. Bird, S.: NLTK: the natural language toolkit. In: Proceedings of the COLING/ACL on Interactive presentation sessions, pp. 67–72. Association for Computational Linguistics (2006)
3. Du Bois, J.W.: The stance triangle. In: Englebretson, R. (ed.) Stance taking in discourse: Subjectivity, evaluation, interaction, pp. 139–182 (2007)
4. Englebretson, R. (ed.): Stancetaking in Discourse: Subjectivity, Evaluation, Interaction, vol. 164. John Benjamins Publishing (2007)
5. Faulkner, A.: Automated classification of stance in student essays: an approach using stance target information and the Wikipedia link-based measure. Science **376**(12), 86 (2014)
6. Ferreira, W., Vlachos, A.: Emergent: a novel data-set for stance classification. In: Proceedings of the 2016 Conference of the North American Chapter of the Association for Computational Linguistics: Human Language Technologies. Association for Computational Linguistics, June 2016
7. Gavagai, A.P.I.: https://developer.gavagai.se
8. Hasan, K.S., Ng, V.: Stance classification of ideological debates: data, models, features, and constraints. In: IJCNLP, pp. 1348–1356 (2013)
9. Hasan, K.S., Ng, V.: Frame semantics for stance classification. In: CoNLL, pp. 124–13 (2013)
10. Hasan, K.S., Ng, V.: Extra-linguistic constraints on stance recognition in ideological debates. ACL **2**, 124–132 (2013c)
11. Hasan, K.S., Ng, V.: Why are you taking this stance? identifying and classifying reasons in ideological debates. In: EMNLP, pp. 751–762, March 2014
12. Kucher, K., Kerren, A., Paradis, C., Sahlgren, M.: Visual analysis of text annotations for stance classification with ALVA. In: Poster Abstracts of the EG/VGTC Conference on Visualization (EuroVis 2016), pp. 49–51. Eurographics-European Association for Computer Graphics (2016)

13. Kucher, K., Schamp-Bjerede, T., Kerren, A., Paradis, C., Sahlgren, M.: Visual analysis of online social media to open up the investigation of stance phenomena. Inf. Visual. **15**(2), 93–116 (2016b)
14. Mohammad, S.M., Sobhani, P., Kiritchenko, S.: Stance and sentiment in tweets. arXiv preprint arXiv:1605.01655 (2016)
15. Pang, B., Lee, L.: A sentimental education: sentiment analysis using subjectivity summarization based on minimum cuts. In: Proceedings of the 42nd Annual Meeting on Association for Computational Linguistics, pp. 93–116. Association for Computational Linguistics, July 2004
16. Rajadesingan, A., Liu, H.: Identifying users with opposing opinions in Twitter debates. In: Kennedy, W.G., Agarwal, N., Yang, S.J. (eds.) SBP 2014. LNCS, vol. 8393, pp. 153–160. Springer, Cham (2014). doi:10.1007/978-3-319-05579-4_19
17. Simaki, V., Paradis, C., Skeppstedt, M., Sahlgren, M., Kucher, K., Kerren, A.: Annotating speaker stance in discourse: the Brexit Blog Corpus, forthcoming (2017)
18. Simaki, V., Mporas, I., Megalooikonomou, V.: Evaluation and sociolinguistic analysis of text features for gender and age identification. Am. J. Eng. Appl. Sci. **9**(4), 868–876 (2016)
19. Simaki, V., Mporas, I., Megalooikonomou, V.: Age identification of twitter users: classification methods and sociolinguistic analysis. In: Proceedings of the 17th International Conference on Intelligent Text Processing and Computational Linguistics, CICLing 2016 (2016, to appear)
20. Somasundaran, S., Wiebe, J.: Recognizing stances in ideological on-line debates. In: Proceedings of the NAACL HLT 2010 Workshop on Computational Approaches to Analysis and Generation of Emotion in Text, pp. 116–124. Association for Computational Linguistics, June 2010
21. Sridhar, D., Getoor, L., Walker, M.: Collective stance classification of posts in online debate forums. In: Proceedings of the Association for Computational Linguistics, ACL 2014, p. 109 (2014)
22. StaViCTA project. http://cs.lnu.se/stavicta/
23. Taboada, M.: Sentiment analysis: an overview from linguistics. Ann. Rev. Linguist. **2**, 325–347 (2016)
24. Walker, M.A., Anand, P., Abbott, R., Grant, R.: Stance classification using dialogic properties of persuasion. In: Proceedings of the 2012 Conference of the North American Chapter of the Association for Computational Linguistics: Human Language Technologies, pp. 592–596. Association for Computational Linguistics (2012)
25. Walker, M.A., Anand, P., Abbott, R., Tree, J.E.F., Martell, C., King, J.: That is your evidence?: Classifying stance in online political debate. Decis. Support Syst. **53**(4), 719–729 (2012)
26. Walker, M.A., Tree, J.E.F., Anand, P., Abbott, R., King, J.: A corpus for research on deliberation and debate. In: LREC, pp. 812–817 (2012)
27. Wiebe, J., Wilson, T., Bruce, R., Bell, M., Martin, M.: Learning subjective language. Comput. Linguist. **30**(3), 277–308 (2004)
28. Witten, I.H., Frank, E., Hall, M.A., Pal, C.J.: Data Mining: Practical Machine Learning Tools and Techniques. Morgan Kaufmann, Burlington (2016)
29. Zheng, R., Li, J., Chen, H., Huang, Z.: A framework for authorship identification of online messages: writing-style features and classification techniques. J. Am. Soc. Inform. Sci. Technol. **57**(3), 378–393 (2006)

The "Retrospective Commenting" Method for Longitudinal Recordings of Everyday Speech

Arto Mustajoki[1]([⊠]) and Tatiana Sherstinova[2]

[1] Helsinki University, Yliopistonkatu 4, 00100 Helsinki, Finland
arto.mustajoki@helsinki.fi
[2] Saint Petersburg State University,
Universitetskaya Nab. 11, St. Petersburg 199034, Russia
t.sherstinova@spbu.ru

Abstract. The paper describes a pilot experiment aimed at revealing the occurrences of miscommunication between interlocutors in everyday speech recordings. Here, miscommunication is understood as situations in which the recipient perceives the meaning of the message in a different way from what was intended by the speaker. The experiment was based on the methodology of longitudinal recordings taken during one day, following the approach which is used for gathering audio data for the ORD speech corpus. But in addition it was enhanced by audition of the whole recording afterwards by the respondent himself/herself and his/her simultaneous commenting on some points of communicative settings with unobservable features. The task of the respondent was to note all occurrences of miscommunication, to explain to the researcher all unclear moments of interaction, to help in interpreting the emotional state of interlocutors, and to give some hints on pragmatic purposes, revealing those aspects of spoken interaction that are usually hidden behind the evident facts. The results of the experiment showed that miscommunication is indeed a rather frequent phenomenon in everyday face-to-face interaction. Moreover, the retrospective commenting method could significantly broaden the opportunities of discourse and pragmatic research based on long-term recordings.

Keywords: Everyday face-to-face interaction · Spoken discourse · Miscommunication · Dialogue · Longitudinal recordings · Stimulated recall · Retrospective interview · Retrospective commenting · Speech corpus · Emotional speech · Pragmatics · Communication strategies

1 Introduction

In recent studies of everyday face-to-face interaction, the concept of miscommunication is increasingly emerging (e.g., [1–3]). In this paper, following [4], miscommunication is understood as situations in which the recipient perceives the meaning of the message in a different way from what was intended by the speaker.

Rather often, miscommunication has a hidden character. For example, if the listener is not very interested in the current conversation, he can just *pretend* that he *is* listening [5].

© Springer International Publishing AG 2017
A. Karpov et al. (Eds.): SPECOM 2017, LNAI 10458, pp. 710–718, 2017.
DOI: 10.1007/978-3-319-66429-3_71

Moreover, it turns out that knowing some rules of spoken dialogue, it is possible to teach an absolutely "deaf" robot to conduct a seemingly successful communication in the form of normal dialogue flow, in which the human interlocutor may not even realize that his cues do not reach the addressee [6].

Taking into account the high communication skill of most people, it is usually quite impossible to understand when miscommunication really occurs without involving the testimonies of the participants themselves. Therefore, it was decided to conduct an experiment, the task of which was to make recordings and to get 'hot-pursuit' commenting on them by the respondent. This paper describes the methodology and some results of the experiment.

2 The Methodology of the Experiment

2.1 Longitudinal Recordings of Daily Interaction

For collecting audio data, the method of longitudinal recording during one day was proposed. This approach for gathering audio data was traditionally used in Japan in studies of "language life" [7]. It was called the method of "the 24 h survey", although in most of the cases the recordings were made from early morning till late evening [8].

Later, this approach was used for collecting data for the JST/CREST Expressive Speech Processing corpus, which was compiled "to illustrate the wide range of speaking-styles that can occur in ordinary everyday conversational situations" [9]. A similar methodology of longitudinal recordings had also been used earlier for collecting data for the demographically sampled part of the British National Corpus [10]. In this case "recruits who agreed to take part in the project were asked to record all of their conversations over a two- to seven-day period" [ibid.].

Recently, this method has been used for collecting data for the ORD corpus of spoken Russian, which is being created at St. Petersburg State University. The recordings are gathered from volunteers who agreed to spend a whole day "with a voice recorder at their neck" which records all their spoken discourse during that day – both in professional and personal settings [11, 12]. All participants are required to fill in a sociolinguistic questionnaire and to undergo psychological testing (Hans Eysenck test, FPI test and Cattell's test).

The ORD recordings provide unique data for diverse linguistic, sociolinguistic, [13], discourse and pragmatic studies [14–16]. However, when interpreting the obtained recordings from a pragmatic point of view, it is sometimes difficult for the researchers (as well as for anybody who did not take part in the conversation) to completely reconstruct the situation on the basis of the audio recording alone. The same is true for miscommunication. We had proposed a hypothesis that many ambiguities could be clarified through commenting and explanations by the participant himself (herself) in combination with a researcher's interview [17, 18]. This was the reason for conducting this experiment.

2.2 Selection of Respondents

The main criteria for selecting participants for this experiment was their willingness to participate in the recording, as well as their readiness to hold a frank discussion afterwards concerning the details and strategies of their spoken communication. Respondents had to be more than 18 years of age, have Russian as their native language, and be open to introspection. For the first experiment, we aimed at choosing a participant who would speak enough during the recording day, both in private settings (either with family members or with friends) and at work. The other important requirement was a full understanding of the aims of the experiment on the part of the respondent.

Finally, preference was given to the following candidate: a 40-year-old woman, with two higher education degrees, currently lecturing on the history of theatre and cinema at the university and also working part-time as an actress. It seemed to us that her experience on the theatrical stage and her skills in the emotional sphere would make it easier for her to look at her own everyday behaviour somehow 'from the outside', while her experience in teaching would help her to judge it quite objectively.

Naturally, participation in the experiment was anonymous. However, the respondent had to sign a consent form regarding participation in the project, which was prepared by the legal service of St. Petersburg University.

2.3 Pre-recording Instructions for the Respondent

Pre-recoding instructions for the respondent were much the same as in the regular procedure for ORD recordings (for details see [11, 12]). The participant was instructed to turn on the recorder in the morning and keep it operating until she went to bed in the evening. She was asked to choose a day for the recording when different communicative situations would be expected. Further, she should be ready to start analysing the recordings on the day following its implementation, and it was expected that the retrospective commenting procedure might take up to three days on average. In addition, the respondent was asked to note (at least mentally) the situations of miscommunication during the day of recording.

2.4 Post-recording and Pre-audition Instructions for the Respondent

The participant was told that the following points were of particular interest for the research:

- **Miscommunication situations** or any other types of communicative failure, e.g., when the recipient understood the speaker in a different way from what was intended by the speaker. Or when she did not understand anything at all, but pretended that she did.
- **The reasons that prompted a person to use this or that dialogue tactic** (e.g., *I am speaking this way because…*). This information is of particular interest for pragmatics studies. In addition, points concerning "recipient design" [1] should also be noted: *I adapt my speech behaviour, speaking with this interlocutor in such a way, because…*

- **Explanations of any communication situations that a stranger could not understand correctly.**
  Consequently, the task of the respondent was to indicate all such moments when listening to the recording and to comment on them.
  Furthermore, the researcher explained that her role as an interviewer was to get information from the respondent concerning what was unclear or incomprehensible from the audio recording. In particular:
- **Description/clarification of the context or word meanings:** *What were you talking about?* It is very often the case in private conversations that some words, names, notions and even the general idea of the dialogue may be difficult (or even impossible) to understand by researchers unfamiliar with the interlocutors' background. Thus, when the researcher does not understand something in the audition, he/she would ask the respondent to explain either the situational context or incomprehensible words, jargon, terms and proper names.
- **Attribution of emotions:** *What was your emotion here? What did you want to express?* Emotionality is inherent in everyday face-to-face interaction [19], but it is often difficult for the researcher, who does not know the respondents personally, to determine whether some phrase is neutral or "emotionally coloured". Therefore, it is valuable to have attributed samples of emotional speech, including the emotional meaning of some paralinguistic phenomena.
- **Pragmatic functions of individual speech acts:** *Why did you say it?* Of course, it is impossible to analyse everything in detail, but the important non-obvious moments should be explained.
- **Recognition of humour, irony, or language play.** These phenomena, too, are not always understandable a priori.
- **Decoding fragments of illegible or slurred speech.** Because they are made in natural conditions, the recordings often have fragments of simultaneous speech, background noise, or poor speech articulation, which makes them difficult to transcribe. Here, it is also possible to resort to the aid of the respondent.

2.5   The Retrospective Commenting Procedure

Both the respondent and the researcher-interviewer listen together to all the sound data that had been recorded shortly before. While listening, the respondent notes and comments on the events, referring to points of interest 1–3, mentioned above in Sect. 2.4. The researcher, on the other hand, monitors the general understandability of the communicative situation, as far as possible, and asks questions related to points 4–8 from Sect. 2.4. The procedure implies a discussion between the respondent and the researcher, which is also recorded on a voice recorder.

The method as such is not new. Some versions of it have been used in teacher training, second language acquisition and intercultural communication research. The general idea of such studies is to ask informants to comment on their own performances in audio or video recordings. It is meant to reveal people's meta-analytic understanding of their attitudes, feelings and interpretations regarding situations in which they have been involved.

Two terms are used to describe this kind of methodology: *stimulated recall* (e.g. [20, 21]) and *retrospective interview*. The latter term has also been applied to research where recordings are not used as a stimulus for reactions, but informants have been asked to describe their recollections of incidents or events they have experienced (see, e.g. [22, 23]). We prefer a more precise name of the method: *retrospective commenting* on one's speech.

In our case, the method is used in a different context from earlier. In research on communication, the method is seen as a complementary means of obtaining more detailed evidence on problems in understanding. The other methods and approaches used include a thorough scrutiny of the dialogue by applying conversational analysis and study of the backgrounds of the participants [24]. As a rule, the participants know each other well and the researchers also know them beforehand. In the case of ORD material, the situation is fundamentally different. During the day there are numerous encounters with various people, in which they talk about all kinds of themes depending on the changing circumstances. The heterogeneous nature of the material makes retrospective commenting a very demanding task for both the researcher and the respondent. The method is at the same time introspective and ethnographic.

3   Some Results of the Experiment

The experiment was held in St. Petersburg in late January, 2017. During her "day of speech", the respondent recorded about 14 h of audio data, of which the fragments containing speech are up to 10 h. They refer to her spoken communication with family members (daughter, mother, and husband), with colleagues (university lecturers), with her students, with partners (actors), with friends, acquaintances, health workers and with herself.

Despite the preliminary agreement, it turned out that the respondent was unable to undertake commenting the day after recording because of family matters. She was able to begin the procedure of retrospective commenting only three days later. However, it seems that this forced delay did not affect the results of the experiment: listening to the recording, the respondent seemed to be able to recall even minor details of the situation.

The joint work of the respondent and the researcher lasted three days, about 8 h each day. The first day was started with a discussion on the objectives of the experiment, followed by the rather detailed pilot commenting. As a result, only 2 h of recordings were analysed on the first day. On the second and third days, the work went faster.

When it became evident to both participants in the experiment that it would be impossible to finish commenting within the three days scheduled for the retrospective commenting if the discussion of each communicative episode continue to be so detailed, it was decided to speed up the process, skipping some fragments during which nothing special took place. This included, for example, most of the 12 examination answers of students taking an exam on the history of theatre.

In general, it turned out that the procedure of retrospective commenting is rather time consuming and needs constant attention from both the side of the respondent and the researcher.

Concerning the primary goal of the experiment, the results are as follows. First, the experiment showed that miscommunication is indead a rather frequent phenomenon in everyday face-to-face interaction.

It is interesting, but when asked about miscommunication episodes before listening to the recording, the respondent could only recall two situations that drew her attention. Both referred to rather difficult conflict situations, in which there was internal opposition between the respondent and her interlocutors that had to be resolved during the conversation (and it really was). The first one took place in a discussion with the doctor of her daughter, and the second occurred in the university with one of her students that had earlier behaved strangely and it felt as though he did not respect his lecturers. The second case relates to miscommunication *in the past* resulting in current tension in relationships.

However, in the process of audition the most frequent types of miscommunication appeared to be the following: (1) *talking past each other*, which frequently happens in domestic conversations, and (2) *not listening to the interlocutor* because of fatigue, lack of interest and some other reasons. These results were fairly predictable [5].

Our respondent seemed to feel quite free to disclose her communication strategies. For example, she explained that when speaking with a doctor, in order to obtain a medical certificate, she pretend to behave like a shy and timid person. Later, she commented on her conversation with her boss thus: *Here I am flattering my directress.* And so on.

Her other comments are also very valuable. Thus, she could explain not only the reasons for her speaking behaviour, but also for many paralinguistic phenomena, and even for singing at home to herself (e.g., *Here, I am singing this song because I'm thinking about my mother – it is "her tune"*).

In most cases, the respondent easily described the emotions of her speech, although sometimes it was difficult for her to find the proper words. It should be mentioned that after the initial training on the first hours of recordings, the researcher-interviewer became able to better understand the emotions and intentions of the respondent's speech. Thus, on the second day of commenting, instead of questions such as *What did you want to express?*, the researcher was able to make his own suggestions, such as: *It sounds like irony, does it not?* In many cases the respondent agreed with the researcher (*Yes, it's irony*), but could also correct (*I would say it's sarcasm*).

The quality of the recording was good enough, so there were not many cases of the unintelligible speech. However, it turned out that there were some fragments when the respondent herself was unable to transcribe her own speech, even of fine quality.

4   Conclusion

The methodology of retrospective commenting was proposed in order to reveal miscommunication situations in everyday dialogues and to clarify some other non-obvious aspects of real communication situations. Besides miscommunication situations or any other types of communicative failure, the following points were of particular interest for the research: the reasons that prompted a person to use this or that dialogue tactic; explanations of any communication situations that a stranger could not understand correctly; description/clarification of the context or word meaning; attribution of emotions; recognition of humour, irony, or language play; revealing pragmatic functions of individual speech acts; and decoding fragments of illegible or slurred speech.

The experiment on retrospective commenting was successfully conducted and showed that miscommunication is indead a rather frequent phenomenon in everyday face-to-face interaction. The most frequent types of miscommunication appeared to be the following: (1) talking past each other, which frequently happens in domestic conversations, and (2) not listening to the interlocutor because of fatigue, lack of interest and some other reasons. The respondent seemed to feel quite free to disclose her communication strategies, easily described the emotions of her speech and in most cases she could freely answer questions posed by the researcher-interviewer.

The experiment showed that the retrospective commenting method could significantly broaden the opportunities of linguistic and pragmatic research based on longitudinal recordings. Moreover, this method can be applied not only to the analysis of longitudinal recordings, but also to all kinds of research on authentic human speech and spoken interaction.

Along with the apparent advantages, this approach also has weaknesses, the major one of which is that, like many qualitative investigations, it is rather time consuming and resource intensive. Despite this drawback, the method of retrospective commenting seems worthwhile and promising, because there are no other possibilities for understanding the nuances of spoken conversations between people whom the researchers do not know personally. For qualitative pragmatic research, it seems worth spending time with respondents in order to clarify the details of interaction, instead of trying to imagine what happened.

Our experience also showed that commenting on one's own linguistic behaviour is a very demanding task. It is evident that not all people are ready and competent to analyse their own actions during a speech day.

Even if a person agrees to an experiment, the researchers cannot be entirely confident that he or she is completely sincere when interpreting the discussed situation with the interviewer (possibly embellishing some details of conversation or concealing others). And even if the respondent is trying to be sincere, one cannot be sure that he or she is not mistaken in interpreting the behaviour of his/her interlocutors. However, a 'sincere informant' can be expected to correctly identify at least his/her own emotions and behaviour strategies.

Our next task is to expand the research and to prove to what extent the experiment is reproducible with participants of diverse social groups and professions. Further, we plan to carry out similar experiments not only on Russian material, but also on other languages. Our main goal is to get a deeper and more reliable understanding of what ultimately takes place in human interaction. Social life in modern society is largely determined by communication between people. In this regard, it is extremely important to understand in more detail the mechanisms that rule and influence its course.

Acknowledgements. The presented research was supported by the University of Helsinki.

The methodology of longitudinal recording was approved during the creation of the ORD speech corpus, which is being created in St. Petersburg State University and was supported by several grants: the Russian Foundation for Humanities projects # 07–04–94515e/Ya

(Speech Corpus of Russian Everyday Communication "One Speaker's Day") and # 12–04–12017 (Information System of Communication Scenarios of Russian Spontaneous Speech), the Russian Ministry of Education project Sound Form of Russian Grammar System in Communicative and Informational Approach. Significant extension of the corpus was achieved in the framework of the project "Everyday Russian Language in Different Social Groups" supported by the Russian Scientific Foundation, project # 14–18–02070.

References

1. Mustajoki, A.: A speaker-oriented multidimensional approach to risks and causes of miscommunication. Lang. Dialogue **2**, 216–242 (2012)
2. Pietikäinen, K.S.: Misunderstandings and ensuring understanding in private ELF talk. Appl. Linguist. 1–26 (2016). doi:10.1093/applin/amw005
3. Roberts, G., Langstein, B., Galantucci, B.: (In)sensitivity to incoherence in human communication. Lang. Commun. **47**, 15–22 (2016)
4. Ryan, J., Roger, B.: Who do you mean? Investigating miscommunication in paired interactions. TESOLANS J. **17**, 44–61 (2009)
5. Mustajoki, A., Sherstinova, T., Tuomarla, U.: Types and functions of pseudo-dialogues. In: Kecskes, I., Weigand, E. (eds.) Pragmatics to Dialogue. John Benjamins, Amsterdam (2017). (in print)
6. Campbell, N.: Machine processing of dialogue states; speculations on conversational entropy. In: Ronzhin, A., Potapova, R., Németh, G. (eds.) SPECOM 2016. LNCS, vol. 9811, pp. 18–25. Springer, Cham (2016). doi:10.1007/978-3-319-43958-7_2
7. Sibata, T.: Studying the language life with the method of the 24 hour survey. In: Alpatov, V.M., Vardul, I.F. (eds.) Linguistics in Japan, pp. 134–141 (1983)
8. Sibata, T.: Consciousness of language norms. In: Kunihiro, T., Inoue, F., Long, D. (eds.) Sociolinguistics in Japanese Contexts. Mouton de Gruyter, Berlin-New York (1999)
9. Campbell, N.: Speech and expression; the value of a longitudinal corpus, LREC 2004, pp. 183–186 (2004)
10. Burnard, L. (ed.) Reference guide for the British National Corpus (XML edition). Published for the British National Corpus Consortium by Oxford University Computing Services (2007). http://www.natcorp.ox.ac.uk/docs/URG/. Accessed 2 Feb 2016
11. Asinovsky, A., Bogdanova, N., Rusakova, M., Ryko, A., Stepanova, S., Sherstinova, T.: The ORD speech corpus of Russian everyday communication "One Speaker's Day": creation principles and annotation. In: Matoušek, V., Mautner, P. (eds.) TSD 2009. LNCS, vol. 5729, pp. 250–257. Springer, Heidelberg (2009). doi:10.1007/978-3-642-04208-9_36
12. Bogdanova-Beglarian, N., Sherstinova, T., Blinova, O., Martynenko, G.: An exploratory study on sociolinguistic variation of Russian everyday speech. In: Ronzhin, A., Potapova, R., Németh, G. (eds.) SPECOM 2016. LNCS, vol. 9811, pp. 100–107. Springer, Cham (2016). doi:10.1007/978-3-319-43958-7_11
13. Bogdanova-Beglarian, N., Sherstinova, T., Blinova, O., Ermolova, O., Baeva, E., Martynenko, G., Ryko, A.: Everyday Russian language in different social groups. Communicative Res. **2**(8), 81–92 (2016)
14. Bogdanova-Beglarian, N.V.: Pragmatic items functions in Russian everyday speech of different social groups. Perm University Herald. Russ. Foreign Philology **2**(34), 38–49 (2016)

15. Blinova, O.: Modeling imperative utterances in Russian spoken dialogue: verb-central quantitative approach. In: Ronzhin, A., Potapova, R., Németh, G. (eds.) SPECOM 2016. LNCS, vol. 9811, pp. 491–498. Springer, Cham (2016). doi:10.1007/978-3-319-43958-7_59
16. Sherstinova, T.: Speech acts annotation of everyday conversations in the ORD corpus of spoken Russian. In: Ronzhin, A., Potapova, R., Németh, G. (eds.) SPECOM 2016. LNCS, vol. 9811, pp. 627–635. Springer, Cham (2016). doi:10.1007/978-3-319-43958-7_76
17. Kvale, S.: Interviews. An Introduction to Qualitative Research Interviewing. Sage Publications, Thousand Oaks (1996)
18. Campion, M.A., Campion, J.E., Hudson Jr., J.P.: Structured interviewing: a note on incremental validity and alternative question types. J. Appl. Psychol. **79**, 998–1002 (1994)
19. Weigand, E.: Emotions: the simple and the complex. In: Weigand, E. (ed.) Emotions in Dialogic Interaction, pp. 3–31. Benjamins, Amsterdam/Philadelphia (2004)
20. Gass, S.M., Mackey, A.: Stimulated Recall Methodology in Second Language Research. Taylor & Francis, London (2000)
21. Lyle, J.: Stimulated recall: a report on its use in naturalistic research. Br. Educ. Res. J. **29**, 6 (2003)
22. Perin, D., Grant, G., Raufman, J., Kalamkarian, H.S.: Learning from student retrospective reports: implications for the college developmental classroom. J. Coll. Reading Learn. **47**, 77–98 (2017)
23. Pratt, S.M., Martin, A.M.: The differential impact of video-stimulated recall and concurrent questioning methods on beginning readers' verbalization about self-monitoring during oral reading. Reading Psychol. (2017). doi:10.1080/02702711.2017.129072
24. Bremer, K., Roberts, C., Vasseur, M.-T., Simonot, M., Broeder, P.: Achieving Understanding: Discourse in Intercultural Encounters. Longman, London (1996)

The 2016 RWTH Keyword Search System
for Low-Resource Languages

Pavel Golik[✉], Zoltán Tüske, Kazuki Irie, Eugen Beck, Ralf Schlüter,
and Hermann Ney

Human Language Technology and Pattern Recognition,
Computer Science Department, RWTH Aachen University, 52056 Aachen, Germany
{golik,tuske,irie,beck,schlueter,ney}@cs.rwth-aachen.de

Abstract. In this paper we describe the RWTH Aachen keyword search
(KWS) system developed in the course of the IARPA Babel program. We
put focus on acoustic modeling with neural networks and evaluate the
full pipeline with respect to the KWS performance. At the core of this
study lie multilingual bottleneck features extracted from a deep neural
network trained on all 28 languages available to the project articipants.
We show that in a low-resource scenario, the multilingual features are
crucial for achieving state-of-the-art performance.

Further highlights of this work include comparisons of tandem and
hybrid acoustic models based on feed-forward and recurrent neural networks, keyword search pipelines based on lattice and time-marked word
list representation and measuring the effect of adding large amounts of
text data scraped from the web. The evaluation is performed on multiple
languages of the last two project periods.

Keywords: Acoustic modeling · Keyword search · Graphemic · Multilingual · Neural networks · Time-marked word list · Recurrent · LSTM

1 Introduction

In the last decades, the research on automatic speech recognition (ASR) has
mainly focused on languages with large amounts of linguistic resources available (e.g. English, Spanish or Mandarin). Meanwhile, the demand has increased
for indexing and searching audio documents in languages, for which only a limited amount of such resources exists. These resources include pronunciation dictionaries, transcribed audio data and large amounts of text data. The IARPA
Babel program aimed at developing robust methods for keyword search in under-
resourced languages that can be rapidly deployed for new languages [2]. One of
its goals was to explore the operating point that minimizes the amount of human
effort required to prepare language specific resources for setting up a KWS system in a new language.

Over the course of four years, the participants of the IARPA Babel program
were provided with a gradually increasing number of languages. Table 1 summarizes the 25 languages released by IARPA. Each year, an evaluation campaign

© Springer International Publishing AG 2017
A. Karpov et al. (Eds.): SPECOM 2017, LNAI 10458, pp. 719–730, 2017.
DOI: 10.1007/978-3-319-66429-3_72

Table 1. Language packs released by IARPA to the project participants. Last row in each of the four period blocks corresponds to the surprise (i.e. evaluation) language

	Language	ID	Language pack version		Language	ID	Language pack version
BP	Cantonese	101	`IARPA-babel101-v0.4c`	OP1	Assamese	102	`IARPA-babel102b-v0.5a`
	Pashto	104	`IARPA-babel104b-v0.4aY`		Bengali	103	`IARPA-babel103b-v0.4b`
	Turkish	105	`IARPA-babel105b-v0.4`		Haitian Creole	201	`IARPA-babel201b-v0.2b`
	Tagalog	106	`IARPA-babel106-v0.2f`		Lao	203	`IARPA-babel203b-v3.1a`
	Vietnamese	107	`IARPA-babel107b-v0.7`		Tamil	204	`IARPA-babel204b-v1.1b`
					Zulu	206	`IARPA-babel206b-v0.1e`
OP2	Kurmanji Kurdish	205	`IARPA-babel205b-v1.0a`	OP3	Pashto	104	`IARPA-babel104b-v0.4bY`
	Tok Pisin	207	`IARPA-babel207b-v1.0a`		Guarani	305	`IARPA-babel305b-v1.0c`
	Cebuano	301	`IARPA-babel301b-v2.0b`		Igbo	306	`IARPA-babel306b-v2.0c`
	Kazakh	302	`IARPA-babel302b-v1.0a`		Amharic	307	`IARPA-babel307b-v1.0b`
	Telugu	303	`IARPA-babel303b-v1.0a`		Mongolian	401	`IARPA-babel401b-v2.0b`
	Lithuanian	304	`IARPA-babel304b-v1.0b`		Javanese	402	`IARPA-babel402b-v1.0b`
	Swahili	202	`IARPA-babel202b-v1.0d`		Dholuo	403	`IARPA-babel403b-v1.0b`
					Georgian	404	`IARPA-babel404b-v1.0a`

was carried out on a new ("surprise") language. In an increasingly short evaluation period, the participants were required to train an ASR system from scratch, extract lattices for approx. 70 hours of audio, search for several thousands keywords and submit the results for scoring.

Depending on the evaluation conditions, the results were evaluated in one of several tracks. In the first two years (BP, OP1[1]), the participants were evaluated on *full* and *limited* language packs (FLP and LLP), that differ by the amount of transcribed training data. In the third year (OP2), the LLP condition was further restricted and is referred to as "very limited language pack" (VLLP). In the VLLP track the participants were allowed to make use of approx. 50 h of untranscribed data. In the final year, the VLLP track had been dropped and the participants were evaluated on the FLP only. The restricted evaluation conditions for VLLP allowed to use data from other languages' FLPs for building multilingual models. Also, the FLP track in the final year (OP3) allowed to use all 24 language packs released in the course of the project and also publicly available data in four additional languages (approx. 200 h each of English, Spanish, Mandarin and Arabic)[2]. Table 2 shows an overview of the different tracks.

It is worth mentioning that the audio conditions are extremely challenging across languages, as the recordings of telephone conversations from both mobile and landline were done in real environments and are of poor quality. Also, the data sets cover a wide range of dialects and other demographic attributes. However the high variability across the 28 languages and the restricted evaluation conditions of the IARPA Babel project have provided an excellent opportunity to explore the effectiveness of multilingual acoustic modeling for under-resourced languages. Please note that the ASR performance (measured in word error rate, WER) has been a secondary objective, since the KWS system is allowed to operate on all hypotheses, while the WER is calculated from the best path only.

---

[1] BP: base period, OP: option period.

[2] see Table 1 in [1] for details on the four additional corpora.

Table 2. Evaluation conditions in each of the project periods. The entries show the approximate amount of *transcribed* training data and whether a pronunciation lexicon and use of multilingual models was allowed

Period	Training data [h]			Lexicon			Multilingual		
	FLP	LLP	VLLP	FLP	LLP	VLLP	FLP	LLP	VLLP
BP	70	10		+	+		−	−	
OP1	50	10		+	+		−	−	
OP2	30		3	+		−	−		+
OP3	40			−				+	

In Sect. 2 we define the keyword search task and the evaluation metric and also describe KWS on lattices. Section 3 introduces the multilingual bottleneck feature extraction. Section 4 outlines the experimental setup and provides the results obtained on the development sets in multiple languages. We report the best results obtained on the languages of the final project period and draw conclusions in Sect. 5.

2 Keyword Search Task

The goal of a KWS system is to detect occurrences of a keyword in large amounts of audio data. According to the Babel program conditions, the KWS is performed on an index built from audio before the keywords are revealed. The index is usually represented by a word graph (lattice) as a compact structure for multiple hypotheses provided by the ASR sub-system. This allows the KWS system to select words that are not necessarily part of the first-best hypothesis. Each query consists of one or multiple words. A hypothesis is accepted if the score based on the word posterior probability exceeds a decision threshold. Given a set of search terms $\mathcal{T}$, a set of hypotheses and the true transcription of the test data, the performance of a KWS system can be measured in Actual Term Weighted Value (ATWV), a quantity based on the negative average value lost per term [5]. The value loss is a linear combination of the probabilities of miss and false alarm errors at a given acceptance threshold θ:

$$V(\theta) = 1 - \frac{1}{|\mathcal{T}|} \sum_{t \in \mathcal{T}} \left\{ P_{Miss}(t, \theta) + \beta P_{FA}(t, \theta) \right\} \tag{1}$$

The threshold is optimized on a development corpus with a development keyword set by maximizing the term weighted value. In this work we only report the maximum term weighted value (MTWV) results, which does not require tuning the decision threshold and allows to evaluate modifications in the ASR component easily. It had been stated by the project organizers, that an ATWV of at least 0.3 is a reasonable operating point. The goal had been further increased from 0.3 to 0.6 ATWV in the final project period. We use a 4-gram count language model (LM) for ASR experiments and a bigram LM for KWS lattice generation, a well-known trick [14] to make the lattice cover more hypotheses.

The queries that contain words unknown to the ASR system at the decoding time pose a fundamental problem to the KWS system, as there are no word arcs in the lattice corresponding to the exact query. A common approach to alleviate this problem is to expand the query and the lattice on the phoneme/grapheme level and to allow for substitutions and deletions by composing the query with a *phoneme-to-phoneme* (P2P) or a *grapheme-to-grapheme* (G2G) weighted finite state transducer (WFST) whose weights are estimated from the training data [17,21]. An alternative approach is to segment the known words automatically in order to obtain a data-driven *morphological* decomposition, where the known words share multiple fragments or *sub-words*. In the decoder, the vocabulary of known words then is replaced by a vocabulary of sub-words. Finally, the out-of-vocabulary (OOV) queries are decomposed in the same manner and the KWS is carried out on the new lattice.

Once the lattice generation is done, the scores can be improved by *lattice rescoring*, e.g. by using a new language model (e.g. LSTM-LM [11]). It is also possible to combine KWS results obtained from different lattices (e.g. full word and sub-word graphs) by weighting the scores and merging the hit lists [15]. Various techniques exist to post-process lists of KWS hypotheses such as smoothing of the scores and applying term-specific transforms in order to make a global decision threshold more suitable [17].

3   Multilingual Bottleneck Features

In order to benefit from the large amount of data from many non-target languages available for acoustic training, we followed the approach outlined in [22]. The idea is to train a deep neural network (DNN) that has multiple language-specific output layers – one per language. As in conventional ASR systems, the output labels correspond to the context-dependent HMM states tied by a classification and regression tree (CART). All other weights in the network are shared across the languages. The training on shuffled samples from all available languages forces the model to learn a hidden representation that is universal for all classification tasks. Similar to our previous work in [26] we use the output of a hidden "bottleneck" layer [7] in order to be able to train a hierarchy of two multilingual (ML) neural networks and to perform feature combination [25].

Our framework consists of a hierarchical topology of two DNNs: the first network is trained on a mix of MRASTA filtered critical band energies (CRBE) [9], voicedness feature [28] and F_0 estimate. The 15-dimensional CRBE features are obtained from three different filtering pipelines that differ in the way the spectral analysis is performed (MFCC, PLP and Gammatone [23]), such that the model performs a feature combination. The input to the second network is similar and is augmented by the bottleneck features from the first network. Also, the features of the first network are spliced such that the second network has an input

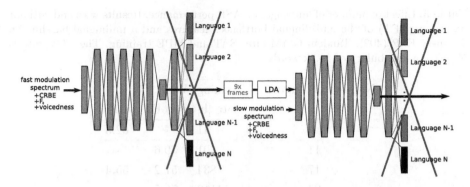

Fig. 1. Topology of a hierarchical bottleneck feature extraction pipeline

context of 9 frames, transformed by LDA. All features are globally normalized w.r.t. mean and variance. In Sect. 4.1 we will also report results obtained by a slightly different topology (no hierarchical structure, simple filter bank features).

Both networks have 7 hidden layers of size 2000 with the sixth layer being the linear bottleneck layer of size 62. The output layer consists of multiple, language dependent softmax layers connected to the last hidden layer. Figure 1 shows the topology of this hierarchical arrangement. Each softmax layer models the 1500 tied context-dependent triphone state posteriors of the corresponding language. Once the training is done, we can *fine-tune* (FT) the DNN on a target language by using the target data only.

4 Experimental Results

4.1 Multilingual Features

In order to explore the impact of the number of languages and therefore, the increased amount of training data, we trained ML features on varying number of languages. Table 3 shows the ASR performance on Javanese FLP. As the amount of training data used to derive these features increases, the WER drops consistently: going from 1 to 28 languages, the relative reduction is 12%. Also, the results show that fine-tuning on the target language is very important.

In the following experiment, we compare two sets of ML bottleneck features that differ by the topology of the extraction network and the input features:

- hierarchical sigmoid DNN trained on MRASTA filtered critical band energies (CRBE) combined from 3 different filter banks (as described in Sect. 3)
- single deep rectified linear units (ReLU) network trained on the output of a 40-dimensional Gammatone filter bank

In order to do this, we evaluate two methods of feature combination: *simple concatenation* and *merger DNN* that is trained on a concatenation of both bottleneck features. The merger DNN produces a new set of bottleneck features

Table 3. Effect of number of languages on ASR performance. Results with and without fine-tuning (FT) of the multilingual bottleneck features and a unilingual baseline on Javanese FLP (402). Tandem GMM after SAT and MPE training. The OOV rate is 5% with a vocabulary of 16.5k words

Number of languages	Training data [h]	WER [%] w/o FT	WER [%] w/FT
1	41	-	62.3
11	601	59.6	-
17	834	57.2	55.4
24	1110	56.5	-
28	1793	56.2	55.1

that is used in the final tandem setup. The new bottleneck features are of same dimension as each of the input features. Table 4 shows that an additional non-linear transform of the bottleneck features improves both the ASR and the KWS performance. Both methods outperform any of the two bottleneck features (not shown in the table). The merger DNN approach, however, comes at the cost of additional DNN training. These results encouraged us to train deep feed-forward and LSTM networks on the first set (sigmoid based) of ML features (cf. Sect. 4.3).

Table 4. Comparison of feature combination strategies: simple *concatenation* vs. bottleneck features from a *merger* DNN. Results obtained on FLPs of OP3 with MPE trained tandem GMM acoustic models that include web data. The KWS pipeline is based on a morphological decomposition of words

ID	Language	WER [%] concat	WER [%] merge	MTWV concat	MTWV merge
401	Mongolian	50.9	49.6	0.5026	0.5105
404	Georgian	42.6	42.3	0.7040	0.7074

4.2 Graphemic Pronunciation Modeling

In RWTH ASR system [20], the tying of context dependent HMM states is done by a classification and regression tree (CART), that is trained using "phonetic questions", i.e. linguistically meaningful subsets of the phoneme set (vowels, consonants, etc.). In the graphemic scenario adopted by the Babel program in OP2 and OP3, this clustering is not available. Thus in [6] we developed a method to generate "graphemic questions" from aligned data. Please note that this is done for each language in isolation, eventhough some languages share graphemes.

The set of graphemes was derived from the training transcripts after converting the text to lower case. Since Amharic has a syllable based writing system, we manually defined a mapping from each character to the consonant-vowel pair, reducing the number of modeled units from 282 to 66. For all other languages, we assumed a one-to-one correspondence between graphemes and phonemes. A simple graphemic lexicon is used to train an initial context independent acoustic model and align the training transcripts. Assuming that every grapheme and, subsequently, each grapheme cluster is modeled by a single Gaussian, we perform a greedy bottom-up clustering of the mean vectors and keep track of all intermediate clusters. This is similar to the approach presented in [3,12]. Each cluster then serves as a potential binary split of the set of graphemes and therefore defines a graphemic question for the CART estimation procedure.

4.3 Acoustic Models

Throughout the course of the project, we have been evaluating and comparing tandem [8] and hybrid acoustic models that operate on ML features. The Gaussian mixture models (GMM) with a tied diagonal covariance matrix are used to calculate emission probabilities in a context-dependent HMM. The hybrid models are based on deep feed-forward neural networks (DNNs) or recurrent neural networks with long short-term memory (LSTM) cells [10]. We use RASR [20] and RETURNN [4] toolkits for acoustic training. We found that sequence discriminative training is absolutely crucial to achieve a high KWS accuracy.

The 115-dimensional input features consist of LDA and CMLLR transformed concatenation of Gammatone, voicedness, pitch and ML features trained on 28 languages. The DNNs take a window of 17 frames as input. In contrast, (bidirectional) recurrent models do not require feature splicing to model temporal dependencies. The output layer corresponds to 1.8k (VLLP) or 4.5k (FLP) tied HMM states. The initial DNN is trained w.r.t. the cross-entropy (CE) criterion by stochastic gradient descent. We train the LSTM-RNN model using Adam [13] for 4–5 epochs. The initial step size is 10^{-3}, the dropout rate is 0.1 and the momentum factor is 0.9. We also penalize large weights with an L_2 regularization factor of 0.01 and clip the gradients if their absolute value exceeds 10.

The DNN consists of 6 hidden layers with 2048 rectified linear units each. In the RNN, we only use 3 layers with 500 bi-directionally connected LSTM units each. This reduces the number of model parameters from 30M to 18.9M. However, when training DNNs w.r.t. minimum phone error (MPE) criterion [19], we only update weights of the output layer (approx. 9.2M parameters), as updating all layers does not improve the ASR performance. In RNNs, we update all layers. We train DNNs w.r.t. minimum phone error (MPE) in the full-batch mode using Rprop, while the RNNs are trained in the mini-batch mode with Adam.

Table 5 shows that the RNNs easily achieve the best word error rates on all five languages (tandem results not shown in table; on average, the LSTM-RNNs outperform tandem GMMs by 0.6% WER relative). Yet only on two out of

Table 5. Comparison of hybrid models trained w.r.t. cross-entropy (CE) or minimum phone error (MPE) criterion. Results on FLPs of OP3 include web data (except Igbo)

ID	Language	Acoustic model	WER [%]		MTWV
			CE	MPE	MPE
104	Pashto	DNN	49.3	48.2	0.4719
		LSTM-RNN	47.7	47.1	0.4679
306	Igbo	DNN	58.9	58.5	0.3715
		LSTM-RNN	57.1	56.6	0.3801
401	Mongolian	DNN	53.4	51.5	0.5059
		LSTM-RNN	49.9	48.8	0.5066
402	Javanese	DNN	53.6	52.4	0.4827
		LSTM-RNN	51.7	51.3	0.4803
404	Georgian	DNN	42.1	41.2	0.7050
		LSTM-RNN	44.0	41.1	0.6978

five languages the RNNs achieve higher MTWV than feed-forward DNNs. Also, Table 8 shows that the best KWS results are often obtained by a GMM.

We repeatedly observed that while LSTM-RNNs clearly achieve a lower WER compared to other acoustic models, the lattice it generates is not always optimal for KWS. Presumably, the long temporal context makes the estimates of HMM state posterior probabilities very sharp, reducing the diversity of hypotheses represented in the lattice. We verified this hypothesis by calculating the ratio of unique word ends to total word ends for each time stamp. In regions with less than 25k total word ends, the tandem GMM had the highest "relative word coverage", i.e. the highest diversity compared to hybrid acoustic models. While other teams have tried to counteract this effect by regularizing the LSTM models via joint (multi-task) training of a recurrent and a feed-forward model [1], we found that combination of KWS hypotheses provides reasonable results.

4.4   Web Data

The web data collected by the Columbia University [18] and BBN [27] teams was made available to all project participants for the VLLP (OP2) as well as FLP (OP3) tracks to increase the lexicon size and improve the LMs. We have evaluated the use of the data in terms of both the ASR and KWS performance. First, a list of 100k to 200k most frequent words is selected and restricted to words with characters that are already present in the audio training data since the graphemic acoustic model requires observations for every character. Then this lexicon is used to estimate and interpolate several separate count-based Kneser-Ney LMs (one for each data source, e.g. *wikipedia*, *blogposts*, *tweets*, etc.).

It is worth mentioning that interpolation assigns the original LM estimated on audio transcripts by far the largest weight (over 0.8).

Table 6 shows the effect of adding web data to the text resources. We report the perplexities (PPL) for the base and the web lexicon for reference, although these are not comparable because of differing vocabularies. The web lexica for Igbo and Dholuo are much smaller than the "target" value of 200k, since the amount of web data turned out to be much lower than for other languages. Clearly, in case of VLLP the impact on MTWV can be tremendous, because the base lexicon is built from the transcripts of approx. 3 h of audio only. Thus adding more words to the recognition lexicon reduces the OOV rate among keywords (denoted as "KW OOV" in the table) and improves the KWS performance.

Table 6. Effect of adding web data to the recognition lexicon and LM. WER is measured on the dev data, the keyword statistics are calculated using dev queries.Results for VLLP (OP2) and FLP (OP3) tracks

ID	Language	Lexicon		PPL		WER [%]		MTWV		KW OOV [%]	
		base	web	base	web	base	web	base	web	base	web
205	Kurmanji	3.2k	97k	169	251	70.2	69.6	0.2340	0.2490	29.2	11.9
207	Tok Pisin	1.9k	99k	67	82	44.8	44.3	0.3950	0.4040	23.8	10.9
301	Cebuano	3.7k	100k	107	151	62.1	60.3	0.3210	0.3490	29.3	12.4
302	Kazakh	5.3k	97k	213	359	61.7	59.9	0.3350	0.4090	35.3	10.6
303	Telugu	7.1k	100k	318	519	75.2	74.0	0.2150	0.2900	43.6	19.3
304	Lithuanian	5.5k	98k	161	347	58.4	52.9	0.4150	0.5490	41.6	12.4
202	Swahili	5.1k	196k	175	491	58.6	54.2	0.4090	0.4920	31.5	12.9
104	Pashto	12.5k	203k	148	161	48.2	48.3	0.4275	0.4471	11.4	5.0
305	Guarani	26.2k	211k	157	183	45.2	45.0	0.5663	0.5723	13.8	9.6
306	Igbo	16.9k	53k	109	112	58.8	58.9	0.3441	0.3304	11.9	9.0
307	Amharic	35.0k	186k	208	296	42.3	41.3	0.6146	0.6362	15.4	9.8
401	Mongolian	24.0k	208k	125	141	51.2	50.8	0.4814	0.5071	12.2	3.8
402	Javanese	16.5k	192k	199	236	52.9	52.6	0.4484	0.4545	12.8	4.8
403	Dholuo	17.5k	63k	155	162	39.5	39.6	0.6140	0.6124	12.2	8.8
404	Georgian	34.3k	209k	274	394	44.4	41.2	0.6740	0.6906	14.9	6.2

4.5   Keyword Search with Time-Marked Word Lists

As an alternative to the lattice-based KWS, we implemented the time-marked word list (TMWL) approach from [16]. The main idea of TMWL is to abandon the graph structure and store the edges from a lattice in a flat list. We compute the word posterior probabilities on the lattice before storing them in a TMWL.

Table 7. Comparison of KWS pipelines on Pashto FLP (OP3) without web data

| KWS structure | MTWV | | | | | |
| | G2G | | | Morph | | |
	IV	OOV	Total	IV	OOV	Total
Lattice	0.4032	0.0345	0.4363	0.4023	0.0370	0.4369
TMWL	0.3940	0.0305	0.4244	0.3940	0.0391	0.4323

It is important to note that the TMWL index requires much less space than a full lattice. Table 7 shows the results obtained by both approaches integrated into two KWS pipelines that differ in the way they handle OOV keywords (*G2G* FST to allow for substitutions of graphemes or *morphological* decomposition of words). We report MTWV split by in-vocabulary (IV) and out-of-vocabulary (OOV) keywords. In this experiment, the TMWL approach lags only slightly behind lattice based KWS. Interestingly, a combination of the KWS results from lattice and TMWL pipelines was not able to improve over the lattice system.

4.6   Performance of Evaluation Systems

Finally, we summarize the best single system results w.r.t. MTWV obtained on the OP3 languages. We report KWS accuracy using dev queries on the dev set. All lattices have been rescored by LSTM language models [24]. Table 8 indicates the best acoustic model (hybrid DNN/HMM or tandem GMM) and whether or not web data and morphological KWS have led to the results.

Table 8. ASR and KWS performance of best single systems on OP3 languages

ID	Language	AM	Web	Morph	WER [%]	MTWV
104	Pashto	DNN	+	−	47.3	0.4719
305	Guarani	GMM	−	+	46.0	0.5903
306	Igbo	GMM	−	+	57.4	0.3806
307	Amharic	GMM	+	+	42.6	0.6501
401	Mongolian	DNN	+	−	50.0	0.5244
402	Javanese	GMM	+	+	52.5	0.4910
403	Dholuo	GMM	−	+	40.5	0.6261
404	Georgian	GMM	+	+	40.2	0.7062

5 Conclusions

In this work we presented an overview of the highlights developed in the final years of the IARPA Babel project. We provided a detailed description of the multilingual feature extraction trained on up to 28 languages and demonstrated its effectiveness in a low-resource scenario. We described the details of neural network training and evaluated the ASR and KWS performance of tandem GMM, hybrid DNN and LSTM based acoustic models on multiple languages. Further on one of the languages we showed that both lattice and time-marked word list based KWS pipelines achieve very similar results. An evaluation of KWS performance is carried out using large amounts of text data scraped from the web. As expected, the improvements in OOV rate and MTWV are especially strong on the *very limited language packs*.

Acknowledgments. Supported by the Intelligence Advanced Research Projects Activity (IARPA) via Department of Defense U.S. Army Research Laboratory (DoD/ARL) contract no. W911NF-12-C-0012. The U.S. Government is authorized to reproduce and distribute reprints for Governmental purposes notwithstanding any copyright annotation thereon. Disclaimer: The views and conclusions contained herein are those of the authors and should not be interpreted as necessarily representing the official policies or endorsements, either expressed or implied, of IARPA, DoD/ARL, or the U.S. Government.

References

1. Alumäe, T., Karakos, D., Hartmann, W., Hsiao, R., Zhang, L., Nguyen, L., Tsakalidis, S., Schwartz, R.: The 2016 BBN Georgian telephone speech keyword spotting system. In: ICASSP, pp. 5755–5759 (2017)
2. Babel: US IARPA Project (2012–2016). http://www.iarpa.gov/Programs/ia/Babel/babel.html
3. Beulen, K., Ney, H.: Automatic question generation for decision tree based state tying. In: ICASSP, pp. 805–808 (1998)
4. Doetsch, P., Zeyer, A., Voigtlaender, P., Kulikov, I., Schlüter, R., Ney, H.: RETURNN: the RWTH extensible training framework for universal recurrent neural networks. In: ICASSP, pp. 5345–5349 (2017)
5. Fiscus, J.G., Ajot, J., Garofolo, J.S., Doddington, G.: Results of the 2006 spoken term detection evaluation. In: Proceedings of ACM SIGIR Workshop on Searching Spontaneous Conversational Speech, pp. 51–57 (2007)
6. Golik, P., Tüske, Z., Schlüter, R., Ney, H.: Multilingual features based keyword search for very low-resource languages. In: Interspeech, pp. 1260–1264 (2015)
7. Grézl, F., Karafiát, M., Kontár, S., Černocký, J.: Probabilistic and bottle-neck features for LVCSR of meetings. In: ICASSP, pp. 757–760 (2007)
8. Hermansky, H., Ellis, D., Sharma, S.: Tandem connectionist feature extraction for conventional HMM systems. ICASSP, vol. 3, pp. 1635–1638 (2000)
9. Hermansky, H., Fousek, P.: Multi-resolution RASTA filtering for TANDEM-based ASR. In: Interspeech, pp. 361–364 (2005)
10. Hochreiter, S., Schmidhuber, J.: Long short-term memory. Neural Comput. **9**(8), 1735–1780 (1997)

11. Irie, K., Golik, P., Schlüter, R., Ney, H.: Investigations on byte-level convolutional neural networks for language modeling in low resource speech recognition. In: ICASSP, pp. 5740–5744 (2017)
12. Kanthak, S., Ney, H.: Context-dependent acoustic modeling using graphemes for large vocabulary speech recognition. In: ICASSP, pp. 845–848 (2002)
13. Kingma, D.P., Ba, J.: Adam: a method for stochastic optimization. In: ICLR (2015)
14. Knill, K.M., Gales, M.J.F., Rath, S.P., Woodland, P.C., Zhang, C., Zhang, S.X.: Investigation of multilingual deep neural networks for spoken term detection. In: ASRU, pp. 138–143 (2013)
15. Mamou, J., Cui, J., Cui, X., Gales, M., Kingsbury, B., Knill, K., Mangu, L., Nolden, D., Picheny, M., Ramabhadran, B., Schlüter, R., Sethy, A., Woodland, P.: System combination and score normalization for spoken term detection. In: ICASSP, pp. 8272–8276 (2013)
16. Mangu, L., Saon, G., Picheny, M., Kingsbury, B.: Order-free spoken term detection. In: ICASSP, pp. 5331–5335 (2015)
17. Mangu, L., Soltau, H., Kuo, H.K., Kingsbury, B., Saon, G.: Exploiting diversity for spoken term detection. In: ICASSP, pp. 8282–8286 (2013)
18. Mendels, G., Cooper, E., Hirschberg, J.: Babler - data collection from the web to support speech recognition and keyword search. In: ACL, pp. 72–81 (2016)
19. Povey, D., Woodland, P.: Minimum phone error and I-smoothing for improved discriminative training. In: ICASSP, pp. 105–108 (2002)
20. Rybach, D., Hahn, S., Lehnen, P., Nolden, D., Sundermeyer, M., Tüske, Z., Wiesler, S., Schlüter, R., Ney, H.: RASR - the RWTH Aachen university open source speech recognition toolkit. In: ASRU (2011)
21. Saraclar, M., Sethy, A., Ramabhadran, B., Mangu, L., Cui, J., Cui, X., Kingsbury, B., Mamou, J.: An empirical study of confusion modeling in keyword search for low resource languages. In: ASRU, pp. 464–469 (2013)
22. Scanzio, S., Laface, P., Fissore, L., Gemello, R., Mana, F.: On the use of a multilingual neural network front-end. In: Interspeech, pp. 2711–2714 (2008)
23. Schlüter, R., Bezrukov, I., Wagner, H., Ney, H.: Gammatone features and feature combination for large vocabulary speech recognition. In: ICASSP, pp. 649–652 (2007)
24. Sundermeyer, M., Schlüter, R., Ney, H.: LSTM neural networks for language modeling. In: Interspeech, pp. 194–197 (2012)
25. Tüske, Z., Golik, P., Nolden, D., Schlüter, R., Ney, H.: Data augmentation, feature combination, and multilingual neural networks to improve ASR and KWS performance for low-resource languages. In: Interspeech, pp. 1420–1424 (2014)
26. Tüske, Z., Nolden, D., Schlüter, R., Ney, H.: Multilingual MRASTA features for low-resource keyword search and speech recognition systems. In: ICASSP (2014)
27. Zhang, L., Karakos, D., Hartmann, W., Hsiao, R., Schwartz, R., Tsakalidis, S.: Enhancing low resource keyword spotting with automatically retrieved web documents. In: Interspeech, pp. 839–843 (2015)
28. Zolnay, A., Schlüter, R., Ney, H.: Robust speech recognition using a voiced-unvoiced feature. In: ICSLP, vol. 2 (2002)

The Effect of Morphological Factors on Sentence Boundaries in Russian Spontaneous Speech

Anton Stepikhov[1(✉)] and Anastassia Loukina[2]

[1] The Russian Language Department, St. Petersburg State University,
7/9 Universitetskaya nab., St. Petersburg, 199034, Russia
a.stepikhov@spbu.ru

[2] Educational Testing Service, 660 Rosedale Rd, Princeton, NJ 08541, USA
aloukina@ets.org

Abstract. The paper evaluates the contribution of morphological factors to the probability of sentence boundaries in Russian unscripted monologue. The analysis is based on multiple expert manual annotations of unscripted speech which allow obtaining fine-grained estimates of the probability of sentence boundary at each word junction. We used linear regression analysis to explore whether there is a relationship between sentence boundaries marked by the annotators and the grammatical features of the text. We focused on morphological factors related to the presence or absence of sentence boundaries.

Keywords: Spontaneous speech · Unscripted speech · Speech perception · Morphology · Sentence boundary detection · Manual annotation · Segmentation · Russian language resources

1 Introduction

Sentence boundary detection in spontaneous speech is one of the challenges in natural language processing [1]. Correct segmentation is crucial for annotation procedures such as, for example, POS tagging, parsing and punctuation prediction, as well machine translation and further processing of automatically recognised speech [1,2].

Human segmentation of speech is usually considered the most accurate way to obtain information about oral discourse structure and therefore it is used as a starting point for models for automatic sentence boundary detection. In the last two decades the large variety of models of automatic speech segmentation was developed. They use different methods and principles of statistical modelling, such as n-gram language models, Bayesian probability, hidden Markov models, decision trees, maximum entropy, boosting, linear and logistic regression, conditional random fields, support vector machines, deep neural networks, k-nearest neighbours etc. [2–6].

Those models are usually based on both textual and prosodic information, though there are also approaches which only use prosodic or textual cues for modelling and machine learning [7–9].

© Springer International Publishing AG 2017
A. Karpov et al. (Eds.): SPECOM 2017, LNAI 10458, pp. 731–740, 2017.
DOI: 10.1007/978-3-319-66429-3_73

While automatic sentence boundary detection models were extensively developed for English and some other languages, e.g. Czech [10], Mandarin [2,3], Japanese [11,12], only some attempts were made for Russian [8,13], and, in spite of the improvement in modelling results, they are still far from perfect.

Previous studies usually reported results based on the application of a certain language model or a classifier to a text corpus. Linguistic analysis of the factors affecting the segmentation was not performed for Russian. This analysis, however, may be useful, on one hand, for better understanding the grammar of spontaneous speech and, on the other hand, for enhancing the models of automatic sentence boundary detection.

The paper explores the effects of morphological factors on sentence boundaries in Russian spontaneous monologue. We report the statistics concerning grammatical features of the words at sentence boundaries. We also perform the regression analysis of the corpus data based on boundary probabilities obtained after expert manual annotation of unscripted speech. Previous models of sentence boundary detection for Russian were based on various classification procedures [8,13]. In this study we use regression rather than classification since multiple expert annotations of the corpus data can be modelled on a continuous scale thus providing a more fine-grained information about sentence boundaries in Russian spontaneous speech than binary classification. For this study we chose OLS Linear Regression as the main learning algorithm since the primary goal of this exploratory study is to better understand the contribution of different morphological factors.

2   Data

2.1   Corpus

Our study is based on the Corpus of Russian spontaneous monologues described in [14]. It consists of 160 monologues of different types recorded from 32 speakers (5 texts from each). The total size of the corpus is about 55 k words, 9 h of recorded speech.

Speakers were asked to read and subsequently retell from memory a story (Ivan Bunin's *Bast Shoes*) and a descriptive text (an extract from Bunin's *Antonov Apples*), to describe a cartoon strip (*The Hat* by H. Bidstrup) and a landscape (Van Gogh's *The Cottages*), and tell about their leisure time or way of life.

The corpus is balanced with regard to speakers' age, gender, educational level and use of speech in everyday life (regular speakers, teachers or lecturers non-linguists/students studying linguistics, lecturers-linguists).

2.2   Manual Annotation of Corpus Data

The corpus also includes manual annotations of sentence boundaries. The transcripts of recordings without capitalisation, punctuation and other signs which could indicate prosodic or syntactic boundaries were given to the group of 20 annotators with at least 1 year background in linguistics or philology (university students and professors). The task was to mark sentence boundaries with a full stop or a slash based on textual information only. There were no time-constraints (for further detail see [14].

After the annotation, we computed boundary confidence score (BCS) for each boundary. This is the number of experts who marked the sentence boundary in a particular position. BCS reflects inter-annotator agreement and ranges from 0 (no boundary was marked by any of the experts) to 20 (the boundary was marked by all experts). In the range of 1 to 20, 1 means the lowest confidence and inter-annotator agreement, and 20 means highest agreement and 100% confidence. Thus, this measure allows for obtaining information about unequal status of annotated boundaries in spontaneous speech and indicates the probability of sentence boundary in a certain position (for the distribution of BCS in the corpus see [15]).

For further analysis, we applied the threshold approach to BCS described in [15]. A position was considered to be a true boundary if BCS was no less than 12 (60% of all experts).

2.3 POS Tagging in the Corpus

The corpus was annotated using automatic POS tagging system released as a part of Sketch Engine [16]. The automatic tags were then checked and corrected manually. Since the main focus of this paper is the analysis of factors that are linked to sentence boundary rather than a boundary prediction system as such, further analysis was performed based on manually corrected data.

3 Data Analysis

3.1 How Does the Sentence Start and End? Descriptive Analysis of the Data

The analysis revealed both lexical and morphological cues to sentence boundaries in the corpus. Table 1 shows 15 most frequent lemmas which occurred in the beginning of a sentence. These represent 46% of all lexical tokens that occurred in the beginning of a sentence in our data. All other lemmas have the frequency of less than 1%.

Table 1 shows that the most frequent words starting the sentence are semantically weak. Discourse markers and particles (27%), conjunctions (27%), and prepositions (13%) constitute 67% of the 15 most frequent lemmas starting the sentence. The share of pronouns within this list is 33%.

Lexical properties of the words which occur in the beginning of a sentence correspond to morphological statistics. Table 2 shows that the most frequent POS starting the sentence is particle (discourse markers are tagged as particles, too). Pronouns and conjunctions also take leading positions.

Table 1. Most frequent lemmas starting the sentence. Percentage is given for the whole corpus

	Lemma	Translation	Percentage
1	ну	well	9.4
2	вот	so	8.2
3	и	and	3.7
4	в	in	3.1
5	он	he	3.1
6	но	but	2.6
7	я	I	2.6
8	да	yes / but	2.2
9	а	but / and	2.2
10	это	it	2
11	на	on	1.9
12	значит	so you say	1.8
13	так	so	1.2
14	когда	when	1
15	она	she	1

Table 2. Most likely parts of speech (POS) in the beginning of a sentence

	Part of speech	Percentage
1	Particle	21.8
2	Pronoun	14.8
3	Conjunction	14.0
4	Noun	13.0
5	Adverb	9.7
6	Verb	8.5
7	Preposition	8.1
8	Modal word	6.1
9	Adjective	3.1
10	Numeral	0.6
11	Interjection	0.3

The patterns of POS at the end of a sentence are very different (χ^2 (8, $N = 5374) = 1570$, $p < 0.001$[1]). Almost 50% of the words at the sentence end are nouns (Table 3) followed by verbs. These two parts of speech constitute almost 70% of all words at the sentence end. These are followed by particles including the discourse markers. Finally, conjunctions and prepositions also often occur

---

[1] Chi-squared statistics was computed without taking into account numerals and interjections.

Table 3. POS frequency at the end of a sentence

	Part of speech	Percentage
1	Noun	48.3
2	Verb	19.2
3	Particle	9.8
4	Adverb	7.5
5	Adjective	6.2
6	Pronoun	5.2
7	Modal word	2.1
8	Numeral	0.7
9	Interjection	0.6
10	Conjunction	0.4
11	Preposition	0.04

at the end of a sentence and in most cases indicate disfluencies such as breaks followed by a boundary mark.

Both pronouns and nouns in Russian take different inflected form depending on what case they are in. There are six different cases. Therefore we next looked at the case of pronouns and nouns when they appear in the beginning of a sentence. These were not the same, even though the pronoun typically substitutes the noun or is in concord with it (see Tables 4 and 5). For both nouns and pronouns nominative is the most common case in the beginning of a sentence, but the frequency of nouns in genitive starting the sentence is five times higher than that of pronouns. The amount of nouns in dative, on the contrary, is more than twice less than that of pronouns. Even though the share of indirect cases for nouns and pronouns is rather small and does not exceed 8%, the difference in case frequencies for nouns and pronouns is statistically significant (χ^2 (4, $N = 754$) = 18.4, $p < 0.001$).

Table 4. Case frequency of pronouns in the beginning of a sentence

	Case	Percentage
1	Nominative	87.0
2	Accusative	7.8
3	Dative	3.3
4	Genitive	1.3
5	Instrumental	0.8
6	Locative	0.0

Table 5. Case frequency of nouns in the beginning of a sentence

	Case	Percentage
1	Nominative	84.7
2	Genitive	6.5
3	Accusative	5.9
4	Instrumental	1.4
5	Dative	1.4
6	Locative	0.0

The distribution of different case forms at the end of a sentence is also different for nouns and pronouns. While nominative is the most frequent case for pronouns and its share is almost three times higher than that of accusative, for nouns accusative takes the leading position. At the same time, the difference in the share of accusative and nominative for nouns at the end of a sentence is less than 1% (see Tables 6 and 7). On the whole, the difference in case frequencies for nouns and pronouns at the end of a sentence is also statistically significant $(\chi^2 \ (5, \ N = 1592) = 25.7, \ p < 0.001)$.

Table 6. Case frequency of pronouns in the end of a sentence

	Case	Percentage
1	Nominative	44.4
2	Genitive	19.4
3	Accusative	16.7
4	Instrumental	7.8
5	Locative	6.7
6	Dative	5.0

POS bigram analysis at sentence boundaries (one word before the boundary and one word after the boundary) showed high variability of bigrams. Almost all possible combinations of bigrams (about 100) were present in the corpus. However, the 14 most frequent bigrams with their amount exceeding 2% cover almost two thirds (63.5%) of POS bigrams in the corpus (see Table 8).

Table 8 shows that the most frequent combinations of content words at sentence boundaries are the combinations of a noun and a pronoun and two nouns. The share of these bigrams is almost the same (the difference is less than 1%). Both bigrams follow similar patterns of the distribution of case forms. Five most frequent case form combinations are the same for both bigrams (see Table 9) and account for 80.4% of all possible case forms for "noun + noun" and 87.1% – for "noun + pronoun". The difference in the share of these combinations, however, is not statistically significant $(\chi^2 \ (4, \ N = 340) = 6.2, \ p = 0.184)$.

Table 7. Case frequency of nouns in the end of a sentence

	Case	Percentage
1	Accusative	28.4
2	Nominative	27.5
3	Genitive	22.2
4	Locative	9.1
5	Instrumental	8.6
6	Dative	4.1

Table 8. POS bigram frequency at a sentence boundary (starting from the amount of 2%)

	Case	Percentage
1	Noun + Particle	8.5
2	Noun + Pronoun	7.7
3	Noun + Noun	7.3
4	Noun + Conjunction	5.6
5	Noun + Adverb	4.8
6	Noun + Preposition	4.8
7	Verb + Particle	4.7
8	Noun + Verb	4.3
9	Verb + Pronoun	3.1
10	Particle + Particle	2.8
11	Verb + Conjunction	2.6
12	Noun + Modal word	2.6
13	Particle + Conjunction	2.5
14	Verb + Noun	2.2

Table 9. The frequency of case form combinations in POS bigrams *noun + noun* and *noun + pronoun* (with the frequency above 5%)

Combination of case forms	Noun + Noun, %	Noun + Pronoun, %
Accusative + Nominative	29.3	25.0
Nominative + Nominative	25.3	23.6
Genitive + Nominative	14.6	21.2
Locative + Nominative	6.1	11.5
Instrumental + Nominative	5.1	5.8

3.2 Linear Regression Modelling

Multiple expert annotations of the corpus data showed unequal status of sentence boundaries. Using boundary confidence scores (BCS) described earlier in this paper, we performed linear regression modelling to evaluate whether probabilistic approach can accurately predict the sentence boundary in new data.

The corpus was split into the training set (75%) and the test set (25%). The partitions were created by recording so that all annotations for the same recordings were always in the same partition. We used BCS at each word junction as a value of interest to be predicted using the following variables: POS of the word immediately before the junction, POS of the second word before the junction, POS of the word immediately after the junction, POS bigram at the junction, POS bigram before the junction.

We started with the full model which achieved multiple $R^2 = 0.151$, adjusted $R^2 = 0.145$, $F_{(284,38132)} = 23.93$, $p < 0.0001$. For the following models we gradually reduced the number of variables. Two models appeared most promising when fitted to the training set. The predictor in the first model was the POS bigram at the word junction. This model showed the following result on the training set: multiple $R^2 = 0.199$, adjusted $R^2 = 0.195$, $F_{(158,38508)} = 60.43$, $p < 0.0001$, predicted $R^2 = 0.16$. When applied to the test set, the model revealed moderate correlation between BCS and predicted BCS (Spearman's $r = 0.390$, $p < 0.0001$).

The second model had two predictors – POS bigram at the junction and POS bi-gram before the junction. The second model achieved multiple $R^2 = 0.213$, adjusted $R^2 = 0.206$, $F_{(302,38364)} = 34.28$, $p < 0.0001$, predicted $R^2 = 0.18$. When applied to the test set, the correlation between BCS and predicted BCS was comparable to that obtained for the first model (Spearman's $r = 0.395$, $p < 0.0001$).

Further analysis of model predictions showed that the models can correctly predict only low values of BCS including 0. Both models regularly underestimate moderate and high values of BCS. A number of correctly predicted highest values of BCS cannot be taken into account since they marked a transcript end. To better understand model predictions, we converted the predicted and observed BCS to binary values using a threshold of 12 as described above and computed precision recall and F-score. These were: precision = 100%, recall = 6%, F-score = 0.11 for both models.

4 Discussion and Conclusions

In this paper we evaluated the connection between the morphological factors and sentence boundary placement in Russian spontaneous speech. The analysis focused on parts of speech (POS) at the end and in the beginning of a sentence and on the case forms of nouns and pronouns which are the most frequent content words at sentence boundaries.

We found statistically significant difference in POS frequency at the end and in the beginning of a sentence. The analysis also revealed different distribution of case forms of nouns and pronouns at sentence boundaries in spite of the fact that pronouns often substitute nouns or reflect their grammatical characteristics.

We also explored the frequency of bigrams at sentence boundaries and case forms of the most frequent combinations of content words at those positions (nouns and pronouns). The shares of bigrams 'noun + noun' and 'noun + pronoun' were about the same, with both bigrams following similar patterns of the distribution of case forms.

Examining the frequency of lemmas in the beginning of a sentence showed that most frequent words in the beginning of a sentence are semantically weakened. Discourse markers, particles, conjunctions, and prepositions constitute two thirds of the most frequent lemmas at that position.

We used linear regression to predict probabilities of sentence boundaries based on inter-annotator agreement which was measured using boundary confidence scores (BCS). The models evaluated the effect of POS on the probability of a sentence boundary (BCS). We also explored how well the model would generalise to new data.

We observed statistically significant correlation between initial BCS and its predicted values (Spearman's $r = 0.4$, p < 0.0001). However, the model could correctly predict only low values of BCS corresponding to the absence of a sentence boundary. In spite of the fact that the model precision for boundary identification was 100%, most of BCS above the threshold established to define sentence boundaries was not predicted by the model, which led to its low recall (only 6%) and F-score of 0.11.

High precision in boundary identification refers to the positions in the transcript end and therefore may be ignored. Low recall shows that morphological factors such as POS are not sufficient for successful sentence boundary detection. In real life speakers perform the segmentation based on the complex of grammatical information of various kind (e.g. prosodic and syntactic structure) and semantics of the text. Adding information about other linguistic features of the text could improve the accuracy of the model.

Acknowledgments. This study was supported by the Russian Foundation for Humanities, project No. 15–04–00165. We thank Keelan Evanini, Michael Flor and three anonymous reviewers for their comments and suggestions.

References

1. Shriberg, E.: How people really talk and why engineers should care. In: Proceedings of the Interspeech 2005, pp. 1791–1794 (2005)
2. Magimai-Doss, M., Hakkani-Tür, D., Çetin, Ö., Shriberg, E., Fung, J., Mirghafori, N.: Entropy based classifier combination for sentence segmentation. In: Proceedings of the ICASSP 2007, vol. 4, pp. 180–192 (2007)
3. Liu, Y.-F., Tseng, S.-C., Jang, J.-S.R., Chen, C.-H.A.: Coping imbalanced prosodic unit boundary detection with linguistically motivated prosodic features. In: Proceedings of the Interspeech 2010, pp. 1417–1420 (2010)

4. Liu, Y., Stolcke, A., Shriberg, E., Harper, M.: Using conditional random fields for sentence boundary detection in speech. In: Proceedings of the ACL 2005, pp. 451–458 (2005)
5. Ueffing, N., Bisani, M., Vozila, P.: Improved models for automatic punctuation prediction for spoken and written text. In: Proceedings of the Interspeech 2013, pp. 3097–3101 (2013)
6. Xu, C., Xie, L., Huang, G., Xiao, X., Chng, E.S., Li, H.: A deep neural network approach for sentence boundary detection in broadcast news. In: Proceedings of the Interspeech 2014, pp. 2887–2891 (2014)
7. Liu, Y.-F., Tseng, S.-C., Roger Jang, J.-S., Alvin Chen, C.-H.: Coping imbalanced prosodic unit boundary detection with linguistically motivated prosodic features. In: Interspeech 2010, pp. 1417–1420 (2010)
8. Chistikov, P., Khomitsevich, O.: Online automatic sentence boundary detection in a Russian ASR system. In: Proceedings of the SPECOM 2011, pp. 112–117 (2011)
9. Momtazi, S., Faubel, F., Klakow, D.: Within and across sentence boundary language model. In: Proceedings of the Interspeech 2010, pp. 1800–1803 (2010)
10. Kolář, J., Liu, Y.: Comparing and combining modeling techniques for sentence segmentation of spoken Czech using textual and prosodic information. In: Proceedings of the Speech Prosody 2010, p. 100021:1–4 (2010)
11. Mori, S., Nishimura, M., Itoh, N.: An automatic sentence boundary detector based on a structured language model. In: Proceedings of the ICSLP 2002, pp. 921–924 (2002)
12. Oba, T., Hori, T., Nakamura, A.: Sentence boundary detection using sequential dependency analysis combined with CRF-based chunking. In: Proceedings of the Interspeech 2006, pp. 1153–1156 (2006)
13. Khomitsevich, O., Chistikov, P., Krivosheeva, T., Epimakhova, N., Chernykh, I.: Combining prosodic and lexical classifiers for two-pass punctuation detection in a Russian ASR system. In: Ronzhin, A., Potapova, R., Fakotakis, N. (eds.) SPECOM 2015. LNCS, vol. 9319, pp. 161–169. Springer, Cham (2015). doi:10.1007/978-3-319-23132-7_20
14. Stepikhov, A.: Analysis of expert manual annotation of the Russian spontaneous monologue: evidence from sentence boundary detection. In: Železný, M., Habernal, I., Ronzhin, A. (eds.) SPECOM 2013. LNCS, vol. 8113, pp. 33–40. Springer, Cham (2013). doi:10.1007/978-3-319-01931-4_5
15. Stepikhov, A.: Resolving ambiguities in sentence boundary detection in Russian spontaneous speech. In: Habernal, I., Matoušek, V. (eds.) TSD 2013. LNCS, vol. 8082, pp. 426–433. Springer, Heidelberg (2013). doi:10.1007/978-3-642-40585-3_54
16. Kilgarriff, A., Baisa, V., Bušta, J., Jakubíček, M., Kovář, V., Michelfeit, J., Rychlý, P., Suchomel, V.: The Sketch Engine: ten years on. In: Lexicography ASIALEX, vol. 1, pp. 7–36 (2014). https://www.sketchengine.co.uk

The Pausing Method Based on Brown Clustering and Word Embedding

Arman Kaliyev$^{(\boxtimes)}$, Sergey V. Rybin, and Yuri Matveev

ITMO University, Saint Petersburg, Russia
kaliyev.arman@yandex.kz, svrybin@corp.ifmo.ru, matveev@mail.ifmo.ru
http://en.ifmo.ru/

Abstract. One of the most important parts of the synthesis of natural speech is the correct pause placement. Properly placed pauses in speech affect the perception of information. In this article, we consider the method of predicting pause positions for the synthesis of speech. For this purpose, two speech corpora were prepared in the Kazakh language. The input parameters were vector representations of words obtained from the cluster model and from the algorithm of the canonical correlations analysis. The support vector machine was used to predict the pauses within the sentence. Our results show F-1 = 0.781 for pause prediction.

Keywords: Speech synthesis · Pause · Prosodic boundaries · Statistical models

1 Introduction

A high naturalness of speech is required for the successful use of speech synthesis systems. Prosodic processing is a key element of the intonational speech synthesis systems, the naturalness of the synthesized speech depends entirely on it. Pauses along with intonation and accent are one of the most important prosodic characteristics of speech, ensuring its naturalness. Correct pausing is necessary for a comfortable perception of speech, and in many cases for a correct understanding of the meaning of the sentence.

An overview of the data available in the literature [1–3] shows that the interaction of factors influencing the pause is poorly understood. Tendencies rather than patterns are revealed, and even for the observed tendencies there are not sufficiently formalized descriptions of text situations, the characteristics of which could serve as keys for automatic pause placing.

In this paper, we propose a method of placement of pauses for the Kazakh language based on the parameters of the lexical representations obtained from the cluster model of Brown et al. [4] and word embedding obtained by the canonical correlation analysis (CCA) algorithm of Stratos et al. [5]. The aim of the research was to simulate the natural style of speakers pausing within the limits of one sentence (syntagma), the pauses between sentences was not considered. Also, for comparison, an attempt was made to predict pausing places for a mixed corpus consisting of records of many speakers.

© Springer International Publishing AG 2017
A. Karpov et al. (Eds.): SPECOM 2017, LNAI 10458, pp. 741–747, 2017.
DOI: 10.1007/978-3-319-66429-3_74

The prediction of places of pauses was carried out at the level of bigrams[1], where the input parameters of the bigram were the vector representations of both of its tokens, their bit string representation in the Brown cluster model, and the words themselves. For the classification of bigrams, the support vector machine (SVM) [6] was used.

For the training and testing of the developed method, two speech corpora were prepared. As a result of this research, a pausing method with an accuracy of F1 = 0.781 is proposed for Kazakh speech synthesis systems in the narrative style.

2 Corpora

The main labeled corpus consists of records of read speech in the neutral tone of a female speaker. 596 sentences were recorded, on average there are 10.4 tokens in each sentence. The total number of pauses in the corpus is 757 or 12.09% in relation to the number of tokens in the corpus. Only pauses within the sentences (syntagmas) were taken into account.

During the recording process, to preserve a single tone of intonation and style, the speaker was given time to rest before and after each session. The duration of each recording session was not more than 2 h.

The second corpus consists of several hours of records of the Kazakh read speech by 47 speakers of different age groups and different genders. Each speaker recorded about 140 sentences.

3 Parameters

Traditionally, for such tasks, the parameters of the input data are POS TAG[2], punctuation and emphases [7,8]. In this study we used the parameters extracted from the context by unsupervised learning.

Brown clustering is a form of hierarchical word clustering based on the distribution of HMM. An example of such a cluster is shown in Fig. 1. As a result

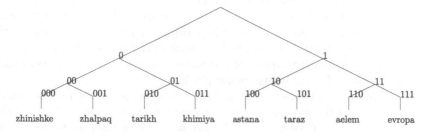

Fig. 1. Bit string representations under the Brown model (Kazakh words were transcribed to Latin characters)

---

[1] The bigram is two words (tokens), which are adjacent in the text box.
[2] POS tagging - automatic morphological marking.

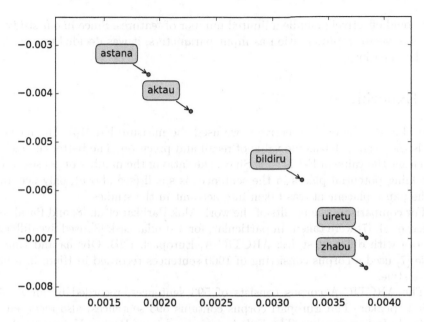

Fig. 2. CCA vector representation (Kazakh words were transcribed to Latin characters)

of clustering, each word in the cluster receives a bit string representation that indicates the path to the cluster from the root.

The bit string representation of words was used to solve many problems of natural language processing, including named entity recognition [9] and dependency parsing [10] (Fig. 2).

Recently Karl Stratos and Michael Collins [11] have shown that deterministic methods of data clustering are capable of qualitatively extracting part of speech information with minimally trained data using the combination of word embedding with the bit string representation. This is partly because the algorithm of CCA computes the statistics of surrounding words, in which the target word appears, then brings together those words in the space of vectors that have a high correlation of the context statistics. Thus, the algorithm effectively groups words in a vector space according to their syntactic behavior.

Considering that the part of speech classifier for the Kazakh language has not yet been developed, it was decided to use the word embedding and bit string representations as input parameters for the classifier. A feature of the proposed method is that the learned parameters were used as input data.

To obtain a word embedding and bit string representation, the textual corpus of the Kazakh Wikipedia, numbering more than 1.7 million sentences, or 20 million words, was used.

Also, tree-based algorithms such as CART [12] and Random Forests [13] were often used as classifiers of such problems. This was due to the fact that the input parameters were pre-processed by various classifiers, including morphological ones. As a consequence, the researcher needed to select an algorithm that could effectively handle a limited number of features. Since in our study we used the vector representation as input parameters, it was decided to use SVM for classifications.

4   Experiments

To evaluate the model objectively, we used the measure F-1 [14]. The measure F-1 is the average harmonic value of recall and precision. The better the model, the closer the value of F-1 is to 1. Since, the ratio of the number of pauses to the remaining potential places in the sentences is small (see above), only accuracy of the pause placement was taken into account in the studies.

For comparison, the results of the work Alok Parlikar et al. [8] and Parakrant Sarkar et al. [7] were taken. In particular, for a similar task [8] used five different corpora with different styles: ARCTIC-A, Europarl, F2B, Obama and Emma, while [7] used a corpus consisting of 1960 sentences recorded in Hindi in a narrative style.

The ARCTIC-A corpus consists of 593 sentences, recorded by an Anglo-Indian speaker. The Europarl corpus contains 595 sentences, also recorded by an Anglo-Indian speaker. The F2B is composed from Boston University Radio News Corpus, the corpus contains 464 sentences. The Obama Corpus consists of two public speeches of the US President Barack Obama. The total number of sentences in the Obama corpus is 465. The Emma case is taken from an audio book (Emma, by Jane Austen), the speech was recorded by a female volunteer. The Emma corpus consists of 9936 sentences.

During the experiments, 80% of the corpus was used for training, and 20% for testing. To obtain an adequate estimate of the model, 10 experiments were performed with the same parameters, and in each experiment the sentences for training and testing were chosen randomly by the program. The final F-1 score is the average estimate of all 10 experiments. The average value of F-1 is 0.781 for the Kazakh speech corpus. Table 1 compares the results with the results of [7,8].

Table 1. Comparison of break prediction accuracy

Data set	F-1
ARCTIC-A	0.851
Europarl	0.776
F2B	0.736
Obama	0.638
Emma	0.829
Kazakh	0.781
Hindi	0.74

In addition, a similar problem was solved by Chistakov et al. [15,16] for the Russian language, using for this purpose a corpus of 38,000 recorded sentences. According to their results, they reached F-1 = 0.76 for pause prediction. Unfortunately, due to the large difference in the procedure for conducting the experiments, we did not include their results in the comparison list.

We also noticed that the increase in the training part of the data positively influenced the results of the classifier. Conversely, a decrease in the training part of the data worsened the results. Table 2 shows the influence of the ratio of training and test parts of the corpus on the results of pausing for the proposed method.

Table 2. Test set performance for different training set sizes

Data set	Recall	Precision	F-1	Training data proportion (%)
Kazakh corpus	0.732	0.824	0.775	70
Kazakh corpus	0.757	0.807	0.781	80
Kazakh corpus	0.770	0.798	0.832	90

Similar studies were conducted on mixed corpus. As expected, the average value of F-1 was much smaller than for homogeneous corpus. In an experiment where the proportion of training data was 80%, F-1 showed a result of 0.406. For more information, see Table 3. Such low results are explained by the stylistic difference in speech of the speakers. For example, young female speakers more often had a tendency to speak quickly, reducing the number of pauses in sentences. When more adult speakers spoke more slowly, inserting more often pauses between words.

Table 3. Break prediction accuracy for mixed corpus

Data set	Recall	Precision	F-1
Mixed Kazakh corpus	0.367	0.454	0.406

5 Results

The proposed method of pausing showed the results comparable to the results of the state of the art systems. For a variety of irregular languages including the Kazakh language, for which the part of speech taggers are not yet developed, this approach is quite acceptable.

We also confirm the need to use homogeneous data to solve such problems. It is important to extract stylistic parameters of speech from one source, in our case from one speaker. Otherwise, researchers risk obtaining parameters that do not correspond to the initially planned goals, namely the modeling of natural human speech.

6 Conclusion

In the near future we expect to develop the proposed method for predicting the lengths of pauses and determining the intonational contours of syntagmas. We hope in the possibility of further use of the vector representation of words and sentences for solving related problems.

The research group aims to create a final method for modeling natural speech, using as far as possible unsupervised learning parameters. Such an approach should open the possibility of creating a high-quality speech synthesis for most languages of the world.

Acknowledgments. This work was financially supported by the Government of the Russian Federation, Grant 074-U01.

References

1. Parlikar, A., Black, A.W.: Modeling pause-duration for style-specific speech synthesis. In: INTERSPEECH, pp. 446–449. ISCA (2012)
2. Norkevicius, G., Raskinis, G.: Modeling phone duration of Lithuanian by classification and regression trees, using very large speech corpus. Inf. Lith. Acad. Sci. **19**(2), 271–284 (2008)
3. Bali, K., Nemala, S.K., Ramakrishnan, A.G., Talukdar, P.P.: Duration modeling for Hindi text-to-speech synthesis system. In: INTERSPEECH (2004)
4. Brown, P.F., et al.: Class-based n-gram models of natural language. Comput. Linguist. **18**(4), 467–479 (1992)
5. Stratos, K. Kim, D., Collins, M., Hsu., D.: A spectral algorithm for learning class-based n-gram models of natural language. In: Zhang, N.L., Tian, J. (eds.) UAI, pp. 762–771. AUAI Press (2014)
6. Cortes, C., Vapnik, V.: Support vector networks. Mach. Learn. **20**, 273–297 (1995)
7. Sarkar, P., Sreenivasa, R.K.: Data-driven pause prediction for speech synthesis in storytelling style speech. In: Twenty First National Conference on Communications (2015)
8. Parlikar, A., Black, A.W.: A grammar based approach to style specific phrase prediction. In: INTERSPEECH, pp. 2149–2152. ISCA (2011)
9. Miller, S., Guinness, J., Zamanian, A.: Name tagging with word clusters and discriminative training. In: HLT-NAACL, pp. 337–342 (2005)
10. Koo, T., Carreras, X., Collins, M.: Simple semi-supervised dependency parsing. In: Proceedings of ACL 2008: HLT, pp. 595–603. Association for Computational Linguistics, Columbus (2008)
11. Stratos, K., Collins, M.: Simple semi-supervised POS tagging. In: Blunsom, P., et al. (eds.) VS@HLT-NAACL, pp. 79–87. The Association for Computational Linguistics (2015)
12. Loh, W.-Y.: Classification and regression tree methods. In: Encyclopedia of Statistics in Quality and Reliability, pp. 315–323. Wiley (2008)
13. Breiman, L.: Random forests. Mach. Learn. **45**, 5–32 (2001)
14. van Rijsbergen, C.J.: Information Retrieval. Butterworths, London (1979)

15. Chistikov, P., Khomitsevich, O.: Improving prosodic break detection in a Russian TTS system. In: Železný, M., Habernal, I., Ronzhin, A. (eds.) SPECOM 2013. LNCS (LNAI), vol. 8113, pp. 181–188. Springer, Cham (2013). doi:10.1007/978-3-319-01931-4_24

16. Chistikov, P.G., Khomitsevich, O.G., Rybin, S.V.: Statistical methods for automatic prosodic break detection in a text-to-speech systems. J. Instrum. Eng. **57**(2), 28–32 (2014). (in Russian)

Unsupervised Document Classification and Topic Detection

Jaromír Novotný[✉] and Pavel Ircing

Faculty of Applied Sciences, Cybernetics, The University of West Bohemia,
Plzeň, Czech Republic
{fallout7,ircing}@kky.zcu.cz
http://www.kky.zcu.cz/en

Abstract. This article presents a method for pre-processing the feature vectors representing text documents that are consequently classified using unsupervised methods. The main goal is to show that state-of-the-art classification methods can be improved by a certain data preparation process. The first method is a standard K-means clustering and the second Latent Dirichlet allocation (LDA) method. Both are widely used in text processing. The mentioned algorithms are applied to two data sets in two different languages. First of them, the 20NewsGroup is a widely used benchmark for classification of English documents. The second set was selected from the large body of Czech news articles and was used mainly to compare the performance of the tested methods also for the case of less frequently studied language. Furthermore, the unsupervised methods are also compared with the supervised ones in order to (in some sense) ascertain the upper-bound of the task.

Keywords: Text pre-processing · Classification · Evaluation · LDA · K-means

1 Introduction

This work deals with the preparation of input text data and consequent document classification using unsupervised methods.

Since a significant portion of the algorithms used for document classification internally utilizes some measures of vector similarity, one of the crucial steps of document pre-processing is the conversion of input text into some kind of a vector representation. The basic approach to such conversion is a so-called Bag-of-Words model(BOW) [4] – in such case, each document is represented by a vector where each element corresponds to a word from a fixed position in the lexicon. The value of such element is usually directly proportional to the number of occurrences of the given word in the given document (term frequency – tf) and indirectly proportional to the number of documents where the given word occurs (the inverse document frequency – idf). The resulting tf-idf model is very successful [2,6,7]. However, sometimes the length and sparseness of the resulting

© Springer International Publishing AG 2017
A. Karpov et al. (Eds.): SPECOM 2017, LNAI 10458, pp. 748–756, 2017.
DOI: 10.1007/978-3-319-66429-3_75

vector, stemming from the size of the lexicon, may hurt the performance of the classification algorithms. Several methods for the reduction of the vector dimension are therefore discussed later and constitute the core of our work.

For the classification itself, we have picked two methods – the "classic" clustering algorithm K-means, which is simple but is known to perform well if we are able to present it with the suitable feature vectors, and the state-of-the-art methods for unsupervised topic detection, the Latent Dirichlet allocation (LDA), adapted for document classification.

2   Datasets

As our basic dataset, we have picked the *20NewsGroups* English corpus[1] which is widely used as a benchmark for document classification [7,9,12,13]. It contains 20 000 text documents which are evenly divided into 20 categories that each contain discussion about a specific topic. The second data set *CNO* is in Czech language and contains also approximately 20 000 articles divided into 31 categories[2]. This corpus was created so that it is at least in size and partially also in topics comparable to the English data set.

In order to compare our results with the ones published previously, we have re-created two subdivisions of the *20NewsGroups* corpus. The first one is created according to [13,14] and consists of the following subsets:

- Set *20NG* consists of all 20 original categories but includes only documents containing at least 10 word tokens (after stop-word removal). This results in approximately 17 000 documents in total.
- Set *10NG* consists of the same documents as the *20NG* above but divides them into 10 categories only – the reduced number of categories was obtained by merging 5 original `comp`, 3 `religion`, 3 `politics`, 2 `sport` and 2 `transportation` categories into one category for each "domain".
- The next group of subsets contains 9 sets for small-scale experiments – there are three *Binary*, three *5Multi* and three *10Multi* sets, each containing 500 documents only and prepared in the following way:
  - Binary subsets (denoted *Binary[0/1/2]*) are created by randomly choosing 2 categories (from the original 20) and randomly drawing 250 documents from each of them.
  - Analogically, the *5Multi[0/1/2]* subsets were created by randomly choosing 5 original categories and randomly drawing 100 documents from each.
  - And finally, the *10Multi[0/1/2]* subsets were created by randomly choosing 10 original categories and randomly drawing 50 documents from each.

---

[1] This data set can be found at http://qwone.com/~jason/20Newsgroups/ and it was originally collected by Ken Lang.

[2] It was created from a database of news articles downloaded from the http://www.ceskenoviny.cz/ at the University of West Bohemia and constitutes only a small fraction of the entire database – the description of the full database can be found in [16].

The other subdivision is created in order to compare the results with experiments described in [12]. This set, denoted as *Binary20NG*, is comprised of 20 bi-classes – each bi-class consists of one class containing all the documents from one of the original categories (i.e., 1000 documents) and the second class containing 1000 documents randomly drawn from the pool of other 19 categories. Two-thirds of each such bi-class documents are used as the training data, the remaining third constitutes the test set.

The *CNO* set was not subdivided in any such way.

3 Preprocessing

First, we removed all the headers from the *20NewsGroups* data, except for the `Subject`. Then all uppercase characters were lower-cased and all digits were replaced by one universal symbol.

As the next processing step, we wanted to conflate different morphological forms of the given word into one representation. This can be achieved by either lemmatization or stemming – even though those two procedures have rather similar outputs, we opted for lemmatization. The MorphoDiTa [15] tool was picked for the task – it works for both English and Czech and is available as a Python package.[3]

Further preprocessing traditionally comprises stop-word removal.[4] Probably the most common approach is to use a pre-defined stoplist, but the stop words can also be determined on the basis of the input data analysis. We use a simple method of detecting stop words from input data. We compute for each lemma its inverse document frequency [6] (*idf*):

$$idf_l = \frac{N}{N(l)} \tag{1}$$

where N is a total number of documents and $N(l)$ denotes a number of documents containing the lemma l. Then we set a threshold θ and classify every lemma l with $idf_l < \theta$ as a stop word and remove it from further processing.

At this point, we have a suitable data for the LDA analysis as it starts from the set of preprocessed documents (see the details in Sect. 4.1).

However, more data processing is needed when preparing input for the K-means algorithm. We need to compute the tf-idf weights $w_{l,d}$ for the lemmas $l \in L$ and documents $d \in D$ using the well-known formula:

$$w_{l,d} = tf_{l,d} * idf_l \tag{2}$$

where $tf_{l,d}$ denotes the number of times the lemma l occurs in document d and idf_l is computed using the Eg. (1).

---

[3] `ufal.morphodita` at https://pypi.python.org/pypi/ufal.morphodita.
[4] The authors of the paper [12] don't use the stop words at all because their feature vector consists only of the top T tokens (lemmas or stems) with highest mutual information (MI).

Besides the basic equations above, there are actually more sophisticated formulas for computing tf and idf available [6]. Many of them are implemented in the Python package `sklearn` [10][5] that we extensively use in essentially all further experiments. The `TfidfVectorizer` takes the set of input documents (preprocessed as described above) and (optionally) a dictionary and outputs the $|D| \times |M|$ matrix, where $|D|$ is the number of documents and $|M|$ is the number of features representing each document (in our case it is of course only the number of distinct lemmas occurring in all the preprocessed documents – L – but the feature set can be much richer – e.g. it can include also the higher order n-grams).

This matrix can be used as input for K-means method directly but it is usually beneficial to lower the dimension $|M|$ in order to lower the computational costs of the algorithm. We have decided to reduce the feature vector dimension using the well-know Latent Semantic Analysis (LSA) [5] which does not only lower the vector dimension but allegedly also captures some of the semantics hidden in the documents. The LSA method is again implemented in the Python package `sklearn` – the concerned module `TruncatedSVD` takes the input $|D| \times |M|$ matrix and produced a $|D| \times |R|$ matrix ($|R|$ being the desired lower dimension passed as a function parameter) that can be consequently used as an input for the K-means method.

4 Classification Methods

4.1 LDA

Latent Dirichlet allocation (LDA) is a generative probabilistic model of a corpus [1]. Marginally, documents are represented as random mixtures over latent topics (the latent multinomial variables in the LDA model are referred as topics). Each topic is then characterised by a distribution over terms (in our case, lemmas).

The LDA model itself and the related data preparation functions are implemented in the Python package `gensim` [11]. The documents preprocessed as described in Sect. 3 are first converted to special gensim's bag-of-words representation called *corpus* using the `doc2bow` function and the special *dictionary* file is also created.

The LDA method itself then uses both the *dictionary* and the *corpus* as its input; the model finds the list of topics (number of topics matches the number of categories of input data) that fits the input data. We set model to classify every document into one cluster only, that is, only the topic with highest probability is a assigned to each document. This model is applied on all prepared corpora (*20NG, 10NG, Binary[0/1/2], 5Multi[0/1/2], 10Multi[0/1/2], Binary20NG, CNO*) and results can be found in Sect. 6.

---

[5] More precisely the `TfidfVectorizer` module from that package.

4.2 K-Means

The classic K-means clustering method [8] is being used here as a classification algorithm. It is generally accepted that even such a simple method is quite powerful for unsupervised data clustering if it is given an appropriate feature vectors. Since we had good reasons to believe that our feature vectors consisting of the tf-idf weights capture the content of the document rather well (and the reduced feature vectors obtained from LSA do it even better), we expected to find the documents with similar topic often in only one of the clusters discovered by K-means.

We have used the version of K-means algorithm implemented in our favorite `sklearn` package. First, we used the full matrix of tf-idf weights; however, given the large dimension of such feature vectors, the clustering was feasible only for a small subset of the documents. The full experiments were performed with the reduced feature vectors obtained by applying the LSA. Again, we applied this model on all the date sets described in Sect. 2 and results can be found in Sect. 6.

5 Evaluation

There are quite a few measures for evaluation of the classification algorithms. In our experiments, we have decided to use accuracy, precision and recall; this choice was guided mostly by the fact that we wanted to compare the performance of our algorithms to the previously published results.

The *Accuracy* measure is applied on *Binary20NG* data set and represents the percentage of correctly classified documents (i.e., show what percentage of the test documents is assigned with the correct topic).

Precision and *Recall* measures are computed according to [13] and are used on data sets *20NG, 10NG, Binary[0/1/2], 5Multi[0/1/2], 10Multi[0/1/2]* and *CNO*. The micro-average type of those measures is applied. One dominant category $c \in C$ is assigned to all output clusters $t \in T$. This is done by computing number of documents which are the same in t and c, the highest value then designate the dominant category c to cluster (output) t. Every $c \in C$ can be assigned only to one $t \in T$. This procedure is done in [13], because of the underlying assumption that user would not have a problem with assigning a dominant topic (if the clusters are relatively homogeneous). We can then define the following quantities: $\alpha(c, T)$ which defines the number of documents correctly assigned to c, $\beta(c, T)$ defines the number of documents incorrectly assigned to c and $\gamma(c, T)$ defines the number of document incorrectly not assigned to c. It is now possible (from those values) to compute micro-average precision P and recall R as follows:

$$P(T) = \frac{\sum_c \alpha(c, T)}{\sum_c \alpha(c, T) + \beta(c, T)} \tag{3}$$

$$R(T) = \frac{\sum_c \alpha(c, T)}{\sum_c \alpha(c, T) + \gamma(c, T)} \tag{4}$$

Since the original corpus and output from algorithms are uni-labeled data sets in this scenario, the $P(T)$ is necessarily equal to $R(T)$ (number of original categories in corpus have to be also the same as the number of output clusters from algorithms) and it is sufficient to report only one of those values. That's why there is only *Precision* reported in Table 2.

6   Results

First, we report the average results achieved on $Binary20NG$ data set in Table 1. This set of results is compared with results of [12]. The mentioned paper employs supervised methods, two of them baselines and the others are those baseline methods improved by semantic smoothing of the kernels. First used method is K-nearest neighbors (denoted by KNN) and the corresponding method with smoothed kernel is denoted by $KNN+P$. The second method is support vector machines (SVM) and the corresponding method with smoothed kernel is $SVM+P$.

The results of our methods are listed in the lower part of the table and denoted as LDA and K-$means$. The K-means method was applied with both the full matrix of tf-idf weights and with the matrix reduced by LSA (reduced feature vectors of size 2). Sice the work reported in [12] concerns supervised training, the data set in question was designed to consist of training and test portion. We have preserved the partitioning but naturally did not use the supervisory information from the training part for our unsupervised methods.

Table 1. Comparison of our results with results achieved in [12]

Method	Accuracy [%]
KNN	71.79
KNN+P	80.13
SVM	86.44
SVM+P	88.52
LDA	56.46
K-Means (tf-idf matrix from all lemmas)	72.19
K-Means (matrix form LSA method, number of features is 2)	75.47

Second sets of results are listed in Table 2; these results were achieved on *20NG, 10NG, Binary[0/1/2], 5Multi[0/1/2], 10Multi[0/1/2]* data sets. Again, we are comparing our results with the values reported in the previously published paper, this time [13]. The authors of the mentioned paper used the (unsupervised) *sIB* and *sK-means* methods. The *sIB* stands for sequential Information Bottleneck method and the *sK-means* stands for sequential K-means method (modification of the K-means). This modification lies in updating the centers of the clusters whenever a feature vector is assigned to one of them (not at the end – after all of the feature vectors are assigned – as in classical K-means algorithm). In our experiments, we run our LDA and K-means algorithms 10 times over each subset (same approach used in [13]). Averaged results from those runs are listed in Table 2. The meaning of the K-means experiment labels listed in the table is the following:

– *K-means* is the algorithm run with full tf-idf weights
– *K-means(LSA)* is the algorithm run with feature vectors reduced by LSA to the dimension equal to the number of original categories (except for sub-set *20NG*, where the number of features is set on 2000)
– *K-means (LSA n features)* states results from K-means method with input matrix produced by LSA method, which lowers dimension to $n = 144$ for large data sets (*20NG* and *10NG*) and to $n = 46$ for small data sets (the rest of data sets in Table 2). The values of n for data sets were computed by using formula listed in [3], which is:

$$n = n_T^{\frac{1}{1+\frac{\log(n_T)}{10}}} \tag{5}$$

where n_T is number of texts (documents).

Table 2. Comparison of our results with results achieved in [13]

20NewsGroups sub-sets	*Precision* of methods [%]					
	sIB	*sK-means*	*LDA*	*K-means*	*K-means (LSA)*	*K-means (LSA n features)*
20NG	57.50	54.10	16.97		38.08	35.81
10NG	79.50	76.30	28.72		45.29	51.04
Average "large"	68.50	65.20	22.84		41.69	43.43
10Multi0	70.20	31.00	30.40	36.68	49.98	51.40
10Multi1	63.80	32.80	23.80	36.72	49.88	52.92
10Multi2	67.00	32.80	32.59	45.22	60.12	63.00
5Multi0	89.40	47.00	43.00	71.76	70.06	76.54
5Multi1	91.20	47.00	46.20	73.50	79.80	84.58
5Multi2	94.20	57.00	36.20	68.64	73.00	79.12
Binary0	91.40	62.40	95.60	94.50	98.80	97.60
Binary1	89.20	54.60	94.00	92.64	93.80	92.90
Binary2	93.00	63.20	93.38	97.48	97.20	97.48
Average "small"	83.30	47.60	55.02	68.57	74.74	77.28

Finally, we list some results from *CNO* data set in Table 3. These are only for the purpose of testing our methods on data in different language than English. This result shows that our approach to the preparation of data can be applied even for the language rather distant from English. We tested different settings on lowering dimension with LSA method. First was set to 2000 and second to 31 (which corresponds to a number of original categories).

Table 3. Results on *CNO* data set

	Precision of methods [%]		
	LDA	K-means (dim. reduced to 2000)	K-means (dim. reduced to 31)
CNO	14.67	42.59	41.72

7 Conclusion

The paper introduced a reasonably effective pipeline for classification of the text documents according their topic. It concentrated mostly on the preprocessing of both the raw input text and the extracted feature vectors. It showed that when applying lemmatization and data-driven stop-word removal to the text documents and consequently reducing the dimension of resulting tf-idf feature vector using LSA, we can get decent classification results even with the most rudimentary classification algorithms, such as K-means. The performance of this unsupervised method was almost on par with some of the simpler supervised algorithms. This is an important finding of our research, since the training data annotated with correct document classification – which are necessary for supervised learning – are often not available.

Acknowledgements. This research was supported by the Ministry of Culture of the Czech Republic, project No. DG16P02B048.

References

1. Blei, D.M., Ng, A.Y., Jordan, M.I.: Latent Dirichlet allocation. J. Mach. Learn. Res. **3**, 993–1022 (2003)
2. Eklund, J.: With or without context: automatic text categorization using semantic kernels. Ph.D. thesis, University of Borås, Faculty of Librarianship, Information, Education and IT (2016)
3. Fernandes, J., Artífice, A., Fonseca, M.J.: Automatic estimation of the LSA dimension. In: Proceedings of the International Conference on Knowledge Discovery and Information Retrieval (IC3K 2011), pp. 301–305 (2011)
4. Huang, A.: Similarity measures for text document clustering. In: Proceedings of the Sixth New Zealand Computer Science Research Student Conference (NZC-SRSC2008), Christchurch, New Zealand, pp. 49–56 (2008)

5. Landauer, T.K., Foltz, P.W., Laham, D.: An introduction to latent semantic analysis. Discourse Process. **25**, 259–284 (1998)
6. Lehečka, J., Švec, J.: Improving multi-label document classification of Czech news articles. In: Král, P., Matoušek, V. (eds.) TSD 2015. LNCS (LNAI), vol. 9302, pp. 307–315. Springer, Cham (2015). doi:10.1007/978-3-319-24033-6_35
7. Liu, Y., Liu, Z., Chua, T.S., Sun, M.: Topical word embeddings. In: Proceedings of the Twenty-Ninth AAAI Conference on Artificial Intelligence, pp. 2418–2424 (2015)
8. MacQueen, J.: Some methods for classification and analysis of multivariate observations. In: 5-th Berkeley Symposium on Mathematical Statistics and Probability, pp. 281–297 (1967)
9. Nguyen, D.Q., Billingsley, R., Du, L., Johnson, M.: Improving topic models with latent feature word representations. Trans. Assoc. Comput. Linguist. **3**, 299–313 (2015)
10. Pedregosa, F., Varoquaux, G., Gramfort, A., Michel, V., Thirion, B., Grisel, O., Blondel, M., Prettenhofer, P., Weiss, R., Dubourg, V., Vanderplas, J., Passos, A., Cournapeau, D., Brucher, M., Perrot, M., Duchesnay, E.: Scikit-learn: machine learning in Python. J. Mach. Learn. Res. **12**, 2825–2830 (2011). http://scikit-learn.org
11. Řehůřek, R., Sojka, P.: Software framework for topic modelling with large corpora. In: Proceedings of the LREC 2010 Workshop on New Challenges for NLP Frameworks, pp. 45–50 (2010). https://radimrehurek.com/gensim/
12. Siolas, G., d'Alche Buc, F.: Support vector machines based on a semantic kernel for text categorization. In: IEEE-INNS-ENNS International Joint Conference on Neural Networks (IJCNN), vol. 5, pp. 205–209 (2000)
13. Slonim, N., Friedman, N., Tishby, N.: Unsupervised document classification using sequential information maximization. In: Proceedings of the 25th Annual International ACM SIGIR Conference on Research and Development in Information Retrieval, pp. 129–136 (2002)
14. Slonim, N., Tishby, N.: Document clustering using word clusters via the information bottleneck method. In: Proceedings of the 23rd Annual International ACM SIGIR Conference on Research and Development in Information Retrieval, pp. 208–215 (2000)
15. Straková, J., Straka, M., Hajič, J.: Open-source tools for morphology, lemmatization, POS tagging and named entity recognition. In: Proceedings of 52nd Annual Meeting of the Association for Computational Linguistics: System Demonstrations, pp. 13–18 (2014)
16. Švec, J., Lehečka, J., Ircing, P., Skorkovská, L., Pražák, A., Vavruška, J., Stanislav, P., Hoidekr, J.: General framework for mining, processing and storing large amounts of electronic texts for language modeling purposes. Lang. Resour. Eval. **48**(2), 227–248 (2014)

Using a High-Speed Video Camera for Robust Audio-Visual Speech Recognition in Acoustically Noisy Conditions

Denis Ivanko[1,3,4](✉), Alexey Karpov[1,3], Dmitry Ryumin[1,3],
Irina Kipyatkova[1], Anton Saveliev[1], Victor Budkov[1],
Dmitriy Ivanko[3], and Miloš Železný[2]

[1] St. Petersburg Institute for Informatics and Automation
of the Russian Academy of Sciences, St. Petersburg, Russia
denis.ivanko@uni-ulm.de, {karpov,ryumin,kipyatkova,
saveliev,budkov}@iias.spb.su
[2] University of West Bohemia, Pilsen, Czech Republic
zelezny@kky.zcu
[3] ITMO University, St. Petersburg, Russia
[4] Ulm University, Ulm, Germany

Abstract. The purpose of this study is to develop a robust audio-visual speech recognition system and to investigate the influence of a high-speed video data on the recognition accuracy of continuous Russian speech under different noisy conditions. Developed experimental setup and collected multimodal database allow us to explore the impact brought by the high-speed video recordings with various frames per second (fps) starting from standard 25 fps up to high-speed 200 fps. At the moment there is no research objectively reflecting the dependence of the speech recognition accuracy from the video frame rate. Also there are no relevant audio-visual databases for model training. In this paper, we try to fill in this gap for continuous Russian speech. Our evaluation experiments show the increase of absolute recognition accuracy up to 3% and prove that the use of the high-speed camera JAI Pulnix with 200 fps allows achieving better recognition results under different acoustically noisy conditions.

Keywords: Audio-visual speech recognition · High-speed video camera · Noisy conditions · Russian speech · Visemes · Multimodal communication

1 Introduction

In recent years, a lot of Audio-Visual (AV) speech recognition technologies have been developed [1]. Nowadays there is no doubt the audio and visual signals supplement each other very well and, when combined, they are capable of improving the performance (both accuracy and robustness) of automatic speech recognition. Although natural speech is the very informative signal, other modalities also convey useful information: the use of video signals makes the system more robust and reliable. Essential attention is paid to the concept of multimodal speech recognition systems and to the multimodal fusion techniques [2–4]. Despite the fact that this area of research is

© Springer International Publishing AG 2017
A. Karpov et al. (Eds.): SPECOM 2017, LNAI 10458, pp. 757–766, 2017.
DOI: 10.1007/978-3-319-66429-3_76

very active, the significance of the use of high-speed recordings (>50 fps) for visual speech recognition has not been investigated.

Preliminary studies on this topic for English and Dutch languages, such as [5] or [6], have reported dependence of speech recognition accuracy to the video frame rate. However, those works did not have a continuation.

In the field of human-machine interaction, high-speed cameras are already used in the tasks of micro-expression recognition [7], facial emotion recognition [8], for medical purposes (e.g. eye blinking detection [9]), etc. But high-speed video cameras are still considered as resource-costly equipment for speech recognition applications [10]. However, at present, some modern smartphones are already equipped with high-speed cameras. For example, Apple iPhone 7 has a camera with the shooting speed of 240 frames per second (fps) at the resolution of 720 × 480 pixels; announced in 2017 new Sony Xperia smartphones has a video camera with the recording speed of 960 fps. Continuing technological progress allows us to assume with a high confidence that in the near future the use of automatic speech recognition systems with high-speed video cameras will be a new direction for multimodal speech recognition.

Recently there were no high-speed audiovisual speech databases available for the Russian language. Such data are necessary for training visual and acoustical models in the scope of statistical methods of speech recognition. In 2016-17, we have collected the HAVRUS corpus [11] (High-Speed Recordings of Audio–Visual Russian Speech) that comprises recordings of 20 native Russian speakers (10 male and 10 female). Our experiments were conducted with an audio-visual Russian speech recognition system [12, 13], which is based on state asynchronous 2-stream Coupled Hidden Markov Models (CHMM).

In this paper, we present the results of our evaluation experiments and show the dependency between the video frame rate and the accuracy of lip-reading and audio-visual speech recognition and try to find an optimal frame rate for the task of robust audio-visual speech recognition. In addition, since the high frequency of video frames allows performing more precise analysis of movements of visible articulation organs we identify new viseme classes for Russian speech.

The remainder of this paper is organized as follows. In Sect. 2, we introduce the collected HAVRUS (high-speed recordings of audio-visual Russian speech) corpus and describe the recording environment; in Sect. 3, we describe a late fusion AV Russian speech recognizer that relies on CHHMs, audio and visual feature extraction mechanism and the used audio-visual speech units; in Sect. 4, we describe the setup and the results of the experiments with our Russian AVSR system; some conclusions are given in Sect. 5.

2 Multimodal Database Collection

Multimodal user interfaces based on audio-visual speech recognition allow organizing natural interaction between users and smart phones, computers, environments. At the moment, there are various audio-visual databases that are collected for this purpose [14–16]. An overview of existing audio-visual speech databases can be found in our recent paper [11]. However, there are almost no audio-visual speech corpora with high-speed recordings. We tried to fill in this gap using developed software-hardware complex for collecting audio-visual databases.

Figure 1 shows an environments setup for audio-visual speech data recording. There are some types of the equipment installed: (a) dynamic microphone Oktava MK-012; (b) high-speed video camera JAI-Pulnix RMC-6740 mounted on a tripod; (c) screen for displaying graphical user interface; (d) speaker; (e) sound board M-Audio; (f) background screen of a homogeneous white color. The distance between a speaker and the camera may be varied base on parameters of lenses installed on the camera. In our study, we use NAVITAR NMV-25M23 lenses with 3.5 mm focal length, 66.9° diagonal angle and –0.04% distortion.

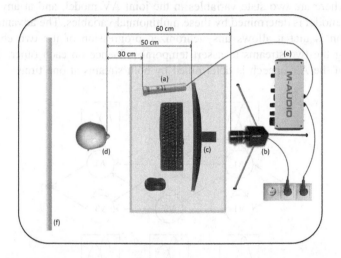

Fig. 1. Scheme of an environment for audiovisual speech recording

20 native Russian speakers (10 male and 10 female speakers) with no language or hearing problems were attracted for the recording. Each of them pronounced (read from the screen) 200 Russian phrases: 130 training phrases are phonetically rich sentences common for all speakers, and 70 test phrases are telephone numbers and are different for every speaker. The content was chosen to maximize the statistical coverage of context-dependent Russian phonemes and visemes. The audio data have sampling frequency of 44 kHz, 16 bits per sample, mono format; the signal to noise ratio (SNR) is not less than 35 dB. The video data have resolution of 640 × 480 pixels and the frame rate – 200 frames per second, uncompressed data in RAW format. The recording session for each speaker lasted about 20–30 min. All the recordings were organized into a logically structured database, that comprises a file with information about all the speakers and recording parameters. More complete description of the framework and characteristics of the collected multimodal corpora can be found in our preliminary works [11, 17].

3   Methodology and Methods

3.1   Fusion of Audio-Visual Speech Modalities

For this study we have implemented own CHMM-based audio-visual Russian speech recognition system with weight optimization [13, 17].

Coupled Hidden Markov Model is a set of parallel HMM, where each HMM corresponds to one data stream [11, 12]. Figure 2 shows the CHMM topology of an audio-visual speech unit (phoneme/viseme pair) with 3 states for each stream of feature vectors. The circles – denote CHMM states, which are hidden for observation, and rectangles show mixtures of normal distributions of observational vectors in states (GMMs). There are two state variables in the joint AV model, and at any time t, the state of the model is determined by these multinomial variables. The advantage of such configuration is that it allows unsynchronized progression of the two chains, while encouraging the two streams to assert temporal influence on each other. The overall dynamics of the AV speech is determined by both streams at one time.

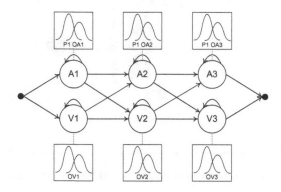

Fig. 2. Topology of the coupled HMM of an audio-visual speech unit

A method to transform the CHMM to an equivalent multi-stream HMM that keeps all the properties of the former model was proposed in [18]. In our recognition system, we used a similar approach, for more detailed explanation see our previous works [12, 13].

3.2   Feature Extraction

For audio signal representation we used 12-dimensional Mel-Frequency Cepstral Coefficients (MFCC) calculated from 26 channel filter bank analysis of 20 ms long frames with 10 ms overlap.

The visual features are calculated as a result of the following processing steps: multi-scale Haar-based face detection in frames of video data with 25–200 fps using a boosted cascade classifier; mouth region detection with cascade classifiers (for mouth and mouth with beard) within the lower part of the face; normalization of the detected mouth images to 32 × 32 pixels; mapping to a 32-dimensional feature vector using a principal component analysis (PCA).

3.3 Audio-Visual Speech Classes

According to our previous studies [12], the best recognition results for AV Russian speech are achieved using only 10 visual speech units (visemes). This number is a language-dependent and for Russian there are 10–14 distinguishable speech units in different works. However, since high-speed recordings much accurately reflect quite fast dynamics of lips movements, in the current study, we researched various sets of visemes of Russian speech. The complete viseme list is presented in Table 1 and recognition results are reported in the experimental section.

Table 1. Viseme classes and phoneme-to-viseme mapping

Viseme class	Corresponding phonemes	Viseme class	Corresponding phonemes
V1	sil (pause)	V11	e!
V2	a, a!	V12	y, y!
V3	i, i!	V13	u, u!
V4	o!	V14	e
V5	b, b', p, p'	V15	s, s', z, z', c
V6	f, f', v, v'	V16	j
V7	sh, sch	V17	h, h'
V8	l, l', r, r'	V18	ch
V9	d, d', t, t', n, n'	V19	m, m'
V10	g, g', k, k'	V20	zh

In our system, as audio-visual speech models we use 48 CHMMs corresponding to all the Russian phonemes. After tying states the output densities of corresponding viseme models according to the mapping in Table 1, we got 60 output densities for the visual data stream and 144 united output densities for the audio stream.

4 Evaluation Experiments

All the audio-visual data were recorded in acoustically clean office environments with audio SNR >35 dB. However, in the real life conditions it is difficult to find an ideally quiet environment. Often, the acoustic environment is mixed with different types of noises of varying intensity and it is not always possible to make a proper sound filtration [19, 20]. In this case, many researches see the solution in relying on video modality that does not deteriorate with acoustic noises [21]. In this context, a more reliable visual speech component leads to a more robust AV system in general.

Our study shows that the use of high-speed video data makes it possible to expand the number of visually distinguishable viseme classes of Russian speech to 20. Experiments carried out with this configuration led to an improvement in the average word recognition accuracy in about 0.5% for all speakers in comparison with previously used 10 viseme classes for a regular 25 fps video data. Further increase in the number of viseme classes did not lead to better recognition results.

4.1   Experiments with the Visual Speech Modality

In our experiments we use a video data of 5 different frame rates: 25, 50, 100, 150 and 200 fps. Figure 3 presents the average Word Recognition Rate (WRR) among all speakers for these cases. As can be seen from Fig. 3, the WRR increases significantly (up to 1.47% absolute) with fps increase from 25 to 50. With a further increase in the frame rate to 100 fps, the recognition accuracy also increases, however, the speed of its growth decreases: only 0.91% for the next 50 fps. This trend continues with the increase to 150 fps and gives only 0.42% gain in the speech accuracy. With the further increase of the frame rate, the improvement in accuracy is even smaller and is about 0.3% for additional plus 50 fps.

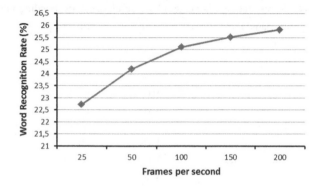

Fig. 3. Average WRR with different frame rates

However, for 3 speakers in our database, the obtained results were a bit different. These results are characterized by the fact that the maximum recognition accuracy was achieved with 100–150 fps and not with 200 fps for these three speakers. Based on this, we can assume that an increase in fps is not always leads to an increase in speech recognition accuracy. There is a certain threshold, after which the information becomes redundant and leads to distortions in recognition results. Presumably, it depends on speaker's speech tempo and this issue deserves more careful study.

There is also an assumption that visual female speech is recognized better than the male one, due to the number of facts, e.g. women have more contrast and visually distinguishable lips, mainly due to the use of lipstick and absence of a beard and moustache on the face, that should allow the system to more accurately detect lips and pronounced visemes. Since in our database the number of male and female speakers is equal, we tested this hypothesis and the results are shown in Fig. 4.

According to the obtained results, the average WRR of male and female speakers is approximately the same and differs by 1–2%, and male speech is recognized even slightly better. The average gain in WRR due to high-speed recordings was 3.12% for male and 3.07% for female speakers. Based on our observations there was no significant correlation between speaker's gender and WRR. However, a certain dependency between the speaker's speech tempo and the resulting accuracy was revealed: speakers with relatively fast speech tempo usually gain more from using high-speed recordings

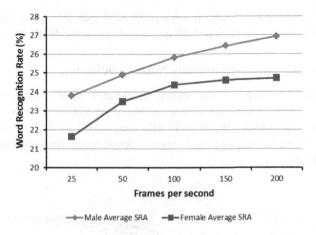

Fig. 4. Average WRR for male and female speakers

than the speakers with a calm and steady speech tempo. Some quick-talking speakers from our database gained an accuracy increase of 7.28% and 5.51%, which is higher than the average result, while slow-talking speakers only gain WRR improvements of 1.5–2%.

4.2 Experiments with Audio-Visual Speech Modalities

It is known from previous studies [12] that CHMM-based AV speech recognition system shows better recognition accuracy results in comparison with multi-stream HMMs due to the ability of CHMMs to process a natural asynchrony between the auditory and visual speech cues (at least, within the model boundaries). Thus, for audio-visual experiments we used CHMMs with 60 common output densities for the visual data stream and 144 common output densities for the acoustical feature stream as described in Sect. 3. The results obtained by this system for a different fps levels can be seen in Fig. 5.

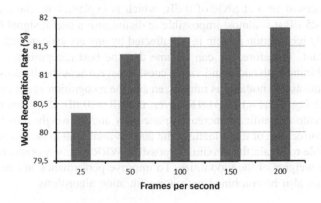

Fig. 5. Average WRR for audio-visual speech recognition with different fps rates

The WRR achieves its maximum value of 81.82% with 200 fps of video data. That is 1.48% higher than using standard 25 fps, which gives the WRR only of 80.34%.

4.3   Experiments Under Acoustically Noise Conditions

Figure 6 shows the results of the speech recognition system under various noisy conditions. Two types of acoustic noises (babble noise and white noise) with different signal-to-noise ratios (SNR from 0 to 40 dB) were added to the test audio data. The audio-only, video-only and joint audio-visual speech recognition systems were tested in these conditions.

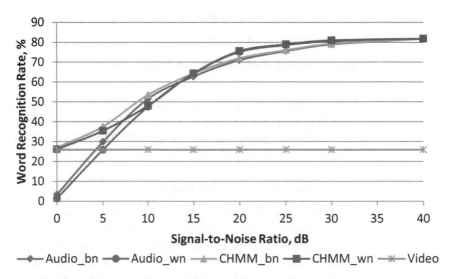

Fig. 6. WRR vs. SNR for different speech recognition models under two types of noises: babble noise (bn) and white noise (wn)

In the audio-only recognition systems the WRR begins to fall rapidly at SNR below 15–20 dB to almost zero at SNR of 0 dB, which is explained by the fact that at the SNR level of <5 dB it is almost impossible to distinguish a useful signal from a noise. The visual-only recognition system is not affected by any acoustic noises, so the WRR remains constant. Therefore, we can assume that the best recognition results can be achieved combining both audio and visual cues. In severe acoustically noisy conditions the weight of the audio modality is minimized and the recognition system relies only on the video modality (SNR <10 dB). However, if SNR >10 dB, the video modality can no longer provide a significant increase in accuracy and its weight must be reduced.

Given to correct use of these features the audio-visual system becomes more robust and it is possible to obtain the maximally possible WRR in any acoustic conditions by modifying the weights of the modalities. To improve performance in real applications this method can also be combined with noise filtration algorithms.

5   Conclusions

In this paper, we presented the results of our evaluation experiments obtained by the CHMM-based Russian speech recognition system. These experiments have demonstrated the positive effect of using high-speed video recordings in speech recognition. In comparison with the regular 25 fps (recording speed used on most devices) using 200 fps high-speed video camera results in an increase of WRR by an average value of 1.48% for all speakers. Experiments with visual-only speech recognizer show an increase of WRR by an average value of 3.10%. For several individual speakers this value even reaches 7.28%.

Despite the existing assumption that female visual speech can be recognized better than male, our study did not reveal such a dependency. According to our observations the speech tempo has more influence on word recognition rate than gender. Speakers with a relatively fast speech tempo had a greater increase in the recognition accuracy and benefit more from using a high-speed camera. The average gain in the recognition accuracy was 3.12% for males and 3.07% for females with 200 frame rate of video data.

Based on the conducted studies it can be concluded that the use of a high-speed camera makes it possible to improve the speech recognition accuracy of continuous Russian speech. Especially under noisy conditions when the accuracy of the audio-only speech recognition system is degraded by acoustic noise. According to our observations, white noise worsens recognition accuracy more than the babble noise with equal SNR values. However, white noise is relatively easy to remove using sound cleaning techniques. While removing babble noise is still a difficult and not completely unresolved task. Since babble noise is quite common in real conditions it is very important to have reliable speech recognition in this case. In our opinion, this can be achieved using audio-visual speech recognition system with a high-speed video camera.

Acknowledgments. This research is partially supported by the Russian Foundation for Basic Research (projects No. 15-07-04415, 15-07-04322 and 16-37-60085), by the Council for Grants of the President of the Russian Federation (projects No. MD-254.2017.8, MK-1000.2017.8 and MK-7925.2016.9), by the Government of Russia (grant No. 074-U01), by grant of the University of West Bohemia (project No. SGS-2016-039), and by the Ministry of Education, Youth and Sports of Czech Republic, (project No. LO1506).

References

1. Katsaggelos, K., Bahaadini, S., Molina, R.: Audiovisual fusion: challenges and new approaches. Proc. IEEE **103**(9), 1635–1653 (2015)
2. Corradini, A., Mehta, M., Bernsen, N.O., Martin, J., Abrilian, S.: Multimodal input fusion in human-computer interaction. Nato Sci. Ser. Comput. Syst. Sci. **198**, 223 (2005)
3. Lahat, D., Adall, T., Jutten, C.: Challenges in multimodal data fusion. In: Proceedings of the European Signal Processing Conference, pp. 101–105 (2014)
4. Shao, X., Barker, J.: Stream weight estimation for multistream audio-visual speech recognition in a multispeaker environment. Speech Commun. **50**(4), 337–353 (2008)

5. Chitu, A.G., Rothkrantz, L.J.M.: The influence of video sampling rate on lipreading performance. In: Proceedings of the International Conference on Speech and Computer, SPECOM 2007, Moscow, Russia, pp. 678–684 (2007)
6. Chitu, A.G., Driel, K., Rothkrantz, L.J.M.: Automatic lip reading in the Dutch language using active appearance models on high speed recordings. In: Sojka, P., Horák, A., Kopeček, I., Pala, K. (eds.) TSD 2010. LNCS(LNAI), vol. 6231, pp. 259–266. Springer, Heidelberg (2010). doi:10.1007/978-3-642-15760-8_33
7. Polykovsky, S., Kameda, Y., Ohta, Y.: Facial micro-expressions recognition using high speed camera and 3D-gradient descriptor. In: Proceedings of the 3rd International Conference on Crime Detection and Prevention (ICDP), Tsukuba, Japan, pp. 1–6 (2009)
8. Bettadapura, V.: Face expression recognition and analysis: the state of the art. Technical report, pp. 1–27. College of Computing, Georgia Institute of Technology, USA (2012)
9. Ohzeki, K.: Video analysis for detecting eye blinking using a high-speed camera. In: Proceedings of the 40th Asilomar Conference on Signals, Systems and Computers (ACSSC), Part 1, Pacific Grove, USA, pp. 1081–1085 (2006)
10. Chitu, A.G., Rothkrantz, L.J.M.: On dual view lipreading using high speed camera. In: Proceedings of the 14th Annual Scientific Conference Euromedia, Ghent, Belgium, pp. 43–51 (2008)
11. Verkhodanova, V., Ronzhin, A., Kipyatkova, I., Ivanko, D., Karpov, A., Železný, M.: HAVRUS corpus: high-speed recordings of audio-visual Russian speech. In: Ronzhin, A., Potapova, R., Németh, G. (eds.) SPECOM 2016. LNCS, vol. 9811, pp. 338–345. Springer, Cham (2016). doi:10.1007/978-3-319-43958-7_40
12. Karpov, A., Ronzhin, A., Markov, K., Železný, M.: Viseme-dependent weight optimization for CHMM-based audio-visual speech recognition. In: Proceedings of the Interspeech 2010, pp. 2678–2681 (2010)
13. Karpov, A.: An automatic multimodal speech recognition system with audio and video information. Autom. Remote Control 75(12), 2190–2200 (2014)
14. Zelezny, M., Csar, P.: Czech audio-visual speech corpus of a car driver for in-vehicle audio-visual speech recognition. In: Proceedings of the International Conference on Audio-Visual Speech Processing (AVSP 2003), pp. 169–173 (2003)
15. Csar, P., Zelezny, M., Krnoul, Z., Kanis, J., Zelinka, J., Muller, L.: Design and recording of Czech speech corpus for audio-visual continuous speech recognition. In: Proceedings of the International Conference on the Auditory-Visual Speech Processing, pp. 1–4 (2005)
16. Grishina E.: Multimodal Russian corpus (MURCO): first steps. In: Proceedings of the 7th Language Resources and Evaluation Conference (LREC 2010), pp. 2953–2960 (2010)
17. Karpov, A., Kipyatkova, I., Železný, M.: A framework for recording audio-visual speech corpora with a microphone and a high-speed camera. In: Ronzhin, A., Potapova, R., Delic, V. (eds.) SPECOM 2014. LNCS, vol. 8773, pp. 50–57. Springer, Cham (2014). doi:10.1007/978-3-319-11581-8_6
18. Chu, S.M., Huang, T.S.: Multi-Modal sensory fusion with application to audio-visual speech recognition. In: Proceedings of the Multi-Modal Speech Recognition Workshop 2002, Greensboro, USA (2002)
19. Stewart, D., Seymour, R., Pass, A., Ming, J.: Robust audio-visual speech recognition under noisy audio-video conditions. IEEE Trans. Cybern. 44(2), 175–184 (2014)
20. Huang, J., Kingsbury, B.: Audio-visual deep learning for noise robust speech recognition. In: Proceedings of the IEEE International Conference on Acoustics, Speech and Signal Processing, pp. 7596–7599 (2013)
21. Estellers, V., Gurban, M., Thiran, J.: On dynamic stream weighting for audio-visual speech recognition. IEEE Trans. Audio Speech Lang. Process. 20(4), 1145–1157 (2012)

Utilizing Lipreading in Large Vocabulary Continuous Speech Recognition

Karel Paleček[✉]

The Institute of Information Technology and Electronics,
Technical University of Liberec, Studentská 2/1402, 46117 Liberec, Czech Republic
karel.palecek@tul.cz

Abstract. Vast majority of current research in the area of audiovisual speech recognition via lipreading from frontal face videos focuses on simple cases such as isolated phrase recognition or structured speech, where the vocabulary is limited to several tens of units. In this paper, we diverge from these traditional applications and investigate the effect of incorporating the visual information in the task of continuous speech recognition with vocabulary size ranging from several hundred to half a million words. To this end, we evaluate various visual speech parametrizations, both existing and novel, that are designed to capture different kind of information in the video signal. The experiments are conducted on a moderate sized dataset of 54 speakers, each uttering 100 sentences in Czech language. We show that even for large vocabularies the visual signal contains enough information to improve the word accuracy up to 15% relatively to the acoustic-only recognition.

Keywords: Audiovisual speech recognition · Lipreading · LVCSR

1 Introduction

It has been well established that visual cues extracted from lip movement can help the automatic speech recognition process mainly in noisy acoustic conditions. With sufficiently small vocabulary, frontal face videos provide enough information for reliable recognition even without acoustic data. Large variety of methods for visual parametrization, feature post-processing and modality integration have been proposed to date. For a comprehensive overview of recent advances in lipreading and audiovisual speech recognition see e.g. work by Zhou et al. [15].

Utilization of automatic lipreading techniques for large vocabulary continuous speech recognition (LVCSR) is rarely explored in the current literature. One of the main obstacles is the lack of freely available datasets, with AVICAR [8] probably being the only option. In [7] Lan et al. used proprietary corpus of 12 speakers and 1000 word vocabulary in order to classify individual visemes, but they did not report the word-level accuracy. Much of the important work on audiovisual LVCSR via frontal face lipreading was conducted in IBM laboratories

© Springer International Publishing AG 2017
A. Karpov et al. (Eds.): SPECOM 2017, LNAI 10458, pp. 767–776, 2017.
DOI: 10.1007/978-3-319-66429-3_77

during the early 2000s [6,11]. The experiments were performed on IBM's proprietary large audiovisual dataset ViaVoice containing 290 speakers and vocabulary size of 10403 words and found the integration of visual features beneficial only for noisy acoustic conditions. Recently, two papers [1,3] using end-to-end trained deep learning systems improved state of the art in lipreading of sentences. Assael et al. [1] trained the system to recognize structured sentences of the GRID corpus [5] by optimizing connectionist temporal classification (CTC) criterion and significantly improved state of the art word error rate (WER) from 13.6% to 4.8% in a multi-speaker split, albeit with still only 51 word vocabulary. Chung et al. [3] designed a first end-to-end trained truly large vocabulary deep learning system for lipreading sentences in the wild. To this end, they utilized watch, listen, attend, and spell framework instead of CTC, and were able to push the results on GRID even further down to 3.3%. Their system was, however, pretrained on a large proprietary dataset of BBC television broadcast with over 100 thousands audiovisual utterances, not available to other researchers.

In this work, we tackle the problem from the traditional feature extraction and classification paradigm, which allows for easier integration and straightforward comparison with existing acoustic-only systems based on hidden Markov Model (HMM) decoding. We evaluate several popular state of the art visual speech parametrizations in the task of audiovisual LVCSR and experimentally investigate their impact on the word error rate. To this end, we utilize moderate sized dataset with 54 speakers and simulate various vocabularies of up to 500 k words. Moreover somewhat non-traditionally, since our dataset is recorded using Kinect, we also evaluate the lipreading performance when depth data is incorporated. Interestingly enough, recognition from the depth stream sometimes yields better results than from RGB, with the advantage of partial complementarity, which makes it suitable for integration with RGB.

The rest of the paper is organized as follows. We describe our dataset in Sect. 2. The visual parametrizations along with our modifications are explained in Sect. 3. System overview is presented in Sect. 4. Finally, the performed experiments and the discussion are described in Sect. 5.

2   Data

TULAVD is our own dataset recorded at the Technical University of Liberec containing data from 54 speakers, of which 23 are female and 31 male with age ranging from 20 to 70 years. Each speaker uttered 50 isolated words and 100 sentences in Czech language, which were automatically selected according to phonetic balance. The sentences were divided into two groups with the first 50 being common to all speakers and the other 50 speaker-specific. The dataset also contains 583 manually annotated images of all speakers in various poses, expressions and face occlusions, which constitute a training dataset for the ESR detector. The audiovisual utterances were recorded in an office environment using Genius lavalier microphone, two Logitech C920 FullHD webcams, and Microsoft Kinect, which also offers depth stream that is fully synchronized with the video.

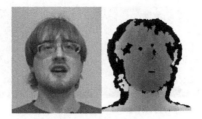

Fig. 1. Sample frame of RGB image and corresponding depth map

Only the microphone and Kinect RGBD data with resolution of 640×480 pixels is used in this work. See Fig. 1 for a sample frame from a frontal face video of a talking speaker. In order to build the language models, we also collected more than 60 GB of texts mostly consisting of online journals and manual transcriptions of television and radio broadcast.

3 Visual Speech Parametrization

In audio visual speech literature, **discrete cosine transform (DCT)** represents a widely used method for visual speech parametrization, and often the first choice. The visual speech features are usually selected as a subset of the full 2D DCT transform computed over the ROI.) Number of feature selection methods have been proposed to date, e.g. zig-zag ordering or selection by mutual information. In this work, we treat the coefficient selection as hyperparameter optimization problem. We sort the DCT coefficients based on an average energy obtained on a training set and then select their optimal number according to validation score.

The Active Appearance Model (AAM) is a well-known method for describing appearance of a deformable object by a hierarchical application of PCA. The appearance is represented by shape and texture that are both modeled linearly using PCA. These modality-specific representations are normalized and concatenated into a single vector, and then subjected to a second-level PCA. In this work, we extract the AAM features using 46 landmarks from the lower part of the speakers face, see the AAM-r in Fig. 2. In addition to the standard AAM, we also evaluate a variant with both video and depth texture included as a form of early feature integration. We denote this case as **DAAM**. The number of AAM coefficients constitutes a hyperparameter that is optimized w.r.t. the recognition accuracy.

For our experiments we also utilize the popular **Spatiotemporal Local Binary Patterns (LBPTOP)** introduced in [14]. Local Binary Pattern (LBP) describes the texture in terms of a histogram of binary numbers that are formed by comparing each pixel of the image to its close neighborhood. Zhao et al. extended the static LBP by considering the neighborhood not only in the spatial domain, but also in the time axis, in order to capture the speech dynamics.

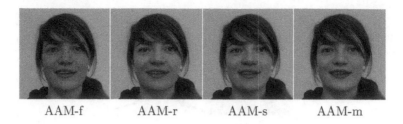

AAM-f   AAM-r   AAM-s   AAM-m

Fig. 2. Possible landmark configurations. We empirically found out that the second configuration (AAM-r) performs best in most experiments

Thus, LBPs are effectively extracted from three orthogonal planes (TOP): xy, xt, and yt. These are then concatenated into a single vector forming the visual speech parametrization. Contrary to the original work [14], we extract the LBP-TOP densely for every frame. We cross validate the parameters of the LBP, i.e. the number of histogram bins and the aggregation method (standard, rotation invariant, uniform, non-rotation invariant uniform).

The last considered parametrization is the **Spatiotemporal Histogram of Oriented Gradients (HOGTOP)**. We proposed this parametrization in [10] inspired by the LBPTOP as a dynamization technique of the standard Histogram of Oriented Gradients (HOG). Normally, the histograms are formed by counting and weighting the gradient orientations in the xy plane. Here, we also add orientations from the xt and yt planes, process them independently, concatenate, and reduce the resulting HOG hypervector by PCA into the final parametrization. Extraction of the HOGTOP features is illustrated in Fig. 3. The only hyperparameter to be cross-validated is the final PCA dimension.

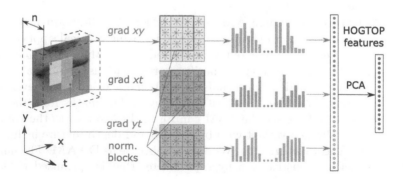

Fig. 3. Extraction of spatiotemporal histogram of oriented gradients

4   System Overview

4.1   Visual Front-end

We pre-process the image in several stages with progressing level of precision. First, an approximate position of the face is estimated using the well known Viola-Jones algorithm. We use the pre-trained model that ships with the OpenCV library. Second, to estimate the facial shape precise positions of 93 facial landmarks are obtained by utilizing the Explicit Shape Regression method (ESR) [2]. The ESR is a discriminative method that iteratively refines the joint landmark configuration (i.e. the face shape) based on the value of only few pixel differences and thus is very efficient (i.e. hundreds of frames per second on regular PC). However, since there is no objective to be optimized, the final landmark positions are slightly different in each frame, which introduces an inter-frame jitter. We reduce it by running the detector from different starting positions 10 times and then taking the median of the fit shapes.

Once the facial landmarks are localized, we define the region of interest (ROI) as a square area barely covering the mouth and its closest surrounding. In order to achieve scale invariance we set its size relative to the normalized mean shape. The geometric transformation for the extraction is estimated by aligning the normalized mean and the detected shapes. To further reduce the inter-frame landmark jitter and stabilize the ROI extraction, we average the fitting results over three neighboring frames in time.

4.2   Feature Extraction and Post-processing

The acoustic channel is parametrized by 39 Mel Frequency Cepstral Coefficients (MFCC) with a 25 ms window at a 100 Hz rate. The visual parametrizations described in Sect. 3 are extracted densely for each frame of the input utterance. Sequences $x_{t-k}, \ldots, x_{t+k}$ of $2k + 1$ feature vectors $x_{t'}$ are concatenated into hypervectors, where k represents the number of left and right adjacent frames, and then reduced by the linear discriminant analysis (LDA) with phonemes as class labels. The k is treated as a hyperparameter for each parametrization separately and therefore is subject to optimization of the validation score. Since visual features tend to be highly speaker dependent, we also perform feature mean subtraction (FMS) with the average computed over the whole utterance. Addition of delta (Δ) features is similarly to k also considered to be a hyperparameter and thus tuned for each parametrization separately. Finally, the video features are linearly interpolated from 30 Hz to 100 Hz frequency to match the acoustic parametrization.

4.3   Acoustic and Visual Models

Due to the limited amount of audiovisual data, we utilize only basic monophone models without context. There are 40 distinct phonemes of the PAC-CZ phonetic alphabet [9] and 13 corresponding visemes [4]. In order to obtain frame-level class labels, we forced-aligned the audio recordings using a separate robust acoustic model that was trained on approximately 300 h of spoken data. The viseme labels were then obtained by a simple phoneme-viseme mapping proposed in [4] and shifted by approximately 0.023 s to synchronize the streams.

Phonemes and visemes are modeled using 3-state hidden Markov model (HMM) with Gaussian mixture emission probability. The main advantage of HMM in our context is that it allows for straightforward weighted combination of acoustic and visual channels via multi-stream synchronous variant of the model (MSHMM), in which each state q has an emission probability equal to the weighted product of the individual streams $s = (1, \ldots, S)$:

$$p\left(x^{(1)}, \ldots, x^{(S)} | q\right) = \prod_{s=1}^{S} p\left(x^{(s)} | q\right)^{\lambda^{(s)}}. \tag{1}$$

We treat the stream weights $\lambda^{(s)}$ as hyperparameters and therefore cross-validate them w. r. t. the recognition accuracy.

We utilized the HTK 3.4.1 toolkit to train the phoneme and viseme models. We followed a simplified procedure by first initializing the models with Viterbi training (HInit) and then reestimating with Baum-Welch in an isolated-unit manner (HRest). We have empirically found out that the more commonly used approach of embedded re-estimation using HERest only degrades the results in our case. This is due to the limited discriminative power of the visual parametrization that makes it unsuitable for alignment on the phonetic level, even when constrained by the acoustic features in the multi-stream model, and as a result, the re-estimation procedure fails to converge.

4.4   Language Models

We evaluate our audiovisual recognition system for four different bigram language models with vocabulary size ranging from 366 up to 500 k words, see Table 1 for the exact numbers. The smallest vocabulary contains only words from the corpus of our audiovisual dataset, whereas the other ones also include the most frequent words in Czech language. The word frequencies and language models are assessed using the 60 GB text corpus described in Sect. 2. We employed the SRILM toolkit [13] with Knesser-Nay smoothing for the language model training.

Table 1. Vocabularies considered in the experiments

LM	min	5 k	50 k	500 k
# words	366	5 182	50 056	499 993
# bigrams	48 338	9 865 k	73 905 k	141 670 k

5   Experiments

Throughout the experiments we follow the k-fold cross validation protocol. The 54 speakers are split into 6 groups of 9, where in each turn of the cross validation 5 groups constitute a training set and 1 is reserved for testing. We then report the average word accuracy (Wacc) achieved over the 6 different test sets.

The phonetic models are learned on all the available training data from each respective fold of the cross validation, which amounts to approximately 5 h of spoken data on average. In order to minimize the number of sources of variability across different folds and to better control the vocabulary, the test data comprise only of the first 50 sentences that are common to all speakers instead of the full set of 100 sentences.

5.1   Isolated Word Recognition

In order to tune the hyperparameters of the visual parametrizations described in Sect. 3, we followed a slightly different approach. For reasons of efficiency, these hyperparameters were optimized using 14-state whole-word models with one or two components per GMM in the task of lipreading of 50 isolated words. The optimized parametrizations were then used for unimodal recognition of the 50 isolated words using phoneme and viseme models. In these experiments we employed the HTK `HVite` decoder. Table 2 summarizes the results of both whole-word and phonetic models.

Table 2. Word accuracy [%] of isolated word recognition and lipreading

Param	Src.	Word	Phoneme		Viseme	
Mixtures:		1/2	8	16	8	16
MFCC	a	99,8	99,5	99,8	97,4	98,0
DCT	v	72,5	42,6	42,8	42,4	43,9
	d	74,4	39,3	42,5	38,6	43,1
AAM	v	74,1	57,5	58,5	59,0	59,3
	d	75,2	54,1	55,0	55,3	56,6
LBPTOP	v	74,2	54,6	56,4	54,6	56,3
	d	64,3	48,7	47,4	45,3	48,2
HOGTOP	v	**86,4**	59,5	61,0	59,8	60,1
	d	84,4	56,6	58,3	56,6	57,7
DAAM	v ∘ d	74,9	**62,0**	**64,6**	**63,0**	**64,7**

The experiment is conducted for both video (a) and depth (d) streams, with v ∘ d denoting their early integration, i.e. concatenation of the feature vectors. Note that in the special case of DAAM, the concatenation of video and depth textures is also followed by coupling via PCA. One can observe that in this simpler scenario, video-based and depth-based parametrizations perform roughly on par, with their combination in the form of DAAM achieving the best results overall.

While the phoneme and viseme models reach similar word accuracies, they perform much worse compared to the whole-word approach. This illustrates one of the issues with the current state of the art in lipreading, where the parametrization and classification algorithms mainly target isolated unit recognition, and the results do not necessarily apply to systems with larger vocabularies.

5.2   Continuous Speech

The results on isolated word recognition show that on average viseme-based models outperformed the phone-based ones. However, the results are inconsistent and the margin never exceeds 2%. This observation may be attributed to the viseme context dependency on the surrounding vowels [12]. For instance, the u-shaped lip protrusion when pronouncing "s" in the word "super" significantly differs from the horizontal extension when pronouncing "s" in "see". As a result, it seems that phonemes cannot be unambiguously mapped to visemes in a surjective many-to-one manner. Considering this issue and potential problems with the score combination, we employed only phone models in the following experiments on continuous speech recognition.

Table 3 presents the achieved results. Due to performance reasons we switched from HVite to the Julius[1] decoder, which is compatible with HTK model definitions. For example, a + v denotes a middle fusion of audio and video channels via MSHMM with optimally set weights $\lambda^{(s)}$ that are cross-validated on a dense grid of all possible combinations with the step of 0.1 and constraint $\sum_s \lambda^{(s)} = 1$.

As expected, with the increasing size of vocabulary, the performance in terms of accuracy and correctness degrades rather quickly, which is mostly due to the relatively small amount of training data. On the other hand, in all experiments the combined audiovisual representations achieved to some improvement over acoustic-only recognition, showing that the visual cues provide useful information even for very large vocabularies with 500 k words. This especially holds for LBPTOP and HOGTOP, as they manage to exploit some of the speech dynamics, which is crucial for phoneme discrimination. The best results overall were obtained by our proposed HOGTOP features extracted from both video and depth, although the difference from video-only LBPTOP is almost negligible.

In contrast to recognition of isolated words, integration of the depth channel does not seem to improve the word accuracy. The only exception to this rule was the HOGTOP parametrization, which in most cases achieved slightly better results in the three modality setting.

For all four vocabularies the highest improvement achieved over audio-only recognition ranged between 5–7% absolutely, i.e. 7–15% relatively. In most cases the optimal weight ratio of audio and video (or depth) channels, which indicates

---

[1] https://github.com/julius-speech/julius.

Table 3. Word accuracy [%] of audiovisual speech recognition by middle fusion of acoustic and visual parametrizations for different vocabularies

Par.	Source	Vocabulary			
		min	5 k	50 k	500 k
MFCC	a	74,0	55,9	43,9	36,3
DCT	a + v	76,8	59,8	47,1	38,9
	a + d	74,3	55,5	43,4	38,3
	a + v + d	77,3	59,6	46,8	38,2
AAM	a + v	76,7	60,5	48,7	40,2
	a + d	76,8	60,0	48,0	39,5
	a + v + d	76,9	60,2	48,3	39,9
LBPTOP	a + v	79,2	62,7	**50,1**	**41,7**
	a + d	77,8	60,8	48,5	39,8
	a + v + d	79,3	62,6	50,0	41,4
HOGTOP	a + v	78,1	60,2	47,8	42,0
	a + d	77,2	58,3	46,2	40,7
	a + v + d	**79,4**	**62,9**	**50,1**	41,6
DAAM	A + v ∘ d	75,2	58,6	48,0	40,7

the relative importance of each modality, was 0.7 : 0.3 or 0.8 : 0.2, with the former being more common for the 500 k vocabulary. Note that the results hold for relatively clean data, i.e. without acoustic noise, and one might expect even higher relative improvement in worse conditions.

6   Conclusion

We have shown that given quality parametrization, the visual cues provided by the lip movement can improve the recognition accuracy even for very large vocabularies with hundreds of thousand words. The best results were achieved using the HOGTOP and LBPTOP features that are designed to exploit the speech dynamics as opposed to static features such as AAM. The relative improvement of audiovisual over audio-only recognition ranged between 7% and 15% when the channels were integrated via multi-stream hidden Markov model with optimally set weights. There might be a potential issue in that improvement observation could be somewhat influenced by the limited amount of data and it is uncertain if the same results would hold for more robust acoustic models trained on hundreds of hours data. In order to verify this, transfer learning techniques could potentially be employed to circumvent the lack of large audiovisual dataset availability.

References

1. Assael, Y.M., Shillingford, B., Whiteson, S., de Freitas, N.: Lipnet: Sentence-level lipreading. CoRR abs/1611.01599 (2016)
2. Cao, X., Wei, Y., Wen, F., Sun, J.: Face alignment by explicit shape regression. In: CVPR (2012)
3. Chung, J.S., Senior, A.W., Vinyals, O., Zisserman, A.: Lip reading sentences in the wild. CoRR abs/1611.05358 (2016)
4. Císař, P.: Application of lipreading methods for speech recognition. Ph.D. thesis (2006)
5. Cooke, M., Barker, J., Cunningham, S., Shao, X.: An audio-visual corpus for speech perception and automatic speech recognition. J. Acoust. Soc. Am. **120**(5), 2421–2424 (2006)
6. Glotin, H., Vergyr, D., Neti, C., Potamianos, G., Luettin, J.: Weighting schemes for audio-visual fusion in speech recognition. In: Proceedings of the 2001 IEEE International Conference on Acoustics, Speech, and Signal Processing (ICASSP 2001), vol. 1, pp. 173–176 (2001)
7. Lan, Y., Theobald, B., Harvey, R., Bowden, R.: Improving visual features for lipreading, pp. 142–147 (2010)
8. Lee, B., Hasegawa-Johnson, M., Goudeseune, C., Kamdar, S., Borys, S., Liu, M., Huang, T.S.: AVICAR: audio-visual speech corpus in a car environment. In: 8th International Conference on Spoken Language Processing, INTERSPEECH 2004 - ICSLP, Jeju Island, Korea, 4–8 October 2004
9. Nouza, J., Psutka, J., Uhlíř, J.: Phonetic alphabet for speech recognition of czech (1997)
10. Palecek, K.: Lipreading using spatiotemporal histogram of oriented gradients. In: EUSIPCO 2016, Budapest, Hungary, pp. 1882–1885 (2016)
11. Potamianos, G., Neti, C., Gravier, G., Garg, A., Senior, A.W.: Recent advances in the automatic recognition of audio-visual speech. In: Proceedings of the IEEE, pp. 1306–1326 (2003)
12. Ramage, M.D.: Disproving Visemes as the Basic Visual Unit of Speech. Ph.D. thesis (2013)
13. Stolcke, A.: SRILM - an extensible language modeling toolkit. In: Proceedings of ICSLP, Denver, USA, vol. 2, pp. 901–904 (2002)
14. Zhao, G., Barnard, M., Pietikäinen, M.: Lipreading with local spatiotemporal descriptors. IEEE Trans. Multimedia **11**(7), 1254–1265 (2009)
15. Zhou, Z., Zhao, G., Hong, X., Pietikinen, M.: A review of recent advances in visual speech decoding. Image Vis. Comput. **32**(9), 590–605 (2014)

Vocal Emotion Conversion Using WSOLA and Linear Prediction

Susmitha Vekkot[(✉)] and Shikha Tripathi

Department of Electronics and Communication Engineering,
Amrita School of Engineering, Bengaluru, Amrita Vishwa Vidyapeetham,
Amrita University, Bengaluru, India
{v_susmitha,t_shikha}@blr.amrita.edu

Abstract. The paper deals with speech emotion conversion using Waveform Similarity Overlap Add (WSOLA) and subsequent linear prediction analysis for spectral transformation. Duration modification is done by taking the ratio between segment durations of neutral and target speech. After performing modification using WSOLA, the duration modified source speech is time aligned with target and further subjected to linear prediction analysis to yield the LP coefficients. The target emotion is re-synthesised by using the prosody manipulated residual and LPCs from source. The waveform similarity property of WSOLA is exploited to give output with minimal distortion. The proposed algorithm is subjectively and objectively evaluated along with popular TD-PSOLA algorithm. The correlation between synthesised and real target shows an average improvement of 60% across all emotions with the proposed technique.

Keywords: Emotion · WSOLA · Linear prediction · Dynamic time warping · Comparative mean opinion score · Correlation coefficient

1 Introduction

Vocal expression is one of the vital components in speech communication. Effective communication enables the intended message to be conveyed effectively by means of linguistic and paralinguistic cues. Over the past decade, researchers have been particularly interested in identifying, estimating and incorporating the vocal features contributing to naturalness in human speech. Naturalness can be attributed to the degree of expressiveness in vocal dialogues relevant to the particular context. According to experiments in [1], acoustic features relevant for perceptive quality are mainly supra-segmental ones like pitch, duration, speech rate along with voice quality parameters like vowel precision. Tao et al. [2] achieved expressiveness in speech by prosody (pitch and duration) modification of the neutral speech using Gaussian mixture model (GMM) and Classification And Regression Tree (CART) methods. Along with prosody modification, incorporation of voice quality parameters to enhance expressivity in speech is

© Springer International Publishing AG 2017
A. Karpov et al. (Eds.): SPECOM 2017, LNAI 10458, pp. 777–787, 2017.
DOI: 10.1007/978-3-319-66429-3_78

demonstrated in [3]. The system operates by manipulating prosodic parameters like pitch, duration and intensity along with characteristics of voice quality like jitter and shimmer using Pitch Synchronous Time Scaling (PSTS).

Rather than modifying the prosody across the entire utterance, selection of emotionally significant regions for prosody modification has yielded better results. A method for dynamically varying prosody at glottal activity regions was proposed in [4]. A method for non-uniform modification of vowel and pause duration using Vowel Onset Point detection and excitation instants (epochs) is described in [5,6]. In emotion conversion, it is important to select regions which are significant in emoting the state of the speaker. Vydana et al. [7] proposed a method based on computation of Strength of Excitation (SoE) at epochs to detect emotionally significant regions in angry speech. PSOLA based prosody modification is restricted only to those regions which are identified as emotionally significant. Recently, attempts have been made to synthesize expressive speech by imposition of pitch, duration and intensity patterns of syllable, word and sentence level segments of neutral speech [8]. Syllable level imposition yielded better results compared to word and sentence-level modifications. A linear prosody modification technique which involves marking vowel, pause and consonant regions in speech by computation of epochs and VOPs and further selection of modification factors based on vowel positions is described in [9].

Most of the literature on explicit control based expressive speech synthesis deals with prosodic and voice quality modifications from knowledge of glottal activity regions. It has been time and again proved that excitation source parameters contribute to the perceptional quality of emotions while statistical similarity is mainly attributed to prosodic factors [10]. Simultaneously modifying excitation and vocal tract characteristics is essential in generating good quality synthesised expression. Also, determination of emotionally significant parameters and segments in speech plays a major role in identifying the positions for incorporation of prosodic features.

This paper describes a method for prosody modification of neutral speech by using principles of WSOLA and linear prediction. The paper is organised as follows: Sect. 2 describes the background theory behind WSOLA analysis. Section 3 illustrates the algorithm in detail while Sect. 4 deals with results obtained using proposed algorithm and performance evaluation with TD-PSOLA. Section 5 concludes the paper with insights into future work.

2 Theoretical Background

2.1 WSOLA

Waveform Similarity Overlap Add technique (WSOLA) [11] is one of the popular algorithms for time scaling of speech. It is especially useful for applications such as voice-mail playback or synchronization of video post dubbing where control of speaking rate is desirable. The challenge associated in time scaling techniques is preservation of other speech features like voice quality, pitch and timbre. The principle of WSOLA is that it should produce a synthetic waveform $s(n)$ with maximum similarity to the original waveform x(m) in corresponding neighbour-hoods of related sample indices specified by a tolerance interval. The overlap add procedure is carried out by finding a segment with maximum similarity to the one that followed a previously extracted segment. The synthesis equation for WSOLA is given as [11]:

$$s(n) = \frac{\sum_k w(n - L_k)x(n + \tau^{-1}(L_k) + \delta_k - L_k)}{\sum_k w(n - L_k)} \tag{1}$$

where L_k are instants used for synthesis given as kL and denominator of Eq. 1 is taken as 1 (symmetric window condition). Figure 1 illustrates the overlap add procedure based on segment similarity. WSOLA yields high quality speech, is computationally very efficient and robust to noises for variety of scaling factors from 0.4–2. Algorithmic complexity is lesser than TD-PSOLA since it involves no pitch synchronous manipulations or pitch scaling and operates on fixed window length.

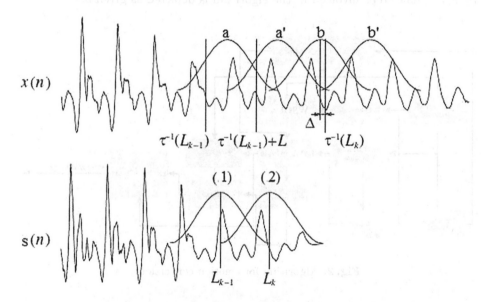

Fig. 1. WSOLA algorithm:Segment 'a' was the last input segment that was extracted and added to output at time instant L_{k-1}, represented as segment 1 in output s(n). The algorithm will then search for a segment extracted from the input around time $\tau_{-1}(L_k)$ that will overlap-add with input segment 1. WSOLA selects a segment 2 which is within a specified tolerance interval around $\tau_{-1}(L_k)$ in the input wave such that it closely resembles a'. The position of the optimum segment 'b' is calculated by maximizing the cross-correlation between the samples corresponding to a' and the input x(n) (Figure used with permission from Werner Verhelst)

3   Proposed Algorithm

In this paper, we implement speech emotion conversion by using a combination of WSOLA and linear prediction. From literature, it is clear that generating expressiveness in speech can be accomplished by conversion of both prosodic and spectral characteristics. Here, only duration is taken as the prosody parameter. WSOLA algorithm allows to do time stretching or compression without affecting the spectral characteristics of the signal. The emotional speech data used in this work is Indian Institute of Technology Kharagpur Simulated Emotion Speech Corpus (IITKGP-SESC). Speech is recorded using 5 male and 5 female experienced professional artists from All India Radio (AIR) Vijayawada, India [12]. For the current study, we have considered 4 basic emotions in IITKGP database viz neutral, anger, happy and fear from both male and female speakers. In each case, we have considered 150 utterances from each speaker. Since parallel data is required, linguistically identical utterances are considered for synthesis. The procedure described below can be illustrated by a block diagram as given by Fig. 2. The steps involved in the algorithm is depicted as given below.

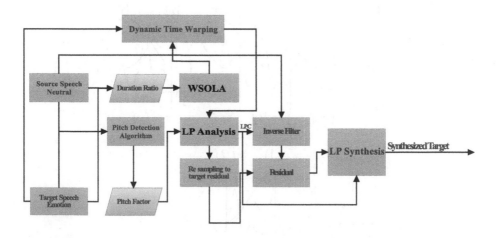

Fig. 2. Algorithm for emotion conversion

1 Read the source signal $X[n] = [x_1, x_2.....x_n]$ and the target signal $Y[n] = [y_1, y_2, ...y_n]$. In the experimentation, we have considered 10 speakers, both male and female from IITKGP-SESC.
2 For performing WSOLA, calculate the ratio of segment duration between source and target and take it as time scaling factor, α.
3 Perform WSOLA with the set duration factor as time scaling/stretch. α is given by Eq. 2:

$$\alpha = \frac{Total\ duration\ of\ neutral\ utterance(sec.)}{Total\ duration\ of\ target\ utterance(sec.)} \qquad (2)$$

An α value greater than 1 implies speeding up the speech and that less than 1 refers to slowing down. A 40 ms Hamming window was used for the analysis with analysis frame shift of 10 ms. Maximum frame offset (δ_{max}) parameter was set as 5 ms.

4 The time scaled utterance after WSOLA is subjected to Dynamic Time Warping along with target utterance to time align the two signals. Let the utterance after WSOLA is represented as S(n). Inter-emotion conversion necessitates the time alignment between source and target utterance. DTW algorithm matches the speech patterns, represented by the sequences of vectors (y_1, y_2, . . . , y_n) and(s_1, s_2, . . . , s_m), where each vector Y_i represents target emotional speech pattern and S_j corresponds to the pattern after time scaling by WSOLA for i^{th} and j^{th} frames, respectively. The two patterns are compared using inter-vector distance through dynamic programming. The minimum distance to any (i, j) is given by Eq. 3 [10] as:

$$D_m(i,j) = d(i,j) + min\{d(i-1,j), d(i-1,j-1), d(i,j-1)\} \qquad (3)$$

where d(i, j) is inter-pattern vector distance between target and time scaled utterances.

5 Dynamic Time Warped utterances are subjected to Linear prediction analysis. The WSOLA scaled utterance is analysed to yield LP coefficients. The target pattern is subjected to LP analysis and subsequent inverse filtering to yield LP residual. Burg's lattice method is used for finding out the coefficients corresponding to vocal tract in both cases [13]. A prediction order of 16 is used, with 25 ms window length and 5 ms window shift. The pre-emphasis frequency is set at 50 Hz.

6 The target is subjected to LP analysis to yield the residual with pitch information embedded in it.

7 Autocorrelation based pitch detection is carried out on both source and target speech segments and pitch modification factor to be applied on the source residual is computed by taking ratio between average pitch period.

8 The source residual is re-sampled using pitch factor obtained and target residual to yield prosody modified residual.

9 Manipulated residual from output signal obtained after WSOLA is subjected to LP synthesis using source LPCs to yield the synthesised emotional utterance.

4   Results and Discussion

The results obtained in all cases showed a good correlation to original target perceptually. The pitch contours for each of the expressions were compared after synthesis using proposed algorithm. The results obtained by using proposed algorithm is compared with that obtained using TD-PSOLA algorithm for pitch and time scaling. Figures 3 and 4 give the comparison of pitch contours in both cases. For evaluating the performance of the proposed algorithm over the existing

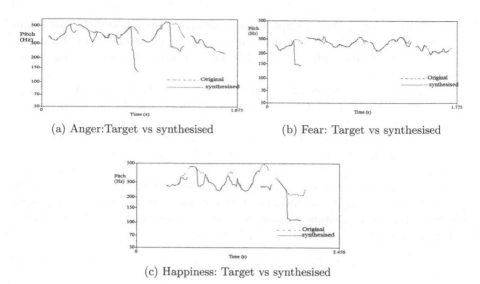

(a) Anger:Target vs synthesised   (b) Fear: Target vs synthesised

(c) Happiness: Target vs synthesised

Fig. 3. Comparison of pitch contours for each converted emotion: in each case, dotted plot represents pitch contour of target and bold line indicates that of synthesised target. It is seen that the synthesised contour closely follows the target

PSOLA based technique, several objective and subjective metrics were considered. In each utterance, Mean Square Error was calculated using Eq. 4 for various combinations of speakers for each emotion.

$$MSE = \sum_k \frac{|x_k - y_k|^2}{N} \tag{4}$$

where x_k represents F0 value of kth target utterance and y_k represents the same for synthesised utterance using proposed algorithm. N represents the number of elements in the sum matrix. From Fig. 5, it can be seen that the highest values were obtained for anger emotion while fear yielded maximum samplewise similarity to target.

Another useful metric for determining the similarity between two utterances is correlation coefficient. In our work, we have used Pearson's correlation coefficient ($\gamma_{x,y}$)(Eq. 5) as an objective measure for contemplating on the accuracy of conversion.

$$\gamma_{x,y} = \frac{covariance(x, y)}{\sigma_x \sigma_y}, covariance(x, y) = \frac{|(x_k - \mu_x)(y_k - \mu_y)|}{N} \tag{5}$$

where $\sigma_x, \sigma_y, \mu_x, \mu_y$ denote the standard deviations and means of selected parameters of target and synthesised utterances, N is the number of observed values in each case. The correlation between utterances for each emotion generated using the proposed algorithm for each speaker has been calculated and plotted in Fig. 6. It is observed that maximum correlation has been obtained for fear in

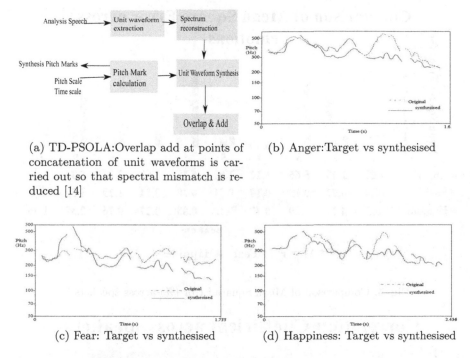

(a) TD-PSOLA:Overlap add at points of concatenation of unit waveforms is carried out so that spectral mismatch is reduced [14]

(b) Anger:Target vs synthesised

(c) Fear: Target vs synthesised

(d) Happiness: Target vs synthesised

Fig. 4. An implementation of PSOLA algorithm is carried out as in Fig. 4(a) [14] and pitch contours have been plotted. PSOLA necessitates pitch marking for analysis using knowledge of epochs which are instants of glottal closure. Synthesis pitch marks are derived from analysis pitch marks by using pitch and time scaling factors provided to the algorithm. Scaling factors are obtained by taking ratio between mean values of F0 and duration of neutral and target utterances. In each case, dotted plot represents pitch contour of target and bold line indicates that of synthesised target using TD-PSOLA algorithm

most cases which coincides with the mean square error trend. Also, speakers 1, 2, 3, 5 and 7 are female while the remaining (4, 6, 8, 9, 10) are male. As per the correlation results, male speech yielded better similarity than female ones. This is because as pitch values are higher in females, extreme variations of modification factors led to higher distortion in voice quality. Correlation coefficient was calculated to estimate the similarity between utterances. Table 1 reflects the results. Fundamental frequency (F_0) was chosen as the parameter for comparison.

From Table 1, it can be noted that in all cases, the correlation between fundamental frequency values is higher for speech synthesised using proposed algorithm than that using TD-PSOLA. In contrast to the findings above, the correlation with respect to fundamental frequency is found to be higher for anger by more than 90% as compared to PSOLA. This is due to the fact that the conversion was based on manipulating the residual with the pitch factor calculated

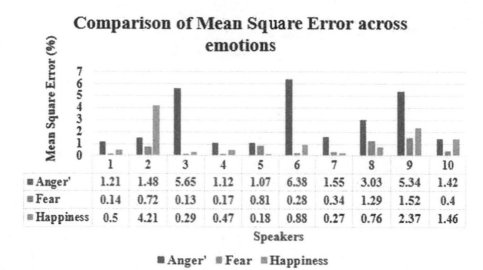

Fig. 5. Comparison of Mean Square Error (%) across speakers

	1	2	3	4	5	6	7	8	9	10
■ Anger'	1.21	1.48	5.65	1.12	1.07	6.38	1.55	3.03	5.34	1.42
■ Fear	0.14	0.72	0.13	0.17	0.81	0.28	0.34	1.29	1.52	0.4
■ Happiness	0.5	4.21	0.29	0.47	0.18	0.88	0.27	0.76	2.37	1.46

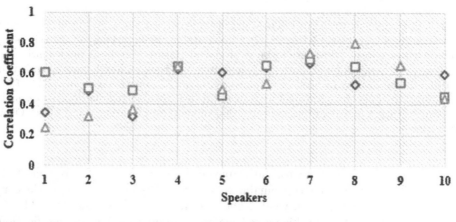

Fig. 6. Comparison of correlation coefficients across speakers

using autocorrelation. An average improvement of 60% is obtained across all three emotions considered.

A better perspective on the perceptual quality of emotional speech synthesis is obtained by conducting a subjective evaluation. For this purpose, 30 speech samples, each of original target, synthesised emotion using proposed algorithm and that using TD-PSOLA were selected for anger, fear and happiness.

Table 1. Comparison of Correlation Co-efficients using F_0 as parameter

Emotion	Algorithm	Correlation Coefficient ($\gamma_{x,y}$)	Improvement (%)
Anger	Proposed	0.79	92.68
	TD-PSOLA	0.41	
Fear	Proposed	0.98	58.06
	TD-PSOLA	0.62	
Happiness	Proposed	0.55	27.91
	TD-PSOLA	0.43	

Table 2. Ranking scale description for perception test

Perceptual similarity with target	Similarity score
Closely similar	5
Some-what similar	4
Sounds little different, little similar	3
some-what different	2
Very much different/no similarity	1

The listening test was conducted in Robotic Research Lab with 11 participants in the age group of 18–30. Table 2 gives the ranking scale used for judging the perception quality of utterances. From the perception experiments conducted, Comparison Mean Opinion Scores (CMOS) were found to be better for proposed method than PSOLA in all cases as in Fig. 7. Listeners experienced difficulty in perceiving the target emotion itself from the database in some cases. Anger showed maximum similarity index as opposed to the objective perception experiments. As anger is associated with higher pitch and intensity, it was easier for the listeners to associate it to the target. A subjective evaluation of database revealed an average CMOS of 3.46, 3.5 and 2.6 for original anger, fear and happiness respectively. The results from objective and subjective evaluations show a promising trend towards generating better expressiveness in speech by using computationally simple signal processing techniques. The most important challenge to be addressed here is that the conversion process requires parallel source-target data and is text dependent. Objective results are better than PSOLA as spectral characteristics are also modified by analysing the target residual. F_0 feature showed highest improvement(evident from Fig. 3 and Table 1) as pitch factor was incorporated into source residual prior to re-synthesis. Correlation factors for fear and happiness can be improved if the database used can depict these emotions with finer details like voice quality.

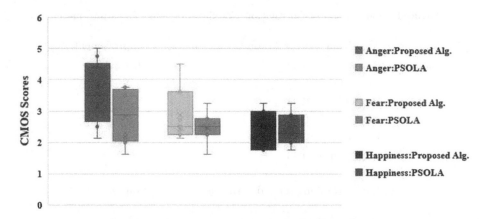

Fig. 7. Subjective comparison based on CMOS obtained for each converted emotion

5   Conclusion

A technique for emotion conversion using explicit control is experimented and evaluated based on both objective and subjective comparison indices. The strength of the proposed algorithm lies in utilising the waveform similarity aspect of WSOLA for effective transformation of time scale. The spectral enhancement is carried out by linear prediction analysis. Here, manipulation of residual is carried out as it embeds excitation source information critical to the required expression. The algorithm mandates availability of parallel data for source and target utterances for linear prediction. Though objective methods give good correlation between emotional samples, subjective results are less convincing. This points to the possibility of inclusion of perceptual features for distinguishing each expression and developing generalised models without the need for a parallel database.

References

1. Burkhardt, F., Sendilmeier, W.F.: Verification of acoustical correlates of emotional speech using formant synthesis. In: Proceedings of ISCA Workshop on Speech & Emotion, pp. 151–156 (2000)
2. Tao, J., Kang, Y., Li, A.: Prosody conversion from neutral speech to emotional speech. IEEE Trans. Audio, Speech, Lang. Pro. **14**, 1145–1154 (2006)
3. Cabral, J., Oliveira, L.C.: Emovoice: a system to generate emotions in speech. In: Proceedings of INTERSPEECH, 17–21 September, PA, USA, pp. 1798–1801 (2006)
4. Govind, D., Prasanna, S.R.M.: Dynamic prosody modification using zero frequency filtered signal. Int. J. Speech Tech. **16**, 41–54 (2013)
5. Rao, K.S., Vuppala, A.K.: Non-uniform time scale modification using instants of significant excitation and vowel onset points. Speech Comm. **55**, 745–756 (2013)

6. Vuppala, A.K., Kaidiri, S.R.: Neutral to anger speech conversion using non-uniform duration modification. In: Proceedings of 9th International Conference on Industrial and Information Systems (ICIIS), 15–17 December, pp. 1–4 (2014)
7. Vydana, H.K., Raju, V.V.V., Gangashetty, S.V., Vuppala, A.K.: Significance of emotionally significant regions of speech for emotive to neutral conversion. In: Prasath, R., Vuppala, A.K., Kathirvalavakumar, T. (eds.) MIKE 2015. LNCS (LNAI), vol. 9468, pp. 287–296. Springer, Cham (2015). doi:10.1007/978-3-319-26832-3_28
8. Yadav, J., Rao, K.S.: Generation of emotional speech by prosody imposition on sentence, word and syllable level fragments of neutral speech,. In: Proceedings of International Conference on Cognitive Computing and Information Processing (CCIP), 3–4 March. pp. 1–5 (2015)
9. Vydana, H.K., Kadiri, S.R., Vuppala, A.K.: Vowel-based non-uniform prosody modification for emotion conversion. Circuits, Syst., Sig. Proc. **35**(5), 1643–1663 (2016)
10. Vekkot, S., Tripathi, S.: Inter-Emotion conversion using dynamic time warping and prosody imposition. In: Proceedings of 2nd International Symposium on Intelligent Systems, Technologies & Applications, LNMIIT, Jaipur, 21–24 September, pp. 913–924 (2016)
11. Verhelst, W., Roelands, M.: An overlap-add technique based on waveform similarity (WSOLA) for high quality time-scale modification of speech. In: 1993 IEEE International Conference on Acoustics, Speech, and Signal Processing, ICASSP 1993, vol. 2. IEEE (1993)
12. Koolagudi, S.G., Maity, S., Kumar, V.A., Chakrabarti, S., Rao, K.S.: IITKGP-SESC: speech database for emotion analysis. In: Ranka, S., Aluru, S., Buyya, R., Chung, Y.-C., Dua, S., Grama, A., Gupta, S.K.S., Kumar, R., Phoha, V.V. (eds.) IC3 2009. CCIS, vol. 40, pp. 485–492. Springer, Heidelberg (2009). doi:10.1007/978-3-642-03547-0_46
13. Makhoul, J.: Linear prediction: a tutorial review. Proc. IEEE **63**(2), 561–580 (1975). IEEE Press, New York
14. Mourlines, E., Laroche, J.: Non-parametric techniques for pitch-scale and time-scale modification of speech. Speech Commun. **16**, 175–205 (1995)

Voice Conversion for TTS Systems with Tuning on the Target Speaker Based on GMM

Vadim Zahariev[✉], Elias Azarov, and Alexander Petrovsky

Belarusian State University of Informatics and Radioelectronics, Minsk, Belarus
{zahariev, azarov, palex}@bsuir.by

Abstract. The paper is devoted to improving the methods of voice conversion (VC) for developing text-to-speech synthesis systems with capabilities of tuning on the target speaker. Such system with VC module in acoustic processor, parametric representation of speech database for concatenative synthesis based on instantaneous harmonic representation is presented in the paper. Voice conversion is based on multiple regression mapping function and Gaussian mixture model (GMM), the method of text-independent learning is based on hidden Markov models and modified Viterbi algorithm. Experimental evaluation of the proposed solutions in terms of naturalness and similarity is presented as well.

Keywords: Voice conversion · Multivoiced text-to-speech synthesis · GMM · GUSLY · Non-parallel corpora training

1 Introduction

The key question in modern text to speech synthesis (TTS) is not about objective features. It is more about characteristics that are more complex such as the naturalness of synthesized speech, support for multiple languages or capabilities of tuning on the specific speaker – multivoiced text to speech synthesis systems (MVTTS). The last aspect is the most important and interesting to study, especially in the context of designing "Photoshop for Audio" – a tool which will allow transforming original speaker voice characteristics online, as well as creating new voices [1].

State of the art in the text-to-speech synthesis systems ("Amazon Polly", "Ivona", "Google TTS", "Siri") are unit selection based systems with rich speech corpus [2]. Such systems often could not be installed locally, due to requirements of permanent Internet connection, since all language resources used for unit selection procedure take up a large amount of memory and are stored remotely [3, 4]. This fact makes it difficult to use corpus based TTS approach in systems with limited computing and memory capabilities: embedded systems, mobile applications or environments without Internet connection.

From our point of view, for such applications, the relevant considerations are the compilation methods of TTS, which concatenate speech from basic elements (units) of small duration and require significantly less memory for storage of linguistic resources. However, the problem is to achieve an acceptable price/quality ratio. In this context questions of personalization and tuning on the target speaker become

© Springer International Publishing AG 2017
A. Karpov et al. (Eds.): SPECOM 2017, LNAI 10458, pp. 788–798, 2017.
DOI: 10.1007/978-3-319-66429-3_79

particularly important. Various strategies such as multiple databases (for several speakers) or voice conversion technology are used to solve the problem.

Voice conversion is a signal processing technique, which transform voice characteristics of source speaker (SS), contained in speech signal to characteristics of target speaker (TS) without changing the meaning of the message [5]. This procedure is performed using the appropriate conversion function, which maps the feature vectors of the SS voice to the corresponding vectors of TS. Objects of voice conversion function are timbre and prosodic parameters.

The paper presents a multivoiced text-to-speech synthesis system with embedded voice conversion module. The architecture of the system includes speech representation model, multiple regression conversion function based on Gaussian mixtures model (GMM) and text-independent algorithm for training.

2 Parameterization of Acoustic Database for MVTTS

The quality of synthesized speech depends on two main factors: speech database itself and accuracy of compilation (concatenation) procedure. Various audible artifacts can be observed when the concatenation algorithm does not work satisfactorily, or speech database does not contain sufficient set of compilation units. The problem is depicted on Fig. 1, where two adjacent compilation units (phonemes, allophones) are plotted. It is easy to see that compared to a smooth transition in natural speech signal a gap (Fig. 1a) occurs between the elements in the range of synthesized signal (Fig. 1b), which leads to audible artifacts. Such distortions become particularly pronounced while using compilation algorithms that fail to account these errors. It can be noted that such phenomenon is difficult to capture, analyze and manage in the time domain.

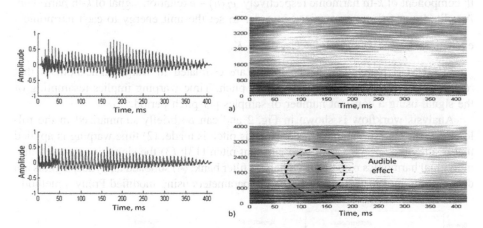

Fig. 1. Audible effects during speech synthesis compilation: a – smooth transition between units in natural speech; b – audible artifacts between units in synthetic speech

In a number of works [6, 7] various approaches are suggested for improving concatenative and unit selection synthesis processes. The most comprehensive review is presented in paper [8]. Basically, the authors propose different special cost functions for solving the problem of choosing the most suitable compilation unit.

In this paper, we focus on the methods of digital signal processing and parametric representation of units in order to attenuate the artifacts. We assume that it is easier to perform compilation and interpolation operations in model parameters space, than implement algorithms that operate in the time domain with raw samples or even doing smoothing in the frequency domain with Fourier, MFCC or LSF coefficients.

Recently, hybrid models of signal representation have become widespread. Among the popular models, we can take out harmonic plus noise model (HNM) [9], STRAIGHT [10], amplitude modulated-frequency modulated speech model with quadratic phase splines and a super-fast cosine generator (VOCAINE) [11].

We use a model based on GUSLY framework [12], that uses an original model of voiced speech, which represents each harmonic as a multicomponent function and provides high quality processing in conditions of partial glottalization.

In GUSLY voiced and mixed excitations are considered as a quasi-periodic process with constant pitch. The pitch period determines how many harmonics are distinguished with the model. The model considers each of them as a multicomponent function and represents signal (n) as:

$$s(n) = \sum_{k=1}^{K} G_k(n) \sum_{c=1}^{C} A_k^c(n) \cos\left(f_k^c n + \varphi_k^c(0)\right) = \sum_{k=1}^{K} G_k(n) e_k(n), \qquad (1)$$

where $G_k(n)$ is a gain factor specified by the spectral envelope, C – number of sinusoidal components for each harmonic, f_k^c and $\varphi_k^c(0)$ – frequency and initial phase of c-th component of k-th harmonic respectively, $e_k(n)$ – excitation signal of k-th harmonic. Amplitudes $A_k^c(n)$ are normalized in order to set the unit energy to each harmonic's excitation: $\frac{1}{2}\sum_{c=1}^{C}\left[A_c^k(n)\right]^2 = 1$ for $k = 1, \ldots, K$.

In GUSLY parameters of the model are estimated in warped-time domain that requires prior estimation of instantaneous pitch. Time warping implies resampling of the signal using a constant number of samples per pitch period.

Analysis workflow is shown in Fig. 2 and can be briefly summarized in the following way: (1) estimation of instantaneous pitch is made; (2) time warping is applied that results in a speech signal with constant pitch [13]; (3) the signal is separated into individual harmonics using a DFT analysis filter bank; (4) subband analytical signals are decomposed into instantaneous harmonic parameters using modified Prony's method.

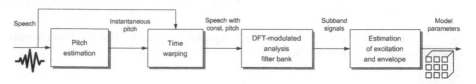

Fig. 2. Speech parameterization with GUSLY framework

The output signal is synthesized using the same functional blocks applied in reverse order as shown in Fig. 3: (1) subband signals are synthesized using (1); the sample rate of the signals varies with target (modified) instantaneous pitch; (2) DFT synthesis filter bank is applied which performs antialiasing filtering of each harmonic component (the subband signals are decimated in order to reduce overall computational cost); (3) inverse time warping is applied to form target pitch contour. Detailed description of the framework along with performance analysis is given in [14].

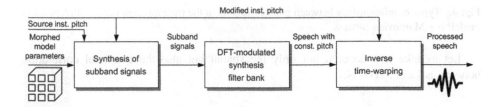

Fig. 3. Signal synthesis with GUSLY framework

3 Voice Conversion with Gaussian Mixture Models for MVTTS

To configure multivoiced speech synthesizer on the target speaker is necessary to choose conversion function and training procedure. The most common paradigms in voice conversion researches now are statistical modeling commonly based on Gaussian mixtures models (GMM) and artificial neural networks (ANN) [15]. Statistical methods have relatively less performance than heuristic models like ANN, but for training procedure they require less computational resources, which is quite important in the context of the application for embedded systems.

Conversion function, taken as a core in our work [16] is based on a linear regression model of the first order, using as their coefficients GMM parameters obtained during the training phase. This function has proven their effectiveness especially when compared with approaches based on hard clustering parameter space [15]. However, a detailed analysis identifies a number of shortcomings. At first the complexity of choice the relevant order of GMM. Inadequate growth of model complexity leads to over smoothing problem. Second shortcoming is connected with a very simple first-order regression function that has limited prediction ability. Statistical relationships are present between only one pair of vectors in each i-th time (Fig. 4a).

Model considers only the spatial correlation between the vectors of parameters, excluding the fact that the parameters of the speech signal does not change rapidly after instantaneous analysis, and have some properties of Markov process. Given this observations we suggest an extended conventional regression function, with multiple factors obtained from GMM coefficient of parameters space (Fig. 4b).

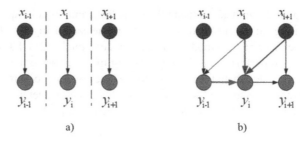

Fig. 4. Types of relationships between pairs of vectors of the training sequence: a – independent model; b – Markovian process

Let us take into account not only the spatial but also the continual correlation between adjacent vectors:

$$y_i = \sum_{q=1}^{Q} p_q(x_i, y_{i-1}, x_{i+1})[\mu_q + \Phi_q \bar{x}_i^q + \Psi_q \bar{y}_{i-1}^q + \Omega_q \bar{x}_{i+1}^q],$$

where i – frame number $i = 1,...,T$, q – number of GMM mixture $q = 1,...,Q$, $x = [x_1, x_2, ..., x_T]^T$, $y = [y_1, y_2, ..., y_T]^T$ – the sequence of parameter vectors of the SS and TS $x_j, y_j \in \mathbb{R}^{1 \times p}$, p – the dimension of the parameter vector, $p_q(x_i, y_{i-1}, x_{i+1})$ – posteriori probability that the input vectors x_i and y_{i-1} and x_{i+1} belongs to q-th Gaussian component, $\mu_q = [\mu_1, \mu_2, ..., \mu_Q]^T$ – vector of the expectations for each component of the mixture of TS $\mu_q \in \mathbb{R}^{1 \times p}$, $\Phi = [\Phi_1, \Phi_2, ..., \Phi_Q]^T$ – the matrix of regression coefficients for all components of the mixture at variable independent variable x_i $\Psi_j \in \mathbb{R}^{p \times p}$, $\Psi = [\Psi_1, \Psi_2, ..., \Psi_Q]^T$ – the matrix of regression coefficients for all components of the mixture of first predictor variable y_{i-1} $\Psi_j \in \mathbb{R}^{p \times p}$, $\Omega = [\Omega_1, \Omega_2, ..., \Omega_Q]^T$ – the matrix of regression coefficients for all components of second predictor variable x_{i+1} $\Omega_j \in \mathbb{R}^{p \times p}$. Then the problem of finding the unknown parameters $\{\mu, \Phi, \Psi, \Omega\}$ is formulated as optimization problem, the solution of which could be found by the least squares method. The weight of the component can be found from the following expression:

$$p_q(x) = \frac{\alpha_q \mathcal{N}(x, \mu_q^x, \Sigma_q^{xx})}{\sum_{j=1}^{M} \alpha_j \mathcal{N}(x, \mu_j^x, \Sigma_j^{xx})},$$

where x – features vector of the source speaker, M – number of component mixture, μ_q^x – expectations vector of the q-th component of the mixture, Σ_q^{xx} – covariance matrix of the source speaker of the q-th component, $p_q(x)$ – posteriori probability vector of x component, $\mathcal{N}$ – multivariate Gaussian distribution. To determine the coefficients of the conversion function, we use the expectation maximization (EM) algorithm, which is based on the iterative calculation of maximum likelihood estimates. To compare the effectiveness of the proposed method, a number of experiments were conducted. Standart statisitical models from [15] where compered with multifactor regression model.

The results are shown in Table 1, where LRM – linear regression model, GMM – joint-density GMM, GMM* – multi factor GMM (proposed). The predecessor model

Table 1. Experimental results for determination coefficient (R^2) of regression VC models

Voice conversion function type		Number of mix. components (diag Σ) test item description							
		16	24	32	64	80	90	100	128
R^2	LRM [15]	0,45	0,57	0,68	0,74	0,74	0,77	0,76	0,74
	GMM [15]	0,47	0,64	0,67	0,75	0,75	0,79	0,78	0,76
	GMM*	0,46	0,62	0,71	0,79	0,78	0,81	0,82	0,79

shows the best results for a number of mixtures exceeding 64 components. During the experiment, diagonal covariance matrices were used. The essence of voice conversion framework in details is considered in work [17].

4 Text-Independent Training Procedure for MVTTS

To find parameters of GMM distribution and conversion function coefficients a training phase is required. Training can be carried out on the basis of text-independent and text-dependent approaches [15]. The key advantage of last approach is the convenience

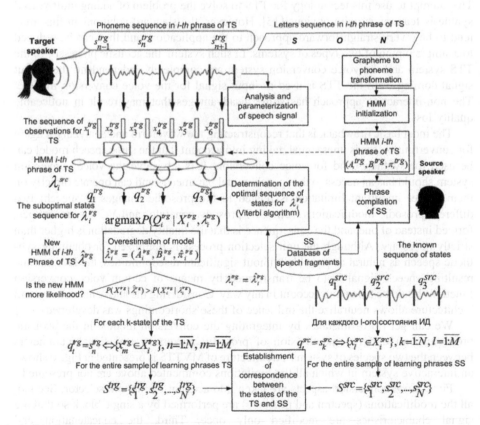

Fig. 5. Text-independent training process in MVTTS

and ease of customization of the system with this type of tuning. In our approach it is not required to record certain corpus of training phrases. The proposed method of text-independent training is based on HMM and Viterbi algorithm (Fig. 5) [18].

User could use any available phonograms, for example but with transcript that could be non-synchronized. Such as interviews, podcasts or programs. The only limitation of the proposed solution is that a text description of the speech material is necessary. However, it is need not be synchronized with speech, for example as subtitles.

Proposed scheme of training involves extensive use of linguistic units TTS to undertake the following stages: normalization of the text, its syntax, morphological processing, phonemic transcription, as well as further accessed synchronization markup phonemic phonogram target speaker based on data obtained from SS, i.e. speech synthesizer. This fact gives the opportunity to subsequently convert phonemic recognition task units in the flow of speech audio synchronization task and phonetic markup and text blocks with a speech synthesizer. A detailed description of the method could be found in [19].

5   Architecture of MVTTS

The attempt to use this technology for TTS to solve the problem of adding multivoiced synthesis features is quite obvious [15]. However, the standard solutions in this area, tend to be a very straightforward approach to the application, and they can be reduced to a simple piping of two types of systems. In such system, the acoustic processor of the TTS system and the voice conversion system are completely independent: the output signal coming from the TTS is used as input signal for the voice conversion module. The non-interactive approach has some disadvantages that may result in noticeable quality loss.

The most basic drawback is that reconstructing the waveform and analyzing it again for converting voices is unessential, taking into account that the same speech model can be used for synthesis and for voice conversion. It is advisable the voice conversion system should has an access to the speech model parameters and can operate directly on them. Other important limitation is related to the prosodic changes of speech: two different prosodic modifications from TTS prosody generator and VC system are performed instead of one, and the consequence is that the quality degradation is higher than strictly necessary. Although the unit selection process is optimized for obtaining synthetic speech as natural as possible without significant discontinuities, the fact that the resulting speech signal is to be transformed by means of certain voice conversion function should be taken into account in any way. Considering the above nuances system architecture allows neutralize the influence of these shortcomings was developed.

We can get rid of mistakes by integrating the conversion module in the acoustic processor unit and rational division of prosody conversion and signal parameters between the two species of systems. Architecture of MVTTS is presented in Fig. 6 shows an interactive system in which all the limitations commented above are not presented.

First, voice conversion aspects are taken into account by the unit selector. Second, all the modifications (spectral and prosodic) are performed by a single block so that the signal characteristics are modified only once. Third, the concatenation and

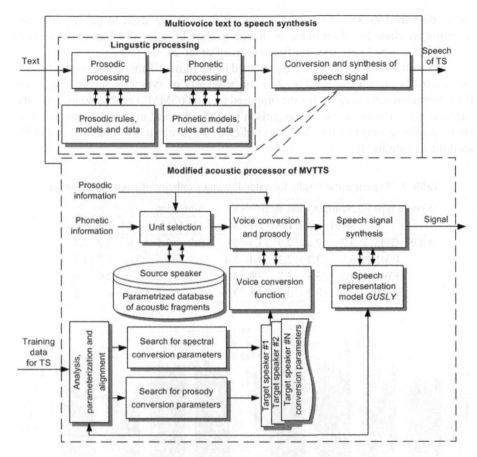

Fig. 6. Architecture of the multivoiced TTS

reconstruction of the synthetic speech signal are performed after having converted the source voice into the target voice.

6   Experimental Results

To assess the effectiveness of the suggested methods as a part of MVTTS system, series of tests to characterize the intelligibility and naturalness were performed. For evaluations mean opinion scores method (MOS) was used.

Experiments were conducted on phonetically balanced set of phrases, including 200 audio recordings of the same proposals for four speakers: two men and two women. In further experiments male speakers conditionally designated as M letter, and female speakers as F letter, respectively. The average duration of one phrase was 5–6 s. The audio files were encoded in wav format, 16000 kHz sample rate and bit depth of 16 bit.

The size of the test sample was twenty phrases that are not included in the training set. Signal analysis and synthesis was produced using GUSLY signal representation model described in Sect. 2. After analyzing the signal was used to parameterize the spectrum envelope based on linear prediction method by using the filter coefficients in the form of vector linear spectral frequencies of order 24.

The results of the experiment are presented in the form of Table 2 and histograms for characteristics of naturalness (Fig. 7-a) and similarity of synthesis speech (Fig. 7-b). Experimental results suggest that the proposed method (GMM*) enables to improve the characteristics of naturalness in comparison with the classical method of conversion on the basis of an average of 10% MOS according to the parameters of naturalness and 5% according to similarity.

Table 2. Experimental results for naturality and similarity of suggested solution

System type		Naturality test item					Similarity				
		M-M	M-F	F-M	F-F	Mean	M-M	M-F	F-M	F-F	Mean
MOS	GMM	3,2	2,6	2,9	3,3	3,0	3,7	3,5	3,6	3,9	3,7
	GMM*	3,5	3,2	3,3	3,4	3,4	3,7	3,6	3,6	3,7	3,7
	FW	4,3	3,3	3,7	3,8	3,8	2,7	2,2	2,8	2,6	2,6
	ANN	3,6	3,7	3,7	4,1	3,8	3,8	3,4	3,8	4,3	3,8

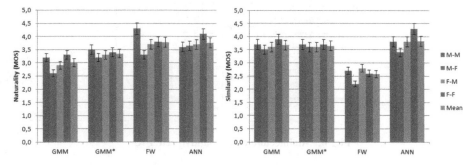

Fig. 7. Quality marks (MOS): a – naturality; b – similarity

Also according to the similarity parameter, this method comes short of approach based on frequency warping (FW) and artificial neural networks (ANN) [15]. This fact can be explained by the fact that proposed method (GMM*) allows to get a stronger, less than the average (more natural) representation of spectral envelope as a result of conversion, while classical statistical techniques (GMM) can significantly average this feature. However, according to degree of similarity, the proposed method exceeds the standard method based on frequency warping and only is slightly inferior to the method based on artificial neural networks, the listed methods in the process of achieving great simplicity in training and fewer resources on preparations. High performance of latest justified by a nonlinear mapping displaying features, but require a preliminary design of a neural network and its learning algorithm selection.

7 Conclusion

The paper investigates the issues of multivoiced speech synthesis systems implementation using concatenation approach. The system architecture includes modified acoustic processor with integrated voice conversion module. To avoid gaps during compilation phase, reduce errors in time of analysis-synthesis and VC transformation stages speech representation model GUSLY was applied. Speech units database were parameterized in the same way. New multifactor regression conversion function with GMM parameterization allowed to take into account the Markov process in the sequence of parameters vector of the speech signal. Text-independent training on HMM and Viterbi algorithm were developed. The proposed solutions have shown their effectiveness in performance in comparison with the known approaches.

Acknowledgment. This work was supported by IT4YOU company (Moscow, Russian Federation).

References

1. Sebastian, A.: Adobe demos "photoshop for audio," lets you edit speech as easily as text. In Ars Technika, electronic resource (2016). https://goo.gl/yCkGyp
2. McTear, M., Callejas, Z., Griol, D.: The Conversational Interface: Talking to Smart Devices. Springer, Switzerland (2016)
3. Dutoit, T.: An Introduction to Text-to-Speech Synthesis. Springer, Netherlands (2013)
4. Taylor, P.: Text-to-Speech Synthesis. Cambridge University Press, Cambridge (2009)
5. Shikano, K., Lee, K., Reddy, R.: Speaker adaptation through vector quantization. In: ICASSP 1986, Japan, Tokyo, pp. 231–237 (1986)
6. Klabbers, E., Veldhuis, R.: Reducing audible spectral discontinuities. IEEE Trans. Speech Audio Process. 9(1), 39–51 (2001)
7. Vepa, J., King, S.: Subjective evaluation of join cost and smoothing methods for unit selection speech synthesis. IEEE Trans. Audio Speech Lang. Process. 14(5), 1763–1771 (2006)
8. Kirkpatrick, B., O'Brien, D., Scaife, R.: Feature transformation applied to the detection of discontinuities in concatenated speech. In: SSW6-2007, pp. 17–21 (2007)
9. Stylianou, Y.: Applying the harmonic plus noise model in concatenative speech synthesis. IEEE Trans. Speech Audio Process. 9(1), 21–29 (2001)
10. Kawahara, H.: STRAIGHT, exploitation of the other aspect of VOCODER: perceptually isomorphic decomposition of speech sounds. Acoust. Sci. Technol. 27(6), 349–353 (2006)
11. Agiomyrgiannakis, Y.: Vocaine the vocoder and applications in speech synthesis. In: ICASSP 2015, Brisbane, Australia, pp. 4230–4234, April 2015
12. Azarov, E., Vashkevich, M., Petrovsky, A.: Instantaneous harmonic representation of speech using multicomponent sinusoidal excitation. In: INTERSPEECH-2013, Lyon, France, pp. 1697–1701 (2013)
13. Nilsson, M., Resch, B., Kim, M-Y., Kleijn, W.B.: A canonical representation of speech. In: ICASSP-2007, Honolulu, USA, pp. 849–852, April 2007
14. Azarov, E., Vashkevich, M., Petrovsky, A.: Guslar: a framework for automated singing voice correction. In: ICASSP-2014, Florence, Italy, pp. 7919–7923 (2014)

15. Mohammadi, S.H., Kain, A.: An overview of voice conversion systems. Speech Commun. **88**, 65–82 (2017)
16. Stylinau, Y.: Continuous probabilistic transform for voice conversion. IEEE Trans. Speech Audio Process. **6**, 131–142 (1998)
17. Zahariev, V., Petrovsky, A.: Voice conversion based on GMM with multifactor regression function and spectral weighting. Speech Technol. **3**, 40–54 (2014)
18. Rabiner, L.: Fundamentals of Speech Recognition. Printice Hall, United States (1993)
19. Zahariev, V., Petrovsky, A.: Text-independent learning in the voice conversion system based on hidden Markov models and the grapheme-to-phoneme conversion scheme. In: DSPA-2013, Moscow Russia, pp. 327–332, March 2013

VoiScan: Telephone Voice Analysis for Health and Biometric Applications

Ladan Baghai-Ravary and Steve W. Beet$^{(\boxtimes)}$

Aculab plc, Bramley Road, Milton Keynes MK1 1PT, UK
{ladan.ravary,steve.beet}@aculab.com

Abstract. The telephone, whether mobile, landline, or VoIP, is probably the most widely used form of long-distance communication. The most common use of voice biometrics is in telephone-based speaker verification, so the ability to operate effectively over the telephone is crucial. Similarly, access to vocal health monitoring, and other voice analysis technology, would benefit enormously if it were available over the telephone, via an automatic system. This paper describes a set of voice analysis algorithms, designed to be robust against the kinds of distortion and signal degradation encountered in modern telephone communication. The basis of the algorithms in traditional analysis is discussed, as are the design choices made in order to ensure robustness. The utility of these algorithms is demonstrated in a number of target domains.

Keywords: Voice analysis · Robust algorithms · Tele-health voice analysis · Voice bio-markers · Voice biometrics · Telephone speaker verification

1 Introduction

1.1 Voice Analysis

Many characteristics of a subject's voice can be measured and quantified. Speech and Language Therapists (SLTs) tend to rely on subjective measures based around concepts such as "breathiness" and "hoarseness" [1–3], while biometric systems concentrate on parameters with a more precisely defined mathematical formulation (most notably various forms of "Cepstral Coefficients") [4–6].

Some voice analysis is applied to sustained phonations (saying "aa", "ee" or "oo") to characterise conditions affecting voice production by the vocal folds, while other sounds, or natural speech, may be used to investigate articulatory or other speech disorders [7].

Considerable research has been performed on automating acoustic measurements in a form useful to SLTs, while conversely, there have also been many attempts to incorporate mathematical correlates of the SLTs' measurements into biometric applications. However of these techniques only operate well on high quality recordings.

© Springer International Publishing AG 2017
A. Karpov et al. (Eds.): SPECOM 2017, LNAI 10458, pp. 799–808, 2017.
DOI: 10.1007/978-3-319-66429-3_80

1.2   Telephone Speech

When speech is collected over the telephone, whether for voice analysis or speaker verification purposes, there are many forms of distortion and degradation in signal quality. There are three main causes:

- Human Factors: subjects rarely hold the handset in the best, or even a constant, position; they may speak too early or too late; there may be other speakers or noises in the background; they may have an extreme accent or cognitive issues which reduce the quality of the recording.
- Hardware Issues: many telephone handsets include quite poor quality analogue circuitry, causing a loss of some frequencies and distortion of others, while others may have audio enhancement such as echo suppression, noise cancellation, or dynamic range compression. All of these can interfere with the correct operation of voice analysis algorithms.
- Network/Codec Issues: analogue telephone networks suffer from restricted bandwidth, hybrid echoes, line noise and other distortions, while digital networks suffer from packet loss and codec distortion (which can vary dramatically within a single call if an adaptive codec switches between data rates in response to network congestion, for example). The sample rate used in the public telephone network also severely limits the bandwidth of the speech signal.

1.3   Sensitivity of Traditional Parameters

To demonstrate the sensitivity of standard algorithms to the nature of the communication channel, we collected a small database of simultaneous high-quality audio recordings and genuine telephone calls, including examples of sustained phonation and spoken sentences[1].

High quality recordings were used to define a baseline against which to compare simulated and real telephone signals. We refer to this type of signal as "hq". The bandwidth-limiting effects of an analogue telephone line were then simulated by resampling the hq signal to 8 kHz, removing frequencies below 250 Hz with a simple 2nd-order filter, and encoding the signal using a-law compression. We refer to this as the "hq-landline" signal.

To replicate some of the effects of mobile phone transmission, we further processed the hq-landline signal by encoding it with a simple GSM encoder, giving the "hq-mobile" signal.

The final signal, that obtained from the simultaneous telephone network recording, was used unaltered and is referred to as the "pq" (phone quality) signal.

---

[1] The database included 7 speakers, each speaking 2 sustained phonations and a number of sentences taken from "The Rainbow Passage", totalling over 5 min of speech. Simultaneous recordings were made: one using a high quality microphone, sampled at 44.1 kHz and encoded using 16 bit PCM, and the other over a standard telephone line, with the handset held in a natural position, chosen by the speaker. The recordings were all processed with an automatic phoneme alignment system, but the resulting labels were not used in this paper.

These signals were analysed using the Praat [8] "Voice Report" function. This yields estimates of many parameters including mean pitch, jitter, shimmer, and Noise-to-Harmonics Ratio (NHR).

For each parameter, the Pearson R^2 correlation (the coefficient of determination) was calculated with respect to the hq baseline. Pearson R^2 values were used in order to allow for different measurement scales, and thus to allow meaningful comparisons between different parameterisations and different algorithms. Three obvious "outliers" were omitted from the analysis: one was the result of an error in the Praat APQ5 shimmer analysis, while the other two were due to the Praat NHR estimate.

The mean pitch was almost identical in all the signals ($R^2 > 0.9999$), but the other parameters were affected to varying degrees (some of the most widely used Praat parameters are included in Table 1).

Table 1. Pearson R^2 values for Praat parameters of sustained phonations, compared with simultaneous hq (high quality) recordings

Signal type	Mean pitch	Absolute jitter	APQ5 shimmer	NHR
hq-landline	1.0000	0.9969	0.8516	0.9378
hq-mobile	1.0000	0.9185	0.9657	0.8483
pq	1.0000	0.9944	0.7914	0.7860

The Praat parameters related to timing (pitch and jitter) are maintained relatively accurately ($R^2 > 0.99$, except for jitter measured on the hq-mobile signals, $R^2 = 0.9185$), while those related to signal amplitudes (shimmer and NHR) are more sensitive to distortion and extraneous noise, especially when a real telephone is used ($R^2 < 0.8$). The other Praat parameters calculated in the "Voice Report" followed a similar pattern.

1.4   Robust Estimation

For many subjective measures, there have been attempts to find automatic methods to generate parameters which are correlated with human evaluations of recorded speech, as reported on scales such as GRBAS and Cape-V. However there has always been some doubt about the use of human-generated baselines in this respect. Some researchers have found a strong correlation within and between individual SLTs' scoring, while others have reported the opposite.

The situation is further complicated by the fact that many SLTs and voice specialists have developed their own variants of the standard scales and assessment procedures, in order to find a system which works well for them.

This lack of a reliable baseline has led us to devise a parameter set with a greater emphasis on the ability to make reliable measurements over the telephone, rather than precisely emulating a specific SLT's evaluation.

Thus we have developed a number of voice analysis algorithms so as to provide a set of measurements which, taken together, will provide a comprehensive parametric description of the speaker's voice and speech, and to do so reliably, even in the presence of distortions due to the use of imperfect telephone channels. These "VoiScan" measurements, or subsets thereof, could be applied in applications ranging from tele-health to speaker verification and forensics.

2 VoiScan Parameters

It is not possible to describe each individual parameter in detail in this paper, but the general principles we have followed, are outlined below:

The pitch and related parameters are calculated using an autocorrelation-based pitch detector, operating on the instantaneous power envelope. By using the power envelope rather than the waveform itself, sensitivity to wide-band noise is minimised.

Similarly, formants and measures of speech dynamics are estimated from an unbiased, non-parametric, power spectrum estimator, which is less sensitive to noise and distortion than (for example) the linear prediction analysis often used for formant tracking.

The algorithms maintain their robustness by (wherever possible) delaying "hard" decisions regarding features of the speech signal [9], or avoiding them completely. Instead, parameter estimates are based on regression curves or weighted averages. The effects of individual values are reduced by performing the regression or weighted averaging over as many samples as possible (the whole of an utterance, or the length of a continuous section of voiced speech, for example).

Weightings are chosen to suit each parameter individually, and to reflect the likelihood that the value is accurate, and thus improve numerical stability.

The results in Table 2 demonstrate that the respective VoiScan parameters are robust, with the only R^2 value below 0.97 being that for the measurement of shimmer in the real telephone recording. The other parameters described in Sects. 2.1 to 2.4 are similar, although obviously there is some variation, especially within the more experimental Articulatory/Dynamics Parameters of Sect. 2.4.

Table 2. Pearson R^2 values for robust VoiScan parameters of sustained phonations, compared with simultaneous hq (high quality) recordings

Signal	Pitch	Jitter	Shimmer	NHR
hq-landline	1.0000	0.9730	0.9828	0.9982
hq-mobile	1.0000	0.9701	0.9848	0.9985
pq	1.0000	0.9722	0.8247	0.9852

Nonetheless we have conducted informal experiments which show a Pearson R^2 value above 0.9 for the major VoiScan parameters, with respect to the Praat equivalents (Table 3, below). In the case of the mean pitch, R^2 was in excess of 0.9999.

Only the jitter value in Table 3 is lower than the corresponding values in the "pq" row of Table 1, indicating that the other VoiScan parameters are closer to the "industry-standard" Praat analysis of the hq recordings, than Praat analysis of the same signals recorded over a real telephone network.

Table 3. Pearson R^2 values for robust VoiScan parameters of high quality recordings of sustained phonations, compared with values derived using Praat

Pitch	Jitter	Shimmer	NHR
1.0000	0.9027	0.9209	0.9007

The most informative parameters we have devised thus far, are listed below. They can be divided into four broad groups: Temporal Parameters, Voice Source Parameters, Vocal Tract Parameters, and Articulatory/Dynamics Parameters.

2.1   Temporal Parameters

These parameters summarise information about the whole of an utterance, in terms of the timing of voiced intervals within the utterance.

Response time: The elapsed time between the start of the recording and the start of detected speech. If this is unusually long, then the speaker may not have heard or understood any instructions for some reason, or have other cognitive issues.

Active duration: The total duration from the start to the end of detected speech. If this is very short or very long, the speech may have been mis-detected or the speaker may not have complied with their instructions.

Total breaks: The number of pitch discontinuities in the voicing of the detected speech. Too many breaks during sustained phonation may simply indicate a poor quality mobile phone line, but can also indicate medical issues such as dysphoria.

Analysed interval: The duration of the segment of the signal subjected to detailed analysis. For sustained phonation this represents the longest continuously voiced interval. For other analyses, it is the total duration of all the voiced segments.

2.2   Voice Source Parameters

Most of these parameters characterise the voice source (the lungs, the vocal folds and the other structures within the larynx). They can be indicative of both physiological and neurological disorders.

Pitch: The mean fundamental frequency of the voiced speech. An unusually low pitch is often associated with increased levels of Creakiness (below).

Pitch (standard deviation): A measure of the range of fundamental frequencies observed during the analysed segment. A low value during sustained phonation indicates that the speaker has good control over their vocal folds, whereas a low value during natural speech indicates that the speech is literally monotonous.

Jitter: The short-term variation in the timing of the vocal folds' vibrations. High values indicate irregularity in the vocal folds' movement which can be due to many factors, including both physical and neurological conditions. In our case, jitter is not calculated from individual pitch epochs (which are prone to error, especially at low sample rates). Instead we take a sample-by-sample estimate of the pitch period, $p(t)$, take the log, and find the magnitude of its deviation from a local mean. This gives an instantaneous log relative jitter value, $j_{\log}(t)$:

$$j_{log}(t) = \left| ln(p(t)) - \overline{ln(p(t_x))} \Big|_{t_x \approx t} \right| \tag{1}$$

These instantaneous values are then averaged over the interval of interest, and converted to a relative jitter value, expressed as a percentage:

$$J_{ave} = \left(exp\left(\overline{j_{log}(t)} \right) - 1 \right) \times 100\% \tag{2}$$

Shimmer: The short-term variation in the amplitude of the vocal folds' vibrations. High values indicate irregularity in the airflow between the vocal folds, which can be due to a range of conditions affecting the control of the muscles within the larynx. Our Shimmer parameter is calculated as for Jitter, above, but on a dB scale.

Noise-to-Harmonics Ratio: The energy in any noise-like components (turbulence) relative to the periodic components (harmonics) during voiced speech. A clear singing voice should exhibit a low Noise-to-Harmonics Ratio (NHR). Conversely, a larger value indicates a roughness to the voice, such as that caused by diseases of the larynx.

Breathiness: An estimate of the perceived breathiness of the voice, calculated using a telephone-optimised version of the Fukazawa Breathiness Index [10]. This is also an indicator of laryngeal pathologies, but designed to reflect similar aspects of the speech to those identified perceptually by clinicians. The original method has been enhanced using modern techniques for high-resolution time-frequency analysis.

Creakiness: A measure which correlates well with perceived creakiness of the voice, but which has been optimised for telephone speech. A high value indicates that there is a periodic irregularity in the voice waveform, such as diplophonia.

Voiced segment amplitude (standard deviation): The standard deviation of the log amplitude during the longest continuously voiced interval. This is analogous to the Modulation Index traditionally used to assess telephone line quality.

2.3   Vocal Tract Parameters

These parameters are based on estimates of acoustical characteristics of the vocal tract, specifically the resonant frequencies (the "formants") and the trough between the first two formants.

F1 (normalised): The frequency of the first vocal tract resonance (formant), relative to that of the third. This normalisation produces values which are relatively independent of the individual's vocal tract length, and so allow detection of abnormalities in the articulation of steady vowels. An unusually high or low value can merely indicate an unusual accent, or possibly a medical condition such as Apraxia of Speech (AoS).

A1 (relative): The energy of the first formant, expressed as a proportion of the first three formants. An unusual value may indicate a medical condition normally associated with Breathiness, but it can also be caused by a poorly located microphone, or other electro-acoustic problem with the telephone.

F1 sharpness: The sharpness of the first formant resonance. This parameter can be high for trained classical singers who are practised in matching the pitch of their voice to the resonant frequencies of the vocal tract. In general, it gives an indication of the perceived clarity of vowel sounds.

F1 variation: The magnitude of the short-term variation in the first formant frequency. During sustained phonation, this value should be small, indicating a stable vowel sound, but during fluent speech, significant variation is normal and unusually small variation can be symptomatic of poor articulation.

A1 variation: The magnitude of variation in the amplitude of the first formant. The same comments as for F1 variation, above, apply here too.

F2 (normalised), A2 (relative), F2 sharpness: The same as the respective F1 and A1 parameters, above, but with respect to the second formant.

F2 variation: The magnitude of short-term variation in the second formant's frequency. As for F1 Variation, this value should be small during sustained phonation, indicating an unchanging vowel sound. However during normal fluent speech, the second formant normally covers a very wide range and a small F2 Variation suggests under-articulation of the vowel sounds.

A2 variation: The magnitude of the short-term variation in the amplitude of the second formant. The same comments as for A1 Variation, above, apply here too.

F1, F2 trough frequency (normalised): The relative frequency of the trough between the first two formants. A value of zero corresponds to the trough being adjacent to F1, while a value of 100% corresponds to it lying next to F2. Most non-nasalised sounds produce a value in the region of 50%, but a value at either end of the range can indicate the presence of unusual nasalisation.

F1, F2 prominence: The normalised energy of the first two formants relative to that of the trough between them. This is related to the F1 and F2 Sharpness measures.

F1, F2 trough sharpness: The sharpness of the trough between the first two formants. A high value can indicate unusual levels of nasalisation.

F1, F2 trough frequency variation: The magnitude of the short-term variation in the F1, F2 trough frequency. If this is large then the estimate of F1, F2 Trough Frequency may have been affected by background noise or other factors.

F1, F2 prominence variation: The magnitude of the short-term variation in the F1, F2 Prominence. Indicates how smoothly the voiced sounds are articulated.

F3: The absolute frequency of the third formant. This is relatively invariant for any given speaker, and is used in the normalisation of F1 and F2.

A3 (relative): The energy of the third formant, expressed as a proportion of the first three formants. This is normally lower than A1 and A2.

2.4   Articulatory/Dynamics Parameters

These parameters describe the articulation and control of the upper vocal tract. They are calculated without explicit identification of formants or pitch, operating on the broad time-frequency structure of the speech signal. They can contribute to the automated analysis of disordered speech, but should be considered experimental at this time, since they are not yet clinically proven.

Frequency-time uncertainty: A telephone-robust version of the Hirschman Uncertainty [11]. A large value indicates that the energy is smoothly spread across large regions of the spectrogram and the recorded speech is poorly articulated, either because of damped vocal tract resonance or imprecise voice source transitions.

Frequency-time orientation: The frequency-domain entropy of the spectrogram relative to the time-domain entropy. If the energy in the spectrogram is spread across a wide range of frequencies, but concentrated in short time intervals (e.g. stutter-like sounds: "p-p-p-...", "t-t-t-...", or "k-k-k...") this value will be positive. If the energy is spread over a long period of time, but concentrated in a small range of frequencies (e.g. when whistling), it will be negative.

Dynamics: The average short-term direction-change of the frequency components in the speech. This value is close to zero during sustained phonation, but negative during natural speech. A more negative value indicates that the formants change direction less often, which can be associated with a slow rate of speaking. A high value indicates frequent changes in direction and a fast rate of speaking.

Dynamics (standard deviation): The standard deviation of the Dynamics parameter over the duration of the speech. Since the Dynamics parameter gives an indication of speaking rate, this value reflects the variation in speaking rate during an utterance.

Dynamics (skewness): The sample skewness of the Dynamics parameter over the duration of the speech. This is derived from the Dynamics parameter. A low negative value indicates that the Dynamics parameter is generally low with brief periods of increased activity, i.e. a slow speaking rate with occasional rapid articulation. This may indicate, for example, a speaker with good motor control and unusually precise speech.

Dynamics (kurtosis): The sample excess kurtosis of the Dynamics parameter over the duration of the speech. It can indicate the presence of outliers in the Dynamics parameter.

3   Example Application

To test the capabilities of the VoiScan parameters, systems were constructed to address the Interspeech 2017 paralinguistic ComParE Cold challenge [12]. This challenge involved the classification of voice recordings into two classes based on the subjects' self-assessed severity of upper respiratory tract infection.

To quantify each VoiScan parameter's ability to indicate the presence of infection, we performed the Z-test on the two classes. The ten most sensitive parameters are presented in Table 4. Under the Gaussian assumption inherent in the Z-test, all the parameters in this table are affected by the severity of URT infection, at a significance level of $p < 0.00001$.

The VoiScan parameters, along with standard MFCCs, were then passed to a Support Vector Machine (SVM) to perform automatic classification, with the results shown in Table 5.

The Unweighted Average Recall, UAR, of the system was approximately 90%. This was significantly higher than the baseline UAR set for this task (71.0%). The baseline system used late fusion of three different classifiers, one based on a recurrent Deep Neural Network, and two based on SVMs. The superior performance of our

Table 4. Z-statistics for top 10 VoiScan parameters using results from the Interspeech 2017 ComParE "Cold" challenge

Parameter	Z-statistic
F1 (sharpness)	14.63
F1 (short-term variation)	13.06
Voiced segment amplitude (standard deviation)	11.98
F1, F2 trough frequency (normalised)	11.70
Shimmer	10.01
Dynamics	9.75
Voice break rate	9.21
F1 (normalised)	8.99
F2 (sharpness)	8.51
Pitch	7.82

Table 5. Accuracy (recall rates) for SVM-based classification in the Interspeech 2017 ComParE "Cold" challenge, using two independent data sets

True class	Data set 1	Data set 2
Healthy	95.09%	95.37%
Cold	86.67%	83.64%
Average	90.88%	89.50%

single system, using VoiScan parameters, confirms that they are indeed able to capture health-related information from the raw audio.

4   Conclusions and Further Work

The extensive set of parameters outlined in this paper has been shown to be useful in identifying voice bio-markers for health and biometric applications. Some of the VoiScan parameters have been shown to be closely correlated with the most widely used clinical voice analysis parameters. They have also been shown to be more robust to the distortions inherent in telephone communication than a widely used alternative.

Work is continuing on refining and extending the VoiScan parameter set, and demonstrating the relevance of each parameter to specific applications in the areas of speaker recognition, health monitoring, and other linguistic and para-linguistic tasks. Our aim is to realise the potential of telephone-based speech analysis, allowing it to provide a complete description of a speaker's voice and speech characteristics.

References

1. Duffy, J.R.: Motor speech disorders: clues to neurologic diagnosis. In: Adler, C.H., Ahlskog, J.E. (eds.) Parkinson's Disease and Movement Disorders: Diagnosis and Treatment Guidelines for the Practicing Physician, pp. 35–53. Humana Press, Totowa (2000)
2. Koreman, J., Pützer, M.: The usability of perceptual ratings of voice quality. In: Proceedings of 6th International Conference: Advances in Quantitative Laryngology, Voice and Speech Research (2003)
3. Kent, R.D.: Hearing and believing: some limits to the auditory-perceptual assessment of speech and voice disorders. Am. J. Speech-Lang. Pathol. 5(3), 7–23 (1996)
4. Dibazar, A.A., Narayanan, S., Berger, T.W.: Feature analysis for automatic detection of pathological speech. Eng. Med. and Biol. 2002: In: 24th Annual Conference and the Annual Fall Meeting of the Biomedical Engineering Society EMBS/BMES Conference, vol. 1, pp. 182–183 (2002)
5. Maier, A., Haderlein, T., Eysholdt, U., Rosanowski, F., Batliner, A., Schuster, M., Nöth, E.: PEAKS – a system for the automatic evaluation of voice and speech disorders. Speech Commun. 51, 425–437 (2009)
6. Godino-Llorente, J.I., Gómez-Vilda, P.: Automatic detection of voice impairments by means of short-term cepstral parameters and neural network based detectors. IEEE Trans. Biomed. Eng. 51(2), 380–384 (2004)
7. Parsa, V., Jamieson, D.G.: Acoustic discrimination of pathological voice: sustained vowels versus continuous speech. J. Speech Lang. Hear Res. 44, 327–339 (2001)
8. Boersma, P., Weenink, D.: Praat: doing phonetics by computer. http://www.praat.org/. Last accessed 15 April 2017
9. Hunt, M.J.: Delayed decisions in speech recognition. The case of formants. Pattern Recogn. Lett. 6(2), 121–137 (1987)
10. Fukazawa, T., El-Assuooty, A., Honjo, I.: A new index for evaluation of the turbulent noise in pathological voice. J. Acoust. Soc. Am. 83, 1189–1192 (1988)
11. Hirschman Jr., I.I.: A note on entropy. Am. J. Math. 79(1), 152–156 (1957)
12. Schuller, B., et al.: The INTERSPEECH 2017 computational paralinguistics challenge: addressee, cold & snoring. Submitted to Proceedings INTERSPEECH 2017. ISCA, Stockholm, Sweden (2017)

Web Queries Classification Based on the Syntactical Patterns of Search Types

Alaa Mohasseb[1(✉)], Mohamed Bader-El-Den[1], Andreas Kanavos[2],
and Mihaela Cocea[1]

[1] School of Computing, University of Portsmouth, Portsmouth, UK
{alaa.mohasseb,mohamed.bader,mihaela.cocea}@port.ac.uk
[2] Computer Engineering and Informatics Department,
University of Patras, Patras, Greece
kanavos@ceid.upatras.gr

Abstract. Nowadays, people make frequent use of search engines in order to find the information they need on the web. The abundance of available data has rendered the process of obtaining relevant information challenging in terms of processing and analyzing it. A broad range of web queries classification techniques have been proposed with the aim of helping in understanding the actual intent behind a web search. In this research, we have categorized search queries through introducing Search Type Syntactical Patterns for automatically identifying and classifying search engine user queries. Experiments show that our approach has a good level of accuracy in identifying different search types.

Keywords: Natural language processing · Query classification · Machine learning · Text mining · Search engines

1 Introduction

The increasing size and diversity of online information has made the process of searching and obtaining information relevant to the information needed, increasingly challenging. Despite being a common fact that search engines have improved the information retrieval methods by looking at different perspectives such as the meaning of words, many difficulties are still present because of the continuous increase in the amount of web content.

Different proposed classifications of web queries have been introduced in several works [1, 2, 5, 6, 14, 16, 22]. Broder's classification of web queries [6] is the most commonly used classification; according to it, web searches could be classified into three categories, namely Informational, Navigational and Transactional. The purpose of informational queries is to find information, merely learn how to do something or just even answer a question. This information is available on the web in a static form and no further interaction is necessary. Topics of this type of queries are commonly broad and general, such as *Los Angeles* or are specific, such as the *Vietnam war*. Usually there is no particular web page containing

© Springer International Publishing AG 2017
A. Karpov et al. (Eds.): SPECOM 2017, LNAI 10458, pp. 809–819, 2017.
DOI: 10.1007/978-3-319-66429-3_81

all the required information needed; users have to gather the information from multiple web pages.

On the other hand, navigational queries have one right result since the purpose of such is to reach a particular site, e.g. *British museum homepage*. In this type of queries, the user usually has a certain website in mind but either does not know the URL or may think that a particular website exists. Finally, transactional queries have as an objective to find a site, so further interaction may be required, such as downloading software or buying a certain product online. The purpose may indeed be to acquire something and not just to find information about it, e.g. to look at it on the screen, such as *song lyrics* or *recipes*.

Many researchers have based their work on Broder's classification regarding user query intent [9,11,13,18,19]. Other works like [15] have used informational and navigational queries only due to lack of consensus on transactional query and also with the aim of making the classification task more manageable. Concretely, in our paper, the web queries classification proposed by Broder [6] will be utilized.

Recent studies classified users' search intent either by analyzing the characteristics of each query types [6,7,11,30], or users' behavior by thoroughly studying the query logs [2,5,10,27,29] and clicking through data [4,16,18,19]. Research alike the ones in [3,28] classified users' intent by analyzing the linguistic structure of web queries, applying techniques from natural language understanding such as part of speech tagging.

Despite their effectiveness, these methods have the specific drawback that they do not take into consideration the structure of the queries. Queries submitted to search engines are usually short and ambiguous and an extended number of them might carry more than one meaning; therefore the use of specific terms for the identification of search intents is insufficient. In addition, the identification of a query could be misleading if depending on users' behavior or users' clicks, as two queries might have exactly the same set of terms but may reflect two totally different intents [29]. Therefore classifying web queries using their syntactical structure along with terms and characteristics may help in making their classification more accurate.

In this paper, we propose a solution that automatically identifies and in following classifies user's queries using their syntactical patterns. Such patterns are created after studying different web queries classification proposals and are based on the examination of various web logs. We have developed a framework to test the accuracy of our solution and the experimental results show that our approach has successfully identified different search types. For the remainder of the paper, we will refer to this new framework as Search Type Syntactical Patterns (STSP).

The rest of the paper is organized as follows: Sect. 2 highlights the different query classification approaches and the different analysis methods used in web query identification. Section 3 presents our proposed STSP method and provides a detailed explanation of the data set and the different methods employed for the analysis of each query type, as well as a description of the analysis of queries. Section 4 covers experiments and results, while Sect. 5 outlines conclusions and future work.

2 Related Work

2.1 Search Types

The works in [11,27] extended the classification of Informational, Navigational and Transactional queries by adding level two and level three sub-categories. Moreover, in [5], authors classified queries into four classes: Ambiguous, Unambiguous but Underspecified, Information Browsing and Miscellaneous. Another similar work is the one in [16], where two new query intents, Commercial and Local, were proposed. According to this work, the query is likely to have a Commercial potential like the query: "commercial offering" or the user might search for information near their current location.

There are also other works like [1,7], which proposed other classification of queries. Authors in [7] classified user intent into dimensions and facets, referring to genre, objectivity, specificity, scope, topic, task, authority sensitivity, spatial sensitivity and time sensitivity. Similarly in [1], query intent is classified into two dimensions; Commercial/Non-Commercial, and Informational/Navigational. Web informational tasks were classified based on three main informational goals, which are Information Seeking, Information Exchange and Information Maintenance [14]. Authors in [2] established three categories for users' search goal, which are Informational, Not Informational and Ambiguous. More specifically, an informational query is triggered when the user's interest is to obtain information available on the web; non informational queries include specific transactions or resources like "buy" and "download"; lastly, ambiguous queries include queries that cannot be directly identified because the user's interest is not fully clear.

Finally, another classification has been proposed in [22], where search goals were classified into Find, Explore, Monitoring and Collect. This classification focuses on three variables: the purpose of the search, the method used to find information and the contents of searched information.

2.2 Classification Methods of Web Queries

Different analysis methods and techniques have been used for the identification and classification of web queries. In works such as [6,11], authors studied web search queries based on their features and characteristics. In [9], a solution that automatically classifies queries based on the features and characteristics described by [6,11,30], is introduced. Works in [7,8,13] analyzed and characterized a variety of query features in order to automatically classify different users' intent.

Users' goals can be deduced from looking at user behavior available to the search engine, such as the query itself and results clicked [27]. Keeping that in mind, authors created a tool that provides this type of information and analyzed three sets of approximately 500 queries that were randomly selected from AltaVista query logs. The limitation of this approach is that the goal inferred from the query may not be the user's actual goal.

Query logs are also used for categorization of the search query [5,10]. Moreover, search logs are introduced for the purpose of enriching a query by mining the documents clicked by users and the relevant follow up queries in a session [29]; the authors use a text classifier to map the documents along with the queries into predefined categories.

Furthermore, similar works used click-through data to identify the user goals behind their queries [1,4,18,19]. A method that has been used by different studies to help search engines better understand what users want so that more effective result ranking could be achieved is discussed in [4]. Query analysis was addressed by using two types of features, past user click behavior and anchor-link distribution in [15], while authors in [16] analyzed click-through data to determine commercial and navigational queries, in addition to a crowd-sourcing approach with the aim to classify a high amount of search queries.

A data-driven methodology is introduced in [10] for disambiguating a query by suggesting relevant subcategories within a specific domain. This is done by finding correlations between the user's search history and the context of the current search keyword. Neural networks and a Naive Bayes classifier were used to learn the category of a given query from a training set.

Natural language analysis techniques were used to examine the structure of web queries by [3,17,28]. For example, in [17], an analysis of the semantic structure of noun phrase queries is presented. The analysis in [28] showed that queries have distinct properties and are not some form of text between random sequences of words and natural language. In [3], analysis of queries was based on the syntax of part of speech tag sequences. Their analysis results showed that query part-of-speech tagging can be used for creating significant features as well as for improving the relevance of web search results and may assist with query reformulation.

2.3 Machine Learning Algorithms

Decision Tree (DT) and *Naive Bayes (NB)* were used as machine learning algorithms for the syntactical patterns classification. More specifically, Decision Tree is considered as one of the most common methods used to create classification models and build them as a tree structure [20]. ID3 [24] is the core algorithm for building decision trees. Several variations of the ID3 algorithm have been proposed over the past decades, such as the C4.5 [25]. In this study, we adopt the J48[1] algorithm with a Java implementation of the C4.5 algorithm.

The main idea behind NB is the estimation of the parameters of a multinomial generative model for instances, while finding the most probable class for a given instance using the Bayes' rule and the Naive Bayes assumption that the features occur independently of each other. In practice, the Naive Bayes learner performs remarkably well in many text classification problems [20,26] and it is often used as a baseline in text classification because of its speed and easy implementation. Less erroneous algorithms tend to be slower and more complex [26].

---

[1] http://www.cs.waikato.ac.nz/ml/weka/.

3   Search Type Syntactical Patterns

In this section we introduce the Search Type Syntactical Patterns (STSP) framework for query classification. The framework mainly relies on Search Type Syntactical Patterns. Therefore, in the first part of this section we introduce our syntactical patterns of web queries and in the second part we explain the structure of the STSP framework.

A total of 712 different Syntactical patterns were constructed and classified to Informational, Navigational and Transactional; each pattern composed of a sequence of term categories. The categorization of terms is mainly based on the seven major word classes in English, which are Noun (N), Verb (V), Determiner (D), Adjective (Adj), Adverb (Adv), Preposition (P) and Conjunction (Conj).

In addition, we added a category for question words (QW) that contains the six main question words: "how", "who", "when", "where", "what" and "which". We have further extended this classification by adding two categories, which are Domain Suffixes (DS) and Prefixes (DP). Some word classes can have subclasses, like Noun (N) has as subclasses the Common Nouns (CN), Proper Nouns (PN), Pronouns (Pron) and Numeral Nouns (NN). In addition, Verb (V) has as subclasses the Action Verbs (AV), Linking Verbs (LV) and Auxiliary Verbs (AuxV).

3.1   Constructing Search Type Syntactical Patterns

A random set of 80, 000 queries has been selected from AOL 2006 dataset[2] for the analysis to take place. This dataset consists of 20 million web queries collected from 650, 000 users over a three month period, where UserIDs were anonymized [23]. The following steps have been taken using pre-developed Java program [21]:

1. Parse the 80, 000 queries and automatically extract terms from the queries.
2. Automatically map terms into their syntactical structure, e.g. "Who is Jane Austen" is mapped as: (a) "Who $--> QW$", (b) "is $--> LV$" and (c) "Jane Austen $--> PN$".
3. Convert each query to its Syntactical Pattern (SP), which is a representation of the original query with each term replaced by a word class (PoS). For example, the query "Free Wallpapers" is converted into the syntactical pattern $[Adj + CN]$.
4. Classify each syntactical pattern into one of the Informational, Navigational and Transactional search types.

Table 1 presents the number of unique syntactical patterns for each of the aforementioned types. We validated the classification of patterns using a subset of the original dataset containing 1953 queries from AOL that were manually classified and used in [19]. In addition, the characteristics of the Informational, Navigational and Transactional search, which have been introduced in [6,11,27], were utilized in our work.

---

[2] http://www.researchpipeline.com/mediawiki/index.php?title=AOL_Search_Query_Logs.

Table 1. Syntactical patterns

Query search types	Total
Informational query	601
Transactional query	108
Navigational query	3
Overall	712

3.2 Proposed Framework

The proposed framework automatically identifies and classifies user's queries by utilizing Search Type Syntactical Patterns and the word classes term categories. The framework consists of three main phases presented in Fig. 1.

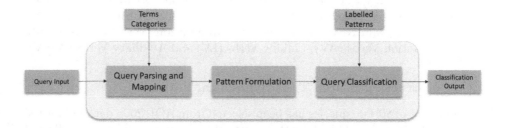

Fig. 1. Query classification framework

For illustrating our approach, we introduce the following two examples: *"Mitch Albom Books Order"* and *"Order Mitch Albom Books"*. One might assume that they have one search intent since both queries have similar terms; but based on the syntactical pattern of the queries, each query has a different search intent. These differences occur because each word in each query may belong to different phrases, reflecting different word classes and subclasses. Hence, word order inside a phrase is one of the major structural ways in which the queries can differ from each other. The position of a word depends on its word class, meaning that each query could formulate a unique pattern. The framework steps are illustrated below:

1. *Query Parsing and Mapping*: this step is responsible for extracting the user's query terms. The system simply takes as input the corresponding query and parses it in order to map each term from the query to its terms category.
   Query 1: **Mitch Albom Books Order**
   Terms extracted: Mitch Albom, Books, Order
   Query 2: **Order Mitch Albom Books**
   Terms extracted: Order, Mitch Albom, Books

As previously mentioned, terms in each query belong to different phrases. More to depth, Query 1 consists of *Noun Phrases*, while Query 2 consists of a *Verb Phrase* and a *Noun Phrase*. As a result, each term in the corresponding query will be mapped into the following:
Query 1 Terms Mapping: Mitch Albom = [PN], Books = [CN], Order = [CN]
Query 2 Terms Mapping: Order = [AV], Mitch Albom = [PN], Books = [CN]

2. *Pattern Formulation*: In this step, the syntactical pattern is formulated after mapping each term in the query.
   Query 1 Syntactical Pattern: [PN + CN + CN]
   Query 2 Syntactical Pattern: [AV + CN + PN]

3. *Query Classification*: In this step, the system matches the Query Pattern with the most appropriate Search Type Syntactical Patterns in order to determine the Query type. Thus, the Syntactical Patterns will be:
   Query 1: Informational
   Query 2: Transactional

4   Experimental Evaluation

4.1   Implementation

To test the accuracy of our proposed approach, 10,000 queries were randomly selected from AOL 2006 data set. The selected queries are different from those used in constructing the query Syntactical Patterns.

As previously mentioned, *Decision Tree* (J48) and *Naive Bayes* were used as machine learning algorithms for the automatic classification. Weka is used for running the algorithms and measuring the classification performance. Since our motivation stems from the fact that our main interest relies on identifying the classifier with the highest performance, the effectiveness of the classification was evaluated based on Precision, Recall and F-Measure, i.e. typical metrics for the evaluation of classifiers, using 10-fold cross validation.

4.2   Results

Tables 2 and 3 present classification performance details (Precision, Recall and F-Measure) of the J48 and Naive Bayes classifiers. Results show that J48 identified correctly (i.e. Recall) 86% of the queries, while Naive Bayes only a percentage of 80%.

Comparing the effectiveness of the classifiers, J48 outperforms Naive Bayes in terms of Precision, Recall and the F-Measure metrics for the Informational and Transactional queries. Regarding the Navigational queries, both J48 and Naive Bayes classifiers exhibit similar Precision, Recall and F-Measure rates. These results clearly indicate that using J48 for query classification is more suitable than Naive Bayes, especially when considering that Naive Bayes does not deal well with large datasets.

Table 2. Decision Tree (J48) classifier performance

Query search types	Precision	Recall	F-Measure
Informational query	0.936	0.680	0.787
Navigational query	0.844	1.000	0.916
Transactional query	0.688	0.920	0.787
Overall	0.820	0.860	0.830

Table 3. Naive Bayes classifier performance

Query search types	Precision	Recall	F-Measure
Informational query	0.854	0.549	0.668
Navigational query	0.848	0.994	0.915
Transactional query	0.597	0.859	0.704
Overall	0.766	0.801	0.762

Taking a closer look at where the errors occur when using J48, 16% of the Informational queries were misclassified as Transactional and less than 1% were misclassified as Navigational. From the Transactional queries, 2.5% were misclassified as Informational and less than 1% were misclassified as Navigational. Surprisingly enough, Navigational queries were 100% correctly classified. Similarly, the Naive Bayes classifier incorrectly classified 23% of the Informational queries as Transactional and less than 1% of the Informational queries as Navigational. Approximately 5% of the Transactional queries were misclassified as Informational and less then 1% as Navigational. From the Navigational queries, 0.05% were classified as Transactional.

In addition, the results validate that using Search Type Syntactical Patterns helps in the improvement of the query classification accuracy overall, as well as in the distinction between different search types compared with other methods used to classify query search types, as outline below.

4.3   Discussion

The method used in [4,15,16] depends solely on past user click behavior and Anchor-link distribution, which could be misleading in identifying a query, especially when the user is looking for something new (i.e. not reflected in their past behavior). In [9], some important linguistic features like verbs and domain suffixes were removed during the identification of user intent, especially for the Navigational queries; in their work these were largely misclassified, i.e. F-Measure of 0.39 for Naive Bayes and 0 for Support Vector Machine (SVM) classifiers. Also, the method used in [10], which was based on the categorization of the search query for medical and travel queries and the time intervals, was not sufficient to be applicable for solving practical query disambiguation problems, i.e.

F-Measure under 0.40. In addition, other studies with similar or higher performance rates such as [1,19], used much smaller datasets, i.e. 1.700 and 2.000 queries, respectively, which cast doubts about the generalization of the results.

5 Conclusions

In this research, we have introduced a framework for automatically identifying and classifying search engine user queries. Unlike other solutions, our solution relies on both query terms as well as the query syntactical structure to determine user's intent. We have categorized search queries through introducing Search Type Syntactical Patterns. Our framework consists of three main steps, namely parsing and mapping user's query terms, formulating Query Patterns, and finally classifying query types. Experiments show that our solution led to a good performance in classifying queries.

As future work, we aim at examining and analyzing more queries from different search engine data sets and extending the analysis of web queries. Another interesting topic of research would be the transfer of the computation to a cloud infrastructure utilizing Big Data techniques. In addition, we will investigate how to support query reformulation strategies [12] to help users gain more relevant results.

References

1. Ashkan, A., Clarke, C.L.A., Agichtein, E., Guo, Q.: Classifying and characterizing query intent. In: Boughanem, M., Berrut, C., Mothe, J., Soule-Dupuy, C. (eds.) ECIR 2009. LNCS, vol. 5478, pp. 578–586. Springer, Heidelberg (2009). doi:10.1007/978-3-642-00958-7_53
2. Baeza-Yates, R., Calderón-Benavides, L., González-Caro, C.: The intention behind web queries. In: Crestani, F., Ferragina, P., Sanderson, M. (eds.) SPIRE 2006. LNCS, vol. 4209, pp. 98–109. Springer, Heidelberg (2006). doi:10.1007/11880561_9
3. Barr, C., Jones, R., Regelson, M.: The linguistic structure of English web-search queries. In: Proceedings of the Conference on Empirical Methods in Natural Language Processing, pp. 1021–1030. Association for Computational Linguistics (2008)
4. Beitzel, S.M., Jensen, E.C., Frieder, O., Grossman, D., Lewis, D.D., Chowdhury, A., Kolcz, A.: Automatic web query classification using labeled and unlabeled training data. In: Proceedings of the 28th Annual International ACM SIGIR Conference on Research and Development in Information Retrieval, pp. 581–582. ACM (2005)
5. Bhatia, S., Brunk, C., Mitra, P.: Analysis and automatic classification of web search queries for diversification requirements. Proc. Am. Soc. Inf. Sci. Technol. 49(1), 1–10 (2012)
6. Broder, A.: A taxonomy of web search. ACM Sigir Forum 36, 3–10 (2002). ACM
7. Calderón-Benavides, L., González-Caro, C., Baeza-Yates, R.: Towards a deeper understanding of the users query intent. In: SIGIR 2010 Workshop on Query Representation and Understanding, pp. 21–24 (2010)
8. Figueroa, A.: Exploring effective features for recognizing the user intent behind web queries. Comput. Ind. 68, 162–169 (2015)

9. Hernández, I., Gupta, P., Rosso, P., Rocha, M.: A simple model for classifying web queries by user intent. In: 2nd Spanish Conference on Information Retrieval, CERI 2012, pp. 235–240 (2012)
10. Højgaard, C., Sejr, J., Cheong, Y.G.: Query categorization from web search logs using machine learning algorithms. Int. J. Database Theory Appl. **9**(9), 139–148 (2016)
11. Jansen, B.J., Booth, D.L., Spink, A.: Determining the informational, navigational, and transactional intent of web queries. Inf. Process. Manag. **44**(3), 1251–1266 (2008)
12. Kanavos, A., Theodoridis, E., Tsakalidis, A.K.: Extracting knowledge from web search engine results. In: IEEE 24th International Conference on Tools with Artificial Intelligence, pp. 860–867 (2012)
13. Kathuria, A., Jansen, B.J., Hafernik, C., Spink, A.: Classifying the user intent of web queries using k-means clustering. Internet Res. **20**(5), 563–581 (2010)
14. Kellar, M., Watters, C., Shepherd, M.: A goal-based classification of web information tasks. Proc. Am. Soc. Inf. Sci. Technol. **43**(1), 1–22 (2006)
15. Lee, U., Liu, Z., Cho, J.: Automatic identification of user goals in web search. In: Proceedings of the 14th International Conference on World Wide Web, pp. 391–400. ACM (2005)
16. Lewandowski, D., Drechsler, J., Mach, S.: Deriving query intents from web search engine queries. J. Am. Soc. Inform. Sci. Technol. **63**(9), 1773–1788 (2012)
17. Li, X.: Understanding the semantic structure of noun phrase queries. In: Proceedings of the 48th Annual Meeting of the Association for Computational Linguistics, pp. 1337–1345. Association for Computational Linguistics (2010)
18. Liu, Y., Zhang, M., Ru, L., Ma, S.: Automatic query type identification based on click through information. In: Ng, H.T., Leong, M.-K., Kan, M.-Y., Ji, D. (eds.) AIRS 2006. LNCS, vol. 4182, pp. 593–600. Springer, Heidelberg (2006). doi:10.1007/11880592_51
19. Mendoza, M., Zamora, J.: Identifying the intent of a user query using support vector machines. In: Karlgren, J., Tarhio, J., Hyyrö, H. (eds.) SPIRE 2009. LNCS, vol. 5721, pp. 131–142. Springer, Heidelberg (2009). doi:10.1007/978-3-642-03784-9_13
20. Mitchell, T.M.: Machine Learning. McGraw hill (1997)
21. Mohasseb, A., El-Sayed, M., Mahar, K.: Automated identification of web queries using search type patterns. In: WEBIST (2). pp. 295–304 (2014)
22. Morrison, J.B., Pirolli, P., Card, S.K.: A taxonomic analysis of what world wide web activities significantly impact people's decisions and actions. In: CHI 2001 Extended Abstracts on Human Factors in Computing Systems, pp. 163–164. ACM (2001)
23. Pass, G., Chowdhury, A., Torgeson, C.: A picture of search. In: InfoScale, vol. 152, p. 1 (2006)
24. Quinlan, J.R.: Induction of decision trees. Mach. Learn. **1**(1), 81–106 (1986)
25. Quinlan, J.R.: C4.5: Programs for Machine Learning. Elsevier, San Francisco (2014)
26. Rennie, J.D., Shih, L., Teevan, J., Karger, D.R., et al.: Tackling the poor assumptions of naive bayes text classifiers. In: ICML, Washington DC, vol. 3, pp. 616–623 (2003)
27. Rose, D.E., Levinson, D.: Understanding user goals in web search. In: Proceedings of the 13th International Conference on World Wide Web, pp. 13–19. ACM (2004)
28. Saha Roy, R.: Analyzing linguistic structure of web search queries. In: Proceedings of the 22nd International Conference on World Wide Web, pp. 395–400. ACM (2013)

29. Song, R., Dou, Z., Hon, H.W., Yu, Y.: Learning query ambiguity models by using search logs. J. Comput. Sci. Technol. **25**(4), 728–738 (2010)
30. Wu, D., Zhang, Y., Zhao, S., Liu, T.: Identification of web query intent based on query text and web knowledge. In: 2010 First International Conference on Pervasive Computing Signal Processing and Applications (PCSPA), pp. 128–131. IEEE (2010)

What Speech Recognition Accuracy is Needed for Video Transcripts to be a Useful Search Interface?

Yang Chao[1] and Marie-Luce Bourguet[2(✉)]

[1] Beijing University of Posts and Telecommunication, Beijing, China
[2] Queen Mary University of London, London, UK
marie-luce.bourguet@qmul.ac.uk

Abstract. Informative videos (e.g. recorded lectures) are increasingly being made available online, but they are difficult to use, browse and search. Nowadays, popular platforms let users search and navigate videos via a transcript, which, in order to guarantee a satisfactory level of word accuracy, has typically been generated using some manual inputs. The goal of our work is to try and take a step closer to the fully automatic generation of informative video transcripts based on current automatic speech recognition technology. We present a user study designed to better understand viewers' use of video transcripts for searching a video content, with the aim of estimating what minimum word recognition accuracy is needed for video captions to be a useful search interface. We found that transcripts with 70% word recognition accuracy are as effective as 100% accuracy transcripts in supporting video search when using single word search. We also found that there are large variations in the time it takes to search a video, independently of the quality of the transcript. With adequate and adapted search strategies, even low accuracy transcripts can support quick video search.

Keywords: Speech recognition · Word accuracy · Video transcripts · Video search

1 Introduction

Informative videos (conference talks, seminar presentations and recorded lectures) are increasingly being made available online. For example, websites such as TED [1], and Massive Online Open Courses (MOOCs) platforms such as Edx [2] and Coursera [3], offer thousands of informative videos on a wide range of topics. For distance learning, videos offer many of the advantages of a classroom-like experience and, in addition, they enable student's control over the pace of their learning. In [4], it was observed that MOOCs learners spend a majority of their time watching videos, and in [5, 6] (for example), video analytics have been used to understand learner's use of videos with the aim of improving video based learning.

However, despite their popularity, informative videos are difficult to browse and search. Viewers must typically scrub back-and forth through a video to gain an overview of the content or find passages of interest [7]. In response, smart video players are being developed, which provide interaction, browsing and search tools,

© Springer International Publishing AG 2017
A. Karpov et al. (Eds.): SPECOM 2017, LNAI 10458, pp. 820–828, 2017.
DOI: 10.1007/978-3-319-66429-3_82

and video digests (e.g. [7, 8]). Some of the most popular platforms, such as edX and TED, let users search and navigate videos via a transcript: clicking a word in the transcript plays the video at that location [7]. Older technologies, such as Windows Media Player, QuickTime, and RealPlayer also support captioning.

Captioning has traditionally been intended for those who cannot hear the audio, but it has also been found to help those who may not be fluent in the language in which the audio is presented. Video transcripts also contribute to making web multimedia content accessible. For example, screen reader users often prefer using the video transcript over the audio because it can be played faster than the time it takes to listen to the actual audio content [9]. Very importantly, transcripts also allow the video content to be searchable, both by computers (i.e. search engines) and by end users.

The formats and techniques for authoring and implementing video transcripts vary. Online services (e.g. [10, 11]) typically accept an audio file as input and return a human produced verbatim transcript of the audio (usually for a fee). The YouTube platform [12] combines Google's Automatic Speech Recognition (ASR) technology [13] with a caption system to offer automatic captions. To improve the transcripts' word accuracy (word accuracy is defined as the number of correct words divided by the total number of words in the transcript), users can provide a text file with all the words in the video and ASR is used to determine when the words are spoken and create the video captions. According to [11], with current ASR technology, the typical word accuracy obtained in transcripts is approximately 80%, which, according to the United States Federal Communications Commission (FCC) standard for close captioning is not acceptable. To guarantee high accuracy (over 99%), a 3-step process is used in [11], which includes a combination of ASR, human cleanup, and a large database of human-corrected, near-perfect transcripts to continually improve the recognition accuracy.

Typically, human input is therefore still used in the creation of video transcripts. Work on how to improve the manual post-processing task of correcting educational video transcripts has been presented in [14]. It investigates different user interface design strategies for the post-editing task to discover the best way to incorporate automatic transcription technologies into large educational video repositories. In [15], lecture transcripts are generated in two ways: (1) using real-time captioning (RTC) for instant viewing during class, and (2) using post-lecture transcription (PLT) with greater word recognition accuracy for download after class. A user study then shows that both RTC and PLT are effective at supporting students learning, but students felt that RTC improved teaching and learning in class as long as word recognition was greater than 85%.

The goal of our work is to try and take a step closer to the fully automatic generation of informative video transcripts based on current ASR technology. In this paper, we present a user study designed to better understand viewers' use of video transcripts for searching a video content, with the aim of estimating what is the minimum word recognition accuracy needed for video captions to be a useful search interface. Our approach has consisted in first developing our own video player (see Sect. 2), which offers a simple search interface based on the video transcripts. We created video transcripts of various word recognition accuracy levels using the CMU Sphinx4 ASR technology [16] (see Sect. 3) and we asked user participants to search a video in order to answer multiple choice questions (see Sect. 4). By analyzing the participants' answers, we estimate the minimum word recognition accuracy needed in the transcripts to conduct a successful video search (see Sect. 5).

2   The Video Player

2.1   The Interface

Figure 1 shows the main interface of the video player and the search results table. The main screen displays the video, and immediately below the video images, a progress bar and control buttons (with pause and play functions) are provided. Users can click on the progress bar to jump to a different part of the video. On the right side of the progress bar is a mute button. The synchronized captions are displayed underneath the progress bar. The captions are extracted from the automatically generated video transcript.

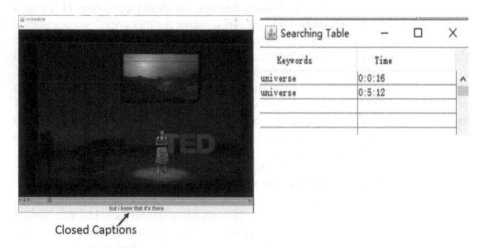

Closed Captions

Fig. 1. The video player interface and the search results table

When the video is playing, the user can input a single word into a search field to search the video content. If the word is found in the transcript, a search results table is displayed that shows all the found occurrences of the word, together with their occurrence time in the video. If the search word cannot be found in the transcript, an error message is displayed.

As shown in the example of Fig. 1, the word "universe" has been typed in the search field, and the search results table indicates that it is pronounced twice in the video, once at time 0:0:16 (this is the video time's format: hh:mm:ss), and again at time 0:5:12. Each word's occurrence in the search results table is selectable. If the user selects the first occurrence, the video player jumps to the frame that corresponds to time 0:0:16 where the word "universe" appears in the captions for the first time.

2.2 Synchronizing the Video and the Transcripts

We used the CMU Sphinx4 ASR technology [16] to automatically generate the video transcripts. Sphinx outputs text transcripts in the format shown in Fig. 2.

```
e her i a a
i am in search of another planet
in the universe
where life exists
i can't see this planet with my naked eyes
or even with the most powerful telescopes we currently possess
but i know that it's there
and understanding contradictions that occur in nature
will help us find it
on our planet
where there's water
there's life
so we look for planets that orbit at just the right distance from their stars
at this distance shown in blue on this diagram for stars of different tempera
planets could be warm enough for water to
flow on their surfaces
```

Fig. 2. A Sphynx generated transcript file

Once a transcript has been generated, the transcript file is given again as input to Sphinx so its content can be matched with the audio and a time stamp assigned to every word in the transcript. Words and their time stamps are saved in a new text file, as shown in Fig. 3(left). Every line indicates a word and its time stamp in milliseconds. For example, the word "her" starts at time 1300 ms and finishes at time 1640 ms.

```
e 170:1060              a 5310
her 1300:1640           consulting 17870
i 1650:2850             demanding 20780
a 2860:5250             teaching 21800
a 5260:5310             math 25610
left 15040:15350        schools 27670
a 15360:15390           teacher 29490
very 15400:15670        tests 31100
demanding 15680:16230   assignments 32710
job 16240:16600         grades 35770
in 16610:16660          me 37880
management 16670:17140  best 42930
consulting 17150:17870  students 44380
for 18380:18540         performers 46860
a 18550:18570           scores 49810
job 18580:18980         kids 51730
that 18990:19150        well 53510
was 19160:19440         thinking 55560
even 19500:19850        math 59040
more 19860:20080        hard 60890
demanding 20090:20780   a 63130
teaching 21260:21800    impossible 66810
i 23330:23390           convinced 69090
```

Fig. 3. Sphinx generated words and time stamps (left); transcript's lines timelines (right)

Using these two files (transcript and individual words with their time stamps), the synchronization is implemented as follows: every line's last word of the transcript file is logged with its accompanying starting time stamp (Fig. 3, right), resulting in every transcript line to be assigned a "timeline". For example, the second line's timeline ("i am in search of another planet") starts at 5140 ms, and finishes at 15130 ms.

When the video is played, a thread is created that reads the player's current playtime every 100 ms. If the current playtime is within a given transcript's line timeline, then this line is displayed as the current captions.

3   Data Preparation

3.1   The Videos

We downloaded five informative videos (four from TED [1] and one from the official White House website [17]) on various topics: (1) other life in the Universe, (2) teaching and learning, (3) internet privacy, (4) paying tax, and (5) animals' internal clock. Each video is between 4 and 7 min long and the presenters are all native English speakers with American English accents.

3.2   Generating Transcripts of Varying Word Recognition Accuracies

Using PCM encoded mono sound files with 16 bits per sample and a sampling rate of 16000 Hz, Sphinx can output transcripts for American English native speakers with, on average, 80% word recognition accuracy. In order to generate transcripts of varying word recognition accuracies, first we manually create 100% word accuracy transcripts for each of the five videos. Then, a digital audio editing software is used to generate 16000 Hz sampling rate, 16 bits per sample, and mono sound tracks of white noise of the same duration as the video audio tracks. The white noise tracks are combined with the video audio tracks in order to generate, using Sphinx, transcripts of the resulting noisy audio. The obtained transcript are then compared with the 100% word accuracy transcripts and their own word recognition accuracy is calculated. The obtained word accuracy is calculated as follows: the number of correct words in the modified transcript divided by the total number of words in the 100% word accuracy transcripts. The operation is repeated until transcripts of approximately 50% word recognition accuracy are obtained for each of the five videos.

In a second step, the 50% word accuracy transcripts are manually modified, by randomly correcting some of the misrecognized words and adding some of the missing words, in order to increase the transcripts' word accuracy to 70%, 80% and 90% respectively. Finally, for each of the five videos, we obtain five transcripts of varying word accuracy levels (100%, 90%, 80%, 70%, and 50%). Each of these transcripts are used as input to Sphinx in order to generate the time stamp files needed to synchronize the transcripts with the corresponding videos in the video player (as explained in Sect. 2.2 of the paper).

4   Experimental Design

Twenty participants (15 male, 5 female) with no prior knowledge about the videos' content were recruited as volunteers. A pre experiment questionnaire confirmed that all the participants have received higher education, have similar abilities to learn and solve problems, and have similar English skills (IELTS test score higher than 6.5 and TOEFL test score higher than 93).

The twenty participants were divided into five groups of four participants each. Given the five videos and the five word accuracy level transcripts for each video, we have 25 different video/transcript combinations to show to the participants. Each group of participants was given to watch five of these combinations following a Latin square experimental design: each participant watched the 5 different videos (in a random order) and each of the video they saw was played with a transcript of a different word recognition accuracy.

Before the start of the experiment, each participant is given time to use the video player in order to understand its functionalities, including the progress bar, the control buttons and the search function.

For each of the five videos, the task consists in answering three multiple choice questions. The participants are shown the questions first and then asked to use the video search function to find the answers in the video content. Each choice provided is a sentence pronounced by the video presenter. The task hence consists in selecting the sentence that answers best the question asked (see Fig. 4 for an example of a multiple choice question).

Q: What conclusion did the speaker reach, after several years of teaching?

    A.   What we need in education is a much better understanding of students and learning from a motivational perspective, from a psychological perspective.

    B.   We need to be gritty about getting our kids grittier.

    C.   Grit is living life like it's a marathon, not a sprint.

    D.   Every student could learn the material if they worked hard and long

---

Fig. 4. Example of multiple choice question for the teaching and learning video

Two computers were used during the experiment: one for playing the videos, and the other for displaying the multiple choice questions. Participants were not allowed to read the questions or play the video until the start of the experiment. A blank piece of paper for writing down the answers to the questions was also provided. The participants were instructed that they had to try and answer the questions as quickly as possible. They were also instructed to notify us as soon as they had completed answering the three questions related to one of the videos. The next questions and video were then prepared for them, and the task was repeated until all five allocated videos had been used. Watching an entire video and then answering the questions was not allowed:

the search function had to be used. For each video, the three questions are independent from each other, and their answers are to be found in different areas of the video.

5   Experimental Results and Discussion

The correctness of the answers, as well as the time it took each participant to answer the three questions related to one video were recorded (time was counted from the moment the questions are shown to the participant, until the moment the participant is signaling that the three questions have been answered).

Table 1 shows the average answer correctness and answer time for each of the five word accuracy levels. We can see that the time it takes to answer the questions and the number of correct answers start to increase and decrease respectively when the word accuracy level reaches 80%. Indeed, a one-way analysis of variance (ANOVA) calculated for the mean answer correctness of the five accuracy levels (from 100% to 50%) shows that the means are statistically different at the $p < 0.05$ level, $F_{(4, 95)} = 7.58$, $p = 0.00$. However, ANOVA calculated for the mean answer correctness of the four highest accuracy levels (100%, 90%, 80%, and 70%) shows no statistical difference at the $p < 0.05$ level, $F_{(3, 76)} = 1.13$, $p = 0.344$. This is an interesting result as it indicates that a single word search using our video player interface can be as effective with a word recognition accuracy transcript as low as 70% than with a higher accuracy transcript.

Table 1. Average answer time and correctness for the five word accuracy levels. Standard deviations are shown in square brackets.

Word accuracy	Answer correctness (Maximum is 3 or 100%)	Answer time
100%	2.4 (or 80%) [0.6]	318 s [78.02]
90%	2.4 (or 80%) [0.5]	333 s [82.06]
80%	2.2 (or 73%) [0.52]	326 s [91.72]
70%	2.15 (or 72%) [0.59]	336 s [72.14]
50%	1.5 (or 50%) [0.76]	364 s [86.49]

With regard to answer times, an ANOVA analysis of the mean answer times for the five accuracy levels (from 100% to 50%) shows no statistical difference at the $p < 0.05$ level, $F_{(4, 95)} = 0.88$, $p = 0.477$; indicating that the time it takes to answer the questions is independent of word accuracy. This can be explained by the fact that the answer time depends both on the number of search results returned (a high number slows down the search and is more frequent with good accuracy transcripts), and the probability that the search results can lead to the right answer (which quickens the search and is also more frequent with good accuracy transcripts). For example, the word "congress" yields 4 search results in the 100% word accuracy transcript, but only 2 results in the 50% word accuracy transcript. If one of the 2 results in the 50% word accuracy transcript happens to indicate the correct answer, the participants using that transcript will be led more quickly to the answer than the users of a 100% accuracy transcript which requires the testing of 4 search results. At contrary, if none of the 50% accuracy transcript results are leading to the answer, then the search must be started again and is likely to take longer overall. T-test analyses to compare answer times for each pair of accuracy levels show that it is only when comparing the 100% and 50% accuracy transcripts, that the mean times are found statistically different (two-sample $t(38) = 1.74$, $p = 0.04$), showing that, in average, a search with a 100% accuracy transcript is a little bit but (marginally) significantly quicker than a search with a 50% accuracy transcript.

During the experiment, we observed that participants tend to use words they find in the questions to initiate their search, and they often start by using proper names, such as people's names, universities' names or the scientific names of animals and planets. In the high accuracy transcripts, this strategy is very effective, as the number of occurrences of proper names in the videos is limited and the search table typically displays at most one or two results, which often and rapidly lead to the correct answer. However, in transcripts with lower word recognition accuracy, proper names have typically been misrecognized, and the search fails to return any result. Participants then change their strategy and start using common words or verbs, such as "atmosphere, right, problem, week, search, share, control", sometimes adjectives are also used.

After trying different search words, some participants combine the results they obtained to improve their chances by analyzing the correlation between different words' occurrence times. For example in order to answer the question shown in Fig. 4, a participant searched two words, "teaching" and "years". When he found that they both appear at time 0:1:18, he decided to watch the video at time 0:1:18 and found the answer to the question there.

When unable to obtain any search results after a few trials, the participants tend to adopt one of two strategies: some participants start using words not from the question but from the choices proposed; others abandon the search and randomly select an answer to the question.

6 Conclusion

We found that transcripts with 70% word recognition accuracy are as effective as higher accuracy transcripts in supporting video search when using single word search. We also found that, lower transcript accuracy does not necessarily mean longer search time. In fact large variations in the time it takes to search a video, independently of the quality of the transcript, were observed. With adequate and adapted search strategies (e.g. avoiding proper nouns), even low accuracy transcripts can support quick search.

Further research is now needed to test different video players and search interfaces. In this study, users were only allowed single word search. We received useful comments on how to improve the video player and the search interface. For example, participants commented that it would be better if, after selecting a word in the search results table, the video could jump to the beginning of the sentence that contains the word (and not just to the word). They also suggested that the results table should display the sentences that contain the search word (and not just the word occurrences).

References

1. TED Homepage. http://www.ted.com/. Last Accessed 12 Apr 2017
2. edX Homepage. http://www.edx.org. Last Accessed 12 Apr 2017
3. Coursera Homepage. http://www.coursera.org/. Last Accessed 12 Apr 2017
4. Breslow, L.B., Pritchard, D.E., DeBoer, J., Stump, G.S., Ho, A.D., Seaton, D.T.: Studying learning in the worldwide classroom: Research into edX's first MOOC. Res. Pract. Assess. **8**, 13–25 (2013)
5. Kim, J., Li, S.W., Cai, C.J., Gajos, K.Z., Miller, R.C.: Leveraging video interaction data and content analysis to improve video learning. In: Proceedings of the CHI 2014, Learning Innovation at Scale workshop, pp. 31–40 (2014)
6. Guo, P.J., Kim, J., Rubin, R.: How video production affects student engagement: an empirical study of MOOC videos. In: Proceedings of the first ACM Learning@scale Conference, pp. 41–50. ACM (2014)
7. Pavel, A., Reed, C., Hartmann, B., Agrawala, M.: Video digests: a browsable, skimmable format for informational lecture videos. In: Proceedings of UIST 2014, 5–8 October, Honolulu, USA (2014)
8. Victor, B.: April 2013. http://worrydream.com/MediaForThinkingTheUnthinkable. Last Accessed 12 Apr 2017
9. WebAim Homepage. http://webaim.org/techniques/captions/. Last Accessed 12 Apr 2017
10. CaptionSync Homepage. http://www.automaticsync.com/captionsync/. Last Accessed 12 Apr 2017
11. PlayMedia Homepage. http://www.3playmedia.com/. Last Accessed 12 Apr 2017
12. YouTube Homepage. https://www.youtube.com/. Last Accessed 12 Apr 2017
13. GoogleSpeech Homepage. https://cloud.google.com/speech/. Last Accessed 12 Apr 2017
14. Miró, J.D., Silvestre-Cerdà, J.A., Civera, J., Turró, C., Juan, A.: Efficiency and usability study of innovative computer-aided transcription strategies for video lecture repositories. Speech Commun. **74**, 65–75 (2015)
15. Ranchal, R., Taber-Doughty, T., Guo, Y., Bain, K., Martin, H., Robinson, J.P., Duerstock, B.S.: Using speech recognition for real-time captioning and lecture transcription in the classroom. IEEE Trans. Learn. Technol. **6**(4), 299–311 (2013)
16. Sphinx Homepage. http://cmusphinx.sourceforge.net/. Last Accessed 12 Apr 2017
17. WhiteHouse Homepage. https://www.whitehouse.gov/. Last Accessed 12 Apr 2017

Author Index

Printed in the United States
By Bookmasters

Printed in the United States
By Bookmasters